View from the Courthouse looking north, circa 1905, showing the old Methodist Church and the jail in the forefront on the left. Note the myriad of telephone lines.

View from the Courthouse looking west, circa 1905. Photo by Frank Medley.

View from the Courthouse roof looking south, circa 1905. Toward the back of the photo is the New McKendree Methodist Church under construction. Photo by Frank Medley.

View from the Courthouse roof looking north, 2002. To the left is the County Jail. On the right, is the John and Vicki Abernathy home built in in 1908 by the Gockel family.

View from the Courthouse roof looking west, 2002: Left to right: Jackson City Hall, Harold's Jewelry, Jones Drug Store, and A-Arrow Bail Bonds.

View from the Courthouse looking down South High Street, 2002.

History of Jackson, Missouri, and Surrounding Communities

TURNER PUBLISHING COMPANY

Turner Publishing Company
Publishers of America's History

Book Commitee Chairman: Catherine Stoverink
Publishing Consultant: Douglas W. Sikes
Book Designers: Emily Sikes and Elizabeth Sikes

Copyright © MMII Jackson Heritage Association
All rights reserved.
Publishing Rights: Turner Publishing Company

Library of Congress Catalog No.: 20022110253
ISBN: 978-1-68162-511-9

Limited Edition, First Printing 2002 A.D.
Additional copies may be purchased from Turner Publishing Company and the Jackson Heritage Association.

This book or any part thereof may not be reproduced by any means, mechanical or electronic, without the prior written consent of the Jackson Heritage Association and Turner Publishing Company. This publication was produced using available information. The Publisher regrets it cannot assume responsibility for errors or omissions.

Table of Contents

Dedication	4
Preface	5
Acknowledgments	6
History of Jackson Missouri	10
Business and Transportation	19
Area Communities	22
Historic Businesses	36
Retail and Industry Today	51
Businesses	55
Agriculture	79
Education	81
Schools	94
Libraries	96
Religion	97
Churches	103
Jackson in The Civil War and Other Military Service	118
Epidemics and Disasters	120
Area Attractions and Activities	123
Organizations	125
Parades and Pageants	143
Tributes	151
References	151
Family Histories	152
Index	300

Dedication

This book is dedicated to the families of Cape Girardeau County. From the pioneers who homesteaded the Louisiana Territory to the newcomers arriving in 2002, their stories are what make this book unique from any previous history and it is they who will continue to make Cape Girardeau County a wonderful place to call home. We thank the families of the past for trusting in the area's future and we welcome all new families to place their roots in the present and future of Jackson, Allenville, Apple Creek, Arbor, Blomeyer, Burfordville, Cape Girardeau, Crump, Daisy, Delta, Dutchtown, Egypt Mills, Friedheim, Fruitland, Gordonville, Gravel Hill, Leemon, Millersville, Neelys Landing, New Wells, Oak Ridge, Oriole, Pocahontas, Randles, Shawneetown, Solado, Tilsit, Whitewater, and areas in-between.

Preface

The Jackson Heritage Association is proud to offer this book as a sampling of the history of Jackson, the surrounding area, and the families that have had a part in making this county such a great place to live. In many ways, this history book project began in 1976 with the founding of the Jackson Heritage Association and its acceptance of the task of renovating the Oliver House at 224 East Adams Street in Jackson. Generous area citizens provided photographs and information about the life and times of the house and its occupants. The donations provided the foundation for an archive of local history files and over fifteen hundred images carefully organized and identified by Bernard Schaper. The history book project seemed a natural extension of the Association's mission "to promote respect and appreciation for historical buildings, landmarks, places and things."

Many more volumes could be written on the history of the towns, government, roads, and buildings of Cape Girardeau County; however, we wish to emphasize that this book is by, about, and for, the families of the area. While we have tried to make the information as accurate as possible, we have had to depend upon outside sources for much of the information submitted to us. Therefore, we cannot claim that all names, dates and places mentioned in the book are entirely accurate. Given the enormity of the project, some errors of fact and omission of information are inevitable. Also, because of limited space and personnel we were unable to include the community of Cape Girardeau. We encourage researchers to use this book as only one of the many sources available for the study of Jackson and Cape Girardeau County history.

Jackson Area History Book Committee
Pat Fosse
Barbara Lohr
Bernard Schaper
Catherine Stoverink

Courthouse Square in the early 1900s. The open area to the west of the old courthouse was the gathering place for wagons and buggies with the city scale being on the left. The large pile of wood was used to heat the many fireplaces of the courthouse.

Acknowledgments

Words cannot express our appreciation to the many individuals and businesses that have supported this project. A special thank you goes to Patty Chiles for endless hours of careful proofreading and continues to Robert Hartle, Mike Hess and Phyllis Seabaugh for contacting businesses; to the business men and women, organizations and churches who purchased pages and took time from their busy schedules to submit histories or patron pages; Jane Jackson and the Cape County Archive Center for assisting researchers; David Bloom and the Cash-Book Journal; Chris Pagano of Jackson USA; the local historians whose names appear with their histories, especially Dr. Alberta Macke Dougan for an updated edition of the history of Jackson; and to patient spouses who have listened to all the stories and worries of the last two years.

We wish to thank the families who worked so hard writing and rewriting their family histories and searching through boxes of photographs to add the finishing touches to their stories. You accomplished a difficult task. Future generations will appreciate that you took the time to share.

- PATRONS -
Dr. T. Wayne Lewis
Barbara Lohr
Philipps Carpet and Decorating
Premium Mechanical Contracting Co.
Rushing Marine Corporation
Bernard Schaper

Homecomer's, circa 1940.

Jackson, Missouri, and surrounding countryside, 1953.

History of the Jackson Area

A Brief History of Jackson Missouri

This history is an updated version of the history previously printed in "Celebrating 175 Years of Tradition, 1814-1819, Jackson, Mo.," by Dr. Alberta Dougan, combined with submitted articles including information from local newspapers of the past.

Jackson, "The City of Beautiful Homes, Churches, Schools, and Parks," became Cape Girardeau County's second town early in the 19th century as European and American immigrants came to settle a rich, untamed wilderness. The history of the settlement and development of Jackson is closely tied to the fate of its neighboring city on the Mississippi River to the east, Cape Girardeau.

The earliest European settler in the Cape Girardeau area was Louis Lorimier, a French-Canadian, who was given the right to establish a home and conduct trade with the Indians "in such lands as may be unoccupied on the Western side of the Mississippi, from the Missouri to the river Arkansas" in 1793 (Houck, Vol. II, 1908, p. 170). In 1795 Lorimier petitioned Governor-General Carondelet for a grant of land where Cape Girardeau is now located. That grant and other lands allowed him on the condition that within one year he make a road and regular improvements eventually totaled about 8000 arpents, roughly 6600 acres (Houck, Vol. II, 1908, p. 177).

Americans began moving into the Cape Girardeau district in 1795. Although Lorimier had aided the British in the American Revolution, he apparently viewed American settlers as important to the growth and profitability of his settlement. The Spanish possibly believed American settlers would be willing allies against the British, who still had troops based in Canada, should they attempt to seize Louisiana. Therefore, the Spanish were willing to offer land to Americans under the conditions that they make improvements in their grants and abide by Spanish law. Thus the first American settlement in the Cape Girardeau District began just to the southwest of Lorimier's post of Cape Girardeau where Andrew Ramsay, a Virginian, and several members of his family established plantations. Most settled close to the Ramsay plantation. However, his son-in-law, William Dougherty, established his plantation in 1798 on Hubble Creek near the present city of Jackson. Other early settlers along Hubble Creek were Ithmar Hubble (sometimes spelled Hubbell), 1797, for whom the creek was named, who built a mill close to where the town of Gordonville is now located; John Summers and his son John, Junior, 1796; Andrew Summers; James Mills, 1799; and Colonel Christopher Hays, 1800 (Houck, Vol. II, 1908, pp. 184-187). Also settling in the Jackson area were the Amos Byrd family, 1799, who came from eastern Tennessee and settled west of present day Jackson; the German-American settlers who came from North Carolina to the Whitewater River with Joseph Niswonger in 1799; and the family of George Frederick Bollinger, of Swiss German descent, who also came from North Carolina to the area of Burfordville in 1800 (Houck, Vol. II, 1908, pp. 184-188). Many of these families would play important roles in the development of Missouri.

The Louisiana Purchase, completed by the United States in December 1803 by paying $15 million to France, brought drastic changes to the Cape Girardeau District. One of the most serious difficulties encountered by many settlers was the question of recognition of land claims made under the auspices of the Spanish government when, in reality, the Louisiana Territory had been returned to France in 1800 in the secret treaty of St. Ildefonso. However the French had never taken formal possession of the territory. Thus when the United States took possession in 1804 and in the Act of Congress that created the "District of Louisiana" of which Missouri was a part declared that all grants of land made after the Treaty of St. Ildefonso should be void unless the grant had been made to an individual according to the laws and customs of Spain and that the individual had settled the land prior to December 1803, many settlers had cause to believe that their land claims would not be honored. In addition, the Act provided that no grant of more than one-mile square (640 acres) would be honored for an individual unless such claim included legitimate grants for

The Cape Girardeau County Courthouse, circa 1900. Photo courtesy Alvin Kamp.

other family members (Houck, Vol. II, 1908, pp. 376-378).

The District of Louisiana was attached to the Indiana territory for administrative purposes with William Henry Harrison as governor. Governor Harrison appointed Colonel Thomas Scott to be Lieutenant Governor of the Cape Girardeau District, which was retained intact under U.S. territorial control. In addition, a Court of Common Pleas and Quarter Sessions was created. In January 1805, Governor Harrison noted that no permanent seat of justice had been designated. He therefore empowered the court to ask for bids for a site. Louis Lorimier offered land in Cape Girardeau and William Dougherty and Jesse Cain offered land along Hubble Creek near the present town of Jackson. Lorimier's offer was accepted, and on January 13, 1806, the governor issued a proclamation designating Cape Girardeau as the permanent seat of justice. The newly created court held its first meeting on March 19, 1806. Christopher Hays was Presiding Judge with Louis Lorimier, Thomas Ballew, Robert Green, John Guthing, John Byrd, and Frederick Limbaugh as associate judges. Joseph McFerron was commissioned as clerk of the court and John Hays as sheriff. The first grand jury was composed of Henry Sheridan, James Earles, Joseph Waller, John Taylor, Daniel Harkelrode, Louis Lathem, John Patterson, Matthew Hubbell, Elijah Whitaker, Ithmar Hubbell, Martin Rodney, Samuel Pew, James Boyd, William Boner, John Abernathy, Samuel Randol, James Currin, Robert Crump, Samuel Bradley, and Frederick Bollinger (Goodspeed, 1888, pp. 316, 318).

In an Act of Congress in 1805, Upper Louisiana was detached from the Territory of Indiana, becoming the Territory of Louisiana. General James Wilkinson was appointed governor and assumed his duties immediately. President Thomas Jefferson removed him from office in March of 1807. His replacement, Merriwether Lewis, arrived in St. Louis in July 1807 (Houck, Vol. II, 1908, pp. 402-409).

Among the acts passed by the Territorial Legislature in 1808 were provisions for incorporating towns by the Courts of Common Pleas and the appointment of commissioners to view and lay out a road from St. Louis to New Madrid. This road followed the old Spanish trace and is today incorporated into U.S. Highway 61. The Territorial Legislature had to make provisions for the building and maintenance of the roads. Thus citizens were required to provide from two to thirty days of road service annually, assessed according to the amount of property owned. In addition, a citizen was required to serve in the militia as needed for defense. Another obligation introduced by the territorial government was assessment of local taxes, a practice unknown under the Spanish. For the most part these taxes consisted of property taxes and merchant licenses (Houck, Vol. II, 1908, pp. 414-415).

An Act of Congress in 1812 created the Territory of Missouri. A territorial General Assembly was to be created by election in each of the five counties, formerly known as districts, of members of the territorial House of Representatives and of a delegate to Congress. The President was to select a nine member Legislative Council, consisting of persons nominated by the territorial House of Representatives. In addition, the Act decreed that schools should be provided for from the public lands of the United States within the territory.

Members of the first territorial House of Representatives from Cape Girardeau County were George Frederick Bollinger and Stephen Byrd. From the names submitted to the President, William Neeley and Joseph Cavender were appointed to the Legislative Council from Cape Girardeau County. William Clark was named as the governor of the newly created Territory of Missouri. Among the action taken by this first General Assembly was provision for taking a census of the male population to determine future representation. Results of that census, taken in 1813, found Cape Girardeau County with 2062 white males (Houck, Vol. II, 1908, p. 106).

Selecting a New County Seat

The present city of Jackson came into being because of the newly acquired territorial status of Missouri. Although Lorimier had been awarded the original site for a seat of justice in the district, a new seat of justice was created for Cape Girardeau County by order of Territorial Governor William Clark in 1813. Thus the seat of justice was moved, partly because of the creation of a new Court of Common Pleas, which replaced the older court structure, and partly because problems with Lorimier's land grant and the legal difficulties associated with probating the will following his death in 1812 brought growth of Cape Girardeau (also referred to as Lorimier's Ferry or Lorimont in some documents) essentially to a standstill. It was apparently decided to move the county seat to an area exhibiting population growth and to which a clear title to land could be obtained.

According to Goodspeed, in February 1814,

Home-Comers and Dedication of the new Courthouse, September 1908. The old Courthouse in front of the newly constructed Courthouse was left standing to accommodate the large crowds.

The Cape Girardeau County Courthouse, 1970s.

Mural depicting Andrew Jackson and symbols representing the town of Jackson, Missouri. The mural was designed by Grant Lund in 1996 and transferred to the Main Street wall of The Andrew Jackson Store by Matt Chubboy.

the commissioners, John Davis, John Sheppard, S. G. Dunn, Abraham Byrd, and Benjamin Shell, were charged with selecting a site. A paper prepared in 1940 by an unidentified student and based on an interview with John G. Putz, former Clerk of Cape Girardeau County and at the time president of the Cape Girardeau County Historical Society, indicated that the commissioners met in the courtroom to hear those who wished to offer their plantations for the courthouse site. Among the sites offered were Thomas Bull's plantation, the site of the Old Bethel Baptist Church, which apparently served as a church and as a community gathering place, and William Ashley's plantation. According to Putz, Ashley urged the commissioners to buy his "improvement," an indication that at least part of the land was cleared. The commissioners purchased fifty acres of land lying along Hubbell (sic.) Creek from William Ashley, who had obtained the land as a wedding present from his father-in-law, Ezekial Able (Goodspeed, 1888, p. 320). County Warranty Deed records, Book C, pages 460-461, show that the commissioners paid $500 for the acreage.

According to the Putz interview, citizens protested the choice of site, claiming that the land was not suitable for building a city. Thus the commissioners purchased an additional site just to the north of the Ashley land from James Mills. Bartholomew Cousins laid out the town and the commissioners began to sell lots. One of the first tasks facing developers was clearing the land. Fortunately they could use the logs to build homes and businesses.

According to Goodspeed, in March 1814 the newly created Court of Common Pleas met in the Bethel Baptist Church. This was to be a temporary meeting place until the new town could be laid out and a court building constructed (1888, p. 319). However, the minutes of the Proceedings of the Bethel Church seem to dispute that claim. According to church minutes of April 8, 1814, members of the church meeting in conference passed the following resolution: "Resolved that no court shall be held in the meeting house and that Bro. John Hitt shall be door keeper of the church." On June 18, 1814, the minutes show passage of another resolution reversing the earlier decision to exclude the court, stating: "Resolved that the meeting house be given up to hold court in until there can be a house built on the permanent seat." In December 1814 the following entry appears: "Brethren McMillin and Bull write to the Association to remove the court from the meeting house. Brethren Sheppard and Bull to write to the committee." (WPA Transcription, 940, pp. 13-14). There is no explanation of the rationale of church members for making the decision to exclude the court, to reverse that decision, then to finally ask the court to leave. It may be that the court did indeed meet in the church in March and take action that displeased the membership. Perhaps pleas of other members or lack of another appropriate meeting place close to the new county seat was a reason to reverse the decision and allow the court to meet in the church. What is consistent is the indication that by 1815 the town of Jackson had been laid out and that there were apparently a few existing structures within the boundaries of the new town.

In 1815 the court structure was further revised, creating the Circuit Court system to handle both criminal and civil cases and to administer the affairs of the county. The first session of this court was held in "the north end of a house attached to what is now the residence of Mrs. Schmuke…" (Goodspeed, 1888, p. 320). This house served as a site for sessions of the court until a courthouse could be built on a public square. This house was located on the north side of Adams Street between South High and South Hope Streets.

There is some dispute about the materials used in construction of the first courthouse and the number of courthouses the court has had. Houck claims the original courthouse was a log structure (Vol. III, 1908, p. 169) and Goodspeed describes it as "frame" (1888, p. 320). According to Goodspeed, John Davis constructed the frame courthouse in 1818 at a cost of $2,450. Ohman (1981) concluded that Houck's log building might have been one of the court's temporary quarters. Since some of the early country records were destroyed in a fire, the records that would clarify this question have been lost. The first jail was built in 1816 at a cost of $1,400. It burned in 1819 and William Byrd was paid $1,994 to replace it. The frame courthouse was old and the Court specified it be removed from the site no later than April 1839. Its replacement, a 45-foot square, two story brick and stone building with cupola completed in 1837 at a cost of $5,000, burned in 1870 and a brick replacement was built in 1871-72 at a cost of $25,000 (Ohman, 1981). According to the *Jackson Herald* (1908), the brick building simply became too small for county business and in 1905 county residents voted to issue $75,000 in bonds to replace it. Total construction costs were closer to $98,000, but the Herald reported that the attractive new building was "worth it." *The Cape Girardeau Republican* (1914) reported the cost to be about $125,000. Although the building was dedicated in 1906, it was not completed until 1908. Many pictures show the old and new courthouses side-by-side. According to the *Herald*, the old courthouse was allowed to stand until after the first Home Comers in 1908 in order to facilitate handling all the visitors expected to come for the event.

As county population has increased, the need for more space and a change in the court structure have given Cape Girardeau County two courthouses and an administrative building. The court system operates out of the Jackson courthouse and the former Common Pleas Courthouse in Cape Girardeau. In 1988 most of the county administrative offices moved out of the courthouse into the nearby Administrative Building, making the primary function of the courthouse fit its name. Completing the courthouse complex is the Cape Girardeau County Archive Center that serves as the repository for Cape Girardeau County records ranging from the 1790s to the present. Jackson is also the site of a county jail, completed in 1978 and expanded in 1999. A county park complex was developed in the 1980s on Highway 61 just inside the city limits of Cape Girardeau.

Naming the County Seat

The town was named for Andrew Jackson, "Old Hickory." There is no dispute about that and Jackson, Missouri, is probably the first town to be named for this military and political figure (Talley interview, 1989). The question is, why? Many had assumed that the name had been selected following the Battle of New Orleans in January 1815. For example, Goodspeed indicates that Jackson was named after the Battle (1888, p. 320). Unfortunately there appear to be no city or county minutes recording a specific date when the town received its name. However, deeds in Cape Girardeau County Warranty Deed Book D, pages 3-4, 23-24, and 28-31, show that land in the town of Jackson was purchased on the seventeenth day of December 1814, thereby indicating that the town was named prior to Andrew Jackson's victory in the Battle of New Orleans.

Apparently the rural pioneer families, such as those settled along Byrds, Randall, Whitewater, and Hubble Creeks and who had settled for a time in the Carolinas or Tennessee, who admired Jackson for his political and military reputation. According to Putz, this group was larger, "animated" and rather noisy. Therefore, "Jackson" it would be. Once again, unfortunately, Putz cites no source for his information and does not indicate "which" Fourth of July. However, considering the sequence of events that had already transpired, the dates of which are contained in county records, this decision would have to have been made on July 4, 1814.

What might there be about Andrew Jackson that would cause such excitement and admiration? By accounts of his biographers, he was a gambler, a dueler, and an opportunist. However, he was also a successful political and military leader who would eventually become the seventh President of the United States. Jackson became well known as one of only a few lawyers in the Tennessee Constitutional Convention in 1796 and was elected Tennessee's first member of the House of Representatives, later being appointed to the Senate after it expelled Senator Blount. Jackson resigned from the Senate after having served only one year because he was not pleased with the way business was conducted in Washington.

Upon returning to Tennessee, Jackson was appointed to a judgeship. However, the real prize, the commission that won him much notoriety, was his appointment as Commander of the Tennessee Militia in 1801. It was in this position that he received the order to march his militia to defend New Orleans in the War of 1812. He received the order in November 1812, but by February 1813, his troops had only reached Natchez, Mississippi. There they were ordered to disband since an attack on New Orleans did not appear imminent. Jackson returned to Nashville where, in September, he learned of an Indian attack on settlers in the area of Fort Mims, about forty-five miles north of Mobile, on the Alabama River. Jackson recalled his troops and began a series of attacks on the Creek Indians. Two major battles took place in November 1813, with the most famous battle, the Battle of Horse Shoe Bend, taking place on March 27, 1814.

Because of the victory at Horse Shoe Bend, Jackson was given the rank of Brigadier-General in the U.S. Army and the command of the entire Gulf region. In December he began serious preparations for the defense of New Orleans. At first it appeared that the British would easily take New Orleans. However, Jackson was able to muster enough troops to stop the British from a quick victory in December 1814, and by January 8, 1815, a combination of preparation, location, and luck gave Jackson the victory. Therefore, if the town of Jackson was indeed named before American victory in the Battle of New Orleans, there would have been just cause for selecting the name to honor Andrew Jackson. He had achieved military fame and recognition, and his record as a political figure shows his support for many ideas that would have been similar to those of area settlers. Seabaugh family records perhaps shed light on one source by which news of Andrew Jackson's victories may have reached this community in a timely manner. According to Seabaugh (1988), Christian Seabaugh carried mail from Missouri to Lincoln County, North Carolina. Although records of one of his trips in 1814 show him to have returned from North Carolina in September, he may have made additional trips earlier in the year.

Jackson Becomes More Than the Meeting Place for the County Court

The town of Jackson rapidly attracted residents. According to Houck, by 1818 Jackson had a population of 300 (Vol. III, 1908, p. 169). Although the Putz interview indicated that additional land was purchased because citizens thought the Ashley land was unsuitable for a

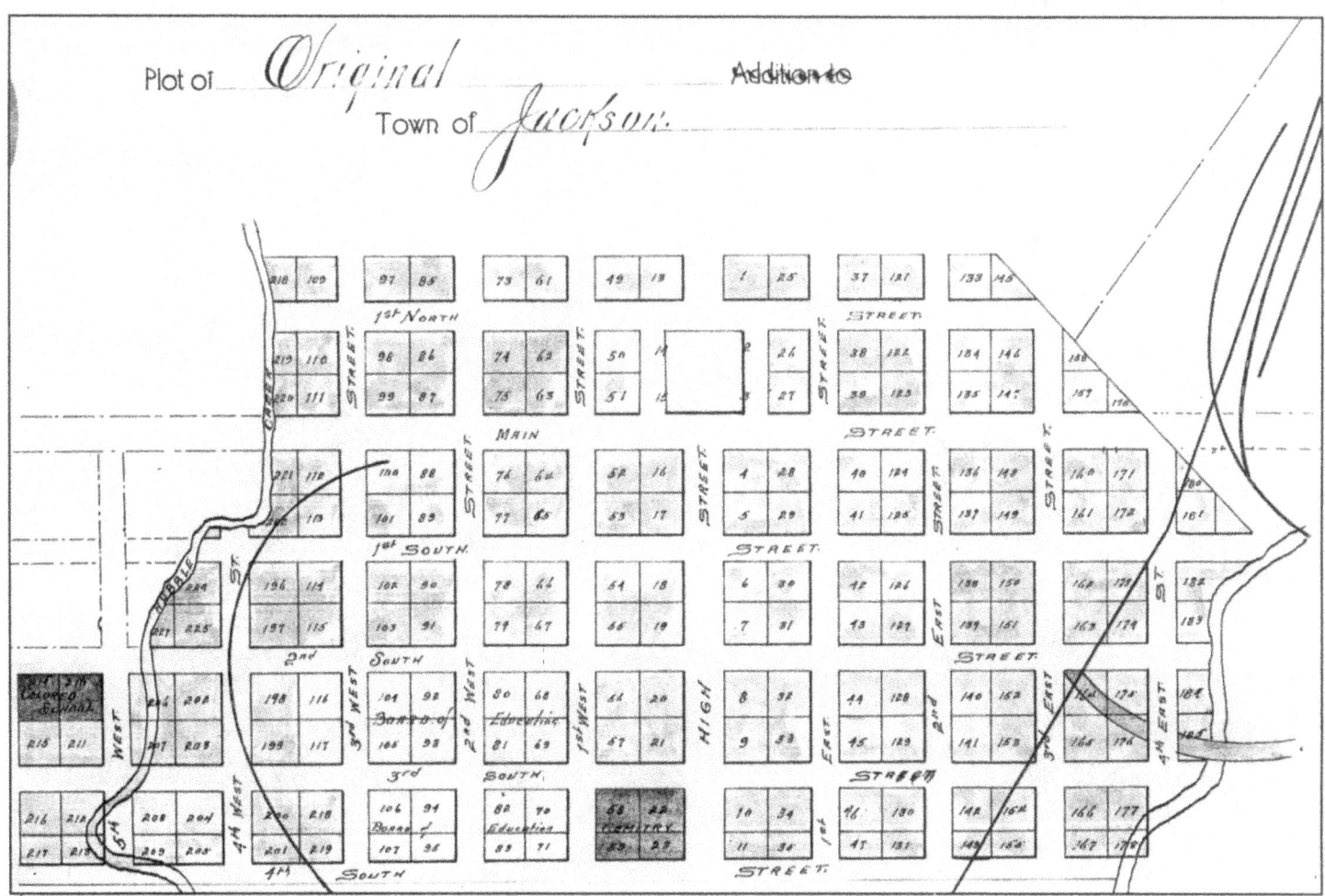

Early plat map of Jackson showing original street names. Courtesy of Cape Girardeau County Archive Center, Jackson, Missouri.

town, Cochran (1965) claims that almost immediately the Ashley land purchase was insufficient and that additional land was obtained from James Mills, whose survey, U.S. Survey No. 2250, is the tract number by which the town is now known. It was on the Mills survey that the new courthouse and jail were constructed.

Soon thereafter two additional surveys were added to the town, the James Earl Survey on the west and the Samuel Pew Survey on the east. Houck cites Peck, a Baptist minister, who in 1818 noted between sixty and seventy dwelling houses, five stores, two shoemaker shops, one tannery, and two good schools, one for males and the other for females. Houck also cites a Major Long who came to Jackson on October 18, 1820. Long noted that after St. Louis and St. Charles, Jackson was one of the largest towns in Missouri. Long claimed that he and his party had difficulty coaxing their animals to come into town since they were "unaccustomed to such displays of magnificence" (Vol. III, 1908, p. 169).

One indication of Jackson's growth and importance is that the news that the Missouri Compromise had been hammered out by Congress, thus allowing Missouri to elect delegates to a constitutional convention, was received in Jackson before residents of St. Louis were told. The welcome news was brought by Thomas Hempstead who passed through Jackson on his way to St. Louis on March 21, 1820. Representatives to the constitutional convention from Cape Girardeau County were Stephen Byrd, James Evans, Richard Thomas, Alexander Buckner, and Joseph McFerron (Houck, Vol. III, 1908, pp. 248-249).

Goodspeed (1888) says Jackson grew rapidly for the first few years, to the detriment of Cape Girardeau, but when steamboats began to ply the river with regularity, Cape Girardeau quickly outdistanced Jackson in population. Another spur to the growth of Cape Girardeau came with the July 4, 1826 recognition of all valid Spanish land claims, thus legitimizing land grants made by Lorimier.

Establishing and naming a settlement is a somewhat different procedure from the formal incorporation process which takes place through the courts. According to Goodspeed, Jackson was first incorporated in 1819 when the county court ordered William Gnatt and Joel Blount to hold an election for trustees. The next mention of this incorporation is made in 1828 when Nathan Vanhorn, Franklin Cannon, G. W. Davis, and Edward Criddle met and organized, with Vanhorn, chairman and C. S. Thomas as clerk. Several ordinances were passed, as were rules governing the boards, but no more meetings are recorded until 1831 when George Juden was made clerk and Welton O'Bannon, town constable. In 1847 the incorporation was revived and the board met regularly until 1859 when a special charter was granted by the Legislature. In a special election held in 1884, citizens of Jackson voted to incorporate as a city of the fourth class (1888, pp. 443-434). Since that time, Jackson has functioned under a mayor-city council form of government with most city offices being elective positions. The *Jackson Herald* (1908) noted that Jackson became a city of the third class in 1907, however, the current city listing in the Missouri State Manual shows Jackson to be a city of the fourth class. Residents of Jackson voted in 1905 to develop a city-owned power plant to produce electricity and a city-owned waterworks. At about the same time two fire departments were organized with the city building a firehouse to store the equipment.

According to the *Southeast Missourian*, 1904 to 1907 were years of real growth for Jackson. In 1904 Jackson's population was 1,980 and by 1906 it was 2,189. The 1950 population was 4,000 and by 1976, it was estimated at 6,454 (July 4, 1976, p. 2D). In 1990 census figures showed Jackson's population to be 9,256. Following the 2000 census, Jackson was recognized as one of the fastest-growing cities in Missouri, a 29% increase reflected in a population of 11,947 living in an area encompassing 10.5 square miles (*Southeast Missourian*, Progress Edition, February 24, 2002, p. 1).

As the above overview indicates, Jackson has expanded over time in population and in geographic dimensions making it imperative that the way in which city services are delivered and the government functions must change as well. Ways to gauge that change other than census figures and boundaries include looking at changes in the infrastructure and in personnel. For example, in 1961 construction was completed on a City Hall building located on the corner of South High and Jefferson Streets to house city offices and the Public Library. By the 1990s the city had outgrown that facility.

In 1995 the city converted a former bank building located at the corner of Main and Court Streets into city offices and space for the Jackson Public Library. The move was completed in 1996. A police and fire complex, located at the intersection of Highways 61, 72, and 25, was completed and occupied on January 15, 1985.

A wagon caravan on the courthouse square in the early 1900s.

Currently renovations are taking place on a former Missouri Department of Transportation building adjacent to the police and fire complex to house administrative offices. Numerous upgrades of the power, water, and sewer systems have been necessary to keep up with the rapid growth of recent years. Over the past five years the city has spent over $15 million dollars on such system upgrades. A southern loop is being added to the water system to improve water pressure and to allow further development of the city to the south. Sewer extensions to property on North High Street, recently purchased by the Jackson Industrial Development Corporation that will become Jackson's newest industrial park, should also facilitate residential development to the north. (*Southeast Missourian*, Progress Edition, February 24, 2002, p. 1. Additional information provided by the City Engineer's office.)

In 1970, as city business became ever more complex, a full-time city administrator was hired to oversee the day-to-day operation of city government. Harry Coleman was hired as the first City Administrator and served until 1972. Carl Talley served from 1972-1994; Steve Wilson, 1994-2001; and James Roach is the current City Administrator. A full-time city staff of 110 attempts to meet the needs of the city by maintaining vital city services such as keeping city records, providing power and water, police and fire protection, street maintenance, and health and sanitation services. Mayors of Jackson and the date of their initial service are: Jefferson W. Limbaugh, 1885; R. P. Wilson, 1887; William Paar, 1889; Charles Pepper, 1891; Ben Gockel, acting mayor, 1893; William Paar, 1893; Edward D. Hays, 1903; Robert W. Russell, 1907; William B. Schaefer, 1909; R. K. Wilson, 1911; E. G. Sibley, 1915; David B. Hays, 1917; H. H. Mueller, acting mayor, 1919; S. F. Rogers, 1919; Sam Vandivort, 1921; J. R. Bowman, 1923; J. E. Schmuke, 1927; J. R. Bowman, 1931; Charles H. Sander, 1941; J. R. Bowman, 1944; J. R. Mabrey, 1949; Larry A. Nowak, 1957; Walter A. Lasten, 1961; Larry A. Nowak, 1963; Russel O. Hawkins, 1969; Paul J. Leonard, 1971; Carlton Meyer, 1973; and Paul Sander, 1993-present.

By Alberta Macke Dougan

City Of Beautiful Homes

The sustained growth of Jackson's population and constant industrial expansion during the Twentieth Century led to a chronic housing shortage. As early as 1922, the newspapers reported "Jackson is still suffering from lack of houses and rooms for rent; ...building is going on but not fast enough to accommodate those who want to come to Jackson and get settled before cold weather." In 1934 the re-opening of the International Shoe Company initiated the "Greatest Building Revival in Jackson's History" with the construction of thirty-one dwellings. That same year the town boasted of having two and one-half miles of paved streets! The economic ups and downs of the area economy and the influence of industries such as the Shoe Company, Jackson Hosiery Mill, Lee-Rowan, and Procter and Gamble from the 1960s through the 1990s kept increasing the demand on the housing market. During that period new subdivisions and additions to the town of Jackson were developed through the

The "Brooks" house built by Major James Francis Brooks in 1877, is located at 219 North Hope Street, and is now the home of Brad and Susan Teets.

The home of Kevin and Debbie Schearf, 425 North High Street, Jackson, 2002. The house was first owned by Joseph and Mary Criddle Williams.

Home of Dr. T. Wayne and Linda Lewis, 742 West Independence, Jackson, 2002.

Home of Tom and Nancy Morris, 624 West Washington, Jackson, 2002.

cooperative effort of individuals, banks, lumberyards, contractors and realty companies. Jackson's developers, contractors and carpenters take great pride in producing beautiful and long-lasting structures. Jackson's homeowners are to be congratulated for the care and attention bestowed upon their homes and neighborhoods.

The Rock House

Several homes within Jackson are noted for their interesting histories. The most notable is known as "The Rock House" located at 119 North Missouri Street.

The house, built by Charles Criddle around 1815, was the first two-story house in townThe original house was built in Southern style: four large rooms and four fireplaces with a kitchen in the back. The stones used to build the house were quarried north of town on Hubble Creek. The walls are twenty-two inches thick. Slaves carried out much of the work, chiseling and hammering the stone to shape, and using oxen to pull the heavy stones to the building site. The two-story rear addition and front porch were constructed when the John Sander family lived in the house. Many Jackson families have made the house their home: Criddles, Cannons, McGuires, Campbells, Mueller, Hartle, and Ellis.

The Frizel-Welling House

Written by Mildred Berenice Granger Hartsfield, circa 1970, and condensed by Mrs. Hartsfield's daughter, Elizabeth Farmer

The house at 209 West Main Street is the second oldest house in Jackson. It was built on a lot purchased by the surveyor, Joseph Frizel, in 1816, shortly after he had helped lay out the town of Jackson. In 1818 Mr. Frizel built a Cape Cod style cottage on the property. The following year he married Sarah Bollinger, only child of Colonel George Frederick Bollinger, builder of the now famous Bollinger Mill and dam, and brought his new bride to this charming house. Elizabeth, the first of their three children, was born in the cottage in 1820.

Although just a story and a half, the cottage was well built and quite different from the log cabins in which many of the early settlers lived. The walls were very thick: brick with weather-boarding outside, and the inside walls covered with thick plaster "about a half inch thick. (This made it delightfully cool in summer and warm in winter- nature's own way of air-conditioning.) The floors were made of wide, smooth poplar boards. On the ground floor was a large living room 15x18 and a dining room 15x20. Across the back porch was the generous kitchen, 20x20, with walls lined with cabinets and shelves. At one end was a large fireplace and an in-the-wall oven. These were used for cooking food for the family until after the War between the States, when a wood cook-stove was purchased.

In the loft above the kitchen the women servants had their living quarters. It was in the kitchen that the children gathered on winter evenings to listen to folk and ghost stories. Sometimes they were afraid to go back across the pitch-black porch to their own rooms. The stories were said to be as good as "Uncle Remus." Two bedrooms on the top floor were small but adequate.

In 1822 Unity Lodge No. 6, the first Masonic Lodge west of the Mississippi, was organized in the Frizel home through the efforts of Alexander Buckner, third senator from Missouri and past Grand Master of the Indiana State Lodge. Mr. Buckner was the first Worshipful Master and young Frizel was Junior Warden. Sarah was very interested in this Lodge and she painted on satin a Masonic apron for each member. One of these was framed and hangs on the wall of the living room.

In 1822, also, Joseph Frizel became ill and the home was sold. The family moved to Whitewater to the home of her father, Colonel Bollinger, where Sarah lived until the close of the War. In 1838 the home came back into the family. Charles Welling bought the property for a home for his bride, Elizabeth Frizel. She came back to her birthplace. The two-story section was added, making it a fine example of early New England architecture. The new part, too, was well constructed. The window and door moldings were mortised (put together without nails). The fireplaces (four of them) matched those in the original section. The floor and side-walls were of brick, and were painted each spring with a solution made from brick dust and water to keep them bright. In the addition, there was a large living room, a bedroom downstairs, and two large bedrooms upstairs. Large white doors opened wide between the living room and bedroom. All the woodwork was painted white, and was thoroughly scrubbed, spring and fall. The floors were covered with carpets, hand-woven from strips of bright woolen cloth. Each spring all the carpets were taken up and thoroughly beaten. Before they were

The "Rock House" circa 1908. Photo by Frank Medley, courtesy of Gerald Venable.

The "Rock House," 119 N. Missouri Street, Jackson, 1994

replaced, the floors were scrubbed and allowed to dry. A fresh layer of straw was put down. Then the carpets would be tacked down again. A wide hall connected the old part of the house to the new.

The front walk and sidewalk were flagstone. The latter is still in use, but the outer walk went the way of all progress and is now concrete. Great flat rock slabs were brought from Whitewater and still serve as front steps. The steps leading from the back porch were of the same heavy rock. The patio beyond was a brick. In the center of this was a large cistern which furnished water so refreshing that it was used until about 1940. There was a shed over this (the cistern shed). Attached to the shed was a large building, approximately 20 x 20. It was plastered and painted and had a door and two windows. It was the quarters for the caretakers of the place, slaves before the war; later paid servants. It was called the cistern room. Next to it was the smoke-house, later used for coal, and beyond that was the ice-house. During the winter, blocks of ice were cut from the creek and stored between thin layers of sawdust in this house (the first method of refrigeration), which lasted only until the warmth of summer melted the ice. At the far end of the lot was the big barn that housed the buggy, a wagon, and the stock. The loft above was filled with hay.

When Mr. Welling built the "big" part of the house, he sent back east for trees and shrubs. Three tiny linden trees were planted. One of these still stands - the famous linden tree in front of the house, now 160+ years old. (The other two fell to "progress" when the street was graded). He planted many other trees, shrubs, and flowers. Even today the yard is lovely in the springtime when it is filled with golden daffodils, relics from his planting, and the lilacs and the syringa are in bloom.

The current owners are great grandchildren of Charles Welling, and great-great grandchildren of Joseph and Sarah Bollinger Frizel. The house was placed on the National Register of Historic Homes on June 25, 1999.

Trisha's Bed & Breakfast

HISTORY OF 203 BELLEVUE STREET, JACKSON, MISSOURI

In 1901 H. H. Mueller Jr. purchased some land from his father in anticipation of building his own home. Mr. Mueller was single at the time, and was a bookkeeper for the family business, a meat packing and processing plant on Goose Creek. Being a frugal investor, H. H. accrued assets and hired a builder to begin construction in 1904. The full two-story Queen Anne was finished in 1905; however, Mueller rented the house out for approximately six years to finish paying the $1500 house price. He and his wife, Rilla, then occupied the house and had one child, Millicent, born in 1912.

In 1924 when Millicent was twelve years old, her father purchased a baby grand piano which sat in the parlor. Millicent and Rilla argued over where to place the instrument; Millicent wanted it in the foyer under the staircase so the sound would carry throughout the house. However, Rilla prevailed because she always decorated a twelve-foot Christmas tree up the center of the staircase. Ironically, Millicent went on to become a piano teacher; in 1932 she married Jim Dean, owner of the Pure Ice Company in Cape Girardeau.

Ms. Rilla wanted to update the house in 1928. Both Mr. and Mrs. Mueller Sr. had passed away, and a second dining room was needed as the Mueller siblings came to dinner often, so the main floor master bedroom had French doors added. Also the original bathroom was removed and changed into a breakfast room and butler's pantry. The staircase had a light added to the newel post and the woodwork and the spindles were painted white. Unfortunately, Rilla had the stained and leaded glass removed to add more light to the house.

Charles Welling, circa 1890.

Mr. and Mrs. Charles Welling in front of their home, 209 West Main Street, Jackson, Missouri, circa 1888.

An apartment was added to the three original second floor bedrooms in 1937 after Mr. Mueller Jr.'s death. Rilla and the tenants shared the upper floor bath; one of the bedrooms was divided into a kitchen for the apartment and a storage area for Rilla. Later Rilla moved her bedroom downstairs to the breakfast room and rented out her 2 _ rooms as another apartment. Renters were always young married couples who enjoyed large homes.

When Ms. Rilla passed away in 1968, Millicent couldn't bear to sell the place. After a year of trying to maintain the house, she and Jim reluctantly sold it to a family. That family only kept it about three years, then the David Berry family with their six nearly grown children moved in and stayed for twelve years. In 1985 Laura Borgfield purchased it and made some improvements, then resold it to the current owners in 1987. Gustav and Patricia Wischmann bought the house with the intention of using it for their home, and making it into a bed and breakfast. They and their family worked on it thirteen months before opening the doors as Trisha's Bed & Breakfast, southeast Missouri's first B&B. They have continued innkeeping for nearly fourteen years and have opened a private tea room for specialty parties and unique dining. After nearly a hundred years, the house is still functioning as a home, and now as a business.

The house features over fifty windows including two bays with three windows each on two floors, six exterior doors, and six transoms. Five bedrooms are on the second floor. There currently are two dining rooms, two foyers, a parlor, a kitchen, and five bathrooms; and the basement has two bedrooms, a family room, and storage and work areas. Outdoors a potting shed, carport, and a new gazebo grace the three-fifths of an acre the house sits on.

Patricia Wischmann

Trisha's Bed & Breakfast, 203 Bellevue Street, Jackson, Missouri.

Southwest corner of Courthouse Square, Jackson, Missouri, circa 1960. Some of the businesses pictured are: Albert Sander Hardware Co., Cape County Savings Bank, Schade's Cafe, Western Auto, and Priest's Store.

Business and Transportation

Public Transportation

In the 21st century, most people take personal transportation for granted. Most families have at least one motor vehicle. Many families have more. Thus it is easy to travel from city to city, to shop, to work, or to play. Because of today's ease of travel, public means of ground transportation have decreased service to most communities. For example, at the start of the Civil War the Cape Girardeau-Jackson Hack Line made daily trips, transporting mail and passengers. According to Snider and Collins, Anton Gockel operated such a line in the 1870s, with William Gockel operating it at the turn of the century. They described William Gockel's operation in the following manner: "During the World's Fair in 1904 he bought a Winston Six 'Red Devil' automobile for the route. It broke an axle, was returned to St. Louis by boat for repairs, placed in service again, but abandoned after a few months as too unreliable" (1956, pp. 247-248). In July 1908 Louis Houck began a motor-car service, making four round trips daily between Jackson and Cape Girardeau and one daily round trip from Jackson to Oak Ridge (*Jackson Herald*, 1908).

From the 1920s until the 1970s several companies offered bus service with stops in Jackson. Most have now gone out of business, or operate abbreviated schedules due to lack of riders. Currently Jackson is served by the Greyhound Bus Line that operates out of a small storage space on the sidewalk outside the County Administration building. The same fate has befallen the railroads. No scheduled passenger service has operated out of Jackson for many years. When the Missouri Pacific Railroad stopped freight service to Jackson in 1984, the Jackson Industrial Development Company purchased the railroad right of way and contracted with the Jackson and Southern Railroad to provide freight service to Jackson. In 1985 a group of investors bought an old steam engine and reintroduced the St. Louis, Iron Mountain and Southern Railroad to Jackson, this time as a tourist attraction.

Business and Industry

Business interests in Jackson have changed over the years as the country has changed. However, for much of its existence Jackson has served as a marketing and supply center for the farming communities surrounding it. To some extent transportation routes played a part in Jackson's development and have influenced the course of businesses that have located here. For example, in 1805 a petition was filed in the Court of Common Pleas and Quarter Sessions that requested a road be built from "Lorimier's Ferry" to William Dougherty's farm. A second petition asked for a road from Dougherty's farm to connect with an existing road running from the upper Delaware Town (at the intersection of Apple and Indian Creeks) to Ste. Genevieve (Houck, Vol. III, 1908, p. 168). Jackson's location in relation to the inland ridgelines, allowing travelers to follow several existing trails, possibly influenced granting these route improvements and later aided in selection of Jackson as the new county seat. Houck further noted that Armour and Juden, merchants in Jackson from 1815-1820, employed Robert Morrison to drive a team to Baltimore to haul goods to Jackson for them. What's more, Morrison was able to complete the trip in three months! (Vol. III, 1908, p. 196). Considering the state of travel in those days, when an "improved road" merely meant the tree stumps could be no higher than twelve inches, that is quite an accomplishment and is an indication of the network of transportation routes providing access to Jackson.

In the early days of Jackson's existence, most businesses existed to serve the needs of area residents who, for the most part, were farmers and relatively self-sufficient. Goodspeed (1888) notes a number of early Jackson merchants, such as a Virginian named Eckhardt who opened the first store but who quickly sold it to Clifton and Charles Mothershead whose business also lasted only a short time. Samuel Cupples was also one of the first merchants. Others included Joseph Frizel, a son-in-law of George F. Bollinger; Armor and Juden; George Scripps; Nathan Vanhorn; and Dr. Thomas Neale. William McGuire operated a tannery on the edge of town and Caleb Fylenwider had a "stillhouse" just west of town. The first persons licensed to keep "houses of entertainment," i.e., taverns or inns, were James Edwards, Thomas Stewart, William Shepard, and John Armstrong. Of the later tavern keepers, Samuel Lockhart was said to have had the principal tavern in Jackson.

John Delap had a shop where he made bells for cattle, hogs and sheep, which Goodspeed reports as being "much in demand." Considering the effort needed to clear land for crops, farmers let most of their livestock run free and the bells, no doubt, allowed them to find their livestock. Of the earliest physicians, including Dr. Zenas Priest and Dr. Thomas Neale (also a merchant), only Dr. Franklin Cannon remained as a permanent resident. Goodspeed also notes Jackson has a saddle maker, Louis Painter; blacksmiths, John Glasscock and Samuel Mitchell; hatter, Edward Criddle; cabinet maker, William Surrell; and carpenter, Scarlet Glasscock. Among lawyers settling in Jackson were Johnson Ranney and Nathaniel Watkins,

View from the southeast corner of the Courthouse roof, 2002. Left to right: Corner of the County Administration Building on Barton Square, "new" Post Office and the Milde Building on Hope Street (Highway 61), and the "old" Post Office building on Main Street which now houses the Jackson Chamber of Commerce and several businesses. Behind the Milde Building is the Oliver house and the steeple of the Evangelical United Church of Christ on Adams Street.

C. H. Wolter Buggy and Harness Shop on the corner and the J. G. Heinberg clothing store on the left. Mr. Wolter's store is the Goose Creek Trading Post in 2002.

View of Highway 61 looking west toward Jackson, 2002.

a half-brother to Henry Clay (1888, pp. 397, 426-428).

Due to its rapid growth, in 1818 Jackson was selected as the site for the third federal land sales office located in the Missouri Territory (Meyer, 1973, p. 238). In 1841 the third branch of the State Bank was located in Jackson. In 1844 it reported a capital of $120,000 and a circulation of $93,660 under the management of A .H. Brevard, president, and Thomas English, cashier. In 1853 it was moved to Cape Girardeau (Goodspeed, 1888, p. 428). By 1819 Jackson had a newspaper, the *Missouri Herald*, published by T. E. Strange. James Russell purchased the press and changed the name to the *Independent Patriot* (Goodspeed, 1888, p. 429).

Growth of the community seems to have slowed almost to a standstill from the 1830's until after the Civil War. Goodspeed reports that "At the close of the war Jackson, in population and commercial importance, stood about where it had thirty years before..." (Goodspeed, 1888, p. 428).

In the 1870's and 1880's two developments improved the business climate of Jackson. The Jackson branch of the St. Louis, Iron Mountain and Southern Railroad line was completed, and the forerunner of the Cape County Milling Company was founded by A.R. Byrd and J.A. Horrell. According to Goodspeed, by the 1880's Jackson had two large flour mills, one producing 300-400 barrels per day and employing about 75 men (1888, p. 429). The railroad line was important to the development of the milling industry. Instead of grinding grain for local use only, flour could easily be shipped throughout the United States, particularly needed in the rapidly growing cities on the eastern seaboard, and overseas. The mills continued to operate until the late 1940s when milling operations were suspended. For a time the business operated as a grain warehouse. The Jackson property was sold in 1953 and Mill B was demolished in 1965. Most of Mill A now houses an antique's shop.

In 1905 Louis Houck completed the basic lines of the Cape Girardeau and Northern Railroad. The line reached Jackson in November 1904. This railroad extended from the Thebes Railroad Bridge through Cape Girardeau, Jackson, Oak Ridge, and Perryville to a connection with the Frisco lines into Chester, Illinois. A spur was built into Farmington in 1912. According to Snider and Collins (1956), most of the line was abandoned during World War I with the Jackson to Cape Girardeau Route the last portion to cease operations.

Cape County Savings Bank on the corner of High and Main Streets, circa 1904.

Just as the railroad extended the industrial markets, the introduction of telephones expanded the communication network. During the 1870s Bernard Ferguson engineered and installed the first telephone in Cape Girardeau County, which connected his home at 224 East Adams to his father's business in uptown Jackson. In 1877 the line was extended to Cape Girardeau and became the first long distance telephone line in Missouri. The Acme Telephone Company, a city-owned company, operated the first commercial telephone service in Jackson from 1897 to 1906. In 1906, the lines were acquired by the Cape Girardeau Bell Telephone Company, providing free service between Cape Girardeau and Jackson. The first telephone was located in the A. C. Schmuke Store (*Southeast Missourian*, July 4, 1976, p. 2D).

The 1850s and 1860s saw a need for improved transportation within the area. One solution to the road-building dilemma was the creation of joint stock companies that were allowed to charge tolls for use of the sections of roads they constructed and improved. The toll road passing through Jackson was the Cape Girardeau Macadamize and Plank Road, constructed in 1853, which extended from the city limits of Cape Girardeau to Bollinger's Mill in Burfordville. There were three tollgate houses located in Jackson. The first, constructed in 1853, was the Cape-Jackson Road Tollgate House, Bainbridge and Highway 61 intersection; the second, constructed in 1861, was the Jackson-Burfordville Road Tollgate House located at Highway 72 and West Main; and the third, constructed in 1890, was the Cape Jackson Road Tollgate House still standing at 816 Old Cape Road, possibly a replacement for the earlier Bainbridge location. According to Morton and Cochran (1976), the last tollgate was taken down in 1908.

The real push for road building and improvement came with the automobile. Missouri's Centennial Road Law, passed by the Legislature in 1921, authorized the Highway Commission to designate as "higher type than clay bound gravel about 1500 miles of roads connecting the principal population centers of the state." (Missouri State Highway Commission, 1969, p. 54). It also provided that a third of a $60,000,000 "Get Missouri Out of the Mud" bond issue and $6,000 per mile from the other two-thirds be devoted to building these hard surface roads. The remainder of the bond issue money was to be used to improve local dirt or gravel farm-to-market roads and to create two state maintained highways in each county (Missouri State Highway Commission, 1969, pp. 75-78). Jackson, by virtue of its position as county seat and its location on existing roads, was a beneficiary of this road building effort. Highway 25 crossed the county north and south through Jackson. Route 9, later to become U.S. 61 (now route 72), entered the northwest portion of the county, passed through Jackson to Cape Girardeau and thus on to the south. By 1925, Jackson was connected to St. Louis by an all-paved road, most of it concrete. Completion of the Mississippi River traffic bridge in Cape Girardeau in 1928 was also of benefit to Jackson (Snider and Collins, 1956). The Federal Highway Act of 1954, which created the Interstate Highway system and brought Interstate Highway 55 within a few miles of the Jackson city limits, has also proven to be beneficial to the growth of the city. It has allowed businesses and industries to transport raw materials and finished products with ease and at less expense to the consumer. Access to I-55 has brought several industries to Jackson since completion of the final link in 1971. Penzel Construction Company was responsible for construction of bridges for this crucial transportation link.

The dilemma for city planners has been how to find ways to move traffic around and within the city. Peak traffic hours bring lines of cars waiting for their turn at four way stops (particularly the intersection of Main and Hope Streets). The addition of electronic traffic signals on Highways 72, 25, and 61 have helped somewhat, but the volume of traffic within Jackson and passing through Jackson on the way to and from Cape Girardeau has brought representatives of Jackson, Cape Girardeau, the Cape Girardeau County Commission, and the Missouri Department of Transportation together to look for solutions. Among the proposals is an additional interchange on I-55. The City of Jackson has completed one extension of East Main Street, with a second phase to be linked to the new interchange. The City of Cape Girardeau is planning for utilization of the interchange as well. The Missouri Department of Transportation has approved construction of the interchange and has placed it on their construction schedule with an anticipated completion date of 2007 (*Southeast Missourian*, Progress Edition, February 24, 2002, p. 1). More problematic are proposals to divert traffic from West Jackson Boulevard (Highway 72) to lessen east-west congestion. The willingness of the cities of Jackson and Cape Girardeau, the Cape Girardeau County Commission, and various state agencies to work together to solve problems such as traffic concerns has been a welcome change from earlier contentious encounters over location of the County Seat or the location of the County Jail (*The Cash-Book Journal*, February 20, 2002, p. 1).

Annexation in the 1980's brought the Jackson city limits to the west lanes of I-55. The widening of Highway 61 from Jackson to Cape Girardeau was completed in the early 1990s. That upgraded thoroughfare (officially named Jackson Boulevard) has become a magnet for high traffic businesses, such as the Wal-Mart Supercenter. As these businesses have changed the shopping patterns of area residents, the "uptown" business district has also changed. While some long-time Jackson businesses, such as the Jones Drug Store, remain, others have joined the move to Jackson Boulevard. The long-time business district has become home to new restaurants and a variety of other locally owned businesses, as well as to county and city offices housed in what were formerly retail business spaces. —amd

Augusta and Jenny Horn, operators for the Acme Telephone Company on South High Street, circa 1918.

Heavy traffic at the intersections of Highways 34, 61, 25, and 72, March 2002.

Area Communities

History of Arnsberg and the St. John Evangelical Lutheran Church

The Evangelical Lutheran St. John Church of Arnsberg has been inactive since about 1890. Only the cemetery remains today and is located over one mile wet of the I-55 exit on Route KK. The cemetery has been restored and a perpetual care fund is being established.

The first information we could find about the church is a deed on file in the Cape Girardeau County Recorder's office. The deed is dated July 22, 1856. According to the deed, Charles Hermann and Louise, his wife, and Henry Pohlmann and Caroline, his wife, sold land to the church. Trustees of the church at that time were: Charles Hermann, Christian Tuschhoff, Henry Pohlmann, and Henry Richter.

At the time the church was built the area was not much more than a clearing. It had been inhabited earlier by the various Indian tribes of the area.

On February 3, 1864, George and Lizette Engelmann sold 110 acres of land to Adolph Tacke. This land bordered the church land and sold for $490. On April 27, 1866, a second deed was made with the Evangelical Lutheran Church. This deed was between Adolph and Lizette Tacke and the trustees of the church who were: Christian Tuschhoff, John Kiepe, and Jacob Klempe.

About twenty-six years after the church was organized, Adolph Tacke built a town nearby. Mr. Tacke was born in Arnsberg, Germany, on April 21, 1833. He served three years in the Prussian Army and in 1857 immigrated to the United States, landing in Philadelphia. In 1859 Mr. Tacke settled in Bollinger County where he built a flour mill. That same year he moved to Cape Girardeau County.

In 1861 he enlisted in the Federal Army of the Civil War. He remained a private in the army for six months with the Fourth Missouri Infantry. He re-enlisted as a first lieutenant and was discharged as a captain in February 1865. He returned to Arnsberg where he built a sawmill in 1882, a flour mill, and a mercantile store. A post office was located within the store. By 1884, there also was a blacksmith shop, a saloon, and an octagon-shaped dance hall.

Mr. Tacke first married Lizette Zoellner, daughter of Ferdinand and Nettie Dolle Zoellner. After her death he married Nancy Caroline Milster. He was the father of four children: William Tacke, Mrs. Mathilde Holmes, Mrs. C. T. Maintz, and Franklin J. Tacke, who married Carrie Long.

Adolph Tacke had a store at Muehleim, Perry County, Missouri, with Ferdinand Zoellner. There are also remembrances of a store just east of Arnsberg on the John Franklin Tuschhoff farm. A store ledger book for Tacke's store in Arnsberg dates from 1867.

Adolph Tacke, founder and owner of the town of Arnsberg, died June 1, 1909. He is buried in the cemetery at Arnsberg. Other family names found buried in the cemetery are: Bailey, Best, Bingenheimer, Dambach, Dickmann, Fiesler, Fulbright, Hoffman, Jaeger, Kaiser, Kayser, Kiepe, Klaus, Kroman, Lowes, Milster, Neislein, Powell, Puntmann, Reinemer, Rhyne, Richter, Rose, Ruppel, Sauer, Schmidt, Schwerdtfeger, Struwe, Thomure, Tuschhoff, Underwood, Wilke, Young, Zimmerman, and Zoellner.

By Mary Daume

The Community of Brookside

Before we had the farm tractor and automobile, a blacksmith shop took the place of our modern machine shop and garage. Located along the south side of Byrd Creek on County Road 439, stood the combination Rapp Store and Wolfenkoehler Blacksmith Shop.

Wilhelm Wolkenkoehler and son Henry, both natives of the Kingdom of Hanover, Germany, and Paul Rapp and son Joseph Rapp were the owners of the shop and store respectively. Joseph Rapp, a Justice of the Peace, was the son-in-law of Wilhelm Wolfenkoehler.

Once a week the owners would hitch a two-horse team to a wagon and go to Jackson for supplies. These supplies consisted of harness, horse shoes, clothing, groceries, medicine,

Arnsberg Cemetery, established 1856.

This small community was referred to as Brookside or Wolfenkoehler Shop Community.

school supplies, and anything sold at a general store or used in the blacksmith shop of that day.

For many years the area was referred to as Wolfenkoehlers Shop, St. John's Church, or Schoenebeck School Community. One day Will Willmann, nephew of William and Mary Kiepe Hoffmann, stopped by and noticed the nearby Byrd Creek and called the place Brookside.

In 1915, apparently sparks from the shop caused the shop and store to burn. Henry Wolfenkoehler rebuilt a shop on that spot and Joe Rapp built a large general store across the road on the west.

In about 1930 Rapp sold the store to a Mr. Zimmith, son-in-law of Theodore Kasten of Pocahontas. Zimmith owned the store a short time before he sold to Adolph and Willie Wilhelm, local farmers. The Wilhelm brothers rented the store to a Mr. Afholter of St. Louis. By this time roads and automobiles were causing business in small towns to be unprofitable.

In the 1930s the Wilhelms were using the store building to store grain. At about that time Albert Wolfenkoehler, son of Henry Wolfenkoehler, took over the blacksmith business along with tending the farm. He kept the shop going for several years until lack of business caused him to close.

The Brookside 4-H Club was organized and flourished from about 1950-1975. They had their meeting place at the St. John's UCC nearby.

The store has been gone for several yars but the shop still stands as a storage shed. The Wolfenkoehler house is still occupied but the Rapp home now stands vacant as a reminder of bygone days.

By Mary Daume

Burfordville and the Bollinger Grist Mill

Major George Frederick Bollinger built his first mill on the Whitewater River in 1800 on a 640-arpent grant from Louis Lorimier, Spanish Commandant of Cape Girardeau District of Upper Louisiana. A German Swiss from North Carolina, Bollinger visited the area in 1796, and returned with twenty families. The families included those of his Bollinger's brothers Matthias, John, Henry, William, Daniel, and Phillip. Other families were those of Peter and Conrad Statler, Joseph Neiswanger, George and Peter Grout, Peter Crytes, John and Jacob Cotner, John and Isaac Miller, Frederick Limbaugh, Leonard Welker, and Frederick Slinkard. Each family received over 400 acres of land in exchange for surveying fees and improvements. (Neumeyer, Jackson Journal, March 19, 1975, p. 11)

Three mills have been built upon the site. In 1825 Bollinger replaced the frame mill with a "more substantial structure" with a limestone foundation and a wooden upper story. His mill became the largest and best in the district. Sarah Daugherty, Bollinger's daughter, inherited the mill upon his death in 1842. During the Civil War, Union troops declared Sarah and her sons Confederate sympathizers and burned the mill.

In 1866 Solomon Richard Burford purchased the mill and surrounding land. He built the mill that stands to this day: three stories of brick placed upon the existing limestone foundation. In 1870 the post office designated the name of Burfordville for the settlement surrounding the mill. Burford was responsible for having the area surveyed to establish an orderly community with lots and streets. Burfordville was incorporated in 1899, almost a century after its settlement.

Ownership of the mill changed hands several times and in 1897 it became part of the Cape County Milling Company. The mill at Burfordville continued its commercial operation until the mid 1940s. In 1953 Clyde Vandivort, a local farmer and descendant of George Bollinger, purchased the abandoned building for storage. The family later donated the mill to the Cape Girardeau County Historical Society. In 1961 the society celebrated the history of the location with a Burfordville Covered Bridge and Mill Marker Dedication. In 1967 the society handed over the property to the Missouri State Park Board, which today is under the auspices of the Missouri Department of Natural Resources.

The covered bridge by the mill is 140 feet long, with a clearance of 14 feet and is 12 feet wide. It is considered the bridge was begun before the Civil War but not completed until 1867. Joseph Lansmon, whose initials are carved over the east entry of the bridge, is cred-

Dedication ceremony at Burfordville, Missouri, of the Bollinger Mill and the Covered Bridge on July 23, 1961.

Bollinger Mill, Burfordville, Missouri, circa 1908. Photo by Frank Medley.

ited with constructing the bridge. Time, automobiles, and floods took their toll on the old bridge, forcing the park to close it even to foot traffic. In 1998 the park began the process of a comprehensive renovation complete with replacement of many of the timbers.

Both the mill and the covered bridge are listed on the National Register of Historic Places. Jack Smoot, Historic Site Administrator for the park, explained that Bollinger Mill has something to offer every visitor, "Technology buffs can admire the intricate machinery and see some of it demonstrated. Historians can study nearly a century of regional history while outdoor lovers can relax and enjoy this rare, rural combination of gristmill and covered bridge in its original, scenic setting." (Smoot, Missouri Resources, undated, pp. 20-22) —cms

Recollections of Burfordville of the 1930s

Let me take you back in time; the year was 1933 and I [Edna J. (Kasting) Ford] was 20. I worked in Burfordville for Marzilla Dockins. One son, 'PAL'mer, and wife Phyllis lived nearby with their two children, Ruth and Bruce. Another son, Francis, was ill with tuberculosis and I was their housekeeper and cook. I became acquainted with most of their neighbors.

Tom and Dorrie Summers operated a grocery store/gas pump, with living quarters within. Several of us would gather there in the evenings to sing and play music. It was cheap entertainment and we had lots of fun? 'Old Tom,' we called him, played the fiddle; Earl Proctor played the fiddle and guitar; and I also played guitar. Dayton Phelps, Earl Smith, Francis Dockins, Ruth Hardy, Charles Hillier and wife, and Dottie Kinder and others would join in the fun.

Mr. and Mrs. Wilson operated a dry goods store/Post Office. The Wilson's young son, W.G. was ten. It later became the Community Building, but is now an antique/collectible shop called 'A River Runs Thru It' operated by John and Kathy Trimble, who live in the house next to it. I suppose they named it due to the frequent floods they must endure from the nearby Whitewater River. After I left the community, the Dockins' house was moved off their property. A new house was built in its place by 'PAL'mer and Phyllis Dockins, I assume. Also erected next door was a grocery store/Post Office.

Chester and Jettie Phelps lived next door to Marzilla with their three children, Virginia, Geneva Lincoln, and Carlin Phelps. Mr. and Mrs. Ben Phelps and children Okle and Dayton lived next door to them. When Earl Smith's parents passed away, he demolished the old house, building a new one in the late 1930s. He also bought the home of school teacher Cora Carvey. Around this time, the Baptist Church burned down. Now the Millersville Fire Station #3 is on this property. Earl and Elaine Smith donated ground where the new church was erected.

John and Alva Acup had a couple of children. John was night watchman at the Bollinger Grist Mill.

Earl and Lillian Proctor had a son, Billy. Earl worked for the County Roads. Mr. and Mrs. Charles Hillier lived down near the river. Next to them lived Mr. and Mrs. Holmes and a daughter who later married Roy Cunningham from the neighborhood. Mr. Holmes worked as a blacksmith with Tom Allen. Their shop was across the street from Tom Summers' grocery. Next door to Summers' (previously the old Fulenwider home) lived Troy and Dottie Kinder and children Elizabeth and Troy, Jr. Troy was a mail carrier. Then there was Willie and Lena Peters' farm (previously the old Bowman home, now the Bangers.)

The schoolhouse burned down and was replaced with one erected in the 1950s. The Hahns lived next door and they sold eggs (now possibly a bed and breakfast.) Hattie Kinder and brother Earl had a farm near Burfordville. As you well know, Burfordville is home to Bollinger Grist Mill and covered bridge and park with the Whitewater River 'running thru it' (literally)! It was always a great place to swing from a rope in the tree, jumping into the water to cool off on a hot summer day (now is the rope still there?)! This little wide space in the road is but a little wider, being a draw to many visitors today as it was back then. Most of these older people are now deceased. Lastly, as you continue through the park, you may walk up a steep hill to the old McGuire cemetery.

By Edna J. (Kasting) Ford

Daisy, Missouri

Drum Town, the place where William Drum, a German emigrant from North Carolina, built his house and store, was located on one of the highest hills in northwest Cape Girardeau County. Drum Town no longer exists, but it is the location of Daisy today.

The first area store, established prior to the Civil War by Andrew H. Kinder and a Mr. Crites, was located east of Drum Town. When the partnership dissolved, Mr. Kinder built a new store closer to town in 1857. After the war, Mr. Kinder closed his store and sold his merchandise to William Drum. One of the next businesses to appear was John Thomas' blacksmith shop.

The exact establishment date for the church is not know, but the Methodist Episcopal South Church (New Salem Methodist Church) purchased 3.94 acres of land from the School District No. D., Township No. 4, range 11 East, on March 22, 1873, for $100. Trustees at that time were Calvin Drum, Marion Drum, and Francis Drum.

Around 1886, Chapman G. and Oliver B. Kinder opened a new general mercantile store in Drum Town. Because of community growth, the residents saw the need for regular postal service and petitioned for a post office. Chapman Kinder, along with Dr. S. S. Harris, circulated a petition suggesting that the new name should be Daisy, the name of the last baby delivered by Dr. Harris. Grass roots efforts worked; Daisy became the name. William W. Drum became the first postmaster in 1887, followed by Oliver B. Kinder in 1889.

Mr. E. W. Harris established Harris General Merchandise, became the postmaster in 1901, and operated a wheat elevator south of his store for the Cape County Milling Company. In 1905 William Ates, who had purchased William Drum's house and store, sold his store's merchandise to C. F. Hahs. Mr. Hahs, along with J. C. Stearns, established Hahs and Stearns General Merchandise. J. Otto Hahs designed and built steam engines for threshing machines in his machine shop. The Houck Cape Girardeau Northern Line came into town. Marshall L. Morton, appointed postmaster in 1895 and operator of the Hotel Morton, became the first agent at the Houck Depot.

From 1905 to 1918, the rail station became a shipping point for livestock, poultry and fruit that was being shipped for distribution in St. Louis or New Orleans. Because of efforts from livestock buyers, T. B. Crites, Bob Hahs, and Bob and Pink Wills, it was not unusual for up to 300 livestock cars to leave this station yearly. After the Houck lines went into bankruptcy, a "bus wagon" used the tracks until 1925. By 1930 the tracks had been removed.

In 1914 the elected officials of Daisy were: Henry W. Hahs, Mayor; David Seabaugh, Marshal, and B. F. Seabaugh, Secretary. If the Marshal were not around when needed, Squire Henry W. Hahs would place offenders in the one-room calaboose. It was also at this time that Christian Frederick Hahs became the postmaster.

A frame bank was built in 1914 on the south side of the square. The second bank building, a brick building, was built in 1917-18 on the west side of the square. The bank dissolved in 1923.

1918 also saw the building of a brick school. It was built to replace a frame school building that burned. After school reorganization in 1956, the school became home to the Daisy Homemakers and the 4-H club. Today it, along with a metal building, has become home to the Cape County Coon Hunters and the 4-H club.

Other businesses established in the first quarter of the 20th century were: Friese Millinery Shop, Edgar Klaus Store, later owned and operated by Darwin Morton and his father; Otis Wills Garage; and Leine (Alvin) and Diefenbach (Ernest) blacksmith, car repair, lumber planing, wood and iron repair, and horse shoeing shop. The Modern Woodmen of America met in the upstairs room of the frame bank building, known as the "Woodman Hall." The Royal Neighbors held their meetings in member's homes.

Once a year there was a picnic held in the community. First it was in a wooded area on the Johnny Drum property; later it was moved to the big hill and became the "Picnic on the Big Hill." Feature of the picnic were the black powder shoots and square dancing. Elmer Kinder called the square dances at the picnic as well as in homes and at the Woodman Hall.

After 1925 Tony Thiele operated a restaurant, store, cream-buying station, and barbershop; C. J. McCauley ran a trucking business that took livestock to St. Louis and brought back merchandise for the stores; and Alvin Leine and Herman Brune operated blacksmith shops facing each other.

Medicine shows added excitement to this farming community. The shows, held on the south side of the square and later between the Sebaugh and Hahs stores, featured flickering films and dancing girls. Who could resist buying a bag of candy to maybe win a lucky token? Of course, liniment and tonic to cure anything and everything was sold.

By 1936, Walter (Bill) Leine bought the garage and renamed it Daisy auto Shop. After his death in 1958, his brother, Eugene, bought the business and operated it under the name of Gene's Garage. The garage became the meeting place for Republican and Democratic Rallies.

Delos Sebaugh bought the brick bank building from Iva D. Hahs. It was from here that he operated an insurance agency (until 1973), and, after buying Mr. Thiele's merchandise in 1939, opened a store and cream-buying station that operated until 1956. In 1946 he added on to the building and converted the bank portion into a residence.

In 1946 Gifford S. Hahs bought out his father, C. F. Hahs, and operated the G. S. Hahs General Store and post office until his death in 1970. His wife, Veda, operated the store until 1971 when the store permanently closed, leaving Daisy with no store for the first time in over 100 years. Also with Mr. Hahs' death came the end of "playing music at Hahs' store" and the Thursday nights' "Egg-buying."

Delmar Crites constructed, on the depot site, a restaurant and pool hall in the late 1940s. He also held shooting matches. In the mid-1900s, Martin and Paul Kaiser had a feed store and trucking line there. The building was sold in the late 1950s to Freeman Siebert who converted the building into a residence and used part of it for a feed store and pool room.

Homes and businesses glowed when electricity finally reached the area at the end of 1950. The first dial phones were installed in 1956. Blacktopped Route B finally replaced a dusty gravel farm-to-market road in the mid 1950s.

In about 1952, Mr. and Mrs. Bill Leine purchased Erby Stearns' restaurant. Their restaurant, Bill's Place, was located in the Woodman Hall and operated for seven years.

In 1970 the post office moved to Gene's Garage with Doyle Leine being the officer in charge; he became postmaster in 1974. Other postmasters have been Margie Leine, 1979, and Janette Hobeck, 1996.

Today, Daisy's businesses have dried up—only the post office remains on the square. Robbie Pennebaker has a body repair shop. But the name of Daisy is kept before the public as Dodie Eisenhauer's Village Designs originals are shipped all over the country.

By JoAnn Hahs

Aerial view of Daisy, Missouri, 1949.

Fruitland, Missouri

"Fruitland" was originally named "Pleasant Hill." A rural village, it was plotted for development by Elam S. Templeton in the 1860s. The name was later changed by Professor J. H. Kerr, who had been called to organize and teach at the first normal school in Cape Girardeau County, the Fruitland Normal Institute. It was housed in the Pleasant Hill Academy Building located on top of the hill east of what is now Highway 61 on a street named "Corns Lane." Mr. Kerr renamed the village because there was another thriving town southwest of Kansas City by that name and his mail was often directed to that place. His neighbors and friends commended the name because of its strength and appropriateness. Mr. J. C. Wallace had successful fruit orchards in the area.

The building had formerly housed a church, built in 1840-41, first named South Apple Creek then changed to Pleasant Hill." In 1854 it was used for a school building. During the Civil War the building was used to house soldiers. It was after the Civil War that Mr. Kerr answered the State Teachers Association's call to establish schools of higher learning.

The Pleasant Hill church now standing at the end of County Road 541 is the third building, built in 1892. It was formerly a Presbyterian church but is not owned and maintained by the Pleasant Hill Cemetery Association. The congregation of the church began as a splinter group from the Apple Creek Presbyterian Church near Pocahontas at the north end of what is now Country Road 541. The Apple Creek hierarchy wanted to modernize its theology. They referred to the move as the "new school." The "new school" proponents stayed at Apple Creek and the opponents moved to Fruitland and started Pleasant Hill. Later in 1891, a group seceded from Pleasant Hill to form the Fruitland Methodist Church because of a disagreement over which literature to use in Sunday School. That building was built on the west side of what is now Highway 61 across the highway from the Cornus Lane entrance. The Methodist building burned in 1975. The new building now houses the Covenant Christian Center. A new church, the Fruitland Community Church, a project of Lynwood Baptist church in Cape Girardeau, was built in 2001.

As you can tell by the map drawn in 1910, Fruitland was once a thriving metropolis. Mrs. Louis Pender Dunn recalls there was a millinery store, a flour mill, and Lodge Hall owned by the Grange which later was a two-year public high school. There were two barber shops, a fee store, two restaurants, and a cannery where vegetables were canned in tin cans. Dr. Hall was the area doctor. The building which housed his office was just recently demolished. The railroad running through Fruitland was what developed it in the early days.

Later, Highway 61 (formerly Highway 25) was what kept it thriving. There was a lot of truck traffic. The Owl Shanty Truck Stop was a dominant name in the area for many years. It was open 24 hours a day, seven days a week, and employed many area residents. Their food was legendary. Mrs. Audrey (Tic) Jenkins, who recently passed away, and her husband ran it for its duration. Originally, they owned it jointly with another couple, but the last several years they owned and operated it on their own. Interstate 55 bypassing Fruitland closed the Owl Shanty and made Fruitland a much quieter community. The post office was formerly housed in the Fruitland Mercantile Store and later moved across the street as a single small building when the State Highway Department decided to enlarge the now 'FF' intersection and take their property. The mercantile store had been run by the Winters family. In later years, Amanda Winters Anderson and her husband Lowry "Caney" operated it. When Amanda retired as postmistress the post office was closed.

But, the building of Procter & Gamble in 1969 revived Fruitland. As the large company started hiring from all across the southern end of the state and Illinois, employees started looking for places to live closer to their work. Construction went wild. The plant manager started petitioning the State Highway Department to improve the narrow blacktop road from Fruitland to Neely's Landing where the plant was built. Their truck traffic was very heavy. The safety factor of employees who worked swing shifts going and coming at all hours and the truck traffic meeting on the curves and hills of Route 177 (previous 'J') was a serious concern. It took seven years, but in 1976 their construction resulted in what is now a wide two-lane span of concrete, flat, with very few curves. Just recently they have added left turn lanes where county roads intersect, making it safer still.

As building progressed and the population of Fruitland grew, so did commercialism. Fruitland is well on its way to being a metropolis again in 2002.

By Ruth Tinnin

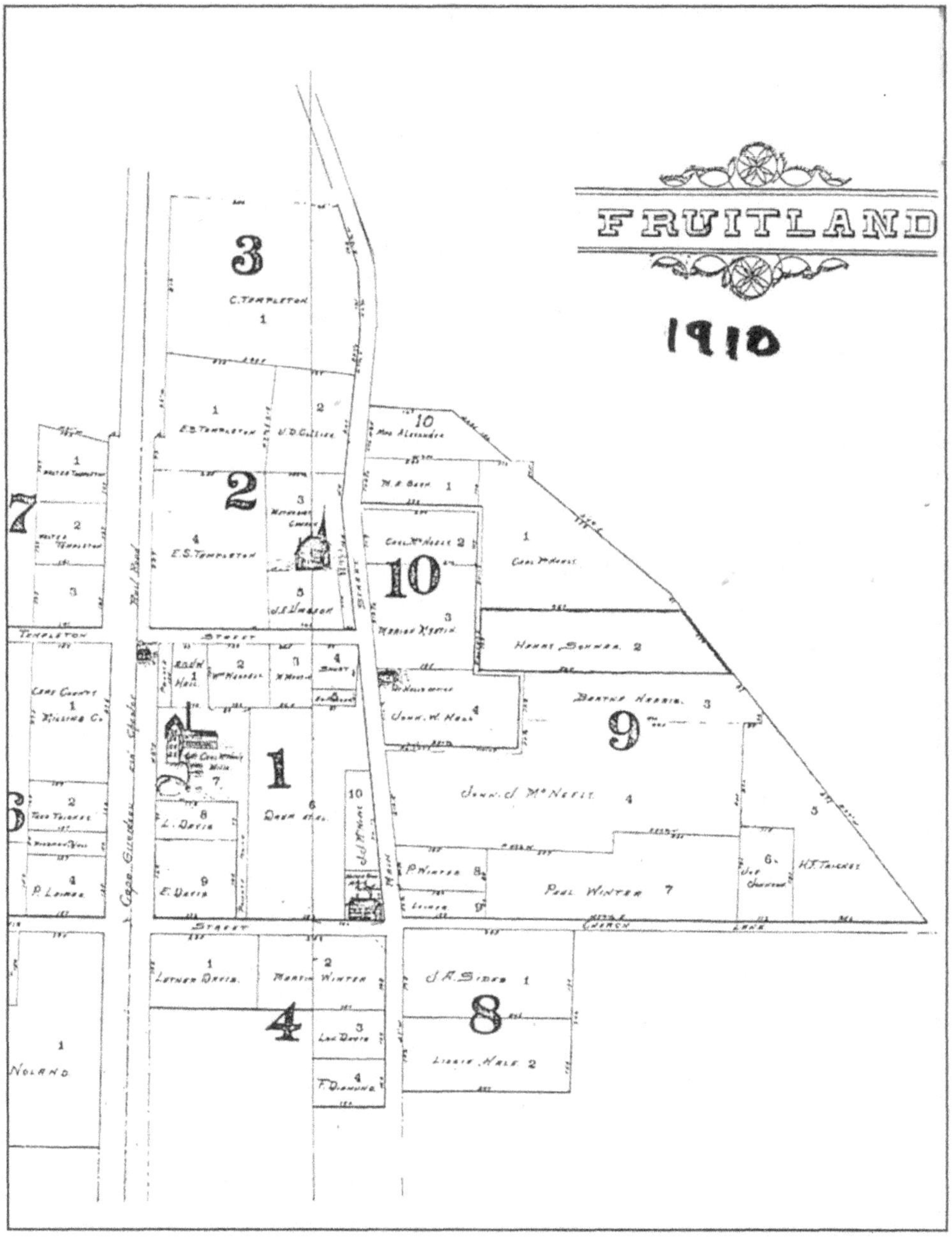

After trains ceased to run on the line through Fruitland, Missouri, a highway bus, converted to travel on the tracks, picked up passengers in front of the depot.

The Town of Gordonville, Missouri

The beginnings of Gordonville are the same as many other towns across the continent. In 1797 the Spanish owned the Louisiana Territory and a man named Ithamar Hubbell settled in the territory on a creek that would one day be known as Hubble Creek. Hubbell established a mill, one of the first in the area, which served as a center for commerce. In the early 1800s several hundred acres were confirmed to John Strong under Ithamar Hubbell and in 1811 Strong sold the property to Louis Lorimier, "founder of Cape Girardeau." The land changed hands several times until 1837 when Baker Gordon purchased the land. He and his son, Samuel, ran the mill for ten years after which Baker Gordon sold the property to Samuel and a relative, Irvin Anderson. The elder Gordon returned to Indiana. In 1857 Samuel Gordon built the first store and the area became known as "Gordonville."

Emigrants from northern Germany and Switzerland settled in the area around 1836 and the population of the area began to grow. The store and mill were the foundation to draw in businesses, a post office was established, and the Jackson Branch Railroad Company built tracks connecting Gordonville to the Iron Mountain Railroad at Allenville. In the late 1800s there was a boom in the community. In 1876 William Winkler purchased the mill, which continued to thrive, shipping flour as far away as Georgia and Texas. The mill also produced cattle feed and bricks were made on the property. The mill had a sawmill and a cooperage plant that produced barrels for the mill's flour. The community added a general store operated by Ahrens (Henry P.) and Volkerding, a livery stable, and a creamery. Henry Kerstner and his sons had a furniture store, where they made furniture and caskets.

In 1904 businessmen of the community organized the Bank of Gordonville with M. H. Lupkes serving as president; J.H. Keller as vice-president; W. O. Medley as cashier; and Henry Kerstner and William Winkler as directors, with Alvin Penzel replacing Mr. Medley in the first year. The town added businesses such as the H. W. Bangert store where clothing and hats were made and the ice cream parlor operated by Jacob Schwab. Around 1910 the mill set up a small electric light plant and the town of Gordonville could boast having electricity long before much of the surrounding area. The Gordonville Telephone Company was established about this time. The town had a physician, a hotel, a saloon and a jail. It is told locally that when the saloon was shut down and liquor was no longer sold in town there was no further need for the jail. The community had a school as well as churches. The first churches established in the area were the German Methodist west of town and the Lutherans south of town. Both of these congregations had German and English speaking services for a number of years. In 1898 some members of the Lutheran church decided that there should be a church in town and started Christ Lutheran Church, which held only English speaking services from the beginning.

The town has seen rapid changes since the advent of World War II. In 1941 the Gordonville Light Company was sold to the Missouri Utilities Company. The two-room school had housed eight elementary grades in one room and a two-year high school in the other room until 1945 when the high school was discontinued. In 1948 many of these small schools began to consolidate and this continued until 1954 when the final reorganization became known as the Jackson R-2 school system. A new school building was built in 1956; it is currently known as the Gordonville Attendance Center. The school has three classrooms and houses local children in grades 1 through 3. The Gordonville Telephone Company sold its lines to Southwestern Bell Telephone Company in 1951. Dial telephones were installed and most people were on party lines with several other households. During this time electricity became readily available to the surrounding farm communities, roads were improved, and cars became more affordable. The businesses in Gordonville began to dwindle and by the 1960s there were not many left in town. The Gordonville Mercantile Store, started by Henry Ahrens, had passed to this grandson, Henry Macke; and his great-grandson, Albert Macke, and was now known as Macke's Store. Albert's widow, Dorothy Macke, and her son, H. Weldon Macke, ran the store until the 1970s. The Bangert store was sold to Norman Eggiman, who in turn sold it to George and Louise Hilpert. The blacksmith shop had become a machine shop operated by John Gast, and Delmar Eggiman had established a garage. The Bank of Gordonville would eventually move to Cape Girardeau in 1961 and become Cape State Bank. After several mergers this bank now exists as US Bank Corp. Several members from the Gordonville community have served on the board until as late as 2001. The post office would remain for several more years and is now located in the most recently annexed piece of property located on Highway 25.

In the 1970s the town would form a Water District, Cape County District #5, and a Fire Department. The city limits remained the same for many years, but were finally extended to the Highway 25 and Route Z intersection. There are still several businesses in Gordonville, but they are mostly housed on or near Highway 25. Some of these businesses include the Gordonville Mutual Insurance Company, Peters Heating and air Conditioning Inc., MacCon Company, SEMO Mustang, Circle S Saddle Company, Gordonville Food and Fuel, and Sparkman Auto Sales. Superior Advertising and Marketing, Inc. is located in the old Macke's Store building in what used to be "downtown Gordonville." The town has increased in population, but it is now primarily a bedroom community with many of the occupants working in Cape Girardeau and Jackson.

By Pam (Macke) Johnson

Millersville, Missouri

The village of Millersville was named after John Miller who settled with his family in the area around 1803. In the early days the name for the town was 'Toad Suck.' The first store was built by John J. and William Miller, grandsons of the original settlers, around 1840 or 1850. In 1860 John J. decided to develop a town around his store and George W. Snider, the County Surveyor, did the survey and the plat of the village. The development of Millersville was delayed until after the Civil War.

In 1865 Wash and Jess Miller, brothers of John J., began a steam-operated mill next to the Whitewater River near the present highway bridge. The first store begun by the Miller brothers became known as Miller & Waller store. Over the years there were many owners of like stores including George H. Miller, Ernest Rieman, Henry Winters, Ernest Miller, E. L. Dockins, and A. A. Townsend. In 1877 John F. Miller opened a store which sold patent medicine, soft drinks, and a few groceries. He also ran a short order restaurant and sold brooms and hats.

The Propst hotel building was constructed in 1874. It was frequented by salesmen (drummers) coming to Millersville. Most of them were clothing and dry goods salesmen who carried large trunks full of samples with them. They would stay two or three days at a time.

The old Gordonville Milling Company, circa 1910.

Mrs. J. W. Propst owned the hotel for more than sixty years.

The first doctors in Millersville were W. C. and J. R. Talley. Other doctors were Drs. Hubbard, Roberts, Crafford, J. A. Horn, Jeff Mayfield and Dayton Seabaugh.

Wesley Miller, older brother of George W. Miller, taught the Millersville School around 1866 or 1867. The next teachers of any record were Joe and Henry Coker. John Calhoun Snider was the Millersville teacher in 1875. The curriculum of the first school was simple. There were no grades and everyone studied the old blue-black spelling book and McGuffey's reader. In those days, school days were about ten hours long. School ran from November 1 until April. The second school was built in 1882. George W. Miller and Wm. Jefferson Miller each gave an acre of ground to construct the building. In 1882 it became a two-teacher school, upper grades and elementary. In 1925 a new two-story brick building was erected at a cost of $11,000.

The Millersville Post Office was established March 19, 1866. John J. Miller was the first postmaster. Some of the later postmasters were John C. Snider, John F. Wilferth, A. A. Townsend, and George Howard in 1955.

The first church in Millersville was a Universalist Church established in 1867. A church building was erected and it later became the Methodist church. At one time the Baptists and Methodists shared one building and took turns leading services. In 1942 the two denominations had outgrown the one building. The Spiritualists, who were no longer holding services in their building, offered it to the Methodists to be kept in good repair. Rev. Paul Fountain led the renovation and developed the new Methodist church. George W. Howard was the first Sunday School Superintendent. The Baptists bought the Methodists' interest in the Union Church and in 1972 a new building was added to the original part and faced with brick. Among the earliest members were brothers Dr. J. R. Talley and Barton Talley.

Blacksmiths in Millersville from the Civil War until the 1940s include William Welty, L. C. Gober, Henry Ramsey, Jim Buchanon, John Calhoun Snider, and Bill Miller. Blacksmith and wagon shops were necessary to horse-drawn vehicular traffic of early Millersville.

School dances were a very important part of early entertainment. Sometimes they were held on someone's birthday or a holiday but on other occasions it was "just time for another shindig." The community had a string band and was addicted to dancing.

A very important occurrence was in 1925. U. S. Highway 61 was constructed through Millersville. The Dale S. Miller garage was located on the hill across from the store. It was a frame building and with the coming of the highway, Dale Miller built a new brick building along the said highway across from George W. Miller's home. Maple Snider Miller, son of Eula and Dale, graduated from Jackson High School and worked for a few years for a cousin in Camden, Arkansas. On returning with a new bride, Gladys Sedare Hale, he became a full partner with his dad in the business. They operated a car agency, sold and repaired automobiles, and dealt in gasoline, tires, etc. Hours were long, from 6 a.m. till 10 p.m. daily.

Millersville has a rich history linking many people in surrounding communities.

By Joan (Mrs. Don) Illers

Oak Ridge, Missouri

As one enters Oak Ridge, Missouri, there are few reminders of what made this town thrive. Time, 20th century inventions, neglect, and fires have destroyed most of what used to make this town a commercial center.

Soon after the Louisiana Purchase, Anglo, Scot, and German settlers from Virginia, Tennessee, and North Carolina began settling on and around a high densely-wooded ridge that formed a natural watershed for Hughes and Byrd Creeks in northwest Cape Girardeau County. There were numerous springs and a natural salt lick there. This lick inspired William Pierce, an early settler, to decide Lizard Lick would be the name for this area. John M. and Edwin M. Wilson purchased four acres of this land for $16.00 from William Clippard in November 1850. They renamed the area based on the natural features. Thus came the name Oak Ridge.

By 1852 Jackson Wilson had established the first store. Shortly, other businesses were established: William Pierce's and Ferdinand Swan's saloon, and Lewis Hinkle's and James Statler's general store.

When the need for a church became apparent, William Clippard donated the land on which a Baptist church was constructed in 1862. He also donated the land for the town's cemetery. The first two burials were Civil War casualties - Methodist ministers, a Southerner and a Northerner. In 1865 the Masons had their first meeting in Oak Ridge.

Once the town plat was surveyed and the village incorporated, Oak Ridge experienced rapid growth. A gristmill and a sawmill began operating in 1869. L. D. Parmenter and Son opened a blacksmith shop in 1870. Oak Ridge became a designated Cape Girardeau County tax collection spot in 1871. Henry Bruihl organized The Patrons of Husbandry, the local National Grange Club Chapter, on November 5, 1873. Oliver Harris became secretary and Dr. Morris Hatler was the first Master. The Masonic Hall was built by R. L. Bowman and James L. Morton. A one-room Methodist church, built on 1.25 acres donated by Lewis Hinkle, was completed in March 1874. R. L. Bowman also built the Oak Ridge School on the land given by William Clippard. Hinkle-Statler Mercantile Company erected a frame store in 1875. Hayes Hotel, the town's first, was erected in 1876. In 1880 the Grange Stock Company built a brick building. Sam Cramer opened the town's first shoe store. Under the leadership of Reverends Beale and Roseborough, a Presbyterian church was organized in 1884. John F. Fulbright began a livery service and stable in 1885. Early doctors in town were Dr. Beauteau, the first, and Dr. John Walker.

The 1890s experienced rapid commercial expansion. Columbus (Kay) Welling, a black man, cut hair. C. C. Penny offered livery and stable services. The Oak Ridge Canning Factory opened on the east side of town in 1896 and on the north side in 1897. The first telephone line from Jackson to Oak Ridge arrived. One phone line was not enough, so a telephone switchboard was installed in the Hayes Hotel with Mrs. Hayes as the operator.

Numerous other businesses operated in the late 1890s. They were: W. O. Meyer Harness Shop, Kassel Brothers Farm Implement Store, Henry Willa Stove and Tinware Store, Fred Kassel Photography Store, A. M. Fronabarger Photography, T. H. B. Williams Furniture, Oak Ridge Furniture Store, A. C. Ford Furniture, Drum and Macon General Merchandise, Willer Nursery, Mr. Case's Tin Shop, George W. Snider Blacksmith, Marshall and Williams Copper Shop, A. B. Ellis Wagon Maker, C. O. Snider Restaurant and Saloon, Cotner and Son Restaurant, J. W. Samuel's Barber Shop, and Cornelius Johnson Blacksmith Shop. William Willer and W. J. Wilson had tinsmithing practices, and Emma Clippard, Gusta Bruihl, Ruby Futrell, the Willer sisters, and the Frizzell sisters operated millinery shops. D. B. Horn operated the first drug store in the first brick building. The Hinkle-Statler partnership ushered in the twentieth century with a modern two-story brick building.

The town continued to thrive during the first two decades of the 1900s. David Peterson and

Miller's Garage. Dale S. Miller in center in front of window. Maple S. Miller in car on the right. The home on the right is that of Dale S. and Eula Miller. The road went from a gravel road to Highway 72 in the early 1920s.

his son, Ed, operated a broom factory and the first hardware store. Scott Reid was the postmaster. Lee Hart, P. M. Hinkle, and J. P. Malone established a lumberyard that used horse and wagon delivery service. J. H. Goodson became an agent for horse-drawn McCormick-Deering equipment. Dr. Ellis, Dr. Futrell, and Dr. Statler practiced medicine in the town. Dix Walker published the first newspaper, The Indicator. Two rural mail delivery route operated from the post office. Benjamin Breckenridge opened a restaurant that featured homemade ice cream on Saturday. C. G. Samuels opened a barber/clock and jewelry repair shop and sold insurance and lightning rods. John Hayes built another hotel. H. H. Wills owned and operated the Central Hotel. C. C. Penny's Paige automobile became a passenger car service. Dr. Walker and Dr. Ellis established a drug store, as did Dr. Futrell. The Oak Leaf Milling company was in its prime, making flour for local customers and shipping products out under the label of Oak Leaf, Belle of the Ridge, O.K. and Tip-Top.

The 1920s brought: $0.05 fountain soda, cherry cokes, or ice cream cones at Walter Trickey's Drug Store; a filling/gas station owned by John Henry Bowers and Frank Clippard; trucking services that hauled livestock to the St. Louis Stockyard and brought back feed, coal, ice, and other merchandise to stock the local stores; and business owners were Emory Harris and Vest Smith, the postmaster. W. D. Clingingsmith's Hardware Store became the Saturday night story-swapping place. Numerous businesses bought or sold agricultural products: R. L. Fronabarger, Will Samuel, John Jenkins, Lawrence Grebe and Earl Probst operated milk and cream-buying stations; Lloyd Snider, J. E. Drum, Drum and Wilson, and Frank Clippard were proprietors of poultry and egg-buying stations; and T. J. Miller and Sons were mule buyers.

A few outstanding events had profound effect on the community. One was the whistle of the first Houck train as it rolled into town in 1905; another was the establishment of a bank. The Farmer's Institute attracted people from miles around. This agricultural, home economic, and livestock fair was held the second weekend every October from 1907 through 1941.

Business operations diminished during the 1930s. J. E. Drum began trucking and later established a feed store. Kenneth Schmidt's barbershop and restaurant opened. The Southeast Missouri Telephone Company's switchboard was installed in Mrs. Hazel Maintz' home. Two firsts occurred: electricity reached Oak Ridge in 1937 and Verta Lou Phelps (Mrs. Dale Fronabarger) opened a beauty shop in 1938.

Landree Carron opened his grocery store in the Hinkle-Statler building in 1947. L. A. Ford and L. L. Moneyhun began operating feed stores. 1954s bright spot was the blacktopping of the Oak Ridge-Jackson Road, making it Route D. Clark Cowan bought the hardware store in 1955. The last resident physician, Dr. R. D. Blaylock, was still practicing medicine in the 1950s.

In 1956 fire destroyed the Hinkler-Statler building. In 1964 fire burned three businesses- a café-tavern operated by Kay Schmidt, a feed store run by L.L. Moneyhun, and the garage owned by E. E. Volz. Only two rebuilt: a grocery store by Eugene Seabaugh and a garage by E. E. Volz.

Bell Telephone Company built and installed automatic telephone service in 1959. Charles and Verla Mangels opened a feed store in 1963. The town obtained a natural gas line in 1967 and a water line in 1968. Rudolph Bohnert was the postmaster when the new brick Post Office was dedicated in 1969. The North Cape County Volunteer Fire District organized in 1977.

Active businesses in 2002 include: Gail and Arlene Curry's "Oak Ridge Market;" Don and June Sides' "June's;" Bill and Billie Criddle's "Bill and Billie's;" Bruce Schoen's "Schoen Construction;" Oda Friese and sons' "Friese Carpentry Services;" "Stahlheber's Woodworking;" Wayne Fronabarger's "Fronabarger Concreters Inc.;" Edward Huffman's "Huffman Auto Sales and Service" and Charles Wilson's "Wilson Auto Sales." The Baptist and Methodist Churches and the school still provide that important stabilizing role needed in the life of a community.

By Jo Ann Hahs

Hinkle-Statler Mercantile Company, Oak Ridge, Missouri, 1910.

Bank of Oak Ridge, 1910.

Oak Ridge Laundry, located in renovated old bank building.

A History of Pocahontas, Missouri

Pocahontas, Missouri, located on Highway C some eight miles north of Jackson, is a peaceful little village with a population of about 125. Though not formally incorporated until 1895, Pocahontas was surveyed and platted in 1861 as the nucleus of a backwoods rural community that was settled many years earlier.

Except for itinerant hunters and trappers, the earliest white settlers began filtering into the Pocahontas area shortly after the united States bought the Louisiana Territory - the lands from the Mississippi River westward to the Rocky Mountains - in 1803. Many of these pioneers were of Scot-Irish ancestry and moved from North Carolina and neighboring states. In 1821, the year Missouri became a state, a group of about fifty of these early settlers organized the Apple Creek Presbyterian Church just east of Pocahontas. The "Apple Creek" designation probably was suggested by members who actually resided several miles to the north on the creek of that name.

Samuel M. Green, a member of the Apple Creek congregation from about 1850 to 1870, paid for the survey and plat of Pocahontas in 1861, the year the Civil War began. He erected a building where the road to Shawneetown crossed the east-west road to Neelys and Oak Ridge and operated a general store there, thus becoming the founder and first merchant of Pocahontas. The Pocahontas post office was established July 3, 1856, with Samuel Green as the first postmaster. Green, who later practiced law in Cape Girardeau and became a judge, was a grandson of Elder David Green, who founded

Pocahontas School, Grades 1 and 2, first year in new addition. James Wolfenhoehler, Paul Wallman, Sammy Swan, Leonard Koeberl, Judy Wolfenkoehler, Carolyn Littleton, Charlotte Dunn, Joyce Sides, Susan Wolfenkoehler, Martha Pinkerton, Connie Leimer, Ruth Pinkerton, Judy Bruhl, Dennis Littleton, Tommy Brunke, James Hope, Richard Mirly, Dwight Craft, Mrs. Vernon Ludwig, 1955-1956.

Jolley Boys Band of Pocahontas. Members: Front Row: Rudy Ruehling. E. W. Ruehling, Wm. B. Ludwig, Joe Engelhart. Back Row: Theo (Pete) Leimer, Joe Leimer, Henry Putz, August Lichtenegger, Charles Leimer, John Kasten, Henry Lichtenegger, Henry Geisendoerfer.

Pocahontas, a healthy place to live, 1950s. Left to right: Joe Randol, August Kasten, Paul Heartling, Jr., Ben Schmidt, Charlie Rauh, R. C. Landgraf, Aug. Reisenbichler, Fred Gerler, all over eighty years old.

the first Baptist church west of the Mississippi River, Old Bethel, near Jackson.

Oral legend has it that Samuel Green fell in love with a Shawnee Indian girl who soon moved west with her tribe. He decided to name his new town for her, but could not spell or pronounce her name. So he chose "Pocahontas," a familiar Indian name from American History.

Another explanation for the town name is related in an historical pamphlet published by the Missouri Cash-Book newspaper and based on an address by John A. Hope in 1926 on the occasion of the 105th anniversary of the organization of the Apple Creek Church. Joseph "Uncle Joe" Abernathy, one of the earliest Apple Creek settlers, had straight black hair, high cheekbones and a dark complexion. He was said to be a direct descendant of Pocahontas, the Virginia Indian princess. Thus, supposedly in honor of the prominent Abernathy family, the town was given its name.

Though founded by Green, a Presbyterian, the village of Pocahontas was settled largely by Lutheran immigrants from Austria, who began arriving in the late 1850s. Immediately seeking brethren of their own faith, the Lutherans attended church in New Wells, about five miles to the north. The Saxon Germans had settled the Altenburg area of nearby Perry County beginning in 1839, and had built several Lutheran churches, including the one at New Wells in 1853. Many Pocahontas area children also were sent to the Lutheran parochial school in New Wells. But the inconvenience of traveling that distance for church and school soon prompted the Pocahontas Lutherans to form their own church.

St. John's Evangelical Lutheran Church in Pocahontas was organized in 1868 and the first building was completed in 1870. The first pastor, the Rev. Joseph Westenberger, immediately started a parochial school. A new brick church was dedicated (on the present site) in 1893, but it burned in 1910. The church was immediately rebuilt and continues as an active congregation today. Many residents of the region are familiar with St. John's Church through its annual kettle-cooked beef suppers.

Zion Lutheran Church-Missouri Synod, also a breakaway from the New Wells church, was organized in Pocahontas in 1889. It, too, remains an active congregation today. One of its most faithful members is Mrs. Esther Macke, the community's oldest resident at age 93 at the time of this writing.

A public school was started in Pocahontas in the late 1800s, and the town had a two-year high school from 1918 until 1944. The school won the countywide basketball championship in 1938. A gymnasium was built by W.P.A. labor in the 1930s, but the structure burned in 1944. The Pocahontas school finally was closed when the area became part of the Jackson reorganized school district in later years.

Pocahontas has had many civic organizations over the years. A Masonic lodge - Wilson lodge - Wilson Lodge No. 191 - was organized on August 17, 1878. The Pocahontas Extension Homemakers Club disbanded several years ago after fifty years of service. The Wonderworkers Extension Homemakers (now known as F.C.E. for Family and Community Education) was chartered in 1967 and is still active. The Pocahontas Jaycees organization was active from 1978 until 1990 with Mark Kasten as charter president. After two earlier clubs disbanded, the present Pocahontas 4-H Club was organized in 1952 by Fred Wachter, Glen Whitledge and Marjorie Swan.

In years gone by, Pocahontas was an active business community. Pocahontas Auto Company, a Chevrolet dealership, was founded by Reginald O. Swan and operated in later years by his sons Norman and Leonard. Other businesses included a bank, doctor's office, barber shop, blacksmith shops, grocery stores, hotels, a funeral home, butcher shop, creamery, furniture store, hat shop, shoe and harness shop, restaurants, a tavern and a lumber yard. Although most of the commercial activity has ended, notable exceptions are the Bowman Milling Company, in continuous operation since 1858, and Reis Meat Processing.

The population of Pocahontas has remained fairly constant for the past half-century. The two Lutheran churches, with many members living in the adjoining rural area, have contributed greatly to the stability of the community. Old Apple Creek Presbyterian Church has not had weekly worship services for many years. But descendants of the founders meet at the church twice annually - in May and September - for worship and business meeting. On the fourth Sunday evening in April, coinciding with the St. John's Lutheran Church annual beef supper, Apple Creek members and supporters gather to sing old hymns, accompanied by an antique pump organ, in the nostalgic light of ancient gasoline lanterns.

Although some of the older family names are disappearing in Pocahontas, they gradually are being replaced as new people move into the pleasant little village. Pocahontas seems destined to hold its own for the foreseeable future as many other towns of its size continue to disappear.

By Marjorie Swan and John Stanard

Tilsit, Missouri

Tilsit is located on a high ridge surrounded by fine farming land about five miles southwest of Jackson, Missouri, in Cape Girardeau County. During the late 1800s and early 1900s, Tilsit was a thriving town with many small businesses serving the surrounding agricultural area. In 1877, John Kerstner built his home a quarter mile southeast

Tilsit Elementary and Junior High School with the William Pensel House in the background.

from the local Evangelical Church. A year later he established a mercantile store. A short time after that shoemaker Fritz Kaminsky and John Schuette also built homes in the vicinity that had become known as Farmers Village.

Louis Kipping came to Farmers Village in 1879 and built a blacksmith shop. Later Kerstner sold his store to Kipping, who in turn sold his blacksmith equipment to his assistant, J.C. Rudert. Road changes brought the main traffic through the village. Tom Kinder built a saloon to serve those coming to town.

An official name had to be found for the town in 1883 when postal service was established and Kipping named the first postmaster. The names of Corola and Dresden were offered but were rejected by the postal department. Fritz Kaminsky, who was a native of Tilsit in East Prussia, suggested the name Tilsit. Kipping sent it in and it was adopted. The first post office was in the blacksmith shop. The first mail carrier to carry the mail from Gordonville to Tilsit was Christian Frisch. Later the route was extended to Tilsit-Houck-Gordonville and still later to Tilsit-Houck-Bean-Whitewater. Kipping remained postmaster for eighteen years, when the office was discontinued on account of being on a rural delivery route. By 1930, Houck, Bean and Tilsit were no longer considered postal entities.

The first public school house in Tilsit was erected in the early 1880s. The small two-room school located directly across the street, to the west, from the store, became a center of activity for the surrounding community. Jeff Ramsey served as the first teacher. Prior to that, students attended the district school located on the Herman Fluegge farm a quarter mile south of Tilsit. The St. James Evangelical Church and the Immanuel Lutheran

Tilsit "Symphonic" Quartet, circa 1905. L to R: Theodore Kipping, Otto Rudert, Steve Kinder, Julius Kipping.

Louis Kipping's General Store and Post Office in Tilsit, Missouri, 1906.

Church each maintained their own parochial schools. The public school was closed during the 1950s when the area was incorporated into the Jackson R-2 school district.

The German heritage of the area is evident in the names of the Tilsit business owners and residents: Kipping, Rudert, Vasterling, Penzel, Werner, Voshage. In 1931 John Putz described the Tilsit of 1900. "It was at one time a jolly crowd who believed in the old turner axim of Vater Jahn,'"Frisch, Froehlich and frei, es lebe the turnerei,' who had among them several musicians of ability, who, old and young, enjoyed a dance occasionally and believed in sociability and unlimited hospitality."

In 1921 Emil and Amelia Mantz and their children moved to Tilsit from Oak Ridge and purchased the general store owned at that time by Henry Kiehne. They ran the store from 1921 until 1938 when Emil died and the store sold to a Wilke family. The building was razed some time during the 1940s. The town began to decline when improved roads and automobiles gave residents convenient access to Jackson and Cape Girardeau. When reporter Steve Robertson visited Tilsit in the 1970s, he found little left of the small bustling community of the 1890s except for the spirit that Mr. Putz had discovered forty years before. Robertson explained "Life in a rural agricultural community can be an experience of joy, peace and happiness— especially if you are surrounded with the good, down-to-earth people who live in this Southeast Missouri town."

By Bernard Schaper

A Brief, Whimsical History of Whitewater, Missouri

Nestled in the southwest tip of Cape Girardeau County, Whitewater endures as a small village boasting 113 residents. Two churches, the Baptist and the Methodist, have served the spiritual needs of the people for approximately one hundred years. The Baptists moved into a new building in 1999, but the old church still stands, a testament to history. The post office, the general store, and the Co-op act as a social centers where folks from the town as well as the surrounding countryside can catch up on the latest news, learning whether a neighbor is still in the hospital or whose grandchild is graduating from college. A new beauty salon is carving out a place of its own, and there is even a boat repair business. The Masonic Lodge and Eastern Star, in existence for many years, continue to attract new members, but suffered a setback when an electrical fire caused extensive damage to the Lodge in April 2002. The Lodge is housed in a large, two-story building. It used to stand beside another very similar structure which no longer exists. One of them was used as a store, the other as the school before the "new" school was built in the early 1900s. The new school, an imposing red brick edifice high on a hill at the edge of town, has been a private residence for many years.

Some residents believe that the loss of the school, which ceased its educational functions in 1958, accelerated the economic decline of Whitewater. But the town had been undergoing a transformation for quite some time, probably dating back to the Great Depression of the 1930s. The village had approximately 350 residents in the first few decades of the 1900s, a number of people large enough to support several businesses. Three stores, an ice cream parlor, a barber shop, a bank, and a flour mill all thrived. There was always at least one doctor in residence, and the railroad depot agent unloaded the day's mail brought into town by one of the town's two passenger trains. A stockyard located close by allowed farmers to ship livestock to distant places. Louis L. Rhodes, my grandfather, ordered leather furniture which was shipped by rail from St. Louis. According to my mother, Loretta P. Crites, "Whitewater was self-contained in those days. You had everything you needed right here, or you could have it shipped in by rail." Few people owned cars, but one could always ride the train to spend a day shopping in Cape or visit a relative in Glenallen. What was once the railroad track has now given way to a park.

Although the Whitewater school stayed open for elementary students until 1958, it saw its last high school class graduate in 1932. The thirties proved to be a difficult time for the townspeople, as well as for the rest of the nation. Sadly, many majestic old homes burned to the ground during the Depression. It was widely believed that arson played a part in most of the fires as people were cash-poor and desperate. A home burned while the family was attending a Christmas program at one of the churches. The preacher saw the flames and quietly brought the pageant to an early close, concerned that if he yelled "Fire," people might

Main street in Whitewater MO, leading to old bridge over Whitewater River. Creamery and Post Office buildings on the left, and the corner of the Devore store on the right, early 1900s. Whitewater photos courtesy of Jackie Devore-Retherford.

John Miles Devore Store, Whitewater MO, early 1890s.

Devore's Feed Store, Whitewater MO, 1953.

be hurt in what was sure to be the ensuing panic. One child, Harrison Rhodes, had not accompanied the family to the church, and the boy's mother, Sophia Rhodes, was hysterical, thinking he was trapped inside the burning house. Luckily, he wasn't home, but tragically for the family, the insurance company refused to pay because so many suspicious fires had occurred. Rumor had it that a rather prominent man in town had a grudge to settle, and had either set the fire himself or had paid someone to do it. However, nothing was ever proven. Fortunately, most of the Christmas programs did not end so dramatically. No matter which church one belonged to, most everyone enjoyed attending revivals, programs, and services at the other churches. Tasty treats were given out by all of the churches after the Christmas presentations.

In the 1930s there were three churches in town. The Little German Methodist church was especially renowned for its Christmas goodies, passed out to eager children and adults alike. This building was later moved to Bloomfield, Missouri. For several decades, Whitewater had only two churches, until the gospel Tabernacle Center held services in the old Fingerhut store in the 1960s and 1970s, perhaps the very early 1980s. When it closed its doors, Whitewater once again was home to only two churches.

In the mid thirties or thereabouts, a new enterprise was started—a funeral home. However, as far as can be ascertained, only one body was ever "laid out" there. Apparently, their embalming techniques left something to be desired, and the poor departed one didn't look so good. The business quickly folded.

For a while in the thirties and forties, Whitewater played host to boxing matches and political speeches, held at "The Gym." Now, of course, this would be called a community building. Someone even flew a small airplane, using a field south of town as a landing strip, and took awe-struck passengers for a short ride. According to Loretta Crites, who remembers riding with her father, "It was very thrilling to be in the air, viewing the landscape."

Revivals were held by a fiery woman preacher on a grass-covered alley. Something seemed to be always going on in those days— an ice cream social, a taffy pull, or a baptism down at the Whitewater River, or Creek, as it was known then. Two mail routes serviced the outlying regions, each mail carrier driving a horse and buggy. One worker would make it a point to stop at Huckstep Springs to eat his lunch. The owner of O'Brien's store often loaded goods onto a poor person's wagon, never expecting any payment.

An unsolved murder from the turn of the century still haunts the village. Mr. Looney was killed in his store. And a young man, Clarence Hunter, died fighting in the Battle of the Bulge in World War II.

Whitewater is a quiet place now. But if one were to look closely, perhaps one could see the parade of vibrant life that has marched by in this little historic town—and is still marching by.

By Marilyn Crites

Fire Service in Rural Cape Girardeau County

Cape Girardeau County Fire Departments- chronological order of the year they were formed: Cape Girardeau, 1880; Jackson, 1908; Delta District, 1972; Gordonville District, 1973; Millersville District, 1977; Fruitland District, 1977; North County-North Station, '7; North County-South Station, 1977; Whit......ter District, 1978; East County District, 1981.

The Civil Defense Fire Department— The first rural fire service in Cape Girardeau County was started by members of the Sheriff's Patrol around 1959. With the approval of Sheriff Ivan McLain, the members started searching for trucks and equipment. A 1950s model GMC truck was acquired and rebuilt into a fire truck. Missouri Department of Conservation loaned a couple of Jeeps to the Sheriff's Patrol to be used for fire service. Fred Shepper was appointed as Fire Chief for the new department.

Several years later the Sheriff's Patrol merged with the Cape Girardeau County civil Defense to create the Civil Defense Sheriff's Patrol. The civil Defense Director was Wib Bangert. About forty people were involved with the program, all being sworn deputies with the Sheriff's Office. They responded to incidents requiring police, fire and rescue operations in the county, and some times were dispatched to the surrounding counties. Trips were made to fires in East Cape Girardeau and McClure, Illinois, and to rescue operations along the river and some of the larger creeks as far south as Sikeston, Missouri.

In May of 1966 Wib Bangert turned in his resignation for Civil Defense Director but continued with the Civil Defense Sheriff's Patrol. On June 1, 1966, Bill Swann was appointed the new Director of Cape Girardeau County Civil Defense. Two years later, on June 3, 1968, twenty members of the Sheriff's Patrol formally split from the Civil Defense organization to work exclusively under the Sheriff's jurisdiction. This left only four or five members to provide fire and rescue service, with Fred Williams being appointed Chief.

A new truck was acquired around this time. The rear mechanics in the old BMC pumper went out while going up 'Snake Hill' north of Cape Girardeau. The truck was full of water and the brakes could not hold it on the hill. The truck rolled backwards down the hill and went off the road. Fortunately no one was injured. The truck was replaced by a 1964 Ford that was built as a pumper using parts from the GMC. The Civil Defense Fire Department also had a truck on loan from the City of Cape Girardeau. It was a 1942 International pumper that was used at the airport and had foam capabilities.

One of the more memorable fires occurred at the Ceramo plant in Jackson. Ceramo makes pots and ceramic items. A tank truck delivering diesel fuel for the furnaces caught fire. Trucks from Jackson, Cape Girardeau and the Civil Defense Fire Departments were called. While fighting the fire, the tank on the delivery truck exploded, sending pieces of debris flying toward the crowds nearby. The local police had been trying to direct the people to stay back and when parts of the tank landed just short of the crowd, the people quickly complied.

In December of 1971 a fire sub-station was established in Delta in the southern part of Cape Girardeau County. A building was donated by Carson Kelley. The 1942 International pumper and a 1953 military Jeep were moved to that site. Larry Umfleet was placed in charge of the station.

Funding had been a problem for a while and an election to form a county-wide fire district had been voted down. Fred Williams resigned as chief and ken Koehler was appointed. The last major fire was a brush fire along I-55 near highway 61. In 1972 the Civil Defense Fire Department was disbanded.

The Cape County Firefighters' Association— This organization of firefighters started out as the Cape Girardeau County Fire Chiefs' Association. Founded around 1978, the rural fire chiefs would meet to discuss problems and work on a way to improve the callout system in the event of a fire. The system at that time would be for the Sheriff's Office to telephone the chief of the fire district and then he would start calling the other firemen in his district. This system was then updated to a page-out system installed by the County Court and the Civil Defense Director Brian Miller. The districts were then responsible for getting the pagers for its personnel.

Also around that time, a van was donated to the Millersville Fire District by Southwestern Bell Telephone. Their Training Officer, David Crites, wanted to build a van with an air compressor and storage bottles on board. The van could then be used at a fire to refill the self-contained breathing apparatus used by the firefighters. Unfortunately the cost of buying the compressor and storage bottles was too much for Millersville Fire District's budget. The Fire Chiefs' Association agreed to take on the project to fund and insure the Airvan. The van is available to any department in the county who needs it.

In the early 1980s it was decided to allow other firefighters into the association instead of just the fire chiefs. In 1985 the association incorporated and was renamed as the Cape County Firefighters' Association. At this time the membership included personnel from the rural fire departments and representatives from the Cape Girardeau County Civil Defense Office.

The Firefighters' Association hosts the Southeast Missouri Regional Fire School held every year in Jackson, Missouri. Noted as the largest regional fire school in the state, it had its start as a joint project between Jackson and Millersville Fire Departments as a way to get fire training in the area. The two departments co-hosted the school for three years, then Jackson hosted it until the association took over. The Fire School has classes and seminars suitable for the beginning firefighter as well as the seasoned veteran. From basic firefighting and water supply techniques to rescue and extrication operations, to how to drive the multi-ton fire trucks safely, are just a few of the classes offered.

For several years the Firefighters' Association and Cape Girardeau County Civil Defense co-hosted a Fire Muster. Patterned after the Fire Muster in St. Louis, area firefighters would get together to compete in events related to fire fighting skills: Moving Ladder Climb, Bucket Brigade, Broken Hose Exercise, Fireball Express, and the Water Fight. Until the fire musters neither Cape Girardeau or Jackson Fire Departments were members of the Association. They thought of the rural departments as farmers acting as firefighters. Two things helped to change their minds. The fire musters showed that the rural departments could handle the equipment every bit as well as the city departments and a Fire Apparatus Resource Book put out each year by the Civil Defense Office, showed that the rural department fire trucks were as good or better than what the city's had. Jackson Fire Department joined the Association and a few years later the Cape Girardeau Fire Department also joined.

In 1987 Marty Schuessler from Fruitland, Carson Kelly from Delta, and Marvin McMillan from North County Fire Districts started a drive to establish a Fire Library in the area. The idea was to establish a local site where film, videos, slides and other training materials could be loaned to departments for training purposes. Jackson Fire Department hosted the site until they ran out of space to store the supplies. The Fire Library was then moved to Cape Girardeau Fire Department Station #1. The library is not restricted to just the Cape County Fire Departments. Any area fire department or district can pay a yearly fee and check out items for their training. A Library Committee made up of members of the Firefighter's Association oversees the operation and purchases for the library.

There is also fire training for children. The Southeast Missouri Homebuilders Association donated a Smoke House to the Firefighters Association. This two story child-sized house on wheels can be used to demonstrate to children the safe way to leave a smoke-filled building. Safe non-toxic smoke can be pumped into the rooms and firefighters show the kids how to "get low and go." The house has been a big hit with both kids and their parents at area schools and during county fairs.

In recent years membership in the Firefighters' Association has been expanded to include fire department in the surrounding counties that respond in Cape Girardeau County. Member departments are: Cape Girardeau Fire Department, Delta Fire District, East County Fire District, Fruitland Fire District, Gordonville Fire District, Jackson Fire Department, Millersville Fire District, North County Fire District, Scott City Fire Department, Whitewater Fire District; also representatives of Cape Girardeau County's Sheriff's Office and the Emergency Preparedness Office are considered as members.

With a goal of providing mutual support, the Association is working to assure that each fire department has the manpower and equipment available to meet their needs. Thanks to the dedication and cooperation of these departments and agencies, the citizens of Cape Girardeau County have a fire service committed to protecting their lives and property.

—The history of the rural fire service is a portion of a book written by Michael Niemeier, 2002, who wishes to acknowledge the "many fire chiefs, board members and firefighters who contributed to this work."

By Mike Niemeier

Aerial view of Whitewater MO, 1979.

Historic Businesses

Many businesses have come and gone through the years with the many changes in the industrial and retail landscape of Jackson. Today, older residents may use businesses such as the Handle Factory, the Hosiery Mill, the Shoe Factory, or the Palace theatre as geographic reference points. Younger residents refer to places as Schaper's shopping center, the old Wal-Mart, Jer's, or Cracraft Furniture store. Below are histories arranged in alphabetical order of businesses ranging from large industries to small mercantiles, from agricultural to urban, that had an impact on the everyday life of their generation.

Cape County Livestock Shipping Association

The Cape County Livestock Shipping Association of Jackson, Missouri, (Missouri Accredited Livestock Shipping Association), was organized in Jackson on April 22, 1921, to meet the needs of farmers and stockmen of Cape Girardeau County to send livestock to market at National Stock Yards in Illinois. The group was incorporated July 25, 1923, and was governed by a Board of Directors. Adolph E. Kies became the second Manager and Secretary-Treasury on May 22, 1925, serving until his death July 21, 1971.

Once there were as many as two hundred Shipping Associations in the state similar to the one in Jackson. This Association not only is the last known to exist, but was the last to use railroad cars for shipments to market. The use of Missouri Pacific cars to reach National Stockyards in Illinois, for sale through Producers Livestock Marketing Association and later Interstate Producers Livestock Association, continued until about 1959.

The Association at one time was the largest of its kind in the state, if not in the nation. Shipments in early days regularly numbered eight rail cars a day. Membership at one time totaled 1300 farmers. From the beginning, the Association made it possible for small shippers to get their livestock to market at carload rates, confident that the animals would get good care and detailed attention at loading time. Shipment was weekly on Wednesday.

In 1928, two thousand persons attended Livestock Day at the stock pen. The purpose of the day was to demonstrate factors governing prices on central markets. Livestock grading contests were held in which farmers of the county judged the cattle. Businessmen closed their establishments to meet the farmers at noon. The Jackson Chamber of Commerce served sandwiches and coffee. The afternoon program included well-known speakers such as: Economist with U.S. Department of Agriculture; Marketing Specialist with the University of Missouri College of Agriculture; Secretary of Missouri Farm Bureau Federation; and Traffic Manager of St. Louis National Stockyards.

On December 17, 1928, the Association was one of the first to be accredited by meeting requirements set by the University of Missouri College of Agriculture, scoring 556 points out of 600, while only 450 points were required. The Association was accredited by the National Livestock Association in Chicago, Illinois, in 1929. There were about 4,500 Associations in the United States but only six were nationally accredited. The Association won the National Producers Shipping Association name slogan: "In the hands of a friend from beginning to end."

"Once Jackson was the major shipping point in the county," Adolph Kies said. "Horses and wagons, as many as 75, would be lined up for blocks, waiting to unload." Kies at one time followed the train as far as McClure, Illinois, to make stop-in transit shipments.

An annual dinner meeting was held for shippers and their wives. Prizes were furnished by Jackson merchants. Gifts were given to the top shippers from the Producers Livestock Association. A trip was made to St. Louis by bus to visit the stockyards each year and see other sights, concluding with a Cardinal baseball game.

The Association celebrated its 50th Anniversary in 1973. In 1977 changing times and increased use of trucks for shipping cattle instead of by railroad cars brought an end to the need for the Association. Because of the effort of Adolph E. Kies in 1939, a Work Projects Administration mural depicting cattle being loaded into a railroad car remains in the Jackson Post Office today.

By Virginia Kies

Cape County Milling Company

Cape County Milling Company was organized in 1895 as a complex of three mill, Mills A and B in Jackson, and Mill C at Burfordville. The organizers of this giant county business were A. R. Byrd, Ruddell M. McCombs, Frederick Tiedemann, J. L. Hinkle, J. C. Clippard, Charles Tiedemann, Hines Clippard, J. A. Horrell, and S. B. Horrell.

Mill A, described by the Cape Girardeau Republican in 1914, "was an immense plant with elevators and warehouses covering several acres of ground." About ninety men were employed regularly in Mill A alone, and many more temporary employees were added during the wheat-buying season. Railroad siding through

Shipping Day. Cape County Livestock Shipping Association. Late 1920s.

Adolph E. Kies, Manager, Cape County Livestock Shipping Association, Jackson, Missouri.

this compound provided ready access for shipping to all forty-eight states and the Caribbean area. Mr. Andrew Delesser of New York City represented the company for sales in the Caribbean area.

All three mills were equipped with the most up-to-date milling machines as buildings were remodeled and enlarged. Mr. Philip Heyde planned the original flow of spouts and rollers. His son, William A. Heyde, Sr., in later years remodeled as newer machinery and equipment appeared. He, in turn, was followed by his son, William A. Heyde, Jr., who continued to update improvements.

The capacity of the three mills at the time of the merger was 700 barrels of flour per day, but by 1914 they were producing 1500 barrels per day. In the elevators 300,000 bushels of grain were stored. These elevators were equipped to turn the grain regularly to prevent the wheat from becoming moldy or stale.

The Cape County Milling Company personnel were innovators of their time. They were the first in the United States to adopt the Hungarian or roller system. In 1903 they introduced the Also Process of bleaching flour by electricity to the milling industry. Heretofore, all flour had had a grayish color. In collaboration with Mr. Philip Heyde, Mr. Nat Alsop, brother of Dr. C. V. Alsop, a local dentist, invented this process. Both of the Alsops were bachelor brothers of Mrs. J. W. Hunter and lived with her and Mr. Hunter in their home on West Main Street. The site is now occupied by the Heritage Building and Loan Association (in 2002, Union Planters Bank.) This process revolutionized the flour milling industry. By 1941 the Alsop Process was used by all wheat-growing countries. Mr. Alsop and Mr. Heyde were awarded bronze medals and citations in 1904 at the Louisiana Purchase Exhibition in St. Louis. Previously Mr. Heyde had received an award for his flour at the Chicago World's Fair in 1893 and again at the International Exposition in Atlanta, Georgia, in 1895.

By 1914 the shipping capacity of the system was 8 train cars of flour and 3-5 cars of feed per day. The company's leading brand of patent flour was "Gold Leaf," a soft wheat flour for cakes and fine pastries. "Capco" was its leading hard wheat flour for bread. "Kitchen Queen" was also a popular brand with several self-rising brands for the market. Much of the popularity of the flour which had withstood tests in stiff competition repeatedly was due to the fact that the mills were located in this region where the best quality of soft wheat is grown. All of the products were tested and analyzed chemically in later years by William A. Heyde, Sr. and his son William A. Heyde, Jr., with Mrs. Helen McCombs Bright directing the baking tests. By 1930, the company produced 1700 barrels of flour and 1500 barrels of corn meal daily.

Officers for the company in 1914 were A. R. Byrd, president; J. W. Hunter, vice-president; John R. Mabrey, secretary; and J. R. Bowman, treasurer. Directors were A. R. Byrd, R. M. McCombs, J. W. Hunter, J. R. Bowman, William A. Heyde, Sr., and John R. Mabrey.

The site of Mill B was originally a flour mill, located just east of the present Main Street bridge over Hubble Creek where Young's Pharmacy and the Greenhouse (2002- Thriftway Drugs and Curves for Women) now occupy the shopping center. J. R. Bowman, Jackson mayor for many years, operated this portion of the company.

Mill C at Burfordville, however, is the plant that gave the company the right to advertise "Doing Business under Three Flags." George Frederick Bollinger, builder of the original mill, came to America from Switzerland in the last quarter of the 1700s and operated a trading post, trading with the Indians in the area later to become Cape Girardeau County, Missouri. At this time Missouri was Spanish territory. In 1797 the Spanish commandant in St. Louis granted Bollinger 640 arpents of land on condition that he develop the land and bring settlers. In 1799 Bollinger brought 20 families from North Carolina into the Spanish territory. Soon after arrival along Whitewater River, Bollinger began construction of a log dam and log mill. It was completed in the early 1800s.

Farmers came from 75-100 miles away to have wheat and corn ground. The mill was not just a place of business, but a way of life. During harvest season, farmers brought their entire families to camp for several days while their turns came to grind grain. It became an occasion for social exchange of new ideas. Settlers became acquainted with others from many miles away while exchanging local, state and world news.

The original mill race was powered by a wooden water wheel. In 1825 Bollinger replaced the log mill and dam with stone. This same heavy stone foundation is still firm, supporting the present turbine-powered mill. Bollinger operated the grist mill for 43 years until his death in 1842.

Mrs. Sara Bollinger Daugherty followed her father in operation of the mill. Sarah, having two sons enlisted in the Southern Army in the War Between the States, was thoroughly sympathetic to the Confederacy and shipped much flour and meal for the Confederate Army. In 1864 the Union troops burned the upper wooden portion of the mill and fired a cannon at the stone dam. Neither the mill foundation nor the dam was destroyed. Sarah sold the mill and all her property for $12,500 (except an acre on the hill for the family burial ground) in 1866 to Solomon Richard Burford, for whom the village of Burfordville was later named.

Burford decided to rebuild the mill. He used clay from nearby to make the brick which can be seen today. He equipped it with 48-inch Buhr stones, quarried in France, shipped to New Orleans and up the river by boat to Cape Girardeau, and carried by oxen to the mill site. Burford operated this grist mill for nearly thirty years until he sold to the newly organized Cape County Milling Company in 1895.

The forces of progress from small mills to the gigantic mills of the 20th century forced insolvency, and Cape County Milling Company liquidated its assets in 1953. It is interesting that the site of Mill C at Burfordville was purchased by Mr. and Mrs. Clyde Vandivort of Cape Girardeau, Mrs. Vandivort having been a direct descendant of

Cape County Milling Company, circa 1910. Photo by Frank Medley.

George F. Bollinger. The Vandivorts promptly deeded it to the Cape County Historical Society. Finally in 1967, both Mr. and Mrs. Vandivort having died, their son, Paul M. Vandivort, represented them as the acreage was dedicated as a State Park. In August of 1981 the mill was reopened to the public as an historic site.

Sources- "Bollinger Mill," <u>Cash-Book Journal</u> Jackson, Mo., March 2, 1983, p. 13.; "Cape County Milling Company," <u>Post & Cash-Book</u> Jackson, Mo., July 11, 1973, p. 8; "Bollinger Mill," Bill Cameron, Point Lookout, Mo., an authority on mills in the State of Missouri; "History of Cape County Milling Company" <u>The Missouri Cash-Book</u>, Jackson, Missouri, May 15, 1941, p. 5; <u>Cape County Post</u>, Jackson, Mo., March 12, 1936, Section C, p. 1; Mrs. R. F. Holden, Jr., Granddaughter of Mr. Philip Heyde.

By Bernice F. Heyde (Mrs. Wm. A., Jr.), October 15, 1983

The Goodwin Company

Leander Allen (L.A.) Goodwin (1864-1943) entered the wholesale poultry and egg business in north-western Indiana in 1885. He moved his operation to Marion, Illinois, in 1887 and in 1893 located in Lutesville, Missouri, (2002- part of Marble Hill, Missouri). In 1894 Mr. Goodwin formed the Goodwin & Jean partnership with Robert F. Jean of Dexter, Missouri. The firm grew rapidly and expanded dramatically.

In 1907 the company began operations in Jackson, Missouri, building the company's headquarters as well as shipping and receiving facilities, a poultry dressing plant, egg processing and cold storage facilities, an ice manufacturing plant and a cream station. The Goodwin & Jean partnership continued until the early 1920s when Jean's interest was purchased and L.A. Goodwin and W.T. Dickey formed a co-partnership which operated as the Goodwin Company. L.A. Goodwin held 75% ownership and Dickey held 25%.

On November 23, 1925, the Company incorporated in the state of Missouri. Officers were L.A. Goodwin as president and majority stock holder, W.T. Dickey as secretary-treasurer, and Andy Stickler and Elmer Finch as branch managers.

By the 1902s the Goodwin Company had become one of the largest dealers in poultry, eggs, and kindred products in the Midwest and was the nation's largest shipper of live poultry to the New York market. On at least two occasions entire trains of 70 or more railroad poultry cars were shipped to the eastern market. The company's gross sales at the time exceeded $3 million a year.

Goodwin Company operated facilities which included buying stations, shipping operations, dressing plants, hatcheries, and cream stations located in Arkansas, Illinois, Missouri, and Tennessee. With more than fifty locations, the company's main offices were located in Jackson, Missouri, and primary shipping locations included: Memphis Tennessee; Paragould, Arkansas; Dexter, Missouri; Jackson, Missouri; and Cairo, Illinois.

The use of the company trademark ABSOGOOD to identify dressed poultry and egg products began in 1916 and was officially registered with the United States Patent Office in 1936. L.A. Goodwin was the Chief Executive Officer of the company until his death in 1943, at which time his son, Robert B. Goodwin, who had served as secretary for the company since 1929, became president.

The Great Depression of the 1930s dealt the company a serious economic blow as a number of the banks which the company dealt with

Goodwin Co. Management, 1936. Standing: Henry Steinhoff, Weston Henderson, Ray Goodwin, Elmer Finch, Orville Godwin, Frank Goodwin, Bob Goodwin, Walter Goodwin, Silas Croll, Elmer Drum. Seated: Henry Stickler, John Stickler, L. A. Goodwin, Andy Stickler. Front: R. B. (Bob) Goodwin II.

failed. Also in the late 1930s the market conditions which had made success possible changed rapidly and dramatically.

The company had provided a local market for poultry, eggs, hides, wool, and furs and were expert at shipping these products, primarily by rail, to eastern markets. With the development of the state and federal highway systems and the trucking industry, markets closer to the producers were developed. At the same time methods for production of poultry and eggs were revolutionized. Although still recognized as one of the largest poultry and egg dealers in 1936, by 1939 the company had begun a rapid selling of its assets to stay solvent. By the end of 1942 the Delta, Missouri, plant was the only Goodwin Company operation remaining.

R. B. Goodwin continued in business very successfully during the World War II years. In 1948 he sold the Delta, Missouri, operation and in partnership with J. R. Bowman, H. J. Bowman, and others, repurchased the Jackson, Missouri, plant and operated the Goodwin Poultry Company until 1950, at which time operations ceased.

L.A. and Fannie Gillespie Goodwin were parents of five sons and three daughters. All five sons, Walter, Robert, Frank, Ray, and Roy, as well as son-in-law Weston Henderson (husband of Leana) worked for the company, as did daughter Mary Jane. Walter served as branch manager at Delta, Poplar Bluff, and Willow Springs, Missouri. Robert served at East Prairie, Missouri, as agent for the company in New York City, as secretary and finally as president. Frank served as branch manager at Cairo, Illinois. Ray served as branch manager at Paragould, Arkansas, and in 1941 purchased that facility and continued its operation into the 1950s. Roy worked in varying capacities at the Jackson, Missouri, plant. Weston Henderson worked at the Delta, Missouri, branch and, like the Goodwins, "ran" poultry cars to the eastern markets for several years. Mary Jane Goodwin Gladish worked as clerk in the Jackson office.

By Jim Goodwin

Illers Jersey Dairy: William A. "Will" and Mabel Rice Illers

Illers Jersey Dairy was started both by accident and necessity for a larger income. One day Will went to town and happened to talk to Mr. Martin Schloss. Will told him that he was thinking about starting a milk route in Jackson and selling bottled milk. Mr. Schloss had been selling milk to several people. He hauled the milk in a tank in a spring wagon. His customers put out containers and he measured the milk they wanted with a cup and poured it into their containers. He told Will he had decided to quit and he could have his customers.

We started Illers Jersey Dairy in 1924. We closed one end of the porch and used it for the milk parlor until we could get one built. We now had a promise for 36 customers. The milk had to be stirred to take the animal heat out of it and bottled in plain bottles. Will put the bottled milk in the metal boxes in the open top buggy. It poured down rain the first three days. He went up the hill with an umbrella over him and the girls and I were standing on the porch waving.

Before the cold winter weather arrived we had to build a dairy barn, a milk house and a garage, just in case we could ever afford a car. The barn had to have a concrete floor for easy cleaning and a stanchion for every cow. Each cow learned to know her name and which stanchion was hers.

The milk house had a cistern under it as large as the house. Water was tested on a regular schedule and chemicals were added to keep it pure. As our customers increased, our water supply was inadequate and we had to dig a well. We also had to have a big ice box built. It held a 300 pound block of ice which had to be put in every day.

We had to hire more help because we also farmed the farm. As soon as Will left on the delivery the hired hands would clean, scrub the barn and take the cows to pasture in the summer. I cleaned the milk house and milking utensils. Will now needed help on the delivery. School boys, Emil and Larry Loos, Jim Frenzel, Jackie Wilson and Bill Zimmer, helped as they could arrange a school schedule. We always had two hired people at the farm and dairy. Albert Fuhrman was with us the longest time.

Our ice box was now too small and we had to build a walk-in cooler. We used two 300 pound blocks of ice each day. They were put on shelves with a pulley. Bottles were washed by hand with a bottle brush. They were rinsed, sterilized and turned upside down in a rack ready to bottle. We had to keep ice and water in our first cooler so that the milk cooled as it ran over the ice. We capped the bottles by hand.

The open top buggy was too small now for the delivery. We managed to buy a four-door Model T Ford. We removed the cushion in the back seat and placed boxes there and on the floor between the seats. For a family car we put the cushion back in.

Will was a popular farmer of the section and his neighbors elected him president of the High Line. Missouri Utilities finally consented to run

Donald Illers and "Old Blue," one of the cows of the Illers Dairy herd.

Wm. A. Illers getting ready to start the sale of his herd of cows. Mr. Illers is in the center of the group of men and has his hand raised.

electricity down here and to Gordonville in 1935. We bought a milk cooler run by electricity. We then capped our bottles, 100 a day, by machinery, converted our milk cooler, washed milk bottles, and bought a milking machine, all run by electricity.

We now had 265 satisfied customers. We added chocolate milk and whipping cream. We now had our own milk bottles made to order. On the bottle it said "Illers Dairy, William A. Illers, telephone No. 6020." Our bottle caps were also made to order with Jersey Dairy and a cow's head on them. They were flashy with red and green on white.

We now had to buy a truck for delivery. The bottles were placed in cases and stacked in the truck. We were now milking 30 cows and had to buy milk from neighbors. These herds of cattle were tested regularly for all required tests. Ours were also tested for butter fat to tell us which cows weren't paying off.

We sold milk to restaurants, schools, Schapers Grocery, and the majority of the people in Jackson and the nearby vicinity. When we started we sold the milk for eight cents a quart. After a couple of years we raised it to ten cents. I was our bookkeeper. As the children became older they all had their chores in the dairy.

Years went by and all of us worked in the dairy. Will and I tried to get to bed by 10:30 p.m. and up again at 3:30 or 4:00 a.m. During World War II family members were leaving for service and rationing was dealt with.

In 1945 Will made a difficult decision. We sold our milk route to Sunny Hill Dairy at Cape Girardeau. We agreed to sell them our milk in ten gallon cans. Our herd would continue to be tested. For about five years we continued with the dairy herd. Will was known far and wide as the owner of fine Jersey cows and his excellent management of what was the oldest dairy in Jackson. The day of the sale of the cows was an emotional day for us all. Will kept "Old Blue." The dairy was hard work and long hours, but we will always be thankful for fond memories of our customers and good friends we acquired.

By Mabel Rice Illers, 1984; deceased 1989, age 93 years and 4 months

Submitted by Mrs. Aleene Illers Sander, daughter of Mrs. "Will" Illers

International Shoe Company

The International Shoe Company plant in Jackson, Missouri was first opened in 1920 in the old Methodist Church building located at the corner of North High and First North (Washington St.), just the north of the Courthouse. The old church proved to be too small and the company was forced to move for lack of adequate facilities.

A new structure built in 1922 on East Main Street, was financed with local funding and leased to the company. This plant operated until 1932 as an auxiliary unit to the Cape Girardeau plant, producing upper parts of the shoe only. In 1932 the company closed the Jackson factory due to the conditions created by the Depression. Two years later in 1934 the company gained full control of the property, production resumed and the factory enlarged to enable the plant to produce a complete shoe. A local headline read "Shoe Factory Locating Gives Jackson New Life." Nearly 2000 men and women registered for the 400 available jobs offering a minimum wage for men of $14 a week and $12 for women.

During World War II, the company was able to remain open even though many of the factory workers were called to active duty. Production of items for the armed services provided ample work. One contract alone was for over 242,000 pairs of gloves for troops in Alaska and the Aleutian Islands.

In 1951 a parking lot was provided by the city of Jackson for the use of International Shoe

View of the International Shoe Company plant at the corner of North Georgia and East Washington Streets, 1965.

International Shoe Company employees with 25 years of employment, December 13, 1965. —photo courtesy of Rosebud Call

and Jackson Hosiery Company employees to reduce the congestion caused by all on-street parking. The paving of Washington Street north of the factory was also accomplished because prior to this, street dust made it inadvisable to produce white shoes. In 1964 the factory was again enlarged by 20,000 square feet to a total of 63,000 square feet of floor space and the other sections of the building completely remodeled and the entire unit air-conditioned.

The supervisory staff worked hard to provide a good working environment for the employees. In 1951 the local paper reported "women and men have almost an equal representation, with age groups almost at a parallel." Many employees remained with the company for well over twenty-five years.

In 1964 the 400 employees with a payroll of approximately one and one-third million dollars, produced almost 900,000 pairs of shoes. Mr. John Hagans was superintendent of the plant on reopening in 1934, and served in that capacity until he retired in 1957 at which time, Mr. Paul Sivia, succeeded Mr. Peil in 1958.

Competition from foreign markets caused the factory's parent company, Interco, to shut down operations in 1988, leaving nearly 300 employees without jobs. —cms

Jackson Hosiery Mill

The Jackson Hosiery Mill was the result of the cooperative effort of the Jackson city government, the Jackson Chamber of Commerce, and the Prim Hosiery Mill of Chester, Illinois. In 1938 the contract was signed between R.K. Wilson, J.V. Priest and A.A. Boss, representing the Jackson Chamber and B.C. Dohn, C.R. Torrence, Pat E. Conner, and Edgar L. Conner of the Chester, Illinois. The contract stipulated that Jackson was to furnish a tract of land, erect a one-story brick building, and furnish funding for the purpose of training fifteen men to become machine operators. The city supported the development of new industry and advanced the $20,000 for the construction of an 80'x 80' building on two acres of land north of Second North Street and east of North Maryland Street (near the present city power plant). Pat E. Conner was named the superintendent. Larry Nowak was hired as plant manager and soon after George Decker as head machinist.

It was a humble beginning in the small factory with just four knitting machines, forty-nine employees and an annual payroll of $65,000. The plant would produce a knitted product which would be shipped to Chester for dying, packaging and marketing. While the plant was originally tooled to manufacture silk hosiery, synthetic materials such as nylon would soon be available. In 1940 the local paper carried the headline "Jackson Hosiery Mill Has Its First Opportunity To Manufacture This Highly Publicized Product;" and went on to explain that nylon "is made from coal, water and air entirely, and years of research work." While the product was accepted and a new market created, World War II was to impact the fledgling company. All but a few of the young men were called to military service. Only Charlie Glueck, George Decker, Ed Howard, and Pat E. Conner, Bern Looney and Larry Nowak remained at the mill. Nylon was needed for parachutes rather than consumer use. The work force at the Hosiery Mill was cut back to thirty. Women began running the knitting machines and rayon was substituted for nylon.

The post-war economy brought opportunity and expansion. At its peak the mill employed more than 350 with an annual payroll of more than $1,000,000. Machines ran around the clock. The building was enlarged to approximately 50,000 square feet to allow for seventy knitting machines. The new addition was referred to as the Cape Addition. The Jackson side of the mill produced full-fashioned hosiery while the Cape side made the seamless style. The Jackson Hosiery Mill later became a division of Wayne Knitting Mills of Fort Wayne, Indiana. Eventually, part of the operation was moved to Humboldt, Tennessee. The factory closed in June 1976.

Interior view of the Jackosn Hosiery Plant. Clarence Bullinger, left, and Frank Hecht, right, work on the full fashioned hosiery machines, circa 1950. Photo courtesy of Alvin Kamp.

Officials of the Jackson Hosiery Mill: left to right, front row: Richard Conner, Larry Nowak, Pat E. Conner, Thurston Taggert; back row: Charles Glueck, George Decker, James Rhodes, Elmer Wather, Arthur Morris, Edward Howard. Photo courtesy of Jessie Kamp.

Jackson Hosiery Mill. Photo courtesy of Jessie Kamp

The development and growth of the Jackson Hosiery Mill was an extremely large undertaking for Pat E. Conner assisted by many loyal employees, but they did an excellent job of providing employment for hundreds of people who were thrilled to have such a nice place to work with above average pay. The employees were like a large family and helped each other. They had a great deal of pride in their jobs. Former employees of the Jackson Hosiery Mill continue to gather for annual reunions.

Information provided by Dorothy Conner and Dorothy Palisch

Kerstner's Drug Store

Mr. Edward Henry Kerstner was born December 26, 1877, in Gordonville. His grandfather, Henry, emigrated from Hanover, Germany, to the United States in 1852. He purchased land and improved a farm where he reared his children. When the eldest of his three boys, Henry Jr., was twenty years old, he went to Appleton and clerked at a store for five years. Then in 1865 he moved to Gordonville and purchased a store. In January 1867, he married Agusta Ahrens and they had five children: Claus, Albert, Martha, Edward, and Laura.

My grandfather was Edward H. Kerstner. As a boy he attended the local schools, and after high school Dr. Hays was responsible for getting him started in the drug business. Ed attended the St. Louis School of Pharmacy and after graduation he and Mrs. Bernard Gockel started a business. Four years later, in 1906, he bought the business and changed the name to Kerstner's Pharmacy, the Rexall Store. Around 1914, the pharmacy moved to 110 South High Street. In addition to selling drugs, he had the Eastman Kodak line. A fountain was installed that would seat sixty patrons. It would open about 7:30 a.m. and close usually between 9:30 or 10:00 p.m. or when the first picture show was over. Saturdays it often ran later as many of the farmers came to town in the evening to buy groceries and supplies. It was a place where children gathered after school, movies, or band concerts; and older customers caught up on local happenings.

Mr. Kerstner married Emma Glueckhertz on December 29, 1901. He built a two-story brick house at 304 N. Georgia where he reared his three children: Cornelia, Edward, and Dorothy. He was an active member in the community, serving on the Jackson Exchange Bank board for forty-one years; he also served as city collector and as an alderman. He was active as a member of St. Paul Lutheran Church.

All three children graduated from St. Paul and Jackson High School. Later, Cornelia married Lawrence Sander. They had one daughter, Carolyn. Edward married Lorene Schlegel, and they are my (Kay Sneed's) parents. Dorothy married Rev. Arthur Brommer; they had two daughters: Joyce and Brenda.

After my dad graduated from Jackson High, he attended Brunswich School Pharmacy and joined his father in the business in 1936. When he married Lorene, she also took an active part in the business; later Cornelia worked there too, making it a family affair.

My memories of the drug store are mostly in the 1960s, of teenagers stopping in for a soda after school. My favorite was always the lemon Coke, but I think chocolate and cherry were the favorites. I also attended St. Paul School and lived in the house at 304 Georgia Street. At Jackson High School I met my future husband, Jerry Sneed. We were married in 1957 and were blessed with two daughters, Pam and Kris. We live on a farm north of Jackson. Now we have two granddaughters, Laura and Lindsey Lynch. Pam and Ed and family live in Knoxville, Tennessee.

My grandfather died in 1956. The drug store remained in the Kerstner family until 1962 when Anita and John Schulte purchased the store.

By Kay Kerstner Sneed

Jackson Movie Theaters

The Gem Theater opened in 1908 on the west side of South High Street. The admission charge was a nickel for children and ten cents for adults. It was an exciting time in 1930, when folks anticipated the addition of

Kerstner's Drug Store in the early 1930s. L to R: Bern Looney, Edward Kerstner, Ben Schade, Emil Kerstner and Eddie Kerstner. It was located on the East side of the first block of High Street south of the courthouse.

Jackson High School students enjoying the soda fountain at Kerstner's Drug Store.

talking machines to the movie theatre. (Missouri Cash-Book 7/17/30) During the 1930s the theater was remodeled and renamed the Palace Theater. The Palace continued to update equipment as new innovations such as Three-Dimension movies were circulated. The theater operated until the 1960s when the building was sold and turned into apartments and businesses. Area movie buffs in the 1950s and 1960s enjoyed the summer fun of the "Sherman's Jackson Drive-In" later known as the "Jackson Drive-In" operated by Gwen Winningham. Two hundred and twenty-five speakers were spread out over ten acres which included a play-ground and refreshment stand. The drive-in was located on the hill now occupied by the municipal swimming pool by the intersection of Independence and North Hope Street. The drive-in was a convenient location for large gatherings of various organizations and churches. In 1953, St. Paul Lutheran Church sponsored the sunrise services to be held at Sherman's. According to the local newspaper, the service was to be held rain or shine, however, "Should inclement weather prevail, the choir would use the concession stand." (Missouri Cash-Book April 2, 1953)

Home of Mrs. & Mrs. Louis E. Kies, Highway 25 South, Jackson, Missouri.

Kimbeland Farm

Kies Farms: 1892-1971

The Kies Farm was located one-half mile south of Jackson, Missouri, on State Highway 25. The home farm of this unit was purchased by Louis E. Kies (1868-1926) and wife Clara (1862-1924), in July 1892. Louis and Clara carried on general farming. Their children were: Adolph E. Kies; Helen K. Blattner; Edwin L. Kies; and Frieda McAdam.

L. E. Kies became a very successful farmer and an outstanding breeder of fine stock. He not only bred pedigreed Shorthorn cattle, Poland China hogs and horse, but he also was a fancier of light harness horses for racing and show horses for exhibition purposes, such as fairs and horse shows.

In 1902 the beginning of the establishing of registered livestock was made when the famous "Cuckoo" 2:16-1/4 was purchased. For a number of years, Cuckoo was Missouri's greatest sire of standard bred trotters and pacers. In 1903 the colt Blacklock was purchased and this colt was developed by William Rash who later gave him the fast mark of 2:04 with a wagon record of 1:59. After two seasons of successful racing, this horse was sold to W. H. Stubblefield who raced him for one year, then sold him to C. K. G. Billings for $10,500. Mr. Billings raced him the following year and sold Blacklock in the Old Glory sale in New York for $17,500. Other noted studs owned on this farm included Milnor 2:28; Allerton 2:09; Belmar Boy and others which were show horses.

For years a number of prominent stallions and jacks were owned at this farm. Imported and American Shropshire sheep were also raised. In 1916 the beginning of the purebred herd of shorthorns was made with the selection of a number of young cows from prominent Missouri breeders. For three generations, purebred livestock of showyard type and breeding were produced from seed stock, obtained from the leading herds in the United States and from animals which were imported from leading herds of Scotland. Registered Poland China hogs were produced on this farm from 1914. The herd contained the blood of many state and national show winners. Breeding stock was sold to many breeders and herds in various parts of the United States.

In 1912 Adolph E. Kies and Edwin L. Kies were taken in on a partnership of the firm name "L. E. Kies and Sons." Adolph managed the farming operations until his death in 1971.

By Miriam Kies

Kimbeland Farm

If you were living in Jackson from the mid 1940s through the early 1970s, you might remember Kimbeland Farm. The big white two-story farmhouse in the upper part of the picture was located on what is now Old Cape Road and Donna Drive. Kimbeland Farm extended south of Highway 61, now Jackson Blvd. Driving along Highway 61, which was then just a two-lane highway, and glancing to the north, you would have seen the big white barns, black angus cattle and lots of white fences.

Kimbeland Farm was owned by George and Lillian Kimbel and managed by Otto Heise.

Otto Heise and his wife Dona lived on the farm with their son, Melvin Heise, and their daughter, LaWanda Heise Werner. George Kimbel and his wife Lillian built their new home on the farm, which is now the Gerald McElrath residence. The farm extended east just beyond Albert Sanders Hardware, and west just beyond Woodard's Restaurant. White fences lined the highway on both sides. A horse barn, which housed show horses, was in the area of the old WalMart. Show horses were shown throughout the Midwest.

Finally, a dream come true was the Kimbeland Golf Course. Convinced Jackson was ready for a golf course, Mr. Kimbel proceeded to make it happen. What was Kimbeland Farm is now Kimbeland Golf Course to the south and Kimbeland Subdivision to the north, with commercial properties lining the highway.

By LaWanda Heise Werner

La Pierre-Sawyer Handle Company

In the early twentieth century M. G. La Pierre, a grocery drummer (salesman) traveling through southeast Missouri and Arkansas, was asked to sell hickory handles. At this time there was a small factory in almost every community. Realizing there was so much hickory timber available and a great demand for handles of all types and sizes, Mr. La Pierre and C. A. Sawyer from Little Rock, Arkansas, conceived the idea to establish a factory to manufacture handles. The spot chosen was at the site of an old stave mill and a lime kiln on the bank of Goose Creek in Jackson, Missouri. The factory was to be run on steam power. It was established in September 1902 with C. A. Sawyer, C. W. Henderson, W. H. Miller and M. G. La Pierre as stockholders. At the last minute Mr. Sawyer decided not to be active in the business.

Pete Weeks was employed as superintendent and to make the patterns. By 1903 the force consisted of M. G. La Pierre, his brother Wilson La Pierre who was finisher, W. G. Niblack, and A. F. Williams who was timber buyer and the superintendent. Later Mr. Niblack became superintendent and continued in that capacity until his death. Ray Randall became superintendent and held that post until he retired in 1975.

The company was incorporated with a paid-up capital of $3,500. By 1936 it had grown to $100,000. The first handles were shaped by hand with a drawing knife. They were then sanded and finished. In 1904 Mr. La Pierre fixed a display of their finest handles and showed them at the 1904 World's Fair in St. Louis. These handles received the Gold Medal Award. From this came the name for their finest grade, Gold Seal. The company eventually reached a position where it had become an important unit in the handle industry.

In 1913 fire destroyed the main part of the factory with its engines and machinery and the city was without water for half a day. The plant was rebuilt, important for Jackson as about sixty men were employed.

Through the years many prominent people have been connected with the company. In 1936 the directors were M. G. La Pierre, President; Henry Puls, Vice-President; A. A. Boss, Secretary; W. G. Niblack, Treasurer; Guild M. La Pierre, Assistant Secretary; Willis Knox; and M. S. Henderson.

In the past, the Northern Woods and those of the Pacific Coast made demands for the Jackson product. Large quantities of handles were shipped to Canada, South Africa and South America as well as different European countries for there is no better wood for handles than hickory, a variety found only in the United States and a very small section of Ontario, Canada. Following World War I most countries erected tariff walls and trade barriers so export business was discontinued. However, in the 1940s handles were shipped to England to be used in the rescue of RAF crews downed in the English Channel.

La Pierre - Sawyer handles were mostly made of hickory. A small percentage of oak was used. Some timber was bought locally but the large proportion came from Arkansas.

Carroll Knox moved to Sheridan Arkansas, in 1946, where he was in charge of buying the timber from 1946 to 1950. Timber was purchased from paper mills which owned huge forests. Then they were loaded on trucks and taken to one of three sawmills. Mr. Knox bought the first power saws in 1946. These logs were sawed into 40-inch pieces, then into various dimensions called blanks or billets. These blanks were loaded into railroad box cars and shipped to Jackson on the Missouri Pacific Railroad, averaging three cars a week. The blanks were turned into different kinds of handles. They consisted chiefly of axe, pick, sledge, hatchet and various kinds of hammer handles. Later, wooden mallets of all sizes were made.

Mr. La Pierre remained president of the company until his death in 1949. His son Guild took over the management, but died suddenly three weeks after his father. The youngest La Pierre son, Tom, took on the task of carrying on the business. With Tom's experience in working with Eastern Wholesale Houses and Steel Companies he was able to modernize the sales department and instill new ideas in the business. In 1963 after the death of Tom La Pierre, the company was sold to E. L. Keathly, owner of IXL Handle Manufacturing Company in Bernie, Missouri, one of nine factories owned by IXL company. They continued to manufacture the higher grade of handles for the IXL group.

The machinery remained about the same as used in the 1920s though run by electricity. The hickory was still purchased in Arkansas. The company operated one sawmill in Sheridan, Arkansas, by that time computer-controlled. The railroads disappeared from Sheridan and Jackson so all timber and handles were moved by truck.

Automation and the recession have cut down the use of handles. In 1983 the Jackson plant maintained a working crew of about thirty men. The handle factory was closed in 1988.

By Susan L. Venable

Loos Sawmill and the Loos Family

Jacob Henry Loos arrived in Cape Girardeau County near Fruitland after being discharged from the Union Army on a medical discharge due to leg wounds. His future wife, Catherine Henry, and her family were beginning a family farm after a tragic experience where her sister Bernice had died aboard ship and was buried at sea as they were emigrating from Austria.

Jacob and Catherine were married near Byrd Township where Jacob had begun his sawmill. The couple had five children: Adam, Louis, Anna, Robert, and Albert. Later they moved the business to the south end of Jackson on Goose Creek. The mill remained on the site until the 1950s when it was destroyed for the third time. The last owners of the mill were Albert and Jacob Loos, the sons of Adams and Betty Loos.

For decades the Loos Brother's mill furnished maple, oak and walnut flooring, as well as fine tongue and groove flooring, to homes, businesses and churches as the area grew and business prospered. The Loos's also leased threshing machinery to the area farmers as the bumper oat and wheat crops flourished in the fields.

The children of Jacob and Catherine Loos

Loos Brothers Sawmill.

were: Adam, Louis, Anna, Robert, and Albert, who died at age 16. They were all buried in the St. John Evangelical Church Cemetery in Oak Ridge.

The children of Adam and Mary Catherine (Betty) (nee Koehler) Loos were: Jacob, Katherine (Kate), Albert, Mary Delia (Dee), Edna, Henry (Heine), Ruth, and Paul Harris. Mary Catherine Koehler Loos' family farm is now the site of the Bent Creek Golf Course. Several Members of the Koehler family were buried in the small cemetery still located on the Bent Creek property. The children of Louis and Ida (nee Black) Loos were: Rika, Charlotte, Anna, Margaret, Louise, and Lloyd. Children of Robert and Anna (nee Loos) Dickson were: Robert, Mary, Roxie, and Victor. Children of Robert and Flossie Loos were Robert and Betty.

The Loos Family is still in Cape Girardeau County with numerous descendants scattered throughout the county and state. My sister Ruth McMullen resides in Cape Girardeau and takes great joy in her children, grand- and great-grandchildren. I am a resident of Holy Cross Retirement Community on the campus of the University of Notre Dame.

By Paul Loos, 81 years of age

McCombs Furniture and Undertaking Company, Inc.

The first written records of 1861 note that a business known as Mooreland and Tobler was located on the east side of south High street in the center of the block where Ross Furniture company now stands in 1984. Gus Tobler, who constructed the original part of what is now known as the "Oliver House," managed the business. All sorts of merchandise, including tinware, cooking utensils, lawn swings, and casket linings, were retailed.

In 1888 Oliver B. Kinder, Joseph E. Schmuke, and Henry Bartels purchased the business and continued with the same type of merchandise; however, as time progressed, caskets with linings were shipped directly from the factory for retail sale.

On April 6, 1906, the company was purchased from Schmuke and Bartles by J. W. McCombs, Jr., who proceeded to fill the three stories of the building with up-to-date goods, principally furniture and undertaking products. Mr. Bartels remained until November of that year when McCombs purchased Bartel's interest. In 1929 the business became incorporated as McCombs Furniture and Undertaking with stockholders being J. W. McCombs, Jr., B. A. Meyer, H. E. Boss, and Hope E. Morton.

John William McCombs, Jr. was born May 11, 1881, on a farm north of Jackson, the son of J. W. McCombs and Adelaide Bray McCombs. He had attended the Jackson schools, being graduated from the old Jackson Military Academy. He has said, "My father saw to it that I didn't loaf. I was at work at my brother's flour mill or the stave factory as a youth when not in school. I did play football occasionally." After finishing school, he worked for a time as a salesman for the milling company, traveling over southeast Missouri, but resigned to enter the furniture business. On January 10, 1905, he married Emma Cyrene Campbell, daughter of Captain (CSA) and Mrs. Stephen Campbell ("Rena" McCombs is not to be confused with Emma Boss McCombs, wife of her husband's brother Ruddell M. McCombs of the milling company).

Both young people were active in the Methodist church, staunch Democrats, and ardent community boosters throughout their entire lives. McCombs always attributed a large measure of his success to Mrs. McCombs (known as Rena) who helped with the business from the beginning, working as a clerk and keeping books.

When interviewed by the Southeast Missourian in 1936, McCombs said, "When I took the business over, the most expensive piece of furniture was a folding bed retailing for $35.00. Now we have single pieces for $550.00. In the undertaking business the highest retail price for wooden caskets was $50.00; a metallic one, $110.00. A bedroom suite —bed, dresser, and wash stand - sold for the princely sum of $15.00 with a spring and mattress or a spring and center table for good measure."

Rugs were practically unknown here. In the "Sunday" room or parlor could be found woven cloth floor coverings. This material came in rolls of 36-inch strips. It was laid on straw or papers. Strips were cut to fit the room and sewed together; outside edges were tacked down with carpet tacks. They were taken up for spring housecleaning and washed by hand when fresh straw was placed on the floor as the carpet was relaid. Another type of covering for floors was straw-mat carpet which came from China or Japan in strips 36-inches wide and rolls 40 feet long. When these wore through, the housewife would clip pieces from the edge and splice them in the hole.

The undertaking business was comparatively new. At one time embalming was considered sacrilegious, akin to witchcraft. When relatives came from a distance, the corpse was preserved in ice to prevent decomposition. The undertaker went by horse and buggy or wagon to the home of the deceased in the middle of the night. He carried a box in which the body was placed and taken to the ice plant. He would call out the iceman, haul it back to the home of the deceased and pack it in. Buckets were placed under the box for water drainage. Later the body was placed in a casket and taken to a church or cemetery in a horse-drawn hearse, rented from the livery stable. These same vehicles were also rented for weddings at times. Jaws of the deceased were tied together with a cloth, while coins were placed on eyelids until rigor mortis set in.

Caskets were wooden or metallic. The wooden type were most frequently used. They were wider at head and shoulders and slanted to a smaller size at the feet. For adults the trimming was black, but children's caskets were white. There were no church trucks on which to place caskets; instead, each end of the casket rested upon two wooden chairs. The casket was lowered into the grave on two lines slung under the box. The four ends were held by four men. Now and again ropes would break or slip from the hands of one or the other men. The funeral director had to be prepared for quick action. The burial was marked by a wooden slab. Badges of black crepe and ribbon were placed on the homes of the deceased.

The firm paid 25 cents a week to have dust in the street sprinkled down each week. A horse-drawn sprinkler came by, but if a business neglected to pay the 25 cents the driver pulled a lever, leaving the street dusty at that point.

Mr. McCombs was the first to introduce to Jackson easy payments and free delivery of furniture. He was not an embalmer himself, but through the years he and his wife provided financial aid to many young men to attend a school of mortuary science. In later years with tears streaming down his face, he would recount one of his first interments of his best friend from days of childhood. This gentleman was Mr. Edward Howard, president of Cape County Savings Bank, married to the former Nettie Ruff, and the father of three small children. Oddly Mr. Howard was killed while on business in St. Louis with Mr. Ruddell M. McCombs, president of Cape County Milling Company. They were in a St. Louis building, talking amicably, awaiting for an elevator to arrive. Howard with his back to the door had punched the button; the door opened and he stepped backward to an empty shaft and fell many stories to his death.

Loos Brothers Sawmill, truck and offices, November 14, 1946.

Mr. McCombs was a warm-hearted optimist who had the knack of making every person he met feel he was exactly the one he was looking for, and he always showed his sincere appreciation for their patronage. Having had no children of his own, he must have given away a boxcar of chewing gum and nickels for ice cream cones to school children passing his store each weekday. As his health declined, he depended on his partners to continue the tradition and standards he had set. His death occurred in May of 1943.

On March 1, 1939, Hope Morton sold his interest in the store to establish the Morton-Hall Lumber Company. Kurre Allen was employed that year and on March 1, 1944, he became a stockholder. On April 28, 1940, Perry Grindstaff joined the staff. He, in turn, became a stockholder in February of 1946. Henry Boss sold his interest in May of 1955. At that time Kurre Allen and Perry Grindstaff purchased most of the stock. Mr. Allen died unexpectedly on Memorial Day of 1956. On August 1, 1956, Elmer Best joined B. A. Meyer and Grindstaff as a stockholder.

Bruce Dockins had worked at the store during the summers of 1957-58, after which he entered the College of Mortuary Science in Nashville, Tennessee. Upon graduation he served his apprenticeship under B. A. Meyer. Shortly thereafter Meyer died and Dockins became a stockholder.

In August of 1942 the McCombs Funeral Parlor was separated from the furniture store on South High Street and moved to the former Presbyterian Manse at 417 N. High Street. The home was completely remodeled for use as a funeral home.

In April of 1971 construction began on an elaborate new funeral home on Route D. After Mr. Best's death in October of 1971, Perry Grindstaff and Bruce Dockins secured all the corporation's stock. The furniture business was sold in November of 1976 to Mr. and Mrs. Wayne Brotherton. The corporate name was changed to McCombs Funeral Home, Inc., located on Route D in the north part of the city. Present (1983) employees are Burce Dockins, Ivan Statler, Oscar Moll, and Perry and Marjorie Grindstaff. Mr. and Mrs. Arthur Musgraves live in the apartment at the funeral home, which still carries the McCombs name.

Sources- Records of McCombs Furniture and Undertaking, Inc.; Records of McCombs Funeral Home, Inc.; Cape Girardeau Republican, 1904-1914, Cape Girardeau, Missouri, p. 12; Cape County Post, Jackson, Missouri, March 12, 1936, p. 5-D; Southeast Missourian, Cape Girardeau, Missouri, 1906.

By Bernice F. Heyde, 1983.

McNeely Foundry and Machine Works

The McNeely Foundry and Machine Works, before it closed its doors for good in 1985, was the oldest continuing business in southeast Missouri. Kay Lamb summarized the following information in the Cash-Book Journal which chronicles its history.

John McNeely, one of the earliest settlers in Cape Girardeau County, moved west from North Carolina in 1828, homesteading a farm north of Pocahontas. President Andrew Jackson signed the papers which originally gave him a 40 acre tract of land. McNeely returned to North Carolina in 1837, marrying Jane Miller and bringing her back to his Missouri farm. The wagon team was drawn by the first team of dapple-gray horses in the entire area.

The McNeelys had three children. Their son John Newton demonstrated talent in work with machinery and tools, and with the help of his father opened the McNeely Foundry and Machine Works at Shawneetown in 1861. Fifteen years later, he moved the business to a site near Fruitland, where he made tools and repaired machinery. He also invented a threshing machine which he sold a few years later to the Belleville, Illinois, Machine Works.

Newton moved his foundry to the growing town of Jackson in 1879, first to the site of the Milde building, which later housed the Coca-Cola plant and Brennecke Chevrolet Company (the corner of Barton and Main Street). It is now the site of county offices. In 1883 Newton returned his business to Fruitland, and after his death in 1895 it was brought back to the county seat by his sons John Jackson and Carl, who operated the business as the McNeely Bros. Foundry until 1900 when John J. bought Carl's interest. John J. moved the foundry to occupy the old wool carding mill on West Main Street in 1908. His was the first business in Jackson to use electric power.

John was succeeded in business by his two sons, Raymond "Bugs" and John Leroy. When Raymond died in 1976, Leroy continued operating the McNeely Foundry and Machine Works until his retirement in 1985.

J. W. McCombs Furniture Store

Rena McCombs, Helen McCombs Harvey on Homecomers Parade Float for McCombs Furniture Store.

The McNeely business was unique in that it was able to reconstruct even the smallest parts for old stoves, clocks, and other items using metal in their construction. It had a brisk business through the years filling orders for manhole covers, anvils, construction castings, fireplace grates, and bells, plus special items for local industries, including Kasten Masonry and La Pierre Sawyer Handle Company. Custom orders for old engine parts, sawdust blowers, or specialty items were sent throughout Missouri, to the southwestern states, and all over the west. Antique patterns, such as the original design for the ball and chain used for prisoners in the county jails and the original frame for the Cape Girardeau Courthouse clock, filled the storage attic.

Many people question the family about the old art of pattern making and producing cast iron items. First the pattern is drafted on paper. The pattern is constructed in wood. Using a jig saw, wood lathe, and even whittling, the wood pattern must be skillfully wrought, even to the extent of making it with the perfect angle when it had been meticulously set into a wet sandpacked mold. The wooden pattern is ever so carefully removed and the whole material bolted together.

One reporter observing a "pour" wrote the following: usually eight men were required to keep the furnace loaded and helped pour the red hot metal into the molds. When the iron cooled and the smoke cleared, the molds were unlatched and the sand removed. The product then received a fine tuning by machinery, painting or whatever was needed for finish. The special sand, from Camden, Tennessee, or near St. Louis, was shoveled through a sifting machine and recycled. The wooden patterns were stacked for reuse and reorder.

To acquire the molten metal, old iron products, such as stoves, motors, sinks, and pipes, were melted down. Sometimes huge pieces were even driven out of town to be blown into usable sizes with dynamite. The iron scraps were placed in a huge, wet, clay-lined bucket that held approximately six hundred pounds of iron, sixty pounds of coke, and two and a half gallons of limestone rocks for flux. The tram car pulled its load to the cupola section of the flue where it dumped the load for melting. The slag, composed of impurities such as mud and rust, floated to the top and was drawn to one side of the stack while the molten iron flowed out the opposite side into a large ladle mounted on a movable hoist.

The furnace had the capability of melting between two and two and a half tons of metal per hour to 3000 degrees. The furnace usually melted continuously for two to three hours in order to pour the entire floor, which was laid with rows and rows of patterns.

To proceed with a pour, a part of the huge smokestack had an inside area lined with protective firebricks. Each time the furnace was used, this area had to be resealed by hand with wet clay, filling any cracks or fissures to assure the extreme heat and molten metal would be contained within the cupola (firebox) part of the flue. Leroy would climb up on a ladder into the firebox area where he would mud, or seal, the firebrick.

Leroy's daughters, Jane Boren and Lawanna Eshbaugh, remember "pour day" when their father was up before dawn to go down to the shop and mud the cupola. When he returned late in the evening from a hot and dirty job with a soot-covered face, shoes full of sand, flash burns and holes in his work clothes from fiery sparks jumping from the bucket of molten metal, they waited for that big hearty laugh as he shared the day's successful casting.

Despite the time spent in hard, specialized work, every site of the McNeely's businesses featured a pot-belly stove in the main work area, surrounded by an assortment of welcoming

McNeely Foundry and Machine Works.

Owner LeRoy McNeely (center) with some employees, L to R: David Pair, Alvin Schwab, Joe Runnels, and Floyd Primm. In foreground are some of the wooden patterns for molding castings.

Leroy McNeely, back to camera, and employee Alvin Schwab pouring castings.

The E. Milde Bottling Works located across from the Cape Girardeau County Courthouse on Barton Street, in Jackson, Missouri, 1908.

chairs. The "shops" were a gathering place for farmers, business people, and those from all walks of life to joke, swap yarns, and enjoy each others' company. "We solve our problems here," said Leroy McNeely.

In 1968 Leroy assumed operation of the gray iron foundry portion of the business, while Raymond concentrated in the welding and machine aspect. Leroy redesigned and modernized the foundry furnace, changing it to charge mechanically and automatically. Over the years, the McNeely foundry had a significant hand in much of the history of Jackson and the surrounding area. A semblance of the foundry is on display at the Black Forest in Jackson.

Leroy's grandson, Rik Boren, who helped his grandpa during the summer, says of the business, "Working at the foundry was a unique experience, bridging the gap between business practices of yesteryears and modern technology. While it was hard work, it was rewarding to take cast iron junk and convert it into valuable commodities. The work ethics of dedication and perseverance I learned there are still with me today as a partner in Price-Waterhouse-Coopers." A pen and ink sketch of the shop and foundry hangs in his office today as a tribute to his grandfather and to the hard-working and inventive men who operated the McNeely Foundry and Machine Works during the 124 years of its history.

By Martha Wagner

E. Milde's Bottling Works

Emanuel Milde, Sr. first bottled his "Milde's Soda" in his E. Milde Bottling Works located across from the Cape Girardeau County Courthouse on Barton Street, in Jackson, Missouri, in 1894. Many people within the community thought there was no future in a soft drink business.

At his death in 1900, Emanuel Milde, Sr. left three children: Alvin D., Emanuel Jr., and Clara, later Mrs. Charles Steck. His sons immediately assumed the operation of the business and enjoyed the rapid growth of the industry in the early part of this century with their Milde's Soda and a new drink, Milde's Cola. The franchise for Coca-Cola was acquired for the Jackson Division in 1924.

This acquisition prompted years of unprecedented growth for the then named Milde Coca-Cola Bottling Company. A. D. Milde expanded his Coca-Cola interest into the markets of Flat River, Cape Girardeau, and Sedalia. The year 1966 brought about the consolidation of its interest under the direction of President Orme S. Kellett; Executive Vice-President Charles W. Sander; Secretary-Treasurer Milde G. Steck, grandson of Emanuel Milde, Sr.; and attorney Robert M. Buerkle. In 1977 Bruce E. Miller assumed the position of General Manager to further assist in the consolidation of company interests. His participation represented the fourth generation of the Milde family in the soft drink business.

Over the period of the next fifteen years, partnership interests were purchased and a major re-alignment of territories was accomplished. The Coca-Cola Bottling Company of Jackson, Missouri as it was then known, purchased the Poplar Bluff (1969) and Kennett (1981) Divisions. With the addition of A&W Root Beer, NuGrape and Sunkist Orange franchises in the early 1980s to a complete line of Coca-Cola products and Milde's Cream Soda, the Company offered a product line second to none. Due to the regional nature of the business, a sixteen county operation, the name was changed to the Coca-Cola Bottling Company of Southeast Missouri in late 1984, further identifying the operation to the region in which its roots were firmly planted.

In the mid 1970s, it became apparent that the Barton Street location was inadequate to accommodate the company's growth into the 1980s and beyond. Ways were explored in which to move the company's headquarters and Jackson Division to more suitable quarters. Cape Girardeau County purchased the facilities on Barton Street to provide additional needed office space. This enabled the Coca-Cola Bottling Company of Southeast Missouri to begin construction of a new and expanded facility on Lenco Avenue.

In the year 1991, the operation was sold to the Coca-Cola Bottling Company of Northeast Arkansas, thus concluding almost one hundred years of the Milde's Soft Drink Bottle Works.

By Billie Sander

History of the Sander Companies:

W. A. Sander Co. 1895-1904
W. A. Sander & Bro. 1904-1933
C. H. Sander Sales Co. 1934-1966
Sanders Appliance Co. 1967-1978

W. A. Sander started a business of selling Plano harvesting machines in 1895. In addition to Plano, he sold Osborn farm machines. In 1904 the firm of W. A. Sander and Bro. was formed with Albert Sander, his brother, joining the firm. In addition to machinery for the farm, they added a line of hardware and paint. Mr. Sander traveled by horse and buggy, often rode horseback, and even walked to conduct his business. According to information recorded, Mr. Sander said those were the days when you had to have a good team of horses to pull a buggy through the mud that graced our roads. Mr. Sander and his brother were in business together until the end of 1933 when the partnership was dissolved.

The C. H. Sander Sales Co., dealers in hardware, paints, and electrical appliances, was established in March of 1934 shortly after the founders of W. A. Sander and Bro. hardware partnership dissolved. They were located on the west side of South High Street in the building now owned by Siemer Sales and Service. This firm was individually owned by C. H. Sander who passed away in 1984 at the age of 92. He and his two sons, Charles W. and Leonard F. Sander, constituted the personnel of the store. Later the store moved to where Ross furniture is now located. In 1945 C. H. Sander sold 2/3 interest in the store to his two sons who formed a partnership which ran until 1966 when Leonard Sander sold his interest in the company to Charles W. Sander. In 1971 Charles W. Sander sold the store to John and Irmgard Siemer.

On June 10, 1967, Leonard F. Sander and his family opened an appliance and electronics store at 107 East Adams known as Sanders Appliance Co. Employees at this store included Leonard Sander, his wife Aleene, and the late Edwin Perdue. Sander's son Fritz spent a couple of summers at the store and his youngest son Paul spent about six years working at the firm. This business was sold in June of 1978 when owner Leonard F. Sander decided to devote his full time to the position of First District County Judge (changed to Commissioner in 1984) a position Sander was first elected to in 1976 and held until 1992. Leonard Sander passed away in 1998.

Schaper's (Grocery) IGA Foodliner

Julius Schaper was born July 29, 1884, on a farm southwest of Jackson. His father died at age 49, leaving his mother with eleven children to rear. The older children had to do the farm work and help take care of the younger ones. Therefore they attended school sporadically and, although Julius completed eight grades, he received very little formal education. Upon reaching age twenty he left the farm and worked for the McAtee Mercantile Company, a grocery and feed business. He later became a partner in this business.

In 1922 Julius had an opportunity to become a partner in a grocery in the 700 block of Broadway in Cape Girardeau with Theodore Roth. Mr. Roth taught Julius basic accounting so that he could do the necessary bookkeeping.

Then came the years of the Great Depression. Since the business was mostly a charge and delivery type of operation, Julius found it increasingly difficult to collect overdue accounts, so in 1931 he sold the business and bought a farm three miles south of Jackson. But again, the depression years were not kind to him there either. He decided to go back in the grocery business and rented the old Peoples Bank building which was located between the Dr. J. L. Jenkins building on the corner of Main and Court Streets and the Jackson Hotel. He had shelves and a counter built, and bought a used Dayton scale and a used National cash register; and that was the extent of the equipment. His capital being very limited, he instructed his son, Bernard, to stock the shelves by "facing" which meant that the shelves looked full but in reality were not. In March 1934 Julius opened his store for business.

At that time none of the numerous grocery stores in Jackson sold fresh meat. Julius' customers urged him to sell fresh meat, preferably young tender beef which they preferred over the heavier beef being sold in the local meat market. Julius then bought his first piece of refrigerated equipment, a Hussman service meat case. He ordered his first beef carcass and had a local man teach him how to "break down" a side of beef. All of this was done with hand tools—a sharp butcher knife, a cleaver and a hand saw.

Fresh milk could not be bought in stores at that time. Having had requests to stock milk and cream, Julius contacted his cousin, Will Illers, who operated a dairy south of Jackson. Will agreed to furnish fresh rich Jersey milk daily in pint and quart bottles. Julius' second major equipment purchase had been a walk-in storage cooler because his meat business had grown, making it a necessity. This cooler had two small glass doors behind which were wooden shelves and this is where the milk was stocked.

In 1937 the corner building owned by Dr. J. L. Jenkins became available. Although it was only 18 feet wide and 75 feet deep, Julius thought it a better location and moved there. Here he installed the first refrigerated produce case in Jackson as well as the first frozen food cabinet. Since frozen foods were new and untried in Jackson, Julius gave Bernard the job of explaining how to use and prepare them. Bernard could not understand why he was chosen instead of his mother, who was an excellent cook.

Schaper's Grocery became an IGA Store in 1936. This was done to gain a competitive advantage as well as a private label and expert guidance. A self-service operation was being planned but World War II interrupted and Bernard left for service in the army on January 19, 1942. Soon other young employees wer inducted, among whom were Richard Davis, Lawrence Schlimpert, Nelson Trickey and Bill Zimmer, all of whom were "Mom" Schaper's boys. However, Julius went ahead with the project and hired the Penzel Construction Company to build and install new shelves and rearrange the equipment. Since this was an entirely new concept, the comment was often heard "I'm not going to push one of those 'baby' carts."

After serving four years in the military, Bernard returned to the business in 1946 and became a partner in 1947. Knowing that the trend was toward larger stores with plenty of parking space, they began planning a building for a supermarket. An added impetus was given when the Jackson Exchange Bank announced that they had acquired the Jenkins building for the purpose of erecting a new bank building on the site. A location at 528 West Main Street was chosen and in 1948 Jackson's first supermarket was opened. It was a 4,000 square foot building. The next year an air-conditioning system was installed- another first for Jackson.

The first few years in the new market were not easy. However, the business grew and another parking lot was added. Bernard remembers that Ray McNeely would come into the store at busy times and say "Huh! Going broke, aren't you!" This became a standard joke stemming from the fact that earlier betting uptown was that the Schapers would "go broke" if they left the courthouse square. Another expression was "that boy is going to break Julius."

After ten years in this first building the Schapers realized that they had outgrown it, so they decided to expand to a new 10,000 square foot building. With the cooperation of the three local lending institutions and a loan guarantee from the Small Business Administration, the building was completed in 1960. The supermarket was designated an IGA Foodliner by meeting IGA Headquarters qualifications. The shelves were arranged diagonally—a new feature - and a bakery-delicatessen was added, another first in Jackson. After ten years in this location the Schapers found that they had again outgrown their facilities. After many meetings with the Wetterau engineering staff, the decision was made to construct a new building to the north and adjacent to the present building. The new building was to be 20,000 square feet — twice the size of the present building.

Julius and Frieda lived to see this large and modern market open on May 5, 1970. They had experienced a tremendous change from a "Pop and Mom" corner store. No doubt they thought back to the days when they dipped country lard into a paper carton and pumped kerosene for lamps and stoves into five-gallon cans, and of selling sauerkraut, herring and fish from open kegs and barrels. They were pleased that their service over the years to their customers, friends, their church, and the community was returned to them in the form of this final accomplishment. Julius continued to work in the store as long as he was physically able. He died June 15, 1971, at age 86, and Frieda died May 1, 1979, at the age of 90. They were unusual products of their time, being conservative yet progressive.

As the business continued to grow and prosper, Bernard came to rely more and more upon two fine young men, Milton Grebe and Lester Maevers. In 1975 Bernard began having eye problems and was told by a specialist that this was caused by stress, so the decision was made that Bernard would eliminate the stress by retiring from the business. In February 1976, the Foodliner was sold to Milton Grebe and Lester

Schaper's IGA Grocery, corner of West Main and Court Streets, circa 1940. Left to right: Julius Schaper, Lawrence Schlimpert, Jacob "Jake" Friedrich, and Bernard Schaper, before self-service.

Maevers. Under their management the business continued to grow and prosper. In 1984 Milton sold his interest to Lester Maevers.

On June 16, 2000, the market was sold to the Food Giant Corporation and Schaper's IGA Market ceased to exist.

By Bernard Schaper

Wagner Machine and Welding Works

The red brick building at 120 South Missouri Street was for many years a familiar sight to Jackson residents. It began as a blacksmith shop of Christian Heinrich (Henry) Wagner. Henry was orphaned at the age of eleven, when his parents died within two weeks of each other. He was taken into the home of Fred Reinecke and raised as a farm hand. As a young man, he was apprenticed to a blacksmith in Burfordville. After completing training in the Jackson shop of Hoffman, Macke & Milde, he opened his own blacksmith shop. Being mechanically inclined, he also developed into an excellent gunsmith and locksmith.

In 1877, on Christmas day, Henry married Fredericka Rasche. Six children were born to them: Alvin August, Louis Robert, Lawrence Jacob, Ruby Charlotte, Frederick William, and Henry Joseph (Harry). Alvin and Harry began working with their father in 1922 in the blacksmith shop which later developed into a machine shop. Lawrence joined his brothers for a short time, as bookkeeper. In 1925 the shop was rebuilt as a one-story, flat-roofed building.

A few years later in 1928, their father Henry having died, Alvin and Harry occupied the building together. Alvin was a well-known gunsmith by this time, specializing in muzzle-loading rifles. Harry was working with electric welding and had fabricated an AC welding machine. He later developed and patented a design for an electrode holder.

Expansion became necessary in 1937 as Harry pursued his interest in welding products. A second story was added to the building and Alvin moved his gun equipment to the new upper floor of the shop. Harry began limited production of welding equipment under the name of Wagner Welding Products.

Harry's son, Kenneth, was employed by the machine shop during summer vacations from high school to do bookkeeping as well as machine work. In 1936 Kenneth attended a business college in St. Louis for one year, and returned to Jackson to work with his dad.

As the welding equipment business grew and the cost of materials increased, others invested in the expanding endeavor and it became essential to move into larger quarters. Harry worked with them for several years. When his health began to fail, he sold his interest in the business and retired in 1956.

The original Wagner Machine shop, under Kenneth's management, continued to flourish and successfully served the community with custom machine work for many of the local factories and in surrounding communities. In the years following Harry's retirement, Kenneth and his brother Roland worked together, upholding their dad's commitment to excellent workmanship and maintaining a good relationship with the customers they served. The Wagner brothers retired in 1989, with time now to reflect upon and remember busy days spent in the place where their grandfather labored as a blacksmith.

By Martha Wagner

Henry A. Ueleke in his Jewelry and Watch Repair Shop located on the south side of the first block of West Main Street in 1905. The building was later demolished to make way for the expansion of the Cape County Bank, now Union Planters

Retail and Industry Today

Locally owned, family operated businesses have been the backbone of the Jackson service community from the early days of the town. During the twentieth century the merchants, lawyers, health professionals, service professionals and tradesmen provided goods and services for the people in Jackson who appreciate the convenience and geniality of trading people from and for the community. The "Saturday Market Days" are gone when four or five hundred cars could be found in the uptown shopping area and yet family owned businesses still thrive in Jackson even with the geographic expansion of the retail community because the "Mom and Pop" businesses have a personal investment in the well-being of the community. The small business men and women support the town several ways. Their support of local charitable and service institutions is invaluable for it is not unusual for a business person to be approached several times a week for a donation of time or money. Revenue from goods sold and sales tax are kept within the area. The business community promotes Jackson through service organizations such as the Chamber of Commerce, Junior Chamber of Commerce, Rotary Club, Optimists, BPWA, Lion's Club and more.

As Jackson and the surrounding area have grown, the character of its businesses has shifted as well. Although serving the needs of the area residents in retail establishments is still important to the Jackson economy, industrialization has allowed the town to support a much larger population.

During the course of the 175th Anniversary Celebration in 1989, the Jackson Chamber of Commerce attempted to locate the oldest existing business in Jackson. Of those companies submitting information, the following were recognized as the oldest within the categories retail business, service business, and manufacturing business: retail business, Jones Drug Store; service business, the *Cash-Book Journal*, and manufacturing business, Kasten Clay Products and the Coca-Cola Bottling Company both founded in 1895.

These industries serve as an indication of how society and Jackson have changed since the days when Jackson was a collection of log cabins on the hill above Hubble Creek. No longer is farming the main occupation of most of the residents of Jackson and surrounding communities. Many small towns have become bedroom communities for industrial workers in Jackson and Cape Girardeau, as well as for employees of retail, medical and educational facilities in the area.

The histories of the businesses on the following pages are an indication of the diversity of the economic base of Jackson and Cape Girardeau County today.

Beussink Brothers Woodworks

Beussink Brothers Woodworks, started by Albert and Hilda Beussink in the 1950s, produces high quality custom cabinets and millwork for homes and offices throughout the region. Nine employees now work in the business, which began as a home workshop.

Albert and Hilda Beussink moved to Jackson from Leopold, Missouri, after their marriage on April 19, 1950. Albert had worked for Elfrink Construction since 1949 roofing houses, pouring concrete, and doing general carpentry. During this time period, Kenny Hager and Leonard Moll operated Jackson Lumber Company and were instrumental in helping Albert start his own business. Albert began building cabinets in the basement workshop of his home in the late 1950s. By 1964 he was doing enough business to start Al's Woodcraft and move into a building next to Jackson Ready Mix at the junction of Highways 61/25/34 in Jackson.

In 1966 Albert's brother Robert (Bob) Beussink Sr. joined the business. "To start the business we each put $1,000 in the kitty and opened a bank account," says Albert Beussink. "We didn't operate on other people's money!" The partnership worked well and the business increased. In 1967 a new building was constructed at Highway 61 and 1311 Gloria between Cape Girardeau and Jackson.

As the partners' families grew and the business expanded, Albert's sons Steve, Don, Mark, Greg, and John, along with Bob's sons Bob Jr., Chris, Matt, and Jeff, all worked in the business at one time or another. In 1992 Bob Beussink, Sr. retired and sold his interest in the business to Albert.

On September 7, 2000, fire destroyed the building on Gloria Street. On the same day of the fire, the business moved into a temporary location on a Gordonville farm owned by Leonard Beussink, another brother of Albert. With tremendous help from family and friends, Notre Dame High School faculty, staff, and students, and the Cape Girardeau and Jackson communities, the cleanup began and the search was underway for a new site for the business. While several sites were under consideration, the Jackson Jaycees came forward and offered to sell property on Old Toll Road that would be suitable for a new location. On March 19, 2001, production began at a new building at 2129 Old Toll Road, Jackson.

Current owners span two generations and include Albert, Steve, Greg, and John Beussink. Current employees include Albert, Steve, Greg, John, Mark, Chris, Matt, and Jeff Beussink and Kevin Ziegler, Albert's son-in-law. The third generation of this family business is represented by the son-in-law of Steve Beussink, Tim Garner, who has also been employed at Beussink Brothers.

By Judi (Beussink) Niederkorn

Central States Coca-Cola Company

In the fall of 1894 Emanuel Milde Sr. invested $1000 in the human powered machinery that would mix, bottle and cap the 6000 bottles of soda he and his sons would produce that year as the E. Milde Bottling Works. With the death of Emanuel Milde, Sr. in 1900, his sons, Emanuel, Jr. and Alvin D., continued the business. With increasing business, machinery was upgraded to gasoline power, then to electric power following the building of the city power plant in 1906. Delivery, originally made to local customers using a small push cart, switched to a wagon and team in 1912, allowing the company to service customers in towns as far as ten miles away.

Soon after the death of Emanuel Milde, Jr. in 1923, a Coca-Cola franchise was purchased and the company line was expanded in 1924, along with the name change, to the Milde Coca-Cola Bottling Company. Over the next forty years, there were a series of changes in partnerships as new territories were added to the company. After the death of A. D. Milde in 1960, the Milde family began to consolidate its interests in 1966. Over the next fifteen years partnership interests were purchased as a major realignment of territories was accomplished. About 1970, the Coca-Cola Bottling Company of Jackson, Missouri, purchased what became the Popular Bluff and Kennett divisions. In the early 1980s the company added the A & W Root Beer, NuGrape and Sunkist Orange franchises to its existing line of Coca-Cola products and Milde's Cream Soda. In order to reflect the regional nature of the business, the name was changed to the Coca-Cola Bottling Company of Southeast Missouri in 1984. It was purchased by the Central States Coca Cola Company in 1993. The company currently employs about eighty people. Instead of the simple pushcart, over 57 trucks deliver the more than 45 million bottles produced annually. (Information provided by the Coca-Cola Bottling Company of Southeast Missouri and Central States Coca-Cola Company)

Ceramo Company, Inc.

Mid-year 2001, saw the 56th anniversary of Ceramo Company, Incorporated. As a company, Ceramo was founded in 1945, beginning with an idea by two Ceramic Engineering students at the then Missouri School of Mines and Metallurgy, now University of Missouri, Rolla, and one of the their professors. A partnership was formed between Vernon L. Kasten, Raymond B. Jones, and Dr. Paul G. Herold for the manufacture of clay flower pots.

Almost a year was spent acquiring clay land, remodeling a large barn on property purchased from Mr. Walter Knox, and preparing the barn to house a manufacturing operation. Securing flower pot manufacturing equipment was a particular challenge. The partners designed a small periodic kiln, and brick for the kiln was laid by Vernon L. Kasten, along with the infant industry's first employee, Irvin W. Rasche.

Vernon L. Kasten's grandfather, father and

uncles were involved in the manufacture of brick in Jackson. Grandfather Kasten had started the production of building brick in 1895, thus there was clay products manufacturing in the background of Vernon L. Kasten.

Because sales potential had outstripped production, it was decided to erect the company's first continuous tunnel kiln. This first expansion came in 1949.

In 1950 the founding partnership was dissolved and Ceramo Company was incorporated. The first Board of Directors elected Vernon L. Kasten president of the corporation. He has continued in that position to the present.

Again, during 1952 and 1953, because of the need for additional capacity, another larger tunnel kiln was purchased from a hotel china manufacturer at Barnhart, Missouri, and was re-erected at Jackson and became the principal firing unit of the Ceramo plant. This kiln was the company's firing "workhorse" until May 1973. At that time, a new kiln was placed in operation. It required eighteen months from the time the company's Board of Directors authorized planning and building, until the new kiln was ready for production. Likewise, manufacturing equipment, including clay crushing and processing machinery, pug mills, presses and driers, followed the same patterns. Equipment was placed in production, re-designed, rebuilt or scrapped, and new, more efficient machines were put into place.

For a period of time, expansion of the company's business took the route of purchase of other companies. Many clay flower pot producers did not modernize their equipment and production facilities. As a result, they became available for acquisition. Ceramo purchased the substantial flower pot manufacturing plant of the Louisville, Kentucky, Pottery in 1959. Later, two smaller plants in St. Louis and a Louisville, Nebraska, plant were acquired. Later, the business and assets of the Wingert Pottery, in Chicago, gave Ceramo access to the Chicago area market. Having purchased the Wingert Pottery, Ceramo set up a warehousing operation in suburban Chicago, which it continues to the present.

In addition to the clay flower pots, all manufactured at Jackson, the company acts as a distributor for many products related to the flower-growing, garden center and retailing businesses. A substantial number of products are imported from manufacturers abroad. These include ware from China, the Dominican Republic, the Philippines, Thailand, Indonesia, Spain, Mexico and Italy.

In 1989, the two sons of Vernon L. Kasten were elected to the Board of Directors of Ceramo Company, Inc. Vernon L. Kasten, Jr., had been serving the company as sales manager, and Lawrence C. Kasten continues his service to the corporation as a member of its Board of Directors.

From a beginning, with one employee, plus the owner, Ceramo presently employs over one hundred persons. From a beginning in 1945 with no production, present production exceeds 50,000,000 pots annually.

By Vernon Kasten

Cracraft Miller Inc. – Furniture and Funeral

The firm began in 1912, formed by Mr. William Wessell. The Wessell Furniture Company sold in 1917 to Mr. William Ruff and Mr. John Talley, who operated it until 1924. At this time S. C. Cracraft purchased the interest of Mr. Ruff and in 1924, Ray G. Miller bought the interest of Mr. Talley, thus forming the Cracraft Miller Furniture and Funeral Home duo businesses, located on the corner of West Main and Missouri Streets. Soon thereafter, they moved across the street into a building known as the Brase building. Here a remodeling put a show window for furniture display in front and a "lay out" room in back for the funeral business.

In 1912 the business was a furniture store with a carpenter shop upstairs. Wood caskets were made and lined in the upstairs shop and transported to the family home by wagon or simply picked up by the family of the deceased. This answers the curious question often asked, how the two businesses were connected and how the Cracraft family got into the furniture and funeral business. In 1918 embalming became a part of the business and a small room for visitation was added to the back of the store.

The funeral business progressed from early wagon transportation to the horse-drawn hearse, rented from the Gockel Livery Stable, to the motor-powered hearse in the 1920s to the ambulance business. Funeral homes had the only equipment to handle a cot to transport sick or accident patients to the hospital. Today there are privately-owned ambulance services equipped with modern technology, EMTs and helicopters for distant transportation.

In 1944 the two businesses still co-existed but at separate locations. The present location of the Cracraft-Miller Funeral Home, 708 W. Main Street, was purchased. It had been a private home known as the Walsh Gladish home. The residence was completely redone by the Armstrong Decorating Department of Lancaster, Pennsylvania. The stained glass windows were purchased in St. Louis, Missouri. Penzel Construction Company did the remodeling, guided by architect Lawrence Luetje. In 1945 Gene C. Cracraft, son of S. C. Cracraft, upon returning from World War II and having completed courses in embalming school, joined the firm. He acquired stock in the businesses, both furniture and funeral.

In 1971 the chapel was built as an addition to the original building, and the back parking lot was completed at that time. At the present the home can accommodate three separate visitations at the same time and offers a variety of services including in-house services, move-to-the-church services, committal only services, and cremations according to a variety of family wishes. A casket display room has been incorporated into the building to offer a display of coffins in an array of prices and designs.

In 1978 Sherman M. Cracraft, son of Gene C. Cracraft, became a partner in the duo businesses. The furniture store remained in the uptown location until 1962, when the new store with ninety feet of glass across the front was built at 615 West Main Street to accommodate an expanding business and to make it a one-level building instead of the three-floor structure uptown. In the 1930s Cracraft-Miller diversified from furniture only, to floor covering, and was one of the first in the area to install wall-to-wall carpeting in 1939.

After the death of S. C. Cracraft in 1972 and the retirement of R. G. Miller in 1973, Gene C. Cracraft assumed the presidency of the firm. Mr. Tom Boudinot became a shareholder in 1962 and Mr. Paul Biri became a partner, and remained with the firm until 1977 and 1978 respectively. Upon selling their shares, for the first time in the history of the firm the Cracraft family was the sole owner of the businesses, and has remained so until the present day.

In 1978 Gene C. Cracraft made the decision to change the image of the furniture store from, in his words, "a tweeds and plaids" to a more up-to-date facility. It ultimately became a complete decorating center within the furniture store. Services included a wallpaper center, and drapery treatments, as well as a full assortment of blinds and alternative treatments, carpeting, hard surface flooring such as hardwood, tile, vinyl, and custom bedspreads and pillows. Gradually the sidewalls were divided into room setting, and decorative items such as artwork, mirrors, table top accessories, floor pieces, screens, area rugs, and silk florals became part of the store's repertoire.

From furniture markets in Chicago to the 1970s, to Dallas through the early 1990s and ultimately to High Point, North Carolina, the furniture store evolved into a one-of-a-kind business, becoming the forerunner for today's furniture store. Mr. Gene C. Cracraft retired in 1999 and Sherman M. Cracraft assumed the presidency. The Cracraft-Miller Furniture Store and Funeral Home combination became the last existing combination in the Cape Girardeau and Jackson area. The furniture store closed in 2000; the funeral home is still owned and operated by Sherman M. Cracraft. From $250.00 in the early years for an entire living room suite to $2000.00 for a sofa only, in 2002, from $250.00 for a funeral with several days of visitation to $5000.00 for a service in 2002, this very respected firm has indeed witnessed the changes over a century.

By Sherman Cracraft

The Devore Family Farm — A Missouri Century Farm

The Devore family farm, located on State Hwy A outside of Whitewater, MO in Cape Girardeau County, was recognized in 2001 as a MO Century Farm. William Miles and Margaret (Strong) Devore purchased 100 acres of the farm in December, 1866. Their marriage produced 10 children. In 1898, William sold approximately 42 acres of the farm to one of his sons, Levi Jack Devore. Levi and his wife, Ella (Hitt) owned the property until February, 1903. At that time, they sold the farm to his brother, John Miles Devore. John Devore and his wife, Alice (Cole) kept the property for five years. They sold the farm in January, 1908 to one of their 7 children, Ira Lee Devore, Sr.

Ira, known by Lee Devore, was born Dec. 2,

John Miles Devore at his farm in Whitewater MO, in 1925. Great-great-great-grandfather to David and Jack Retherford. Photo courtesy of Jackie Devore Retherford.

Jackson Frozen Food Locker, 2002.

David, Jr. & Jackie Devore-Retherford and their sons: L to R, Jack David and David Jack Retherford, Dec. 2001.

1881. He married the former Annie Eakins in June of 1903. After their marriage they added more rooms onto the original farmhouse. They lived their entire marriage on the farm. During this time, they row cropped the land and raised chickens, hogs and cattle. The farm had two barns, a machine shed, a granary, several chicken houses and a smokehouse. Lee and Annie had 5 sons. Three of the sons, Robert, Wilson, and Wilburn died in infancy. Their oldest son, Cecil Devore, born in 1907, lived his entire life on the farm. He died in 1986. Their youngest son, Ira Lee Devore, Jr. was born in 1917. He married the former Glenda Azalea Slinkard and lived in Whitewater until his death in 1996.

Upon Ira's death, his son and daughter-in-law, Jack Lee and Janice (Copman) Devore began extensive renovations of the old family farm house. All of the original fixtures that could be salvaged were refurbished and restored. The old smoke house that stood next to the house for many years was torn down at this time. The cypress wood in the smoke house was then used inside the newly remodeled home. Family folklore was that this original structure was a log cabin, but there was no evidence of this found when this restoration process was done. Jack and Janice Devore currently reside in this home.

In 1953, Lee and Annie Devore sold the State of Missouri the right-of-way for the relocation of State Hwy A. At this time a new bridge was built across the Whitewater River and the road was moved, splitting the farm. The road was moved to a higher location and a new bridge built to prevent flooding of the roadway, which was a recurrent problem. The road was relocated right next to the farm pond which is why the pond is currently located right next to the highway with no shoulder right-of-way.

The Devore farm currently consists of 200 acres, of which approximately 153 is tillable and 7 is mowed for hay. One tillable field, known as the "Island," is located where the Whitewater River ends and empties into the Diversion Channel. It is bordered by both these waters and also a slough, making it almost completely surrounded by water, thus the name "Island."

In 1989, David and Jackie (DeVore) Retherford, Jr., formerly of Jackson, MO, rented the farm ground from Ira and Jack Devore. Jackie is the daughter of Jack and Janice Devore, and the great-great-great- granddaughter of William Miles Devore. David, Jackie and their two sons, David and Jack Retherford still farm the Devore ground. David and Jack Retherford make seven generations of Devore descendants to work this family farm.

Also, recognized in 2001 as a MO Century Farm was another farm owned by David, Jr. and Jackie (DeVore) Retherford. In 1873, Jackie's great-great-grandfather, John Miles Devore purchased 332 acres in Whitewater, MO, of which 180 were under cultivation. Mr. Devore had one the first steam threshers in the area, with which he did a large business during the threshing season. During the winter he used his engine for sawing lumber. He also owned a blacksmith shop and mercantile store in Whitewater and was a member of the Agricultural Wheel.

In 1906, John sold the farm to one of his sons, William A. Devore. William was married to the former Viola Kinder. They lived their entire married life on the farm, raising two sons, Russell and Glen. David and Jackie purchased 78 acres of this farm from the family in January 1997. They still farm the ground today along with their two sons, David and Jack Retherford of Advance, MO.

By Jackie Devore-Retherford

Jackson Frozen Food Lockers

In 1949 William Daniels, with Carlton Meyer as the General Manager, founded Jackson Frozen Food Lockers at 400 South High Street. Mr. Daniels also opened the Cape Frozen Foods business on Broadway in Cape Girardeau until its closing in the 1970s. The Lockers' main business is custom processing of locally raised beef and hogs. In the 1960s the business attempted to put a slaughterhouse in the basement of the building, but the City Council voted against allowing it, due to concerns of "the smell."

In 1972 Carlton purchased the Locker from Mr. Daniels. Beginning in the late 1970s, Charles Meyer, Carlton's oldest son, began managing the business. He continued in this position until 1993. In 1993 Carlton's youngest son, Craig, began managing the business. Over the years, almost all members of the family have worked at the Locker in some capacity.

In the 1970s deer hunting became more prominent in the area, and the Locker offered deer processing. Since that time, the Locker has processed over 9000 deer and made over 150,000 pounds of deer sausage. The Locker is the oldest meat processing plant still operating in Cape Girardeau County.

The Locker has offered many different services over the years. Until 1993, locker rental was quite popular. At one time, over four hundred freezer lockers were rented, each holding two hundred pounds of meat and vegetables. It was common to have a waiting list of months to obtain a locker. Up until the early 1970s, the local students enjoyed stopping by the Locker to purchase different ice cream and soda products that were offered.

Each August a fully loaded tractor-trailer unloaded its fruits at the Locker.

The Locker also sold tons of frozen fruits each August up until the late 1980s when the demand for wholesale frozen fruits diminished. Things have changed over the years at the Locker.

In 1997 the Locker began retail selling of their own beef summer sausage, and in 1998 also sold their own beef jerky. In 2000 they put up their website, Ask The Meatman.com, and began advertising and selling over the Internet. In 2002, the Locker is still in business and looking forward to finding new ways to serve customers in the local area and across the United States.

By Craig Meyer

Jones Drug Store

Jones Drug Store was founded in 1871 by James F. Edwards and Henry L. Jones and located in a building on the corner of Main and First West Streets. When Mr. Edwards retired from the firm, the business was renamed H.L. Jones Drug Store. When the brick building next door became available, Mr. Jones purchased it and increased his stock of medicines and merchandise. When the City of Jackson adopted plans to beautify the uptown area following the building of the "new" courthouse in 1908, and in the process to change the street pattern to create the courthouse square, Jones Drug Store was among those buildings scheduled for demolition. However, Mr. Jones contracted with a St. Louis firm to have the building turned to face the new street on the east. When the work was completed, using horses and wagons to rotate it, this became the first brick building west of the Mississippi to be moved and turned in another direction. The building still stands today, a testament to good construction. The business remained in the Jones family, passing from H.L. Jones's sons Murrary and Duree to his grandson Henry L. Jones, who operated it with his mother, Tom Rahm, and John Schulte, Jr., until it was sold in 1968. The business retained the name "Jones Drug Store" and is operated today by Gene Brockett and Don Brown in the Court Street location, one of the few drug stores in Missouri having the same name and the same location for over a hundred years. (Information provided by Jones Drug Store).

Kasten Masonry Sales, Inc.

That the ancient and honorable science of brick making has a long history in Jackson, Missouri, is evidenced by the fact that the Kasten Clay Products, Incorporated, celebrated its 106th anniversary in 2001. In 1895 R. C. Kasten moved from Uniontown to Jackson, when he purchased a one-half interest in the William Oldenhoener Brick Company. In 1896 R. C. Kasten moved from Uniontown to Jackson, when he purchased a one-half interest in the William Oldenhoener Brick Company. In 1896 Kasten bought the other half of the Oldenhoener Company and moved the manufacturing operations to the area of Highway 61.

The method of producing brick in that plant entailed using horses to mix the soft red surface clay, placing it in a sand-lined mold, and "bumping" the clay in the shape of a brick, out to dry. Firing the brick was done in rectangular periodic, or beehive, kilns. The kilns were first fired using wood, and later, coal was used to fuel the kilns.

In 1898 H. R. English started the Jackson Brick and Tile Company. In 1908 this company became bankrupt. Two entrepreneurs purchased the company and operated it about a year. At this time, R. C. Kasten and Jos. Schmuke, who had bought a half-interest in Kasten's company, bought the Southeast Missouri Brick and Tile Company and operated both companies until 1914. At this time all the equipment was moved to a location near the present-day bowling alley. In 1920 the four sons of R. C. Kasten- Arthur, Louis, Walter and John -purchased the Schmuke interest in the brick plant.

In 1926 ground was broken for a new manufacturing facility. A continuous tunnel kiln was built, the first in the state. This kiln continues as the firing facility for the company. Today the kiln operates using sawdust as fuel, instead of coal or gas, because of the costs involved.

In 1959 Arthur, Walter and John Kasten sold their interest and Kasten Clay Products, Incorporated, came into existence, replacing the Kasten Brothers Brick Company. Also, in 1959, the company established the Kasten Concrete Products, Incorporated, for the production of concrete block, brick and other concrete products, in Cape Girardeau. To sell the output of both the brick and concrete products plants, Kasten Masonry Sales, Incorporated, was established. This latter company also sells brick made by other manufacturers and has diversified to sell spas, wood burning stoves, fireplace inserts, gas logs, gun safes and many other products.

That the growth of this industry as been little short of phenomenal is attested to by the fact that the present location of the brick manufacturing facility was a corn field. Today the large area, with its surrounding clay deposit and fleet of twenty-three highway tractors and thirty trailers used to deliver products, gives evidence of broad scale activity. Since 1895 the brick-making facility has produced well over a billion bricks to serve the needs of builders in southeast Missouri and nearby Arkansas, Illinois and Tennessee points.

In 1988, to aid in the distribution of products, Kasten Masonry Sales, Incorporated, established a full service warehousing and distribution center in Carbondale, Illinois. All products manufactured and sold by the three Kasten Companies are warehoused and delivered from the Carbondale facility.

Since 1959, Vernon L. Kasten has been president of the three corporations, Kasten Clay Products, Incorporated; Kasten Concrete Products, Incorporated; and Kasten Masonry Sales, Incorporated. John David Kasten is general manager of the three corporations and his son, Quentin Kasten, serves as production manager.

By Vernon Kasten

Other Jackson Industries

Other Jackson industries include ACF (American Car Foundry), a manufacturer of parts for railroad cars, 149 employees; Wahlco D. W. Tool, outsourcing and custom packaging, 270 employees; and RAPCO Manufacturing Company, customized electric cables, 140 employees. Northeast of Jackson is the Proctor and Gamble Paper Products plant manufacturing disposable diapers, feminine hygiene products, and other paper products. P&G employs 1,600 workers. Its associated companies, such as Defender Industry and Nordenia, employ hundreds of Jackson residents. (*Southeast Missourian*, Progress Edition, February 24, 2002, p. 2-5 and Jackson Chamber of Commerce website).

Premium Mechanical Contracting Co., 3185 North High Street, Jackson, 2002.

Businesses

ANDREW JACKSON BRIDAL & TUXEDO

The Andrew Jackson Bridal and Tuxedo Shop in Jackson, MO was founded in January 1992. Originally the store sold fine men's clothing and offered alterations. The store began phasing out fine clothing and became a men's formal wear store. From men's formal wear, the store began to offer candelabra rentals, invitations, lattice, and church and reception items.

Gina Cook Janson purchased the store from Tom and Pam Schulte. After owning the store for a year, an expansion was needed, and at that time we expanded to include prom wear, then bridal wear, with men's formal wear still remaining an important part of the business. Today, we are happily serving the second generation of men, as we have so much repeat business.

Today's brides and grooms are very informed and very busy, so we try to meet their needs by being able to furnish everything for a wedding. We have a larger selection of wedding gowns, bridesmaids dresses and men's tuxedos. Prices vary greatly, according to the style and color. However we try to fulfill everyone's needs and dreams for "that special occasion."

Bank of Missouri

"We're new to Jackson, but you've known us for a long time," stated John M. Thompson, community bank president of The Bank of Missouri in Jackson.

The Bank of Missouri has been serving southeast Missouri since 1891 and now has five full-service banking centers and two branches. The bank began in Perryville where a small group of men saw the need for a bank in their town, thus began Bank of Perryville. In 1997 Bank of Perryville opened another full-service facility and changed its name to The Bank of Missouri. This change was the first step in an effort for the bank to expand into other markets.

In January 1998 another full-service bank opened at 1622 N. Kingshighway in Cape Girardeau, and was soon followed by a loan production office in Jackson. The banking center at 233 W. Jackson Boulevard in Jackson opened for business on Dec. 18, 2000. In May 2001 another full-service banking center opened in Marble Hill. The Bank of Missouri also operates branches at Chateau Girardeau in Cape Girardeau and TG Missouri in Perryville, in addition to owning and operating Banc of Missouri Mortgage in Cape Girardeau and Banc of Missouri Investment Services in Perryville.

The Bank Of Missouri Timetable

November 1891 – Bank of Perryville opens.
November 1991 – Bank of Perryville celebrates 100th anniversary.
April 1997 – Bank of Perryville opens loan production office in Cape Girardeau.
August 1997 – Construction is complete on a new full-service bank in Perryville.
January 1998 - Construction is complete on a new full-service bank in Cape Girardeau.
April 1998 – Loan production office opens in Jackson.
September 1998 – Bank branch opens inside Chateau Girardeau in Cape Girardeau.
April 1999 – Bank branch opens inside TG Missouri in Perryville.
December 2000 – Construction is complete on new full-service bank in Jackson.
May 2001 – Full-service bank opens in Marble Hill.
November 2001 – The Bank of Missouri celebrates 110th anniversary.

The Bank of Missouri

The Cash-Book Journal

The *Cash-Book Journal* (CBJ) has been providing news to the Jackson community and the surrounding area for well over a century. The news has come under a variety of names and publishers, but the continuing thread has been to provide readers with a quality newspaper.

The Missouri Cash-Book was established in 1871 by W. L. Malone. Other newspapers were established in Cape Girardeau County before and after the *Cash-Book,* but most lasted only several years; indeed, some stopped operation after just months. The one newspaper that published longer than the others was *The Deutscher Voksfreund,* which began publishing in 1886 under Rev. Frederick Kies.

Rev. Kies sold his interest to his sons, J. G. and Fred, six years after publication began. In 1910 the brothers began an English newspaper, *The Jackson Items.* In 1917, J. G. sold out to his brother to pursue other interests; the load of publishing two newspapers proved to be too much and on July 4, 1918, Kies changed to *The Cape County Post.* It was bilingual, with five pages printed in English and three in German.

That all changed, however, when WWI broke out. Despite the area's large German ancestry population, there were a number of anti-German acts of violence. Despite the armistice signing in 1918, a mob gathered at the newspaper office on Aug. 29, 1919, threatening to destroy all German type in the office. To prevent any violence, Kies agreed to stop publishing in German. On that night, *The Cape County Post* became 100 percent English and continued to publish for several years.

Until 1833, there were several owners of *The Missouri Cash-Book;* it was then that F. A. McGuire became sole owner of the paper. He operated the publication until 1915, when he sold out to C. C. Oliver who then founded the Cape Girardeau *Morning Sun.* Oliver retired in 1922 and the Jackson newspaper was operated by Joe Myer, who published it for just 16 months before selling his interest to R. K. Wilson. Wilson served as editor until his death in 1955.

That same year Wilson's then son-in-law, Marvin Proffer, was discharged from the service and returned to Jackson to take over as editor. Oliver came out of retirement for a brief time to advise Proffer, who was new to the publishing business. The Proffers purchased *The Missouri Cash-Book* from Wilson's estate in 1960.

1962 was an important year for Jackson newspapers. In April John Hoffman purchased *The Cape County Post* from then-editor Leo Schade and also purchased *The Missouri Cash-Book* from the Proffers. He then merged the two newspapers and named the new publication The *Jackson Pioneer.* Around that same time, Ward Denman began publishing the *Jackson Journal. The Pioneer* was sold to Wayne Freeman, who resurrected the two previous names of the newspaper, christening the new publication the *Post and Cash-Book.*

In 1967 Marvin Proffer returned to the publishing industry, purchasing the *Post and Cash-Book* with partner Joyce Peerman. Proffer and Peerman served as co-editors as well as co-publishers. At that time the newspaper was printed in Corning, AR. As Proffer had recently been elected to the Missouri Legislature, the weekly job of delivering the paper to Corning to be printed fell to Peerman. Several years later they were able to have the paper printed in Sikeston, saving Peerman a lot of time and miles. In 1970 Proffer and Peerman joined with the publishers of three area newspapers (Perryville, Charleston, and Chaffee) to form Cape Central Publishing Company, which still today prints *The Cash-Book Journal* and several other weekly newspapers. Peerman sold her half-interest to Proffer in December 1976 but remains a special part of the newspaper, writing her weekly *Potpourri* column which receives high praise from readers. In 1974, current CBJ publisher Gerald Jones and three friends purchased the *Jackson Journal* from Gary Rust, now owner of *The Southeast Missourian.* Jones became general manager of the newspaper and soon bought out his three friends. In January 1977 he and Proffer merged their two publications and renamed the newspaper *The Cash-Book Journal,* taking a part of the name of each of their papers to maintain the continuity. The headline in the Jan. 5, 1977 issue read "NEWSPAPERS CONSOLIDATE: PROFFER AND JONES ARE EDITORS."

The partners proceeded to improve the newspaper and increase its circulation. In 1968, when Peerman and Proffer first purchased the *Post and Cash-Book,* circulation was at 1,600; today circulation stands at 5,875. More than three years ago, the CBJ expanded with a second publication called *The Weekender,* bringing total circulation to more than 11,000.

Jones and Proffer remained partners until November 1984, when Jones became sole owner *of The Cash-Book Journal.* Jones was elected as Cape Girardeau County Presiding Commissioner in 1995, which meant he needed a dependable, experienced staff working at the newspaper offices. Among them, the staff has over 100 years of newspaper experience.

Newspapers in Jackson and Cape Girardeau County have come and gone, and most have been forgotten. Through name and ownership changes, *The Cash-Book Journal* has remained constant for well over a century ... providing its hometown with the best source for community news and advertising.

The McAtee Mercantile Company in the first block of West Main Street. The owners, clerks and grocery delivery wagon drivers were from the left: Alvin Kneibert, Fred Schneider, Julius Shaper, driver of second wagon was Ed Rose, lady under Cash-Book sign was Lulu Rose, and the man with vest and tie was J. Haisten Poe. The Cash-Book Printing office apparently was upstairs and the Jackson Exchange Bank next door, circa 1915.

Eye Care Center Of Jackson

Dr. Kenneth C. Detring, established Eye Care Center of Jackson in 1980. Eye Care Center was first located at 1404 Old Cape Road in the former Goodson Building. Phyllis Thompson was his first optometric assistant. A few years later this office underwent remodeling and expansion to include an enlarged optical dispensary and an additional exam room. Terry Timpkins, Cheryl Cook, and Sarah Stearns Fadler were added to the staff as well as Dr. Detring's wife, Dawn.

In 1990, the office was moved to 810 E. Jackson Blvd. into a newly constructed office building. The practice continued to grow and Kim Fritsche Dost was added to the staff.

In 2000, Eye Care Center celebrated its 20th anniversary with the opening of the newly remodeled office at 1014 East Jackson Blvd. The new facility has easy access to Jackson Boulevard, has a large parking area, and is handicapped accessible. Cheryl Cook, Kim Dost, and Dawn Detring are the current optometric assistants with combined experience of over 40 years. Today, computers are networked together to handle patient records and accounts.

Dr. Detring and his staff attend Vision Expo in Las Vegas to see the latest product development in the optical field. The mission statement reads: "Our Mission is to always be a leader in the ophthalmic profession for those who choose personal, professional, quality eye care."

By Kenneth C. Detring, O.D.

Blumenberg Homesite circa, 1900 near Allenville, MO. L to R with birth year noted: Louis Lee (1888), Monroe Columbus (1896), Louis Henry (1847), Wilson Ernold (1898), Mary Herzog (1857), Anna Meta (1892), Walter William (1894), and Albert (1890). July 26, 1906 SE Missourian: Best wheat heard of so far this year is reported by old German Farmer, Louis Blumberg, who lives 1-1/2 miles north of Allenville; he has 33 acres of wheat which average 22 bushels per acre and tested 65 pounds to a bushel; Whitewater Milling Co. pays him 85 centers per bushel premium of 5 cents for extra weight.

Fronabarger Concreters, Inc.

In 1980 when Glenn and Marilyn Fronaberger started the Fronabarger Concrete Finishing business, most of the work performed by a few employees was residential. In 1983, a full time estimator was hired. In 1986, the company incorporated and the name was changed to Fronabarger Concreters, Inc. In 1999 we moved to a new office located in Oak Ridge, MO and a full time office manager was hired.

Through the years, we have purchased more advanced equipment including a laser screed in 2000. Today we have around 50 employees and most of the work done is commercial and industrial flatwork

Some of the work that we have done in the Jackson area includes: all of Bent Creek, Adams Street, Rosewood Subdivision streets, Savannah Ridge subdivision, Ridge Road, Shawnee Street, Warren Place subdivision, Morgan Street extension, all of the concrete work at Shawnee Square Carwash and Storage and all of the concrete work at Independence Square Carwash.

Fronabarger Concreters, Inc. Oak Ridge, MO

Fronabarger Concreters pouring Morgan Street extension, 1995

Hebo USA and Indasia

In 1996 Henning and Brigitte Bollerslev founded Old Bavarian Sausage in Jackson, MO. With Henning coming from a family with three generations of master sausage makers and Brigitte also an experienced sausage maker; it seemed to be a natural choice. They bring more than generations of sausage recipes; they also bring the German technology of today's history to the American market.

The rich German heritage in the community was among the reasons for living here. Henning is a native of Denmark and Brigitte was born and raised in Munich, Germany. They met each other in Germany and there they married and lived, until moving to America with son Daniel Herzog in May of 1996. Brigitte has family that lives in the States and friends in southeast Missouri, which is another reason they chose the Jackson area.

Soon after operations started at Old Bavarian Sausage, the Bollerslevs attained a contract with the U. S. Military to deliver their authentic German sausages to the commissaries. This gave the military personnel who had been stationed in Germany or their native spouses the opportunity to purchase authentic German products. Bratwurst, knackwurst, wiener, braunschweiger, leberkaese and German bologna are just a few items among the varieties that the company offers.

In conjunction with the office in Jackson, there is an outlet store which offers the same products that are in the commissary. Also available is a large selection of spices, seasonings and marinades. For those hunters or home butchers in the area, they will find natural and sterile casings along with spice compounds to make their own sausage. The store also carries a selection of German knives and equipment for sausage making.

All products at Old Bavarian Sausage are made with German spices and overseen by Brigitte who insures that the original recipes, which have been passed down from generations of master sausage makers, are followed to produce an authentic quality product. Providing this authentic taste requires them to import spices and seasonings from Germany. For this reason Indasia USA was founded in 1998.

While the name is little known here, in Europe the Indasia spice mills are renowned for very high quality spices and seasonings. The company has been in existence for 52 years and was started by master sausage makers who wanted to make their own seasonings for their products. There are now a total of seven spice mills in Europe which produce approximately 200,000 tons of spices each year.

Indasia USA brings these quality spices to America. Henning Bollerslev provides consulting to the meat and sausage industry, and introduces them to the Indasia spices and seasonings along with a wealth of knowledge available through technology to help them produce a better meat product. Henning, who travels nationwide, offers personal attention to all of his clients.

The Bollerslevs decided after six years of experience in the meat market and industry to change the company noame from Indasia USA to Hebo USA (derived from Henning Bollerslev), effective on October 1, 2002, therefore giving the customer a larger variety of products from different suppliers.

Today, customers appreciate the knowledge that the Bollerslevs share to experience the authentic taste of Germany. Indasia, which translates, "for the love of flavor," truly is the inspiration of this business.

Henning Bollerslev

2370 N. High Street, Suite 3, located in the North High Mall, Jackson, MO 63755, 573-243-5222, fax # 573-243-8723

Henning and Brigitte Bollerslev and son, Daniel Herzog

A sampling of line Old Bavarian Sausage

Kimbeland Country Club

On July 16, 1962, five members of the Jackson community formed a corporation to start a golf course and country club. These five gentlemen, Robert Wulff, Robert Hartle, Kenneth Kasten, Paul Mueller and John Schulte Jr., each spent $100.00 so the corporation could be started. With the help of Paul Mueller, a lawyer from town, they drew up the original by-laws and articles of incorporation for the club to govern their rules and regulations.

These original shareholders met with a gentleman named George Kimbel. Mr. Kimbel owned the Kimbeland Farm, which is the land the golf course currently occupies. Even though Mr. Kimbel was not a golfer and didn't have any interest in playing, he and his wife, Lillian, liked the idea that they could sit on their porch and watch the players enjoying their rounds of golf. George Kimbel agreed to lease the land to build the golf course and loan any monies that were needed at an interest rate of 6.0%. The original plans were to build a nine-hole golf course with a clubhouse, swimming pool and tennis courts, with an additional nine holes to be added as funds became available. The construction of the original nine holes began in the fall of 1962 on approximately 78 acres of ground. A five-acre lake was added to the property to serve as the water source for the golf course. With the help of many Jackson citizens and businesses, the farmland started to turn into what looked like a golf course.

To gather funds together to help pay for the expenses, many of the charter members began traveling around the area trying to sell stock in the corporation. Each share of stock was sold for $100.00, which enabled the owners to obtain a membership without paying an initiation fee into the club. The Board of Directors set the dues for an annual membership at $100.00 per year. They were able to get 90 members before the golf course was opened. George Kimbel funded any other monies that were needed to help build the course. Mr. Kimble did not believe in investing his money in stocks or bonds, but he was very generous with his money if he could have his name placed on his investment.

Including the help of the original members, many others, including Jack and Jim Litz, Jim and Billy Joe Thompson, Wib Bangert, Palmer Hacker, Hassle Looney, Kelly Blackman, Bill Call, R. O. Hawkins, J. E. Hecker, Gene Cracraft and Bill Heyde Jr., began to put in the effort to take the farmland and turn it into a golf course. Many companies, including Kasten Clay Products, Calvin Phillips Excavating, Cape County Commissioners, Charlie Meyer Excavating, Litz Brothers Poultry, and Bangert Auto Wrecking Service, also donated their time and equipment to help. Fencerows and trees were removed, land was tilled, the lake was constructed and the road and water lines were put in. With the assistance of Albert Linkogel and Ray Freeburg, a golf course design company from St. Louis, the course was laid out over hilly, wooded land of southeast Missouri. With recommendations from Linkogel and Freeburg, bent grass greens would be built which ensured that the members would be able to enjoy their golfing season year round. Bob Wulff was instrumental in overseeing the construction of the greens.

After the golf course opened in the spring of 1963, designs for a clubhouse were drawn. The Board of Directors decided to issue more stock to help fund the construction of the clubhouse. It was built in the fall of 1963 with plans to open in the spring of 1964. Now that the nine-hole golf course had a clubhouse, a motion was made to build a pool. Mr. Kimbel informed the Board of Directors that he would pay for the construction of the pool if he could design the shape. With approximately 300 members in the fall of 1965, the stockholders voted to build an additional nine holes to make the first eighteen-hole golf course in Cape Girardeau County.

The membership was flourishing and the golf course was improving due to the hard work of the people involved. The golf course superintendents and their staffs kept the golf course in such shape that it was voted the best golf course from St. Louis to Memphis. Mr. Blevens, a greens keeper from Sikeston, was the first superintendent, but due to his lack of experience with bent grass greens, Earl Siebert replaced him. Earl served as the superintendent until 1970, when Sherry Baker took over.

George and Lillian Kimbel celebrating their 25th wedding anniversary

One of the beautiful lakes on the Kimbeland Golf Course

Sherry continued to work for Kimbeland as the greens keeper until 1996. David Chasteen took over the helm and still serves as the superintendent to this day.

An integral part of having a country club with a clubhouse is to have somebody run the operation. The club hired a man named Penny Crabtree to oversee the business of the clubhouse and pro shop. Penny was replaced by Henry Vogel and then by Jim Thompson. Jim was the first person to own and operate the clubhouse on his own. He hired a young man named Bill Wampler to work for him, who went away to a Professional Golf Association School in Florida. When Bill came back, he took over for Jim and became the first P.G.A. member to be hired as the golf professional at Kimbeland. Many others have succeeded Bill, including Jess Simpson, Wes Duperier, Bill Curry, John Alexander, Brad Krutz, Larry Emery, Doug Dunbar, Todd Eastin, and now Jim Davey, but the club has always kept the tradition of having a P.G.A. member serve as its golf professional.

A long-standing tradition of Kimbeland has been the associations that sponsor and help run the tournaments for members and outside guests. The Men's and Ladies' Associations were formed and their support for golf and the club has continued to this day. Both associations have formed leagues and tournaments as well as a bridge club for the ladies. Thursday has been ladies' day since the club started and has played an important role in the social atmosphere the club has provided to its members and guests. Kimbeland Country Club sponsors an Annual Children Fishing tournament; begun by Hartford Hill, the event has been coordinated by Ed Schwent for the last 15 years.

The golf course stayed the same until 1996, when a group headed by Jack Litvay laid out a new and improved golf course with larger greens and a more challenging layout. The course continues to improve with the help of the current Board of Directors and the members, but all of it can be attributed to the young men who decided to dedicate their time and money to build a golf course and country club in the town of Jackson. And as they all know, without the financial help of George Kimbel, there would be no Kimbeland Country Club.

2002 Board of Directors: Clarence Ackman, Mike Hess, Gordon Feeney, Sam McCune, Wayne Nesslein, Bob Phillips, Carroll Williams, Pres., Jim Walker, Treas.

Aerial view of Kimbeland Golf Course, circa 1975

Lichtenegger, Weiss & Fetterhoff, LLC

It wasn't always the same partners, but the Law Firm has its origins in 1974. John Lichtenegger had just completed serving as the campaign manager for John Ashcroft who was running for State Auditor of Missouri. Lichtenegger and his wife, Donna, of just six months decided to leave politics behind and return home to Jackson to start a family and practice law. They have two children; Brent and Leigh. Leigh will graduate from the University of Colorado School of Law in May of 2003.

John, the son of Melvin and Norma Lichtenegger, grew up on Russell Street next to the City Park, right next door to the home of Judge Osler and Erma Statler. The Judge's son, Peter, had completed law school and was serving in the Navy. Judge Statler wrote a letter of recommendation to dean Joe Covington at the University of Missouri on behalf of John. John was admitted and three years later in 1972 received his law degree. Judge Statler swore John in as a member of the Missouri Bar Association.

John practiced a few years with Ken Waldron, who was then City Attorney. The first office was located at 128 West Main, Jackson, MO.

In 1978, John decided to start his own law firm. The first office was in the "Goodson Building" located at Highway 61, Shawnee and Old Cape Road. Within a year, Jack H. Knowlan Jr. joined John to form the firm of Lichtenegger and Knowlan. Cheryl Amos, formerly Cheryl Pender, served as legal secretary the first day and for 20 years thereafter.

In 1980, John and Jack built a beautiful building designed by local architect Keith Cracraft. Cracraft created a strong functional building with iron spot brick and unique window treatments. The building continues to serve as the main office of the firm located at 1210 Greenway Drive, Jackson.

John was appointed to the Board of Curators of the University of Missouri System in 1985. He served 10 years on the Board, serving two consecutive terms as President of the Board in 1992 and 1993.

In 1998, Jack Knowlan was named by Governor John Ashcroft to be the Chief Administrative Law Judge for Workers Compensation in Southeast Missouri. In that same year, Chris Weiss joined the firm.

Chris N. Weiss was born and raised in the Jackson, MO area. He is the son of Norman and Viola Weiss. He is married to Lesa J. Weiss. They have three children; Jennifer, Andrew and Abigail.

Scott Fetterhoff is the son of William G. and Carol Fetterhoff of Marble Hill, MO. He is married to Tracy Fetterhoff. They have two children, Evan and Sarah.

Current Partners of the firm are: John P. Lichtenegger, Chris N. Weiss, Scott Fetterhoff and Nathan D. Cooper. Wayne M. Keller is an associate with the firm. In addition to the Jackson office at 1210 Greenway Drive, the firm has offices in Marble Hill and St. Louis. The firm employes 11 para-legals and assistants.

John P. Lichtenegger – University of Missouri-Columbia Law School – 1972

Chris N. Weiss - University of Missouri-Columbia Law School – 1988

Scott Fetterhoff - University of Missouri-Columbia Law School – 1990

Nathan D. Cooper – St. Louis University – 1999

Wayne M. Keller – University of Missouri-Kansas City – 1997

John Lichtenegger

Chris N. Weiss

Scott Fetterhoff

Nathan D. Cooper

Macke's Store, Gordonville, MO

This is the story of not only a general store, but also a family and a way of life. However, it begins not in Gordonville, MO, but in Ellierode (Ellisrode), Germany. Heinrich Ahrens the elder was born about 1811 and in 1836 he married Johanne Siemers. Mr. Ahrens was a tailor by trade. A son, Heinrich P. Ahrens, was born to the couple on Oct. 18, 1837. A daughter followed in 1840 and she was named Fredericka. Heinrich's first wife died and he married Johanne Fredericka Wilhelmine Louise Sackman. A daughter, Wilhelmina, was born on Nov. 27, 1843. In November of 1845 the couple and their three children boarded the ship *Charlemagne* and set sail for the Port of New Orleans. The youngest child died during the journey and was buried at sea. The Ahrens with their remaining children traveled up the Mississippi River to Cape Girardeau and settled on a farm near the town of Gordonville, MO.

Henry P. Ahrens farmed with his father and Judge Hager until he was old enough to marry and begin farming on his own. On Feb. 7, 1860 he married Christine Mueller and the couple had seven children. In 1881-1882 Henry purchased some land and buildings from Albert Feszold. He went into business with Volkerding and a store was built near Hubble Creek. Later Ahrens sold this land to the railroad, which built a depot on the land, and the store was moved to higher ground. It is believed that at this time Ahrens bought out Volkerding. He ran the business until his death in 1916 after which his grandson, Henry Wesley Macke, inherited the business. Henry Macke was the only child born to Julius Macke and Caroline Ahrens (see Macke/Ahrens) and was reared by his Ahrens grandparents.

The family business was originally known as the Gordonville Mercantile Company. Mr. Ahrens eventually purchased the Gordon Store on Main Street and combined the merchandise. The town of Gordonville was a thriving community and served as a center of trade for much of the surrounding territory. Mr. Ahrens' grandson, Henry Macke, worked with him, learning the business, and took over when Mr. Ahrens passed away. Henry Macke married Rosena Ueleke on May 29, 1904, and they had one son, Albert Henry Macke. At some point the family purchased the Kerstner's Furniture business building. Henry began constructing a new brick building next door and it is told that after a day of hauling roofing materials Henry suffered a heart attack and died in November of 1928. Henry and his son Albert did not work together like Henry had worked with his Grandpa Ahrens. Albert had worked in the office at a cement plant and sold cars for a living. When Henry died Albert took over the business and the business expanded into new areas of endeavor during the next 30 years.

Albert married Dorothy Elsie Probst on Oct. 23, 1929, and they worked hard to make the business a success in hard times. During the Depression years the Mackes managed to keep their business alive and helped others in their community. Early on Albert established a milk route and during WWII this was considered an essential service. Those driving the routes were not necessarily obligated to serve overseas. He also began a livestock hauling venture. The store would send stock trucks to local farms to pick up the livestock, bring it back to a holding facility, and then haul the animals to St. Louis to the stockyards. The livestock business was in competition with the railroad and was successful, because the animals lost less weight on their way to market. There are many interesting tales amongst the family about hauling livestock. The store started early on hiring young men from the community and for many this may have been their first paying job. It continued in this practice until the family sold the business.

During Albert and Dorothy's tenure as owners of the business it was known as Macke's Store. In the 1950s the decision was made to build a new larger building next to the brick structure. The Kerstner building, a wooden structure that was probably the original Gordon Store, was taken down. The story is told in the family that there were hand-hewn logs in the structure that had secret compartments in them designed to hide valuables in when raiders would come during the Civil War. Once the new store was completed the brick building next door was taken down. When the brick building was taken down there were "coins" found in the structure, but they turned out to be store tokens. In the 1950s a mobile milling service was added to the business. This service took a feed grinder to the farms and ground the feed on site as opposed to purchasing large quantities of feed in bags. As had been the case in the past, family members often worked in the store. Albert and Dorothy had three children, Henry Weldon (1930), Dorothy Ann (1932) and Alberta Louise (1945). Weldon married Bonnie Bierschwal in 1954 and continued to work in the store. In December of 1957 Albert Macke died of a stroke and in 1958 the business became Macke's Store Inc. In the early 1960s the Mackes opened a small store on Independence in Cape Girardeau selling eggs, processing cream and selling other items like fertilizers. This business was open for about 10 years.

Dorothy Macke and Weldon continued to work together with Mrs. Macke focusing on the General Store business and Weldon working more with the Farm Services. Dorothy Macke was always generous with her time and service to her community. She was active in the Gordonville 4-H for 40 years as a project and a community leader. She worked with the University of Missouri Extension Council, the Gordonville Homemakers, and the Southeast Missouri Hospital Auxiliary. The family sold the store in 1975 to Roy Brown and Mrs. Macke retired. Weldon kept the farm equipment portion of the business and operated it at the corner of Hwy 25 and Route Z until he sold the business to Dan Buessink in the 1990s.

The Macke children remember many days of working and playing in the store. Weldon's daughters, Pam and Karen, enjoy telling the story of picking up a load of hogs at a local farm with their parents. On the way back to the store the girls were looking out the back window and giggling because the hogs had gotten the gate up and were jumping off the back of the truck, rolling, getting up and running off. The hogs were eventually rounded up, reloaded and hauled to market. Some of the jobs taken on by family members were learning to grade eggs, sort soda bottles, take inventory, stock shelves and wait on customers. For many years the store would open before the farmers went to the fields and stay open until well after dark with Sunday being the only day off. The store was often a gathering place where the locals could get a fresh lunch meat sandwich, a cold soda from the cooler, and visit with friends and neighbors. Improvements in the roads and cars made it easier for families to travel to larger towns, and the advent of supermarkets would spell the end of the profitability of general stores. It would also be the end of a way of life, as the town of Gordonville is now primarily a bedroom-community.

Albert Macke (left) and cousin, Alvin Ueleke (right) across street from Gordonville Mercantile owned by Henry Macke. Note Post Office designation on front of store, circa 1910.

Old-time grocers. Carol Ann Wachoski (left) got assistance at the checkout counter of Macke's Store in Gordonville in this Sept. 18, 1971 photo. Behind the counter were Mrs. Dorothy Macke, store owner, and Mrs. Albert Wessell.

McCombs Funeral Homes, Inc.

The first written records of 1861 note that a business known as Mooreland and Tobler was located at 112 South High Street in uptown Jackson. Today it is known as Ross Furniture Company. Gus Tobler, manager/owner, carried all sorts of merchandise: tin ware, cooking utensils, lawn swings and casket lining.

In 1888 Oliver B. Kinder, Joseph E. Schumke, and Henry Bartels purchased the business. On April 6, 1906, J. W. McCombs Jr. purchased the business and filled the three-story building with furniture and undertaking products. In 1929 the business was incorporated as McCombs Furniture and Undertaking with stockholders being J. W. McCombs Jr., B. A. Meyer, H. E. Boss, and Hope Morton. In 1939 Mr. Morton sold out and established the former Morton-Hall Lumber Company.

John William McCombs Jr. was born May 11, 1881, north of Jackson, the son of J. W. and Adelaide Bray McCombs. On Jan. 10, 1905, he married Emma Cyrene Campbell, daughter of Captain (C.S.A.) and Mrs. Stephen Campbell (known as "Rena"). Ruddell M. McCombs, brother of J. W., and his wife, Emma (Boss) McCombs, owned the milling company in Jackson.

When interviewed by the Southeast Missourian newspaper in 1936, Mr. McCombs said the most expensive piece of furniture he had was a folding bed for $35.00. In the undertaking business, the most expensive casket was $50.00. A metal one was $110.00. McCombs was the first to introduce easy payment and free delivery in the furniture business. The logo was "Easy to Buy and Easy to Pay." Mr. McCombs was not an embalmer himself, but he did provide financial aid to various young men to attend embalming school in St. Louis. Mr. Kurre Allen became a stockholder in 1944. In February 1946 Perry Grindstaff became a stockholder. Henry Boss sold his interest in 1955 and became a banker. Kurre Allen died unexpectedly on Memorial Day 1956. Elmer Best became a stockholder in August that year. In 1959 Bruce Dockins became a stockholder. It was company practice that women were not working partners.

In August 1942 the McCombs Funeral Parlor was separated from the store and moved to the former Presbyterian Church parsonage located at 417 North High Street. The parsonage was completely remodeled to become the first funeral home in Jackson. After the death of Elmer Best, Mr. and Mrs. Perry (Marge) Grindstaff and Mr. and Mrs. Bruce (Donna) Dockins became the owners. Mr. Grindstaff passed away in 1996. Today, Bruce and Donna Dockins are the owners. Also working with them are their children, Christi and Rick Guilliams, both of whom have their funeral director's license, and their son, Jamey Dockins, who is a licensed embalmer and funeral director. Other employees include Ivan Statler, Embalmer/Funeral Director; Lonnie Stroder, Funeral Director, Renee Gambill, Preplanning Consultant; and Raymond McAfee, Chaplain.

In April 1971, construction began on a new and modern funeral home on Route D. Upon its completion, an open house was held in January 1972 and the name of the company was changed to McCombs Funeral Home, Incorporated. For several years, Mr. and Mrs. Arthur (Rose) Musgraves lived in the funeral home apartment. The McCombs Furniture Store was sold in 1976 to Mr. and Mrs. Wayne Brotherton. On Nov. 1, 1995, open house was held for the new McCombs Funeral Home in Cape Girardeau, located at 1425 Kurre Lane.

The McCombs Funeral Home of Jackson sits on four acres across from the city park and is of colonial design. The building consists of 13,000 square feet with two complete chapels with pews, all very appropriately decorated. The McCombs Funeral Home of Cape Girardeau sits on approximately two acres with one chapel with pews and two parlor rooms and over 10,500 square feet. Each funeral establishment's parking lots will facilitate over 125 automobiles.

McCombs has always strived to be a leader in the funeral service and will continue to be prepared to meet the needs of those they serve with compassionate professionalism, industry knowledge and affordable pricing.

McCombs Funeral Home, 417 North High Street, Jackson, MO

McCombs Funeral Home, 640 West Independence, Jackson, MO

New Lenco Company, Inc.

On April 1, 1948, a charter was issued by the state of Missouri to create a corporation, known then as Wagner Manufacturing Company, Inc. The incorporators were Harry Wagner, Paul Leonard, and Matt Schuch. The objective of the corporation was to engage in the manufacture of quality products and their distribution and sale throughout the world.

Mr. Schuch and Mr. Wagner withdrew from the company and in 1956 the name of the corporation was changed from Wagner Manufacturing Company, Inc. to Lenco, Inc., and the trade name for electrode holders and ground clamps of "HI-AMP" was adopted and registered. Paul Leonard remained as Chairman of the Board and President until his death in 1981.

In September 1955, the first step was taken to diversify the manufacturing facilities of Lenco, Inc. Andrew Perrin, formerly Vice-President of Koch Plastic Manufacturing Company, joined Lenco with the direct responsibility of organizing a department for the custom molding of plastic, straight compression, transfer and injection molding. This department grew into a valuable division with an excellent reputation for quality molded products at reasonable prices.

In June of 1961, Roy W. Poe joined the staff as Sales Manager of the Welding Accessory Division, bringing with him over 12 years of sales management experience in the welding field. He was charged with the responsibility of organizing and directing a sales force to expand sales worldwide. This he did in organizing an effective sales organization which Lenco believed was second to none.

In October 1964 Lenco's third division was started for manufacturing a series resistance spot welder (the PANELSPOTTER) to repair bodies on wrecked automobiles. It produced two welds at one time from one side of twenty-gauge metal, enabling the automotive body repair shops to spot in fenders, door skins or quarter panels to repair damaged parts of an automobile body.

In July 1971, Lenco purchased the Aljay Safety Clothing Manufacturing Company of Philadelphia. The facilities were moved to Jackson to become the fourth division, the Lenco Leather Division Industrial leather clothing and other items used in the protective field of welding and other industries were offered to the distributor and consumer through this division. Products such as leather jackets, overalls, aprons, sleeves, spats, curtains, etc. were produced with excellent quality at fair and reasonable retail prices.

In August of 1971 the company purchased a new modern foundry from Decatur, IL, built a new building and moved the equipment to Jackson. Lenco had been doing molding of nonferrous metals since 1950 in a small "captive" foundry, making parts for its own use. With the addition of the new modern foundry, the fifth division was established which equipped the company to "custom" mold parts for other industries.

In September 1971, the assets of Mustang Electronics Company of Dallas, TX, were purchased and moved to Jackson to establish the sixth division. A complete redesign of the manufacture of video equipment was undertaken. The Electronic Division engaged in making advanced quality equipment for television broadcast, closed circuit television and CATV. Included in the items manufactured were black and white cameras, color encoders meeting NTSC requirements, sync generators, distribution amplifiers, and many other items used in generating good clear video pictures.

Over the years the company expanded from its original location at 350 West Adams Street to cover 1-1/2 blocks of West Main Street, and has approximately 100,000 square feet of manufacturing and office space.

After Paul Leonard's death, the company was eventually sold to Jerry Ford, a local businessman, who ran the company from 1984 until 1989. In late 1989 the assets of Lenco, Inc. were purchased by NLC, Inc. (New Lenco Company, Inc.), a new company formed by Associated Equipment Company of Pearland, TX, and David Hoelscher of Midland, TX. At that time several of the divisions were sold or discontinued.

NLC, Inc. manufactures and sells a complete line of LENCO arc welding accessories which includes electrode holders, rod ovens, ground clamps, cable connectors, international dinse type machine plugs, lugs, splicers, and chipping hammers.

In March of 2000, NLC, Inc. completed the purchase of the Duro line of electrode holders from Duro Engineering, Inc. located in Connecticut, and moved all manufacturing to their plant in Jackson. The Duro holder had been a recognized brand in the industry since the 1930s.

NLC, Inc. manufactures an updated version of the original series resistance spot welder, dent pulling systems used in auto body repair, and a wide variety of auto and body repair equipment. Two resistance spot welders were added to the line which work with more modern methods of body work because of the higher power required.

A standout in the educational market is the LWT-3200 Weld-Trainer, a welding simulator which develops necessary skills for MIG, TIG and stick welding.

The Plastics Division still produces custom molded parts for a limited number of customers. NLC, Inc. primarily uses this division to manufacture parts utilized in its other divisions. The foundry, like the Plastics Division, is used to make parts for internal use.

NLC, Inc. is positioned to continue to meet the needs of the marketplace in the welding industry. Its products are sold through the welding supply distribution network throughout the United States and world markets. Since NLC, Inc. purchased Lenco 13 years ago, it has made investments in updating the equipment and manufacturing facilities and plans to be part of the Jackson Community for at least another 54 years.

Lenco, Inc., circa 1960

NLC, Inc., 319 West Main St., Jackson, MO, 2002

Pocahontas Lumber and Hardware, Inc.

Clarence Saupe purchased the business called R. C. Landgraf Lumber Co. in 1949. He changed the name to Pocahontas Lumber and Hardware. At this time the business was located in Pocahontas, MO. Clarence Saupe was the only employee and he had one delivery truck. In 1958 Mr. Saupe bought Morton-Hall Lumber Co. in Jackson, which was located at 210 West Main Street. At this time the business was in Jackson as well as the original location in Pocahontas. It was incorporated in 1963. The company built a new store at its present location at 410 West independence in Jackson in 1965. Then the other two locations were closed. The company became an Ace Hardware dealer in 1974. Mr. Saupe died in 1985.

The company continues with Earl Saupe, President; Orville Fluegge, Vice-President; Rick Saupe and Ken Fluegge, also Vice-presidents; Marlene Saupe, Treasurer; and Loretta Fluegge, Secretary. Earl is Clarence's son and Loretta is his daughter. Marlene is married to Earl and Rick is their son. Orville is married to Loretta and Ken is their son.

In 1985 the business completed a 7,600 square foot expansion, which gave the business 15,000 square feet of display space. There are more than 30,000 square feet of storage on five acres. Equipment in 2002 includes four forklifts and seven delivery trucks. The business employs thirty people, and one salesman spends much of his time on the road.

Originally Pocahontas Lumber offered items such as nails, roofing, lumber and miscellaneous hardware items. Today, the business offers one-stop shopping. It has everything you need to build or remodel a house, including tools, as well as lawn and garden supplies and a large selection of Christmas decorating items. The store's mission is to provide the best possible service and satisfaction to our customers, by offering a wide selection of quality products at good value, adhering to the highest retail standards, supporting this community and our country, and encouraging sound environmental practices. Pocahontas Lumber and Hardware has been noted for its excellence in hardware retailing for several years by Ace Hardware Corporation.

Top Left: *Pocahontas Lumber and Hardware, Inc., aerial view, June 2001*
Above Left: *Members of the family-owned business are, from the left, Ken Fluegge, vice president; Loretta Fluegge, secretary; Orville Fluegge, vice president; Earl Saupe, president; Marlene Saupe, treasurer; and Rick Saupe, vice president*
Above Right: *Orville Fluegge, Clarence Saupe, Earl Saupe*
Bottom: *In January of 1949, Pocahontas Lumber opened for business when Clarence Saupe purchased the R. C. Landgraf Lumber Company and changed the name.*

Rosewood Estates, Jackson, Missouri

Rosewood Estates subdivision is a fine example of the growth and development of Jackson during the 1990s. Jackson's population was growing steadily and there was a need for housing. In 1990 there were few new subdivisions in the area. Land on the north side of Route D, now Independence, provided an ideal location for a subdivision and city expansion. Beginning in 1991 over a period of eight years, Gerald E. Stoverink Construction developed Rosewood Estates in five stages over ninety acres divided into one hundred and ninety-eight lots. From Primrose Lane to North Farmington, Rosewood Estates I, II, IV and V are neighborhoods of beautifully landscaped substantial brick homes and proud homeowners. Rosewood Estates III contains over forty rental units, a duplex, and several commercial establishments to serve the area. The neighborhood is enhanced by its proximity to several Jackson schools and the City Park. The entire development is an excellent example of what can be accomplished in an atmosphere of cooperation that exists in the community between the developer, the landowner, the financial community, and the City of Jackson.

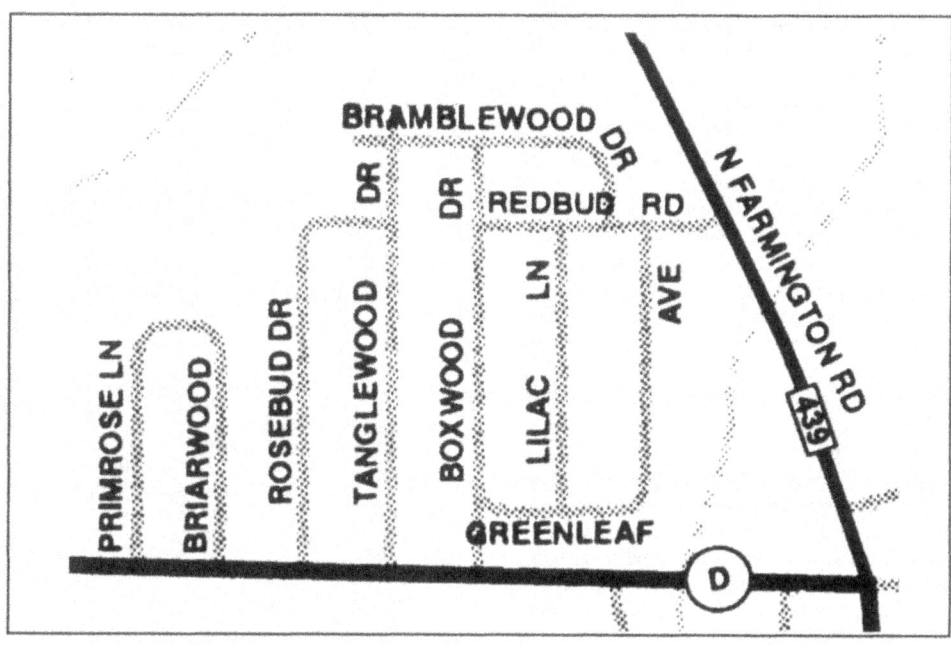

Rosewood Estates I – V, Developed by Gerald E. Stoverink Construction. Gerald E. and Catherine Stoverink, continuing Jackson's tradition of fine homes

RW IV, Lot 110, 1639 Boxwood Dr., Jackson

RW V, Lot 198, 1363 Greenleaf, Jackson

RW IV, Lot 125, 1611 North Farmington, Jackson

RW V, Lot 139, under construction

Ross Furniture

In 1979 Charles and Eddie Ross founded Ross Furniture. In September of the same year Ross Furniture opened for business at 116 South High Street in uptown Jackson.

In the early years of business, Charles and Eddie purchased, sold, and even delivered the furniture. As business grew, a second store was opened at the Perryville Plaza in Perryville, MO. In 1987 Ross Furniture became incorporated. Ross Furniture now consists of 15 employees.

In 1994, after 40 years in the furniture business, Charles retired, selling his half of the business to Eddie. In 1995 Jeffery Moore joined Ross Furniture as a stockholder and vice-president. Moore began working at Ross Furniture in 1992.

The Jackson store has remained in its original two-story High Street location, just a half-block from the courthouse square. The building has been home to a variety of Jackson's past businesses. At one time there were three separate storefronts at this location. Past businesses that were located in one or more of these storefronts were Mooreland and Tobler, Town & Country Home Furnishings, McCombs Furniture, McCombs Funeral Home and C. H. Sander Sales.

Ross Furniture in Jackson and Perryville carry such name brands as Lane Action, Justice, Cochrane, Riverside, Northern Harvest, Peters Revington, Best Chairs, Vineyard, Webb and Crawford. These lines include recliners, bedding, curios, dining room, living room and bedroom suites.

Ross Furniture continues to back all of its quality home furnishings with the same exceptional service that they have been providing Jackson and surrounding communities for nearly a quarter of a century.

Eddie and Charles Ross during the opening week of Ross Furniture, September 1979

Ross Furniture, 116 South High Street, Jackson, MO, 2002

Rubbermaid Closet And Organization

December 1999 marked an ending to an era. It also marked the 35th anniversary of the opening of the LeeRowan plant, Jackson, Missouri.

LeeRowan was founded in 1939 by Edgar D. Lee and John V. Rowan. Desmond Lee and James P. Rowan, sons of the founders, began working for the company that year.

Over the years LeeRowan has grown from a one-product company to a multi-divisional corporation. We design, manufacture, and distribute over 600 storage and organizational products which are sold world-wide. These products are produced with the help of over 1,100 LeeRowan associates in three modern manufacturing facilities located in Jackson, MO; Vista, CA; Watford, Ontario Canada with headquarters in Fenton, MO. The Jackson plant has been expanded 11 times and now totals approximately 719,240 square feet or 16.48 acres in the existing building. In November 1999, an 80,000 square foot expansion was completed.

The company's first product was a Trouser Creaser that was sold to leading department stores throughout the United States. The product line was quickly expanded to include hangers, shoe and garment racks, which were designed and merchandised for mass marketers and discounters, as well as department stores.

In 1970, LeeRowan entered department stores, catalog houses, bath specialty stores and discounters with our bath line.

In 1985, LeeRowan took its most significant step forward with the introduction of a full line of ventilated, epoxy coated wire storage systems, featuring the patented FastSet installation hardware system. Unlike vinyl coating, epoxy coating is truly maintenance free. It will not warp, discolor, crack and peel, or collect moisture and dust.

Today, LeeRowan products can be found in department stores, mass market and discount stores, catalog houses, specialty retailers, home centers, hardware stores and drug/super market chains throughout the United States and many countries around the world.

LeeRowan products are designed for Total Home Storage. Our products can be used to organize the home; kitchen, bathroom, laundry room or office. They can transform a cluttered closet into beautifully organized space, even doubling your storage capacity. We offer the widest range of flexible storage and organizational systems on the market today, with solutions to meet any special needs.

Because purchases made for a home are important investments we make sure LeeRowan products are designed and built to last. Our storage systems are made from strong industrial grade steel and are finished with state-of-the-art baked on epoxy coating.

To keep pace with the 21st century, LeeRowan will constantly develop new products and strive to remain competitive in the market place. These goals will only be reached through the help of each and every associate.

- **1939** LeeRowan Company is founded to manufacture Trouser Creasers.
- **1942** LeeRowan manufactures arming wires for bombs to support war effort.
- **1945** LeeRowan moves operation to Etzel Avenue, St. Louis, MO. 1950
- **1950** LeeRowan enters closet accessory business with the innovate "Adda-Hanger" feature.
- **1964*** LeeRowan Jackson, MO plant is built with 49,000 square feet.
- **1969** Expansion - 42,500 square feet.
- **1970** LeeRowan begins producing bath furniture. Expansion - 13,000 square feet
- **1972** Expansion - 12,500 square feet.
- **1983** Expansion - 47,700 square feet.
- **1985** LeeRowan develops the Storage Systems ventilated wire product line. Expansion - 52,500 square feet.
- **1987** Expansion - 60,600 square feet.
- **1988** Expansion - 86,440 square feet
- **1989** LeeRowan celebrates its 50th Anniversary!
- **1990** LeeRowan purchases the Space Solvers Line. Expansion - 100,000 square feet.
- **1991** LeeRowan introduces New Under Cabinet Organizers Line.
- **1992** LeeRowan introduces New Sports & Lawn Organizers, Solid Oak Shelving, and the Max- Track Adjustable Shelving System. Expansion - 93,000 square feet.
- **1993** Expansion - 80,000 square feet.
- **1998** Relocation of Wood line from Memphis facility.
- **1999** Expansion - 80,000 square feet.
- **Dec. 1999** Acquired SPUR, USA. Relocated SPUR operations from Cincinnati, OH to Jackson, MO
- **2001** LeeRowan officially changes name to

Closet & Organization Products

1901 Lee Avenue • Jackson, Missouri 63755 U.S.A.

Rubbermaid Closet and Organization Products, A New Beginning. A local sign company installs the new Rubbermaid Closet and Organization Products sign on the front of the main building at 1901 Lee Ave., Jackson, MO

The New Rubbermaid Closet and Organization Building

Shawnee Car Wash & Storage

Shawnee Square Car Wash & Storage is located at 560 S. Shawnee. We opened for business on July 1, 1995. We started out with one Automatic wash and four self service bays. We also have two vacuum islands where you can shampoo your carpets,, make your car smell like a new car and you can vacuum it. We started the storage units with 62 units.

In 2000 we added another Automatic bay. We have added units every year since. We now have a total of 274 units. Our storage unit sizes are 5x5, 5x10, 5x15, 10x10, 10x15, 10x20, 10x25, 10x30.

The manager is Mary Smith. The owners are Wayne and Marilyn Fronabarger.

Southeast Missouri Hospital Main Street Family Fitness Center

July 1995

Southeast Missouri Hospital Buys Main Street Fitness Center

Seven years ago on July 1, 1995, Southeast Missouri Hospital assumed ownership and operation of the Main Street Family Fitness Center in Jackson that had opened in 1992 by Jim Maevers and Maevers Enterprises, Inc.

Since 1992, Southeast had worked in association with Main Street Fitness to coordinate and provide fitness and wellness classes for children and adults.

Though the Hospital purchased Main Street Fitness Center, the Maevers family continued to operate the Main Street Center Complex, management office and Super Video with Southeast as the major tenant and owner of Main Street Fitness

July 2000

Main Street Fitness Hosts Open House

Two years ago, Main Street Family Fitness celebrated its five-year anniversary under ownership of Southeast Missouri Hospital with a public open house that offered refreshments and activities for children and adults. These include body composition testing, short classes and tours. There were prize drawings as well, with the top prize being a one-year family Gold Membership valued at over $700.

July 2002

Center Adds Member and Physical Therapy Services

Main Street Family Fitness Center has grown tremendously in the past seven years. Currently there is a membership of over 2,300 men and women of all ages from throughout the area.

Since January of 2002, Physical Therapy services have been offered by Southeast Missouri Hospital's Outpatient Rehabilitation Services at Main Street Fitness Center in Jackson.

Patients with physician referrals to Southeast Outpatient Rehab may schedule appointments at the Hospital's primary outpatient rehabilitation facility in Doctors' Park or at Main Street Fitness by calling 339-1188.

If you haven't stopped by to see what Main Street Fitness can offer you and your family, please do – we love to meet our neighbors!

2003

Southeast To Celebrate 75 Years of Service to the Region

As Southeast Missouri Hospital prepares to commemorate 75 years of providing health care services to the region, we salute our Jackson neighbors and thank the good citizens of Jackson for their support and use of the Hospital since it opened in January of 1928.

Main Street Family Fitness Center, located at 410 W. Main Street in Jackson, MO.

Southeast Missouri Hospital, located at 1701 Lacey St. in Cape Girardeau.

Main Street Family Fitness Host Center offers the following:

Free weights & Circuit Training
Sauna and Whirlpool
Cardiovascular Equipment
Indoor Walking/Jogging Track
Aerobics Room & Classes
Racquetball & Walleyball
Fitness Assessments/Screenings
Information/Health Education
Childcare for Members
Community Meeting Room

Southard TV

In 1948 Elmer Southard, using his G. I. Bill, ordered and started a correspondence course in electronics from the National Radio Institute NRI, while employed by Central Packing Company. When Pevely Dairy opened routes in Cape Girardeau, Elmer had an early route, giving him an opportunity to do part-time radio service work in a home basement shop. In 1950, under a work-assistance program, he started working for Earl and Jesse Kamp as a service-sales technician. The Zenith Radio franchise became available in Jackson in 1955 and Mr. Southard opened Southard Radio and TV. Southard and Zenith are still partners in 2002.

Southard Radio and TV opened its doors Feb. 15, 1955, at 404 S. Hope Street in a converted filling station, rented from J. V. Priest, with two televisions and an assortment of radios. In 1959 Southard purchased a lot at 220 E. Monroe from Mr. and Mrs. Arthur Kasten and constructed a 30 x 50 foot shop. In 1965 a 28 x 30 foot addition was added to the east end of the building for storage and in 1972 a 30 x 50 foot display room was added to the west side of the original building.

Bob Helderman started working with Elmer in 1956-57 and was with the business until 1994. Son Jay Southard attended United Electronics Institute after graduating from Jackson High School in 1969, and joined his dad in 1971. Jay's son Josh helped part-time while in high school but remarked that "family business wasn't for him," choosing instead to be a mechanic. Merlin Schultz worked part-time and several high school students worked under work-study programs. In 1994, after being semi-retired for several years, Elmer handed the front door keys to Jay Southard and his wife Jari. The advertisement announcing the change read "Responsibility Changes Hands; Quality Service Remains the Same."

The Jay Southard service truck delivers and services your Zenith merchandise. Jay services all brands of electronics and fencers in the shop, and does outside antenna work. His dad assists him part-time. Through the years Elmer Sr. has accumulated a large number of antique radios and phonographs, which he enjoys sharing and sharing knowledge about. Elmer Southard was a familiar face at the Jackson Homecomers celebration for over 40 years, as he furnished and operated the stage sound equipment.

Southard TV has seen a lot of change in almost 50 years in electronics. We've gone through 78-, 45-, and 33-RPM records, 8-track tapes, cassette tapes, video discs, and black and white television, and watched video grow from a Pong-Pong game. We've watched microwave ovens progress from the size you had to haul in a pickup truck (our open house in 1972) to the tiny efficient ones of today; satellite from a ten-foot monster to a tiny dish; and computers that filled an entire room to today's laptops.

Southard TV is proud to be a part of the Jackson community, and their motto, "Your Sight And Sound Center, The Quality Goes In Before The Name Goes On," is as sincere today as it was in 1955.

Southard TV 1964

Elmer Southard adjusts the loudspeakers on the stage of the county courthouse at Jackson, for the 84th annual Jackson Homecomers

Jay Southard, Bob Helderman, Elmer Southard, Merlin Schultz

40th Anniversary Open House

Southard TV 1970

Southard TV in 2002

BILL WALLACE INSURANCE

George Jacob Mecherle founded State Farm Insurance in the state of Illinois on June 7, 1922 and served as its president from 1922 until 1937. The company originally offered automobile insurance but added life insurance in April 1929; fire insurance in June 1935; the State Farm Bank Plan in April 1939; and health insurance in August 1965.

Bill Wallace is the current agent of State Farm Insurance in Jackson, which is located at 231 Main Street. The company today offers State Farm Federal Savings Banks with checking, savings and money market accounts; certificates of deposit; auto loans; home mortgage loans; home equity loans; and credit cards. The most popular services include auto, homeowners, life and health insurance, as well as State Farm Bank products.

Bill Wallace Insurance, 231 East Main Street, Jackson, MO

Union Planter's Bank

The oldest bank in Cape Girardeau County was organized on May 15, 1888. On May 17, 1888, the local newspaper, *The Cash-Book*, reported: "Jackson now has a bank - the Cape Girardeau County Savings Bank, with a capital of $15,000. The stockholders are J. H. Schaefer, J. B. Shaner, F. Tiedemann, W. H. Miller, H. W. Howard, S. D. Williams, and J. E. Franklin, with Mr. J. E. Franklin as business manager."

Started in a building at the corner of South High and Main Streets, the bank was first located in the rear of Jacob Schaefer's hardware store. Later the bank moved to the front corner of the building, sharing space with Kuellmer's Saloon. A barber shop was located upstairs and tellers had an alarm system that would ring a bell in the shop.

In 1907 the bank changed its name to Cape County Savings Bank and continued to grow. In order to expand its facility, the bank purchased in 1920 the Oliver Building, which had been used by Garry Sibley as a restaurant. The bank then went on to acquire the Peoples National Bank in 1927 and the Bank of Pocahontas in 1930.

On Dec. 15, 1932, during the midst of the Depression, *The Cash-Book* ran an article stating: "In banking circles, Cape County Savings Bank is known as one of the strongest and best managed banks in the State. The bank has a capital stock of $50,000 and a surplus and undivided profits totaling practically $100,000."

In 1942 the Jones building was acquired by long-term lease. A large vault was built and the first night depository in Jackson was constructed. A complete remodeling of the building was done in 1952, including the replacement of the old brick exterior with limestone and the removal of the cupola from over the front entrance. The front portion of the Jones building, occupied by the Hoffmeister Barber Shop, was remodeled in 1964 to provide a board room, offices, and storage. The Hoffman building, containing Ueleke's Jewelry and Jackson Realty, was purchased in the same year to provide room for future expansion.

In 1970 the drive-in window was installed followed by the opening of the drive-through facility at 402 West Main Street in 1971. On Nov. 1, 1977, the bank changed its name to Cape County Bank. Early in 1983, the bank opened a new facility in Jackson at 2210 East Jackson Boulevard.

On Nov. 14, 1983, County Bancorporation, Inc., a bank holding company, was formed. By the end of the decade, County Bancorporation operated banking offices in Jackson, Cape Girardeau, Sikeston, Perryville, Columbia, and Clayton, Missouri.

With the acquisition of First Federal Savings and Loan Association on May 18, 1990, Cape County Bank gained another location in Jackson at 727 West Main. In August of that same year, the company changed its name to Capital Bancorporation, Inc. and Cape County Bank became Capital Bank of Cape Girardeau County.

In 1995 Capital Bancorporation, Inc. obtained the milestone of $1 billion in assets. On Dec. 31, 1995, the company became part of Union Planters Corporation, a multi-state bank holding company headquartered in Memphis, TN. Capital Bank of Cape Girardeau became Union Planters Bank.

The three Jackson offices of Union Planters Bank are now part of a 12-state network of 764 banking offices and 964 ATMs offering a full range of services from traditional banking products to investments and insurance. Union Planters is one of the 30 largest bank holding companies headquartered in the United States, with assets of $33.2 billion as of Dec. 31, 2001.

Cape Girardeau County Savings Bank. Capital, $50,000; Surplus and Profits, $12,500

Union Planter's Bank, 101 West Main, Jackson, MO, 2002

Circle S Saddle Co.

When Greg and Lisa started out in 1989 selling new and used saddles and tack from the car-lot at Sparkman Auto Sales, nothing was organized. Customers shopped out of boxes on the floor. When the business moved to the new building, the customers followed.

Circle S now carries: many major brands of boots, clothing, hats, saddles and tack; men's, ladies' and children's lines of jewelry, purses, pictures and statues; all kinds of miscellaneous and more. Plus horse trailers, living quarters, cargo trailers, of aluminum and metal of Sooner, Kiefer Built, Delta and Doolittle.

Today Circle S is the largest full-line Western store between St. Louis and Memphis, filled with stock items in everyone's price range. While their most popular items are boots, hats and jeans – if they don't have it, they will order items for you. Owners Greg and Lisa Sparkman's plans for the future are that "with a lot of prayer, a little luck, and a grateful appreciation to all our customers from Missouri, Kentucky, Tennessee, and Arkansas, we plan to be here for many years to come."

Greg and Lisa Sparkman, 5728 State Highway 25, Gordonville, MO 63752

Dutch Guttering, Inc.

Dutch Guttering Inc. was founded by Vernon L. Werner in 1968. At that time, Dutch Guttering was a branch of Vernon L. Werner Plumbing, Heating and Air Conditioning Inc. The business was located at 210 W. Main, in Jackson, MO (now the home of *Cash-Book*).

Dutch Guttering is now owned and operated by Vernon's son, Mark Werner, and is located at 4903 Old Cape Road East, Jackson, MO 63755, telephone number 573-334-1664. The company does all kinds of guttering repairs, including taking down the old guttering and installing new seamless aluminum guttering.

In addition to seamless aluminum guttering, Dutch Guttering is a Gutter Helmet dealer. Gutter Helmet is a gutter and roof protection system that fits over your existing gutters, keeping out leaves, snow, ice and other debris, while protecting and prolonging the life of your gutters and roof edges. This product came on the market approximately 20 years ago and more then 10 million feet have been installed across the country.

Another fine service offered by the company is blown fiberglass attic insulation. Call for free estimates. Your home is a valuable investment. Take care of it!

Lakenan Insurance Agency

Lakenan Insurance Agency was started in Perryville, MO, in 1938 by William Lakenan. In 1960 the Gene Koeppel Agency in Jackson was purchased by Lakenan with William Lakenan's son-in-law Bill Williamson being the office manager. Offices were later opened in Ste. Genevieve and Crystal City.

Bruce McClard started Midland Insurance in 1978 and purchased the Danny Day Insurance Agency that same year. Midland later purchased Boss and Puls Agency which was started in 1898 by Alvin A. Boss and Henry Puls. Bill Poe started working for Boss and Puls in 1958 and continues to sell for Lakenan now.

In 1996 Chad and Geneva Hartle purchased the Jackson Lakenan office with Doug Mueller being the office manager. In 2000 Chad and Geneva also purchased the Midland Insurance Agency in Jackson and Cape Girardeau from Bruce McClard and combined the two agencies, keeping one office in Jackson and one in Cape Girardeau.

Current producers in Jackson and Cape Girardeau are Doug Mueller (office manager and shareholder), David Hamm, Jim Abernathy, Kevin Stanfield, Bill Poe, Bruce McClard, Doris Dirnberger, and Lisa Brooks. Lakenan Insurance Agency offers all lines of commercial and personal lines insurance as well as life and health, individual, and group policies.

Peoples Bank Of Altenburg

The first recorded meeting of the BANK OF ALTENBURG was held on February 28, 1910. At this time, officers and directors were appointed and the initial list of stockholders prepared. In March of that same year, a lot was purchased and a committee formed to begin selection of a contractor. The initial building was constructed and remained in use for almost 41 years.

The BANK OF ALTENBURG opened for business on July 5, 1910, with capital stock of $10,000.00. Total assets at that time were $26,761.87. The bank has enjoyed substantial growth throughout the 92 years of its existence and today has resources of more than $40,000,000.00.

In 1993 BANK OF ALTENBURG was purchased by Lincoln County Bancorp located in Troy, MO. A few years later the Board of Directors of BANK OF ALTENBURG agreed to a slight change in the name, which is now PEOPLES BANK OF ALTENBURG. In addition, in 1997 a branch was opened in Jackson, MO.

The bank has enjoyed growth and success over the years, due to the many good, solid customers we have served and continue to serve. We are a full service bank offering top dollar for deposits with low rates on loans of all types. Our motto has been "Small Enough to Know You, Large Enough to Serve You." Give us the opportunity to be your bank.

SEMO Specialties And Sports

Butch Schneider and Paul Sander opened SEMO Specialties and Sports in January 1991 at 131 South High Street, Jackson, MO. Originally the business concentrated on AD specialty products, trophies and screen printed shirts.

In early 1994, Butch purchased Paul Sander's interest and became the sole owner.

Now they have a retail store front, have a computerized art department, provide automated custom screen printing and embroidery, engraving and made to order trophies, plaques and awards, promotion products such as mugs, pens, etc., and embroidered patches.

Sparkman Auto Sales

In August 1987, Greg and Lisa Sparkman opened Sparkman Auto Sales used car-lot with only four cars and wondered if they would be able to sell even one. Before the first week was over, they had sold all four cars and had nothing to drive themselves. They borrowed Greg's grandfather's truck until Greg could purchase more cars.

Sparkman Auto Sales now has an inventory of around 150 used cars and trucks, 4-wheelers, boats, trailers, and tractors. While customers never know what they may find in the wide range of older and later models, they do know that they will find quality used cars at affordable prices. Greg will go out of his way to provide customer service and trade for almost anything. He considers cars are like eggs. They are cheaper in the country. Sparkman Auto Sales is looking forward to a bright future and a move to larger facilities in order to better serve their customers.

Greg and Lisa Sparkman, 5728 State Highway 25, Gordonville, MO 63752

Agriculture

Agriculture has long been the economic base for Cape Girardeau County and the city of Jackson. The earliest settlers, drawn by the Spanish offer of free land, settled along the waterways to farm. Their first task was to fell the native oak, hickory, sweet gum, elm, ash, walnut, and many other varieties of trees from which they built their homes and whatever outbuildings they might need, and to prepare their fields for planting.

The first "industry" to follow the settlers was the milling industry. Houck reports that Lorimier constructed the first mill, known as the "lower mill," on Cape LaCroix Creek close to the present Cape Girardeau-Scott County line. His second mill was built on Hubble Creek some time later. The millstones were reportedly brought from Ohio (1908, Vol. II, p. 179). Other mills were built by Hubble near Gordonville and Bollinger in Burfordville, with many others located throughout the district as population increased. These mills, the first "Agribusiness," in the area, at first met the need of the population to turn grain into a usable commodity. When farming became more than a subsistence activity, farmers increased their wheat acreage and local milling companies produced tons of flour for shipment across the United States and to Europe.

One of the earliest agriculture reports come from a census taken at the time the Louisiana Territory was sold to the United States. Out of a total population of 1,206 in the Cape Girardeau District, there were 180 slaves. Crop production was reported to be 2,950 bushels of wheat, 58,990 bushels of corn, 3,100 pounds of tobacco, 9,200 pounds of flax, and hemp, 39,000 pounds of cotton and 19,000 pounds of maple sugar. There were 2,380 head of horned cattle and 674 horses. The district exported 371 barrels of salt pork, 14 barrels of unrefined lard, 8,675 pounds of beef, 1,800 pounds of cotton, and 7,000 pounds of bacon (Houck, Vol. II, 1909, p. 407).

Once Jackson was founded, the earliest businesses catered to the needs of the surrounding farm community and utilized the goods that they produced as well. Thus we see Delap making bells for livestock, McGuire's tannery using hides from local farms, and Fylenwider distilling grain.

In the 1870s farming began to change. Farmers began to utilize horse-drawn machinery to allow them to farm more acreage more efficiently. Although the technology was developed from farming the vast expanses of the Great Plains, it changed the way local farmers operated as well. In the 1880's local farmers began to feel the competition from the wheat fields of the Great Plains. The flat expanses made efficient use of the McCormick Reapers and the railroads could easily transport the grain wherever it was needed. Therefore local farmers began to look for more profitable crops.

The *Jackson Herald* (1908) reported that the Goodwin and Jean Company bought eggs and poultry from area farmers, putting $50,000 per year in farmers' pockets. The coming of refrigerated railway cars made it possible for local eggs and dressed poultry to be shipped to city markets. The Old Reliable Poultry firm of Southeast Missouri and Arkansas had its headquarters in Jackson. It also bought and slaughtered poultry for shipment, as well as producing the ice for packing in its own ice plant. The article states that these businesses caused area farmers to raise more poultry.

The 1910 census shows that of the 371,200 acres in Cape Girardeau County, 329,867 acres were in farmland, with 224,850 acres "improved," farmland, i.e., cleared and in production. Value of the land was estimated to be $15,292,154. In 1912 Cape Girardeau County farmers received assistance from a new source, the Missouri Agricultural Extension Service. The Cape County Extension Service was in place for at least two years before its statewide establishment in 1914. A 1919 narrative report by County Agent Seth Babcock states that in August 1911 the County Court of Cape Girardeau County, in cooperation with the University of Missouri and the U.S. Department of Agriculture, hired C. M. McWilliams as County Agent. Other sources use the date August 1912. In a report of its first ten years in Cape Girardeau County, the Extension Service outlined some of the changes made in county agriculture due to the work of its agents: introducing four new crops, alfalfa, soybeans, sweet clover and hairy vetch; gathering seed corn in the fall and testing it before planting; growing corn for silage; vaccinating hogs for cholera and establishing other animal testing procedures; and introducing purebred dairy cattle to firmly establish the dairy industry. In addition, the Extension Service helped organize the Cape Girardeau County

Goodwin & Jean Company was established in 1907, located on West Main Street.

John Rudert, standing behind the tractor, was a blacksmith in Tilsit, Missouri, who began selling farm equipment. He appears to be demonstrating one of the first gasoline powered tractors in Cape Girardeau County, circa 1908.

Farm Bureau, as well as livestock breeders associations and livestock shipping associations to aid farmers in improving animal breeding and in obtaining better prices when marketing livestock. Beginning in 1918 County home economics agents worked to improve health and living conditions for all citizens of Cape Girardeau County through such activities as school nutrition clinics and organization of clubs for businesswomen. The home economics agents also introduced improved methods of poultry and egg production, encouraging farm women to cull flocks. The agents concluded that the formation of the Farm Bureau was the most significant accomplishment because it was through the dues farmers paid to that group that many projects were made possible (Ten Years of Extension Work in Missouri, 1924, and annual reports of County Extension agents).

Throughout the 1920s and 1930s, Extension Service reports stress the attempts to make farming a more profitable venture in Cape Girardeau County. Farmers were encouraged to diversify crops, to terrace and use other soil conservation measures, to make use of local limestone as an applied fertilizer, and to improve animal husbandry practices to increase their value at market time. Dairy farmers were taught to improve testing methods for cream, the major form in which milk was marketed.

Among the projects carried out by the home agents was encouraging parents to allow their children to drink milk. Youngsters were encouraged to join the 4-H Clubs being organized around the country as a way to develop awareness of good agricultural practices at an early age. An extension report prepared February 9, 1937, shows the population of the county to be 33,203, with 14,010 county residents living on farms. In 1937 farmers were encouraged to "market their grain through livestock," this being seen as more profitable than selling grain. The 1939 report shows 2806 farms in the county, with 1600 of them selling milk or cream and 900 hatching or buying baby chicks by April 15. By 1962 there were only 450 farmers with five or more cows. Most of the milk was to be processed for direct consumption as milk, not for creamery purposes, and farmers were using pipelines and bulk milk holding tanks. 1987 found 103 farms with dairy herds. To a large extent this change came about as farming became more specialized in the 1940s and 1950s, allowing farmers to focus on the techniques and the technology of one or two areas of commercial farming, rather than more generalized subsistence farming. Some area farmers began to experiment with "tree farms," "fish farms," and other specialized uses of their land. With this specialization, marketing had to change as well. In addition to local milk and meat processing industries, local farmers were shipping these products to larger, more competitive markets in St. Louis. Several area businesses provided access to the St. Louis markets to area farmers. Improved transportation also allowed area farmers to market directly to consumers.

By the 1970s farmers were looking not only to St. Louis markets, but to foreign markets as well. Many Missouri farm products were now being shipped overseas and farmers, along with other businessmen, were looking anxiously, not at the "price of tea in China," but at the price of soybeans in Japan.

Throughout the existence of the Agricultural Extension Service, Cape Girardeau County farmers have been encouraged to develop sound farming practices based on the most recent research or on time-honored methods. Continuing themes have been land conservation strategies such as terracing and other erosion control measures; fertilization techniques to boost the productivity of the soil; improvements in animal husbandry, ranging from introduction of purebred animals to artificial insemination and embryo transplant technology; improved marketing strategies, from aiding farmers in organizing to give them greater marketing power to analysis of farming techniques to assist in developing individual marketing strategy; introduction of record keeping strategies to assist in farm management decisions; and always a focus on better health and sanitation practices for farm animals, the people who tend them, and the people who consume them. According to the U.S. Department of Agriculture's 1997 Census of Agriculture, Cape Girardeau County had a population of *67,200 and 1,161 farms. Only 541 individuals indicated that their main occupation was farming, with 620 farm operators indicating some other enterprise as their main occupation. Of Cape Girardeau County's 371,200 acres, 260,931 acres were still in farmland. Although the local economy is no longer solely dependent on the prosperity of local farmers nor is the local farmer solely dependent on local businesses for his purchases or on local markets for his products, farming is still big business in Cape Girardeau County and many Jackson businesses still cater to those needs.
*(The 2000 U.S. Census figure was 68, 693.) - amd

H. Roy Meier plowing on the family farm, circa 1940.

Shelby Brown on his 1923 Case steam engine, 1965.

EDUCATION

Early Township Schools were established by the Missouri General Assembly in each "congressional township as soon as practicable and necessary, where the poor shall be taught free." The Township schools in Cape Girardeau County were not organized until the 1840s. According to research by local school historian Mary Daume, the schools were governed by the 1839 and 1845 "act to provide for the organization, support and government of Common Schools." Fifteen township schools were established within the present boundaries of Cape Girardeau County. New schools could be organized if there were twenty or more children within the district. The increases and shifts in population led to newer buildings and the abandonment of the old township schools.

District Schools developed from the redistricting of the old township schools as required by the 45th Missouri General Assembly. Counties were directed to assign numbers to the schools by March 1, 1910. Local names accompanying the numbers seemed to have come from extended families or landowners who settled in the area. Most alumni remember the old schools by their name rather than the assigned number. By 1925 there were 80 different school districts in Cape Girardeau County: Old Appleton, Millersville, Allenville, Whitewater, Oak Ridge, Burfordville, High Hill, New Wells, Shawneetown, Buckeye, Apple Creek Valley, Arnsberg, Hilderbrand, Critesville, Daisy, Goshen, Liberty, Pocahontas, Oak Hill, Neelys Landing, Iona, Oriole Indian Creek, Horrell, Schoenebeck, Clippard, Fulbright, Old Salem, Kurreville, Niswonger, Riemann, Big Spring, Roerts, McFerron, Clover Hill, Plainview, Egypt Mills, Brooks, Coker, Brick School House, Williams, Cane Creek, Link, Stroder, Gravel Hill, Sandy Ridge, Juden, Kage, Oak Grove, Poplar Grove, Tilsit, Helderman, Hickory Grove, Crump, Poplar Ridge, Gordonville, Campster, Rock Levee, Abernathy, Needmore, Maple Grove, Snider, Stroderville, Dutchtown, Pecan Grove, Blomeyer, Collins-Moore, Round Pond, Randles, Arbor-Hickory Ridge, and Rum Branch. Enumeration lists were used to prove the necessary student population required to receive state and local tax support for providing and maintaining a school in an area.

The lists for 1925 indicate there were approximately 10,000 children of school age in the county with 4,300 in Cape Girardeau, and 766 in Jackson, with the remaining student population being divided among the one room rural schools. The percentage of students actually attending school varied by district anywhere from twenty to sixty percent of those listed (Cape County Post, October 15, 1925).

During the 1950s, redistricting and consolidation ended the era of the one-room schoolhouses. The state and local educators saw reorganization as a means to increase educational opportunities for the area students. Under the program, all of the individual rural districts were eliminated and high school pupils transported to Jackson, Cape Girardeau, Oak Ridge or Delta. Grade school pupils were transported to conveniently located grade school centers in each of the three enlarged districts. The abandoned rural school buildings were turned over to neighborhoods for community centers. (Southeast Missourian, January 29, 1949)

Even though few of the schoolhouses remain standing, alumni and faculty of the one-room schools have fond memories of the difficulties and delights associated with the limited facilities and small student populations.

Campster School

Campster School, according to the old district records, was built about 1858 on Bloomfield Road where it stood until it was so dilapidated that it was torn down in 1940.

The school had a pot-bellied furnace surrounded by a round metal shell. Coal was dumped in along with wood to keep the far corners of the room warm for the boys and girls. The desks were double so two pupils could sit in them. The desk of the teacher was so the pupils were under his eye at all times. A rack holding the many books of all eight grades sat on the top of the desk. No grade could be taught long or some grades would be missed. When George Smith was teacher, it was a delight to get him off the subject for he could keep the pupils wide-awake with his interesting stories. Blackboards lined all but the back wall. It was for coat hangers, bookshelves, and the wooden barrel with its drip-bucket. Until the hand pump was installed outside at the back of the schoolhouse, water had to be carried from the spring at William Schwab's house about a quarter mile down the hill. Much playing would go on along the way.

The outhouses were some distance from each other. Each had three holes or so, for there were at times as many as sixty-four pupils. Every Halloween the big boys of the community had a gay time turning the boys' outhouse over. The last time they were caught and that was the last turnover.

The board decided that sixty-four pupils were too many for one teacher. They built a partition through the middle of the room. George Smith had the upper grades and Leah Slinkard had the bottom four. It was said that Leah Slinkard could teach anyone to read. Mr. Smith had other duties. He prepared contes-

Pupils and teacher of Horrell School near Oak Ridge, 1910. Left to right. Front row: Tom Sawyer; John J. Ludwig; Ellis Reid; Frank Samuels; Ella Goforth; Agnes Sawyer Kistner; Virgie Reid Kieninger; Emma Criddle Baker. Second row: Vince Goforth; Ella Reid Walker; Smith Criddle; Elmer Ludwig; Arthur Ludwig; Ethel Samuels Propst; and teacher Eursa Cauvey Wilkinson. Third row: Ruth Samuels Drum; Rose Ludwig Kuehle; Helen Criddle Thompson; and Bertha Ludwig Koenig.

Students at Campster School in the spring of 1957. Left to right. Front row: Stephen Golden, Stephen Schonoff, Kermit Melton, Richard Golden, Danny Niswonger, Bonnie Schwepker, Kathy Compas, John Melton, Darrel Hobbs, Patrick Suzuki and Terry Juden. Second row: Brenda McElroy, Linda Armstrong, Larry McElroy, Norman "Butch" Golden, Martin Dubs, Terry Keller, Denise Keller and Ronnie Propst. Also pictured are, on left, teacher Mrs. Clark Ervin, and on right is cook Miss Lena Schwepker.

tants for ciphering, spelling, history, and drama. Early in the spring he coached outdoor events. Competition was fierce with other schools. One treat was when the whole school walked several miles to the Pleasant Valley black school to hear the students in concert.

Not too far past Pleasant Valley is a cemetery where a man named Campster is buried. Campster School is named after him.

When F. J. Armstrong was president of the school board, Frank James and William Schwab were board members, and Robert Keller was clerk, it was voted to build a new school to be built by the WPA. Armstrong made many trips to Jefferson City to consult with the WPA officials concerning the blueprints. The new limestone school was completed in 1940. There were two teachers. Lena Schwepker as cook was a new addition. Mulligan Stew suppers were given by the ladies of the Campster Welfare Club in order to buy needed items for the school children. The combination gymnasium, cafeteria, and stage was the ideal place for the Campster 4-H Club's dances, plays and suppers.

Due to annexation of land from the Campster District by the City of Cape Girardeau, the school closed its doors in May of 1965. The Schriners' had previously rented the building. After it had been vacant for some years, Jane Cox purchased Campster School for use as an antique store with its large playground from the Cape Girardeau Public School.

The limestone Campster School still stands. Oh, Campster School, many were the pupils who learned lessons for a better life inside your walls. You will not be forgotten.

By Bonnie Ludwig

Horrell School

Long ago on February 18, 1849, James and Elizabeth Russell, for the sum of one dollar, sold a parcel of land by Horrell Creek to Benjamin B. (unknown), Thomas Horrell, and John Russell as Trustess of Horrell School. This Horrell School stood on a hillside by Horrell Creek on the land owned by Herman Ludwig. His farm was next owned by Oscar Ludwig and now by Vernon Ludwig. The current owner found Indian artifacts in the area. Today only a foundation stone shows where the school stood.

Willis Ludwig remembered that his dad, Charles Ludwig, born in 1868, attended the old school in the first and second grades before going to Liberty School. The only other known pupils were Herman Ludwig, born in 1855, and Louis Brown.

In 1881, it was decided to dissolve Horrell School and form two districts because of the crowded conditions in the one room. The northern part on County Road 432 was called Horrell No. 22 and the southern district became Schoenebeck No. 23 on the banks of Byrd Creek east of County Road 439. The records of this dissolution were kept by the patrons of Schoenebeck School.

The second Horrell was probably built in 1881. Pupils who attended Horrell recall how things used to be. Betty Cowan and Martha Ludwig Wilhelm remember the time Jimmy Sadler fell through the ceiling and landed on the stove pipe. They played ball games with other schools and at pie suppers boys bought the girls' boxes for 25 or 50 cents. Marvin, Leonard, and Verna Ludwig recalled fried egg and sugar-cured ham in their lunch boxes. when the teacher wasn't in sight during recess the boys sometimes engaged in fierce wrestling matches. The pupils loved to play ball with Miss Lydia (Eisenberg) Meyer. Not even the biggest boys could knock a ball farther than she could.

Verna Engelhart taught during 1937-38. A tornado approached the school. She decided to keep the 20-25 frightened children in the school- a good choice, for the tornado swerved. Worried parents soon arrived to pick up their children.

Miss Eisenberg was Vernon Ludwig's first teacher. On the morning of his first day at school she was brought around the road with her suitcases as she was to board with Vernon's family. Vernon was to lead the new teacher along the path by the branch to return home. Instead he headed straight through the shoulder-high weeds in the field. He could see the roof of the house. The new teacher even climbed over the fence with her long skirt.

According to Verda Moore, scarlet fever, a sometimes fatal disease, closed the school in February 1925. The building was fumigated and most of the books were burned. Willis Ludwig did not get to finish the fifth grade that year, so he spent almost nine years at Horrell. It is claimed that was why he was so bright.

Oscar Ludwig, one of the older pupils, recalls going to the stove to warm up. He would leave a note for a certain girl. She would collect it and leave him one. Many a heart fluttered at the old wood store.

When Bonnie Ludwig was teacher, 1949-1950, typhoid pollution was in the cistern water. A man and woman were hired to pump out the great amount of water. They wisely paid the older students 25 cents per hour to pump out the water. All were happy.

In 1951 Mary Estes was teacher. Board members were Willis Ludwig, Henry Puchbauer, and Vernon Ludwig. The school consolidated with Oak Ridge. The building was sold to Walter Hennecke, then to Carl Reimann. Now no building remains. Only the memories of the former occupants linger on. Some of the teachers were: Oscar Sample; John Daume; Ellis Caldwell; Ersia Caldwell Wilkerson; Iva Wills; Erma Simpson; Mary Gholson 1922; Mrs. J. C. Clippard 1924; Fred Statler 1925; Mayme Penny 1926; Lydia Eisenberg 1927; Mrs. Paul Fronaburger 1930; Mae Sample 1935; Herb Schaper 1936; Verna Engelhart 1938; John W. Kuehler 1939; Emille Schmidt 1942; Norma Richter 1943; Kenneth Englehart 1947; Mrs. Vernon Ludwig 1949; and Mary Ann Estes 1950-51 closed the school doors.

By Bonnie Ludwig

Pictured by the old school bell are Shirley and Melvin Sievers, with teacher Bonnie Ludwig, 1947-48 school year.

The original Campster School.

The Old School Bell

When the old school bell rang in the morning neighbors knew their children were safe.

Long ago children, Lincoln, Jefferson, were called by the bell to learn.

Men and women listened to the bell and learned to guide our nation.

Under the bell knowledge of war and peace was dispensed.

Many a school bell and many who obeyed it are gone.

Its sound is fading away.

It was made of iron and so must our lives be strong like iron.

—Bonnie Ludwig

Schoenebeck School

Schoenebeck was once a part of what has been called the old Horrell School, District A., Township 7, Range 12. It stood on the farm now owned by Vernon Ludwig, on a hillside along Horrell Creek. The log school was twenty by fifteen feet with long wooden benches. The deed to the land was made February 18, 1849.

Onc traveling teacher, Friedrich Kies, taught mostly catechism. Other teachers were the Byrd, Russell, Horrell and Anderson families. Pupils recalled as attending the old school were: Charles and Herman Ludwig and Louis Brown.

The district was large with many pupils. The Rev. Frank Eschenfeld, first pastor of the St. John's Evangelical Church in 1877, took some of the younger pupils into his home near Brookside. He taught them until the old district was divided into the new Horrell and Schoenebeck Districts in 1881.

The first meeting of the new E District was held April 15, 1881, in the home of Charles Wilhelm. Directors elected were: George Kaufmann, Charles Tuschhoff and Miles A. McLard. It was voted to borrow #305 to buy land and build a log building 20x26 feet with a height of ten feet. A stove with drum and piping was to complete the building.

On July 30, 1881, the Board of Directors borrowed $25 from William Deimund to pay John Schoenebeck for the one-acre schoolhouse site. Interest on this note was at eight percent.

On September 22, 1881, the directors met at the new school building to investigate the work and found it complete. Payment was made to the carpenters, Gustav Penzel and R. C. Kneibert; with one hundred and sixty-five dollars in cash and sixty dollars on note.

At the meeting of June 13, 1881, Mrs. Ellen McKenney was hired to teach for four months at $35 a month. The property of the old Horrell School was divided. Schoenebeck got two blackboards and eighteen benches. A bucket was bought for 15 cents and a dipper for five cents.

The Farmer's Mutual Benefit Association used the Schoenebeck School as a meeting place. Sunday School classes and various other community activities were also held in the school.

In 1898 a 24-foot extension was added to the school building. In 1922 Mary Schoenebeck, widow of John, was paid $60 for the three-fourths acre that the school yard was extended.

Lloyd Schoenebeck remembered that during the tenure of Miss Lillian Anderson, hot lunches were cooked on the heating stove. The children would each bring something to put in the pot. Some days it was vegetable soup, mush, beans, etc. Lloyd's father, Joe Schoenebeck, remembered that no one dared chew gum. The paddle was four feet long and an inch thick. Pupils who talked too much in a week were set on a table, and dunce caps were placed on their heads. The other children laughed at them.

The following teachers served the Schoenebeck School: Ellen McKenney, Fannie Fox, Charley Sawyer, Robert Sawyer, Charley Harris, Will Bowers, John Phillips, Dewitt Sawyer, Bennett Welker, Ida Metje McFerron, Charlie Sample, Minnie Steele, Willis Caldwell, Karl Schoenebeck, Oscar Sample, Eula Caldwell, Andrew Caldwell, Erp Dickmann, Rufus Byrd, Ernest Ford, Cletus Ford, Lillian Anderson, Lucy Clippard Unger, Carl Fronabarger, Sue Burch Owens, Evelyn Schweer Ludwig, Hester Frissell Myers, Elda Bowers Ellis, Dorothy Wilkening, Lorene Puchbauer, Sylvia Kayser, Geneva Brown Nance, Alice Schaper Godwin, Mrs. D. L. Mowery, Kenneth Englehart, Janet Bartels Talbert and Bonnie Armstrong Ludwig.

The school was closed in 1953 and the pupils were transported to Jackson R-2 North Elementary in Fruitland. The Schoenebeck School building at the present time is owned by Gene and Gloria Kimbel.

By Bonnie (Mrs. Vernon) Ludwig

The 1947-48 Class of the Schoenebeck School: Back row from left: Donald Ludwig; Shirley Sievers; Mrs. Bonnie Ludwig, teacher; Wayne Wolfenkoehler; Raymond Pensel; Charles Sievers. Front row: Freddy Petzoldt; Gerald Pensel; Melvin Sievers; Marylyn Smith; Harold Pensel.

Oak Ridge School, 1874.

Oak Ridge Schools

Grass root efforts are always interesting and many startling surprising results occur because of these actions. The story of Oak Ridge High School is no different.

By the mid-1800s, the Oak Ridge area had five of the nine public schools in Cape Girardeau County, so when the state legislature voted to create a Normal School in southeast Missouri, the Oak Ridge area led by Dr. Morris Hatler vied for the school. Even though the school was eventually located in Cape Girardeau, the progressive, influential area citizens (Dr. Hatler, the town's physician; W. T. Wilson, a merchant; C. C. Clippard, a miller and large scale farmer; Elam Russel, State Legislator; Nathan Frissel, Civil Engineer and surveyor; J. M. Siebert, sheriff and collector; C. M. Pepper, county clerk; R. B. Oliver, Prosecuting Attorney; Ashley Coker, editor of the Cash-Book; Ruddle Byrd, large land-owner; and Robert Drum, merchant at Sedgewickville) organized and decided to build their own school by asking the citizens to vote a tax of $600 and then they raised $2000 more by subscription. The subscribers were: Dr. Hatler, Wiley Statler, Tom Roberts, Harvey Kinder, Calvin Drum, Lewis Hinkle, J. R. Evans, William Clippard, G. D. Statler, W. L. Turner, O. S. Harris, Morton Hines, Richard Swan, and C. C. Clippard.

This being accomplished, a large two-story frame building was built by R. L. Bowman on land donated by William Clippard. When classes began in November 1874 the enrollment of 80 students included Miss Almarinda "Minnie" Steele, the first student to enroll and who gladly paid the $0.20 per day tuition.

Oak Ridge's first superintendent, D. T. Stanley, was hired at $100 a month, taught twelve 30-minute classes, and worked with three young men for an hour after school to teach Virgil and calculus. He had one full-time assistant, one part-time assistant, and four student helpers who taught classes. Because Mr. Stanley diligently sought students, the district erected a large room on to the back of the school in 1875. The lower grades then occupied the lower floor, the upper grades were on the second floor, and the high school was in the large new room.

An interesting surprise awaited the students in 1876. During school hours and in the presence of the students, Nelson B. Henry, the second superintendent and organizer of the southeast Missouri Teachers Association, married Mill Lou Thompson, a primary teacher.

W. T. Carrington, the fourth superintendent who later became the State Superintendent of Schools and President of Southwest Missouri State University, wrote that the high school students were among the best he had ever known. They were comparable to those enrolled in Cape Normal School at the time and to those enrolled in the Springfield school thirty years later.

1878 saw the first graduates: T. D. Hines, J. W. Malone, Marcus Robb, and W. A. Wills. The next year D. A. Drum, Ed Wilson, W. G. Wilson, and Tom D. Drum graduated.

After the turn of the century, the district felt the need to make the two-year departmental high school into a three-year program. Efforts by Superintendent L. McGee led to the school's first basketball team in 1910. by 1921 the high school became a four-year graded system offering 16 units for graduation under the leadership of R. E. Ford, superintendent, and Glen C. Smith, principal.

The need for a larger and more modern building prompted the district to build a two-story brick building in 1924. The lumber from the

The old Oak Ridge Gymnasium.

Oak Ridge School, 1930.

Oak Ridge R-6 School, 2000.

first school was donated to the community by the school board to use in building a combined community hall and gymnasium. "The Old Barn," as it came to be called, was completed in 1925 by school and community-spirited contractors who worked for $0.30 an hour instead of the usual $1.25.

Disaster befell the community when on March 17, 1932, the new brick school burned during an electrical storm. After the school burned, the citizens voted a $15,000 building proposal to rebuild. This third school building, the oldest on the campus today, is located approximately where the first two stood. In his dedicatory speech, Sen. R. L. Dearmont credited the community's early citizens with being the instigators of the educational movement in southeast Missouri.

In the years before modern facilities were available, it was not unusual to see water being carried to coolers and buckets of coal being carried to fire stoves. A hum could be heard as a light plant ran to recharge batteries for electricity. Students could be seen making regular trips to the "outhouses' that stood at the back of the school yard. Plus, every morning and evening the students could be seen trudging toward their destinations carrying their books and lunch pails.

By the year of 1937-38, electricity was installed in the school buildings. The first "shop-made" body school bus transported high school students from the Lixville, Sedgewickville, Millersville, and Daisy areas, but hot lunches were still a dream. They were in place by 1950 and before the time of reorganization in 1953.

Several building programs have been overwhelmingly approved by the voters of the Oak Ridge R-IV School district since 1953. Starting in 1954, additional classrooms and a gymnasium were completed, followed by a new elementary school in 1959. 1974 brought a new music room and industrial arts area. A new cafeteria, and math and social studies classrooms were added in 1985. 1996 saw the completion of a new high school building.

To keep abreast of, or ahead of, educational trends, the district instituted an all-day Kindergarten program in 1969. Again with that all-important community support, local volunteer builders constructed an early Childhood Center for three- and four-year-olds in 1999.

In the spring of 2001, a 1.95 million dollar bond issue was passed by the district patrons. This bond issue allowed the district to purchase 30 additional acres of land, build a new middle school and a new multipurpose building, and create additional parking area.

Oak Ridge is proud of its school and its heritage. It is the oldest public high school in southeast Missouri and its history shows it truly believes in "Our Children: Our Future."
By JoAnn Hahs

EDUCATION IN JACKSON, MISSOURI

The earliest records of formal education in the Jackson area show the establishment of the Mount Tabor School near the Ramsay plantation as the first English school west of the Mississippi River. James McFerron is believed to have been the first teacher in that school. An English school was established in the Byrd settlement and a German school in the Burfordville area (Houck, Vol.II, 1908, p. 182).

The first schoolhouse in Jackson was a small building built on the site of the present Central Elementary building soon after the town was established. The building lot was set aside for the purpose of education in accordance with an 1817 act of the Territorial Assembly. Three years later the Jackson Academy was incorporated, but no one put this institution into operation. According to the *Cape Girardeau Republican* (1914, p. 7), the charter was allowed to lapse. Houck (1908) notes that a number of subscription schools were started. Henry Sanford started the first grammar school, while Mrs. John Scripps, Mrs. Edward Criddle, Mrs. Wathern, and Miss Rhoda Ranney operated primary schools. Dr. Barr was also another early teacher (Vol. III, pp. 69-70).

In 1839, a two-story brick elementary school building was constructed and the Jackson Academy was again incorporated. J. G. Gardiner was principal, with Miss Elmira Gregory as his assistant. According to The Republican, during Gardiner's tenure the school established a good reputation. After he resigned the school continued to exist until after the Civil War, with frequent teacher turnover and inconsistent quality of education. For a time the school was even operated by the Methodist church. After the Civil War the building and grounds were transferred to the public schools. -amd

Carlisle Training School and the Jackson Military Academy

Two private institutions were part of the development of secondary education in the Jackson area- the Carlisle Training School and the Jackson Military Academy.

On October 1, 1892, the Methodists of Southeast Missouri elected a board of curators and established the groundwork for what would become the Carlisle Training School. Tuition, room and board cost $150 per semester. The course of studies covered a great deal of reading, declamation, religion, and music. Physical education was promoted and a well-outfitted exercise room provided. The first graduates were Miss Margaret Ruff, Miss Adelaide LaPierre, Glen Seibert, Miss Christine Medley, Miss Emma Howard, Joseph H. Byrd, and A. R. Byrd. A major portion of the school burned in October 1897, but the local citizens assisted the institution with funds sufficient to build a three-story building housing dormitory rooms and classrooms. The 1898-99 Carlisle Training School Catalogue and Announcements outlined the high ideals and stiff guidelines expected for parents and students and explained that the school's mission was to establish a co-educational boarding school in Southeast Missouri - a school where brother and sister may receive a good education, fitting them either for life or college. Our experience is that boys and girls ought to be educated together; they each have a refining influence on the other. We want no boy or girl who has been unmanageable at home. Do not send such to us: it will cost you their fare to Jackson and return. We require and must have STRICT OBEDIENCE. We reserve the right to punish, when, and how, and as severe, as we think best. If you are unwilling to trust this to our discretion, sent to another

Jackson Military Academy, 1908.

Maj. Byrd and Capt. Hartle, Co. B

school. When you send to us you thereby relinquish your claims upon us and the boy for that time. When he is placed with us we propose to answer for his conduct, his lessons, his morals, and his advancement, and we cannot do satisfactory work without our hands tied. He must go to church and Sunday school at least one each Sabbath. He is not allowed to leave the campus without permission. He must deport himself gentlemanly at all times. He is expected to bathe regularly and keep neat—not foppish. He must practice the manners of a gentleman; learn to be considerate of the welfare of others; in short, he comes into a well-regulated family, and he is expected to contribute his part toward keeping it so.

The shortage of funds and a lack of enrollment caused the school to close after the spring term of 1899, and the buildings were leased to a new educational institution- the Jackson Military Academy.

The Jackson Military Academy and School of Fine Arts for the education of young men and women above the age of twelve, began in 1899 on the former campus of the Carlisle Training School. The enrollment was 85 students: 55 male cadets and 25 women. Tuition was $250 per year for tuition, room and board. The directors were proud of their campus and equipment as described in the 1908 school catalog.

The Academy building is a handsome, steam-heated brick structure, three stories high, perched on the crest of a lovely knoll overlooking the city of Jackson. During the past year we have installed a thoroughly modern acetylene gas lighting plant. A large campus abundantly supplied with fine shade trees furnishes ample space for drill, recreation and sports. A dormitory has been attached to the main building in late years, so that rooming facilities for about 50 cadets are afforded. The sleeping rooms are well aired and large, and each furnished with an iron bedstead, a mattress, wash stand, bowl and pitcher, two chairs, a table and a mirror. The chapel occupies the third floor of the Academy building and furnishes an excellent place for recitals, and other entertainments, while elegant double parlors are found on the first floor. Classrooms are equipped with blackboards and modern school furniture, maps, charts and the like. Laboratory equipment for work in science, library facilities, and instruction are the best.

The course of study allowed for students in college preparation, commercial life, or fine art. The four year study course covered classical and modern subjects: English, Latin, Arithmetic, History Geography, Physiology, Rhetoric, Caesar, Greek, Botany, Algebra, Cicero, Geometry, a living language such as French, German, Spanish, American Literature, Trigonometry, Physics or Chemistry, the Iliad, and Virgil. Students leaning toward the business studies could also take Commercial Law, Typewriting, Stenography, Letter Writing, Book Keeping and Accounting. The Department of Fine Arts offered classes in Vocal Culture, Art and Elocution. While the course above offered exercise for the mind, the Military Department stated that it was an "essential matter to have some form of exercise which is conducive to health, thereby developing, enabling, and qualifying the mental faculties to comprehend and retain the knowledge imparted to them."

The day began at 6:00 a.m. with Reveille and ended at 9:30 p.m. with Taps. The daily routine and rules for the school and dormitory were strictly enforced. A demerit system tracked student violations for unkempt rooms, untidy appearance, yelling, whistling, or creating disorder in the classroom. While cigarette smoking was strictly forbidden, students with parental permission could smoke or chew tobacco in their rooms during recreational periods. A student could be expelled for cheating on exams, leaving campus without permission, intoxication, gambling, and "or having cards in his possession, either in barracks, or grounds, or in city."

The Jackson Military Academy laid a strong foundation for the future of school sports in the area. The athletic department of the school had a strong following among the local sports fans. The rosters for the 1904 football, and baseball, and basketball teams read like a who's who of Cape Girardeau County families: Taylor, Bacon, Byrd, McGee, Medley, Hines, Morton, Hartle, English, Litzelfelner, Williams, Kipping, Hoffman, Limbaugh, Colyer, Horrell, Obermiller, Moore, Oliver, and Bingenheimer. The 1906 football record showed that in thirteen games only Perryville High School was able to score any points against the JMA squad. True to the ideals of good sportsmanship, the 1908 catalog noted that the football team had won the Southeast Missouri championship and that "The pleasing feature of the games was that there was no rough work, only clean, clever plays." The school was advanced in its acceptance of women's sports and provided the female students with a basketball team of their own.

The Jackson Military Academy closed its doors after the commencement of May 1909. According to the Missouri Cash-Book newspaper, the directors, Col. T. W. Birmingham and Col. T. L. Hamlin, having fulfilled the terms of their ten-year contract to provide a "school of such a grade that pupils graduating from it could enter the state university without examination" decided to sell the property and "seek more remunerative and less arduous employment in other fields of educational work." The Jackson School Board accepted a proposal to purchase the property because of the reasonable asking price for a well-maintained building, the necessity of finding a proper high school facility, and the proximity of the property to the existing Jackson Public School.

Jackson Public Schools

The public schools of Jackson were established in 1867. According to *The Magnet* (1915 and 1921), the yearbook of Jackson High School, a three-year high school program began in 1903 in a single classroom with one teacher. The first graduate of that program, Lewis Reed, graduated in 1906. In 1909, high school classes were moved into the old Jackson Military Academy building where a four-year program with multiple teachers was established. Elementary classes continued in the existing elementary building until 1881 when a new building was constructed. In 1870 a school was organized for black children with Prof. William Brooks as the teacher. This school met in a one-story frame building, on Union Avenue. In 1944, the Board of Education, realizing that facilities for black students were inadequate, built a two room modern brick school with a basement and an auditorium. The building was completed in 1947 and was in use for classes until integration of black students into the public school system in 1954 following the Supreme Court decision in the case *Brown v. Board of Education of Topeka*. This building then became the Administrative building for the district.

As the population of Jackson increased and the desire for formal education became greater, the school district changed to meet those needs. In 1920 the first part of the present high school building was constructed, with an addition completed in 1929. The football stadium was constructed in the 1930s as a WPA project, with a community cannery located in part of the space under the bleachers. The current Central Elementary Building was constructed in 1939. Over the years as the district has expanded, buildings were added or remodeled to meet the changing needs of the curriculum.

A real change came about in the 1950s. Nationwide, the trend was to do away with small, rural school districts to provide a program more academically sound, particularly at the secondary level, than most rural districts could afford. Wisdom of the times stressed that pooling tax resources of many small districts would be practical and beneficial. Thus, in 1954, after having received approval of the State Board of Education for its reorganization plan combining the Jackson Public Schools with seventeen smaller districts, an election was called to approve the plan creating the Reorganized School District R-2 of Cape Girardeau County (commonly known as the Jackson R-2 District).

The measure passed and a second election was called to select a six-director board for the new district. The Board of Education of the newly created district met for the first time April 8, 1954. Within a year five more districts would join the system with the final addition, the Millersville R-7 Elementary District, coming in 1957 (Lacy and White, 1985).

Reorganization brought new challenges. As a district covering approximately 550 square miles, transportation to centralized attendance centers became a major concern. Decisions regarding which existing buildings to utilize, which to replace and which to offer for sale had to be made, not always to the satisfaction of residents of the former school districts.

As the population of the district has increased over the years, it has become necessary to add buildings to the district. Within the city limits of Jackson the district has developed a high school complex consisting of the original 1920s structure; a music, home economics, and agriculture building; two gymnasiums; and a science and math building, as well as converting the Central Elementary Building for use of the High School. In addition, an Alternative Learning Center was developed in 1997. There is also a Junior High School, currently under expansion, and a Middle School. Elementary buildings include the Primary Annex, West Lane Elementary, Orchard Elementary, and South Elementary. The district also operates the Gordonville Elementary Attendance Center, North Elementary at Fruitland, and Millersville Attendance Center.

In 2000 the district purchased an existing building on East Main Street as an administration center, moving offices for support services, transportation and maintenance into the space they vacated. In addition, the district has purchased land on the East Main Street Extension for future elementary school needs. With a district population estimated to be 27,799 and growing, a school population of 4,657 as of September 30, 2001, and a staff of 563 employees, the district has come a long way from the small log cabin that served as Jackson's first school. Enrollment figures were given here with as much accuracy as can possibly be recorded after the passing of many years. Information taken from the district's web site with other information provided by the school district staff.) -amd

STUDENT ORGANIZATIONS AT JACKSON HIGH SCHOOL

In addition to their everyday studies, the students at Jackson High School have a long list of extracurricular activities to choose from by the year 2002. Some of the organizations offered to the students include, but are not limited to, Student Council, National Honor Society, The Squawler (the Senior High Newspaper), French and Spanish Clubs, Speech Team, Drama Club, Photography Club, Scholar Bowl, Quill and Scroll (encourages students interested in journalism and creative writing), DECA (Distributive Education Clubs of America), FBLA (Future Business Leaders of America), FHA (Future Homemakers of America), FFA (Future Farmers of America), SADD (Students Against Drunk Driving), J-Club (for the Varsity Lettermen), History Club, Hi-Step (High School Taught Elementary Program), Silver Arrow Staff (the staff the coordinates the pages in the yearbook and the Silver Arrow Dance), Just Say No, Junior Rotarians (student body elected students that participate in Jackson Rotarian meetings), Jam (Jackson Acting Motivators), FCA (Fellowship of Christian Athletes), and Peer Tutors. SADD, Jam and Just Say No are beneficial to the community by providing education to area youth on how to prevent drug and alcohol abuse. The Drama Club presents a different play each year to display their acting talents to the public.

The large number of music organizations entertain the community throughout the year: Jackson Marching Chiefs, Jazz Band, Pep Band, Hand Bell Choir, Concert Band, Symphonic Band, Chamber Choir, Mixed Chorus, and Girls' Choir. Their wonderful music can be heard at various concerts throughout the year, most notably at football games, Christmas concerts, and the Annual Pop Concert.

Aside from the many clubs offered, the Jackson High School students may also try out for a number of sports teams. The young men can participate in football, baseball, soccer, cross-country, basketball, wrestling, golf, and track. The young women can participate in volleyball, fast-pitch softball, tennis, cross-country, basketball, golf, soccer and track. Not only can the student athletes be rewarded by winning throughout the season in their respective sports, but they can also receive notoriety through their academic achievements by being named Scholar Athletes. On the sidelines or at halftime, a spectator can always rely on the support of the Cheerleading squads, the Pep Club, or the Jackson Marching Chiefs for team spirit.

By Katy Liley

Jackson R-2 High School, 2002.

Jackson High School Science/Mathematics Building, 2002.

Jackson High School's "Fine Arts"

To help develop a well-rounded, productive young person, a community must be involved. It must have a vested interest in the education of each child, an education that stimulates the mind, body, and spirit. It must then support the activities and endeavors of that child. Such is the community in which we live, Jackson, Missouri.

Jackson has always been a supportive partner in the development and nurturning of her children. The citizens of this community promote academic excellence by building and maintaining quality schools. Year after year, they fill the stadium, the ballparks, and the gymnasiums in support of the athletic programs. The performing groups never want for an audience, for our community citizens have always encourage and support the "Arts."

Our high school's Fine Arts programs have excelled throughout the years, not just on a local level, but on the district and state levels as well. Entertainment, amusement, and joy have been brought to the thousands who have attended concerts, musicals, parades, and dinner theaters. The raw talent of an artist is of course inherent; the life-blood is drawn from an appreciative and enthusiastic audience; but the training, instruction and often the inspiration of the artist is found in his or her teacher.

Jackson High School has been fortunate to have among its Fine Arts faculty, some of the best and most dedicated in their field. Through these teachers, thousands of young minds have developed an eye for visual beauty, an ear for the harmonies and emotions of music, and a desire to incorporate the arts into their daily lives. Jackson High School teachers, in the area of Visual Arts, include the renowned Jake Wells, a master sketch artist and painter. His famous "Missouri Mills" watercolor collection is in constant demand for museum exhibits and tours. Mr. Wells began his teaching career in Jackson in 1944. He taught art to grades 1 through 12, and coached football, baseball and basketball. In 1960 he became a professor of art at Southeast Missouri State University where he taught until his retirement. Mr. Herbert Wickham followed in the fall of 1960, introducing the students to a world of creative endeavors. His own artistic skills are famous throughout the area and state, as well as his wit and humor. Mr. Wickham's sketches, chalks, and oil paintings of area landmarks hang in numerous homes, banks and prominent buildings. He retired from public school teaching in 1991, but stays by working in his private studio, and teaching occasional workshops and adult classes. Mrs. Wanda Young began teaching at Jackson High School in 1976. She and Ms. Andrea Talley are the current art instructors at the high school level, still encouraging the students to see the world with the creativity and appreciation of an artist's eye.

In the Fine Arts vocal department, the goal has always been to teach, train, and develop not only young voices, but young musicians. Through the years, the Jackson High School choirs have earned many honors and awards, and have entertained literally thousands of area residents. Mr. Leroy Mason served as the first full-time choral/band director, beginning his career at Jackson in 1939. The choir library, started years ago by Mr. Mason, is today a storehouse of classic treasures. Many of those early arrangements are now priceless (no longer in print), many were copyrighted in the early 1920s and 1930s at the incredible price of 10 - 25 cents per copy, and may are written in Mr. Mason's own hand. After some eighteen years, he moved to Southeast Missouri State University, where he served as chairman of the Music Department, organizing and developing the nationally known Golden Eagles Marching Band. Back in Jackson, Mrs. Leona Kinder had taken the reins as choral directory in 1957, following Mr. Mason. She taught at Jackson for only three years before moving to Arizona for health reasons, but she was a wonderful, vivacious teacher, vocalist, and pianist. Mr. Alan Rowland, who had student taught with Mrs. Kinder, took over the vocal program in 1960. Under his direction the choirs grew in numbers and expertise. He taught at Jackson High until 1968, continuing his teaching career in Festus, Missouri. Mr. Nick Leist, already busy as the sole Jackson High School band director, picked up the vocal program for one year. In 1969 Mrs. Ernestine Kirk took the position of Choral Director. During her seventeen years at Jackson, she introduced the choirs to district and State Music Contest, put on a number of Broadway Musicals including *Showboat* and *Sound of Music*, and started the renowned *Pop Concert*. Mrs. Jean Schwean followed in 1986, after having taught elementary music for a number of years. Her choirs achieved recognition by earning #1 State Contest ratings for twelve consecutive years, along with numerous All-District and All-State honors. The annual mid-winter Dinner Theater took shape under her direction, the most popular being the Madrigal Christmas Feasts, a banquet/musical/play celebrated in the ancient traditions of Merry Old England. Mrs. Christy Shinn joined the high school staff in 2000, and will take over as Jackson High School Choral Director following Mrs. Schwean's retirement in 2002. The instrumental music program has always been the very backbone of the school's fine arts department. It has been recognized on every level, continuing to earn top honors throughout the District and State. Again, Mr. LeRoy Mason's name pops up as one of the founders of the high school band program. He began teaching in 1939, building a solid music program during his eighteen years at Jack-

Marching Band Festival formation, 1947.

son. Mr. Mason was the founder and organizer of the annual "Marching Band Festival" which remains a popular high school event to this day. After Mr. Mason moved to Southeast Missouri State University in 1958, Mr. Ed Carson served as band director for the next two years followed, in 1960, by Mr. Richard Partridge. Mr. Alan Rowland took over as band director in the fall of 1963, adding to his already busy choral schedule. Mr. Nick Leist began his long tenure as Jackson High Band Director in 1964. His famous marching theme song, "Everything's Comin' Up Roses," entertained thousands of parade watchers and football fans over the next thirty-plus years. His Co-Director and friend, Mrs. Patricia Schwent, joined the high school staff in 1975, and became the Director of Bands in 1999 following Mr. Leist's retirement. Her expertise in the field of Jazz is known throughout the state. She retired in 2001, handing over the baton to Mr. Scott Vangilder, who continues to teach high school bands, along with Mr. Tom Broussard, Mr. Paul Fliege, and Mr. Chris Crawford.

The Jackson community continues to be involved in the lives, the activities, and the endeavors of its children, and the children, in turn grow up to become respected, productive community citizens. Thank you, Jackson, for a heritage of excellence.

By Jean Schweain

Jackson High School Sports

HISTORY OF JACKSON HIGH SCHOOL WRESTLING

Jackson High School actually had wrestling teams in 1961-62 and 1962-63 coached by Bill Daniels. However, these were not sanctioned teams as they only had two matches with official teams - Sikeston and Charleston. In order to be considered a sanctioned team and compete in district tournaments, a team had to have ten meets with other sanctioned teams. Wrestlers qualified for district competition by winning 50% of their matches.

When Bob Lohr was hired by Jackson for the 1963-64 school year as social studies teacher, assistant football coach and the wrestling coach, a full wrestling schedule was part of the school's commitment. Since Coach Lohr had no wrestling experience, he spent the summer with several wrestling books, learning the different holds and how to counter them. Sikeston, Charleston, and Bell City were the only wrestling teams in the area so a full schedule included matches with more experienced teams for Carbondale, Murphysboro, and the St. Louis area. For one of the matches the team had to take their own mats as Bell City did not have their own.

Bob Lohr coached this fledgling team of hard-working, dedicated young men through the 1967-68 season. During the 1964-65 season, wrestlers Fred Seabaugh, Terry Ladreiter, and Van Hitt qualified for district competition. Terry Ladreiter qualified to go to the sectionals tournament. There was much support for these young teams on which a 95 lb. wrestler such as Lee Gladish could be as productive as wrestlers weighing over 200 lbs. Because of the enthusiasm of team members, the number of individuals on the team grew. During the 1965 to 1967 seasons, the teams won many dual matches and began to compete and place in tournaments. Ladreiter and Seabaugh won medals in several tournaments and Ladreiter qualified for state competition, was named team captain, and chosen outstanding wrestler in his senior year. Nelson Morrison coached the team from 1968 through the 1969-70 season. In 1969-70, Jackson had three state qualifiers. Dave Riney, Rich Seyer, and Rodney Roshek, a wrestler from Nebraska who transferred to Jackson, all competed at State, with Roshek placing 3rd.

For the 1970-71 season, Paul Webber became head coach with Bob Sink as his assistant and junior varsity coach. At this point, Jackson teams began to dominate in southeast Missouri. The team was undefeated in duals, and had twelve regional qualifiers and three state qualifiers: John Wilson (2nd), Rich Seyer (3rd), and Dave Riney. In 1971-72, Webber and Sink coached the team to a district championship and qualified Stanley Bowers, Dave Ramsey, and Dave Reiminger for state. Dave Reiminger had an undefeated season, captured the state championship, and was elected team captain. In 1972-73, the team was again undefeated in duals, won the Conference and Regional championships, and sent three wrestlers to state. The team won their first state trophy as they placed fourth in state competitions. During the 1973-

Wrestling Team 1961-1962. Back row: Lonnie Davenport, Pat Horrell, Don Schaefer, Ray Schweain, Dennis Seivers, Jim Wallis, Van Hitt. Front row: Jesse Kinder, Ron Hovis, Steve Byrd, Mike Seabaugh, Mike Kasten, John Wessel, Tony Kirn. Seated: Dave Hitt, Dave Wendel.

Row 1: T. Ladreiter, R. Eakins, T. Smith, G. Wilke, H. Crites, R. Richter, V. Hitt, S. Hager (lying), M. Sides. Row 2: F. Seabaugh, D. Hoffman, Coach Lohr, C. Wachter, R. Meyr, J. Seabaugh, D. Meyr. Row 3: M. Conley, M. Lincoln, R. Conner, L. Gladish.

74 season, the team won Conference and District championships, sending six wrestlers to state. John Goodson had a 27-0 record in the heavyweight division, Jim Welker was 2nd at state, and Butch Wright was 3rd.

In 1974-75, the team won Conference and District tournaments, with Butch Wright and Bruce Collier qualifying for the State tournament. In 1975-76 state qualifiers were Steve Skelton, Rich Weith, Kevin Rampley and Bruce Collier, who won 1st at state and had an undefeated season.

The highlight for Jackson wrestling came in the 1976-77 season when the team was undefeated in duals, won District and Regional championships, and qualified ten of twelve team members for state competition. Mark Collier and Curt Davidson won 2nd and Kevin Rampley was state champion. **The team won the Class A State Championship.**

The next school year, Jackson moved up to Class AA so was unable to defend that state championship. However, they were undefeated in duals and won the conference Championship in 1977-78. They had their 100th team victory in 1978-79 and were Conference champions in 1979-80. In 1980-81, Bruce Thomas joined Coaches Webber and Sink. In 1981-82 the team was again competitive at the state level, having eight state qualifiers and winning second as a team in Class AA.

Due to serious illness, Coach Webber turned the team over to his assistants Bruce Thomas and Bob Sink for the 1982-83 season. That year they were undefeated in duals, and were District champions and sent twelve of thirteen team members to the Regional Tournament. District champions were Steve Schreiner, Scott King, Kyle Wright, Lane Lohr, and David Sievers. In 1983-84 the team won the Conference and district Tournaments, sending eight qualifiers to state competition.

Coach Bruce Thomas took over the reins, with Steve Wachter as his assistant, for the 1984-85 season. They were again undefeated in duals, won District, and sent twelve wrestlers to sectional competition. The team won the Conference title in 1985-86, 1986-87 and 1987-88. Dane Baker won Conference championships all three of these seasons. In 1987-88 Brandon Norman set the record for most wins (34-0) in a season and won a state championship.

The team won 2nd in Conference and District competition in 1988-89, but fared better in 1989090, winning district Tournament and sending six wrestlers to state competition. Bill Britzman was a district champion and Brent Young and Chris Jaco placed at state.

In 1990-91, the team won 2nd at the Conference Tournament and was District champion. Chris Hinze was a District Champ. Eight wrestlers qualified for state competition, with Chris Jaco placing 2nd. This was also a memorable year for the Junior Varsity—even though they didn't know it. During the latter part of the season, the Junior Varsity started a winning streak in dual competition that continues to this day —with over 100 wins.

In 1991-92, the team won the Conference championship and sent six wrestlers to state. Todd Reiminger placed 3rd at state. The 1992-93 team again was undefeated in dual competition and placed 2nd in Conference and districts. Eight wrestlers qualified for state competition, with Gary Newman winning a state championship and the team placing 6th in state. The team was again undefeated in dual competition, Conference and District champions, and had eight wrestlers advance to state competition in 1993-94.

Steve Wachter became head coach of the team in 1994-95. Brandon Norman was his assistant. The team was undefeated in dual competition and won the District title. District champions were Joe Wiseman, Travis Reiminger, Stacy Langston, Nathan Norman, and Kit Eifert. Norman placed 2nd in state competition. The team had another outstanding season in 1995-96, being undefeated in dual competition, Conference champions, and 2nd in Districts. The team had eight state qualifiers with Nathan Norman winning a state championship. The team placed 4th at state.

In 1996-97 the team moved up to the AAAA division, but still managed to place 6th in state competition. The team was undefeated in dual competition and qualified four wrestlers for the State Tournament. Lance Schlick placed 3rd, Joe Wiseman placed 2nd, and Travis Reiminger was state champion, setting a new school record with 38 wins-0 losses. In 1997-98 the team had six state qualifiers, with Lance Schlick and Kyle Watson placing 6th.

As the number of wrestlers grew, additional coaches were added to help with the team. These included Neal Glass, Jerry Golden, and Matt Wendel. In 1998-99, five wrestlers qualified for state, with Lance Schlick placing 2nd. This made him a four-time state placer. Cyle Huck also placed. In 1999-2000, seven wrestlers qualified for state. Adam Wachter was state champion in the 140 lb division; the team placed 9th. The team continues to do well in the AAAA Division in 2000-01 as they sent eight wrestlers to state competition. Mike Wright placed 2nd and Ray Goodson was state champion in the 215 lb. division, setting a new school records for most wins with 42 wins and 0 losses.

In the current school year 2001-02, seven wrestlers qualified for state competition with James Love placing 2nd, Ricky Feiner placing 4th, and Brock Howard placing 5th. The team placed 9th at State Tournament. Those young men who were willing to try this grueling new sport forty years ago have seen the Jackson High School wrestling program become a legend in southeast Missouri and well-known around the state as they consistently place in the top ten in Missouri in the AAAA Division. When they first started the program, it was difficult to field a full team so they had to forfeit matches in some weight classes. Now there is a varsity team, a junior varsity team, a 9th grade team, and an 8th grade team with Jeff Scott as coach.

By Barb Lohr

GIRLS' SPORTS AT JACKSON HIGH SCHOOL

Jackson High School Principal Jim Nelson was proud to introduce the first Jackson Girls Track Team on April 1, 1974. Mr. Nelson started the process of developing a track team in November 1973 when he proposed the idea to the Superintendent and Board of Education as a way to comply with the Title IX ruling that high schools receiving federal education grants could not restrict use of facilities for reason of race, religion, or sex. Mr. Nelson would need to find girls interested in running, teachers willing to coach, and convince other schools to develop teams for the Jackson girls to compete against. Many female students were excited by the idea of running, competing and getting in shape.

Eighteen girls signed up and remained the entire season. Lloyd Banks, assisted by Charles Koch and Bob Sink, agreed to coach the girls in addition to the boys. However, there were no other girls' track teams in the Southeast Mis-

State Champions, 1976-77. Row 1: Rich Weith; Russ Jackman; Kevin Rampley; Steve Wachter; Kevin Bolen; Steve Powell; Doug Brown; Jim Lohr. Row 2: Coach Paul Webber; Joe Reiminger; Mark Collier; Jimmy Williams; Curt Davidson; Doug Goodson; Kirby Mirly; Coach Bob Sink.

souri conference. The Jackson track squad had to travel north and run against the Lead Belt schools in Desloge, Farmington and Flat River. By June of 1974, Cape Girardeau Central and other area schools took notice of the serious effort made by the Jackson Girls' Track Team.

With one program successfully on its way, Mr. Nelson again approached the Superintendent and Board of Education, this time with a proposal to develop a girls' basketball team. The Board requested more information about the provisions necessary for a coach, cost of uniforms and transportation, number of games, time sharing arrangement for the practice gym, and names of other participating schools. Once again, finding other schools with which to schedule games proved to be the most difficult aspect in achieving his goal. In 1975, Mr. Don Illers (whose daughter attended Jackson High School) presented a petition to the Board requesting a team be organized. With the cooperation of the local administration and a few area schools, Girls' Basketball began in the Fall of 1975. Even though the program was new and the team's uniforms did not arrive until late in the season, the team finished the season with seven wins and five losses. With so few schools having girls' teams, they played four schools twice and then had to travel to play a school in Illinois twice.

Sporting programs for female students have come a long way during the last thirty years. The girls' volleyball and basketball teams rotated practice hours with the boys basketball and wrestling teams until the construction of the Multipurpose Building. The girls' sports have their own following of loyal fans. It is not unusual for Jackson's girls' teams to win their way through the season, districts and sectionals to compete at the state level. The Lady Indians squads in cross-country, basketball, golf, tennis, track, volleyball, softball, and most recently soccer are comprised of dedicated, bright students whose names often appear in the paper not only for their athletic achievements but also for their academic accomplishments.

By Jim Nelson

JACKSON CROSS-COUNTRY HISTORY, 1959-2001

Many outstanding athletes have come through the Jackson Cross-Country program and the history of the sport reflects the extreme sacrifice and determination that these athletes have demonstrated throughout the years.

The program was the brainchild of then High School Track coach Herb Marshall, when, in the fall of 1959, he asked former JHS distance runner Gerald Jones to start a Cross-Country program. Jones was, at that time, a sophomore Cross-Country runner at Southeast Missouri State College, but he agreed to coach the Jackson runners during their 7th hour Study Hall period. He then would have time to rush back to Cape Girardeau to run his own collegiate practice. Herb Marshall was attempting to get Jackson's track program up to speed with other schools in the state, as Cross-Country had a State sponsored Championship meet as early as 1944, but no Southeast Missouri schools had ever run a Cross-Country program. Jones went to Study

Jackson High School Girls' Track Team. Left to Right. First row: Karen Dost; Ramona Hary; Brenda Cattron; Monica Reisenbichler; Beth Weis. Second row: Susan Illers; Cathy Allen; Pam Vinyard; Cheryl Carlton; Lanny Landgraf. Third row: Joyce Aufdenberg; Patty Litz; Lesa Brockett; Dina Kurre; Sheri Sievers; Paula Dow. -photo by Tom Neumeyer

Seven members of the Girls' Cross-Country Team, 1997. Left to right: Annie Stoverink, Julie Wunderlich, Christy Thoma, Sarah Stiegemeyer, Sarah Strack, Jennifer Brown, Sarah Schlick.

Hall, recruited boys who were not out for football, and said "You're running Cross-Country," and nine boys followed their recruiter to their first practice. Coach Jones' first team consisted of Don Mason, J. C. Bond, Rex Henderson, Jerry Estes, Carl Smith, Eddie Schreiner, Milton Mouser, Bill Short, and Allen Crader.

In 1960, the boys competed in full schedule. During home football games the boys ran a 2-mile race. Starting their races out on the roads they ended on the cinder track that circled the football field, finishing during the halftime show. In 1961 the team blossomed to seventeen boys and Jackson had their first ever State Qualifiers in Larry Schloss who placed first in every regular season race he entered and placed 15th at State.

Since Jackson was the first southeast Missouri school to start Cross-Country and needed competition, Coach Jones set out to convince other area schools the value of Cross-Country. Jones' former running teammate Rex Miller then started a team at Cape Central. Enough schools were competing by the mid-1960s that a district meet could be held. Each school would host an Invitational so the schools competed against each other many times. Gerald Jones continued to coach through 1966. He was suc-

ceeded by Leroy Johnson in 1967, Coach Godwin a few years later, and Lloyd Banks in 1973.

In 1977 a new change came about with the addition of a Girls' Cross-Country team. Andrea Talley set the tone for the girls program with excellent times in the 1 1/2, 2, and 2 1/2 mile runs.

New coaches came during the next three years: Dwight Garris, 1979; Steve Burk, 1980; Tim Sutton, 1981. Coach Sutton ran the program until 1987. The fall of 1987 saw the beginning of a coaching era in which Jim Stoverink coached from 1987 to 2000. Stoverink's assistant coaches were Tracy Stockton Williams in 1993 and Andrea Talley in 1998. In 2000, Coach Stoverink stepped aside to become assistant coach and Andrea Talley assumed the head coaching duties. Coach Talley recruited large teams in 2000 and 2001, and expects the same in 2002. The future of Cross-Country looks to be growing stronger with each passing year.

So many changes have taken place in the sport of Cross-Country over the years— race distances, training required for the sport, the addition of female athletes, just to name a few. Gerald Jones probably had no idea that the sport he started, not only at Jackson High School, but in the entire southeast Missouri area, would grow in numbers and interest to the point that it has. He, along with the many coaches and athletes, parents and community members that have made this program thrive, should be commended for their tremendous dedication to the sport and their intense desire for success. What these athletes have gained, and the lessons learned by their participation in this great sport, will stay with them forever. We are grateful this outstanding program is available to the youth of our community.

Condensed from comprehensive history by Coach Andrea Talley.

HISTORY OF JACKSON HIGH SCHOOL FOOTBALL

Football was begun in Jackson in 1895, when some of the students of the Carlyle Training School, a combination senior high and junior college, organized a football squad without the help of a coach. This was the first football team organized in Missouri south of St. Louis. The team played its first game in Jackson with Oak Ridge town team. In 1896 the Jackson team played the Carlton College team of Farmington for the first football game between schools in Southeast Missouri.

In 1897 the Carlyle Training School became the Jackson Military Academy. The JMA, as it was commonly called, continued football. Jackson won the championship of Southeast Missouri in the year 1900. The 1910 yearbook states, "The most successful period of Jackson football history was the fall of 1909, when our team won the championship of Southeast Missouri among the high schools." From Jackson's early academy beginnings to the present day, football remains a community passion and, win or lose, people of the community support and follow the high school team.

According to the school yearbook "The Magnet," teams from 1914 to 1925 had few rules, recruited new players weekly, had players ranging in age from 15 to 20 years old, and one year almost had no team when parent permit slips were required from the players. The Board rescinded this requirement so a team was fielded. Travel at the time was difficult and tiring, and the yearbook mentioned that the team was worn out from the long ride over rough and muddy roads—to Perryville.

Early opponents included Cape Girardeau High, Charleston, Perryville, 2nd team from the Teacher's College, Will Mayfield College, Caruthersville, and Poplar Bluff. In 1923 and 24, opponents included Oran, Morley, Morehouse, and Blodgett. In 1921-22, the school had no money for equipment or funds to operate a football team. Citizens gave donations so we would have a team that year. This may have been the first record of a "Benchwarmers Club."

In 1922-23, the name of the yearbook was changed from "The Magnet" to "Silver Arrow." Ten football contests became the norm for a season. E. F. Kimbrell coached the football team from 1923-24 to 1925-26. In his final season as coach, the team won the championship of the Southeast Missouri League—Northern Division. They played Gideon, winners of the Southern Division. They played to a tie! Under Coach J. S. Crabtree in 1926-27, the football team won the Northern Division of the Southeast Missouri League again.

In 1929-30 the schedule included contests with Chaffee, Diehlstadt, and Sikeston. That year three games had to be cancelled due to sore arms of players from smallpox vaccinations. Coach Ryland Milner was football coach from 1933-34 to 1936-37. He had an impressive coaching record that included the first undefeated season in 1935-36. This team was not only undefeated, but were never scored on. They had 311 points to 0 for their opponents. Coach Milner started the next season with seven victories giving the Jackson Indians a 17-game winning streak. At the end of that school year, Coach Milner accepted a coaching position at Maryville College, offering scholarships to five of the football players: M. and R. Rogers, Larry Loos, Dean Walker, and Stubby Wilhelm

Elmer Seefeld coached from 1937-38 to 1939-40. In 1937-38 the Jackson Indians were again Southern Division champs with a record of 7-0-1. On September 23, 1938, the new stadium was dedicated during the Jackson vs. Chaffee contest. One of the members of the football team was Bill Deck, who enlisted in the Marine Corps and was later killed on Iwo Jima.

The next four years showed losing records but fighting spirit, and the Indians again won the Conference trophy in 1943-44. After three losing seasons, Coach Wallace Hicks took over as head coach in 1949-50. He coached for four years but never had a winning season. In 1953-54 the contract of Coach Hicks was not renewed. When players and students learned this, they organized a protest and paraded through town at lunch time. Coach Ralph (Bogey) Harrison

The 1935 S.E.Mo. Conference Champs. Left to right. First row: L. Crites; M. Rogers, Co-Captain; M. Meier; O. Litzelfelner; L. Loos; Milton Nothdurft. Second row: L. Cracraft; C. Wessell; C. Wilhelm, Co-Captain; R. Rogers; D. Sneathen; G. Niswonger. Third row: M. Godwin; A. Godwin; E. Loos; Robert Hartle; C. Davis; P. Kurre. Fourth row: Jr. Weiss; H. Bollinger; S. Cracraft; D. Walker; E. Cracraft; N. Gockel. Fifth row: Coach R. N. Milner; Marion Nothdurft; W. Crites, Manager.

Top: 1910 Football Team: Professor J. H. Goodin; Fred Masters, Coach; Clyde Mabrey; Weston Henderson; Emerson Spradling, Capt.; Paul Mueller; Lester Taylor; Tom Boon; William Schwab; Clarence Litzelfelner; Ed Slack; Harrison Boon; Henry Mueller.
Middle: Jackson High School Football Team, 1994.
Bottom: Jackson High School Football Team, 1995.

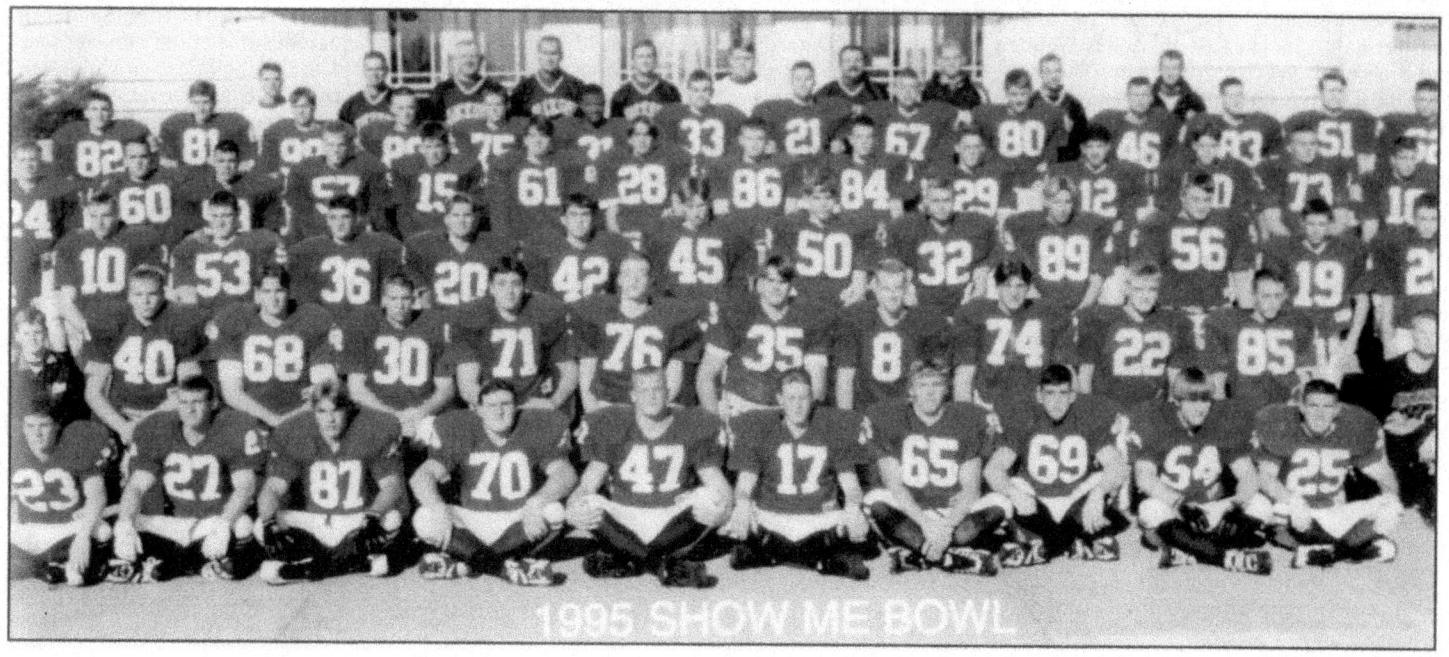

coached the team in 1954-55. They had a record of 7-3. Bogey left at the end of that year to take a position at SEMO.

The next four years were also losing seasons. However, the 1956-57 team, coached by Herb Marshall succeeded in defeating Cairo, who was tied with Sikeston for the conference title. By beating Cairo, it gave the title to Sikeston. The Sikeston coach sent Coach Marshall a dozen roses. Coach Marshall threw the roses on the floor and stomped on them. Coach Marshall got his revenge in 1959-60 when the Indians won the Big Eight Conference.

The period from 1960-61 to 1968-69 was a "roller-coaster" with up and down seasons and a series of different coaches. Jim Lee, assisted by Bob Lohr, coached the team for four years from 1963-64 through 1966-67. One of their outstanding players was Van Hitt, who currently coaches football for the Jackson Indians.

In 1969-70, Paul Webber, affectionately nicknamed Beasto, began a 20-year tenure as head coach. He was ably assisted by Bob Sink, who is still with the school as assistant football and head track coach. During the early years, Webber and Sink did a lot of rebuilding. They won the Conference title in 1975-76 with a record of 9-1. From then on, Webber and Sink never had a losing season. In keeping with the rich tradition of Jackson football, many former Jackson players have served as assistant football coaches. Some of the former Indians who have been with the program at various times are Van Hitt, Steve Decker, Mike Gohn, Dave Riney, Steve Wachter, Brandon Norman, Jerry Golden, Reagan McDowell, Nathan Norman, Neil Glass, Jim David Lohr, Kent Gibbs, Eric Venable.

In 1981-82, Carl Gross joined the Jackson football staff as an assistant coach. That year's team won the District championship, went to the semi-finals in state playoffs. The following year John Paul Webber and Lane Lohr, referred to by teammates and newspapers as "the Connection," were the leading passer and leading receiver in the state. In 1983-84 the team had a 9-3 season, were 4A District champs and went to state quarterfinals. In 1984-85, Coaches Webber and Sink recorded their 100th win. The team won the District championship and went to state playoffs again in 1991-92. The 1994-95 Indians made JHS history as the first team to play for a football state championship. This phenomenal 12-2 season included SEMO Co-Conference Championship and the 4A District Championship. With the school and community enjoying football fever, most of the town traveled to Columbia, leaving signs declaring, "Last one out of town, turn off the lights." The team repeated their success the following year, again winning the District Championship and taking second place at state, losing by a score of 20-19.

The Indians moved up to Class 5A in 1996-97. Even in the largest school division, the team ended with an 8-2 record and a District championship, but lost in the first game of sectional playoffs.

The 1997-98 team was undefeated in regular season play. This was only the second time for an undefeated season—the first being in the 1935-36 school year. After winning the Conference and District championships, the team lost in the second round of state playoffs. The 1999-2000 season indicated that Jackson football is a powerhouse in the 5A Division as the team had a 9-2 record, a District championship, and made it to the first round of state playoffs.

In 2000-01 the Jackson Indians had a third undefeated season in regular play. With a record of 12-1, they were Conference and District champions, and played three playoff games making the team 4th in state. Mario Whitney set a state record for most rushing yards in a single game. With excellent coaching and consistent team improvement from first to last game, the football tradition and community support will continue.

By Barbara Lohr and Richard Decker

Immaculate Conception School

After the Immaculate Conception Roman Catholic Church was formed in 1874, a small classroom was located in the rear of the church. However, in 1879 or 1880 the congregation was allowed to collect money for a school. The Uz McGuire residence was purchased and, when Ursuline Nuns came to Jackson to instruct the children in 1882, the building became both a school and a convent. About a year later a two-room frame school was constructed on the east side of the convent. In 1927 Father H. J. Eggiman supervised the building of a one-room frame school building on the corner of Hope and Jefferson streets. The school closed when he was transferred.

Father F. E. Sommerhauser reopened the school in 1943 with the assistance of two Sisters of Notre Dame. Classes were held in the convent. Later in the year the schoolhouse built by Father Eggiman was converted to two rooms and the school was moved into that building. In addition, a temporary schoolroom was built east of the school due to an increased number of students. A small school bus was purchased to transport students from as far away as Dutchtown.

In 1945 a drive was begun to raise funds to build a brick school. This school, dedicated in December 1949, was enlarged in 1970 with the addition of new classrooms and a multipurpose auditorium. The 1970s saw the beginning of a gradual shift from clerical to lay teachers as fewer young people entered religious orders. Due to rising enrollment, the building was again expanded in 2001. Currently Immaculate Conception has eleven full time teachers and three part time teachers. There are 291 pupils in grades K-8. *(100 years of Immaculate Conception Parish, 1974 and school staff, 2002).*

St. Paul Lutheran School

When the first church was constructed to house St. Paul Lutheran Church in 1893, the building was to serve as both church and school. After a parsonage was built in 1894, the school was moved to the basement of the parsonage. In 1908 the congregation built a new brick church and the old frame church was converted to house the school.

In 1935 a brick school building was constructed and used until 1951 when the present building was completed. The original brick school then became the church Parish Hall. Additional classrooms have since been added to the school, with an Activity Center/Gymnasium constructed in 1977 to be used jointly by the church and the school. An expansion completed in 1998 added still more classrooms to accommodate increasing enrollment. School enrollment in 2002 is 291 in grades K-8. *(Information provided by the church and the school staff).*

Other Schools in Jackson

It is obvious that educational institutions in Jackson have expanded both in school population and physical facilities. In addition to the schools within the city limits, educational opportunities in surrounding communities have drawn the children of Jackson residents as well. Notre Dame Regional High School moved into a new facility on Route K on the western outskirts of Cape Girardeau in the fall of 2000. This move was necessitated by an expanding enrollment and the interest of families in the surrounding area to provide secondary students with the opportunity for a Catholic education. The founding of Saxony Lutheran High School in 2000 came about for some of the same reasons that motivated the Catholic congregations to support expansion of Notre Dame, the desire for their children to be able to pursue secondary education in a Christian atmosphere. They have purchased a building site northeast of Jackson on which they plan to construct their school. At the present time classes are being conducted in the St. Andrews Lutheran Church in Cape Girardeau. Other schools drawing area residents are the Eagle Ridge Christian School and the Cape Christian Academy. There are also families in the area home schooling their children. -amd

Schools

SAXONY LUTHERAN

The Jackson, MO area has been rich in Lutheran heritage since the Saxon immigrants settled in Perry County, MO in 1839. Part of that heritage is one of providing for the education of our young people. Five vibrant Lutheran elementary schools in southeast Missouri, including St. Paul Lutheran School in Jackson, continue to provide a Christ-centered approach to education in the early years. However, until recently a Lutheran high school education was only available by sending students hundreds of miles from home just when they were facing ever-increasing changes and challenges in their lives and to their faith. Today we have the opportunity to enrich our Lutheran heritage of education by extending grade offerings through high school.

On Aug. 4, 1998, a meeting was held to discuss interest in a Lutheran high school for southeast Missouri. Preliminary surveys completed by Lutheran Church-Missouri Synod congregations from Sikeston to Perryville indicated an interest and need for a Lutheran high school by a positive response of over 80%. What has developed is Saxony Lutheran High School. On Aug. 22, 2000, the first year of classes began at Saxony Lutheran High School. On that first day, one sophomore and six freshman students boldly stepped out in faith and became the first enrollees. At the beginning of the next school year, they were joined by 14 additional students to bring total enrollment to 20.

Saxony Lutheran High School strives to provide a quality, college-preparatory education in an atmosphere centered in Christ and His Word. Our mission statement reads: Saxony Lutheran High School, centered in Christ and His Word, stresses students' life skills education, fosters mutual respect, and strengthens their faith with Christ as their Savior and Guide.

Looking forward, 40 acres of land have been purchased at the 1-55 and Highway 61 interchange near Fruitland, to provide the permanent location of Saxony Lutheran High School. Future needs are being assessed which will determine the physical structure needed to provide for growth. The location is not only central and accessible to all 20 Lutheran congregations in the area, but will be a tangible sign of our commitment to Christ in our lives. Saxony Lutheran High School will also serve to unite our churches into a community of Christ.

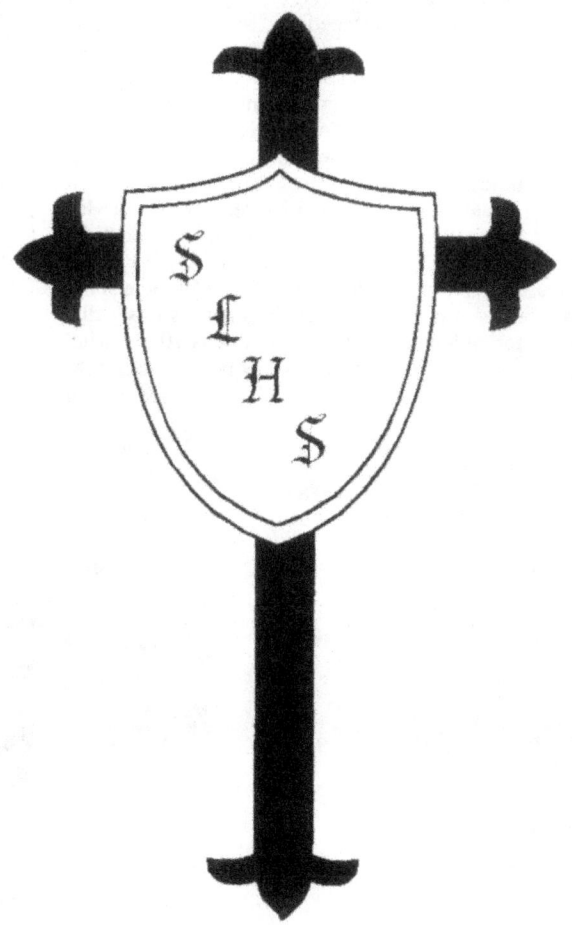

LIBRARIES

Jackson is fortunate to have the services of two public libraries within its city limits, the Jackson Public Library and Riverside Regional Library.

Riverside Regional Library

Riverside Regional Library came into being following the election of April 5, 1955, when citizens of Missouri voted to levy a one-mill tax (ten cents per one hundred dollars valuation) to form county libraries. Such libraries were to serve rural areas of the state and therefore came under the jurisdiction of the county courts, which were given authority to appoint a library board. The counties of Cape Girardeau, Perry and Scott combined their resources to form the Riverside Regional Library with its headquarters to be in Jackson because of its central location within the three county region.

The library's first home was the basement of the Cape Girardeau County Courthouse which housed 7,000 books donated by the state library. The library was later moved to the McDowell building on Highway 61 north of Jackson and finally, in 1958, moved into its present facility at 204 South Union in Jackson.

Much of the circulation of materials was done through visits of the bookmobile to rural schools and community centers. Following the school consolidation movement of the 1950s, the bookmobile was discontinued and branch libraries were established in Scott City, Benton, Morley, Oran, Altenburg, and Perryville. The library is particularly known for its genealogical collection and for its collection of audiovisual materials. *(Information provided by the library staff).* -amd

Jackson Public Library

No history of Jackson Public library can be written without a bow to the Thursday Literary Society which in 1923 began the work that would lay the foundation for the present institution. Most of the books in the very first collection were volumes discarded by St. Louis Public Library, selected by a committee of club women including Miss Bess Litzelfelner, Mrs. E. A. Mason, and Mrs. D. I. L. Seabaugh. Funds, begun by members contributing $1.00 each per meeting for two years, were given a boost when the club presented a play, and other organizations including the D.A.R. and P.E.O. added their support. Beginning as a Subscription Library with membership cards at one dollar per year, checkouts began March 25, 1925; hours were two to five p.m. Tuesdays and Thursdays. Housed in a room provided by Peoples Bank, the library was staffed by members of the Literary Club.

Popularity of the Subscription Library led to a petition being presented to the City Council asking that a small (one mil) tax be placed on the next election ballot for library financing. The tax carried and Jackson Public Library opened officially on January 1, 1927, in the historic Frizel-Welling-Granger-Wilson house. Material had been carried across the street by Joe Wagner, Jess Stewart, and Glenn Luetje in wash tubs belonging to Mrs. Martin Wagner, a Literary Club member. Appointed members of the Library Board were William Bruening, Kent Wilson, Frank Hines, Rosco Pierce, Miss Clara Mueller, Mrs. William Schwartz, Mrs. D. I. L. Seabaugh, Mrs. Clarence Grant, and Miss Bess Litzelfelner, who resigned to become the first librarian. Mrs. R. M. McCombs was appointed to this place on the board.

Librarians succeeding "Miss Bess" include Mildred Brown, Claire Decker, Gloria Kiehne, Elizabeth Link, and Sally Pierce. Karen Kramer, Gwynn Noe, and Judy Holmes have served as children's librarians. Michelle Poe, Terri Noland, and Sue Mouser have served as part-time children's assistants. Mrs. R. G. Goodwin was assistant librarian for several years and Mae (Mrs. Walter) Keisker was long-time part-time librarian.

Jackson Public Library has overcome some serious challenges including moves to six different locations; its present one is 100 N. Missouri Street. The library has been at this location since April 1, 1996. The collection, which in 1926 could be moved "across in wash tubs" has grown to include over 29,000 titles.

Jackson Public Library received its first computer in 1987, but it was in 1993 that cataloging was first done using a computer. The library became a part of the REAL (Remote Electronic Access for Libraries) Project with a dial-up modem. It was after the move to the present location that a computer was added for public access to the Internet. There are now four public access computers for the Internet. With a gift from Walt and Sally Pierce and funds from the City of Jackson, Jackson Public Library began automated circulation in March 2001.

Automation and public Internet-accessible computers have brought Jackson Public Library into the informational age, but the library staff believes in friendly, personal service and is proud of the long history of the library.

By Gloria Kiehne

Faith Crutsinger checks the book return for the Jackson Public Library.

Riverside Regional Library, 2002.

Third grade class and teacher from Immaculate Conception School choosing their favorite reading material at the Jackson Public Library, May 2002.

Religion

Although religion and religious affiliations have played an important part in the development of Jackson, its earliest days in the Cape Girardeau District were weak. Records show that no churches existed in early Cape Girardeau. Houck (Vol. II, 1908) notes that Father James Maxwell occasionally held services in a small chapel located near the present intersection of Lorimier and Independence Streets but that under Spanish law, no Protestant churches were to be established. However, that did not stop enterprising residents from attempting to circumvent the law. For example, Houck also notes the baptism of Mrs. Agnes Ballew in the waters of Randall creek in 1799 by Reverend Thomas Johnson, a Baptist preacher (Vol. III, 1908, p. 205). This is reported to be the first Protestant baptism administered west of the Mississippi River.

George Frederick Bollinger, on a visit to his former home in North Carolina, persuaded Reverend Samuel Weyberg, a minister of the German Reformed Church, to return to Missouri with him in 1803. Weyburg preached the first German Protestant sermon in upper Louisiana in the home of a German Settler about a mile south of the city of Jackson. He continued to preach in settlers' homes until the purchase of the territory by the United States (Houck, Vol. III, 1909, pp. 204-205).

After the acquisition of Louisiana by the United States, Reverend Daniel Green, a Baptist minister, came into the Cape Girardeau District. Although he preached in various settlements, on July 19, 1806, he organized Bethel Baptist church at the house of Mr. Thomas Bull. In October 1806 the congregation built a small log meeting house on land donated by Bull. Thus, the first Protestant church west of the Mississippi was built just south of Jackson. In 1816 Bethel Church would found a new association of Baptist churches in Missouri. (Houck, Vol. III, 1908, pp. 206-207). The minutes of the Bethel Church still exist. Although they provide a colorful account of life in early Jackson, they give little insight into reasons for some of the more important acts of the church. For example, why was a new meetinghouse constructed in 1812? Why did a church that had so diligently worked to establish new congregations throughout southeast Missouri eventually take an anti-missionary stand, an act to which Begley (n.d.) attributes the decline and eventual closing of the Bethel church. Following a three-year gap in the minutes, apparently due to suspension of church activities during the Civil War, the church membership may have declined. The last minutes of the church are dated September 1867. Begley concluded that the church must have been closed soon afterward. The church building is no longer standing.

Methodists also established a congregation in this area in the early 1800s. The first Methodist society west of the Mississippi was organized about three miles east of Jackson sometime about 1806. (The Old McKendree Board of Trustees uses the date July 1809 for organization of the congregation, a date inconsistent with Houck's research.) Houck (1908) reports that when Reverend John Travis came west in 1806, he found two Methodist congregations in existence, one in the Cape Girardeau District and one on the Meramac River. In 1808 the Reverend Jesse Walker was appointed preacher for the Cape Girardeau circuit. On Good Friday in 1810 the first Methodist camp meeting was held at the "Old Camp-ground" at McKendree Chapel. The first conference of the Methodist Church west of the Mississippi was held at McKendree Chapel in 1819. Thereafter, three additional conferences were held there (Vol. III, pp. 243-241).

According to the Old McKendree Board of Trustees, the church was built in 1819 of poplar logs on land donated by William Williams and named for William McKendree, a Methodist bishop highly regarded by the congregation. The first service held in the chapel was the 1819 church conference, the first session of the Missouri Conference of the Methodist Episcopal Church. Regular services were held in the chapel until the split in the Methodist Church brought on by the Civil War. At that time the chapel was gradually deserted and the road closed.

In 1926 a movement began to save the chapel. The Old McKendree Memorial Association was formed and over the years completely restored the chapel, ultimately constructing a metal canopy over the building to protect it from the elements. Although no longer used for regular worship services, the chapel is open to the public and is the site of special religious events.

Women, though by most accounts not in the majority in early Jackson, played a big part in the founding of the area churches. In addition, Jackson was one of the early locations of a Women's Mite Society, an organization founded to aid in spreading the gospel. In 1818 such a society was established in Jackson with Jason Chamberlain as president and in Cape Girardeau with Hiram Davis as president, although the Cape Girardeau society met at the New Bethel Church in 1819 and 1820. These were among the first of such societies in Missouri. (Houck, Vol. III, 1908, p. 223).

According to Houck (1908), the earliest Presbyterian presence in Jackson came with the forming of the Columbian Bible Society, with Jason Chamberlain as president in 1819. On Sunday, June 4, 1820, the Reverend Timothy Flint preached at the courthouse. He was followed by Reverend C .S. Robinson on June 25, who met with a group of people at the home of Joseph Frizell to arrange to support a Presbyterian church (Vol. III, p. 232). However, a church was not firmly established until 1864. -amd

Today, the many churches of Cape Girardeau County are alive in the spirit of their past and present. Church congregations and clubs work to serve individuals and the community. The Jackson Ministerial Alliance is one example of the cooperative spirit among the area churches.

The Jackson Ministerial Alliance has been serving the local area since October 1942. The minutes of the first meeting recorded those present: Rev. W. L. Meyer of the Methodist Church, Father Felix Sommerhauser of the Catholic church, Rev. H. A. Selves of the Baptist church, Rev. Herman G. Borne of the Evangelical church and Rev. D. C. Boyd of the Presbyterian church. The group's constitution states it was founded for the purpose "to further Christian witness in the community, and fellowship among the churches and ministers." The Alliance usually has several ecumenical services annually: the Baccalaureate service, a Thanksgiving service, a Good Friday service, and a live Nativity scene during the Christmas season.

During its history, the Ministerial Alliance has offered emergency financial aid in the form of "Good Samaritan" help to transient people who need food, gas, or overnight lodging while traveling through the area. The Jackson Ministerial Alliance Food Assistance Program began in 1996 to give local families in need a helping hand by providing food, vouchers for gas, and other necessities during times of short term need. The food pantry is housed in Cox Memorial Hall, next door to New McKendree United Methodist Church. -cms

Apple Creek Presbyterian Church, Pocahontas, MO

Apple Creek Presbyterian Church was started by two groups of Scot-Irish Presbyterians from North Carolina who settled in Cape Girardeau County early in the 1800s, one near Shawneetown and one in the Indian Creek area east of Fruitland. With help and encouragement by the Rev. Salmon Giddings, a Presbyterian minister assigned to the missionary field, the two communities joined forces and established the Apple Creek Church at a point about midway, so the church was located just east of Pocahontas near a large spring. This became the mother church of Presbyterianism in Cape Girardeau County and is revered for that reason.

The church was organized on May 21, 1821, and is the third oldest Presbyterian church west of the Mississippi. The Rev. Salmon Giddings officiated at the organizational meeting held on the Hope farm within sight of the present church. The meeting took place at the Baldridge Spring, known then as "Uncle Joe Abernathy Spring." The Rev. Giddings used a two-foot high limestone rock as a rostrum while acting as moderator at this first meeting place, which is about one-quarter mile west of the present church. The spring still flows.

On the same day the congregation voted that Mitchel Fleming, Oliver Harris, John Gilliland and Samuel Anderson be ordained as elders by the Rev. Giddings. The following March, Ebenezer Flin and James Hope were ordained as elders by the first minister of the church, the Rev. Edward Hollister.

The first marriages recorded at Apple Creek Church were in 1821, Joseph McClain and Jean Gilliland, and Robert McFarlin and Agnes Fleming. The last marriages performed were Robert J. Hope and June E. Barber on February 21, 1946, and Robert Bruce King and Margaret Grace Peterson on October 15, 1982.

The first church was built of logs cut from timber felled on the property. It was erected in 1822 and contained 24 pews. The building served for ten years but was too small and was replaced in 1831 by a large wooden structure covered on the outside with wooden shingles. In 1873 the old frame building was torn down and replaced by the present church.

An organ was purchased for the church in 1878. It was later sold when a piano was bought. The organ was bought from A.C. Stephenson by the Robert Yancey family. Mr. Sam Hartman later acquired the organ, which was restored and returned to the church in 1969. A special re-dedication service was held in 1971. The organ is still in use at each church service.

As a result of the diminishing congregation of Apple Creek Church, Presbytery on May 20, 1962, dissolved the church as an active congregation and established the Apple Creek Presbyterian Memorial Association, which perpetuates the memory of the Apple Creek Church, its members of years ago and the historical cemetery.

It is not known exactly how many persons have been buried in the large cemetery adjoining the church grounds. We are told that in one section many were buried without grave markers during the cholera epidemic. An early count of gravestones made by Rev. William G. Gammon and one also made by Mrs. A.D. Ferguson, gives the names on 516 tombstones. The present count is 814. The earliest burials recorded are of Robert Steel and Charles H. Harris, about 1822. It is also known that at least three Revolutionary War veterans are buried in the cemetery.

The Apple Creek Memorial Association holds two annual church services, the "Third Sunday in May" at 11:00 a.m. and a Vesper Service the third Sunday in September at 3:00 p.m. Each service has a guest speaker and a basket dinner following. The public is cordially invited to attend, bringing food, drinks and lawn chairs.

Apple Creek Church is located one-half mile east of Pocahontas, Missouri, on County Road 532. The 175th anniversary was celebrated the "Third Sunday in May," 1996.

Apple Creek Presbyterian Memorial Association, P.O. Box 3, Pocahontas, MO 63779

By *Todd Rushing*

Calvary Baptist Church, Jackson, Missouri

Calvary Baptist Church was organized in 1933 with Rev. Emmitt Cross as pastor. Charter members were: Mr. and Mrs. Loy L. Barks; Mr. and Mrs. Clyde Baugh; Mr. and Mrs. Ellis "Doc" Hahs; Mr. and Mrs. Willis Orrell; Mr. and Mrs. C. A. Graves; Mr. and Mrs. Warren Hale; Mr. and Mrs. Henry Barks; Mr. and Mrs. Frank Hager; Mr. and Mrs. Will Hager; Mr. and Mrs. August Gartung; Joe Hager; Homer Bollinger; Marvin Goehman; Otto Goehman; Lynn Allen; Mr. and Mrs. Robert Watkins; Mr. and Mrs. Ira Walker; Mr. and Mrs. Bill Hager; and Rev. and Mrs. Emmitt Cross. The first meetings were held in Clyde and Sadie Baugh's home.

Apple Creek Presbyterian Church

Left to right. Front row: Velberta Hayes, Harlena Henson, Hays' girl, Jackie Hager, Roberta Smith, June Martin, Shirley Martin, Jerry Henson, Joyce Henson, Unidentified, Paul Brown, Jr., Carolyn Orrell, Reatta Maloney, Kenneth Maloney, Harold Williams, Jim Martin, Doyle Riehn, Robert Smith, Bobby Barks, Dewey Riehn, Billy Hager, Williams' boy. Second row: Rev. Velbert Hayes, Helen Hayes, Will Hager, Bode Hager, Betty Brown, Mary Baugh, Floyd Bollinger, Alice Walker, Clyde Baugh, Sadie Baugh, Elva Smith, Rev. Robert Smith, Mrs. Clarence Graves, Clarence Graves, August Gartung, Anna Gartung, Willis Orrell, Sarah Barks, Henry Barks, Betty Loos at end of bench. Third row: Mary Martin, Hattie Henson, Glenda Henson, Agnes Hohler, Opal Henson, Ernest Riehn, Effie Riehn, Ollie Hager, Bill Hager, Gladys Bollinger, Mrs. Luther Williams, Eldon Maloney, Luther Williams, Maude Hahs, Ellis "Doc" Hahs, Buddy White, Mrs. Calvin Williams, Baby Williams, Calvin Williams, Addie Martin, Richard Martin, Gladys Baker, Wanda Martin, Flossie Loos. Fourth Row: Jo Smith, Ruth White, Oscar Henson, Paul Brown, Zola Hayes, Margie Hager, Allen White, Jessie Williams, Allene Hager, Wilma Maloney, Bernard Carr, Pearl Carr, Millie Hayes, Unidentified, Ira Walker, Josephine Henson, Bob Loos.

The first church building (the old Tabernacle) was located on South Georgia Street across the railroad tracks from the current Jackson Bowling Lanes. In 1951 the congregation finished their new building at 611 Blanch Street where services were held until 1995 when the church disbanded.

From its inception until the closing of its doors, Calvary Baptist Church stood for the gospel according to the Original King James Version of the Bible. Their basic belief has always been that each human being is a sinner and that Jesus Christ, the Son of God, shed his blood on an old rugged cross so that each individual who is willing to ask forgiveness for their sins and accept Jesus Christ as their own personal savior will have eternal life.

Pastors down through the years have included: Rev. Emmitt Cross; Rev. I. M. Rainey; Rev. H.G. Richardson; Rev. R. P. Mitchell; Rev. Will Bess; Rev. Turner; Rev. Robert Smith; Rev. Everett Baidy; Rev. Chappel; and Rev. Loy L. Barks.

Rev. Loy L. Barks was ordained as a Baptist minister on March 27, 1946, at Calvary Baptist Church in the old Tabernacle. From 1939 until 1994 he had the live radio broadcast "The Bible Baptist Fellowship" which aired at 9:00 a.m. every Sunday originally on KFVS (Cape Girardeau) then ended on KUGT (Jackson).

During Rev. Barks' tenure at Calvary Baptist Church he served as president of the Missouri/Arkansas Baptist Bible Fellowship Association in the late 1950s. The church supported missionaries in Argentina, Old Mexico, Lebanon, and Formosa, as well as the Baptist Bible College in Springfield, Missouri, which prepared missionaries for their call to the ministry.

Rev. Barks served as pastor of Calvary Baptist Church from 1951 until 1995 when failing health forced his retirement. He will be 98 years old on October 15, 2002, and is currently residing at Jackson Manor Nursing Home.

By *Hazel (Barks) Henson*

Fairview United Methodist Church

Fairview United Methodist Church of Millersville began in 1893. Before this time, the people of the surroundings community did not have a church house except for a small log schoolhouse in which all denominations went to worship. Mr. I. T. and Maria Louise (Criddle) Summers wanted a church built on their farm. They donated one acre of their land to the Methodist Church South for a church to be built there. The site and the name were selected by Mrs. Summers. The deed was given and the building was started February 1892.

When the cornerstone was laid, Mrs. Summers placed the Testament beneath it. Reverend John Haynes, a local Methodist preacher, gave the first sermon on the Sunday evening after the foundation was laid. All the lumber was donated by the general public and sawed on I. T. Summers' farm by W. M. Welty's Saw Mill, except for the finishing lumber. John Summers and C. C. Summers cut the first tree, and the stump is under the church house to this day. The finishing lumber was acquired in Marquand, Missouri. Those who made the two-day trip were William Nienstedt, I. T. Summers, C. C. Summers, and Louis Brenecke. The church was completed and dedicated in 1893.

The First Annual Conference was held in September of 1893. The first bishop was Bishop Galloway. J. L. Kendell was the presiding elder. W. M. Boutwell was the pastor. The first two weddings took place March 11, 1894. Rev. Hy Hanesworth officiated at the union of Tennessee Summers to John H. Limbaugh and Emma Runnels to Robert Kinder.

With the exception of a short duration, Fairview has never been without a minister. There have been fifty circuit riders. The shortest stay of these ministers was Rev. Suffold, staying only one quarter. F. L. R. Crooke finished his time. The longest stay was Jack Byrd. The pastors who served Fairview since 1893: Bishop Galloway, J. K. Dickson, W. T. Barnhouse, O. Dodson, T. W. Glass, McBee, J. E. Martin, J. L. Stamper, H. J. Charlton, Jim McDonald, Ola Bowers, Suffold, G. L. R. Crooke, W.A. Fulbright, K. Probst, M. M. Blease, I. W. Sherrow, C. R. Baker, W. S. Tussey, H. E. Corbin, J. B. Kincaid, J. P. McDonald, T. P. Ralph, F. A. Hearn, P. F. Newton, S. C. Headrick, M. A. Garrison, Leo M. Willard, W. A. Edmundson, Sam Bohnenkamp, Cyril Ashton, P. L. Prichard, C. R. Baker, Ernst Slovensky, Elosie (James) Hahs, E. M. Cook, Leroy Tillman, H. E. Horner, Fred Shurm, Jimmy Corbin, Richard L. Combs, Dale Emery, Kenneth Elders, Jesse James, J. Michael Hanna, Wayne Koehler, Stella Turner, Jack Byrd, Dr. David Stewart, and Calvin Brown.

In 1975 new pews were purchased, replacing the original ones that were handmade locally. The new furnishings were largely made possible from money willed to the Church Building fund by the late Mr. and Mrs. Silas Welker, longtime members. In 1981 a multipurpose building was constructed on the church property. In 1993 a piece of ground was donated by Quentin and Virginia (Summers) Felty for a parking lot. Mrs. Felty is the great-granddaughter of Ira T. Summers and now takes care of the church and cemetery. Over the years, numerous improvements have been made to the church, keeping it a beautiful historic structure.

In 2001, marking the 108 years in God's service, Fairview church is still going strong. Serving Jesus Christ and His people continues to be the mission of the Fairview United Methodist Church, a place where everybody makes a difference.

Submitted By the Fairview United Methodist Church and Marilyn Fronabarger

Rev. Loy Barks

Fairview United Methodist Church of Millersville

German Evangelical Church

From Goodspeed's History of Southeast Missouri I found "the oldest German Evangelical Church in Southeast Missouri is at what is known as Dutchtown, in Cape Girardeau County. Its history dates back to about 1836, when several Swiss families located in the vicinity of Rodney's Mill, which was purchased by two of the colony, Benedict Schneider and Benedict Mullet. The colonists had been meeting together at private residences to sing hymns and to listen to the reading of a sermon by one of their members. This was kept up until the year 1846 or 1847, when a church was organized by Rev. Jacob Kobler. Services were continued at private residences until the winter of 1850-51, when a small log building was erected. This was occupied as a house of worship until the completion of the present brick building, which was dedicated on May 15, 1887. The original officers and members of this church were John Eggiman, Christian Kuss and Andrew Suedekum, trustees; Chr. Kothe, Hy. Butz, John Schneider, H. Homburg, Benedict Buetiger, Carl Allers, Henry Achterman, George Keller, Henry Steimel, Chr. Bohnsack, Benedict Mullet and Benedict Eggiman. The present membership is about twenty. The pastors have been Revs. Jacob Kobler, Unbeck, Ulrich, Brunner, Herman, Jacob Schwab, Christian Frey, G. Press, Stoerker, Ludwig, John Thaal and John Koletschke" (Goodspeed History of Southeast Missouri, 1888, p. 581).

After other churches were organized in the area and the road in front of the German Evangelical Church was relocated to the present day Highway 74, these events cause a decline in membership and in the early 1900s services were discontinued. In 1909 the cemetery association was organized and incorporated (applied for a proforma decree at Cape County Circuit Court, file March 8, 1909). The members of the association were: Wm. G. Schneider, B. S. Schwab, Chas. Blattner, Chas. R. Kuss, W. Feuerhahn, G. C. Siermers and wife, H. F. Ueleke, Henry Bethe, R. R. Schwab, J. C. Keller, J. W. Siemers, Em. Geiser, J. O. Keller, Herman Schwab, Robert Keller, C. F. W. Daume, Mary M. Nebels, John S. Schwab, Eds. Schneider, N. F. Chostner, Anna Meyer, Geo. H. Obermann, Henry Brakebusch, Albert J. Schwab, H. M. Siemers, Johan Schwab, A. E. Feuerhahn, Jacob Gluekhertz, John H. Keller, Jacob Schwab, Christian Frey, Ernst Steinhoff, Wm. Geiser, Wm. Ringwald, Henry Senn, Wm. Blank, John A. Lang, Herman Schulenburg, Rudolf Nussbaum, Scharlott, Lucke, John Eggimann, Arnold Geiser, Wm. Steinhoff, J. H. Fisher, John Rider, Henry Wessell and Jacob Eggimann. In 1912 additional members H. W. Beers, Oscar Geiser, Albert Schrader, Hy. Schlegel, Edwin Geiser, Charles B. Enderle, T. J. Pearson, Hilda Obermann and Mrs. John Bentley, joined the association. After a few years, some of the officers of the cemetery association had passed away and because of lack of funds and of interest in the association, the cemetery and building were neglected.

The German Evangelical Cemetery Association was revitalized in 1953-54 and extensive work was done to clean the cemetery and repair tombstones and Church building. In 1996 the German Evangelical Church and Cemetery Association was incorporated by the State of Missouri and a new constitution was adopted. We have several families that are interested in the upkeep of the church and cemetery. A lot of work has been done on the church, tombstones have been repaired and the cemetery is neat and clean. In June 1851 William and Wilhelmina Willer conveyed 1.55 acres to the German Evangelical Church. This land was used for the church and cemetery. The oldest marked grave is for Christain Kuss dated 1852. The brick buidling that was dedicated May 1887 is used for the annual association meeting.

By Dorothy Rowley, Association Treasurer

The Millersville Methodist Church

The Millersville Methodist Worship began in the town of Millersville together with a small group of Baptists. For several years these two denominations continued to worship in the same building, known as the "Union Church." The Methodist denomination has been in Millersville officially since 1915. Rev. J. C. Ward, sent by the Methodist Board of missions, held a revival in October, and the following twelve charter members were baptized on October 24, 1915, by the Rev. Wilburn. Together they organized the Methodist Worship. The charter members were: Mr. and Mrs. J.C. Snider, Mrs. Catherine Thompson, Mr. and Mrs. Baylis Statler, Dr. D. I. L. Seabaugh, Mr. and Mrs. Andy Hendrix, Mrs. Oma C. Miller, Mrs. Pete Sawyer, and Mrs. Kate Thompson.

The two denominations continued to worship together in the Union Church until 1942. By 1942 the two congregations had outgrown the one room church. They dissolved their union and the Methodists sold their interest to the Baptists. It was then that the Spiritualist Church, which sat on top of the hill overlooking the Baptist Church, the site of the present Methodist Church in Millersville, offered their church to the Methodists. The Spiritualists had discontinued services there for several years. Repairs on the church were needed and the building was wired for electricity. All of this work was done under the supervision of the Rev. Paul Fountain, who was pastor at that time. The Methodists moved to their new church on the last Sunday in August 1942. The church has undergone extensive remodeling and survived a tornado in 1957.

August of 2002 will mark the 60th anniversary year of the separation from the Baptists and the Union Church and the beginning of the separate Methodist Worship and Church in Millersville, Missouri.

By Rodney Miller

Old Bethel Church

Old Bethel Church in Jackson has long been documented as the "first permanent non-Catholic church west of the Mississippi River." On October 11, 1806, the congregation voted to erect a meeting house and a small log house was built on the farm of Thomas Bull. In 1812 the small church was replaced by a log building 30 x 24 feet. All that remains at the site now is a cemetery, a monument and a few stones that may have been part of the foundation at one time.

It is not known what happened to the building, whether it burned, was razed or simply abandoned and deteriorated. A marker bearing the names of the charter membership that organized the church is located in the Old Bethel Church cemetery at the spot where the church once stood. The tract of ground, now held by the Missouri Baptist Convention, is located about 1 _ miles south of Jackson, south of the William A. Lowes farm.

The original business session minute book, which contains entries from throughout the church's 61-year history, beginning with its es-

German Evangelical Church, Dutchtown, Missouri, 1996. Drawing by Nancy Riehn.

tablishment in 1806, has been preserved for many years by Truman Lewis, a great-great-grandson of Isaac Sheppard. Sheppard was one of a group of Old Bethel members who left the church on April 10, 1824, to form what is now the First Baptist Church of Jackson. Another Ancestor active in Old Bethel was John Sheppard. Chesley D. Ford was the church clerk in 1850.

While this area was still owned by the French and the Spanish, who maintained the Roman Catholic faith as the established religion, Baptists moved into the district and secretly held worship services in defiance of the law, which made such services illegal. When Bethel was organized, Upper Louisiana was the most western section of the United States, the farthest outpost of settlement. Naturally it attracted the wild and adventurous, and a small but very noisy class of lawless men, and they lived rather peaceably with the Indians. Many of the early settlers were farmers, lead miners, fur hunters, trappers and river men. They were famous for their wild sprees and brutal fights. Old Bethel used a heavy hand in dealing with the early settlers, and the most powerful tool was excommunication. Disciplinary action often was taken against members for offenses ranging from gossip and card playing to drunkenness and adultery.

Old Bethel was known as a Regular Baptist Church, the forerunner of what are now Missionary Baptist Churches, affiliated with the Southern Baptist Convention. It grew to a total membership of an estimated 350, including its many 'arms' in nearby communities and counties. The New Madrid earthquake of 1811 apparently brought a great spiritual revival among the membership. Wilson Thompson, pastor of the church for two years, credited God for the quake to get the church back to "prayer and short exhortations." Records reflected a large influx of new members following the quake. Bethel's ministers spread the gospel throughout Upper Louisiana long before Missouri became a state in 1821. Records show the first court to be held in the area was convened in the Old Bethel Church building.

When Missouri became a state in 1821, new ideas were demanding consideration. It was a time of great religious excitement. It was recorded that there were "many disorders existing amongst us" and members were not reporting "disorderly conduct" of fellow members. New measures were needed to control the membership. To remedy this, four committees were formed on January 12, 1822, to study the problem and report back to the church. Serving on these committees were: Thomas P. Green, Samuel K. Parker, John Daugherty, James Massey, William Hitt, W. Abernathy, Abraham Randol, Simon Poe, Benjamin Hitt, James Holcomb, Robert Looney, Benjamin Thompson, James Randol, John Randol, Thomas English, John Sheppard, Thomas Bull, William Surretts, E. Hill, H. C. Davis, and John Dowty.

From the strict new rules which followed, they appear not to have set too well with many of the members and four months later, on May 11, 1822, some of the church's stalwart leaders asked for letters of dismissal to form the Hebron Church: Polly Green, Abraham Randol, Rebecca Randol, Mary Randol, Simon Poe, James Randol, Nancy Randol, Samuel K Parker, Rebecca Poe, James Holcomb, Francis Holcomb, Susannah Williams, Matilda Williams, Benjamin Hitt, and Sarah Hitt. Two years later, on April 10, 1824, another group asked for dismissal letters to form a new church at Jackson: Isaac Sheppard, William Surretts, John Juden, Sr., John Juden, Jr., James Massey, John Daugherty, and Francis Thomas; forming the First Baptist Church on April 30, 1824, they being the charter members. The new Jackson church was organized and built on a lot belonging to John Sheppard, the first judge of the district.

From the Sheppard/Ford Family History Book, submitted by Ella Jean Pleasant

St. James United Church of Christ

St. James is the oldest existing United Church of Christ congregation in the area. Some of the early records about the church have been lost or destroyed but it is believed that as early as 1843 a group of settlers were meeting together in their homes for worship.

In 1848 Henry Nothdurft filed in the land office at Jackson, Missouri, for forty acres of land. In the year 1849 this group of people who had been meeting together for worship, which was a number of Cape Girardeau County citizens from the Jackson community, met in the Tilsit School in order to deliberate about building a German church and school. This group constituted the local congregation that became St. James Church. A council of ten members was chosen. At the front of this enterprise were two laymen, Jacob Kneibert and Jacob Tobler. On January 29, 1849, Henry Nothdurft and his wife, Caroline, sold to the church twenty acres of land for $36.50. The trustees of the church at that time were: Jacob Kneibert, Jacob Tobler, Henry D. Brennecke, Henry Flintge, Julius Nothdurft, Ferdinand Kuehle, Henry F. Brennecke, Henry Nothdurft, Frederick Macke and Christian Sander.

On January 18, 1858, Jacob Kneibert and his wife Elizabeth sold forty acres of land to the church for $110.00 for the purpose of a school. The trustees of the church at that time were: Jacob Rasche, Henry Bose, Henry Ahrens, Frederick Wedekind and John Reitmann. The first church was built about 100 feet west of the present church buidling.

The constitution was adopted and signed by fifty-seven members on March 12, 1858, and the name chosen was "German Evangelical Lutheran Reformed Whitewater Congregation of St. James Church." However, the church was known by a shorter name, St. Jacobi (James) German Evangelical Church. Two pastors, Jacob Kobler and F. W. Umbeck, served the

Old Bethel Church

St. James United Church of Christ, Tilsit, Missouri, July 13, 1997.

congregation from 1850 to 1857. In the year 1866, during a turbulent time in the life of the early church, a large group seceded or withdrew to form the neighboring Lutheran church.

Pastor W. C. Kiesel served the congregation from 1866-1871. Other pastors were: John Kaminiski, Fred Kies, Fred Delvean, L. Reinert, Ed. Pinkert. In 1891 the congregation adopted a new constitution and became a member of the Evangelical Synod of North America. An additional sixty acres of land was purchased from August Voges. Pastor Gustav Pahl served St. James Congregation from 1892-1896, followed by Pastor Theo, C. M. Kugler. In 1896 the congregation built a new house of worship. Then in 1898 a new school was built adjacent to the church. In January 1902, the congregation decided to build a new parsonage. Additional pastors were: Albert J. Winterick 1902-1905; Kugler 1905-1909; Horst Suppe 1909-1911; Salinger 1912-1914; Adolph Kalkbrenner 1914-1917; Julius Symanski 1917-1919; E. Roglin; G. Viehe 1921-1925; H. Schroeder; G. Schmeiser 1931-1934; and F. W. Weltge 1934-1940.

In 1934 the Evangelical and German Reformed Churches united to form one new denomination. Services were held in the German language, but in later years held only once a month and finally discontinued. Pastors A. A. Kanzler served 1941-1947; Herman Borne 1947-1949; J. M. Hertel 1949-1954; and E. J. Moritz 1954-1961. In 1957 the Evangelical and Reformed churches merged with the Congregational Churches forming the United Church of Christ. Since 1957 the congregation has been known as St. James United Church of Christ. Pastor E. C. Budlong served 1963-1967. St. James Congregation was served by retired pastors, lay speakers and student pastors from Eden Seminary 1968-1981. Pastors Dr. Don Hartman served 1982-1984; Jesse Perry 1986-1987; Jeffrey Jackson 1988-1996; and James Schultz 1996 to present.

By Dorothy M. Rowley, member St. James UCC

St. John AME Church

St. John African Methodist Episcopal Church is located at 329 Cherry Street in Jackson, Missouri. No written records remain of the church's early days, but tradition dates the church back to the year of 1886. The first church was erected on a small plot of ground overlooking River Zenon, now known as Hubble Creek, at the west end of Cherry Street. Funds for building the first church came from Burrell Wade, Thomas Wade, Joseph Green, James Wheeler and others who donated $100 each. The structure served as church and school. The first minister was Rev. George Gaines. The new church building erected in 1888 when Rev. O. Plumer was pastor was destroyed by fire in 1931. The existing building was finished in 1932 under the pastorate of Rev. W.R. Davis.

Information from the Cash-Book Journal, March 2, 1983. pg 8.

St. John African Methodist Episcopal Church

An interior view of the Burke and Hobbs Revival held in 1915 in a tabernacle adjacent to the New McKendree Methodist Church. This appears to be a choir assembled for the occasion.

Churches

First Baptist Church, Jackson

God has worked His many wonders in the 175-plus years of First Baptist Church of Jackson. This church, with His guiding care, has a remarkable and lengthy historical record rich with mission and ministry. First Baptist Church is the only current church still meeting that is directly descended from the first permanent Baptist church west of the Mississippi River. The church has been a stalwart in the Jackson area and with Southern Baptists throughout the state of Missouri.

Bethel Baptist Church, now referred to as "Old Bethel," was organized in July of 1806. The acquiring of the Louisiana Purchase from France in 1803 had opened the door to non-French Catholic congregations. Baptists from Georgia, Kentucky, and Virginia organized Bethel Baptist Church as the country began to move across the Mississippi. Bethel Baptist Church grew as it established new congregations as "arm" or "daughter" churches. The First Baptist Church of Jackson was the ninth church organized from Bethel and the only one to continue in ministry today. Bethel and the other congregations were strongly anti-mission, which greatly limited their growth and reaching new people. First Baptist Church was formed in April of 1824 by eight mission-minded believers.

First Baptist was the smallest among the ten churches that drew together to form an association of Baptist churches in June of 1824 called the Cape Girardeau Association. Because no records exist from the first 32 years of the church, little is known about the first pastors, but they probably include Rev. Wingate Jackson and Rev. Thomas Green. Many of these men served as either lay pastors or pastored several different churches at the same time. For a time there was only one house of worship in Jackson used by all denominations. First Baptist built a new church building on the site of its present location that opened for worship in April of 1858. An interesting sidelight in the church records is the suspension of worship from June to November of 1861 as the building was used to quarter Civil War soldiers.

The first Sunday School was organized in 1868 as a Bible study for adults as well as youth and children as a vital part of the church. As the church grew, Sunday morning Bible study space was at a premium. Additional properties, including the previous sanctuary, homes around the church, the Wilson Apartment Building, and even a former beauty salon, were purchased and/or renovated for education space. The proclamation of the good news of our hope of salvation through Jesus Christ has continued to be a vital part of the church. As early as 1868 and then again in 1878 church records record the church experiencing great revivals as "...many souls were saved and a great number added to the church." Throughout the historical records are sprinkled reports of life-changing revivals and "Roll Call" and "Covenant Services" to "conserve the results of revival."

A new church building was constructed in 1901 on the same High Street location. A parsonage was added during the pastorate of Rev. F. W. Carnett from 1913 to 1916. On March 11, 1923, a windstorm swept through the city of Jackson, destroying many of the structures, including the sanctuary of First Baptist Church. The following Sunday the church voted to rebuild the church building. Meetings were held in the courthouse just up the street until the new building was completed in May of 1924. It was during this time that the church began using the "Single Budget System of Finance" in which the first annual budget was devised and followed. An educational building that is still being used was constructed at the back of the sanctuary in 1956. The 1924 sanctuary building continued in use for worship and then education until it was razed in 1993 for additional education space that was built and dedicated in 1994. The present sanctuary on the corner of High and Jefferson was built in 1966 and then remodeled in 1980.

An individual pastor provided the ministerial leadership of the church for over 140 years. The church staff grew to include an Associate Pastor in 1967. The staff has now developed to include a Senior Pastor, Minister of Education, Minister of Music and Senior Adults, Minister of Youth, and a part-time Minister of Single Adults. First Baptist Church has recorded 40 pastors and 16 associated ministers who have served over 146 years of recorded history of the church. There were untold others who pastored as a volunteer, on an itinerant basis, or in association with other churches in the formative years of the church. The membership has grown from 8 in 1824 to 284 in 1910, the year the church first started keeping a "uniform church letter," to a present membership of 1770.

The concept of missions and reaching out beyond its own walls has been a vital part of First Baptist Church. The church has continued to be interested in church development, from the support of the Niswonger Church in this area in 1907 through the present support of a church in Belarrus, formerly a part of the Soviet Union. Members have served as full time and mission volunteers. Over the years members have assisted churches to minister throughout the United States and the world. Recent trips have included Wyoming, Kentucky, Rhode Island, Illinois, Indonesia, India and Lesotho. Historically over 20% of all undesignated receipts have been given to mission endeavors.

The church has adopted the maxim "changing lives forever." This is also a good historical description of the church. First Baptist Church has been at the center of the Jackson Community for over 175 years. We believe it was the desire of those eight members in 1824 to reach out and minister to the community with the good news of Christ. That is what led them to form the church. Today it continues to be the heart of First Baptist Church to reach out to our community with the good news of Christ as we strive to serve the Lord in "changing lives forever."

First Baptist Church, Jackson

First Presbyterian Church

The Presbyterian Church in Jackson, MO, was organized on May 15, 1864. The following persons were the first persons admitted as members:
 1. Mrs. Sarah Daugherty, from Pleasant Hill Presbyterian Church;
 2. Charles Welling, by letter from First Apple Creek Presbyterian Church;
 3. Miss Mary J. Welling, by letter from Cape Girardeau Presbyterian Church;
 4. Mrs. Emily Anderson, by letter from Cape Girardeau Presbyterian Church;
 5. Miss Ann Taylor, by letter from Cape Girardeau Presbyterian Church;
 6. Irvin Anderson, on profession of faith;
 7. Mrs. Hannah McGuire, from the Methodist Episcopal Church;
 8. Mrs. Mary Davis, by letter from the Presbyterian Church of Shelbyville, KY.

Charles Welling was elected Ruling Elder. He served in this capacity for 35 years. Founder and father of the church, he was its sole elder for 23 years. He was superintendent of the Sunday School and carried on the work of a deacon, as well as any other duties necessary to keep the small church functioning. He was also a member of the first Jackson public school board and was elected president; he was also on the first board of the Jackson Military Academy, and a trustee of the town when it was incorporated. Six of his daughters became loyal members of the church: Misses Mary J. (Mrs. Z. M. LaPierre), Frederica (Mrs. Samuel Williams), Ann Guild (Mrs. C. P. Medley), Juliette Gayle (Mrs. M. B. W. Granger), Elizabeth (Mrs. W. H. Miller) and Berenice.

Worship services were held in the homes of members until 1870 when the first church, a frame building, was built on the northwest corner of West Adams and South Russell Streets, during the pastorate of Rev. W. W. Faris. The building seated 500, proof of the faith of its early members, since communicants numbered only 11 at the time.

Membership in 1874 rose to 36 and in 1891 to 83. The first full-time pastor was Rev. Charles W. Latham in 1898. Under his direction, plans were made to erect a new church. It was erected on the site of the former church. Services were moved to the Courthouse during construction. Services were first held at the new church, a brick building, on Oct. 8, 1905.

Another family stands out in the history of the church. The Knox family are descendants of John Knox, founder of Presbyterianism in Scotland. Walter Knox served as elder for 50 years, the longest term in the history of the church. His son, Carroll Knox, was deacon for the longest period of time, 40 years, from 1921 until his election as elder in 1961.

In 1910, membership was 209. During Rev. Lynn Ross' pastorate (1911-1917), membership rose from 221 to 311, the largest gain in the church's history. During WWI, at least 15 young men who were members of the church were enrolled in the armed forces. Ray Medley died in service.

On Aug. 9, 1925, the lot upon which the present church stands was purchased. An Episcopal church which stood upon the site had been destroyed in the tornado of 1921. The brick edifice built in 1905 was no longer adequate. In fact, the west wall of the church collapsed and a portion of the pulpit alcove had to be removed. In 1938 a building committee was elected consisting of Rev. Stuart H. Salmon, M. G. LaPierre, A. A. Boss, C. W. Knox, F. E. Williams, J. R. Short, G. M. Cobble, Mrs. Willis Knox and Mrs. J. R. Henderson. Plans of the architect Theodore H. Steinmeyer were accepted and a contract let to the Penzel Construction Company for the erection of a building of Wisconsin Lannon stone. The cornerstone was laid Sept. 24, 1939, on the birthday anniversary of Charles Welling. Mr. Welling's grandson, M. G. LaPierre, and Elder A. A. Box presided at the ceremony. Mr. Charles Steck sealed the copper box of mementos placed in the cornerstone. (Special Note: In 1999 descendants of Theodore H. Steinmeyer visited this church to view the architectural style.)

The new church was dedicated June 23, 1940. When the first service was held in the new church, the old bell, which had hung in the belfries of both the frame and brick churches, summoned the congregation. In the west wall was the familiar stained glass window of the Good Shepherd, a memorial to Charles Welling, bought by the young people of the church when the brick building (second building) was erected. The original pulpit was also moved to the new church, and now stands in Fellowship Hall.

In 1969 Julia LaPierre and Betty McDowell became the first women elected as elders in this church.

First Presbyterian Church, Jackson, MO

Immaculate Conception Parish Church and School, Jackson, MO

The first Mass celebrated in Jackson was in 1850, in the basement of the courthouse. The celebrant was Rev. Joseph Timon CM, a Vincentian missionary from Perryville. A few years later, the citizens of Jackson decided it was time to build a church. The parish archive contains the following explanation of the fundraising. "The citizens of the township of Jackson wanted a church but were equally divided as to whether it should be a Catholic Church or a Baptist Church. It was decided to build both a Catholic and a Baptist Church. To raise money, collectors called on the citizens of Jackson for contributions. The solicitors had a "Catholic" and a "Baptist" pocket in their coats and the contributions were equally divided between the two pockets. Two brick churches were constructed, each with a capacity of 125 and both were debt free."

The church built from "the Catholic pocket" was constructed on property purchased in 1854 at the intersection of East Adams and South Hope Streets. Shortly after its completion, the church was dedicated to the patronage of Our Lady of the Immaculate Conception. Mass was celebrated once a month by a priest from St. Vincent's College. The mission in Jackson attained parish status in 1874, and the pastor, Father Rheingold, began to keep official records of baptisms, marriages and deaths. The first baptism in the parish records was that of Joseph A. Wiley, Dec. 13, 1874, and the first death, also of Mr. Wiley, Dec. 14, 1874. The first wedding was of Louis Lorimier and Mary Freeze on Dec. 8, 1874.

In 1881 the church building was enlarged. In 1889 the pastor and the parish began constructing the first rectory. The parish continued to grow during the twentieth century and by the 1960s it was evident that a new church was needed. On Aug. 15, 1962, the parish celebrated the dedication of its current church and rectory. In August 2000 the parish celebrated the 150th anniversary of the first Mass in Jackson, with a celebration culminating with an outdoor Mass in front of the present-day courthouse.

A tradition of service and action abounds in the parish as members volunteer to support programs such as Vacation Bible School, the school of Religious Education, Christmas Novena, Birthright, Teens Encounter Christ, the Jackson Ministerial Alliance, Cursillo, Camp Re-New-All, RCIA, Church sports' leagues, Eucharistic Ministers, Musicians, Quilters, and the St. Ann's Sodality, sponsor of the Annual IC Turkey Dinner.

Catholic education began in the parish when the Ursuline Nuns directed a parish school from 1880 to 1913. From 1922 to 1927, a one-room Catholic School operated under the direction of a lay teacher. In 1943 the parish school reopened with the School Sisters of Notre Dame as teachers. A new school facility was constructed at 308 South Hope Street to serve Grades 1-8. By 1970 more space was required and four classrooms and a multi-purpose room were added. In 1988 the curriculum was expanded to include Kindergarten.

The 1980s and 1990s were decades of rapid growth for the church and school. After studying available options, the decision was made for the Parish to remain at its current site rather than attempt to relocate. In 1999 the Parish embarked upon a multi-year program to enlarge both its educational and worship spaces to serve the children in the School of Religious Education program, students in the parochial school program, and the families of Immaculate Conception Parish. The year 2000 brought many changes to the parish physical plant. Property was purchased and cleared in order to expand limited boundaries and make room for new school buildings. The parish, faculty and school children look forward to the dedication of the new classrooms in the fall of 2002.

Immaculate Conception Catholic Church, 1854-1962

Drawing of bas-relief for entry area of new school to open Fall 2002

Immaculate Conception Catholic Church, 1962-present

Jackson Church of Christ

The Church of Christ which meets at 310 Shawnee had its beginning when about 20 believers from various communities, such as Gordonville, Millersville, Sedgewickville and Delta, met at 1034 Old Cape Road in a building which they had procured from a Baptist group. The first service was in August of 1969 when Gerald Cowan from Caruthersville, MO, held an evangelistic meeting and helped get the congregation organized. The first minister to preach on a regular basis was Melvin Elliott who came to Jackson from Dexter each Sunday. One of the earliest programs, Bible Call, was an announcement on radio stating that questions concerning the Scriptures could be asked by telephone. These inquiries were answered by volunteers from the church.

As a result of church growth the building became too small to accommodate the worshipers and was also lacking in classroom space. An undeveloped tract was found on Shawnee and was secured for development. A new building was constructed and was ready for occupancy in May of 1986. This building had sufficient classroom and office space, a full basement with an outside doorway, and an auditorium which would seat approximately 325. At a future time some interior walls may be moved which will give a seating capacity of 500. A dwelling for the minister is also on the premises.

Churches of Christ have a local government by which each congregation is responsible for its own leadership and finances. The control is by appointed overseers, also called elders. Those presently serving in such capacity at Jackson are Ray Duffey, Larry Dowdy, and Steve Simmons. Two charter members, both widows, are still in regular attendance.

Ministers or preachers who have served include: Melvin Elliott; Jim Norville; Paul Sain; Harold Luscombe; Dane Todd; Sonny Preslar; Noel Quinn; Don Cox; Kenneth Dinkins; Jerry Culbertson and the present preacher, Bryan McAlister.

Current programs consist of a personal counseling and evangelistic program for any individual in the area; local benevolence; support of missionary efforts in Recife, Pernambuco, Brazil and Thursday school. The Thursday school attracts pre-school children from the community whose parents are members of the congregation, as well as those whose parents have no ties with the church. *Submitted by Murray Dunn*

Jackson Church of Christ, 310 Shawnee, Jackson, MO

St. John's Lutheran Church, Pocahontas, MO

Before, during and after the Civil War, emigrants from Upper Austria began to settle around Pocahontas. These industrious Austrians toiled, sowed and harvested, and reared their many children. They practiced goodwill and neighborliness toward others for they were free men and women in a land of opportunity and freedom. One of these freedoms was the right to worship. Lutherans by birth and convictions, they had been oppressed by the Roman Catholic Church in Austria.

The Saxons from Germany had settled in Perry County some 20-30 years earlier. They had established congregations in and around Altenburg, one of which was at New Wells in 1853. The distance to New Wells of five to eight miles presented problems in travel, especially for children attending parochial schools. Nearly all Lutherans from Pocahontas attended church at New Wells.

About the middle of the 1860s, the number of children had grown large enough that parents asked the New Wells congregation to establish a school in Pocahontas. The request was denied. About a year later the request was made a second time with the addition of preaching services to be held in Pocahontas. Again the request was denied. Many felt that it was disadvantageous to make a third request. They invited Pastor Koeberle of the Lutheran Church in Altenburg to conduct services in Pocahontas. These services were held in homes of members.

In the year 1868 or 1869 the building of the church was begun. The church was completed in 1870 and a lot for the parsonage was purchased. With the coming of Pastor Joseph Westenburger, the keeping of records was begun. Parochial school was conducted regularly with the pastor being the teacher. At that time and for some years later the parochial school was attended by children of families who lived near Pocahontas but attended New Wells church.

In 1892 the congregation was incorporated and on December 1892 the building of a new church was begun. A site of two acres was purchased and the Methodist church at Old Appleton served as a pattern for the style and size of the new church. It was completed and dedicated within the year. The entire cost was $3157.00.

During the night of May 4, 1910, lightening struck the spire of the church, setting it on fire, and the church was destroyed. The furnishings were saved and only the blackened brick walls remained. A committee was appointed and on Oct. 30, 1910 the rebuilt church was dedicated. With the insurance payment, and donated labor and materials, the church was completed at a cost of $2600.

Sunday School was organized in 1920 and two years later the Lutheran League was formed. In December 1928 a new pipe organ was dedicated at a cost of $1500.00. In 1989 the organ was refurbished at a cost of $12000.00. In April 1938 the Ladies Aid was established and continued until 1974 when it disbanded. In its place the St. John's Church Women was organized.

A new parsonage was built and dedicated on May 23, 1951. Groundbreaking services for a Parish Hall was held May 4, 1958, and it was dedicated on Nov. 23, 1958. An addition was dedicated in 1998.

In 1968 St. John's, along with two Lutheran Churches in Metropolis, IL, and one from Harrisburg, became involved in sending campers and counselors to Bible Camp at Dixon Springs State Park in Illinois. The facilities were outgrown and the camp moved to a Methodist Church Camp at K Little Grassy Lake. The present location is a United Church of Christ Camp, DuBois in Illinois.

Two sons of the congregation became ministers: Rev. Frank Engelhart, who migrated to Missouri as a small child in 1875, and his nephew, Rev. Edward Kasten. The 125th anniversary was held during 1993 with former pastors taking part in the celebration throughout the year.

Throughout the history of St. John's, members have faithfully taught Sunday School and Bible School, served on church councils and committees, and attended organizational meetings, Bible Studies, and Bible Camps. St. John's is presently served by Pastor John Kiehl.

St. John Lutheran Church, Pocahontas, MO

Altar and pipe organ

Parish Hall

Old McKendree Chapel

Old McKendree Chapel was completed in 1819. At that time, before Missouri was a state, this area was considered the edge of civilization.

The Chapel is listed in the National Archives of the Methodist Church, the National Federal Register of Historic Places in the United States, and as one of the sixteen Historic Shrines of the United Methodist Church. It is the oldest Protestant church building still standing west of the Mississippi River.

Before the Chapel was built, as early as 1806, Methodists from miles around traveled by horse or wagon to this spot on the William Williams property for camp meetings, as it was covered with oak, maple, and poplar trees and had a good spring located at its base.

The Chapel was constructed by builder Charnell Scarlet Glasscock and assisted by James Giboney as well as a man known as Mr. Shelby. The structure was considered to be well built with huge hand-cut poplar logs, a wood plank floor (not earthen), and glass windows. It was a very modern structure for the times.

As far as the Chapel's name, theories range from the thought that Bishop William McKendree may have visited the area and sparked an interest to build the chapel, or it may have just been named in his honor as a well-respected Methodist.

The first Annual Conference held west of the Mississippi River met at McKendree Chapel on Sept. 14, 1819, as well as in 1821, 1826, and 1831. For a long time, McKendree Chapel was the only meetinghouse in the Cape Girardeau Circuit. Before public schools existed, classes were held in the Chapel for many years.

The Civil War caused a gradual decline of the Chapel. Church services were held there until about 1888 or 1890. After that time, the Chapel was home to only special interest services. In 1910, and again in 1916, the Annual Conference met at McKendree. The participants were brought to the Chapel by a special train on the Houck Railroad, which passed close by the property.

However, without regular use, the elements took their toll on the building and grounds. In 1926 Rev. William Stewart, of the New McKendree Church, initiated an interest in renovating and restoring the Chapel and surrounding property. The McKendree Chapel Memorial Association was formed and with the funds raised, stone piers were placed under the Chapel and a new plank floor was laid, the fireplace was rebuilt, rafters were replaced, windows were repaired, and a new roof of handmade shingles was put on the building. A rededication service was held on Oct. 15, 1933, with an attendance estimated at 2000.

Since that time, the original logs that had previously been covered with clapboard, have been restored and the building is protected from the elements by an all-steel canopy. A small home has been built from the logs of the original William Williams homestead.

Today the Chapel is used for weddings and the Easter sunrise service, and the annual Old McKendree service is held each September.

Directly across the road from the lane leading to the Chapel is the Old McKendree Cemetery, where several hundred area residents and church members are buried.

Submitted by Terri Tomlin

Old McKendree Chapel under protective covering, 1998

Old McKendree Chapel circa 1940

New McKendree United Methodist Church

In 1840 the first Methodist church was erected as a log building on Lot 13 on the corner of High and Washington Streets in the town of Jackson, MO. Civil War soldiers destroyed this church when they used it as a stable to shelter their horses.

In 1868 a building committee met and later in 1870, a frame building was erected on this same lot. In 1895, this church was updated with brick veneer and with an additional outside entrance. Church papers, including a list of all the 1895 members, were placed inside the cornerstone.

Due to rapid growth resulting in crowded conditions, the members of the Methodist congregation resolved to build a new church on a more desirable location. Mr Louis Houck was the owner of a beautiful corner lot on First South (now Adams St.) and High Streets, and willingly exchanged this valuable corner lot for the old church site and building. The cornerstone was laid in 1908. The church bell was moved from the old church to the new one. The new church was constructed of Bedford stone, with Gothic stained glass windows, three of which are beautiful works of art. The main auditorium is a large room with a cone-shaped ceiling forming an almost perfect pyramid. The congregation erected a magnificent church costing about $30,000.

On March 7, 1909, the congregation, led by Rev. Marvin T. Haw, marched from the old church to the new one. Mr. W. D. Henderson carried the pulpit Bible. The members walked two abreast while singing hymns and were accompanied by the church orchestra. At the time, the new church was large and elegant for a community of Jackson's size, and was capable of seating two-thirds of the population of Jackson. As a whole, the church was one that the congregation and the whole city of Jackson could be proud. The congregation was a large and live one, numbering 475 in 1910.

Sunday, Sept. 25, 1910, is a day long to be remembered by the Methodists of Jackson as the culmination of one of the greatest undertakings ever attempted in a town of this size. The event marks the dedication of one of the most handsome and substantial houses of worship in the state irrespective of town or wealth of congregation.

The church continued to grow through the years. In 1952 plans were begun for an educational building, completed in 1958 under the pastorate of Rev. Chester Yoes. In 1972 an extensive remodeling was undertaken and a new 16-rank organ was installed.

In 1995 the church acquired the old City Hall on the corner of High and Jefferson Streets. This building, which houses the church's administrative offices, the Child Development Center preschool, a community Food Pantry and a banquet hall was named Cox Memorial Hall after John Cox whose estate benefacted the purchase of the building.

Senior pastor, the Rev. John Rice has been at New McKendree since July 1999. Other members of the staff are: Associate Pastor: Richard Northcutt; Outreach Minister: Jimmie Corbin; Christian Education Director: Bob Zoll; Educational Assistant: Betty Henry; Office Manager: Sue Jones; Membership and Financial Secretary: Sue Jones; Administrative Secretary: Kim Martin; Chancel Choir Director: Sheila Cunningham; Treasurer: Kim Martin; Organist: Linda Thompson; Kids Choir and Bell Choir Director: Julie Walker; and Custodians: Cecil Chiles and Benny Wade.

Today New McKendree has grown from its small beginning in 1840 to a membership of more than 1200 members. Worship services average approximately 450 in weekly attendance and around 200 children; youth and adults attend Sunday School each Sunday morning. Wednesday evening activities were added in 2000 with a fellowship meal from 5:30 to 6:30 p.m. followed by activities for the whole family from 6:30 to 7:30 p.m. All are invited to attend the church services on Saturday at 5:00 p.m. Sunday at 8:00 a.m. and 10:00 a.m. Sunday School is from 9:00 to 9:50 a.m. Sunday; New McKendree is truly "A Historic Church with a Great Future."

New McKendree United Methodist Church, 1895

New McKendree United Methodist Church, circa 1920

St. John's United Church of Christ

The St. John's United Church of Christ, located at 781 State Highway FF in Jackson, MO, was organized in 1877 under the name German Evangelical Lutheran St. John's Church. The constitution was adopted that year. The early secretary records are lost, but legend is that the first services were held in the home of the first minister, the Rev. Frank Eschenfeld. The Eschenfeld home still stands on the east side of road 439, between Horrell and Byrd Creeks.

The early church members included Henry Borgfield, Louis Goehmann, Jacob Hanselmann, Wilhelm Heider, George Kaufmann, Henry Koechig, Henry Koehler, George Loos, Henry Loos, Jacob Loos, Ernst Mantz, Karl Mueller, Friedrich Pensel, John Pensel, Wolfgang Pensel, August Puchbauer, Henry Puchbauer, Paul Rapp, John Schoenebeck, Charles Sievers, Ludwig Sievers, Charles Tuschhoff, Albert Wilhelm, Henry Wilhelm, Charles Wilhelm, Adolph Willa, Henry Willa and Wilhelm Wolfenkoehler.

The present six acres of church land was purchased Feb. 8, 1878, from Charles and Henrietta Wilhelm. A church, parsonage and German parochial school were soon erected.

We joined the Evangelical Synod in 1890. In 1934 we became the St. John's Evangelical and Reformed Church with the merger of those two denominations. On June 25, 1957, a larger church union was effected with the Congregational Church. St. John's officially became known as the United Church of Christ in 1964.

The first frame church building was destroyed by a tornado on June 12, 1922. The bell, weather vane and as much lumber as possible from the old church was used in the present church building. The new church was dedicated on Oct. 22, 1922, by the Rev. Titus Lehmann, at a cost of $1791.26. A splendid musical program was presented and in the afternoon not one-half of those present could get inside the house of worship.

The log parsonage was razed in 1947 and the present parsonage was begun. Logs from the old parsonage were used in what is now dental offices at 3130 East Jackson Blvd. in Jackson, MO. A basement was added to the church in 1934, the kitchen area in 1970, and the fellowship hall in 1999. The church members have done much of the carpentry work themselves.

Henry Koechig was leading carpenter for the first church, parsonage and school. Daniel Tuschhoff, Barney Tuschhoff and Clarence Templeton led in building the present church; Barney Tuschhoff and Adolph Ludwig the parsonage; the Ruben Landgraph Construction Company the basement; Adolph Ludwig and Carl Wilhelm the kitchen; and Craig Yount the fellowship hall.

Ministers serving the church have been Frank Eschenfeld, Edward Werner, Albert Santner, William Goertner, Fritz Weber, Hugo Friedrich, A. Winterich, John Fismer, E. Rudolf, W.F. Hermann, Robert Neumann, Richard Lehmann, George DuVal, G. H. Jurick, Titus Lehmann, Karl Benkendoerfer, Carl Jankowsky, Adie Petzoldt, Ernst Nolte, Karl Albers, Paul Piepenbrok, Fritz Deuschle, Joseph Mayer, Charles Franke, John Hertel, Martin Torbitzky, Emanuel Moritz, Peter Schmiechen, Edwin Budlong, Fred Brandenburg, Don Hartman, Jesse Perry and several other supply students and pastors. The present pastor is the Rev. David E. Schaffner.

The old Parsonage of the St. John's United Church of Christ

The above photo shows the first log parsonage of the St. John's United Church of Christ. The church is located at 781 State Highway FF in Jackson, MO. The building was built in about 1878 and contained three rooms downstairs and two upstairs. There was a walled rock cellar with a dirt floor, under the south front room. The parsonage stood about where the present one stands and faced east. The building was razed in 1947.

The Rev. Dr. S. E. Stringham, former pastor of the New McKendree Methodist Church in Jackson, purchased the logs for $113.75. Dr. Stringham used these logs, along with material from other historical buildings, in the construction of the log house named "Weonah Ranch," located at 3130 East Jackson Blvd. in Jackson, MO. Today this log building has been converted into dental offices.

Submitted by Mary Daume

St. John's United Church of Christ

St. John's United Church of Christ Parsonage. Photo by Johnny Daume about 1937

St. Paul Lutheran Church, Jackson, MO – 1893-2002

St. Paul today enjoys a vital place in our community, but its beginning was hesitant and even discouraged. The inception of St. Paul began with a simple inquiry in the early 1890s by Henry Gerlach. Mr. Gerlach, employed by the Cape County Milling Company, was a miller who had moved from Perry County to Jackson. He wrote to his pastor, the Rev. J. Roesnor of Altenburg, about the lack of a Lutheran church in Jackson.

When Rev. Roesnor inquired of the Cape County Pastoral Conference about possible Lutheran services in Jackson, he was told, "There is no Lutheran church in Jackson. Moreover, there is no material to form a congregation. Besides, the organizing of a church in that place would be detrimental to the neighboring congregations such as New Wells, Altenburg, Cape Girardeau and Gordonville." Rev. Roesner and Rev. Emanuel Mayer of New Wells persisted and persuaded the Pastoral Conference to investigate the possibility of starting a church in Jackson. Rev. Herman Flachsbart of Cape Girardeau and Rev. Mayer were appointed to the committee. This event led to the founding of St. Paul and to 109 years of growth and service of a Lutheran church for Jackson.

This growth began simply in the fall of 1892 with Rev. Flachsbart preaching at Jackson, alternating with Rev. Mayer and Rev. J. Pflantz of Zion near Gordonville. Early services were first held at a gymnasium (Turner Hall), later in the old Cape Girardeau County Courthouse, and even in the Methodist Church.

The Jackson mission was placed in the care Of Rev. Charles Rehahn of Hanover Church as a temporary solution until the arrival of a resident pastor. A constitution was signed on May 18, 1893 by six charter members, William B. Schaefer, William Paar, August Illers, Henry Haase, R. M. Timenstien, and August Hennecke, marking the official beginning of St. Paul Lutheran Church.

In 1893 the congregation began a commitment to permanence by purchasing the "Grant Lot" on which to build a church and school, and received bids for a church building. On Oct. 1, 1893, the first church building, located at West Main and South Russell, was dedicated. The first resident pastor, Rev. John Gassner, was installed on Dec. 3, 1893, and he served until October 1897. In January of 1894 a parochial school began its first session.

The next 40 years of change was presided over by Rev. W. G.. Langehennig. He also taught school. Instruction was in English and German as were the services until German services were discontinued in January 1942, as a casualty of the war. A second new church was dedicated on Feb. 23, 1908. St. Paul expansion continued with both the acquisition of land and the increasing size of the congregation.

On Nov. 20, 1938, Rev. Walter Keisker was installed as the new pastor. Progress continued and by the invigorating growth accompanying the 1950s and 1960s, St. Paul also began to make long-range plans for future goals. After the 1951 school building debt was liquidated, a new church building fund was undertaken beginning in 1957. The new and present church building was dedicated on Dec. 2, 1962. Pastor Keisker retired on Oct. 6, 1968, after serving almost 30 years at St. Paul. Paster Keisker continued to assist in the ministry of St. Paul for many years after his official retirement.

On Oct. 13, 1968, Rev. Earl Weis was installed as pastor. On Nov. 27, 1977 Leslie Mitkos Jr. was installed as associate pastor and served until Dec. 2, 1981. On Aug. 21, 1983, Rev. Lawrence Eatherton was installed as associate pastor. When Rev. Weise retired on Nov. 2, 1986, Rev. Eatherton assumed duties as administrative pastor. Rev. Rollie Meyer was installed as associate pastor on Jan. 11, 1987, and served until Dec. 17, 1989. Rev. Robert Henrich was installed as associate pastor on Nov. 18, 1990, and continues to serve. Rev. David Johnson was installed as administrative pastor on Aug. 28, 1994 and continues in that capacity.

St. Paul Lutheran Church, Jackson, MO

Zion Lutheran Church, Gordonville, MO

Early in the year 1865, just as the Civil War was ending, a group of farmers in the Gordonville area met to organize Zion Lutheran Congregation. During the formative stages, Pastor Polack of Trinity, Cape Girardeau assisted in the organization and conducted services. On Aug. 13, 1865, the congregation was formally organized and the constitution for the church was adopted. Signers of the original constitution, and therefore charter members, included William Hager, Ludwig Siemers, William Gerecke, Friedrich Schwab, William Schneider, George Keller, George Siemers, and Samuel Nussbaum. Many of these family names still appear in the current membership list of Zion.

Following the formal organization, a three-acre tract of land was purchased from Samuel Nussbaum. The first church building was erected and served the members until 1915 when it was replaced by the brick structure now in use. In 1875 and again in 1887 additional land was purchased and Zion Cemetery occupies a portion of this acreage.

Members of the church were deeply concerned about the education of the congregation's children and therefore established a Christian Day School with the pastor as teacher. The school was in existence until 1937.

The first official acts recorded for Zion included: the baptism of William Henze in 1867; the confirmation of Heinrich Bohnsack, Wilhelm Wessell, Wilhelm Sander, Wilhemina Ackermann, Marie Siemers, and Augusta Hager in 1867; and the funeral of a son of a Mr. Volkerding in 1867.

During the 137-year history of the congregation, 13 pastors have served, including the present pastor, Rev. Wayne Schwiesow (since 1997). Others were Rev. F. Doederlein (1865-1866); Rev. H. L. Luecker (1867-1869); Rev. F. C. Basel (1871-1875); Rev. W. L. Fishler (1877-1878); Rev. H. M. Kreuter (1878); Rev. Heinrich Birkner (1880-1886); Rev. J. G. Pflantz (1886-1898); Rev. C. C. E. Brandt (1901-1912); Rev. Valentine Hennig (1913-1918); Rev. Valentine Walthers (1919-1937); Rev. G. B. Seboldt (1938-1973); and Rev. Karl Leeman (1974-1997).

Through the years, exterior and interior renovations to the church building have been done to maintain the house of worship in good repair. The construction of the Parish Hall in 1978 provided space for Sunday School classes, confirmation instruction, meetings, and Vacation Bible School. Currently, the congregation is involved in a project of a complete restoration of the Hinners pipe organ which was originally placed in the first church building in 1904. When the project is completed, the appearance of the organ will be as it was in 1904.

Members of Zion also participate in a variety of organizations to further growth in God's Word and growth in Christian fellowship and service to others. The Sunday School Bible classes, Youth Group, Vacation Bible School, and the Ladies Aid provide avenues for learning and service.

Since Zion Lutheran Congregation exists to minister to individuals and families as it shares the love of God and the message of salvation in Jesus Christ, its members rejoice in the opportunities provided in this community and pray that God will continue to use the members of Zion for service in His Kingdom.

Zion Lutheran Church, Gordonville, MO

Zion Lutheran Church, Pocahontas, MO

Early in the year of 1889 a number of members of Immanuel Lutheran Church at New Wells, MO, living in the vicinity of Pocahontas, met for the purpose of establishing a parochial school and a church at Pocahontas, MO. This was the beginning of Zion Lutheran Church. The reason for this move was to make it more convenient for their children to attend school. After all, these were horse and buggy days and the four miles from Pocahontas to New Wells was a long way, especially in the winter season.

A Constitution was drawn up and signed. The following were the family names of the charter members who signed the first Constitution: Dost, Gaebler, Gerth, Jahn, Kieninger, Kranawetter, Landgraf, Lehner, Reisenbichler, Schneider, Steiner, and Vogel. These early members set to work immediately to erect a school building which would also serve as a house of worship. The contract for this first building was awarded to Adolph Landgraf and Johnny Kieninger for the sum of $640.00. This building was dedicated in September of 1889.

The first teacher of the new school was Miss Anna Koepel. Her salary was $10.00 per month plus room and board. Upon her resignation in 1894 it was decided to call a pastor who would also teach the schoolchildren. Rev. Fred Geske accepted the call to be the first pastor of Zion. His annual salary was $295.00. This same year the congregation made plans to build a parsonage. Mr. Adolph Landgraf was the builder.

The first children to be baptized in the new congregation were Bertha Koenig and Roland Starzinger. The first marriage was performed in 1896, that of Fred Gerler and Bertha Lehner.

In April of 1912 plans were begun for a new church building. During the next two years the new church edifice was built. Adolph Landgraf was the builder, along with the help of many of the church members. This church was dedicated in September of 1914. This building still serves as our house of worship today. Also in the year 1914 the Ladies Aid Society was organized with eight charter members.

1935 was when our small pump organ was replaced with a pipe organ. What beautiful music this added to our church services.

Sunday School for our children was introduced in 1947. Through the years many children have been students in our Sunday School. It is still a large part of our parish ministry today.

In the year 1948 it was decided to raze the first church and school building. A new parish hall and school 32 x 100 feet, was built for $23,000.00. What a wonderful addition this building has been to our parish. This hall still serves as a meeting place for various organizations, Sunday School, church suppers, and other activities. This building served as a parochial school until the year 1969 when we resolved to send our primary school children to St. Paul School at Jackson, MO.

Divine services continue to be held every Sunday as it has been since our early beginning. Vicar Robert Mann is our spiritual leader at the present time. We look forward to serving our community as the population of our area grows. Everyone is certainly welcome.

Zion Lutheran Church and School, Pocahontas, MO, 1914, soon after church was built.

Zion Lutheran Church, Pocahontas, MO, 2001

Zion United Methodist Church of Gordonville, MO

Standing tall and strong amid the low rolling hills of rural Cape Girardeau County is a powerful symbol of a way of life, ever-enduring peacefully against the strong and boisterous winds of time. Yes, in fact, it is a church with a story. Indeed it is a church with many stories; a bastion of strength, a haven of rest, a place to begin and a place to end, in the eternal pilgrimage of life. It is the story of a people woven together over the years into a community of faith.

The immigration of many Germans to Missouri is in large part due to Dr. Gottfried Duden. Duden came to Missouri in 1824 and lived along the Missouri River in Warren County, near the present-day town of Dutzow, from 1824-1828. He wrote letters home which were eventually published in Germany in 1829 in an account entitled, *Report About a Journey to the Western States of North America and a Several-Year Visit on the Missouri (in the years 1824, 25, 26, and 27)*. Duden painted a picture of a wonderful place for those Germans who dreamed of a new start in a land free of the almost constant turmoil, limitation, and drudgery of the old world. It is no coincidence that many of the founding members of Zion United Methodist Church came to Missouri directly from the Kingdom of Hanover and Braunschweig, or Brunswick, in north central Germany. In the 1840s and 1850s, many of Zion's families braved the ocean voyage from Germany to the port of New Orleans, after which they traveled up the Mississippi River directly to Cape Girardeau County. A number of Zion's founding members traveled on board the *Bark Diana*, which embarked from Bremen, Germany, and arrived in New Orleans on Nov. 11, 1844.

The families of Conrad Boettcher, Conrad Deneke, Henry Meyer and Frederick Stoffregen had migrated from Germany and in 1844 settled in the community west of Gordonville. They were invited to the home of Frederick Schlueter, where these newcomers decided "they did not want to live in this new country without God and without the study of the Bible." They continued to hold religious services in their homes, with Frederick Stoffregen in charge of interpreting the Scriptures. In 1846 a young German missionary from St. Louis, Karl Hollman, came into the community and preached his first sermon. On June 5, 1847 the first Quarterly Conference was begun under the presidency of the Rev. Henry Koeneke, District Superintendent. In the same year the first Church School was organized. Christian Bartels, Conrad Boettcher and Henry Doere were elected the first stewards of the congregation. The following are listed as charter members:

Pictured here are the Old Parsonage Building, the Church and the Old School Building in the extreme background. This photograph captures the buildings around 1900. The church operated a German School, which provided a complete elementary education until WWI.

The Charter Members of Zion Church

Christian Bartels
Elizabeth Bartels
August Guenter
Frederick Vasterling
Sophia Vasterling
Johann Stoffregen
Johanna Stoffregen
Conrad Boettcher
Heinrich Ahrens
Johanna Plagge
Magdalene Deneke
Frederick Oberbeck
Maria Oberbeck
Heinrich Doerris
Maria W. Doerris
Heinrich Meyer
Elizabeth Meyer
Christian Bierschwal
Doretta Bierschwal
Wilhelm Phillips
Conrad Rouse
Dietrich Brase
Maria Brase
Johann Antonsen
Heinrich Dralle
Dietrich Kuehle
Dorotea Kuehle
Gottfried Urbann
Caroline Urbann
Heinrich Ische
Louise Antonsen
Louise Dralle
Wilhelmina Ische
Thomas Triller

The first church was built in 1848 and the congregation was officially organized.

In this same time frame, German Methodism formed three districts within the Methodist Episcopal Church. Zion was a part of the St. Louis District with L. S. Jacoby, presiding elder, and 13 preachers. Due to a disagreement on the issue of slave ownership, the newly created St. Louis German District became part of the Illinois Conference and many of those of German descent enlisted in Illinois Regiments during the Civil War. In 1876 the congregation erected a new brick church, with the bricks being made on the site. The only major addition was constructed in 1892 and was built on the west end of the church. This happened to be the site of the original log church. A two-story parsonage was built in 1895 and in 1896 a Parish House was built to house the Sunday School. These buildings would serve the congregation into the 1960s.

Zion Methodist was an active and growing church in the late 1890s and early 1900s. The advent of WWI and anti-German sentiment began the process of merging the German Methodist Church with the English-speaking Methodist Church. The congregation has a long history of active organizations that continues to this date. The Loyal Temperance League was a youth organization that was formed to teach the youth the harms of tobacco, alcohol, profanity and immorality. The League would evolve into the Epworth League in 1912, the Methodist Youth Fellowship in 1948, and is currently known as the United Methodist Youth Fellowship. Today's United Methodist Women began as two groups. In 1923 the Ladies Aid Society was established, Mrs. William Winkler as president, and the Women's Foreign Missionary Society followed in 1924 with Mrs. Ferdinand Kuehle as President. In 1940 the women's organizations merged six groups into The Women's Society of Christian Service (WSCS) and the Wesleyan Service Guild. In the 1960s the WSCS helped to form a Circle that was named for Anita Allison, a missionary from St. Louis, who was stationed at the Methodist Girls School of Kauntan in the Malay Islands as a teacher. Ms. Allison visited Zion on June 20, 1965. In 1973 the WSCS became the United Methodist Women (UMW) and this unit is still very active in the church today. The United Methodist Men was organized in 1954 and continues today. They have raised sugar cane, broom cane and watermelons to help fund different activities. They have an annual Wildlife Supper and participate in district and conference events like the Men's Retreat held at the church camps near Arcadia, MO.

In 1989 the church published a history book entitled *Marching to Zion* that contains much more information about the church. In 1998 Zion celebrated its 150th Anniversary with a yearlong celebration. The congregation recently renovated the sanctuary and the pipe organ. The organ had been purchased used in 1892 and many of the church's older members related fond memories of hand-pumping the organ. While it no longer has to be hand-pumped, it is still serving the congregation well today. Zion is still a place to worship God and study the Bible. It holds as its mission "to make disciples for Christ by introducing and teaching the Gospel, and providing a spiritual home for our community, through which we can grow in faith and reach out into the world in love." As Zion moves through its second century, it still stands tall and strong and is marching into the future with plans for expansion and growth.

Zion United Methodist Church near Gordonville as it is today

Emanuel United Church of Christ – Our Heritage

The Emanuel Evangelical Church was founded in May 1867 with 28 German-American residents as members. Emanuel is one of four U.C.C. congregations in this area. St. James U.C.C. of Tilsit is the oldest active congregation, dating back to 1843; St. John's U.C.C. of Fruitland was organized 10 years after Emanuel; and Evangelical U.C.C. of Cape Girardeau is the youngest of the four.

Emanuel U.C.C. has grown from 28 members in 1867 to 500 in 1990. The congregation has been served by 17 resident ministers along with a number of additional persons who conducted services when there was no resident pastor. Today the average church attendance is 150-175 and 90-100 in church school. Twenty-two pastors have served Emanuel in 135 years. Rev. Samuel E. Roethemeyer has been pastor since 1988.

The present church was erected in 1927. The parsonage across the street from the church was erected in 1956. An Educational Building was erected in 1963 on the lot adjoining the church. An elevator was installed in 1989.

One member of our congregation, Miss Lydia Kies, devoted her life, after graduating from Moody Bible College in 1921, to missionary service in the Central Province of India. She now lies buried among the ones she loved and served.

Another member of Emanuel, Paul Lehmann, grandson of Rev. Reinhart Lehmann, was ordained into the Christian Ministry on May 28, 1975. He studied at Eden Theological Seminary in Webster Groves, MO.

Emanuel United Church of Christ

New Bethel Baptist Church

The church that was to become New Bethel Baptist Church was founded on Jan. 18, 1873. In accordance with a call from brethren who had agreed to unite together in a church organization, a council was convened at Oak Hill schoolhouse. Those on the council were as follows: John F. Ford, William H. Walker, John F. Godwin, John Chaferman, James Cameron, Hiram Childs, and Benjamin H. Chaferman. Council members were from Gravel Hill and Goshen churches.

The council organized by electing Elder John F. Ford as moderator and John F. Godwin as secretary. Elder B. L. Bowman was selected by the brethren to present the member letters, Articles of Faith, Church Covenant, and statement of reasons for wishing to constitute a new church. The council unanimously agreed to recognize the church as a regular church of Christ.

In the evening after the founding, the church was called to order by Elder B. L. Bowman. After a short conference, the church agreed to postpone the election of pastor, deacons, and church clerk, as well as selection of the name of the church, until the next regular meeting. A committee was appointed to draw up rules of deacons, time and place of meeting, and time of stated communion.

Due to rain, the next meeting was postponed until the Saturday before the first Sunday in March of 1873. After divine services by Elder B. L. Bowman, the church was called to order. Visiting brethren were invited to membership in the newly formed church. Minutes of council were read, approved, and adopted. Isaac Ackman was elected as church clerk. Benjamin Bowman, Rowland Childs Sr., and John Medlock were elected as deacons. New Bethel was selected as the church's name.

The original church building was built in 1880 on a two-acre plot purchased from Elizabeth McCain. This building was a log structure, which later burned. Services were then held in homes until 1899, when a one-room frame structure was built with the aid of members. In 1963, the church voted to construct a new building. The building was completed in 1966, and is the same structure that is currently standing. The old church building built in 1899 was torn down in 1967. Additions were made to the current church building in 1979 and 1992.

New Bethel Baptist Church is located at 6137 County Road 525, four miles east of Pocahontas. Visitors are welcome. Sunday School is at 9 a.m., with worship following at 10 a.m. Sunday evening service is at 6 p.m. from the beginning of September until the end of May, and at 7 p.m. from the beginning of June until the end of August. Wednesday evening service is at 7 p.m. year round. New Bethel's web site is www.newbethelbaptist.net , and the e-mail address is nbbc@showme.net. *Submitted by David Golightly, Church Historian*

Recent photograph of New Bethel Baptist Church

Pleasant Hill Presbyterian Church, Fruitland, MO

In 1838 a little band of Scots-Irish Presbyterians seceded from the Old Apple Creek Presbyterian Church near Pocahontas, MO to organize a church of their own where they might worship God according to "dictates of their own conscience."

A meeting was held by the Session near a big spring along Indian Creek on land owned by James Woods. The site of the building was changed to land owned by Robert Caldwell. Ebenezer Flinn, a ruling elder, offered to trade a strip of land two rods wide and one-half mile in length on a hill just east of Fruitland for land of equal value on the farm of Robert Caldwell.

The first church building was erected in 1840 and the congregation held their first worship service on June 15, 1841. On Oct. 1, 1841, the name was changed from South Apple Creek to Pleasant Hill. This building served until 1854, then was used as a school building. The second church building was built in 1855 and was used until 1892. The third building was built in 1892 on the same site as the first church and was dedicated Nov. 13, 1892, free of debt.

This church had an active women's organization and youth group. A piano was used in this church. In 1965 an addition to the classroom/kitchen was added to the back of the building and an electric organ was purchased from the First Presbyterian Church of Jackson when that church received a new organ.

Many ministers served this church. The first minister was Rev. J. L. Frary in 1841 and the last was Rev. Joseph Mayer who was also the pastor of St. John's UCC Church west of Fruitland.

In the mid-1900s this church was yoked with the Brazeau Presbyterian Church. In the 1960s it was yoked with the First Presbyterian Church of Jackson, then finally it was yoked with St. John's UCC Church. Due to dwindling numbers of the congregation, the church disbanded as of Nov. 30, 1982, and joined the First Presbyterian Church of Jackson on Dec. 1, 1982.

Many of the old "hitching trees" are still alive on grounds of the church as of this writing in 2001. The cemetery next to the church holds lots of dear and faithful citizens of this church and the surrounding area. A cemetery association first met in December 1969 and is keeping the cemetery and church grounds in beautiful shape. The former congregation and friends of the church hold a homecoming worship service once a year on the fourth Sunday in May at 11:00 a.m., with a basket dinner following.

A more detailed report of the history of this church may be found in the Riverside Regional Library in Jackson, MO genealogy room, entitled Pleasant Hill Presbyterian Church, Fruitland, MO. *Compiled by Carolyn Thompson*

Pleasant Hill Presbyterian Church, Fruitland, MO

Jackson In The Civil War And Other Military Service

To some extent Cape Girardeau County resembled the make-up of the rest of the state in the Civil War era. The early American settlers coming into the area had been from southern states, such as Virginia, Tennessee, and the Carolinas. Many of them were slave owners or were opposed to the coercion of the southern states. They tended to side with the Confederacy. Later immigrants to the area, particularly the German immigrants of the 1840s and the 1850s, tended to side with the Union. Thus when the split in the Union finally came, Cape Girardeau County provided almost equal numbers of troops to each side. As Snider and Collins (1956) explained, "Soon troops were being recruited for local duty, in state units for Confederate service, in state units for Federal service, and in the regular Union Army." (p.38).

Although much of the action in Southeast Missouri during the Civil War was preparation for a major Southern offensive that never came, there was also a considerable amount of guerilla activity in the area. This was due, in part, to proximity to Arkansas, and, in part, to the varied backgrounds and loyalties of the population.

In May 1861 the Missouri Legislature passed an act providing for organization of the Missouri State Guards. This volunteer militia generally supported the Confederate cause. The governor appointed N. W. Watkins of Cape Girardeau County as Brigadier-General in the First Military District, which encompassed southeast Missouri. Watkins soon found himself to be unsuited to this assignment and resigned. He was later to become a General in the Confederate Army. A colorful successor, General Jefferson Thompson of Bloomfield, was appointed. According to Snider and Collins (1956), about 1500 men responded to Thompson's call to arms in 1861. Those troops would harass the Southeast Missouri area and the occupying Federal forces until 1863. Goodspeed (1888) noted that prior to the beginning of the war a company of militia, known as the "Marble City Guards," was formed in Cape Girardeau. With Lincoln's call for troops in 1861 and Thompson's call to arms, those with Confederate sympathies went to Jackson and joined a battalion of State Guards organized by Samuel J. Ward (p. 505).

Another Confederate force formed in Jackson at about the same time was W. L. Jeffers' "Swamp Rangers." Jeffers commanded the Cape Girardeau Company of this cavalry unit of the State Guard. This company mustered out after six months. Later Jeffers would form a regiment designated the as Eighth Missouri Cavalry. Six of the eight companies of this unit were from Cape Girardeau County. Although most of the action this group saw during the war consisted of hit-and-run guerilla raids, it did participate in all the battles during General Marmaduke's Missouri raid in 1863 (Goodspeed, 1888, pp. 506-507). According to the *Jackson Herald* (1908), a monument dedicated to Jeffers was unveiled at the first Home Comers celebration, indicating the admiration many Jackson residents felt for him more than forty years later. The monument still stands in the city cemetery.

There were five categories of Union units organized in the Cape Girardeau area: Home Guards with three months' enlistment; the Six Months' Militia; the Missouri State Militia; the Missouri volunteers, who saw the most service; and the Enrolled Missouri Militia (Snider and Collins, 1956, p. 42). In June 1861, four companies of Home Guards were recruited in Cape Girardeau for three months' service. All their service was in this vicinity. In August 1861, the "Fremont Rangers" battalion was recruited by Lieutenant-Colonel Lindsey Murdoch to defend Cape Girardeau. It served until Christmas Day, 1861, without pay or government issued clothing. Its primary task was scouting in Southeast Missouri. (Goodspeed, 1888, p. 511).

The Third Company of the Engineer Regiment of the West Missouri Volunteers was recruited and organized in Cape Girardeau in 1861 and was charged with building the defense works of Cape Girardeau and Birds Point. They saw service throughout the South until the end of the war. Battery F of the Second Illinois Light Artillery was organized in Cape Girardeau in December 1861. It served in Cape Girardeau until March 1862, when it was moved to Tennessee and Mississippi, serving in the battles of Corinth and Shiloh. It spent the remainder of the war in Louisiana. (Goodspeed, 1888, pp.519-520).

Only one regiment of the Missouri State Militia was organized in southeast Missouri. In February 1862, Captain Lindsay Murdoch recruited Company A of the Twelfth Cavalry. This unit was later to become Company K of the Third Cavalry. It performed guard and escort duty, much of it between Cape Girardeau and Pilot Knob, and fought the guerilla units operating in southeast Missouri. (Snider and Collins, 1956, p.43).

In October 1862, the 56th Regiment of the Enrolled Missouri Militia was raised in Cape Girardeau County. In that same month the Twenty-ninth Infantry was organized in Cape Girardeau. It performed some local service but then served in many battles throughout the South. According to Goodspeed, up to January 1, 1864, regular army volunteers in each command from Cape Girardeau County were Second Infantry, 58; Eighth Infantry, 33; Twenty-ninth Infantry, 186; Second Artillery, 68; Tenth Cavalry, 52; and Engineer Regiment, 116 (1888, p. 514).

Prior to the end of the war, two additional units were recruited in Cape Girardeau, Company C Fiftieth Regiment of the Missouri Infantry and the Thirty-ninth Regiment Missouri Enrolled Militia. The latter regiment manned Fort D in Cape Girardeau until the end of the war. (Snider and Collins, 1956, p. 43-44).

Because of Cape Girardeau's strategic location as the first high ground north of the Ohio River and the presence of many residents with known Confederate sympathies, Federal forces occupied the city from July 10, 1861 until August 14, 1865. Their orders were to stop any attempt of Confederate land or naval vessels from invading the North along the river and to keep the river open for use by Federal forces. In addition, they were to establish a base of operations from which Union troops could control Confederate guerilla activity.

Camp Fremont, as Cape Girardeau was

Left to right: Woodrow Seabaugh, Bernard Schaper, John Fred Hartle, J.E. Hagans, Gene Himmelsbach; July 22, 1989.

known, consisted of four forts, two artillery batteries, and the main Union camp located at the Old Fairgrounds, just south of Good Hope Street and west of Sprigg Street. According to Snider and Collins (1956), these forts saw little or no action. Forts A and D were located on bluffs overlooking the Mississippi River. Fort C was located to the southwest of the city, roughly at the present intersection of Pacific and Bloomfield streets, to defend against attack from the Commerce, Bloomfield or Gordonville roads. This fort attempted to shell the right flank of the Confederate force in the Battle of Cape Girardeau, but its location prevented it from providing much assistance. Fort B, located on what is now the campus of Southeast Missouri State University, saw most of the action in the war. Its location was selected to cover the Perryville and Jackson roads and it was from this direction that attack came April 26, 1863. In addition to the forts, two artillery emplacements were located on the west side of the city. Dittlinger (1976) states that the Battle of Cape Girardeau would never have happened if General John McNeil, the Union commander of Camp Fremont, had not accidentally come across a Confederate force under Colonel Carter as McNeil was returning from a recruiting expedition. Carter's forces pursued McNeil, stopping about four miles outside the city to wait for reinforcements from General Marmaduke, who had been on a foraging expedition in southeast Missouri, and General Joe Shelby. The battle itself lasted only about four hours. As word reached the Confederates that Federal reinforcements had arrived, they retreated into Arkansas.

Jackson's role in the Civil War was slight. However, its location on the major transportation routes made it a perfect place to watch troop movements and thereby was reputed to be an intelligence center, particularly for the Confederates, since the major routes north and west from Cape Girardeau passed through Jackson. Lines of the Pacific Telegraph Company, used to maintain communication between the various Union headquarters, also passed through the town. The *Jackson Herald* (1908) noted that the B. M. Morgan house was used as a hotel, office and telegraph station by Union solders and that his farm fences were burned three times and many of his cattle and hogs were slaughtered to supply the needs of the military.

According to Brown (1976), a skirmish that took place on August 8, 1862, was typical of the kind of action that took place in Jackson. On that date some of the local young men, members of Jeffers' Swamp Rangers, had slipped home to visit family and friends. A patrol of Union cavalrymen from the Wisconsin Cavalry Regiment came to Jackson to investigate reports that an employee of the telegraph company had been captured by Confederate troops and was being held at the Turnbaugh Hotel. When the patrol was unable to find the Confederate force reported to be in Jackson, they split up and began to search the town. In the process, they came upon several of the young men attempting to return to their unit and followed them to the Fairgrounds, located south of Russell Heights Cemetery. A brief skirmish followed, with several injuries and one Union casualty.

In April 1863, Shelby's Rangers camped overnight in Jackson prior to the Battle of Cape Girardeau. In 1864, when marching to Pilot Knob to participate in Price's final attempt to take Missouri, Jeffers and his cavalry skirmished in Jackson with a Federal force under Captain Tacke (Goodspeed, 1888, p. 503). However, neither of these events had much effect on the course of the battles or the course of the war. Thus, Jackson's involvement in the war really consisted of the service provided by the many young men who fought in the war and the families who supported them.

While there is much fascination with Civil War, young men and women from Jackson and the surrounding region have served in the many other military ventures in which the United States of America has been involved. The Memorial to All Veterans, located in Brookside Park, has allowed the community to become more aware of the number of area residents who served in the ten officially recognized wars: Revolutionary War, War of 1812, Mexican War, Civil War, Spanish-American War, World War I, World War II, Korea, Viet Nam, and Desert Storm. The memorial, dedicated in 1991, was created through the efforts of members of the American Legion Auxiliary. The American Legion Altenthal-Joerns Post #158 has been an active part of the community since it was founded in 1919. The Legion and its Auxiliary are sponsors of the annual Homecomers celebration. The Veterans of Foreign Wars also has a Post in Jackson. -amd

On The Home Front

During the conflicts of the Twentieth Century, from World War I to Desert Storm, area clubs provided moral support for the servicemen by sending them a touch of home.

The citizens of Cape Girardeau County became one large family concerned with the care and safety of its sons and daughters serving in the military.

Even though the area weekly papers did not carry news of the day-to-day battles, the news of military transfers, injuries, furloughs, and deaths brought home the tragedy of war. During World War I, the Missouri Cash-Book reported "Walter Sams of Neely's Landing received a message last Tuesday that his son Clyde was very sick of influenza at Camp Funston. He had also received word that another son who is in France was in a hospital after having been in two battles." (Missouri Cash-Book, October 17, 1918). Also in 1918, ambulance driver Robert Vinyard's letters home reminded Jacksonians of the "stearn realities" of war, of being captured, recaptured and eventually left in "No-Man's Land" with many wounded. "I have seen the bad side of war. I don't think there is any other side. It is hard for a fellow to learn of nice chaps that he has met and made friends with being killed." He missed the folks back home and wished he could be with them at Christmas. A later letter thanked his family for sending a package of personal items from home.

In 1966, the Jackson Jaycee Wives undertook a care package program much as the women's clubs had done during World War I and II. The local papers published the club's requests for fund-

Monument on the south side of the Cape Girardeau County Courthouse, "In memory of those from Cape Girardeau County who gave their lives in defense of Liberty in The World War [WWI]."

ing and supplies and praised their work, "Doubtless, in spite of the hard work, not a one of them regrets a moment's effort. The controversy rages in this Nation about whether American should be fighting in Vietnam, but these young women know that America's servicemen are there, and they are backing them with actions, not words alone." (Jackson Post and Cash-Book, 2 March 1966 and 8 November 1967)

Other service clubs, such as the PEO, the DAR, and Old Salem Homemakers in Millersville aided the Jaycee wives. The Wonderworkers Homemakers of Pocahontas "donated their Christmas gifts of silver to the Jaycee Wives' project and decided to bake cookies for the February boxes." (Jackson Post and Cash-Book, 28 December 1967). Smaller organizations sent parcels to the sons and brothers of members.

The club secretaries made copies of the servicemen's thank you letters to be printed in the paper. Marine Ron Lowes, serving as a photographer in Chu Lai, explained that items such as soap, toothpaste and candy sent by the Jaycee Wives were scarce in Vietnam. "Things you take for granted in the states are treasured items over here. It is great to come out of the field and find a package from home. I shared it with my buddies and now quite a few guys have heard of Jackson, Mo." (Jackson Post and Cash-Book 14 December 1966) Sgt. Orville L. Thoma, stationed at Phy-Cat Air Base in Vietnam, complemented the Sunday School Class at the Oak Ridge Baptist Church. "I want to thank you for that fine box of cookies you sent me. It's good to know the people of the community are thinking of us over here, and one of these times soon we hope to be back home and part of it." (Jackson Post and Cash-Book, 27 March 1968, pg. 2)

Epidemics And Disasters

Cholera Epidemics in Jackson

When it comes to the treatment of communicable diseases there is no doubt that the Twenty-first Century should be considered the "good old days." Jackson and Cape Girardeau County are blessed with two hospitals and fine physicians. In times past, the only weapons available against disease such as cholera and influenza were quarantine and tender loving care. Many citizens of Jackson died during two cholera epidemics to strike the town, the first in 1833 and the second in 1852. The first epidemic started with a family south of town and spread northward. The area doctors tried all means to stop its progress but there were few means available to them aside from quarantine. One hundred and twenty-eight citizens fell victim.

In 1852 the second round of the sickness began within the city limits in a house near the jail by the public square. Only the sick and those tending them remained in town. As before, families of every race and creed in the area were affected. Forty years later, The Missouri Cash-Book newspaper published a list found in the Circuit Clerk's office. The list, dated June 11-24, 1852, included members of the following families, their servants, and their slaves: Innman, English, Harris, Cordell, Dennis, Wheeler, Costner, Flin, Russell, Horrell, Ranney, McCombs, Snider, Russell, Harris, Flenzi, Hickman, Masterson, Cowen, Beatties, Cannon, Limbaugh, Tolson, Kuehle, Warren, Reeves, Fulenwider, Welling, Daniel, Green, Hager, Davis, Turnbaugh, Clodfelter, Linch, Hale, Short, Taylor, Will, Randol, Williamson, Hughey, Grayson, Cole, Flowers, Dennison, McNeely, and Daugherty. Over eighty people died during the thirteen day period. The newspaper also related the story of an old gentleman named Sion Adams who claimed, as one of the few who remained in town to bury the dead, that several of the cholera victims were buried "in one of the lots back of the row of buildings on the south side of the public square."

Information from The Cash-Book Journal, March 2, 1983 and The Missouri Cash-Book, June 1892.

Spanish Influenza

In 1918 influenza swept through Europe and the United States, killing almost as many citizens and soldiers as the guns of World War I. The residents of Cape Girardeau County were not spared. The newspapers carried weekly updates on the progress of the epidemic. In one week during October 1918, Julian Dearmont, Ray Medley, Arthur Graden and Otto Winters, four soldiers from this county stationed in various training camps, died from influenza. The young men were given full military burials even though "it was not given to them to go to the front and there battle for their country and human liberty with their comrades in arms, but because of this their sacrifice is no less." (Missouri Cash-Book, October 17, 1918).

Meanwhile at home in Jackson, "All Public Meetings Forbidden - Influenza Scare" read the headline October 17, 1918. Jackson was under quarantine, schools and churches were closed, and "all citizens are ready to obey orders if it will save the people from the scourge." The quarantine was short-lived, school resumed and hopes were high that the epidemic would pass quickly. Such was not the case. A December edition of the newspaper stated, "The epidemic of influenza does not improve with age. There are perhaps as many cases of it in Jackson as there have ever been at one time since it started." At its peak one hundred and fifty pupils and several teachers were absent due to illness. Substitute teachers were brought over from Cape Girardeau where the schools had been shut down due to absenteeism. Without the benefit of modern medicines and antibiotics, citizens of all ages died from complications of the Spanish influenza.

View of the south side of the first block of East Adams Street after the tornado of 1923. The two story brick house in the center is the home of Frank Medley, the photographer. In the background is the old Immaculate Conception Catholic Church.

The Great Fire of 1888. The Robb Hotel is ablaze and men are on the roof of the Henry Boss building trying to keep the fire from spreading.

Smallpox

During the fall of 1929 schools and churches cancelled meetings and activities because of the presence of smallpox in Jackson. Area physicians reacted quickly to limit contact with infected persons; eighteen families in town had to be quarantined. Children could not return to school unless they presented a certificate of vaccination. At that time, vaccination was a painful procedure with various side-effects. Even strapping young football players were laid low, "Members of the Jackson high school football squad have been having vacation the past two weeks as far as practice on the gridiron is concerned but a number have received more punishment from the effects of vaccination than from the infliction of strenuous workouts this season. This brings about reasons for the majority ailing with sore arms." One gentleman indicated that that were it "not for the inconvenience of quarantine, the kind of smallpox that appeared here would be preferable to vaccination."

The Fire of 1888

On April 17, 1888, fire swept through the principal business section and wiped out the buildings on the entire first block of West Main Street. Church bells and steam whistles sounded the alarm. There was no organized fire department in Jackson at the time. Bucket brigades did their best to keep the fire from spreading. Bucket lines formed and nearby shopkeepers like Henry Boss and Charles Welling placed wet quilts and curtains on the shingled roofs of their stores in hopes of extinguishing flying embers.

After three days of effort the only business left on the block was Fritz Obermiller's store on the corner of Missouri Street. Barrels of whiskey and beer were the only inventory of any value that could be saved. Lost in the blaze were the J. M. Schmuke harness shop, William Washington Taylor's cabinet and wood working business, saloons operated by Jim Jenkins, Robert Hoffman and Sam Lail, the Robb Hotel owned by John and Iva Robb, a building owned by F. A. McGuire, two restaurants and a meat market. While the fire was no doubt a blow to the owners of the lost enterprises, some residents considered it a boon to the uptown area that had been nicknamed "Battle Row" because of the rowdy saloon clientele.

Source of information— The Cash-Book Journal, March 2, 1983

The Cyclone of March 1923

Missouri weather changes are rapid and at times, costly. Such was the case on Sunday, March 11, 1923, when a tornado blew through Jackson's business district. The capricious nature of the twister left most of the uptown businesses damaged and yet not one window in the courthouse was broken. The wind first struck the cemetery, overturning monuments and ripping trees from the ground. The chimneys of the Baptist church were blown down causing damage to the roof and creating alarm among the Sunday evening churchgoers. The Masonic Hall (at the northeast corner of High and Adams) was destroyed when the wreckage of the upper floor fell through to the garage on the first floor owned by Brennecke and James. The twelve cars housed in the garage were relatively unharmed.

The tin roof over the Jackson Mercantile Company was left twisted and crumpled in the street. The homes of the Dalton, Medley, Schmuke, Fulenwider, Ritter, Sutton, Gockel, and Hunter homes sustained serious damage with the second floor of the Hunter home a complete loss. The walls of the Episcopal church were blown out of alignment tearing out a corner and destroying part of the roof. Hail and a blinding downpour followed the terrific winds of the storm soaking furniture and inventory left in the damaged buildings (Missouri Cash-Book, March 11, 1943, 20 years ago). The Masonic Hall and Corinthian Baptist Church were considered total losses and were razed to make room for new structures.

The damages totaled over $100,000 and yet the citizens of Jackson considered themselves extremely fortunate for there were no lives lost. On the same day, a tornado struck Jackson, Tennessee, killing twenty people and injuring forty more.

Floods

Floods come in many forms. Flash floods, street flooding and cresting rivers all add up to the possible loss of homes, lives and livelihoods. Waterways abound in Cape Girardeau County: Hubble Creek, Goose Creek, Byrd Creek, Whitewater River, Indian Creek, Cane Creek, Williams Creek, Rocky Branch, Neal Creek, Randol Creek, and the Mississippi River. This is only a partial listing of the streams intersecting Jackson and the surrounding farms and towns. When contained within their banks streams are a delight to fishermen, children, and all who appreciate a peaceful afternoon by run-

One of the Union Street homes destroyed by the Hubble Creek flash flood of 1958.

Cleaning up after the flood of 1958.

ning water. However, sudden heavy rains or prolonged rainy seasons can turn the local creeks and streams into forces of destruction.

Residents of Jackson keep a watchful eye on Hubble and Goose Creek. The flood of January 1950 developed in the Goose Creek area with widespread damage to the various industries. LaPierre Handle Company had three feet of water in the boiler room and four to six inches of water in the rest of the mill. Several stacks of lumber and logs floated away from Loos Sawmill. Due to the industrial nature of the vicinity financial losses were low (Cape County Post, January 1950).

The waters of Hubble Creek rise quickly and furiously when heavy rains blow through the area. The floods leave debris scattered along the creek banks and fences from the Fruitland area through the Jackson City Park and south. The area south of the park was particularly vulnerable until the Union Street levee was built. In June 1958, an overnight rain of 6.5 inches caused both East and West Hubble Creeks to overflow their banks. Businessmen and homeowners could only watch as a wall of water roared through the Hubble Creek district leaving a wake of mud and debris and damaging or destroying over fifty buildings. Water reached a height of thirty-eight inches inside Riverside Regional Library while the McNeely Brothers Foundry had over four feet flooding the heavy equipment room. Schaper's IGA was forced to close temporarily while they shoveled mud and damaged goods from the store. Homeowners on Union and Daisy Street had to be evacuated by boat. (Missouri Cash-Book, June 12, 1958)

The Mississippi River affects many of the residents far away from the river's edge. Area creeks and the Diversion Channel have nowhere to drain when the mighty river floods. The flood of May 1943 set new records for the river. Major highways closed north of St. Mary's and south of Dutchtown, effectively isolating Jackson from the rest of the state. The International Shoe Company had to close temporarily because shipments could not get through. (Missouri Cash-Book, May 27, 1943, p.1). New records were set fifty years later. The flood of 1993 will long be remembered for the amount of water distributed from Neelys Landing, Egypt Mills, Cape Girardeau, and inland to Dutchtown via the Diversion Channel, and on south. It was a time when the residents of Cape Girardeau County pulled together, filled sandbags and aided their neighbors with supplies such as drinking water and medical supplies.

In the spring of 2002, runoff from persistent heavy rains in Missouri and Illinois once again caused the river to rise and backwaters to creep toward Dutchtown. The flooded Diversion Channel turned Allenville into an island accessible only by boat and an abandoned railway trestle. A six-inch rainfall in the north Jackson area forced Hubble Creek from its banks and two feet of water poured through the City Park. Even the Union Street levee could not keep street flooding from making its way into the lower level of Riverside Library, homes and businesses in the Union Street area.

The Big Snow of 1918

From year to year Cape Girardeau Countians never know what winter will bring. Temperatures plummet from fifty degrees to ten degrees below zero in a matter of a few days. Precipitation changing from sleet to snow to freezing rain coating trees and power lines creates treacherous conditions for pedestrians and automobiles. Today when the local weathermen predict heavy snow, residents scurry to buy groceries and children hope for school closings. Accurate advanced warnings of heavy snow have not been available at least twice in the county's history. The snowstorm that befell Jackson on Wednesday, January 11, 1918, qualified as "The Big Snow" for many years.

Even the United States Post Office could not make its appointed rounds for several days. The local newspaper described the scene. "The snow is at least fourteen or fifteen inches deep on a level, and in many places has drifted to a depth of several feet. Drags, scrapers, shovels and other tools have been used in an effort to open up the streets and public roads in many parts of the county." Train service between St. Louis and Cape Girardeau was suspended. Motorists who tried to travel between Cape Girardeau and Jackson were blown off the road into ditches and drifts. On Friday, the temperature dropped to twenty degrees below zero where it remained until Sunday. More snow fell on Monday hindering road clearing. While several rural schools closed, the schools in town continued to hold classes even though several members of the school board were in favor of closing for a day or two until the streets and sidewalks could be cleared!

The Blizzard of 1979

The record for "The Big Snow" lasted until February 25, 1979. Area residents went to sleep on Saturday night to the sound of heavy rain and high wind. Early Sunday morning the rain turned to a driving snow accompanied by thunder and lightning leaving two feet of snow and drifts as deep as eight to ten feet. The Sunday morning blizzard gave new meaning to the phrase "rude awakening." Church services were cancelled. The local television weatherman tried to explain how a chance for flurries had turned into the worst blizzard on record for the area. The deep drifts buried cars and trapped motorists. Interstate 55 and all major highways through the county were closed. The National Guard was called in to rescue stranded motorists and to assist families in rural areas to get needed supplies and emergency transportation. The St. Paul Lutheran Church congregation turned their school gymnasium and cafeteria into an emergency housing center for over four hundred and fifty stranded motorists. School children had a long break in which to look forward to spring.

Southard's TV on Monroe Street during the Blizzard of 1979.

Uptown Jackson following the "Big Snow of January 1918."

Area Attractions and Activities

"In building a modern city with all conveniences, good schools and churches, the citizens of Jackson have not overlooked social life which enables one to enjoy the conveniences provided." *Missouri Cash-Book, 2 August 1934*

Social life in the Jackson area comes in as many forms as there are individuals to enjoy the good life. Religious, civic and social organizations provide camaraderie while serving their members and the community. Parades, pageants, festivals, music, and sports are a part of the heritage of Cape Girardeau County. Life can be fast paced and sometimes hectic for citizens willing to participate in the activities of town and country.

The holidays provide the opportunity for young and old alike. During the Easter season, churches honor the day with prayer services, the Baptist Church Passion Play and area Sunrise services. Organizations sponsor Easter Egg hunts in the park for the younger crowd. On Memorial Day, service men and women of the past and present are remembered at honors ceremonies hosted by the local Veterans of Foreign Wars and American Legion organizations. The Fourth of July festivities at the Jackson City Park start off with a 5K race followed by an antique car show, mud volleyball, craft displays, rides for the young children, concert by the municipal band, and a spectacular fireworks display. Fall is highlighted with craft shows, picking apples, football, and Halloween. Several annual events marking the beginning of the Christmas season are the local Dairy Queen parking lot turning into the Optimist Christmas tree lot, the lighting of the Christmas displays in the Courthouse Square, the annual merchants' Christmas Parade bringing Santa Claus to town, Christmas Swim Team tour showcasing area homes, the R2 Madrigal feast, and the live Nativity scene sponsored by the Ministerial Alliance.

Almost every week is a holiday at one church or organization or family reunion as they serve a feast of good company and good food with menus varying from pancakes to kettle beef or chicken and dumplings accompanied with fresh vegetables and thick slices of homemade cakes and pies. Several groups are known for their specialties. The Rotary Club and Junior Rotarians serve Pancake Day and Ham and Beans Day. Immaculate Conception Church has Sausage breakfasts and an annual Turkey Dinner with all the trimmings. The Masons' serve Chili during the Christmas Parade and the DeMolay delight the Homecomer's crowd with home-made ice-cream. Family gatherings may be culinary delights with potluck and basket supper tables laden with casserole dishes and trays filled with salads, fried fish or chicken, ham, slaw, tomatoes and green beans fresh from the garden, iced tea and lemonade, barbecue, baked beans, home-made ice-cream with strawberries, and rolls warm from the oven, or the family may enjoy the simpler fare of hotdogs and buns followed by s'mores cooked over the fire. Either way, good food followed by the good fun of a rousing game of volleyball, horseshoes, badminton or softball makes for moments of caring and sharing that have long been a part of Cape Girardeau County's heritage.

Music fills the air around town with performances by church vocal and bell choirs, and the Jackson Municipal Band. The Jackson High School Music Department sponsors the fall Band Festival, a concert and Madrigal feast at Christmas, and the annual spring Pop Concert. Generations of proud parents and grandparents enjoy annual Christmas and spring programs by the kindergarten and grade school children around the county. More music and festivities abound with the annual Band Festival Parade, Veterans Day Parade, Fourth of July Parade, and Christmas Parade.

For individuals interested in the more historic aspect of the area there are music and tours at Bollinger Mill, tours and displays at the Oliver House Museum, and military re-enactments at the St. Louis and Iron Mountain train. The quiet hills surrounding the visitor's center of Trail of Tears State Park are filled with the history of the Cherokee removal.

At one time or another in Jackson, church socials, picnics, the bowling alley, the skating rink, sporting events, and the movies were all possibilities for young couples looking for a place to socialize. In years past, Jackson had not one but two movie theaters: Palace Theater uptown for year round enjoyment and the Jackson Drive-In for summer fun.

Every month of the year finds sports en-

Young people enjoying the fun at the Jackson Roller Rink during the 1960s. -photo courtesy Mrs. Woody Seabaugh.

St. Paul Lutheran Band members, 1910. G. Siemers, left front with drum. Left to right- front row: L. W. Kasten; A. Roloff; A. Diefenbach; A. Kasten; M. Schloss; C. Boehme; G. Rabold; Wm. Diefenbach. Back row: Wm. Engelmann; Hy. Sievers, R. Sawyer; Hy. Engelmann; Wm. Bruening Sr.; R. C. Kasten. The band practiced on Sunday afternoons at the home of Hy. Engelmann. - photo submitted by Lillian Harmon.

Santa Claus comes to town during the annual Christmas Parade, 1967. Driver of the truck is Warren Wilson of the Jackson Coca-Cola Co.

Hunting, 1894. Left to right: C. Henry Wagner, City Marshal for many years; J. R. Jenkins; Dogs Lou and Sport; John Macke, City Marshall at the time; John Snider, lawyer and later Judge of Common Pleas Court. Photo taken about one mile south of Highway 72 in bottom land of Goose Creek between England Slinkard house and that of Andy Kinder. -photo courtesy of Ken Ruff

thusiasts of all ages from three to eighty involved in some form of sporting activity either as participant or spectator. Local churches, the park department, organizations like the Optimists, the Amateur Athletic Union and others sponsor soccer, basketball, baseball, volleyball, fast-pitch softball, slow-pitch softball, football, and bowling leagues. Other popular activities include skating, running, hunting, fishing, swimming, shooting matches, dog trials, horseshoes, and golf. Tournaments and competitions add even more excitement. Newspaper reports of early parochial school and church leagues demonstrated the ecumenical good-natured competition between denominations.

Until the 1970s sporting teams were usually reserved for men and boys. Women and girls were eager to enjoy the active life. Jackson R2 High School introduced their first women's track team in 1974 followed by women's basketball and cross-country. Now, a whole generation of women has grown up with the opportunity to compete in all leagues.

School sports also carry through the year. Summer camps offered by Jackson R2 or the parochial schools give young people practice and instruction in the proper form for their chosen sports. The seasons criss-cross from cross-country, volleyball, softball, men's soccer, and football in the fall, to basketball, cheerleading, spirit dancing, twirling, and wrestling in winter, to baseball, golf, tennis, women's soccer, and track in the spring.

Long-time residents and newcomers to the area need to take a look at what the area has to offer and join in the fun of the organizations, parades and pageants, area attractions and activities.

ORGANIZATIONS

The Cape Girardeau County 4-H Program

The 4-H Program celebrates its 100th Anniversary in 2002. In 1902 the 4-H program began in response to young people and their need for agricultural education — "Learning by Doing." The idea of starting 4-H clubs cannot be credited to one person but instead is a result of many people's ideas. 4-H clubs initially started as corn clubs for boys and canning clubs for girls. The first two 4-H clubs in Missouri were founded in Iron County in October 1915. The first two boys and girls clubs in Cape Girardeau County were organized in 1919 with a membership of eighty youth. In 1932 Art Siemers and Albert Schabbing organized the first 4-H Club in Cape Girardeau County based on the "community model" club which was a co-ed, multiple project club — the Campster 4-H Club.

The first 4-H emblem was a three-leaf clover, introduced some time between 1907 and 1908. The three "Hs" represented Head, Heart, and Hands. In 1911 the fourth "H" was added representing "Hustle" which was later changed to "Health."

The 4-H pledge was written in 1927. The words "my world" were added to the pledge in 1973 and this has been the only change ever made to the 4-H pledge: "I pledge: My HEAD to clearer thinking, My HEART to greater loyalty, My HANDS to larger service, and My HEALTH to better living, For my club, my community, my country, and my world." While maintaining its strong agricultural tradition, 4-H has diversified into a wide range of subjects. Today, 4-H participants can choose from over 150 project areas. 4-H offers youth opportunities in communications, leadership, career development, livestock, home improvement, and computer technology. During its first 100 years, 4-H changed from an organization primarily concerned with improving agriculture production to one dedicated to the development of young people.

In 2002 the Cape Girardeau County 4-H Program has 243 club members ages 5 - 18 in eleven 4-H clubs. There are 165 adult volunteers who serve as club leaders, assistant club leaders, project leaders, or special events volunteers. The 4-H club membership has fluctuated through the years from a low of approximately 200 members in 10 clubs to a high in the 1970s of approximately 30 4-H clubs with 650 members. The RYO, Rural Youth Organization, was organized in Cape Girardeau County in 1953 as a joint sponsorship between 4-H and Farm Bureau. The RYO later developed into the present day 4-H Junior Leaders Club for 4-H members ages 14 - 21.

The Cape Girardeau County 4-H Program has also been very active in the IFYE (International 4-H Youth Exchange) program. From 1958 to 1990, Cape Girardeau County has sponsored twenty 4-H members who have traveled and lived with 4-H families oversees in countries ranging from the Netherlands, Finland, Denmark, Wales, Switzerland, German, Trinidad and Tobago, Ceylon, India, Australia, and New Zealand. Cape Girardeau County has the highest number of IFYE exchanges from a single county in the state of Missouri.

By Donna Taake

Campster 4-H Club, First in Cape Girardeau County

Campster 4-H club started as a "calf" club for boys, led by Ernest Lihn and Robert Cunningham. The meeting in 1932 was held at 12:30 p.m. at the original red brick, one-room Campster School located along Bloomfield Road. Early members of the 1934 dairy group were Arthur Siemers, L. C. "Bud" Blattner, Harry Siemers, Robert Kiehne, Louis Haman, and a Burford boy.

The next year a sewing club was started for area girls under the leadership of Mrs. George Schwab. Members were: Ruth Schwab, Margaret Geiser, Dorothy Schabbing, Georgia Schwab, Dorothy Schwab, Allene Siemers, Edna Job, Wilma Schrader, Agnes Brown, Alberta Schrader, Celeste Cantrell, Ruby Marie Kiehne, and Rose Schabbing. Each girl made a 4-H dress using the traditional green and white colors. The girls used the same pattern, but in the right size for the wearer.

The two clubs merged, taking the name of the school. They chose to meet the first Friday of each month at Campster School. Other special meetings were held in the homes and at the farms of the members of project leaders.

On June 13, 1982, at 12:30 p.m., a fifty-year basket dinner reunion was held outdoors during a beautiful Sunday afternoon. The old school had been torn down. In a spot just east of the old site, W.P.A. workers built an attractive limestone structure during 1940-1941, including two school rooms, two bathrooms, two cloak rooms, and a large basement with a stage, kitchen, furnace, and pump room. A well was dug to serve the completely modern building. The basement was a wonderful meeting place for the 4-H club, Campster Ladies Club, family gatherings, Mulligan stews and a place to vote.

4-H wasn't all fun. One young girl happened to think that it was time for the meeting and she was responsible to bring the drink...no Kool Aid! There was no time to drive to a store. Her mother opened up canned cherries and strained them. How embarrassing to take cherry juice! Sewing leader, Marie Cunningham, sampled the juice. "Ah, this is

Names of girls, using married changes: left to right; Ruth Schwab, Margaret Geiser Moore, Dorothy Schabbing, Georgia Schwab Bierschwal, Dorothy Schwab Sprenger, Allene Siemers Ainsworth, Edna Job Schabbing, Wilma Schrader Grossheider, Agnes Brown Hente, Alberta Schrader Loos, Celeste Cantrell Watson, Ruby Marie Kiehne Moore, Rose Schabbing Gregg.

Early members of the Campster 4-H Club were the 1934 Dairy Group, left to right, kneeling: Art Siemers, L, C. "Bud Blatner; standing: Harry Siemers, Bob Kiehne and Louis Haman.

Some of the members of the R-II Retired Elementary Teachers, 1998. Left to Right. Front row: Sue Smith, Dorothy Ramsey, Jennie Allgood. Second row: Mabel Smith, Bonnie Ludwig, Elda Ellis, Wilma Grossheider, Kathryn Hagans. Third row: Nina Arnhart, Marcella Green, Dorothy Conner, Virginia Paul, Evelyn Brase, Mary Morton. Back row: Martha Stickler, Miriam Wallenmeyer.

much better than Kool Aid," she said. The young 4-Her was quite relieved. Marie had a sharp eye for detecting mistakes. One member came to the meeting ready to join the skirt to the top. Marie didn't think it looked right. She soon found the darts in the front should have been in the back. She carefully ripped them, and the 4-H member corrected the mistake. The dress won several blue ribbons.

Leader Russel Armstrong would see that 4-H wasn't all work. He would hitch up a wagon to his tractor, pile on some hay and pick up 4-H members and leaders at the school, then away they went the "circle" to Benton Hill Road, to Silver Springs Road, back to Bloomfield Road to the school where marshmallows and wieners were soon roasted. This all took place before I-55 was constructed during the early 1960s, cutting off our "circle," and while traffic was sparse compared to hundreds of cars whizzing by these days.

Campster School closed its doors at the end of the 1965-66 school year. The dwindling enrollment of pupils were taken by bus to town schools. The building was taken over by the school system of the city of Cape Girardeau, and leased to several organizations, including Cerebral Palsy association. Campster 4-H was allowed to sue the basement, and in turn their families kept the lawn mowed. Sadly, membership declined as the young people grew past 4-H age. Some moved away. Those remaining joined the Young Americans 4-H Club, and to this day (year 2002) some of the younger generation of Campster families are members there. The Campster building was sold to the Jerry Cox family some years ago.

Early Campster leaders and council presidents, all working under the guidance of County Extension Agents, in some way, led 4-H members toward receiving honors at fairs and county, state and national competitions. Some of those agents of years past were: Florence Carvin, Helen Hanson, Sydney Karondo, Aleta McDowell, T. P. Head, Roger Wilcoxin, A. D. Arnhart and other. Well known Campster 4-H family names are as follows: James, Kirchdoerfer, Lewis, Siemers, Priest, Koerber, Farrar, Schabbing, Armstrong, Snider, Keller, Etherton, Lihn, Stoll, Eddleman, Hitt, Steimle, Cunningham and Seyer, to mention a few.

The scene has changed, but the 4-H spirit is always there, as was observed Saturday night, March 16, 2002, when present-day interested families gathered at the new extension office at Jackson, Missouri, to celebrate 100 years since the founding of 4-H. There were faces from early days as well as those from the present. It was a memorable event, especially for some of us that were in 4-H years ago. There was an abundance of pictures and mementoes on display to bring back treasured memories. Among those honored during the program was B. W. Harrison, a great benefactor of 4-H work for many years.

By Bonnie Ludwig and Olive Keller

Jackson R-II Retired Elementary Teachers

The Jackson R-II Retired Elementary Teachers Organization was formed in August of 1980. It began as the result of a need to help newly retired teachers adjust to life without school children and yellow buses.

Ruby Reitman was feeling lonely and let down as she realized a new school year was fast approaching. Her husband, John, noticed that she was not herself. One day when he was in Jackson he saw Elsie Jenkins, another retired teacher. He told Elsie that she and her retired teacher friends should get together and perhaps this would help Ruby. Elsie met with Mabel Smith at the Harvest House Restaurant. The two of them discussed plans for a group organization. They proceeded to notify other retired teachers of a forthcoming meeting.

Eight teachers were present at the first called meeting. These charter members were: Mabel Smith, Chairperson; Fay Settle, Secretary-Treasurer; Elsie Jenkins; Ruby Reitman; Viola Neilson; Marguerite Wallis; Marie Kinder; and Bonnie Ludwig. At this time it was decided to hold the meetings at 9:00 a.m. on the fourth Tuesday of each month at a public eating establishment. Of the eight charter members, only two are still living - Mabel Smith and Bonnie Ludwig.

The main objective of the group is social. It is a time of fellowship which holds the group together. The members learn news of interest, send cards and memorials, and learn of pending legislation. In the past, guests have been invited to eat and speak to the group. These were usually the superintendent or principal at the Jackson schools. Other guests have included college students wishing to gather information.

To date the group has met at four restaurants: Harvest House, Ranch House, Jer's, and Woodards. At least twice, they met elsewhere; once at the Lutheran Home and once at Chateau Girardeau. This was one way to bring the meeting to those unable to attend.

At the end of each school year, an invitation is extended to each newly retired elementary teacher to join the organization.

Only two leaders have presided over the meetings: Mabel Smith (first chairperson) and Sue Smith (present chairperson). Their main duties are to telephone and remind each teacher of the meeting once a month. Three Secretary-Treasurers have served: Fay Settle (deceased), Kathryn Hagans (presently living in Springfield, Missouri), and Marcella Green.

The Jackson Municipal Band on the front Courthouse steps, August 31, 1939. Left to right. Row 1: Drum Major J. C. Steinhoff; Director Albert Roloff; Vernon Kasten; Jack Howard; Jake Loos; Jack Obermiller; Melvin Kasten; Herbert Scates; Bernard Schaper; Edward Cracraft. Row 2: Wm. C. Hines; Alvin Bodenstein, Jr.; Paul Mueller, Jr.; Paul Bruening; Edwin Puls; S. C. Cracraft, Jr.; Lynn Illers; Bill Sides; Wilson Steck; Vinyard Kies. Row 3: Leroy McNeely; Hines Wolters; Milde Steck; Leo Roloff; Paul Kasten; Alber Tindal; Gene C. Cracraft; Robert Hartle. Row 4: Clyde Baugh, Jr.; Richard Davis; Carl Sievers; Bill Moll; Wilbert Froemsdorf; Manford Schwab; Jerry Friedrich; Herman Lee Hardy. Row 5: Clarence Neumeyer.

At least twice the members were presented a booklet containing information collected from each one of them. Mabel Smith and Jeanie Allgood gathered and typed the information.

At the present time, the group has over thirty members, both active and inactive.

By Marcella Green, Bonnie Ludwig, and Mabel Smith

Jackson Municipal Band

The Jackson Municipal Band had its beginning in 1920, when the Jackson Chamber of Commerce asked Mr. A. W. Roloff to form a band. The band practiced in Mr. Roloff's woodworking shop using sawhorses for benches. The citizens of Jackson passed a band tax, and the little gazebo on the courthouse lawn was completed in 1932. The gazebo served as the stage for the group until July 1976, when the present and shell, located in the city park, was dedicated. Each year, for their final concert, the band returns to the gazebo, where audience members sit in their cars and honk their horn to show their appreciation. The band has had a total of eight conductors, A. W. Roloff, Leroy Mason, Ed Carson, Richard Partridge, Linton Luetje, Alan Roland, Jim Rhodes, and Nick Leist, who is completing his 34th year as conductor. The membership of the band is made up of primarily adult community members, and also includes a few talented high school students.

David Thompson is President of the Municipal Band Board, Steve Meier is Vice-President, and Pat Schwent serves as Secretary-Treasurer. Other Board Members are Mike Grebing, Kenny Fluegge, and John Thompson. The Jackson Municipal Band provides free concerts every Thursday evening at 8:00 p.m. throughout the summer months. They also provide special concerts for community Memorial Day services, July 4th celebrations, and various other special community functions.

By Nick Leist

A Boy Scout troop from Jackson, Mo at Camp Lewallen, circa 1936. From left: Gene "Rusty" Cracraft, Jack Priest, L.R. Seabaugh, J.T. Allen, Bob Kibler, Paul Mueller, Jr., Bill Kibler.

Jackson American Legion Post #158

During the final days of the Great War (1914-1918), thousands of American servicemen talked of forming a veterans organization and once the fighting stopped that morning, Nov. 11, 1918 at 11 o'clock, the idea was discussed again. When Col. Theodore Roosevelt (son of Teddy Roosevelt) returned to this country, the movement was started among the men who did not go overseas, and on May 18, 1919, 1100 veteran delegates assembled in St. Louis. The group adopted the name "The American Legion," and proposed to hold a national convention. It was at this convention that the American Legion was officially formed with President Woodrow Wilson and General "Black Jack" Pershing declared members.

Locally, on Sept. 13, 1919, a large number of people, including a strong delegation of veterans, met at Pocahontas for the purpose of organizing an American Legion Post. The organization was completed after a prolonged and exciting meeting which even continued the following week. The veterans who had returned from service were acquainted with some of the conditions that had prevailed in the area during the war and felt that some explanations and promises were due from some of the local citizens.

The meeting was held in the town hall at Pocahontas which was packed with close to 500 people. When the meeting was called to order, several names were called to see if they were present. Several were missing, so a committee of veterans was appointed to go and extend a "special invitation" to those person to attend. A number of persons were questioned as to their loyalty and patriotism. People were asked to discontinue in their business places the use of the German language.

The following were elected officers of the Pocahontas Caldwell-Snider Post 115: Paul Kaiser, Commander; Claud Devenport, Assistant Commander; Paul McNeely, Secretary; and Linus Morton, Treasurer. The post was short-lived, and in 1923 the Caldwell-Snider Post 115 of Pocahontas sold its meeting hall to Fred Lichtenegger. At the same time, Oak Ridge attempted to organize a post.

A week after the organization of the Pocahontas Post, a meeting was held on Sept. 18, 1919 in the courthouse in Jackson to organize an American Post. Here too, a large group attended with a delegation of the Pocahontas group in attendance to show the Jackson veterans how to conduct a "quizzing bee." The meeting was called to order by J. Frank Caldwell. C. W. Knox was elected chairman and he called upon Major Warren Mabrey to give the address. He stated the cardinal principles of the Legion:

• There must be but one flag – the Stars and Stripes;

• There must be one language and that language must be the one the Constitution was written in; and

• There must be but one loyalty and that to America.

Here too at the Jackson meeting, a number of people were questioned as to their patriotism and the use of another language.

The Jackson Post was named in honor of two men from the area who made the supreme sacrifice—Clarence G. W. Altenthal and Clark Adams Joerns—the Altenthal-Joerns Post 158. Officers were: C. W. Knox, Commander; Harry Williams, Vice Commander; Lawrence Morton, Adjutant; Ryland Short, Finance; Lemon Gladish, Historian; and Ed Slack, Chaplain.

Jackson Post 158 continued in 1919 and 1920. However, due to a general lack of interest, the Post did not meet again until 1924 at which time, under the leadership of C. W. Knox, Roscoe Pierce (Jackson Superintendent of Schools form 1922-1928), and C. W. Medley, the Post reorganized and has continued to the present with more than 700 members.

Commanders Of Jackson American Legion Post 158

In the 84 years since the National American Legion has been formed (1919), it has had 76 commanders. During the years 1921, 1922 and 1923, there was not an American Legion post in Jackson.

1919-Carrol Knox; 1920-Robert Goza; 1921, 1922, 1923, 1924-Roscoe Pierce; 1925-C. W. Medley*; 1926-C. W. Medley*; 1927-Lawrence Snider; 1928-Frank Hines; 1929-Paul Mueller; 1930-Joe Myer*; 1931-Ryland Short; 1932-S. T. Daley; 1933-Lyman Steele; 1934-S. C. Cracraft; 1935-C. W. Medley*; 1936-Hy. A. Illers; 1937-George Seybold; 1938-Floyd McManus; 1939-Manning Davis; 1940-Louis Mantz; 1941-E. L. Crader; 1942-Allen Reed; 1943-Eldon Roberts; 1944-J. R. Henderson; 1945-Joe Myer*; 1946-J. R. Kibler; 1947-Osler Statler; 1948-Cotton Meyer; 1949-Glenn Lewis; 1950-Perry Grindstaff; 1951-Milde Steck; 1952-Gene C. Cracraft; 1953-Gilbert E. Sewing; 1954-Paul A. Muller; 1955-Hubert Seabaugh; 1956-Bill Schloss; 1957-W. E. Miller; 1958-J. W. Poe; 1959-Marvin F. Proffer; 1960-Manford Schwab; 1961-Leonard Moll; 1962-Oscar Hoffmeister; 1963-Kermit Nations; 1964-Nelson Meyer; 1965-Leonard Dambach; 1966-Milton Nitch; 1967-Louis A. Loos; 1968-Joe W. Smith; 1969-Earl F. Clifton; 1970-Carl A. Barrett; 1971-Robert B. Beissink; 1972-Lloyd Law; 1973-Verlin Puchbauer; 1974-H. Jim Schnurbusch; 1975-Glen H. Thompson; 1976-Vincent H. Schwartz; 1977-Troy Hartle; 1978-Roy Woeltje; 1979-Jerry H. Hinkebein; 1980-Charles P. Hutson; 1981-Albert J. Beussink; 1982-Robert G. Kurre; 1983-Rupert F. Fiehler; 1984-Donald K. Lewis; 1985-Marvin H. Meier; 1986-Thomas F. Sperling; 1987-E. Glenn Bollinger; 1988-Albert S. Hines; 1989-Harold E. Landgraf; 1990-Harlan E. Siebert; 1991-Jim Nelson; 1992-Raymond Willer; 1993-Tom O'Loughlin; 1994-Leon Laurentius; 1995-Mike Proctor; 1996-Milford P. Kirn; 1997-Norman H. Sebastian; 1998-Kacl Latimer; 1999-Robert L. Hartle; 2000-Keith Seabaugh; 2001-Bill Sillivan and 2002-Richard Augilar. *Two people have had multiple terms; C. W. Medley, three times, and Joe Myer, two terms.

The 1999 Jackson American Legion Post 158 Honor Guard

Front row from the left, Dale Smith, Boyd Summers, Glen Bollinger, Wilbert Ruesler, Virgil Whitener, Oscar Hoffmeister, Dale Hartle, Jack Lattimer, Vencent Schwartz and Jim Nelson; second row are Roy Robins, Carlton Meyer, Bob Beussink, Harold Landgraf, Norman Sebastian, Milford Kirn, Milton Nitsch, Jerry Hinkebein, Albert Beussink and Bob Hartle; third row are Richard Aguilar, Paul Myer, Lou Crites, Tom O'Laughlin, Charles Hutson, Joe Smith, Leon Laurentius, Harlan Siebert, Bill Sullivan and Mike Proctor. Not pictured are Don Darnell, Mike Hyson, Rupert Fiehler and Don Lewis.

Members of the Jackson American Legion Post 158, ca. 1920

American Legion Auxiliary Jackson Unit #158

The veterans organized soon after the end of WWI. They gathered in Paris, France creating the first American post. Subsequently the veterans of each community all over the United States formed their own posts. The Legion soon found the need of forming an auxiliary. The Legion sent out more than 200 invitations to wives of veterans, setting the date of Oct. 19, 1937.

The headquarters were in a hall on South High Street (over Blicks) and they were willing to share the hall with the Auxiliary. Bathrooms had been installed along the southeast corner and a bandstand was built on the west wall. Local musicians provided the dance music.

It was a custom in Jackson to serve the local clubs to raise money to contribute to worthy causes such as the Red Cross, youth programs, scholarships, the less fortunate, and Boys and Girls State.

There was no cooking stove. When the Auxiliary was chosen, the food was prepared in the home, brought to the hall and served. The Auxiliary members complained because carrying the food had become a burden.

The post bought the present home when the Jackson Implement Company moved. A new kitchen was built and stocked with equipment. The other hall was abandoned on South High Street for the floor was certainly unsafe, especially at dances.

The night of organization, only about 15 eligible ladies came. The first order of business was to elect a chairperson. Margaret Henderson was chosen and the following officers were elected: President Helen (Mrs. C. C.) Conrad, Vice President Margaret (Mrs. J. Ryland) Short, Second Vice President Margaret (Mrs. J. R.) Henderson, Secretary-Treasurer Dorothy (Mrs. R. W.) Illers, Chaplain Claire (Mrs. Herbert) Scates, Historian Ima (Mrs. George) Seybold and Sergeant-of-Arms Ora (Mrs. Lyman) Steele.

It was voted to hold the membership open for one year for mothers, wives and daughters of veterans.

The charter members are: Malinda Allen; Irene Beattie; Olinda Birk; Anita Bodenstein; Rose Bollinger; Louise J. Caldwell, Ruth Clingsmith; Helen Conrad; Berniece M. Cracraft; Ethel G. Davis; Grace Dickerson; Maudree Dickerson; Frieda Gerecke; Nadine Goza; Ella Hahs; Margaret Henderson; Lena G. Henderson; Comfort P. Heyde; Grace Hines; Lauia Hohler; Eda Hopkins; Hilda Huckstep; Dorothy C. Illers; Nina W. Illers; Hattie Kasten; Lola Klaproth; Mary Lape; Lennie Mayfield; Bessie McGuire; Pearl McLain; Alma McManus; Hester Miller; Minnie Paar; Coral Probst; Meta Probst; Bertha Puhbauer; Elizabeth W. Reed; Eula Roberts; Claire Scates; Mary Shelton; Margaret Short; Sadie Slinkard; Ima Seybold; Maggie Smith; Rika Smith; Mary Lewis Steele; Ora Steele; Velma M. Stickler; Elsie B. Tibbs; Katherine Tuschoff; Leona Voshage; Lillian Wagner; Mabel Waller; Nona Wilkinson; Chloree Williams and Mary Jo Williams

Mrs. Dorothy Illers, a charter member of the American Legion Auxiliary Unit #158, compiled this history in the year 2000 and it was turned in to historian Betty Myer on March 23, 2000.

American Legion Auxiliary Supports Numerous Causes

American Legion Auxiliary Unit #158 of Jackson was organized on Oct. 19, 1937. The first officers were Helen Conrad, President; Margaret B. Short, First Vice President; Margaret F. Henderson, Second Vice President; Dorothy C. Illers, Secretary-Treasurer; Claire Scates, Chaplain; Ora Steele, Sergeant-at-Arms; and Ima Seybold, Historian. At present the Unit has 319 members, with a goal of 335 members, said Malinda Hope, Unit Historian, and a charter member of the Unit. The Unit belongs to the 14th District and is the largest unit in the district.

To be a member of the American Legion Auxiliary, a woman must be a mother, wife, sister, daughter or granddaughter of a member of the American Legion, or of a man or woman, living or dead, who served in WWI, WWII, the Korean conflict, or the Vietnam era.

American Legion Auxiliary Unit #158 is a very active organization with many service projects throughout the year. The Unit awards scholarships to graduating Jackson High School seniors each year, as well as supports the district with scholarship funds. It also sponsors trips to Girls State for selected Jackson High School girls each year, where they have a chance to learn about and participate in a working government system.

The Unit also supports many community organizations, including the Muscular Dystrophy Association, Multiple Sclerosis Society, Community Chest, the American Cancer Society and the American Red Cross.

Another program the Auxiliary helps sponsor is the annual Christmas Gift Shop at the Veterans Administration Hospital in Poplar Bluff. The Unit donates gifts and members volunteer to assist in the operation of the gift shop where patients may "shop" for their families. All packages are wrapped and can be mailed at no charge to the veteran patients.

The Unit sponsors bingo parties at the hospital as well, donating money for prizes and fruit for refreshments. They also hold bingo parties every month at the American Legion Hall in Jackson.

The Auxiliary holds a family Christmas dinner and party each year, and prepares and serves the annual American Legion birthday banquet each March.

One of the biggest projects of the year for the Auxiliary is Poppy Day. The American Legion Auxiliary adopted the National Poppy Program in 1921. "By wearing the poppy," Mrs. Hope said, "one shows he remembers the war dead and honors the living servicemen." We have just ordered 4,000 poppies to be distributed on Poppy Day in Jackson. The Auxiliary members distribute the memorial poppies, made by veterans in hospitals and workshops during the month of May.

They also organize queen candidates for the annual Jackson Homecomers celebration.

Present officers are Verna Lee Nitsch, President; Geneva Schwartz, First Vice President; Rosalee Sides, Second Vice President; Ruby Friedrich, Secretary; Shirley Kessler, Treasurer; Marjorie Grindstaff, Chaplain; Dorothy Siebert, Sergeant-at-Arms; and Malinda Hope, Historian. The organization meets the first Tuesday of each month and dues are $10.00 per year.

In July 1990, the Missouri State Convention of the American Legion Auxiliary met in Cape Girardeau. This history was compiled on Feb. 10, 1990 by Mrs. Malinda Hope (a charter member of the American Legion Auxiliary (now deceased) and her daughter, Mrs. Rosalie Moeller.

First row, seated, left to right, Rosalie Moeller, Betty Myer, Rosalie Sides, Lavern Bangert and Daisy Long. Second row, seated left to right, Bonnie Smith, Ida Ruesler and Verna Lee Nitsch. Third row, standing, left to right, Norma Proctor, Vickie Moore, Marjorie Grindstaff, Naomi McClard, Marie Hinkebein and Dora Mantel

Jackson Chamber of Commerce History

The Jackson Chamber of Commerce grew out of an earlier Commercial Club, an organization of merchants active in the city in the early 1900s. The Chamber of Commerce was chartered by the state of Missouri in 1955, with a reported membership of 86 members. Membership has steadily increased to our current strength of 385.

The first Chamber office was opened and staffed with a full time secretary in April of 1974 at the intersection of Highways 61 and 25. In October 1984 the Chamber of Commerce purchased the old Post Office building at 125 East Main (our current location). In 1998 the city of Jackson and the Chamber of Commerce entered into an agreement to assist in funding of the Chamber for Economic Development and to hire an Executive Director to manage the day to day operations. A valuable partnership was formed and continues to flourish between the city and the Chamber.

The Chamber's mission is to serve and promote the business and civic interests of the Jackson area. Some of our objectives include:

Advance commercial, industrial, retail, agriculture, educational, civic, and other interests in the city of Jackson and surrounding area.

Provide a forum for members to meet and discuss common concerns.

Promote expanded education for membership, keep members current on new and ever changing technology and consumer needs.

Assist existing commercial, industrial, retail, and agricultural community to meet current and expanding needs.

Promote the Jackson area as the place to live, work, and play.

The Jackson Chamber of Commerce has grown considerably since 1955, as has the community of Jackson. We strive to keep our membership up to date through our web site, weekly memos, and monthly newsletters. We will continue to provide a quality service for all concerned. The Jackson Chamber of Commerce is the organization to belong to if you want the best return on your investment. We don't just do things, we make things happen.

John Guild Chapter, Jackson, Mo.

Guild Chapter (changed to John Guild Chapter in November 1949) National Society Daughters of the American Revolution was organized March 16, 1914, at Jackson, MO. "God, Home, and Country" is the motto of the National Society. The organization was formed "to perpetuate the memory and spirit of the men and women who achieved American Independence."

There were 16 charter members; they were: Miss Mabel Henderson, Mrs. Edward Howard (Nettie Ruff), Mrs. J. W. Hunter (Ada Alsop), Miss Winifred Jones, Mrs. A. H. Kneibert (Anna Harris), Miss Adelaide LaPierre, Miss Martine B. LaPierre, Miss Mary LaPierre, Miss Christine B. Medley, Miss Conway Medley, Miss Elizabeth L. Medley, Miss Frederica Medley, Miss Ruth Medley, Miss Elizabeth Ranney, Miss Gayle Ranney and Miss Berenice Williams. The first Regent was Miss Winifred Jones. Eight of the Charter members were descendants of John Guild. Those descending from other Revolutionary soldiers or patriots were Ada Alsop Hunter from Col. George Taylor; Winifred Jones from Jesse Dean; Amy Nell Henderson, Nettie Howard, and Anna Kneibert from Robert Harris, Jr.; and Elizabeth and Gayle Ranney from Stephen Ranney.

John Guild Membership - 2001

Martha Adams (Alexander Beggs), Sally Adams (Jacob Van Metre), Donna Allen (Capt. Rudolph Conrad), Ethel Baker (Col. Frederick C. Hambright), Carole Baugh (Capt. John Ware), Anne Brock (William Godsey), Mildred Brown (Capt. Henry Whitener), Suzanna Clippard (Thomas Costner), Dorothy Conrad (Henry Bollinger), Cheryl Cook (George Perkins, Peter Hockenberry, Pvt. Lambert Van Dyke, Henry Van Dyke, Pvt. Patrick Cassidy, Pvt. John Shirley), Kim Crimmins (Absalom Blair), Doris Davault (Thomas Costner), Edith Davidson (Samuel Greer/Sylvester Greer), Elizabeth Farmer (Capt. Timothy Langdon, Rev. John Guild, Henry Bollinger), Eleanor Fenner (John Stephen Hill), Wanda Fitzpatrick (Simon Poe, Moses Jones, Enos Randol), Pam Friedrich (William Uriah Brock), Juliet French (Capt. Timothy Landon, Rev. John Guild, Henry Bollinger), Nancy Gillette (John Hunt), Clara Nell Griffith (James Eubank), Jan Hankinson (Thomas Humphry), Becky Heuer (Thomas Wicker, Sr.), Olga Hill (John Stephen Hill), Mary Ada Hopper (Alexander Beggs), Martha Howell (John Stephen Hill), Linda Hutson

The John Guild Chapter of the Daughters of the American Revolution, 1989. Sitting, left to right: Mrs. Billie Sander; Mrs. Doris Davault; Mrs. Cheryl Cook; Mrs. Mildred Brown (Regent); Mrs. Carmen Below. Standing, first row: Mrs. Stacia Kasten, Mrs. Pat Puls, Miss Ethel Baker, Mrs. Mable Sample; Miss Martha Wagner; Mrs. Dorothy Illers; Mrs. Terri Tomlin; Mrs. Dorothy Griffy. On steps, beginning at bottom left: Mrs. Kim Crimmins; Mrs. Nancy Gillette; Mrs. Gretchen Birk; Mrs. Olga Hill; Mrs. Ada Kurre; Mrs. Yanna Crites; Mrs. Becky Heuer; Mrs. Marjorie Swan; Mrs. Alma Lee Slinkard; Mrs. Shirley Young; Mrs. Pam Johnson; Mrs. Esther Wagner and Mrs. Juliet French

(Capt. Amos Byrd), Dorothy Illers (Thomas Wicker, Sr.), Mary Kate Johnson (Capt. Timothy Langdon, Ambrose Gaines, Rev. John Guild, Benjamin Frizel, Johannes Hunsaker, Henry Bollinger), Pam Johnson (Thomas English), Patsy Johnson (James Marks), Stacia Kasten (Wilson Hunt), Morgan Lake (Constantine O'Neal), Delma Loftis (William Magill Jr., Michael Holt, Samuel Lochart), Mary Meyer (Walter Whitney), Marybelle Mueller (Christian Butz), Adelaide Parsons (Richard Bull), Joyce Peerman (Anthony Dibrell), Carolyn Peterson (Robert Harris, Lt. Henry Heath, Kern Henderson, Moses Shelby, Elisha C. Smart), Pat Puls (Capt. Henry Whitener), Francis Reid (Christian Shuman/Schumann), Carol Rene' Robinson (Alexander Beggs), Elizabeth Ross (Simon Poe), Neva Kay Ross (Simon Poe), Susan Ross (Simon Poe), Mable Sample (Col. Frederick C. Hambright), Marsha Miller Sander (Stephen Mayfield), Rosamund Sander (Green Spurrier), Ruby Schrader (Ebenezer Snow), Kelly Lynn Shields (1st Lt. Robert Mosley), Judith Sneathen (Pvt. Nicholas Caillot), Earlene Sokolowski (Capt. Rudolph Conrad), Erma Statler (John Call, Joseph Mackey), Marjorie Swan (Capt. Randolph Conrad, Johannes Casper Schell), Terri Tomlin (Mitchel Fleming), Martha Vandivort (Daniel Sanford), Lisa Vogel (Richard Bull), Jane Wagner (John Stephen Hill), Martha Wagner (John Henry), Shirley Young (Capt. Rudolph Conrad, Johannes Casper Schell), and LouAnn Zoffuto (Obediah Hooper, Sr.).

JOHN GUILD DISTRICT OFFICERS, STATE OFFICERS, AND STATE CHAIRMEN

Southeast District Directors. Mrs. C. M. (Ruth) McWilliams (1948-49), Mrs. William H. (Doris) Davault (1982-1984), Mrs. James R. (Carmen) Below (1984-1986), Mrs. Donald (Cheryl) Cook (1986-1988), Mrs. Michael (Terri) Tomlin (1996-1998), Mrs. Lloyd (Shirley) Young (1998-2000).

State Officers. Mrs. William H. (Doris) Davault, Corresponding Secretary (1989-1992); Mrs. Donald (Cheryl) Cook, Historian (1992-1994), Corresponding Secretary (1994-1996); Mrs. Stanley (Pam) Johnson, Historian (1998-2000); Mrs. Lloyd (Shirley) Young, Organizing Secretary (2000-2002), Corresponding Secretary (2002-2004).

State Chairman, Speakers, and Coordinators. Mrs. David (Lynn) Moll, Motion Picture, Radio and Television (1983-1985); Mrs. William H. (Doris) Davault, Membership (1984-1989); Mrs. Donald (Cheryl) Cook and Mrs. Davault, National Committee Missouri Transportation and Safety (1987); Mrs. James R. (Carmen) Below, Good Citizen (1986-1989); Mrs. Donald Cook and Mrs. Lloyd Young, Conference Co-Chairmen (1990-1991); Mrs. Donald Cook, Page Chairman (1989-1992), Magazine Chairman (1996-1998), National DAR Speakers' Staff (1995-1998) and (1998-2000), National Vice Chairman South Central Division Magazine (1995-1998), DAR Services – Veteran Patients (1998-2000), Flag of the U.S.A. Chairman (2000-2002); Mrs. Stanley Johnson, Junior Membership (1992-1994), Chairman of Pages (1994-1996), National Vice Chairman Magazine (1995-1998), Honor Roll Chairman (1997-1998), National and State Chairman Coordinator (2000-2002); Mrs. Lloyd Young, Columbus Quincentennial Chairman (1989-1993), Commemorative Events (1993-1996); Mrs. Charles P. (Linda) Hutson, Jr. Co-Chairman Missouri Church and Cemetery (2000-2002).

REGENTS OF JOHN GUILD CHAPTER

Miss Winifred Jones, Mrs. J. W. Hunter, Miss Winifred Jones, Mrs. D. C. Hope, Miss Gayle Ranney, Mrs. D. C. Hope, Miss Conway Medley, Mrs. T. E. Wilson, Mrs. W. J. Gammon, Mrs. J. E. Schmuke, Miss Martine LaPierre, Mrs. C. L. Grant, Mrs. W. H. Wagner, Miss Frederica Medley, Mrs. W. A. Heyde, Jr., Mrs. Paul A. Mueller Sr., Miss Irene Wilson, Mrs. C. M. McWilliams, Mrs. H. G. Cooke, Mrs. J. R. Henderson, Miss Christine Medley, Mrs. J. D. Mackey, Mrs. Paul Mueller Sr., Mrs. Eugene Wilcox, Mrs. J. R. Short, Mrs. J. V. Priest, Mrs. Paul Mueller Jr., Mrs. George Walker, Mrs. C. M. McWilliams, Mrs. J. R. Henderson, Mrs. L. H. Schrader, Mrs. O. S. Hartsfield, Mrs. William H. Davault, Mrs. James R. Below, Miss Mary H. Schmuke, Mrs. David Moll, Mrs. Donald Cook, Mrs. Shelby Brown, Mrs. Van Puls, Mrs. Richard Wagner, Mrs. Donald Cook, Mrs. Michael Tomlin, Mrs. Stanley Johnson, Mrs. Lloyd Young, Mrs. Charles P. Hutson Jr.

The objectives of the DAR are historic preservation, promotion of education, and patriotic endeavor. These objectives are carried out with the following activities and programs: (1) Constitution Week is celebrated every September with speakers on the Constitution and framers of the Constitution; (2) National defense reports at monthly meetings and a yearly program by speakers; (3) Scholarships (certificates/monetary awards) presented to outstanding Junior and Senior High School history students at Jackson, Woodland (Marble Hill), and Meadow Heights; (4) Good Citizen pen, certificate, and monetary gift to Jackson High School senior; (5) Gold ROTC medal and certificate to a Senior Air Force Cadet, Southeast Missouri State University, since 1973; (6) Participated 100% with monetary gifts toward state and President General's projects including historical preservation of state and national DAR buildings; (7) Slide programs on "Making Local History Live" to organizations and elementary students; (8) Marked graves of Revolutionary War heroes as well as deceased John Guild members graves; (9) Gifts presented each year to the Poplar Bluff Veterans' Hospital, and Veterans Home, Cape Girardeau, as well as members volunteering at Veterans Home; (10) Monetary gifts for DAR and Indian Schools; (11) Good Citizenship Medals to outstanding students; (12) Books to public library as memorials to deceased members; (13) Family histories and genealogy books to local, state, and national libraries; (14) Patriotic float in Jackson's 4th of July celebration on their 175th birthday; and (15) Chapter participated in commemorative events.

Immaculate Conception Church Quilting Club

Quilters from Immaculate Conception Church have been stitching together beautiful quilts and long-lasting friendships since the 1930s. Initially, most of the quilting took place in the homes, with Edna Hawthorne coordinating the effort. During the 1960s, with the encouragement of Reverend E. G. Stolle, the ladies formed the Immaculate Conception Church Quilting Club. During the 1960s and early 1970s, the group produced more than 100 quilts per year when the club sponsored the Quilt-of-the-Week fundraiser for church and school projects.

In 2002, people continue to appreciate the beauty of a hand-quilted quilt. Since fewer people seem to have the time or patience for hand stitching, there is a waiting list to get a top quilted. As in the past, there are often two quilts "in the frame" in an effort to keep up with demand. The time required to finish a quilt has increased because more families use queen and king size beds. Approximately 120 hours are needed to quilt an average queen size quilt, providing ample time for a generous amount of sharing and caring among friends.

The quilters also enjoy sharing with the parish. In 2000, their earnings purchased a large outdoor Nativity scene which enhances the church's and community's Christmas spirit. Today's 12 members quilt tops for individuals and supply the quilts needed for the support of church activities such as the annual church Turkey Dinner, St. Ann's Craft Fair, and the Immaculate Conception Home and School Spring Fling. *Donated by friend of the IC Quilters*

1990 quilters around the "big frame:" Marguerite Elfrink; (unidentified); Viola Peak; Frieda Scheffer; Mary Weisbrod and Evelyn Friedrich

1990 members of the quilting group relax after finishing a quilt. Seated left to right are: Viola Peak; Louise Hulshof; Geneva Schwartz; Dora Koehler; Viola Randol; and Evelyn Friedrich. Standing are Frieda Scheffer and Opal Laurentius

Quilters 2000, seated left to right: Frieda Scheffer, Dora Koehler, Loretta Arnzen, Monica Lewis, Marie Hinkebein, Irene Stoverink, Gladys Thompson

The Jackson Heritage Association

The Jackson Heritage Association is a not-for-profit corporation organized in 1977 by a group of citizens interested in historic preservation. The organization's mission is "to function as an historical club; to conduct a civic organization for the common benefit of the members and the community; to develop, locate, preserve, acquire, maintain, and manage real and personal property in the Jackson, MO area for the benefit of the community and future generations; to promote respect and appreciation for historical buildings, landmarks, places, and things."

Primarily, the Association came into being to accept responsibility for completing the restoration of the Oliver House Museum. In 1976 the Jackson Industrial Development Corporation transferred the deed of the Oliver House to the Jackson Heritage Association. The Association then proceeded with the monumental task of replacing floors damaged by termites, repairing fallen plaster, repairing and re-glazing 29 windows, opening and repairing fireplaces, and providing heating and air-conditioning. Community support came in many forms. People were willing to donate labor, materials, money and their knowledge and expertise. In December of 1981, the house was opened for a Christmas tour with only the parlor completely renovated and furnished. This was done to acquaint local citizens with the project so they could see what had been accomplished and what still needed to be done.

In 1985 the Bennett-Tobler-Ferguson-Oliver House was placed on the National Register of Historic Places for the significance of its Federal-style architecture and the importance of its early occupants. Bernard Ferguson engineered and installed the first telephone in Cape Girardeau County, which connected the house to his father's business. In 1877 the line was extended to Cape Girardeau and became the first long distance telephone line in Missouri. In 1881 Robert Burett and Marie Watkins Oliver purchased the home. Mr. Oliver had practiced law in Jackson since 1878 and was elected to serve as Prosecuting Attorney in the same year. The next year he was elected to the Missouri State Senate. The senator also gained prominence for his service on the Board of Curators for the University of Missouri at Columbia and was among those who were instrumental in the establishment of the Little River Drainage District in southeast Missouri. Several distinguished guests visited the house during Mr. Oliver's political career including William Jennings Bryan and David R. Francis. Marie Oliver would be hailed as "Missouri's Betsy Ross" when she, along with Mary Kochititsky, designed and made the first and only official state flag.

Just as the early members of the Jackson Heritage Association labored to insure a sturdy foundation for the Oliver House, the present membership is working to insure its future by expanding the endowment fund and increasing community awareness. Membership in the Association is open to anyone interested in the preservation of our local heritage. While the Oliver House Museum has been the highest priority of the Jackson Heritage Association, other projects have been undertaken in the researching and recording of Jackson's history with the Jackson History Book, and the collection, identification, and preservation of old Jackson pictures and photographs.

Marie Oliver, 1911.

R. B. Oliver, 1909

The Oliver House Museum, Jackson, MO

Jackson Heritage Association Officers and Board of Directors - 2002

Pat Fosse, president
Cathi Stoverink, vice-president
Bonnie Macke, secretary
Carlton Meyer, treasurer
Phyllis Seabaugh
Vicki Lane
Vicki Abernathy
Kevin Schearf
Debbie Schearf
Mike Hess
Grace Wille
Barbara Lohr
Kyle Mabuce
Bernard Schaper, director emeritus
Justin Gibbs, youth representative

JACKSON MEMORIAL VETERANS OF FOREIGN WARS AUXILIARY #10495

Jackson Memorial VFW Auxiliary #10495 is an organization that aids veterans and veterans' families and promotes patriotism.

The VFW Post and Auxiliary are co-sponsors of the Veterans of All Wars Memorial located in Brookside Park, Jackson, MO. Auxiliary members assist in displaying flags of deceased veterans on several holidays throughout the year. Auxiliary members also assist the Jackson Park Department with upkeep of the flower gardens in the area of the Memorial.

Auxiliary members volunteer at the Missouri Veterans Home in Cape Girardeau. Wings A, B, and C at the home are decorated by the Auxiliary for major holidays. Tray favors are made for most holidays for the veterans. The Auxiliary has "adopted" several veterans who reside at the home and also provides Christmas gifts for indigent veterans. Members assist the veterans with bingo monthly, take veterans shopping as needed, donate supplies regularly, and pay for breakfast on Veterans Day for those vets able to attend. Each year the Auxiliary presents scholarship checks in the amount of $200.00 to one to two graduating Jackson High School students. The Auxiliary donates flags to area schools and other non-profit groups.

The Auxiliary contributes to nationally-sponsored VFW Auxiliary programs, some of which are cancer research, the hospital fund, the National Home for children of veterans, the Voice of Democracy speech contest, the Missouri past president scholarship fund, Junior Girls fund and Health and Happiness fund.

The Auxiliary uses emergency funds to aid needy community families. We have placed several fire alarms in the homes of elderly people and have donated funds to the Police Department and Fire Department. We donate regularly to the community food pantry. We have raised funds from tasting bees, food stands, raffle ticket sales, yard sales, an auction and Best Choice labels.

We assist the Post by helping with the Veterans Day breakfast, selling buddy poppies annually, and many other functions. We participate in community parades. We are responsible for conducting the POW/MIA walk and program and also the Loyalty Day program conducted at the Memorial.

The Auxiliary was organized Jan. 21, 1990, with the following officers presiding:
President Jean Latimer
Senior Vice President Dorothy Siebert
Junior Vice President Evelyn Brase
Secretary Fern Shultz
Treasurer Becky Klob
The 2001-2002 officers are as follows:
President Barbara Slinkard
Senior Vice President Betty Wiggins
Junior Vice President Rosemary Smith
Secretary Bernice Haynes
Treasurer Becky Klob

JACKSON MEMORIAL VFW AUXILIARY POST 10495

Ann Adams
Myrtle Allen
Laverne Bangert*
Ruth Bartlett
Christine Becker*
Cherry Sue Birk*
Shirley Bishop
Dorothy Blackman*
Evelyn Brase*
Juanita Brazel
Barbara Burnette
Sandy Cromer
Marjorie Deneke
Lois Edwards*
Maxine Fluegge
Darlene Fluegge
Lucille Frederick
Coletta Garland
Sheila Garland*
Louise Getts
Shelby Gilmore*
Laverne Gross
Betty H. Hahs
Betty L. Hahs*
Bernice Haynes
Pat Hill*
Helen Humes*
Joann Johannes*
Virginia Jones*
Kim King*
Margaret King
Becky Klob*
Inez Knott
Margaret Kracke
Jean Latimer*
Virginia Latimer
Ceil Law
Bernita Leadbetter
JoNelle Lingo*
Mildred Lohmann*
Peggy Luehrs
Freda Madison
Lou Maevers*
Cecilia Margrabe*
Carol McCauley*
LaVerne McGuire*
Darlene McLemore
Wanda Mouser*
Betty Myer
Kathryn Nations
Pauline Nitsch*
Marilyn Nussbaum
Edna Peetz
Betty Rampley*
Mary Renne
Cheryl Rhodes
Debra Riehn
Erna Schattauer
Hazel Schloss*
Fern Shultz*
Dorothy Siebert*
Gladys Siebert*
Mabel Skinner
Barbara Slinkard*
Rosemary Smith
Edna Sneathen
Lucreda Spears
Katherine Stueve
Mary Talley*
Roberta Ulrich
Martha Vandivort
Vera Wagner
Judy Wendel*
Betty Wiggins
Grace Wille*
Gwen Winningham
*Charter members

Memorial to Veterans of All Wars rests on terrace greens at Brookside Park, Jackson, MO.

Bethel #60 Job's Daughters

The International Order of Job's Daughters was founded in 1920 by Ethel T. Wead Mick. The organization is open to girls between the ages of 11 and 20 who have a link to a Master Mason. The teachings of the organization are based on the 42nd Chapter, 15th verse of the Book of Job that tells us "In all the land were no women found so fair as the daughters of Job, and their father gave them inheritance among their brethren." The organization strives to develop poise, self-confidence, leadership and friendship amongst the girls. Its objective is to teach respect, commitment, patriotism, reverence, love and service to the members. In 1969 Rev. Ronald Wood brought up the idea of having a Bethel in Jackson. The group received permission from the members of Excelsior Lodge 441 to meet in their temple.

Girls with Masonic relationships were visited, petitions were filled out, and on a cold snowy day, the 11th of January, 1970, the Grand Guardian Council of Missouri, International Order of Job's Daughters instituted a new Bethel in Jackson, MO. The ceremonies were held in the Jackson High School gymnasium, as the lodge hall was too small to accommodate the crowd. The following girls were initiated that day.

Karen Borgfield
Susan Brown
Pat Cracraft
Susan Craiglow
Mary Kay Craiglow
Sally Crites
Susan Davault
Sherry Davenport
Kathy DeClue
Glenda Estes
Linda Estes
Beverly Fowler
Jennifer Friedrich
Manota Friedrich
Karen Gohn
Terri Gohn
Jane Hahs
Connie Harris
Paula Hawkins
Nancy Henderson
Andrea Hughes
Elizabeth Hughes
Linda Kasten
Wendy Litzenfelner
Pamela Macke
Carol Masterson
Brenda Meyer
Debby Montgomery
Kathy Morton
Doris Neilson
Donna Neilson
Jeanna Palmer
Susan Palmer
Mary Beth Prill
Marian Proffer
Carol Sander
Patricia Sander
Bonita Seabaugh
Susan Thompson
Clarinda Unger
Lanette Unger
Suzanna Unger
Debbie Williamson
Lois Williamson
Patricia Wood
Karen Wright

Four others soon joined the group to become charter members. They were Jane Niswonger, Laura O'Neill, Sherri Ulrich and Lynn Wilcox. On May 23, 1970, the Bethel received its charter and officially became Bethel #60. Since that time Bethel #60 has been an active organization in activities at the local and state level. Several of the members have served as appointed officers on the Grand (state) level.

The girls currently attend Mini Session, which is held in the spring and is a more informal event, and Grand Session, which is held in June and is the regular business session of the Grand Bethel. The daughters participate in raising funds for HIKE, a program designed to help hearing impaired kids. The Bethel has had the privilege of having a local child selected to receive help from this fund. They visit shut-ins twice a year and help the Masons and Eastern Star when asked. Their fundraising activities over the years have included bake sales, car washes, sacking groceries, selling cookie dough and most recently making and selling apple dumplings at Pioneer Orchard's Harvest Days Celebration.

The girls elect their top five officers, Honored Queen, Senior Princess, Junior Princess, Guide and Marshall. Each year consists of two six-month terms. The following young women have served as Honored Queens of Bethel #60 from January of 1970 to June 2002.

Pat Sander Smith
Donna Neilson
Susan Brown Mayfield
Lanette Unger Whitford
Brenda Meyer Reed
Clarinda Unger
Debby Montgomery Lohman
Jennifer Friedrich Cook
Pat Cracraft Walker
Connie Harris Mantia
Kath Declue Newell
Manota Friedrich Cowell
Judy Allmon Smith
Benita Daniel Limbaugh
Mary Friedrich Thompson
Teresa Lape
Charlene Henry Underwood
Cynthia Pittman Hazelwood
Kathy Rampley Heckt
Danita Lowes
Phyllis Propst Sander
Kathy Friedrich
Patty Athey Anderson
Allison Louden Trischler
Kim Niswonger King
Cindy Holloway Oliver
Jenny Switzer James
Pam Kuntze Eggiman
Julie Henry Lohman
Julie Schreiner Phillips
Yolanda Barnes Steinberg
Stacy Sandin Ross

These are the young women who were initiated on Jan. 11, 1970 when the Bethel was instituted

Job's Daughters emblem

Stephanie Gable
Tonya Moyers
Traci Tuschoff Branscum
Brenda Thompson
Jody Wardron
Debra Glenn
Rebecca McClard Kluesner
Sherry Langford
Laura Flannery Keller
Melissa Sterner Schwab
Emily Fulenwider
Angela Flannery
Sara Hurst
Kami Sneed
Dawn Makins
Emily Sterner
Carolyn LaRue
Heather Butler Donner
Jessica Jones Kinder
Maegan Miller Jensen
Amanda Crouch
Amber Miller
Beth Johnson
Erica Masterson
Jennifer Hrabik
Kara Koeberl
Kim Straedey
Ashley Hobeck
Cynthia Cobb
Michela Steinmeyer
Victoria Adams

These daughters have been assisted by Bethel Guardians that have included: Marilyn Proffer, 1970-1972; Sylvia Gellately, 1972-1974; Jerri DeClue, 1974-1977; Betty Rampley, 1977-1980; Joyce Baker, 1980-1984; Betty Henry, 1984-1996; and Ruth Masterson, 1996-Present. Associate Bethel Guardians have included Joe Masterson, 1970-1978; Wayne Pitman, 1979; and Joe Masterson, 1979-Present.

Brenda Thompson, PHQ served as Junior Miss Missouri Job's Daughter in 1988-1989. Amanda Crouch served as Scottish Rite Youth Ball Queen in 1997-1998. In 1995 the Bethel celebrated its 25th Anniversary and conducted its first Majority Ceremony, with a number of its Past Honored Queens and Majority Members returning to take part in this ceremony. The Bethel currently has an active membership of girls and council members. Bethel #60 IOJD has seen many young girls enter the organization as shy and uncertain only to leave as confident and caring young women. Truly the young women who pass through this Bethel strive to live up to the scripture the founder chose as the cornerstone for this organization. "And in all the land were no women found so fair as the Daughters of Job; and their father gave them inheritance among their brethren." Job 42:15.

The group currently meets on the second and fourth Tuesdays and anyone who would be interested in finding out more about the organization can contact the Guardian via Job's Daughters Bethel #60, Masonic Temple, 204 South High, Jackson, MO 63755. Come join the fairest in the land.

Current active members of Bethel #60 are pictured at Mini Session 2002 held in Springfield, MO. Front row, left to right: Brittany Meyer; Victoria Adams; Kara Koeberl; Caitlin Burress; Shyanna Riehn. Back row, left to right: Kim Straedey; Beth Johnson; Amanda Crouch; Cindy Cobb; Erica Masterson. Not present for the picture were Michaela Steinmeyer and Jenny Hrabik.

KNIGHTS OF COLUMBUS LADIES AUXILIARY BISHOP TIMON COUNCIL 6405

The Knights of Columbus Ladies Auxiliary had its first organizational meeting on Wednesday, March 7, 1979. The meeting was held at the old Knights of Columbus Hall located in the basement of Beussink Brothers Woodworks, 1311 Gloria Street in Jackson, MO. Several things were accomplished that night: Officers were elected, dues were set at five dollars per year, and all those who paid dues by April 25, 1979, would become charter members (there were 42). The meetings were to be held on the third Wednesday of each month. The purpose was to assist in promoting the welfare of the men's council and to promote some charitable activity.

The first officers were: Nancy Pleiman, president; Marie Bradford, vice-president; Agnes Boitnott, secretary; Audrey Humes, treasurer; Beulah Beussink, sergeant-at-arms; Louise Milde, three-year trustee; Johanna Broshius, two-year trustee; and Evelyn Clippard, one-year trustee.

A few memories from the past include fashion shows, tasting bees, Easter egg hunts, Jackson Homecomer's stand, CPR training, craft demonstrations, craft fairs, Christmas parties, cookie swaps, dance instructions, Dumplin' Day, and many, many more activities. Some meetings in the winter were held in members' homes because the Knights of Columbus Hall was too cold. Those were the days!

The 2001-2002 officers are: Kathleen Huck, president; Susan Hinkebein, vice-president; Cindy Beussink, secretary; Cheryl Scheffer, treasurer; Sue Craig, parliamentarian; Carolann Beussink and Marlene Strieker, sergeants-at-arms; Dolores Bohnsack, chaplain; Debbie Pinkston, one-year trustee; Alice Isaac, two-year trustee; and Brenda Bartels, three-year trustee. The auxiliary meets on the third Monday of every other month. Its current membership is 92 and dues are two dollars per month.

Knights Of Columbus Bishop Timon Council 6405

The Bishop Timon Council 6405 Knights of Columbus organization has been in the Jackson area for 30 years. Thirty years is not a long time by Knights of Columbus standards. The first group of Knights of Columbus was founded in 1882 by Father Michael McGivney and a small assembly of young Catholic men. From those few dedicated men, the Knights of Columbus has grown to an organization of more than 12,000 councils, an international organization of 1,700,000 members, and over 36,000 members in the state of Missouri. The local council, Bishop Timon Council 6405, is approaching a membership of nearly 400 men and continues to grow.

Council 6405 began in the basement of Beussink Bros. Woodworks, a local cabinet shop located at that time at 1311 Gloria Street in Jackson. The first slate of officers for Council 6405 in 1972 were as follows: Chaplain, Father Alois Stevens; Grand Knight, O. J. Bradford; Deputy Grand Knight, David Elfrink; Chancellor, Mike Stoverink; Recorder, David Reiminger; Financial Secretary, Gary Evans; Treasurer, John Horrell Jr.; Advocate, Ronald Badger; Lecturer, John J. Scharenborg; Warden, Joe Don Randol; Inside Guard, Pat Horrell; Outside Guard, Kenny Koehler Sr.; three-year Trustee, Herman Beussink Jr.; two-year Trustee, Paul Prokopf; one-year Trustee, Steven Friedrich. The group agreed to meet twice a month, on every second and fourth Wednesday at 7:30 p.m.

The Council soon outgrew this location as their membership and activities expanded rapidly. In 1984 land was purchased on Highway 61 North at 3305 North High Street. Construction was begun soon thereafter and Council 6405 moved into its new and much larger facility. This move allowed the Council to be host to many community activities and allowed for continued growth in its membership. The council still remains at this location and the site has been expanded with the purchase of an adjoining tract of land. The extra land allowed for the construction of a small lake and provided needed space to host large activities such as the Missouri State Knights of Columbus Horseshoe Tournaments.

Council 6405 follows the Knights of Columbus tradition of service. Among the greatest of these is to serve the Catholic Church and the community in which it resides. In all things, the Knights of Columbus places its greatest focus on "charity." To this end, Council 6405 members are involved in many local and national service projects including the "Tootsie Roll Drive" for the handicapped, manual labor for those in need locally, cash contributions where needed, sponsoring youth programs such as the boys and girls Free Throw Contests, hosting charitable events, and much more.

Council 6405 is proud to have had the following men serve as Grand Knights during the last 30 years: O. J. Bradford, Joe Don Randol, Bill Boitnott, Tee Trankler, Bernard Beussink, Glenn Elfrink, Jack Martin, Jim Dohogne, Wes Bartels, Leonard Beussink, Ennis William Hinkebein II, David Murphy, Tim Beussink, Tony Mier and John Mautino. Through the years, several local members have had the honor of being selected to serve at the state level of the Knights of Columbus. Bill Boitnott held several positions: District Deputy 1979-1982; Family Life Chairman 1982-1983; Membership Chairman 1983-1984; Program Chairman 1984-1986; State Deputy 1986-1988; and State Ceremonials Chairman 1994-2000. Ennis William Hinkebein II also held multiple posts: First Vice President State K.C. Softball Association 1982-1985; President State K.C.-Softball Association 1986-1989; and District Deputy 1994-1996. Other state level appointees were: Father David Hulshof, State Chaplain 1986-1988; David Beeson, State Advocate 1979-1981; Bernard Beussink, District Deputy 1982-1986; and Rick Sauer, District Deputy 1990.

For more information about the Knights of Columbus contact any member or come by the Knights of Columbus Hall at 3305 North High Street in Jackson, MO. Meetings are held at 7:30 p.m. every second and fourth Wednesday of the month.

The Optimist Club of Jackson

The Optimist Club of Jackson has been in existence since 1939. The Evening Optimist Club of Cape Girardeau was the sponsoring club and an affiliate of Optimist International. The Optimist organization has as its motto "Friend of Youth." In keeping with that theme, our club activities are youth oriented. All money raised by our fundraisers go 100% for these activities and are spent here in the Jackson community.

The purposes of the Optimist club are: to develop optimism as a philosophy of life utilizing the tenets of the Optimist Creed; to promote an active interest in good government and civic affairs; to inspire respect for the law; to promote patriotism and work for international accord and friendship among all people; and to aid and encourage the development of youth, in the belief that the giving of one's self in service to others will advance the well-being of humankind, community life and the world.

In keeping with the purpose of our organization our club sponsors or has sponsored the following activities: the Soap Box Derby on Mill Hill; the Thanksgiving Turkey Chase on the football field; "Toys for the Needy;" the Boys' Baseball League; the Jackson Optimist Soccer League; Boys Basketball; Girls' Basketball; Wrestling; the Optimist Oratorical Contest; the Optimist Essay Contest; Chartering Organization for Boy Scout Troop #311; Fishing Rodeo; Respect for Law; Boys' State and Girls' State; the Junior Optimist Club; Youth Appreciation week the first week in November; Youth in Government Day; built a picnic shelter in the park on Optimist Hill; and a scholarship to Southeast Missouri State. This is not meant to be an all-inclusive list.

Fundraisers for these programs have been varied. In 1944 the Tennessee Playboys were in town; in 1949 the first Minstrel Show was held; in 1951 "The Optimist Fashion Show" was held; in 1956 the Optimist fish stand was built; in 1959 Christmas tree sales began; in 1967 dog-on-a-stick stand was built; in 1982 the Bald Knobbers from Branson were here; in 1997 Optimist Spaghetti Day was held; and in 2001 Optimist Bingo at Bingo World was held in Cape Girardeau.

The Optimist Club of Jackson has helped spread optimism as a way of life, as stated in the purpose of Optimist International, by establishing seven clubs since its existence. The Perryville Club (1946) co-sponsored with the Cape Girardeau Club, the Flat River Optimist Club (1949), the Ste. Genevieve Optimist Club (1953), the Sikeston Optimist Club (1967), the Breakfast Optimist Club of Jackson (1975), the Lutesville-Marble Hill Optimist Club (1981), the New Madrid Optimist Club (1983), the Optimist Club of Fredricktown (1990), and the Noon Optimist Club of Jackson (1991).

Our club has furnished the Missouri District and the international organization with some leadership. In the year 1999-2000 Don Sievers served as Optimist International Vice-president, John Mabrey and Don Sievers served as Past District Governors, and Walt Pierce and Chuck Gorton served as past District Secretary-Treasurers.

Serving the Zone Level of Missouri District were Walter Kasten, John Mabrey, Larry Nowak, Harold Engelhart, Adolph Borgfield, Roy Savers, Bill Thompson, Louis Rohlfs, Don Sievers, Paul Hoffmann, Walt Pierce, Larry Ream and Al Franke as Lieutenant Governor.

Throughout 60-plus years of existence our club has strived to not only furnish money to support our many programs but actually become very involved in the activities of these programs. Our club is always ready to welcome anyone for membership who has a love for the youth of our country, our future leaders, and who enjoys working with the programs that support them.

Top: Christmas Tree Lot Fundraiser for youth and Boy Scout Troop 311, sponsored by Optimist Club
Center: General Membership, 1999
Right: Homecomers Fish Stand fundraiser for the youth

Jackson Rotary Club

The Jackson Rotary Club was organized March 12, 1929, and its Charter Night was held March 28, 1929. Twenty-two members comprised the original roster. The Charter President of the club was M. G. LaPierre. Fred Kies was the Vice-President and Lawrence Snider was Secretary-Treasurer. Other Charter members included: A. A. Boss, J. R. Bowman, W. L. Essmann, C. L. Grant, Max Keyser, Louis Kies, Adolph Kies, J. W. McCombs, A. D. Milde, C. G. Macke, Ray G. Miller, J. V. Priest, Henry Puls, J. E. Schmuke, Dr. D. I. L. Seabaugh, Sam Vandivort, Will H. Wagner, and Kent Williamson.

The first year saw 11 new members join the club, including Bob Henderson, Herman Obermiller, Frank Hines, John Sachse, Rev. Hugh Isbell, James McDonald, Roe Warren, William Schwartz, C. C. Conrad, Maurice Thompson, and Herman Wolters. Over the years, the club has experienced steady growth. Current membership totals 73.

Rotary is the first service club. Its purpose is service. Rotary worldwide renders service in four areas: Club Service, Vocational Service, Community Service and International Service.

The 25th anniversary celebration of Jackson Rotary was held April 23, 1954. The club's president for 1953-54 was Paul Bruening and the club's secretary was Melvin Lichtenegger. Dr. Willard E. Goslin, a member of the Department of Education of Peabody College, gave the principal address. A paragraph from the program booklet from this occasion stated, "The youth who dives into the refreshing waters of the Municipal Swimming Pool doesn't know the Object of Rotary." "The Boy Scout who weekly meets with the Rotary-sponsored Scout troop is not aware of our motto, 'he profits most who serves the best,' but he does recognize that the majority of the community projects planned for his benefit have had the sponsorship and support of the Jackson Rotary Club."

On Feb. 9, 1979, the Jackson Rotary Club celebrated its Golden Anniversary. The President-Elect of Rotary International, James Bomar, of Shelbyville, TN, was the principal speaker. James Moore was the club's president during this year, and Weldon Macke was club secretary.

On March 28, 1989, the Jackson Rotary Club celebrated its 60th anniversary. Duane R. Sterling of Warrensburg, MO presented the principal address. Sterling is General Manager of The Rotary Foundation. David Beasley was president during Jackson Rotary's 60th year, Dennis Sievers was the club's secretary. The club has at least 200 Paul Harris Fellows who have given over $200,000.00 to support international programs. These programs include efforts to "Stamp Out Polio in the World" and "Helping People to Regain Sight."

The Jackson Rotary Club has provided many outstanding projects for the community. One of the first projects involving the Rotary Club was the sponsorship of Boy Scout Troop 11, in 1929. The troop continues to be sponsored by Jackson Rotary to the present. They have also sponsored the high school international exchange program, which has sent and received many students from abroad. Individual scholars from India, Brazil, Australia, Holland, Sweden, Russia, Latvia, Denmark, Finland and France have studied in Jackson. High school students from Jackson have studied for an academic year in France, Belgium, Denmark, Sweden, Japan, Holland, and England.

Through the Rotary Foundation Graduate Scholars program the Jackson Rotary Club has sponsored the following students to attend universities abroad for an academic year: Mark Doberenz, University of Belgium; Hank Birk, University of Bath, England; Andrea Rigdon Seabaugh, University of Southhampton, England; Mark Steiner, University of Klagenfurt, Austria; Drew Burke, University of Lyon, France; and Jon Mark Milde, Institute of Political Studies, Paris, France.

The Jackson club continues to sponsor the Junior Rotarian Program and Camp Enterprise for local students, which are designed to promote interest in business and leadership.

While youth programs are important to Rotary, the local club has also sponsored International Exchange Teams. This program is designed to promote an exchange of ideas amongst young individuals who are in a business or a professional field. Locally the club has sponsored the following programs: Service to the Senior Citizens Center; Partners in Service-provides leadership in community development projects; and Coat and Food Collections - to help the needy.

A major community service project done by the Jackson Rotary Club was the building of Rotary Lake in the City Park. Over a number of years, this project included paving a jogging path around the lake and lighting the area to extend hours of use of the facility. Their promotion of environment and safety is designed to make Jackson and the surrounding community a good place to live and work.

The club has supported the ideas of Rotary by providing leadership. Less than ten years after being chartered, the Jackson Rotary Club was responsible for chartering a new Rotary club at Marble Hill. This club was chartered on Oct. 18, 1938. During this year, Will Wagner was the Jackson club's president and S. H. Hardy was club secretary.

They have also supported the following members who have served as District Governors, including: William Meyer, Lee G. Cochran, Stone Manes, Carlton G. Meyer and Marvin Adams.

The Jackson club currently meets at noon every Tuesday at the Highway 25 Diner. The current officers are President Mike Seabaugh; President Elect Tim Walker; Secretary Rick Shultz; Treasurer Bob Grebing; and Past President Vanita Jones. The club will celebrate its 75th year in 2004 and it continues to be proud of serving Jackson and the surrounding areas. Jackson Rotarians continue to recognize as guiding lights, their two mottoes, "HE PROFITS MOST WHO SERVES THE BEST," and "SERVICE ABOVE SELF."

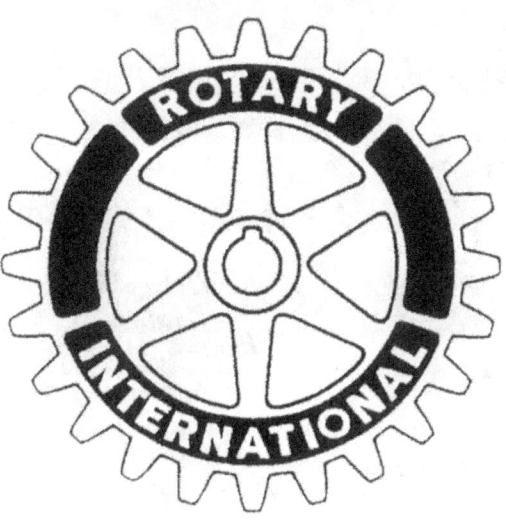

St. Louis Iron Mountain And Southern Railroad Company Steam Powered Tourist Train

The first railroad company that actually built a railroad in southeast Missouri was the St. Louis Iron Mountain and Southern Railroad Corporation. This was in 1851 by a special act of the Missouri Legislature. Its purpose was to make available the great quantities of iron ore around Iron Mountain, MO, to the river and other areas. The line was from St. Louis, MO to Pilot Knob, later south into Bollinger County (the Belmont branch) and connecting at Allenville. Later this was acquired by the Missouri Pacific Line, now Union Pacific, and then abandoned in 1984. The Jackson Industrial Development Corporation purchased the seventeen miles of track and right-of-way from Delta to Jackson and operated the Jackson and Southern Railroad Co., keeping rail service open to Jackson.

A group of investors with dreams of owning their own steam-powered train was organized. The following 15 people were the original stockholders: President John Lorberg, Vice-President John Lichtenegger, Secretary-Treasurer Walter Drusch, Shelby Brown, Ralph Edwards, Gene Penzel, B. W. Birk, Bruce Miller, Jim Drury, Robert Landgraf, Robert Adams, Leo Kohlfeld, F. E. Rhodes, Ora Masters and E. Desmond Lee.

They found at Crab Orchard and Egyptian Railroad in Marion, IL, an engine being used as a switch engine along with several commuter cars. The engine known as Number 5 is a 1910 model and carries five tons of coal and 7,000 gallons of water. The coaches are 1920 vintage and were used as commuter cars in Chicago. The 1929 cupola caboose ran on the Missouri Pacific Line and was donated by The MoPack, fully refurbished.

A home for the tourist attraction was found at the intersection of Highways 25 and 61, some four acres formerly known as the Loos Saw Mill. Bringing the equipment from Marion, IL, to Jackson was a major involved task. It was 100 miles by rail. This was a two-day trip. After equipment was in Jackson, the renovation work then began. There were many hours of volunteer work sand-blasting the coaches inside and out. The engine and tender were completely overhauled. After one year's extensive work, Number 5 was ready to roll. The inaugural run was April 18, 1986. The two coaches were named for John Hall and Scott McDowell, who donated their talent and many hours of labor.

The tourist train operates from April through October with regular scheduled runs on weekends, and many weekday charters have been run. The two coaches carry 160 passengers with some of the original flipseats and also one coach has the original light fixtures. Additional riders can enjoy the caboose or on nice days the open air flatbed car. Special events such as Craft Shows, Railfan Weekends, Civil War re-enactments, Hobo parties, mock Jesse James train robberies and Western Days have attracted many out-of-state visitors to Jackson. Other events for which the train has been chartered have been receptions, private birthday parties, weddings, bachelor parties, school groups, senior citizens and side trips for conventions coming to the area.

The train travels to Gordonville, Dutchtown, Allenville, and over the Diversion Channel into Delta. Having no turntable, the train backs up the entire trip home. The train operates under regulations of the Federal Railroad Administration. The operation is supported by a not-for-profit organization, "Friends of Steam Railroading," which provides volunteer workers as well as monetary contributions. The purpose of this group is to promote railroading as an industry. It is the intention of both organizations to keep rail services open to Jackson for generations to come.

The St. Louis Iron Mountain is still operating since its inaugural run in 1986. **Engine #5, "The Shelby Brown," sits at the front of the line.** FRA regulations requiring updating and special inspections have taken the engine out of operation temporarily. The coaches are being pulled by a 1953 E-A diesel unit originally from Pennsylvania. It ran on the Pennsylvania Railroad until the 1970s, from 1970 to 1985 on Amtrak, and then was sold to Blue Mountain & Reading Railroad in Reading, PA. There it was restored to its original color of deep maroon and gold striping and its original cal #5898. A 1971 Chassis System bay window caboose and an air-conditioned New York Central Coach have been added. Documentation for a non-profit organization is currently being submitted to allow that charitable donations made to the train qualify as tax deductions.

Children ages 1 to 100 enjoy riding the antique equipment and reliving the past on this historic tourist train. Portions of this article were included in the book *Celebrating 175 Years of Tradition, 1814-1979* honoring the 175th anniversary of Jackson, MO.

The St. Louis Iron Mountain and Southern Railroad Company, steam-powered tourist train, 2002

Parades and Pageants

Homecomers

Edward D. Hays, the probate judge for Cape Girardeau County in 1907, decided the dedication of the new county courthouse should be an occasion for a celebration. Hays promoted the idea of a "homecoming" reunion for all of the county residents, past and present. In December 1907, preparation began with the establishment of the Cape Girardeau County Home Comers Association headed by Judge Hays as president; F. A. McGuire, Vice-president; Henry Puls as secretary and Julian B. Miller, treasurer, with the executive committee comprised of C. L. Grant, John G. Putz, M. G. LaPierre, and F. E. Kies.

The Homecomers' 50th Anniversary program gives the following description of the first day of the "First Annual Reunion of Cape Girardeau County Home-Comers' Association," held September 24, 25, 26, 1908.

Everything possible was done to make the visitors and home folks comfortable. A reception room, once the office of the Circuit Clerk, was fixed up with M. G. LaPierre in charge. John G. Putz was in charge of the exhibits of historic objects and relics ...

Contests were held, the Band gave Concerts, there was a Ball game as well as a Balloon Ascension and Parachute Leap each day. Political Candidates, seeking support in the coming elections were on hand. A soldier from both the Union forces and Confederate forces were speakers. Carnival amusement stands were open all day lending an air of gaiety to the festivities.

Uptown Jackson during Homecomers, 1950s. Businesses shown are Wagner Bakery, Rozier's, Cox's 5 & 10 Store, Jackson Decorating Center, C. H. Sander Sales Company, Ideal grocery, Jackson Studio, Kerstner Drug, Sander Hardware, and the Air-Conditioned Palace Theatre.

At 8:30 a.m. on September 24th, according to the programme, Home-Comers officially opened with all of the steam whistles and bells going full blast! The Band presented a short concert and Judge Edward D. Hays delivered the welcoming address; Judge Thomas Mabrey of Doniphan gave the response…

A mixed chorus sang America and the Star Spangled Banner, and the school children passed in parade. Governor Joseph Wingate Folk arrived at noon, lunched with the Missouri Guard Officers, made a political speech at the school park and then left for Marble Hill.

Dedication of the new $90,000 Court House came next. The Hon. Linus Sanford made the address from a platform on the north side of the Court House. Presiding Judge William B. Schaefer accepted the building on behalf of the County. The doors swung wide and the beautiful building was open for inspection. History does not relate the number of people inspecting the new courthouse that day, but we can assume many did, for there were about 16,000 persons attending the opening day that first Home-Comers Reunion.

Homecomer activities were suspended several times during its history. There was no reunion in 1918 because of World War I. The 1919 reunion was planned in honor of returning veterans. During Homecomers, war hysteria created an air of unrest and a large crowd bordering on a mob stormed the Volksfreund newspaper office and demanded that editor-owner Frederick Kies no longer print the paper in German. Homecomers attendance began to decline and the event ceased in 1922. In 1935 the Jackson Chamber of Commerce voted to revive the reunion. A committee comprised of A. D. Milde, Ruben R. Schade, and Paul Bruening worked hard to regain the community's interest in the original idea of an annual reunion. Except for a period during World War II, the Homecomers Reunion has been an annual event ever since.

The 50th anniversary committee recommended that the local residents "put aside your worries and cares," and "let the carnival spirit of fun be the rule." Whether 1908 or 2001, Homecomers has been a source of various forms of entertainment. Live entertainment was a must before the advent of sound systems and recorded music. In 1935 Homecomers featured an extensive line-up. Jack Stalcup and his band of the Southland were at Home-Comers, with a large open air dance floor for five nights with dancing from "8:30-'til?" The Meyn Concert Group provided a concert of instrumental and vocal classical and semi-classical selections (Cape County Post, August 1935). The Stars of 1950 programs presented children of pre-school and primary age in a concert of readings, dancing, solos and novelty features. A licensed pilot operating a new Robin Plane appeared three days in a row at 1:45 for a demonstration of stunt flying. Various contests covered Harmonica playing, scouting events, a children's parade, and more. Families still take blankets and lawn chairs to the Courthouse lawn to watch the local talent show and queen contest. The first Homecomer's queen contest was held in 1935 with the crowning of Miss Isabella Johnson of Burfordville. Jackson Municipal Band has been a popular attraction for young and old since 1939. The band closes its summer season with their Homecomers' concert.

Homecomers requires a cooperative effort between the residents, organizations and business community of Jackson and surrounding area. The Altenthal-Joerns Post 158 of the American Legion of Jackson has sponsored Home-Comers since 1938. As the 1958 program explains, "Each year the Home-Comers chairman, with many assistants appointed by the American Legion Commander, have worked untiringly to assure Jackson a successful celebration. Understanding wives willingly become 'Home-Comers widows' for a good part of the year, thus adding their part to the success of each reunion. Yes, weeks and months of preparation are necessary to contract for carnival attractions, arrange Queen contests, Home Talent shows, arrange for food stands, etc."

Since the first Homecomers, local merchants and organizations have provided raffle and contest prizes ranging from a gold watch to a car. Homecomers' programs and advertising read like business directories of the day. In 1935 cash contributions for contest prizes and event costs were received from over ninety businesses in the Cape and Jackson area: Palace Theatre, Jackson Mercantile Co., Kerstner's Pharmacy, Schade Bros. Café, Rozier's Cash Store, International Shoe Co., Wagner Bakery, McCombs Furniture, Bruening Company, Herbert Sachse of the A&P Store, LaPierre-Sawyer Handle Co., Jackson Oil Co., Bowers Motor Co., Coca-Cola Bottling Co., Blick's Café, Ott's Café, Hotel Jackson, Gem Café, Falstaff Brewery Co., Sinclair Oil Co., Missouri Cash-Book, Cracraft

Members of the "Brothers of the Brush" during Jackson's Sesquicentennial celebration."

& Miller, Roy Seabaugh of Kroger, Cape County Post, Jackson Lumber Co., C. R. Query of Ice and Coal., Brennecke Chevrolet Co., W. A. Sander Sales Co., Loos Brothers Sawmill, Roloff's Cash Market, Meyer-Albert Grocery Co., Midwest Dairy, Kieninger's Barber Shop, Jackson Electric Co., Hoffmann's Shoe Shop, Kurre & Putz Produce, L. E. Schmidt-Butcher, Marquette Oil Co., C. W. Boutin, Thomas & Son Trucking, Kneibert's Variety Store, Steele's Stationery Store, Post Office staff, Kasten's Grocery, Wagner Machine Shop, Jess Huckstep, Tucker Truck Lines, Traveler's Café, Cape County Savings Bank, Dr. D. I. L. Seabaugh, Wides Oil Company, Dalton Grocery, Rilla Mueller, Jackson Beauty Shoppe, Jackson Cleaning Co., Ideal Grocery, Jones' Drug Store, Jackson Exchange Bank, Goddard Grocery Company, Kelso Oil Company, Hoffmeister Barber Shop, Sander's Hardware Store, Model Grocery, Marice Thompson Insurance, Chas. Leimer Farm Implement, Wm. A. Illers Dairy, Dr. A. M. Estes, Chas. Steck Plumbing, Dale Reed Barber, Adams Coal Co., Schaper Grocery, Obermiller Floor Co., H. A. Ueleke Jewelry, Bob Illers Service Station, L. C. Martin Service Station, Geo., Frissell Service Station, Dr. D. L. Mowery, Frank Hines -Attorney, Dr. E. R. Schoen, and Dormeyer's Drug Store. Thirty years later, the August 20, 1969, the Jackson Journal newspaper would list the businesses of that era. Many names were gone from the previous list, but the small businesses' generosity remained unchanged. The prizes to be given away included "a deep freeze on Monday; a bedroom suite on Tuesday; an automatic washer on Wednesday; a set of watches on Thursday, a riding mower on Friday, and a color television on Saturday." Tickets for the drawings could be obtained from "Fashion Fabrics, Kasten's Building Center, Lichtenegger AG Store, The Allen House, Sebastian Sales & Service, Schaper's IGA, Jackson Variety, McCombs Furniture, Jackson Rexall Drugs, Ladies Toggery, Ideal Grocery, Fulenwider Drugs, Cape County Savings Bank, Leonard's Seeds, Schwab and Eakins, Western Auto, P. N. Hirsch, Harold's Jewelry, Kefauver's Big Star, Lohman's Shoe Store, C. H. Sander Sales, Albert Sander Hardware, Dalton Florist, Sander's Philco Ford, Cash-Book Printing, Rozier's Cash Store, Cracraft & Miller, Jackson Savings & Loan, Jones Drug Store and the Jackson Savings Bank."

Often, travel to, from and around Homecomers was and is an adventure. In the early days, travel was a slow process. Days, instead of hours, were required to travel by horse and buggy and early motor cars. Local residents housed relatives coming from faraway towns such as Perryville and Ste. Genevieve. Almost one hundred years since the first Homecomers, residents still must adjust their traffic route to accommodate the closing of the courthouse square. The patient motorist is especially appreciated during the years when Homecomers coincides with the first few days of the new school year.

Folks from near and far continue to attend the annual gathering even with the competition from school starting before Labor Day, modern air-conditioning, and television. For time seems to stop in Jackson for one week in August every year. One day the streets are as usual. The next day Homecomers' stands and the carnival rides appear with the promise of entertainment, family gatherings, a chance to be queen, the prospect of prizes, funnel cakes, barbecues, taffy, scary rides, and carousel horses. Then just as suddenly on Sunday morning, every trace of Homecomers is gone and empty streets greet the early morning. Homecomers and summer are both gone for another year.

Every 25 years-

Several celebrations highlighted the Twentieth Century for Jackson. Every twenty-five years Jackson pauses to commemorate another quarter century of peace and prosperity. The Centennial, the 126th anniversary also known as Jacksonian Day or Jackson Day Fete, the Sesquicentennial, and the 175th anniversary were all occasions to celebrate. The May 1941 Jackson Day Fete was a weeklong celebration which included a parade with several marching bands and twenty floats, the pageant "Jackson Marches On," a beauty contest, and a "Whisker Club" competition. The Southeast Missourian newspaper reported "Jackson Day, May 14, will be more than an advertising stunt for the city; in fact, the advertising feature is a minor consideration. It is the urge to have a spring play day, to which the citizens invite the country round about, that actuates those who give time and money to make it a success. The histrionic talent developed in the city astounds even the most optimistic. Women with cares of household and society, staid business men whose time is usually taken up with the daily grind, have laid aside these things for the time being, and have entered into the festive spirit in a way that is remarkable" (Southeast Missourian, May 10, 1941).

Twenty-four years later, in 1965, an equally enthusiastic Jackson greeted the town's Sesquicentennial. The occasion was incorporated into the annual Homecomers Celebration. An Old-Timers Baseball Game and Ice Cream Social set the tone for the week. "Sisters of the Swish" and "Brothers of the Brush" patrolled the streets to catch folks not wearing "proper attire."

Various events were held: the Longest Resident of Jackson Contest; Parents with the Largest Family Present Contest; Homecomers Queen Contest; Talent Show; Sisters of the Swish Contest and Fashion Show; Person Coming the "Furtherest" Contest; a Beard Shaving Contest; Band Concert; and the Sesquicentennial Arts Festival Week.

In 1989 the 175th Anniversary committee's plans began in March with a Mayor's Proclamation and the Burying of the Razor, the 175th celebration on the 4th of July, and carried through to December and the annual Christmas Parade. The activities in the Jackson City Park on the Fourth of July included a fishing derby, mud volleyball, horseshoe tournament, live music, auto show, greased pig contest, watermelon eating contest, pie eating contest, hog calling, skil-

Four members of the Sesquicentennial Committee in period costume, left to right: Mrs. Neil Schuknecht, chairman of the headquarters; Mrs. F. E. Keene, vice-chairman and chairman of the "Sisters of the Swish;" Wib Lohman, chairman of the "Brothers of the Brush;" and Marvin E. Proffer, general chairman of the Sesquicentennial.

Soap Box Derby cars racing to the finish line at the lower end of Mill Hill.

let throwing, children's games, Queen crowning, and a fantastic fireworks display. Soon Jackson will be anticipating its Bicentennial and more fun will be had by all.

Jackson's First Soap Box Derby- June 29, 1939

Jackson's first Soap Box Derby racer event was held Sunday, June 29, 1939, at 2:00 p.m. The Jackson Municipal Band under the direction of A. W. Roloff led a parade prior to the race. The parade formed at Jackson High School. This was the first time for an event of this type to be held in Jackson. All Jackson and surrounding community area children were asked to join in the parade.

The race was held on West Main Street known as Mill Hill to most citizens of Jackson in 1939. It started at the intersection of Missouri Street and West Main Street. A wooden ramp with a 45-degree angle held two Soap Box Racers at a time. The two were released and the finish line was 1,000 feet down the hill and beyond Hubble Creek bridge. It was reported racers sped down the 1,000 foot course in 29 seconds. Over 3,000 people watched the event.

It was described as a race between amateur-constructed miniature cars without motors. The construction cost of the car was not to exceed $10.00. The Optimist Club and the Cape County Post sponsored the event which was held in conjunction with a district event sponsored by the Cape Girardeau News to be held in Cape Girardeau on Sunday, July 16, 1939. The winner in Jackson advanced to enter that race for a chance to go to Akron, Ohio, for the National race.

All vehicles were serviced and examined before the start of the race to insure the driver was staying within the rules. No vehicle and

Early morning sunshine on the dock at Rotary Lake, Jackson City Park.

Winners of the Jackson Optimist Club Soap Box Derby and members of the Jackson Optimist Club. Third-place winner was Roland Wagner standing second from left in first row. Next in front is Professor Buckner with Buster Meehan, second-place winner. Next in front is Estes Caldwell, and next is Billy Reisenbichler, first-place winner, and Bernard Schaper.

driver was to exceed 250 pounds. Test runs were conducted on Wednesday evening before the Sunday, June 29, 1939, race. There were nine Soap Box Car entries steered by the following young men: Roland Wagner, Buster Meehan, Glenn Edward Wilson, Billy Reisenbichler, Jerry Venable, Elwood Hitt, Bryce March, William Allen and Harold Grant.

There were several close races especially when Jerry Venable lost to Roland Wagner. However, the last two racers left in the event for first place were Bill Reisenbichler and Buster Meehan. In their first race Buster had the north lane headed west and Bill had the south lane. They tied in their first race. A tractor towed their cars, as it did all of the cars after their races, up the hill to the starting ramp. Their cars were reversed on the starting ramp. Bill's car was placed in the north lane and the car Buster drove was placed in the south lane. This time there wasn't any doubt. Bill Reisenbichler was the winner of the first Soap Box Derby held in Jackson, Missouri.

Final results were Bill Reisenbichler, 1st; Buster Meehan, 2nd; and Roland Wagner, 3rd. On July 11, 1940, the second race was held in Jackson. Buster Meehan won the second Soap Box Derby and Gene Clifton was runner-up. Buster was Jackson's entry on July 25, 1940, in the race at Cape Girardeau for a chance to go to Akron, Ohio. There were 35 youth, seeking the trip to Akron in the Cape Girardeau race. Buster Meehan tied for third place.

By Jerry Venable

Parks

The latest version of the signs welcoming visitors to Jackson have added "Parks" to the long-time "Welcome to Jackson, The home of beautiful homes, churches, and schools." Jackson's city parks have long been a matter of pride to the community. In the early 1930s the City paid $5,000 for approximately twelve acres of land on North High Street, and sold $1,000 worth of lots off the tract, and $5,000 was spent out of CWA funds in developing it. (Missouri Cash-Book, August 2, 1934, pg. 2)

The park was expanded over the years from its original boundaries of Park Street on the south and Hubble Creek on the north to its current boundaries, which extend to Independence Street (Route D) on the north and west to Union Street where it connects to the American Legion Ball Field. The park contains the city swimming pool, sports fields, tennis courts, basketball courts, play areas for young children, and many sites for group gatherings. In 1976 a band shell was constructed on the north side of the park and the Municipal Band moved its weekly summer concerts from the gazebo on the grounds of the County Courthouse to the new location. The Rotary Club funded construction of a lake and walking path near the band shell and the swimming pool. The Noon Opti-

Pedestrian bridge crossing Hubble Creek in the Jackson City Park.

The tree arch on Highway 61 between Cape Girardeau and Jackson was a lovely sight in the summer but created icy conditions during the winter months, 1968.

mist Club created a Safety City to assist children in learning safety rules for riding bicycles and other wheeled vehicles.

The city has added parks as the community has grown. Brookside Park, accessible from Goodson Drive, contains the Memorial to All Veterans and ball fields. Litz Park, accessible from Odus Street, contains basketball courts and a nature trail along Goose Creek that is currently under development. The newest park, Jackson Soccer Park, accessible from Jackson Boulevard or South Farmington Street, was developed on fourteen acres of land donated by the Jackson Industrial Development Corporation. It contains multiple soccer fields.

The "Road from Cape to Jackson"

The road between Jackson and Cape Girardeau has had numerous names during its long history: Camino Real, No. 9, No. 61, Highway 61 East, Highway 34, North Kingshighway, East Jackson Boulevard, the road to Jackson, the road to Cape. Today the boundary lines of Jackson and Cape Girardeau meet. Not so long ago, before the widening of Highway 61, the trip from Cape Girardeau to the county seat in Jackson made an interesting drive through the country. The two-lane highway curved between gently rolling hills and patches of woods. The following is part of a "Motor Guide" written by the Automobile Association of America in 1910 explaining how to travel from the Jackson courthouse over the gravel "highway" to the Cape Girardeau courthouse (Jackson Journal, June 29, 1966, page 2).

0.0   JACKSON. Court House on Public Square. Turn right.
0.1   Turn right, then turn left. Go south one block, then turn left (east)
1.4   Turn right.
1.5   Cross railroad. Cross iron bridge. Straight ahead.
4.1   Cross iron bridge. Straight ahead.
6.2   Straight ahead.
8.2   Cross iron bridge.
8.4   Slow. DANGER. Bend left. Cross railroad, then turn right.
10.1 Cross concrete bridge.
11.0 Cross car line. Straight ahead.
11.2 Straight ahead to right.
11.3 Straight ahead on Broadway.
11.9 Turn right.
12.0 CAPE GIRARDEAU. Court House on Lorimier St.

Dangerous road conditions were a constant source of concern for travelers and the highway patrol. The weekly papers were persistent in their warnings:

"Driving on the paved road at a fast speed is a dangerous proposition unless the driver keeps a firm grip on his steering wheel and his eyes on the road, far more so now than in a year or two when the right-of-way will have been leveled off, packed and covered with a sod" (Cape County Post, December 31, 1925).

Fatal accidents were frequent, given the conditions of the road and the lack of safety measures in early automobiles. Unsafe bridges were another source of concern. The many creeks in and around Jackson created the need for numerous bridges to allow for easy access in all directions. It was difficult for the city and county to keep up with the demands of newer, heavier vehicles and increased traffic that came with the improvement of Highway 61. The urgency of the situation was brought to light in 1929, when

A very serious accident happened yesterday morning at 4 o'clock, when a large A. & P. bus, north bound, loaded with 22 passengers and having an extra driver along, crashed into the West Main street bridge in Jackson, causing the structure to crumple and fall into the creek while the bus reached the bank at the southwest corner of the bridge and remained on solid ground. As a result of the crash three persons were seriously hurt and quite a number of passengers received minor cuts from splintered glass. If the bus had slipped back or failed to make the west bank, a real catastrophe might have followed. As it is, a happening of this kind has been dreaded for some time, and there is another similar danger point in the bridge on the east side. The west bridge, just collapsed, carried signs warning vehicles weighing more than 3,500 pounds, and the east bridge carries a limit of 7,000 pounds, yet the bus, according to an official of the company, weighs between 15,000 and 16,000 (Cape County Post, November 14, 1929).

Citizens of the county called for the improvement of Highway 9 from Jackson to Cape Girardeau. In 1926 the name of the road was officially changed from No. 9 to Highway 61 in compliance with the national numbering system. It was big news when the paving was finally completed as part of the "Get Missouri Out of the Mud" program. On October 16, 1930, headlines read "No. 61 to be thrown open Saturday." Folks would be able to travel on pavement all the way from St. Louis to Ancell, Missouri, except for the section in Jackson where the bridge had collapsed. In 2002 signs remain of the early road crews. Local historian Murray Dunn relates:

"Hidden among honeysuckle vines beneath a cedar tree near the old KFVS radio tower on North Kingshighway lies a pair of ancient tractor wheels. It has been reported that they are from a Fordson which had been used in construction of the road in the late 1920s or early '30s. The lugs had been removed and another set of extension rims added, then filled with concrete. It is assumed that the tractor was used as a roller. When the road was completed, the tractor was left on the site and later scrapped. These wheels, being filled with concrete were unfit for scrap, and have been left as a monument to the construction of the road connecting Cape to Jackson."

Following the paving, a group of citizens from Cape Girardeau decided to make the ten mile stretch between the towns "the most beautified stretch of Highway in the state of Missouri." Between 1931 and 1938, several hundred elm, spruce, pine, redbud, dogwood and native trees were planted. In 1939 local garden clubs and W.P.A. workers, supervised by D. M. Scivally, planted 10,000 rose bushes along the road that became known as the "Ten-Mile Gar-

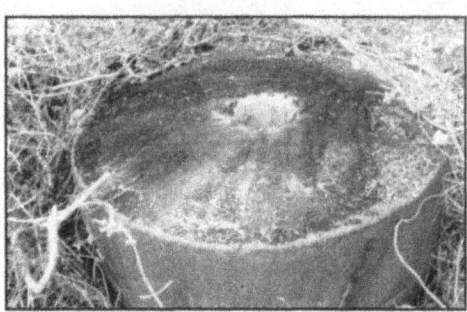

Fordson tire left behind after highway construction. Photo by Murray Dunn

den." A Better Homes and Gardens Magazine editor declared, "There's nothing of the kind to equal it in the United States" (Jackson Homecomers," Program, page 24). The "garden" attracted thousands of tourists to the area and was featured in Reader's Digest magazine in 1961. (Celebrating 175 Years of Tradition, 1814-1989, Jackson, Mo). Members of the highway department of Jackson maintained the garden for over twenty years. Hungry and tired travelers could stop at Wedekind Roadside Park on Highway 61 (just east of present Interstate 55); surrounded by the trees and roses, it was a lovely spot for a family picnic. Occasionally remnants of the lovely garden could be seen until the highway was widened during the 1970s and 1980s.

Traveling west from Wedekind Park, a visitor to Jackson was greeted by the shade from trees intertwined over the two-lane highway. In 1968 the local paper noted the well-known arch was considered "A familiar sight that is eagerly awaited each spring by young and old alike is this natural arch between Cape Girardeau and Jackson. Although the ten-mile rose garden may have lost part of its charm, the natural arch still guards all travelers as they pass beneath its shade" (The Jackson Journal, June 19,1968, pg. 1).

The intersection of Highways 61, 25, 34, and 72 became a point of reference for residents trying to give directions to visitors. Until the middle of the 1970s, residents simply referred to the intersection as "the four-way stop." Increased traffic finally necessitated a stop-light be installed. It was the only stop-light in town for almost a decade. Stores in the vicinity could use "by the stop-light" in their advertising to describe their location. The intersection is now known as the intersection "by the train and the police station."

The widening of Highway 61 to four lanes during the 1980s permanently changed the landscape between Jackson and Cape Girardeau. The trees, flowers, and Wedekind Park picnic area no longer grace us with their color and comfort. However, beauty is in the eye of the beholder. The North and South Cape County Parks offer picnic shelters, a fishing lake, large green spaces to enjoy in the summer and a fantastic lighting display during the Christmas season. Modern conveniences are offered along the road in the form of easy access shopping, strip malls and fast food restaurants. As for the road itself, the modern daily commuters cannot help but appreciate the "beauty" of four lanes of straight safe concrete road.

The Ten-Mile Rose Garden between Jackson and Cape Girardeau.

Lydia Kuntze Wedekind, Ella, Laura, Gus, and Emil standing in front of the Wedekind barn. The wooden barn has been incorporated into the Rainbow Auction barn on Highway 61 East. Photo courtesy of Don Kuntze.

A special thanks to Jackson High School, particularly the following teachers, for their inspiration and the difference that they made in both my personal and professional life:

Mrs. Mary Ellen Berkbigler

Mrs. Marie Harbison

Miss Sarah Jenkins

Mr. Leroy Mason

Mr. Jim Nelson

Mrs. Fern Snider

Mrs. Esther Wagner

Submitted by Bill Heyde

REFERENCES

Begley, Terry, "The Old Bethel Church," n.d.

Bethel Church Book: Minutes of Proceedings of the Bethel Church, 1806-1867. Prepared by Missouri Historical Records Survey Division of Professional and Service Projects, Work Projects Administration. St. Louis, 1940.

"Bollinger Mill," Cash-Book Journal Jackson, Mo., March 2, 1983, p. 13.

"Bollinger Mill," Bill Cameron, Point Lookout, Mo., an authority on mills in the State of Missouri.

Brown, Mildred, "The War Comes to Jackson." In J.E.Thilenius, (Ed.), Biography of Historic Cape Girardeau County. Bicentennial Commission of Cape Girardeau, Missouri, 1976.

Cape County, in Ten Years of Extension Work in Missouri. Columbia, Missouri: Missouri Agricultural Extension Service Project Announcement 16, 1924.

"Cape County Milling Company," Post & Cash-Book Jackson, Mo., July 11, 1973, p. 8.

Cape County Post, Jackson, Missouri, March 12, 1936.

Cape County Post, Jackson, Mo., March 12, 1936, Section C, p. 1.

Cape Girardeau Republican, Tenth Anniversary Edition. Cape Girardeau: Naeter Brothers, Publishers, 1915.

The Cash-Book Journal. 114 (12) July 5, 1989.

The Cash-Book Journal. 141 (46) February 20, 2002.

Cochran, Katherine H. A History of Jackson, Missouri. In Jackson Sesquicentennial: 150 years of Progress. Jackson: Cash-Book Printing Co., 1965.

Curtis, James C. Andrew Jackson and the Search for Vindication. Boston: Little, Brown & Co., 1976.

Dittlinger, D., "The Battle of Cape Girardeau." In J.E. Thilenius, (Ed.), Biography of Historic Cape Girardeau County. Bicentennial Commission of Cape Girardeau, Missouri, 1976.

History of Southeast Missouri. Chicago: The Goodspeed Publishing Co., 1888.

"History of Cape County Milling Company" The Missouri Cash-Book, Jackson, Missouri, May 15, 1941, p. 5.

Houck, Louis A History of Missouri: From the Earliest Exploration and Settlements until the Admission of the State into the Union, (3 vols). Chicago: R.R. Donnelley & Sons, Co., 1908.

Houck, Louis. The Spanish Regime in Missouri, (2 vols.) Chicago: R.R. Donnelley & Sons, Co., 1909.

Jackson Herald. Souvenir Edition, First Annual Reunion Cape Girardeau County Home Coming Association, Jackson MO., Sept. 24, 25, 26, 1908.

Lacy, Christabel & White, Bob. Rural Schools and Communities in Cape Girardeau County. Cape Girardeau Missouri: Center for Regional History and Cultural Heritage Southeast Missouri State University, 1985.

The Magnet. Yearbook of Jackson High School. Jackson, MO Kies Brothers Printers, 1915.

The Magnet. Yearbook of Jackson High School. Jackson, MO Cape County Post Printing Co., 1921.

Meyer, Duane. The Heritage of Missouri: A History. St. Louis: State Publishing Co., Inc., 1973.

Missouri Cash-Book July 17, 1930

Missouri Cash-Book April 2, 1953

Missouri State Highway Commission. Roads and their builders. Jefferson City: Division of Public Information, n.d.

Morton, Virginia T. & Cochran, Katherine H., Toll Roads Things of the Past. In J.E. Thilenius, (Ed.), Biography of Historic Cape Girardeau County. Bicentennial Commission of Cape Girardeau, Missouri, 1976.

Neumeyer, Tom. "Burfordville," The Jackson Journal. March 19, 1975.

Ohman, Marian M. Encyclopedia of Missouri Courthouses. Columbia, Missouri: University of Missouri Extension Division, 1981.

Oliver, Allan L. History of Missouri Flag. In J.E. Thilenius (Ed.), Biography of Historic Cape Girardeau County. Bicentennial Commission of Cape Girardeau, Missouri, 1976.

100 Years of Immaculate Conception Parish. 1974.

Reorganized School District R-2 Cape Girardeau County website.

Seabaugh, Otto. From Seebach to Seabaugh 1123-1988. Jackson, Missouri: Cash-Book Printing, 1988.

Smoot, Jack. "Bollinger Mill State Historic Site" Missouri Resources, undated.

Snider, Felix E., & Earl A. Collins. Cape Girardeau: Biography of a City. Cape Girardeau, Missouri: Ramfree Press, 1956.

Southeast Missourian, Cape Girardeau, Missouri, 1906.

Southeast Missourian. July 4, 1976

Southeast Missourian, Progress Edition, February 24, 2002.

Talley, Carl. Personal interview, June 1989.

U.S. Department of Agriculture, Census of Agriculture 1997. (http://www.NASS.USDA.gov/)

University of Missouri Extension Service. Annual Reports. Cape Girardeau County, 1914-1925, 1937-1942, 1962-1963.

* This history is an updated version of the history previously printed in "Celebrating 175 Years of Tradition, 1814-1819, Jackson, Mo.," combined with submitted articles including information from local newspapers of the past.

Family Histories

ABERNATHY – Mrs. Bertha Sides Abernathy and her children: Ellen Clippard; Virginia A. Seabaugh; Wilson Abernathy; Paul Abernathy; Hilda Mae Trimble; Norma Leigh Tompson, Joe Elem Abernathy, and Betty Lou Collishonn. Father Fred Abernathy died in 1932 at age 52. All lived and went to school in the Leemon and Jackson areas. *Submitted by Virginia Seabaugh*

Mrs. Bertha Sides Abernathy and her children: Joe Elem Abernathy, Norma Leigh Tompson, Hilda Mae Trimble, Betty Lou Collishonn, Paul Abernathy, Virginia A. Seabaugh, Wilson Abernathy, Ellen Clippard, 1979.

ABLE – Ezekiel Able, an early pioneer to Cape Girardeau County, arrived in Cape Girardeau in 1801. He was a veteran of the Eighth Virginia Regiment of the Continental Line in the War for Independence.

The book, *History of Southeast Missouri*, by Robert Sidney Douglass, A.B., LL.B., (Volume 1), states that "Ezekiel Abel (this spelling was often used instead of the correct spelling of Able) was another one of the prominent citizens of the old town (Cape Girardeau). By trade he was a blacksmith, but his principal business during the years he lived in Cape Girardeau was trading in land and land grants. He erected the first public buildings in this district. He had some financial difficulties, but finally became wealthy. In 1811 he constructed the first brick house in the town. It was finished just in time to be badly damaged by the earthquakes of that year. He left a large family, consisting of four sons and two daughters. His eldest daughter, Mary, became the wife of Gen. W. H. Ashley. The younger daughter, Elizabeth, married W. J. Stevenson."

Ezekiel Able was reputed to own thousands of acres of land in Cape Girardeau County. On Nov. 17, 1807, his daughter, Mary Able, married General William H. Ashley. Shortly after their marriage, Ezekiel Able transferred to the newly married couple's 480 arpens of land in what became Jackson, MO. Mary and General Ashley formed a plantation on this land, which contained lot No. 527 between the waters of Hubble and Goose Creek. The book, *A History of Jackson, Missouri*, compiled by Katherine Hinchey Cochran (Mrs. Lee G. Cochran), states that a section of this land "was on elevated ground and free from high water during the rainy season." On Feb. 8, 1814, the Ashleys sold 50 acres of this land to the Commissioners of the Court House and Jails of the County of Cape Girardeau Territory, for a sum of five hundred dollars.

Together with land purchased from three surrounding plantations, this ground became the site upon which the settlement of Jackson, MO, the county seat of Cape Girardeau County, was established. General Ashley later became a famous fur trader and the first Lieutenant Governor of Missouri.

Descendants of Ezekiel Able, his son Wilson, and his grandson Captain Dan Able, the well-known riverboat captain and Wharf Commissioner of St. Louis, now live in Jackson, MO.

Joseph Tado, his wife Mary Ellyn Nelson, and their son, Zachary Alexander Tado, have lived in Jackson since 1994. Both Joseph and Mary Ellyn received degrees in criminal justice from Southeast Missouri State University. Joseph is currently a detective with the Cape Girardeau Police Department's Scientific Investigation Unit and Mary Ellyn is employed by the Southeast Correctional Center in Charleston, MO. *Submitted by Jane Able Tado.*

ADAMS – John August Oberbeck Sr., grandfather of Anna Louise Overbeck Adams, was born in Hanover, Germany, on Oct. 15, 1837. He arrived in America some time prior to 1861 and married Carolina Vogelsang on Dec. 22, 1861. He died Feb. 20, 1888, leaving a widow and ten children (ages 26 to 2), which included twins John August Jr. and Carl Albert (father of Anna Louise). At some period in time, the spelling of the name was changed from Oberbeck to Overbeck.

Carl Albert, known as Albert or C. A., and his wife Bessie Wise were married in 1905. They were parents of six children: Wise, Hunter, Reba, Mabel, Carl and Anna Louise. Albert purchased a farm six miles west of Jackson and farmed until his death in 1953. Anna Louise and her mother continued living on the farm until 1956 when they sold the farm and moved to Jackson.

The Albert Overbeck family. Left to right, front row: Anna Louise Overbeck Adams, Albert Overbeck, Bessie Overbeck, Carl Overbeck. Back row: Reba Overbeck Dow, Hunter Overbeck Jones, Wise Overbeck, Mabel Overbeck Yancey.

Wise (May 19, 1906 – 1991) married Vera Grebe; he farmed and Vera taught school. They had a son Jerry, who graduated from the University at Rolla, MO. He was offered a position in Seattle, WA, and is still employed there by the City of Seattle. Vera died in 2001.

Hunter (Nov. 3, 1907 – 1987) married Ramon Jones; she was a school teacher and housewife. Ramon worked for an auto supply company in Cape Girardeau and died in 1992. They had three children. Nina died in infancy, Jane was killed in 1967, and James married Renee Cobble and lives in Indiana. They have three children and two grandchildren.

Reba (Aug. 6, 1910 – 1997) married Ray Dow, a farmer; Ray died in 1976. They had three children: Paul Ray, Clinton and Judith. Paul Ray married Bettie Godwin and had two children; Steven and Paula, and two grandchildren. Paul Ray was a farmer and Bettie a secretary for the First Baptist Church. They are retired and maintain a home in Jackson. Clinton married Flossie Wilkinson and they have two sons, Eric and Curtis. Clinton was employed by Cape Girardeau County and died in 1992. Flossie is employed by Cape Girardeau County and lives north of Jackson. Judith married George Cozby and they have four children: Kevin and Darin Werner and Nick and Katie Cozby. Judith is employed by Lee Rowan (now Rubber Maid) and George by the Marion, IL Federal Prison. They live in Jackson and have four grandchildren.

Mabel (Nov. 14, 1912) married Robert Yancey and they have two children, Donna and Roger. Mabel worked at the Jackson Hosiery Mill and Robert at Shell Oil Company; they live in Jackson. Donna married Mike Rushing and they have two children, Carmen and Todd. Donna is a teachers' helper in the Jackson School System and Mike and son Todd own and operate Rushing Marine Corporation. Roger married Darlene Tibbs. They have two children, Marsha and Warren. Roger works for Betchel Corporation. Darlene is a teacher and lives in Georgia.

Carl married Bonnie McBride and farmed west of Jackson; he was killed in a car accident in 1988. Bonnie lives on the farm and raises and shows sheep.

Anna Louise (Oct. 19, 1920) married Woodrow Adams. Woodrow had a son Michael by a prior marriage; he died in 1973. Woodrow was a construction worker and died in 1989. They maintained a home in Jackson. Anna Louise worked for USDA in an ASCS office until her retirement in 1983. She is a member of New McKendree United Methodist Church, and since her retirement and Woody's death, she has stayed active in church activities, numerous clubs, and maintaining a home, garden, and yard. *Submitted by Anna Louise Overbeck Adams*

ALLEN – Clarence Washington Allen was born Jan. 25, 1910 and died Oct. 12, 1991; he was the first child of Albert Martin Allen (b. 1887; d. 1918) and Nora Belle (Devore) Allen (b. 1890; d. 1967). They lived in the rural area of Whitewater-Crump, where his grandparents, John Henry Allen (b. 1852; d. 1940) and Fansey Elizabeth (Barks) Allen (b. 1863; d. 1939), and William Washington Devore (b. 1863; d. 1928) and Sarah Elizabeth (Lessley) Devore (b. 1871; d. 1939) also lived. His sister, Lucille, was born on Aug. 28, 1913, and they attended Hickory Grove School.

Clarence and Noma Allen, Fiftieth Anniversary, January 1983. Front row, left to right: Elouise Forrest, Martin Allen, Marie Ruester, David Allen, Debbie Freund. Back row, left to right: Roy Allen, Marilyn Mayfield, Noma Allen, Clarence Allen, Helen Cook, Tom Allen.

After his father died, they moved to Cape Girardeau, and they attended Washington Grade School. Nora married Frank Neader in 1921, and they moved back to the country. He had two half-brothers, Clyde Neader (b. 1924; d. 1991) and Boyd Neader (b. 1926; d. 1991). They attended Hickory Grove School again and would walk or ride a horse to get to school. He decided to go to Hog Creek School to finish his eighth grade. Sometimes he would use stilts, that he had made, to cross the creek if the creek was too high. After finishing the eighth grade, he went to live with his grandparents "Devores" at 929 North Frederick in Cape Girardeau, and went to the old Normal School-University College High, graduating in May 1929. His grandfather was a streetcar operator which was owned by the city at this time.

On Jan. 7, 1933, he and Noma Marie Crites (b. July 11, 1913; d. Aug. 30, 1995), daughter of Thomas B. Crites (b. 1872; d. 1945) and Louvina J. (Hartle) Crites (b. 1871; d. 1922), were married at the county courthouse in Jackson. Judge McDonald performed the ceremony and it cost $3.00 for the marriage license and to pay the judge. They had nine children: B. Marie (b. Jan. 14, 1934), M. Elouise (b. Dec. 27, 1935), C. Martin (b. March 3, 1938), Helen L. (b.. Feb. 1, 1940), Marilyn E. (b. Sept. 19, 1941), Roy L. (b. March 26, 1945), David M. (b. Nov. 17, 1946), Tom S. (b. June 21, 1951) and Debbie K. (b. Sept. 7, 1955).

They lived in the Jackson area and bought their first home at 124 S. Bast Street. In 1942, they moved to a 40-acre farm about seven miles west of Jackson, which is now County Road 347. In November 1952, they moved to a farm about five miles northwest of Jackson. In the fall of 1954, the family bought a 265-acre farm on Little Whitewater Creek between the Mayfield Community and Highway 72 in Bollinger County, from Dr. D. I. L. Seabaugh, which had been in the Seabaugh family for several generations.

The children attended Jackson, Big Springs, Roberts and Patton schools. The family attended Burfordville Baptist and First Baptist in Jackson, and were members of Little Whitewater Baptist Church, where Clarence was a Deacon. Clarence and Noma both worked at International Shoe Factory in Jackson and he also worked part-time as a meat cutter at the Kroger Store. Clarence, Noma and family spent long hours farming, making sorghum (which he was widely known for) and maple syrup, and doing other farm chores to make the payments on the farm in Bollinger County. Planting corn, wheat, beans and sugar cane, hog killing and curing the meat, milking cows, slopping the hogs, gardening, canning, cutting wood, harvesting crops in the fall, baking and quilting were only a few of the chores that were done to just live from day to day. Even though there was always work to do, they took time to visit family and friends. Clarence won several trophies pitching horseshoes and bowling in his later years.

The children remembered Christmas as a more simple time when they were little. "We had fruit and candy and a present, but we didn't have dozens of packages for each of us as so many people do today, but we have the memory that the family was happy, they enjoyed what they had, and they didn't feel any sense of being deprived. The love and warmth of the gathered family was what was most important." *Submitted by Marilyn Mayfield*

ALLEN – Vincent Allen was born May 11, 1756 in Essex County, VA. He married Virginia Elizabeth, maiden name not known, Jan. 27, 1776 in Culpeper County, VA. He served in the Revolutionary Army. He died May 30, 1834. His wife died Oct. 19, 1848 in Lincoln County, NC. They had three children; John Stanly, Margaret and Vincent Allen, who resided in Gaston County, NC in February 1858.

Vincent Hale Allen, son of Vincent Allen, married in North Carolina. His first wife died in Cape Girardeau County, MO. They had five children: Benjamin, Vincent, Albert, Rosie and Nancy. He married a second time in Cape Girardeau County and had children Sarah, Caroline, Jim and Fred.

Benjamin Frank Allen was born in North Carolina and is buried at Birds Grave Yard, Birds Creek, MO. He married Jane Bast from Cape Girardeau County, MO. Children were: Phoenix, Frank, Harve, George Thomas, Anne, Mary Jane and James Edward.

George Thomas Allen married Matilda Kurre on March 30, 1890. The couple had seven children: Georgia, Gale, Lucy, Joe, Charles, Gus and Kurre. They lived in Burfordville, MO for a few years, where he was a blacksmith by trade. They moved to Jackson, MO and bought the old Kneibert home. The home was large with many rooms. It was later bought by the First Baptist Church and torn down, which was very unfortunate since it was built in the 1850's and was one of the true historic homes in Jackson. George Thomas passed away in 1941 and Matilda Allen passed away in 1962.

George Thomas and Matilda Allen home, built in 1856 by Jacob Kniebert Sr., razed in 1963.

Thomas Kurre was born Dec. 30, 1904 in Jackson, MO. He married Olga Mae Dow on Aug. 10, 1932 in Jackson. He served on the Jackson School Board as President and was President of the Optimist Club. He was part owner of McCombs Furniture and Funeral Home. He died on May 30, 1956 in Jackson. Olga Mae Allen passed away in 1984. They had two children, Kurre Wayne and Nancy Lou. Nancy married Byron Luber, who is an Associate Judge for Pemiscot County, MO. Nancy is a school teacher in the school system at Caruthersville, MO. They have two sons, Byron Allen and Kurre Thomas, who are married with one son each. Kurre Wayne and his wife, Ava, have five sons: Aaron, Alex, Greg, Barry and Matthew. Kurre Wayne has been an insurance salesperson for over 30 years and his wife, Ava, has been an insurance staff person for over 20 years. *Submitted by Kurre S. Allen*

ALLEN – On June 21, 1951, a son was born to Clarence Washington Allen and Noma Marie (Crites) Allen. He was named Thomas Stanley after his maternal grandfather, Thomas Benton Crites. Tommy, as he was called, was the eighth of nine children, and the first to be born at a hospital. His older siblings were Marie Ruester, Elouise Forrest, Martin Allen, Helen Cook, Marilyn Mayfield, Roy Allen and David Allen, and his younger sister was Debbie Freund. When Tom was born at Southeast Missouri Hospital in Cape Girardeau, his parents lived on what is now County Road 347 off Highway 34. At the age of three, Tom's family moved to a farm at Patton, MO. Being from such a large family, Tom was no stranger to chores and farm work. His family was noted for making maple syrup and sorghum molasses. The family attended Little Whitewater Baptist Church at Mayfield, MO, where Tom was baptized.

Tom attended school in the Patton-Sedgewickville school district. He participated in high school sports and was the first class to graduate from Meadow Heights High School. The district was so named for the new school building in which he attended for one month in 1969. While in high school, Tom started dating Tandra Yamnitz, daughter of Harold Edgar Yamnitz and Rose Marie (Backler) Yamnitz of Patton. Tandra graduated from Meadow Heights High School in 1970. Both Tom and Tandra were attending Southeast Missouri State University, with Tom working at Rose Can in Cape Girardeau and Ceramo in Jackson, MO, and Tandra working at the University, when they decided to get married. The wedding took place on Jan. 23, 1971 at Mt. Zion Lutheran Church at Yount, MO. They became members of St. Paul Lutheran Church in Jackson, MO. With one car, they continued working and going to school while living in a trailer rented from Willard Tally at 207 East Monroe in Jackson. In September 1972 they bought their first home in Seabaugh Acres on Highway 72, and moved to their present home at 1208 Augusta Drive in December 1996.

Tom continued his interest in sports by bowling, golfing and playing softball. He joined the Missouri National Guard and left for basic training on Jan. 28, 1972, at Fort Leonard Wood, MO, and remained a member for six and a half years. Tandra remained in Jackson, attending college and graduating in July 1972 with an Associate of Arts degree in Computer Science. She went to work at Hardware Wholesalers, Inc., which is now called Do it Best Corporation, where she still works today. Tom returned to school in the fall of 1972 and graduated in May 1974 with a B.S. in Education. He received his Master's Degree in Administration in 1983 and his Specialist Degree in 1988. He has worked to New York Life Insurance Company and Modern American Insurance Company. Tom has taught and coached at the former St. Vincent's Seminary School in Cape Girardeau, Jackson Junior High School, Meadow Heights High School and Oak Ridge High School. He has been an administrator at Oak Ridge Elementary, Woodland High School, Greenville Elementary, Richland Elementary and Kelly High School, and is currently superintendent of schools at Delta, MO.

On March 9, 1977, the couple was blessed with a daughter, Tara Marie, born at Southeast Missouri Hospital. She attended St. Paul Lutheran Church and School. Tara graduated from Jackson High School in 1995. In 1999 she graduated from Southeast Missouri State University with a B.S. in Business Education and is currently teaching at Jackson High School.

Tom Allen, Tandra Allen, Tori Allen and David Mirly, Tara Allen, June 3, 2000.

On April 3, 1978, another daughter was welcomed. Tori April was born at Southeast Missouri Hospital. She attended St. Paul Lutheran Church and School, and graduated from Jackson High School in 1996. Tori graduated from Southeast Missouri State University in 2000 with a B.S. in Marketing. She currently teaches computers at Jackson Junior High School. On June

3, 2000, Tori married David Wayne Mirly, son of Kenny and Joann Mirly of New Wells, MO. David was a 1995 graduate of Jackson High School and a 1999 graduate of Southeast Missouri State University. He is currently teaching and coaching at Chaffee High School. They live in Jackson. *Submitted by Tandra Allen*

AMELUNG/AMELUNKE – Heinrich "Christian" Amelunke (son of Johann Heinrich Amelunke and grandson of Johann Christof Amelung) was born Sept. 18, 1796 in Klein Rhüden am Harz near Seesen, Braunschweig, Germany, and died between 1852 - 1853 in Gordonville, Cape Girardeau County, MO. He married Johanne "Marie" Friederike Klusmann (or Clausmann) on Nov. 11, 1823, daughter of Christian KluBmann and Marie Habekost. She was born March 4, 1800 in Germany, and died between 1860 - 1870 in Gordonville, MO.

As to when the family arrived, the ledger of Dr. J. W. Cramer, MD indicated that he treated Christian Abelunke primarily by emetic and purging from Dec. 26, 1847 to May 19, 1849 in Jackson, MO. This ledger is presently in the possession of the Bollinger County Historical Society. How amazing it is that medical records should exist this far back.

After Christian's death, Maria had a hard time keeping the farm running. She and her son, Henry, took out a mortgage on the property with Andrew Suedekum, her son-in-law, recorded in Cape Girardeau County on May 16, 1857. But for all her work, the farm was put up for sale by the court to pay the debts due to Clamont Freeza. The property was auctioned on the courthouse steps with Henry Amelunke being the highest bidder. This is how the farm came to fall into the hands of his son, Henry Amelunke, who managed it until 1903 when he died.

Christian Amelunke, born Klein Rhüden A. Lesen Am Harz (Germany)

Children of Christian Amelunke and Maria Klusmann are: (1) Johanne Christine Wilhelmine Amelunke was born Aug. 6, 1824 and died Nov. 20, 1842 in Klein Rhüden, Braunschweig, Germany. (2) Conradine Amelunke was born Feb. 27, 1827 in Germany and died Sept. 4, 1883 in Gordonville, MO. She married Andrew Suedekum. (3) Caroline Luise Amelunke was born Aug. 4, 1829. (4) Johann Heinrich "Christian" Amelung was born Sept. 26, 1832 in Germany and died Aug. 6, 1903 in Pilot Knob, Iron County, MO. He married Johanna Marie Magdalene Bodenstein on Jan. 5, 1854 in St. Francois County, MO; she was born Feb. 9, 1833 in Hahausen, Braunschweig, Germany and died Dec. 4, 1918 in Pilot Knob, MO. (5) Johann Heinrich Amelunke was born Nov. 25, 1835 and died July 26, 1836 in Klein Rhüden, Germany. (6) Johann "Heinrich" Amelunge was born June 8, 1837 in Klein Rhüden, Germany, and died July 26, 1903 in Gordonville, MO. He married first Johanna Overfert in 1855; she was born in 1828 in Braunschweig, Germany and died after 1867. He married second Catherine Schmie on June 15, 1871. He married third Rosena Schweer between 1871 – 1877; she died Feb. 6, 1924 in Gordonville, MO. (7) Johanne Christine Juliane Amelunke was born Nov. 18, 1839 and died Jan. 19, 1841 in Klein Rhüden, Germany. (8) Johanna S. W. Amelunke was born Feb. 17, 1842 and died Feb. 11, 1884 in Gordonville, MO. She married Benedict Walperswiller Sr. on Feb. 3, 1865 in Cape Girardeau County; he was born May 1827 in Switzerland and died 1909 in Cape Girardeau County, MO. (9) Andreas "Wilhelm" Amelunck was born Jan. 14, 1846 in Klein Rhüden, Germany and died after 1860. *Submitted by Marcine Lohman*

ARMSTRONG/RAMSEY – In 1795, eight years before the Louisiana Purchase, Andrew Ramsey (also sometimes spelled as Ramsay) came to what is now Cape Girardeau County and built a two-story log cabin which still stands today. Ramsey, along with his wife Eva and ten children, were the first English settlers in the area. Ramsey fought in the Revolutionary War and also in the French and Indian War under Braddock. The following account of the Ramsay settlement is given in it *The History of Southeast Missouri* page 271 following:

"As has been stated the settlement at Cape Girardeau was purely American, there not being more than five French families in the entire district. Of this settlement Andrew Ramsay was the pioneer. Attracted by the liberal offers of land, the salubrity of climate and fertility of the soil, as well as, no doubt, by the personality of the commandant, or more properly speaking by the personality of his able, accomplished and intellectual secretary, Andrew Ramsay, in 1795, settled immediately adjacent to the grant of the commandant, and for many years his home was the point to which the hardy pioneers of Virginia, Kentucky, North Carolina and Tennessee directed their course. An eye-witness, Jesse Friend, now dead, but who as a boy remembers the encampment around Ramsay's plantation, gave a graphic picture of these hardy pioneers, who, under the inducements offered by the Spanish Government, now crowded across the Mississippi. Every day, he said, new settlers would arrive from the States, and after a long and weary journey, rest along the bank of a creek that meandered through his plantation, and yet known as Ramsay's Creek, and allow their cattle to pasture in the open and park-like woods, filled in summer with luxuriant cane and grass, while they themselves, accompanied by Ramsay, prospected the country for eligible locations. On Sundays, especially, the whole settlement would congregate at Ramsay's to hear the latest news from the latest immigrants, and to pass the day in such enjoyments as a new country afforded .... Andrew Ramsay was a man of substance and the owner of a goodly number of slaves. He exercised a decided influence in the settlement, and so early as 1799 an English school, the first west of the Mississippi, was established at what was called Mount Tabor, a mile from his plantation, and in the center of the new settlement. He was one of the largest landholders in the district." [Southern Historical Preservation ISBN: 089308431X]

Andrew Ramsey Sr., who was from Dalhousie Castle in Scotland, had the property from 1795 to about 1813 when it was taken over by descendants William and Eleanor Ramsey. Ramsey Sr. went to Batesville, AR where he died from an arrow in an Indian war. The "Wood" and "High Hill" houses were built by descendants of Ramsey. Subsequent owners of the property were: Rebecca Harbison (April 14,1818); John Cross (Sept. 28, 1833); William Cross/Miriam T. Cross (Oct. 10, 1864); Robert Wilson (taken over for debt on Dec. 7, 1882); Miriam T. Cross (March 25,1887); L. R. and E. R. Johnson (March 25, 1887); Horeph and Ella Johnson (March 22, 1895); Benjamin F. Davis (April 6, 1899); daughter Olivia W. Davis (Sept. 20, 1918); Otto F. and Caroline Willa (Dec. 26, 1918) and Bowman Brothers Co., realtor - Florian James and Lula Jane Armstrong (April 6,1925). F. J. Armstrong died Aug. 14, 1992 and left the house to four descendants: Olive (Mrs. Albert) Keller of Cape Girardeau; Bonnie (Mrs. Vernon) Ludwig of Jackson; Eileen (Mrs. Martin) Gannon of Stillwater, NY and Carl D. Armstrong of Alvin, TX. Another son, Russel Armstrong of Cape Girardeau, preceded his father in death. The house is located on Silver Springs Road between the Shawnee Parkway (SH 74) and Mount Auburn Road (about one-half mile east of Interstate 55).

The original two-story log cabin still stands today and is said to be one of the oldest houses between Ste. Genevieve and Memphis. A larger house was built around it. F. J. Armstrong's father, James Alexander Armstrong, came from Glasgow, Scotland. He was the son of a wealthy doctor, who disinherited him for changing his career from medicine to engineering. He worked on the Suez Canal, Ead's Bridge in St. Louis, and at the glass plant in Crystal City, where he started up one of the world's largest steam engines. He died of pneumonia on March 4, 1898, exactly three months before F. J. was born. F. J.'s mother, Matilda (Gasche) later married Bernard Schneider and moved to Marquand, MO.

Armstrong-Ramsey House on Silver Springs Road, September 2001.

There F. J. met and married Lula Jane Smith (of English and Cherokee descent from Lenoir, NC) and had their firstborn, Russell Edwin. F. J. and family then moved to Puxico, MO. Here, Olive Marie was born. F. J. cropped the rich farmlands and sold meat, milk and garden produce in Puxico. With two neighbors, he groveled fish in the Mingo Swamp and sold them to the Houck Railroad. Lula was with child (Bonnie Mae) but the pregnancy was complicated with the onset of malaria. The doctor warned F. J. that she must leave the Mingo Swamp area or die.

On March 4, 1925, F. J. scouted for a new home. The cattle and machinery were loaded on two cars on Houck's railroad. The furniture rode by team and wagon driven by a hired boy and the Armstrongs navigated the dirt roads to Cape Girardeau County in a Model-T Ford. On March 23, 1925, F. J. drove on the dirt road leading to the old Ramsey house and showed Lula a large unpainted house that would be their home. It had no running water and no electricity, but work galore to be done. However, the farm did have two all-weather springs and F. J later registered the farm name "Silver Springs Farm" with the state. Milk was kept cool in the spring water.

The original two-story log cabin house had been expanded over the years to a colonial-type house with four large rooms and a hall in front, and then a wing was added in the back with a kitchen and bedrooms. The inside was plain farmhouse structure. Two large brick chimneys are on each side of the house. It was not until many years later that the Armstrongs became aware that the old original log cabin hidden in the structure has a rich history dating back to the Andrew Ramsey settlement. Scott City historian Edison Shrum was instrumental in this discovery. The original logs can still be viewed.

The Armstrong family over the years found many Indian artifacts on certain parts of the farm and have set aside a small area that was once was an Indian campground. It is said that the Shawnees and Delawares were once on the land. Also, a number of Civil War cannon balls have been found on the farm.

Bonnie Mae, Opal Eileen, and Carl David were additions to the Armstrong family after they moved into the old Ramsey home. F. J.'s mother and step-father, Bernard, joined them to live in the house. Bernard was an expert fiddler and played on KFVS radio station. From time to time there were parties in the house. The family struggled through the depression years and F. J.'s loan fell into default. The banker would ride out to the farm to receive butchered pork, beef, chickens and vegetables, eggs and dairy products. This saved the farm from foreclosure.

The Armstrong family of Silver Springs Farm, circa 1939. Front row left to right: F. J., Carl, Lula. Back row left to right: Russell, Bonnie, Olive, Eileen.

Over the years the house (which came through the 1811 New Madrid earthquake) has been repaired many times. Open porches were finally enclosed, the roof tinned, chimneys tuck-pointed and a long support log added under the house to shore up the flooring. The house even has a concrete "tornado/atomic fallout shelter" cellar which F. J. added. It has a heavy metal door that was obtained when the Common Pleas Courthouse "dungeon" was dismantled.

The farm has undergone rapid change. Highway I-55 and Mount Auburn Road have cut the farm in two. Silver Springs is changing into a wide, modern road. Southeast Missouri Hospital now owns 21 acres north and west of the house. The large red hay-barn that F. J. built still stands on the property. F. J.'s heirs have incorporated the land as Armstrong Heritage, Inc. The house is now the Armstrong-Ramsey House. The land of which it now resides is the Silver Springs Historical Trust. *Submitted by Bonnie Ludwig and Carl Armstrong*

BAKER - Mary Jane Baker was born July 2, 1848 near Millersville, MO, and died in 1927. She was married Jan. 27, 1867 to Charles Benton Stearns who was born Feb. 8, 1844 in Bollinger County, MO, and who died 8 Feb. 1921. Both are buried in the Snider Cemetery. He was the son of Joseph Marion Stearns and Sarah Sally Seabaugh. Charles and Mary Stearns were the parents of Cecilia, Andrew Lee, Odie, Charles Jefferson, Effie Miller, and Sarah Sally Allen, the wife of William Harve Allen.

The Stearns were members of the Spiritualist Millersville Church. Mary Jane Stearns was the daughter of Joseph Baker Jr. who was born Nov. 2, 1806, a twin, and who died Jan. 7, 1849. He was married Dec. 15, 1831 to Ann Young who was born July 24, 1814 near Oak Ridge, MO. Both are buried in the Baker Cemetery. She was the daughter of Phillip Young and Betsy Elizabeth Byrd. Joseph and Ann Baker were the parents of Peter, Clara, Sarah, Catherine, Mary, Levi, Hanna, Polly, and Mary Jane Stearns.

Joseph Baker Jr. was the son of Joseph Baker Sr. who was born 1777/1778 and who died June 24, 1848. He was married Jan. 27, 1805 in Cape Girardeau to Catherine Niswonger who was born in 1788 in North Carolina and who died in 1850. Both are buried in the Baker Cemetery. Catherine was the daughter of Joseph Niswonger Sr. and Eva Katherine Statler. Joseph and Eva Catherine Niswonger were the parents of Elizabeth Martin, Joseph Jr., and Catherine Baker.

Joseph Baker Sr. was the son of Peter Baker Sr. who was born in 1735 in Lancaster County, PA, and who died in 1819 in Bollinger County. He was married in Pennsylvania to Mary Miller. Both are buried in Deck Cemetery. It is said Mary Miller was a sister to John Miller and Martha Clay, the founder of Millersville, MO. The Baker family goes back to 1450 when Jacob Baker was married to Abigail. The Baker-Becker family came from the southern part of Germany along the Rhine River.

Joseph Niswonger Sr. was born in 1745 in Switzerland and died April 15, 1833 in Cape Girardeau County. He was married about 1783 to Eva Katherine Statler who was born Nov. 5, 1759 in Goshenhoppen, Berks County, PA, and who died in June 1821 in Cape Girardeau County. He was the son of Ulrich Neighswonger-Niswonger. *Submitted by Andrea Nicole Slinkard*

BANGERT – Wilhelm and Catherine Eichmeyer Bangert emigrated from Waldeck in 1848 and settled near Lixville, MO. Wilhelm signed a citizenship declaration on June 1, 1849. They were early members of Trinity Lutheran Church at Friedheim. The Bangerts, along with Mr. and Mrs. Freidrich Sewing, donated the land for the first log cabin church. Wilhelm and Catherine had nine children: William (Tilda Kester), Caroline (Ernest Yamintz), Louisa (George Kester), Anna, Catherine (Henry Mecker), Frederick (Matilda Moeller), Henry (Hannah Seabaugh), Wilhelmina (Jefferson Statler), and Mary (Henry Leonard).

Frederick Bangert and Matilda Moeller were married on Nov. 25, 1880. They lived on a farm near Lixville. They had four sons: Christian (Martha Bangert), William (Myrtle Blaylock), Robert (Caroline Pohlman), and Walter (Leona Ruesler). All four sons lived on farms near Lixville, but Walter later moved to Perryville. Christian, known as Fritz, lived to the age of 104. He is buried in the cemetery at Friedheim, along with many other family members.

William Bangert and Myrtle Blaylock were married on Nov. 28, 1907. Myrtle was the daughter of Columbus and Belinda Barks Blaylock. Columbus's grandparents, Thomas and Elizabeth Blaylock, arrived in Perry County sometime in the early 1800s. Belinda's great-grandparents, Hunteel and Sarah Masters Barks, settled in Cape Girardeau County around 1800 on a land grant on Whitewater Creek. Hunteel is listed in the census of 1803 as a landowner in what is now Bollinger County.

William and Myrtle lived on a farm near Lixville. They had seven children: Sidonia (Earl Seabaugh); Edgar (Reva Statler); Dewey (Lyla James); Ruby (Elmer Stearns); Wilbur (LaVern Meyer); Dorothy (Calvin Phillips); and Pervis. In 1925 a tornado hit the area, damaging or destroying many structures in the area. The Bangert home was one of the first hit. The barns and outbuildings were demolished, and most of the livestock killed. Most of the house was blown away, leaving only the original log cabin room. William and Myrtle ran into that room, carrying 6-month-old Wilbur, and were unharmed. The tornado next struck Garner School, where Sidonia was teaching. Edgar, Dewey and Ruby were among the students. All four were injured, Dewey the most severely.

Dewey served in the military in WWII in the 101st Airborne. His company was released by glider into enemy territory and was captured the next day. He spent seven months in a prisoner of war camp. Pervis joined the Navy after the war (he was too young to join during the war), and was sent to a base in Alaska. He was on a plane that was lost on Aug. 7, 1948. It was never located. Wilbur "Wib" joined the Navy, and was stationed on the aircraft carrier *Hannock*. He was part of the crew that helped with airplane landings, and was present at the Battle of Midway. After the war, Wib opened Bangert Body Shop and later Bangert Ford Tractor Sales. He enjoyed playing golf and was one of the first members of Kimbeland Country Club. *Submitted by Peggy Luehrs*

BARKS – My first remembrance of Jackson was coming to shop; it was larger than the Marble Hill-Lutesville area. My granddad Otto W. (O. W.) Reutzel had gone to school at McFeron School north of Jackson. We would take a picnic lunch on a Sunday afternoon to McFeron School; we loved the big flat rocks and grapevines to swing on.

On one occasion, with my grandparents in the car, my dad Wendell Barks stopped the car on north Farmington and announced to O. W. and Dora Reutzel that he and Clodine had bought nearly eight acres on the corner from Billy Green (1945). O. W. Reutzel was not too pleased and said "you kids could have bought a big farm in Bollinger County for less in price." Wendell and Clodine Barks developed that into Barks Mobile Home Park. Clodine was the third child of the Reutzels, Ruby Kirkpatrick and Orville Reutzel being older, and Bonnie Grindstaff and Cletus Reutzel being younger.

Wendell and Clodine first built a granite house and we moved to Jackson for a couple of years. We loved the branch behind the field, jumping across it going to Burne's Orchard (now Strawberry Lane). Dad's love for the farm in Glen Allen won out and we moved back to Bollinger County for years, knowing we would come back to Jackson. There are four of us children: I, the oldest; Glenda married E. D. Francis; Wanda married Kelly Francis; Mary Barks Barnes and James Barks.

I had always wanted to live in Jackson. We moved here in 1975. Our daughter Deana finished high school here and is still teaching fifth grade at West Lane. She married Jerry Myracle and they have two daughters, Mandy and Frannie. Our son Steven teaches at Marquand. He married Dianna Robins and they have a daughter and son, Stephanie and Trevor. *Submitted by Glenda Barks Francis*

BARTELS – Wilhelm August Bartels was born Nov. 12, 1851 in Kohnigrich, Hanover Germany, came to America June 10, 1860 with his parents Friedrich and Louise Bartels, along with a sister Louise born in 1849 and a brother Friedrich born in 1855. Wilhelm Bartels married first on Feb. 25, 1877 to Anna Lange, born May 17 1859. This union was blessed with two children, daughter Mena who was born Dec. 24, 1877 and died February 7, 1878 at age 7 weeks, and August Friedrich Bartels who was born Feb. 16, 1880. Anna (Lange) Bartels died April 21, 1880.

Wilhelm A. Bartels married second to Wilhelmina (Lange) Meier Hauenschild on Nov. 25, 1880, she was a sister to his first wife. This union was blessed with three children; William, Anna and Friedrick. Wilhelmina Bartels was born March 19, 1845 and died June 11, 1911. Wilhelm A. Bartels died June 9, 1916.

Left to right: Mary, Emma, Minnie, Bertha, August Bartels

August Friedrich Bartels was married August 11, 1907 to Bertha Johanna Sternberg who was born June 17, 1879. They were the parents of three daughters; Minnie was born Oct. 1, 1908 and who died Feb. 10, 2000; Emma who was born Sept. 25, 1910; and Mary who was born June 30, 1912. Mary was married Sept. 30 1945 to George Vrbosky, born July 15, 1913, and they were the parents of Joe, Paul and Betty (Vrbosky) Phillips. Mary died Feb. 22, 1994, and George died April 18, 1996.

On May 5, 1925 August Friedrich Bartels bought the Oliver House from August Flenge. Minnie, Emma and Mary lived there and worked at the Jackson Shoe Factory. On March 11, 1937, August Bartels was killed in a logging accident when he was hauling logs to the August Voshage sawmill on the Bartels farm. Minnie, Emma and Mary moved back to the farm to be with their mother but continued to work at the shoe factory. Minnie and Emma worked there for a combined total of 83 years. Their mother died Feb. 19, 1954, at the age of 74 years. Emma just celebrated her ninety-first birthday and still lives on the family farm. *Submitted by Emma Bartels*

BAST - Mary Elizabeth Bast was born Nov. 5, 1830 near Gravel Hill, MO. She died Aug. 18, 1923 and is buried in the Russell Heights Cemetery in Jackson, MO. She was married to Benjamin Franklin Allen who was born in 1829 in North Carolina. He is buried in the Byrd-Delph Cemetery. Benjamin was a descendent of Vincent Allen of South Carolina and Virginia.

Mary Elizabeth Allen was the daughter of George Washington Bast Sr. who was born Aug. 25, 1795 in Lincoln County, KY, and who died July 3, 1874. He was married Jan. 4, 1827 in Davies County, KY, to Ruth (Bell) Taylor who was born in 1806 in Berkeley County, VA, and who died in 1890. Both are buried in Gravel Hill Cemetery. Bast Street in Jackson, MO, was named for the Bast family.

Ruth Bast was the daughter of Benjamin Bell who was born in 1700 in Berkeley County, VA. He was married in Berkeley County, VA, on Sept. 2, 1799 to Margaret Fanny Southwood who was born in 1775/1778 and who died in 1829 in Davies County, KY. George and Ruth Bast were the parents of George Washington Jr.; Margaret; Virginia; Thomas Jefferson; Benjamin; Anna; and Mary Elizabeth Allen.

George W. Bast Sr. was the son of Thomas Peter Bast who was born in 1754 in Pennsylvania and who died in 1816 in Lincoln County, KY. He was married Feb. 17, 1785 in Baltimore, MD, to Catherine Illspach who was born in 1760 and who died in 1820 in Lincoln County, KY. They were parents of David, Valentine, Abraham, Isaac, Moses, Adam, Thomas, Catherine, Mary, Elizabeth, Peter, Rebecca, Sarah, and George Washington Sr.

Thomas Peter Bast was the son of Valentine George Bast who was born about 1725 in the Palatine and who died about 1785 in Frederick County, MD. He married Mary Felty and they were the parents of Michael, Ferdinand, Felty, and Thomas Peter.

Benjamin Bell was born in 1770 in Virginia and married Margaret Fanny Southwood who died in Davies County, KY. They were the parents of Joseph, Benjamin Jr., James, Edward, Rebecca, and Ruth.

Margaret Fanny Bell was the daughter of Edward Southwood who was born about 1740 in Virginia and who died in 1824 in Berkeley County, VA. He married Miss Washington. *Submitted by Donald Ray Slinkard*

BEGGS – James Edward Beggs was born in 1933 in Fornfelt, MO, the son of Ora Greenlee and Barney Beggs. James became known as Jim. Jim served in the U.S. Army active duty from 1953-1955 and served inactive duty for six years.

James Beggs with his four children and five grandchildren. Left to right, back row: Brenda, Theresa, Tammy and Jimmy; James in middle. Front row: Cyndi holding Lucas, Nicki, Paul holding Brooke. October 2000

In January 1959 Jim married Shirley Ann Martin of Kelso, MO, the daughter of Virginia Smith and Edward Martin. Jim and Shirley resided in Scott City after their marriage. Together, Jim and Shirley had four children: Theresa; Jimmy; Brenda and Tammy. In 1973 the family moved to Jackson for a better life and a nice place to raise their kids. The family moved to a subdivision just outside of town called Grandview Acres. The kids attended the Jackson Schools.

Jim and Shirley were divorced in 1988. Shirley now works and resides in Cape Girardeau, MO. Jim remarried in 1988. In 1992 Jim moved into the town of Jackson. He retired in 1996 from 40 years with the Cotton Belt Railroad. Jim once again divorced. Jim continues to live in Jackson today.

Theresa married Dennis Horst, also of Jackson; the couple resides in Jackson and has a son. Jimmy married Kim Webb of Cape Girardeau; they reside in Cape Girardeau and have a daughter. Brenda married John L. Reed of Wilton Center, IL; Brenda has two children from a previous marriage and the family resides

Brenda, Shirley, Jimmy, Theresa, Tammy, Jim. 1981

in Wilton Center, IL. Tammy resides in Cape Girardeau and attends Southeast Missouri State University. She has a daughter. They all continue to visit Jackson often. *Submitted by Stanley Beggs*

BEUSSINK - Albert Beussink and Hilda Thiele were married on April 19, 1950, at St. John's Parish Church in Leopold, MO, and moved to Jackson because "that's where the work was," said Albert Beussink. When they moved to Jackson, Mr. and Mrs. Beussink joined Immaculate Conception Catholic Church.

Albert was born on Sept. 6, 1926, the son of Herman Sr. and Mary (Holzum) Beussink of Leopold, MO. Hilda was born on Jan. 21, 1929, the daughter of Fred and Lena (Elfrink) Thiele of Leopold. Albert served in the U.S. Army during WWII, and worked for the phone company when his tour of duty was over. In 1949 he started working for Philip Elfrink Construction Company in Jackson.

With the help of family and friends, they built their home in a field on the east side of Jackson. They had a small farm with a cow, pigs and chickens. A gravel road named Highland Drive was constructed, and the area began to develop with the addition of Forest Acres and Indian Hills Subdivisions. In the 1960s the couple developed Beussink Subdivision (Oakland Drive) in this area on three acres purchased from Johnny Seiler.

Front row, left to right: Judi Beussink Niederkorn, Albert Beussink, Hilda Beussink. Second row: Don Beussink, Steve Beussink, Sheila Beussink Ziegler, John Beussink, Cindy Beussink Poston. Back row: Mark Beussink, Greg Beussink

Albert and Hilda are the parents of eight children: sons Steve; Don; Mark; Greg and John and daughters Judi Niederkorn; Sheila Ziegler and Cindy Poston. All eight children graduated from Immaculate Conception Grade School in Jackson and Notre Dame High School in Cape Girardeau. The couple has 16 grandchildren.

Albert founded Beussink Brothers Woodworks, builders of custom cabinets and millwork. He and his brother Robert "Bob" Beussink Sr. formed a partnership in 1966 that continued until Bob's retirement in 1992.

Albert belongs to the American Legion, Knights of Columbus and Fourth Degree Knights of Columbus, VFW, Chamber of Comemrce, Cursillo and Capaha Antique Car Club. He served on the Immaculate Conception Parish Council and School Board for several years. He was a member of the building committee in charge of construction of the IC School gym in 1970. Mr. Beussink is semi-retired and enjoys working with antique cars.

Hilda is a member of the Knights of Columbus Auxiliary and St. Ann's Sodality, and was a dedicated volunteer many years for the IC and Notre Dame schools. Both are members of the Notre Dame Booster Club. Mrs. Beussink retired in 1990 after working for ten years as a cook at Notre Dame High School. She enjoys gardening, reading, and quilting.

The Beussinks moved to a new home at 146 Borax Lane outside Jackson in January 1999. *Submitted by Judi Beussink Niederkorn*

BEUSSINK – Johannes Beussink was born in Bibergen, Netherlands on Nov. 1, 1862. His mother died in Holland, and his father went back to Germany. This left Johannes an orphan, so he went to work on a farm in 1879 as a servant to the Broshius family. This was next to the Landewe farm. Johannes got acquainted with the Landewe twin girls, whose family then moved to the United States.

Johannes Beussink migrated from Haaksbergen, Netherlands in 1888 to Cincinnati, where many people migrated. The trip was often very dangerous, taking 40 to 60 days by ship, costing 30 and 45 guilders, taking enough food for two months and sleeping between decks on hay sacks. Their valuables were sold for the trip. They carried personal memories or small items. Father Luytenaar, a Catholic priest, moved with 12 families, including John "Johannes" Beussink, via ship on the Ohio River, then the Mississippi River to Cape Girardeau, MO, settling in Vinemout, which was later named Leopold. Pioneering was very difficult. In 1848 Herman Vrielink (no relative) wrote home to Holland after living in the United States seven years. He worked with two horses and earned $3.00 a day. The horse feed was expensive.

In 1858 he wrote how he earned $7.00 a day working from 3 a.m. to 10 p.m. He said to keep this up, one had to drink as much beer and gin in one week as they did one year in Holland.

They built a church in Leopold consecrated to St. John. The first homes were a hole in the ground with a roof on it. More people moved to the new location. Lots of property cost 12-1/2 cents per acre.

John Beussink again met the Landewe twins. He was to marry Diana, but she died with typhoid fever. John then married the other twin, Mary. Shortly after they settled, the American Civil War broke out. Missouri belonged partly to the North and partly to the South. On Aug 24, 1862, there was a fierce battle at Crooked Creek in Bollinger County, located between Leopold and Laflin.

John and Mary Beussink had eight children: Drika; Henry; Herman; John; Anthony; August; Bernard and Marie. They lived on a farm near Leopold. Anthony "Tony" and Mary Arnzen were married May 27, 1924. They lived three miles south of Leopold. They had 12 children, but Joseph lived only a few hours. The others were Bill, Adele, Philip, Catherine, Fred, Charles, Franklin, Harold, Pat, David and Linda. Franklin passed away Feb. 23, 1991. Charles passed away in December 1997.

Philip was born April 11, 1928. He walked three miles to school with his sisters and brothers. He worked on his dad's farm, and cut logs during the winter months. He also worked as a carpenter until Nov. 11, 1950. He was drafted into the Army and served in the Korean War. He married Angela Wubker on May 17, 1952. They lived in Jackson after Philip's discharge in August 1952.

Philip and Angela had five children. Karen was born Dec. 14, 1953, married Rick Kubb on April 17, 1982 and had three children; Charlotte, Ashley and Brandon. Kathy was born Sept. 15, 1955, married Tim McNamara on Aug 6, 1979 and had children Meghan and Jamie. Scott was born Jan. 21, 1960, married Sharon Atchley on April 6, 1991 and had one daughter Tracy, who married T. J. Martin and had children Kaylin and Krista. Tina was born Feb. 24, 1964, married Larry Blattel on April 16, 1983 and had children Emily, Elaine and Nicole. Vickie was born Aug. 16, 1965, married Mike Bollinger on Oct. 27, 1984 and had children Jessica, Sarah, Rebecca and Monica.

After Philip's discharge, he worked at Cape Florsheim Shoe Factory for six years, then worked in construction work for other companies. He eventually had his own construction company until he retired, when his son Scott took over, under the name Scott Beussink Construction Co. Angela worked at Jackson Hosiery Mill for six years, then stayed home with the children until they were in school. She then worked at Cape County Nutrition Center until she retired. *Submitted by Angela Beussink*

BEUSSINK - A significant part of Jackson's history is the construction industry. An important part of that industry for over 30 years has been a successful cabinet shop known as Beussink Brothers Woodworks. Co-founder and one of the "brothers" is Robert "Bob" H. Beussink Sr.

Bob Beussink was born on July 22, 1928, outside the small Bollinger County town of Leopold. He was the second son of Herman and Mary (Holzum) Beussink. On Oct. 25, 1950, he married Evelyn Marie Nenninger at St. John's Catholic Church in Leopold. Evelyn was born on Nov. 25, 1929, and was the daughter of Henry and Martha (Elfrink) Nenninger. Barely a month after their marriage, Bob was called to serve his country in the Army and was sent to fight in Korea. Bob was recovering from a wound in a hospital in Japan in July of 1951 at the same time Evelyn was in a hospital back home delivering them a son, Robert Jr. Bob returned from Korea in April of 1952. He, his bride and young son then moved to St. Louis. Tragically, Evelyn, who had been battling cancer while Bob was away, finally succumbed to its ravages and died on Oct. 3, 1953.

Bob continued to work in St. Louis, making frequent trips back to southeast Missouri. On one of those trips he met Irma Catherine Ziegler. Irma is the daughter of John and Coletta (Scherer) Ziegler and was born on Dec. 8, 1936, in Benton, MO. On May 30, 1958, Bob and Irma were married at St. Dennis Church in Benton. The couple took up residence in St. Louis (Overland), where Bob worked as a carpenter for Vatterott Construction, and then for Fred Terbrock Construction. They lived there for the next eight years with Bob, Jr., and new additions, Karen, Chris and Marsha.

In 1966 Bob and Irma had the opportunity to change their lives. They had done well in Overland, but their hearts and families were in southeast Missouri. Bob made the decision to leave his job in the city and start a partnership with his brother Albert in the cabinet shop in Jackson. This partnership was the beginning of Beussink Brothers Woodworks. It was a difficult decision, but both Bob and Irma felt that the big city was not the place to raise a quickly growing family, and Jackson looked to be the ideal place to continue their lives. Their first move was to the old Immaculate Conception Convent located on the corner of the school parking lot on Hope Street. This 100-year-old building served them well until they purchased a house and property on what was then called Highway 61 North (now North High Street) in the spring of 1967.

Bob and Irma Beussink family

Several additions to the family brought on several additions to the house. Since moving to Jackson, Bob and Irma have added a girl and three boys to their family bringing the total to eight: sons Bob Jr., Chris, Matt, Jeff and Chad; and daughters Karen Rigdon, Marsha Williams and Janice Long. The children are all married and live in Jackson or the immediate area. Bob and Irma currently have 13 grandchildren.

After over 40 years in the construction business, Bob finally retired from Beussink Brothers Woodworks in 1992 (three of his sons still work there) for what he thought would be a well-deserved rest. But quality woodworking skills and difficulty in saying no to folks have Bob constantly busy doing custom jobs for people. He does find more time now to spend with his grandkids, and is always ready to lend a helping hand when one of his children needs help on a "project."

Irma's life has slowed a little too. Being a housewife and mother for eight children was quite a career in itself, but Irma also found time to provide childcare for several of her grandchildren and a few other boys and girls along the way. Her door and her arms are still always open for a grandchild "a little under the weather."

Bob and Irma Beussink have been an important part of Jackson history for almost 40 years. Besides being a successful business man, Bob has also been active in Immaculate Conception Parish, serving on the parish council and numerous other positions. He was president of the Immaculate Conception Home and School Association, and devoted much time to Notre Dame High School where he served on its main board, as president of its ways and means committee,

Angela and Philip Beussink, Karen Kubb, Kathy McNamara, Scott Beussink, Tina Blattel, Vickie Bollinger

as a member of its building committee, and as a long time member of the Booster Club. Bob belongs to the VFW and the American Legion where he is a past Commander and Captain of the Color Guard. He is a 4th Degree member of the Knights of Columbus and belonged to the Carpenter's Union for many years.

Besides all of her homemaker and childcare duties, Irma is an active member of the Knights of Columbus Auxiliary and the Immaculate Conception St. Ann's Sodality. The Immaculate Conception and Notre Dame Booster Clubs and their Home and School Associations have also benefitted from Irma's time and efforts. When she is not helping out with the grandkids, she enjoys reading and crocheting beautiful works of art for relatives and friends. *Submitted by Bob Beussink Jr.*

BIERSCHWAL/BAUMGARDT/BRAKEBUSCH/ DAWSON/GREBE – The Bierschwal family migrated from Lafferde, Germany which is now knowr as Lahstedt, on Nov. 11, 1844, aboard the *Bark Diana*, along with many other families that settled in Cape Girardeau County. The family included Christian (a weaver), his wife Doretta (Kelpe) and four children. They settled near Dutchtown and were charter members of the German Methodist Church (Zion United Methodist Church) near Gordonville. Their son Conrad (b. May 27, 1838; d. Apri 21, 1916) married (1855) Wilhelmine Henriette Grebe (b. Aug. 21, 1839; d. Oct. 22, 1904), the daughter of Johann Heinrich Grebe (b. April 8, 1807; d. Nov. 29, 1842; Schleweke, Germany) and Johanne Sophie Louise Christiane Philips (b. July 23, 1807; d. circa 1870). Conrad and Henriette Bierschwal had five children of which two died as infants. John Henry married Dorothea Sander in 1880, Anna married William Bartles in 1882, and John C. "Conrad" (b. Nov. 6, 1861; d. March 25, 1932) married Alvina Brakebush (b. Dec. 26, 1860; d. Aug. 17, 1935) on May 5, 1887. Alvina was the daughter of Johann Christian and Caroline Wilhelmine (Brinkman) Brakebush, who migrated from Germany in 1858.

John C. and Alvina Bierschwal operated a store and restaurant in Dutchtown for 30 years. They had three children; Selma who married John Randolph, Laura who married Robert L. Hager and Herman "Walter (b. July 16, 1890; d. Feb. 21, 1946) who married Bertha May Baumgardt (b. July 3, 1889; d. July 19, 1974) on Jan. 1, 1913. Bertha was the daughter of Peter Baumgardt (b. Aug. 25, 1861, Ohio; d. Jan. 11, 1928) and Louise Josephine Dawson (b. March 17, 1868; d. April 9, 1954), daughter of John and Sarah (Wagner) Dawson from Ohio.

Walter Bierschwal was a blacksmith; he and Bertha had nine children. Cecil Webster (b. March 26, 1916; d. April 28, 1983) was their third child and he married Marjorie "Margie" Rebecca Webb (b. Oct. 2, 1918; d. Jan. 1,1992) (see Howard/Webb entry) on Feb. 29, 1936. Cecil worked in the foundry in St. Louis, making war supplies during WWII. He was also employed in the trucking business, driving for Cauble & Fields and Day Transfer for 25 years. He then worked for the city of Cape Girardeau for a number of years. Margie worked at the Osteopathic Hospital and later at the Ratliff Nursing Home, both located in Cape Girardeau. He and Margie resided in Cape Girardeau and had seven children: Bonnie Sue (b. July 5, 1936); Gracolyn Mae (b. Aug. 9, 1937); Forrest Glenn (b. Sept. 19, 1940; d. Dec. 24, 1993); Michael Webb (b. Jan. 3, 1943; d. Aug. 21, 1943); Charles Roger (b. Aug. 20, 1944); William Hunter (b. Sept. 30, 1949) and Danny Webster (b. May 13, 1951).

Bonnie married Henry Weldon Macke (b. Aug. 16, 1930) on July 11, 1954, and moved from Cape Girardeau to Gordonville. They have always attended Zion United Methodist Church of Gordonville, which her ancestors helped to found. They have three daughters, of which Karen Kay Macke (b. Jan. 1, 1959) is the second child. Karen graduated from Jackson High School in 1977 and married Rick Welker, with one child, Rachel Ann Welker, being born to them on July 22, 1977. Rachel married Garrett Thorne (b. Dec. 2, 1977) on Jan. 15, 1999. On Sept. 21, 2000 Cameron Vaughn Thorne was born. Karen later married Kevin Yarbro (b. March 1, 1958) on Sept. 27, 1982. They have a daughter, Erica Michelle Yarbro (b. Nov. 7, 1984) who is a junior at Jackson High School. Karen recently retired from Wal-Mart and is currently employed by Beussink, Hey, Roe, Seabaugh and Stroder, L.L.C., and Kevin works for Austin Periodicals. They reside in Cape Girardeau County north of Pocahontas. *Submitted by Karen Macke Yarbro*

BIERSCHWAL – Heinrich "Christian" Bierschwalen was born Sept. 16, 1794 in Gross Lafferde, Germany. Christian was listed as a farmer from Werder when he married on Oct. 17, 1822 to Joh. Maria "Dorothea" Schrack, who died about 1838. According to Glen C. Randolph, the author of *The Study of the families Bierschwalen, Bierschwale, Bierschwall, and Bierschwal*, Christian second married Charlotte Doretta Kelpe between 1838 and 1844. They arrived on Nov. 11, 1844 on the *Bark Diana* at the Port of New Orleans with his four children. They immigrated with many other Germans who settled in the German area of southern Cape Girardeau County. Christian Bierschwall was listed as a weaver from Hannover on the passenger list. He became a charter member of the Zion Methodist Church near Gordonville, MO. Christian had the following children: Charlotte (1823-1899) who married Theodor Happle; John (1829-1861) who married Rosina Nabe; Louise (1836-?) who married Christian Kothe Jr.; and Conrad (1838-1916) who married Wilh. Henriette Grebe. Christian died in May of 1856.

Conrad Bierschwal farmed near Dutchtown. He and his wife Henriette had five children. They were Albert (1855-1856); John "Henry" (1858-1910), who married Dorothea Sander; Louise (1859-1861); John Conrad (1861-1932) who married Alvina Brakebush; and Anna C. (1863-1942), who married William H. Bartels. Conrad served in Co. B of the 56th Enrolled Missouri Militia during the Civil War. Conrad died April 21, 1916, and Henrietta died Oct. 22, 1904. They are buried with their infant children, Albert and Louise, in the Eggiman Cemetery. This cemetery is located on the old Bierschwal farm on Gopher Lane on Highway 25 south of Gordonville. It is now the Emil Nussbaum farm.

John "Henry" Bierschwal married Dorothea Sanders on April 29, 1880 and had eight children as follows: Bertha (1881-1946) who married John S. Neumeyer; Amanda (1883-1940) who never married; Emma (1885-1965) who married Steve Searcey (see Searcey sketch); Meta (1886-1906); Mary Henrietta (1889-1973) who married William George Kaschner; Henry Albert (1892-1968) who married Ada French; Clarence (1895-1954) who married Ida Dankel; and Charles Weston Bierschwal (1898-1954). The family took a covered wagon to Kansas to find work during the wheat harvest, but being unsuccessful, they came back to Whitewater, MO. Henry Bierschwal, John Neumeyer, and a Schlimme ran a grocery store called "Bierschwal's and Co.," dealer in general mer-

Left to right: Mary Bierschwal, Emma Mary Bierschwal, Amanda Bierschwal, friend, St. Louis, MO, 1904.

chandise. Apparently the store went bankrupt about 1908. Dorothea died April 27, 1909, and John died Nov. 29, 1910, both of tuberculosis. They are buried in the Whitewater Methodist Church Cemetery. The three younger children resided in the homes of older siblings after their father died. *Submitted by Dawn Dement Detring*

BIRK – John Birk was born about 1822 in Baden from Wieniech, Germany (Weisbaden). He married Augusta Sander on Sept. 18, 1849 in Madison County, MO. She was born Dec. 11, 1832 in Grossichern, Brunswick, Germany, and died Jan. 25, 1893 in Tilsit, MO. John Birk came to America in 1844, and according to the 1850 Madison County census, he was a miner and lived at Mine Lamotte, MO. John Birk abandoned his family some time after 1853. Although there are several theories about where he went, speculation is that he went to the California gold rush; no one knows for sure. He was never heard from again.

John Birk and Augusta Sander had two children: John Henry, born Aug. 31, 1851 in Mine Lamotte, MO, and died March 1, 1926 and Thomas Marcus, born Oct. 21, 1853 in Mine Lamotte, MO, and died Oct. 12, 1929 in Tilsit, MO. John Henry Birk married Caroline Aufdenberg on June 11, 1874 and they had 10 children: William; Bertha; Marcus; John; Herman; Albert; Theodore; Paul; Joseph and Louis. This family of 10 children produced 37 children. Thomas Marcus Birk married Louise Nagel on Jan. 4, 1877 in Tilsit, MO. Both are buried at Immanuel Lutheran Cemetery, Tilsit, MO. They had seven children: Emma; Otto; Rosa; Clara; Alvin; Walter and Oscar Birk. This family of seven children produced 41 children.

Otto John Birk was the second child of Thomas and Louise. He was born April 2, 1884 in Tilsit, MO and died Dec. 31, 1963 in Cape Girardeau, MO. He married Marie Caroline Frieda Lange on Feb. 3, 1907 in Tilsit, MO. She was born Jan. 28, 1885 in Tilsit, MO and died April 28, 1975 in Gordonville, MO, at the home of one of her sons. Both are buried at Russell Heights Cemetery at Jackson, MO. Otto and Frieda Birk had five children: Martin; Edwin; Anton; Viola and Richard. They had 20 grandchildren and 41 great-grandchildren.

Martin married Martha Best and had six children: Loyd; Orville; Glen; Alice; baby boy and Donald. Edwin married Alma Fluegge and had six children: Charles; Roy; Ellen; Larry; David and Joyce. Anton married Alene Neumeyer and had five children: Gene; Sharon; Carol; Cheryl and Martha. Viola married Willie Sides and had three children; Rena, Stanley and Ronald. Richard was killed in France during WWII in 1944.

Loyd Birk, son of Martin and Martha (Best) Birk, was born March 15, 1931 at Tilsit, MO and married Vera Mae Bock at St. Paul Lutheran Church, Chaffee, MO on July 3, 1960. She was born April 18, 1935 at Route 1, Advance, MO. They had two children; Christine Diane married Richard Buttram and they had two children, Nathaniel and Rachel Buttram of Camdenton, MO. Philip Loyd married Pattie Peel and they had three children; Chastity, Alexandria and Keaton Birk of Jackson, MO. The Thomas Marcus Birk family lived and farmed in the Tilsit, MO area, and the John Henry Birk family lived in the Cape Girardeau, MO area. *Submitted by Loyd Birk*

BIRK – Theodore Charles Birk was born Dec. 27, 1888 and died April 7, 1982. His ancestor, John Birk, was a native of Baden from Wieniech, Germany, born about 1822. He married Augusta Sander on Sept. 18, 1949 in Madison County, MO. She was born Dec.. 11, 1832 at Groszrhilten in Braunschweig, Germany. She came to America in 1844 and died Jan. 25, 1893.

John Birk was a miner and lived at Mine LaMotte; he disappeared after 1853 and was never seen again. There were several theories about what happened to him. John and Augusta had two children, John Henry who was born Aug. 31, 1851 in Mine LaMotte, MO and died March 1, 1926; and Thomas Marcus, who was born Oct. 21, 1853 and died Oct. 12, 1929. Augusta married Henry Werner in 1857.

John Henry married Caroline Catherine Aufdenberg on June 11, 1874. (She was previously married to Charles Huter on April 18, 1872; he died on Dec. 31, 1872.) Ten children were born to John and Caroline, who was born March 7, 1854 and died March 26, 1923.

William was born Feb. 24, 1875 and died June 18, 1945; Bertha was born Feb. 10, 1877 and died April 14, 1960; Marcus Henry was born Jan. 7, 1879 and died Aug. 7, 1911; John Henry Jr. was born Nov. 30, 1880 and died March 12, 1945; Herman was born Jan. 11, 1883 and died April 27, 1967; Louis was born Jan. 16, 1885 and died Nov. 13, 1975; Albert was born Dec. 13, 1886 and died July 23, 1937; Theodore was born Dec. 27, 1888 and died April 7, 1982; Paul was born 1891 and died 1920; Joseph was born March 3, 1896 and died Jan. 14, 1990; and one half-brother, August Huter was born May 15, 1873 and died September 1954.

Adeline "Addie" and Theodore Birk, June 10, 1950

Theodore Charles married Adeline Isabelle Bennett on Dec. 26, 1920. She was born Feb. 1, 1895 and died Aug. 18, 1954. They had six girls and one boy. Evelyn married Edwin Puls and had two sons, Van and Russell "Eddie," who died Aug. 5, 1993. Van married Patricia Wulff and had two sons, Shannon married Katrina Bolen and they have two children, Miles and Megan. Drew married Tracy Miller and they have two children, Gage and Addison.

Doris Lenora married Ray Williamson and had four children: Barbara; Robert; Daniel and Doris Patricia. Doris Patricia married a Caldwell. Barbara married a Hoelscher and had two children. Susan married a Manley and had three children; Cheryl, Shannon and Kaitlyn; and Michael married Katrina Baumann.

Mildred Theodore married Robert Finley and had three children; Terry, Sharon Lynne and Robert Charles. Terry married Patricia McClintook and had two sons, Sean and Mark. Sean has two daughters, Hanna and Haley. Lynne married a Vallacher and has one daughter, Christina.

Marjorie Adeline married Perry Grindstaff and had two children, Bradley and Brenda. Bradley married Chiyoka Tanabe and had three children; Melanie, Amanda and Christopher. Brenda married Steve Ferst and had one son, Joel Perry.

Betty Jean married Lee "Ebby" Myer and had three sons; Michael, John and Mark Edward, who was born and died July 3, 1955. Michael married Kathy Johnson and had one daughter, Rachel Leigh. John married Terri Wilcoxson and had three sons; Justin, Tyson and Jonathan. John married a second time to Sylvia Davies and has four stepchildren: Lee; Christina (who has two children); Dannell and Daniel.

Mary Helen married Howard Reynolds and had four sons: Randy; Robert; Howard Douglas and David Scott. Randy married Janet Caldwell and they have two children, Matthew and Kathryn. Robert married Julie Thompson and they have one son, Robert Samuel. Howard Douglas married Kay Masterson and they have one daughter, Adaline "Addie." David Scott married Dorothy Elizabeth Bledsoe and they have two sons, Jacob and Chrision Elie.

Jimmy Charles Birk married Judy Popp and they have three sons; Jimmie Charles II; Byron and Robert Anthany, who married Amy Werner. Jimmie Charles II married Shelia Statler and they have two sons, Jimmie C. III and Jessie. Byron married Jackie Ebson and they have one daughter, Jacqulyn, who has a daughter Daphine.

Theodore was very proud of his family. There was a lot of love and togetherness in the family. He was also protective of his girls living on a farm. He let them stomp hay down on the wagon while hauling hay, which they enjoyed very much. *Submitted by Betty Jean Myer*

BIRK – John Birk was born about 1822 in Baden from Wieniech, Germany (Weisbaden). He married Augusta Sander on Sept. 18, 1849 in Madison County, MO. She was born Dec. 11, 1832 in Grossichern, Brunswick, Germany, and died Jan. 25, 1893 in Tilsit, MO. John Birk came to America in 1844, and according to the 1850 Madison County census, he was a miner and lived at Mine Lamotte, MO. John Birk abandoned his family some time after 1853. Although there are several theories about his disappearance, including going to the gold rush, no one knows for sure what happened to him. He was never heard from again.

In 1857 Augusta (Sander) Birk married Henry Werner and had six more children. John Birk and Augusta Sander had two children: John Henry, (born Aug. 31, 1851 in Mine Lamotte, MO; died March 1, 1926) and Thomas Marcus (born Oct. 21, 1853 in Mine Lamotte, MO; died Oct. 12, 1929 in Tilsit, MO).

John Henry Birk married Caroline Aufdenberg on June 11, 1874 and they had 10 children: William; Bertha; Marcus; John; Herman; Albert; Theodore; Paul; Joseph and Louis. This family of 10 children produced 37 children.

Thomas Marcus Birk married Louise Nagel on Jan. 4, 1877 in Tilsit, MO. Both are buried at Immanuel Lutheran Cemetery, Tilsit, MO. They had seven children: Emma; Otto; Rosa; Clara; Alvin; Walter and Oscar Birk. This family of seven children produced 41 children.

The Fritz Bock family: front row, left to right: Otto, Lydia and Ida on mother's lap. Back row: Fritz Bock, Anna Frieda, Clara (Sparfield) Bock.

Otto John Birk was the second child of Thomas and Louise. He was born April 2, 1884 in Tilsit, MO and died Dec. 31, 1963 in Cape Girardeau, MO. He married Marie Caroline Frieda Lange on Feb. 3, 1907 in Tilsit, MO. She was born Jan. 28, 1885 in Tilsit, MO and died April 28, 1975 in Gordonville, MO, at the home of one of her sons. Both are buried at Russell Heights Cemetery at Jackson, MO. Otto and Frieda Birk had five children: Martin; Edwin; Anton; Viola and Richard. They had 20 grandchildren and 41 great-grandchildren.

Martin married Martha Best and had six children: Loyd; Orville; Glen; Alice; baby boy and Donald. Edwin married Alma Fluegge and had six children: Charles; Roy; Ellen; Larry; David and Joyce. Anton married Alene Neumeyer and had five children: Gene; Sharon; Carol; Cheryl and Martha. Viola married Willie Sides and had three children; Rena, Stanley and Ronald. Richard was killed in France during WWII in 1944.

Loyd Birk, son of Martin and Martha (Best) Birk, was born March 15, 1931 at Tilsit, MO and married Vera Mae Bock at St. Paul Lutheran Church, Chaffee, MO on July 3, 1960. She was born April 18, 1935 at Route 1, Advance, MO. They had two children; Christine Diane married Richard Buttram and they had two children, Nathaniel and Rachel Buttram of Camdenton, MO. Philip Loyd married Pattie Peel and they had three children; Chastity, Alexandria and Keaton Birk of Jackson, MO. The Thomas Marcus Birk family lived and farmed in the Tilsit, MO area, and the John Henry Birk family lived in Cape Girardeau, MO area.

All Birks living in southeast Missouri are descendants of the first John Birk. *Submitted by Loyd Birk*

The Thomas Marcus Birk family home, about 1900. Left to right: Alvin, Clara, Otto, Walter, Louise (Nagel) Birk holding Oscar, Rosa, Marcus Birk and Emma.

BLAYLOCK – Richard Dalmerine Blaylock was born Jan. 15, 1873, in Cape Girardeau County. He was the son of James Alexander Blaylock and Luvicy Dorey Penny. He had three broth-

161

ers, Charles, Thomas, and George. His father was from Tennessee and his mother from North Carolina. The name Blaylock is Scottish. Penny is Dutch-Irish.

R. D. and his brother George wanted to become doctors, so they entered Barnes Medical School in St. Louis, MO. R. D. drove a streetcar to pay his way through medical school. When he graduated from medical school in 1903, he opened his first office in Sedgewickville, MO. In 1910 he moved to Pocahontas where he stayed for 26 years before moving to Oak Ridge where he had his office. During those 26 years, he also had an office in Altenburg, which he kept open two days out of the week, and an office over Jones Drugstore in Jackson for a short time, as well as one in Matthews, MO. Dr. Blaylock traveled the country on horseback, buggy, and then a Model-T Ford. He delivered over 1000 babies, white and black, and all were delivered in their homes. He handled everything: curing a cold, pulling teeth, delivering babies, sewing up cuts and taking out splinters. His pay was very little but he always said "I am here to care for the sick, not to make a lot of money." He was called "Old Doc Blaylock" by all who knew him.

Dr. R. D. Blaylock, center, talking with Reverend in Oak Ridge

Dr. Blaylock was the mayor of Pocahontas and also was a Mason. He loved roses - red ones. On the south side of his office in Pocahontas, he had 12 red rose bushes. He cared for them as patiently as he did his people.

After the death of his first two wives, he met Sallie Ann Bowers and they became close friends. On April 17, 1910, he married Sallie Bowers. The marriage took place in Oak Ridge, MO, in the home of John and Sarah Bowers, parents of Sallie. Doc had a child from his second marriage, so right from the start Sallie had a 3-year-old son. Two years later a son, Cecil, was born, and three years later came a daughter, Trula. Trula loved to sit on Doc's lap and listen to him tell of his day's work with the sick.

Howard worked on a farm for a Mr. Bruihl and then went to St. Louis and worked at Liggit Meyers Tobacco Company. He married Pearl Cook and they had one daughter, Norma Jean.

Cecil graduated from Jackson High School and worked for Southwestern Telephone Company. He married Chola Statler and they had a son, Richard, and a daughter, Sally.

Trula married Vernon Ladreiter and they had four sons: Rodney; Richard; Wayne; and Terry. Trula was very active in her community. She was a Boy Scout Den Mother, Room Mother, Band Mother, chaperone for seniors who went to Niagara Falls and Washington, D.C., city-wide chairman for the Jackson Heart and Cancer Friend Drive, on the Community Betterment Committee, president of West Jackson Extension Clubs, sponsor for the first "trash and treasure sale" ever held in Jackson, soloist for the tri-state horse show, and lead singer and seamstress for the Sweet Adelines Girardeau Rose Chapter. At one time she played the piano for her Sunday School class, was a cook for her church, Secretary of the United Methodist Women of New McKendree Church, and chairman of several church circles; she won the Bible slogan for her church in 1966, and has been singing in the church choir for over 66 years. *Submitted by Trula Blaylock Ladreiter, condensed version*

BLUMENBERG – Louis Henry Blumenberg was born Feb. 20, 1847 in Sehnde, Germany, the oldest son of Ludwig and Christina Bartels Blumenberg. His father was born Jan. 10, 1821 in Oldenrode, the son of Hennies Albrecht and Marie Sophie (Klusmann) Blumenberg, and died Feb. 2, 1889 in Scott County, MO. His mother was born Dec. 7, 1823 in Sehnde, the daughter of Just Conrad and Ilse Marie (Klunder) Bartels. The Bartels family lived in Sehnde for many generations. Ludwig and Christina and their two small sons, Louis and Henry, set sail for America on Dec. 5, 1849 on the *Bark Mississippi* from Bremen. They traveled with her brother, Henry Conrad Bartles (1826-1918) and the Christopher Kluender family. The family likely stayed the winter months with Henry and Augusta Henze Blumenberg near Jackson, MO. In the spring of 1850, the Kluender family traveled up the Mississippi River and settled in Lee County, IA. Ludwig Blumenberg owned land in Byrd Township form 1851-1856.

Another son, August Blumenberg, was born March 17, 1850/51 near Jackson, MO. A fourth son, George, was born on Dec. 16, 1858 near Commerce, Scott County, MO. Ludwig enlisted in the Civil War in 1861 at Cape Girardeau in Co. F, 2nd Regt. IL Light Artillery. His wife died while he was away at war, so Henry C. Bartles took care of the children. Ludwig remarried in 1864 to Mrs. Elizabeth Weidmann and had an additional son, John (1865-1890). Son Louis left the family around this time and stayed with John Bock and relatives in Cape Girardeau County. He worked in Iowa and Illinois on a farm and made $25.00 a month, coming home only once a year.

Louis Henry Blumenberg (1847-1920)

Louis married Anna Maria Herzog on Feb. 14, 1882 at her parent's home near Bell City, MO. She was born Sept. 29, 1857 near Commerce, MO, the daughter of Albert Caesar and Barbara (Thomen) Herzog. The Blumenbergs settled on a farm near Allenville, MO. They raised turkeys, cattle, chickens and hogs. They also had a fruit orchard. They raised five sons and one daughter. The Blumenberg children were Louis Lee (1888-1974); Albert (1890-1957); Anna (1892-1948) who married Herman Bock; Walter (1895-1991); Monroe (1896-1984) and Wilson (1898-1980). All the children resided in Cape Girardeau County, except for Louis who lived at East Prairie. Louis Sr. died June 24, 1920 of cancer of the mouth. Wife "Mary" died June 18, 1918; they are both buried at Zion Methodist Cemetery near Gordonville, MO.

Wilson married Doraretta Searcey on Dec. 20, 1922 in Jackson, MO. They had three daughters: Mary (1923-) who married Burl R. Statler; Betty (1928-) who first married James F. Dement and then Kenneth Hudson; and Louise (1930-1999) who married Lewis W. Brown.

Betty Blumenberg and James Dement had three children: Dawna who married Kenneth Detring; James who married Donna Olson and David Dement (1961-1993). Ken and Dawn Detring reside in Jackson with their three daughters; Amanda, Meredith and Sarah. James and Donna Dement reside in Tulsa, OK with daughters Dana and Megan. Betty married Kenneth Hudson in 1988 and they reside in Jackson. *Submitted by Dawn Dement Detring*

BOCK – Johann Thomas Bock (first Johann) came to America as a stowaway, to avoid the German military draft. Born in 1793 in Brunswick, Germany, he married Doettey (last name unknown and born in Prussia) in Germany. She and their son (second Johann) later came to America with friends named Hornbergs. The 1850 census states that Johann was a shoemaker and the 1860 census states he was a farmer from Berel', Germany being 67 years old.

Their son Johann (second Johann) was born Nov. 22, 1824 in Berel', Germany and died April 1899 at Tilsit, MO. He married Wilhelmine Warneke and was a farmer south of Jackson, MO. He was a Private in Company B of the 56th Enrolled Missouri Militia, which was organized in July of 1862, and was made up of men from Cape Girardeau County, MO. Company A was a cavalry unit and the rest was infantry. The last record of the 56th was for December 1864.

Johann (second Johann) and Wilhelmine Warneke had seven children: Carolina; Johann (third Johann); Frederick; August; Dorethia; Baby Wilhelmine and Hanacon. The two children who remained in this area were Frederick and August.

Frederick (Fritz) was born March 6, 1856 and first married Nina Loss on July 27, 1870. They had two children, Emma (married John Henry Birk Jr. of Tilsit, MO and lived in St. Louis, MO) and Heinrich Bock, who never married. After Nina Loss died, he married Clara Sparfeld of Allenville, MO. They lived on the Sparfeld homeplace and had nine children: Frieda; Anna; Friedrich; Lydia; Otto; Ida; Martin; Linda and Viola.

Otto Wilhelm Bock (father of Vera Birk), son of Fritz and Clara Bock, was born Oct. 19, 1898 at Allenville, MO. He married Martha Augusta Christine Tuschhoff at Trinity Lutheran Church, Friedheim, MO. They lived on the Sparfeld-Bock homeplace, Route 1, Allenville, MO and had four children: Nora Nelda Seabaugh; Wesley Bock; Lela Hahn and Vera (Bock) Birk.

August Bock (brother of Fritz) was born Dec. 6, 1857. He first married Anna (Bruns) Ristig and had three children; Anna, Friedrick and Elsie. The latter two died as children. August Bock later married Willielmina Ristig and had nine children: Wilhelmine; Lydia; Frieda; Herman; Albert; Alma; Minnie; Alvin and Carolina. Minnie married Albert Schloss and they had three children; Kay Francis, Larry and Jerry Schloss. Alvin married Ruby Willa and their three children were LaDonia Beggs, Donald and Larry Bock.

The Johann Thomas Bock (first Johann family) were farmers, and almost all of the people mentioned above grew up on area farms. Fritz Bock's family grew up on Hickory Ridge, Route 1, Advance, MO, and August Bock's family grew up south of Jackson, MO. *Submitted by Vera (Bock) Birk*

BODENSTEIN – The Bodenstein family that resided in Gordonville, MO and extended to Pilot Knob, MO, came from a small village in Germany near the Harz Mountains. Johann "Heinrich" Bodenstein, born in 1793 in Ortshausen, Braunschweig, Germany came to America in

1853. Previous to this time, he married Johanna Marie "Dorothee" Achtermann (born April 6, 1802, the daughter of Heinrich Jacob Achtermann and N. N. Reinecke) on Feb. 8, 1829 in Bornum, Germany, and they had three children (Christian, Johanna and William). Family stories written down in an old Bodenstein Bible tell that Heinrich was the mayor of the city they came from and that it took them three months to make the trip across the ocean to America. This trip began with his youngest son, Wilhelm, who came to America first, most probably to purchase the land. Immigration records show that William, age 20, a servant, arrived in New Orleans on Oct. 26, 1852 aboard the ship *Rebecca* from Bremen, Germany. Because many people were leaving Germany without paying their debts, it was required that all persons place a notice in the newspapers to allow bill collectors a chance to regain their money. As documented in Fritz Gruhne's book, Heinrich Bodenstein, residing in Jerze, along with his wife, a service maid, announced to leave Germany in 1853 to America with the following children; Friedrich Christian, born Jan. 13, 1830 and Johanna Marie Magdalene, born Feb. 7, 1835. This book also indicated that Adolf "Wilhelm," born Oct. 19, 1831, announced to leave in 1852 and is the son of the aforementioned.

Christian and Johanna (Bodenstein) Amelung

Not long after they arrived in America, the children married and started families of their own. Johanna married Christian Amelung on Jan. 5, 1854 and moved to Pilot Knob, MO. Wilhelm married first Mina Eps on Aug. 22, 1854 and second Christiana Niemann on March 3, 1869. Christian married Elisabeth Beiser on Feb. 25, 1857. Whether it was fate or perhaps a spread of disease, Johanna's brothers and parents all died between 1870-1872.

Heinrich worked as a laborer and died on Oct. 13, 1871. He was buried in the St. James UCC Cemetery in Tilsit, MO. His wife, Dorothee, died April 23, 1870 in Pilot Knob, MO at the home of their daughter, Johanna.

Christian died Jan. 8, 1872, in Tilsit, MO. His wife Elizabeth, married second Gottlieb Graulich (b. March 9, 1831; d. July 8, 1886) on Sept. 10, 1874. Elizabeth died on May 21, 1891. Christian and Elizabeth had the following children: Maria; Caroline; August; Herman and Mina.

William died Oct. 23, 1871. As indicated in the newspaper, "...he had chopped down a tree, and in descending, it fell upon and killed him ... he was about 40 years of age." William and Mina had the following children: Mina; William; Heinrich; Christian; Maria and lastly August, born 1868. William and Christiana had one son, Frederick, born July 1871.

Johanna lived a long life and died Dec. 4, 1918 from influenza complicated by pneumonia. There was a terrible nationwide influenza epidemic at the time and several people died from it. Her obituary indicated that she was born in Hahausen, Germany. *Submitted by Marcine Lohman*

BOEHME – Carl Wilhelm Joseph Boehme moved to Jackson by wagon in the winter of 1902 from Wittenberg, MO, bringing his wife Bertha, with 3-month-old daughter Adelia and mother-in-law Marie Magdalin Loebs. This account begins with the memory of miseries of that first winter in Cape Girardeau County.

Carl purchased 160 acres where the original town of Jackson had first located. Their house consisted of two huge rooms. The weather was bitterly cold, so the first item moved into their home was a stove for warmth and cooking. Since space was limited, pieces that didn't fit into the two rooms were stored in a woodshed. After all this was completed, the worst scenario happened. Tiny bugs warmed and started crawling out from under the wallpaper, the house was infested with bed bugs! Extinction of pests had to be dealt with immediately in spite of cold weather and a new baby. The wallpaper was soaked off and the bugs exterminated

Carl Wilhelm, self-conscious of his German name, changed it to Charles William. He purchased a coronet, took lessons, and after long days of farm work, walked two miles to practice with a beginning band in Jackson The family became actively involved with St. Paul's Lutheran Church, which had been founded about ten years before the Boehmes' arrival in Jackson. Bethel Baptist Church and cemetery bordered the Boehme farm, and the cemetery remains with some headstones still readable. Court sessions were held in the church in 1814. Charles recalled that a jail was located where he built his barn. Homes possibly surrounded this area, accounting for the many pieces of beautiful broken china Lillian collected while playing in fields here. There was also an abundance of arrowheads, indicating the land was occupied by Indians in the past.

Charles Boehme was an innovative farmer who took great pride in caring for his land. Although he had a minimal formal education, he was well versed in several agricultural techniques which became popular during his early farming years. He was among the first farmers in his area to use terraced farming to protect his rolling land from the effects of wind and water erosion. And earlier than most of his peers, he started to rotate his crops to retain soil vitality and improve the productivity of his farm.

Corn, wheat and hay were major crops. Charles Boehme loved raising cows, pigs and mules. Each was given a name, cows usually according to their personality. One was called "Funny," another "Kickin' Minnie" sent many pails of milk airborne. Mules were special to him. All fieldwork was accomplished with a team of mules. Charles often said they were hard-working and highly intelligent - no mention about being stubborn as a mule! He bred 'em, broke 'em and worked 'em.

Neighbors worked together during times of harvest, illness or trouble. An outstanding example of this was the Boehme's house fire. Tongues of flame were licking at the wooden shingle roof when discovered. Lillian cranked that phone wildly, telling the telephone operator to send the chemical fire department. The operator couldn't understand, but neighbors knew the house was on fire, as they listened on the party line because of the wild ringing. Soon Billy Lowes, swinging five-gallon buckets, came running. Next a car, driven by Leonard Sanders with then girlfriend, Aline Illers, came. Men dressed to attend a funeral jumped out of the car and, not fearing soiled dress suits, all joined in a bucket brigade. As arms tired cranking water from the cistern, turns were taken. The house was saved by the concern of neighbors!

The farm was owned by Boehme until 1952, when it sold to Meir whose land bordered his property. The present owner is Byron Lang.

Charles Boehme was born in 1869 and died

Charles Boehme family, 1944. Left to right, front row: Charles Boehme, Lillian Harmon, Bertha Boehme. Back row: Norma Doering, Louis Boehme, Adelia Shoults, Frieda Schaefer.

in 1958; his wife Bertha was born in 1878 and died in 1951. Their children were: Adelia (Mrs. Erroll Shoults), 1902-1986; Norma (Mrs. Arnold Doering), 1905-2000; Frieda (Mrs. G. A. Schaefer), 1908-1969; Louis, 1910-2000; Cordelia who died in infancy and one remaining daughter, Lillian (Mrs. Vyron Harmon), born in 1920 who now lives in Scott City, MO. *Submitted by Lillian Harmon*

BOLLINGER – James "Jim" and Laura Bollinger moved to Jackson, MO in 1961 after selling their farm near Marble Hill. They decided it was time to retire from the farm, so they bought a house with 13 acres at 2110 Bainbridge Road in Jackson. They kept a few cattle and some chickens for a while. The 160-acre farm had been purchased from his father, Henry Bollinger. The 7-room house had been built by his father when James was 15 years old.

Laura and James Bollinger, 50th Anniversary, June 2, 1970

James and Laura were married on June 2, 1920. Laura was an elementary schoolteacher near Advance, MO. They lived with her parents the first year, while she taught school. James worked on the Highway Department and helped her father on the farm. James was the son of Henry and Pernecie Bollinger of Marble Hill. Laura was the daughter of John G. and Bertha (Schrock) Hartle of Advance.

The Bollingers moved several times in their early years. They lived on farms at Crump, Jackson, Leemon and Neelys Landing before buying the old homeplace from his father.

The Bollingers had six children. They were Lee Elvis, born July 8, 1921; Hester Virginia, born July 8, 1925; Grace Elaine, born June 16, 1923; Bonnie Ruth, born Oct. 5, 1927; James Junior, born Nov. 2, 1930 and Bertha Bernice, born May 18, 1933. Grace Elaine died in 1926 at the age of 3 years.

Both sons served in the U. S. Army. Lee was in WWII for three years, stationed in Italy. James was in the Korean War for two years. They were thankful that both sons returned without any serious injuries.

James and Laura were active members of the County Line Baptist Church in Bollinger County. James was ordained as a Deacon there. After moving to Jackson, they moved their membership to the First Baptist Church in Jackson.

Their son Lee was married to Marylou Reimann on June 22, 1946. They moved to Park Hills, MO, and had two daughters, Becky and Sally. Daughter Hester moved to Los Angeles, CA, and married Don Lynch. They had four children: Diane; Gary; Donna and Mary. Daughter Bonnie moved to Cape Girardeau. She married Cecil Pletcher on Aug. 29, 1947. They had two sons, Richard and Randy. Son James married Anna Mae Gibson on Jan. 21, 1950. They had two daughters, Jamie and Laurie. They moved to Park Hills, MO. He later married Peggy Mayor on Nov. 1, 1980. Daughter Bernice was married to Keith Haynes on Jan. 27, 1952. They had two children, Connie and Michael. They live in Jackson, MO.

Jim and Laura celebrated their 50th Anniversary on June 2, 1970. They had 12 grandchildren at this celebration. Many relatives and friends celebrated this anniversary with them.

Jim was diagnosed with A.L.S. (Lou Gerig disease) in 1972, and only lived two more years. He passed away Nov. 27, 1973. Laura passed away May 5, 1992. Burial was in Russell Heights Cemetery in Jackson for both. *Submitted by Bernice Haynes*

BOLLINGER - Roy Alvin Bollinger Jr. was born May 24, 1952, the son of Roy Alvin and Alene Goehman Bollinger. On Feb. 19, 1972 he married Carol Sue Kamp, the daughter of Elmer and Martha Daume Kamp. Carol was born May 15, 1952. The couple have one son, Landon Roy Bollinger, who was born Aug. 22, 1981. Roy, Carol and Landon all graduated from Jackson High School.

Roy and Landon have been mechanics since high school, Landon taking shop training from his father. In 1979, Roy purchased his present Bollinger Auto Repair Shop at 802 West Main Street in Jackson where father and son work.

Carol Bollinger attended Office Training School in Cape Girardeau. She worked as a teller for the Jackson Exchange Bank for 22 years. Since 1994 she has worked in the County Collector's Office.

Roy, Carol and Landon Bollinger

The family moved into their new rural Jackson home in 1992. From their home northeast of Tilsit they can see the steeple of the St. James U.C.C. where E. F. William and Dorothea Suedekum Daume and Frederick and Sophia Edell Suedekum, great- and great-great-grandparents of Carol are buried.

They can also see the steeple of the Immanuel Lutheran Church where August and Mary Schrock Kamp, great-grandparents of Carol, are buried. August Kamp and his father, Peter Joseph Kamp (1817-1886), were born in Ahweiler, Germany. Peter is buried in St. Joseph Cemetery, Cincinnati, OH. Peter's first wife was Christina Koch and the second was Helena Antwerpen (1823-1849).

Roy is a descendant of the Bollinger family that settled along the Whitewater River in the late 1700s. Roy Bollinger Sr. was the son of Pearl and Emma Penny Bollinger and grandson of John and Elizabeth Friese Bollinger. Robert and Mary Penny were his maternal grandparents. Roy Sr. worked at the International Shoe Factory and Alene, his wife, was a cook at West Lane School in Jackson.

Elmer Kamp was a superintendent at the Jackson Hosiery Mill and Martha, his wife, was secretary of St. Paul Lutheran School and Church in Jackson from 1964-1992. Elmer Kamp was the son of Albert and Nora Bodenstein Kamp of Burfordville, and Martha was the daughter of John and Meta Engelmann Daume of Oak Ridge. *Submitted by Carol Bollinger*

BOWERS – Henry and Sarah Cobble Bowers moved to Missouri in 1854 from East Tennessee and settled on a farm north of Oak Ridge. Henry enlisted in the Union army and served about one year. He was wounded by accident and was mustered out of service.

In October, 1862, John A. Bowers, son of Henry and Sarah, also enlisted in the Union army and served until the close of the war as a non-commissioned officer in battles around Nashville. In 1867 he was united in marriage with Sarah Beal. They purchased a farm north of Oak Ridge where they lived for several years. They were the parents of eight children, one of whom was John Henry. They were members of the Methodist Episcopal Church South and drove a two-horse wagon to attend church. Sunday was a holy day and the family never went into the fields to work on the Sabbath and there was no fishing either. The family farmed and operated a sorghum molasses mill.

Mr. Bowers was a member of the A. O. U. W. and the Farmers' Mutual Benefit Society. John Henry Bowers, son of John A. and Sarah Bowers, was born in 1881. He married Ina Penny, daughter of Jefferson and Ida Penny. They lived their early married lives in Oak Ridge and were the parents of two children, Leon and Elda. John and his brother, Oliver, owned and operated a harness shop in Oak Ridge where they made harnesses and sold buggies.

In 1908 John built a "wood sawing rig" powered by a 3-horsepower gasoline motor mounted on wheels. He drove from place to place to saw wood for people. When automobiles were invented, John became interested in them and purchased the first car in Oak Ridge. This car had a fold-down top and isinglass curtains. The tires were solid rubber eliminating flats, but contributing to bumpy rides. John closed the harness shop and opened a garage and service station. He sold cars and maintained them. When someone purchased a car, John would teach them how to drive.

Left to right: John H. Bowers, Ina Bowers, Leon Bowers, Jeff Penny, Ida Penny.

In 1931 the family moved to Jackson where John, along with Frank Clippard, established Jackson Auto Parts Company in 1935. Elda married John Ellis of Bollinger County and they had two children, John and Nancy. In 1947 Leon and John Ellis bought Frank Clippard's part of Jackson Auto Parts. The business was expanded to include a machine shop. Leon was an electrical engineer employed by McDonnell Aircraft Company in St. Louis until his retirement. He died in 1982. Elda taught music in the Jackson Schools for many years and John was cashier of Cape County Savings Bank. John died in 1986.

John and Ina were active members of New McKendree Methodist Church and the Order of Eastern Star. John was a 50-year Mason and Ina was a member of the Women's Christian Temperance Union (WCTU) and United Methodist Women. Ina died in 1970; John in 1973. *Submitted by Elda Bowers Ellis*

BRASE – Evelyn Brase, the former Evelyn Lowes, daughter of William and Lydia Lowes, has been a resident of Jackson, MO for 80 years. She was born and grew up on the Lowes home place. In 1943 she was married to Emil W. Brase of Gordonville.

In March 1945 Emil was called into service for WWII. He joined the navy. He was sent to Japan but got off the ship at Hawaii to attend radar school. While there, the war ended and he was transported to Okinawa, where he was assigned to a destroyer tender called the *Henry A. Wiley* in the Sea of Japan and swept mines for a couple of months.

The Brase family: Emil, John and Evelyn.

While Emil was in service, Evelyn was teaching school at Delta, MO. Emil was in Shanghai, China, when he received a letter from the Delta School Board offering a coaching and teaching position upon his release from the Navy. In 1946 he was discharged from the Navy and returned to Jackson and the teaching and coaching job at Delta. They lived in an upstairs apartment at the Lowes home for two years and then built their own home next to the Lowes home. Emil had very good basketball teams at Delta and missed going to the state playoffs by one game two times.

In 1953 Evelyn accepted a position as kindergarten teacher at Jackson, MO. Two years later Emil was also hired at Jackson as an elementary physical education teacher and 7th and 8th grade basketball coach at the Junior High. In 1955 he was asked if he would accept the head basketball coaching position for the boys at Jackson High School. He accepted and coached for seven years.

Emil W. Brase

In 1957 the Brases' were blessed with a son, John William. He was a joy to them and has led a very successful life. At present he is a computer analyst with Southwestern Bell Telephone in St. Louis, MO.

Coach Brase, as he came to be called, had a very good record at Jackson with many talented players. He coached the freshmen boys' basketball team for 13 years and assisted Ron Cook with the girls' basketball program for seven years. He retired in 1988 and Evelyn retired in 1986.

Emil and Evelyn are active members of New McKendree Methodist Church. Emil was Methodist Men's president and chairman of the Administrative Board several years. He has also been a Sunday School teacher at New McKendree for 50 years, a position he still fills. Evelyn has also served as choir member for 50 years, a Sunday School teacher, and chairman of the Wesleyan Circle and the United Methodist Women. She also belongs to the Thursday Literary Club and the Beta Iota Chapter of Alpha Delta Kappa. They also attend the retired teachers' organization meetings in Jackson and Cape Girardeau.

Emil is also very active in the Veterans of Foreign Wars Organization and has served as Chairman of the Voice of Democracy Program.

Emil is well-known in Jackson as Coach Brase and has touched the lives of many Jackson students. Together Emil and Evelyn have taught 85 years. Emil is still doing some basketball coaching. He has coached the Lutheran 5th to 8th grade girls' basketball teams for 13 years since his retirement in 1988. *Submitted by Evelyn Brase*

BRAUN – F. F. Braun was born March 28, 1877 in Jackson, MO and died Sept. 17, 1950. He was the son of Ferdinand Frederick Braun (born Oct. 6, 1834 in Renchen, Germany; died July 20, 1900 in Jackson, MO) and Caroline Hoeckele Braun (born Aug. 8, 1852; died Oct. 7, 1932).

In the early days, Ferdinand acquired business properties in Jackson, originally living in the Main Street location and operating a saloon in the store front. He also acquired a double building around the corner on High Street. These properties remained in the family until recent years.

It was April 1865, immediately after Palm Sunday, that Ferdinand Braun was enroute to Cape Girardeau in the company of other recruits to replenish the quota of soldiers needed from Jackson for the Federal Army. Others like Ferdinand had only recently become citizens of the United States, and they knew that leaving home would create a hardship on their families. He was disheartened, downcast and submerged in melancholy when news broke out that the Civil War had ended. The following year he purchased the Abel farm on Bainbridge Road, which remained in the family for over a century.

The Braun homestead, originally a double log cabin, received substantial additions, making it one of the more attractive homes in the rural area. It was a showplace of Jackson, but the many years took a heavy toll on the old house and it was torn down July 1967 due to extensive termite damage. It was located a couple miles from Jackson on the Old Cape Road, and protected from the road by a grove of sugar maple trees planted shortly after the house was built in 1866. On the rolling land north of the house there was a vineyard that covered two and a half acres producing the most tasty wines. Also the Braun children used to find quantities of Indian relics in the woods

Grandmother Braun's husband, Ferdinand, died at age 65 years, leaving four boys, August Braun, Arthur Braun, F. F. Braun and Charles Braun; and four girls, Lillian Braun Sanders, Molly Braun Lowes, Helen "Dolly" Braun Greene and Mary Braun who died in infancy. He and his family attended the Catholic Church in Jackson and was one of the first members to be present

The Braun family: F. F. and Delia with daughters Bessie Braun DeLisle and Charlotte Braun McCrate

at its cornerstone laying in 1857. F. F. Braun used to tell how he and the family had to walk several miles in all kinds of weather to attend church in Jackson.

One of F. F. Braun's first business ventures was that of an itinerant map salesman. In this pursuit, he traveled by buggy throughout much of the Bootheel in Missouri, where he encountered plagues of mosquitoes and was glad to return to Jackson.

F. F. Braun was married in 1903 to Delia L. Deevers at Saint Vincent's Seminary, Cape Girardeau, MO. They had two daughters, Bessie Braun DeLisle (deceased) and Charlotte Braun McCrate. F. F. Braun opened a grocery store on Broadway and a few years later opened a larger grocery store in Harrig (Good Hope Street) about 1910. At this time, his brother Charles Braun joined him in the business, which he later purchased when F. F. Braun went into the real estate business.

Charlotte and Mike McCrate have six children: Carolyn Hadjuk; Mary Catherine Anderson; Charles Mike McCrate; Janet Hafernik; Margaret Parrish and Sean McCrate and 21 grandchildren. Mike and Charlotte live in Cape Girardeau, MO, where they have been engaged in various aspects of the real estate business. *Submitted by Charlotte (Braun) McCrate*

BRAUN - Ferdinand Frederick Braun sailed from La Havre on the ship *Sahrah Purington*, arriving in the port of New Orleans on May 9, 1853. He made his way to the Jackson area, supposedly to look for his father, Ignaz Braun, who had emigrated earlier. The story is that he found his father, but he had remarried, although he had left a wife and two children in Germany.

F. F., as he was known, was born in Renchen, Baden, Germany, on Oct. 6, 1834 to Ignaz Braun and Klara Hoeckele Braun. He was the fifth of seven children, but the only one to survive and have a family. His mother and sister, Amelia, also came to America, and settled in Jackson, but Amelia died shortly after arriving, in 1855, at the age of 17. Ferdinand was naturalized as a citizen on Nov. 29, 1858 in the Circuit Court of Cape Girardeau County, MO.

He worked in Ignaz Milde's blacksmith and buggy shop in Jackson. They built buggies, and during the Civil War they made wooden coffins for both sides. He was on his way to Cape Girardeau to join the Union forces, when he met a rider who told him, and the other recruits, that the war was over. No doubt this was welcome news.

He later bought a farm two and a half miles east of Jackson on the old Cape Rock Road, where he lived with his mother, Klara.

In 1869 Caroline Hoeckele, his mother's niece, and his half cousin-they shared the same grandfather, but had different grandmothers-

sailed to America on the ship *Paraquay*, arriving in New York on Sept. 20. Caroline was born Aug. 8, 1852, in Renchen, Baden, Germany. The story is that Ferdinand went to visit his aunt Ludovica, Caroline's mother, when she and her twin brother, Charles, were infants, to tell her that he was leaving for America. Now she too had come over. Caroline stayed in New York for several years, then came to Jackson to help care for her aunt Klara. The cousins fell in love and were married Nov. 20, 1873.

Ferdinand and Caroline had eight children. Gustav was born in 1874 and died in 1904, never married; Arthur, born 1875, married Emma Baumgarth and had nine children; Ferdinand, born 1877, married Delia Deevers and had two daughters; Charles, born in 1878, married Anna Milde, the daughter of Frank Milde, and had two daughters; Lillian, born in 1880, married Herman Sanders; Amelia, born in 1882, married William Boone and was stepmother to his children, and later married Emory Lowes; Helen, born 1885, married Warren Green and had five children; and Mary, born in 1887, died as an infant.

Ferdinand Frederick Braun Sr.

Ferdinand was a successful farmer and businessman. On his death in 1900, he owned the farm and several buildings in Jackson. His obituary said that he was well-known and esteemed, and his funeral was one of the largest ever seen in Jackson. Caroline lived until 1932 on the farm. Her body was discovered by her daughter, Amelia Boone, who lived on a farm directly across the road. They are buried in the Jackson City Cemetery. *Submitted by Helen Horvath*

BRENNECKE – August and Wilhelmine Brennecke, born 5 Nov. 1801, and 5 Dec. 1806, respectively, and their six children from Sebexen, Germany, sailed from Bremen, Germany, on the *Bark Diana* (small three-masted ship), arriving in New Orleans, LA, Nov. 11, 1844. They then traveled up the Mississippi River to Cape Girardeau and settled west of Jackson, MO. The ship's list included August, a weaver, his wife Minnie (Wilhelmine), and children Heinrich, Friedrich, Wilhelm, Louise, Carl, and Caroline. One child had stayed in Germany and one had died there earlier. Three more children were born in America: George, Franklin, and Jacob. August died 8 Oct. 1856 and Wilhelmine 20 March 1871; both were buried in the Zion Methodist Church Cemetery at Gordonville, MO.

Three months and 17 days from the date they arrived in America - Feb. 28, 1845 - August applied to the Circuit Court of Cape Girardeau County for citizenship. On Dec. 18, 1850, citizenship papers were presented to him. The original citizenship papers are in the possession of Doris Davault and a copy hangs on the wall of her home.

The first Brennecke History and Genealogy was originally begun by the late Herbert Schaper, a great-grandson of August. Doris Brennecke Davault, also a great-grandchild, joined Herb in the writing and they published the book in 1977. Mr. and Mrs. Norman Brennecke of Rockwell, TX, and the late Carl Pensel of Jackson, did more research in Germany and found additional information on the family, and Norman and his wife updated the book and republished it in July 1988.

165

Eight of the nine descendants of August and Wilhelmine remained in this area and were prosperous farmers. They settled in the Gordonville, Burfordville, Jackson, Cape Girardeau, and Kelso areas; Justin Louisa moved to Litchfield, IL.

August and Wilhelmine's children were Heinrich August Julius (1825-1901; remained in Germany) who married Louis Wilhelmine Emelie Mathilde Neinstaedt or Louisa Philomena Emelia Mathilda Neinstaedt, and they had five children. (2) Georg Heinrich "Henry" Ludwig (1829-1856) who married Wilhelmine Amelie Aftenthal and had two children. (3) George August Friedrich (born and died in Germany - 1831-1831). (4) Carl August Friedrich "Fred" (1833 –1907) who married Dina "Deana" Hunze and had eight children. (5) Georg Friedrich Wilhelmine (1834-1910) who married Carolina Nothdurft and had eight children. (6) Hanna Justine Louisa (1837-1899) who married Henry Meyer and had six children. (7) Johann Heinrich Christian Carl "Charles" (1838-1884) who married Caroline Martens and had five children. (8) Johanna Caroline Friedrike (1841-1921) who married Karl Neumeyer and had eleven children. (9) George H. "Schoose" (1845-1924) who married Christina Ludwig/Johanne Reitman (Redman), Louisa Criddle and had seven children. (10) Franklin "Frank" (1848-1902) who married Anna Kuehle and Alvina Kuehle and had five children. (11) Jacob "Jake" (1853-1935) who married Henrietta Peetz and had six children. *By Doris Brennecke Davault*

BRENNECKE – Clarence (19 March 1907 - 31 Jan. 1975) married Ruth Desselman (19 Dec. 1908 - 7 Oct. 1966) in 1931. Clarence attended Jackson schools and Southeast Missouri College. He and Ruth had two daughters. Ruth Jane married Dr. Joe Hecker from Independence, MO. They have five children: Dr. Cynthia Brown in Asheville, NC; Laurie Whitely in Collierville, TN; Missy Madare in Luling, LA; Julie Boresow in Leewood, KS and Brian Hecker of Poplar Bluff, MO. They have 13 grandchildren: Samuel; Melissa and Joey Brown; Brandon and Lindsey Whitely; Michael, Jennifer and Jessica Madare; Elizabeth, Emily, Mathew and Jacob Boresow and Alexis Hecker. Jane and Joe lived in Jackson, MO from 1960 – 1965, then moved to Poplar B1uff, MO, where they currently reside.

Patricia Ann married Allen Welker. They have two daughters, Elizabeth Schnurr and Annette Ellenberger, and five grandchildren: Sarah and Jonathan Schnurr. Kristen and Adam Mikesch (from Annette's first marriage) and Jacob Ellenberger. They all reside in Festus, MO.

Ruth and Clarence Brennecke

During WWII, Clarence took a leave of absence from working with his father in the Chevrolet business to work for the federal government laying gas pipelines in the east. He, his wife and daughters lived in Lancaster and Westchester, PA and also Cincinnati, OH. After the war he came home to resume work at Brennecke's. His daughters have found correspondence regarding the business, which passed between him and Edna Grossheider during this time. Edna became synonymous with Brennecke's having started with Henry in 1931 and retiring in 1974.

In 1957 Clarence bought Johnny Wagner's shares of the dealership and continued to manage the business when they moved to the present location on Highway 61 in 1969. The dealership was sold after his death in 1975, but the name "Brennecke" is still in use after 70 years. It is the oldest in its field with continuous service in Jackson. After his father, Henry's death, Clarence took an active interest in his brother Marvin's farm. He had a close friendship and working relationship with Raymond and Betty Rampley, who lived on and operated this farm since the middle 1950s. *Submitted by Patricia Welker*

BRENNECKE – Henry was the second son of Jake and Henrietta, (20 Sept. 1878 - 23 Oct. 1952). Henry married Anna Amos (20 May 1881 - January 1919). They lived in a frame house on West Main near Hubble Creek. The first of their children died in infancy. (2) Marvin A. became a medical doctor and lived in Waimea, Kauai. (3) Clarence Jacob joined his father in the Chevrolet dealership and married Ruth Desselman of Cape Girardeau. (4) Allene married Cornelius Biegner of St. Louis. They have four children. Allene is still living in St. Louis. (5) Evelyn married Louie Tomlinson. They have three children and have lived in Greenwood, IN most of their married life.

Henry Monroe and Anna (Amos) Brennecke

Henry grew up on the family farm west of Jackson, which is now Lakeview Acres. In 1928 the Brennecke name rested on an auto repair shop near what is now the Masonic Lodge. Henry's granddaughter, Pat Welker, has an advertising picture that reads, "Brenneckes Service Station, Phone no. 158," given to her by her sister-in-law Mrs. Dee Welker.

In 1931 Henry and J. D. Bowers acquired the Chevrolet franchise and moved to a site next to the old Coca-Cola plant on Barton Street. It is now the Cape County Administration Building. In 1932 Mr. Bowers sold his shares and Clarence "Fritz" Brennecke, Henry's second son, joined the dealership. A short time later, Johnny Wagner bought into the business. Henry's second marriage to Alma Wagner took place in 1930

After Henry retired, he managed a farm on County Road D for his son, Marvin. All of Henry's grandchildren have fond memories of going to the farm with Grandpa in his old black Chevy.

Marvin graduated from Washington University Medical School in 1930. After a year of internship at Missouri Baptist Hospital in St. Louis, he moved to Waimea, Kauai. He became a physician for a Lihue plantation in 1931 and served as a Public Health Official from 1933 to 1958. Marvin served as a medical director of the Waimea Hospital for a while and then entered in partnership with another doctor in the Waimea Clinic group from 1963 to 1975. He also had a beach home built in 1934 at Poipu on the southern end of the island. It became such a landmark that the beach in front was named Brennecke Beach. On Nov. 23, 1982, hurricane "IWA" totally destroyed Marvin's beach house and he decided not to rebuild. He donated the land to the state of Hawaii. All that remains is part of the sea wall and a plaque on the east corner that states "He wishes everyone will enjoy the beach as he did." In 1994, when he died, he left an endowment to Washington University Medical Center. *Submitted by Patricia Welker*

BRENNECKE – Jacob "Jake" Brennecke (14 July 1853 – 30 Dec. 1935) and Henrietta Peetz (6 April 1855 - 4 July 1936) were married Feb. 6, 1877 and were the parents of six children: August; Henry; Anna; Alvin; Joseph "Joe" and Benjamin. Jake was the eleventh child of August and Wilhelmine Brennecke, and Henrietta was the daughter of Heinrich and Henrietta Peetz. Both Jake and Henrietta's parents were immigrants from Germany. They lived all their lives in the Jackson area.

August Frederick (29 April 1878 - 6 Sept. 1957) married Ida Emma Hinck (1879 - 1964) from Gordonville. They lived in Gage, OK and their children were: (1) Anna Bertha (died at age 1); (2) Freda Maude who married Arno Eldred Haines and they had two children, Sandra Lynn and Diane; and (3) George Frederick.

Jacob and Henrietta Brennecke

Henry Monroe was born 29 Sept. 1878 and died 23 Oct. 1952; he married Anna Amos, who was born 20 May 1881 and died 10 Jan. 1919. He married Alma Wagner later in life.

Anna Caroline Henrietta (26 Jan. 1881 – 27 Nov. 1974) married Louis Herman Frederick Schaper (7 July 1878 - 31 March 1958). He was a prosperous farmer.

Alvin Brennecke (1 March 1883 - 30 Aug. 1978), a farmer, was never married.

Joseph "Joe" Henry (21 Aug. 1866 - 7 April 1970) and Cora Chostner Brennecke (8 Aug. 1886 - 3 Jan. 1975) were married Sept. 11, 1912.

Benjamin (l Aug. 1890 - 19 April 1891).

One cold day, many years after Jake and Henrietta had children, Jake went to Jackson in his buggy. He went into the saloon to get warmed up (had a drink or two). A farm was being sold on the courthouse steps on a tax sale, and Jake bought it for $800, sight unseen. The family went down to see what he had bought; he wanted to move his family there, but Henrietta would not hear of it. She said she wouldn't take their children there to die of typhoid and malaria.

Jackson, MO was very much divided between the north and south during the Civil War; the Brenneckes were northern sympathizers. After the Battle of Cape Girardeau, a wounded Confederate soldier rode to the Brennecke home. Jake, his mother and grandmother took him in. They got Dr. Pace from Jackson to take care of him, hid him out and nursed him until he recovered. When the Confederate was ready to leave, he insisted on leaving his horse as payment for their kindness. The Brenneckes kept Major, the horse, for many years. *Submitted by Doris Brennecke Davault*

BRENNECKE – Joe was the fifth child of Jacob "Jake" and Henrietta Brennecke. He was born

Aug. 21, 1886, at the family home near Jackson. He died April 7, 1970 while living at Jackson. Joe married Cora Chostner on Sept. 11, 1912, at Marble Hill. Cora was born Aug. 8, 1886, in Scopus, MO and died Jan. 3, 1975, in Cape Girardeau. She was the daughter of Frank and Louvenia Hopkins Chostner from Scopus, MO.

Joe was a farmer during his early years and Cora taught school in Missouri and Oklahoma seven years before they were married. The year following their marriage, they went to California and lived and worked there three years. Cora often talked about the department store where she worked and seeing some of the women movie stars come in and trade. Joe went up to Oregon and Washington the last summer before leaving the west and worked for cattle and sheep ranchers and wheat farmers – an experience he never forgot.

Cora and Joe Brennecke

Joe and Cora returned to the Jackson area and farmed the home place (now Lakeview Acres) a few years. Their first child, Carmen, was born there May 30, 1919. They soon bought a farm on the historic old Bloomfield Road between Dutchtown and Allenville and built a new house on the farm. He raised high-bred Leghorn hens, Hampshire sows, and the best of Holstein cows.

Their second daughter, Doris, was born Oct. 25, 1920. The family moved to Cape Girardeau for a year (1925) and Joe worked for Ford Groves. They came back to the farm the next year and Joe farmed until he became postmaster in the fall of 1931 and they moved to Allenville and opened a general store. Joe retired from the post office in 1957 but remained in the store business until January 1964, when they moved to an apartment in Jackson where they could be close to their daughter, Doris, and her husband, Hughes Davault.

Joe and Cora's older daughter, Carmen, married James R. Below on Aug. 18, 1939. Carmen taught school 28 years, nine of those as Delta High School principal. She was a very outstanding member of her community and her church. Jim was a long-time construction worker. They had five children: (1) Sam (divorced) had the following children: Scarlet; Allen; Samuel Aaron and Rebecca. (2) Martha married Darris Dalton; their children are Mark, David and Lesley. (3) James "Jim" Joseph married Suzie Dooley (divorced); their children are James Joseph II, Lynn, Timothy, Kimberly and Andrew. (4) Mary Lou married Mike Dobron; their children are Lauren and Erica. (5) George married Debbie Peterson; they have one child, Ryan.

Joe and Cora's youngest daughter, Doris, married William Hughes Davault on Nov. 20, 1941. *Submitted by Doris Brennecke Davault*

BRITT – James O. Britt Jr. was born Feb. 17, 1950 in East Prairie, MO to James O. Britt Sr. and Frances Jeannette (Tyler) Britt. Jim grew up in East Prairie and attended East Prairie schools, graduating in May 1968. Jim joined the U.S. Navy and went to Naval Training Center Great Lakes. Jim was a Gunners Mate and served on several destroyers, including the USS *Zellars*.

Jim married Betty Carolyn Blumenberg on March 20, 1971 at Pulltight Church of God near East Prairie, MO. Carolyn, the daughter of Roy Richard Blumenberg Sr. and Mollie Callie Arington, was born Oct. 5, 1953 at St. Mary's Hospital in Cairo, IL. Carolyn's father, Roy, was originally from Cape Girardeau County. Roy's parents were Louis Lee and Ella Sophia (Eggimann) Blumenberg from the Whitewater area. Carolyn lived in the Pulltight Community, southeast of East Prairie, and attended school at East Prairie, except 4th grade at Anniston, MO. Carolyn graduated May 1971 and joined Jim in New York City, where he was stationed at the Brooklyn Shipyards. Upon Jim's discharge from the U.S. Navy, Jim and Carolyn moved to Memphis, TN, where they made their home until June of 1984, when they moved to Jackson, MO. Jim is employed by the Internal Revenue Service and Carolyn is employed by FedEx Corporation.

Christopher Alan Britt made his arrival April 28, 1977 at Methodist Hospital in Memphis, TN. Chris attended Evangelical Christian School (ECS) in Memphis through 1st grade. Chris began 2nd grade at Jackson, MO and graduated May 1995. Chris was a member of Chamber Choir and President of FBLA, as well as a member of other clubs. Chris was accepted into and graduated from the United States Military Academy at West Point, NY in May 1999. Chris was commissioned a 2nd Lieutenant upon graduation and his first post of duty was Fort Carson, Colorado Springs, CO. In 2000, Chris achieved the rank of 1st Lieutenant. On Sept. 1, 2001, Chris was sent for a 6-month tour of duty to Eskan Village, Saudi Arabia. Ten days later, life in the United States would change for all Americans with the bombing of the World Trade Center in New York City. This was difficult for parents of all military personnel, not knowing the outcome of such an attack on our country.

The Britt family: Chris, Carolyn, Jim and Matt at the West Point Ball at Regal Riverport, St. Louis, MO, December 1997

Matthew Tyler Britt was born Sept. 29, 1979 in Memphis, TN. Matt attended school in Jackson, MO and graduated in May 1997. Matt sang in Chamber Choir and was a member of FBLA and FCA. Matt auditioned for and was chosen, as a freshman, to be in Southern Exposure, a Jazz/Show Choir. Matt had the privilege of touring Europe with a Missouri Southern Choir in May 1999. In June of 2001, Matt enlisted in the U. S. Army with a delayed entry. Little did Matt know the attack on America was coming Sept. 11, 2001. Matt attended Basic Training at Fort Benning, GA and graduated from AIT – Advanced Individual Training, Fort Bragg, NC on March 28, 2002.

The Britts are members of First Baptist Church in Jackson, MO, where Jim serves as a deacon and fifth grade Sunday School teacher. Jim and Carolyn also sing in the church's Sanctuary Choir. Jim enjoys golf and watching sports, especially Jackson Indian football and basketball. Carolyn enjoys reading and music. *Submitted by Carolyn Britt*

BROCK – Robert Cooper Brock II was born on Jan. 27, 1920 on a farm in Benton, of Scott County, MO. He was the fifth son and the ninth child of Robert Cooper Brock and Amelia (Steimle) Brock. He grew up on the farm helping his dad with farm chores. But as one of the youngest in his family, he had the privilege of being his mother's helper as well. He worked by her side in the garden and kitchen learning the arts of cooking and canning.

He attended St. Dennis Catholic Church in Benton with his family, and was also a student at St. Dennis Catholic School. St. Dennis and St. Henry Catholic Church of Charleston, MO cohosted many youth dances. It was at one of these gatherings that Robert met the girl who would one day become his beloved wife.

Seated: Alma and Robert "Bob" Brock. Standing: Patricia, Robert III, Pamela

That girl was Alma Josephine Brown. She was born April 16, 1922, the second daughter of Joseph Earl Brown and Helena (Sampson) Brown. She and her family were members of St. Henry Catholic Church and the children attended St. Henry Catholic Grade School. Alma graduated from St. Henry's Catholic High School, then attended St. Mary's School of Nursing in Cairo, IL. After graduation, she moved to Nashville, TN to work at Vanderbilt Hospital as a nurse in surgery.

Meanwhile, Robert answered the call of his country and joined the U. S. Navy. He was in the Navy for four years and fought in WWII. Once he was discharged from the Navy, he and Alma continued their courtship and decided to marry. They were married on Nov. 3, 1945 in Nashville, TN. They moved back to Benton the day after they got married and Robert got a job at Miller's Store. He and Alma had three children. Robert Cooper Brock III was born on Aug. 31, 1946; Pamela Rose on Dec. 12, 1948; and Patricia Lynette on June 30, 1950. All three children were born at St. Francis Hospital in Cape Girardeau, MO.

In 1951 Bob, as he was known to friends, was hired by the Associated Natural Gas Company. He then moved his family to Jackson, MO. The family first lived on South High Street in the Dalton house next to Jackson Auto Parts. Later they moved to 109 East Jefferson. The Brock family were members of Immaculate Conception Church, and all three children attended Immaculate Conception Grade School from grades 1 through 8. The family home on Jefferson Street was very conveniently located. The Brock family could walk to church, school and town. The children spent much time at the public library (now Cox Memorial Hall) visiting with Miss Bess

Liztelfelner, Mildred Brown and Mrs. Goodwin. They also loved to go to Saturday afternoon matinees at the Palace Movie Theatre (where Jer's was located), and often walked to Dairy Queen for ice cream treats. They walked through town to Ideal Grocery and the A&P Store for groceries. The Associated Natural Gas Company was located on Adams Street in an office south of the Rozier store. Bob could walk to work, then back home for lunch every day.

Alma continued her work as a registered nurse at St. Francis Hospital and Southeast Hospital. She preferred working as a night nurse. She took a few years off to help her husband start a catering business, but returned to work in 1968 at the Cape LaCroix Manor as a night nurse supervisor. She worked there until her retirement in 1978.

Bob and Alma were excellent cooks. Bob was especially known for his barbecue talents. The Brock family opened a barbecue and catering service in 1960 called "Brock's Bar-B-Que" located in a building where Wille's Bakery now stands. The business was open on weekends for carry-outs and catering services. All members of the family (Bob, Alma and the children) were involved in its operation.

In 1964 Robert Brock III graduated from Jackson High School and entered nursing school in Chicago that fall. That same year Patricia Brock graduated from 8th grade at Immaculate Conception. In the fall, she moved to St. Louis to attend Notre Dame High School. She graduated from Notre Dame High School in 1968, then Notre Dame College in 1972. She was a School Sister of Notre Dame, teaching and working as an administrator in the Jefferson City and St. Louis areas until 1996. She presently lives in St. Peters, MO and works for a private company.

Robert Brock III was drafted in the U. S. Army in 1968. He served two years at Fort Sam Houston in Texas. He returned to Chicago to finish nursing school and then went to California to work in a hospital. Later he returned to school in Sioux Falls, SD to become a nurse anesthetist. On Feb. 27, 1971, he married Patricia Ashworth from Tulare, CA, who was a pharmacist at the hospital where he worked. Robert and Pat are parents of three children; Robert Cooper Brock IV, born May 31, 1972; Sara Lynn, born Aug. 6, 1973; and Cynda Roselle, born Aug. 16, 1976. In 1971 Robert and Pat moved to Rogers, AR, where they raised their family and still live today.

Pamela Brock graduated from Jackson High School in 1966 and attended Southeast Missouri State University while living at home with her parents. She continued helping with the family catering business until 1968, when they closed the business on Hope Street. Pamela graduated from college in 1970 with a degree in elementary education. She moved to Crystal City, MO to teach third grade in the fall of 1970. She returned home to Jackson the following summer and got a job teaching kindergarten in the Jackson R-2 school district, where she taught for 30 years, retiring in May 2001.

Pamela married Stephen Randol Friedrich, son of Chester and Evelyn Friedrich, on Aug. 7, 1971. Stephen grew up on a farm near Oak Ridge, MO. He graduated from Oak Ridge High School in 1966 and served in the U. S. Army (including a tour of duty in Vietnam) from 1967 to 1969. Stephen graduated from Southeast Missouri State University in 1976, also with a degree in elementary education. He taught grades 3 through 6 in the Jackson R-2 school district. Stephen and Pamela had four children: Erin Patricia, born Feb. 19, 1977; Brock Thomas, born Jan. 2, 1979; Zachary Stephen, born June 2, 1982 and Joseph Matthew, born March 25, 1988.

Their daughter Erin married Dennis Robert Wilson, son of Robert and Marlene Wilson of Jackson, on Oct. 7, 2001.

In 1968, Bob Brock was promoted to general manager of the Associated Natural Gas Company. At that time he closed his weekend catering business. In 1971 the house on Jefferson Street was sold to the Baptist Church, and was later torn down to make room for a parking lot. Bob and Alma moved to Grandview Acres, a subdivision south of town, where they lived for the rest of their lives. Bob retired from the gas company in 1985 and resumed barbecuing and catering meals until 1996. Bob and Alma Brock continued to make Jackson their home until their deaths. Alma died on May 14, 1992 and Bob died on Nov. 27, 1996, both peacefully in their sleep. *Submitted by Pam Friedrich*

BROSHUIS – Bernard "Ben" John Broshuis was born Oct. 2, 1920 in Lutesville, MO. His parents were Bernard Sr. and Elizabeth (Wubker, Holzum) Broshuis. There were five children born to them, Bernard Jr. being the youngest. Bernard Sr. left Holland Jan. 8, 1887, and his parents, Lambert and Berndina and their three other children came later and settled on a farm south of Lutesville, MO.

Elizabeth's first husband, George Holzum, died in December of 1905, leaving Elizabeth with two children. She married Bernard Sr. in late 1907 or early 1908. Her parents were Henry and Gesena (DeBrock) Wubker. Henry Wubker was born in Germany. Gesena was born in this country, possibly of Native American heritage.

Johanna (Holzum) Broshuis was born Nov. 29, 1921. Her parents were Robert G. and Hannah (Lenderink) Holzum. Robert's parents were of German and Dutch lineage. Hannah's parents came from Holland in the early 1880s.

Johanna and Bernard Broshuis, 1978, 30th wedding anniversary

Bernard Jr. went to St. Louis in 1940 where he worked for Masman Construction Company until he was drafted into the U. S. Army on Aug. 28, 1942. In 1943 he was assigned to the 161st Airborne Engineers at Camp Carson in Colorado. Bernard came home on leave and he and Johanna were married Feb. 27, 1943 at Guardian Angel Church in St. Louis, MO. Johanna joined her husband in Colorado until he was transferred to North Carolina in November 1943. Johanna returned to live in St. Louis and to her work at St. John's Hospital. She later went to live with her dad near Leopold, MO. Bernard spent the last year of his service on Luzon in the Philippine Islands, being discharged Jan. 26, 1946. In March 1946 he went to work for Elfrink Construction Company and remained with them for over 50 years.

In March of 1950, Bernard, Johanna and daughters Betty and Brenda, moved from Leopold, MO to Jackson, MO. They became members of Immaculate Conception Church. In June Johanna joined the St. Ann's Sodality and Bernard joined the Holy Name Society. They also were members of the home and school organization. Their daughters attended Immaculate Conception Grade School and both graduated from Notre Dame High School. Bernard served on the building committee for the new church, which was dedicated in 1962. Bernard, a long time member of the Knights of Columbus Council #6405, is a 3rd degree Knight. Johanna is a charter member of the Knights of Columbus Ladies Auxiliary.

Bernard and Johanna have two daughters, Elizabeth Joann "Betty" married to Michael A. Elfrink and Brenda Francis married to Norman H. Grass. They also have four grandchildren, eight great-grandchildren and three step-great-grandchildren.

Bernard is a semi-retired construction worker, but would prefer to "pick up a lunch box and go to work." Johanna is a homemaker and a retired seamstress. She enjoys doing volunteer work. *Submitted by Johanna Broshius*

BROWN – Mildred and Shelby Brown were married in 1933 and moved to Jackson in 1934 after living a short time in the Perryville area, where Shelby's father had a saw mill. Shelby (March 18, 1910 – Aug. 29, 1998) was the son of William Dellon Brown (1886-1959) and Nellie Tennessee Condor (1888-1970) of Bollinger County; they were married March 18, 1905 and had 17 children. Mildred was also born in Bollinger County on June 18, 1911. Her parents were Phil E. Bollinger and Azie Myrtle Limbaugh.

Shelby's family came to Bollinger County from North Carolina. The following are his sisters and brothers: Ovo (1907-1976); Opal (1908-1991); Orpha (1912 -); Otto (1914-1914); Lillian (1915 -); Lottie (1917-1988); Hobert (1918-1984); Essie (1920 -); Jessie (1920 -); Paul (1921 -); J. W. Brown (1924-1925); Oleta (1925 -); Nellie (1927 -); Idell (1929 -); John Henry (1931-1998) and Mary Lou (1933-1933). Shelby's sister, Mrs. Jerry (Idell) Dockins, depicted the Brown Family History in a quilt fashioned from photos of the family. A picture of the quilt and article were featured in the *Jackson USA Signal*, March 8, 1998.

Mildred and Shelby lived most of their lives at 1001 West Main Street, where Mildred still lives. She attended Bollinger School near Scopus; Will Mayfield College and Southeast Missouri State University. Prior to marriage, Mildred taught in rural schools, but when coming to Jackson, they worked at the shoe factory until Shelby went into service during WWII and spent time in the South Pacific.

After the War, Mildred completed her degree at Southeast Missouri State University, became librarian at Lutesville High School, then Assistant Librarian at Jackson City Library (1955) and head librarian in 1960 until her retirement in July 1976.

They became members of New McKendree Methodist Church on April 20, 1941; Mildred became active in the Fellowship Sunday School class, United Methodist Women, and taught in the children's Sunday School many years. Shelby was an active member of the

Mildred and Shelby Brown

Masonic Lodge in Jackson and Mildred the Order of the Eastern Star. Mildred and Shelby gave of their time and resources toward Old McKendree many years, serving as Trustees, and Mildred is still a Trustee (2001). Mildred was active in John Guild Chapter DAR for 30 years serving as Regent from 1986-1989; she was also active in the Thursday Literary Club for that many years.

Mildred's great-grandfather Mathais Bollinger was a brother of Col. George Frederick Bollinger. Mathais and family were one of 20 families that migrated from North Carolina with Col. Bollinger (ca.) 1800; they settled in the Burfordville area. Mildred had one brother, John Bollinger of Scopus (deceased), and two sisters, Velda Bollinger (deceased) and Melba Bollinger, Jackson Manor, Jackson.

Shelby was a prosperous business man and spent most of his life in the timber business. Shelby and Mildred worked with the "Train" of Jackson, giving of their time and resources. Mildred is still an asset to them. The old steam engine bears the name "Shelby Brown." *Submitted by Doris Brennecke Devault with information from Mildred Brown and Shelby's sister, Idell Dockins*

BRUHL – Ernst Hermann Theodore[3] Bruhl (*Jacob Ernst[2], Johann George[1] Brudl*) was born Aug. 7, 1859 in Apple Creek, Cape Girardeau County, MO and died Sept. 3, 1938 in Oak Park, Cook County, IL. He married Emma Virginia Daniel Feb. 19, 1887 in Fruitland, Cape Girardeau County, MO, daughter of Christopher Daniel and Cecelia Alexander. She was born June 2, 1864 in Kentucky, and died June 10, 1940 in Oak Park, Cook County, IL.

Children of Ernst Bruhl and Emma Daniel are: Robert Roscoe Bruhl; Emma Irene Bruhl; Benjamin Neil Bruhl; Ernest Helene "Helen" Bruhl and George Daniel Bruhl.
Generation No. 2
Robert Roscoe Bruhl was born Nov. 20, 1887 in Fruitland, Cape Girardeau, MO and died Oct. 10, 1978 in Lakeland, Polk County, FL. He married Sylvia Stroner June 14, 1913 in Chicago, Cook County, IL. She was born Dec. 28, 1894 and died June 3, 1960 in Lakeland, Polk County, FL. Their children were Harry Bruhl and Maria Virginia Bruhl.

Bruhl family: little boy center front, George Daniel Bruhl; second row: Benjamin Neal Bruhl, Emma Virginia (Daniels) Bruhl, Ernst Hermann Bruhl, Ernst Helene (Bruhl) Young; third row: Robert Roscoe Bruhl, Emma Irene (Bruhl) Hall

Emma Irene Bruhl was born June 17, 1890 in Fruitland, Cape Girardeau County, MO and died Feb. 2, 1965 in Oak Park, Cook County, IL. She married Thomas W. Hall April 23, 1912 in Chicago, Cook County, IL. He was born June 19, 1886 in Monaghan, Ireland and died Dec. 23, 1960 in Hertell, Brunett County, WI. Their children were Thomas W. Hall Jr, born 1914, Chicago, Cook County, IL; died 1916, Chicago, Cook County, IL; Margaret Hall, Chicago, Cook County, IL; and Virginia Hall, Chicago, Cook County, IL.

Benjamin Neil Bruhl was born Aug. 31, 1893 in Fruitland, Cape Girardeau County, MO, and died Sept. 15, 1976 in St. Louis, St. Louis County, MO. He married first Mary Schaefer about 1918 in Illinois. She was born in Missouri and died in Illinois. He married second Octa Vera Bollinger after 1942 in Cape Girardeau County, MO, daughter of David Bollinger and Mahala Bowers. Octa was born Oct. 23, 1906 in Oak Ridge, Bollinger County, MO and died Jan. 19, 1981 in St. Louis, St. Louis County, MO. He married third Ethel McMillian. Children of Benjamin Bruhl and Mary Schaefer are: Harold Benjamin Bruhl, born May 4, 1919, Illinois, married Dorothy, who was born in Illinois; Virginia Bruhl, born June 10, 1921, Illinois; and Genevieve Bruhl, born Oct. 23, 1922, Illinois.

Ernest Helene "Helen" Bruhl was born June 6, 1900 in Fruitland, Cape Girardeau County, MO and died June 19, 1994 in St. Charles, Kane County, IL. She married Eugene Clayton Young Feb. 20, 1923 in Cicero, Cook County, IL, son of Daniel Young and Annie Petterson. Eugene was born June 28, 1900 in Berwyn, Cook County, IL and died July 23, 1993 in Aurora, Will County, IL. Their child was Clayton Cullbertson Young, born July 11, 1930, died Feb. 11, 1959.

George Daniel Bruhl was born Nov. 30, 1902 in Fruitland, Shawnee Township, Cape Girardeau, MO. He married Eliza "Alice" Frances Kostal Oct. 19, 1928 in Clement Presbyterian Church, Cicero, Cook County, IL. She was born Nov. 19, 1905 in Chicago, Cook County, IL and died July 24, 1993 in Boca Raton, Palm Beach County, FL. Their children are: Paul Daniel Bruhl, born Dec. 3, 1934, Berwyn, Cook County, IL; died Sept. 12, 2000, Naperville, DuPage County, IL; and Robert Edward Bruhl, born Feb. 28, 1932.
Generation No. 3
Harry Bruhl was born May 7, 1914 in Chicago, Cook County, IL and died Feb. 2, 1987 in Mt. Prospect, Cook County, IL. He married Margaret, who was born about 1940. Their children are: John R. Bruhl, born Nov. 12, 1941; Jimmy "James" Bruhl, born Dec. 2, 1942; Jeff Bruhl, born Feb. 12, 1945; and Jay Bruhl, born Dec. 14, 1945.

Virginia Bruhl was born June 10, 1921 in Illinois. She married Mr. Sticka about 1944 in Illinois. Their children are: Jimmy Sticka, born Feb. 24, 1945; Richard Benjamin Sticka, born Jan. 19, 1951; and Larry Sticka, born Feb. 15, 1958.

Genevieve Bruhl was born Oct, 23, 1922 in Illinois. She married Albert Kec May 17, 1941 in Illinois. Their children are Jerry Kec, born Jan. 8, 1944 and Kenneth Kec, born March 3, 1947.

Clayton Culbertson Young was born July 11, 1930 in Chicago, Cook County, IL and died Feb. 11, 1959 in Chicago, Cook County, IL. He married Patricia Stancik Sept. 8, 1956 in Cicero, Cook County, IL. She was born July 19, 1934 in Chicago, Cook County, IL. Their children are Ronice Jo Young, born Sept. 4, 1957 and David Daniel Young, born Dec. 25, 1958.

Robert Edward Bruhl was born Feb. 28, 1932 in MacNeal Memorial Hospital, Berwyn, Cook County, IL. He married Carol Georgene Schaefer July 20, 1957 in St. Andrew Lutheran Church, Park Ridge, Cook County, IL, daughter of Edward Schaefer and Louise Dockter. Carol was born Dec. 31, 1934 in Chicago, Cook County, IL. Their child is George Daniel Bruhl, born March 21, 1961, Mac Neal Memorial Hospital, Berwyn, Cook County, IL.
Generation No. 4
Ronice Jo Young was born Sept. 4, 1957 in Batavia, Kane County, IL. She married Robert Kenny Nov. 19, 1983 in Batavia, Kane County,
IL. Their children are Christopher Clayton Kenny, born Nov. 19, 1983 and Sean Kenny, born Oct. 21, 1987

David Daniel Young was born Dec. 25, 1958 in Chicago, Cook County, IL. He married Denise Michell Dupuis in 1977 in Batavia, Kane County, IL. Their children are Kevin David Young Brown, born June 23, 1978 and Kristina Ann (Young) Brown, born June 4, 1980. *Submitted by Carol Bruhl*

BRUHL - George Daniel[4] Bruhl (*Ernst Hermann Theodore[3] Bruhl, Jacob Ernst[2], Johann Georg[1] Brudl*) was born Nov. 30, 1902 in Fruitland, Shawnee Township, Cape Girardeau, MO. He married Eliza "Alice" Frances Kostal Oct. 19, 1928 in Clement Presbyterian Church, Cicero, Cook County, IL. She was born Nov. 19, 1905 in Chicago, Cook County, IL and died July 24, 1993 in Boca Raton, Palm Beach County, FL. Their children are: Paul Daniel Bruhl, born Dec. 3, 1934, Berwyn, Cook County, IL; died Sept. 12, 2000, Naperville, DuPage County, IL; and Robert Edward Bruhl.
Generation No. 2
Robert Edward Bruhl was born Feb. 28, 1932 in MacNeal Memorial Hospital, Berwyn, Cook County, IL. He married Carol Georgene Schaefer July 20, 1957 in St. Andrew Lutheran Church, Park Ridge, Cook County, IL, daughter of Edward Schaefer and Louise Dockter. Carol was born Dec. 31, 1934 in Chicago, Cook County, IL. Their child is George Daniel Bruhl, born March 21, 1961, Mac Neal Memorial Hospital, Berwyn, Cook County, IL. *Submitted by Carol Bruhl*

BRUHL – Johann George (Prudl)[3] Bruhl (*Jacob Ernst[2], Johann George[1] Brudl*) was born July 2, 1833 in Lahn, No. 6, Austria and died Aug. 8, 1907 in Perryville, Perry County, MO. He married first, wife's name unknown. She was born in Austria and died in Austria. He married second Elizabeth Lehner April 27, 1858 in Altenburg, Perry County, MO, daughter of Matthias Lehner and Theresa. Elizabeth was born November 1840 in Austria and died Sept. 1, 1913 in Frohna, Perry County, MO.

Children of Johann Bruhl and Elizabeth Lehner were: Johann Heinrich (Brul) Bruhl, born Aug. 31, 1859, Cape Girardeau County, MO; died Nov. 9, 1903, Frohna, Perry County, MO; married Marie Rhyne April 15, 1903, Perry County, MO; Wilhelm August Christian Bruhl, born Aug. 12, 1861, married Maria (last name unknown); Juliana Elizabeth Bruhl; Josephine Theresia Brul; Carl (Karl) Ludwig Brul.
Generation No. 2
Juliana Elizabeth Bruhl was born Jan. 5, 1864 in New Wells, Perry County, MO. She married August Ludwig Roth May 8, 1887 in Concordia Lutheran Church, Frohna, Perry County, MO. August was born Nov. 4, 1862 in Germany and died April 1, 1924 in Frohna, Perry County, MO. Their children were: Johannes "John" George Roth, born April 2, 1888, Frohna, Perry County, MO, died 1903, Frohna, Perry County, MO; Dorthea "Dora" Elisabeth Roth, born Nov. 10, 1889, Frohna, Perry County, MO; Joseph Wilhem Roth, born April 7, 1890; Hedwig "Hattie" Juliane Roth, born Nov. 5, 1893, Frohna, Perry County, MO.

Josephine Theresia Brul was born Jan. 20, 1866 and died 1918 in Frohna, MO. She married first Theodore Ernst Palisch May 6, 1888 in Frohna, Perry County, MO, son of Ernst Palisch and Julianne Hoffstadter. Theodore was born 1864 and died 1896 in Cape Girardeau, Cape Girardeau County, MO. She married second Andreas George Dietrich Hilpert June 22, 1902 in Frohna, Perry County, MO, son of Georg

Hilpert and Anna Ross. Andreas was born 1853. Their children were: Ernst Rudolph Palisch; Baby Palisch, born 1890; Richard J. Palisch, born March 1891, married Grace Mueller; Otto T. Palisch, born June 1895, Frohna, Perry County, MO, married Ida Muller; Joseph Ernst Palisch, born 1896; and Norma Amalie Palisch, born 1896.

Carl "Karl" Ludwig Brul was born May 22, 1869 in Brazeau Township, Perry County, MO and died April 12, 1940 in La Junta, Otero County, CO. He married Juliana "Julie" Brigett Popp Nov. 5, 1891 in Frohna, Perry County, MO, daughter of William Popp and Caroline. "Julie" was born July 1870 in Brazeau Township, Perry County, MO. Their children are: Lydia Brigitta Brul; Hugo Bruhl, born 1893; Rudolf "Rudolph" Bruhl, born 1895; Paula Elenora Bruhl, born Sept. 26, 1897, Frohna, Perry County, MO, died after 1920, MO, married Theobold A. Mueller April 7, 1915, Altenberg, Perry County, MO. Theobold was born October 1891, Altenberg, Perry County, MO, died after 1920, MO; Hilda Bruhl, born Jan. 23, 1900, Frohna, Perry County, MO; Elsa Josephine Bruhl, born April 9, 1905, Frohna, Perry County, MO; Georg Herbert Brul, born Feb. 22, 1908; and Gertrude Bruhl, Nov. 14, 1915, Altenburg, Perry County, MO (per letter from Carl W. Brul, May 10, 1999).

Generation No. 3

Ernst Rudolph Palisch was born Sept. 17, 1889 in Frohna, Perry County, MO and died April 29, 1949 in Brazeau Township, Perry County MO. He married Cora J. Mueller Sept. 22, 1910 in Brazeau Township, Perry County, MO, daughter of Benjamin Mueller and Johanne Sommer. Cora was born July 25, 1888 in Perry County, MO and died Oct. 21, 1985 in Brazeau Township, Perry County, MO. Their child is Wilbert Theodore Palisch, born July 14, 1913.

Lydia Brigitta Brul was born Sept. 20, 1892 in Frohna, Perry County, MO. She married Robert A Gerler April 27, 1913 in Frohna, Perry County, MO, son of Friedrick Gerler and Lina. Robert was born Nov. 26, 1887 in Missouri and died February 1977. Their child is Ewrin Gerler, born 1915.

Rudolph "Rudolph" Bruhl was born April 1895. Child of Rudolf Bruhl is Marcie Bruhl

Georg Herbert Brul was born Feb. 22, 1908 in Frohna, Perry County, MO and died June 4, 1992 in La Junta, Otero County, CO. He married, wife's name unknown, between October 1934 and February 1935 in La Junta, Otero County, CO. Their children are: Nancy Brul married Bob Palo; Tom Brul married Connie; Carl W. Brul, born April 19, 1936, married Diane; Sylvia Brul, born Aug. 20, 1938, married Tom Frankmore; Susan Brul, born Aug. 3, 1940, married Frank Reeves. *Submitted by Carol Bruhl*

BRUHL – Johann Heinrich (Brul)[4] Bruhl (*Johann George (Prudl)[3] Bruhl, Jacob Ernst[2], Johann Georg[1] Brudl*) was born Aug. 31, 1859 in Cape Girardeau County, MO and died Nov. 9, 1903 in Frohna, Perry County, MO. He married Marie Rhyne April 15, 1903 in Perry County, MO. The following was found in the Recorder of Deeds, Jackson, Cape Girardeau, MO: 1871 – Personal Property, #1397 – Land valued at $650. 3 horses - $100, 2 cattle - $20, 14 hogs - $25, other property - $105 for a total value of $900. *Submitted by Carol Bruhl*

BRUHL – Robert Edward[5] Bruhl (*George Daniel[4], Ernst Hermann Theodore[3], Jacob Ernst[2], Johann Georg[1]*) was born Feb. 28, 1932 in MacNeal Memorial Hospital, Berwyn, Cook County, IL. He married Carol Georgene Schaefer July 20, 1957 in St. Andrew Lutheran Church, Park Ridge, Cook County, IL, daughter of Edward Schaefer and Louise Dockter. She was born Dec. 31, 1934 in Chicago, Cook County, IL. The other residences Robert and Carol lived at were Cicero, IL, Downers Grove, IL and Lisle, Du Page County, IL.

Robert and Carol were Scouters when they lived in Lisle, IL; Carol was a den leader with two other mothers and had 24 Cub Scouts. She had a great time working with these boys. This was the time their son, George, joined Scouting. Robert and Carol continued their scouting experience when they moved to Oak Park, IL. They both earned the Wood Badge Award, the highest training award in the program. Robert worked with Troop 16 as an assistant scoutmaster, Awards Chairman for the Trailside District, Thatcher Woods Council located in Oak Park, IL. Carol worked with both Cub and Scout and Leaders, and also for Trailside District, training and attending various camping activities. At one point, Carol joined her son in a campout with Troop 16, along with other parents, to Colorado and took a whitewater raft trip down the Colorado River. When they moved to Jackson, MO, they gave up their scouting experience.

Robert worked at various jobs throughout his life. He started as a delivery boy for Western Union in Riverside, IL; Cook Manufacturing Company, Chicago, IL; Western Electric – Hawthorne Works, Cicero, IL (where he met Carol) and downtown Chicago; First National Bank, Chicago, IL (downtown Chicago); Velsico Chemicals, Chicago, IL; and Railroad Retirement Board, Chicago, IL where he retired on Nov. 22, 1996. Shortly afterwards they moved to Jackson, MO.

The following is a listing of churches the family belonged to: Immanuel Lutheran Church, Downers Grove, IL; Bethany Lutheran Church, Naperville, IL (both in Du Page County); Bethany Lutheran Church, Chicago, IL; St. John Lutheran Church, Forest Park, IL; and St. Paul Lutheran Church, Jackson, Cape Girardeau County, MO (1997).

Bob suffered a minor stroke, call TIA. His right eye was affected only. So far he is fine. This happened on June 7, 1996 while at work.. One summer they were camping at Trail of Tears Campground in Cape Girardeau, MO, and Bob came down with a case of the shingles. They had a hard time locating a doctor on the weekend. They did find one and medication was taken and it disappeared. After they moved here permanently, he had a macular pucker of his left eye. He had it operated on in 1997 by Dr. Krummenacher in St. Louis, MO. The operation was a success. In 2000 Bob had a cataract removed and another in 2001.

The following is a listing of schools attended by Carol Georgene Schaefer: Grace English Lutheran School, Wrightwood and Parker, Chicago, IL; Holy Cross Lutheran School, Wrightwood and Lemond, Chicago, IL; Our Savior's Lutheran School, 6035 N. Northcott Avenue, Norwood Park, IL (a suburb of Chicago, graduated); and Taft High School, Chicago, IL (graduated). The reason for attending these schools was that her parents moved around while living on the northwest side of Chicago.

The following is a list of places of work attended by Carol Georgene Schaefer: McMaster-Carr, Forest Park, IL; a motel for Western Electric employees (training school); North British Insurance Company, Chicago, IL; Pettibone Manufacturing, Chicago, IL; Western Electric Co. – Hawthorne Works, 22nd and Cicero, Cicero, IL and downtown Chicago; and Playboy Enterprises, 919 Michigan, Chicago, IL (computer work, May 1980). All of these jobs were clerical in nature except for the motel job; there she did housekeeping.

She was a member of the following churches, either as a child or adult: Grace English, Holy Cross, Our Savior's; Bethany Lutheran Church, Narragansett and North Avenue, Chicago, IL, St. John Lutheran, Forest Park, and St. Paul Lutheran, Jackson, MO. While attending Bethany Lutheran Church, the church started a program whereas lay persons were asked to sign up to be readers. She signed up for at least two Sundays a month.

Her middle name was spelled Georgine instead of Georgene. Her bible verse was Psalms 37:5 – Commit thy way unto the Lord, trust also in Him; and He shall bring it to pass. Aunt Florence and Uncle Martin presented a confirmation card that read: Whatever future days may hold, Or coming years impart, May all His love abide with you forever in your heart. Aunt Clair Schaefer (wife of Arthur Schafer, her father's brother) presented her with a baptismal card that had her birth and christening dates, the names of the church and pastor listed. The verse on the card was: Thou calleth the little one, Oh Lord! Thou, the friend of Children, Blessest them all. This little one too take to Thy Heart, Preserve it from care and sorrow In all the days of its life.

On July 2001, she had a cataract removed from her left eye. On July 18 she entered St. Francis Hospital, Cape Girardeau, MO for a complete knee replacement, being done by Dr. Kapp, Cape Girardeau, MO.

The witnesses to the marriage of Robert Bruhl and Carol Schaefer were Georginian I. Kruger and Roy Mitchell. The pastor was Paul Mehl.

The child of Robert Bruhl and Carol Schaefer is George Daniel Bruhl, born March 21, 1961, Mac Neal Memorial Hospital, Berwyn, Cook County, IL.

The following is a list of schools George attended: 1966-1968 – Lewster Elementary, 311 Lincoln, Downers Grove, Cook County, IL; (teachers: Mrs. Judith Crowell, Kindergarten and Alma Campbell, First Grade); 1968 – 1969, Beebe Elementary and 1969 – 1971, Bethany Lutheran, both located in Naperville, Cook County, IL; 1971 – 1972, Grace Lutheran, River Forest, Cook County, IL; 1972 1977, Whittier Elementary and 1977 – 1981, Oak Park/River Forest High School, both located in Oak Park, Cook County, IL. He also took truck driving lessons from Franklin College Truck Driving School, 3360 Park Avenue, Paducah, KY, on Apri 22, 1997 and graduated May 12, 1997. This did not work out well for him, even though today he misses it.

The following is a list of places where George worked: 1981 – 1993 Sears & Roebuck, George Street, Melrose Park, Cook County, IL; 1984 – Wilson Pet Supply Company, Wood Dale, DuPage County, IL (this was in between Sears); Midwest Sterilization, Rt PP, Jackson, Cape Girardeau County, MO (sterilized medical supplies and milk containers); and other various small jobs here in Jackson. Most of his work consisted of warehouse work – shipping and receiving.

George was a member of Boy Scout Troop 16, Oak Park, IL. He reached only the level of Life, but was an assistant scoutmaster along with his mother and father, who were on the roster as members of the committee. *Submitted by Carol Bruhl*

BRUHL – Johann Georg Bruhl was born about 1700 in Litzlberg, Austria. He married Barbara Eichhorn. She was born in Austria. Children of Johann Bruhl and Barbara Eichhorn are: Johann Bruhl and Jacob Ernest Bruhl.

Generation No. 2

Jacob Ernst Bruhl was born May 9, 1811 in Lichtenburg, Rutzenmoos, Austria and died July 26, 1895 in Pocahontas, Cape Girardeau County, MO. He married first Anna Maria Reuter (Reither) March 5, 1832 in Rutzenmoos, Austria (Jacob was 21 and Anna was 28 and the witness was Jacob Reuter), daughter of Franz Reuter (Reither) and Elisabeth Schirl. Anna was born 1804 in Austria and died in Austria. He married second Theresa Roither Jan. 15, 1849 in Rutzenmoos, Austria, daughter of Andre Roither and Magdalena Gneissl. She was born Sept. 10, 1827 in Parschall, Upper Austria, and died Dec. 16, 1903 at 3011 Arch St., Chicago, Cook County, IL.

Children of Jacob Bruhl and Anna Reuter (Reither) are: Johann George (Prudl) Bruhl, b. July 2, 1833, Lahn, No. 6, Austria; d. Aug. 8, 1907, Perryville, Perry County, MO; Elizabeth Bruhl, b. about 1838; Julianna Bruhl, b. March 14, 1841, Rutzenmoos, Austria, married Christian John Schaefer, b. July 17, 1835; and Franz "Frank" Bruhl/Brul, b. April 6, 1844, Lichtenberg, Austria; d. May 7, 1918, Shawnee Township, Cape Girardeau, MO.

Children of Jacob Bruhl and Theresa Roither are: Theresa Bruhl, b. Nov. 12, 1849; Joseph Christian Bruhl, b. Nov. 17, 1854, Apple Creek, Shawnee Township, Cape Girardeau, MO; d. Sept. 10, 1932, Jackson, Cape Girardeau County, MO; Amelia "Emilie" Ernstine Bruhl, b. Aug. 21, 1857, married Christian Hoeger, born Sept. 1854; Ernst Hermann Theodore Bruhl, b. Aug. 7, 1859, Apple Creek, Cape Girardeau County, MO, d. Sept. 3, 1938, Oak Park, Cook County, IL; Jacob Christian Bruhl, b. May 28, 1864, Apple Creek, Cape Girardeau, MO, d. Jan. 27, 1928, Illmo, Scott County, MO: Minna Bruhl, b. 1865; Georg Andreas Bruhl, b. Aug. 8, 1867, Altenburg, Perry County, MO, d. Sept. 11, 1931, Chicago, Cook County, IL. *Submitted by Carol Bruhl*

BURNS – Richard B. Burns was born in 1831 in St. John's, Newfoundland, Canada. His parents were William Burns and Mary Hemsdale, both born in Scotland. Richard arrived in Jackson, MO about the year 1853. Richard married Ann Gayle Tooke, probably in 1855. Ann Gayle Tooke had been born in England and was a member of the well-known Tooke family. Nearly a century later, a great-nephew of Richard, Howard Tooke, became Mayor of Cape Girardeau.

Tollgate and house, Richard B. Burns, Custodian

It appears that Richard's wife insisted that Richard be baptized before they were married. He was baptized in 1855 at the age of 25, in St. Vincent's Catholic Church, Cape Girardeau. Their daughter, Julia Elizabeth, was born in 1856, and also was baptized in St. Vincent's Church.

In 1861 a son, Charles Maple Burns, was born to Richard and Ann Gayle. By this time it appears that Richard was attending the Jackson Baptist church and was a very good friend of the pastor, J. C. Maple. In all likelihood, Charles' middle name was in honor of J. C. Maple. Around the age of 30, after working as a printer in Jackson, Charles M. Burns moved to Carsonville, St. Louis County, MO, where he worked many years as a proof reader on the *Globe-Democrat* newspaper.

On Sept. 20, 1863, Richard enlisted as a Private in the Union Army assigned to Company I of the Cavalry. He served honorably and was discharged on July 8, 1865 at the age 35.

About 1870 Richard had custody of the tollgate for the East Cape-Jackson toll road connecting Cape Girardeau with Jackson. This toll road, today called the Old Cape Road, was developed by the Cape Girardeau MacAdamized Plank Road Company. This company had been formed in 1851 prior to the Civil War, but had not been active during the Civil War Period. The company was reorganized in 1866, and road construction started. Tollgate houses were built for the tollgate family to live there. The house, in which Richard Burns lived with his family, was the second tollhouse built by the company and was larger than the usual tollhouse. This one contained comfortable living quarters for the family. The address was 816 Old Cape Road, Jackson. The accompanying photo, taken Sept. 4, 2001, shows the toll office attached to the house.

There was another toll road connecting Cape Girardeau with Jackson. This toll road was called the "West Cape-Jackson" toll highway. Mrs. Julia Elizabeth (Burns) Simpson, who was a daughter of Richard B. Burns, operated this tollgate house. Her husband was called Doc Simpson because he sold patent medicines. The Simpsons lived in their tollhouse until about 1906, which was three years after Richard died. Their daughter, Birdie, was born in 1887.

In December 1900, Isaac E. Kincaid, a very good friend of the Burns' who lived with the Burns family, died. Isaac Kincaid was a well-known candy drummer (salesman). In honor of his friend Isaac, Richard Burns made arrangements for Kincaid to be buried in a Burns family cemetery plot located in the City of Jackson Cemetery.

In 1901 Ann G. Burns died and was buried in the family plot in the City of Jackson Cemetery.

In 1903, after about 30 years as a tollgate keeper, Richard gave up his custody of the tollgate and house. He stayed in Cape Girardeau a few weeks and left there in May for St. Louis, MO, to make his home with his son, Charles Maple Burns. Within a week of arriving in St. Louis, Richard was stricken with apoplexy. With good medical help he was feeling much better until on April 30, he was stricken again and died in the home of his son. His remains were shipped by boat to Cape Girardeau, where they were taken charge of by his brethren of the Masonic fraternity and escorted to Jackson.

He was buried alongside the grave of his beloved wife. His Masonic brethren purchased a very large grave marker/monument, shown in the photo, which features the Masonic emblem on the side where Richard and Ann are buried. On the other side of the monument, a letter "K" is used as an emblem to designate the Isaac E. Kincaid gravesite. The funeral for Richard Burns was one of the largest ever witnessed in Jackson. Services were held in the Baptist church where, in the absence of a pastor of the denomination to which he belonged, Rev. C. W. Latham of the Presbyterian Church preached the funeral sermon.

Grave marker, Richard B. and Ann G. Burns, 1903, Jackson City Cemetery

Richard was plain spoken and had ideas and convictions on every question that came up, and possessed the moral courage and the ability to defend them. Many years before his death, he united with the Baptist Church and lived a zealous, consistent Christian life. He was always an active, industrious man, scrupulously honest and fair in all his dealings with his fellow man. He was a Mason high up in the knowledge of that order, past master of the lodge in Jackson and as faithful to obligations and duties imposed upon him by Masonry as he was in his church relations and every other obligation he had taken upon himself to perform. The large funeral was an evidence of the high esteem in which Richard B. Burns was held in the community in which he had lived so long.

Noteworthy is a Resolution of Respect printed in the Jackson Cash Book for 11 June, 1903. "Whereas, It has pleased the supreme grand Master of the universe to remove from the lodge below to the celestial lodge above our esteemed brother, Richard B. Burns, therefore, be it Resolved, That while we humbly bow in submission to the will of our Supreme Master we feel that in the death of Bro. Burns Excelsior Lodge, A.F.&A.M., has lost a worthy member, his children a kind and indulgent father, and the community good man and an honorable and upright citizen. Also, That as a token of our respect for Bro. Burns the charter and jewels of the lodge be draped in mourning for thirty days."

Another unusual event took place shortly before Richard died. Richard made application to be restored to the Union Army pension list. His attorney at Cape Girardeau received notice from the Commissioner of Pensions that the certificate had been allowed, giving Richard a pension of $8 a month from Feb. 4, 1898 to Nov. 5, 1902, and $10 a month from Nov. 5, 1902. Richard died on May 30, 1903. The letter to the pension attorney notifying him of the allowance was dated May 22, showing that the matter had been passed upon before Richard died. There was about $500 due him, which should have been awarded to his estate. However, the government attorney, through whom the pension was granted, stated that the money couldn't be recovered.

Charles Maple Bums learned the printing trade in Jackson. However, he moved to St. Louis and worked for over 30 years as a writer and proofreader for the *Globe-Democrat* newspaper. Charles married Lillian Maude Patchin in 1890. They had three children: Robert Maple Burns, Una Maude Bums and Paul Patchin Bums. Robert Maple Bums was a salesman and had one daughter. Una Maude Bums married Ebbert Matthew Webber and had three children. The Webbers moved to California during the early 1930s. Paul Patchin Bums served as a Marine in WWI. He received a Purple Heart medal as a result of being wounded. He married Mary Emily Knowles and moved to Tulsa, OK. Paul P. Burns was a concrete contractor, which later led him to being a building General Contractor. They had four sons. The oldest, Paul Yoder Burns, has had a very distinguished career in education, specializing in forestry management. He received a Ph.D. degree from Yale University, CT. He served in the Army Air corps during WWII. The second oldest son, Robert Charles Burns has had a rewarding and captivating career in avionic engineering. He served in the Navy during WWII. He received a M.S. degree from Stanford University, CA. The third son, Gene Crandall Burns, has had an interesting career concerned with mathematics and accountability. He served in the Navy during WWII. He received a B.S. degree in math from Oklahoma State University, OK. The fourth son, Donald Kincaid Bums, performed outstanding work as a general contractor in the construction business, schools, churches, office building, etc. He served in the Marine Corps during WWII. He completed his mechanical engineering college work at Oklahoma State University, OK. *Submitted by Robert "Bob" Charles Burns, great-grandson of Richard B. Burns*

BYRD - Amos Byrd, the founder of the Byrd family in Missouri, was one of the first settlers in what is now Cape Girardeau County, having come with his family in 1799. He was born in 1737, by tradition in the disputed territory between Virginia and North Carolina, and quite early was on the frontier with his wife, Sarah Ruddell, and his growing family. He was prominent in the early history of Tennessee before deciding to move west, and founded "Byrd's Fort" south of Knoxville. Gillespie's Fort was close by, and three of Amos' sons married daughters of fellow Revolutionary War soldier William Gillespie and his brother John.

When he was 62, Amos decided to immigrate to the wild lands to the west, evidently persuaded by the liberal land policies of the Spanish who controlled what is now Missouri. When he did so, he came with his entire family and connections including his sons John, Stephen, Abraham, Amos Jr., and Moses and their wives, and daughters Polly with husband William Russell, Sarah and Clarissa (the latter two later married George Hays and James Russell respectively). According to family tradition, they came by flatboat down the Tennessee River to the Ohio, and then up the Mississippi to what is now Cape Girardeau County. They settled on Byrd's Creek and tributaries, and all except Stephen remained in Cape Girardeau County until their deaths.

Amos did not live to see Missouri become a state, as he died on June 5, 1818. His son Stephen however was at the Constitutional Convention for the state of Missouri, and Abraham represented Cape Girardeau County as a Senator for 20 years in the Missouri legislature. At the time, Jackson was considered the chief source of political power south of St. Louis.

Abraham Byrd (1772 - 1857) in later years built his home out of rock, and carved his initials over the door in 1827. The then new home presided over marriages of Abraham and wife Elizabeth Gillespie Byrd's children, and a number of their grandchildren - the children of his son Stephen (1815 - 1866) and wife Nancy Isabella Moore - were born there. The "old rock house" was inherited by Stephen, and later by his son Abraham Ruddell Byrd. It saw great changes - marriages, privation during the Civil War, and many births and deaths.

Abraham Ruddell Byrd (1851 - 1922) was born in the old rock house, and it was there that he brought his college sweetheart and bride, Sallie Hunter, in 1878 - although she did not want to live there. They did, however, and their two eldest sons, Joseph Hunter and Abraham Ruddell, were born there before they sold the home and eventually moved to Jackson in 1887 (the old rock house still exists - cared for lovingly by its current owners). Abraham Ruddell Byrd lived and raised his family in Jackson, but poor health forced him to move to New Mexico and then Texas in about 1904.

By this time most of the Byrd name - always restless and lured by new lands and adventure - had moved elsewhere, although many descendants are still in the County today.

There are many stories:
-of Abraham's wife Elizabeth Gillespie, born the day Cornwallis surrendered, who survived Indian massacres and lived to be 87, surrounded by grandchildren who could hardly understand her thick Scots accent, and who was blind late in life and had the children read the Bible to her;
-of Abraham Byrd's son Stephen, wrongfully imprisoned (for "secreting slaves") for most of the Civil War by the Union Army, returning in broken health and dying shortly thereafter;
-of Stephen Byrd's family, left facing death by starvation or freezing (all they had -even bedding - had been confiscated and the eldest remaining male in the family was 9 years old), but who survived because of former slave Matthew Jackson Alligood. He plowed the fields by night and hid in the woods or haystacks by day, and kept the family fed;
-of Stephen's son Will, who went off at 16 to join the Rebel Army, and got so exhausted he fell asleep during a battle and was captured by the Yankees;
-of the same Will Byrd in later years building a fine new home in Jackson but refusing to have it wired for electricity, because he "had too much money invested in lamps;"
-and of how Abraham Ruddell Byrd and Sallie Hunter Byrd happened to join the McKendree Methodist Church: since he was Presbyterian and she a convert to Catholicism, they compromised on the church where they felt people were the happiest. Not bad theology, actually.

Although I never lived in Jackson, I am the lucky recipient of stories and memories related to me by my aunts and uncles, of a Jackson and a Missouri of 100 years ago, and am happy to share them. *Submitted by Abraham Ruddell Byrd III*

BYRD - Betsy Elizabeth Byrd was born May 22, 1786 in Tennessee and died March 17, 1860. She was married to Phillip Young who was born Aug. 9, 1780 in New Jersey and who died Aug. 19, 1853. Both are buried in the Byrd-Delph Cemetery near Oak Ridge, MO. Phillip went with Louis Lorimier to New Madrid in 1803 and was granted 300 arpens for his service, survey #814 on Byrd's Creek.

Their daughter Anna Young was born July 24, 1814 and died Dec. 21, 1893. She was married on Dec. 15, 1831 to Joseph Baker Jr., who was born Nov. 2, 1806, a twin, and who died Jan. 7, 1849. Both are buried in Baker Cemetery. He is the son of Joseph Baker Sr. and Catherine Niswonger.

Mary Jane, the daughter of Joseph Jr. and Anna Baker, was born July 2, 1848 and died Sept. 21, 1927. She was married Jan. 27, 1867 to Charles Benton Stearns who was born Feb. 8, 1844 in Bollinger County and who died Feb. 8, 1921. Both are buried in Snider Cemetery. He was the son of Joseph M. Stearns and Sarah S. Seabaugh. Joseph and Sarah were playmates in childhood.

Sarah Stearns, daughter of Charles and Mary Stearns, was born Aug. 15, 1873 in Millersville, MO, and died Nov. 30, 1927. She was married June 14, 1895 to William Harve Allen who was born Nov. 6, 1862 in Gravel Hill, MO, and who died July 2, 1948. Both are buried in Russell Heights Cemetery.

Their son, William Lynn, was born June 25, 1896 in Oak Ridge, MO. He was married Aug. 3, 1916 to Alta Idler Hall who was born Feb. 9, 1899 in St. Francis, AR, and who died May 8, 1985. She was the daughter of George A. Hall and L. Celia Scholl Lane. Lou Celia was a Cherokee Indian. Both are buried at Arbyrd, MO. Lynn and Alta's children are J. C., Lee, George William, Tommy Gene, Oscar, Joe, Anna Rumfelt, Mary Niswonger, and Hattie Ferne.

Hattie Ferne was born Nov. 25, 1919 in Jackson, MO, in her Uncle Baker's house on Georgia Street. She was married Aug. 19, 1939 in Jackson, MO to Boyd Loren Slinkard who was born Oct. 16, 1915 in Crump, MO, and who died Dec. 31, 1966. He is buried in Russell Heights Cemetery. He was the son of Ora C. Slinkard and Arra M. McGuire.

Boyd and Hattie had two sons. Richard Dean Slinkard was born Nov. 19, 1945 in Cape Girardeau. Donald Ray Slinkard was born July 14, 1940 in Jackson, MO. He was married in November 1966 to Carol M. Picou who was born May 6, 1947 in St. Marys, MO. She is the daughter of Andrian Picou and Helen M. Clery. Donald and Carol Slinkard have three sons. Jeffery Allen was born Oct. 26, 1967 and is single. Christopher Boyd was born March 12, 1978 and is single. Mark Wayne was born Oct. 31, 1969 and was married Sept. 21, 1991 to Julie Marie Lueder who was born Dec. 6, 1970. She is the daughter of Arthur Lueder and Marion Pierce. Mark and Julie have three daughters: Amanda Marie was born June 27, 1992; Ashleigh Lauren was born Feb. 14, 1995; and Andrea Nicole was born Dec. 27, 2001.

Betsy Elizabeth Young was the daughter of John Byrd Sr. who was born in 1770 and who died in 1819 in Cape Girardeau, and his first wife

Anna Gillispie of Gillispie Fort, TN. She was the daughter of William Gillispie.

John Byrd Sr. was the son of Amos Byrd who was born in 1737 in North Carolina. He was in the Revolutionary War and he died June 5, 1818 in Cape Girardeau County. He married Sarah Ruddle who was born in 1744/1745 in Augusta County, VA, and who died in 1792 in Cape Girardeau County.

Amos Byrd was the son of Andrew Byrd who was born in 1718/1719 in Shenandoah, VA, and who died Feb. 26, 1750 in Augusta County, VA. He was married about 1735 to Magdalene Jones. The Byrd family goes back to Thomas Lebrid-Byrd who was born in 1565/1567 and who died in London, England. *Submitted by Christopher Boyd Slinkard*

BYRD – James Commodore Perry Byrd was born May 20, 1829 in Western Kentucky, one of several children of William R. Byrd, born 1793 in South Carolina, and Charlotte Williams, born in 1802 in Georgia. James came to Cape Girardeau County, MO and married Arcadia "Arcada" Mizell on Aug. 3, 1848, daughter of William Mizell III, born 1800 in North Carolina, and Susan Green, born 1802 in Kentucky. He traveled to Izard County, AR and lived in that area until about 1857, when he returned to Cape Girardeau County and settled in the Neelys Landing and Egypt Mills neighborhood. Eight children were born to James and Arcadia. They are: Frances S.; Irene "Rene;" Mary Elizabeth; Sarah C.; William Henry; Martha E. "Matt;" Laura and Ada.. James' signature has been found on a document dated Nov. 21, 1887, as a petitioner to have Cape Girardeau County Court build a public road or highway from Neelys Landing to Pocahontas, starting at Neelys Landing and Jackson Road. James C. P. and Arcadia are both buried in McLain's Chapel Cemetery in Cape Girardeau County.

James Commodore Perry and Arcadia (Mizell) Byrd, about 1890

The only son, William Henry, was born Sept. 3, 1858 in Cape Girardeau County, and married Hilah Jane Wampler in October 1893, daughter of John A Wampler and Caroline. William Henry and Hilah were the parents of four children: James Rufus; Lela Avis; Carol Elliot and William Lee. William Lee "Bill" Byrd was born July 29, 1907 and married Ethel Lloyd June 20, 1931, daughter of John "Bart" Lloyd and Nellie Virginia Dixon. William Lee was well known in the Jackson and surrounding area as a sign builder and painter, including the first City of Jackson municipal signs, as well as painting signs over 11 counties. He also worked 33 years for Coca-Cola Bottling Company and the former Milde Bottling Company. William Henry, Hilah, William Lee and Ethel are all buried in Old Salem Methodist Church Cemetery in Cape Girardeau County.

One son, Jack, was born to William and Ethel. Jack married Carole Jo Crites on Sept. 21, 1952, daughter of Dr. W. W. "Woody" Crites, a well-known Jackson native and optometrist, and Jo Ellen Shelby, daughter of Dr. M. H. and Lucy Shelby of Cape Girardeau. To Jack and Carole Jo were born four daughters: Deborah; Carole; Lucy and Lisa. In 2001 Jack and Carole Jo were grandparents of 10 grandchildren and one great-grandchild.

In 1970 Jack and his father William "Bill" and their wives started Tri-State Swimming Pools. One year later David Myers, husband of Deborah, entered the company and in 1980 Jack, David, Carole Jo and Deborah incorporated the business and opened, "The Swimming Pool Shop."

As in all family history, the Byrd name has mixed and spread in many directions and buried in many other names that are not listed here. It is not possible to list here all the descendants of William R. and Charlotte Byrd, only one small thread. *Submitted by Jack Byrd*

CALDWELL – Ernest Caldwell was born Dec. 30, 1880 in Delta, IL, the son of Horace Lee and Sarah Ann (Sitton), who were married on Nov. 14, 1867 in Cape Girardeau County, MO. Sarah Anna Sitton's parents, Issac Bowen Sitton and Elizabeth Cox were married on March 26, 1844 in Cape Girardeau County, MO. Edith Lyle Lightner was born April 16, 1883 in Thebes, IL; her parents were Nathaniel William Lightener and Mattie Belle Boles. Ernest and Edith were married April 12, 1905 in Cairo, IL. Eight children were born to Ernest and Edith Caldwell.

Clifford Lightner, born Feb. 23, 1906 in McClure, IL, married first Edith King of Thebes, IL and had one daughter, Patricia; and second, Sally Rukkila of Michigan.

Elvis Lavern was born June 16, 1908 in Anna, IL and died Sept. 12, 1982. He married Ruby Wagner of Cape Girardeau, MO and had two children, JoAnn and Jerry Caldwell. Ruby died in 1951. Elvis married second Marie Bradley, and third Clara Shelton Russell.

Helen Pauline Caldwell was born Aug. 1, 1911 in McClure, IL. Her first marriage was to Jake Reiger and they had one son; her second marriage was to Paul Walburg; and her third marriage was to Bob Brune in Cape Girardeau, MO. Pauline lived and worked in Cape Girardeau, MO since 1948. She worked at the Colony Club and the Montgomery Ward Store. Pauline died in 1996 in Cape Girardeau, MO.

William Horace was born March 2, 1914 in McClure, IL and died Feb. 15, 1980. His first marriage was to Rosella Rhodes and they had one daughter; his second marriage was to Alice Drum in Rhode Island, and they had one daughter and three sons.

Jack E. Caldwell was born Dec. 17, 1916 in McClure, IL and he died unmarried on Nov. 25, 1972 in Cape Girardeau, MO.

Don Boyd was born Aug. 27, 1918 in McClure, IL and died in June 1979. He married Charlene Nothdurft on Feb. 9, 1952 in Cape Girardeau, MO and had two sons, John Kent and Stuart L. Caldwell.

Robert Levi, born on July 17, 1921 in McClure, IL, married Billie Jean Allgier in Cape Girardeau, MO in May 1947. They had one daughter and three sons.

Mary Lou, born June 17, 1927 in Cape Girardeau, MO, married Thomas H. Lett and had one daughter and two sons. Mary Lou worked for Southwestern Bell Telephone before her marriage.

Ernest, as a young man, ran a livery stable in Thebes, IL, at the time they were building the railroad bridge across the Mississippi River. He rented out horses and carriages to the men working on the railroad bridge. After the couple's marriage, they moved to McClure, IL, and bought the Day Farm one year before moving to Anna, IL, due to floods in McClure. They moved back to East Cape Girardeau, IL and bought the Billingsley farm, and lived in East Cape Girardeau until 1925. They then bought the Devils Island partnership with Dr. Duncan to farm. They moved the family to Cape Girardeau, MO to educate the children. Mary Lou was born in Cape Girardeau, MO on June 17, 1927. Living in Cape Girardeau proved to be difficult, traveling back and forth across the river without a bridge, and they moved the family back to McClure, IL. Ernest had a duck hunting club on Devils Island. One year the famous Jimmy Doolittle, who flew the first air raid over Japan, was our guest to hunt ducks with Mr. Brady from Cape Girardeau, MO. Mr. Doolittle at the time was working for Standard Oil Company in St. Louis, MO. Ernest Caldwell died on April 18, 1934 in McClure, IL and is buried in Lorimier Cemetery in Cape Girardeau, MO.

Edith Lyle Lightner Caldwell taught school before her marriage. She taught school in Searcy, AR, where her parents had moved due to the many floods in McClure, IL; she taught at Cotner School in McClure, IL until her marriage. After Ernest passed away, Edith and her son Elvis continued to farm for three years. She then worked as a cook at the McClure, IL grade school, until she moved to Cape Girardeau, MO in 1944. Edith worked in Cape Girardeau at the Darsa Dress Factory. She also worked at Southeast Missouri College as a cook. In 1952 Edith started a nursing home at 1305 Broadway and continued to run the nursing home, with the help of her daughter, Pauline Brune, until 1972. Edith Caldwell died on Feb. 14, 1980 at the age of 97, and is buried in Lorimier Cemetery in Cape Girardeau, MO. *Submitted by Mary Lou Caldwell Lett*

Ernest Caldwell holding son Bill Caldwell, Elvis Caldwell, Clifford Caldwell, Pauline Caldwell and Edith Lightner Caldwell holding Jacob Caldwell on her lap

CALDWELL – Robert Caldwell was born Nov. 24, 1794 in Campbelltown, Scotland, to John and Jane (Armour) Caldwell. John and Jane were married July 9, 1793 at South End Church in Campbelltown, Scotland. They had four children: only three boys lived to manhood, Robert, Andrew and John.

John and Jane and three boys left for America about 1800. Robert's father, John, died on the ship and his widow and children were met in Charleston, SC by relatives and taken to Mecklenburg County, NC. Jane and family stayed in North Caroline until about 1833. Jane, Robert and Andrew came to Fruitland, MO. Robert had land allotted to him for service in the 1812 war. The other son,

John, stayed in Mecklenburg, NC, but traveled to Missouri on horseback to visit his mother and brothers. Some of John's descendants settled in Bedford County, TN. Robert and Andrew were married while in Mecklenburg, NC. Robert married Mary Emily Shields and Andrew married Peggy McClard Query. Robert and Mary Emily Shields were married March 20, 1819 in North Carolina. Robert's first wife, Mary Emily Shields, died Dec. 21, 1838 and is buried in the Apple Creek Cemetery.

Robert and Mary Emily Shields had eight children: John A., born Jan. 14, 1820 in North Carolina, married Martha Cochran on Oct. 28, 1845; David Shields, born Oct. 29, 1821 in North Carolina, married his cousin Lamaria Caldwell; my ancestor, Marcus Layfayette, a shoemaker by trade, born in North Carolina on Nov. 4, 1823, married Sarah Lee on May 1, 1845 in Cape Girardeau County, MO, and he died Jan. 15, 1856 and is buried in the Pleasant Hill Cemetery at Fruitland, MO; William, born Feb. 3, 1826 in North Carolina married Darcas Cochran in Cape Girardeau County, MO on May 24, 1849. William moved to Jasper, MS, fought in the Civil War and was killed and buried at the Military Cemetery in North Springfield, VA. His wife and children moved back to Fruitland, MO; Isabel E., born April 29, 1828 in North Carolina, never married and died Aug. 17, 1848 in Cape Girardeau County, MO; Robert N., born March 27, 1830 in North Carolina, married Louisa Snider in Cape Girardeau County MO and is buried near Ash Hollow, KS; Andrew A. Caldwell born Aug. 5, 1832 in North Carolina, married Mary Miller in 1861 and died in June 1916; and Mary J. Caldwell, born in Cape Girardeau County, MO, married Phillip Sutherland and died July 2, 1867.

Robert married a second wife, Narcissa Alexander, the daughter of Ambrose Alexander of North Carolina. Narcissa is buried in the Pleasant Hill Cemetery in Fruitland, MO, along with Robert who died Sept. 14, 1856. Three children were born to this union; Charles Samuel Caldwell (born in Missouri in 1842; died Feb. 10, 1907 in Fruitland, MO), married Virginia Alexander; Martha Ellen (born in Missouri on May 22, 1845) married Robert Query; and Henry Lauren (born in Missouri May 23, 1848) married first Mollie Chastner and second, Mary C. Crosby.

Robert was active in the Presbyterian Church. He served on the board, taught school in the church, and donated the land for the cemetery and lived close to the church. The Presbyterian Church holds church once a year in May, and many of the descendants of the church come back every year for church and a basket dinner. My ancestors are John, Robert, Marcus, Horace and Ernest Caldwell.

Marcus Layfayette Caldwell was born Nov. 4, 1823 in North Carolina and moved to Fruitland, MO about 1833. He married Sarah Lee on May 1, 1845. Marcus was a shoemaker. They had three children; Mary F., born March 23, 1846 in Jackson, MO; Horace Lee, born July 29, 1848, married Sarah Anna Sitton on Nov. 14, 1866, the daughter of Issac Bowen Sitton and Elizabeth (Cox) Sitton; and Ella R. Caldwell, born Dec. 23, 1850 in Jackson, MO. Mary F. and Ella R. died before adult age. Horace Lee Caldwell and Sarah Ann Sitton were married in Cape Girardeau County, MO on Nov. 14, 1867. They were parents of 13 children altogether, including two sets of twins. The first four children were born in Missouri, then they moved to Alexander County, IL about 1874. Ernest Caldwell's sixth child was my father, born Dec. 31, 1880 in Delta, MO, who married Edith L. Lightner in Cairo, IL on April 12, 1905. They had eight children. *Submitted by Mary Lou (Caldwell) Lett*

CANNON – Dr. Franklin A. Cannon came to Jackson in 1819 from North Carolina in a covered wagon. He was one of Jackson's early doctors and set up a practice on Nov. 18, 1819 on Main Street in Jackson. Dr. Cannon believed in the importance of education and also in purchasing properties in and around the county seat, one being the rock house at 119 North Missouri.

In between his land dealings and medical profession, he found time to get into politics. His first political venture was in the local area serving on the Jackson Board of Trustees in 1820. In 1832 he was elected to the Missouri Senate, but in 1833 was in Jackson, along with other doctors, trying to fight the cholera epidemic. In 1834 he served a second term in the State Senate. It was during this term as senator that he married Mary Dunklin, the oldest daughter of Governor Daniel Dunklin, in Jefferson City, MO, in 1835. Dr. Cannon went on to serve two terms on the Democratic tickets, as Lt. Governor in 1836 and 1838 under Governor Daniel Dunklin.

Some time after his second term, Dr. Cannon and his family moved to Jackson, around 1840. They built a home they named "Poplar Grove" on what is now Route D, two miles north of Jackson, where they raised their family of 10 children. Their seventh child, Ella Eliza, born in 1851, later became the mother of Dr. J. L. Jenkins, dentist, a prominent member of the Jackson Community in the 1900s. Many political leaders of Missouri continued to be guests of Dr. Cannon and his family after they left Jefferson City. As a southerner by birth, Dr. Cannon was the owner of slaves, who fashioned the home's native clay bricks in kilns on the property.

Following the death of his wife, Mary, during the cholera epidemic of 1852, Dr. Cannon continued on as father, doctor and head of this home at "Poplar Grove." He was a charter member and elder of the Presbyterian Church in Jackson. Even thought Dr. Cannon was sympathetic to the southern cause during the Civil War, he helped northern and southern soldiers alike. Dr. Cannon passed away at his home on June 13, 1863. His will made generous provisions for his surviving children, allowing them to continue farming operations on the "Poplar Grove" estate. He had believed in the importance of education for men and women alike. He made certain in his will that there be ample funds for the education of his heirs. The three youngest daughters would be given the same opportunity for higher education that the older siblings had received. Dr. Cannon even provided for his former slaves, now servants, Sam and his wife Millie, specifying that they not be sold or made to leave "Poplar Grove," and that they be provided for in their old age. Dr. Franklin Cannon and his wife Mary are buried in the Old Jackson Cemetery. For more information see the J. L. Jenkins family history. *Submitted by Nancy Ware Ladreiter*

Dr. Franklin Cannon

CHILES – Ernest Samuel Chiles II was born June 11, 1939, in St. Louis, MO, the only son of Ernest Samuel Chiles (b. Jan. 20, 1899, Longtown, Perry County, MO; d. May 5, 1959, Bloomfield, Stoddard County, MO) and Mamie Eudora Butler Chiles (b. July 20, 1896, Stoddard County, MO; d. Sept. 16, 1968, Cape Girardeau, Cape Girardeau County, MO), the daughter of David Oliver and Nartisia Leila Welch Butler. He grew up in Bloomfield, where his father, grandfather and aunt owned and operated the Chiles Undertaking Company. Upon his graduation from Bloomfield High, he attended and graduated from Southeast Missouri State College in 1962 with a B.S. degree in education. On April 2, 1960, he married Dorothy Anne Evans (b. Oct. 12, 1940), the daughter of Thomas Herbert and Dora Winifred Bryant Evans of Dexter, MO, to which union were born two sons, Ernest Samuel Chiles III (b. Sept. 2, 1970, Vincennes, IN) and James Thomas Chiles (b. March 27, 1973, Vincennes, IN).

After graduation from Southeast Missouri State College, Ernest was employed by the Cape Girardeau Public Schools as a senior high school science teacher. After three years of teaching, during which time he obtained a private and commercial pilot's license, as well as flight instructor certificate, he began working full time as a flight instructor and charter pilot for Cape Central Airways. After two years he returned to teaching in the Jackson Public School system as a junior high school science teacher. In 1969 he joined the faculty of Vincennes University at Vincennes, IN, and after two years was promoted to Director of Programs and Services for the Aviation Flight Technology Department. He was also a designated flight test examiner for the Federal Aviation Administration. After five successful years operating the university's airport at Lawrenceville, IL, he went into business for himself, operating first a Western Auto franchise in Albion, IL; then a Sonic drive-in restaurant in Jackson, MO; the Frontier restaurant and convenience store in Fruitland, MO; and finally the Gordonville Gas and Grocery in Gordonville, MO. Upon the sale of the Gordonville store, he was employed by Larron Laboratory in Cape Girardeau as Director of Underground Storage Tank Services. He has lived north of Jackson, MO since 1976, where he now resides with his second wife Patty Jo (nee Johnson) Chiles.

Patty Jo (Johnson) Chiles and Ernest Samuel Chiles II, 1999

Ernest's father, Ernest Samuel Chiles, was the son of James Andrew Chiles (b. Sept. 1, 1868, Pocahontas, Cape Girardeau County, MO; d. May 27, 1946, Bloomfield, Stoddard County, MO) and Jennie Leonard Clifton (b. March 30, 1873, Crosstown, Perry County MO; d. Oct. 30, 1952, Bloomfield, Stoddard County, MO), the daughter of Bartholemew Stanhope and Ann Elizabeth (Pinkerton) Clifton. James, or J. A., as he was known, was the son of Confederate veteran Isaac Gonce Chiles (b. July 28, 1842, Benton County, MO; d. Nov. 20, 1928, Bloomfield, Stoddard County, MO), who served with the 8th Missouri Cavalry, Company

D, Jeffers' Regiment, and Frances L. Abernathy (b. August 1845, MO; d. Oct. 27, 1918, High Prairie, Klickitat County, WA), the daughter of Robert and Rebecca S. Morton Abernathy and granddaughter of Joseph and Glaphyra Abernathy of Pocahontas. Isaac was the son of Roland Chiles (b. 1813, Tennessee; d. 1890, Cape Girardeau County, MO) and Sarah Gonce (b. 1808, Tennessee; d. 1886, Cape Girardeau County, MO), the daughter of Isaac and Frances Ann Wilson Gonce. Roland was a veteran of the War of Florida, 1837-38 (Volunteer, North Alabama Cavalry); the Mexican War, 1846-47 (Missouri Mounted Volunteer, 2nd Regiment); and the War Between the States, 1861 (Missouri State Guard, Company C, 1st Regiment). Roland and Sarah, after living in Benton and Perry Counties in Missouri, moved to the northeastern part of Cape Girardeau County in 1854, where they lived until their deaths. *Submitted by Ernest Samuel Chiles II*

CHILES – Patty Jo Johnson, daughter of Ralph Meryl Johnson (born March 26, 1906, Piedmont, Greenwood County, KS; died Feb. 8, 1998, Eureka, Greenwood County, KS) and Hazel Orrel Houghton (born Nov. 3, 1915, Severy, Greenwood County, KS), was born May 8, 1953, in ElDorado, Butler County, KS. She had six brothers: (Elwin Olan, born Feb. 27, 1933; Sharon Shadrach, born Aug. 13, 1935; Roy Alvin, born Oct. 29, 1938 and died Jan. 23, 1972; Meritt Keith, born May 9, 1940; Marion Sydney, born Aug. 9, 1942; and Douglas Michael, born Feb. 17, 1956) and two sisters (Nancy Jean, born and died Oct. 20, 1937; and Peggy Jane, born Sept. 22, 1946). Patty grew up in Eureka, KS, where she graduated from Eureka High School in 1971.

On May 29, 1971, she married Jerry Lee Snider (born Oct. 26, 1952, Eureka, KS; died Dec. 15, 1973, Kingfisher, OK), son of Elwood Evander Snider and Wanda Lucille Osborn, in Eureka, KS. Their daughter, Laura Kay Snider, was born on March 10, 1972, in Goodland, Sherman County, KS. After Jerry's untimely death, Patty and Laura moved briefly to Eureka, KS, and then moved to Ankeny, Polk County, IA, where they lived for several years. There, Patty met David Jay Shaffer (born Sept. 25, 1951, Cambridge, NE), whom she married on Aug. 19, 1978, in Eureka, KS. David adopted Patty's daughter in November of 1978, in Polk County, IA, and she was thereafter known as Laura Kay Shaffer.

Patty (Johnson) Chiles, Laura (Snider Shaffer) Stants, 1993

Patty and David lived eight years in Union Grove, WI, and two years in Omaha, NE, where Patty graduated with a B.S. degree in Chemistry from the University of Nebraska-Omaha. The couple moved to Cape Girardeau County, MO, in 1989, where they were divorced in January of 1991.

Laura graduated from Lincoln Christian School in Lincoln, NE, in 1990. She attended Cedarville College, Cedar-ville, OH, for one year, and then transferred to Vincennes University in Vincennes, IN, where she graduated with an A.S. degree in Aviation Flight Technology in 1993. She later attended Purdue University in Lafayette, IN, and graduated in 1997 with a B.S. degree in Aviation Administration with an Aviation Flight Emphasis. While working as a flight instructor in Kokomo, IN, she met Steve Harold Stants (born Sept. 15, 1959, Marquette, MI), whom she married on May 24, 1996, in Gatlinburg, TN. Two sons and one daughter were born to this union. Devon Richard Stants was born May 16, 1998, in Kokomo, IN, and he died June 22, 1999, in Indianapolis, IN. Sidney Houghton Stants was born and died August 28, 1999, in Indianapolis, IN. Both boys died with Type I Spinal Muscular Atrophy and are buried in Logansport, Cass County, IN. Kaylee JoAnn Stants was born Jan. 23, 2001, in Kokomo, IN.

Patty has worked as an analytical chemist for 12 years. She married Ernest Samuel Chiles II (born June 11, 1939, St. Louis, MO) on May 6, 1994, in Paducah, KY, and the couple resides at their home north of Jackson. *Submitted by Patty Jo (Johnson) Chiles*

CHRONISTER – Abraham Chronister was born in 1791 in Lincoln County, NC, the son of James and Susanna (Earhart) Chronister. Abraham's grandfather came from Germany in the early 1700s and settled in Pennsylvania. They were called "Pennsylvania Dutch" and they traveled from there to Lincoln County, NC. In the early 1800s they migrated to Cape Girardeau County, MO. Abraham Chronister signed a petition in 1828 that there was not a minister for the German Lutheran and Reformed Church in the wilderness of Cape Girardeau County, MO. Other Chronisters on this petition from Cane Creek include: James and Maria Julian Chronister, Mary Chronister, John Chronister and Daniel Chronister.

The name of Abraham's first wife is unknown. They had the following children: Thomas (b. 1814) who married Ms. Mahanney; Rebecca (b. 1821 in Missouri) who married John Steward; Alfred (b. 1821); Eliza (b. 1824); Sally (b. 1826); and Maria (b. 1828). On Oct. 9, 1831, Abraham second married Nancy Martindill in Cape Girardeau County, MO. They had the following children: Anderson (b. 1832) who married Lucinda Revelle; Polly (b. 1835) who married Alfred W. Revelle; and Nancy (b. 1837). Abraham died early in 1840 in Cape Girardeau County, MO. The 1840 census lists "Mary Cronester" with three sons and four daughters. Nancy second married James M. Revelle on June 22, 1848 in Cape Girardeau County, MO. James died before 1860, but Nancy is on the 1860 and 1870 Bollinger County, MO census. Alfred and his sister, Rebecca (Chronister) Steward, went to Stoddard County, MO by 1850. *Submitted by Dawn Dement Detring*

CLIFTON - Robert L. Clifton, age 72 years as of March 25, 2002, is the son of Opal Clifton Wille who married Ernest Wille (deceased). His grandparents were Alexander and Sherilda Louizia (Louise) Jackson Clifton. He is the half-brother of Norman Wille (deceased), who married Grace Gilliland and had sons Jeffery and Robert Todd; and Pearl E. Wille (deceased).

Opal Clifton Wille's siblings include: Roscoe Clifton, who married Elsie Brown; Mary Lou Clifton, who married James Hughey (deceased); Betty J. Clifton, who married Claude G. Jaco; Margaret Clifton, who married Gary Niswonger; John Alex Clifton, who married Debbie Kamp; and Jewel D. Clifton, who married Walter (Pete) Hoffmeister (deceased) and had a daughter Betty J. Hoffmeister who married James A. Palmer.

Robert married Joyce A. Lindsay on Nov. 4, 1950. Joyce is the daughter of Rufus and Cora Slinkard Lindsay (deceased). Her grandparents were John and Cora J. Hobbs Lindsay, and Leo and Emma Ervin Slinkard. She is the sister of William J. Lindsay, who had children Randy Lindsay, Teri Lindsay Birk, Marc Lindsay, Suzanne Lindsay Duplissey, and Jeffery Lindsay; Judith Lindsay, who married Willis Smith and had children Christal Smith Falk and Shanon Smith Pettifer; and Kenneth Lindsay, who married Roxie Robinson and had children Douglas, Kurt, Scott, Greg, and Lorie Lindsay Siebert.

Chief of Police Robert "Red" Clifton

Robert and Joyce are the parents of Penny, Joana, Julie, and Joseph. Penny A. Clifton Meyer married Bernard L. Meyer and had children Bernard W. Meyer and Laura A. Meyer. Penny's granddaughter Paige A. Meyer is soon to be married to Nathan Ernst. Joana L. Clifton Popp Hoffman married Richard Hoffman and had children Tera L. Popp, Cody Hoffman, and Casey Hoffman. Julie M. Clifton Smith married Michel Hugh Smith and had sons Travis H. Smith and Brandon Smith. Joseph A. Clifton married Lisa Gale Medlock and had children James, Lacie J., and Jacob Clifton.

Robert L. Clifton is sometimes known by different relatives, friends and co-workers as Red, Bill, (on Sundays) Chief, or Sarge, He is a man of honor, compassion, and determination, a loving husband and father, and very giving of his time. He served in the Naval Reserve from about March 28, 1948 to July 24, 1949. He joined the National Guard on July 25, 1949, and served until Jan. 18, 1990, retiring as a Sergeant First Class.

Robert started working at the International Shoe Factory at the age of 16 and worked there for about 10 years before he was hired by the city of Jackson as Night Marshal on July 22, 1957. He was appointed Police Chief on Aug. 6, 1974, retiring on Dec. 31, 1990. Robert was the Police Chief and his cousin's husband, Gary Niswonger, was Fire Chief when they helped in the design of the first Public Safety Complex Building.

Robert's awards include: Sergeant Major award from the National Guard; the Exchange Club of Cape Girardeau presented by Judge Stanley A. Grimm to Robert the 1978 police officer of the year award; and numerous other awards and recognitions. Robert is a member of the Jackson Evening Optimist Club, the New McKendree United Methodist Church, and the Gideons. *Submitted by Joyce Clifton*

CLINGINGSMITH/CRAFT/WALKER/ WILLIAMSON/ACKMAN/COTTNER/MCCAIN – The Clingingsmith, Craft, Walker, Williamson, Ackman, Cottner and McCain families gathered for a fish fry at Neelys Landing, MO, circa 1911. Photographer William "Bill" Wiggins captured the moment at the old Craft home on Neilstadt Road, east of New Bethel Church, Neelys Landing, MO. This photograph shows several generations of Evelyn Myer Wright who received the photo after her parents, Charles and Helen Clingingsmith Myer, died in 1981. The Myers are buried in New Bethel Cemetery. *Submitted by Evelyn Myer Wright of Hillsboro, MO*

*Clingingsmith, Craft, Walker, Williamson, Ackman. Cottner, McCain
Left to Right, 1st row: 1. Ella Clingingsmith, born in 1903 and died at age 15 in 1918; 2. Helen Clingingsmith Myer, "Evelyn's mother," born 1905, died 1981 at the age of 75; 3. Viola Cottner McCain, wife of Bill McCain; 8. Barbara Craft Walker, wife of Irwin Walker; 10. Mae Craft Williamson, wife of Russel Williamson. Second row: 1. Henry Craft; 4. Susan Craft; 5. Sarah Jane Brown Clingingsmith, "Evelyn's grandmother," wife of Marion Clingingsmith; 7. Sally Ackman (buttons on dress); 8. Julia Brown Craft, with baby on lap, wife of Hiram Craft; 11. Eliza Craft Cottner, baby on lap, wife of John Cottner; 19. or end of second row, Nora Clingingsmith, baby on lap, wife of Carl Craft. Third row: 1. Hiram Craft, husband of Julia Brown Craft; 6. Tom Craft; 8. Charlie Craft (by porch post) husband of Katie Clingingsmith Craft; 11. Marion Clingingsmith, husband of Sarah Jane Brown Clingingsmith; Evelyn's grandfather. Fourth row: 5. Katie Clingingsmith Craft, wife of Charlie Craft.*

CLIPPARD - Daniel Clippard, son of John Clippard, from Lincoln County, NC was born Oct. 26, 1795. Daniel immigrated to the Burfordville area, MO in Cape Girardeau County at the age of 22. He had very little material resources when he arrived but, having learned the blacksmith trade in his native state, he soon started a shop on Whitewater near Burfordville. When land came on the market he "entered" 79 acres.

Elizabeth, daughter of Peter Crites Jr., was born Sept. 18, 1796, in North Carolina and came to the Burfordville area with her father in a covered wagon at the age of 6. Peter was one of 21 families that migrated from North Carolina to the Cape Girardeau District in Missouri with Col. George Frederick Bollinger ca 1800. Most of them settled around what later became Burfordville, MO, where Col. Bollinger built the "Old Mill" and made flour and meal for the settlers for miles around. They came to settle Spanish land grants obtained for them by Louis Lorimier, Commandant of the Spanish forces at Cape Girardeau.

Daniel Clippard and Elizabeth Crites were married July 16, 1818. After their marriage, Daniel and Elizabeth located on a farm near Oak Ridge, MO. When other land became available he "entered" at different times until he had large tracts of land. He owned at the time of death 850 acres, after having given 60 acres to each of his sons. For the first few years, Peter was compelled, on account of Indians, to seek protection for himself and his family in a blockhouse at Major Bollinger's Mill at Burfordville. Children of Daniel and Elizabeth and their spouses were: Peter (died young); John Franklin and Elizabeth Sadler; Andrew Jackson and Mary J. Wilson; and Sarah Susan Lloyd; William A. and Arta M. Crawford; Martha Ann and John Snider; George Washington and Cordelia Minerva Snider; and Sarah Armagost; Christopher Columbus and Elizabeth Wheeler; Margaret Caroline and Julius Snider; Mary Elizabeth and W. Frank Kinder; and Minerva and Sandy H. Wilson.

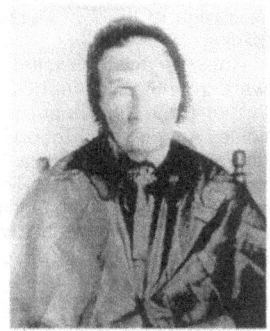
Elizabeth (Crites) Clippard

Many of the families of Daniel and Elizabeth settled in the Oak Ridge, Jackson, and nearby areas, and many of their descendants still live in the Jackson area. Daniel died July 18, 1865, and Elizabeth Jan. 6, 1875. Both are buried, as well as many other members of that family, in the Clippard Cemetery on land he originally settled - now owned by Chug Crites, Jackson (also a descendant). Daniel gave an acre of land for the Clippard Cemetery and an acre for the Clippard School, both near Oak Ridge, MO. *Submitted by Doris Brennecke Davault*

COLMAN – William Henry Colman, son of Sterling Price Colman and Elizabeth Shaw, was born in Mine la Motte, MO in 1895. He grew up in Palmer, MO, where his father was superintendent of the St. Francis Lead Co. and also ran the company store. Bill, his brother Ben and his sister Stella had a tutor in their home until time to go to high school in Columbia, MO, where they lived with a cousin while attending high school and then college at the University of Missouri.

In 1919 Bill became a 2nd Lieutenant in the U. S. Army Balloon Corps. After discharge, he returned to Missouri University to get his degree in Agriculture. It was there that he met Geraldine Harper, daughter of Dr. George Albert Harper and Hattie Hamilton. George had his degree in dentistry, and Hattie, who had grown up in Gallipolis, OH, had a degree from the Conservatory of Music in Dayton, OH. Geraldine was born in Bonham, TX, but grew up in Shreveport, LA. She received her degree in Home Economics and taught in Byrd High School in Shreveport before she and Bill were married in 1925.

They lived in Salem and Walnut Ridge, AR, where Bill served as County Agent. When the county went bankrupt, they moved to Farmington, MO, where Bill helped his father run a Red and White Grocery. They had three children; Harriet Elizabeth (1927), William H. Jr. (1930) and Geraldine May (1934).

When the Soil Conservation Service was formed by the U. S. Department of Agriculture in 1935, Bill was sent to head the office in Fulton, MO. In 1942 he was transferred to Cape Girardeau. The family settled in Jackson and lived on West Main Street in what is now the Cracraft Funeral Home. The children attended school in Jackson for two years and then the family moved to Cape Girardeau where the SCS office had been relocated.

Harriet, Bill Jr. and Gerre graduated from Central High School and then attended Southeast Missouri State College. Harriet graduated in 1949 with a degree in English and then taught school in Hammond, IN. After one year in college, Bill Jr. enlisted in the Navy, where he studied electrical power and reached the rank of EM2. Gerre received her degree in marketing and went to St. Louis to work.

In 1951 Harriet married Eugene Shorb of North Canton, OH. He had served four years with the Navy Seabees in the South Pacific. He graduated from Purdue University with a degree in Mechanical Engineering. He and Harriet had three children; Janet (1952), William (1958) and Thomas (1959).

Bill Jr. married Evelyn Milas of Forest Park, IL in 1957. They have two children, Jonathan (1958) and Elizabeth (1960). Bill worked for Lenco, Inc. as chief engineer and safety director, before retiring after 31 years. Evelyn has worked at the Cape County/Capital/Union Planters Bank.

Gerre married Todd Dudley of St. Louis and has three children, Elizabeth (1961), William Todd (1963) and Susan (1968).

William Sr. died in 1974 and Geraldine died in 1995. *Submitted by William and Evelyn Colman*

COOPER – Roy Cooper was born June 19, 1902 and died Sept. 5, 1995. He was the son of Henry Thomas Cooper and Elizabeth Whitener. He married Bessie Hendrix Sept. 30, 1925 at Cape Girardeau; she was born Oct. 24, 1901, the daughter of John William Hendrix and Katie Cordelia Allard. They lived on a farm at Grassy, MO, until he retired in 1965; they then moved to Fredericktown.

Daughter Dorothy was born Feb. 2, 1928 and married William Earl Morton. When he returned from the service, they moved to St. Louis. They had one daughter, Teresa, born July 19, 1962, who married Andrew Hunt from England.

Son Gary Lee was born Oct. 28, 1931 and married Mary Charlene Freeland; they lived in St. Charles. They have one daughter, Lisa Cooper, born Jan. 2, 1965, who married Philip Barringer, and had one son, Blake Andrew Barringer.

Son Aldo Cooper was born Sept. 14, 1933 and married Dorothy Sitze. They had four children: Jeffery, born April 8, 1961 and died Dec. 22, 1986; Sheree Elaine Cooper, born Sept. 22, 1966 and married Larry Light; Shelia Darlene Cooper, born Oct. 2, 1971 and married Kevin Cooper, and Kevin Ray Cooper, born Sept. 4, 1973.

Daughter Shirley Janice Cooper was born Aug. 2, 1935 and married Dean Wilson Kirkpatrick, who was born Dec. 5, 1935. They had four children. Randy was born Nov. 12, 1953; Bradley was born March 10, 1955; Connie was born Feb. 28, 1963 and married James Crook; and Shawn was born April 28.

After the children married and left home, Bess started making Raggedy Ann and Andy dolls for her grandchildren. She started receiving orders from friends who would see the dolls. She soon was in the business of making and selling these dolls far and wide. She also was making many quilts for her children and grandchildren. Soon that became a business for her.

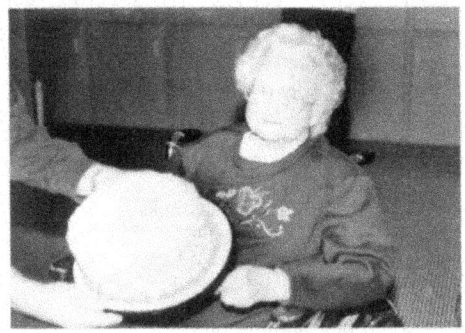

Bessie V. Cooper, 100th birthday

She made many friends and enjoyed visiting with her newfound friends. She did all kinds of needlework while they lived in Fredericktown.

Her husband, because of ill health and because he was almost blind, went to live with a son. She continued to live alone and do needlework until she fell and broke her hip. In 1997 she had to go to a nursing home in Fredericktown. Then she was moved to a nursing home in Desoto to be near her children.

Bessie celebrated her 100th birthday in October, receiving a birthday greeting from President George W. Bush and Laura.

Happy 100th Birthday to a Great Lady, Bessie Hendrix Cooper. *Submitted by Gary Cooper*

CRACRAFT - The Cracraft name dates back to 1203 in Lincolnshire, England, and to 1720 in this country when Joseph Craycroft came to the new world (the oldest known spelling of the family name is Creacraft, but it has also been spelled Crecraft, Craycroft, Cracroft, Creycraft, Creicraft (possibly erroneous) Craycraft, and Cracraft. Today it is most commonly spelled either Craycraft or Cracraft). Joseph settled in Frederick County, MD and had six sons there. One son, Joe Jr., went to Prince George County, MD, where he had four sons.

One of the sons, William, came to Kentucky and later to New Madrid County, MO. During the events of the New Madrid Earthquake of 1812, he may have migrated north to Cape Girardeau County, as many others did, settling south of Jackson near what was the Old Bethel Baptist Church. William married Elizabeth Howard and had one son, Andrew Henderson Cracraft, born in 1821 (the 1840 Missouri census lists four men and two women in the William Cracraft household. One of the women may have been a daughter, and one of the men may have been another son).

Andrew was married to Margaret Deland Lewis on Dec. 23, 1850. They lived and farmed the family farm south of Jackson, and were later buried in the family cemetery there. To this marriage was born at least four children, possibly six: William Cooper; Andrew Lewis; Martha; and Althea. Also buried in the cemetery between Andrew Henderson and Andrew Lewis are two baby graves, marked Albert and Martin, probably the brothers of William Cooper and Andrew Lewis.

William Cooper married Annie Summers and had one son, John. Shortly after, Annie died and William Cooper married Mary Hester Tucker and had four children: Harry; Sherman Cooper; Grace; and Lucille. William Cooper left the farm in 1913, moving to Jackson after retiring from farming. During his working career he held several county offices, including judge (He may have been presiding justice). It was while he was a judge that the new courthouse was designed and built in Jackson.

Of William Cooper's children, only Sherman Cooper's descendants remain in the Jackson area. He was married to Bereniece Miller (of Cape Girardeau) and they had three sons: Sherman "Mike" Cooper Jr., Edward Miller, and Gene "Rusty" Carlyle. In 1924 Sherman Cooper Sr. moved to Jackson off the farm and started Cracraft-Miller Funeral Home, which is still in the family today. Gene Carlyle married Mary Jane Thompson and had three children: Keith Winfield, Sherman "Mike" Miller, and Pat. Today, only Gene Carlyle's son Sherman Miller remains in the Jackson area, running the funeral home and the farm.

Sherman Miller Cracraft married Nancy Joyce Pfeiffer (of Gordonville) and have two children, Ashley Elizabeth and Michael Andrew. Michael Andrew recently married Amy Marie Aufdenberg (of Burfordville). To date, the Cracraft family has been in the Jackson area for seven generations and 189 years. *Submitted by Sherman (Mike) Miller Cracraft and Michael Andrew Cracraft*

CRIDDLE – Donna Marie Ludwig was born Jan. 26, 1949 at Cape Girardeau, MO. Her parents were Vernon Ludwig, born in 1921, and Bonnie (Armstrong) Ludwig, born in 1925. Donna's ancestors were of German, French, Swiss, Cherokee and Scottish origin. She grew up on a farm seven miles north of Jackson, or 3-1/2 miles southeast of Oak Ridge. Grandpa Oscar and Grandma Tillie lived on the other side of the duplex house, so Donna and her older sister, Cherry Lou, born Nov. 1, 1946 always had plenty of help and attention while Vernon was out on the farm or Bonnie was teaching.

The two sisters loved animals. They found a helpless little pigeon on the ground in front of the barn. They fed it and played the clarinet while it ate. Finally it was turned loose to be on its own but when the clarinet was played it would circle over their heads to give thanks.

Donna was active in the Brookside 4-H Club. She was Farm Bureau Queen, and participated in choir, band, and drama in Oak Ridge High School. She was active in St. John's Youth Fellowship. The family, along with the Albert and Olive Keller family, enjoyed camping in various states for the Keller cousins, Terry and Denise, were almost Cherry and Donna's age. The sisters spent many happy hours riding their horses. The birth of colts was great excitement.

The Criddle family: front row: Travis, 14; Jamie, 12; Beth, 10. Back row: Danny, Donna, Kim, 16, December 1988.

A new boy, Danny Charles Criddle, came to Oak Ridge High School. He was born Aug. 30, 1949, at Segue, TX. His parents were Charles William "Bill" Criddle, born in 1930, near Oak Ridge; and Billie McCanless Criddle, born in 1931, at Cooter, MO. Bill was born on the adjoining farm to the Ludwigs. Danny graduated from South Dade High School in Homestead, FL, in 1967. He enlisted in the Air Force and was stationed for a year in Thailand. While he was in service, Donna completed a B.S. degree in Elementary Education at Southeast Missouri University. When Danny was on leave, he and Donna were married March 20, 1971, at St. John's United Church of Christ near Fruitland, MO. They lived at Shaw Air Force Base in Sumpter, SC.

Donna and Danny have four children: Kimberly Ann, born Dec. 22, 1971; Charles Travis, born Feb. 26, 1974; Jamie Austin, born Oct. 15, 1976; and Beth Eileen, born Oct. 28, 1978.

Danny worked at Procter and Gamble and with his dad, hauling and setting up new furniture and attending auctions to stock memorabilia supplies for Billie's Place in Oak Ridge. Danny also helps in the operation of his father-in-law's farm. Donna's occupation has been homemaker for the family and four grandchildren. She has been primary teacher and music leader for the women's organization in her church. A nice tribute of Donna is that she always gives praise and encouragement to others. *Submitted by Bonnie Ludwig*

CRITES – When you think of the Crites family, think education and automobiles. John "Jack" Crites immigrated to Missouri from Switzerland in the early 1800s, bringing with him the firm belief in the value of education. His grandson, John Henry Crites (1858-1940) married Julia Ann Seabaugh (1855-1943) of Critesville, six miles north of Jackson. John Henry served on the Critesville School Board for many years and farmed in that community. Four of his seven children

Grover Cleve Crites

(Cleve, Dennis, Walter and Mellie) graduated from Will Mayfield College in Marble Hill. Cleve, Walter and Mellie became rural schoolteachers. The sons, Grover Cleveland "Cleve," Dennis and Walter moved to Jackson.

Cleve Crites and his future wife, Rhoda James, also a Will Mayfield graduate, taught in rural schools, beginning in 1907. They moved to Jackson in 1913, when Cleve became a different kind of teacher, a driving instructor. Driving's biggest challenge was keeping the newfangled automobiles running. Only the livery stable and blacksmith shops sold gas or oil. Many towns had no facilities to repair the contraptions. Seeing the need for an automobile repair shop, Cleve and his friend, Tom Harris, from Oak Ridge opened the Jackson Garage in 1914, with Tom Jones as the mechanic. In August of 1915, they opened the Jackson Auto Company, selling the brand new Ford Model T. The Model Ts, all painted black, sold for $300 and could reach the amazing speed of 30 mph.

Left to right: Florence James, Dennis Crites, Cleve Crites, Emerson Seabaugh, July 2, 1914

Peyton Miller, Albert Overbeck and three rural mail carriers, Maurice Short, G. H. Friedrich and J. E. Russell, were the first customers.

McDowell South. Left to right: Kyle and Ronald McDowell

There was a lot more to running a car dealership in those days. The cars, shipped by train from Michigan to Jackson, arrived unassembled in huge crates. Horse-drawn wagons transported the crates from Jackson Depot to Jackson Auto on the second floor of the Milde Building, where workers reassembled them and drove them down the back ramp to the sales lot. In addition to selling cars, Crites and Harris also had to teach the buyers how to drive! At Christmas, 1915, Santa arrived in a new Model T and awarded it to the lucky holder of the most sales receipts from Priest and Behrens' Clothing Store. Crites and Harris continued to sell cars in southeast Missouri for 50 years. The family tradition continues with Cleve's grandson and great-grandson, Ronald and Kyle McDowell, who run McDowell Ford in Perryville and McDowell South in Jackson.

Cleve and Rhoda had six children: Viola; Woodrow; Grover; twins Lorene and Loren; and James. Viola wed Woodrow Godwin, who became superintendent of shoe factories in Jackson, Cape Girardeau and Anna, IL. He also served as an advisor to shoe factories in Puerto Rico and Poland. In addition to raising a family and working in the shoe factory, Viola took correspondence courses from the Baptist College in Jefferson City, attaining the equivalent of an A.B. degree. Their daughters graduated from Jackson High School. Patty worked as a secretary at McDonnell-Douglass. Colette and Carolyn became teachers in the St. Louis area. Viola died in 1993.

Rhoda Adaline James, Will Mayfield College, April 2, 1908

Woodrow Crites, who married Jo Ellen Shelby of Cape Girardeau, became Jackson's first optometrist, practicing from 1947 to 1996. He also served on the Jackson School Board for eight years. His children, Carole Jo, Mitchell and Wilson, graduated from Jackson High School. Carole Jo married Jack Byrd, a lay minister from Oak Ridge. They, their daughter Deborah and her husband David Myers, have been co-owners of Tri-State Swimming Pools for 31 years. Mitchell is a teacher, an archaeologist and an antiquities dealer in Delhi, India. He collaborated in writing two books, one on Persia and one on modern Iran. Wilson served in the National Guard and is a building contractor in Jacksonville, FL.

After graduating from Jackson High School and Southeast Missouri State University, Grover became a teacher, coach and principal in Advance, Perryville and Belleville, IL. His wife, the former Helen Hard, and their daughters, Nancy and Linda, were also teachers. Grover now resides in Phoenix, AZ.

After two years at Southeast Missouri State University, Loren enlisted in the Royal Canadian Air Force and became a pilot in 1941. He transferred to the Army Air Corps after Pearl Harbor. Married to Mary Jane Miller of Cape Girardeau, he died when his plane crashed on a New Mexico training mission, just before he was to go overseas. A son was born posthumously.

Grover Cleveland Crites, Will Mayfield College, April 2, 1908

After graduating from Jackson High School and attending Southeast Missouri State University, Lorene became a teacher in a rural school near Oak Ridge. She and her husband, Allen McDowell of Fruitland, ran a successful dairy equipment business for many years. Their son, Ronald, graduated from Jackson High School, then served in the National Guard. He opened his first car lot in 1969. Daughters, Donna and Cheryl, became teachers. Donna taught school in Kentucky for 30 years, while Cheryl currently teaches at Jackson Middle School. Cheryl's husband, Darrell Hanschen, operates Medicap Pharmacy in Jackson.

James, the youngest, served in the Army during WWII, fighting in both the European and Pacific theaters. After the war, he became an optometrist, working first in Fredricktown, then in Cape Girardeau from 1949-1986. He attained the rank of Brigadier General in the Missouri National Guard. He and his wife, Margaret Cook of Cape Girardeau, had one daughter, Jane Ellen, who graduated from Central High School, then worked in the family business. James died in 1987. Janey followed in death in 1993.

"Cleve" Crites with 1923 Dodge car

Cleve's brother, Walter Crites, was a rural schoolteacher and farmer in the Cane Creek Community near Jackson. His seven sons and one daughter graduated from Jackson High School. Otto, Don and Ralph worked in the Jackson Hosiery Mill and later became food inspectors. Tom worked at the natural gas pipeline near Jackson. Clarence, superintendent of Jackson Power and Light from 1928-1936, served as general superintendent of the City of Jackson for eight more years. Wilbur worked at Milde Coca-Cola for 40 years, becoming its manager. He also owned Jackson Tavern. Rusby served as Cape Girardeau County Clerk from 1958-1978.

Dennis, Cleve's second brother, became a doctor of veterinary medicine, serving the Jackson Community from 1920-1970. His son, John, was sheriff of Cape Girardeau County from 1956-1966. He served as Postmaster until 1990. Dennis' daughter, Maxine, and her husband, Bill Eakins, operated Eakins Jewelry on Main Street for many years. Their son, Roger, works at the University Extension Office in Jackson.

The Crites family is very proud of their Jackson heritage. *Submitted by Lorene (Crites) McDowell and Cheryl (McDowell) Hanschen*

CRITES - In late autumn of 1927, my mother, Loretta Pearl Rhodes (later Crites) was 12 years old, almost 13. It was shortly before Thanksgiving, and Loretta had been feeling quite ill. Her father, Louis L. Rhodes, bought a can of pineapples at Brase's store, thinking perhaps the refreshing fruit would make her feel better. However, after only one or two bites, Loretta grew violently ill. Louis walked quickly down the railroad tracks to Allenville to fetch Dr. Davault, better known as "Doc" Davault. Upon arriving at the Rhodes farm just outside of Whitewater, Doc quickly diagnosed appendicitis. "We have to get her to the hospital as soon as possible," Doc Davault informed her parents.

Arnold F. and Loretta P. (nee Rhodes) Crites at 1984 Eaker reunion. Reunion is known as "Shoecobbler's Kin."

The long, arduous trek to Cape Girardeau was about to begin. Back in those days, the roads to Cape Girardeau were muddy, and the mode of travel was quite different from today. First, Louis and Doc loaded Loretta onto a wagon pulled by a team of mules. They placed her on a featherbed to cushion the jarring as much as possible.

After a relatively brief ride, they stopped at the home of George Hinck, who lived a little farther up the road from the Rhodes farm. He owned a fairly large touring car, so Loretta was transferred to it, and another part of the journey began.

For some reason, which Loretta can't remember, Mr. Hinck was unable to take them all the way into Cape Girardeau, so they traveled to the home of Martin Hampton, who lived still farther up the road. Mr. Hampton's son, Dan, owned a one-seated Model-T Ford. Loretta sat between Dan and Doc Davault, and her father stood on the running board.

The next stop was at Mr. Rowe's, who lived just outside of Dutchtown. Loretta was placed in his large touring car, and Mr. Rowe, my mother, my grandfather, and Doc Davault made their way over the muddy, bumpy, and most likely narrow path known as the Old Bloomfield Road.

Finally, they arrived at the old St. Francis Hospital on Good Hope Street. At 7:00 p.m. Dr. Fuerth, a young surgeon, operated on my mother. He told my grandfather that it was a very good thing that they had not delayed in bringing her in. A few more hours, and she would not have made it. Her appendix had either ruptured or was on the verge of doing so.

My grandmother, Mary Jane Hedge Rhodes, did not accompany the group on their wild ride. But she went to Cape Girardeau right away and stayed with her sister, Lennie Sams Fluegge. Every day, she walked up several streets in the cold weather to catch a streetcar in order to be with her daughter.

The hospital stay turned out to be a long one. Loretta spent Thanksgiving, Christmas, New Year's, and her birthday, January 4, as well as several weeks afterward, at St. Francis. She recalls with fondness and gratitude the capable young surgeon, the caring nuns, and the young girls who were nurse assistants. They all took very good care of her.

Loretta is also deeply grateful to her family and all the people who made sure she arrived at the hospital in time. She grew up, married my father, Arnold Francis Crites, and had three children, Louis Francis, Sheriann, and Marilyn Marie. Sadly, my father passed away in 1989, but my mother is still going strong, 87 years young, and lives in Whitewater. *Submitted by Marilyn M. Crites*

DAUME – John William Daume and Meta Lydia Engelmann were married Feb. 17, 1912 by the Rev. Henry Idel, in the bride's parents' home north of Oak Ridge (now the home of Mary Daume). Attendants were John Engelmann, the bride's brother, and Mrs. Albert (Selma Daume) Sievers, sister of the groom. The couple, along with their attendants, celebrated their 60th wedding anniversary at the St. John's United Church of Christ, near Fruitland.

Mary Meta Daume was born April 16, 1926 on a farm north of Cape Girardeau on Engelmann Road. Her father, John Daume, was principal of the Egypt Mills School for seven years. He taught in the Cape Girardeau County Schools for 21 years. John and Meta Daume had six children: Meta, John, Mrs. Lloyd (Louise) Schoenebeck, Mrs. Lawrence (Dorothy) Heise, Mary and Mrs. Elmer (Martha) Kamp.

Great-great-grandparents of Mary Daume were Christopher and Wilhelmina Engelmann, natives of Schlemm, Germany. Their son Henry married a widow, Mary Kraegel Woeltje. Widowed again, Mary married Friedrich Pohlmann; widowed a third time, she married William Boeller. Her children were: William and Minnie Woeltje; Henry; Mathilda and Charles Englemann; and August Boeller.

Charles Engelmann married Louisa, daughter of George and Dorothea Philipp Krattli, natives of Untervatz, Switzerland. Children of Charles and Louisa were: Mary; Henry; John; Alvin; Ida; Annie and Mrs. John (Meta) Daume.

Paternal great-grandparents of Mary Daume were Conrad and Charlotte Strube Daume, natives of Brunswick. Left a widow, Charlotte married Wentzel Maschka, after whose death she married Mathias Gratz. Her children were: August; Annie; Charles; Wilhelmina and Ernest Daume; Ida and Joseph Maschka; and stepchildren Katharine; Elisabeth and Michael Gratz.

Ernst Daume married Dorothea, daughter of Friedrich and Sophia Edel Suedekum, natives of Gross-Rhuden. Dorothea had a brother, Friedrich II and a sister, Annie Amos. Children of Ernst and Dorothea were: Friedrich; Josephine; John (married Meta Engelmann); Charles; Selma; Minnie; Harry; Leo and four who died young.

Mary Daume is a caregiver, poet and historian. She received 12 years of education at Oak Ridge. She served as chairman of the Historical Committee of the Oak Ridge School Centennial in 1974. This project, along with Section 16 of her abstract, helped her begin searching the old Township Schools.

John and Meta Daume

She was chairman of the St. John's UCC Centennial in 1977. With help from the Rev. and Mrs. Emanuel Mortiz, and the Rev. Walter Keisker, she translated and indexed the church record book, including photos of charter members and pastors.

She is an active member of the St. John's Church, Cemetery Association, Women's Fellowship and Sunday School, and writes an article for the monthly newsletter. She is serving as secretary and historian of the Arnsberg Cemetery Association and is on the committee of the Cape Girardeau County Township School Project.

A poem entitled *The Life of a Flower* has appeared on the front cover of *Farmland News Magazine*. It can be accessed at www.mmsucc.org or jacksonmo.com by clicking on local churches, then on St. John's UCC, Jackson, MO. *Submitted by Mary Daume*

DAVAULT – Hughes and Doris Davault, accompanied by their two children, Webster Joe and Suzanna, moved to Jackson in August 1956. The Davaults were both high school teachers; Hughes teaching vocational agriculture and Doris teaching business subjects. Both retired from teaching in 1976. Doris finished out her career as a business teacher for a short time at Southeast Missouri State University. Doris had received her B.S. and Masters Degree from Southeast Missouri State University. Hughes received his degree from the University of Missouri in Columbia.

Hughes was born at Shawneetown, MO on June 14, 1916, but lived most of his early years in Whitewater and Allenville. He was the son of Dr. W. W. and Anna Jenkins Davault. Doris was born Oct. 25, 1920, on a farm between Dutchtown and Allenville. Her father became postmaster in Allenville in 1931 and also went into the store business so Doris grew up there. She was the second daughter of Joseph "Joe" Henry and Cora Chostner Brennecke. Hughes and Doris were married Nov. 20, 1941.

Hughes and Doris Davault

Hughes was inducted into the service in May 1942 and spent about 6-1/2 months in the states and 34 months on active duty in the 13th Air Force in the South and Southwest Pacific as a medic with the Army Air Force.

Hughes was active in the District and State Vocational Agriculture Association; he was a public speaker, master of ceremonies, Little League umpire, author, Sunday School teacher, member of the Methodist Men organization, member of the Chamber of Commerce, member of the Masons and Scottish Rite, charter member and past president of the Bell City Rotary Club, and was involved in many more activities in his early life before and after coming to Jackson.

Doris was also active in many organizations: District and State Business Teachers associations; the local and district Methodist Women; local, district and state National Society Daughters of the American Revolution; author; Sunday School teacher, and many others. Hughes and Doris were active members in New McKendree United Methodist Church and served on many committees the past 45 years. Hughes is serving at the present as a Trustee of Old McKendree Chapel. Hughes and Doris have been members of the Jackson Heritage Association many years and Doris served as chairman of the weekend volunteers during the early years at the Oliver House.

Webster Joe (born Aug. 30, 1946) and Suzanna (born June 15, 1949) both graduated from Jackson High School in 1964 and 1967 respectively. They also both received degrees from the University of Missouri at Columbia. Webster first married Brenda Niswonger and they had two boys, Dax and Ian. He has been married to Gail Prichard 22 years and has been manager of plants in Texas and Georgia. Suzanna, a nurse, married David Clippard and they have three children, Matthew, Kristen and Mark. Hughes and Doris have one great grandchild, Dax Alexander Davault, born Aug. 5, 2001. *Submitted by Doris Brennecke Davault*

DAVIS – John C. Davis was born at Crosstown, MO on Jan. 2, 1880. He was the son of Franklin Davis and Susan Rhyne. At one time, Franklin was a butcher at Crosstown. The story told by the family is that Susan was a Cherokee who was left here for some reason during the march on the Trail of Tears and was adopted by Sarah (Hoffman) and Daniel Rhyne

John and Esther Cox were married March 5, 1907 at the home of her parents. The ceremony was performed by her father, a Baptist minister, near Longtown. The bride made her own dress and hair bow. The groom immediately took his bride to Perryville for a wedding photo and a meal. Esther was the daughter of Reverend William Marion Cox and Elizabeth Cottner. She was one of 13 children.

John and Esther became the parents of 12 children: Amos; James; Mildred; Homer; Vera; John; Henry; Zeta; Percy; Lillie; Lillian; and Melva.

Life was hard for the family in those days. John farmed with the help of the children as they became old enough. They would get up at the crack of dawn to begin each day. The cows were milked, chickens fed, breakfast was made by Esther and the girls, the dirty dishes were washed, and then off to the fields they would go, both boys and girls. They hoed crops and pulled weeds during the growing season. They returned to the house at noon. The girls helped to cook a full farm dinner. After eating, the boys would be off again, with the girls following after the kitchen was cleaned. They would work until supper, cook, clean, and then fall into bed exhausted.

Some days were spent picking, cleaning, canning, and drying produce. Sauerkraut and pickles would be "put up" in stone jars and stored in the smokehouse. Apples and peaches were dried under window screens on large wooden tables. Food was rationed. When it ran out,

John C. and Esther Davis family at the Davis home in Oak Ridge, June 21, 1959. Back row, left to right: Amos Davis, James Davis, Mildred Davis Brown, Homer Davis, Vera Davis Farrow, John M. Davis, Henry Davis, Zeta Davis Putz, Percy Davis. Front row, left to right: John C. Davis, Esther Davis, Melva Davis Floyd, Lillian Davis Weber, Lillie Davis Kraemer.

they ate cornbread and drank wheat coffee. Clothes were washed on a washboard with lye soap made in a kettle outdoors. A heavy iron was heated on a wood stove to press them. If a garment was worn out, it was not cast away. It was made into a towel, potholder, apron, rag, or quilt scrap. To get to school or church, they walked three miles. Once, they lived in a small house where chickens could be seen through the floor. Sometimes there was ice in the kitchen for a week.

The children grew, began to marry, and leave home. Five of the six boys served in the armed forces on active duty during WWII. The parents received a letter in 1943 praising them for the "personal sacrifices" they were making in giving the services of five sons to the armed forces.

John retired from farming in the fifties and moved to Oak Ridge. He died in 1969 at age 89. Esther followed in 1982 at age 94. Several of the Davis children moved to Jackson during the forties. Vera, Zeta, Henry, and Lillie still reside here. *Submitted by Vera Davis Farrow*

DAVIS - Richard Greenwood Davis, a lifelong resident of Jackson, MO, was born on Dec. 3, 1920, to Manning Oliver and Ethel (Greenwood) Davis. His sister, Mrs. Harold (Maxine) Buxton, lives with her husband in Cape Girardeau, MO. He attended Jackson Public School and Southeast Missouri State Teachers College. He served in the U. S. Army during WWII. In 1945 he married Betty Lou Windsor, daughter of William L. and Bernetta (Davis) Windsor. Mrs. Davis resides in Cape Girardeau. They had two children, William Windsor (born in 1948) and Mary Maxine (born in 1951).

Mr. Davis was elected to the Jackson R-2 School District Board of Education in 1956. He was active in Jackson Community Betterment and numerous civic affairs, and served on the Governor's Commission on Education and the Jackson Development Corporation.

Mr. Davis was in the banking industry for 35 years. He served as Executive Vice-president of the Cape County Bank and as Vice-chairman of the Board of Directors of the Cape County Bancorp. He was a Past President of the Tri-County Bankers Association and a member of the Missouri and American Bankers Association.

He was a life member of the First Presbyterian Church in Jackson, where he chaired many committees and was elected to both the Board of Directors and the Session. He was a lay minister as well. Mrs. Davis was also very active in her church, New McKendree United Methodist Church, and was President of the Women's Organization and served on other committees.

In 1968 Mr. Davis received the Community Leadership Award from the Cape Girardeau Chamber of Commerce. In 1981 the Jackson Chamber of Commerce honored Mr. Davis with the R. A. Fulenwider Award for Meritorious Service to the Community. In 1987 he was presented the Jackson Heritage Award, due largely to his large contributions to the restoration of the Oliver House Museum. Mr. and Mrs. Davis and their son were all Paul Harris Fellows in Rotary International.

The Davises were always very interested in civic and church affairs, but their greatest pride and joy were their children and grandchildren, Bill and Julia Davis and children Beth, Katherine, Joshua, and Claire, and Gerald and Mary Linnenbringer and children Charles and Gerald. *Submitted by Betty Davis*

Richard and Betty Davis

DAVIS – Maxine Davis Buxton was born on Oct. 19, 1922 in Jackson, MO, daughter of Manning O. Davis, who was born in 1892 and died in 1961, and Ethel (Greenwood) Davis, who was born in 1895 and died in 1981. Manning served as a Corporal in WWI and became a barber for a short time following his discharge. Then for many years, he delivered gas and oil to farmers in the area. Many times he was asked to stay and eat the noon meal with them. Manning and his three sisters, Bernice Wessell Wagner, Ethel Obermiller and Maggie Pender, were born on a farm near Fruitland, which their grandfather, George Washington Davis, homesteaded in 1829 after coming to Cape Girardeau County from North Carolina by ox wagon. Their parents, James Cicero and Virginia (Alexander) Davis, later occupied the family farm, moving to Jackson in 1916.

Maxine had one brother, Richard Greenwood Davis, who was born Dec. 3, 1920 and died Feb. 26, 1988. Richard lived all his life in Jackson. He was an active supporter of the Jackson Community and his church. On Aug. 4, 1945 he married Betty Windsor and they became parents of Bill and Mary Davis.

On March 6, 1948 Maxine and Harold Buxton were united in marriage at the First Presbyterian Church in Jackson. They have lived in Cape Girardeau since then, and are the parents of Kirk and Dick Buxton.

Maxine and Richard both started the first grade in the Jackson public schools and both graduated from high school there, Richard in 1938 and Maxine in 1940. Richard attended Southeast Missouri State University until he was called into the service. Maxine received her B. S. from Southeast Missouri State University and began teaching in the new Jackson Elementary School, a beautiful new building built by the W.P.A. The Jackson High Stadium was also built by the W.P.A. During WWII a cannery was set up underneath the stadium where residents could take their vegetables and fruits from their gardens and can them in tin cans.

Maxine and Richard lived across from the high school, so therefore they could wait until hearing the opening bell, and then run across the street without begin tardy. R. O. Hawkins was Superintendent and Mark Scully was Principal during those years.

Maxine and Harold moved 2-1/2 years ago into an independent living apartment at Chateau Girardeau, where they have made many new friends and are living a relaxed lifestyle. *Submitted by Maxine Buxton*

DECKER – George and Ruby (Grosvenor) Decker came to Jackson in April 1939 from Chester, IL. George was employed by a group from Chester to start the Jackson Hosiery Mill in Jackson. Their oldest son, Richard A. "Dick" Decker was born in October of that year. George and Ruby had a total of five children. Larry F. was born in September 1943; Steven B. was born in April 1947; Martha R. was born in March 1951 and Lisa A. was born in July 1961.

George worked for the Jackson Hosiery Mill for over 40 years and then for the Jackson School District until his retirement in 1985. George and

The Buxton family, left to right: first row: Andrew Buxton, Maxine Buxton, Harold Buxton, Kent Buxton. Second row: Sarah Buxton, Kirk Buxton, Teresa Buxton, Mary Buxton. Third row: Dick Buxton. Children and grandchildren of Maxine Davis Buxton and Harold Buxton. Christmas 1998.

The Decker family, standing left to right: Steven, Larry, Richard. Seated: Ruby holding Lisa, Martha and George

Ruby were active members of St. Paul Lutheran Church and all their children attended St. Paul Lutheran Parochial School. George served on the Jackson City Council. As a WWII U. S. Army veteran, he became a member and was active in the American Legion Post. All the Decker children graduated from Jackson High School and participated fully in the school's sports programs and other extracurricular school activities. George and Ruby could be expected to be in the audience witnessing most of these events. George died in 1990.

All of George and Ruby Decker's five children graduated from Southeast Missouri State University. All living members of this family consider Jackson as their home. Currently, only Ruby and Richard reside in Jackson. *Submitted by Richard Decker*

DELAPP – John Delap was born 1780-1790 in Kentucky and was in Missouri territory in t he village of Jackson in 1819 as a blacksmith. He married in Lewis County, KY on March 1, 1813, Matilda Mitchell; the bondsman was Thomas Mitchell and both were of lawful age. The Delap and Mitchell families were early settlers in Kentucky. One family history says he had three wives and his last wife was Cynthia Mitchell; however, the death certificate of John's son Samuel Jackson, born in 1829, gives Matilda Mitchell as his mother. John's brother Richard died in Cape Girardeau County, MO in 1837. It is unproven, but three descendants' branches claim there was Indian blood through the wife of John Delap.

In Lewis County, KY in August 1817, James Mitchell brought suit against John G. McDowell and John Delap, claiming that an agreement was made that they were to lay a line of pipes from the salt wells to the furnaces in 1817.

The History of Missouri by Houck states, "John Delap advertised that he makes bells for cattle, sheep and hogs, at Jackson." In the *Jackson Herald Newspaper*, dated Aug. 26, 1820, John asked persons owing him to pay up. In Douglas' *History of Southeast Missouri*, it states, "In 1797 the first settlement was made on Hubbell Creek. The creek was then known as River Zenon…" and under the heading of Founding of Jackson, it states, "A Mechanic shop was conducted by John Delap." In Goodspeed's *History of Southeast Missouri, 1888*, it states, "John Delap-his shop near Hubbell Creek where Howells Mill now stands."

On May 24, 1819 John Delap bought from John Davis, 24 acres and 75 poles of land on Hubble's Creek and across the creek on the west bank of the creek, the haven of Jackson, MO in the territory of Missouri for $120 and $173. On Sept. 4, 1819 John Delap sold to James Burns the deed for the undivided half of 24 acres and 75 poles of land in Byrd Township, for $611.50, the land on River Zenon. On Aug. 18, 1822 John Delap sold the other half of 24 acre and 75 poles to John Mitchell, being part of the John Davis Mill tract for $1.00. This small payment suggests a family connection. This John Mitchell died in Perry County; his estate file names children but no Matilda or Cynthia.

In the 1830 census of Missouri, page 453, John has nine children under the age of 20. John died in Cape Girardeau before Aug. 23, 1839, when his son John Mitchell Delap had Samuel W. Mitchell (son of John Mitchell) appointed guardian. No estate file has been found for John Delap or his wife.

The children of John Delap and probably Matilda Mitchell Delap are as follows.

Rebecca Jane Delap was born 1814 in Kentucky and married James Smith in 1838; they lived two to three miles south of Burfordville, and are buried in the Smith Cemetery near Akers on Road 25, Cape Girardeau County, MO. The couple had seven children.

Granville Wright Delap was born between 1815-1820 and married in 1848 Nancy Jane Lincecum, daughter of Asa and Malinda Nurls Lincecum, in Cape Girardeau County. Granville enlisted in 1846, with his brother John, in the Mexican War. He died Dec. 20, 1848. Nancy is buried at Fairview Cemetery in Cape Girardeau County, MO. They had one child.

Francis Henry Gaines Granville Delap was born in 1817 in Kentucky and married in 1848 Susan Caroline Walker; he lived in Perry County, MO and was a blacksmith, cabinet builder and farmer. She was the daughter of Osbirn Walker who is considered the son of old John Walker, the Revolutionary War veteran who is buried in Apple Creek Church Cemetery. The couple had nine children.

Elizabeth Julia Delap was born about 1819 in Kentucky and married in 1843 James Thomas Mitchell. They moved to Texas and then to California where he was a placer miner and farmer. She had no children; he had a son by an earlier marriage.

Emily E. Delap was born about 1820 in Missouri and married William Henry Walker, born in 1824 in North Carolina. She lived and died in Perry County, MO. Henry was also a son of Osbirn. The couple had nine children.

Andrew G. Delap was born in 1822 in Missouri; no record of him has been found after the Missouri census of 1850.

John Mitchell Delap was born in 1824 in Missouri and moved to Moran and Scott County, Illinois. He was married twice to Eliza Jane Black and Mary Frances Headen. He served in the Mexican War in the battle of Buena Vista. He died in Huntington Beach, CA, while visiting family. He had six children.

Artilla Rachael Delap was born in 1825 and married Peter I. Hinkle in Cape Girardeau County. He died and she married William J. Robert N. Mitchell. They sold their Perry County, MO land in 1858. Both died in Dutch Mills, Washington County, AR and are buried in Summers Cemetery. Oral history says they adopted a Choctaw Indian girl.

Samuel Jackson Delap was born in 1829 in Missouri and died in 1915 in Plumas County, CA; single; a placer miner. *Submitted by Ivy Baebler*

DETRING – Kenneth Charles Detring was born at Farmington, MO, the son of Walter Charles and Geraldine Shannon Detring. Ken grew up on the Detring farm south of Libertyville in St. Francois County. He attended the two-room Libertyville School through the eighth grade. He spent summers baling hay and helping on the neighboring farms. He graduated from Farmington High School in 1970, Mineral Area College in 1972, and Southeast Missouri State University in 1974 with a B. S. in Secondary Education, majoring in mathematics.

Ken married Dawna Dement on Aug. 17, 1974 at Grace Methodist Church in Cape Girardeau. Dawn was the daughter of James Felton and Betty Blumenberg Dement. She graduated from

Dawn and Ken Detring

Holcomb High School in 1972 and Southeast Missouri State University in 1975 with a B. S. in Chemistry. Ken taught junior high math and science from 1974-76 at Scott Central School at Morley, MO.

In 1976 they moved to Chicago where Ken attended the Illinois College of Optometry. Dawn worked at the Institute of Gas Technology as a research chemist in their analytical lab. Living in the city was a cultural awakening after residing in rural Missouri. They visited museums and ethnic restaurants. They became friends with people of diverse backgrounds.

Amanda Detring

Their first child, Amanda Rose, was born at Michael Reese Hospital overlooking Lake Michigan on Ken's birthday during his senior year. Ken graduated in 1980 and they headed to Jackson, MO.

Ken opened his optometric practice at 1404 Old Cape Road. Dawn was hired as manager/chemist for Larron Laboratory. They joined New McKendree United Methodist Church. Ken also joined Rotary and the Kimbeland Country Club. Dawn became active in the Mary and Martha church circle and the Cape Girardeau Genealogical Society. They resided at 307 Francis Drive in Jackson, MO.

Meredith Detring

Two more daughters were born. Meredith Dawn will be a senior at Jackson High School in 2003 and Sarah Elizabeth will graduate in 2007. They moved in 1990 to their current home in Broadridge subdivision in Jackson. Oldest daughter Amanda is a senior at Southeast Missouri State University, majoring in business education in 2002.

In 1999 they celebrated their 25th wedding anniversary by taking a family trip abroad to London, Paris and Germany. They visited the family of their former Rotary exchange student, Lena Steinberg, in Nachrodt, Germany. They visited the ancestral towns of the Detring and Blumenberg/Bartels families while in Germany.

Sarah Detring

Ken's practice, Eye Care Center of Jackson, moved to 1014 E. Jackson Boulevard in 2000. He is currently a trustee with the Missouri Optometric Association. He enjoys golfing and traveling in his spare time. Dawn is busy with school and church activities and works part time in the office. She continues to work on genealogical research projects. *Submitted by Dawn Dement Detring*

DIRNBERGER – Jerry Dirnberger and Carol Stoverink were married Sept. 10, 1966 at Immaculate Conception Catholic Church in Jackson, MO. Carol, daughter of Irene (Thiele) Stoverink of Jackson, and the late Alphonse Stoverink, was born Jan. 9, 1945. Jerry, son of Evelyn Dirnberger (b. Nov. 2, 1917) of Oran, and the late Arthur Dirnberger (b. May 21, 1913; d. May 11, 1992) was born Nov. 11, 1937. Jerry and Carol are the parents of two daughters, Donna (born Oct. 16, 1967) and Janis (born March 9, 1970).

Jerry has lived his entire life at Oran – first on the family farm, located 1-1/2 miles outside of town, then in Oran for 28 years. In March 1993 he and Carol moved back to the farm.

Carol moved several times, namely to Leopold, Jackson, Cape Girardeau, Blomeyer, Laflin, Gordonville and Oran. She attended St. John's School in Leopold, MO for grades 1 and 2. Grades 3-8 were at Immaculate Conception School in Jackson. In 1962 Carol graduated from Notre Dame High School in Cape Girardeau.

After graduation, Carol worked at Jackson Hosiery Mill. That fall, Metropolitan Life Insurance Company employed her in Cape Girardeau. In the fall of 1967 Carol became a stay-at-home mom. She re-entered the work force in 1980 at Dirnberger Feed Store in Oran. In 1989 Carol became a rural carrier substitute for the post office, first at Chaffee and then at Oran. Currently, she is a full-time postal clerk at the Mail Processing Center in Cape Girardeau.

Jerry attended Guardian Angel Catholic School in Oran, and graduated from Oran High School in 1956. He farmed with his father until March 1966, when he became employed as a truck driver for Montgomery Ward in Cape Girardeau. Scott County Milling Company in Oran hired him in 1968. Cargill, Inc. later bought out the company. In October 1979 Jerry and Buster Bollinger formed a partnership known as BeeJay Supply, selling Gristo Feed in Oran. In 1980 Jerry became sole owner, and changed the name to Dirnberger Feed Store. He first sold Gristo Feed and then Nutrena Feed until July 31, 1999, when he sold the business to Animal Nutrition Center. Jerry became semi-retired in November 1999. He continues to work part-time at Animal Nutrition Center in Oran.

The Dirnbergers, standing left to right: Donna, Jerry and Carol. Seated, Janis

Jerry played rhythm guitar for The Varieties Band and Dirnberger Brothers Band. For over 20 years they provided music for various occasions such as public dances, weddings, anniversaries, picnics, and Christmas parties. Their repertoire included waltzes, polkas, two-steps, country and light rock.

Donna Dirnberger attended Guardian Angel School and Oran High School. She graduated from the University of Missouri-Columbia in 1990 with a major in Computer Science. She lives in Ballwin, MO and is employed by CIBER as a computer consultant.

Janis Dirnberger Gosche attended Guardian Angel School and Oran High School. She graduated from the University of Missouri-Columbia in 1992 with a degree in Agricultural Journalism. She is Administrative Assistant for the Missouri School Counselor's Association in Jackson. Janis married Dennis Gosche (born June 12, 1966) in February 1997. Their daughter Amanda was born Jan. 11, 2000. The Gosches live in New Hamburg, MO, where Dennis is a self-employed farmer. *Submitted by Carol Dirnberger*

DOCKINS – Palmer Bruce Dockins (DOB Nov. 1, 1938), son of Columbus Palmer and Phyllis Elizabeth (McManus) Dockins, married Donna Lee Malone (DOB Aug. 25, 1938), daughter of James Lloyd and Linda (Pensel) Malone on Feb. 14, 1960 in Jackson, MO, at the New McKendree United Methodist Church by the Reverends Rex Henderson and John Glassey.

Two children, Christi Leigh Dockins (DOB April 29, 1966) and Jamey Bruce Dockins (DOB Dec. 7, 1970), were born from their marriage. Christi married Rick Guilliams on Jan. 15, 1987 and gave birth to their daughter, Rebecca Christine, on April 23, 1990. Jamey Bruce Dockins has one daughter, Madalyn Palmer Dockins, born Aug 9, 1997.

Bruce has one sister, Ruth Marguerite (Dockins) Colyer, the wife of Woodrow Colyer. They have three sons; Brennan, Gregory and Scott Colyer. Donna was an only child.

Bruce was reared in Burfordville (home of the Bollinger Mill and dam) and attended the Burfordville School where all eight grades were taught. He grew up in his parents' store, Dockins Produce, along with his parents, who were both postmasters of the community. In his last year of grade school, his parents transferred him to the Jackson public school, which was the first year the eighth grade was held in the high school building.

Donna grew up in Jackson and attended both grade and high school. Bruce graduated in Jackson in 1957 and Donna in 1956. Their courtship lasted for five years before their marriage. Donna's parents' home was located on North Farmington Street; and behind their house, they operated a strawberry field, now Malone Sunny Slope Subdivision, which her parents developed.

Bruce and Donna Dockins, Christmas 1999

In 1964 Bruce and Donna built their first house on 742 Donna Lane, named after Donna. Their first apartment was in the Wilson Apartments located on South High Street, now owned by the First Baptist Church. At the writing of this article, their home is located at 204 Harmony Lane, where Donna enjoys attending the family racking horses.

Mr. Malone, Donna's father, worked for the Pevely Dairy out of St. Louis, the Wulff's Hatchery in Jackson, and drove a school bus for Jackson R-2 for a number of years. Lloyd was instrumental in developing the conservation areas in and around St. Louis in cooperation with the Missouri Conservation Commission. Linda, Donna's mother, worked for the Jackson Hosiery Mill a number of years and the Tarrace Restaurant across from Brennecke Chevrolet dealership.

Donna attended Southeast Missouri State University and worked for the Cape County Bank a number of years. Bruce graduated from Gupton Mortuary School in Nashville, TN, in 1959 and returned to work for the McCombs Furniture and Undertaking Company that same year. In 1998 Bruce and Donna became the sole owners of McCombs Funeral Home located in Jackson and Cape Girardeau. From 1959 until 1998, the various partners were Bern Meyer, Perry Grindstaff, Elmer Best and Ivan Statler. Bruce and Donna were co-owners of Radio Station KJAS and Q-99 of Jackson, Chiles-Cooper Funeral Home of Bloomfield, MO, and the Lorberg Funeral Home of Cape Girardeau. *Submitted by Bruce Dockins*

DRUCKENMILLER – Roxie Tina Loberg Druckenmiller was born in Washington County, OH on Sept. 4, 1943. Her mother's name is Marjorie Sample Loberg Swan, born on May 16, 1923, whose parents were William R. Sample and Reva Niswonger of Bollinger County. Her father's name is Denver Loberg, born on June 17, 1923, and died on Dec. 24, 1944 (killed in action in WWII). His parents were Jesse Loberg and Meta Barks of Bollinger County.

As an infant she lived in Ohio and then lived with her grandparents in Bollinger County until October 1946, when she moved to Pocahontas, MO. Her mother married Norman R. Swan, born on July 9, 1919, the son of Reginald Swan and Alma Schoen. He was a very kind and loving man and raised Tina and her older sister, Vida Loberg Stanard, as his own children. Her three younger siblings are Norman R. Swan Jr., born July 5, 1948; William R. Swan, born Feb. 13, 1950 and Nina Swan-Kohler, born Jan. 18, 1952.

Tina Druckenmiller

Tina attended elementary school at Pocahontas Public School and then went to Jackson, MO for junior high and high school, graduating in 1961. Some of her favorite memories as a young child in Pocahontas are walking home from school with her brothers and sisters, and knowing that her mother would always be home to greet them. She also enjoyed going uptown to see her dad at his work (Chevrolet dealership). They would usually be treated to Pepsi and peanuts. She loved going to church picnics and chili suppers. Tina is thankful to have grown up in a small loving community.

As a young child, she was raised in St. John's Lutheran Church. The whole family enjoyed many activities together, and they were all involved in Pocahontas 4-H Club. She won many awards and ribbons for projects during the 12 years of 4-H. In school she played in the Jackson High School band and she especially loved the football games and band festival.

In 1961, Tina went to the University of Missouri in Columbia to study Home Economics and Elementary Education. She met her husband, Arthur E. Druckenmiller, and was married on Jan. 24, 1965 in Sedgewickville, MO. They were an Air Force family, and lived in Texas, where their first son, Richard Arthur, was born on Nov. 30, 1965. Then they lived in Topeka, KS and Cape Girardeau, MO. In January of 1967, they moved to Clark Air Force Base in the Philippine Islands where Tina's husband was stationed during the Vietnam War.

In 1969 they came back to live in Smyrna, TN and their second son, David Earl, was born on May 20, 1969. Tina's husband left the military and they moved to Nashville, TN. Tina went to cosmetology school, and was very involved with church and raising her children, while also learning the skill of cake decorating. On Dec. 29, 1975, their third child, Elizabeth Ann, was born.

In 1980 they moved to Marietta, GA where they currently live. Tina worked as a teacher's aide for 15 years in the public school system in Cobb County. She retired early so that she could spend time with her grandchildren: Joseph; Connor; Hope; Anna; and Rachel. She still makes beautiful wedding cakes, teaches Sunday school and enjoys helping her husband with his work. *Submitted by Tina Druckenmiller*

DRUM – Verna Marie Mouser, daughter of Glen Allen and Vertis (Sitze) Mouser, was born on New Year's Day 1934, in Bollinger County, MO. When Verna was only 4 years old, she contracted spotted fever and nearly died. As a young girl, she attended the Randol Brick, Williams Creek and Jackson schools. At the age of 16, she began working at the Shoe Factory in Jackson, where she met her future husband, Arnold Drum Jr.

Arnold Drum, most often called "J. R." was born Jan. 10, 1928 to Arnold and Bertie (Brown) Drum in rural Cape Girardeau County, MO. J. R. grew up in the Kurreville area and went to school at Oak Ridge until he was 16 years old. At that time he went to work at the Shoe Factory in Jackson and remained there until it closed its doors. In addition, he worked part-time at the Bunny Bread store in Cape Girardeau for several years and also worked as a self-employed painter.

After a brief courtship, J. R. and Verna were married on Oct. 24, 1952 at the New McKendree Methodist Church in Jackson. They built a home in Kurreville just across the street from his parents. While living in Kurreville, two children were born to them. Ricky Gene was born April 14, 1961 and Deborah Ann was born Jan. 7, 1965.

Verna and Arnold "J. R." Drum on their wedding day, Oct. 24, 1952

As a small baby, Rick became very sick with pneumonia and bronchitis and was placed in the hospital. At this time, Verna quit working at the Shoe Factory in order to better care for her son. About a year after Debbie was born, J. R. and Verna moved from their home in Kurreville and built a new house on Highway 72 between Millersville and Jackson. In 1967 Verna started a new job at Lenco, Inc. and worked there until 1993.

Rick married Lisa Lynn Liley, daughter of Lyndall and Daphine (Kirkpatrick) Liley, on Nov. 21, 1981. Two daughters were born to them; Danielle Nicole, born May 24, 1985, and Caitlin Ranae, born Nov. 14, 1989

Debbie married Douglas Dale Osborn, son of Dale and Virginia (Cox) Osborn, on Aug. 28, 1987. They are the proud parents of Nathan Lee, born Dec. 25, 1995, and Rachel Marie, born Jan. 27, 1999. Nathan (Park Sung Chul) and Rachel (Choi Young Sook) were born in Korea and adopted by Debbie and Doug as infants.

The Drum family attended the Old Salem United Methodist Church and the Millersville United Methodist Church before becoming members of the First Baptist Church in Jackson in 1978.

Verna, in addition to working outside of the home, was a remarkably proficient homemaker and talented seamstress. She will always be highly regarded for lovingly and sacrificially caring for her family.

J. R. was diagnosed with melanoma and died on March 29, 1989 at St. Francis Hospital in Cape Girardeau. He is remembered fondly and loved deeply by all who knew him. He was small in stature but big in heart, always ready to help someone in need, and always with a smile on his face. *Submitted by Lisa Drum*

DRUM – Ricky Gene Drum was born to Arnold "J. R." and Verna Marie (Mouser) Drum on April 14, 1961 at Southeast Hospital in Cape Girardeau. He grew up in rural Cape Girardeau County, living in the Kurreville and Millersville area. He went to elementary school in Millersville and Burfordville and graduated from Jackson High School in 1979. While in high school he participated in football and track and played the alto saxophone in band. Upon his graduation, he went to work for Lenco, Inc.

Ricky's high school sweetheart, Lisa Lynn Liley, was born to Lyndall Ledo and Jean Daphine (Kirkpatrick) Liley on Aug. 15, 1960, also at Southeast Hospital. Lisa went to school in Jackson, where she was a percussionist in band and graduated in 1978. Lisa also learned to play the piano and has used that talent throughout her life. She has given piano lessons, accompanied many high school students at district and state music contests, and played for many weddings. After graduation, she attended Southeast Missouri State University and worked part-time for First Baptist Church in Jackson as music secretary. In February 1980 she went to work for Cape Girardeau County in the Data Processing office.

Rick and Lisa were married on Nov. 21, 1981 at the First Baptist Church in Jackson with Dr. Anthony Jordan officiating. They have two daughters, Danielle Nicole, born May 24, 1985, and Caitlin Ranae, born Nov. 14, 1989. Danielle is in the class of 2003 at Jackson High School, works part-time at Tanfastics in Jackson, and hopes to become a court reporter. Caitlin attends Jackson Middle School and plays on area soccer and basketball teams.

Rick and Lisa Drum, Nov. 21, 1981

In January 1990 Rick changed jobs and began to work for Dana Corporation. He was employed as a tool and cutter grinder and later was promoted to process engineer. While he worked for Dana Corporation, he was able to continue his education at Oakland Community College in Auburn Hills, MI. In June 1999 he graduated Summa cum Laude with an Associated in Applied Science degree in Manufacturing Technology.

Rick, Lisa and daughters are active members of the First Baptist Church in Jackson, where Lisa has played the piano for various choirs and worship services since she was in junior high school. She also has taught Sunday School in their Senior High Department for many years. Their family hobbies include camping and canoeing. Rick also loves to hunt and scuba dive. Lisa has an avid interest in scrapbooking and genealogy and is a member of the Cape Girardeau County Genealogical Society. *Submitted by Lisa Drum*

DUNN/PENDER – Louise (Pender) Dunn, the daughter of Clarence and Margaret (Davis) Pender, was born Sept. 25, 1915 on a farm between Fruitland and Leemon. The farm was a land grant issued to James Henry McNeely on Aug. 9, 1859 for $1.25 per acre. James (b. 1828) married Sarah Mitchell (b. 1826) in 1854 and they had one daughter, Eliza (b. 1859). Eliza married John L. Pender (b. 1853) in December 1882, and they had three children; Clarence, Eva and Helen.

Clarence (b. 1884) married Margaret "Maggie" Davis (b. 1884) in 1909. A respected church and community leader, Clarence farmed the land passed down from his father and grandfather during his entire life. He built a new house on the farm in 1910, and the couple's only child, Dorothy Louise, was born there in 1915. Louise lived in the house for 77 years before moving to Jackson in 1992. Her life was shaped by the three communities of Leemon, Fruitland and Jackson.

Clarence and Maggie Pender at family home, 1946

Louise attended Leemon Grade School from 1920-1926 and graduated from Fruitland High School in 1933. She received her two-year teaching certificate from Southeast Missouri State Teachers College in 1935, taught school in Leemon, Fruitland, Pocahontas and Jackson for the next nine years, and finished college during the summers. She was principal at Fruitland School in 1942-43.

In 1943 she married Lyman Hamby Dunn (b. 1918), from Wayne County and Cape Girardeau, who was in the U. S. Army. Although she boarded during the week while teaching in Pocahontas and Jackson, the two years in Texas, where Lyman was stationed during the war, was the only time that she did not reside where she was born. After the war, Lyman and Louise returned to the farm to live with her parents while Lyman established Dunn Dental Laboratory in Cape Girardeau that he ran for 34 years. Louise maintained the business accounts.

Lyman and Louise's two sons, Joe Pender (b. 1945) and Keith Alan (b. 1948), attended Fruitland Grade School and graduated from Jackson High School, where both where athletes and honors students. They each graduated from Southeast Missouri State College, and each received Ph.D.'s in history from the University of Missouri in 1973. Both served in the Army – Joe, a sergeant in Vietnam, and Keith, a lieutenant colonel, who later was a senior civilian NATO Officer. Joe is a college professor and Keith is a Senior Defense Department official.

When Lyman and Louise moved to Jackson, Keith purchased the family farm. Louise was a lifelong member of Pleasant Hill Presbyterian Church, near Fruitland, until the church dissolved in 1982. Following in her grandfather's, father's and husband's footsteps, she was an elder (the first woman) at Pleasant Hill Church, and she served as church treasurer as had her grandfather and father. Lyman and Louise were later active in Jackson's First Presbyterian Church.

Lyman and Louise moved to Spartanburg, SC in November 1998 to be near Joe's family. Lyman died on Feb. 7, 1999 and is buried in Pleasant Hill Cemetery. Louise lives in Spartanburg, but will return someday to Pleasant Hill. *Submitted by Joe P. Dunn*

EGGERS – Myron Eggers (1898-1971) was the son of William and Sarah Jane (Hitt) Eggers. His grandparents were Herman and Susan (Greer) Eggers, longtime residents of the Jackson area, and Clark and Cynthia (Quade) Hitt, also of Jackson. He had one brother, Charles, and one sister, Ruth. He married Flora Koehler (1899-1984), daughter of W. H. and Katie (Kneibert) Koehler, in Jackson, MO. Her grandparents were Henry and Lena (Loos) Koehler of Jackson, and Jacob Henry and Fredericka (Rehkopf) Kneibert. Fredericka came from Nordheim, Germany, and married Jacob in 1866. They lived in Jackson all their married life. Jacob served in the Civil War. They had nine children. Flora had six sisters: Caroline; Fredericka; Tessie (Charles) Harrison; Katie (Richard) Wynn; Agnes (Ben) Keslar and Nellie (Leslie) Davis. Myron lived in the Clover Hill and Hanover Community and Flora lived in the city of Jackson. They were members of New McKendree United Methodist Church. They were married on Oct. 4, 1917, in Jackson. Myron worked at the Cape County Milling Company as a packer. He farmed during the day and worked at the mill on the night shift until he built up his dairy herd. He sold milk to Pevely Dairy Company in St. Louis, MO. They purchased their family home in May 1936, and lived there until their deaths. They are buried in Russell Heights Cemetery in Jackson.

There were seven children born to this union. William (1918-1996) married Edith Mehrle. Bill served in the U. S. Army during WWII. He worked on the dairy farm with his dad, later purchasing the farm, and lived there until his death in 1996. William and Edith were members of New McKendree United Methodist Church. They had four children: Ben (Darla); Richard (Marica); David (Kathleen) and Diane (Lanny) Schweer. Ben lives in Mexico, MO; David lives in Kansas City, MO; Richard lives on an adjoining farm; and Diane's home is built on the family farm. Richard and Marica have one son, Gabriel. Diane and Lanny have two children, Victoria and Gary.

Joe Eggers is married to Nelda McLain. Joe served in the U. S. Army for four years. He worked at MFA and farmed. He still farms on their farm, adjoining the family farm. Joe and Nelda are members of New McKendree United Methodist Church. They have three daughters. The oldest daughter, Saundra (Joe) Miller, has two daughters, Heather (Scott) Crow and Rebecca Miller. They live in Granbury, TX. Their second daughter, Patricia (Harold) Rubel, lives in Egypt Mills, MO and has two sons, Joseph and Hunter. The youngest daughter, Martha (Mark) Skinner lives next to her parents and has a daughter, Ashley.

Myron and Flora's oldest daughter, Evelyn (Harold) Berberich (1921-1996) moved in the early 1940s to Chicago, IL, retiring in Oxford, WI. She worked at an aluminum company in Bensenville, IL until she retired. She and Harold had six children: Juanita (John) Schlage; Jeanne (Wayne) Mech, whose children are Rob (Melissa) and Tina (Evan) Kallies. Harold Daniel, who has five children: Laurie; Connie; Jonathan; Harold and David. Kathy (Jim) Brand who has two sons, Ed (Danielle) and Scott. June (Paul) Vargas who has four children: Pablo (Lori); Tony (Lisa); Harold and April Vargas. Larry (Luann) Berberich has three children, Tonya, Andy and Evelyn.

Myron and Flora's fourth child, Sarah (Harold) Kesterson (1924-1979) worked for Southwestern Bell Telephone Company until her retirement.

The fifth child is Mary Elizabeth (Earl) Szwabo of Florissant, MO. She is employed in retail sales. She and Earl have three children, Peggy (John) Forbis and son, Wesley; Michael; and Mark and his two sons, Nikolas and Jozef.

The sixth child, Madonna (James) Englehart, resides at Jackson, MO. She is retired as an elementary teacher. She and Jim have one son, James Brent. He has two children, Paige and James Brent.

The youngest child of Myron and Flora is Dorothy (Leonard) Pfeiffer of Jackson, MO. She worked at the Jackson Hosiery Company and later as a librarian's assistant. They are members of New McKendree United Methodist Church. Dorothy and Leonard have one daughter, Linda (Jerry) Mowery, who has two children, Christopher and Caroline Leimer. *Submitted by Madonna Englehart*

ELLIOT – John Elliot married his wife Nancy in North Carolina around 1827. Nancy was a widow with three children on the 1840 census of Cape Girardeau County, MO.

The oldest child was Elizabeth T., who was born on Dec. 18, 1828 in North Carolina. Elizabeth married Francis M. Murray on July 19, 1847 in Cape Girardeau County, MO. They had five children: Nancy J., born 1848; Lovey Ann, born 1850; James M., born 1852; Julia Ann, born 1854; and S. Q. Murray, born 1864. Elizabeth T. died May 31, 1881 in Alexander County, IL, where she is buried in the Hazelwood Cemetery.

The second child was Ann Elizabeth, who was born on Jan. 30, 1831 in North Carolina. She married Benedict Burtles Knott on Dec. 20, 1850 in Cape Girardeau County, MO. When Benedict died on Aug. 27, 1860, Ann was pregnant with their fifth child. (See Knott sketch for information on their children.) Ann died April 9, 1887 and they are both buried in Old Salem Cemetery with a single stone.

The third child was John Elliott, who was born in 1833 in North Carolina. No additional information is known about him.

Nancy Elliot then second married Elijah Musgroves about 1842 in likely Stoddard County, MO. They have the following three children; Henderson (born 1843) who married Margaret Helderman; Mary V. (b. Jan. 17, 1845) who married Jacob Rhodes; and William H. (b. April 4, 1849 in Cape Girardeau County, MO).

Nancy then married Joshua Scruggs Pair on Dec. 15, 1852 in Cape Girardeau County, MO. Joshua left a large family by his first wife, Catherine McAllister. If there was a record of divorce, it likely burned in the courthouse fire in Bollinger County, MO, where records of his first wife and 11 children were found in 1860. Nancy and Joshua had two daughters; Nancy M. Amanda and Martha Margaret J. Pair (b. 1853). The Elliot daughters raised their baby half-sisters, since Nancy and Joshua Pair died around 1857 in Cape Girardeau County, MO. Daughter Amanda married a man named L. H. Ewing. Margaret married Charles A. Merrill and they lived in Alexander County, IL in 1880. *Submitted by Dawn Dement Detring*

ENGELHART – Joseph Engelhart, the immigrant, was born Aug. 21, 1840, to Joseph and Maria Nussbaumer Engelhart near Gmunden in Austria. Joseph's grandfather was also Joseph Engelhart, who farmed in a neighboring section called Goberg.

In 1843, when he was three years old, his father died. His mother married a farmer named Matthais Kirchmeyr. Because there were no Protestant schools or churches in Gmunden, he attended a Catholic school until age ten. The following years he lived with an uncle and attended a Protestant school. After his confirmation, he returned home to work on the family farm. At age 21, Joseph was drafted into the military, where he served as a secretary to officers, serving in Salzburg and in the northernmost sections of Italy.

His stepfather died in 1866 and he was granted a discharge to help his mother and young stepbrothers. However, under Austrian law only the youngest son could inherit land, so within a year or two he established himself on another farm, which had been owned by an aunt and uncle who were given a lifetime home. In 1867 Joseph married Theresia Gumplemeyr.

Joseph Engelhart with grandchildren, Harold Engelhart, Verna Engelhart Vogel, Charles Engelhart, c. 1929.

What makes a man leave a country? Joseph had been exposed to the "American Fever" by young men he had gone to school with and by letters from Austrian communities in America encouraging him to come. In addition, the farm was not productive enough for his growing family. He sold his farm in late 1874 or early 1875. The family sailed third class on the steamer *Oder* in the spring of 1875. Fourteen days later they arrived in Hoboken, NJ, with three children: Theresia, age 7; Engelbert, age 5; and Franz, not yet age 3. They went by rail to St. Louis, leaving there by boat to Wittenberg, where they were met by Joseph Oberndoerfer of Frohna. They eventually bought 135 acres west of Pocahontas for $2000. That farm is recognized as a Century farm by Missouri as it has been owned and operated by the Engelhart family since 1875. Joseph Carl and Alvinia Engelhart owned the land until 1964, when it was sold to Joseph Charles and Joy Engelhart. In 1992 the farm was sold to their son Paul and Carol Engelhart.

In 1981 Erna Kirchmeyr, age 21, came to Missouri to visit her Engelhart relatives, and visits between Missouri and Austria have continued. In 2000 Charles and Joy visited with Austrian relatives and worshipped in the Lutheran Church in Rutzenmoos where his grandfather was baptized, confirmed and married. In 2001 Robert and Christian Hallerweger, sons of Erna Kirchmeyr Hallerweger, came to spend three weeks with their American relatives. *Submitted by Joy Engelhart*

ENGELHART – William "Herbert" Englehart (1897-1975) was the oldest son of William Phillip (1868-1943) and Lou Verna (McDowell) Englehart (1872-1954). They lived in the Jackson-Fruitland Community all of their lives as farmers. Herbert had one brother, Melvin (Ruth) Englehart (1902-1976), and two sisters, Grace (John) Stevenson (1911-1985) and Onas (1895-1896), who died in childhood. They were members of the Fairview and Fruitland United Methodist Churches.

Herbert married Agnes Estelle Bandy (1905-1988) of Portageville on June 16, 1922. She was the daughter of Robert and Ida (Morrison) Bandy. She had one sister, Inez (Earl) Rogers (1907-2000). Mr. Bandy died when Agnes and Inez were very young. Mrs. Bandy then married Robert Gilmore (1872-1949). They had a son, John Woodrow (Evelyn Ackman) Gilmore (1913-1986) of Jackson, MO.

Herbert and Agnes were both teachers. They taught at Canalou, Wardell, Hayward, Indian Creek, Whitewater and Fruitland. They also farmed and lived on the Englehart family farm all their married lives after the first few years. They were both active members of Fruitland, now Wesley United Methodist Church. Mrs. Englehart was a member of Pleasant Hill Cemetery Association of Fruitland, MO.

The Engleharts had three sons who were all in the field of education. The oldest son, William Dale (1926-1996) was married to Carol Austin. Bill joined the U. S. Army at the end of high school. He graduated from Peabody University in Nashville. He taught at Shepard, Indian Creek, Egypt Mills and Pocahontas Elementary Schools, later becoming elementary principal at Jackson R-II Schools. He then became a textbook salesman for American Book Company and later, McMillan Book Company. Carol was an elementary librarian in Mehlville, MO, where they resided. Bill and Carol had two children. Ed (Donna) and two children, Katie and Phillip, reside in Indianapolis, IN. Their daughter, Karen Kay, (Allen Adam (1956-1977), (Paul) Schwarz and two children, Amy Adam-Schwarz and Eric Schwarz live in Mehlville, MO.

W. H. and Agnes Engelhart and their three sons, Bill, Bob and Jim

Herbert and Agnes' second son was named Robert Phillip (1931-). He married Shirley Ann Jones of Jackson, MO. Upon the completion of high school, Bob served in the U. S. Air Force. He was a graduate of Southeast Missouri State University. Bob taught at Pocahontas Elementary School and Advance Schools, and then moved to O'Fallon, MO as elementary principal in the Fort Zumwalt School District until he retired. Shirley was a school secretary in one of the elementary schools in O'Fallon. Bob and Shirley had three children. James Phillip (Pat) (1954-1998), (Marilyn) and their children, James Robert (Melanie) and two children, Alexia and Ethan; and Mindy (Scott) Gorman and son Kane, live in St. James, MO. Jim also has two stepchildren. Barbara (Tim) Schwane and her two children, Jill and Allen, live in O'Fallon, MO. Their youngest daughter, Connie (Rod) Snyder and their two sons, Nicholas and Jeremy, live in Jackson, MO.

The youngest son, James Burnell Englehart (1933-) married Madonna Eggers. They reside in Jackson, MO. Both Jim and Madonna were teachers. After graduating from Jackson High School, Jim served in the U. S. Air Force. Returning home, Jim graduated from Southeast Missouri State University and Missouri University. Jim was high school principal at Puxico R-8 High School, Portageville High School, and Poplar Bluff High School, where Madonna taught in those elementary schools. Jim came to Cape Girardeau Public Schools in 1970, first as junior high school principal and then as Director of Secondary Education, until he retired in 1994. Madonna taught at Jackson R-II, Advance, Scott County Central and Delta during those years. Jim and Madonna have one son, James Brent Englehart, who resides in Jackson on what remains of the Englehart family farm. He has two children, Paige and James Brent Englehart. *Submitted by Madonna Englehart*

ENGLISH – According to family history, the first English to migrate to America was a Thomas English, who came from England. My great-great-great-grandfather, Thomas English, was born in Virginia on Oct. 13, 1851. He married Jane Wicker, place and date unknown, but the event may have been about 1775 in Anson County, VA. She was a daughter of Robert Hester and Hannah Simmons (Holley) Wicker. Thomas English served in the Revolutionary War, and their first son, also named Thomas, was born in a fort during that time.

Sometime between 1803 and 1806 the English family, along with other related families, including Holland, Holley, Renfroe, Sheppard, Tennille and Wicker, left Georgia and moved to Cape Girardeau County, MO. Most of these families settled first in the Jackson, MO area. According to Bethel Church Records, Thomas English died May 16, 1829 and Jane (Wicker) English died April 5, 1842.

Thomas and Jane's son, John, my great-great-grandfather, married Sinai Ballew. Her father, Thomas Ballew, was one of the first justices of the Court of General Quarter Sessions of the Peace of the District of Cape Girardeau, Territory of Louisiana. John English was one of the first judges of Court of Common Pleas in Hempstead County, AR. His home served as the first courthouse and the first post office. He was a representative to the Arkansas legislature and introduced the cotton gin to southwest Arkansas. He died in 1821 in a cotton gin accident.

The Henry R. English home, Jackson, MO

After John's death, his brother, Simeon English, took John's children to Cape Girardeau to be raised by relatives. One of these six children was my great-grandfather, Thomas Ballew English. Thomas B. English was born July 15, 1811 in Harrisonburg, LA and died Nov. 10, 1866 in Jackson. He married Sarah Cone Joyce on Sept. 17, 1834 at St. Vincent's Catholic Church. Sarah, daughter of Hannah (English) and Edward Joyce, was born in Louisiana on April 24, 1815 and died July 31, 1895 in Jackson. Thomas B. and Sarah are buried at Jackson Cemetery. Thomas B. English was educated at St. Mary's of the Barrens in Perryville and studied law under Colonel Ranney. After being admitted to the bar, he began his law practice in Jackson.

Thomas B. and Sarah C. (Joyce) English had 10 children, one of them being my grandfather, Henry Randolph English. Henry was born April 10, 1850, and died in 1919 in Tulsa, OK. He was brought back to Jackson on the "Iron Horse" and buried in Jackson City Cemetery. Henry married Margaret Judith Scherrer, daughter of Major John Jacob and Elizabeth Beattie Scherrer, in 1883 in Jackson. Due to Elizabeth's death, William and Martha Cordell Warren raised Margaret. Henry and Margaret's children were Margaret Ursula, Henry (Harry), Grace, Maude, Celeste, Frank and Martha. They lived near New McKendree Methodist Church.

Henry served as Clerk of Circuit court and Ex-officio Recorder for 16 years. He established the English Mining and Manufacturing Company and served as president of Jackson Exchange Bank. *Submitted by Patricia (Russell) Pat Nance*

FARROW – Once a year the grandchildren of Alfred Farrow get together and reminisce about the beginning of their grandfather's life in Missouri. The Farrow saga began in America when Christopher and Rachael (Smally) Farrow boarded a ship from Wales bound for a new world. They had a son, Alfred, born Feb. 15, 1859 in Louisiana. Rachael died in childbirth. Since Rachael's parents were against their daughter's marriage to Christopher, he decided to take Alfred and run away when Alfred was two years old, leaving a daughter and twin sons behind. Christopher and Alfred wandered the country. During this time Christopher married several women and never divorced. When he got wanderlust, he took off. Chris was often called "Doc" Farrow because he peddled patent medicine.

Alfred came to "Pinkroot Hollow" near Jackson and stayed to build a home and raise a family. He ran a sawmill and farmed. In the beginning, he had 40 acres and a log cabin. He bought land whenever he could until he had 251 acres and a large house on a hill. Alfred married Elizabeth Welty, daughter of Peter Welty and Bertha Dunn. They became the parents of George, Edward, Emma, Bertha, Minnie, John Henry, Charley, Claude, Burette, Mollie, and Bill.

John Henry Farrow, son of Alfred and Elizabeth, married Lillie Kraemer in January of 1917. John Henry and Lillie farmed and peddled produce in Cape Girardeau. They became parents of Arnold, Viola, Leroy, Dora, Lillian, John, Jr., Delia and Lyman. In the early 1940s, they bought a large two-story house located on Russell Street in Jackson known as the Judge Snider place. John and Lillie did not move to their new home for several years, deciding to rent it instead.

Their son, Arnold, was one of the renters. He had been drafted into the army in April of 1945 and needed to move his family from the farm into town. Arnold had married Vera Davis on March 12, 1937. He and Vera had two daughters, Marcella and La Fern. Arnold was discharged from the army in November of 1946 after WWII ended. His family remained in Jackson and he began building a small home on Mary Street on a lot he had purchased from his father. Arnold had farmed and worked at various jobs but preferred doing carpentry work. He worked for his cousins with Farrow Construction Company. Arnold was well known for designing and building clocks, especially Grandfather clocks and clock shelves, and fixing clocks. He died Feb. 15, 1985.

Alfred and Elizabeth Farrow on the farm, 1920s

Arnold and Vera's oldest daughter married J. D. Green on June 21, 1959. She graduated from Southeast Missouri State College in 1961 and taught school for 30 years, retiring in 1992. The Green's have three children: Jennifer Elliott (Jay) of Sikeston, Christopher (Racquel), and Stephen (Julie) of Jackson, and two grandchildren, Justin and Braxton Green. The youngest, La Fern Judd, is a secretary at NLC. She has two daughters, Deborah Schearf (Kevin), and Michele Housman (Robert), and a grandson, Brandon Housman.

Vera and other family members still reside in Jackson. *Submitted by La Fern Farrow Judd*

FREUND – Debra K. (Allen) Freund was born Sept. 8, 1955, the ninth child of Clarence and Noma (Crites) Allen. Debbie was raised in Patton, MO and graduated from Meadow Heights School in 1973. She worked as a secretary at Perryville International Shoe Company, First Baptist Church of Cape Girardeau, Bollinger County Extension Office, Kimbeland Country Club, H & R Block and Farm Service Agency in Marble Hill. On Dec. 4, 1976 she married Robert F. Freund at Little Whitewater Baptist Church in Mayfield, MO. Robert was born Jan. 29, 1944 to Robert and Juanita (Paubel) Freund in St. Louis, MO. He graduated from Normandy High School and attended the University of Missouri at Columbia and Ranken Trade School. He began working for Otis Elevator Company in 1963 and transferred to Cape Girardeau in 1969 with Otis Elevator Company, as a local representative. In 1977 they established SEMO Elevator Company, a passenger elevator service company. SEMO Elevator Company serviced the elevators at the Cape County Courthouse and Jail, Jackson Exchange Bank, Lenco Company, Buerkle, Beeson and Ludwig, Jackson High School, Jackson City Hall and Library, and many others within a 90-mile radius.

Bob and Debbie Freund, 2001

The Freunds moved to Jackson in 1981 and continued to run their elevator company. In 1989 they purchased 403 acres of hunting property in Bollinger County. They sold the business to Otis Elevator Company in 1992 after many years of being on call seven days a week, 24 hours a day. Their motto was *"We understand your ups and downs."* Bob was fortunate enough to retire at this time. He is now able to hunt deer and turkey whenever he chooses. He also likes to chase a little white golf ball at Kimbeland Country Club, where he plays with what is known as the "10:00 Group."

They have three children: Kimberly A. (Freund) Brinkopf (born Jan. 20, 1966) of Cape Girardeau; James F. Freund (born June 9, 1970) of Chicago, IL; and Jennifer L. (Freund) Thurman (born Jan. 22, 1978) of Festus, MO. Jennifer graduated from Jackson High School in 1996. Their first grandson, Zachery Allen Thurman, was born July 7, 2000 and a granddaughter, Macie Elizabeth Brinkopf, was born April 6, 2001. The Freunds presently attend the First Baptist Church in Marble Hill. They have been members at First Baptist Church in Jackson, Lynwood Baptist, and First Baptist Church in Millersville.

Although they enjoyed living in Jackson very much, they decided in 2000 to sell their home and move to the country. They are now able to look out their back door and see turkey and deer grazing on clover planted in their pasture field. They feel truly blessed. *Submitted by Debbie Freund*

FRIEDRICH – Johann Carl Samuel Friedrich, a master horseshoer blacksmith, who resided at Tiefendorf, Germany, married Kunigunde Hoffman of Wallbetendorf on Jan. 30, 1806. Three of their sons who immigrated were Johann Andreas Jacob, born March 9, 1817 in Tiefendorf, Ober Bayern; Johann Christian Elias, born April 23, 1820 in Diesendorf, Foringe Bairn; and George Peter, born Jan. 29, 1823 in Bavaria.

Jacob married Anna Marguretha Rogler on Jan. 20, 1850. Jacob, Marguretha, their son Johann Nicol, and his brother Peter, immigrated for religious freedom. They sailed from Bremmen on Aug. 22, 1852 on the *Ruchan*. When food ran out, the Captain appropriated Jacob's sheep to feed the passengers. Jacob never received compensation for his sheep. They landed at New Orleans, LA on Oct. 11, 1852. They collected their two pieces of luggage in which were packed their Bible, their baptismal, marriage and emigration certificates, and Johann's smallpox certificate. They intended to join friends in Iowa, but ran out of funds at Cape Girardeau, MO. Jacob, a shoemaker, purchased lot #63 in Jackson on July 18, 1854. On March 27, 1865 he purchased lot #75. These lots are the present even-number block of 200 W. Main Street. Their children included Lina Barbara Bertha, Matilda (Stumpp), George Jacob, Albert Carl Christian, Jacob Heinrich, Bertha Sophie (Wagner), August Heinrich, and Anna (Hartmann). In May 1867 the Friedrichs became founding members of Emanual United Church of Christ. On July 25, 1873, Jacob purchased 100 acres on the present Greensferry Road. Jacob died Oct. 31, 1886 of typhoid and Marguretha died Jan. 7, 1901. Both are buried in the Jackson City Cemetery in lot #105.

Christian tangled with the German law for cutting wood. Christian fled and settled at Monroeville, IN. He married Sophie Schlemmer, who had a son Christian. Here, their children, George Herm Peter, George Phillip and Maria Katherine (Schleger) were born. In 1858 the family moved to Jackson, MO. Christian purchased 40 acres near Allenville on Feb. 16, 1870. The children, Jacob Peter Ernest and Johann Heinrich, were added to the family. Unable to pay for their property, the family moved near Illmo after 1872. Christian died Oct. 11, 1889 of abdominal inflammation and is buried in Eisleben Lutheran Church Cemetery in Stoddard County.

Peter, a blacksmith, married Apolonia Sutter on March 24, 1856 at Hanover Lutheran Church. He purchased lot #110 in Jackson on Jan. 22, 1859 and sold it on May 9, 1859 to a Litterer. The family moved to Cape Girardeau, where Peter purchased lot #9 on Oct. 9, 1866 and lot #10 at a later date. These lots are the present 24 North Fountain Street. In 1867 Peter was one of 11 blacksmiths in Cape Girardeau. Their children included Anna Marie Sophie (Huebel), Anna Fredericka Margaretha (Ollar), Frederika Caroline Elisa (Bedhe), Emma (Kraft), Ada (Schmitt), and Carl Wilhelm. Peter died of a heart attack on Feb. 3, 1887 and Apolonia died of paralysis on Jan. 16, 1912. Both are buried in the New Lorimier Cemetery. *Submitted by Mrs. Vernon Ludwig*

Johann Andreas Jacob Friedrich (March 9, 1817- Oct. 31, 1886), brother of Christian and Peter Friedrich, came to America in 1852 on the ship Ruchan from Germany

FRIEDRICH – August Henry Friedrich was born Feb. 21, 1867 in Jackson, MO, the son of Jacob A. J. Friedrich, born in 1817 in Germany and died Oct. 31, 1886 in Jackson, MO. His mother, Anna Marguarita Strunz, was born in 1827 in Germany and died in 1901 in Jackson, MO. Jacob was a founding member of the Emmanuel Evangelical Church. Jacob and Marguarita sailed on the *Bremmen* in 1852 to New Orleans. They were so poor by the time they had almost reached Jackson, they had only a loaf of gingerbread to eat. August's father was a shoemaker on Main Street. During the Civil War, he would hide the leather shipment that he used for making shoes for the Union soldiers. Once he did not get the leather hidden. A Confederate soldier cut the leather into small pieces with his sword.

While his parents lived on West Main, two blocks from the courthouse, August and seven siblings were born. They, except John who was born in Germany, were: Matilda, 1854; Abert C., 1859; Jacob H., 1862; Bertha, 1866; August H., 1867; and Anna, 1869. Two infants that died were unnamed. In 1876 the family moved to Greens Ferry Road.

August inherited half of his parents' farm, now Sunset Subdivision, and Jacob inherited the

The August Henry Friedrich family, ca. 1943. Back row: Ray, Gus, Margaret, Irene, Valla, George. Front row: Tillie, August, Martha, Elsie

other half, now Brookside Memorial Park. August, as a young man, met a spunky orphan girl who was raised by the Charley Dankels of Tilsit. She only knew that she was born at Dongola, IL. Her mother was Cherokee and her father, Sneider by name, was a Frenchman. He passed away, leaving five young children whose names she believed to be John, Minnie, Rose, Marie and her name, Martha Ann Sneider. Their mother could not care for five children, so they worked outside their home. August and Martha were married June 3, 1897 in Jackson.

Their first child was Valentine Carl, born April 17, 1898 (he had one daughter). Martha did not know the date of her birth, so she acquired that of her first son. The children were in order of boy-girl: Hilda Matilda Ludwig, born 1900 (three children); August Alvin, born 1902 (two children); Irene Sophie Wolfenkoehler, born 1906 (two sons); Ray Henry, born 1907 (two sons); Martha Margaret Goodson, born 1911 (two sons); George William, born 1917 (three children) and Elsie Amanda Barrett, born 1920 (two daughters).

A livelihood was made by dairying. The cows were milked by hand. The children would carry the fresh milk uptown where the customers filled their containers. One customer bought one cup just for his cat.

August played jolly tunes on the accordion, violin and harmonica. Martha presided over a table of fresh bread, butter and cheese for the many children, grandchildren and neighbors who sought her company. She went to the third grade, but she managed the money, was sharp in games, kept boarders, and was in urgent demand when the women of the neighborhood needed a midwife. She was loyal to her church, then Evangelical, and urged that the Friedrich family attend church and family reunions. At mealtime, all 10 sat around the table and held hands while Dad said the prayer in German. *Submitted by Elsie Barrett*

FRIEDRICH – Dorothy Lee (Friedrich) Mayfield was born Aug. 22, 1927 on Greensferry Road in Jackson, MO. She was the daughter of Volla C. and Maud (Kasten) Friedrich. The following year her father purchased a farm one mile north of Jackson, MO and moved his family there. This is where he lived until he passed away at the age of 99. He farmed and also was a rural mail carrier by horse and buggy before improved roads and the Model T car replaced the buggy. He was among the early farmers to practice soil conservation through terrace-building and contour farming. In 1948 and 1950 they received certificates of merit at Jefferson City, MO for this achievement.

Dorothy grew up on this farm. When the harvest season came sometimes she would help out by driving the John Deere tractor that was pulling the grain binder that made bundles of grain for the threshing machine. She helped with the other farm chores also. They had beef cows, dairy cows, hogs, turkeys, chickens, ducks and geese. They also grew corn, oats, wheat, and hay.

Dorothy Friedrich Mayfield

She attended school at the Mcferron School and graduated from Jackson High School in 1945. She graduated from the Cape Girardeau School of Beauty Culture in 1946. She was a member and leader in 4-H club work, and was baptized and confirmed at the Emanuel Evangelical church in Jackson, MO.

Dorothy and Juel Dean Mayfield were married in 1949. They have the following children: Joe Daniel; Deborah Faye; David Lee; Dennis Rodney and Douglas Wayne. After marriage they lived on and farmed land adjoining her homeplace that her father had purchased in 1947. In 1963 they bought the farm and replaced the farmhouse with a new home. The farmhouse was taken down so the same building site could be used.

"Sunday Morning." Juel Dean Mayfield, Dorothy, Joe Daniel with book, Debby, Douglas with white coat, David in center, Dennis with bow tie and sweater, September 1959.

They farmed and milked Holstein cows until Juel was hired as a diesel engineer to work on riverboats. This job experience came through his time in the U. S. Merchant Marines before marriage. On his leave time away from the boat, he was able to continue to farm so the Holstein cows were replaced with Angus beef cows. Dorothy and the children cared for the cattle and farm when Juel was at work on the boat. On his time away from the boat, he would put up the hay for winter-feeding and care for the cattle.

The Mayfield Angus Farm received a lifetime membership certificate from the American Angus Association in 1967. As the children grew up you would find them at the SEMO-District Fair at Cape Girardeau, MO, with some livestock, first Holsteins and then Angus. They won some blue ribbons, did lots of work, and had lots of fun. The children also all played musical instruments in the High School Marching Band and were all graduates of the Jackson High School in Jackson, MO.

Dorothy's ancestors came from Germany. Jacob Fried-rich came from Hanover, Germany. Jacob and his wife Margurita and son John sailed from Bremen, Germany in 1852 on the ship *Rucan*. They sailed to New Orleans and settled in Jackson, MO. He was a shoemaker by trade and German Evangelical by faith. He was one of the 28 founding members and served on the first church council of the German Emmanuel Evangelical Church in Jackson, MO. Twenty-eight German-American residents who united to worship and study together organized this church in May 1867. Today this church is Emanuel United Church of Christ in Jackson, MO.

Jacob was Dorothy (Friedrich) Mayfield's great-grandfather. Her grandfather, Jacob's son, was August H. Friedrich and his wife's name was Martha Ann Schneider. They had a dairy farm on Greensferry Road in Jackson. Dorothy's mother was the daughter of Phillip C. and Catherine (Richter) Kasten born in Old Appleton, MO. Phillip was a farmer and in 1919 became a county judge for Cape Girardeau County and moved to Jackson, MO. While he was a judge, the railroad bonds that had been purchased in 1869 by Cape Girardeau County were retired and burned. Phillip was the son of Christian and Mary (Schriner) Kasten. Christian Kasten immigrated from Germany to Old Appleton, MO. He was a wagon maker by trade. *Submitted by Juel Mayfield*

FRIEDRICH – In Diesendorf Foringe Bairn, Hanover, Germany, Jacob Friedrich was born in 1817. At a young age in Germany, Jacob learned the trade of shoemaking. Jacob married Anna Marguarita Strunz, who was born in December of 1827. In 1851 their son John was born. Jacob, Marguarita, and John migrated to the United States on Aug. 22, 1852 from Bremmen, Germany on the ship *Ruchan*, and landed in New Orleans, LA, on Oct. 11, 1852. Their personal belongings were packed in two pieces of luggage. They traveled up the Mississippi River to Cape Girardeau, MO. Jacob and Marguarita eventually settled in Jackson, MO, Randol Township, in Cape Girardeau County. Jacob and Marguarita lived in a house on West Main Street, two blocks west of the courthouse. Here were born their children Matilda, Albert C., Jacob H., Bertha, August H., and Anna. Jacob continued his trade of shoemaking by opening a shop in Jackson. In May 1867 the family became founding members of Emmanuel United Church of Christ in Jackson. Jacob served on the first church council. In 1867 the family moved to a farm on Greensferry Road. Jacob died in 1881 and Marguarita died Jan. 7, 1901. Both Jacob and Marguarita are buried in the old Jackson City Cemetery.

Jacob H. Friedrich, 1909

Left to right, first row: Mrs. Alvin Reitzel, son Edwin Reitzel, mother Mrs. Henry Reitzel, son Wm. Reitzel, father Henry Reitzel, granddaughter Clara Friedrich, daughter Mrs. Jake Friedrich. Back row: son Alvin Reitzel, son Henry Reitzel Jr., grandson Tony Friedrich, Jacob Friedrich. Summer 1893

Left to right, standing: Jerry and Helen Friedrich, Otto Friedrich, Miss Clara Friedrich, Tony Friedrich, Jake Friedrich, Robert Friedrich, Ima Friedrich Seybold, George Seybold, Marven Campbell, Chester Friedrich. Sitting: David Friedrich, Barbara Jean Friedrich, Jacob H. Friedrich holding Bob Friedrich, Mrs. Jacob H. Friedrich, Ollie Friedrich, Mary Friedrich, Barbara Friedrich, Libby Friedrich Campbell. Missing from the family picture of Mr. and Mrs. Jacob H. Friedrich is Ralph Friedrich. Picture taken in 1938

Jacob H. Friedrich, the third son born to Jacob and Marguarita Friedrich, was born in 1862. Jacob H. Friedrich and Bertha Reitzel were united in marriage on May 27, 1888. The couple had six children: Anton (1889); Clara (1891); Otto (1894); Jacob (1896); Ima (1902) and Robert (1908). In 1903 Jacob H. received the appointment of rural mail carrier out of the Jackson office on what was then Jackson RFD No. 2, Cline Hensley having been made carrier on Route 1. These were the first rural mail carriers out of the Jackson office. The mail route ran through Tilsit and Houck when road conditions were bad and in the horse-and-buggy days. Jacob H. retired from the post office after 43 years of service. Upon retirement he bought property on the Greensferry Road. Jacob H. Friedrich died in 1946.

Robert C. Friedrich, son of Jacob H. Friedrich and Bertha Reitzel, was born in 1907. Robert C. Friedrich attended Jackson High School and after graduating got a job working for the Pierce Petroleum Corporation in St. Louis. In 1933 Robert married Ollie M. Seabaugh. Robert and Ollie had three children, Robert Jr., Mary Ruth, and John Phillip. Robert owned and operated the West Side Shell and Uptown Shell Stations in Jackson. During WWII, Robert was drafted at the age of 38. Robert went overseas to the European Theater and served during the Battle of the Bulge and the crossing of the Rhine River. Robert was discharged from the service in 1945 with two Silver Stars, a Purple Heart and the rank of T5. In 1946 Robert and Woodrow Seabaugh became co-founders of Jackson Electric. The company served as one of the main electrical contractors in the southern part of Missouri for nearly 40 years. Robert was a lifelong member of Emanuel United Church of Christ and a former board member. Robert was one of the original chapter members of the Jackson VFW Post and the Jackson DeMolay chapter. Robert C. Friedrich Sr. died in 1990 at the age of 82. In August of 2000, Ollie Friedrich died at the age of 88.

Robert C. Friedrich Jr. married Patricia Ruth Schulte in 1959. Robert and Patricia had three children, John, Eric, and Robert. Robert C. Friedrich was an electrician by trade, retiring in 1995. Robert C. Friedrich served two years in Berlin, Germany, as a member of the occupational forces of the U. S. Army. Robert has been active in the Boy Scouts of America for nearly 50 years and was the founder of Explorer Post 211. Robert was an original charter member of the Trail of Tears committee. This committee made it possible to retrace by automobile the original trail taken by the Cherokee Indians during their forced removal from North Carolina during the 1800s. Former Missouri Governor John Ashcroft appointed Robert to this capacity. Patricia Friedrich died in May of 1995. Robert C. Friedrich Jr. lives on Greensferry Road on land which is still considered part of the original family farm purchased in 1867. *Submitted by Robert Friedrich*

FRIZEL – The Frizel - Welling family traces their roots in Missouri back to George Frederick Bollinger, who settled on the Whitewater River (site of the present Bollinger Mill State Historic Site) in the year 1800. Mr. Bollinger had one daughter, Sarah, who was born in 1799 in North Carolina, and came to live with her father four years later. When Sarah was 16 years old she was sent back to North Carolina to Salem College. Upon her return to Missouri Territory, Mr. Bollinger purchased for her the first piano brought west of the Mississippi River. Sarah's piano is now on display in the Jackson Heritage Museum.

Frizel – Welling house

Mr. Joseph Frizel, who was a surveyor and a civil engineer by trade, was born in 1794 in Wiscassett, ME, and came to Jackson prior to 1816. By 1818 he had built a Cape Cod style cottage near the center of town, and brought his widowed mother to live with him. This home still stands at 209 West Main Street. In 1818 the first Masonic Lodge, Unity Lodge No. 6, was organized at Mr. Frizel's home. He opened one of the early general stores in Jackson prior to 1819. Joseph Frizel married Sarah Bollinger, daughter of George Frederick Bollinger, on Jan. 21, 1819. Joseph and Sarah Frizel had three daughters: Elizabeth, Mary, and Sarah Josephine, prior to Mr. Frizel's untimely death in 1823. The Frizel girls grew up and were sent back east to a Moravian College in Bethlehem, PA.

Mr. Charles Welling was born in Pennington, NJ in 1812 and came to Jackson in 1832 to help in the general store of his uncle, Mr. Ralph Guild. Mr. Welling bought out Mr. Guild and became a very successful merchant in Jackson. On July 5, 1838, he married Elizabeth Frizel, the oldest granddaughter of George Frederick Bollinger. That same year Mr. Welling added a two-story addition to Mr. Frizel's Cape Cod cottage to produce a Greek Revival style house that was the latest rage in architecture back east. The house was also furnished with the latest style furniture from back east.

Charles and Elizabeth Welling were Southern sympathizers during the Civil War. Sarah Bollinger, Elizabeth's mother, would secretly meet Confederate officers at night at their home to discuss getting flour from her mill through the Union lines. Mr. Welling was very active in civic affairs in Jackson. He was president of the first Jackson School Board. He was County Treasurer for two terms. He was the first Cashier of the Cape County Bank (presently a branch of Union Planters Bank). He served as Jackson Postmaster. The First Presbyterian Church of Jackson was organized at the Welling home on May 15, 1864.

Mr. and Mrs. Welling had many children who grew up to become prominent citizens. Their youngest daughter, Juliette, married the Rev. M. B .W. Granger (born 1856 in Maryland), who was pastor of the Presbyterian Church on Jan. 15, 1890. The Grangers had four children: Marion; Charles; Elizabeth; and Mildred. Elizabeth married Dr. T. E. Wilson (Aug. 30, 1930), who practiced dentistry in Jackson for many years. Mildred married Olin S. Hartsfield of West Palm Beach, FL (Dec. 22, 1933). The Hartsfields had three children: Juliet, Elizabeth, and Benjamin, who are the present owners of the Frizel-Welling home. The home was placed on the National Register of Historic Places in 1999. *Submitted by Ben Hartsfield*

FULBRIGHT - Jacob Fulbright was born in 1778 in North Carolina. He married Barbara Plunk in about 1802. In 1814 he migrated to Missouri and settled on a farm near Oak Ridge, MO. Jacob died in 1844 and Barbara died in 1858 and both are buried in Fulbright Cemetery near Oak Ridge, MO.

Jacob and Barbara had seven children, one of whom was John, Dorothy Fulbright Schaper's great-grandfather. John was born in 1818 and married Matilda Mayfield. He became a wealthy man, at least land-wise, owning 1200 acres of land, enough to leave each of his 12 children 100 acres. He was a lover of race horses and bred his own horses, racing them on a track near his home. John died in 1888 and Matilda in 1902, and both are buried in Fulbright Cemetery.

Apparently it was the custom for every family member to have a nickname. John's children nearly all had nicknames. Jacob F. was "Jack," Peter Horry was "Pete," Philip was "Coose," John Jasper was "Cap," Margaret was "Marg," Nancy was "Nance," George Washington no doubt had one but it is unknown, Andrew Jackson was "Cot," Mary was "Mollie," Barbara was "Bill," and Evangeline was "Bipps." John's grandson, George Donald Fulbright (Dorothy Fulbright's father), was called "Put," because he had seen a picture of Civil War General Putnam and played as though he was the general riding his horse.

One of John's sons was George Washington Fulbright, who was Dorothy Fulbright's grandfather. He was born in 1857 on the family farm a few miles west of Oak Ridge, MO. In 1884 he married Louisa Katherine Pair. To them were born nine children, eight growing to maturity. George Washington farmed in the Oak Ridge area until the year 1901, when he moved his family to Oklahoma near Cache where they shared the home of his brother, Andrew Jackson "Cot" Fulbright, along with "Cot's" wife and five children. "Cot" Fulbright's ranch was near the Comanche Indian reservation and the Indians often stopped by to help themselves to a freshly baked loaf of bread.

Quanah Parker was the chief of the Comanches and he and George Washington became friends. The story was told that after the birth of the ninth baby, Quanah begged to have the boy, saying that he would make him a chief and give him a pony. Mother "Kate" Fulbright told Quanah that she couldn't do that because the baby needed to nurse. Quanah replied that his wife "Toonicy" would nurse him. To placate the chief the boy was named Andrew Quanah. After they had been in Oklahoma less than a year, George's health began to fail and the family moved back to Oak Ridge where he died in 1903 and was buried in Fulbright Cemetery.

George Washington Fulbright and "Kate" Pair had nine children, eight of whom reached adulthood. The third child was George Donald, Dorothy's father. He was born in 1888 on the family farm west of Oak Ridge. After the family moved to Cape Girardeau, he started working in the timber business and worked for many years as a lumber inspector, earning the respect of all who bought lumber there because of his honesty and accuracy in grading lumber.

The George Washington and "Kate" Pair Fulbright family, circa 1899. Back row: George Donald (1888-1962), Grace (1890-1972), John Miles (1885-1949). Front and sitting: Ruth (1898-1913), George Washington (1857-1903), Louise Katherine Pair (1867-1955), Nick Amos (1895-1972), Hester (1897-1962).

In 1915 George married Grace Cleveland Nicholas. Although lacking a formal education, he was very intelligent and was proficient in mathematics. To amuse his children and grandchildren he would compose clever poems and carve wooden figurines that were well-proportioned. He died in 1962 and was buried in Memorial Park Cemetery near Cape Girardeau. They had two children, Dorothy Grace, born June 28, 1919, and George William, born Feb. 5, 1924.

Dorothy Grace Fulbright married Bernard Julius Schaper on April 20, 1947 and they established their residence in Jackson, MO. They had two daughters, Nancy Ellen, born Oct. 15, 1949, and Teri Lee, born Aug. 7, 1951. Teri married Thomas Allen on Dec. 27, 1971 and they had three children; Thomas Peter, born July 6, 1976; John Henry, born Oct. 8, 1979 and died Jan. 28, 1980; and Mary Katherine, born Aug. 31, 1989. Dorothy Grace died Oct. 24, 1992.

George William Fulbright married Dorothy Kammrath on Dec. 25, 1946. They had two children, George Edward born Feb. 28, 1951, and Joyce Ann, born Aug. 30, 1953. George Edward married Phyllis Gail Bean in 1972 and they had two children, Diane Louise, born Oct. 14, 1981, and James Edward, born June 27, 1985. Joyce Ann married Peter Anthony Cardell in 1985. They had three children, Katherine Louise, born Dec. 31, 1987; Matthew William, born June 19, 1989, and Margaret Elizabeth, born March 26, 1991. George William died June 5, 1999. *Condensed from the Fulbright family history compiled by Dorothy Fulbright Schaper*

FULENWIDER – Caleb Pinkney Fulenwider, an early settler of Cape Girardeau, MO, and a founder of the city of Jackson, was born Aug. 31, 1798 in Rowan County, NC. He was the youngest son of Henry Fulenwider and his second wife, Elinor Leonard (daughter of Henry and Elizabeth Leonard), who were married on Aug. 20, 1783 in Rowan County. Caleb's paternal grandparents, Jacob and Esther Walder Fulenwider, were married on Jan. 7, 1737 in Mettmenstatten Parish, Rossau, Switzerland, and the above-mentioned Henry was born there on July 4, 1745. Jacob and family immigrated to America, sailing from Rotterdam on the ship *Priscilla*, and arriving on Sept. 11, 1749 in Philadelphia. On that day, Jacob took the Oath of Allegiance to the English king, signing "Jacob Folenweider."

After a stay in Pennsylvania, the Fulenwiders migrated to Rowan County, NC, where Jacob received a grant of 449 acres from the Earl of Granville on Aug. 26, 1762. Jacob was a prominent and successful planter and member of his community, serving as Constable and Justice of the Peace. He was a Lutheran and provided land to build Hickory Church, which served Lutheran and Reformed congregations. Jacob's children were Henry, Jacob, Margaret, Barbara and John. At his death in May of 1771, he left no will, and by law of primogeniture his plantation was inherited by his eldest son Henry, who as a prosperous planter, tripled the size of his landholdings.

This Henry Fulenwider, a member of the Committee of Safety of Rowan 1774-76, was chosen to represent the Committee in the Provincial Congress. He served as an Ensign in the First Regiment of the Rowan County Militia in the Revolutionary War, and fought in the Battle of King's Mountain, near the Fulenwider plantation. Henry had two children by his first wife (name unknown): John, 1772-1811 (married Mary Fulenwider) and Ann, Oct. 8, 1776-1853 (married Jacob Boshart).

The children of Henry's second marriage were: Esther, June 23, 1784 to 1869 (married Peter Casper); Elisabeth, born 1788 (married Jacob Rendleman); Henry; Isaac; Jacob, March 4, 1792-Jan. 22, 1859 (married first Ann Cauble, next Mary Casper); Barbara, Feb. 17, 1799-before 1815; and Caleb. After their father died on Oct. 13, 1800 they lived with their mother, who died in 1815. Caleb Fulenwider migrated in 1817 with his sisters Esther Casper and Elisabeth Rendleman and their husbands, to Union County, IL where he stayed until 1820. He then went to St. Louis, MO where he bought land, but family tradition is that the next day he sold it back to the Frenchman from whom he had bought it. From there he went to Cape Girardeau County, MO, where he bought land and was a teacher, farmer, businessman and public servant. A prominent member of his community, he served as judge of the Court of Common Pleas 1824-31 and 1836-40, and as Clerk of County Court from 1840 until his death.

In Cape Girardeau County, on June 10, 1830, Caleb married Margaret Atwell, member of an early family of the county, formerly of Maryland. The Fulenwiders had a number of children, and some of their descendants continue to live in this area. Their son Franklin B., born in 1831 (married Caroline Barr), served as a Major in the Confederacy in the Civil War, and later lived in Boone County, MO. Sons Thomas H., Dec. 24, 1832 – March 17, 1853; Charles W., Jan. 30, 1837 – Jan. 2, 1853; and James L., Oct. 10, 1842 – Oct. 20, 1846; predeceased their father and are buried in Jackson City Cemetery near him. Son John W., June 10, 1835 - after 1879 (married Anna Rowland) served in the Confederacy. Daughter Sarah J. was born in 1839. Son Richard P., 1841 – 1902 (married Balma Virginia Smith) is buried in Dexter, MO. Son Caleb P. Jr., Aug. 27, 1846 – Dec. 30, 1914 (married Missouri E. Morgan) died in Denver but is buried in Jackson. Son Robert O., born about 1848, inherited the family home from his mother. Daughter Margaret Elmira, born February 1851 and died about 1910 (married Bernard Morgan).

Caleb Sr. died Aug. 27, 1853 and Margaret died Sept. 25, 1879. Caleb's tombstone in Jackson City Cemetery praises him for having served many important trusts honorably. *Submitted by Barbara Longwell, descendant of Caleb's sister, Esther Fulenwider Casper*

FUTRELL – William Mack Futrell was born in Jackson, TN on Dec. 12 1888, the oldest of five children. The death of his father at an early age forced him to abandon any educational pursuits as a second-grader. He often spoke of plowing fields behind two mules as a young boy, so small that he had to reach high above his head to grab the plow handles. As a young man he migrated to St. Louis, MO, in search of work and a better way of life. He held

Rev. William and Beulah Futrell

a variety of jobs including working as a railroad worker, in the steel mills, and then as a chauffeur and caterer for wealthy Webster Groves, MO families during the early 1900s.

In 1918, he met and married his wife of 63 years, Beulah Elmira Stone. Beulah was his soulmate, companion and confidante until his death in 1981. She passed away in 1988.

The Futrells, shortly after their marriage, joined the congregation of the newly established Church of God in Christ in Webster Groves, where Mr. Futrell became an ordained minister. The church soon became the cornerstone of the Futrell's lifelong religious commitment. As an assistant pastor at the Webster Groves church, Mr. Futrell was sent to start a church in Jackson, MO in 1942. In the beginning, he commuted each weekend from Webster Groves to Jackson, not an easy task in the days before interstate highways and such. But he persevered and got the church underway before moving to Jackson permanently about 1944 with his wife and daughter, Susie.

Susie married Jackson native Raymond Lewis in 1945, a union that produced eight children, five boys and three girls: Larry; Bobby; Wayne; Billy; Rodney; Jackie; Janet and Kathy. All attended and graduated from Jackson High School.

Under Reverend and Mrs. Futrell's guidance, the church prospered and has been a steady influence in the Jackson Community to this day.

Affectionately known by many as "Pop Mack" and "Granny," the Futrell's became leaders of the community, loved and respected throughout the area. Although not a formally educated man, Reverend Futrell served on various boards including the Tuberculosis Society and was a longtime member of the Jackson Ministerial Alliance.

Reverend Futrell pastored the Jackson church, which was rebuilt and renamed Futrell Memorial COGIC in early 1982, for 45 years. He also founded and served as pastor of another church in Cape Girardeau, MO, now known as Greater Dimension COGIC. Although Reverend Futrell didn't live to see the new church, his memory was honored by many in the Jackson Community with donations and gifts to aid its construction.

A familiar figure in uptown Jackson, he was custodian of the Cape County Savings Bank - now Union Planters - for more than 30 years. A smile and his trademark tip-of-the-hat greeting was offered to all. Reverend Futrell touched the lives of many and left behind a legacy that is respected and admired by all who had the pleasure of meeting this wonderful, kind man. *Submitted by Susie Lewis*

GLUCKHERTZ – Jacob and Frederika Loffel Klugsherz started their journey from Baden, Germany on Oct. 1, 1853, along with their seven children: Frederika, 18; Ursula, 12; Carolina, 10; Catherine, 9; George, 6; Jakob, 5 and Christina, 2. They arrived at the Port of New Orleans in a sailboat. The name was changed to Gluckhertz, probably because it was written and spoken the way it was heard.

George Gluckhertz married Elizabeth Hopper, daughter of Andrew Jackson and Harriet Cox Hopper on Sept. 2, 1875. They had 11 children, four dying as small children. The children were named George Jr.; Albert; William Ozro; Louis J.; Jasper; Mary; Jacob Amada; Rosella; Ida Della; Carrie and Charlie. William Ozro married Laura Belle Poston, daughter of Louis T. and Mary Ervin Poston, on Dec. 14, 1899. Laura gave birth to two sons, Harry W. and Lewis L. Lewis died Oct. 24, 1905 and Laura died March 19, 1907. Harry was five years old when his father remarried on Feb. 17, 1908 to Lula Ann Redrick. Harry W. married Lillian Lamar on Dec. 13, 1930. They were parents of Harry Jr. (infant death); Barbara Louise (Mrs. Farris Wallace); Laura Mae (Mrs. Raymond Moore) and Charles Robert (died as a child from an accident). Harry had a daughter from a previous marriage, Monda Drucilla (Mrs. Paul Kuntze).

The Gluckhertz family, left to right, back row: Jacob Amada, William Ozro, Rosella. Middle row: George, Elizabeth, Charlie. Front row: Ida Della, Carrie

Jacob became a prominent farmer in Cape Girardeau County and married twice, to Wilhelmina Schneider Grossheider on April 24, 1875, and to Augusta Kerstner on Nov. 24, 1912. The children born to Jacob and Wilhelmina were Pauline "Polly"; Emma Marie; Louise; Ida Sophia; Laura; Lemore; Ludwig Robert and a foster son, Fred Nischwitz who married Ida Sophia.

An interesting excerpt from a book on the history of Tilsit follows: The marriage Wednesday of Jacob Gluckhertz and Mrs. Augusta Nolde Kerstner has put Ed Kerstner, druggist, in a peculiar position. The bride is Ed's mother and the groom is the father of Ed's wife, making Ed's mother his mother-in-law, his wife his mother's step-daughter, his father-in-law his stepfather, his wife his stepsister, his own daughter his niece.

Christina married Michael Zapf on Nov. 12, 1874. Michael was a prominent cigar manufacturer in the city of Cape Girardeau. They lived in Cape Girardeau and raised four children: Emma; Ella (Mrs. George Popp); Rosa (Mrs. John Meystedt) and William.

Carolina married Fred C. Bender and lived in St. Louis, where she died at the age of 57 and is buried in Concordia Cemetery.

Information on Frederika, Ursula and Catherine remains elusive. The daughters Frederika and Ursula are believed to be step-sisters to the other children. *Submitted by Laura Gluckhertz Moore*

GOHN – Our first ancestor in America was Phillip Johan Gohn Sr. He was married in Germany to Maria Sophia Bracher. They had six children: Philip Johan Jr., born in 1739; Maria Catherine, born prior to 1738; Catherine Elizabeth, born in 1741 and died before 1744; Catherine Elizabeth, born in 1744; and Adam and Johannes, both born prior to 1738. Phillip Gohn Sr. died in 1747 and Maria died in 1769. They arrived on the ship *The Thistle of Glasgow* in 1738. They came to America from Rimschweiler, Germany, because of religious persecution. They arrived via Plymouth and then settled in Pennsylvania. The family is supposedly one of the smallest Pennsylvania Dutch families.

Phillip Johan Gohn Jr. first married Elizabeth Dellinger, then a woman named Anna Elizabeth, and finally Elizabeth Oberdorff. He had the following children: Johannes "John," born in 1767; Johan Jacob, born in 1769; Johann George, born in 1772; Maria Sophia, born in 1774; Maria Elizabeth, born in 1780; Henry, born in 1801 and Johan George, born in 1777.

It is thought that Johan Jacob Gohn had six children: Phillip, born in 1790; Anna Maria, born in 1798; Susanna, born in 1801; Jacob and Samuel, born in 1807; and John (date of birth possibly prior to 1790).

John Gohn is believed to have had four children by his first wife: Samuel; John; David and Elizabeth; and five children by his second wife: Harrison; Noah; Josiah; Rebecca and Sarah.

David Josiah Gohn Sr. was born in Pennsylvania about 1813. He was a shoe cobbler and family history states he ran away from home at the age of 15 and traveled down the Ohio River on a flat boat to Cairo, IL, then on to Missouri about 1835.

He first married Anna Madden and then in 1846, married Mary Walker Dempsey, who was born about 1817. David and Mary's children are listed as: John, born about 1845; Nancy E., born about 1848; Mary C., born about 1850; Samuel H., born in 1853; Emily J., born about 1855; and David Josiah Jr., born in 1858. Mary had three children from her previous marriage to Joseph Dempsey: Van Dempsey, born in 1835; Larkin Dempsey, born in 1838; and Mary Dempsey, born in 1842. David Josiah Gohn Sr. died after 1880 and his wife Mary died by 1880.

David Josiah Gohn Jr. married Martha Evelyn Byrd in 1878. David died in 1941 and Martha died in 1932. Their children are listed as: Bertha, born in 1879, married Alfred Craft in 1901; Burley, born 1882, married Ellen Garner in 1905; Edgar, born in 1884, married May Littleton in 1918; Kelly, born 1886, married Hettie Kilbues in 1907; Gilbert, born in 1888, married Florence Littleton in 1911; Stella, born in 1893, married Webster Head in 1923; Willie Blanche, born in 1894, married T. J. Seabaugh in 1919 and died the same year; Dale, born in 1898, married Maude Medlock in 1924; and Byrd, born in 1904, married Henry Steinhoff in 1926.

The following were born to Gilbert and Florence Gohn: Dean; David; Dayton; Marjorie; Eugene; Marian and Wilma. Stella and Webster Head had two children; Webster Jr. and Martha. The following were born to Bertha and Alfred Craft: Guy; Cecil; Roscoe; Betty and Dorothy. Kelly and Hettie Gohn had seven children, among them Helen and Lester. Dale and Maude Gohn had two daughters, Virginia and Ruby. Two children were born to Burley and Ellen Gohn, Hope and Thelma. Byrd and Henry Steinhoff had five children.

Edgar and May Gohn had four children: Hazel, who married Arthur Duhaime and had one son, Timothy; Mary Dell, who married Milton Frentzel; Donald and his wife Lynnette, who had five children: Donnie; Gary; Tommy; Jimmy and Mary; and Joseph, who married Helen Masterson and had two daughters, Terri and Karen, as well as a son, Michael, from a previous marriage. *Submitted by Terri Gohn Tomlin*

GOLIGHTLY – Harold Clifton Golightly is a descendant of Jackson pioneers Milas Niblack and Mary Louisa Knott. Milas came to Missouri as a child, about 1818, from Rowan County, NC. In 1842 he married Mary Louisa Knott, daughter of John Knott and Louisa Burtles, who came from Maryland about 1836.

In 1855 Miles bought an old water mill on Goose Creek in Jackson, MO, and by 1861, he had a steam grist and saw mill operating. Milas bought up land until he had accumulated almost 700 acres. He also owned and operated a rock quarry off Bainbridge Road. In 1868 he sold the mill and became a full time farmer.

Milas and Mary built their home on a hill overlooking the mill and started a family. The house grew to about 17 rooms and it is reported that they had about 20 children, not all of them surviving. After Milas had died and all the children had grown, Mary sold the house in 1885. Later, it was struck by lightning and burned. The house was located on the Reiminger property on Michael Anna Street.

Milas died in 1869 at age 52 and Mary died in 1890. They are both buried at Old Bethel Church Cemetery. Milas and Mary's children that married and had families were: Mary Lucy (Long); Nancy Elizabeth (Dryden Morrison); Benedict Miles; George Washington; Joseph; Queen Victoria (Hickson) and Lilly.

Lilly Niblack, the youngest, was born in 1862 and in 1886 she married James Albert Baugh, son of Joel Tolbert Baugh and Frances Isabel Myers. He was born in Illinois in 1865. One day James just walked away from home and was never seen again. Lilly had two surviving daughters to care for; she worked as a cook for a Sikeston hotel and also for the Cape Girardeau County Jail. She died in 1928 and is buried at Jackson City Cemetery.

Lilly's oldest daughter, Mary Belle Baugh (1887-1943), married Henry "Uncle Bud" Clement Koehler (1878-1968), son of Fred Koehler. They had a large farm and raised 10 children. Mary and Henry are buried at Koehler Cemetery, once on their farm but now in the middle of Bent Creek Golf Course.

In 1913 Lilly's youngest daughter, Irene Baugh (1897-1966), married William Hubbard Golightly (1881-1956) of Mississippi County, MO, son of Isaac Sanford Golightly and Martha Lett. They are also buried at Koehler Cemetery.

Harold Clifton Golightly, the seventh of 11 children born to Bill and Irene, was born in 1924 in

Scott County, MO. He joined the Navy during WWII and served for 20 years. He worked for Proctor & Gamble until his retirement, and he owned and operated Golightly Greenhouse near Fruitland for 15 years.

In 1951 he married Delores Marlene Barks (descendant of Jacob Barks of Bollinger County), daughter of John Burlen Barks and Maggie Gertrude Ramsey. They had four children: Brenda; Barbara; Gary and David, and they live near Fruitland, MO. In August 2001 they celebrated their 50th wedding anniversary. *Submitted by Brenda Reynolds*

Harold and Delores Golightly, 2001

GOODWIN – Leander Allen Goodwin, the patriarch of the Goodwin family of Jackson, MO, was born in 1864 on a farm near Greenville, IL, only weeks following his father Leander Goodwin's death. He attended Valparaiso University in Indiana. There he taught school for a short time and then entered into the poultry and egg business. In 1887 he moved his business to Marion, IL, where he met and married Fannie Gillespie. In 1893 he moved his business to Lutesville, MO, where he had a home built and in which five of his eight children were born: Leana (Henderson); Helen; Walter; Robert and Frank.

In 1894 he formed a partnership with Bob Jean of Dexter, MO. The Goodwin and Jean Co. grew rapidly, becoming one of the largest wholesale poultry and egg businesses in the United States with locations in Missouri, Illinois, Kentucky, Arkansas and Tennessee – some 50 in all. In 1908 Mr. Goodwin moved to Jackson and built a modern poultry and egg processing plant at the present location of the Lenco Co. on West Main.

He purchased property in East Jackson and built his home (now a Bed and Breakfast called "The White House"). It was designed by Theodore Link, the architect for the St. Louis Union Station. Here, three more children were born; Mary Jane (Gladish) and the twins, Ray and Roy.

In 1925 Mr. Goodwin bought out his partners and the Goodwin Co. was incorporated in the state of Missouri and continued to operate following his death in 1943, until 1950, when it ceased operations.

L. A. Goodwin was a landowner with large tracts in the Delta, MO area. Mr. Goodwin and partners founded the town of Delta on land purchased from the railroad. He was active in civic affairs, as president of the Byrd Township Road District and the Jackson School Board. He was an active member of the Presbyterian Church in Jackson.

All Goodwin's sons, his son-in-law, and daughter Mary Jane worked in the Goodwin Co.: Walter at Willow Springs and Poplar Bluff; Robert in New York and Jackson; Frank at Cairo, IL; Ray at Paragould, AR; Mary Jane and Roy at Jackson; and Weston Henderson at Delta.

Two of the Goodwins were elected to public office: Roy to the State Legislature in 1948 and Robert Bryce "Bob" to Clerk of the Circuit Court in 1952. The last members of the Goodwin family to reside in Jackson were Mary Jane (Mrs. Troy Gladish) and Robert Bryce II of Cape Girardeau. Others born and raised here are: Jim Goodwin, Alton, IL; Lane Goodwin, Lacrosse, WI; L. A. Goodwin, Jonesboro, AR; Fannie Goodwin, Colorado; and Lee Gladish, Springfield, IL. *Submitted by James L. Goodwin*

GRAY – William Ronald Lynn "Ron" Gray married Esther Marie Windisch Gray on Dec. 21, 1963 in Cape Girardeau, MO. Ron and Esther both graduated from Central High School in Cape Girardeau, MO in 1961. Ron went on to obtain his B. S. Degree, Specialist Degree and Master's Degree from Southeast Missouri State University. In 1989 he received his Doctorate Degree in Administration from Southern Illinois University. He was a superintendent of schools at various schools in southern Illinois, leaving education after many years. He then began a new career with Edward Jones as an investment representative. Esther received her A.A. Degree in Nursing from the Lutheran Hospital School of Nursing, St. Louis, MO in 1964. She worked at both local hospitals and was School Nurse for Jackson R-2 School District for nearly 27 years, retiring in January 1999. Ron and Esther Gray have three sons and one daughter.

Gary L. Gray, a graduate of Jackson High School, received an Industrial Engineering Degree from the University of Missouri in 1988. He worked for Contel Communications in Alma, AR for five years, then changed careers and has been an investment representative for Edward Jones in Herrin, IL for seven years. He married Julie D. Fronabarger on June 16, 1990. She was a graduate of Jackson High School and a graduate of the University of Missouri with her B. S. Degree in Education. They have two children, Megan Lyndale and Max Lyndale Gray. They make their home in Herrin, IL.

Sean A. Gray graduated from Jackson High School and received a B. S. in Agri-business from Southeast Missouri State University in 1989. He previously worked for Skyview Animal Clinic and at present is farming and working for Dana Corporation in Cape Girardeau. He married Mary E. James on March 9, 1991. She is a graduate of Central High School and received her B. S. Degree in Elementary Education in 1991 from Southeast Missouri State University and now is a teacher at the Junior High in Cape Girardeau. They have two daughters, Micayla Colleen and Jessica Mae Gray. They make their home on their farm in Whitewater, MO.

Ron and Esther Gray with their children and grandchildren, and Esther's mother, Esther Windisch

Brian W. Gray graduated from Jackson High School, received his B. S. Degree in Criminal Justice at Southeast Missouri State University in 1991 and his Master's in Administration from Southeast Missouri State University in 1994. At present he is a Federal Probation and Parole Officer. He married Joanna Joy Allen from Sikeston on Aug. 6, 1988. Joanna received her A.A. Degree in Nursing in 1990 from Southeast Missouri State University and at present is a school nurse for Jackson R-2 School District. They have two children, Brianna Marie and Joseph Allen Gray. They make their home in Crystal Springs Estates between Cape Girardeau and Jackson, MO.

Angel M. Gray Niswonger graduated from Jackson High School and received her B. A. Degree in Art Education from Southeast Missouri State University in 1992. She married Jaime K. Niswonger, also a graduate of Jackson High School on July 7, 1990. Jaime received a Computer Engineering Degree from the University of Missouri at Columbia in 1993. They have three children; Colten Kieth, Rachel Erin and Braden Lynn Niswonger. They make their home in Lee's Summit, MO. *Submitted by Dr. Ron and Esther Gray*

GREEN – On a cold Thursday, March 2, 1939, a baby daughter was born to Arnold and Vera (Davis) Farrow at the family farm in "Pinkroot Hollow" near Leemon. The child's grandparents were John Henry and Lillie (Kraemer) Farrow of Oriole and John C. and Esther (Cox) Davis of Neely's Landing. She was named Marcella after a singer her mother had heard on the radio. Marcella was the first grandchild for both the Farrow and Davis families. Her aunts were delighted and, according to them, she became the "apple of their eye." When she was about 17 months, her Aunt Zeta Davis took her to Homecomers, where her first picture was taken. About 2-1/2 years after Marcella's birth, a new baby sister, La Fern, joined the family.

When Marcella was about 5, she began helping her parents on the farm. She would walk up a dry creek bottom and bring the cows from the fields to the barn in the late afternoon. She rode old "Red," the horse, with her daddy's help and together they went fishing. She especially liked it when he took her "coon" hunting one night and she got to hold the lantern when the dogs treed a "coon." She also liked to watch her mother milk and use a separator to skim the cream from the milk. When her daddy got a job delivering ice, she rode along and watched as he took the big tongs, lifted the block of ice from the truck, and took it to a house with a sign in a window that indicated ice was needed for their icebox.

In April 1945, Arnold was called into the service. He moved his family into Jackson and he asked the girls' Aunt Lillie Davis to live with them until he could return home.

In the fall of 1945, Marcella entered school. After living in the country for six years, the "big" city of Jackson, and especially the "big" school were frightening. She wore her flowered feed sack dresses and when winter came, she wore long cotton socks held up by garters. Marcella was so skinny that her socks kept falling down. Her mother got her a garter belt to help hold them up. Finally, in third grade, she was allowed to wear anklets.

Marcella's first picture; Marcella Farrow, Homecomers 1940

Marcella grew and made many friends. In high school, she became interested in writing and art. She worked on the *Squawler* newspaper and took as many art classes as possible. She was awarded an art achievement medal at the graduation ceremony her junior year. She graduated from Jackson High in 1957.

After much encouragement from her parents, she began attending Southeast Missouri State College. In 1961, she became the first grandchild from both sides of her family to graduate from college. Her degree was in Elementary Education. Marcella taught elementary school for 30 years, mostly in Jackson. She retired in 1992.

She, her husband J. D., and two of their three children and families reside in Jackson. *Submitted by Marcella (Farrow) Green*

GREEN - Many times, while enjoying a Sunday afternoon drive in and around the Jackson area, I've admired a stately old house no longer in use, and often in desperate need of repair. I've tried to imagine its first occupants, the people whose dream it was to build a home on that particular plot of land. I look for obvious signs that it was built with love and anticipation; that the family was excited to inhabit such a dwelling. I see strategically placed shade trees, now bowed and gnarled with age, and envision children climbing and swinging from their branches. I notice unkempt, but still beautiful rose briars and day lilies persistently climbing along the feeble remains of a yard fence, and imagine the hands that lovingly planted and nurtured the young seedlings. The old outbuildings, clothesline posts, smokehouses, and the occasional ancient implement reminds me that life was hard, and survival depended on the family's cooperation and work ethics. The old houses seem somehow lonely now.

Such is the old log house that sits atop the hill of my parents' property. The trees, the roses, the outbuildings, the obvious signs of a hardworking family remain. The difference, however, is that its past and its inhabitants are not a mystery, for the home was built by my great-grandfather, John Green.

Front row: John Green, Matilda Green, Martha Stovall Green. Back row: Bert Green and William Fred Green

John Green was born July 3, 1865 near Millersville. In his late teens, he moved to a tiny community called "Terrapin Neck" (about three miles south of Burfordville) to work at the old Snider Mill. It wasn't long before he met and fell in love with Miss Martha Stovall (b. Sept. 4, 1868). They were married in 1887, and John began building the two-story poplar log home for his bride. The young family stayed busy carving a "life" out of the wilderness. John ran a blacksmith shop, repairing wagons and equipment for the area farmers. Martha stayed busy with household chores, gardening, preserving food for the winter months, and raising the children: Bert, born in 1889; Fred, born in 1891; Mary, born in 1893 (died at age 2); and Matilda, born in 1895.

The house, though not fancy, was built for a family. A porch stretches across the front, another one off the kitchen in the back. There is a window and an outside door for each room on the first floor, allowing the summer breezes to flow gently throughout the house. A stove placed between the bedroom and parlor warmed the chilly winter nights. The second-story loft was bedroom to the boys. The kitchen, just large enough to prepare the meals and seat the family, was most certainly a favorite gathering place.

Living in a somewhat remote area did not keep my great-grandmother from exposing her children to music. She ordered an old-time pump organ and great-grandfather built on a "parlor" room to house it. Their son Fred, (my grandfather) played guitar, fiddle, and banjo. Everyone sang. I can only imagine the fun-filled family entertainment pumped from that old parlor organ. The organ is still in the family, having been passed down to Matilda's heirs who live in Oak Ridge.

Of course, every farm must have a barn. The original barn burned to the ground after having been struck by lightning, so great-grandfather and the boys built a large new barn in 1914, a strong, sturdy structure. The boys, Bert and Fred, carved the date in one of the beams, preserving that bit of history still today.

Bert and Fred moved to St. Louis as young men, married and raised their families there. My grandfather (Fred) worked as a foreman for Valley and Florsheim Shoe Companies in St. Louis and Chicago, but always kept close contact with his southeast Missouri roots. His daughters, Viola and Mildred, often spent their summers on the Green farm, hiking across the fields, fishing along Whitewater River, and helping their grandmother with the cooking and canning.

John Green died in November 1921. Martha lived alone on the farm until the 1940s. She died in April 1949. Both are buried alongside their baby daughter, Mary, in the McGuire Cemetery near Burfordville.

The old log house, barn, and farm had been out of the family for several years when Fred's daughter Mildred and her husband Bill Smith (my parents) purchased some of the property in 1974. They built a new home on the west side of the farm, and still use the old barn built by her grandfather. My dad (Bill) continues to mow and maintain the old log house, using it to store bits and pieces of our past.

The roses still climb on the fence, the day lilies still bloom, and children still romp and play in the yard ... but now they are Mildred's grandchildren and great-grandchildren. Perhaps the old house is not so lonely after all, for she has sheltered many through the years. Six generations (all descendants of the Green clan) have played in her yard, and conversed idly on her front porch. *Submitted by Jean Smith Schweain*

GREEN – The Robert George Green family moved into Jackson in 1952. Robert was the son of George and Hulda (Bailey) Green. On Nov. 21, 1923 he married Maggie Elizabeth Grindstaff, daughter of Jefferson and Mary Elizabeth Seabaugh. Six children were born to this union: Robert Junior; Virgie; Annie Jean; J. D.; Dayton and Ruth Ann.

Prior to living in Jackson, the Greens had lived on various farms where Robert helped the owners with their crops and livestock. In return, housing was provided as well as a share in the proceeds when the livestock was sold. They had a plot of ground to plant a garden and they raised their own hogs and chickens. The last farmer Robert worked for was Linder Miller. The Millers provided them a house near Cane Creek school and this is where they began their education. They hunted in the woods, fished and swam in the nearby creek.

When they lived on the farm, the Green family loved to come into Jackson to sell eggs, shop, and visit with all of the other area farm workers. One of the highlights in town was the Palace Theater. Robert Green became acquainted with Robert K. Wilson, owner of the theater. Mr. Wilson learned that Robert Green liked to joke around and always seemed so happy. He also knew Mr. Green liked western movies and even though movie tickets were 5 to 10 cents for children and 15 cents for adults, R. K. Wilson also knew Robert Green often could not afford to buy the tickets. Many times he gave the whole family free passes.

The Greens also liked to visit Roloff's Store. If they had a nickel, the children would buy a double dip ice cream cone. Orange and green pineapple were among their favorites. Robert Junior and J. D. remember at least 12 homemade flavors were sold.

Robert and Maggie Green

In December of 1944, Robert Junior entered the Army during WWII. He was shipped to the South Pacific. While he was there, he ran into a fellow Jackson resident, Leo Roloff, who was a cook aboard one of the ships. Once, his ship sank not far from shore. He held onto his duffle bag and swam to land. The war was over before he could participate. After he returned home, he married Nellie Statler and they moved into Jackson.

In the fifties and early sixties, three of the Green family, Robert, Robert Junior and J. D., all worked at La Pierre-Sawyer Handle factory. Robert retired from the factory, but the boys went on to other employment.

Robert Junior and Nellie became parents of a daughter, Alice. They have one grandchild. Virgie married Raymond Smith and moved to the St. Louis suburbs. After Raymond retired, they returned to Jackson. Annie Jean married Harold Pruitt. They have two daughters, Christine and Donna. They live in Cape Girardeau. J. D. married Marcella Farrow. They have three children, Jennifer, Christopher and Stephen, and two grandchildren. Dayton married Katie Runnels. They have a son, Kenneth, and a daughter, Kristal. They have two grandchildren. Dayton has a daughter, Teresa, from a previous marriage. Ruth Ann married Wayne Mayfield. They have three sons, Danny, Gary and Kevin, and five grandchildren. They live in Delta. *Submitted by J. D. Green*

GRINDSTAFF – Frank Grindstaff was a descendant of the Jacob and Christina Barks family. Jacob Grindstaff (b. 1790-d. 1867) was born in Burke County, NC. According to statistics, there are Grindstaffs living in 38 of the 50 states, with the majority of them living in the Tennessee area.

Henry Frank Grindstaff (b. March 1885, d. July 1970) was the son of Joseph Grindstaff (b. 1857, d. 1895) and Sarah A. Barks (b. 1864, d. 1936). The family lived in the Patton and Sedgewickville Communities most of their lives.

Frank married Ida Catherine Fellows (b. January 1887, d. March 1986) on Oct. 25, 1906 in Perryville, MO. Ida and Frank lived in the Sedgewickville and Patton areas most of their lives, with the exception of a few years when they lived in the St. Louis area. Frank was a farmer most of his life until his later years, which were spent in the town of Sedgewickville. He enjoyed fishing and hunting until ill health kept him from being able to enjoy these pleasures. Ida was a housewife and homemaker. She enjoyed all types of needlework including quilting, crocheting and embroidery. During her life she made dozens of quilts that she shared with her children and grandchildren. To this day, her descendants are still enjoying her beautiful handiwork and keeping warm, as well as proudly displaying the splendidly crafted works. Ida lived to be 99 years and 2 months old.

Ida was the daughter of Emmanuel Fellows (b. 1861, d. 1938) and Luviesa Statler Fellows (b. 1861, d. 1964). Luviesa Fellows lived to be 102 years old and was still active baking bread, coffee cakes and such until she was 95 years old and fell and broke a hip. Then she was bedfast most of the time until her death. Ida had two brothers, Robert and Harvey Fellows, and two sisters, Mary Statler and Rosa Propst. Her two sisters and brother Robert all lived to be in their late nineties. Harvey was the youngest in the family and passed away at the age of 69.

Frank and Ida Grindstaff, 1910

Frank had two brothers, Daniel and Jesse Grindstaff, and one sister, Rosa. He also had a half-brother, William Pridemore.

Frank and Ida had two sons, Loy E. (b. May 1911), who now lives in Festus, MO and Perry Harvey (b. August 1920, d. September 1996), who resided in Jackson, MO. Loy married Edna Richey. They have two daughters, Pat Blow and Kathy Mason, and four grandsons, Steve and Aaron Blow and Marshall and Dalton Mason. Perry married Marjorie Birk of Jackson, in 1947. They have one son, Bradley Grindstaff, of Osaka, Japan; one daughter, Brenda Sue Grindstaff Ferst of Tallahassee, FL; two granddaughters, Melanie and Amanda Grindstaff; and two grandsons, Christopher Grindstaff and Joel Perry Ferst. *Submitted by Marjorie Grandstaff*

GRINDSTAFF – Perry Harvey Grindstaff was born Aug. 16, 1920 in Alliance, MO, son of Henry Frank Grindstaff (March 21, 1885 – July 22, 1970) and Ida (Fellows) Grindstaff (Jan. 9, 1887 – March 2, 1986). Perry lived in the Jackson and Sedgewickville areas most of his life, except when the family lived in St. Louis for a few years when Perry was a young child. He remembers his mother speak of the "old Indian trail," known commonly as the Trail of Tears, which was Route K near their Sedgewickville home. Perry had one brother, Loy Grindstaff, who lives in Festus, MO.

Following graduation from Oak Ridge High School in 1938, Perry began a lifelong career at McCombs Furniture and Funeral Home. He became a partner and co-owner in 1955. Although not formally introduced, Perry and Marjorie Birk (born Nov. 11, 1925) would speak almost daily, as Perry stood in front of McCombs Furniture Store, 116 South High, and Marjorie walked to town for lunch from Jackson High School.

After graduating from Jackson High School in 1943, Marjorie worked at the Jackson Hosiery Mill five years until she and Perry married on Nov. 22, 1947. She then worked part-time at McCombs. Daughter of Theodore Charles Birk (Dec. 27, 1888 – April 7, 1982) and Addie (Bennett) Birk (Feb. 1, 1895 – Aug. 18, 1954), Marjorie has five sisters and one brother.

On leave from McCombs, Perry served in the U. S. Army, 378th Infantry, 95th Division, from July 1942 until November 1945, seeing action in Northern France, Rhineland, and Central Europe during WWII. In December 1946 he helped organize the Jackson National Guard, Company E, 140th Infantry, and served as Company Commander. In September 1963 he retired with 20 years combined service from the Guard and Army.

Left to right, top row standing: Steven and Brenda Ferst. Seated: Brad and Chiyoka Grindstaff, Melanie and Amanda Grindstaff, Marjorie and Perry Grindstaff

Marjorie formally met Perry after he returned from WWII. Materials to manufacture automobiles were scarce so Perry sometimes borrowed his father's coupe or, for 35 cents, hired a taxicab to travel the three miles to Marjorie's home. After a Gene Autry or Roy Rogers movie at Jackson's Palace Theatre, admission about 30 cents, they'd head to Roloff's Grocery for a 10 cent double-dip cone.

At the time of their marriage, the funeral home was located in the former Presbyterian Parsonage, 417 North High Street. They lived in the funeral home's upstairs apartment until 1965 when they built a new home at 614 Morgan Street. After they retired in January 1988, they built a new home on Pecan Lane, where Marjorie still resides. Perry passed away Sept. 20, 1996 at age 76.

The furniture store was sold in 1976. Now called Ross Furniture, it's still at the same High Street location. McCombs built a new funeral home on Route D in 1971, its present location. Before 911 and paramedics, funeral homes provided emergency ambulance services as well, including positioning themselves at Jackson High School's football games. Normally not an amusing profession, the Grindstaffs once received a 3:00 a.m. telephone call from county authorities that a man had hung himself from the I-55 overpass. Perry rushed to the scene only to discover that it was a prank, probably by local college kids, and "the victim" was a dangling dummy.

Standing: Christopher, Melanie and Amanda Grindstaff, children of Brad and Chiyoka Grindstaff. Seated: Joel Perry Ferst, son of Steven and Brenda Ferst, and Marjorie Grindstaff, grandmother of the four children

The Grindstaffs were active members of Jackson's St. Paul Lutheran Church, American Legion Post 158 and its Auxiliary, Girl Scouts, Boy Scouts, Rotary, the Chamber of Commerce, and many other community organizations. Marjorie was a charter board member of the Cape Girardeau County health unit and an American Cancer Society volunteer for over 45 years. She's still active in church and many community projects. They each received the Jackson Chamber of Commerce's R. A. Fulenwider Meritorious Community Service Award.

They were blessed with two children and four grandchildren. Brad Grindstaff lives with wife Chiyoka and children Melanie, Amanda and Christopher in Osaka, Japan. Brenda and husband Steven Ferst and son Joel Perry live in Tallahassee, FL. *Submitted by Marjorie (Birk) Grindstaff*

GUTH – The development and expansion of Guth Brothers Block and Brick Company of Cape Girardeau years ago has been tangible proof of the opportunities in private enterprise for those who visualize, plan and work the plan. Vernon Harry Guth and his brother began in 1947 with a hand operation which produced 25 concrete blocks a day.

Vernon was born in 1920 in Raddle, IL, the son of Otto and Paula (Fuehler) Guth. His father died when Vernon was 1 year old, and he was then raised by his grandparents in the Shawneetown, MO area. Mr. Guth attended local schools and then worked for local farmers in the area until 1946.

In that year, he and his brother started a small garage business on Highway 61 north of Jackson. It was at this location a year later, with a hand-operated block machine, that they first produced 25 blocks a day. As the demand for blocks increased, more modernized equipment was purchased. In 1957 the plant was moved to Cape Girardeau, where in an 8-hour shift 7,000 blocks could be produced daily, completely automated, a long way from the hand operation which produced 25 blocks a day. In 1961 a total of two million units were manufactured. As the demand for concrete blocks increased, more modern equipment was purchased and the company continued to grow.

Vernon Harry Guth

In August 1973, Guth Brothers Block and Brick Company was sold to Max Stovall, who continued the operation for years. Mr. Guth and his wife, Jacqueline, then fulfilled Mr. Guth's dream to travel the United States, Canada and Mexico in their Airstream travel trailer.

Vernon and first wife, Mabel, lived in Jackson. They are parents of Margaret (wife of Bob Pfeiffer), Jackson residents; Laverne (wife of Jerry Krauss) of Perryville, MO; and Richard (Anita) Guth of Charlotte, NC. All were educated in Jackson schools. The grandchildren include Tim Pfeiffer, Melissa Pfeiffer Spiegel, and Kirby and Kelly Krauss. There are two great-grandchildren, Mallory Krauss and Melinda Pfeiffer.

Mr. Guth and his wife, Jacqueline (daughter of Gus and Frieda Schaefer), have enjoyed retirement in Arizona for the last 25 years. *Submitted by Jacqueline Guth*

HAHN – Lucinda Stroder, daughter of Daniel and Matilda Caroline Wells Stroder, married John J. Hahn on July 2, 1885. Lucinda was born May 3,

1867 and died Aug. 11, 1952. John was born March 13, 1863 and died Jan. 25, 1933. They are both buried at Stroder Cemetery.

Children of John and Lucinda were: Daniel, born April 5, 1886, died as an infant. Elijah Cornelius, born Dec. 9, 1887, married Sarah Ellen Welker on Dec. 24, 1922. Their four children were Wilma Eileen, Lela Lorene, Johnny J. and Virginia Lou. John Amos, born March 4, 1890, married Charity E. Slinkard on Oct. 5, 1911. Emma, born April 12, 1892, married Joe Cummins on Dec. 24, 1921. Cloly, born May 6, 1894, married Mark York. Jesse L., born July 10, 1896, married Mattie E. Rhodes on June 24, 1933. Dewey, born Aug. 2, 1898, married Ruby Angle on Jan. 30, 1926. Lewis Albert, born Aug. 20, 1900, married Zenobis Summers on March 26, 1927. Joseph S., born Nov. 5, 1901, married Opal Brown on Nov. 13, 1926. Martha J., born Nov. 20, 1903 married Bert Kinder on Feb. 11, 1928. Lester, born March 12, 1906, married Ora Lee Filer on Aug. 24, 1932. Eula Virginia, born July 20, 1909, married Marvin Bollinger on Aug. 27, 1932. Luther Ed, born May 28, 1912, married Lillian Brown on July 13, 1932. *Submitted by Marilyn Fronabarger*

HAHS – John Conrad Hahs came to Missouri in 1801 with the pioneer, George Bollinger, from Lincoln County, NC. He was granted 640 arpens of land on Big Whitewater, according to the *History of Missouri* by Louis Houck. The German/Swiss families who came with Bollinger from the Carolinas, were a sturdy stock who were good farmers and used to hard labor. John Hahs' family was no exception. Houck's census of Nov. 1, 1803, for John "Hoss" inventory, Cape Girardeau County, was the following: 10 bushels of wheat, 200 bushels of corn, 80 lbs. of flax and hemp, 400 lbs. of cotton, 500 lbs. of maple syrup, 10 head of cattle and 4 horses.

Writings show that one of the oldest and most primitive mills erected by the early settlers in the area was located 1-1/2 miles from Sedgewickville at the foot of a hill. This mill erected by John Hahs shortly after settling here was known as the "pounding mill." A strong spring supplied the power for the mill, which could crush one-half bushel of grain at a time. Four families who resided in the vicinity used Hahs' mill to get their wheat ground. It is believed these were the Conrad Statlers, Peter Statlers, and a family of Seabaughs, along with the John Hahs.

The interior of this home is a log cabin built by John Conrad Hahs' grandson, John Hahs, in 1853. It was enlarged and is presently the home of the great-great-grandson of John Conrad, Cletus and wife Stella Hahs

According to several accounts of the day, the journey to America made by the Hahs family began in the country of Switzerland, probably moving to the Rhine Valley of Germany before starting the long trek by way of the Netherlands to America. The immense migration from the Palitinate area was the result of William Penn encouraging the German people to settle his land of Pennsylvania given to him by the King of England. The long arduous journey took months to float the Rhine River to the Netherlands and await a ship in England for the long ocean trip to America. It's amazing anyone survived, as the worst horrifying segment of the journey was the months on the open seas. Disease and crowded conditions took its toll.

It is not exactly certain when John's ancestor, Jacob Hahs, landed in Philadelphia; however, it is recorded that he moved from Pennsylvania before 1770 as he bought his first North Caroline land on Oct. 13, 1770 on Clarks Creek. With other land purchases made over the years, Jacob's land holdings grew to a total 1000 acres. Jacob had a brother Christian who also traveled the Great Philadelphia Wagon Road to North Carolina.

Jacob and his wife Elizabeth had four sons in North Carolina: Francis; Anthony, (both of whom remained in North Carolina); Christian who moved to Brown County, OH; and John (born c. 1754) who journeyed by wagon to Cape Girardeau County, MO in 1801. John's first wife, Christina Susanna, died and is buried in North Carolina. Records show John remarried an Elizabeth James (b. 1760 or 1770) on July 7, 1801 before coming to Missouri. John and Christina Susanna had three daughters and five sons: Barbara; Maria; Margaret; John; Jacob (born c. 1780s); Adam (born c. 1790); Francis; and Daniel (born 1800). It is believed John and Elizabeth were parents of Christopher in 1805 after moving to Missouri. Eleven people were living on John's farm in Houck's *History of Missouri* in 1803.

John Conrad Hahs' will, dated February 1809, reveals names of three daughters, Maria, Barbara, and Margaret, with the boys listed as minors. The will stated each daughter would receive one spinning wheel, a feather bed, dutch oven, and two cows. As the boys came of age, it was John's wishes they settle upon "the plantation" with the land divided upon the death of his wife Elizabeth. At that time, a public auction would take place and the money equally divided among the daughters and sons. Elizabeth and John's neighbor and friend, Peter Statler, were executors. Listed as witness was Samuel Weiberg, the minister brought by Bollinger to serve the new inhabitants of the Whitewater area.

It is wise to assume all "Hahs" families of Missouri and other states are a part of the lineage of John Conrad Hahs, pioneer who traveled by wagon from the North Carolina piedmont. *Compiled by Beverly K. Hahs*

HALL - Jane Hall was the daughter of John Irby who was born Feb. 5, 1791 in North Carolina. He was in the War of 1812 and he died May 13, 1870. He was married Aug. 30, 1817 in Wilson County, TN, to Nancy Harris who was born Oct. 15, 1800 and who died Dec. 30, 1868. Both are buried in Little Spring Cemetery in Hamilton, IL.

James Russell Hall was the son of James Mathew Hall who was born in 1788 in Anson County, NC. A farmer, he loved his church. He died in 1828 in Saline County, IL. He was married in Tennessee to Amanda Boone, who was born 1799/1800.

James Mathew Hall was the son of John Hall who was born in 1765 in Anson County, NC. He was in the Revolutionary War and died Aug. 26, 1822. He is buried in the Old Ruff Cemetery in Illinois. He was married in September 1784 in Anson County, NC, to Mary Polly Broadway who was born in 1767 and who died Aug. 31, 1855. John and Mary Hall were the parents of Patty Eaton, Joseph, William, Henry, John Jr., Sarah Williams, Mary McFarland, Archibald, Elizabeth Betsy Rodgers, Rebecca Flint, and James Mathew.

John Hall was the son of Henry Hall who was born about 1735. He was a farmer and he married in Anson County, NC.

John Irby came from Wilson County, TN, to Illinois, in 1838. He was the son of Hennesy Henry Irby who was born in 1775 and who died in 1793 in Newberry, SC. He married Mary Polly Henderson who died in 1802. She was the daughter of James Henderson and Nancy Ann Dunlap.

Alta Idler Hall was born Feb. 9, 1899 in St. Francis, AR, and died May 8, 1985 in Cape Girardeau; she is buried in Russell Heights Cemetery. She was married Aug. 3, 1916 in Kennett, MO, to William Lynn Allen who was born June 25, 1896 in Oak Ridge, MO, and who died April 2, 1961 in Whitewater, MO, in the old schoolhouse, the home of his daughter Hattie. He was the son of William Harve Allen and Sarah Sally Jean Stearns. William Lynn and Alta Allen were the parents of Lee Roy, J. C., George William, Tommy Gene, Oscar Ray, Hattie Slinkard, Mary Niswonger, Anna Rumfelt, and Joe Lynn.

Alta Idler Allen was the daughter of George Allen Hall who was born April 4, 1858 in Benton, IL, and who died Nov. 12, 1932; he is buried in the Lulu Cemetery in Arbyrd, MO. He worked for the railroad and was also a farmer. He was married Oct. 31, 1878 to Lou Celia Priscilla Scholl Lane who was born Aug. 6, 1850 in Washington County, IL, and who died Oct. 15, 1912 in Arbyrd, MO. She was a Cherokee Indian and the daughter of William Isaac Lane who was born in 1829 in Tennessee and who died in Illinois. He was married Nov. 6, 1848 to Sylvai Silvy Stricklin who was born in 1831 in Washington County, IL.

George Allen Hall was the son of James Russell Hall who was born Jan. 13, 1814 in Maury County, TN. He was in the Civil War and he died April 30, 1879. He married Jane Janitha Irby who was born in 1821 in Tennessee and who died March 3, 1883. Both are buried in Sullen's Cemetery in Franklin County, IL. James Russell and Janita Hall were the parents of Nancy Carter, Mathew Boone, Mahula, Martha, Mary Ann, John Russell, Hanna, and George Allen.

Hennesy Irby was the son of Joseph Lafayette Irby who was born Sept. 7, 1738 in Culpepper, VA, and who died Nov. 19, 1798 in North Carolina. He was married in 1752 to Mary Francis Carter at Haynes Station. She was born in 1736 in Newberry County, SC, and she died in 1797.

William Isaac Lane was the son of Thomas Lane who was born in 1795 in Tennessee. He married Milly Celia Scholl who was born in 1792 in South Carolina. She was a Cherokee Indian and the daughter of Joseph Scholl who was born in 1755 and died in 1835. He was married in 1785 to Levina Boone who was born in 1766 and who died in 1802. Joseph Scholl was the son of William Scholl and Leah Morgan.

Levina Scholl was the daughter of Colonel Daniel Boone who was born Oct. 22, 1734 and who died Sept. 26, 1820. He was married in North Carolina on Aug. 14, 1756 to Rebecca Bryan who was born Jan. 9, 1739 and who died March 18, 1813. She was the daughter of Joseph Bryan who died about 1805 and who was married to Alee.

Amanda Hall was the daughter of Enoch Morgan Boone who was born Oct. 16, 1777 and who died March 8, 1862. He was married Feb. 8, 1797 to Elizabeth Lucy Goldman who was born in 1775. Enoch Morgan Boone was the son of Squire Boone who was born in 1744 and who died in 1815. He married Jan VanCleve who was born in 1744 and who died in 1829. Squire was a brother to Daniel Boone. *Submitted by Hattie Ferne "Hap" Slinkard*

HARTLE – Emanuel Hartle was born Feb. 17, 1838 on the family farm west of Millersville, that has been in the Hartle family since the early 1800s when his grandfather, Peter Hartle, and family settled here. Emanuel's parents were Jesse and Sarah Sally Seabaugh Hartle.

Emanuel's grandfather was Peter, born 1745/1750 in the Germanic Lowlands of Germany. He arrived on the ship *Minerva* Sept. 17, 1771 in the port of Philadelphia. After a brief period in Lancaster, PA, he acquired a farm in Cumberland County near the town of Carlisle, staying there for the next 10 years. On a visit to Hagerstown, MD, he met Elizabeth Reiter. They were married Feb. 25, 1778 in Washington County, MD.

Peter served in the Continental Army in 1780 and 1781, participating in the battle of Yorktown. After his wife died, he married Elizabeth Masters and brought his family to the Whitewater Township where the Hartles lived for many years. Peter died in 1819; it is said he was the first one buried in the Hartle Cemetery.

Peter's grandson Emanuel, after completing a common school education, became a farmer. At one time he owned over 1000 acres in Cape Girardeau and Bollinger Counties. In the Civil War, he became a member of Col. Kitchen's Regiment, Price Brigade in 1864, and was in several historic battles. When he returned to his home, he resumed farming.

Emanuel and Sarah Adeline (Yount) Hartle

Emanuel married Sarah Adeline Yount March 21, 1867; she was the daughter of John S. Yount and Annie Elizabeth Schell (Shell). They were the parents of seven children: Carrie married Dr. John Jefferson Mayfield Aug. 9, 1887; Revie married Warren Smith; Katie Maggie married Dr. Amon Mayfield Aug. 27, 1893; Jessie M. married Lorenzo Miller April 5, 1895; Cora married Brown Clippard; Fred married Jacie Gladish Feb. 9, 1910; and Myrtle married Ernest Miller.

Emanuel retired from farming, purchased a home in west Jackson and took life easy. On April 14, 1919 he died at his home in west Jackson, a few days after his wife died. Both are buried at the Hartle Cemetery. The cemetery is located eight and one-half miles west of Jackson on Highway 72 to Millersville, one and six-tenths miles past Millersville, left on the gravel road (352), and in two miles turn right in a small lane (100 yds.) leading to the cemetery. *Submitted by B. J. Knehans*

HARTLE – John Fred Hartle was born April 28, 1912 on the family farm west of Millersville, the same farm his great-great-grandfather Peter Hartle settled on in 1801. He was the son of Fred and Jacie (Gladish) Hartle. His great-grandfather was Mastin Gladish, born in 1812 in Kentucky, the son of Richard R. and Marian (Lampley) Gladish. He moved his family to Illinois in 1849. The next year they moved to Burfordville, MO.

Mastin's son, Washington, married Mary Strong, daughter of Samuel Augusta and Lavina Helderman Strong. Their children were William, Jettie and Silas. Lavina died in 1882. In 1885 Washington married his first wife's sister, Margaret Elizabeth Strong. Their children were Jacie, Zaida and Troy.

John Fred married Maxine Seabaugh in 1942, the daughter of John Otto and Sally Caroline (Green) Seabaugh. They had one daughter, Judy Kay, born in 1946. She married first J. C. Bond, and second Robert A. Leuthold. John Fred and his brother, Troy, attended the Hartle School on the farm until the family moved to Jackson in 1924.

His father, Fred, was sheriff of Cape Girardeau County from 1936 to 1940. The family lived above the jail and Jacie, his mother, cooked for and fed the prisoners.

John Fred graduated from Jackson High School as big chief. He went to the University of Oklahoma for two years on a sports scholarship during which time he excelled in football, basketball and track. When in a football game and extra points were needed, they called for "Automatic John" (John Fred) to set the kick for extra points. He seldom missed and the crowd cheered! He transferred to St. Louis University, again with a sports scholarship. After graduating he returned to Jackson, where jobs were scarce. He went to work in the International Shoe Factory. J. F. purchased his uncle's farm for delinquent taxes earned from working in the factory and farming. He served in the U. S. Navy from 1942 to 1945 with the rank of Chief Petty Officer. He and Maxine lived on the farm west of Jackson city limits. Today the R. O. Hawkins Junior High and other schools are on the Hartle's original farm.

J. F farmed and also had a dairy, and he was the first to introduce Charlois cattle in Cape Girardeau County. This thrilled him greatly! He was on the Jackson School Board when the Jackson R-2 School District was formed. J. F. retired from the Soil Conservation Service as a technician in 1983; he was a member of the First Presbyterian Church, Althenhal-Joern American Legion Post 158, Jackson Optimist Club and Jackson Bowling League.

John Fred was always interested in sports. He was in many Senior Olympics. He overcame many health complications to enjoy physical and athletic competition in his 70s. He was an amazing gentleman. In his early sixties, Hartle had surgery to correct a problem with his aorta, by Dr. DeBakey at M. D. Anderson Hospital in Houston TX. John Fred and Maxine lived wonderful family-oriented lives and passed away four months apart in 1992. Both were buried in Russell Heights Cemetery. They were missed by many, as they contributed much. *Submitted by Judy Hartle Leuthold*

HARTLE - The first Hartle in Cape Girardeau County arrived in 1802, ending a long journey that had begun in Holland. Born about 1750, Peter Hartle emigrated from Holland to Philadelphia in 1771. After serving in the Revolutionary War, Peter married Maryland's Elizabeth Reiter. Peter and Elizabeth started their family in North Carolina before the long trek to Missouri. In 1819, Peter was buried in the Hartle cemetery just west of Millersville.

Among Peter's many grandchildren was Ransom Bettis Hartle (1840-1917), who married Mary Elizabeth Welty. Four of Ransom and Mary's nine children (Verbit, Ernest, Eva, and Odney) have descendants still living in the Jackson area. Verbit Bettis Hartle worked at Harris Motor in Cape Girardeau, where his daughter Pauline Rawlings continues to live, having survived her brother Cauvey and husband Jack Rawlings. After banking in Sikeston for a while, Ernest returned to work the Hartle farm west of Millersville. His children include Harold (deceased), Janice Miller, Margie Risha, and Ransom Bettice (RB). Eva married Fred M. Burford and lived in Burfordville with her children Paul, Seibert, and Hubert.

Dr. Odney Willis Hartle, shown in the accompanying photograph, practiced medicine in Fornfelt and Ancel (now Scott City). He died in 1914, leaving his young widow Mary Crites to care for three children, Wilma, Harry, and Homer Bettis. Mary Crites Hartle stayed in Millersville till her death in 1976, eventually living in a four-generation household with her daughter Wilma and Wilma's husband George Miller, their daughter Mary Don and her husband Jack Randol, and Mary Don and Jack's children. Wilma and George's son Mac also still farms in Millersville with his wife Sue Hanners Miller. Annabelle Wofford Hartle, the widow of Harry Hartle, lives in Millersville. Annabelle and Harry's children Roger and Shirley (Mrs. Roy) Holmes and their children live and work in the Jackson area. Homer B. Hartle was in education and construction. In his retirement, he became an amateur historian, chronicling the Hartle family among other topics of interest, and writing weekly columns for the Jackson Journal from 1966 to 1971. He married Lois Houk, with whom he had two daughters, Kathlyn and Betty. Kathlyn (Mrs. Archie) Hahs recently moved from Cape Girardeau to Wisconsin, and Betty (Mrs. Bob) Goza is retired in Jackson after a 35-year career as the Secretary of the Jackson R-2 School Board.

Dr. Odney Willis Hartle

This is only one of many branches of the descendants of Peter Hartle. The Hartle descendants have continued their cross-country trek, and now populate the states of Wisconsin, California, Washington, Illinois, and North Carolina. *Submitted by Betty Goza*

HARTLE – Robert Hartle is the son of John Fred (1882-1976) and Jacie Cheatum Hartle (1886-1966). Robert was born Nov. 3, 1918 on the farm that his great-great-grandfather, Peter Hartle, settled on in 1801. Peter is one of the first buried in the Hartle Cemetery that was located on Peter's farm. Many of his descendants are buried there.

Robert's family, Fred and Jacie, moved to Jackson in 1924. Fred owned about 1200 acres in Cape Girardeau and Bollinger Counties at that time. Fred and Jacie had three boys, all born on the Hartle Farm; John Fred (1912-1992), Troy Emanuel (1913-1997) and Robert. After graduating from Jackson High in 1937, Robert went to Southeast Missouri State University for two years. He worked at various jobs in the area. He then went to St. Louis and worked at small arms, a defense plant.

In 1942 Robert enlisted in the Naval Reserves (Naval Air Corp) and graduated from Corpus Christi as Naval Aviator with the rank of Ensign. He was sent to New Orleans Naval Air Base and trained to be a flight instructor. From there, he went to N.A.S. at St. Louis, MO, teaching British cadets to fly. He was transferred to N.A.S. at the Atlanta, GA Instrument Flight School. From there he went to the Alameda, CA Naval Air Station, flying 4-engine sea planes (PB2Y) to Honolulu, Johnston Island, Kwajalein, Saipan, Samor and Manila. He would return to Alameda, CA. This Naval Air Service was called "Naval Air Transport Service or NATS. He was stationed at Moffit Field to be checked out on R5D. He was stationed on Guam, flying 4-engine land planes with NATS. He would fly from Guam to Iwo Jima, Tokyo, and Atsugi, return to Guam and then fly to Peleliu and Manus. He would go back to Guam and fly to Okinawa, Shanghai and Tsingau, return to Guam and fly to Samar and Manila. He was released to inactive duty in October 1946. He joined the Naval Reserves Squadron in Cape Girardeau when it was formed about 1948. He went on active duty from 1948 to 1952. He had 2200 total hours of flying time as a pilot. He was in a passenger plane crash with Osler Statler, as pilot, at Cape Girardeau Airport in 1948.

Robert and Adell Hartle

In 1947 Robert became a State Farm Insurance agent in Jackson. In 1950 he married Adell Hendrix, daughter of John and Katie Cordelia Hendrix. Adell worked in the office with Bob. They had two children, Barbara Jo married Gene Thomas Huebel. They live in Smyrna, TN and have two sons, Daniel and David. Robert Chadwick married Geneva Sides. They have three children, Jacie, Lindsey and Robert Chadwick II.

On July 9, 1990 Robert received the R. A. Fulenwider Award presented by the Jackson Chamber of Commerce. The recipient of the award is the person deemed to have made important contributions and given much service to the community. Hartle is a retired emeritus with State Farm Insurance Company, where he served as an insurance agent from 1947 to 1984. He obtained his real estate license in 1950 and in 1960 began a partnership with Riverside Lumber Company and developed the Indian Hills Subdivision.

Hartle's community service and contributions included the following. He was president of the Jackson Rotary Club in 1967; a Paul Harris Fellow in Rotary International, District 609 Conference Chairman in 1977; and secretary, vice president, and in 1965 president of the Jackson Industrial Development Corporation. He was the recipient of the Community Leadership Award at Jackson from the Cape Girardeau Chamber of Commerce and president of the Chamber of Commerce in 1969. He helped organize the Southeast Missouri Medical Center and served on its board of directors; he was active in the Jackson Community Chest Board, and he participated in the organization of Kimbeland Country Club in 1962 and served as president in 1964. He was a past member of the administrative board of New McKendree United Methodist Church and past president of the Methodist Men's Club. He served as president of Post "M" of the Travelers Protection Association, served as state director, and also served on the national board of directors from 1980-1982. He was a member of the Excelsior Masonic Lodge #441 AF & AM since 1948 and received his 3rd degree in October 1949. He was a member of the Sword of Bunker Hill and a member of the SEMO Seniors Golf Association and served on the board of directors. He joined the Jackson American Legion Post 158 in 1946 and was adjutant in 1948. He was a member of the honor guard and was commander of the post in 1999. He was a member of the Veterans of Foreign Wars, Clippard-Wilson-Taylor Post in Cape Girardeau, MO. He was named a Kentucky Colonel during the term of Gov. John Y. Brown in 1982. *Submitted by Robert L. Hartle*

Jacie Gladish Hartle and John Fred Hartle on their Golden Wedding Anniversary, February 1960

HARTLE - Robert "Chad" Hartle was born May 1, 1955 at St. Francis Hospital in Cape Girardeau, first and only son to Robert L. and Adell M. Hartle. Chad spent most of his childhood fishing and swimming at Kimbeland Country Club in Jackson. He lived in the same home at Indian Hills from 1960 to 2000. His father co-developed the Indian Hills Subdivision

Chad graduated from Jackson High School, then received a Bachelor of Science in Business Administration from Southeast Missouri State University in 1977 where he also completed some graduate work. After graduation Chad worked at Crown Finance in Cape Girardeau, then moved to Los Angeles to work for Security Pacific Finance. In 1979 he moved back to Jackson to work at his father's State Farm Insurance Agency.

In 1982 he married Geneva Sides. Geneva was born in 1960, also at St. Francis Hospital in Cape Girardeau, to Norman Hadley Sides and Minnie Sides. Geneva graduated in 1978 from Jackson High School and attended college at Murray State University in Murray, KY and Southeast Missouri State University in Cape Girardeau.

Adell and Robert Hartle, 9 June 1950, parents of Barbara Hartle Huebel and Chad Hartle

Following in his father's footsteps, Chad started investing in real estate in 1977. He began a full time career developing real estate in 1990 after working at the Jackson Exchange Bank for seven years and leaving as Vice President. Currently Chad and Geneva own rental properties in Missouri, Illinois, and Florida.

Geneva was employed as a Savings Administration Coordinator and Retirement Accounts Administrator at First Federal Savings and Loan Association before she began her full time career in real estate in 1987. Geneva is president of their real estate management company, which also specializes in relocating tenants during the preservation and rehabilitation of apartment complexes.

Utilizing his background in finance, Chad and four other individuals founded Alliance Bank in Cape Girardeau in 1997. Currently Alliance Bank has two locations in Cape Girardeau and one in Sikeston. Chad and Geneva also own Midwest Cash Advance. They have offices in Cape Girardeau and Jackson.

Also following a family tradition, Chad and Geneva purchased Lakenan Insurance in Jackson in 1996. Lakenan Insurance Agency is the oldest insurance agency in Jackson. In 2000 they purchased Midland Insurance in Jackson and Cape Girardeau and combined it with Lakenan Insurance Agency.

The Hartle family, front: Geneva, Robbie. Standing: Chad, Jacie, Lindsey

Their first child, Jacie Katlyn, was born Oct. 8, 1986. Jacie was named after Chad's grandmother Jacie Cheatam Hartle. Jacie is a student at Jackson Junior High School, where she is a member of student council, plays flute in the band and plays on the Freshman and Junior Varsity volleyball teams and runs track. Jacie started dancing when she was two years old and has competed in and won various dance competitions. She was a member of a dance team that captured first place at StarPower National Dance Competition in Orlando, FL. She also loves to swim, but is most at home in the great outdoors. Jacie loves 4-wheeling and taking the family dog to their "farm" near Marquand, MO.

Their second child Lindsey was born Dec. 28, 1989. She shares her middle name, Marie, with Chad's mother. Lindsey enjoys reading, gymnastics, swimming, basketball, and track. She also loves riding 4-wheelers and going to the family farm with their dog JJ. But Lindsey is best known for her ability to operate electronic devices. From computers to VCRs, she is quite at home pushing buttons. She loves researching on the internet, especially researching about dolphins.

Robert Chadwick Hartle II was born April 11, 1986. Robbie's favorite pass time is fishing and playing soccer. Robbie also enjoys riding 4-wheelers, bicycling, rollerblading, and anything to do with sports. All Robbie needs is a ball, any ball, and he will keep himself entertained for hours.

Their favorite vacations include Maui, Hawaii, Colorado, Kentucky Lake and Florida. The children's most memorable and enriching vacation experience is their private session, swimming and interacting with the dolphins in Florida's Gulfarium while visiting their condo in Destin.

Chad and Geneva and their children are members of New McKendree United Methodist Church. Both Chad and Geneva have been very active in the community. In 2000, the family moved into their newly constructed home in Bent Creek Subdivision. *Submitted by Robert "Chad" Hartle*

HARTLE – Rusby Hartle was born Nov. 22, 1915 in Sedgewickville, MO to Robert and Clara Hartle. He attended school at Sedgewickville and Oak Ridge, graduating in 1935 from Oak Ridge High School. He worked on the family farm with his father. On Nov. 22, 1937 he and Gladys Seabaugh were united in marriage. They lived at Sedgewickville, farming, and Rusby was employed by the Sedgewickville School as a bus driver. Their daughter Ruth Ann was born on Sept. 27, 1939.

In 1954 the family moved to Jackson where Rusby and Gladys both were employed by the Jackson School District, Rusby as a bus driver and Gladys as a cafeteria cook. Some time later Gladys was employed for a number of years at Schaper's IGA in the bakery department. Rusby worked for the school district for 27 years, retiring in 1981. During their retirement they enjoyed traveling and spending time with their three grandchildren and great-grandchildren.

Rusby and Gladys Seabaugh Hartle

Gladys Hartle passed away Oct. 31, 1990. Rusby became very involved with the Jackson Senior Center where he enjoyed the fellowship with many friends. In 2000 he received the Unsung Hero Award from the Jackson Heritage Association. He was surprised by the award and shared the evening with his family and many of the teachers and students he came in contact with during his time at Jackson School district.

Rusby passed away June 6, 2001 at the age of 85. He and Gladys are survived by their daughter and son-in-law, Ruth and Lester Maevers, three grandsons and wives, Tim and Patty Maevers, Jim and Deb Maevers, and Kenny and Jane Maevers; and eight great-grandchildren, Kyleigh, Landon, Trey, Hailey, A. J., Shayna, and Kimberly Maevers and Nate Kennon. *Submitted by Ruth Maevers*

HARTLE – Troy E. Hartle, the son of Fred and Jacie Gladish Hartle, was born Nov. 6, 1913 on a farm west of Millersville, MO. He and Ida Hahn, daughter of Roy M. Hahn and Bernice Jenkins Hahn, were married June 26, 1948. Troy was in failing health in 1996 and was a resident of the Missouri Veterans Home in Cape Girardeau from Feb. 26, 1996, until his death on May 31, 1997. He was employed by the City of Jackson as an electrical engineer from 1934-54. He then was employed by the Natural Gas Pipeline of America, retiring in 1976. He was a member of the New McKendree United Methodist Church, VFW Post 3838 in Cape Girardeau, Scottish Rite of Free Masonry Valley of St. Louis, Sword of Bunker Hill, Disabled American Veterans in Cape Girardeau, Altenthal-Joerns American Legion Post 158, Altenthal-Joerns American Legion Honor Guard, Past Commander of the American Legion Post 158, and Past Master of Excelsior Masonic Lodge 441 AF & AM in Jackson. He served in the Navy in WWII.

Ida Hartle was born on a farm on Millersville Route. She worked at Jackson Shoe Factory and is a homemaker, member of New McKendree United Methodist Church, American Legion Auxiliary Post 158, VFW Auxiliary Post 3838 and Disabled Veterans Auxiliary.

Hartle family, standing: Ida Hahn Hartle, Troy E. Hartle; seated: Larry W. Hartle, Terry L. Hartle, Brenda J. Hartle

Troy and Ida had three children: Larry W. Hartle was born June 8, 1949. He drowned July 25, 1965, while swimming at the Old Mill Covered Bridge at Burfordsville, MO. It had rained earlier on the head of the Whitewater Creek and the sudden rise of the water swept him over the dam. He was a member of New McKendree United Methodist Church, Order of Demolay, Future Farmers of America, Jackson 4-H Club, and the Jackson football, basketball and tennis teams.

Brenda J. Hartle Knehans was born Jan. 7, 1951. She married Jon Knehans on July 6, 1974. They have one daughter, Jill Knehans, born March 9, 1981. Jill is a junior at the University of Orlando, FL. Brenda attended Jackson High School, graduating in 1969. She was a drum majorette and a member of the chorus and the Jackson 4-H Club. She went to business school in Kansas City, MO, working in banking for 30 years. She is now employed at Mac Dill Federal Loan Co. and lives in Port Richey, FL.

Terry L. Hartle was born May 28, 1953 and died May 2, 1996 in Chicago, IL. He graduated from Jackson High School in 1971. He was in band and chorus and was on the Student Council his senior year. He belonged to the Order of Demolay, Jackson 4-H Club, and the New McKendree United Methodist Church where he sang in the choir. He went to vocational school in Cape Girardeau for two years. He worked at the Jackson Shoe Factory, went to beauty school in St. Louis and moved to Chicago, IL, where he was employed at a beauty supply store. *Submitted by Ida Hartle*

HAYNES – Keith and Bernice Haynes celebrated their 50th anniversary on Jan. 26, 2002. They were married in Marble Hill, MO on Jan. 26, 1952. Bernice graduated from Lutesville High School in May 1951 and was employed in the office of Vocational Footwear. Keith was co-owner of Thomas-Haynes Service Station in Marble Hill.

Keith was born on Sept. 22, 1930, son of Ulus and Maude Haynes. Bernice was born May 18, 1933, daughter of James and Laura Bollinger. Keith was born at Lowndes, MO and Bernice was born in Jackson, MO.

Six weeks after Keith and Bernice were married, Keith was drafted into the U. S. Army. He was sent to Fort Eustis, VA for his basic training. After three months, Bernice was able to join him for the next three months of training. They had an apartment and lived near Virginia Beach. The summer was spent enjoying the beach and touring the many interesting places like Williamsburg, VA. In September of 1952 he got his orders to go to Korea. He served there until March 1954. Bernice got her old job back in the office of Vocational Footwear while he was gone.

After Keith received his honorable discharge, he and Bernice moved to Cape Girardeau. Keith went to work for a construction company, and Bernice went to work at the State Employment office. They had their first new home built in 1954 on North Main Street in Cape Girardeau. Two years later they moved to Jackson and sold the house in Cape Girardeau. Their first home in Jackson was on Michael Anna Street.

On May 11, 1957 their first child, daughter Connie Sue, was born. Bernice had quit working in March and enjoyed staying home as a full-time mother. In 1959 they had a new home built on Legion Drive in Jackson, and sold the house on Michael Anna. On July 31, 1960, their second child, son Michael Keith, was born.

In 1961 they purchased a 24-acre farm on Bainbridge Road. They had a new home built on this property. He continued working on construction as a heavy equipment operator until retiring in 1993. Bernice went to work in 1962 for Uregas, now Ferrellgas, as a secretary, and retired in 1997 as office manager.

Connie and Michael were involved in many activities such as tap dancing, piano lessons, softball, basketball and swimming. She was active in Jobs Daughters and Girls Auxiliary at church. Both children were active members of First Baptist Church.

Keith has belonged to the American Legion Post #158 for 45 years, and V.F.W. Post #10495 for 10 years. Bernice is active in the V.F.W. Auxiliary where she is presently serving as secretary. Brookside Memorial to Veterans at Brookside Park was a project which the Haynes helped develop.

The Haynes took square dance lessons in 1964 and were members of Hilltoppers Club. They made many good friends while dancing. Many dances were attended, including state and national dances. They also held various offices, including president of the local club.

Bernice and Keith Haynes, May 1, 2001

Connie and Michael graduated from Jackson High School and Southeast Missouri University. Connie got her degree in Elementary Education and has completed 20 years of teaching. Michael's degree was in Business Administration and Marketing. He is presently a sales manager with Ocean Spray Company.

Connie was married on July 26, 1980 to Mike Bradford, and they have three children, Sarah, David and Melissa. On June 23, 2001 she married Robert Gregg Clippard, who is also from Jackson. They live in Maryland Heights, MO. Michael married Linda Kluesner on April 27, 1985. They have two children, Michael Keith II and Lauren Lynn. They live in Ste. Genevieve, MO. *Submitted by Bernice Haynes*

HENDERSON – Judge John Robinson Henderson, judge of Cape Girardeau County for 20 years (1850-1866 and 1868-1872), was born in Mecklenburg County, NC, the "Cradle of Free-

Kneibert-Henderson Lumber Yards, Jackson, MO

dom" in 1818. When he was a year old, his parents, Cyrus and Jane Henderson, and his grandparents, Carnes and Lilly Parks Henderson, settled in northern Cape Girardeau County, and with other families of Scotch Presbyterian ancestry, established the Apple Creek Church

During Judge Henderson's term as presiding judge, Jackson's first courthouse burned, and a brick structure was built. The cornerstone (now on view at the Heritage Association) is inscribed:
County Judges
J. R. Henderson pr.
R. M. Wood
M. Dittlinger
E. D. Baldwin, Arc't
Jos. Lansmon, Ctr.
A.D. 1871

Goodspeed's *History of Southeast Missouri*, 1888, records: "Judge Henderson holds honest, liberal views and has a good library with which he is well acquainted."

His sons and daughters moved to Jackson from their New Wells farm. Dr. George Henderson, a dentist, had offices above the local bank as did Dr. Robert T. Henderson, a physician. Mrs. Emma Camp, a daughter, and two granddaughters, Mrs. Nettie Howard and Mrs. Margaret Haupt, established Jackson homes. Charles Weston, another son, accepted a position with the county clerk and in 1884 was elected county surveyor. He and his wife, Carrie Klein, built a home on Mary Street for their five children, Hazel, Amy Nelle, Mabel, C. W. Jr. "Weston" and John Robert "Bob." Carrie's brother, Daniel, owner of a harness shop, lived close by. At one time two blocks of Mary Street were occupied by Henderson kin. Northwest of Jackson were the farms and orchards of William and Mosa Henderson. Active church leaders, they served as elders, deacons, choir members and teachers.

A local newspaper wrote, "C. W. Henderson is a live wire in the affairs of the city and is ever ready to lend assistance in any improvement project that may be of value." In 1889 he co-founded the Henderson Lumber Company located on West Main. His son, Bob, wrote of its early history, "Jackson had a population of 1,500 and there was no place to purchase dry, dressed lumber. C. W. and his partners each deposited $200.00 and pine lumber was purchased from an Ozark sawmill. Cement was manufactured in Germany, shipped in barrels (as ballast) to New Orleans, to Cape on the Mississippi River and hauled by wagon to Jackson. The lumber was stacked on a lot; a blacksmith shop was the office." Bob, as a small boy, spent summers "hanging around" the yard ($3.00/week) and later became a "hired-hand" ($12.00/week). He unloaded rail cars of lumber and cement, and was a salesman, bookkeeper, draftsman and architect. At the time of Mr. Henderson's death (1926), he was president of Cape County Savings Bank, a member of Sawyer Handle Company, a director of Southeast Trust, and, "a moving spirit in the development of the area serving as a director on the first board of the Little River Drainage District." (*Cash-Book*).

In 1919 Bob Henderson purchased a one-fourth interest in the Henderson Lumber Company. He married Margaret Ferguson, daughter of Dr. and Mrs. A. D. Ferguson of Fulton, MO in 1925 and became sole owner of the company which he continued to operate until his retirement (1963). In partnership with J. V. Priest, Elmwood Heights subdivision was developed. Like his father and grandfather, he was an active citizen, serving as president of the Lumber Dealers, Chamber of Commerce and Rotary Club. A charter member of the library board and American Legion Post, he also represented the Boy Scouts in many areas and was an elder in the Presbyterian Church. He participated in choirs and, as a pianist, was a favorite guest at civic and social events. Margaret, prior to her marriage, was an English teacher at Jackson High School. She edited a poetry magazine, *The Bard*, was president of Women of Potosi Presbytery, and served on the first Missouri Council of Arts. Their home, "Henderson Hill" west of town, was a popular place for family, friends and organizations. Their children, Bob Jr. and Carolyn, attended Jackson schools. Bob, a graduate of M.I.T. and a retired architect, lives in Hawaii. He has two sons: Tom of Sacramento, CA and Greg of Albuquerque, NM. Carolyn, married to C. Charles Peterson, graduated from Northwestern University. They live in Milford, CT. Chuck retired as Vice-President, Sikorsky Aircraft. They are the parents of Robert of Elgin, IL; C. Jeannan of Bethesda, MD; Margaret of Chaplin, CT; Charles of New Haven, CT; and Jim of Hinesburg, VT. *Submitted by Carolyn Henderson Peterson*

HENDRIX – Andrew "Andy" Monroe Hendrix was born 1870 near Imboden, AR in Randolph County, the son of James K. Polk Hendrix and Charity Louise Kinder. They came to the Burfordville area in 1878 and settled near the Kinders. There were three sons, Andy, Frank and John. Andy married Sarah Summers, the daughter of Perry and Sophia Houk, a direct descendant of the pioneer Miller family of Millersville, John

Sarah Summers Hendrix and Andy Hendrix, ca. 1930

Miller and Martha Clay. They had six children: William; Dora; Lula; Sarah; Robert and Tom.

Andy and family lived near the Fairview Church between Millersville and Burfordville. They were the parents of two daughters. Hazel Pearl was born in 1899. She taught school in Millersville until she married Russell Nelson. He had the general store in Millersville and was postmaster. She then worked with her husband. They had three children; two died as infants. A son Russell "Dub" married Mary Ann Dockins of Burfordville. They had two children, Cynthia Lou and William Russell III. Dub was killed in an automobile wreck in 1965.

Helen was born in 1907 and married Rev. Theodora Probst, a Methodist minister. She was a teacher for 22 years. They had a daughter, Judith, who married Milford Fluegge; they live in Millersville.

Andy was a rural mail carrier until he retired. He attended the Methodist Church in Millersville and helped get the Union Church, Baptist and Methodist, started in Millersville in the year around 1915.

They took Madonna Reitman, a niece of Sarah Hendrix, and reared her as their own daughter until she married in October 1936. Madonna's father died when she was 2 years old and her mother, Lula Summers Reitman Hersinger, was ill with tuberculosis and at Mount Vernon for nine months.

Madonna (Reitman) Fellows

Andy died of a heart attack in his sleep on June 27, 1946. Sarah died with a stroke on July 9, 1949 after being ill three days. Both are buried in the Fairview Cemetery.

Madonna Reitman married Edgar E. Fellows Oct. 17, 1936. They lived in Millersville. She worked at the ASCS Office in Jackson 15 years before retiring. She was active in the community, belonging to the Homemakers Club and working with the 4-H Club. She was a member of the UMW Methodist Church in Millersville and played the piano for 55 years. She kept many scrapbooks of Cape Girardeau County. She lived alone after her husband died June 7, 1993. When her eyesight failed, she thought it best for her to go to the Monticello House in Jackson, where she is very alert and enjoys friends visiting her. *Submitted by Madonna Fellows*

HENDRIX – Isaac Frank Hendrix was born Oct. 6, 1873 in Imboden, AR, in Randolph County, the son of James K. Polk Hendrix and Charity Louise Kinder. His paternal grandparents were Andrew J. Hendrix, born in 1807 in South Carolina and married Sept. 9, 1829 in Williamson County, TN to Jane Rebecca Ann Cosby, the daughter of Garland and Nancy Cosby. His maternal grandparents were Adam Kinder and Sarah Sally Devore.

In 1878 James brought his family to the Burfordville area to be near his wife's family, the Kinders. They had three children; Andy, 8; Frank, 5; and John, 2. Within two years, James died and was buried in the Stroder Cemetery. The 1880 census lists Charity with her boys, living next door to her mother and brothers; Sarah Sally Kinder, age 62 and two sons, G. F., age 23, and Levi Monroe, age 23.

Frank's mother later married Dan Felty and they had a daughter Goldie. Both are buried in the McGee Cemetery in Bollinger County. His brother Andy had married Sarah Summers and lived in Millersville. John had married Katie Allard and Frank came to live with them. They left Cape Girardeau County and moved to Scott County

Katie Allard Hendrix and Frank Hendrix, son of James K. Polk Hendrix

near Chaffee in the very small town of Bleda. There Frank met and married Ida Hunt Ferguson, a widow with two sons, Harold and L. F. Frank and Ida had two children while in Scott County. Margaret was born in 1908 and she married Truman Hopkins. Warren Russell was born 1911 and he married Juanita Cato.

Frank and family moved to Stoddard County near Greenbrier and was a very successful farmer for 30 years. He died at home April 19, 1949. Ida died in 1963 at the home of her daughter, Mrs. Truman Hopkins, in Dexter. Both are buried in Memorial Park Cemetery, Cape Girardeau. *Submitted by Brent Hendrix*

HENDRIX – Gary Don Hendrix was born on Nov. 2, 1944 at St. Mary's Hospital, Cairo, IL. He is the son of Lala Virginia Sue Pennybaker Hendrix of Jackson and the late Isom Troy Hendrix who passed away Nov. 2, 1995. Gary has two brothers and two sisters: Rosalee; Troy Dean; Stephen and Becky.

Gary attended grade schools from 1950 to 1959 in Charleston, Rush Ridge and Wyatt, MO and Barlow, KY. Gary attended high school from 1960 to 1963 at Ballard Memorial in Kentucky and Caruthersville High School in Missouri. Gary attended computer technology school in 1964 at Memphis, TN. At the completion of school, Gary moved back to Charleston, MO and worked as a carpenter. In 1965 Gary joined the U. S. Army Corps of Engineers in the Memphis District. From 1965 through 1981 Gary was a Construction Inspector, promoted through GS-3 to GS-7, working on several river projects and the Memphis Bulk Mail Center.

On March 24, 1967 Gary married Donna Jean New of Diehlstadt, MO, daughter of the late Talmadge Henderson New who passed away January of 1987 and her mother, Wanda Ruth Watson New who passed away May of 1991. Donna has two brothers and two sisters: Connie; Jimmie; Kenny and Sheri. Gary and Donna are of the Baptist denomination. All of Gary and Donna's three children were born at Missouri Delta Community Hospital in Sikeston, MO. The eldest daughter was born in December 1969 and named Tammy J. Hendrix. Gary became a full-time employee with the Corps of Engineers as a GS-3 in 1970 and moved his family to West Memphis, AR. In May of 1974 Gary and family moved to Minor, MO because Gary had transferred to the Cairo Area Office located on the fifth floor of the Post Office building in Cairo, IL. In June 1974 another daughter was born named Kimberlee A. Hendrix. Gary's continued dedicated work for the Corps of Engineers earned him a position as GS-7. In March 1978 Gary and Donna had a son named Jeffrey D. Hendrix. In 1981 Gary was promoted to GS-9 Construction Representative and transferred to the St. Louis District to work on the Melvin Price Lock and Dam. In May of 1985 Gary and family moved to Bethalto, IL. Donna went to work at J. C. Penney in Alton, IL as a sales representative where she became top sales leader within one year. Donna was also top sales leader in the district and regional level. Donna worked as a Girl Scout leader in the community. Donna was chairperson over the cookie sales and was the distributor of cookie merchandise to each troop.

In May of 1988 Tammy married Stephen Harris and moved to California. They had a son named Stephen Harris II in July 1989. Tammy and Stephen divorced in April 1995. Tammy attended Southeast Missouri State University at Cape Girardeau, MO. Tammy was a member of the Alpha Lamda Sigma National Honor Society. In April 1998 Tammy married James Unterriner, son of Robert and Dolores Unterriner of Jackson. In December 1999 Tammy and James became the parents of a son named Dominique Unterriner.

Kimberlee married Brian Powell. They have four children: Brittani; Tiffani; Kaleb and Ashlee. Kimberlee attended Southeast Missouri State University at Cape Girardeau, MO. Kimberlee was on the Dean's List and a member of the Alpha Lamda Sigma National Honor Society.

Front row: Brittani, Stephen, Tiffani, Kaleb, Ashlee, Dominique. Back row: Gary, Jeff, Brian, Kimberlee, Tammy, Donna

Jeffery graduated from Jackson High School in May of 1996. Jeffery obtained his CDL license in October of 2001 and chose to work in the construction field.

Gary transferred to the Cape Girardeau Area Office in 1993 where Gary worked as a Construction Representative GS-9. In 1997 Gary was promoted to Resident Manager of the Cape Girardeau Area Office as a GS-11. In 1999 Gary retired from the Corps of Engineers with 32 years of service. *Submitted by Donna Hendrix*

HENDRIX – Arthur Franklin "Jack" Hendrix was born Feb. 6, 1903 near Burfordville, the son of John William and Katie Cordelia (Allard) Hendrix, and grandson of James K. Polk Hendrix and Charity Louise (Kinder) Hendrix; Charity was the granddaughter of Adam Kinder who settled around Burfordville in the 1880s.

Jack and his sister Bessie went to school at Gravel Hill. As a young man he went to Flint, MI, with his younger brother Joe. His sweetheart, Opal Strong of Whitewater, joined him and they were married Oct. 8, 1926 at Flint, MI. Jack was working at the Flint General Motors Fisher Body

Four generations, standing: father John and son Jack Hendrix. Seated: Grandma Charity Felty with baby Art Hendrix.

Plant. Opal ran a boarding house where she kept nine boarders. Their first son, Arthur Franklin Jr., was born Aug. 3, 1927 and a few years later another son, Donald Lee, was born.

The stock market crashed in 1929. The depression was about to begin. The good times were over. Jack brought his little family back to Missouri where they lived with his parents for a few months; he thought maybe he could get back on at the plant and send for his family to join him in Flint. That didn't happen. There were sit-down strikes at the plant and the depression was real. He came back to Missouri and worked at any job he could find to support his family. He later moved to St. Louis during the war. He and Opal worked in defense plants. The boys went to school. World War II was declared and their oldest son, Art, was called up on the draft and served in the Army. The family moved to Charleston where Jack worked in the timber.

Art married Pauline Browning and they had a son, Delbert. Donald Lee married and moved to Texas.

Jack was working on the Island of Bird's Point with his brother Troy and son Art, when he died with a heart attack. He died Oct. 4, 1965. She continued to live in Charleston until her death Sept. 21, 1969. They are both buried at IOOF Cemetery in Charleston, MO. *Submitted by Art Hendrix*

HENDRIX – John Allard Hendrix was the great-grandson of Adam and Sarah Sally Devore Kinder. The Kinders settled around Burfordville in the 1800s. He was the son of John William and Katie Cordelia (Allard) Hendrix, and was born near Burfordville, MO, where his ancestors settled. In 1940 he married Gladys at Oran, MO. They were divorced and he then married Mrs. Fern Bogan in Houston.

John Hendrix and sister, Bessie, 1916

In 1963 they moved to Kingston, MO and bought a 240-acre farm. For four years the farm was flooded out, and knowing he couldn't keep farming, he decided to start raising pigs. He went to southern Missouri and bought 10 brood sows and had such good luck raising them that he bought 50 more. Now he was in the business of hogs, and he made good money. The winters were so cold, however, with lots of snow. He said, "this is not for me." Even though he was raising 1000 head of hogs per year, he sold out and moved back to Texas.

John was back in carpentry work. He and his wife, Fern, built beach houses around Lake Livenston, TX, and other places. He would say "I am a lock and key man; from start to finish I build the homes." He retired in 1997 and built their home in a subdivision in Splendora, TX. This was in 1980.

In November 1985 they took their pop-up trailer and vacationed in Gila Bend, AZ. All winter they prowled the desert looking for old mines and rocks. Always with them was "Little Man," their little poodle. He took about 500 pounds of rock back to Texas with them. He made his own machines and cut and polished rock for a year. He also made grandfather clocks. The one he made for his home is now in the home of his nephew, Chad Hartle and family in Jackson. He was an expert at woodwork. His home had many pieces of furniture he had made.

In 1986 he had a stroke but wouldn't go to the doctor. In November he and Fern went back to Arizona. He got sick and they took him to Casa Granda Hospital the day before Thanksgiving. Tests were taken and the results were bad. A highway patrolman took the bad news to his wife. She was to return to the hospital at once. They sent him by ambulance to St. Joseph in Phoenix, AZ. He underwent surgery the day after Thanksgiving, where they removed a brain tumor. Doctors didn't know what caused it. He spent ten days in the hospital and then was taken home to Splendora, TX. A few days later he was back in the hospital with cancer of the lung. He died in September 1987. *Submitted by Fern Holland*

HENDRIX – Roy Hendrix was born Jan. 18, 1918, the son of John William Hendrix and Katie Cordelia (Allard) Hendrix, near Burfordville, MO. He also had a twin brother, Troy. There were four other children in the home: Bessie, 16; Jack, 14; Joe, 12; and John Allard, 4. Dad always said Katie couldn't have handled the babies and a 4-year-old without the older daughter's help. He hired a lady for two dollars a week to help; that was big money in 1918, when Dr. Vanamburg only charged 10 dollars to deliver the twins.

They looked so much alike only the mother could tell them apart. They had a very close relationship throughout their lives. Whenever you would see one, the other was nearby. When they entered school they would drive the teachers wild. If she called on Roy to answer, maybe it would be Troy answering. Perhaps they didn't know their names apart.

The family moved to Charleston. Roy met a lady by the name of Mildred Melton. They were married Dec. 3, 1938 and lived in Charleston, where Bobby Wayne was born Jan. 13, 1940 and a daughter Susie was born Dec. 13, 1944. Soon after her birth Roy was drafted into the Army and was sent to Germany. When he returned, another daughter, Saundra, was born April 7, 1949. They moved to Texas where he worked in his own construction company, building homes.

Back row: John and Katie Hendrix. Front row: Roy and Mildred Hendrix

Mildred had cancer during this time. She recovered and life was good. Cancer again came to the family, but this time it was Roy. He died Nov. 16, 1980 in the Veteran's Hospital in Houston, TX. Again cancer raised its ugly head and Mildred had cancer again. She died Aug. 10, 1985; both are buried in Forest Park Cemetery in Houston, TX. *Submitted by Bob Hendrix*

HENDRIX – John William Hendrix was born in 1876 in Imboden, AR. He was the son of James K. Polk Hendrix and Charity Louise Kinder, the daughter of Adam Kinder, born in 1805 in North Carolina, and Sarah Sally Devore. In about 1810 four Kinder brothers, Adam, Conrad, Jacob and John, came from North Carolina to Missouri. They settled around the Gordonville, Burfordville and Gravel Hill area, known as the Whitewater Settlement. Adam and Jacob married sisters, the daughters of Revolutionary War Captain Lewis Linebarger and Barbara Spanheimer. Adam, born in 1773 in North Carolina, married Susan Linebarger. Jacob's wife was Mary.

Adam and Sarah had nine children: Martin Van Buren; Julia; Adam B.; Charity Louise; Nathan; Rodice; Joel Franklin; Jasper and Levi. Martin Van Buren left Missouri and went to Arkansas where he met James K. Polk Hendrix. They became friends. Both would ride horseback to Missouri to visit Kinder's family. James and Charity, Martin's sister, married and returned to Arkansas. There they had three children; Andy, Frank and John.

John and Katie Hendrix, 1938, Charleston, MO

In 1878 when John was only 2 years old, the family joined a wagon train and moved to Missouri to be near Charity's family, perhaps because of James' health, as he died shortly after moving to Missouri. He is buried in the Stroder Cemetery near Burfordville in an unmarked grave. Martin Van Buren Kinder, after going to Imboden, AR, married Nancy Jane Hendrix, daughter of Andrew J. Hendrix and Rebecca Cosby. Andrew and Rebecca had six children: Isaac; Nancy Jane; Fal; Mary; James K. Polk and Andrew. The Kinder, Hendrix and Cosby families are related in many ways. This seems to be the custom years ago.

John Hendrix married Katie Cordelia Allard on June 29, 1900 at Jackson, MO. She was the daughter of Milo Allard and Barbra Ann Liley, the daughter of Maston and Angeline Hartline Liley. John and Katie lived near Burfordville, where eight of their nine children were born. Mamie died when a baby. Bessie was born in 1901 and married Roy Cooper, who died in 1995. They had five children: Dorothy married Bill Morton; Gary married Charlene Freeman; Aldo married Dorothy Sitze; Shirley married Dean Kirkpatrick; and John Henry Cooper died as an infant. A. F. married Opal Strong and had children A. F. and Donald. Joe married Ruth Fellows. John married Gladys Wendel. Troy married Lala Virginia (Sue) Pennybaker and had five children: Rosalee married Jimmy Pate; Troy Dean married Kay Jones; Gary Don married Donna New; Steven married Marcia Stoner; and Becky married Kenneth Eftink. Roy, a twin to Troy, married Mildred Melton and had four children: Bob married Diana Kilby; Susie married Howell; Sandra married Billy Dousay; and Adell married Robert Hartle and had children Barbara Jo and Robert Chadwick. Elton Reed died when an infant. *Submitted by Donna Hendrix*

HENDRIX – Isom Troy Hendrix was born on Jan. 18, 1918 at his home in Burfordville, MO during a blizzard. Troy was the son of the late John William Hendrix (born in Imboden, AR on Feb. 3, 1876; died Nov. 27, 1954) and Katie Cordelia Allard (born in Piedmont, MO on Jan. 16, 1882; died July 14, 1977). Isom Troy's parents were married on June 29, 1899. Troy is the sixth child of nine children. Troy had a twin brother named Andy Roy Hendrix. Troy grew up around Bell City and Advance, MO. Later in life his family moved to Charleston, MO. Troy worked as a carpenter and also at Brown Shoe Company in 1939.

Troy met Lala Virginia Pennebaker in January of 1939. They were married on March 24, 1939 at Charleston, MO. Lala's parents were the late Eddie Wade Pennebaker (born in Calloway County, KY on Feb. 27, 1879; died Oct. 12, 1964) and Frocie Lee Smith (born in Kentucky on Oct. 3, 1891; died Feb. 22, 1965). Lala's parents were

Troy and Lala Virginia Hendrix

farmers and owned a bakery in Charleston, MO.

Troy and Lala had five children: Rosalee; Troy Dean; Gary; Stephen; and Becky. Lala's first job at the early age of 17 was at Brown Shoe Company. Troy and Lala purchased a farm near Grassy, MO in 1946, where Troy was a logger. In 1947 Troy and Lala sold their farm and moved back to Charleston, MO, where Troy continued to farm on Jack Stallings' plantation as a foreman and later farmed land at Wolf Island, MO.

In 1952 Troy moved his family to Barlow, KY where he farmed Swan Lake and land in the Barlow River bottoms, approximately 800 acres. In 1957 a tremendous flood from the Ohio River destroyed their crops. At that point Troy quit farming and went back to logging for a living. Troy moved his family in 1963 to Caruthersville, MO, where he worked for Best Tipton Saw Mill as a self-employed logger. In 1964 Troy and family moved back to Charleston, MO. Troy and Lala purchased a commercial tree-removing machine and they traveled around Missouri removing tree stumps for local farmers.

In 1970 Troy and Lala purchased a farm outside of Jackson, MO on County Road 458. In 1971 Lala went to work at Roziers Department Store in Jackson, MO and continued to work there until 1979 as a sales clerk. In 1974 Troy and Lala were involved in forming the square dance club named "Roll-A-Way."

In 1980 Troy and Lala retired from their tree removal business and spent several winters in Florida and Texas, enjoying the warm weather and retirement. Troy and Lala celebrated their 50th wedding anniversary on March 24, 1989, while they were with family and friends. Troy and Lala continued square dancing after retirement. Isom Troy Hendrix died on Nov. 2, 1995 after having open-heart surgery at Saint Francis Hospital at Cape Girardeau, MO. *Submitted by Donna Hendrix*

HENDRIX – Troy Dean Hendrix is the second child of five born to Troy I. And Lala V. "Sue" Hendrix. He was born in Charleston, MO in September 1942. In April 1965 he married Kay Jones at her home in Charleston. She is the second daughter of five born to Stan and Marie Jones. She was born in December of 1946 in the Dixon, MO area.

Troy and Kay lived in the Charleston area until October 1967, when the moved to Mississippi. They returned to Missouri in 1971, and settled in Jackson. In December 1980 their first child, Ginger Marie, was born, followed by Christopher Dean in February 1983. Ginger became a student at Southeast Missouri State University in the fall of 1999. In December 2000, Ginger married Jason Rhea, father of Devon Rhea and son of Terry and Donna Rhea. Chris became a student at University of Missouri – Rolla in 2001. Troy and Kay Hendrix moved to Bollinger County in June 2000. *Submitted by Kay Hendrix*

Left to right: Troy Hendrix, Kay Hendrix, Devon Rhea, Ginger Rhea, Chris Hendrix, November 2001

HENLEY - Mary Catherine "Kate" Henley was born July 4, 1871 in Gravel Hill, MO. She was married Dec. 22, 1887 to Daniel Franklin Slinkard who was born Oct. 27, 1856 in Scopus, MO, and who died Feb. 19, 1935. Both are buried in Lesley Cemetery, He was the son of John Slinkard who was born Dec. 28, 1812 in Scopus, MO, and who died Jan. 14, 1877. He grew up on his parents' farm located on little Whitewater Creek. He ran a sawmill and wheat-threshing mill. He was married Feb. 9, 1851 to Sarah Margaret Fox who was born Jan. 30, 1832 near Gravel Hill, MO, and who died Dec. 21, 1916. Both are buried in Lesley Cemetery. She was a very religious woman and a Cherokee Indian. She made her own herbs and smoked a pipe. She was the daughter of William Isaac Fox and Mary Warren Coyler. They were the parents of David Alex, Hanna Elizabeth, Sarah Angelin, Mary Ann, Vidda Marzilla, Nancy, William Jefferson, John Marshall, Ramson Bettie, James Henry, Elbert Pinkney, and Daniel Franklin. Daniel Franklin married Mary Catherine Henley and were the parents of Charity Hahn, Olga Limbaugh, Ruth Stroder, Jesse Limbaugh, Charle Wilson, Verb Austin Smith, and Ora Cleveland, who married Arra Mae McGuire and adopted a son Earl Wiseman.

Mary Catherine "Kate" Slinkard was the daughter of Thomas Henley who was born in 1824 in Virginia and who died Jan. 28, 1905. He was known to everyone as Uncle Tom; he had bright red hair and a long red beard. He married Sarah Jane Rice who was born in 1838 in Tennessee. Both are buried in Gravel Hill Cemetery. She was the daughter of John Rice who was born in 1816 in North Carolina. He married Louise Wyatt who was born in 1821/1822 in South Carolina or Kentucky. Both are buried in Gravel Hill Cemetery. She was the daughter of Zadock Wyatt who was born March 1, 1778 in Prince William County, VA, and who died Feb. 27, 1843 in Caldwell County, KY. He was married to Mary Carmack who was born in 1784/1785 in Kentucky and who died in 1859 in Caldwell County, KY.

Zadock was the son of William Wyatt Jr. who was born in 1742. He was married to Frances Newton who was born in 1745/1746. William was the son of William Wyatt Sr. who was born in 1707 and who died in 1775 in Virginia. He was married to Lettice Nicolls. William was the son of Edward Wyatt who was born in 1671. He was married to Frances Newton who was born in 1685/1686 and who died in 1753 in Westmoreland County, VA. Edward was the son of Conquest Wyatt, and Conquest was the son of Edward Wyatt, born in 1619, who married Jane Conquest; she was born in 1622/1623.

Thomas Henley was the son of William Henley who was born in 1784/1789 in Lynchburg, VA. William was the son of Leonard Benjamin Henley who was born in 1750. He was a colonel in the Revolutionary War under General George Washington, and he died in 1798. He was married to Elizabeth (Danridge) Aylett who was born in 1749. Elizabeth was a sister of Martha (Danridge) Curtis who married George Washington, the first president of the United States. They were daughters of Colonel John Danridge who died in 1756 and who married Francis Jones, the daughter of Orlando Jones, who was the son of Rev. Rowland Jones.

Leonard Benjamin Henley was the son of Turner Henley of James County, VA, who was born about 1730. He married Miss Goode. Turner Henley was the son of Leonard Henley who was born about 1710. He married Miss Richardson, the daughter of Eliza Richardson. Leonard Henley was the son of Reynolds Henley who was born about 1680. He married Miss Keeling, the daughter of Leonard Keeling, who was the son of Captain George Keeling and Ursula Fleming, the daughter of Charles Fleming. The Fleming family is related to the Bollinger-Rolfe-Page-Henderson families. *Submitted by Ashleigh Lauren Slinkard*

HESS – Mike Hess was the youngest of three children born to Ben and Flora Friedrich Hess who lived and worked at Oran for many years. When they "retired," they bought a farm on Star Route in Burfordville. Flora still lives west of Jackson, but has sold the farm since Ben passed away.

Mike met Sandy in 1967 and they married the next year. She was originally from Commerce, but finished high school at Scott City. Her father, Elois "Red" Simmons, was a farmer for years in Scott and Mississippi Counties. He and Alfreda Smith Simmons had five children, of whom Sandy is the oldest. Her father was later a deputy sheriff in Charleston and the jailer before he died. Mrs. Simmons still lives there.

Mike, Sandy, Pamela and Janice Hess

Mike served in the Navy during the Vietnam era aboard the *USS Coral Sea* aircraft carrier. Sandy accompanied him to Alameda, CA for two years. This was a very strange time in our nation's history. There were many very patriotic military people there, but the bank where Sandy worked during this time was across from the regional induction center where new draftees were processed from the Pacific coast. There were regular peaceful protests almost daily here and in the Berkeley campus nearby.

They returned to Jackson in 1970 where both were employed by Procter & Gamble. Mike was an electrician there, and Sandy worked in the accounting office. They had two daughters, Pamela born in 1971 and Janice born in 1975, who both attended Jackson public schools and Southeast Missouri State University. Pam still lives in the Cape Girardeau area, working in the health care field as an insurance specialist. Janice lives in the Manchester, MO area and is a data processing manager for Southwestern Bell.

Mike and Sandy both retired in March 2002 after 32-year careers with Procter & Gamble. *Submitted by Mike Hess*

HEYDE - Arriving in Jackson in 1899 to become superintendent of the Cape County Milling Company, Philip Heyde, along with Mr. Nat Alsop, developed and perfected the process for bleaching flour. Previously the flour produced by mills across the country had been gray. For the quality of their flour, the two men won medals at the Chicago World's Fair (1893), the Atlanta Exposition (1895), and the St. Louis World's Fair (1904). After planning and installing the original flow of spouts and rollers, he left the mill and returned to Mascoutah, IL in 1912, and his son, William A. Heyde Sr., replaced him as superintendent and continued improvements that increased the mill's capacity from 700 barrels of flour per day to 1500 barrels per day in 1914. By 1930 the three mills in the system produced 1700 barrels of flour and 1500 barrels of corn meal daily, and the Gold Leaf brand had won national and international honors. Philip Heyde, married to Gertrude Tiedemann, the granddaughter of two eminent Heidelberg University medical professors, had four children who grew to maturity: William (Bill) A. Heyde Sr.; Mrs. J. G. (Frieda) Kies, Mrs. W. J. (Elsie) Kies and George "Hap" Heyde, all of whom resided in Cape Girardeau County.

Bill Sr. married Tom Ella McCombs on Dec. 31, 1912 and in the 1920s participated actively in Masonic groups, including The Scottish Rite Consistory and the Excelsior Blue Lodge #441 in Jackson. In 1933 the York branch of the Shriners conferred upon him its Thirty-Third Degree. In Jackson he took an active role in organizing the local Demolay chapter and served as Dad to the group as well as on the school board that oversaw the construction of Jackson High School. In 1938 he left the mill after 35 years and purchased land in Stoddard County, where he farmed for the rest of his life. In his years as a Mason he did not hesitate to travel hundreds of miles to help numerous children get needed medical assistance from Shriners' Hospital in St. Louis. He and his wife had two children, Bill Jr., who married Berenice Fitzpatrick, and Lilly, who married Jack Yount and lives in Sikeston where they own and operate farms. The Younts have two children, Jane Ella Potashnick (teacher) and Heyde (teacher).

After playing in high school on championship football teams and winning all-conference honors and attending Southeast Missouri State College, Bill Jr. replaced his father as superintendent and continued to lead the mill through various stages of production improvements until 1946, when he left to serve as an insurance inspector and salesman for Millers Mutual of Alton for 26 years. Also a staunch Mason, he had his Thirty-Second Degree conferred upon him by the Ancient and Accepted Scottish Rite. He loved hunting and fishing until he lost an eye in an accident; after that, he became an ardent golfer. He and Berenice, who taught English and French for 23 years at Jackson High School and took an active role in the Thursday Study Club, the Jackson Public Library Board, the Jackson Park Board, the Federated Women's Clubs, the Cape Girardeau County Red Cross, the Daughters of the American Revolution, the Jackson Human Relations Committee, the P.E.O., and New McKendree Methodist Church, had four children: Bill III (teacher); Tom (Air Force Colonel); Adelaide (college professor); and Phil (corporate lawyer).

Frieda Kies married Gottfried Kies on Jan. 11, 1906. Her husband's family had founded the

Philip and Gertrude Heyde, 50th wedding anniversary. First row, left to right: W. A. Heyde Jr., W. A. Heyde Sr., George "Hap" Heyde, Norma Kies Blattner, Gertrude Heyde, Philip Heyde, Betty Kies Chesley, Frieda Heyde Kies, Elsie Heyde Kies, Ruth Kies Trost, William "Bud" Kies. Second row, left to right: Lilly Heyde Yount, Tomella McCombs Heyde, Comfort Dickey Heyde, Phil Heyde, Ruby Heyde, Gertrude Kies Holden, J. G. Kies, William Kies, unidentified, unidentified

Deutscher Volks Freund, a German language newspaper, which in 1918 became the *Cape County Post* with her husband as the editor. Frieda, a passionate reader, a skilled researcher into family history, a tireless homemaker, and an Evangelical church member, lived in Jackson for most of her life, retiring to St. Louis and later Wichita, KS, after her husband's death. The Kies's had one daughter, Gertrude, the wife of Dr. Ray Holden.

Elsie Kies, who married William J. Kies, the brother of Gottfried, on Sept. 12, 1912, had five children: Betty Chesley (teacher); Martha Louise (who died at the age of two); Bill Jr. (businessman who worked with his father); Ruth Trost (missionary); and Norma Blattner (homemaker). She resided in Cape Girardeau. A member of the Evangelical Church, she was a warm, caring, sensitive mother who was an active member of her church circle and a quilters group and worked as a bookkeeper with her husband at Riverside Lumber Company.

George L. "Hap" Heyde, County Clerk

G. L. "Hap" Heyde, Philip's second son, married Comfort Dickey of Lutesville on May 23, 1917. After attending the Jackson Military Academy and St. Louis Business School, he served in the U. S. Navy in WWI, as a Wells Fargo telegraph operator for several years in Colorado, as the owner of dry cleaning business in Cape Girardeau, and as an owner of a dry cleaning business in Cape Girardeau, and as an employee of the Lutesville Milling Company. In addition, he served three terms as Cape County Circuit Court Clerk (1935-1947), as chairman of the Cape County Draft Board during WWII, and as bookkeeper for the Jackson Oil Company. A member of Althenthal Joerns Post #158 of the American Legion and the Scottish Rite Consistory, Hap volunteered for many years as a cooking and camping merit badge counselor for local Boy Scout troops. An ardent fisherman and hunter and an accomplished amateur cartoonist, he and his wife were members of the Presbyterian church. *Prepared by William A. Heyde, III*

HINDERBERGER – Cherry Lou Ludwig was born Nov. 1, 1946 near Jackson, MO, the daughter of Vernon Ludwig, born 1921, and Bonnie Armstrong Ludwig, born 1925. Cherry attended first and second grades at Schoenebeck, a one-room schoolhouse, where her mother was the teacher. Grades 3-12 were completed at Oak Ridge R-6 where Cherry enjoyed choir and drama activities. Her class had a variety of money-making projects, including picking apples at Begg's Orchard, to raise money for the senior trip to Washington, D.C.

The Hinderberger family: Ed, Cherry, Gina, Jon

Cherry graduated from Southeast Missouri University with a degree in Elementary Education on Aug. 11, 1967. On Aug. 12, 1967 she married Edward John Hinderberger Jr. Following a wedding trip to Niagara Falls and the Montreal's World Fair, they made their home in Columbia, MO, where Ed was working toward a Master's degree in Chemistry. Cherry completed her M. Ed. in Curriculum and Instruction in 1985. Cherry taught two years in the Mexico Public Schools and 29 years in the Columbia Public Schools.

On July 2, 1975 Gina Lyn Hinderberger was born. Jon Vernon Hinderberger was born on Nov. 13, 1978.

Cherry toured France and Switzerland in the summer of 1998 at the invitation of one her fifth grade students, Sally McKibben, and her family. Ed and Cherry are active members in the First Christian Church in Columbia, where Cherry teaches Sunday school, sings in the choir, and helps with the jail ministry outreach.

Following retirement from public school teaching in 1998, Cherry began traveling with her husband to Chemistry conferences, bowling and golf tournaments. In 2001 Ed won the gold medal in the national Senior Olympics in Baton Rouge, LA in doubles bowling. Cherry enjoys tutoring English as a second language to students. Studying with students from around the world has helped her learn new cultures and new places. *Submitted by Cherry Hinderberger*

HOPE – One of the pioneer families of Pocahontas was the Hope family. The family farm is located just east of Pocahontas right off County Road 532. This farm has been passed down to members of the family. It has been in the Hope family 100 years or more.

Robert Hope (born 1918), the son of James R. Hope and Bertha Thompson, still resides on the family farm. The James R. Hopes also had five other children: Cline; Avis; Hazel; Thomas and Paul. The Hope family has always been good citizens, an asset to the Pocahontas Community.

Robert married June Barber of the Brazeau Community on his 28th birthday. They have four children: James Hope; Robert Hope Jr.; Barbara Hope Taylor and Gary Hope. They also have eight grandchildren and five great-grandchildren.

Robert has always been a very community-minded person. He has been very active in the Apple Creek Presbyterian Church and now in the Apple Creek Historical Society. He is always available to help visitors locate graves of their family. He answers a lot of correspondence from people locating ancestors. He keeps a watchful eye over the church property and is in charge of keeping the grounds in good order, being assisted by his sons and grandsons.

Robert and June Hope

In August of 1948 the Conservation Department put on a Soil Security Demonstration on the farm. In one day they moved in with all of the equipment, built terraces, dug ponds and seeded the grounds for conservation. It was called Hope day and people came from far and near and observed this project.

Robert attended two years of high school in Pocahontas and moved on to Jackson to complete his next two years. Robert was a good basketball player and even after graduating from Jackson, he visited the Pocahontas School and assisted with the basketball teams. He was a member of the board for a number of years. Robert remained on the family farm after graduation. Robert has served as Democratic Committeeman in the Pocahontas Precinct. He always attended basketball games at Jackson High School and Southeast Missouri State University.

Robert is a great support to bereaved families, always there for them in the time of need. He enjoys coming to the post office in Pocahontas each day after his mail. He shares his words of wisdom with the postmistress and meets other friends there – always with a smile.

A great tradition on the Hope farm was wheat-threshing day. The neighbors always helped each other thresh. The Hope family always served a special dinner. Robert's Uncle Cross Hope, from Fruitland, arrived early in the morning and slaughtered a sheep. He cooked the meat outside in a kettle. An hour or so before noontime, it was carried into the kitchen where it was placed in the oven of Grandma Bertha's Home Comfort oven and browned, and gravy was served with it along with all the other vegetables. There were always a variety of pies on hand to serve the threshing crew. Robert always enjoyed the pies – June says he still likes his pie (especially cherry pie). The young girls from Pocahontas were always invited over to Robert's threshing.

Robert has been a good all-around community member, a son that Mr. and Mrs. J. R. Hope would have been proud of. He has well preserved the farm his ancestors passed to him. *Submitted by Margie W. Reisenbichler*

HOWARD – Henry Howard, a native of England, moved from Kentucky to Cape Girardeau County sometime between 1799 and 1804 and settled three miles northwest of Jackson on a Spanish land grant. He fathered no less than 13 children, including Zedekiah and Henderson.

Zedekiah (b. 1783, d. 1836/7) married Jane English (b. 1789/92, d. 1850/60), daughter of Thomas and Jane (Wicker) English on Dec. 13, 1808 and eight children were born to them. Their daughter Elizabeth (b. 181?, d. 1870/6) married Wiley J. Webb (b. 1807, d. Dec. 17, 1881) on Dec. 24, 1835. Wiley moved from the Carolinas to Cape Girardeau County with his father, John C. Webb (b. 1770/80, d. Nov. 16, 1836) in 1825. Wiley and Elizabeth had at least nine children with William Wiley (b. June 18, 1838, d. Dec. 11, 1882) being the oldest. On Oct. 12, 1866 William married Rebecca Ann Hendricks (b. Oct. 10, 1843/4 in Tennessee), daughter of Nelson Hendricks (b. 1805 in Georgia). The Hendricks moved from Tennessee to Missouri in 1865. William and Rebecca had six children, one of whom was Charles Andrew Webb (b. Sept. 16, 1880).

Henderson Wilson Howard was a younger brother to Zedekiah. Henderson was a twin (b. April 15, 1807, d. Aug. 18, 1867) and on Feb. 5, 1856 he married Mary Pauline Huston (b. Nov. 10, 1847, d. May 13, 1870). Their son John Henderson (b. Feb. 24, 1859, d. Feb. 13, 1929) was married on June 6, 1884 to Emma Gabriel Roussell (b. July 5, 1859, d. April 3, 1943). Emma's father was Duveral Roussell, whose tombstone says he was born on the Isle of Guadeloupe (Caribbean Isle). Roussell (b. Nov. 13, 1832, d. May 31, 1887) married Mary Tooke in 1854/5. Mary emigrated from England with her parents, William (b. 1796, d. Dec. 19, 1871) and Ada (Holman) (1803) Tooke in 1838/9. John and Emma (Roussell) Howard had five children, one of whom was Emma Grace Howard (b. June 6, 1889, d. Jan. 20, 1972).

Charles Webb married Emma Howard on Dec. 18, 1904 and they lived near Jackson, MO, until Charles' death in a car accident on Sept. 23, 1929. The couple had nine children, one of whom was Marjorie Rebecca Webb (b. Oct. 2, 1918, d. Jan. 1, 1992). Marjorie and Cecil Webster Bierschwal (b. March 26, 1916, d. April 24, 1983) were married on Feb. 29, 1935 (leap year).

The Bierschwals had seven children, five of whom are still living and are in the southeast Missouri area. Their eldest daughter Bonnie Sue Bierschwal married Henry Weldon Macke of Gordonville and they have three daughters. Barbara was born April 2, 1969. She graduated from Jackson in 1987 and from Southeast Missouri State University in 1992 with a B.S. in Political Science. On Feb. 27, 1993 she married Jeffrey C. Stroder (b. Sept. 26, 1970), son of Shelby C. and Anna Marie Stroder, of Sedgewickville, MO. Jeff received his degree in Accounting from Southeast Missouri State University in 1992. The couple moved to Jefferson City, MO for four years, where Jeff was employed with the State Auditor's Office and Barbie worked for the department of Economic Development's Professional Registration division. The couple returned to Jackson in 1997 when Jeff took his current position as audit manager with Beussink, Hey & Roe, P.C. Barbie returned to school and received a B.S. in Middle School Education in 2000 and is presently working with the Woodland R-IV school district in Marble Hill, MO as a junior high social studies teacher. *Submitted by Barbara Jo Macke-Stroder*

Charles and Emma Grace Howard Webb

HOWARD - Louisa Jane Howard was born in 1818 and died in 1881. She was married on Sept. 6, 1838 in Cape Girardeau to William Madison McGuire who was born in 1820 in Virginia, and who died Jan. 12, 1901. Both are buried in Howard Cemetery. They were the parents of Malinda Tucker, Charles, Ezekial, John, Milton, Emery, Samuel, Rachel Crafton, Alice Knaup, and William Franklin.

William Franklin was born in 1854 near Crump, MO, and died March 3, 1931. He was married on May 25, 1882 to Artelda Tilda Berry who was born in 1854 near Crump, MO, and who died in 1887. Both are buried in Allen Cemetery. She was the daughter of Robert Port Shibley Berry and Nancy Jane Allen. William Franklin and Artelda McGuire were the parents of Berdie Strong, Felty, Dill, Bill, Luther, and Arra Mae, who was married to Ora Cleveland Slinkard.

Louise Jane McGuire was the daughter of Zedekiah R. Howard who was born in 1789 in Kentucky and who died Jan. 31, 1839. He was married Dec. 13, 1808 in Cape Girardeau to Jane English who was born in 1789 in Georgia and who died April 5, 1842. Both are buried in Howard Cemetery. Zedekiah R. Howard's father gave him 80 acres on June 11, 1818, three miles west of Jackson, MO. When he died he had 410 acres.

Zedekiah R. Howard was the son of Henry Howard whose family was from England. He purchased 100 acres from Joseph Young Jr. on May 24, 1804. He was married to Nancy Allen. Henry and Nancy Howard were the parents of Elizabeth, John, Sarah, Lucy, Henry Jr., Susannah, George, Mary, James, Nancy, Aramita G., Henderson, Hamilton, and Zedekiah R.

Zedekiah R. Howard married Louisa Jane English; they were the parents of Richard, Susan, Thomas, William, Simon, Nancy, Elizabeth, and Louise Jane McGuire.

Jane Howard was the daughter of Thomas English Sr. who was born Oct. 13, 1751 and who died May 16, 1829. He was married in Macon, GA, to Joan Jane Wicker who was born May 27, 1760 and who died April 5, 1842. Both are buried in English Cemetery. Thomas English Sr. was the son of William English and Mary Elizabeth Bettie Draper. Richard Dean Slinkard of Whitewater, MO, a member of the Sons of the American Revolution, set the first ceremony to mark the grave of a Revolutionary War soldier; the SAR chapter in Cape Girardeau put up a Revolutionary War marker for Thomas English Sr. His regiments included the 8th, 4th, and 12th Virginia Regiments. His father-in-law was also in the Revolutionary War; his ceremony was held June 29, 1991.

Thomas and his wife Jane were both dismissed by letter from Bethlehem Baptist Church in Washington County, GA, on Feb. 15, 1806. After arriving in Missouri territory he purchased 600 arpens; on June 6, 1806 he purchased 231 arpens; and in 1811 he purchased 240 arpens. Thomas was a charter member of Bethel Baptist Church in Jackson, MO. He was a deacon for 36 years. He and his wife faithfully served the church until their deaths.

Jane English was the daughter of Robert Wicker who was born in 1748 and who died in 1821 in Cape Girardeau. He married Hannah Simmon Holly who was born in 1741 and who died Aug. 12, 1818 in Cape Girardeau. Robert Wicker was the son of Thomas B. Wicker who was born in 1717 in New Kent, VA and who died in 1781 in North Carolina. He married Mary Hester, who died in 1784. *Submitted by Mark Wayne Slinkard*

HUEBEL – Julius Huebel, Gene Thomas "Tom" Huebel's great-great-grandfather, came to America in 1850 from Waldeck, Germany, and married Mary Kraft from Hessel Cassel, Germany. They lived in Cape Girardeau in 1854 and had three sons; Julius, Adolph and William. Tom's great-grandfather, Gottfried Hartung, was born in 1854 in Germany and came to America in 1881. In 1898 he purchased a corner lot on Broadway and Frederick Streets in Cape Girardeau, where he owned a business handling guns, bicycles, sewing machines, paint and gramophones and records. In 1890 he married Minnie Phillips, a native of Germany, and had two sons, William C. and Emil, and a daughter Clara. Clara married William Huebel, Tom's grandparents who lived on Washington in Cape Girardeau. They had three sons, William who died as an infant, Raymond C., and Eugene William. All families were members of Trinity Lutheran Church in Cape Girardeau.

Tom, born Oct. 1, 1951 to Marcella Jane Morgan Huebel and Eugene William Huebel, lived on Cape Rock Drive in Cape Girardeau with his sisters, Katherine Rae and Elizabeth Ann. He was awarded the rank of Eagle Scout in 1967 and graduated from Central High School in 1969. He graduated from Southeast Missouri State University in 1973 with an industrial technology degree.

Barbara Jo Hartle, born Aug. 22, 1952 to Adell Marie Hendrix Hartle and Robert Lee Hartle, lived in Indian Hills in Jackson with her brother Robert Chadwick. A 1970 Jackson High School graduate, she received a degree in home economics in 1974 from Southeast Missouri State University. She was a member of Alpha Delta Pi and Kappa Delta Pi.

Barb, Dan, David and Tom Huebel

Tom and Barbara were married on New Year's Eve, 1974 at New McKendree Methodist Church. Through Tom's careers as a teacher, manufacturing engineer, distribution and manufacturing manager and sales representative, the family has lived in St. Louis; Mountain Home,

ARK; Parma; Malden; Lexington, TN; and since 1985 has lived in Smyrna, TN. He received Tennessee 2000 Salesman of the Year from the Jefferds Corporation. Barbara taught family and consumer sciences, and after additional training at University of Tennessee, Martin has been teaching culinary arts at Smyrna High, where she has been Rutherford County's High School Teacher of 1995 and awarded Tennessee's Program of the Year in 2000 by TACTE. Her students have received scholarships and competed in national FCCLA STAR Events throughout the United States.

Barbara and Tom have two sons, Daniel Thomas born Feb. 19, 1981 in Sikeston, and David Lee born March 6, 1984 in Jackson, TN. Dan graduated from Smyrna High School in 1999 where he played varsity soccer all four years. He is a junior majoring in science at Middle Tennessee State University where he is a third year defensive starter on the soccer team and a member of Beta Theta Pi. David will graduate from Smyrna High School in 2002 where he has been a varsity wrestler for the past four years in the 130 to 140 weight classes. Tom's family are members of Smyrna First United Methodist Church where he has taken several leadership roles and has been an active choir member. *Submitted by Barbara Hartle Huebel*

HUGHES – Malinda and Charley Matthew Hughes left Raleigh, NC and came to Missouri by covered wagon, settling in the Leeman-Fruitland area. Malinda (b. July 16, 1826; d. Sept. 14, 1902) was buried in the McLains' Chapel Cemetery about a quarter mile from the old house in the photograph. The McLains' Chapel Cemetery land was given by Malinda's daughter and husband, David and "Lizzie" McLain. Four of her daughters and one son are buried at McLains' Chapel, as is Malinda.

Front row: Tennessee Hughes Abernathy, Missouri Hughes Shelton, Mother Melinda Hughes, Sarah Hughes Harris. Back row: Hettie Hughes Armstrong, her son Charles Hughes, Ludi Hughes Davis, "Lizzie" Hughes McLain Simmons

The house in the picture was Lizzie's home located in the McLain Chapel, Indian Creek, Oriole Community. In the front row: 1. Tennessee Hughes Abernathy (b. July 24, 1855; d. May 24, 1918); 2. Missouri Hughes Shelton (b. 1860; d. 1948); 3. Mother Melinda Hughes; 4. Sarah Hughes Harries, buried at Neelys Landing, MO. Back Row: 5. Hettie Hughes Armstrong (b. June 26, 1862; d. May 24, 1937, buried in McLains' Chapel Cemetery); 6. son, Charles Hughes (b. June 4, 1865; d. Dec. 29, 1917, buried in McLains' Chapel Cemetery); 7. Ludi Hughes Davis, buried at Pleasant Hill Cemetery, Fruitland; 8. "Lizzie" Hughes McLain Simmons (b. Nov. 30, 1850; 3. May 23, 1928), buried at McLain Chapel Cemetery. Lizzie lived in this house with her husband David McLain until he was killed while hunting in the woods. He chopped the tree down and it fell on him, killing him. They had five boys: David; Ivy,; Monroe; Mark; and Charley, who was born after his father's death.

Later, a cookstove salesman, Mr. Simmons, came into Lizzie's life and they married and lived in this house until 1914. A new house was built and still stands at the Indian Creek School location. Lizzie and Simmons had two daughters; Mattie (b. July 17, 1887; d. Sept. 13, 1943) and Kate (b. 1889; d. 1915). Mattie married Ivan Marlin, who came to teach at the Indian Creek School. They had one daughter, Mary Beth, born July 3, 1915, who taught at the Indian Creek School during the depression of the 1930s. Kate married Charley Noland and had two daughters, Norma and Marjorie. Kate died during childbirth when Marjorie was born. Marjorie died a few months after her daughter Carol was born and Carol died shortly after her daughter's birth.

Those around here from the Malinda Hughes family are Gene and J. O. Sides and Hazel Sides Schloss; Virginia Seabaugh and Ellen Clippard, grandchildren of Tinnie Abernathy; from Missouri (Aunt Dood) Shelton, Judy Hines of Cape Girardeau, Shirley Montgomery and Mary Ann Austin of Arnold, MO. From Hettie Hughes Armstrong are granddaughters Nelda Eggers of Jackson and Evelyn Woods of Granite City, IL. From Lizzie Simmons are granddaughter Mary Beth Vogt and great-granddaughter Harriet Vogt Martin of Jackson and Frederick Vogt of Indian Creek, Jackson. Others are Ivan and Bill McLain of Cape Girardeau. Ivan was sheriff of Jackson for a number of years; also, Mary Wissman, Carrie Wilhelm and Clara Mahy of Cape Girardeau; Loida Gilbert of Herrin, IL; Dorothy Sides of Pacific, MO; and grandsons Gene Brockett, druggist at Jones Drug Store in Jackson, and Charles Brockett of Cape Girardeau. These two grew up in Oran, MO.

This picture is the closest thing of history that is left anywhere. I am proud that I know this much of Malinda and Charley Hughes and can share it with you. *Submitted by Mary Beth Marlin Vogt, great-granddaughter of Malinda Hughes.*

HUTTON – Walter William Hutton was born Aug. 7, 1923, in Willow Bunch, Saskatchewan, Canada. He was the sixth of seven children born to Winnie (Sinden) Hutton and the first son of William John Hutton. His father was of Irish descent; grandfather Samuel Hutton immigrated to Quebec during the potato famine of the 1840s. His mother's ancestors were of English-German descent. His parents were farmers and Walter remembers they used horses exclusively until he was 15 and his Dad finally bought a used tractor!

Walter graduated from high school in Kelvington, Saskatchewan and shortly thereafter joined the Canadian Army. He served in the European theatre from 1944 to 1946, part of that time being spent in the Medical Corps. One of Walter's sisters served in the Canadian Women's Army Corps (CWACS) and another in the Canadian Air Force.

Dr. Walter and Shirley Hutton

After discharge from service, Walter graduated with an Associate in Arts degree from the University of Saskatchewan, Regina campus, where his mother had moved following his father's death when Walter was 17 years old. He enrolled in Kirksville College of Osteopathy in 1948 and graduated in June 1952. His interest in the osteopathic profession had been sparked by two osteopathic physicians who had attended KCOM, which was founded at Kirksville in 1892 by Dr. Andrew Taylor Still, M.D.

Two weeks before his graduation, Walter married Shirley Jean Finney on May 24, 1952. She is a north Missouri native from Linn County. To this union, three sons were born: William Kirt, who presently lives in Scott City, MO; Scott Glenwood (born in November 1954 and died in November 1966); and Evan Lee (born and died in November 1957).

Walter interned at McCormick Osteopathic Hospital, Moberly, MO, and in 1953 moved with his family to Saskatoon, Saskatchewan, where he had a limited practice. In 1954 he moved to Keytesville, MO where he had a family practice — including many home deliveries!

In September 1956 the Hutton family moved to Jackson, MO, where Walter had been made aware of the availability of a home/office combination. This was the Gockel home, which is on East Washington Street just north of the courthouse (Lot One) and is presently owned by John and Vickie (Litzenfelner) Abernathy. Walter maintained a family practice in Jackson from 1956 until 1989 when he closed his office due to health problems. During the years Walter spent in Jackson, he also served as anesthesiologist for Cape Osteopathic Hospital (1956-1969) and later for Chaffee General Hospital (1969-1983).

After moving to Jackson, the Huttons joined First Presbyterian Church where Walter has been active in many capacities. Having been a farm boy during his early years, Walter chose to move to the country following retirement. He and Shirley built an earth-sheltered home in north Cape Girardeau County near Oak Ridge, where they currently reside. *Submitted by Dr. Walter and Shirley Hutton*

ILLERS – Joan Hale Miller was born to Maple S. Miller and Gladys Hale Miller on April 9, 1930. She attended school in Millersville until beginning high school in Jackson where she met Don Illers, son of William A. and Mabel Illers. They graduated from Jackson High School in 1947 and 1948. After attending Southeast Missouri State University for 2-1/2 years where she majored in elementary education and belonged to the Clio Society, Don and Joan were married at New McKendree United Methodist Church on June 5, 1949.

The first few years were spent on the farm, where Don was a partner in the dairy business with his father and Joan taught in a rural school and later substituted in the Jackson school system. Don worked for Natural Gas Pipeline of America. Joan and Don were active in church organizations and belonged to various clubs such as Jackson Jaycees and Jackson Homemakers Club. Don enjoyed coaching sports teams for his children and later the grandchildren. Joan liked to sew and enjoyed making things for her family.

Four children were born to the family: David; Denis (now deceased); Susan and Chris. They, like their parents, graduated from Jackson High School and participated in various activities and sports. There are seven grandchildren: Julie; Kelly; Staci; Ami and Colby Illers; and Kyle and Danielle Wells, who live in South Carolina. There are two great-grandchildren, Cori and Riley, children of Staci Illers.

The Illers have lived on Highway 25 south of Jackson for years. Joan and Don celebrated

Joan and Don Illers, June 5, 1999

their 50th wedding anniversary on June 5, 1999 at New McKendree United Methodist Church Cox Hall with a large number of friends and family attending. *Submitted by Joan Illers*

ILLERS – On Dec. 12, 1915, William August Illers and Mabel Luella Rice were married in the Lutheran Parsonage in Jackson, MO, by Rev. W. G. Langenhennig. "Will" was a member of St. Paul. His father was one of the five founders of the church. I was a member of New McKendree Methodist.

Will's mother died when he was 9 years old and his father, when he was 14. He was the oldest of six children and he had to quit school to farm. We borrowed money from the Federal Land Bank to purchase 144.4 acres joining the Iller's home place. This was located 1.5 miles south of Jackson on Highway 25. There was a three-room house on this land and Will had it refinished. We were happy to move into it without modern conveniences. For our wedding gifts, Will's family gave us $2000, a cow, and a team of mules. My parents gave us two cows, two heifers, a cream separator and $500, to furnish our home.

Will tilled the farm land and I planted a large garden. I canned several hundred quarts of vegetables, fruits and meat each year. Our home was the "Friendly Inn." My father, Alvis Rice, was co-owner of Behrens-Rice Grocery. He advertised groceries at your own price.

On March 24, 1918, our twin daughters were born. Everyone was excited. Then we realized Edna Ruth had a heart problem and she died 10 days later. Ruby Aleene survived. On Oct. 9, 1921, Doris was born. Aleene now had a sister and a playmate.

We continued our life on the farm. We were now raising chickens, hogs and selling cream. As time went by we decided our income was not what we wanted it to be. Illers Dairy became a part of our life.

On June 28, 1926, our son Harold was born. A son was a new and fun experience. When Harold was about 6 months old, we decided to build a larger home. Trees were cut from our woods and hauled to the mill to be sawed into lumber to build our home. We moved into temporary quarters.

William A. and Mabel Luella Rice Illers, wedding picture, Dec. 12, 1915

While living there the children had chicken pox and measles. During that winter I cooked for six carpenters, our family and the hired help on the farm. We moved into our brick bungalow in December 1927. Our new home had eight rooms, a bath, two porches and a basement. We continued to do finishing in the house and I finished all of the woodwork.

On Dec. 6, 1928, Evelyn was born. An employee had whooping cough and didn't know it. Evelyn became ill with the disease and died Jan. 29, 1929. It was another sad time in our life.

Soon after this my widowed grandmother, Sarah Rice, came to live with us. She watched the children while I worked. She told them stories about going in a covered wagon to hear Abe Lincoln speak and how they made ink out of berries. Later, my parents, Alvis and Florence Hightower Rice, came to live with us. They were a joy and a help to all.

On March 4, 1930, our son Donald was born. Harold now had a brother and playmate.

As the children were old enough they attended Jackson Public Schools. When school buses were put into service they could not ride them because we lived within two miles of school. The children had a horse, a pony, a small red wagon, little cars and dolls. They swung on grapevines in the woods and would slide down haystacks in the fields. In October, they'd gather nuts in the woods. As they grew older, they had chores. They had many friends who loved to come to the farm. Chocolate milk was their favorite treat.

Box and pie suppers were held at country schools. They were sold to the highest bidder. Dances were held in neighborhood homes. We continued to be active in our churches. We also did what we could for school activities. During harvest time neighbors formed a wheat "threshing ring" and "silo ring." They went from farm to farm helping each other. They did the same thing with hog butcherings.

We had happy times with weddings. Aleene married Leonard Sander (deceased), Doris married Herman L. Hardy (deceased), then Edward Eltzroth. Harold married Rebecca Schlegel of Cape Girardeau. Donald married Joan Miller of Millersville. In WWII, Leonard served in the North and South Pacific as a Radar Technician attached to the U. S. Navy. Harold served in the Army Air Force.

Grandchildren are Leonard Fritz Sander Jr. and Paul Sander; Greg and Lisa Illers; David, Susan, Chris and Denis Illers (deceased); and Marsh Hardy (deceased).

Our life was a story of hard work but just before Will died, he said he'd live his life the same way.. He died Sept. 30, 1964. In 1984, I am still living on the farm. *Written by Mabel Rice Illers in 1984; Submitted by Mrs. Aleene Illers Sander*

JAEGER – Dr. Joseph Nicholas Jaeger was born on Morgan Street in Jackson, on Nov. 30, 1916. He had an older brother, Jesse Howard, who was born in 1915. Their younger sister, Irene Ray (1921-1933), lived to be only 12 years old, having died of scarlet fever. Joe's father, Charles Boniface Jaeger (1869-1930), was the first generation of Jaegers born in this country. Joe's mother, Floy Dean Howard (1884-1968), was from Jackson and was one of the oldest members of the First Baptist Church when she died at age 84. The young family moved to a house on Main Street and the children attended the Lutheran Elementary School. Charles Jaeger served two terms as Clerk of the Circuit Court in 1918 and 1922. In 1928 he was elected Coroner. He was ill a few years before he died at age 61.

Howard worked at the Palace Theater in Jackson and at a theater in Lutesville. He served in WWII as a supply sergeant in England. Later, he belonged to the National Guard in Jackson from 1947 to 1973. Howard never married. He died of a heart attack in 1977 at age 62.

While attending Jackson High School, Joe was the student manager for the championship football team of 1934. He worked at Fulenwider's Drug Store and Rozier's Department Store until his mid 20s, when he attended Southeast Missouri State University for two years. From 1945 to 1949 he attended Washington University School of Medicine. He helped with autopsies in exchange for room and board. He then spent a year at Rush-Presbyterian Hospital in Chicago for his internship before establishing his medical practice on High Street in Jackson. Joe married Harriet Reisenbichler of Pocahontas in 1954 and they lived in west Jackson before moving to Forest Acres. There Joe had a beautiful azalea garden. Joe and Harriet have five daughters. They divorced in 1974, and he retired from practice in 1984, after 34 years. He currently lives at the Lutheran Home Apartments in Cape Girardeau and enjoys his daughters and 12 grandchildren.

J. N. Jaeger and family, 1992

The Jaegers are from Germany. The profession of milling flour was passed down though several generations. Sebastian Jaeger (1807-1887), Joseph Nicholas' great-grandfather, had eight children. Tradition was that the oldest son, Peter, would inherit the family property. Thus, four of the eight children moved to the United States. Nicholas, Sebastian's second oldest son, emigrated and settled in St. Louis about 1870. In 1872 two other brothers, Joe and John, came to the United States. They settled in Cape Girardeau, where they were millers and helped run a saloon on Broadway. Nicholas Jaeger married Elizabeth Karrillon, also from Germany. Charles Boniface was the oldest of their 11 children, who eventually moved to Jackson where he married Floy Howard.

Joe Jaeger recalls visiting his grandparents, Nicholas and Elizabeth, on Sydney Street in St. Louis. Elizabeth was hard of hearing so didn't learn much English. This is where Joe must have begun his life-long study of the German language, which he continues to enjoy. *Submitted by Jo Jaeger Bonner*

JAMES – Iva and Henry had both been teachers in neighboring country schools in Oklahoma. On April 4, 1910, Iva Fisher, age 18, and Henry James, age 26, were married by Judge Grahm in the courthouse at Kingfisher, OK. The next day they went to spend a few days visiting with Iva's parents on their farm near Hennessey, OK. Then the next week they went by train to Watona, OK to visit with Henry's mother and his brothers.

While they were there, Henry received a letter for his appointment for a traveling salesman's job in Cape Girardeau County, MO. Henry bought a team of horses and an old wagon that they drove to where Iva's parents lived. Then Iva's father and Henry put bows and a tarpaulin on the wagon, making it a covered wagon. Iva's mother gave her eight feed sacks that Iva filled with wheat straw and sewed shut to use in the wagon as their bed. Iva's mother also gave them a wooden cracker box that her father fashioned to the outside of the wagon. In it they put sand and then filled it with radishes, onions and lettuce from her mother's garden. They were told to water it each day so the vegetables would stay fresh and last throughout the trip to Missouri.

Frances James, Henry James, 1913

It rained on the fourth day of May when they started on their trip to Missouri. It took 30 days for them to drive the 600 miles. Henry and Iva arrived in Jackson on June 4, 1910, where they rented a house and barn for $7.50 a month. They had $2.50 left to live on, and since Henry's contract wasn't signed properly, he went to work at Mill "B" in Jackson for 15 cents per hour earning $9.00 a week for the ten weeks until his contract was straightened out. They lived in that rented house for several years, then bought a house at 213 South First West Street - now South Missouri Street,.

For a number of years Henry was a traveling salesman for the S. F. Baker's Medicine Company, which furnished him a wagon for that purpose. Henry then served as Jackson City Collector for eight years and then was Jackson Grade School custodian for 20 years.

The James' attended services at the First Presbyterian Church. Henry was a 32nd degree Mason, a member of Excelsior Lodge 441, and a member of Chapter 91 Order of the Eastern Star of which Iva was also a member.

Iva and Henry lived out the rest of their lives in Jackson, where they raised their seven children: Iva Fisher James (Jan. 30, 1892 – Dec. 17, 1970); Henry James (Nov. 16, 1881 – April 14, 1962); Frances Taplin (Jan. 6, 1911 – June 13, 1985); Clara Mae Oster (March 29, 1912 – April 9, 1994); LeRoy James (April 8, 1914 – Nov. 8, 1989); Lyla Bangert (Feb. 2, 1919 – Nov. 6, 1999); Joseph James (Jan. 13, 1923 – June 5, 1986); Mabel Hufstedler (Nov. 20, 1924) and Milton James (Aug. 25, 1928). Grandchildren: Ruth and Richard Oster, from Clara; Carol and David James from Leroy; David Bangert from Lyla; Joe David, Janet, and John James from Joseph; Paul, Karen and Nathan James from Milton. *Submitted by Milton James*

JANSEN – Katherine Marie Lohr, a life-long resident of Jackson, MO, and Gregory Louis Jansen of Kelso, MO, were united in marriage on June 18, 1994. As a couple, they made their home in Jackson. They bought and totally refurbished a 100-year-old farmhouse on a 10-acre tract on Greensferry Road, just inside the city limits.

Kathy was born Nov. 19, 1966, the daughter of Barbara and Bob Lohr. She has two older brothers, Jim David and Robert Lane. At the time of her birth, Kathy was the first girl born in the Lohr family in over 120 years. She attended Jackson schools and was a 1985 graduate of Jackson High School. While in high school, she was a member of the girl's cross country and track teams. She was selected captain of both teams.

Kathy attended Southeast Missouri State University from 1985 to 1988. She received a Bachelor of Science degree with a major in Elementary Education and Early Childhood Education in December 1988. Following graduation, she taught at Woodland and Jackson Elementary Schools. She earned her Master's Degree in Administration from Southeast Missouri State University in 1999.

Greg Jansen was born in Kelso, MO, on March 21, 1969. He is the son of Mary Jane (Drury) and Martin Jansen. Greg has four brothers and four sisters: Mrs. Ronald (Patricia) Bradshaw; Mike Jansen; Susan Jansen; John Jansen; David Jansen; Mrs. William (Krista Kay) Keesee; Mrs. Mark (Deborah) Perry and Tom Jansen.

Left to right: Greg Jansen, Katherine Jansen, Bobby Jansen, Megan Jansen

Greg attended Notre Dame High School where he was involved in athletics. Following graduation in May 1987, Greg enlisted in the U. S. Army where he was stationed in Germany. Following a two-year stint in the Army Greg attended Southeast Missouri State University, receiving a degree in Finance in 1994.

Greg worked at Columbia Construction Company, a family-owned business, during high school and college. He is currently the construction manager and a part owner of Columbia Construction. Kathy and Greg are the parents of Robert Louis Jansen, born Nov. 24, 1996 and Megan Lohraine Jansen, born June 14, 2000. They attend Immaculate Conception Church and Greg is a member of the Knights of Columbus. *Submitted by Kathy Lohr Jansen*

JENKINS – Edward R. Jenkins (b. 1804; d. 1874) of Virginia married Martha L. Kenne (Keen) (b. 1804, d. 1877), also of Virginia. They came to Cape Girardeau County in 1851 and settled five miles southwest of Cape Girardeau. In 1857, they moved to Jackson, and there ran a hotel. They were the parents of the following known children: William F.; Luther E.; Edward F.; James R.; Martha P. and John H.

William F. Jenkins was born in 1829 in Maryland and died in Cape Girardeau County in 1871. He is buried in Old Bethel Church Cemetery. Luther E. Jenkins was born in 1839 in Virginia; his death date is unknown. He and his wife, Susan, had one known child, Luther, born in 1868. Edward F. Jenkins was born in 1840 in Virginia and died in 1925 in Jackson, MO. He is buried in Jackson's Old City Cemetery. James R. Jenkins was born May 5, 1842 in Virginia and died March 13, 1920 in Jackson. He and Ella E. Cannon (b. May 16, 1841; d. Aug. 7, 1922) were married on Oct. 31, 1867. She was the granddaughter of Missouri Governor Daniel Dunklin. James R. and Ella E. were the parents of five children: Frederick; James L.; John H.; William M.; and Elbert. (See James L. Jenkins family history for more information). Martha P. Jenkins was born in 1845 in Virginia. No further information is available. John H. Jenkins was born in 1848 in Virginia and married Martha Emma Harrison (b. 1860). John H. died on Jan. 20, 1908. Martha passed away on Jan. 25, 1908, five days after her husband.

During the Civil War, all five of the Jenkins brothers joined Company F of the 8th MO Cavalry under Col. William L. Jeffers of the Confederate Army. William F. achieved the rank of 1st Lieutenant and Edward F. was a Corporal. Luther E. and James R. were privates. No official record has been found about John H. joining the Confederacy. He likely joined toward the end of the war because of his young age. Perhaps he joined his brothers after Company F had a skirmish in Jackson, MO on Sept. 24, 1864 before the company headed on to the Battle of Pilot Knob. On May 26, 1865, the 8th MO Cavalry of the CSA surrendered at New Orleans and received their paroles on June 7, 1865 at Shreveport, LA. All the brothers survived the many battles and miles of Company F and returned home to Jackson. For more information, see the J. L. Jenkins family history. *Submitted by Nancy Ware Ladreiter*

JENKINS - James Linton Jenkins was born Feb. 8, 1871 on a farm owned by his parents on Highway 25 South. James was the second of five sons born to James R. Jenkins (b. May 5, 1842; d. Oct. 1, 1867) and Ella Cannon Jenkins (b. May 16, 1851; d. Aug. 6, 1922). James and his brother, Freddie Bates Jenkins (b. 1869 - d. 1884) loved to hunt and fish in the woods behind their home (now known as Forest Acres). The home place was torn down and a new home built across from the L. E. Kies barn on Highway

Left to right: Luther Jenkins, Edward Jenkins, James R Jenkins, John R. Jenkins. Sons of Edward R. and Martha Jenkins

25 S. In 1881 they moved to Jackson and built a home on the corner of Greensferry Road and North Hope Street.

James received his academic education in the original public school building. In October 1890 he began the study of dentistry at Washington University in St. Louis, graduating in 1893. On April 25, 1893 he opened a dental office over Jones Drug Store on Court Street. In 1899 he bought the Alvin Boss building on the corner of Main and Court Streets and had his dental office upstairs in the cupola and rented the downstairs to Julius Schaper for his grocery store. Dr. Jenkins was known to most people as "Lynn" or "Whistling Doc" because he loved to whistle, was a fun-loving person, and enjoyed helping people. In 1948, J. L. Jenkins retired and sold the building to the Jackson Exchange Bank (currently the Jackson City Hall).

In 1898 Dr. Jenkins married Emma D. Hope (b. Sept. 16, 1881, d. September 1944), who was the daughter of David and Margaret Frances Hope. David owned Shawneetown Photography. He died when Emma was 12 and she and her mother then moved to Jackson.

In 1904 Dr. J. L. Jenkins and Emma moved into a new home, presently 541 N. Hope Street. That same year, Dr. Jenkins won a contest at McAtee Mercantile and received a completely decorated revolving feathered Christmas tree with a silver-plated wind-up base that played two Christmas songs. Emma loved music and poetry and J. L. Jenkins loved history and took a great interest in the Jackson public school system. Together, they instilled this love for education, music, and poetry in their three daughters, Ella Frances, Martha and Sarah. They were all members of New McKendree United Methodist Church.

541 North Hope Street, Jackson, MO, 1908. Standing: Dr. J. L. Jenkins and wife Emma Hope Jenkins. Seated in the middle, Margaret Frances Hope, mother of Emma; she was known as Fannie Hope and lived here and helped raise the three girls. She sewed for people all over Jackson and Hope Street was named for her. Seated on left, Ella Frances Jenkins. Seated on right, Martha Linton Jenkins. Sarah was not born yet.

Their first daughter, Ella Frances (b. Sept. 11, 1899; d. Aug. 28, 1915), was artistic and enjoyed writing poetry and short stories. She died of spinal meningitis just two weeks before her sixteenth birthday.

The second daughter, Martha Linton (b. Aug. 29, 1904; d. June 22, 1947), attended the University of Alabama and taught in Orlando, FL. It was there that she met McDavid Ware (b. Aug. 29, 1894; d. May 1, 1950) originally from Huntsville, AL and a veteran of WWI. They were married in Birmingham, AL in May of 1929. Martha was a fine seamstress and homemaker. They belonged to the Highland Methodist Church in Birmingham. The couple had one daughter, Nancy Jane, born Nov. 28, 1935.

The youngest daughter, Sarah Adelaide (b. March 1, 1910; d. Jan. 28, 1977) graduated with honors from Jackson High School in 1927 where she was crowned Silver Arrow Queen. She received a B. S. in Education from Southeast Missouri State Teachers College in 1930 and taught at Jackson High School for 36 years, teaching English most of those years. For many years she was Junior class sponsor, directed the Junior play and coordinated the Junior/Senior prom activities. In May 1973 she retired from teaching.

In 1947 when Martha Jenkins Ware passed away, it was Martha's and McDavid's wish that their only child, Nancy, come to Jackson to be raised in Martha's family home by her grandfather, Dr. Jenkins, and his daughter Sarah. Sarah had never married and Nancy's grandmother, Emma, had passed away in 1944. Nancy spent some summer vacations with her father and relatives in the south until her father passed away in 1950. Nancy graduated from Jackson High School. In 1952 Nancy married Robert Rodney Ladreiter and the couple lived in the family home with Sarah, where they raised their family of four children. Sarah greatly influenced her niece, Nancy, and Nancy's children, and was an inspiration to all those who knew her. Sarah passed away in 1977. Rodney and Nancy are still living in the family home today. (See Rodney Ladreiter family history) Submitted by Nancy Ware Ladreiter

Sarah Adelaide Jenkins

JOERNS – Maple E. Joerns was born Sept. 25, 1895 in Cape Girardeau (died January 1976). His father August, a blacksmith and harness maker, passed away at an early age leaving his mother Minnie with five small children: Maple, his older brother Clark, and sisters Claire, Mildred and Venita, the oldest of the girls and married. The boys and the two youngest girls attended Jefferson School in Cape Girardeau until 1916 when the family moved to Jackson to live with their married sister, Venita, on North Hope Street.

Meanwhile, the brothers found work on the Mayfield farm north of Jackson and remained there to support the family until the war began in Europe. Enlisting together, and along with others, Maple and his brother served in France, though in separate units. Clark was killed in the Argonne Forest.

Maple E. Joerns, Frances Joerns, Eleanor (standing), Margaret (youngest), 1923

Mape, as friends and acquaintances sometimes referred to him, returned home, finding work first at Cape County Milling Company's Mill A in east Jackson and later at Mill B in west Jackson for a total of 25 years, where he remained until 1940, at which time he became Custodian at the Jackson Post Office, retiring from there in 1960.

An only child, Frances Strong was born Sept. 15, 1895 (died 1974), and grew up on the family

Maple E. and Frances Joerns, 1967

farm near Oak Ridge, MO. In later years she reminisced about the trips she took from Oak Ridge to Jackson with her own horse and buggy, a surrey, and receive compliments from folks saying they thought she "handled the rig, being a young woman alone and all."

One such admirer was Maple and after a whirlwind courtship, they married on April 4, 1917, only to see him ship overseas in August of the same year. After his return from Europe, the family grew by one with the birth of their first child, Eleanor Elizabeth, in a small frame house on Adams Street, Oct. 1, 1918 (died February 1994). She had five children: Sandra (died less than a year old); Richard; Bradley (died 1996); Donna and Eddie Brown.

Maple and Frances had a second daughter, Margaret, born Dec. 26, 1922 (died March 1986). She had three children; Peppie, William and Tammy Kassel.

Maple was a member of the Altenthal-Joerns American Legion Post 158 in Jackson and the World War I Veterans Barracks 1311 in Cape Girardeau. He and Frances were members of the First Baptist Church of Jackson. Submitted by Richard E. Brown

JONES – Edgar O. Jones was born March 24, 1912 in Dexter, MO, the son of Columbus J. Jones (1875-1922) and Dora (Ruffner) Jones (1878-1965). Columbus' ("Lum") parents were Jeremiah Jones (1840-1874) and Martha (Baker) Jones (1847-1929), all from the Whitewater/Stroderville area. Dora's parents were William A. Ruffner (1852-1917) and Mary (Hunter) Ruffner (1850-1885). Edgar and Kathleen Jones had four children, Gerald Wayne (b. 1940), Fred Owen (b. 1944), Nancy Delaine (b. 1946), and Joseph Michael (b. 1950). The family moved to Jackson in 1955 and all four children graduated from Jackson High School.

Edgar joined the Navy in 1932 and served in both WWII and the Korean War. He retired from the Navy in 1953 as a Chief Petty Officer power plant engineer. He served on four aircraft carriers (USS Boxer, Lexington, Saratoga, and Ranger) plus several cruisers, destroyers, and transports. He saw battle in the South Pacific and off the coast of Japan during WWII and was with MacArthur's Inchon landing during the Korean War. After his retirement from

Kathleen and Edgar Jones, 1939

the Navy he worked in power plants for both the National Lead Company of Fredericktown and Western Electric Company in Lee's Summit, MO. He died at the age of 86 on Nov. 4, 1998.

Kathleen Rhodes was born Jan. 7, 1922 in Whitewater, MO, the daughter of George W. Rhodes (1892-1982) and Belle Dora (Proffer) Rhodes (1895-1976). George was the son of William Pinkney Rhodes (1848-1926) and Mary (Griffith) Rhodes (1848-1926). Belle's parents were Francis Marion Proffer (1856-1934) and Bettie (Aldrich) Proffer (1863-1917). Supposedly, Bettie Aldrich's parents were American Indians and part of the Cherokee Nations' Trail of Tears journey through southeast Missouri in 1838.

Gerald, Fred, Nancy and Joe Mike Jones in Whitewater, MO, 1953

Kathleen (Rhodes) Jones attended Delta High School and played on the varsity girls' basketball team. All four of her children were born during the difficult time when America was involved in WWII and the Korean War. When her husband, CPO Edgar O. Jones, USN, was at sea the family made their home in Whitewater, MO. When he was stationed stateside, the family moved to either the east or west coast. Two of her children, Gerald and Nancy, were born in Whitewater and the other two, Fred and Joe Mike, were born in California. She also worked for the Jackson Hosiery Mill when the family moved to Jackson in 1955. With her husband often away serving in the Navy or working away from the family home in Jackson, she managed to rear four children who all completed university masters degrees. Her youngest son, Joe Mike, received a Ph.D. in Economics from the University of Missouri and is a college professor in Fargo, ND. Her oldest son, Gerald, is the Presiding Commissioner of Cape Girardeau County and owns the Cash-Book Journal newspaper in Jackson. Her son, Fred, is a retired assistant superintendent with the Jackson R-2 School District, and her daughter, Nancy, is a counselor and administrator in Janesville, WI. Kathleen Jones has 11 grandchildren and nine great-grandchildren. *Submitted by Fred Jones*

JONES – Fred O. Jones was born May 11, 1944 in San Francisco, CA, the son of Edgar O. Jones (1912-1998) and Kathleen (Rhodes) Jones (born 1922). Edgar was the son of Columbus J. Jones and Dora (Ruffner) Jones/Bartles. Kathleen was the daughter of George W. Rhodes and Belle (Proffer) Rhodes. All families were from the Whitewater area. Edgar Jones was on active duty in the U. S. Navy (1932-53) and was stationed in San Francisco when his second of four children, Fred, was born. Fred attended grades 1-4 in a one-room schoolhouse in Whitewater. After moving to Fredericktown for one year, his family moved to Jackson in 1955. He attended Jackson schools from the sixth grade until he graduated from Jackson High School in 1962.

He attended Southeast Missouri State College, graduating in 1966 with a degree in education. He taught junior high art from 1966 until 1985 when he was appointed as assistant principal and athletic director at Jackson High School. He served in that position until 1990 when he was appointed assistant superintendent for the Jackson R-2 School District. He retired in June 2000 after 34 years as classroom teacher and administrator with the Jackson schools. He also served as president of the Southeast Missouri Teachers Association (1981-82) and was elected to serve on the Jackson City Council (1976-86) for five terms. Fred Jones and Pamela Hahs were married while both were students at Southeast Missouri State College. They have three children; Jolie Ann (b. 1965), a speech pathologist for Jackson R-2 Schools; Frederick Christopher (b. 1968), a professor in the mass communications department at Southeast Missouri State University; and Polly Ann (b. 1972), a speech pathologist for the Delta School District.

Pamela Ann Hahs was born Sept. 6, 1945 in Cape Girardeau, MO, the daughter of Ernest L. Hahs (1921-1991) and Anna Mae (Amos) Hahs. Ernest was the only child of John Hahs and Ara (Niswonger) Hahs/Hency, who were born in the Sedgewickville/Daisy area and moved to Jackson before he was born. Anna Mae's parents were Robert Amos and Myrtle (Byrne) Amos, both born in Allenville. Ernest was co-owner of Prill-Hahs Motor Company in Jackson. In 1964 he opened Hahs Office Equipment in Cape Girardeau where he and Anna Mae worked until his retirement. They had one other child, Gregory Hahs (b. 1942).

Pamela (Hahs) Jones graduated from Jackson High School in 1963. She lived all her life in Jackson and attended Jackson schools from first grade until high school graduation. She attended Southeast Missouri State University and was a full-time homemaker until her three children were in school. She then worked as a newswriter and advertising manager for the *Jackson Cash-Book Journal* newspaper.

Jolie, Fred, Pamela, Polly and Frederick Jones 1990

Fred and Pamela Jones are members of New McKendree Methodist Church in Jackson and have three married children and six grandchildren: Jolie and Brian McCallister (daughters Mallory Ann, Madeline Belle, and Mabrey Joie); Frederick and Shirlee Wilson Jones (daughter Jasmine Elise); and Polly and Kent Koch (daughters Brittney Morgan and Khloe Ann). *Submitted by Fred Jones*

JONES – Gerald W. Jones was born Jan. 4, 1940 in Whitewater, MO, son of Edgar O. Jones (1912-1998) and Kathleen (Rhodes) Jones (born 1922). Edgar was the son of Columbus J. Jones and Dora (Ruffner) Jones/Bartles. Kathleen is the daughter of George W. Rhodes and Belle (Proffer) Rhodes. All families were from the Whitewater area. Edgar and Kathleen Jones had four children. Gerald was the oldest. He had two younger brothers, Fred and Joe Mike, and one younger sister, Nancy. Gerald attended elementary grades in one-room schoolhouses in Whitewater and Stroderville. He attended Delta High School and Fredericktown High School. His family moved to Jackson in 1955 and he graduated from Jackson High School in 1957.

He attended Southeast Missouri State College, graduating in 1962 with a B. S. degree in

Gerry, Sarah, Clarice, Gerald and Gina Jones 1990

education. He earned seven varsity letters in collegiate track and cross county teams, held the school record in the mile run, and received the Outstanding Athlete Award (track) in 1961. He received a masters degree from the University of Missouri in 1966. He taught biology and science and was the varsity track and cross country coach in the Jackson R-2 School District from 1962-1967. He then worked with the Missouri Department of Education for six years before becoming the owner and publisher of the *Jackson Cash-Book Journal* newspaper. He was also the owner of Associated Inventory Specialists. He was elected as president of the Missouri Jaycees in 1971-72. He served in the U. S. Army and Missouri National Guard for nine years. He has been the Presiding Commissioner of Cape Girardeau County since 1995.

Clarice L. McDowell was born Nov. 4, 1942 in Granite City, IL, the daughter of Cecil McDowell (1910-1993) and Uvalde (Lassen) McDowell (born April 1, 1915), who lives in Jackson. Clarice has a sister Gloria who lives in Kansas City, and a sister Carol who lives in Nashville. Her brother Ronnie died when he was 24.

Clarice (McDowell) Jones graduated from Doniphan High School in 1960 and Southeast Missouri State College in 1964 with a B. S. degree in elementary education. She earned her masters degree in English in 1984. She has taught elementary classroom grades in Washington Elementary School in Cape Girardeau and in the Jackson R-2 School District. She has taught high school English at Perryville High School since 1985.

Gerald and Clarice Jones were married in 1964. They are members of the First Baptist Church in Jackson. They have three children. Gerald W. Jones II "Gerry" is married to Amy (Graff) Jones and they have a son, Jed (Gerald W. Jones III). Gina K. (Jones) Bader has a son, Kyle Patrick Bader. Sarah E. (Jones) Wilson is married to Steve Wilson. Gerry is an attorney with the Limbaugh law firm in Cape Girardeau. Gina is the Assistant Publisher of the *Cash-Book Journal* newspaper. Sarah is an occupational therapist at Vanderbilt Medical School, pediatric department, in Nashville. *Submitted by Gerald Jones*

JONES – Joseph Michael Jones was born July 14, 1950 in San Diego, CA, the son of Edgar O. Jones (1912-1998) and Kathleen (Rhodes) Jones (born 1922). Edgar was the son of Columbus J. Jones and Dora (Ruffner) Jones/Bartles. Kathleen is the daughter of George W. Rhodes and Belle (Proffer) Rhodes. All families were from the Whitewater area. Edgar Jones was on active duty in the U. S. Navy (1932-53) and was stationed in San Diego when Joe Mike was born. Joe Mike is the youngest of four children. He has two brothers, Gerald and Fred, and one sister, Nancy. Joe Mike attended Jackson schools from kindergarten until he graduated from Jackson High School in 1968.

Joe Mike received a B. S. in Mathematics from Southeast Missouri State University in 1972. He also received a Master of Business Administration from Southeast Missouri State University, graduating in 1975. He received his Ph.D. in Business Administration - Marketing in 1991 from the University of Missouri at Columbia. He is an Associate Professor of Marketing at North Dakota State University in Fargo, ND. He teaches graduate and undergraduate courses in marketing research and strategic marketing. He has presented numerous scholarly papers and has been a guest lecturer at conferences and universities throughout the United States.

Joe Mike and Helga Jones with their sons Nicholas and Andrew, 1992

Joe Mike and Helga I. Lehmann were married in 1981. Helga was born Oct. 12, 1957 in Caracas, Venezuela, the daughter of Burkhard F. Lehmann (1923-1999) and Helga V. Lehmann (born 1922). Helga is an elementary school teacher and author of children's books. She has published two children's books.

Joe Mike and Helga Jones have two sons, Nicholas Owen Jones and Andrew Burkhard Jones. Nicholas was born Aug. 3, 1986 in Jefferson City, MO. Andrew was born June 5, 1990 in Potsdam, NY. Both Nicholas and Andrew enjoy participating in several sports, including hockey, soccer, and track. Both are good students and have won awards for both athletics and schoolwork.   *Submitted by Joe Mike Jones*

JONES – Nancy D. Jones was born Nov. 27, 1946 in Whitewater, MO, the only daughter of Edgar O. Jones (1912-1998) and Kathleen (Rhodes) Jones (born 1922). Edgar and Kathleen Jones had four children: Gerald Wayne (b. 1940); Fred Owen (b. 1944); Nancy Delaine, and Joseph Michael (b. 1950). Nancy attended her first elementary grades in a one-room schoolhouse in Whitewater. After moving to Fredericktown for one year, her family moved to Jackson in 1955. While in Jackson she was a member of the First Baptist Church where she was active in the choir and Girls' Auxiliary. She attended Jackson schools from the fourth grade until she graduated from Jackson High School in 1964.

She attended Southeast Missouri State College, graduating in 1968 with a B. S. degree in education, majoring in English and social studies. She taught high school English for one year in Morley, MO. She converted to Roman Catholicism in 1966 and married John Gruenloh in 1967. During the next 12 years she moved to several cities with her husband and family. Her son, John Aaron Gruenloh, was born in 1970. Daniel Joseph Gruenloh was born in 1974, and her daughter, Stephanie Kathleen Gruenloh, was born in 1980.

While in Sedalia, MO, she founded the Birthright of Pettis County in 1975, a volunteer orga-

Daniel, Stephanie, and Aaron Gruenloh, with their mother, Nancy Jones, 1999

nization that is still in existence. She developed the first high school counseling program for Sacred Heart High School, also in Sedalia, MO. After moving to Janesville, WI, she earned a Master of Science degree in social work from the University of Wisconsin-Madison. She developed a statewide Employee Assistance Program for the State of Wisconsin Transportation Department in 1988. Later she became the Executive Director of the Stateline Area YWCA in Wisconsin (1990). In 1999, as Director of Education of a Wisconsin hospice, she created and produced a CD for the purpose of assisting in counseling those who have experienced personal loss. Since 2001, she has been the Director of Human Resources at a large regional Janesville skilled nursing facility.

Her marriage ended in 1986 and she reared three children alone. She remained in Wisconsin, with her children all living in the same area of Wisconsin. Aaron is a computer technician in Marshfield, WI with his wife Debbie, and son, Timothy John. Daniel is an accounting supervisor with Kallista, a subsidiary of Kohler Manufacturing in Sheboygan, WI. Stephanie is an honor student at the University of Wisconsin-Milwaukee, majoring in microbiology.

Nancy is currently writing a book on personal spirituality and is interested in neighborhood and family activities. *Submitted by Nancy Jones*

KAMP – Earl Kamp was born May 4, 1923 at Tilsit, MO, the son of Albert Kamp Sr. and Nora Bodenstein Kamp. Earl graduated from Jackson High School and received a degree from the National Radio Institute in 1942. He worked on the family farm until 1943, at which time he came to live in Jackson and started a radio shop above the Western Auto Store on West Main Street, just across the street from the Old Jackson Hotel, where he roomed for $3.00 a week.

His first big success was converting battery-powered radios to electric and vice versa during the war. Later he built radios, taking blank cabinets and installing five-tube radio chassis. They sold about as fast as Earl could make them. There was a great demand for them at that time. He later moved his small shop to ground level on Court Street, west of the Courthouse, which formerly housed the Hoffman Shoe Repair Shop.

Shortly after WWII was over, appliances became available and Earl started handling appliances and needed more space, at which time he moved to the new building John V. Priest built at 119 S. Hope Street in Jackson. He rented the building at first and later bought it in 1947.

On June 24, 1945 he married Jessie Evans, the daughter of Sam Evans and Malinda Lehman Evans. They were married at St. Paul Lutheran Church in Jackson and are still members of that church. Jessie was also a graduate of Jackson High School.

At the time of their marriage, Jessie was Secretary and Payroll Clerk at the Jackson Hosiery Mill and worked there 11-1/2 years. She discontinued her employment there in 1956 to work in her husband's appliance store. At that time, television was new to this area and lots of televisions were sold and installations made. Jessie took special training in St. Louis and Louisville, KY, to design G. E. kitchens. Later, they installed many G. E. kitchens in Jackson and Cape Girardeau. In July 1957 the store won the "Kitchen of the Month" contest from General Electric for the best-designed kitchen. This contest covered the St. Louis and surrounding areas. The kitchen was the Mr. and Mrs. Adolph Borgfield

Earl and Jessie Kamp

Earl and Jessie Kamp at beach dinner party in 1968 in the Bahamas

kitchen located in Indian Hills in Jackson. The name of the store was then "Kamp's Sales and Service" and the store continued in operation until 1959, when Earl and one of his employees invented a welder and named it MOR-AMP. They manufactured welders under the name of MOR-AMP, INC. for approximately five years and it was then discontinued.

When in the appliance business, the Kamps won several exotic trips, based on quantity of

Commercial Building at 119 South Hope Street, Jackson

sales. Some of their memorable trips were to Las Vegas, Miami, Three Lakes, Wisconsin and the Bahamas.

When the Kamps purchased the commercial building at 119 S. Hope, it housed the appliance store (later Kamp's Koin Wash), two rental apartments (where Earl and Jessie later lived for 17 years), Jessie's Income Tax Service office, a woodwork shop where Earl made grandfather clocks in his spare time, and also another rental outlet. See picture below.

Earl Kamp and grandfather clock in 1994

In the woodwork shop, Earl spent many spare hours making grandfather clock cabinets, and some furniture, and repairing some antique furniture. Earl has handcrafted over 50 grandfather clocks.

Earl started a land clearing and farming business in 1964 which last approximately 30 years.

On Feb. 15, 2001 Earl and Jessie sold their commercial building and laundry business and are retired at their home at 603 N. Russell, Jackson, MO. As of this writing, they have been married 57 years and have been in business in Jackson over 55 years. Of all the many places they have been in the United States and outside the country, they say they would still pick Jackson as their choice place to live. *Submitted by Jessie Kamp*

KAMP – William and Bertha (Pensel) Kamp had four sons: Louis; Ray; Otto and Alvin. We spoke German most of the time, and at other times English. Dad had the trade of cement mason, carpenter and jack of all trades. In the early 1920s he drove a 1911 Model T Ford to Jackson to work at Millers Garage as a mechanic.

We had the only filling station in Tilsit. A customer would come and ask for a couple gallons of gas. Mom or Dad would go to the garage to the 100-gallon tank which had a spigot on the bottom. One gallon at a time was drained out in a one-gallon container which in turn was poured, using a funnel, into a five-gallon can. This was then poured into the customer's tank. It was cash and carry, no credit or barter of produce.

Sometimes in the summer a family would have a Saturday night dance. My parents usually attended. They would send me to my grandparents, John and Karoline Pensel, about three blocks from our home, who would babysit with me. Grandma could only speak German, but Grandpa could speak some English too.

Almost in the center of the village lived a black man called George Lacey. He could be hired by the day doing hard work such as tilling the soil, splitting wood, cleaning fence rows, etc. It is unknown if he was a widower or a bachelor. He was treated with respect and fitted in well with all.

My first grade teacher was Viola Hoffman and since I was brought up speaking mostly German, I had a little difficulty with English, learning the 3-Rs.

Dad got rid of the potato bugs by using a rusty pan with a small amount of kerosene in the bottom. He would use a stick to shake the potato plants, catching the bugs in the pan of kerosene. No chemicals were used, as this cost too much money.

In the wintertime Dad had a problem getting the old Ford started. Mom would put two cast iron kettles filled with water on the wood-fired kitchen stove until they boiled. Dad would raise the hood on the car and Mom would slowly pour the boiling water on the intake manifold

William and Bertha (Pensel) Kamp, circa 1904

while he used his left hand to pull the choke and then crank the car with his right hand. By using boiling water it helped to vaporize the gasoline and if it fired once they had it made.

We lived in a small two-story house and had a small cellar which was used to store potatoes, homemade wine and things that Mom canned. Butchering day around the first part of December was quite an event. Four persons were hired and my uncle August Huter was the butcher or boss because he always knew by heart the recipes to make summer sausage, liver sausage, and blood sausage. The day usually started around 4:00 a.m. by lighting a fire under the two large iron kettles in order to have boiling water. The day usually ended around 10:00 p.m. The pay was $2.00 for the butcher and $1.00 for other help for the entire day. Around midmorning and mid-afternoon Dad passed around a jug of bootleg whiskey for everyone to take a swig. This was done for everyone to stay warm. We moved to Jackson in 1926. *Submitted by Alvin Kamp*

KASTEN – The oldest known ancestor of Vernon Kasten was Christoph Kasten, a Dragoneer of Royal Braunschweig, who was born in Germany in 1721. He and his wife had three children, one of them named Ludolph.

Ludolph was born in Sudheim, Germany in 1775, and he and his wife had four children, one of them named Heinrich Christoph, born in 1809. Ludolph was a musketeer in the 2nd Inf. Reg. (Hannover) and later became a woods "Aufseher." Ludolph's wife died in Sudheim in 1840 and he died in Uniontown, MO in 1843.

Heinrich was married in Sudheim in 1837; three of his children were born there before April 7, 1842, and six later in Uniontown, MO, where the family arrived in mid-1842. Heinrich and his wife died two days apart in Uniontown, Dec. 9 and Dec. 11, 1898 at the age of 89, and were buried in the same grave.

Christian Kasten, the great-grandfather of Vernon Kasten and the first of the six children born in America, was born in 1845. He and his wife had seven children, the oldest being Rudolph Carl, born in Uniontown in 1868.

Rudolph was an apprentice brickmaker in Uniontown, and in 1895 he bought the William Oldenhoener Brick Company and moved to Jackson. He married Augusta Bingenheimer in 1891 and they had four sons: Arthur; Louis W.; Walter A. and John M. C. and two daughters, Edna and Emilie. R. C., as he was known, was active in his church and community and served on the City Council. His wife died in 1924, and he died in 1929. The four sons bought the half-interest of Joe Schmuke in 1920. This half-interest had been sold to Mr. Schmuke in 1905. Upon the death of their father, Rudolph, they acquired the other half and the brick plant became known as Kasten Brothers Pressed Brick Company.

Louis W. Kasten graduated from St. Paul Lutheran School and attended Jackson High School. He wanted to be a Lutheran School teacher, and was accepted at Concordia Teachers College at River Forest, IL. Upon arrival he was informed that teachers had to be able to play a foot pump organ for school singing, and they could not accept him because he was crippled as the result of falling into a buggy wheel at the age of 6. He then attended and graduated from the Cape Girardeau Business School and went to work for the Little River Drainage District in Cape Girardeau. He later accepted an accounting position with the War Department in Washington, D. C. during WWI where he met Francis Philpott of Findlay, OH. Her family had immigrated to Ohio from Kent County, England in 1853. They were married Dec. 28, 1919 in Ohio and had three children; Dorothy, Vernon and Kenneth. Francis died of pneumonia on May 27, 1927, leaving three children; a 9-month-old, a 4-year-old and a 6-1/2-year-old. She died the day after Vernon's fourth birthday. The children were taken care of by Louis' sister, Edna, until he married Edna Langehennig in 1939, the daughter of the Lutheran Minister in Jackson for many years. She died in 1995 at the age of 101. Louis Kasten was very active in the community, serving on many boards at Southeast Hospital, St. Paul Lutheran Church, and several state associations; he also served several terms as an alderman for the City of Jackson. He died in 1990 at the age of 94.

Vernon Kasten was born in 1923, and graduated from St. Paul Lutheran School and Jackson High School. He attended Southeast Missouri State College for two years before transferring to Missouri School of Mines and Metallurgy, now known as UMR, where he received a B. S. and M. S. degree in Ceramic Engineering in 1945. He and a classmate and the head of the Ceramic Engineering Department founded Ceramo Company in 1945 for the purpose of manufacturing red clay flower pots from the local clays. Vernon married Stacia Lawrence of Fayette, AL in 1957 and they have two sons, Vernon Louis Jr. and Lawrence. Vernon Jr. has a degree in Business Administration and is a vice-president at Ceramo Company. He is married to the former Stephanie Ruff and they have a 4-year-old daughter, Chloe, and live in Jackson, MO. Lawrence has an LLD Degree and is an Associate Hearing Judge with the Workman's Compensation Division of the State of Missouri. He is married to the former Alison Lane and they have a 7-year-old daughter, Laurel, and live in Cape Girardeau, MO.

The Kasten family: Chloe, Stacia, Vernon, Laurel, Vernon Jr., Stephanie, Alison, Lawrence

Vernon has been president of Ceramo Company, Inc. since its beginning and is president of Kasten Clay Products, Kasten Concrete Products, and Kasten Masonry Sales. He has been President of the voters assembly of St. Paul Lutheran Church, President of the Easter Seal Society, President of the Jackson Industrial Development Board, President of the Jackson Rotary Club, and Chairman of the Rotary District Youth Exchange Committee. He was a recipient of an UMR-MSM Entrepreneur Award in 1994 and later received an Honorary Professional Engineering Degree from the University of Missouri-Rolla. He is still active in the business at Ceramo Company, and he and his wife reside at 1220 Broadridge Drive in Jackson. *Submitted by Vernon Kasten*

Willie T. Kasten and Mary N. Morton, married May 20, 1923

KASTEN – Willie Kasten was born July 29, 1900, near Pocahontas, MO. His parents were of German descent so he did not speak English until he started to school. At age 21, Willie and his father, Theodore, bought the Vogel Brothers' store in Pocahontas. It was a general merchandise store.

On May 20, 1923, he married Mary Morton. Mary lived on a farm near Fruitland at the time. She was the daughter of Robert and Nellie (McNeely) Morton. Mary joined Willie's church (Zion Lutheran) and attended the services every Sunday even when they had German services and she couldn't understand anything. Was that love or what? This couple had two children, Eugene and Ruth. They grew up in Pocahontas. Eugene married Evelyn Rauh on May 9, 1948, and Ruth married Eugene Sample on Oct. 17, 1948.

When Willie was a teenager, he was driving a team of horses one day and the horses got scared. They started running with the wagon and he couldn't get them stopped. He fell and broke his collarbone. A Dr. Sample was practicing medicine near Pocahontas at the time, so he set the bone in place.

Later Willie bought a grocery store of his own in Pocahontas and operated it for many years. Mary stayed home with the children, tended a large garden, milked a cow, sold cream to neighbors, and did the general work at home. In later years Willie bought a grocery store and meat market in Ste. Genevieve, MO, leaving Mary to run the store in Pocahontas. After a few years he bought a store in Jackson, MO and another one in Cape Girardeau. They moved to Cape Girardeau where he retired.

Mary died April 3, 1973, and Willie passed away April 25, 1977. *Submitted by Ruth Sample and Marge Swan*

KAUFMAN – Palma Lee Kaufman Owens was born Jan. 14, 1923, the daughter of Albert Kaufman (born 1877; died 1950) and Rettie Thompson Kaufman (born 1880; died 1968). Albert and Rettie lived in Jackson on Jefferson while he was a rural mail carrier and sold fruit trees until he purchased a dairy farm in Fruitland in 1904, where he was respected as a diversified farmer, participating in all community affairs. He assisted a few people in building the first Methodist Church in Fruitland. The Kaufmans and Owens have been Methodists since the 1900s. Dad Kaufman played the violin and accordion for Saturday night country dances in private homes. Pam and her sisters Iona, Verda, and Odene assisted with farm chores. While young they enjoyed the community "hog-butchering" days as well as the hot summer wheat-threshing activities in the home.

Pam's elementary and high school years were in the Fruitland District until the school was consolidated with Jackson in 1940. Her last year she graduated from Jackson High School in 1940. Following graduation she obtained a business degree from the Steimle Business College.

Albert and Rettie Kaufman, October 1902

She was employed by United Shoe Machinery, Inc. in Cape Girardeau, where she met her boss's nephew, Dr. Vern E. Owens, which led to a war correspondence. World War II started Dec. 7, 1941 and girls at home started writing letters to servicemen to cheer them and inform them of activities on the homefront.

A true courtship began with Vern's romantic messages to Pam from the Pacific via APO free mail. His naval ship the *USS Bismarch Sea*, was sunk at Iwo Jima on Feb. 21, 1945, by two Japanese kamikaze (suicide) pilots. Two-thirds of the Navy men were lost at sea while the others were being strafed in the water by other Japanese pilots. Hours later they were rescued by a Merchant Marine ship.

Vern and Pam were married in Yuma, AZ on June 29, 1945. They returned to Cape Girardeau where Vern and Pam worked while he attended Southeast Missouri State University. In 1947 he transferred to the University of Missouri Veterinary School and Pam transferred her job to the Missouri Employment Office in Columbia, MO; she also worked for the Missouri State Teacher's Association and the U. S. Production and Marketing Administration. In 1953 Vern received a Doctorate in Veterinary Medicine and a B. S. Degree in Agriculture. They returned to Jackson for Vern to open the Oak Ledge Veterinary Hospital. They had five children: Dustin; Mark; Nanette; Toni and Debra.

Dr. Vern E. Owens, U. S. Navy, 1942

After Dr. Owens' death on July 4, 1975, Pam has worked for the Social Security Administration and the Southeast Missouri State University Museum. At the time of his death, the five children were in college, subsequently obtaining these goals: Dustin attended Missouri University and received degrees from Southeast Missouri State University in Biology and Art, and he owns Oak Ledge Dental Lab; Mark obtained

Kaufman home from 1904 to 1950, two miles east of Fruitland, 1999

a B. S. degree from Missouri University and his Masters and PhD. From the University of Utah in Psychology and has a private practice; Nanette attended Missouri University and received a B. S. degree in Education at Southeast Missouri State University and is teaching in a Christian school; Toni obtained a B. S. degree in Nursing at Southeast Missouri State University (worked in St. Francis Hospital 12 years) and a Masters in Communications from Sagamon University; and Debra obtained a degree in Graphic Arts at Southeast Missouri State University and worked in their print shop for over 20 years. *Submitted by Pam Owens*

KEENE – Francis Everett Keene (Frank E.) was born in St. Joseph, MO on Jan. 5, 1921 to Frank and Hilda Katherine Chequer Keene. Frank's (Sr.) paternal ancestry was English, while his maternal grandfather Kiene (note spelling) emigrated from Bavaria, Germany to the United States accompanied by Adolphus Busch in the 1850s. Hilda's father, Samuel Chequer, arrived from England in the 1890s.

While in college, Frank E. learned to fly, and with WWII brewing, he enlisted in the Aviation Cadets in 1941, receiving his Lieutenant's commission in the U. S. Army Air Corps on Jan. 14, 1942. In 1942 he was transferred to India to fly the Hump (over the Himalayan Mountains) to China, where he earned the Distinguished Flying Cross with two Oak Leaf Clusters and the Air Medal with three Oak Leaf Clusters before returning to the air base in Memphis, TN in September 1943.

Mysie Statler was born in Bollinger County to Louis W. and Emma Conrad Statler on Dec. 16, 1918. Her family moved to Cape Girardeau in 1920 where she attended Franklin and Central High Schools and graduated from College High School after her family moved to Jackson. After graduating from Rubicam Business College (she later earned credits from Stephens College) she became office manager of the Memphis, TN office of Copperweld Steel Company where she met Capt. Frank E. Keene. They were married Sept. 8, 1944 in Hernando, MS.

For the next 10 years they led a fascinating life, transferring from air base to base from Mem-

Frank E. and Mysie Statler Keene, 1944

phis to Manchester, NH; to Presque Isle, ME; to Hamilton Field and then Travis Field, CA; to Tinker Field, OK; and to Prestwick, Scotland, usually with some interesting twists. For instance, they were in Presque Isle, ME, ten miles from the Canadian border in the far northeast corner of Maine, when WWII ended and Frank E. received orders to Okinawa to fly troops into Japan. Frank E. handed Mysie a stack of gas ration coupons and said, "See you at Hamilton Field in 60 days, and by the way, it's just north of San Francisco across the Golden Gate Bridge." This was almost 3,500 miles away, with no interstates, and the farthest Mysie had ever driven alone was from Jackson to Memphis! When orders came for Scotland, Frank E. flew off and six weeks later Mysie drove their car to New York and put it on a ship for England before sailing on the *Queen Mary*. In 1948 and 1949 Frank E. flew the Berlin Airlift in Germany for six months. He ended his military career as a Lieutenant Colonel. Frank E. became a pilot with Ozark Airlines in 1955. He flew with that airline until his sudden death from a heart attack on Oct. 27, 1975. He had amassed 28,000 hours flying time when he died.

Frank E. and Mysie had a daughter, Kimberley Susan, born Aug. 11, 1954. She graduated from Jackson High School in 1972, from Stephens College, magna cum laude in 1976 and received her MBA from Washington University, St. Louis She and Steven Bollinger were married at New McKendree Methodist Church on May 21, 1977. Steven received a degree in Mechanical Engineering cum laude from the University of Missouri, Rolla, MO in 1977. On July 27, 1991, they had a son, Ross Alan Bollinger. After college Kimberley worked for McDonnell-Douglas and was manager, Contracts and Pricing, Advanced Systems and Technologies when she resigned to move to South Bend, IN. She is Director of Finance, CNA Unisources and Steven is a professional engineer with EFI.

Mysie was very active in civic affairs, serving as president of the Jackson R-2 PTA, 1962-64; Girl Scout Leader and Neighborhood Chairman; co-chairman of the Jackson Sesquicentennial celebration in 1965; and was named president of the Jackson Community Betterment Committee (1965-1969). Since the latter was sponsored by the Jackson Chamber of Commerce, she was told to join the Chamber to give monthly reports, so in 1965 she likely became the first woman member of the Chamber and is still a member. She helped organize the Jackson Heritage Association and served on the Board of Directors 1977-1980. Appointed to the City Park Board in 1970, she served as president 1973-1978 during the establishment of the newly-purchased north 50 acres of the City Park and the new swimming pool. She was on the Board of Directors of the Chamber of Commerce 1976-1985 and 1987-1989 and was elected Chamber president 1982-1893 and was the first woman to hold that office.

She was on the Board of Directors of the Jackson Industrial Development Company 1981-1990, president 1984-1985 and 1987-1988, and was on the Board of Directors of the Jackson Industrial Development Authority 1981-1990. Mysie was a member of the Southeast Missouri Medical Center Board seven years, Community Chest Board three years, and Cape County Park Board. On Jan. 1, 1981 she was appointed a commissioner on the Southeast Missouri Regional Port Authority, and held every office including chairman (1993-1994) before retiring in 1994.

On the state level Mysie was appointed by Governor Teasdale to the Governor's Advisory County on Inter-Governmental and Community Services Program (1977-1981), and by Governor Bond to the Missouri Private Industry Counsel (1981-1983) and to the Missouri Job Training Coordinating Council (1982-1991).

Mysie also served on dozens of committees and compiled a 62-page Fact Book for the J.I.D.C. Among the awards she received was the Governor's Leadership Award for Community Betterment for 1971-1972 (one statewide award given annually), the R. A. Fulenwider Meritorious Community Service Award in 1984, and the Jackson Heritage Association Award in 2001. Mysie still lives in Jackson. *Submitted by Mysie Statler Keene*

KEISKER – Walter J. Keisker was born July 10, 1899, at Jarvis, MO. One of seven children, he was the son of dairy farmer John and Magdalene Keisker.

At the age of 13 Walter realized he wanted to become a minister when he heard a young seminary student speak at a youth gathering. He entered Concordia High School at Concordia, MO, and shortly thereafter to begin his studies. He graduated from the seminary in June of 1923 and married Zola Mae Fikuart of Farmington on Nov. 29 of that year. They lived in Flat River (now Park Hills) where he was pastor of Trinity Lutheran Church for 15 years. Those years were shadowed by the Great Depression which affected the entire county, and living conditions were sparse for everyone.

Rev. Keisker served churches in Flat River and Bonne Terre and spoke to miners at noon at the St. Joe National Lead Company Mines. He took an elevator 300 feet underground and would speak to workers during lunch and then he would go to another area and talk with supervisors.

On Nov. 17, 1938, the Keisker family moved to Jackson where Rev. Keisker became pastor of St. Paul Lutheran Church. He said, "I found Jackson with its population of 3000 to be a very solid community," and at the age of 102, still found that to be the case, adding that people in the community have to be convinced, but when that is accomplished, they move forward without hesitation. This was evident when, under his guidance, St. Paul built a new school in 1951 and a new church which was dedicated in 1962.

There are many memorable events which Rev. Keisker recalled during his years in the ministry. These include church services held on VE Day and VJ Day, both of which were held on short notice to a full church. He recalled the blizzard of Feb. 25, 1979, when I-55 was closed and St. Paul Church became "an inn by the roadside" for 75 stranded travelers. No church services were held that day, however, Keisker walked to church and telephoned the pastor, Rev. Earl Weis, to warn him of the blizzard.

Mae and Walter Keisker were married 69 years before her death on July 2, 1992. They had two daughters, Ruth Illers of Jackson and Virginia Goodwin of Cape Girardeau.

During his long years of service, Rev. Keisker was instrumental in bringing Lutheran Family and Children's Services to the area. He was always community-oriented and was a 50-year member of Jackson Chamber of Commerce. He also served as chairman of Cape County Historical Society and was a member of the Appleton Bridge Committee.

In 1993 Rev. Keisker was given the honorary degree of Doctor of Divinity from Concordia Seminary and in October of that year entered the Lutheran Home Residential Care Facility in Cape Girardeau where he conducted Bible classes, held services at various times and called on residents.

Keisker family, 1933. Mae and Walter with daughters Virginia Mae, 1 year, and Ruth, 5 years

He was humble, unassuming and faithful to his beliefs for over 102 years, a stalwart member of the community, a true-blue American and a loving example to friends and family.

With his mind sharp and his concern and prayers for the country he loved following the terrorist attacks being uppermost in his thoughts, Walter Keisker died peacefully in his sleep on Sept. 18, 2001. *Submitted by Ruth Illers*

KEY - John Key, the son of Martin Key, married Martha Tandy and had five children: Martin Key II, born in 1715 in Virginia, married Ann Bibb and had twelve children; Mary Key, born in 1717, married Robert Dalton; Henry Key, born in 1730, married Mary Clark; John Key Jr., born in 1731 in Albemarle County, VA, married first, Agnes Witt, and second, Susanna Watts; and George Key, born in 1733, married Nancy Edwards. John Key died in 1764

John Key Jr. and Agnes Witt, the daughter of William Witt (1675-1754), had five children. After Agnes' early death, John married Susanna Watts and had eight more children. Their first son, William Waller Key, was born about 1760 in Amherst County, VA. William married Elizabeth Alford (born 1765-66 in Frederick County, VA) and had 10 children. Their youngest son, Martin Green Hill Key, was born in Olneyville, Davidson County, TN, on Oct. 27, 1809.

Martin G. H. Key and Elizabeth Dunkin Shumate were married in Olneyville on May 26, 1831. Elizabeth, the daughter of William Willis Lawson Shumate and Sarah Caroline Felts, was born on Sept. 3, 1813, in Fauquier County, VA. Martin and Elizabeth had 14 children, all of whom were born in Olneyville except the youngest son, Thomas, who was born in Roanoke, AR. Martin died on July 4, 1864, when he was robbed and murdered in Fruitland, MO.

The children of Martin Green Hill and Elizabeth Shumate Key were: Louisa Frances Key, born May 5, 1832; William Willis Key, born August 1833, married Eliza Ann Willis on Feb. 17, 1861 and had seven children; Sarah Elizabeth Key, born Sept. 6, 1835, married W. A. Rodgers on Oct. 28, 1858, and had three children; Mary Mariah Key, born March 5, 1837, married William Brightwell on Aug. 23, 1858; John Taliferro Key, born Jan. 22, 1839; Martha Jane Key, born Sept. 26, 1840, married William W. Cagle on May 11, 1859; Elvira Caroline Key, born Dec. 31, 1842, married Joseph Swann on Nov. 27, 1860; Elvirus Lawson Key, born Dec. 31, 1842; Frances "Frank" Josephus Key, born Oct. 4, 1845, married Mary Jane Rodgers and had eight children; Julius Shumate Key married Polly Ann Eaker Baker and had one daughter, Louisa Key; Fannie Shumate Key, born Nov. 19, 1849; Joseph Addison Key, born Feb. 18, 1852, married Aletha W. Atchison on Sept. 3, 1877, and had 10 children; Ann Isabelle Key, born Oct. 6, 1855, married Soloman C. Bud Baker and had four children; and Thomas Walter Key, born Aug. 27, 1860, married Alice Marie Noel and had 11 children.

After Elvira's first husband, Joseph Swann, was killed in the Civil War, she married William Watkins and had three children, only one of whom lived to maturity. Daughter Emily Jane Watkins, born in 1869, married Marcelles W. Hunt on Oct. 12, 1886. Marcelles was the son of Mathew Hunt (born 1813-14; died March 15, 1890) and Sampian Lesseldine Hudgins (born 1825). Marcelles died young and after his death, Emily Jane left her three children, Russell (born July 29, 1887, married Irene Slater), Mamie Elizabeth (born Jan. 22, 1888, married Clarence Berry), and Beulah (born March 31, 1892, married Ed. Dial), with their grandmother Elvira Watkins to raise.

Beulah and Ed. Dial had seven children. Their second child was Pauline Dial, who was born in 1914 and who married Emmit Gaither. *Submitted by Catherine Gaither Allison, daughter of Emmit and Pauline Dial Gaither*

KIES – Adolph E. Kies (1894-1971) married Grace Vinyard (1895-1986) at the home of Dr. and Mrs. G. W. Vinyard on March 15, 1917. They built a home near the Kies Farm on Highway 25 South.

Adolph studied Business at Marvin College and Agriculture at the University of Missouri. He was Manager and Secretary-Treasurer of the Cape County Livestock Shipping Association in Jackson from 1925-1971. He was Secretary-Treasurer of the National Farm Loan Association in Jackson, retiring in 1959. He served 15 years on the Jackson Board of Education, seven years as President. He was a charter member of the Southeast Missouri District Fair Board and served 13 years as President, and was President of the Missouri Fair Association.

Grace graduated from Stephens College, Columbia, MO, majoring in music. She was gifted musically. She played the organ for the church hymns at 9 years of age, the piano and organ for the First Baptist Church throughout her lifetime, playing consecutively for 30 years. She played ragtime and other popular music for her high school classmates at Stephens College, and at many other social events.

Grace and Adolph Kies

The couple had five children: Harriett, at age 16, was "Miss Jackson" and the first female majorette of the Jackson High School Band. She attended Southeast Missouri State College and studied at a secretarial school in St. Louis. She married Fred H. Abbott Jr. and they had four children: Fred III; Bruce Vinyard; Judith Bailard and Deborah Hawke. They reside in California. After retirement, Harriett became an artist and traveled.

Vinyard L. Kies was a well-known dentist in Jackson for 44 years. He was an Eagle Scout in his youth. He was a graduate of the University of Missouri at Kansas City School of Dentistry. He married Margaret Matvy, R.N. They had three children: Richard L. Kies, M.D. of Cape Girardeau; Jane Kies of Seattle, WA; and Judy Junk, R.N. of Lenexa, KS. Dr. Kies served as the 100th President of the Missouri Dental Association 1968-69. He also served as President and Secretary of the Southeast Dental Society and helped organize that group. In addition, he served as a member of the Governor's Commission on Dental Treatment of Handicapped and Crippled Children, and as President of the Missouri Dental Board of Examiners.

Left to right: Dr. Vinyard Kies, Virginia Kies, Harriett Kies Abbott, Sue Kies Horne, Miriam Kies, 1951

Miriam J. Kies was Carnival Queen her sophomore year of high school. At the age of 16, she was "Miss Jackson." She attended Southeast Missouri State College and graduated from St. Luke's Hospital School of Nursing in St. Louis.

Virginia L. Kies was Basketball Queen in high school. She attended Southeast Missouri State College majoring in music and business. She was employed by Southwestern Bell Telephone Company in Cape Girardeau as secretary to the District Manager for 39 years. She has been a soprano soloist.

Marguerite Sue graduated from the University of Missouri with a major in art. She married William Earl Horne. Their children are; William Earl Jr.; Cynthia Sue and Robert Bruce. They reside in Jacksonville, FL. *Submitted by Virginia Kies*

KINDER - Adam Kinder, born in 1773, along with his brothers, Conrad, Jacob and John, came to Cape Girardeau County from Lincoln County, NC around 1800. Adam and Jacob had married sisters, the daughters of Revolutionary War Captain Lewis Lineberger. Adam married Susan Lineberger and settled in an area southwest of Gordonville. Their son, Joel Lee Kinder, born in 1804, married Sarena Irene Thompson and also lived in that area. Joel and Serena's son, Levi Jackson Kinder, born in 1829, married Martha Jane O'Neal and they homesteaded land along the present County Road 231 and built a log house and barn buildings. Levi farmed the 200 acres which later became the home for his son William Martin Kinder, born in 1854. A second frame home and barn buildings were built in 1887.

William Martin Kinder married Louisa Nussbaum, daughter of John Jacob Nussbaum who, along with his two brothers, Samuel and Henry, came from Aarau, Switzerland in the 1840s. John Jacob lived in the Gordonville area, south of Zion Lutheran Church. He married Wilhelmina Achtermann in 1849. John Jacob Nussbaum and his family sold their farm and home and went west by covered wagon to the gold fields of California during the days of the gold rush. After losing their claim due to flooding they returned to Cape Girardeau County and settled near Stroderville, south of Whitewater. Louisa was born in 1854 while the family was in California.

William Martin Kinder and Louisa had four children. William Leo, who married Della Lou Smith and with their children, Ruth Caroline, Howard Leo, Charles Russell and Dorothy Mae, lived in Jackson, where William Leo worked at and retired from the Cape County Milling Company. John Levi never married and lived with his brother Roy. In 1922 Roy married Alma Clara Krueger of the Hanover Community. The youngest of William Martin and Louisa's children, a daughter, Lera Mable, married John Quade and with their children Ruby, Linus, Cleman and Norman lived and farmed west of Jackson off the present Route 34.

Roy and Alma lived on the home place where Roy and his brother John Levi farmed and owned and operated a steam tractor-driven sawmill and threshing machine during the 1920s and 1930s. Roy and Alma had three children. Lorene Alice married Delmar Keller; Arlene Joann married Roby Kight, and Elroy Frederick married Mary Susan Sciortino.

Levi Jackson Kinder and his wife, William Martin Kinder and his wife, and Louisa and son John Levi are buried in the Thompson Cemetery off County Road 222 on the Samuel Thompson farm, now owned and farmed by Larry and Bernice Lukow. The cemetery was restored in the 1960s by Leeman Kinder, Cecil Devore and Glenn O'Neal along with others. The Thompson Cemetery Association, with chairman Elroy Kinder, now administers the cemetery and recent documentation has been found to affirm that Adam Kinder, Joel Kinder and other family members are buried there in unmarked locations.

Elroy Kinder attended the one-room Liberty School, the second building, now in very poor condition, along County Road 231. His teachers were John Devore, Doris Brennecke (Davault), Vivian Lemly and Doris Trickey. The school closed in 1945 due to declining enrollment. Elroy and his family moved from the farm in 1942 to South Kingshighway near Cape Girardeau where he attended Marquette School, then College High School. After two years in the U. S. Army serving as a Battalion Personnel Clerk in Stuttgart, Germany, he returned and attended Southeast Missouri State University, graduating in 1960 with degrees in Education, Biology and Geology, and later a masters degree in Counseling and postgraduate work in Historic Preservation. He taught in the Cape Girardeau Public Schools for 30 years, retiring in 1992. He presently works as Parish Assistant for Hanover Lutheran Church. Mary Susan retired as a R.N. in Cape Girardeau Public Schools and area hospitals. They have four children. David Frederick, married to Cheryl Lynn nee Pogue; John Joseph; Kathy Jane; and Jill Suzanne, married to Chris Haman. Elroy has written several family histories and researched and has written the history of Hanover Lutheran Church, the first Lutheran church in Cape Girardeau County. He has served on the Historic Preservation Commission of Cape Girardeau and wrote the 1987 nomination for inclusion of Old Hanover Lutheran Church on the National Register of Historic Places. In addi-

Elroy and Mary Susan Kinder

tion to the Thompson Cemetery Association, he also serves as Chairman for the German Evangelical Church and Cemetery Association, east of Dutchtown, and Arnsberg Cemetery Association, near Friedheim. Elroy and Mary Susan live at 3227 Bloomfield Road and enjoy their one grandson, Jared Eli Kinder. *Submitted by Elroy F. Kinder*

KINDER – Robert Kinder was born June 22, 1939 in Peoria, IL, the son of Lonnie Kinder (born 1899; died 1979) and Marie (Miller) Kinder (born 1899; died 2000).

Lonnie Kinder, a 1919 Cape Central graduate, attended Southeast Missouri State University, where he played football for the Southeast Missouri State University Indians. Two years later he transferred to St. Louis University where he was recruited on a football scholarship. After graduation, Lonnie accepted a position with Caterpillar Company and moved to Peoria, IL. Lonnie had two brothers, Andrew, who resided in Jackson and was the owner of Kinder's West Side Grocery and James, who resided in the state of California and was an author of psychology and audio-visual books.

Marie Kinder, a 1918 Jackson High School graduate, completed an elementary education degree from Southeast Missouri State University in 1929. She taught at Crystal City, MO, then at Washington, MO and finally at Jackson, MO. Marie was an only child.

Lonnie and Marie were married in 1935 and resided in Peoria, IL. After a 10-year stay and a 5-year-old son, Robert, the Kinders returned home. Lonnie took over the Burfordville family farm, and Marie taught first and second grade in the Jackson School District. They lived in the city of Jackson from 1945 to 1965. They built a home on the family farm in 1965. They were members of the First Presbyterian Church in Jackson.

Linder Miller farm, 1944. Left to right; Lonnie Kinder, father; Robert Kinder, son; Linder Miller, grandfather

Robert was a member of the Future Farmers of America for three years and worked part time at Schaper's IGA while attending high school. He graduated from Jackson High School in 1957. After high school, he worked with his father on the family farm where they raised cattle and row cropped. He was a member of the Army National Guard in Jackson, 81st MM Mortar Section from 1958 to 1963.

At the 1960 Jackson Homecomers, Robert met Shirley Kester, his wife-to-be and daughter of Albert and Bertha Kester of Friedheim. The couple married May 19, 1962 at the Friedheim Lutheran Church, and settled on the Kinder property.

Robert pursued a career as an over-the-road truck driver, while both he and Shirley ran the family farm and raised four children, all of whom reside in the Jackson area. Cynthia married Mike Mirly and is the mother of Ryan (14), Ashley (13), and Deanna (2). Rodney married Vicki Neace and is the father of Breanna (3). Deborah married Aaron Abernathy and is the mother of Zachary (6) and Megan (2). Timothy married Crystal Mungle and is the father of Tyler (5) and Gage (2).

Robert and Shirley have enjoyed traveling to Alaska and touring Mt. McKinley, Denali National Park, Seward, and Anchorage (where their daughter, Deborah, was living at the time). They took a road trip to Colorado Springs for the birth of their grandson, Zachary, who was born at the Air Force Academy. They have also visited Yellowstone National Park, Niagara Falls, Mt. Rushmore, Pikes Peak and several other places. After retirement, they hope to travel to many other historical landmarks. *Submitted by Robert Kinder*

KING - Gail W. King Jr. and Gale Allen King grew up in Puxico, MO. Their parents were Gail King Sr. and Leona Phelps King and Ellsworth Allen and Virgie Tucker Allen. Gail and Gale graduated from Puxico High School. They were married in 1948. They had three children, Sue, Kathryn, and Scott. Sue and Kathryn graduated from Truman High School in Independence, MO. Scott graduated from Jackson High School in Jackson, MO. Gail, Gale, Sue, Kathryn and Scott attended the University of Missouri.

Gail received a Bachelor of Science degree and a Masters degrees from the University of Missouri in Columbia, MO and a second Masters degree from the University of Missouri in Kansas City. He worked for the University of Missouri Extension Service as County Agent in Perry County, MO, as Area Director in the Metropolitan Kansas City, MO area, and as Agronomy Specialist in Cape Girardeau County, MO. He retired from the University after 33 years and began a second career in banking and appraisal work. Gail now manages his farm in Stoddard County.

Gale's first job after college was with the University of Missouri Extension as a Home Economist in Crawford County, MO. While they lived in Perryville, MO, she taught school. She taught all eight grades at Cashion in rural Perry County; then she taught Home Economics at Oak Ridge High School, and then elementary school in Perryville. After the family moved to Independence, MO, Gale taught elementary school in the Independence Public School System. In 1977 the Kings moved to Jackson, MO where Gale taught in the elementary school until her retirement.

The King family, front row: Gail, Scott, Gale; second row: Sue, Kathryn, October 1966

Sue and Kathryn graduated from Truman High School in Independence, MO. Sue attended college at the University of Missouri in Columbia, MO, and graduated from the University of Missouri at Kansas City with a B. A. degree and Master's degree in Music. She taught choral music in the Kansas City public school before moving to Tacoma, WA, where she teaches high school choral music.

Kathryn attended the University of Missouri in Columbia and the University of Missouri in Kansas City, majoring in Business. She worked several years for Hallmark in Kansas City before moving to Jackson. She now works for KFVS TV as an account executive. Kathryn has one daughter, Madalyn Bruegging. Madalyn is now a freshman in the Jackson school system.

Scott graduated from Jackson High School in 1983. He attended Southeast Missouri State University for two years before transferring to the University of Missouri where he received a Doctorate of Veterinarian Medicine. He is now Director of Equine research for Purina. He resides in the St. Louis area with his wife and two sons, ages three and six. *Submitted by Gail King*

KING – The King family history is a story of Scot and Irish people who escaped the harsh rule of English royalty to immigrate to North Carolina in the 1700s. Some moved to southwestern Virginia before making the trek to Missouri. The first of this group settled near Leemon in 1814. Others might have scouted the area earlier but this is the earliest known documented date of settlement. Others, notably Kings and Abernathys, moved onward to Madison County where there was news of greener pastures.

Henry and Nancy Mclard King were among those early pioneers in the area. Married in 1816, they raised seven children. These children grew up and married Dunns, Sides, Abernathys, Garners, Reynolds and Daughterys. Henry and Nancy's son, James, married Sophia Daugherty. Their children attended Martin School, one of the earliest schools in Cape Girardeau County. It was constructed of poplar logs and provided a place for learning until it was replaced by Leemon School before 1900. Many of the people in the Leemon area attended Draby Chapel in the 1800s. It was one of the two early Methodist churches in the Indian Creek valley. McLains Chapel stood at the eastern end and served those in the Neelys Landing area. Both were built in the early 1850s and McLains remains today. Although the cemetery there has been maintained, the Draby Cemetery went through years of neglect and many grave markers are no longer there.

The King homeplace was a short distance east of Leemon and south of Indian Creek. Records show Samuel (son of James) and Catherine (Dunn) King living there in 1901. This 40-acre rocky hillside farm was mostly wooded and incapable of supporting a large family. The 1910 census shows a family of 11 residing there, including oldest daughter, Sarah, and her two children.

Harrison and Tavie (Wills) King, 1914

Among those children in Samuel's family was Harrison. Born in 1890, he married Tavie Wills in 1914. Harrison and Tavie moved to Neelys Landing early in their married life. The lumber and quarry industry was flourishing along with the railroad. Neelys was a busy community at this time, supporting two general mercantile stores and various smaller businesses. It was a major shipping point for livestock and provided employment for over one hundred families.

Harrison and Tavie were parents of eight children but only one son would survive to adulthood. One would drown in Indian Creek and another from a childhood intestinal infection. Robert, the oldest, was born in early 1916. He attended Iona School near Oriole and Sheppard School at Neelys but dropped out before graduating to help support the struggling family. His first job was helping Ivie McLain, the town "Justice of the Peace." Ivie was a fisherman. Robert would control the oar boat while Ivie pulled in the nets. While still a teenager, Robert was working in the quarries at Neelys and working at sawmills during the winter. His father played the fiddle at local dances. Robert had learned to play the instrument as a young lad and by now was in demand for the big gatherings.

In 1936 he married Geneva Morton, a very attractive young lady from Neelys and an accomplished pianist. This couple's "Home Place" was across the road from Sheppard School and one mile north of Neelys. Most of their eight children would be born while they lived there.

In the 1950s land was being purchased by the state for the proposed Trail of Tears Park. By this time Neelys was in a rapid state of decline. Eager to move closer to Jackson, the couple sold the home to one of the displaced families from the park. In 1952, Robert purchased a service station and tire service in Jackson. He had been taught the art of tire vulcanizing during WWII when there were shortages and the repair system gave added life to rayon tires of that era. This business is still family-owned, celebrating 50 years of continuous operation in 2002. In the late 1960s the family would be living in Jackson. All eight of their children would graduate from Jackson public schools. Today, they reside within a few miles of one another and are parents of another generation. But that's another story. *Submitted by Gene King*

KNOTT – John and Louisa Burtles Knott were from Charles County, MD. They came to Jackson, MO about 1835. John was born in 1790, the son of Justinian Knott. He died shortly after arriving in Missouri. Louisa was born in 1791, the daughter of William Burtles and Sarah Wathen. Louisa died on May 1, 1857. They had the following children: William Valentine (1813-1860); Sarah Lee (1815-?); John "Jack" Richard (1817-aft. 1880); Benedict "Dick" (1820-1860) who married Ann E. Elliot; Sarah Ann (1822- 1886) who first married Johnson Ranney and then Erin McFerron; Mary Louisa (1824-1890) who married Miles Niblack; Jane Catherine (1826-1889); George Andrew (1829-died 1899 in CA); Ellen (1831-1905); and Margaret Elisa (1835-1873) who married Henry Sperling. Daughters Jane and Ellen never married.

Benedict Burtles Knott was born Jan. 13, 1820 in Charles County, MD. He married on Dec. 20, 1850 to Ann Elizabeth Elliot in Cape Girardeau County. They had the following children: Lucretia E. (1852-?); Lucy Ann (1855-1922) who married Robert William Searcy; Charles (1856-?); Stephen A. (1858-after 1930 in AR); and Elizabeth B. (1860-1930) who married David Ellington Talley in 1881.

Benedict died on Aug. 27, 1860 and his brother William Valentine Knott died a week or so later. Benedict owned 200 acres of land that was part of Survey 2203 in Township 31 N and Range 12 E. His log cabin was approximately six miles west of Jackson, a short distance from Byrd Creek in Link School District. Elizabeth Knott Talley inherited the cabin and surrounding 40 acres of land. *Submitted by Dawn Dement Detring*

KRAEMER – Arthur Claude Kraemer was born July 3, 1921 to Edwin Otto Heinrich Kraemer and Mollie (Farrow) Kraemer in a log house near Egypt Mills, MO. His grandparents were John A. and Louisa (Froemsdorf) Kraemer and Alfred and Elizabeth (Welty) Farrow.

Arthur was always thinking up ideas and inventing things. Around age 12 he made a two-wheel scooter similar to the ones sold in stores today. Next he decided a threshing machine was needed, so he spent hours making one approximately two feet wide and six feet long.

Arthur asked his father to get him a gasoline engine, but he put him off. One day as Arthur was walking along Highway 177 he found a bulldozer piston in the ditch. As he walked home, he began thinking about making an engine. He had never seen the inside of an engine, although he knew how it should work. He took a straight piece of rod and made a crankshaft. Other parts were fashioned using a small metal lathe. It was finished by the time he was 17 and it ran perfectly.

Arthur graduated from Jackson High School in 1940. While in school, he was especially interested in photography and math. He helped his dad on the farm and also helped other farmers while attending school.

Arthur entered the service in 1942 and was stationed at Camp White in Oregon. He was sent to North Africa and later to Italy, where he fought in three major battles. He received numerous decorations: Infantry Rifle Badge, Good Conduct Medal, a Bronze Star, and three battle stars. The U. S. Army honored him in Italy with the Bronze Star for rescuing a two-ton truck which was under fire by the German Army.

He returned home from military service in 1945 and continued farming. He was a self-taught tractor mechanic, well known by farmers throughout Cape Girardeau County. He was called to many farms to work on tractors between 1947 and 1955. During this time Arthur took an interest in woodworking. A cedar tree was cut up by hand and turned into a clock shelf. Later a walnut tree from the farm was into a grandfather clock, which stands in his living room.

In 1951, Arthur was asked by Ruben Landgraf of Landgraf Construction Company to make new clock faces for the Cape Girardeau County Courthouse in Jackson. Landgraf Construction was reconstructing the dome and needed the work done precisely. Arthur constructed four clock faces, six feet in diameter, and made each face a waterproof door twelve inches by six inches under the numeral twelve for setting the hands on the clock. Arthur also extended the shafts of the clock works to reach the hands on all four faces. This is only the second set of clock faces, with the first set being stored in the dome of the courthouse.

In 1955, Arthur was hired by Jackson R-II school district as the first bus mechanic and also as a bus driver. He performed this job for 14 years. In 1970, he joined the work force at Proctor and Gamble (P&G) and retired in 1983. Since retiring, he has kept busy making parts for machinery in his workshop and constructing a working sawmill. He has continued some farming, giving his abundant produce to others, and has enjoyed planting different kinds of trees from other states.

Arthur married Lillie Davis on Nov. 27, 1947 and they have three children: twin sons Garry and Larry, born Sept. 8, 1948, and a daughter Cheryl, born July 2, 1954. Garry and Larry graduated from Southeast Missouri State University with B. S. degrees in Mathematics and enlisted in the Air Force in June 1970. They went to Officer Training School at Lackland Air Force

Left to right: Garry, Lillie, Cheryl, Arthur and Larry Kraemer, 1961

Base (AFB), TX and then Williams AFB in Arizona, where they earned their pilot wings. Both have flown the B-52. Larry is currently an electrician at P&G. Garry is a Senior Software Engineer for L-3 Communications at Luke AFB, AZ. Cheryl graduated from Southeast Missouri State University with a B. S. degree in Business Administration. She is assistant manager at Hancock Fabrics in Cape Girardeau.

Grandchildren are: Krystyn (Kraemer) Jenkins; Jason Kraemer; Vicki (Kraemer) Rubel; Natalie Tuschhoff; Nathan Tuschhoff and Nicholas Tuschhoff. Great-grandchildren are Ashley Jenkins and Hannah Rubel. *Submitted by Arthur Kraemer*

KRANAWETTER – Leo Kanter, my husband, has an "inquiring mind." He knew his great-grandmother, Theresia Kranawetter emigrated from Austria to America with her son Joseph, settling in southeast Missouri. Since many immigrants of that area arrived through New Orleans, LA, the search began there. At the Archives – Port of Entry in New Orleans, LA, we found (and copied) the manifest of the ship *Ernst Moritz Arndt*, which arrived June 13, 1853; it listed Theresia's family and city of origin as Halle, Austria. Can you imagine the bewilderment Leo experienced when he called the local library to inquire where Halle, Austria is located and was told "there is no city in Austria by that name." There is no Halle, Austria!

Throughout the ensuing years, Leo still was determined to find his "roots." In 1997, two bits of information came serendipitously: the name of the home town of Theresia's husband and the knowledge of the "International Registry of Names." With this new information, a "letter of inquiry" – giving names, dates, details and an international reply coupon – was mailed to the 107 names on the "Kranawetter International Registry." One letter was addressed to "Pastor – Lutheran Church, Neukematen, Austria."

A miracle happened. Within three weeks, a reply was received from a Pfr. Friedrich Lages, pastor of the church in Neukematen, Austria. He had taken the information provided, checked the church records, verified it, and found and detailed the ancestry-line of Theresia Kranawetter. What a joyous day! Descendants of Theresia's youngest brother still live in the ancestral home – purchased by their parents in 1831. These descendants are members of Pfr. Lages' congregation. Through marriage, the name is no longer Kranawetter, so these people had not received the "letter of inquiry." Pfr. Lages told them of their "American cousins." Numerous letters, telephone calls and e-mails followed. Pfr. Lages is fluent in the use of the English language.

In October 1998, Leo and I traveled to Upper Austria. We were guests in the home of Pfr. And Mrs. Lages, we met the "cousins" in the ancestral home and worshipped with them in the ancestral church. We were welcomed with open

This picture August 1913, on the Joseph Kranawetter Farm, four miles east of Pocahontas, MO. First row left to right: Reuben Boganpohl, Loren Boganpohl, Wm. (Bill) Boganpohl. Second row: Bertha Kranawetter, Paul Kranawetter, Mrs. Paul Kranawetter, Ester Kranawetter, Lena (Kranawetter) Boganpohl, Hilda Kranawetter, Joseph Kranawetter, Vera Kranawetter. Third row: Henry Stueve, Reinhold Kranawetter, Roland Starzinger, Benjamin Kranawetter, Ernestine (Ruehling) Kranawetter.

arms, love and warm hospitality. After 145 years of silence – a new beginning! The experience was truly an emotional one for all.

In May 2000 our daughter and grandson, Brenda and Mark Turpin, traveled with us to the ancestral area in Austria, so Brendan and Pfr. Lages could complete plans for a July 2001 "Kranawetter descendant reunion in Austria." After much preparation and anticipation, on July 19 – 31, 2001, a group of 25 descendants from the United States visited their ancestral church in Neukematen, Austria. We stayed in the homes of Austrian relatives and members of the congregation. We were treated to a gala celebration at the ancestral home – 85 people attended. We took part in local festivals, bus tours in Austria and Germany, family gatherings and worship services. Again, all were welcomed with open arms, love and warm hospitality.

I'm happy that my husband has an "inquiring mind." Many people have shared in the results of the search for his roots.

Paul Harvey, radio commentator, is known for saying: "Here is the rest of the story." Approximately 100 years ago – the name of the town of Halle, Austria was changed to Bad Hall! *Submitted by Gladys (Mrs. Leo) Kanter*

KRANAWETTER – Not many people nowadays go on a transatlantic voyage to immigrate to a new land, but 150 years ago that method of transportation was standard. Imagine being 9 years old, leaving friends and family, not speaking any English, and traveling on a wooden three-masted sailing ship for 2-1/2 months to a place called America. That was what my great-great-grandfather Joe experienced in 1853.

The trip was no Carnival or Royal Caribbean sailing cruise. The 297 passengers on board the *Ernst Moritz Arndt*, which sailed from the harbor of Bremen, Germany, in March of 1853, existed in cramped quarters. The ship was built by a shipbuilding firm in Bremen and was launched on Oct. 23, 1847. The first captain, Albert Haake, had made a number of voyages to America, but now Captain Luder Rust was commanding the square-rigged ship for the first time in March 1853. The ship was bound for New Orleans, and by the end of the voyage, ten people died on board.

Joe traveled with his mother, Theresia, 29 years old; her husband Paul, age 39; and their three children, Paul, 7 years old; Martin, 5 years old; and Theresia, 3 years old. They had originally traveled from Halle, Austria, a small village that was over 500 miles from Bremen. Joe had said goodbye to grandparents, aunts and uncles, school friends, and the farmhouse where he had been born. He did not know if he would see them again, since they would be separated with 3000 miles between them.

Joe's family simply had not taken their belongings and left at a minute's notice; but had planned for the immigration to America. The house the family lived in prior to leaving was sold. They lived in temporary quarters for three months until final preparations to emigrate were made. The time for departure came in March 1853.

When the ship set sail it traveled through the English Channel. From his geography, Joe knew that they would sail past the English, French, and Portuguese coasts, even though he couldn't see them. The passengers ate their meals as if sitting on a seesaw, watching the tableware roll back and forth. To be sure, Joe and his family experienced the usual difficulties of seasickness, with spells of illness and discomfort. But they tolerated these hardships, because of their optimistic view of what lay ahead: a land where one is free to believe as his conscience dictates, and where the soil is fruitful and sold for $2.00 per acre.

All this opportunity lay past the open delta of the Mississippi and past the port of entry of New Orleans. After going through customs and the required health check, Joe and his family boarded a steamboat to carry them up the Mississippi River. It would be another 10 to 14 days before they arrived at their final destination, Missouri.

This voyage was quite an adventure for a young boy and his family. Joe came not knowing his stepfather and a brother and sister would die within three months of their arrival. He also came not knowing that he would be the Patriarch of a large family with hundreds of descendants, a family that has increased these 148 years and thrives today. *Submitted by Brenda Turpin*

KRANAWETTER – Joseph Kranawetter (Jan. 30, 1843 – Nov. 20, 1923) emigrated from Austria in 1853 with his mother, Theresia. They settled in eastern Perry County, MO. Joseph matured, served in the Civil War and married Ernestine Ruehling in 1871. Joseph and Ernestine purchased a farm four miles east of Pocahontas, MO. Their marriage was blessed with nine children: Martin (1872-1939); Emma (Bendel) (1874-1967); Paul (1876-1960); Adolph (1878-1921); Herman (1881-1962); Reinhold (1883-1975); Lena (Bogenpohl-Weber) (1885-1932); Bertha (Schlimpert) (1887-1969); and Benjamin (1889-1970).

Most of these children settled in the Altenburg, Frohna, Pocahontas and Jackson areas of Missouri as farmers and/or businessmen. Several located in Jacob and Chester, IL. Many descendants still live in those locals.

A law enacted June 27, 1890 gave a pension to all honorably-discharged Civil War veterans. Joseph Kranawetter (47 years old) applied for his pension, only to find he was not a "citizen of the United States of America." The necessary "Certificate of Citizenship" was procured, whereby Joseph Kranawetter became a citizen of the country he had served in the Civil War.

Certificate of Citizenship for Joseph Kranawetter

Joseph Kranawetter (1843-1923) and Ernestine Kranawetter (1848-1930) are buried in the Zion Cemetery, Pocahontas, MO.

I am proud of my heritage! I am one of hundreds of descendants of Joseph and Ernestine Kranawetter. *Submitted by Brenda Turpin, great-granddaughter*

KUEHLE – August Ferdinand Kuehle was born Dec. 7, 1798 in Brunswick, Germany. He came to Missouri in the early 1840s and settled in the Tilsit Community. On Jan. 27, 1846, he married Christina Johanna Dorrie. They had the following children: Frederike Rachel was born Dec. 11, 1847; Mena was born in 1848; Anna was born Jan. 3, 1850; Augusta was born Jan. 26, 1854; Alvina was born Aug. 6, 1856; Ferdinand was born Sept. 5, 1858; Emma was born Aug. 16, 1861; and Paulina was born May 25, 1867.

Frederike married Charles Wm. August Nothdurft; Mena died as a child; Anna married Franklin Brennecke; Augusta married John Schuette; Alvina married Franklin Brennecke (Anna died soon after their second son was born; Alvina went to stay with Frank and care for the two sons. Later, Frank wed Alvina; Ferdinand

Joseph and Ernestine Ruehling Kranawetter 50th wedding anniversary, July 13, 1921, in front of their home located approximately four miles east of Pocahontas, MO

married Emma Naumeyer; Emma was married to Julius Macke; and Paulina married Ferdinand Hargens.

August Ferdinand Kuehle was a farmer. Records show that he received a land grant from the U. S. Government, signed by President James K. Polk. The grant was for 40 acres of land, and was issued Feb. 1, 1848. That particular parcel of land is still a part of the Kuehle farm west of Gordonville.

August and Christina were active members of the German Methodist Church west of Gordonville, MO. It is said that August was among those who made the bricks for the current church building, which is still in use today.
Submitted by Don Kuehle

KUEHLE – Donald Lawrence Kuehle was born Jan. 13, 1934, the son of Lawrence H. Kuehle and Louise Roloff Kuehle. He grew up in the Tilsit Community, and attended Tilsit Grade School. Don graduated from Jackson High School in 1951. He farmed with his father and later inherited the family farm. Don was active in Future Farmers of America, 4-H, and Rural Youth Organization. Don answered the call to the ministry, receiving his license to preach in 1959. He graduated from Southeast Missouri State University in 1961. Don attended Garrett Theological Seminary in Evanston, IL; he received his Seminary Degree in 1964. In 1980 Don earned his Doctor-of-Ministry Degree from Drew University in New Jersey. Don pastored local congregations in eastern Missouri for some 40 years, retiring in 1999. He has been active in the United Methodist Church's Camping Program, serving as a camp director since 1967. Since 1989, Don has been writing a weekly column, "Good Thinking," for area newspapers.

Don married Karen Ruth Nothdurft on May 26, 1968 at Zion Methodist Church west of Gordonville. They have two children. Laura Ruth was born on June 16, 1970; she is married to Alan Stanfill and lives in St. Charles, MO. Aaron Don was born on July 14, 1973 and lives on the Kuehle family farm. He is a Physical Therapy Assistant at Southeast Hospital in Cape Girardeau, MO.

Back, left to right - Aaron Kuehle, Laura Kuehle Stanfill; front, Don Kuehle, Karen Kuehle

Karen was born on Aug. 22, 1942 and grew up on a farm west of Gordonville. She is the daughter of Sylvester Nothdurft and Marguerite Deneke Nothdurft. Karen has two brothers and two sisters: Joan (Sebaugh); Glenn; Paul and Donna (Taake). Karen is active in United Methodist Women and sings in the church choir.
Submitted by Donald Kuehle

KUEHLE – Ferdinand August Kuehle was born on Sept. 5, 1858 in the Tilsit Community. He farmed with his father; he later inherited the family farm west of Gordonville. On June 19, 1884 he married Emma Maria Neumeyer. They were

Front, left to right – Lawrence Kuehle, Ferdinand Kuehle, Emma Neumeyer Kuehle. Back, left to right – Albert Kuehle, George Kuehle, William Kuehle, August Kuehle, Mary Kuehle Fingerhut

married at the German Methodist Church, west of Gordonville, by Rev. Stoffregan. Emma Neumeyer was born in the Tilsit Community on Jan. 26, 1866. Her parents were Johannes W. Neumeyer and Johanna J. H. Stoffregan. Emma's brothers and sisters were: Caroline; Charles Henry; Rosena Wilhelmina; August; Lisette Rosine; Frederick Wilhelm; Lena and John F.

Seven children were born to this union: Mary Johanna was born July 6, 1888; August Ferdinand was born Dec. 5, 1889; Frieda Anna was born Jan. 5, 1892; William John was born July 14, 1895; Albert Edwin was born Feb. 9, 1899; Lawrence Herman was born Jan. 4, 1904; and George Henry was born Feb. 22, 1907.

Mary was wed to William Fingerhut on Nov. 4, 1909; August married Edith Arnold on June 23, 1920; Frieda died as a child; William wed Rosa Ludwig on Oct. 7, 1917; Albert married Anna Meyer on Sept. 22, 1921; Lawrence was wed to Louise Roloff on Sept. 20, 1931; and George married Della Voges on Oct. 27, 1929.

Ferdinand and Emma were active members of Zion Methodist Church, west of Gordonville; they are both buried in the cemetery there.
Submitted by Don Kuehle

KUEHLE – Lawrence Herman Kuehle was born in the Tilsit, MO community on Jan. 4, 1904. He attended school at Tilsit Grade School. Lawrence farmed with his father and later inherited the family farm west of Gordonville. Lawrence married Louise Johanna Roloff of Jackson, MO on Sept. 20, 1931. Three children were born to this marriage: baby Kuehle (stillborn); Donald Lawrence was born on Jan. 13, 1934; and Marilyn Ruth was born on April 1, 1937. Don married Karen Ruth Nothdurft on May 26, 1968. Marilyn married Gaylon Ray Stutts on Dec. 7, 1958.

Lawrence was the son of Ferdinand A. Kuehle and Emma Neumeyer Kuehle. His siblings were Mary (Fingerhut), August, William, Albert, and George. Louise was the daughter of Albert W. Roloff and Emma Rose Roloff. She had a brother, Leo, and a sister, Helen (Moll).

The Kuehles were engaged in farming until their retirement in 1967; they moved to Donna Lane in Jackson, MO at that time.

Lawrence owned the first tractor in Cape Girardeau County, an iron-wheel John Deere. He also operated a Hammermill, grinding wheat, corn and other grain for feed for his farm animals; Lawrence also ground feed for many of the neighboring farmers.

Lawrence was a member of Farm Bureau, was active on the Livestock Shipping Association Board. He also served on the Board of the Gordonville Mutual Insurance Company, as well as selling insurance for Columbia Insurance Company. Lawrence served on the Tilsit School Board for many years and was actively involved in the school consolidation that resulted in the formation of the Jackson R-2 School District. Lawrence was a faithful member of Zion Methodist Church, serving on the Church Board and also as a Trustee. Lawrence died June 14, 1993 and is buried in the Zion ME Cemetery.

Marilyn Kuehle Stutts, Louise Kuehle, Lawrence Kuehle, Donald Kuehle

Louise was a city girl, growing up in Jackson, MO. She attended school in Jackson, and worked as a sales clerk in her father's store. She grew up in the Evangelical Church, and was baptized and confirmed there. Louise was a superb homemaker; she enjoyed cooking, sewing, and gardening. Louise served Zion ME Church as Sunday School Superintendent, she sang in the church choir, and was a member of Methodist Women. Louise died Sept. 16, 1984 and is buried in Zion ME Cemetery. *Submitted by Don Kuehle*

KUNTZE - Wilhelm Kuntze (1841 - 1907), a shoemaker in Germany, arrived in Baltimore, MD, in 1869. Wilhelm, his first wife Wilhelmine, and 3-month old William (1869-1949) left Baltimore for Altenburg, MO in 1870. William grew up in Altenburg and as a young man went to work for Mr. Sander in Tilsit. In December 1904 William married the widow of Heinrich Sebastian, Louise W. Warner - Sebastian. Louise had four children: Hugo; Lawrence; Louis; and Elsie with Heinrich Sebastian; and three children; Louise (1906-   ), Albert (1909-1974) and Alvin (1912 - 1979) with William Kuntze. William and Louise Kuntze owned a farm just south of Jackson.

Albert Kuntze married Lydia Wedekind (1905 - 1995) in 1932. Albert, who was a carpenter, built their first home at 508 Nellie Street in Jackson. They purchased this lot from Louise and Albert Voges, who were Albert's sister and brother-in-law. Albert also served as the night marshal for the city of Jackson until 1940. For a short period of time, Albert and Lydia owned the Coronado Cafe on Highway 61 (now Highway 74 and 25), where Rhodes is now located. Albert and Lydia had three children; Marge (1934 - died at birth), Shirley (1935 -), and Donald (1937 -). In 1940 Albert and Lydia divorced and Albert moved to Los Angeles, CA. In California Albert served as a policeman and worked in construction. Albert later married Eva Masters, formerly of Jackson, and had two girls, Dorothy and Mary, and one son, Carl. Albert died at the age of 64 in California and was buried in Russell Heights Cemetery in Jackson. Carl now lives in Cape Girardeau with his wife Karen and their children, Kevin and Keith. Carl works for Procter and Gamble.

After the divorce and serious medical complications, Lydia decided to rent out the house at 508 Nellie Street and to move back home to the Wedekind farm, which is located at I-55 and Highway 61. Donald still remember the change from oil lamps to electric lights and the digging of a well on his grandparents' farm.  *Shirley, Lydia and Donald Kuntze, circa 1941* The digging went on for weeks until they had dug down 850 feet for the third hole that they hit clear water. Lydia and her two children stayed at the farm for about two years before they moved back to Jackson. The move was necessary because the little school bus would not pick the children up in 1942. Once back in Jackson, Lydia enrolled Donald in St. Paul's grade school at the age of 5. Their new home was a small one-story flat with an outside toilet at Cherry and Russell Street. They rented one room and shared the kitchen with the owner of the flat. With the war on, there was no available housing and there was a rent freeze. When school was out they moved back to the farm. For the next two years, Shirley and Donald were able to ride the Jackson High School bus to their school. Then in 1945 the people who were renting Lydia's house at 508 Nellie Street moved out and so Lydia and her children moved back in. They lived in different parts of the house for the next several years due to the necessity of having to rent out part of the house. At one time there were two other families living with them, the Birks and the Sieberts.

Donald attended Jackson High School where he was on the football team. In January 1954, at the age of 17, Donald joined Jackson's Army National Guard Company E, where he served for four years. In 1956 Donald began working for the *Southeast Missourian* newspaper as a printer. Later that same year, Donald married Dorothy Margrabe (1937 -) of Cape Girardeau. They had four children: Donald; Mark; Debra and Shari.

In 1962 Donald left the *Southeast Missouri*, a newspaper, and worked for a number of newspapers. He worked for newspapers in Atlanta, GA; Birmingham, AL; Terre Haute and Indianapolis, IN; and Springfield, IL. Donald retired from the *St. Louis Post Dispatch* newspaper in St. Louis, MO, where he worked for 32 years. Donald moved his family to St. Louis in 1964 and still resides in the same home today. Donald and his wife enjoyed coaching their children's sports teams. Dorothy was also very active in the Girl Scouts.

Donald has been active in Jackson for several years and is currently building a home in Jackson on land that has been in his family for about 150 years. The barn, which is home to the Rainbow Auction, was built in 1904. Donald's great-grandparents, Frederich and Maria Wedekind, purchased the Wedekind farm in 1851. Frederich purchased 320 acres of land in the center of Cape Girardeau County; their land was to the west of the county farm/poor farm. At this time it was one of the largest farms in the county. The Cape Girardeau - Jackson Road passed through the middle of the farm. *Submitted by Don Kuntze*

KURRE – Herman Monroe Kurre's story starts with his father, Henrich Christoph Kurre, leaving Hanover, Germany and immigrating to America. He came to this area to live with relatives. Henrich "Henry" bought land and started a farm. He married Amelia "Mollie" Haupt. Three children grew to adults from this marriage; Caroline, Mary and Fred. Sophie Martin became his second wife in 1862. From this union there were nine children: Josphine Heidelbarger; Emma Evans-Crites; Bertha; Henry; Mathilda Allen; Sophie Baudendistl; Gustav; Hulda Mayer; and Herman Monroe.

During these years the farm became a little village called Kurreville. The village consisted of a general store and post office, a blacksmith shop and several other buildings. A Lutheran Church was built as was a one-room school.

A story is told that after the Civil War, Bushwhackers were terrorizing the area, forcing men to join their group or be killed. Henry's little store was a good target. To save some supplies and valuable things, he filled his wagon bed, camouflaged it, and drove to his in-law's in Perry County and hid things in caves. While he was gone, the Bushwhackers did come, demanding keys for the store. Sophie, left behind with the three children, handed over the keys. The store was ransacked but not burned. Upon checking the store, Sophie discovered the Bushwhackers had left the lamp burning. Afraid of a fire, she hoisted little Fred through an open window to blow out the lamp.

Henry and his two sons farmed the land until his death in 1887. Gustav kept the homestead. Monroe received 175 acres about one-half mile away as his inheritance. Monroe married Albine "Binnie" Clingingsmith in 1902. They built a home on their property and lived there until 1928. They had three daughters; Mabel (Ritter), Hazel (Miller), Viola (Putz) and a foster son, Dean Walker. In 1928 they moved to Jackson. Monroe had several businesses at this time. One was a restaurant with Mr. Schade located on High Street. Another business was a creamery at the corner of Main and Russell. Milk was brought in, separated into milk and the cream then sold. Chickens and eggs were also sold. Binnie helped with the killing and dressing of the chickens. During this time, the house they lived in on East Adams caught fire. Monroe was burned when he went back into the burning house to retrieve some receipts and money from the creamery.

 *Monroe and Binnie Kurre*

Monroe died in 1946 of a heart attack. Son Dean was just returning from his tour of duty after WWII. Binnie lived until 1962. She loved gardening, quilting, sewing and visits from her grandchildren. Mabel married Clarence "Brick" Ritter of Jackson. They had two children, Mary Sue Niemann and C. John Ritter. Hazel married Payton Miller of Oak Ridge. They had two children, Betty Smith and June Hulsey. Viola married Dillman Putz of Pocahontas. They had two children, Barbara Loyd and Nancy Kettner. Dean Walker married Wilma Godwin. They had two children, Jim Walker and Joe Walker. *Submitted by Mary Sue Niemann*

LADREITER - Robert Rodney Ladreiter and Nancy Jane Ware were married in 1952. Rodney, born on May 1, 1935, is the son of Vernon and Trula Blaylock Ladreiter. Nancy is the daughter of McDavid and Martha Ware and granddaughter of Dr. James L. and Martha Jenkins (see J. L. Jenkins family history). Rodney and Nancy moved into the Jenkins family home at 541 North Hope Street in Jackson, where they still live. Rodney is very active in the New McKendree Methodist Church and Nancy is a member of the Mary and Martha Circle. Rodney has been assistant director of Recreational Sports of Southeast Missouri State University for 15 years. Nancy has been very busy for the last 20 years providing child-care in their home.

Front row, left to right: Martha Austin, Robert Ladreiter, Brock Austin, Sarah Ladreiter, Rodney Ladreiter, Nancy Ladreiter. Second row: Alex Austin, Maggie Baugh, Carole Baugh, and David Ladreiter. Back row: Gabe Baugh. Christmas 1998.

Rodney and Nancy are the parents of four children: Carole Jane, Martha Ann, Robert Brent and David Charles. Carole Jane Ladreiter was born July 14, 1953. She graduated from Jackson High School in 1971, and Southeast Missouri State University in 1975 with a B.S. degree in education, and received her Masters Degree in education from Webster University. Carole has been a teacher in the Jackson School District for 26 years and manages the Jackson City Pool during the summers. Carole married Robert Joe Baugh on Oct. 15, 1977. They are the parents of two children: "Gabe" and Maggie. Joel Gabriel "Gabe", born April 23, 1984, is a member of the Jackson High School class of 2002; a defensive cornerback for Jackson High's football team, and runs in the track program. He is also an avid hunter and fisherman. Maggie Jenkins Baugh, born Jan. 5, 1990, is a sixth grade student at Jackson Middle School, and active in softball and basketball.

Martha Ann Ladreiter was born Sept. 16, 1955. She graduated from Southeast Missouri State University in 1978 with a B. S. degree in business administration and management. She has been associated with St. Francis Medical Center for 18 years, and presently is the office manager for the Center for Health and Rehabilitation. Martha teaches Sunday school at the First Baptist Church in Jackson. On Nov. 3, 1979, Martha married Kenneth Clyde Austin. They are

Gabe, Carole, Bob and Maggie Baugh, Christmas 2001.

the parents of two sons, Alex and Brock. Alex Kendall Austin, born Nov. 25, 1989, is a seventh grade student at Jackson Middle School, and plays football and basketball. Brock Taylor, born May 31, 1994, is in the first grade at South Elementary and plays baseball and the piano.

Robert Brent Ladreiter was born April 30, 1958. He graduated from Jackson High School in 1976 and Southeast Missouri State University in 1981 with a B. S. degree in computer science. After 9 years in the U.S. Navy, Robert is now employed by Procter and Gamble. Robert and Debbie Lottes Doemel are the parents of Sarah Ann Ladreiter, born June 3, 1979. Sarah graduated from Marquette High School in 1997, and will receive a degree in accounting from the University of Missouri-St. Louis in May 2002. She is currently in the intern program with World Wide Technologies in St. Louis.

David Charles Ladreiter was born May 5, 1970. Since graduating from Jackson High School in 1988, David has worked in the restaurant business and is presently owner of DC'Z Café in Cape Girardeau.

Rodney loves to travel by vehicle, and one of the first family vacations was a tour of Missouri, camping as they traveled. This was followed by a vacation to the World's Fair in New York and a visit to Washington, D.C., camping in a homemade truck camper. The second time out was to Smoky Mountain National Park in the same camper.

The first family vacation in a factory built truck camper, in 1966, with the kids riding in the back playing games while they traveled, was to Mount Rushmore; Yellowstone Park; Grand Teton Park; Rocky Mountain National Park; Pikes Peak and the Royal Gorge.

After that they traveled to the World's Fair in San Antonio, TX, and Toronto, Canada; visited Big Bend National Park; Glacier National Park; Key West and Disney World, FL, and in 1971 when David was 1 year old, the family traveled to Disneyland; Yosemite National Park, and Kings Canyon National Park in California.

The Austins: in back- Martha, Brock, Kenny and Alex in front. May 2001.

In 1993 Rodney and Nancy along with Rob, his daughter Sarah, and their grandson Gabe Baugh, traveled to Yosemite National Park; Bodie, CA, a true mining ghost town; Crater Lake, OR; Mt. Rainier, WA, and left Yellowstone Park on July 4 for home in a snow storm.

Rodney and Nancy continue to travel and in 2000 traveled to Stow, VT, home of the Trapp family; Bar Harbor, ME; and on to Halifax, Nova Scotia, where they saw the world celebration of the Tall Ships and toured the Titanic Museum.

For nearly 30 years Rodney has wanted to travel the Alaskan Highway and visit Alaska. On June 8, 2001, Rodney and his oldest son, Rob, left for a 23-day exciting, memorable trip to Alaska, vowing to return again some day, along with other family members. *Submitted by Rodney and Nancy Ware Ladreiter*

LADREITER – Ernest J. Ladreiter was born in the Shawneetown Community and married Hattie (Hedwig) Gerharter in 1908. Ernest had a brother in Nezperce, ID, where there was a homestead program, and he asked Ernest to join him. Before Ernest and Hattie arrived, the program was over and he subsequently took a job at Ramy's Lumber Camp. After several years, Ernest and Hattie moved back to Jackson, MO, where he became a painter and janitor for St. Paul Lutheran Church and she became a seamstress. While in Idaho, Ernest and Hattie had two children, Mildred and Vernon. Mildred married Otto "Pete" Hanschen and had one daughter, Judy; Vernon married Trula Blaylock and they had four sons.

Vernon helped his father as a house painter, and by milking cows and delivering the milk. He also worked at the local Phillips 66 service station. In 1933 he went to work for Wilson Lewis at the new Mobil Gas Station. In 1958 he and Wilson's brother, Richard Lewis, purchased the station. In 1960 Vernon's oldest son, Rodney, purchased Richard's interest of the business. In 1966 they began a recreational vehicle dealership and in 1970 the business was moved to Highway 61. Vernon retired in 1975.

Trula and Vernon Ladreiter

Vernon had also joined the Volunteer Fire Department in 1934 and was Fire Chief from 1959 until his retirement in 1975. He was called "Chief" by his fellow firemen and friends until his death in 1996. His most memorable fire was in April 1974 when 10,000 gallons of gasoline spilled and caught fire at the Jackson Ceramo plant and blew the top of a storage tank to the opposite side of Highway 72. The fire burned for 14 hours. The first fire truck he drove, a Diamond T Pumper, led his funeral procession. As they passed by the new Fire/Police complex, the firemen stood at attention and the flag flew at half-staff on its route to Russell Heights Cemetery.

Vernon was past president and past secretary of the Jackson Optimist Club, past president and secretary of the Jackson Retail Merchants, chairman of the Jackson Horse Show, and a member of the Chamber of Commerce and Jackson Industrial Development Board. He worked at the "Egg and You Day," forming the Kroger Egg Grading Plant. He was a member of the St. Paul Lutheran Church, serving on many committees. He and his wife, Trula, had four sons: Rodney, Richard, Wayne and Terry.

Rodney, born May 1, 1935, graduated from Jackson High School where he played football, ran track, and was a member of the 880-yard relay team that took first place at the state track meet in Columbia, MO, in 1953. Because he was so fast, he was nicknamed "Zip" by his football and track coaches and it has stuck with him over the years.

Rodney and his father owned a service station and recreational vehicle sales and rental business and in 1978, Rodney purchased the local Western Auto business and operated it until 1982. Today Rodney is employed as assistant director of recreational sports at Southeast Missouri State University. He is a charter member of the Jackson Jaycees where he held several offices, received the local DSA Award in 1964, and was later presented a JCI International Membership, a lifetime membership in the Jaycees. He has been a member of the Jackson Rotary Club and the Jackson Chamber of Commerce, and a member of the Planning and Zoning Committee as well as other community committees. Rodney is very active in the Methodist Church. He has served as president of the New McKendree Men's Club and president of Cape/Farmington District Methodist Men; he is a member of Camps and Conference Committee of Missouri East Conference; a member of the Wesley Foundation Board located at Southeast Missouri State University; and past president and current board member of Old McKendree Chapel and various other committees.

Rodney married Nancy Jane Ware in 1952 and they have four children, Carole, Martha, Robert "Rob," and David (see Rodney Ladreiter family for his children's information)

Richard, born Aug. 8, 1940, died at 2 months and 14 days.

Wayne, born July 10, 1942, graduated from Jackson High School where he played in the band for four years and was voted Big Chief of Jackson High his senior year. He attended art school in Kansas City, MO, and New York. He worked as an interior decorator at Cape Girardeau, Poplar Bluff, and Atlanta, GA, where he resided when he passed away in August of 1987.

Terry, born Aug. 22, 1948, also graduated from Jackson High School where he played on the Jackson football team. He served in the Marines for two years after graduation, was married, and opened T & S Cleaning Service in Jackson. He later moved to Colorado where he was employed with Telephone Express Long Distance Service. Later he moved back to Jackson and now works for the southeast quarter of the state of Missouri for CGI. He is currently married to the former Pam Patten and they have a daughter, Christina Munden, a son-in-law, Charles Munden, and a grandson, Kaleb. *Submitted by Trula Blaylock Ladreiter*

LANE - Gary G. Lane and Vicki R. Crites were married on Feb. 10, 1962. Their parents are Rusby C. and Margie G. Crites of Jackson, MO, and Paul and Erma Lane of Fredericktown, MO. They moved to Festus, MO, where their son Gary II was born on April 29, 1964.

Gary was in the insurance adjusting business and began climbing the corporate ladder when they moved to Connecticut with The Hartford Insurance Group. Vicki was a stay-at-home mom and taught ceramic and oil painting classes.

Their next move was to Buffalo, NY, with The Hartford. Gary was regional claims manager and Vicki kept right on painting. Then they moved on to Naperville, IL, where Gary was in charge of the Chicago regional claims department. Vicki continued painting and began working in a gift shop called "My Attic" until they moved once more.

Young Gary II graduated from high school and then from Purdue University in Indiana. He met and married Deborah Roberts, where they live today. They own and operate a management corporation in Lafayette, IN. They have three children; Gary 6, Ashley 16, and Jeremy 18.

Gary had been with The Hartford for 30 years when he retired in 1995. He and Vicki now live in Jackson, MO. *Submitted by Vicki Crites Lane*

LANG - The Lang family began when Henry Bruihl, born in Germany in 1831, and wife Anna, also born in Germany in 1840, immigrated to America. They settled in North Cape Girardeau County on a farm approximately five miles west of Old Appleton, on the banks of Apple Creek. Their property extended from near what is now State Highway KK along County Road 501, which crosses Apple Creek into Perry County. Henry operated a flour mill on the bank of Apple Creek, which was in use for several years. Sometime later a friend, Dr. David Lang, also born in Germany, came to America to visit the Bruihl family. While here, Mr. Bruihl died and later Dr. Lang married his widow Anna.

Dr. Lang acquired land joining the Bruihl land to the south and east. His tract of land was some 360 acres. This land is still owned by his descendants. Dr. Lang had two sons and a daughter; August A. Lang, William E. Lang and Mary Tuschhoff. August migrated to western Kansas, now Wilson, KS, approximately 50 miles south of Interstate 70. He acquired a large acreage in the wheat country and became quite wealthy.

William E. Lang remained on the Lang homestead. The picture of his family is the enclosed picture. He had a family of nine children. Those in the family picture are named as follows: On the upper porch is son Edward H., who migrated to California and established an orange grove; Emma Wilson, who married a doctor of Old Appleton and moved to California; Carrie Tacke, wife of Franklin Tacke of Arnsberg who operated a mill, a store, a harness shop, etc., in the small town of Arnsberg; and Bertie Lischer, who with her husband later moved to Sparta, IL, where he operated a store. On the downstairs porch is William E. Lang and daughter Willie Sadler, whose husband was a dentist and who later moved to Cape Girardeau; John H. Lang who became a doctor and moved to Fullerton, CA; Mary C. Lang, nee Schultz; and Oscar H. Lang, who kept and farmed the old homestead. In front is Mabel Westover and Myrtle Wilkening.

The Lang Homestead

Oscar Lang and his family lived on and maintained the Lang homestead until the present time. This house was replaced by another in 1923 in approximately the same spot. Oscar and his wife Roxie (Kurre) had seven children: Virgil A. became a mechanic and operated a garage in Old Appleton; Leona P. married Julian Tuschhoff of Arnsberg (both were teachers) and they later moved to Wentzville, MO; Margaret married Melvin Leimer, also a teacher, and they later moved to Keokuk and Burlington, IA; William K. remained on the farm, farming and raising livestock; Mary Dell married Adrian Clingingsmith and she taught school in the area for 38 years; Byron L. married Margaret Nitsch and they lived, farmed and operated a trucking service in Jackson; and Robert D., who later moved to Idaho with his family.

The Lang farm is now owned by William's son, David, and the farm is still in operation. *Submitted by Mary Dell Clingingsmith*

LA PIERRE - Zephrin La Pierre (born 1820 in Vercheres, Canada), son of Bazil Mazuret de La Pierre (born in St. Sulpice, France) and Marguerite LaDue (born in Chambly, France) came to the Jackson area sometime between 1850 and 1853. He and Mary Josephine Welling, daughter of Charles Welling Jr. and Elizabeth Bollinger Frizel, were married in 1855. Their seven children were: Martine; Mazuret Guild; Adelaide; Frederick; Wilson C.; and Charles H. He operated a grocery store in Jackson where his son Maz helped, before becoming a salesman.

Mazuret Guild La Pierre (1870-1949) and Marguerite Struthers (1876-1956) married in 1899, and had five children: Guild Mazuret; Margaret S.; Cramer Wilson; Mary Jeannette; and Thomas H. Her father, Thomas Struthers, came from Scotland before 1874 and married Margaret Townsend, who was born in England and immigrated as a child. He was a miller. On the advice of his doctor that a sea voyage might benefit his health, Thomas went to Scotland in early 1879 where he died. After her husband's death in 1879, Margaret took training in millinery in St. Louis and opened a shop in Jackson. She later married Wilson Cramer. Her daughter Marguerite was also a milliner.

In the early twentieth century M. G. La Pierre, a grocery salesman traveling through southeast Missouri and Arkansas, was asked to sell hickory handles. He and C. A. Sawyer from Little Rock, AR, conceived the idea to establish a factory to manufacture handles, which was established in 1902, with Mr. La Pierre made president of the company.

Mazuret was one of the organizers of the Jackson Chamber of Commerce and was a charter member of the Rotary Club and its first president installed March 1929. He was active in the Presbyterian Church, for 68 years, an officer alternating between deacon, Sunday School superintendent and elder. He also served for a number of years as a member of the Jackson Building and Loan Association and the City Board of Aldermen.

Guild Mazuret La Pierre (1899-1949), as well as his brothers and other young teenaged boys, worked at the handle factory making wooden crates for shipping handles. Upon his graduation from high school in May 1918, he volunteered for the Army, serving in the tank corps. In France, he was assigned to go to the front lines on November 11. Following the signing of the armistice, he remained in Europe in the Army of Occupation and was discharged after 15 months' service in time to enter Southeast Missouri State Teacher's College. In 1920 he joined his father in the operation of the handle factory. Over the years he gradually assumed more of the management responsibilities, becoming general manager in 1949. He died suddenly that April, three weeks after his father's death.

Guild and Julia Mueller, (1900-1988), daughter of H. H. and Ida Brass Mueller, were married in 1925. Following graduation from the Lyceum Arts Conservatory of Chicago, she was accompanist for the Temple Singers, a mixed quartet booked by the Lyceum, and toured the United States for two years. Returning home, she began a 60-year piano teaching career and was much in demand as an accompanist. Their two daughters are Susan and Margaret.

Guild served on the City Council from 1928 to 1932 and on the Board of Education for five years. Both were active members of First Presbyterian Church, both serving as officers and Julia as organist for 35 years. She was active in civic clubs and was one of the organizers of the Cape Girardeau Community Concert Association and its predecessor. Following her husband's death, she became a bookkeeper at the handle factory until her retirement. *Submitted by Susan L. Venable*

LATIMER – In 1957 Jack and Jean Latimer were looking for a good school system in which to enroll their oldest child, Pat, for kindergarten. Like many young parents, they chose Jackson. They became members of the New McKendree United Methodist family. Jack, a skilled crane operator, went to work for Penzel Construction where he stayed until his retirement in 1987. He and Jean built a house in Daily Heights subdivision and made a home for their children, Pat, Greg, Stan, and Sheila. Jean was active in many community organizations such as the American Legion Auxiliary, VFW Auxiliary, Elks Ladies, and the Eastern Star. She was a loving wife and mother, but sadly passed away in August of 1998.

Pat graduated from Southeast Missouri State University, became an interior designer, married Phil Hill, and had one daughter, Felicia, who is currently pursuing a degree in education at St. Louis University. Tragically, Pat's life was cut short by Multiple Sclerosis. She passed away in December of 2000. Greg is an antiques dealer in Illinois. Stan served in the Air Force, retired as a Master Sergeant and brought his wife, Lois, and three children, Jessica, Ashley, and Matthew, to live in Jackson. He and Lois went to work for Proctor and Gamble and Ashley and Matt attend Jackson High. Their oldest daughter, Jessica, a graduate of Jackson High, now attends University of Missouri at Columbia, studying pre-med. Sheila married Jeff Garland, an Air Force man like her brother, and has one son, Ryan. They currently live in Washington, D.C., where Jeff works for the White House Communications Agency and Sheila works as an assistant controller for a real estate developer.

Jack continues to be active in various community organizations such as the Elks, American legion, and VFW. He married Virginia Bohnsack, a former resident of Jackson, in 2000, and they reside at the homestead on the corner of John and Corinne Streets. *Submitted by Sheila Garland*

LEE – Joseph Lee's grandfather, William Henry Lee, was born in Hunterdon, NJ in 1740 and lived there until about the Revolutionary War time. Then he served in the Maryland Militia in Washington County under Captain Daniel Cresap in Colonel Lemuel Barret's Battalion (Maryland Revolutionary War Militia lists, copies compiled by the Daughters of Founders and Patriots of America, p. 225). The family kept moving west in 1780 to Gooden's Fort in Nelson County, KY.

Joseph Lee's father, David Lee, was born Jan. 27, 1766 in New Jersey, and married Mary Asborn in Ohio County, KY at Barnetts Station on July 11, 1785. David Lee fought in the Revolutionary War on the western front of Kentucky in 1781. His wife, Mary Asborn, was born June 16, 1764 in Vermont. David and Mary moved to Hamilton County, OH, and stayed a few years, then received land for Revolutionary War duty in Monroe, Tippecanoe County, IN. David died Jan. 10, 1852 in Monroe, IN.

They had seven children: Katherine, born Dec. 27, 1788 in Nelson County, KY, married

Ebenezer Griffing; Ezra was born in Nelson County, KY; David Lee Jr., born Sept. 16, 1791 in Nelson County, KY, married first Emily Hamilton, and second, Martha O'Henry; William Lee was born Dec. 17, 1793 in Nelson County, KY; Joseph Lee, born March 8, 1796 in Nelson County, KY, married Francis "Fanny" Hutchinson; Mary Ann Lee was born in Hamilton County, OH and married Frank Hawthorne; and Nathan Lee, born July 18, 1801 in Hamilton County, OH, married Jerusha Phoris.

Joseph Lee, before he left Monroe County, IN, prepared his father, David's, application for his Revolutionary War pension. Joseph Lee and Fanny Hutchison moved to Jackson, MO, sometime after 1835. It is thought they followed the Brooks family here, as they were related through William Henry Lee's children. Joseph Lee was a bricklayer and had a brick home on Greensferry Road.

Joseph and Fanny had seven children: Matilda Lee, born in 1821 in Hamilton County, OH, married John Hicks in Jackson, MO; Sarah Lee, born Sept. 25, 1824 in Hamilton County, OH, married Marcus L. Caldwell, a shoemaker, in May 1845 in Jackson, MO; Mary Lee, born in 1826 in Hamilton County, OH, married John Gholson July 12, 1855 in Cape Girardeau County, MO; Robert Lee, born in 1830 in Hamilton County, OH, married Temperance English in 1859 in Cape Girardeau County, MO and he died in 1868 in Jonesboro, IL; Joseph Lee, born in Tippecanoe County, IN, married Sarah Francis Dickerson on Dec. 5, 1853 in Cape Girardeau County, MO and he died about 1877 in Cape Girardeau County, MO; Louisa Lee, born in 1835 in Tippecanoe County, IN, married first Jr. T. Burns and second Henry Hardin in Cape Girardeau County, MO; and Fedila Lee, born in 1840 in Jackson, MO, married Charles M. Slack in Cape Girardeau County, MO in September 1860. *Submitted by Mary Lou Caldwell Lett*

LETT – Thomas H. Lett Jr. was born in St. Louis, MO on April 12, 1924. His parents were Thoms H. Lett Sr., born at Bertrand, MO, and Evelyn Miller of Oran, MO. His parents moved to Morley, MO, where his mother taught school and his father worked for Dunn and Bradstreet.

Tom attended school in Morley, MO and College High and college in Cape Girardeau, MO, until WWII. He enlisted in 1942 in the Navy, attended flight school in Iowa, Kansas, Kirksville, MO, Texas and Sandford, FL, where he crashed in an F-4 Wildcat plane on Feb. 10, 1943. After the war, he attended the University of Missouri at Columbia, MO, and the Miami, FL University and graduated with a B.S. degree in Vocational Education from the University of Missouri at Columbia, MO in June 1955.

Tom married Mary Lou Caldwell in December 1952 in Piggott, AR. Her parents were Ernest and Edith Caldwell. She was born June 17, 1927 in Cape Girardeau, MO.

Tom first taught vocational agriculture in Delta, MO from 1955 to 1957, then moved to Benton, MO in the fall of 1957 and taught agriculture at Kelly High School, from 1957 to 1960. Then he took a job as County Office Manager for ASCS farm programs for Scott County, MO, from 1960 to 1965, and transferred to the state office USDA – ASCS as employee Development Specialist. He transferred in 1966 to the Washington, D.C. Agriculture Department and was detailed to the Executive Office of President for one year. They lived in Springfield, VA from 1966 to 1971 and transferred to Kansas City, MO ASCS Field Office. Then in October 1978, he retired and moved to Cape Girardeau, MO, and bought part of the Juden farm on Bloomfield Road and started a tree nursery. He retired from the nursery in 2000.

Mary Lou Caldwell Lett and husband, Thomas H. Lett Jr., Cape Girardeau, MO

Children of Tom and Mary Lou Lett are Tom Lett III, Scarlett Lynn and Paul Allen Lett. Thomas H. Lett III was born in 1953 and served in the Navy in the 1970s. He worked for the NASA Project Manager at NASA Tracking Station in Dekar, Africa, then transferred to the USDA Research Laboratory in Peoria, IL. He graduated from Southeast Missouri State University in Cape Girardeau, MO in the summer of 1991. He developed cancer in 1991 and died on Jan. 7, 1994 in Cape Girardeau, MO; he is buried in Memorial Cemetery in Cape Girardeau, MO.

Scarlett Lynn Lett was born in 1957 in Cape Girardeau, MO and attended school in Benton, MO, Columbia, MO, Springfield, VA and Kansas City, MO. In 1976 she graduated from Stephens College in Columbia, MO with a B.F.A. in Graphic Design. She is a sales representative with Southwestern Bell. She married Henry Charles Puls of Jackson, MO on June 11, 1983 in Cape Girardeau, MO. Henry Charles Puls is Vice President of Union Planters Bank in Clayton, MO.

Paul Allen Lett was born in October of 1967 at Fort Belvoir, VA while the family lived in Springfield, VA. He attended school in Kansas City, MO and Cape Girardeau, MO. Paul has worked in construction and maintenance work. He married Dina Marie Dempsey Santos in August 1998 in Ft. Walton, FL. She was born in 1977 in St. Maries, ID. Her parents are Diane Marr and Mitchell Santos. Their daughter, Selina Marie Lett, was born on Oct. 26, 1999 in Cape Girardeau, MO. *Submitted by Thomas J. Lett Jr.*

LIGHTNER - Levi Luther Lightner was born Dec. 25, 1793 in Lancaster County, PA to Nathaniel and Elizabeth (Wike) Lightner. His ancestors left Germany in 1709, fleeing religious persecution and went to Holland, to England, and to America, settling in 1723 at Leacock Township, Lancaster County, PA. In 1814, when Levi was 21 years old, he came down the Ohio River on the first steamboat that ever came to Cairo, IL and decided to come on to Cape Girardeau, MO, where there were only a few white families, between 1814-1826.

Levi Luther Lightner, first judge of Alexandria County, IL, Thebes, IL. Born Dec. 15, 1793, Lancaster County, PA, died Nov. 17, 1869. Buried at Thebes, IL.

He built and operated a still house just north of Cape Girardeau, he also erected and occupied the house. Later it was the residence of Rev. Mr. Mooney and also for a time in 1831 - 1834, he engaged in business with Charles G. Ellis. The Lightner-Caldwell family still has old ledger where many old members of the community shopped.

In 1830 Levi L. Lightner was one of the elected trustees to purchase a lot to build a schoolhouse. They obtained a lot at the corner of Fountain and Merriwether Street and erected a small building which was used for several years. He also served as temporary Postmaster in Cape Girardeau. In 1835, later in the year, he moved to Clear Creek (McClure), IL where he operated a sawmill and engaged extensively in farming. In 1844 he joined Jonathan Freeman and plotted the town of Thebes, IL was the first county judge to serve at Thebes. He also served as County Clerk, School Commissioner, Probate Judge, and Justice of the Peace in Thebes, IL. While a resident of Thebes, IL, he had the honor of entertaining Abraham Lincoln in his home. Lincoln had been at Jonesboro, IL, debating Stephan A. Douglas, and went by horseback to Thebes. A settee upon they sat is still in the family, a valued relic to the family. In 1860 when Cairo became the county seat, he was appointed to the office of Public Enry and remained there till his health failed, then returned to Thebes, IL. He died Nov. 17, 1869 at age 74, and is buried in the old Lorimier Cemetery in Cape Girardeau, MO by his first wife Elizabeth (Godair) Lightner and two daughters, Elizabeth Julia (born 1824) and Julia Elizabeth (born 1831, Cape Girardeau, MO).

Granddaughters of Levi Lightner, 1904. Sitting, Edith Lightner; standing, Pearl Lightner. Daughters of Nathaniel William Lightner and Mattie Belle Lightner.

Judge Lightner was married three times. His first wife was Elizabeth Godair, the daughter of Peter Godair. She was born about 1803 in Pittsburg or Philadelphia, PA and died April 13, 1831 at age 28, in Cape Girardeau, MO; she is buried in old Lorimier Cemetery. They had five children: Matilda, born in Cape Girardeau, MO, married Anthony Randol Feb. 27, 1845 in Cape Girardeau County. Anthony died and she married Andrew Mifflin in Cairo, IL. Elizabeth Julia Lightner was born in Cape Girardeau, MO in 1824. Julia Elizabeth Lightner was born in Cape Girardeau, MO. Both daughters are buried in old Lorimier Cemetery by their parents. Louisa Lightner, born in Cape Girardeau, MO, married Washington McRaven in McClure, IL. John Lightner was born in Cape Girardeau, MO; there is no further record of him.

Judge Lightner's second wife, Mrs. Eleanor Desha (nee Shelby) was a niece of ex-Governor Shelby of Tennessee. Son Alfred Shelby Lightner, born March 23, 1835 in Cape Girardeau, MO, married Amanda M. Crouse in St. Louis on April 12, 1859; he died Nov. 8, 1916 in Akron, OH and is buried in St. Louis, MO. Son Levi Luther Lightner Jr. was born about 1838 in Cape Girardeau, MO and died Nov. 8, 1863. He is buried in Thebes, IL. Both sons were pilots during the Civil War on the Mississippi River and Arkansas River, ferrying soldiers to different locations.

Judge Lightner's third wife, Susan W. Wilkerson (nee Mansfield) was born May 12, 1828 in Todd County, KY and married Levi Luther Lightner in November 1848 at Benton, Scott County, MO. They moved to Thebes, IL. Susan died in December 1905 at McClure, IL. They had seven children: E. Julia Lightner, born in Thebes, IL, married Roy Breeze and died in 1930; James C. Lightner, born in Thebes, IL, married Josephine Stewart; Euginia, born in Thebes, IL, married Albert Brown; Eleanor for whom there is no further record; Nathaniel William was born July 4, 1861 in Thebes, IL, married Mattie Belle Boles (born Feb. 14, 1867, Tennessee) on Oct. 22, 1882 in Thebes, IL; Lilly Lightner, born in 1865 in Thebes, IL, married C. P. Spann in Thebes, IL and died Jan. 27, 1892; and Pearl Lightner, who died as an infant. Judge Lightner's stepson, George Alexander Wilkerson was born in Louisiana and died March 9, 1848. Nathaniel William Lightner who died March 25, 1949 in St. Louis, MO, was grandfather to Mary Lou Caldwell Lett.

Nathaniel William and Mattie Belle had nine children. Edith Lyle Lightner, born April 16, 1883 in Thebes, IL, married Ernest Caldwell on April 12, 1905 in Cairo, IL; they were the parents of Mary Lou Caldwell Lett. Ernest died April 18, 1934, and Edith Caldwell died Feb. 14, 1980; they are buried in New Lorimier Cemetery in Cape Girardeau, MO. They lived in McClure, IL and Anna, IL, then moved back to McClure. They moved to Cape Girardeau, MO in 1925 and back to McClure in 1927, then back to Cape Girardeau, MO in 1943.

Nathaniel William Lightner and Mattie Belle Boles Lightner, 1932, 50th Anniversary, Themis Street, Cape Girardeau, MO; son of Levi Lightner.

The other eight children were: Pearl, born March 28, 1885 in Thebes, IL, married Chance McRaven on March 9, 1911 in Cape Girardeau, MO; Mossie L., born Oct. 22, 1887, died as an infant; Helen, born Feb. 28, 1890, married Joseph LeRoy in Reynolds, IL; Will Alma, born Aug. 6, 1893, married Joe Hobbs in Cape Girardeau, MO; Levi Luther Jr., born Jan. 21, 1896 in McClure, IL, married Clara Taylor in Murphysboro, IL in 1917; Jewel E., born Nov. 25, 1898 in McClure, IL, died as an infant; Ruth Lightner, born Feb. 5, 1900 in McClure, IL, married Albert Blattner on Oct. 23, 1919 in Cape Girardeau, MO and she died June 3, 1970 in St. Louis, MO; and Susan Lightner, born Oct. 30, 1903 in McClure, IL, married Merel Taylor in 1927 in Illinois or Missouri and she died Aug. 15, 1981 in Los Angeles, CA.

William N. Lightner died March 25, 1949, and Mattie Belle died June 4, 1934; they are buried at Thebes, IL. *Submitted by Mary Lou Caldwell Lett*

LILEY - Jason Scot Liley was born to Carol Joe (Masterson) and Michael Dane Liley of Jackson on Feb. 1, 1971. Mike Liley, a current resident of Grassy, MO, is the son of Lyndall Ledo and Gene Daphine Liley of Jackson. Carol Keen, the daughter of Hazel and Joe Masterson of Cape Girardeau County, married C. Michael Keen of Jackson on June 11, 1988.

Jason attended First Baptist Church where he participated in youth choir. He completed grade school at Jackson Public Schools and continued on to Jackson High School. He competed as a member of the Jackson Swim Team. In high school, he participated in activities such as Chamber Choir and football. His senior year, he received a scholarship to play football for Southeast Missouri State University. Jason began his college career in the fall of 1989. During his freshman football season, he was named Southeast Missouri State University's starting quarterback against the University of Missouri-Rolla.

Jason met Katy Stoverink the summer of 1993 while working at Bent Creek Golf Course. Jason attended one more year of classes and graduated from Southeast Missouri State University in December of 1994 with a Liberal Arts Degree.

Katy (Kathleen Marie), the first daughter of Gerald E. and Catherine M. Stoverink, was born in Jefferson City, MO, on April 23, 1975. Gerald, Catherine and Katy's older brother Fred moved soon after to Cape Girardeau County.

Katy attended Immaculate Conception Church and School. She then attended Jackson High School where she was active in softball, basketball, and French Club. She took piano lessons for eight years from Pam Raney and Susan Venable until her junior year of high school.

Katy graduated high school in May of 1993 and continued on to college in Southeast Missouri State University's pre-engineering program that fall. By August of 1995, she transferred to the University of Missouri-Rolla to complete her schooling. She graduated from University of Missouri-Rolla in December of 1997 with a B.S. degree in Civil Engineering and immediately began her career at Koehler Engineering and Land Surveying, Inc. of Cape Girardeau the following week.

Jason and Katy were married the following month on Jan. 10, 1998 at First Baptist Church in Jackson, by Father J. Friedel. Jason and Katy's father contributed to the construction of their first home on the north side of Jackson, completed in March of 1998. Jason is currently self-employed by Liley Construction Company through which he builds homes and installs ceramic tile, skills he learned from working with his father-in-law Gerald Stoverink. They have since moved to a home built by Jason two blocks south of their first home.

Jason, Katy and Mikala Liley, February 2002

Jason and Katy started their family on Nov. 12, 2000 with the birth of their daughter, Mikala Marie. Father J. Friedel baptized Mikala in February of 2001 at Immaculate Conception Church. Mikala's godparents are Mike and Carol Keen and Nathan and Alisha (Liley) Turley. Jason, Katy and Mikala currently attend First Baptist and Immaculate Conception Churches of Jackson. *Submitted by Katy Liley*

LILEY – Lyndall Ledo Liley, son of William "Wild Bill" and Leona Adeline (Gatlin) Liley, was born April 1, 1926 in Grassy, MO. He attended the Zalma, Gregory and Lutesville schools until WWII interrupted his education. He was called to serve in the U. S. Army from Sept. 9, 1944 to July 24, 1946. While he was in the Army he frequently corresponded with a friend from home. When he returned home he completed his education, graduated from Lutesville High School, and went to work at the Shoe Factory in Lutesville. He also married his friend, Jean Daphine Kirkpatrick, on July 13, 1947.

Daphine, daughter of Russell Marvin and Ora Lea (Smith) Kirkpatrick, was born April 10, 1928 in Grassy, MO. She attended the Grassy and Pounds elementary schools and graduated from Lutesville High School in 1945. After graduation she attended the Southeast Missouri Teachers College in Cape Girardeau and taught school at the Grassy and Buchanan Schools. She also worked at the Shoe Factory in Lutesville for a brief period.

Lyndall and Daphine moved to Jackson in June 1952. Lyndall worked at Rozier's from 1952 until 1963. In 1963 he began to work for the United States Postal Service as a letter carrier, retiring in 1989. Daphine worked for the Jackson R-2 School District in food service from 1968 to 1990. During those years she served at the Primary Annex and West Lane Elementary schools.

Four children were born to them at Southeast Missouri Hospital in Cape Girardeau. Michael Dane, born Dec. 12, 1950, lives in Grassy, MO and is married to the former Laura Reta Barnett Borgfield, widow of Larry Gene Borgfield. Rodney Lane, born June 30, 1954, lives in Evansville, IN and is married to the former Karen Sue Osborne. Lisa Lynn, born Aug. 15, 1960, lives in Jackson and is married to Ricky Gene Drum. Sandra Jean, born Aug. 1, 1963, lives near Whitewater, MO and is married to Brooks Howard Moore.

Lyndall and Daphine Liley

Lyndall and Daphine are the grandparents of Jason Scot Liley and Alisha Anne Liley Turley, Michelle Lea, Katie Ellen and Cameron Michael Liley; Danielle Nicole and Caitlin Ranae Drum; Madison Glenn and Graeme Gatlin Moore; and Wesley Gene and Wendy Lee Borgfield.

While Lyndall and Daphine lived in Grassy, they attended Grassy Friendship Church. In Jackson they have been faithful members of the First Baptist Church. Camping, fishing, hunting, reading, gardening and walking are some of their favorite pastimes. Upon returning from a camping trip, the Lileys found themselves in a newspaper editorial, where they had been dubbed "Minnow Man" and "Mrs. Minnow Man." Lyndall had befriended the editor and shared with him his love of catching minnows in a gallon mason jar filled with cracker crumbs. The author, quite perceptive, was able to capture the essence of Lyndall and Daphine. He wrote, "this tall, soft-spoken Minnow Man was not only a true gentleman, he truly was a gentle man." He also wrote of the "simple joy that glowed on his face as he talked about life's many pleasures" and "relishing his journey through life, a trip that obviously had no room for strangers." And he was "reminded that the best things in life - minnows included- really are free." *Submitted by Lisa Drum*

LIMBAUGH/CALDWELL - In 1809, Henry Limbaugh and family arrived in Missouri from North Carolina and settled on a farm near Sedgewickville. Henry's son Daniel married Elizabeth Statler; their eldest son, Jefferson Wilson Limbaugh, born Oct. 15, 1826, became a lawyer and in 1850, the publisher of the *Southern Democrat* based in Jackson. He married Hannah Adelaide Wilkinson but left her a widow with a small daughter and a baby on the way when he died in the cholera epidemic in June 1852. The baby who was born Dec. 7, 1852 and named Jefferson Wilson Limbaugh, grew up to become a lawyer and the first mayor of Jackson after its incorporation in 1885. When he died in 1905, the city declared a memorial holiday for his funeral. In November 1881, he married Anne Moon, the daughter of Dr. Henry Buckman Moon, DDS, and his wife Martha Davis. Jefferson Wilson and Anne had six children, including Phoebe Davis Limbaugh, born Dec. 28, 1890 and died Sept. 4, 1990. She worked in the office of Judge Hayes and was Clerk of the Probate Court before her marriage on July 25, 1914 to Alban Berne Caldwell, whom she met while he was working for his father in the Tax Collector's Office.

Alban Caldwell's family came to Missouri from South Carolina around 1840 and settled on a farm near Laflin. His grandfather, James Faulkner Caldwell, married Sarah Snider Morgan, a widow with a son; they had two children before Sarah died shortly after their daughter was born. He then married Mary Elizabeth Estes with whom he had six children. When the Civil War began, he joined Colonel Jeffers' Regiment, CSA. After the war, he moved his family to Arkansas briefly before returning to Missouri and settling in Millersville, where he was a farmer and brick maker. His third son, James Franklin Caldwell, was born Dec. 18, 1862 and died Nov. 9, 1931; he married Lydia Christine Schlueter, the daughter of Andrew Henry Schlueter, in 1889. James Franklin Caldwell served as county tax assessor for eight years and then was elected tax collector and served eight years in that capacity. In 1911, he moved his family to Jackson where he bought the house which had been built by Jefferson Wilson Limbaugh in 1900. Frank and Lydia had 10 children; Alban was their second son, born May 8, 1892.

Jefferson Wilson Limbaugh, date unknown. Original photography by Gilliland's Photo Gallery, Main Street, Cape Girardeau.

After Alban Caldwell and Phoebe Limbaugh were married., they had two children while living in Jackson. In October 1917 they moved to Washington, D. C. and later to Chevy Chase, MD. They had three more children, one of whom died in 1918 flu epidemic. They never severed their ties to Jackson but were limited to visits with relatives and friends. Alban worked at the General Accounting Office until his death June 2, 1941. Phoebe then found employment at Woodward and Lothrop's Department Store where she worked until retiring in 1956. Phoebe and her youngest daughter, Anne, shared a home until her death. *Submitted by Elizabeth Anne Caldwell, youngest daughter of Phoebe and Alban*

LINCOLN - On a frosty Christmas Eve morning in 1910, Miles Olen Lincoln and Ruth Adeline Long rode in an open wagon near Patton, MO. After a brief marriage ceremony, they traversed rough roads that led to the studio where they had their wedding portrait made. Little did this couple imagine that this union would span over 63 years and that they would parent 18 children, 10 sons and eight daughters.

The Lincoln family. Back row, left to right: Dwel, 1918; Miles J., 1922; Clinton, 1923; Floyd, 1924; Ralph, 1926; Kenneth, 1933; Gerald, 1936; Clifford, 1938-2001. Front row: Lorene Walter, 1928; Isabel James, 1917-1985; Miles O., 1888-1982; Ruth A. (Long), 1893-1974; Freida Long, 1915; Jean Rogers, 1920-1970; Pauline Statler, 1929.

Increments of five seemed to follow this family. In 1932 a typhoid epidemic hit the neighborhood and the Lincolns found themselves with five critically ill children. They were told three of those five might not survive, but only one, the oldest, Lillard, succumbed to the fever. Three years later the youngest daughter, Janice, became ill with whooping cough. She faded away in a few days, leaving the grieving family to cope with the loss of four children (the first two deaths were the only set of twins who had died at birth in 1914.) Nearly four decades would pass before Jean, a 50-year-old daughter, would be taken with cancer in 1970, making a total of five children lost.

WWII called five of the remaining sons. Three were stationed in Europe, two in the Pacific. A son, Clinton, took a German bullet that caused him to nearly bleed to death before he was rescued by his commanding officer. However, it was three weeks from the first telegram delivery informing the family of the severe injury until news came that Clinton had survived. All five boys, Dwel, Miles J., Clinton, Floyd, and Ralph, came home. Later, Kenneth served the Army in France during the Korean conflict.

Carpentry and farming were the mainstay of this rural family who lived in the Scopus area. They lived off the land, feeding the family with a large vegetable garden, an orchard, a sugar maple grove, livestock, and crops. Raising kids, crops, and livestock was a way of life. Some cash was produced by selling milk cows and cream, hogs and chickens, and eggs. Miles never owned a car so he walked to work sites. His specialty was rafters and shake shingles and many times he would be gone a week at a time, leaving the farm and home responsibilities to the very frugal Ruth. She controlled money and children well, and was not necessarily the winner of popularity contests at home, but her oversight got many jobs done! She did this by assigning specific chores to everyone, whether they liked the chores or not!

Life wasn't easy, work was hard and the hours long, but Sunday was a day of rest, except for all those hungry mouths to feed, and that included people and animals! It took some real effort and organization to feed, dress, and get the family to church. Before sunrise Miles had fired up the stoves and Ruth had breakfast prepared. Then it was off to the barn to feed all the animals, do the milking, gather the eggs, and slaughter a couple of chickens for Sunday dinner. Then the children were awakened, dressed, fed breakfast and packed into the wagon for the ride to church services. In the earlier years of the marriage, they attended Coles Chapel, than later, the church of Christ at Scopus.

The Miles Lincoln family can trace its roots back to 1540 when Robert (Linkhorn) Lincoln dated his deed in Norfolk, England. Ten generations later, Abraham Lincoln was born and went on to become the sixteenth president of the United States. Miles Lincoln was a sixth cousin (once removed) to Abraham. *Submitted by Lorene Walter*

LINGLE - Odie Lingle was born May 15, 1951, son of Ralph and Doloris Lingle of East Prairie, MO. Odie's great-grandparents, Thomas and Mary Lingle, farmed near Goreville, IL, as did his grandfather, Rollie Virgil Lingle. The Lingles moved near Charleston, MO in the early 1900s. At this time there were no bridges across the Mississippi River. Legend has it that they crossed in a horse-drawn buggy during the winter when the river was frozen. Ironically Odie's great-uncle, for whom he was named, Otis Lingle, would later work in construction and help build the bridge that connects Cairo, IL and Charleston, MO.

Left to right: Fay, Amy and Odie Lingle

Odie's father's other grandparents, Ralph and Florence Golightly, also came from southern Illinois to Charleston, MO. Ralph Golightly was a large farmer near Charleston and reportedly owned the first tractor with caterpillar-type tracks in southeast Missouri. They farmed south of what is now the Charleston Country Club. The school their daughter, Myrtle (Odie's grandmother) attended still stands just south of Highway 60. Today the school is used as a church.

Doloris Lingle's family moved to Missouri from Alabama in the 1930s. Her mother Essie Laura Barker was born Feb. 17, 1896 in Cleburne County, AL, the only daughter of Rev. Wesley Jackson and Nancy Emma Bowman Barker. She married Francis Newton Taylor, a farmer, on Oct. 26, 1913. Doloris was the youngest of their seven children.

223

Ralph Lingle served in the Navy at the end of WWII. He was a lifelong farmer and also worked for the East Prairie Post Office. He and Doloris had three sons and one daughter, Odie being their second child.

Odie graduated from East Prairie High School in 1969 and Southeast Missouri University in 1973. He worked five years for the Internal Revenue Service in Chicago and Southern Illinois before moving back to Missouri in 1978. For the past 23 years he has owned and operated the H&R Block Income Tax Office in Jackson. In addition to preparing tax returns, they offer accounting and financial services. Odie married Faye Parker on June 6, 1970.

Faye Parker was born Feb. 27, 1952 in East Prairie, MO, daughter of George and Celia Parker. She is the seventh of nine children. Her father's family came from Kentucky and Tennessee in the early 1900s and worked as farmers and laborers. Her mother's mother is of Scottish origin and settled in Arkansas, coming to Missouri in the early 1900s as well. Faye graduated from East Prairie High School in 1970 and attended Olney Central College in Olney, IL receiving an A. S. degree in Art. Moving to Jackson in 1979, she worked for 20 years with husband Odie in his business.

Odie and Faye have one child, Dr. Amy Lingle, an optometrist in Lake Havasu City, AZ. Amy graduated from Jackson High School in 1989. She received her Bachelor's degree from Indiana University, Bloomington, and her Doctor of Optometry degree from Illinois College of Optometry in Chicago.

Personal Note - I cannot imagine a nicer town to live and work in for the last 20 + years. *Submitted by Odie Lingle*

LITTLETON - William Littleton was born Nov. 23, 1852 at Newport, KY, the son of John Littleton and his wife Elizabeth, who was the daughter of James Winton. She died in 1856, along with an infant girl. The Littletons also had a son, Evan, born in 1854.

After Elizabeth's death, Evan was reared by an aunt Mary (Mollie) and her husband Evan Morgan in Newport, KY. As an adult, he came to Perry County and Cape Girardeau County, MO until his death. He is buried in Lorimier Cemetery in Cape Girardeau.

William was brought to Wittenburg, MO by his grandfather, James Winton, and was raised by his aunt Caroline Winton Dryden and her husband James. James Winton remained in Perry County, MO until his death. He was buried in the Dryden-Littleton family cemetery.

Wilhelmina Johanna "Mina" Blattner was born Aug. 22, 1860, at Breese, IL. She was the daughter of Gottlieb and Francis Delporte Blattner. It is thought that the Blattner family had close friends of the same Swiss descent in the Wittenburg, MO area and visited often, where she met William Littleton. Mina and William were married on Aug. 27, 1878 on Tower Rock in the Mississippi River. The ceremony took place during low-water river stage when they could walk from shore across the shale to the "Rock." It was a civil ceremony performed by Judge Greenwell from Grand Tower, IL on the east slope of the "Rock" facing Grand Tower.

William and Mina Littleton had 13 children; however only seven lived to adulthood. Smallpox, cholera, and meningitis plagued the family. The children were: Richard, born in 1878; Elizabeth, born in 1880 and died at 11 months of age; James, born in 1882 and died in 1899 from meningitis; Irene, born in 1884; Robert, born in 1886; May, born in 1888; Evan, born in 1889; William Jr, born in 1892; Florence, born in 1894; twin girls born and died in 1896; Joseph, born in 1897 and died in 1899 from meningitis; and a stillborn son died in 1899 as Mina had the disease as well.

In 1906 the Littletons moved from Wittenberg, MO, where William had farmed land and worked at the silica pits, both owned by the Dryden family, to Pocahontas, MO. William died in 1917 and Mina died in 1940. Both are buried at Old Apple Creek Presbyterian Church, located east of Pocahontas, where they were among the earliest members.

Richard Littleton married Minnie Ruppel in 1908 and had four children: Oliver; Winton; Ralph and Edith. Richard died in 1953.

Irene Littleton married L. A. Quinn in 1908 and had six children: James; Marie; Margaret; Tom; Billy; and Geraldine. Irene died in 1968.

Robert Littleton married Clara Milner in 1908 and had four children: Allen; Mildred; Roberta and Inez. Robert died in 1942.

William Littleton Jr. married Katherine Jocob in 1920 and had four children: Wilanna; Maxine; Clara and Robert. William died in 1963.

Florence Littleton married Gilbert Gohn in 1911 and had seven children: Eugene; Marian; Wilma; Marjorie; Den; David and Dayton. Florence died in 1972.

May Littleton married Edgar Gohn (brother of Gilbert) in 1918 and had four children: Hazel; Joseph; Donald and Mary Dell. Hazel married Arthur Duhaime and had one son, Timothy; Mary Dell married Milton Frentzel; Donald and his wife Lynette had five children: Donnie; Gary; Tommy; Jimmy and Mary; and Joseph married Helen Masterson and had two daughters, Terri and Karen, as well as a son, Michael, from a previous marriage. May died in 1986. *Submitted by Terri Gohn Tomlin*

LITZELFELNER - Joseph Litzelfelner was born in March 1803 in Austria. He, along with his wife Anna and their children, immigrated to America in 1853 via New Orleans. They traveled the Mississippi River to Cape Girardeau, MO, where, under the Homestead Act, they staked out claims and preempted 160 acres of dense woodland located between New Wells and Pocahontas, MO. Joseph and Anna had five children: Andreas (Andrew) born in 1832; Katharina born in 1835; Louis born in 1841; Karl born in 1846; and Theresia born in 1848.

Joseph served in the Civil War from October 1861 until June 1862, serving in the Fourth Missouri Regiment as a second lieutenant in Company I under Captain Tackey of the State Militia. Joseph Litzelfelner died in 1874 and Anna died in 1860. They are buried in the Brothers of Jerusalem cemetery one mile south of New Wells, MO.

Andrew Litzelfelner married Eva M. Meyr, who with her mother Catherine, immigrated to America in 1853. They lived on his father's farm and had 10 children: Emilie, born in 1866 and died in 1881; Joseph C., born in 1857; August H., born in 1859; Teresa Martha, born in 1860; Maria Louise, born in 1862; Kathrinea, born in 1864 and died in 1865; Bertha, born in 1868; Robert, born in 1870 and died in 1878; Wilhelm, born in 1873; and Benjamin born in 1876.

August Herman Litzelfelner left the family farm in November 1882 to clerk in a store at Neelys Landing for two years. Then, along with his older brother Joseph, he formed a partnership known as Litzelfelner & Bros. On June 14, 1885, August married Willie Manervia Hansel in Shawneetown, MO. Willie was born in 1866 and was the daughter of William Hansel. Their farm at Neelys Landing is now the site of the Procter & Gamble plant. They had eight children: Bessie Clyde, born in 1886, never married and was a librarian in Jackson for many years; Thomas Dick, born in 1888 and died in 1907; James Andrew, born in 1890 and died in 1899; Otis Cleveland, born in 1892 and died in 1949; Glenn David, born in 1894; Maggie Inez, born in 1897 and died at age 9 months; Myra Emma, born in 1898; and Virginia Ruth, born in 1904, was married to Lawrence Leutje and lived in the original family home.

August left his warehouse business and began buying land surrounding his farm at Neelys Landing (which is now part of the Trail of Tears State Park); he also bought a farm west of Fruitland, MO. August bought a house in Jackson, MO (now located on North Hope Street), so his children could attend school, although the family returned to the farm in the summer. August bought more land around Jackson and become one of the largest landowners in Cape Girardeau County. Willie Litzelfelner died in 1907 and her eldest daughter, Bessie, helped raise the younger children. August died in 1929.

Odus Cleveland married Ethel Myree Masterson, daughter of Robert and Ella McDonald Masterson. Ethel was one of four members of the first graduating class from Cape Central High School in 1912. Odus died in 1949 and Ethel died in 1966. The family farm is now the site of Bent Creek Golf course and subdivision. Odus and Ethel had 12 children, all of whom graduated from Jackson High School: Dorothy LaDonne, born in 1914; Kathleen Ruth, born in 1916; O'Deen Elaine, born in 1917; Odus Charles, born in 1918; Ralph Lee, born in 1920; Margaret Myree, born in 1921; Rosemary, born in 1925; James Reed, born in 1927; Jackson Madison, born in 1928; Joe Gene, born in 1930; Phyllis Sue, born in 1932; and Barbara Ann, born in 1937.

Dorothy LaDonne married William Wilson and resided in California. Kathleen Ruth married Edward Gebhard and had one son. O'Deen Elaine married Royal Harrison Wier and had two children. Odus Charles married Dorothy Bernice Davis and had one daughter. Odus was killed in 1945 during WWII. Ralph Lee married Helen Juanita (Leggett) Goforth, who had one daughter. Margaret Myree married Paul Christian Miltenberger and had six children. Rosemary married Buddy Bradsher and had twin

The Odus and Ethel Litzelfelner family.

boys. James Reed married Belva Jean Niswonger and had three children. Jack Madison married Julia Ann Thompson and had five children. Joe Gene married Betty Rose Gilbert and had five children. Phyllis Sue married Charles Edwin Vickrey and had three children. Barbara Ann married William Gorski. *Submitted by Victoria Litzelfelner Abernathy*

LOHR - Robert E. "Bob" and Barbara (Clinton) Lohr moved to Jackson in July 1963, following his discharge from the United States Marine Corps and completion of his Master's Degree. He accepted a teaching/coaching position with Jackson High School. Coach Lohr was assistant football coach and coached the first wrestling team for Jackson.

Bob previously lived in Colchester, IL; Poplar Bluff and Sikeston, MO. Barbara lived in Sikeston, MO. Both graduated from Sikeston High School and Southeast Missouri State University. While Bob was in the Marine Corps, they lived in Virginia and California.

Bob's parents were Loren L. and Katherine (Jarvis) Lohr from Nakomis and Colchester, IL. Barbara's parents were Gilbert N. and Marie (Grojean) Clinton from Plainville, IN and New Hamburg, MO. Bob has one brother, Jim L. Lohr; Barbara has a brother and a sister, Roy Jay Clinton and Bonita Clinton Eaglin.

While stationed at Camp Pendleton, CA, the couple's first child, Jim David Lohr, was born on Jan. 5, 1962. Two other children were born while the couple resided in Jackson, Robert Lane on Sept. 10, 1964 and Katherine Marie on Nov. 19, 1966.

The Lohr family. Parents, Barbara and Bob Lohr; children: Lane, Kathy and Jim.

Bob was an outstanding athlete. He was an all-conference, all-state, and all-American football player for Sikeston High School. He was selected to play in the Polio Bowl and the All-American game in Memphis, TN. He also played on the basketball and baseball teams. He attended college on a football scholarship. Following his teaching/coaching career at Jackson High School. Bob worked for the State Department of Education as a Disability Determinations Counselor, and he was the Area Supervisor for the State Schools for the Severely Handicapped. Bob was also active in the Optimist Club and coached several flag football teams. He was also an avid fisherman. Bob died on Jan. 26, 1991.

Barbara is also active in community affairs, being a past member of the Progressive Homemakers; secretary for the Home and School Association of Immaculate Conception Church; vice-president of the Parent-Teacher Organization for Jackson Junior High; Senior Girl Scout leader; Brownie and Cub Scout leader; and Neighborhood Girl Scout Chairman. She was instrumental in organizing the first Day Camp for Girl Scouts held in Jackson and in starting a Sunday School program for pre-school children of Immaculate Conception Church. Barbara taught at the Vocational-Technical School in Cape Girardeau for 28 years. She was active in professional organizations and served as Treasurer, Secretary, Vice-President and President of the Missouri Business Education Association.

She was selected the Outstanding Business Educator for the Southeast District and for the state of Missouri. She was also selected an Outstanding Educator by the Cape Girardeau Chamber of Commerce.

Jim, Lane and Kathy were all outstanding athletes while attending Jackson High School. Jim attended Southeast Missouri University on a track scholarship; Lane attended the University of Illinois on a track scholarship. Kathy also attended Southeast Missouri University. All three children are teachers. Lane is married to the former Jill Garvey. They have two girls, Lindsey and Erin. Kathy is married to Greg Jansen. They have a boy and a girl, Bobby and Megan. Kathy and Greg live in Jackson. *Submitted by Barbara Lohr*

LORBERG – It's not as if the Lorberg Family was in Cape Girardeau County all the way back during Creation (giving God pointers on what types of soil He should lay down for good farming), but they have been around these parts a long time. Andreas Lorberg actually came with his wife and two small daughters to America and Cape Girardeau in 1846 based on the encouragement of other earlier arrivals. He came from Edesheim, a small town in Germany near Hanover, where he had been a butcher.

Andreas Lorberg was a prominent member of that early community, being a charter member of Hanover Lutheran Church. He was also quick to help whenever needed, and this characteristic was described in a letter Heinrich Lueder of Egypt Mills wrote to his family back in Germany in 1846. After Lueder and his wife got very sick earlier that summer, Andreas first went to summon a doctor to treat them, and ultimately took them there himself in his wagon to get medical treatment.

About two years after Andreas' arrival with his family in the United States, another child, a boy, Friederick Andreas Lorberg was born. Andreas continued his trade as a butcher and eventually passed the skills down to his son. Frederick married Anna Marie Fassold in 1876, and in 1897 the couple bought a farm outside of Gordonville from Herman and Minnie Siemers. This farm has remained in the Lorberg family now for over a hundred years.

In addition to being productive farmers, Frederick and Anna Marie were also fruitful in offspring, having six children. One of them, Leo C. Lorberg, purchased the 67-acre farm from his parents in 1907 for $3600, a deal on land that we all wish we could find today.

Leo Lorberg and son, Walter, butchering, January 1930, Gordonville, MO

The following year, Leo married Mathilda "Minnie" Sander and the two farmed for a number of years. The butchering tradition - brought from Germany and so necessary for farm life in those days - continued. In fact, a photo of Leo butchering hogs was on the cover of the *Southeast Missouri Telephone News* in January 1930.

Though somewhat gruesome for a magazine cover by today's standards, this scene showed real life on the farm, how a good many made their living at that time.

Leo and Minnie were blessed with the birth of a son, Walter, who was born in 1914. Walter married Edna Sander in 1935, and in 1943 ownership of the farm transferred to them.

Walter and Edna had four children between 1937 and 1945: John; Jerry; Joan and Janet. John and Jerry still farm the original property, along with other acreage added over the years. Joan lives in Florida and Janet in St. Louis. Each of the four children has been blessed with lasting marriages and good health, and also with children and grandchildren. They are all active in church and community, and are ever grateful to God for the courage, faith and example of their forefathers, who came to southeast Missouri so many years ago. *Submitted by David Fiedler, son of Leonard and Janet Lorberg Fielder, great-great-great-grandson of Andreas Lorberg*

LOWES - Christian and Wilhelmina Fornkahl Lowes emigrated from the Kingdom of Hanover in 1851 on the ship *Ernestine*, along with their seven children. They arrived in New Orleans on Nov. 8, 1851. Christian signed a citizenship declaration on Feb. 20, 1852. They lived in Cape Girardeau for a short time, and then purchased a farm near Arnsburg (a small town that was east of Friedheim). They were members of the Lutheran Church that was located in Arnsburg. The cemetery is still there, but the church building is not. Many of the family members are buried there. Christian died on March 16, 1865. He was a prosperous farmer, as can be seen by the will he left on file in probate documents. Son Peter was bequeathed the family farm near Apple Creek. He was to give his mother Wilhelmina "the third part of all the produce growing on the said land during her natural life." Wilhelmina also received all of Christian's personal estate. She also likely lived with Peter and his family until her death in 1895. The oldest daughter Johanna received $300. The eldest son, Christian, was bequeathed "one plantation on the Benton Jackson road worth about $600." Daughter Christine received $300. Son Conrad was given $1000 to "pay for a plantation." Son Henry received $1200 "to pay for a plantation on the stream of Apple Creek." Henry and Peter were to pay $200 each to their sister Mina, who at the time was unmarried.

Christian (the son) and wife Wilhelmina (Graeve) purchased a farm near Cape Girardeau. They were members of Hanover Lutheran Church, and donated the land that was used for the church cemetery, with the stipulation that his descendants could be buried there at no cost. The first to be buried there was his wife Wilhelmina, who died April 9, 1895. Christian and Wilhelmina had seven children: Minna; Henry (Emeline Steinborn); Karoline (George Meyer); Augusta (Friedhoff); Anna (Strack); Charles (Minnie Stoffregen); and Johanna (Frederick Krueger).

Charles Lowes married Minnie Stoffregen, daughter of August and Julia Dormeyer Stoffregen. They had five daughters: Helena (Arthur Fassold); Ardena (John Kasten); Erna (Charles Meyer); Elsie (Theophile Grebing); and Hazel (Harold Hitt). They also raised Minnie's niece Thelma (Edwin Strack) after the death of Mina's sister Helen. Charles died in 1937 and Minnie died in 1955. *Submitted by Peggy Luehrs*

LOWES – The Christian Lowes Sr. family left their home in Seesen, Kingdom of Hanover, Germany, in early fall of 1851. They traveled by wagon to the Weser River where a riverboat took them north to the port of Bremen where they boarded the German ship *Ernestine*. Their crossing took about three months reaching New Orleans in November. On the ship were other families that settled in Cape Girardeau County including the Krueger, Niemeier, Brinkopf, Hunze, Allers, and Koechig families.

Christian Lowes Sr., born in 1802, his wife Wilhelmina nee Fornkahl, and their family came upriver by steamboat and landed on the Cape Girardeau riverfront. They visited with friends in the city, and then traveled on to buy land north of Oak Ridge, near the junction of the present Route KK and I-55. They raised a family of seven children. Johannah married Henry Buchterkirchen; Christian Jr. married Wilhelmina Grebe; Conrad married Maria Klaus; Henry married Mary Louise Kiepe; Peter married Johannah Fornkahl; Wilhelmina married George Weiss; and Christine married William Brinkman. At the passing of Christian Sr. in 1865, his will provided for each of his children to receive a farm or a generous inheritance. His son Peter Lowes lived on the home place and his mother lived with them until her death in 1895. Christian Lowes Sr., his wife Wilhelmina, Peter and his wife, Johannah, and other relatives are buried in the Arnsberg Cemetery.

Christian Lowes Jr., born in 1831, and his wife Wilhelmina nee Grebe, lived on the farm, now the 5-H ranch, where they raised seven children. Henry married Emilie Steinborn; Carolina married George Meyer; Wilhelmina married Henry Heise; Charles married Wilhelmina Stoffregen; Augusta married Christian Friedhof; Annie married Anton Strack; and Johannah married Frederick William Krueger.

The Roy Kinder family, 1969, left to right: Lorene, Roy, Alma, Arlene and Elroy.

Frederick William Krueger, born in 1869, and Johannah, born in 1874, were married in 1892 in the Hanover Lutheran Church. They settled in the Hanover Community on a farm near the Boutin Drive area, and they attended the Hanover Lutheran Church. Frederick was an organist at the church for some time. Frederick William, Johannah, and their family moved to a farm near Whitewater where Frederick died at the early age of 45. Johannah and children returned to the Hanover Community, buying a small farm on County Road 621. Their children were: Arthur Christian, who married Annie Bartels; Alfred August, who served in and was missing following WWI; Anna Johannah, who married Elmer Hamilton; Alma Clara, who married Roy Kinder and moved to a farm southwest of Gordonville; Allen Martin, who married Frieda Meyer of St. Louis County; Alvin Anthony, who married Edith Moore of Cape Girardeau; and Arnold Frederick, who married Clara Greer of Cape Girardeau.

Alfred August Krueger served with the American Expeditionary Force in WWI. He was in the trenches during the battle near Flanders, Belgium. His letters told of the experiences in "no man's land" and the assault by armored tanks, and of the chemicals used by the enemy.

Roy Kinder, born in 1888, and Alma, born in 1903, had three children. Lorene Alice married Delmar Keller of Gordonville; Arlene Joann married Roby Kight Jr. of Bell City; and Elroy Frederick married Mary Susan Sciortino of Cape Girardeau. A number of pictures and books, including a family Bible, and family memorabilia of the Christian Lowes Sr. family were passed down to the grandmother of Elroy, who has done extensive genealogy on the Lowes family line along with the Krueger, Lorberg, Nussbaum, Achtermann, and Kinder family lines. He presently serves as chairman of the Arnsberg Cemetery Association organized in 1998, which has done much work to restore and preserve the burial places of Christian Lowes Sr. and Wilhelmina, and also many other early settlers in northern Cape Girardeau County. *Submitted by Elroy Frederick Kinder*

LOWES - Christopher Lowes was born in Hanover, Germany in 1831. His son Peter was born in 1842 and came from Hanover, Germany. He was the father of William Lowes. William A. Lowes was born Aug. 1, 1882 on a farm near Apple Creek School, four miles southwest of Appleton and one and one-half miles west of Arnsberg.

William did farm work and went to Apple Creek Valley School until he was 18. At 19 he took a preparatory and freshman course at Cape Girardeau Normal School. After Christmas he went to Jackson Military Academy where he enrolled in a business and a literary course. He also received a commission from Gov. A. M. Dockery as 2nd Lieutenant on May 25, 1915. He went back to the farm for a year and the Houck Railroad built through the nearby towns. He was offered a job as station agent at Pocahontas for $15 per month and had to pay $14.50 per month for board. After about 9 months he went back to the farm and took the county teachers examination and taught his home school, Apple Creek Valley in 1910-1911.

In 1913 his father bought a house in Jackson. William decided to rent out the home place which his father deeded to him and also move to Jackson. He bought 131 acres one mile south of Jackson and sold his home place. The farm was formerly owned in 1807 by Thomas Bull, an Englishman, and later by Thomas English, Joel Sheppard, and John Jenkins. They were members of Bethel Baptist Church in 1818. The farm was later bought by Gotthold Rabold who sold it to William Lowes in 1914. The first protestant church west of the Mississippi River, Old Bethel, occupied a half-acre of his farm and for years William tended and protected the site. He said that at one time the old Bethel site was considered to be a part of Jackson.

William married Lydia Bartels from Whitewater, MO on April 18, 1918. They joined New McKendree Methodist Church. She became a great church worker and he became an active member of the Men's Bible Class. Three girls were born to this union; Mildred, Evelyn and Mabel. Mildred married Roger Schreiner from Oak Ridge. He was in the service of our country during WWII doing commissary work. He served time in Germany, France, Japan, and Korea. After his discharge Mildred and Roger built a home on the farm south of Jackson. He died of a heart attack in 1977. Mildred has worked for a lawyer, a probate judge, Jackson Exchange Bank, Jackson High School secretary, and secretary at New McKendree Methodist Church. They have two children, Robert and Donna.

Robert married Carolyn Hilpert and they have three children; Elizabeth, David and John. Robert and Carolyn live in Palmyra, MO and Donna is a nurse and lives in Portland, OR.

Evelyn married Emil Brase from Gordonville in 1943. They adopted a son, John, in 1957. He is a computer analyst with Southwestern Bell in St. Louis. Emil was in the Navy for two years. When he was discharged from the Navy he taught school and coached basketball at Delta, MO for 9 years. Evelyn also taught at Delta for 9 years. They were both employed at Jackson where Emil coached and taught physical education for 33 years and Evelyn taught 29 years. They built a house next to the home place. Evelyn retired in 1986 and Emil retired in 1988. Although retired Emil is still coaching 5th to 8th grade girls' basketball at St. Paul Lutheran Church.

W. A. Lowes family, left to right: Mildred Schreiner; Lydia Lowes; Evelyn Brase; William A. Lowes; Mabel Illers.

Mabel married Albert Illers Jr. They have two children, Mark and Marilyn. Mabel was an office worker at the Jackson Shoe Factory and Kasten Brick Yard. Albert was associated with his father in dairy farming. Mark is chief maintenance foreman at Kasten Brick Yard. Marilyn has worked as a secretary for the Junior High and Middle School of Jackson R2 school district. Mabel died in 1983 after a long siege of cancer and Albert died four years later.

Mr. Lowes wrote many prayers, meditations, and inspirational messages. One of his meditations was published in the Methodist publication of *The Upper Room*. His message ended with the following prayer: "Heavenly Father, help us to be humble, to help someone in need. Help us to be kind to neighbors even though our kindness may not be accepted. Help us to strive to keep on and doing something for others in need. Amen." He lived this prayer and died Aug. 4, 1967. Lydia Lowes died Oct. 19, 1987. *Submitted by Evelyn Brase*

LUDWIG - The Ludwig family came to the United States of America and landed at the port of New Orleans on April 21, 1855. They sailed on the ship *Nurinburg* and were numbered 194 to 198 on the ship listing register. Johannas Ludwig and his wife Maria purchased a farm 2-1/2 miles east of Oak Ridge, MO from Samuel and Mahala Jane Turner for $25.00. The Warranty Deed was dated Sept. 2, 1859.

Peter Ludwig's parents had immigrated to the United States in 1855, locating in Cape Girardeau County, MO. They bought land and improved the farm where their son, Peter Ludwig, resided. His father lived on the farm until his death in October 1885, at the age of 81 years and 6 months old. He lived to see two of his god-grandchildren. The mother died soon after arriving in America.

Peter Ludwig was born on Feb. 29, 1840, in his native country of Germany. He was the son of John and Mary (Karben) Ludwig, both natives of Germany. Peter was 15 years of age when he came to Missouri with his parents. He had received a good education in Germany.

In August 1861 he enlisted in the Union army, joining Company I, Eighth Missouri infantry, under Colonel Morgan Smith. He served with that regiment for three years and participated in all of its engagements. The most important battles were Pittsburg Landing (in which he received a slight wound), Corinth, all of the battles around Vicksburg, Jackson, MS, Chattanooga, Lookout Mountain, Missionary Ridge and Knoxville.

After his discharge, he returned home on May 30, 1865, and was united in marriage with Elizabeth Grutz, daughter of Mathias Gartz (deceased). Mrs. Ludwig was born in Germany and came to Cape Girardeau County during her youth.

Peter's sister, Apollonia, had returned home from the Civil War and was given a share of the family farm. Later she sold her portion of the farm to Peter. Apollonia had married a Civil War soldier named Flavious J. Jordon on July 14, 1864. Later they went to Chillicothe, MO, then in 1876 they moved to Colorado.

John Ludwig came to the United States from Germany in 1855; he is the father of Peter Ludwig.

After his marriage, Peter Ludwig took charge of the family farm from his father, Johannas Ludwig, for $200.00. The warranty deed was dated June 2, 1865. He was a successful farmer and raised livestock on the family farm. He had 140 acres of land with about 90 acres under cultivation. He had a good residence with buildings and all necessary machinery for farming. He and his wife had a family of six children: Ferinand; M. J.; Mary K.; Henry W.; Minnie R.; William B.; and Ida M.

Later, Peter sold the farm to his son Henry W. for $2,090.00. The warranty deed was dated July 22, 1902. Next, Henry W. sold the farm to his son Adolf Ernest. The warranty deed is dated Nov. 10, 1923. A. Ernest sold the farm to his son Marvin. The warranty deed is dated Jan. 22, 1965. Currently, Marvin and Dorothy Ludwig reside on the farm. *Submitted by David L. and Janet L. Ludwig, Thomas A. and Christina D. Ludwig*

LUDWIG - Oscar Charles Ludwig was born March 9, 1896 on a farm about seven miles north of Jackson. His father, Herman Robert, and his mother, Minnie Sophia Kiepe, were of German descent. His father bought the farm, built a house and barn, and had his first child, Cora, in 1881. The other children were Anna, Emma, and Cora.

Oscar graduated from Horrell School and went back for algebra and literature during winter months when farm work was slack. He helped his dad shear sheep, butcher, plow, and gather corn. He early learned to train horses and mules. When he was 9 years old, his dad insisted that Oscar drive his four sisters in the buggy to dances. He was the one who could take care of horses. Once he saw a horse he always knew it. He learned to dance and call dances. One dance was a great disappointment. His buggy whip was stolen.

He met a dairy maiden, Hilda Mathilda Friedrich, who was French, German, and Cherokee. She was called "Tillie." She was born July 27, 1900, the oldest daughter of August and Martha Friedrich. The other children were: V. C.; August; Irene; Ray; Margaret; George; and Elsie. Tillie took care of the younger children. She baked a bushel of cookies every Saturday for a neighbor's large family. When the flu hit the household, only V. C. and Tillie were well. Suddenly V. C. fell over but Tillie nursed the family and some neighbors.

Oscar and Mathilda "Tillie" Ludwig. Children, standing; Evelyn Schoenebeck, Martha Wilhelm and Vernon Ludwig.

On March 9, 1919 Oscar and Tillie were married and moved into a second house on the farm. Vernon Oscar was born Feb. 24, 1921. His sister, Evelyn Lucille, was born May 28, 1923. They were both christened at St. John's United Church of Christ. When Oscar's parents became unable to watch the cattle, they exchanged houses so Oscar would be near the barn. Twin girls were born, Martha Irene and Marjory Eileen on Feb. 3, 1933. Marjory lived only a few hours.

The family attended church regularly. Oscar sang tenor in the choir. Tillie would ask three or four families for dinner, (that meant supper, too). Oscar would slice a ham or jars of sausage, plus vegetables and fruit came out of the cellar. The ladies peeled potatoes. Tillie always had a cake baked.

At threshings, Tillie's specialty was pies. The 26 pies were made with soft runny lard and baked on a wood stove. The pies were so delicious that they didn't last the day out.

Oscar and Tillie were respected by their children and neighbors. She passed away at the age of 68. Oscar passed away at the age of 88 on Jan. 7, 1985. They were buried side by side in St. John's United Church of Christ Cemetery near Fruitland, MO. *Submitted by Vernon Ludwig*

LUDWIG - Vernon Oscar Ludwig was born Feb. 24, 1921 seven miles north of Jackson, MO. He was the son of Oscar Ludwig (born 1896; died 1985) and Hilda Friedrich Ludwig (born 1900; died 1968). Vernon went to nearby Horrell rural school and, as did his sisters Evelyn and Martha, graduated from Oak Ridge High School. During his freshman year he rode his favorite horse to school. The next three years he drove a Model T and hauled passengers.

On Easter Sunday, April 9, 1944, Vernon went on a double blind date. His date lived in the Armstrong-Ramsey house built in 1795-1811 on Silver Springs Road in Cape Girardeau. Vernon's date was Bonnie Mae Armstrong, born Aug. 18, 1925 at home. Her father was F. J. Armstrong, who was born June 4, 1898 and died Aug. 14, 1992. He was of Scottish descent and owned Silver Springs Dairy. His wife, Lula Jane Smith Armstrong, was born Feb. 14, 1901 and died Jan. 2, 1970. Lula's mother was one-half Cherokee and had Walker and Hildebrand ancestors in North Carolina. Other family members were Russell, Olive, Eileen and Carl.

There were many happy dates which ended when Vernon went to Great Lakes Naval Station. He was next stationed at Peru, IN. The box of chocolates he mailed to Bonnie contained a diamond. At his next weekend pass they would be married by the Reverend Joseph Mayer in the old Log room. Vernon's sister Martha would sing "Always." It didn't happen. Vernon was shipped to Clinton, OK. Bonnie arrived by train in Clinton, OK on Oct. 20, 1945. The Rev. E. W. Parker drove them five miles to Arapaho for the license and at six p.m. they were married in the Methodist parsonage. They lived in one room on Route 66. Bonnie worked at Bestway Grocery. For entertainment they went to movies, to the U.S.O., and hitchhiked 90 miles to Oklahoma City.

Vernon was being transferred to Hitchcock, TX, so he took Bonnie home. Parting was very sad for she was with child. His discharge came in July 1946. The couple went to the home of his parents where several rooms were later added. Cherry Lou was born Nov. 1, 1946. In 1947 Bonnie began teaching at Schoenebeck. On Jan. 26, 1949 Donna Marie was born. The two girls graduated from Oak Ridge High School and from Southeast Missouri State College. Cherry went on to get a Masters degree.

Vernon and Bonnie Ludwig seated in center. Standing, Ed and Cherry Hinderberger, Kim, Donna and Danny Criddle. Three boys from left: Jon Hinderberger, Travis and Jamie Criddle, granddaughters Gina Hinderberger and Beth Criddle. Ludwig's 40th wedding anniversary, Oct. 20, 1985.

Bonnie taught at Schoenebeck, Horrell, Pocahontas, and Sheppard for a total of 28 years. She received her B.S. in 11 summers and a Masters degree from the University of Missouri. Vernon bought his first tractor the day Cherry was born. He attended Veteran's Agriculture class to learn how to improve farming methods. He also completed a course sponsored by Ford Motor Company from LaSalle University on farm management and mechanics. He became a modern farmer. *Submitted by Bonnie Ludwig*

LUETJE - Charles Marion Luetje and his family moved to Jackson from the Old Appleton area in 1920. Charles purchased 40 acres of farmland within the city limits of Jackson. Charles was born March 28, 1880 and died Sept. 13, 1962. His wife Rosa died in 1946. Charles and Rosa's two sons were Lawrence (March 16, 1907 – Aug. 23, 1976) and Glenn (March 2, 1911 – Oct. 26, 1967).

The Old Appleton farm was a land grant to John Henry Lutge (Charles' grandfather) by President Franklin Pierce on Jan. 3, 1856. Henry (Charles' father) was born in Hanover, Germany in 1842 and immigrated at the age of two.

Lawrence was the cashier at the Jackson Exchange Bank and ran an insurance agency. He spoke German before he learned English.

Lawrence was also a history buff, interested in world events that made lasting changes in history. Glenn was an architect in Jackson. While attending Washington University, he was a member of the fencing team. He attributed his fencing skills to his strong wrists obtained by milking cows as a teenager on the family farm.

The farm was located on the west bank of Hubble Creek, north of Washington Street. Around 1950, some of the land was obtained by the American Legion for a baseball field. Upon Charles' death, the remainder of the farm was used to expand the city park and for residential lots. The current Luetje Street, two blocks in length, was once the cow pasture and the spring located in the park was the site of the pigpen. The family house (at the corner of Elm and Parkview) faces south and provided a good view of the farm. The house is still in use. The barn was just west of the house. A favorite family story was the world-famous aviator, Charles Lindbergh, during his barnstorming days, landed north of the house in an open field. Lawrence and Glenn did not go for a ride.

The Luetje family was very active in the New McKendree Methodist Church.

Left to right: Don Luetje, Charles Luetje, Linton Luetje, April 2001

Lawrence and his wife Virginia had two sons, Linton and Charles. They lived at 535 Hope Street. Linton (March 16, 1939) is a retired music educator living in Alton, IL, with his wife Donna. They have two children, Mim and Matt. Charles (May 28, 1941) is a physician and founded the Midwest Ear Institute. He has been featured in *Time* and *Parade* magazines. Charles and his wife Sandy have three children, Charles, Kevin and Andrew.

Glenn and his wife Mildred had one son, Don. They lived at 946 W. Main Street. Don (Sept. 7, 1938) is retired from Southwestern Bell and lives in Kirkwood, MO. He and his wife Virginia have two children, Greg and Linda.

During the mid 1950s Linton, Charles and Don would go sled riding on Washington Street. The Street Department would close off the street from the old county jail down to the creek. This became the sledding hill for Jackson. *Submitted by Don Luetje*

LUTTRULL – Pamela Henley Luttrull
March 9, 1953 – Aug. 29, 2000
    Born in Odessa, TX.
    Moved to Jackson, MO January 1987
    Married to Larry Luttrull.
    Mother to Regina Lee Mouser, Coye Lyn Moore, and Steven Jeremy McCarty.
    Nana to Adam Jeremy Mouser, Olivia LeAnn Mouser, Jessica Erin Mouser, Meagan Christina Moore, Christy Lynn Moore, Shaddow Hawk Moore, Heaven Lee Moore, and Austin Tyler McCarty.

We, her children, dedicate this page in the loving memory of our mom.

Pam was loved by all.
She gave even when there was nothing or very little to give.
She believed in putting people before herself, especially her family and children.
Family was everything to her. It was more important to her than anything else in this life, with the exception of God. She loved the Lord. She was a very spiritual person, and this is one of the many reasons people were so drawn to her. She had a very magnetic personality, a certain glow about her.

Pam was also very funny. One of her favorite things to do was make people laugh. She loved to laugh. And to be around her when she was laughing, you couldn't help but laugh too. She was very silly, unlike a normal mom. She loved speaking in her many different accents (which she proudly passed on to her kids). She enjoyed the friendship she had with us kids and with her grandbabies. She believed in discipline as well, and we completely respected her with all of our being. She was simply the best in every aspect of the word, the best friend, the best mom, the best counselor, the best advisor, the best teacher, and the leader we all looked to.

Pamela Henley Luttrull

Whether you knew her from Delmonico's and Bully's as your waitress, Country Mart as your deli person (or as the young people called her - "Mom"), whether she may have been your neighbor, your friend, or just someone you may have only met once, I, as her child, am sure that you agree:
She is truly missed by all.
Her smile and laugh will be remembered by everyone.
I believe that Pam brought something very unique and special to Jackson, MO in January of 1987. HERSELF.
Losing her was a devastation to us all. I pray that she will live through us. All of us.
We love and miss you, mom. *Submitted by Coye L. Moore*

MABUCE – The Mabuce family is descended from Ludwig Emil Mobius, a brick mason from Aarhuss, Denmark, who immigrated to America in April of 1866. He had four children: Jacob; Hans Hansen; Anna and Neils, all of whom were born in Denmark. Upon immigration, Mobius was changed to Mabuce. The family settled immediately in Bollinger County, MO, near the small town of Bessville. Ludwig Mabuce was later the first person buried in Liberty Methodist Church Cemetery in Bollinger County.

Hans Hansen Mabuce married Katherina Miinch of Patton in 1879. To them were born nine children. One daughter, Ethel Mabuce Soelberg, served as a missionary to Burma from 1916-1921. While in Burma she did not keep a journal, but instead wrote long detailed letters home to her parents and siblings. These letters were published in a book entitled *I Always Wore My Topi* in 1973.

The couple's second son, Emil Augustus Mabuce, became a carpenter in the Bessville area and married Mary Jane Murray. They had five children: Estel; Benton; and triplets Delwin, Audell, and Monell. Due to health reasons, only Benton participated in WWII, serving as an engineer. The other siblings all worked on the home front, Estel and Delwin as teachers and Audell and Monell in a munitions plant in St. Louis. During the war, Delwin married Juanita Parson and in 1944 had one son, Freddie Delwin Mabuce.

During WWII, Delwin and Juanita settled in Millersville, MO, close to his sister Audell, who had married Roy Robins and operated a general store. In Millersville, Delwin began a successful carpentry career and later helped rebuild Millersville United Methodist Church after a tornado severely damaged the church in 1957. His father, Emil, who had also moved to Millersville, served as assistant foreman for the reconstruction of the church. Delwin continued to believe in education, serving as a school board member for the Millersville School, prior to incorporation with the Jackson school system.

Fred D. Mabuce attended Jackson High School, where he was active in both basketball and baseball. After attending barber school in St. Louis, Fred married his childhood sweetheart, Cheryl Ann Martin, also of Millersville. Fred is the owner of Varsity Barber Shop in Cape Girardeau, while Cheryl is a past vice president of Union Planters Bank. They have two children, Kyle W. Mabuce, born April 30, 1972 and Nicole S. Rhodes, born July 20, 1977. Nicole married Craig Rhodes in 2001 and they live in Chicago, IL. Fred and Cheryl live near Jackson.

The Mabuce family, back row: Emil and Mary. Front row: Benton, Audell, Delwin, Monell, Estel, ca. 1923

Kyle attended Jackson High School, graduating in 1990, and Southeast Missouri State University, graduating in 1994 with a degree in Secondary Education, Social Studies. He is currently a history teacher at Jackson Junior High School, where he sponsors Student Council and National History Day. He married Misty A. Cates in 1997. Misty graduated from Advance High School and Southeast Missouri State University with degrees in Historic Preservation and Elementary Education. She currently teaches at Meadow Heights Elementary. Kyle and Misty live in Jackson. *Submitted by Kyle W. Mabuce*

MACKE – The oldest resident in Pocahontas, Esther (Rauh) Macke, is the beloved and gracious lady who lives in the white house at the top of the hill, across from Zion Lutheran Church. And this is her story.

Esther Emma Elizabeth was born June 24, 1908, to Charles and Louisa (Bergmann) Rauh at their farm home near Longtown. She was the fourth of five daughters, and was a sister, also, to three dear brothers (listed in their birth order: Oscar; Alma; John; Lela; Anna; Esther; Herbert and Lorna). Like most of the children in her day, Esther received limited schooling beyond the seventh grade. But be assured that she made the most of her education and gave freely her love and talents as a devoted wife to Wiley and mother to their four children: Thomas; Mary Lou; James and Paul.

Married on June 12, 1927, Wiley and Esther spent their first years of married life in Jackson, where their children attended St. Paul Lutheran School. In 1945 the family moved to Pocahontas where they became involved in the community's continuing progress.

Wiley, who passed away in 1995 at age 96, was well known as a top-notch auto mechanic in Jackson and Cape Girardeau. A veteran of WWI, he saw four years of active duty with the U. S. Navy, traveling around the world on the USS *Wilmington*, the USS *Samar*, the USS *Pelos*, and his last ship assignment, the USS *Detroit*. Wiley was one of three children (Owen and Daisy were the others) born to William and Hittie Belle (Sachse) Macke, natives of Jackson.

Esther Macke is admired by neighbors and friends in this rural community. She continues to enjoy her personal interests of handwork (particularly crocheting), baking, cooking, and gardening, as her health permits. Throughout her 93 years, Esther has served the Lord with gladness in her role as Sunday School teacher, Ladies Aid and L.W.M.L. member, and with faithful attendance at Zion Church. Her friendship to families, especially to her numerous parsonage neighbors (the Kueckers, Janks, Wesches, Brusses, Koenigs, Warrens, Muellers, and Vicar Mann) has not gone unnoticed. Letters and cards from former Lutheran pastors and their families continue to reach her door, not just at Christmas time, but throughout the year. When Jim, who resides with his mother, makes his daily walk to the post office, he is always overjoyed to bring back still another greeting from a friend or relative.

The Charles F. Rauh family of Longtown posed for this photograph (circa 1913) at a studio in Perryville. Little Esther sits beside her sister, Lela (front and center). Other family members are their mother Louisa (left) and father Charles, holding the youngest child, Herbert; back row: Alma, eldest daughter; Anna; John; and Oscar, eldest son. The picture was made before their fifth daughter Lorna was born. Mr. and Mrs. Rauh were married Nov. 27, 1894 at Peace Lutheran Church in Friedenberg. They were parents of 10 children and one foster son, Louis Vogel. Two daughters, Melva and Evelyn, died in childhood.

Photographs of Esther's extended family line her walls, shelves, and tables. Included are snapshots of her four grandchildren, six great-grandchildren, and one great-great-grandchild. She is quite proud of the five-generation picture of herself, daughter Mary Lou Haertling, granddaughter Susan McClain, great-grandson Justin McClain, and great-great-granddaughter Billie Ann McClain.

Being the only surviving child in a family is a "bittersweet experience," as anyone who is the last-of-the-line will agree. For Esther Macke, it is a humbling and often, lonely place to be. "Family and friends, along with a firm faith in God, make all the difference in greeting each new day!" *Submitted by JoAnn Bock*

MACKE – Heinrich Friedrich Ludewig Macke was born Feb. 10, 1795, in Kirchberg, Germany, and on Nov. 18, 1824, he married Hanna Marie Sophie Elisabeth Bose (Aug. 2, 1800 – March 9, 1871), daughter of Heinrich and Marie (Rese) Bose of Muchenhof, Germany. The Mackes left Germany from the port of Bremen and arrived aboard the *Richman* on Dec. 16, 1847, in New Orleans. They purchased land in Cape Girardeau County on May 25, 1848, from Jno A. Brimmer. Friedrich died on Sept. 23, 1869, and Marie passed away on March 9, 1871. They had six children, five sons and a daughter, Louise (see Sander/Bartels/Illers). The sons included Wilhelm, Frederich (1828), Henry (1835), Charles (1836) and Louis (1842).

Heinrich Friedrich Wilhelm Macke (Feb. 7, 1825 – March 11, 1878) was the oldest son and on April 11, 1850, he was married to Johanna Caroline Rose (Jan. 26, 1824 – Dec. 11, 1875). She was the daughter of Heinrich Julius (1798-1868) and Friedricke (Enbrecht) Rose (1799-1832) of Wiershausen, Germany. The couple had eight children: Johanna, Carl, Henry, Julius F., Fredericke, Adolph, Herman (see Sander/Bartels/Illers), and Lena.

Julius F. (Feb. 6, 1856 – April 21, 1914) was married three times, the first being on April 17, 1881, to Caroline Ahrens (Nov. 22, 1862 – Sept. 16, 1882), daughter of Henry P. (Oct. 18, 1837 – Nov. 20, 1916) and Christine (Mueller) Ahrens (June 21, 1839 – April 8, 1924). Mr. Ahrens was born in Ellisrode, Germany, and immigrated in 1845, establishing a mercantile business (see Macke's Store). This marriage produced only one son, Henry Wesley Macke (March 5, 1882 – Nov. 13, 1928), who was raised by his Ahrens grandparents. Julius next married Emma Kuehle, with whom he had four children: Charles, Alma, Mina and Albert. His third marriage was to Bertha Schwab and their children were Manda, Herman, Ida, Otto, and Rethor and Rudolph (twins).

Henry Macke married Rosena Ueleke (see Ueleke/Schlueter) on May 29, 1904, and they had one son, Albert Henry (Dec. 21, 1905 – Dec. 23, 1957). Rose passed away in 1915 and on Aug. 31, 1916, he married her sister Emelia Ueleke.

Albert would remain an only child and on Oct. 23, 1929, he married Dorothy Elsie Probst (Oct. 22, 1906 – June 11, 1999). Albert took over the mercantile business that had been passed on from his Grandpa Ahrens. He was a prominent businessman. He and Dorothy had three children: Henry Weldon (Aug. 16, 1930), Dorothy Ann (see Ueleke/Schlueter), and Alberta Louise (see Probst/Bartels).

Henry Weldon was married on July 11, 1954, to Bonnie Sue Bierschwal (July 5, 1936) and they had three daughters: Pamela (English/Wicker entry), Karen (Bierschwal et al entry), and Barbara (Howard/Webb entry). Weldon graduated from Jackson High School in 1948 and went on to college, two years at Southeast Missouri State College and two years at the University of Missouri, where he earned a degree in agriculture and was a member of Pi Kappa Alpha. He returned to work the family business with his mother until 1974 when they sold the general store and he retained the farm service portion of the business. Weldon taught agriculture classes at Jackson High School for a couple of years and in 1968 he became county auditor of Cape Girardeau County, serving a two-year term. He has won re-election eight times, but will retire in 2002. Weldon has served the community in many capacities that include the following. He served on the Board of the Bank of Gordonville, which went on to become Cape State Bank and is now First Star Bank. He has been a long time Rotarian; he has served as president of the Jackson Club and he and Bonnie are Paul Harris Fellows. He serves on the Boards of Southeast Hospital and Southeast Missouri University Foundation. He has chaired the Southeast Regional Planning Commission since its beginning. He has served on the Southeast Missouri District Fair Board and the Agriculture Committee of the Cape Chamber of Commerce. Weldon served as a president of the Missouri Association of Counties and served on the Finance Committee of the National Association of Counties. He has also served the United Methodist Church, at the local, conference, and general church levels for many years.

Bonnie worked in the family store and later she worked 25 years at Southeast Hospital. She has been active as a leader in 4-H, the United Methodist Women, and the Methodist Church Mission work area, and is Secretary of the Jackson Heritage Association. They are members of Zion United Methodist Church and reside just outside of Gordonville. *Submitted by Bonnie and Weldon Macke*

MAEVERS - Lester August Maevers was born Sept. 7, 1935 at Tilsit, MO to August and Amanda Nagel Maevers. The family lived on a farm before moving to Jackson in 1941. August Maevers worked at the Handle Factory and Amanda worked as a cook at various restaurants in Jackson. Lester is one of five children. His sisters are Mildred Lohman and Jerlene Hutteger of Jackson. His brother Arlen Maevers resides in Sikeston, MO, and Norman Maevers of Jackson passed away in 1995. August Maevers passed away in 1968, Amanda Maevers passed away July 30, 1988.

Lester attended school in Jackson, graduating in 1953. During his high school years he worked part time at Schaper's IGA in Jackson. He also joined the Missouri National Guard in September 1952. On Jan. 12, 1957 he and Ruth Hartle were united in marriage at St. Paul Lutheran Church in Jackson. Lester and Ruth are the parents of three sons; Tim and Jim of Jackson and Kenny of Sedgewickville.

Lester and Ruth Hartle Maevers, 1989

Lester continued working at Schaper's IGA as meat department manager. In 1968 he became co-owner of the business with Milton Grebe. The family all worked in the store in various departments. Tim, Jim and Kenny worked part time while attending high school. Lester was a member of the Missouri Grocers Association, serving as a board member for many years and as president of the association in 1987. Lester served in the Missouri National Guard for 24 years, retiring in 1976. Lester and Ruth purchased Schaper's IGA in 1984 and the Shopping Center in 1981.

Tim continued to work in the store after graduating from Jackson High School. Jim joined the U. S. Marine Corps and was stationed in Twenty-Nine Palms, CA and Japan during his four-year tour, before moving back to Jackson in 1987. Kenny works for Landgraf Construction Company.

During the years in the grocery business the Maevers family has owned seven grocery stores. In 1998 they sold the IGA store and joined the Save-A-Lot program. Tim and Jim now own three Save-A-Lot stores. Jim also owns Super Video in Jackson. The family still owns Schaper's Shopping Center, Main Street Center, and other properties in the area.

Lester and Ruth enjoyed the years in the grocery business. They are now involved in various civic clubs and organizations. They are members of St. Paul Lutheran Church. They enjoy traveling, bowling, spending time with friends and their eight grandchildren. *Submitted by Ruth Maevers*

MAINTZ - Ernest Maintz was born March 13, 1786 in Opperhausen, Germany. He lived his entire life in German and died in the fall of 1845. He married Elizabeth Boohnsacker. In their marriage, eight children were born. Their children were: Wimens; August; Fredrick; Ferdinand; Charles; William; Ernest and Henry.

Four brothers immigrated to the United States, landing at New Orleans in the fall of 1843. They were Charles, William, Ernest, and Henry. William and Henry settled in Whitewater Township. Ernest settled in Byrd Township. Charles was a soldier in the war with Mexico. He was wounded and returned to Cape Girardeau County. Ferdinand immigrated to the United States in Cape Girardeau County with August Maintz in 1883.

Henry Maintz married Johanna Behrens. They had six children: Mary; Henry; John; Charles Christian; August and Caroline.

John Maintz married Augusta Haupt on May 15, 1892. They had two children, Bertha and Henry Charles Maintz.

Henry Charles Maintz married Lena Luecreshie Seabaugh on May 10, 1928. They had a farm on County Road 471 between Daisy and Millersville. The farm was on 329 acres. Henry was born in this house. They had four children: Hoover; Geraldine; Marie Roselee and Dorothy May Maintz. Henry was a farmer. Lena stayed home and helped with the farm. They lived on the farm until 1978. August Maintz lived across the road from Henry Maintz.

Henry and Lena Maintz and children: Hoover; Dorothy; Rose and Geraldine

Hoover Maintz married Lurena Niswonger on Nov. 22, 1947. They lived across the road at an angle from Henry and Lena Maintz. They had three children; David Lee, Kathryn and Carol Ann. Geraldine Maintz married Leroy Seabaugh on Aug. 29, 1953. They had one son, Gary Edward Seabaugh. Dorothy Maintz married Truman Horn on July 12, 1968. They had two children, Vickie and Teresa Horn. Marie Roselee Maintz married John Moneyhun on May 15, 1954. They had one daughter, Connie Sue Moneyhun.

In 1957, Henry and a group of men interested in cooperative marketing, spent the day at the National Stockyards Market in St. Louis. They went to the G. M. plant and went to a Cardinal and Braves baseball game.

They sold the farm in 1978. They moved closer to the town of Jackson. The Missouri Conservation bought the farm and August Maintz' farm also. The Conservation made Maintz Preservation. They moved on West Lane in Jackson.

Henry Maintz died Sept. 30, 1992. Lena Maintz died Oct. 15, 1999. Their son Hoover Maintz died on Jan. 24, 1981. A grandson, David Maintz, died on March 6, 1995. All are greatly missed. Henry and Lena Maintz had four children, seven grandchildren, 10 great-grandchildren and six great-great-grandchildren. *Submitted by Vickie (Horn) Ford*

MANTZ - Ernest Mantz was born in 1786 at Opperhausen, Germany. He lived his entire life in Germany and died in 1845. He was married to Elizabeth Boohnsack. She was born in 1785 in North Germany. To this union eight children were born, seven sons and one daughter. Four of these brothers immigrated to the United States, landing at New Orleans, LA in 1843. They came up the Mississippi River to Cape Girardeau County, MO.

Emil and Amelia (Wilhelm) Mantz, wedding May 7, 1908

One of these brothers was also named Ernest (1819 - 1899). Upon his arrival to the United States he became a tailor in the town of Cape Girardeau and was an organizer of the Trinity Lutheran Church there. He was married to Marie Bodie (1833 – 1917) of Braunschweig, Germany. Ernest and his wife Marie later settled on a farm located west of Fruitland, MO. They had five children, all boys. Both Ernest and Marie are buried in the St. John's United Church of Christ cemetery west of Fruitland.

Two of Ernest and Marie's children, Emil and William, were married and also lived on this farm. There were two separate houses and barns on the farm. Emil (born Aug. 28, 1875) and his wife Amelia (Wilhelm) (born July 3, 1881) lived in a frame house located toward the back of the farm on a hill several hundred yards off what is now county road 436. It was in this house that their three children; Ernest William, Nora Lena and Albert Edwin Martin, were born.

In 1916 Emil and Amelia Mantz and the three children moved to a farm located between Oak Ridge and Jackson, MO. The three children attended the one-room Roberts' School while living there. In 1921 the Emil Mantz family moved to the town of Tilsit, MO, where they bought the general merchandise store. They ran this store in Tilsit from 1921 until 1938, when Emil Mantz died. They lived in a house immediately next to the store. The house and store were located directly across the street from the Tilsit School. This was a small two-room school where the three Mantz children attended elementary school. The Mantz' attended the St. James United Church of Christ in Tilsit. Ernest and Albert built the altar, pulpit and lectern for this church, which is still in use today. After the death of Emil Mantz in 1938, Amelia Mantz moved to Jackson, MO, where she lived until her death in 1975.

Ernest Mantz spent a large part of his life in the state of Tennessee. He was married to Edna Fluegge. Nora Mantz was married to Charles "Butch" Neumeyer and they spent their life on a farm near Tilsit, MO. Albert Mantz was married to Hilda (Neumeyer) and a second wife Marie (Sadler/Schweer). They resided in Jackson where they ran a small grocery store for a number of years.

Numerous descendants of the Mantz' still live in the Jackson area. The original property in Opperhausen, Germany is still occupied today by Mantz descendants. *Submitted by Harold C. Mantz*

MARLIN - Ivan E. Marlin was born March 18, 1886, near Herald, IL. From Herald, IL, the Marlin family moved to Ripley County, MO, near Naylor and Doniphan. As a young man Ivan came to Cape Girardeau to attend the Normal School, and he lived in Albert Hall. He became a rural schoolteacher and taught for 19 years. In 1911 he taught at the Indian Creek School near Oriole, MO. He met Mattie Simmons and they were married April 25, 1914. They moved to Ripley County and he taught school and farmed.

Their daughter, Mary Elizabeth Marlin, was born July 3, 1915, at Naylor, MO. In 1920 they moved back to Cape Girardeau County and he taught at the Plainview School, later teaching in the Indian Creek School again in about 1923. The last school in which he taught was the Sheppard School at Neelys Landing in about

Ivan Marlin, teacher on left, with students from Sheppard School, Neelys Landing, MO, circa 1925-26

1925. He had a new Model T Ford but rode many days from Indian Creek to Neelys Landing by horseback because of weather and road conditions. He had all eight grades with as many as 60 or more enrolled. That was such a hard year that he quit teaching and started raising registered cattle and leghorn chickens. He bought a Delco light plant and had a two-story chicken barn, and would get the chickens up at 4:00 a.m. to start eating.

This was the start of the great depression and money was hard to get. He had $200.00 and bought 100 pounds of sugar, 100 pounds of beans, a 50-pound can of lard, and a few other store items and a pair of store scales, and started the Marlin's Grocery at the Indian Creek School location. The business grew enough that he made a good living with the store, the livestock, and the chickens until his death on Feb. 28, 1958. During WWII he cut timber from the farm and built a new store building which still stands.

The Indian Creek School closed and consolidated and is now the Nell Holcomb School. The McLain Chapel Church closed and built a new church building near Leemon, which is the Wesley United Methodist Church. Though the church, school, and store closed, Mary Beth Marlin Vogt and family still maintain the farm and buildings.

The McLains Chapel Church cemetery is maintained by a well-organized group that functions for the McLains Cemetery, the Iona Baptist Cemetery near Oriole, and the Bray Cotter Cemetery near Neelys Landing. In the early days, Ivan Marlin would sharpen the blades of the horse-drawn mowing machine and cut the weeds and grass in the McLains Chapel Cemetery. Now it is kept in beautiful, well-kept condition all because someone cared. *Submitted by Mary Beth Marlin Vogt*

MARTIN - Elmo Cline Martin was born May 16, 1917, in Leemon, MO, the son of Tony and Daisy Martin. His mother was the former Daisy Garner of Leemon. Mr. Martin was known by all in the vicinity as a kind and loving man, devoted to his family, church and community. He was committed and cooperated with every phase of community betterment. Mr. Martin was graduated from Fruitland High School. He was a veteran of WWII, having served in the Navy in the south Pacific on Admiralty Island. Prior to WWII, he worked at Wagner Electric in St. Louis. While in St. Louis, he served his apprenticeship under his brother-in-law, Leslie Braig, learning the jewelry trade.

While there he met and married Miss Virginia Knoll on Nov. 23, 1946. They later gave birth to one son, Gary Anthony Martin, on May 5, 1948, and one daughter, Susan Lynn Martin, on April 12, 1955.

On completion of his training, they moved to Jackson and opened a jewelry store (Elmo C. Martin Jeweler) in the old Mueller building in 1949. Later they moved into the Steck building. Recently a clock that had been displayed in the front lobby of Mr. Martin's store was found by his daughter, Susan, at the United Cities Gas Company in Jackson, where she purchased the clock from them in December 2001. This business was sold in 1960. Mr. Martin then

Elmo C. Martin

devoted his full time to his insurance agency, until the time he sold it in 1963.

To list all of his activities would be impossible. A list of the organizations with which he was actively associated is as follows. He was Past President of the Chamber of Commerce; he was Associate Patron and Past Patron of the Jackson Chapter of the Order of the Eastern Star; he served in the Missouri State Legislature in 1958 and 1959; he was a member of the Excelsior Lodge #441 of the Masonic Lodge and a member of Scottish Rite of Missouri Valley; he was a member of the Moolah Shrine and a member of the Knights Templar of Cape Girardeau Commandry #55; he was vice-president of the National Association of Postmasters of Missouri and a member of the New McKendree Methodist church; he was a member of the Althenthal-Joerns of the American Legion and a member of the Wilson Chapter #75 of the Royal Arch Masons; he was a member of the Cape Council #20 R. & S. M; he was a member of the Southeast Missouri and State Democratic Club and was on the Advisory council of the Order of the Demolay; he was past-president of the Men's Club of the New McKendree Methodist Church; he was counselor for the Boy Scouts of America, and he was an active member of the Kimbeland Country Club.

In 1962 Mr. Martin was appointed postmaster of Jackson, after serving as an assistant for two and one half years. Mr. Martin, acting Postmaster, lost his life at the early age of 47, on Dec. 20, 1964. Mr. Martin was survived by his wife, Virginia Martin; son Gary; daughter Susan; two brothers, Clyde Martin of Jackson and Nelson Martin of Cape Girardeau; and two sisters, Mrs. Leslie Braig of St. Louis and Mrs. Bill Hollenbeck of Cape Girardeau. Mr. Martin's wife, Virginia Martin Tierney and his daughter, Susan Martin Seabaugh, both reside in Jackson; his son, Gary Martin, resides in Rock Hill, SC. *Submitted by Virginia Martin Tierney and children*

MARTIN - Jack Duree Martin Jr. was born October 21, 1947 in Cape Girardeau, MO. He was the son of Jack Duree Martin Sr., born 1911 and died 1959, and Lorraine Creamer Martin, born 1917 and died 1978. Jack's parents were farmers living in the Pocahontas, MO area. When Jack's father died, the family moved to Jackson in March 1960. Jack's mother had various domestic jobs to provide for herself, Jack and Jack's brother, Thomas Dale Martin.

Jack went to Immaculate Conception grade school and graduated from Jackson High School in 1965. During his teen years Jack worked for Southeast Dairy owned by Thomas O'Loughlin, delivering milk to local homes, schools, and businesses in the Jackson area. After graduating from Jackson High School he attended Southeast Missouri State College for one semester in the fall of 1965. In August of 1966 he went to work for Southwestern Bell Telephone Company.

In June of 1971 Jack married Mary Anne Welker. She was born Oct. 20, 1949 to Wilbert E. and Stella Brands Welker who were dairy farmers in the Gordonville area. Mary Anne was one of five children. She graduated from Notre Dame High School in 1967 and received an Associate of Arts Degree in nursing from Mercy Jr. College, and St. John's Hospital in St. Louis in 1969. She received a Bachelor of Science degree in nursing from Southeast Missouri State University in 1986. She worked at St. Francis Hospital as a staff nurse and part-time supervisor and taught nurses aides at the area Vocational School. In 1979 she started working for Dr. Jean Chapman, a local allergist, until he retired in 1997. She continued working for Mississippi Valley Allergy Partners. Mary Anne received an international certification in Asthma Education in January 2001.

Jack and Mary Anne had three children; John, Michael and Sarah. All three of their children went to Immaculate Conception Grade School and graduated from Jackson High School. All three of their children attended Southeast Missouri State University and are involved in elementary and secondary education. John married Keely Donaldson in 1997. Their son Brayden was born in 1999.

Jack and Mary Anne were members of Immaculate Conception Church. Jack became a member of the Knights of Columbus in 1977. He was Grand Knight in 1985 and 1986. Mary Anne became a member of the Knights of Columbus Ladies Auxiliary. Jack received the Distinguished Graduate Award from Immaculate Conception School in 1996. He also served on several boards for immaculate Conception School and Parish.

Front row, left to right: Jack and Mary Ann Martin, grandson Brayden. Back row: John Martin, Keely Donaldson Martin, Michael Martin, Sarah Martin

Jack retired from Southwestern Bell Telephone Company in 1991 and did contract work for them until 1996. In January 1997 Jack started working for the city of Jackson in the Park Department. *Submitted by Jack Martin*

MASON – The family of Edwin Augusta "E. A." Keeble Mason and Alice Faye (Burdette) Mason was not an old family of the area, coming to Jackson in 1920-21 after moving several times early in their marriage. It is believed they found Jackson when traveling back and forth between Arkansas and Tennessee to St. Louis to visit family. They saw the potential of a growing peaceful community (population about 3000), which would be a good place to raise a family.

Edwin "E. A." was from an old political family on his paternal and maternal sides. His maternal great-grandfather Colonel Richard Henry Keeble (1831-1864) was killed at the battle in Petersburg, VA. His paternal grandfather, William Newton (1827-1916) was a judge until 87 years of age; his father, Pleasant Peyton (1860-1941), was a prominent lawyer first for the "Cotton Belt" Railroad in Tennessee and Texas and then he moved to St. Louis around 1898 to open his own successful law firm where he practiced until he was 84 years old. E. A.'s only brother, Richard Henry Keeble, "Dick," was also a lawyer for the Arkansas Division of the Frisco Railroad and later was a member of the House of Representatives, a Lieutenant Governor and a State Senator of Arkansas.

E. A. was born Sept. 2, 1888, in Murfreesboro, TN, and attended the private Mooney's Prep School. He then went to Barnes Business College in St. Louis. He married Alice Faye Burdette (1892-1949) in 1911, who was a teacher in Colfax, IL. They had their first child,

William Newton (1912-1992), in Danvers, IL. E. A. then became secretary to the superintendent of Brown Shoe Company and began night school at City College in St. Louis. After passing his bar exam he worked in his father's law firm for a few years. In 1915 their second son, Edwin Augusta Jr. "Teddy" (1915-1935) was born in St. Louis. In 1919 E. A. moved his small family to Memphis where he worked as a claims agent for the Frisco Railroad. About a year later they moved to Jackson where E. A. became a prominent lawyer with his office in the old Cape County Savings Bank. In 1926, Alice Faye (Thompson, 1926-1999) was born in Jackson. E. A. was later appointed city attorney for Jackson and was serving in his second term at the attorney time of his death at age 51.

In the short time they were in Jackson they were active in numerous community activities. Both were members of the Christ Episcopal Church in Cape Girardeau. He was a member of the Cape County Bar Association, the Masonic Lodge and the Republican Party. Alice Faye was very active raising the children; being a journalist for the local paper and The Southeast Missourian; president of the PTA, Tuesday Culture Club, Republican Women's Club; Worthy High Priestess of the Calvary Shrine; Worthy Matron of the Eastern Star; member of the Civil Defense and Red Cross and member of the County Welfare Board that helped raise funds for the county tuberculosis home. Her enthusiasm along with other members of the Tuesday Culture Club helped bring about bathrooms in the county courthouse, drinking fountains in the public schools, lights around the courthouse entrances, establishment of the loan library (in 1925), and cleanup days for Jackson. In 1947 she was active in planning the campaign to pass a bond to erect a Memorial Library Building on the Dougherty property next to the Methodist Church.

Alice Faye also wrote several plays and essays, some that were published. Two of these were used for the celebration of Jacksonian Day in 1940 and 1941. Proceeds from her play, "Let Freedom Ring," added to the increasing funds to obtain new band uniforms for the high school. The cast of the play was 350 and told a history of the town combined with a patriotic theme. Admission for the play, which was held at the high school stadium, was 25 cents for adults and 15 cents for children. About 6000 people attended from the area.

The town mourned the loss of these two special people who contributed so much to this community. They along with most of their family are buried at Russell Heights Cemetery in Jackson. They have passed along their belief in community commitment to their children, grandchildren and future generations. *Submitted by Susan Thompson Hahs*

MASTERSON - This branch of the Masterson family originated in Virginia and North Carolina and migrated to Kentucky. David Masterson was born in Nelson County, KY. He later came to Missouri and settled in the Cape LaCroix Creek area.

His son, Elijah Masterson, was born in 1809 in Kentucky and was brought to Missouri as an infant. He married Rebecca Hall and fanned land just north of his father's land. Elijah died during the cholera epidemic in 1862 and Rebecca died in 1842.

His son, Medad, the eldest surviving of the family's three children, was born Nov. 25, 1829. He married Lucinda Carolina Phillips, the daughter of Moses Phillips, who was born in Alexander County, IL on Dec. 25, 1829. Medad and Lucinda both lived to be 67 years old. They had eight children; five sons lived to adulthood. The oldest child died in infancy and two girls died in early childhood.

William E. Masterson was born March 1, 1854 and died in 1910. He and Millie F. Thompson were married on Sept. 28, 1882, and had one child, Lucy, born March 20, 1886. Samuel Linn Masterson was born Jan. 5, 1858 and died in 1890. He and Mary Ellen Hitt were married on Nov. 16, 1882 and had two children, Luella, born Oct. 6, 1883 and Emory, born July 15, 1886. Robert Jackson Masterson was born Aug. 19, 1867, and died in June 1936. He and Mamie Katherine Eggers were married July 16, 1893. Mamie died in July 1946. They had four children: Hazel, born Nov. 1, 1894; Ruth, born Dec. 18, 1896; Robert, born Nov. 29, 1900; and Herman, born Feb. 13, 1903.

Nathaniel Forrest Masterson was born Feb. 16, 1874. He never married and he died in 1923. John Franklin Masterson was born March 3, 1858, and died in 1905. He and Mollie Elvira Campbell, born Oct. 9, 1862, were married on Feb. 18, 1886. They lived on a farm on the Clover Hill School road, about three miles northeast of Jackson. They had three children; Garnett Edward, born Dec. 8, 1886; Samuel Duree, born Aug. 10, 1891; and Grace Margaret, born June 30, 1895.

Garnet Masterson and Rispa Johnston, who was born Feb. 13, 1891, were married on June 3, 1909, and they had six children: Goldie Geneva, born July 22, 1910; Ruby Helen, born Oct. 4, 1913; Dorothy Ann, born July 21, 1917; Inez Elvira, born April 16, 1920; Carl Edward, born Jan. 21, 1923; and Maggie Ruth, born Jan. 14, 1928. Garnett died March 3, 1936, and Rispa died April 27, 1965. Grace Masterson and Paul Byron McNeely, who was born Feb. 16, 1892, were married on Dec. 4, 1920 and had three children; Troy Franklin, born Nov. 28, 1921; Margaret Pauline, born July 19, 1930; and Paul Wilson, born Dec. 18, 1936. Samuel Duree Masterson and Lenora Rosetta Weltecke, who was born March 8, 1890 were married on Dec. 26, 1919. They had four children: Samuel Duree, born May 8, 1921; Patricia Jean, born Nov. 19, 1924; Joe David, born April 9, 1928; and Helen Elvira, born Jan. 27, 1932.

Samuel Masterson and Thelma Owens, who was born April 17, 1924, were married on June 30, 1945. They had one daughter, Catherine, born March 4, 1954. Patricia Masterson and James Monroe Davenport, who was born Dec. 6, 1921, were married on Dec. 29, 1949. They had two children, Sherry, born Feb. 18, 1951; and Kirk, born Sept. 6, 1955. Joe Masterson and Hazel Lee Meyer, who was born Feb. 16, 1935, were married on June 17, 1951. They had two children, Carol, born May 24, 1952; and Mark, born May 11, 1955. Helen Masterson and Joseph Gohn, who was born July 2, 1923, were married on Aug. 14, 1953. They had two children, Terri. born Oct. 14, 1954 and Karen, born March 19, 1957. *Submitted by Terri Gohn Tomlin*

MAYFIELD - Dale and Alpha Mayfield were married on Nov. 9, 1930. They moved to Jackson in 1946 from Mayfield, MO. Dale was born July 5, 1904, in Mayfield, MO, and died Jan. 11, 2001. His parents were John H. Mayfield and Tilda Seabaugh Mayfield. Alpha Allen Mayfield was born May 11, 1903, in Gravel Hill, MO, and died March 27, 1989. Her parents were Barney B. Allen and Amanda Elizabeth Hanners Allen. Dale retired from Kasten Brick Company in Jackson, MO at the age of 66. While living in Mayfield, MO, he worked for the General Motors Company in Michigan; he also worked in St. Louis, Cape Girardeau, and the handle factory, Lapier and Sawyers, in Jackson, MO. Dale also farmed some in Mayfield, MO.

Dale graduated from the American School of Music in Chicago on April 18, 1927. He could play the harmonica, guitar, and violin. He could still play the violin at the age of 93. His mother, father and grandfather all had musical talent. In the late 1800s his mother, Tilda Seabaugh Mayfield, his grandfather, Joseph Seabaugh, and other members of the family traveled to St. Louis, MO, by horse and wagon from Sedgewickville, MO, to play at a concert there.

Alpha attended the Will Mayfield College in Marble Hill, MO. She was an elementary school teacher in Crump, MO. She also worked at Lenco in Jackson. In later years she was a homemaker. Date and Alpha liked going to church and reading their Bible. They were members of the First Baptist Church in Jackson. They enjoyed gardening, and they also enjoyed taking care of their grandchildren.

Alpha and Dale Mayfield on their wedding day, Nov. 9, 1930

Dale and Alpha had four boys. One died as an infant, unnamed. Ralph E. Mayfield has two sons, Kenneth E. and Douglas L. Kenneth has a daughter Ashley and a son Chad. Douglas has two girls, Leslie and Rachel.

Glenn W. Mayfield has three children, Angie, Kieth, and Kyle. Angie has two children, Luke and Lacy. Kieth has twin boys, Blake and Cody.

Clarence A. Mayfield has two sons and two daughters. Jeffery has two girls, Megan and Haley. Carla has two boys, Dereck and David. Karen has two girls, April and Malisa. Greg has two children, Creg and Kala.

All of the families live in Jackson or the surrounding area. *Submitted by Ralph Mayfield*

MAYFIELD - Marilyn E. (Allen) Mayfield was born Sept. 19, 1941 at 124 S. Bast Street in Jackson, MO to Clarence W. Allen and Noma M. (Crites) Allen. When she was 1 year old, the family moved to a farm west of Jackson on what is now County Road 347. She attended school for five years at Big Springs School, a one-room school with first through eighth grades attending. Mrs. Carrie Wallis was the teacher of the school, which had a big wood stove in the front of the room, the only heat source at this time. They had to walk to school, as there was no school bus at this time.

In the fall of 1952 the family moved to a farm five miles northwest of Jackson on County Road 442, and her brothers and sisters walked through the fields to attend the one-room Roberts' School. Mrs. Hanners was the school cook and this was the first time a hot lunch had been served to the Allen children at school. In the fall of 1954 they moved to a farm near the Mayfield Community where she attended Patton High School. There were 41 in her class when she graduated in 1959. They didn't have to walk to school anymore; the school bus picked them up in front of their home.

They started attending Little Whitewater Baptist Church and she was baptized at the age of 14. This is where she met her husband Donald H. Mayfield (born March 08, 1938), the son of Homer H. Mayfield (born May 25, 1903, died Feb.

3, 1980) and C. Marie (Mayfield) Mayfield (born May 11, 1905, died Dec. 25, 1996). His family had lived in the Mayfield Community for several generations. He was the youngest of five children, including Algerene, Gerald, Verda Mae and Jerry. They all had attended the Mayfield School in Mayfield Holler. Donald graduated from Patton High School in 1956. He was a member of the Missouri National Guard from 1959 to 1965, training at Fort Leonard Wood in Waynesville, MO, and at Fort Ord in California. They were married at Little Whitewater Baptist Church on Nov. 24, 1960 by his uncle Rev. Edward Mayfield, a Baptist minister.

They moved to Cape Girardeau and lived there eight years. They had three children; Patty (born Nov. 30, 1961); Pam (born Aug. 14, 1964) and Brian (born Jan. 26, 1968) and were members of Lynwood Baptist Church. Patty first attended Alma Schrader School in Cape Girardeau and after they moved to Jackson, County Road 618, in 1969, they attended Jackson schools.

Donald and Marilyn Mayfield with children and grandchildren.

Patty married Tom Schlosser on April 20, 1985 and with their three children, Cody, Kyle and Kati, live in the Jackson area. Patty has worked in the County Clerk's office for 10 years where she is Election Supervisor. Pam married David Olson on July 2, 1988 and with their three children; J. D., Chelsea and Courtney, live at Marble Hill; the children attend Jackson Schools where Pam is a Kindergarten teacher at the Primary Annex. Daryl Olson, their oldest son, attends college in Houston, TX. Brian married Kristi (Allen) on April 19, 1990 and with their three children, Brandon, Kara and Brady, live in Tulsa, OK where he works for William's Pipeline as a Manager, Business Planning and Analysis.

Donald retired from Union Electric in 1997 after working 36 years in the electric line department. Donald now enjoys helping friends and family with small projects and riding his horse. Marilyn enjoys flower gardening and crafts, and they both enjoy spending time with children and grandchildren. *Submitted by Marilyn Mayfield*

MAYFIELD - John Jefferson Mayfield Jr. was born Aug. 13, 1862, in Mayfield, MO. He received the degree of Doctor of Medicine from the St. Louis College of Physicians and Surgeons of St. Louis, MO, on March 7, 1885. He received certificate number 3029 from the State Board of Health, State of Missouri on May 17, 1886, which authorized him to practice medicine and surgery in the state of Missouri.

Dr. Mayfield moved to Jackson, MO in 1890. This is where he lived and practiced medicine until his death May 21, 1923. He was buried in the new Lorimer Cemetery, Cape Girardeau, MO.

He married Carrie Adele Hartle in 1887. They had four children: Francis; Roy Emanuel; Emory Jefferson, and John Jesse.

Dr. Mayfield was the son of John Jefferson and Sarah "Micky" (Williams) Mayfield. He had one sister, Sarah Adaline, and nine brothers: Dr. Eli Marion; Colombus James; George Washington; Francis; Dr. Amon Arvel; Marshall Hamilton; Adam Lee; Dr. Pinkney Martin, and Stephen Hesikie.

Dr. Mayfield's grandparents were George Washington and Mary "Polly" (Cheek) Mayfield. Their children were: Dewitt; John Jefferson (Senior); George Washington Jr.; Dr. Andrew Jackson; Cynthia "Sally" M.; Margret; Mary Ann "Polly;" Dr. William Henderson; Dr. Amanuel Benton;

Erin Mayfield, Dec. 27, 1991, age 6 years

Dr. Stephen A.; Dr. Randolph L. and Dr. Eli Burton. Dr. William Henderson Mayfield is remembered for his work in the Missouri Baptist Sanitarium, Missouri Baptist Hospital, and Barnes University and Hospital in St. Louis, MO. He was president of Barnes University in 1911. Dr. H. J. Smith and Dr. William Henderson Mayfield started the Smith-Mayfield Academy located in Marble Hill, MO in 1878. The name was changed to the Will Mayfield College in memory of Dr. Mayfield's deceased son, William H. (Jr.). The college was chartered in 1903, and it was closed in 1934. Dr. Andrew Jackson's sons who became medical doctors were George Franklin and Cary Boyd. Dr. Eli Marion's son, Maud Dean, became a medical doctor. Doctor Eli Burton had two sons, Eli Burton Jr. and George Conrad, who were medical doctors. Dr. Stephen A. Mayfield's son, Lee Stephen, was a medical doctor. Dr. John Jefferson and 15 of his relatives were medical doctors in the states of Missouri, Illinois, Arkansas, Kansas, and Texas.

Timothy Paul Mayfield, a 1996 graduate of Cape Girardeau Central High School, started at the University of Missouri School of Medicine in the year 2001. He is a descendant of Dr. John Jefferson Mayfield's brother George Washington and Sarah Ann (Samples) Mayfield.

Ben Mayfield, March 29, 2000, age 10 years

The Mayfield history was researched and written by Timothy's grandparents, Juel Dean and Dorothy Mayfield. Juel and Dorothy wish to thank the Cape Girardeau County Archive Center and Glenn W. Mayfield, editor of the book, *MAYFIELDS*, published in 1997. The publisher's address is P. 0. Box 452, Sallisaw, OK 74955. Another valuable information source was the biography of William Henderson Mayfield written by Wiley B. Patrick and published in 1912. The Will Mayfield Heritage Association is restoring the buildings. *Submitted by Juel Mayfield*

McCLARY – Jackson, the "city of beautiful homes, churches and schools," came into view as the Ed McClary family drove into Jackson in 1954 to make the town their home. Eight-year-old Laura added "- and the McClarys." Her sister, two brothers and parents all applauded.

They moved into the John Kasten home in east Jackson and were influenced by the helping hands of many Kastens during their lives here. They soon became involved in the activities of the Methodist Church, the schools and the community. Jane was born the next year. Lynn, Laura, Robb and Eddie were all in school.

Ed, an Agency Manager for State Farm Insurance Company, found time to teach Sunday School, be active in Rotary Club, and serve on the Kasten Brick Board and The Jackson Exchange Bank Board.

In 1959 Elizabeth was named "Jackson's Leading Lady." She has been active in PEO, Thursday Study Club and church school groups. She remembers with amazement that she was a room mother and a band mother for 20 years in a row. She remembers an amusing incident that shows Jackson as it was. About 10 years after they moved here, she was asked to speak at a Literary Club function and the lady prefaced her introduction with "Although she is a newcomer here.."

Front row: Elizabeth and Ed McClary. Back row: Robb, Laura, Lynn, Jane, Ed, Christmas 1996

Music was an important part of the McClary lives. All of the children sang in the school music groups and the Methodist choir, and played musical instruments in both the high school and Muny bands. The boys formed a rock band called "The Mustangs" that played on their carport and at the roller rink. Today, son Eddie is a professional musician and Robb plays his saxophone as a hobby with the "Contors," a St. Louis Motown band. They all remember Leroy Mason, Dick Partridge, Al Rowland, Nick Leist, Elda Ellis and Ernestine Kirk, all who influenced their love of music and their lives.

Among Jackson's favorite attractions for the family was the city park where the children learned to swim and enjoy every day in the summer, and attended meetings in the Scout Hut under the direction of outstanding leaders like Hutz Grossman, Cotton Meyer, Dorothy Phillips and Marge Grindstaff. The children particularly enjoyed skating at the roller rink under the loving, watchful eyes of Woody and Jean Seabaugh who also spent many pleasurable hours with them water skiing at Lake Wappapello. Homecomers was a much-anticipated event every year. The boys, as high schoolers, got up early to help erect the carnival rides, and Laura won a contest guessing how many beans were in a jar in Rozier's window.

The values and activities, as well as the love of neighbors, teachers and friends, shaped the futures of the children. Although their professional lives have taken them far from Jackson, Lynn Hawkins, who completed her Ph.D., is a writer and college teacher in Florida; Laura Avakian is human resources vice-president for the Massachusetts Institute of Technology in Cambridge, MA; Robb has had a successful career in city management; Eddie owns a music company and plays professionally in San Francisco; and Jane is a TV producer in New York.

The McClary family includes 10 grandchildren and five great-grandchildren.

Jackson was — and is — a special place for the family. It is, indeed, "the city of beautiful homes, churches, schools — and the McClarys." *Submitted by Elizabeth McClary*

McCOMBS – Born on August 17, 1845, John William McCombs, Sr. became a steamboat pilot on the Mississippi River between St. Louis and Memphis, owned a ferry, and piloted another at Veneil's Landing. After marrying Berry Byrd in 1868, he came to Jackson where they had two children, Ruddell Monroe McCombs and Martha Elizabeth "Mattie" Twogood. After operating a brick and clay business and working for the Cape County Milling Company, he moved to Bowie, TX, after his wife had died. He remarried Addie Bray in 1879, who bore him two children, John W. Jr. and Tom Ella. He and his family returned to Jackson in 1884 where he remained until his death at 87, working until retirement for the Cape County Milling Company, eventually serving as superintendent.

Ruddell, whose mother died when he was 3, returned to Jackson at 18 and graduated from Jackson schools, after which he attended St. Louis Business College before becoming secretary of the Horrell and Byrd Milling Company. Shortly thereafter, in 1895, he took the lead in organizing the Cape County Milling Company. During his tenure as president, the company ran two flour mills in Jackson (Mills A and B), one in Burfordville (Mill C), and one in Oak Ridge, selling internationally the brands developed by the company—Gold Leaf, Capco, and Kitchen Queen. By 1914 the mill had, according to the *Cape Girardeau Republican*, "an immense plant with elevators and warehouses covering several acres of ground." About 90 men worked, in 1914, at Mill A alone. In 1896 Ruddell became a member of the Methodist Church; he served as a member of the Board of Stewards for 57 years and superintendent of Sunday schools for 40 years. Emma Boss, his wife for over 50 years, and Ruddell had one daughter, Helen McCombs Bright, a Mary Institute graduate, who worked at the mill, testing the flour chemically. Ruddell, Emma, and Helen-passionate about Methodism—took active leadership roles in New McKendree Methodist Church. Present at the laying of the cornerstone in 1908, Ruddell had served on the building committees. The family donated the stained glass windows, still in the church today, after purchasing them for $1700 from a closing church. A close friend of Bishop Ivan Lee Holt, he served on the board which restored Old McKendree Chapel. Known as a hard-driving businessman and a devout churchman, he left his mark on the church and the community. After economic pressure from gigantic mills forced the company into insolvency, it liquidated its assets in 1953, the year Ruddell died. Emma served as president of the WSCS (later called United Methodist Women) and secretary of numerous committees, directed the church choir, and taught Sunday School. In addition, she became a charter member of the Thursday Literary Club. Helen served on a plethora of committees and taught Sunday School for years.

Born in Bowie, TX, on Feb. 14, 1884, Tom Ella "Ella" McCombs moved to Jackson in 1897. On Dec. 31, 1912, she married the superintendent of the milling company William A. Heyde, Sr. A member of New McKendree Methodist Church, the Eastern Star Lodge, and the Thursday Literary Club, she was a kind, generous, caring wife, who loved her children, Lilly and Bill, Jr., and who, in later years, doted over her six grandchildren. She divided her time, after the 1930s, among Jackson, the Heyde Farms in Stoddard County, and Sikeston where Lilly, her daughter, lived.

Born in Jackson on May 11, 1881, John William "Will" McCombs Jr. attended Jackson Military Academy. After graduation, he said, "My father saw to it that I didn't loaf. I was at work at my brother's flour mill or the stave factory as a youth when not in school. I did play football occasionally." Later he sold county maps after which he became a Cape County Milling Company salesman. On June 10, 1905, he married Emma Cyrene "Rena" Campbell. In 1906 he purchased a furniture and undertaking business which he, with his partners B. A. Meyer, H. E. Boss, and Hope E. Morton incorporated in 1929 under the name McCombs Furniture and Undertaking, the first to use easy payments and free furniture delivery in Jackson. A warm-hearted optimist, Will had "the knack of making every person he met feel that he was exactly the one he was looking for and always showed his sincere appreciation for their patronage." Though he had no children, he made up for it by giving chewing gum and nickels for ice cream to the many young people who crossed his path. In addition, he had farming interests. An active member of New McKendree Methodist Church, he served on the Board of Stewards for 35 years, two of them as chairman. Later, heart trouble forced him to curtail his business activity until he died at 62.

J. W. McCombs Sr., W. A. Heyde Jr.

Will credited Rena with much of the success of the business. She worked as a clerk and bookkeeper from the beginning. She, the daughter of Mary E. Horrell and Captain Stephen Campbell (C.S.A.) who had fought under the command of General Sterling Price during the Civil War, was born on Jan. 31, 1879. After her husband had died, Rena's mother moved to Jackson because of its superior schools. Active in the community, she was, with Ella Heyde and Emma McCombs, a charter member of the Thursday Literary Club which made her an honorary life member, and in 1967 a tree was planted in her honor at the Jackson City Park. In addition, she was a member of the West Jackson Homemakers (for 40 years), the UDC, and the WCTU. A proud member of New McKendree for 70 years, she took an active role in the WSCS (later the United Methodist Women), serving as treasurer many terms. The WSCS also made her an honorary life member. Moreover, she became an affectionate and generous mentor for her adopted grandchildren, the Yount and Heyde children. She died at home at the age of 93. *Prepared by William A. Heyde, III*

McDONALD – Matthew and Ann McDonald emigrated from Ireland in the 1820s. They first settled near Vincennes, IN in 1826 lived there until 1834 when they moved to Natchez, MS, where they lived until 1841. Matthew and Ann McDonald arrived in Cape Girardeau County in February 1841 with their children: Margaret; James; John; Eliza and Matthew, Jr.

Margaret married Abraham Penn. James and John served the Union during the Civil War. John drowned near Hickman, KY returning from the war. James married Anastasia Ervin in 1857. Matthew Jr. died in 1840. Eliza married and moved to St. Louis.

James McDonald worked as a brick mason. He worked on the original Normal School, the Cape Girardeau Courthouse, and the Jackson Military Academy. James and Anastasia McDonald had eight children. Charles had a business in Cape Girardeau and served as city marshal. Ella married Robert Masterson. Her many descendants include the Hitt and Litzelfelner families in Jackson and Cape Girardeau County. Emma McDonald married Dan Fennell. Frank McDonald married Ida Brooks. He lived north of Cape Girardeau and is said to have donated land for Hobbs Chapel. He was a schoolteacher and cattleman. Arthur McDonald married Betty Arnold. His son, Clyde, began McDonald Cement of Cape Girardeau. John McDonald married Samantha Sides. He was a minister and served several local churches. His descendants include the Thompson family of Jackson. Olive McDonald married Thomas Haddock. Their farm was near the intersection of McDonald and Haddock Streets in Cape Girardeau. James T. McDonald was their youngest. He married Elizabeth Huntley of Caruthersville. He served as Cape Girardeau County Superintendent of Schools and was Probate Judge until his death in 1936. James T. and Elizabeth had five children.

James Huntley McDonald married Lucille Brue. He taught auto mechanics at Caruthersville, IL for Southern Illinois University, and lived in Jackson after retirement. Joseph and Eugene McDonald were twins. They were well-known athletes at College High and Southeast Missouri State University during the 1930s. They were co-captains on Southeast Missouri State University's first MIAA championship basketball team in 1936. Joseph married Margarite Johnson. He had a Doctor of Theology degree and served as a minister. He retired from the University of Rolla as a counselor. Eugene married Marjorie Ludy from Emporia, KS. He served as a medical officer in France during WWII. He was a Doctor of Medicine in Jackson. Evelyn married Hart Donnell, M.D. and lived in Crystal City. They had five boys. Elizabeth married David Mitter and had five girls. They lived in south St. Louis County. The family of Eugene and Marjorie McDonald grew up in Jackson. They had four children: Eugene Jr.; Susan; Cheryl; and Janet. *Submitted by Dr. Eugene McDonald Jr.*

McDOWELL - James McDowell was born May 1, 1845 and died Feb. 24, 1890. James and his mother immigrated to America from Ireland. He was a Confederate soldier in the Civil War and was at the Battle of Vicksburg. He was wounded while in the military.

James married Nancy Ervin (born May 3, 1845; died June 23, 1908). They made their home in the Leemon Community. James and Nancy became the parents of five sons: Lynn; Eli; William; Charles and James. They had two daughters, Lou Verna and Bertha. Bertha never married and died at the age of 17.

Lynn McDowell married Louie Sides. The children born to this union were: Ira; Frank; Robert; Raliegh; Grace; Mary; Vergie and Bessie. They left this area and raised their family in the Bonne Terre area.

Eli Ervin McDowell (Jan. 7, 1875-April 30, 1959) married Effie Noland (Jan. 7, 1884- Jan.

5, 1956). They made their home on a farm in the Leemon Community. The farm was located along what is now Highway 177. They were the parents of six sons and five daughters. Their sons were Robert; Roy; Chester; Harry; Edward and Eugene. Adah, Mabel, Hazel, Virginia, and Maxine were their daughters. Virginia died in infancy. Robert, Roy, Chester and Harry were all farmers or livestock dealers in the Fruitland and Leemon Communities. Ed operated a filling station and later an appliance store in Fruitland. Eugene made his home in Jackson and was engaged in the construction business. The four daughters all became teachers. Mabel, Hazel and Maxine all retired from that profession.

James McDowell family: back row: Eli, Will, Charles, Phillip and Verna Englehart. Front row: Lynn, Louie holding Grace, James, Nancy, Bertha and Aunt Ann McDonald and daughter.

William Henry (July 6, 1877 - April 5, 1955) married Hettie Noland (Jan. 7, 1884-Jan. 15, 1951). Hettie was the twin sister of Eli's wife Effie. They made their home on a farm adjacent to Eli and Effie's farm. They became the parents of Paul, Fred, Wilson, Allen, Lou and Lora. Paul, Fred and Allen owned and farmed land in the same community as their father.

Charles Jami was born Oct. 13, 1877, and married Nellie Mae Howard (Dec. 3, 1889). They had a farm that bordered both Eli's and William's farms. Their children were James, Elliot, Lloyd, Orville, Ruby, Wilma and Genevieve. James and Wilma lived and raised their families in the area.

Lou Verna McDowell (1872-1954) married Phillip Englehart (1868-1943) and they owned a farm to the southeast of her three brothers. Four children were born to this union. Onas, their first child, died in infancy. Their other children were Herbert, Melvin and Grace. Herbert lived on the family farm, taught school and lived in the Leemon Community.

James McDowell was born after his father's death on March 20, 1890 and died in 1972. He married Carolyn Snider and they had one daughter, Elaine. He taught school in southeast Missouri, became a lawyer and later was judge of the Springfield Court of Appeals.

Today there are numerous descendants of James and Nancy McDowell living, working and raising their families in the Jackson, Fruitland and Leemon communities. *Submitted by Mary Morton*

McDOWELL - Robert Lee McDowell was born Sept. 2, 1901 in Leemon, MO. He was the oldest son of Eli and Effie Noland McDowell. Robert received his education at Leemon Grade School, Fruitland High School, and Cape Business College. On Dec. 31, 1931, he married Ilda Shaner (Aug. 4, 1911), daughter of Lawrence and Ella Heuer Shaner. Ilda attended the Dogwood Grade School, Fruitland High School and Southeast Missouri Teachers College.

In February 1934, Robert and Ilda moved to a farm they had purchased in the Leemon Community. Their farm was next to his father and mother's farm on the "Farm to Market Road" that is now known as Highway 177. Crops and livestock were raised on the farm. Two creeks ran through the farm, one on each. They provided the family with great recreation. Later, Robert and sons started a dairy operation on the farm.

Robert and Ilda McDowell, 40th wedding anniversary

Robert and Ilda had four children: Mary Ella (November 1932); Robert Lawrence (February 1935); Gary Lane (January 1938) and Brenda Joyce (December 1944). Mary married Robert J. Morton and had two children, Michael Robert and Sherrie Lynn. Brenda married Johnie D. Keene and had one son, John Devin.

Robert and Ilda were interested in promoting better education facilities for the children of the community. They worked along with many others to promote the consolidation of Dogwood, Sawyer, and Leemon schools into Fruitland Consolidated District No. 2 in 1940. Children were then transported to school for the first time in what had previously been the Fruitland High School. Later, Robert and Ilda would work with others to get a hot lunch program started at the school. They let a piece of their farm be used for a garden to help supply vegetables for the lunches.

The family was affiliated with the Fruitland Methodist Church. In 1966 members of three churches (Fruitland, Fairview and McClain's Chapel) united to form the Wesley United Methodist Church. This church was built on land donated by Robert and Harry McDowell from the corners of their adjacent farms. *Submitted by Mary Morton*

McGUIRE – Arra Mae McGuire was born July 12, 1893 in Burfordville, MO, near Snider Mill, and died Feb. 27, 1963. She was married on May 16, 1912 in Cape Girardeau to Ora Cleveland "Dude" Slinkard who was born Nov. 19, 1888 in Gravel Hill, MO, and who died July 18, 1975. Both are buried in Memorial Park Cemetery. Arra was a housewife and she loved flowers. She was a member of Whitewater Methodist Church and of the Eastern Star. Ora loved to do garden work. He was a Mason and Eastern Star at Whitewater. He was known as "Dude" to his friends.

Ora Cleveland Slinkard was the son of Daniel Franklin Slinkard who was born Oct. 27, 1856 in Scopus, MO, and who died Feb. 19, 1935. He was married Dec. 22, 1877 to Mary Catherine "Kate" Henley who was born July 4, 1871 near Gravel Hill, MO. Both are buried in Lesley Cemetery. Ora and Arra Slinkard were the parents of Woodrow Wilson, Glenda Azalee DeVore, and Boyd Loren "Dick."

Arra Mae Slinkard was the daughter of William Franklin McGuire who was born Aug. 12, 1854 near Crump, MO, and who died March 3, 1931. He married Artelda "Tilla" Berry, who was born in 1855 near Crump, MO, and who died May 25, 1883. Both are buried in Allen Cemetery. William Franklin and Artelda McGuire were the parents of Berdie Strong, Felty, Dill, Bill, Luther, and Arra Mae Slinkard.

William Franklin McGuire was the son of William Madison McGuire who was born in 1820 in West Virginia and who died Jan. 12, 1901 at the home of his son, William Franklin McGuire. He owned a tanner business. The McGuire Cemetery near Burfordville, MO, was named after William M. McGuire. He was married on Sept. 6, 1838 to Louise Jane Howard who was born in 1818 near Jackson, MO, and who died in 1881. Both are buried in Howard Cemetery. They were the parents of Charles, Ezeikial, Emanuel, Elizabeth, Mary Ann, Elnora, Rachel, and William Franklin.

Louise Jane McGuire was the daughter of Zedekiah R. Howard and Jane Joan English. William Madison McGuire was the son of Hugh McGuire who was born in 1776 in Virginia and who died in 1849 in Wayne County, MO. He was married in Virginia to Betty Elizabeth Trotter who was born in 1779 in West Virginia and who died in 1848 in Cape Girardeau. She is buried in McGuire Cemetery.

Hugh McGuire was the son of John McGuire from Ireland, who married Elizabeth Lewis. She was the daughter of Colonel Fielding Lewis of Virginia, who married Betty Washington. Colonel Fielding Lewis of Warner Hall of Gloucester County was married to Elizabeth Warner. She was the daughter of Augustine Warner Jr. who was the son of Augustine Warner Sr.

Colonel Fielding Lewis was the son of John Lewis of Gloucester County. John and Elizabeth McGuire were the parents of John, Samuel, Rebecca, Anna, Polly, Rachel, and Hugh. John McGuire was the son of James McGuire. *Submitted by Jeffery Allen Slinkard*

McGUIRE - Eleanor "Aunt Sis" Seabaugh was born on Sept. 3, 1923 in a log house in Millersville, but moved to Jackson with her family when she was very small. Her parents were Ora and Eula Vanilla (Statler) Seabaugh. Ora was born June 12, 1903 and died Aug. 7, 1976. Eula was born Nov. 7, 1900 and died Sept. 9, 1982. Eleanor also had two younger sisters, Mary Lou and Helen Leona.

Billy Fred McGuire was born on April 27, 1906, and was raised by Frank and Jennie McGuire in the Gordonville area. As a teenager he had to walk to Jackson High School, where he graduated in 1926.

Bill and Eleanor were married on Oct. 11, 1946 in the home of the Methodist preacher. During WWII, Bill served in the Medical Corps in Walla Walla, WA, where he injured his back. When Bill returned home, he worked at Brennecke Chevrolet as a mechanic and wrecker driver for 19 years. He then drove a wrecker for Wib Bangert. After graduating from Jackson High School in 1941, Eleanor went to work at the Shoe Factory.

On May 31, 1948 Billy Fred McGuire Jr. was born to Bill and Eleanor. It became increasingly difficult for Eleanor to leave Little Bill, as he became known, to go to work each day so she decided to open a nursery school in her home, called Aunt Sis' Day Nursery. When her hus-

Bill and Eleanor McGuire

band, Big Bill, retired in 1973, he began to help Aunt Sis with the kids, so they renamed the business McGuire's Nursery School. Through almost 50 years of daycare the McGuire's cared for more than 400 children in the Jackson area. Aunt Sis quickly became famous for her goulash and sweet rice. She was also known for her witty poems. In 1992 she put together a book that included her famous recipes, poems and experiences in childcare.

Bill passed away on May 12, 1988, after a long battle with cancer. Aunt Sis continued to care for children for 12 more years. During those years, macular degeneration began to affect her eyesight and she reluctantly retired in June of 2000.

Bill was a member of the American Legion. Aunt Sis was active in the American Legion Auxiliary, serving as chaplain, historian, 2nd vice-president, 1st vice-president and president, respectively. The McGuires were members of First Baptist Church in Jackson where Aunt Sis taught Sunday School for more than 50 years. She also served many years as a Girls In Action leader and a Baptist Young Women leader.

Aunt Sis has been featured in the *Missouri Farmer, Southeast Missourian,* and the *Cash-Book Journal* publications, as well as KFVS Channel 12 News. On October 22, 1980 the Missouri House of Representatives passed a resolution honoring her for her many accomplishments in childcare, church and community activities. *Submitted by Lisa Drum*

McLAIN - Charles was born to David M. and Elizabeth Hughes McLain, in the Oriole Indian Creek area in north Cape Girardeau County. He was the youngest of their five children: Ivy and Dave of Neelys Landing, Monroe of Oriole, and Mark, a Spanish American War veteran of San Diego, CA. David D. died accidentally while out hunting with his son, Ivy. Charles was only a few months old. He was still crawling. Charles' mother remarried "Mr. Simmons," by whom she had two daughters, Kate and Mattie.

Charles was encouraged by a cousin, J. D. McLain, as well as by his stepfather, Mr. Simmons, to seek higher education. J. D. McLain was a prominent merchant in Oriole who spoke with authority. Cape College was nearby so Charles accepted the challenge. His mother, "Lizzie," had simply named him "Charley." One of Charley's professors advised him to change his name to Charles and to add a middle name, making him more dignified. Henceforth he became Charles I. McLain.

Armed with a teacher's certificate, Charles taught in small schools in southeast Missouri. However, in 1912 he was teaching in south St. Louis County in Afton, MO, when he met and married Mamie Henson. They survived and enjoyed 59 years of marriage during which they reared six children: Helen; Loida; Dorothy; Jeanette; Norman and Herbert. Charles finally earned his B. S. Degree from Southeast Missouri State University in 1929. His teaching career lasted 35 years.

Charles and Mamie McLain

Mamie always dreamed of owning a business. This venture started with a very small grocery store and developed into a variety store. The business was located in Eureka, MO, which is in west St. Louis County. It was "smack dab" on Highway 66 (now 44). Every so often, down home people would stop by for a chat or to remember school days. Charles and Mamie fit in the village of Eureka just like they had wherever they lived; church, school, and community. However, heart and home was Indian Creek.

McLains Chapel Cemetery is the resting place for many family and friends. Charles' great-grandfather, Alexander McLain, is buried in Apple Creek Presbyterian Church Cemetery, Cape Girardeau County, MO. Alexander McLain is a documented veteran of the Revolutionary War.

Charles I. and Mamie are buried in the same community where they met and married. Grandpa Henson had the foresight to purchase several lots in the church cemetery. Charles and Mamie shared a full life together. Lest we forget. *Submitted by Loida McLain Gilbert, daughter*

McLAIN - Ivory "Ivy" McLain was born Aug. 14, 1870 at Indian Creek, and died May 15, 1943. He is buried at McLain's Chapel Cemetery. He was the oldest son of David M. McLain and "Lizzie" Hughes McLain. His brothers were Dave, Monroe, Mark and Charles McLain, and his two half-sisters were Mattie and Kate Simmons. Ivy and Dave were squirrel-hunting in the woods at Indian Creek with their father when their father chopped down a tree and it fell and killed him. Ivy was only 12 years old but was a loving and helpful son who helped his mother raise his brothers until she was finally remarried to Alexander Simmons.

Ivy and Lillie McLain and son Elmer, about 1906

Ivy married Lillie Statler on Nov. 4, 1896, and they lived in the house in the photograph, across Indian Creek from his mother. They had five children: Elmer (1898-1951); Earl (1902-1975), and Ruby (1906-1989) were born in the old house. Hazel McLain Parker (1913-1978) and Eileen McLain Groves (1915-1985) were born at Neelys Landing.

As a young man Ivy was legally named Justice of the Peace, so he could perform all legal matters of the community. We found a wedding certificate of the marriage of Pearl Sides and Jeffie Abernathy dated Feb. 12, 1902. The couple was married in Ivy's office at Indian Creek, MO in Cape Girardeau County, signed Ivy McLain, Justice of the Peace, with witnesses being J. H. Young and Fred Abernathy. This certificate now hangs in the home of Hazel Sides Schloss of Jackson, MO.

In about 1909, Ivy built a new house at Neelys Landing, and moved his office there and lived there until his death. Neelys Landing was on the Mississippi River, with the Frisco Railroad running along the side of the river. In the early 1900s a depot and a water tower were added in the heart of Neelys Landing just across the road from Ivy. The train made regular scheduled stops for both passenger and freight service. Also, boats made regular stops for cattle, ties or whatever needed to be shipped. A boat with a store made stops so people could shop for their needs. Also, a show boat with a calliope made regular visits. Every day was exciting in Neelys Landing with a church, school, three grocery stores, post office and other short-term businesses, one being a commissary owned by Ivy McLain, with groceries and a good selection of women's hats.

Ivy owned a skiff, river safe, from which he fished for the commercial market. Loida Gilbert remembers when Uncle Ivy would gladly row them into the river for a treat. She remembers his story of him rowing up the river to see a new baby and telling them to name it Neely. Neely Sams Triplett is now over 90 years old and lives in Herrin, IL. Ivy served the law for many years with honor and dignity, always fair-minded and always available to the public. *Submitted by nieces, Loida McLain Gilbert and Mary Beth Marlin Vogt*

McLAIN – J. D. McLain was a descendant of one of the pioneer families of the Oriole Community. His great-grandfather, Alexander McLain (1753-1851), established a homestead on the banks of Indian Creek before 1815. He had fought with the Carolina Militia during the Revolutionary War. J. D.'s grandfather, David D. McLain (1799-1855), gave land to McLain's Chapel and cemetery. His father, John Alexander McLain (1831-1898), went to California as part of the gold rush. When he returned, he married his beloved, Susan McLaughlin. Most of their sons were given names of people who had honored the Confederacy. Jefferson Davis (1861-1929) lived his entire life in the Oriole Community.

On Nov. 6, 1889 he married Minnie Shaner (1864-1954). They had two children, Maude (1892-1951) and Lawrence Jefferson (1898-1993). In 1897, J. D. and Jack Armstrong purchased the Oriole Store from J. Benton Comer, who had built the store. In 1898 Jeff bought Mr. Armstrong's share of the store, and he managed it with the help of his son until his death.

Jefferson Davis McLain and his granddaughter, LaFern. Photo taken about 1925.

Maude married Clarence Watkins and they had three children: Hazel (1914), Denzel (1918-1995) and Delbert Lee (1923). Lawrence married Pearl Noland (1902-1992) and they had one daughter, LaFern (1928). On Nov. 8,1929, the telephone rang its two long rings signaling the Oriole Store. The news was dreadful! Clarence Watkins had been killed in a quarry accident at Neelys Landing. Minnie, Jeff's wife, was watching the baby for Lawrence and Pearl to enable Pearl to help at the store that day. When Jeff McLain heard the news of Clarence's death, he went next door to their home to tell his wife. He took the baby from her arms because he was afraid she would be so upset that she may drop the child. As soon as he had told his wife the news of the accident, he began to fall. As he fell, he carefully laid the baby down, so his granddaughter would not be harmed. He never regained consciousness from the heart attack. In Oriole at that time, funeral homes were seldom used. Both coffins were placed in the Jeff McLain home over Saturday and on Sunday a double funeral was held at McLain's Chapel. It was the largest funeral service they had in that community.

Oriole Store was a general merchandise store that thrived from about 1890 to after 1940 when it burned. Gas pumps were across the gravel road. You could buy yard goods, hardware, medicine, groceries, shoes and clothing.

Shortly after Jefferson's death, while Lawrence and Pearl were managing the store, Lawrence had written a check for store supplies, drawn on the Sturdivant Bank of Cape Girardeau. The Depression had hit Cape Girardeau! When he got the call that the bank could not open, he counted their money. They had $7.04. He had suddenly become the man of three grief- stricken households and a business; but, he didn't have enough money to cover the check he had written. The Cape Girardeau Banks would not lend him any money on land during this disastrous period in our history. He was able to borrow $500.00 from Cape County Bank by mortgaging the store, his home, his mother's home and his sister's farm. As long as he lived, Lawrence was grateful to this Jackson Bank. In 1940 he sold the store to his niece, Hazel and her husband Paul McLaird. *Submitted by LaFern McLain Stiver*

McLAIN - The family of Monroe and Myrtle McLain began with their marriage in 1906 at Jackson, MO. Into this family 13 children were born and the picture includes all, left to right. Front row: Carrie Wilhelm, Mary Wissmann, Monroe and Myrtle McLain, Clara Mahy, Susie Bryant. Back row: Carl, Glenn, Woodrow "Woody", Frank, Roy, Paul, Ivan, Bill and Jack. This picture was taken next to the family home in 1953, when Jack was home on leave from the Navy.

Monroe was born near Indian Creek on his family's farm. His family had five boys: Ivy; Dave; Monroe; Charlie and Mark. This family was responsible for the McLain Chapel, the Indian Creek store, the Indian Creek School and the cemetery that is still in the family. Monroe was raised within three miles of where they lived for nearly 60 years. His wife, Myrtle May Comer, was born at Greenville, MO. Her father moved to Oriole where he taught at several schools in the area. He also built and ran a store at Oriole when Myrtle was a young girl. Her dad had another daughter when Myrtle was 11, she was later married to Henry Fornkohl.

When Monroe and Myrtle were married in 1906 they moved to a farm about a mile from the Oriole store. This was where they raised their family of nine boys and four girls. The family made their living by farming, raising most of their food on the farm. The farming was done with a team of horses raising corn, wheat and cane. In the fall they took the corn and wheat to the mill to be ground for their corn meal and flour. They cut and processed their sorghum on the farm, trading the extra for things at the store. They raised cattle, hogs and chicken for their meat, dairy and eggs. Some of the garden produce was taken to town where it was sold for money to help with the family expenses. What food could be keep was stored in a big concrete root cellar hand-dug into a hillside behind the house. Next to the cellar was the cistern that caught rainwater for drinking and washing. It was a three-mile walk to Indian Creek School. The kids walked until one of the older brothers bought a Model T for $15 and left it at the farm for them to use. Monroe couldn't keep it out of the ditches so he left it for the older kids to drive. Myrtle died on Dec. 24, 1953 and Monroe died on June 2, 1970. *Submitted by Mark Wissman*

McSPADDEN - Harley McSpadden was born in Freemont, Carter County, MO on July 21, 1920 to Moses Murman and Stella Mae (Kinnard) McSpadden. He married Eula Mae Martin of Mammoth Springs, AR in Van Buren, MO. During WWII Harley served in Italy and Eula Mae stayed in Mammoth Springs; after the war they made their home in Cape Girardeau County. They have one daughter, Gwendolyn McSpadden Nussbaum, born July 27, 1942 in Mammoth Springs, AR, who graduated from Jackson High School and Southern Illinois University-Carbondale and retired from Waltonville School District in 1997.

Harley worked for E. C. Rains in the timber business for many years, then became an independent timber cutter and buyer. He retired from the timber/wood cutting business at the age of 76, but continued to assist in the buying of timber. Eula Mae received her cosmetology license in 1954 and as of the writing of this history (2001) is still operating her own shop, "Eula's" outside of Jackson, MO.

Harley's brother/sisters are: Robert McSpadden (his mother is Jossie Allen McSpadden), born in 1899; Emma Gladys (Chilton), born Jan. 24, 1906, died July 1, 1969; Cleo Ardna, born March 26, 1908; Samuel Leo "Lee," born Nov. 14, 1910, died July 13, 1977; Earl Edward, born Dec. 16, 1912, died Jan. 24, 1989 in Cape Girardeau; Glenn Kinnard, born April 21, 1915, died May 25, 2000; Lola Elzetta "Sis" (Brame), born Nov. 17, 1917; and Lillian Marie (Sanders), born Sept. 9, 1923, living in Cape Girardeau County.

Moses Murman McSpadden was born February 1875 in Carter County, MO and died Nov. 15, 1944. He was a life-long farmer in Carter County. He married Stella Mae Kinnard, his second wife, on Jan. 8, 1905 (she was born March 14, 1885).

Moses was the son of Samuel Dillard McSpadden, born April 12, 1846 in Calhoun, GA, who married Amanda Caroline (Neal) of Maury County, TN in 1867/69. Samuel served in the Civil War, in Company G, 1 Georgia Infantry, and after the Civil War around 1869, he moved his family (parents and children) to what is now Carter County, MO. Samuel and Amanda's children are: Julia Evaline (Hurst) born Sept. 27, 1868; Georgianna Mahalia (Hill) born March 21, 1871; Cordelia J. (Keaster) born Dec. 28, 1873; Mosus Murman; John Elvins born June 9, 1877; Lewis "Luke" born June 16, 1879; Dallas "Barto" born May 14, 1881; Alsey Catherine (Durham) born Feb. 25, 1883; Cornelius Franklin born May 16, 1885; Lola Estell (Kinnard) born Oct. 9, 1889; Hendricks "Henry" born Nov. 14, 1889; Bessie and twin sister Elsie born Jan. 24, 1892; Ernest; and Frank McSpadden.

Harley and Eula Mae (Martin) McSpadden

Samuel's father was Joseph B. McSpadden, born Oct. 16, 1820, and married to Edith C. Dillard, born Oct. 1, 1827. Joseph B. McSpadden served in the Civil War in Company G, 1 Georgia Infantry. Their children are: Helen Victoria (Snider); Samuel D.; John W.; Cornelius Andrew Dale; Elize Jane (Jacob); Sarah (Kinnard); and Joseph Franklin.

Joseph's parents are Samuel McSpadden and Phoebe "Phebe" Butcher or Boucher. *Submitted by Gwen Nussbaum*

MEDLEY - John O. Medley came from England to Maryland in 1635. The next generation, Ignatius Medley, married Sarah Boone, Nov. 13, 1797. His second wife was Francis Bickett. The next generation, John Sylvester Medley, was born Dec. 19, 1802 and the only child of Ignatius and Sarah Boone. He married Barbara Wathen Sept. 29, 1829. Through the influence of Ignatius R. Wathen, his brother-in-law, of Cape Girardeau, he moved from Marion County, KY to Cape Girardeau County in 1855. He bought a farm of several hundred acres, three miles from Jackson, from Frank Allen. In 1957 it was occupied by the third generation of the Charles Medley family. None of them are with us in this life as of this writing. Mrs. Martha Williamson told of the arrival of the Medley family in Cape Girardeau by steamboat from Louisville. "It was a sight to behold!" Mr. Medley was dressed in his voluminous black broadcloth cape and high silk hat (he had been a State Senator in Kentucky). He was accompanied by wife Barbara Ann; sons Charles Pius, Ignatius Edward and Richard James; and daughters Christine Benedicta and Isabella Amanda. Their son Joseph Francis preceded him to Jackson. Son John Marshall Medley and family remained in Kentucky.

Jackson had a small population. It had not constructed a formal place of worship prior to 1858. Father Joseph J. Timon attended to the needs of Catholics in Cape Girardeau County in

Left to right, front row: Carrie McLain Wilhelm, Mary McLain Wissmann, Monroe McLain (father), Myrtle McLain (mother), Clara McLain Mahy and Susie McLain Bryant. Back row: Carl, Glenn, Jesse Woodrow, Frank, Roy, Paul, Ivan, Bill and Jack McLain

Cape Girardeau, the nearest church. He often preached in the courthouse at Jackson. Community interest grew in building a mission church. One of the men that helped generate enthusiasm was John Sylvester Medley. His desk is in his great-great-grandson Gerald and Susan Venable's home. Cape Girardeau was the nearest Catholic Church.

It was a time when few roads cut through the wilderness. Tracks of mud by wagon or horseback was the means of transportation. John S. Medley and some community members favored a Catholic Church. Others desired a Baptist Church. To raise money for two new churches, each collector had a Baptist and a Catholic pocket. Jackson residents gave equal donations to each pocket. The result was two new churches.

His son Joseph Francis Medley was the father of Francis Newton Medley. Francis Newton, known as Frank, married Emaline "Lina" Shorter. Edward, Lucile, Paul and Elsie were their children. Frank Medley worked for the U. S. Postal Service and was a photographer. He

Francis N. and Emaline "Lina" Shorter Medley

made many postcards with his pictures. They were of buildings in the business district of Jackson as well as of manufacturing. The handle factory and saw mills were some of his postcards. He made several postcards of different years of Jackson Homecomers.

The location of his home for his family was the lot next to and west of Mouser's used car business on East Adams Street. The home was a two-story stucco. Son Edward married Elda Ross. They had no children. Lucile married Fenton L. Venable and had Gerald F.; Paul married Lucy Clippard and had Paul B. and Martha Ann. Elsie, their youngest, never married.

He never thought of himself as a historian. His postcards preserved history. He was Captain of Jackson's home guard. A picture of the guard hangs in the American Legion Hall basement. *Submitted by Gerald F. Venable*

MEDLEY/WILKINSON - After Sarah Katherine (Medley) Shively Gohn died on Dec. 29, 1947 near Apache Junction, AZ, her son, Ed Shively, went to Arizona to take care of her affairs. Some of the things that he brought home were his baby book, seven photograph albums, and a very old scrapbook. The scrapbook belonged to Kate's mother, Emma Teresa (Wilkinson) Medley and was full of newspaper clippings, death notices, invitations, announcements and advertising items, most involving Jackson people and events.

Emma Teresa Wilkinson, the daughter of Teresa J. (English) and Joel R. Wilkinson, was born in Jackson, MO at the home of her grandparents, Thomas B. and Sarah Cone (Joyce) English, on June 8, 1859. Her mother, Teresa, was born Sept. 4, 1835 in Cape Girardeau County, MO. Her father, Joel R. Wilkinson, was born west of Jackson on Dec. 29, 1830. His parents were William and Jemima (Sheppard) Wilkinson. Emma's mother and father were both descendants of Robert Hester and Hannah Simmons (Holley) Wicker. Teresa and Joel were married on April 3, 1856, probably at the home of her parents in Jackson. Teresa died on Feb. 21, 1860, leaving Emma to be raised by her English grandparents while Emma's father, Joel Wilkinson, served as a clerk in the Quartermasters, 8th Missouri Cavalry Confederate. He died Aug. 16, 1883, and he and Teresa are buried in Jackson Cemetery.

Emma Wilkinson married William Medley on Dec. 25, 1878, in Jackson, probably at the home of her Grandmother English, and the marriage is recorded in St. Vincent's Catholic Church records. William Henry Medley born in Marion County, KY, on Sept. 19, 1856, to John Marshall and Mary Josephine (Livers) Medley. It is unknown when he moved to the Cape Girardeau County area but his grandparents, John Sylvester and Barbara Anne (Wathen) Medley, are found in the 1860 Cape Girardeau census.

Emma and William Medley had two daughters, Sarah Katherine and Natalie Teresa. Kate was born on May 13, 1888 in the Jackson area. Kate married Loren Stanford Shively on Nov. 6, 1906 at St. Vincent's Catholic Church. Their only child, Edward Medley Shively, was born on Sept. 15, 1907 in Cape Girardeau.

Natalie was born April 27, 1893 in the Jackson area and died April 18, 1929 at St. Marys, St. Genevieve County, MO. She married Emmanuel Sylvester Lawbaugh on Nov. 23, 1911 in St. Marys. They had four boys.

After Emma's death on Sept. 20, 1900, William Medley married at least two times. On Feb. 11, 1902 he married Catherine "Katie" (Burgett) Bogy, widow of Leon Bogy and daughter of John and Mary (Flynn) Burgett. Then he married Emma (Houck) Walker Giboney in 1935. She was the daughter of Julius and Eva (Bishop) Houck. She had previously been married to Peter Walker and Robert Giboney. William H. Medley died on May 25, 1940. Pallbearers included Buddy Tlapek and William's five grandsons: Edward Shively; Sylvester; Medley; LaViel and James Lawbaugh. Emma and William Medley are buried at Jackson Cemetery. *Submitted by Patricia Shively Elmore*

MEHRLE - Werner Christ Wilhelm Mehrle was the son of John and Anna (Fette) Mehrle. John and Anna came to the states from Germany, met and married. Zetta Virgin (Unger) Mehrle's family came from New Wells, MO and Illinois. There were five boys and two girls in Werner's family, and six boys and seven girls in Zetta's family.

Werner served in WWI, but never went overseas. Werner and Zetta were married on Sept. 16, 1924, in Marble Hill, MO. First and foremost, Werner was a farmer. He was also a grocer and a school bus driver, and he worked for Jackson Lumber Company. He was also a carpenter.

They lived for a short time with his parents. This is where their first daughter was born. Then they moved to an apartment on Spanish Street, where their second daughter was born. Then they moved to Cape Rock Drive, about a half-mile from the water plant. The next three daughters were born at this location. In September 1936 they moved to Jackson on Greensferry Road. In January 1941 they moved to the farm they purchased on Route W, where their sixth daughter was born. They and their six daughters grew up in the Southern Baptist faith.

They farmed until Werner passed away in 1975. Zetta then sold the farm and moved to an apartment in Jackson, then to her daughter's at DeSoto. Later she resided at the Baptist Home in Ironton, MO until her death.

The oldest daughter, Virginia Leah, was married to Robert Heuer. They have two children, Brian and Kelli (Shawn) Preston, and they have two granddaughters. Bob and Virginia both retired from National Lock Company in Rockford, IL. They are now resting at Cape County Memorial Park.

Edith Marie married William M. Eggers. Their four children are Ben (Darla); Richard (Marica); David (Kathleen) and Diane (Lanny) Schweer. Their three grandchildren are Gabriel Eggers and Victoria and Gary Schweer. Bill served in Korea during WWII. Bill was a dairy farmer most of his life and Edith is a homemaker. Bill is laid to rest at Russell Heights Cemetery in Jackson, MO.

Mary Ellen is married to Homer Lamb. They have four daughters: Robin; Terri (David) Ball; Jeanneane (Bob) Palezewski; and Linda (Brian) Thompson. Homer is retired from National Lock Company of Rockford, IL. They have eight grandchildren.

Margaret Ann was united in marriage with Bob Stroder in Jackson, MO. They have a son, Perry (Regina), and a daughter Kenda (Keith) Jones. They have six grandchildren. Bob was in the Korean War. He is retired from McDonnell-Douglas in St. Louis. Margaret is a beautician.

Zetta and Werner Mehrle and six daughters: Virginia Heuer; Margaret Stroder; Edith Eggers; Alice Robertson; Mary Lamb and Carolyn Ragsdale at the Mehrle's 50th wedding anniversary, 1974.

Alice Mae is married to Wade Robertson. Their children are Mark; Bruce (Kathy); and Melanie. They also have three grandchildren. Alice and Wade graduated from Golden Gate Baptist Theological Seminary in California. Wade is a Baptist minister.

Carolyn Sue is married to Bill Ragsdale. Their children are Jonathan and Debbie. Bill was in the Army in Korea. He graduated from East Texas State University. Bill is a CPA. *Submitted by Edith M. Eggers*

MEIER – Frederick and Fredericka Meier came to this country in the winter of 1849 from Klein-Rueden, in the grand duchy Braunschweig, Germany. Frederick was born Sept. 10, 1813. After paying the passage of his family, he still had enough money to purchase 40 acres in the forests surrounding the present Tilsit. He died Nov. 24, 1879.

His son, William F. "Boss Bill," later purchased a farm at the junction of Cane and Byrds Creeks. He was born May 13, 1841. He married Amelie Wessel on Feb. 21, 1864. He served in the Enrolled Militia under Capt. Tacke and afterwards as teamster in government supply service from Pilot Knob south to the Missouri Pacific Mountain Railroad. The couple lived on this farm until 1893 when he purchased the fine farm on Highway 72, three miles west of Jackson, from Senator John Mogler, on which his grandson now lives. Mrs. Meier died July 1894. To them six children were born, with three dying at a tender age and one son, Gustav B. Meier, a hardware and implement dealer in Jackson, dying when in the prime of life. The surviving sons were Henry R. Meier of Jackson and Alvin F. Meier of Mt. Clemens, MI. At the time of his 99th birthday, he was the only remaining Civil War veteran in Cape Girardeau County. He was confined to a wheelchair in later years. He suffered a paralytic stroke a few days before the end. He died June 7, 1940.

On, April 21 1895, William F. Meier married Wilhelmine, nee Sperling, Wettengel, who died Aug. 3, 1928. Wilhelmine was born at Hauschausen, Braunschweg, Germany. At the age of 7 years she emigrated with her father, Henry Sperling. The Sperlings settled on the place formerly owned by Andrew Howard, where the father died in 1884 leaving his wife with one son and three daughters. The son was killed accidentally in young manhood. In April 1895 Wilhelemine became the wife of William F. Meier. Mr. Meier was a most successful farmer and became quite wealthy. The 244-acre farm was transferred to Henry R. Meier on May 17, 1918.

Home of Wm. F. "Boss Bill" Meier, built by Senator John Mogler, ca. 1850

Henry R. Meier was born March 30, 1877. He was a farmer and served on the Cape County Savings Bank board; he was a Republican County Chairman and City Police Judge. He purchased the first angus cattle in 1905. They became the foundation for a commercial herd which developed into one of the top commercial herds in southeast Missouri. During the Depression, he acquired several farms in Cape Girardeau County. He married Rosie Heise Feb. 17, 1903. One son, Oscar, was born Nov. 30, 1903. He died Aug. 10, 1975. On Dec. 11, 1911 he married Annie Wettengel. They had two sons. Gilbert died at the age of 8 years and 4 months on Dec. 8, 1929 of meningitis. Henry Roy was born March 23, 1917. Annie Meier was born Jan. 20, 1884 and died Dec. 28, 1952.

After graduating from Jackson High School, H. Roy farmed with mules. He was one of the founders of the SEMO Cattle Association and Sales, serving as secretary. He served on the Missouri Angus Board from 1943-1976 and was president. He and Rosemond Oberbeck were married Oct. 31, 1937. In the early days they raised chickens and sold them to Schaper's Grocery. They were instrumental in breeding and showing purebred Angus cattle and were one of the famous herds in the United States, winning many championships. On Nov. 12, 1969, Rosemond died of cancer. Their children are Robin Ann and Karen Kay. In 1969 Roy was elected to the National Angus Board where he served six years; he was elected to two terms as vice president and in 1975 was elected president.

On April 3, 1971, Roy married Betty Ann Smith, nee Grossheider. She had a daughter, Beth Annette, and a son, Jory Len Smith. The three daughters showed cattle all over the United States. Today the farm still has Angus cattle but is slowly becoming subdivisions: Bull Meadows, Meier Meadows, Meier Lake Estates, and Indian Spring Estates. *Submitted by Betty Meier*

MEYER - Julius Henry and Caroline Schweiger Meyer emigrated from the Duchy of Braunschweig in 1847, coming through the port of New Orleans. He signed a citizenship declaration form on April 29, 1851. Once in Missouri they bought a farm near Cape Girardeau. By the time of the Civil War their farm had prospered, but they were virtually wiped out by Confederate raids and were forced to start over. The Meyers were early members of Hanover Lutheran Church and are listed on some of the earliest Communion lists found in the Church records of 1848. They had seven children: Charles (Caroline Ude); Julius (Anna Happel); Christina (Haase); George (Karoline Lowes); Dorothy (Strack); Henry; and Henrietta (Hunze). Henry left home in 1853 at the age of 18, after telling his parents that he was discontented with life in Cape Girardeau. He told them that they would never hear from him again unless he decided to return home. He probably went to California to join in the Gold Rush, but no one here knows for sure. Julius died in 1872. Caroline died in 1916 at the age of 96, after a fall at the home of her son George.

The second son, Julius, was born in 1848. In 1872 he went to Mississippi and worked for several years as a blacksmith. Upon returning to Missouri he married Anna Happel, and purchased a farm near Cape Girardeau. He was also a livestock dealer, and had a blacksmith shop on his farm. Julius and Anna had four children: Charles (Erna Lowes); William (Rosa Windeknecht). Anna died in 1919. Julius died in 1934 in Jackson, where he lived with his son Charles.

Charles Meyer was born in 1885 and married Erna Lowes in 1913. After living on a farm near Cape Girardeau for several years, they moved to Jackson. They had seven children: Altha (Glenn Smith); Dorothy (Lou Ficken); Carlton (Clemency Horn); Nelson (Dorothy Pohlmann); LaVern (Wilbur Bangert); Betty (F. J. Hessenflow); and Harold (Peggy Fornkohl). All three sons served in the military. Harold served in Korea and in Vietnam. Nelson "Butch" was in a medical detachment and served active duty in the Pacific during WWII, including the Battle of Guadalcanal. Butch was well-known in Jackson as the owner of Meyer Brothers Plumbing and Heating. Carlton "Cotton" was stationed in Europe and the Middle East during WWII. He flew 50 missions as a radio operator and air gunner in a B-17, in submarine patrols and bombing missions. He has owned the Jackson Frozen Food Locker for over 50 years. Cotton was on the Jackson Board of Alderman, and was mayor of Jackson for 22 years. *Submitted by Peggy Luehrs*

MEYR - The Meyrs established roots in Cape Girardeau County when Josef Meyr and Anna Maria Starzinger Meyr, married Feb. 4, 1850 in Rutzenmoos, Austria, immigrated to the United States in 1852. Upon arriving in Missouri, the Meyrs purchased land east of New Wells and began farming. Josef and Anna Meyr had six children: Anna Maria; Mattias Ernst; Theresa; Pauline; Johan and Gustav.

Johan Wilhehn Meyr, son of Josef, was born May 20, 1862. He married Miss Emilie Mirly, daughter of Karl and Anna Maria Pechmueller Mirly on Nov. 23, 1882. Johan and Emilie engaged in farming and trading, operating one of the largest farms in New Wells successfully. When Johan passed away Oct. 24, 1927, he was described in the newspaper as "endowed with a rugged body and a strong constitution together with a keen mind, he was always industrious." They had five children together: Bertha; August; Otto; Hedwig and Amelia.

Otto Friedrich Meyr, their youngest son, was born Oct. 2, 1890. He married Flora Adeline Koenig, daughter of Alvin and Martha Schrumpf Koenig on Oct. 11, 1891, and remained on the family farm. Otto farmed, traded cattle and horses, and advertised stud horses and jacks. He became an innovator in the area, purchasing the first rubber-tired tractor in New Wells. The couple had two children: Ruben Oscar and Evelyn Martha.

Ruben O. Meyr, born May 16, 1915, married Gertrude Alida Schlimpert, daughter of Charles Benjamin and Dora Magdilene Starzinger Schlimpert, on Feb. 19, 1939. They had seven children: Ryland; Doris; Larry; Dennis; Glen; Loretta and Rex. Ruben and Gertrude lived and raised their children on the farm in New Wells until February 1952. One hundred years after Josef Meyr came to New Wells, Ruben moved the family, including his parents, to Chaffee, MO, in Scott County, and continued their farming operations there. Even at that time, the family primarily communicated in German. The seven children and 16 grandchildren of this close family mourned together when Ruben passed away July 3, 1988.

Four generations of the Meyr families, summer 1941. Left to right, standing: Ruben Meyr, Otto Meyr. Seated: Ryland Meyr, Emilie Mirly Meyr.

Gertrude's family traditionally gathers every December 23, overflowing her kitchen on Dame Street with food, laughter and great-grandchildren.

The oldest child of Ruben and Gertrude, Ryland "Dutch" Meyr, attended Southeast Missouri State University where he earned All American honors as a lineman. After receiving his degree in 1962, he coached football for 15 years at Cape Central High School and Southeast Missouri University. Today, Dutch owns and operates Fruitland Dressed Meats in Jackson as well as manages his farm and cattle. He and his wife Sharon have developed some of their land into Touchdown Estates, a subdivision which boasts "country living at its best."

His oldest daughter Morgan Lynn Meyr graduated from Jackson High School in 1987, and received her bachelor's degree in 1992. She married John Thadeus Lake on Feb. 20, 1993, and they currently live outside Jackson with their two sons, John Ryland and Peter Burgess. Thad is a board certified psychiatrist and Medical Director of the Psychiatric Unit of Southeast Missouri Hospital.

Lindsey Michelle Meyr, his youngest daughter, graduated in 2001 from Jackson High School, where she received All-State honors in softball and track. She is now attending Southeast Missouri State University on a track scholarship. *Submitted by Morgan Lake*

MIER - Anthony Joseph "Tony" Mier was born Oct. 23, 1964 to Leroy and Dolores (Hopkins) Mier. Tony was raised on the family farm in Oran, MO. Leroy and Dolores had eight children: Steven; Madonna; Mary Sue "Susie;" Patrick; Jeffrey; Chris; Julie and Tony, the youngest. Madonna died in 1950 at almost 7 months of age. Patrick, Jeffrey, and Julie died in their teen years from a genetic disease called Hurler's Syndrome. They are all dearly missed. Steven, Susie, Chris and Tony survive.

Tony grew up helping with the family farm where they grew wheat, corn, and soybeans and raised hogs, cattle, horses, and chickens. He spent many hours before and after school milking cattle and feeding livestock as well as helping neighboring farmers. Tony was a member of Guardian Angel Catholic Church in Oran, MO and attended Guardian Angel Grade School. He graduated from Oran High School in 1983. He attended two years of college at Southeast Missouri State University with a focus in agriculture and then was hired full-time at Procter and Gamble of Cape Girardeau in 1985. He has been employed at Procter and Gamble for 16 years. Tony became a member of the Knights of Columbus Guardian Angel Council 4311 in 1984 and transferred to Bishop Timon Council 6405 when he moved to Jackson, MO in 1986. He became knighted as a Fourth Degree member in 1990. He served as Faithful Navigator for the Fourth Degree from 1993 to 1996 and served as Grand Knight from 1998 to 2000. He continues to be an active member of the Knights of Columbus. Tony also enjoys hunting and is a handyman around the house and for others. Tony married Ruth Ann Wencewicz on Aug. 1, 1992.

Tony, Ruth Ann, Theresa and Paul Mier, Nov. 2, 2001

Ruth Ann (Wencewicz) Mier was born Aug. 31, 1968 in Cape Girardeau, MO to Thomas and Dorothy (Bergfeld) Wencewicz. Thomas and Dorothy were born and raised in St. Louis, MO and moved to Cape Girardeau, MO after they married. Ruth Ann is the oldest of eight children, with six surviving. Surviving siblings include Amy, Sara, Katie, Tommy, and Timmy. Mary Catherine was born July 10, 1973 and died a day later. Another child was lost to miscarriage in 1976.

Ruth Ann grew up in Cape Girardeau, MO and was a member of St. Vincent de Paul Catholic Church. She attended St. Vincent de Paul Grade School and graduated from Notre Dame High School in 1986 as Valedictorian. She obtained a Bachelor of Science degree in Secondary Education in 1990 and a Master of Arts degree in Psychological Counseling in 1992 from Southeast Missouri State University. She is a Licensed Professional Counselor and is certified by the National Board of Certified Counselors. She has been employed at Community Counseling Center in Cape Girardeau, MO since 1992, working in psychiatric rehabilitation and crisis response. She is the contact person for NAMI Cape Girardeau, a local affiliate of the National Alliance for the Mentally Ill (NAMI). Ruth Ann was a Girl Scout for 11 years and has been a Birthright volunteer since 1987. She is also a member of the Knights of Columbus Bishop Timon Council 6405 Ladies Auxiliary. Ruth Ann enjoys sports, gardening, decorating, singing, and gatherings of family and friends.

Tony and Ruth Ann currently reside north of Jackson, MO and are members of Immaculate Conception Catholic Church in Jackson. They have two children. Theresa Rose was born on May 6, 1996, and Paul Anthony was born April 23, 2000. Theresa is in Kindergarten at Immaculate Conception Grade School and Paul is an active one and a half year old boy! They enjoy living in the Jackson area and think it is a wonderful place to raise a family! *Submitted by Ruth Ann Mier*

MIER - Dolores Hopkins Mier was born Oct. 4, 1927, to Barbara Diebold Hopkins and Virgil Hopkins. She was raised in Ancell, MO, attended St. Augustine Grade School in Kelso, MO, and the Precious Blood Convent High School in Ruma, IL.

She worked briefly in a defense plant, and married Leroy Mier on June 25, 1947. Eight children were born to this marriage: Stephen; Madonna; Mary Sue; Patrick; Jeffrey; Chris; Julie and Anthony. Madonna died in infancy and Patrick, Jeffrey, and Julie died as teenagers from Hurler's Disease. Stephen, Mary Sue, Chris, and Anthony were raised on the family farm in rural Oran, MO.

Dolores Mier, 1999

After the death of the four children, Dolores became active in parish activities at Guardian Angels Church in Oran, MO; she served on the Parish Council Parish School Board, and taught a Wednesday evening religion class for teenagers of Guardian Angels parish.

In 1986 Dolores and her youngest son Anthony "Tony" moved to Jackson, MO. She immediately became active in various activities at Immaculate Conception Church. These activities include Cursillo, St. Ann's Sodality, Parish Council, and R.C.I.A.

Dolores has been active with Birthright since 1973, being part of the original group that started Birthright. She served as director of the Cape Girardeau Birthright organization for 21 years. She did much to contribute to the stability and growth of the Birthright office. Dolores started a regular newsletter to give updates on the work of Birthright and to obtain financial support. Dolores recruited and trained volunteers and was active in public relations, giving many Birthright presentations. Although she is now retired as director of Birthright, she remains active as senior advisor.

Children of Dolores Mier: back row, Stephen Mier, Mary Sue Mier McBride; front row, Chris Mier, Dolores Mier, Anthony Mier, July 12, 1986

In January 1998 Dolores was asked to minister to patients of the Catholic faith who resided in the Monticello Nursing Home in Jackson. Every Sunday morning she visits with these patients and brings Holy Communion to them. Some of these residents have become a second family to her. In May 2001 Dolores was asked to lead an interdenominational Bible study among the residents of Monticello. This Bible study session is held every Wednesday and is a great source of inspiration to participants. Dolores is assisted in conducting these Bible study sessions by Pat Rushin and Janet Lakner.

Dolores has had a lifetime love of growing things. She still plants a large garden, has several flower beds, and raises her own annuals and perennials. These are nourished by all the compost produced in her back yard.

Dolores' remaining children are her pride and joy. The oldest son Stephen now resides with her in Jackson, MO. Her only living daughter, Mary Sue McBride, lives at Vanduser, MO. Chris lives at Scott City, MO, and Tony lives in Jackson. Her children have gifted her with nine grandchildren and four great grandchildren. *Submitted by Dolores Mier*

MILDE - Our Milde history began in the county of Bohemia, which was the largest of the Czechoslovakian provinces. Johann Michel Milde, born Oct. 9, 1790, was the father of Joseph, who immigrated to this country in 1858. Joseph grew up on his father's farm and must have farmed the fields much as his father had. He married Rosalia Herrman, who was born June 20, 1822.

Joseph and Rosalia were the parents of four sons: Frank X., born on Sept. 11, 1845; Ignatz, born Nov. 3, 1847; Emanuel, born Feb. 22, 1852; and Daniel, born Dec. 3, 1857. It is believed that Joseph and Rosalia left Europe so their sons could escape the military. Joseph sold his farm in 1857. They took the ship *Borrusia* for America. It has been stated that Rosalia had $50,000 sewn in the hem of her petticoat, and also had a money-belt around her waist. What a rustling noise she must have made on the ship!

Joseph, wife, and four sons landed in New York Port on July 1, 1858. We know they went to Chicago. They probably chose this particular city because Frank had studied music at the Berlin Conservatory and his parents wanted him to continue, and at the time there was a good chance that he could further his education in music there.

They lived in Chicago for approximately two years and because of the severe cold winters decided to move farther south and settled in Jackson. Joseph farmed, was a good furniture maker, and raised bees. Milde's had the first bowling alley ever built in Jackson; it was called Nine-Pins at that time and was popular in Europe and therefore known to the other Germans who settled in the area. When the courthouse was built in Jackson, the Milde farm furnished most, if not all, of the lime.

Emanuel Milde Sr., the founder of E. Milde Bottling Works in 1894 in Jackson, MO. It later became the Coca-Cola Bottling Company in Jackson.

Emanuel Milde, third child of Joseph and Rosalia Herrman Milde, had a carefree, happy type of personality and married Wilhelmina Caroline Illers "Lena." Of this union three children were born; Alvin (1879-1960), Emamuel Jr. (1882-1923) and Clara (1888-1979).

The Emanuel Milde Jr. family – front left, Gretchen, next Eugenia "Jean," back left, Rosamond "Billie," Emanuel and Mrs. Emanuel Milde, circa 1919.

Emanuel Milde decided to go into the soft drink business in 1894. Shortly before his death on Feb. 2, 1900, he instructed his sons to stay in the soda business as he felt a good living could be made from it.

Emanuel Milde Jr. married Lillian Marie Armstrong (Dec. 26, 1888-1965). Three daughters were born, Gretchen Armstrong (April 16, 1912-1967), Eugenia Adela (Nov. 8, 1914-2000), and Rosamond Spurrier (Jan. 5, 1916). Of the three daughters of Emanuel Jr., Gretchen married Henry A. Loos. No children were born of this union.

Eugenia "Jean" married Orme S. Kellett. To them three children were born, Orme Morgan, Eugenia, and Christopher. Jean and Orme were blessed with seven grandchildren.

Rosamond "Billie," the third daughter, married Frank Miller. Two sons were born, David Brian Miller (Sept. 8, 1945-1996) and Bruce Miller (Dec. 24, 1950-1991). Bruce married Marsha Dement. This union was blessed with two sons, Frank Emanuel Miller (Nov. 30, 1979) and Trentis Miller (Feb. 19, 1982). *Submitted by Billie Sander*

MILLER - The evidence is strong that John Miller and his family came to the area around Whitewater River from North Carolina. They accompanied a group led by George F. Bollinger to the Spanish territory. The journey from North Carolina through the wilderness was a hazardous one and even a seasoned frontiersman would have had an experienced guide such as George Frederick Bollinger. The Millers became a part of a community composed of Swiss-Germans located four or five miles up the Whitewater River. It was one of the farthest west settlements in America. John Miller's wife was said to be Martha Clay, a first cousin of the American statesman Henry Clay.

Congress passed an Act in 1805 granting titles to all persons who were residents in the territory prior to Oct. 1, 1800. The Millers' land claims were under this group. According to the Spanish Land Grants, the northern edge of John Miller's 640-acre tract was one-quarter mile south of the present Millersville. John and Martha Clay Miller had 12 children, many of whom are buried in the Old Miller Cemetery west of Millersville along with their parents.

There are many interesting stories told of the early Miller settlement. In the early days there were many Indians in Cape Girardeau County especially along the bluffs of the Whitewater River. One day an Indian came to the home of Henry Miller and made it known that he was hungry. After enjoying a meal, the redskin went on his way. Sometime later Andrew Miller, who was a tiny boy, strayed in the woods. Suddenly he came face to face with an Indian. It was the one who the family had fed. The grateful Indian took little Andrew by the hand and led him back to the Miller cabin.

George W. Miller reported that in his youth there were many wild animals such as panthers and bear in the woods.

George W. Miller lived to be 92 years old and left a family of four children: Dale S.; Ray; Gale and Eula Miller Penzel. Dale operated a garage; Ray was a partner in the Cracraft-Miller furniture and funeral business; Gale was a newspaper man in Dexter; and Eula Miller Penzel was a homemaker, teacher and wife of a local banker. All were educated in the Old Normal School.

The George W. Miller farm has been in the family since the original Spanish Land Grant. The present location of The Illers Top of the Berry Farm is part of this farm. It is operated by Don and Joan Miller Illers and son, Chris. *Submitted by Mrs. Don Illers*

MILLER - It was first thought that John Miller and his family arrived with George Frederick Bollinger the first of January 1800. A definite proof of the date the Millers arrived is found in the testimony of John and Issac (John's son) Miller, George Frederick Bollinger, and Joseph Neyswanger (Niswonger) before the Board of Land Commissioners appointed to adjust the Spanish land claims in the Louisiana Territory. Their testimony stated that the Millers arrived in Cape Girardeau County in October of 1803.

The Millers settled along the western banks of the Whitewater River. The bulk of the early American settlers were of German, Swiss and Dutch ancestry. Although the Millers became a part of a community composed almost entirely of Swiss and German settlers, the Millers seem to have been of Scot-Irish descent.

Left to right, seated: Dorothy Miller Marks, John Dale Hosking, Ray Miller, Jr., Joan Miller Illers, Charles Hoskey. Standing: Eula Miller Penzel, Effie (Mrs. Gale) Miller, Geo. M. Penzel, Grace (Mrs. Roy) Miller, Alvin Penzel, Geo. Washington Miller, Roy Miller, Mrs. Geo. W. Miller, Charles Penzel, Geo. Wm. Miller, Judge J. C. Snider, Gladys Hale (Mrs. Maple) Miller, Dale S. Miller, unknown, Gale Miller, Eula Snider Miller, Lucille Miller Hosking. Picture taken at home of Dale and Eula Miller, celebrating 90th birthday of Geo. W. Miller,

When the Millers arrived in the Cape Girardeau District in October of 1803 the area was a frontier wilderness. These settlements in the western territory of Cape Girardeau County constituted some of the farthest western settlements in America. The City of Cape Girardeau had not been laid out and Jackson did not exist.

Little is known of John Miller before he came to Cape Girardeau County from Lincoln County, NC. His birth date on his tombstone says 1763, but evidence seems to indicate that he was born somewhat earlier. During the Revolutionary War John was in his early 20s; whether or not he participated in the Revolutionary War has not been proven conclusively.

John married early in his life to Martha Clay. It was thought that Martha was a sister of Henry Clay, although this still remains in question. Martha Clay bore John Miller 12 children, eight boys and four girls. The boys were: Jacob; Issac; Henry; Abraham; Don; Joseph; Nicholas and John Clay. The girls were: Hannah; Katie; Sophie and Susie. All of the 12 children did not remain in Cape Girardeau County. Nicholas moved to Illinois and Jacob moved to the vicinity of Bloomfield about 1825 and became one of the pioneers of Stoddard County. The remaining 10 children of John made Cape Girardeau County their home and from them comes the large Miller family tree of Cape Girardeau County.

John Miller and his sons Jacob and Issac received land permits from Louis Lorimier to settle on land in the Whitewater Bottoms. The area that John Miller claimed was nearly two square miles in area. The Miller homestead was a cabin built by John and 40 acres he had cleared. His new home was located on the east side of Big Whitewater River about three-quarters of a mile south of the present location of the town of Millersville (the town of Millersville received its name from John J. Miller, grandson of John Miller, who platted the town in 1860). The house of John Miller was on the extreme northern border of the extensive tract belonging to John Miller.

A family burial ground was established on a hill overlooking Big Whitewater River just south of the old homestead on the west bank of the river. The Miller Cemetery is now located on the Fred R. "Rockne" and Judy Wilferth farm. Fred R. (Rock as he is known) is a descendent of John Miller.

The Miller family tree is quite large as you would expect and the following is just one branch of Henry Miller, one of John's sons. Henry Miller was the father of William Miller who was married to Sallie Eaker. They were the parents of Jim Henry Miller. Jim Henry and his second wife, Marada, were the parents of my grandfather Truman Blaine Miller. Truman married Alice Estes and they were parents of my father Winfred, brother Kelly, and sister Rada Lou. Winfred (known as W. E. or Winnie) married Mable Stearns. Winfred and my mother Mable had two children, Rodney and Greta. Greta married Bill Meyers and they have three daughters, Celeste, Jessica, and Kirsten. Rodney Miller married Janet Hanlin and they have two sons, Blaine and Branden. Blaine has a son Nicholas and is married to Anna Marie Morley, and Branden is married to Karen Wright.

Rodney and Jan Miller now own and live on the Truman Miller Farm, which was part of the original Spanish Land Grant John Miller received in the 1800s. Jim Henry Miller, my great-grandfather, built the eight-room farm house we now live in and the large barn that stands north of the house.

It is with a proud Miller heritage that I (Rodney Miller) submit this short history of the Miller family, beginning with John Miller and Martha Clay. *Submitted by Rodney Miller*

MILLER - Truman Blaine Miller, a native of Whitewater Township, Cape Girardeau County, youngest son of James Henry and Marada Elizabeth Edinger Miller, was born Oct. 13, 1893 on the family farm south of Millersville. After attending a rural school at Millersville, he attended high school and also three years at the old Normal Teachers College in Cape Girardeau. He returned to the farm where he spent all his life.

After courting a young lady at Burfordville, MO, on May 3, 1914, Truman Blaine and Alice Ruth Estes, daughter of Joseph Hezikah and Louraine Bast Estes, were married at the Estes home. Alice's mother passed away when she was 7 years old; a short time later Mr. Estes married Lorada Hutson, who was a wonderful mother to the five Estes children and her two Hutson children. Truman and Alice's marriage license was witnessed by J. H. and Rada Miller, and J. H. and Rada Estes, very unusual.

Truman operated the fertile, well-stocked and well-equipped farm successfully, and thus he and his family enjoyed many prosperous years. For many years he was one of the leading livestock shippers in Cape Girardeau County. There were always one or two families that lived in extra houses on the farm that the men worked with Truman on the farm. Alice was a good cook, and always had clean clothes ready for the family. She was active in the First Baptist Church in Millersville, and the Homemakers Club. In 1939 they attended the World's Fair in California with Truman's cousin and wife, Dale and Eula Miller. They enjoyed taking trips.

On July 6, 1915, a son, Winfred Eugene, was born. He attended the Rieman Rural School and Millersville High School, and graduated from Jackson High School. He and Mabel Stearns were married on Feb. 3, 1936. Winnie (his nickname) worked for Kroger Grocery Company in Jackson.

Left to right: Truman Miller, Rada Lou Miller, Kelly Miller, Alice Miller and Winfred Miller. Rada Lou is now Kamp. Photo taken in 1936.

On Sept. 24, 1940, a son, Rodney Eugene, was born, the first grandchild of the Truman Millers. In 1943 Winnie was drafted into the Army, and was stationed in Texas before serving overseas in France and England. After returning home he was selected as the rural mail carrier out of the Millersville Post Office. On Nov. 4, 1948, a daughter, Greta Sedare, was born to Winnie and Mabel. They attended Mail Carrier Conventions each year that took them all over the United States, and they also visited WWII friends in England. They enjoyed their family. Rodney married Jan Hanlin, Loganport, IN, and they had two boys, Blaine and Branden. Greta married Charles "Bill" Myers, Oak Ridge, and they had three girls, Celeste, Jessica and Kirsten. Winfred Eugene passed away Dec. 1, 1992, and Mabel passed away June 26, 1996.

The Truman Millers' second child, another boy born Feb. 28, 1918, was named Dayton Hugh, but the hired hands nicknamed him Kelly after a Cape Girardeau County Judge Kelly. He was known by that name the rest of his life. He attended Rieman Rural School and Millersville High School, then stayed on the farm with his dad until January 1942, when he was drafted into the Army. He was stationed In Wyoming and California before serving overseas in England where he and his brother Winnie met. After returning home in August 1945 he decided to go back to Stockton, CA to live. He retired after working for Civil Service for 30 years. He never saw a stranger, always enjoyed talking, and had many friends. He suffered a stroke on June 11, 1999 and passed away July 22. It was his wish to be cremated and his ashes thrown in the mountains where he spent many hours taking pictures.

On Sept. 13, 1924, Alice Miller had been making kraut, and then scrubbed the kitchen floor; at 6 o'clock that evening a baby girl was born. They named her Lou Rada Blaine after her grandmothers and her dad, but in a couple of weeks they changed it to Rada Lou Blaine. Being the only girl, she could have been a little spoiled. When she was 4 or 5 years old, and was called to come to eat, she'd climb on a chair in the living room and holler "come get me" until someone carried her to the table. Is that being spoiled?

Rada Lou attended the Rieman Rural School and Millersville High School, and graduated from Jackson High School, attending Southeast Missouri Teachers College a short time. She taught in the rural schools at Burfordville, Big Spring, and Rieman. On Sept. 3, 1947 she married Odus Lee Fronabarger, Oak Ridge. They had a son, Lee Miller, born Oct. 12, 1949. On Sept. 12, 1951, Odus Lee passed away. Rada Lou and son Lee Miller lived with her parents and worked at the Nelson Store and Millersville Post Office. On Dec. 19, 1958, she and Alvin Kamp were married. Alvin worked at the Hosiery Mill and Rada Lou went to work for the County Clerk, Rusby Crites. They are retired now. She has always been active in the Millersville Baptist Church where they both attend. They enjoy collecting glassware and antique kerosene lamps.

The Miller family keeps increasing; now there are great-great-grandchildren, Nicholas Blaine, Whitney and Natalie Wheeler, Owen Myers, and Nadia Sedare. Truman and Alice would have been so proud of them. *Submitted by Rada Lou Miller*

MIZELL - The Mizell family originally came from Luxembourg, France. It seems that William has been a family name for many years. William Mizell, born in 1800 in Kentucky, was one of our earliest ancestors. William was a farmer. He was married to Susan Greene and they were the parents of four children: Louisa; William Charles; Aluis and Galden.

William Charles was married to a lady named Scharlattia Rentfloe. To this union were born four children: Montlebert; Theodoshia; Rosa and William Jeffers Mizell. In researching my family history, I found William Charles was enrolled in the 56th Regiment of the Missouri Militia, which was a Cape Girardeau unit. William was also found on the list of Confederate soldiers in Company K, 8th Missouri Cavalry, which was Lieutenant Colonel William L. Jeffers' regiment.

William Charles Mizell, 1834-1912

William Jeffers and Mary Bell Davis were married and continued the generation with six children: Zita Marie; Paul Franklin; Grace; Maude; Gladys and Noah.

Paul Franklin and Nola Ethel Reed were married on May 15, 1928. To this union were born six children: Veda; Earl; Verna; Leona Paulene; an infant and Paul William. I, Leona Paulene, married Earl Cook and we were the parents of two children, Melinda and Allen William. After Earl's death some years later, I married Royal Mueller.

Most of my family were farmers in and around the Jackson, MO, area. It is with much appreciation for my ancestors, and the hardships they endured, that I write about my family history. *Submitted by Leona Paulene (Mizell) Cook Mueller.*

MOELLER - Rosalie Allen Moeller was born June 19, 1924, three miles west of Jackson, MO, at the house of her grandparents, Wilham Birk and Emma Maevers Birk. Her grandfather, a farmer, was cutting wheat that day. Rosalie's father was Henry Gale Allen, born July 22, 1893. Her mother, Malinda Elizabeth Birk Allen, was born March 28, 1905.

Henry Allen was a WWI veteran, and had the influenza while he was in the service. Later he developed sleeping sickness. Rosalie was two years old when he became ill with it. Henry would go hunting with his dog and friends found him sleeping. He went off and on to different veterans' hospitals for 21 years. He was at Jefferson Barracks Veterans Hospital, close to St. Louis, MO, and Veterans Hospital at Wadsworth, KS. At times he would be able to spend as much as a year and a half to two years at home. He was at Marion Veterans Hospital, at Marion, IL when he passed away on Oct. 2, 1945, because the sleeping sickness had paralyzed the nerves in his throat and he was unable to swallow. Mr. Allen had been a member of the Altenthal-Joerns American Legion Post 158 and attended the First Baptist Church in Jackson.

Rosalie's mother, Malinda Birk Allen, was a charter member and three-time president of the American Legion Auxiliary. Rosalie was and is still a member of the auxiliary. Malinda Allen worked for the International Shoe Company in Jackson for 46 years, and at the Ely Walker garment factory at Illmo, MO for one and a half years. Mrs. Allen and Rosalie belonged to the St. Paul Lutheran Church in Jackson. In 1951 Mrs. Allen and Rosalie built the Rosalie Apartments in Jackson. In 1969 Malinda Allen married Brainard Hope; the couple divorced in 1992. Malinda Elizabeth Birk Allen passed away Aug. 11, 1996 at the Deal Nursing Home in Jackson, MO.

Rosalie began school at the Jackson Public School in Jackson, studied for one and a half years at the Fornfelt Missouri Public School, attended the St. Paul Lutheran School for four years, was confirmed by Rev. Walter Keisker in 1939, and then went on to four years at Jackson High School, graduating in 1943. She then worked for International Shoe Company for 16 years. On June 1, 1957, Rosalie married Glen Martin Moeller, from Emblem, WY. They met through the Lutheran Walther League pen pal program. Mr. Moeller was born May 5, 1917. He could not get work in Jackson, and so worked in Cape Girardeau at the Southeast Missourian and Southeast Hospital from June 1, 1957 to Oct. 7, 1958. He was laid off at these two places. He then went to St. Louis to work at the Concordia Publishing House where he worked for 21 years.

Henry Gale Allen, Malinda Elizabeth Birk Allen, and daughter, Rosalie, in front of their home in west Jackson.

He took ill with stomach cancer and passed away on Nov. 14, 1979 at Lutheran Medical Center. Rosalie brought him back to Jackson for burial. Rosalie Moeller quit the International Shoe Company on May 1, 1959, when she was 65 years old, after completing the 16 years necessary to get her pension. On April 18, 1960, she went to work at the Lutheran Medical Center in St. Louis and worked there until Jan. 11, 1983. Rosalie belonged to Our Redeemer Lutheran Church and the Holy Cross Lutheran Church in St. Louis. She bought and owned her apartment while living in St. Louis, selling it when she came back to Jackson to be close to her mother. *Submitted by Rosalie Moeller*

MOORE – Rebecca Ann "Becky" Stoverink-Moore was born Oct. 17, 1979 at Southeast Hospital of Cape Girardeau, MO. She is the third child of four born to Gerald E. and Catherine M. Quatmann-Stoverink of Jackson, MO. Becky attended Immaculate Conception Catholic School and Jackson High School for her education. After graduating from high school in 1998 she went on for one year of college education at Shawnee Community College.

On Oct. 20, 2001 Becky married Christopher Lynn Moore, oldest son of Lindel and Julie Moore of Jackson, MO. They have three children: their daughter, Kari Jo Moore, born Oct. 8, 1999; Ali Nicole Moore born July 26, 2002; and Christopher's son, Christopher Lynn Moore II, born July 4, 1997.

Christopher and Becky Moore holding Kari Jo and Christopher Lynn II; inset, Ali Nicole

Christopher grew up in Sikeston before moving to Jackson with his family. He attended and graduated from Jackson High School in 1993. After high school, he joined the United States Marine Corps until 1996. Christopher is now a police officer for Scott City Police Department of Scott City, MO and Becky is a customer service representative for Big River Telephone Company of Cape Girardeau, MO. *Submitted by Becky Moore*

MOORE - Peter Moore was born Feb. 9, 1804 in Greene County, TN. The Moore name first shows up in Greene County in 1782 as com-

Left to right: Andrew Moore and sons, Albert, Bob, Elick, Charlie and Tom

ing from Pennsylvania. Peter Moore and Susan Farmer were married Dec. 22, 1836, and traveled to Missouri in 1844. They homesteaded land in what is now the Caney Fork Community, located in the western part of Cape Girardeau County. No further information on Susan Farmer is known. The children coming to Missouri were William, born in 1838; Andrew, born Feb. 1, 1841; and Alfred, born in 1845. Peter and family would cross the Caney Fork River in middle Tennessee at some point in their journey. Today Caney Fork River meanders around and would be crossed five times coming to Missouri from Greene County. Peter's sons, Andrew and Alfred served with the Union Army during the Civil War. Alfred never returned. It is not known if he was killed in the war or simply did not come home.

Andrew returned home and married Caroline Canzada Poston on Oct. 2, 1876. Andrew with a very limited education became a successful farmer and father to 12 children, nine that reached adulthood. Andrew and Canzada lost two children as infants and another daughter died at 10 years of age. Peter Moore and many of his descendants are buried in the Caney Fork Baptist Church Cemetery. The original cemetery was a part of the Peter Moore homestead and deeded to the church by his daughter-in-law, Canzada. The remaining land was in the homestead of 1856, while Franklin Pierce was President, and is still owned by a Moore.

Five generations lived in the house built by Peter Moore: Peter, son Andrew, grandson Thomas, and great-grandson Milford, and Milford's daughters. The property is still in the Moore family and owned by Mrs. Milford Moore. The house is no longer standing but holds many special memories for the children that visited there for Sunday dinners at Grandma's house.

The Peter Moore descendants each year have a family reunion with as many as eight generations being listed in the genealogy books. There are still several family members in the middle 80s and two who still come to the reunions, Truman Ernest Moore and Dessie Viola Moore Drum. Truman, son of Albert and Maggie Statler Moore, lived his entire life in the house he was born in. He married Verda Loos and brought his bride to the Kurreville, MO farm community. They raised four children: Raymond; Wayne; Lonnie; and Bonnie, and are grandparents to five and great-grandparents to eight. Dessie, daughter of Robert and Mary Fulbright Moore, lived in the Randles area as a young girl and now resides in Oak Ridge, MO with her husband, John Francis Drum. They have one son and two grandchildren. The family reunion in 2002 will be the 50th straight year for the family to gather. *Submitted by LaRae Moore Leimer*

MOORE – Dixie Lee Gregg was born July 2, 1938 in Milo, IA. She was the daughter and only surviving child of Orval Adelbert Gregg (deceased) and Eleanor Virginia (Bales) Gregg (deceased).

Orval's work for the Texas-Illinois Natural Gas Pipeline brought the family to Jackson, MO, where she attended school the last few months of her eighth grade year. Her parents divorced, and she returned to Indianola, IA with her mother. Dixie graduated from Indianola High School in 1956. After graduation, she returned to Jackson, MO to attend Southeast Missouri State University for two years. Cape Girardeau was her home while she worked various office jobs.

After a couple of years of courtship, Dixie Lee Gregg and James F. Moore were married on Feb. 12, 1960. They made their home in Jackson. This union brought two sons into the world, Jeffrey James Moore was born April 19, 1961, and Jay Joseph Moore was born March 30, 1964.

James was the son of Eugene Paul Moore and Erma Grace (Sander) Moore (both deceased). James was from the Tilsit/Gordonsville area. He and his family were members of the Zion United Methodist Church of Gordonville.

After graduating from Jackson High School, Jim, as he was being called at this time, began working for Brennecke Chevrolet. He worked from the service department, to parts, to parts manager, car salesman, sales manager, vice-president, and dealer with the purchase of half of the business.

Jim was also a former company commander of Company A, 1140th Engr. Bn., and retired from the HHC 135TH Eng gp Mo (National Guard). He served from October 1956 until his retirement in December 1976 with the rank of Captain. Jim graduated from Infantry Officer's *Jim and Dixie Moore with sons, Jeff and Jay* Candidate School in Fort Benning, GA in 1967. He received various awards during his duty: Certificate of Appreciation for Outstanding and Dedicated Service from O. T. Dalton, Brigadier General, for service as O. T.'s aide; Army Reserve Components Achievement Medal; and a State of Emergency Medal, to name a few.

Jim was a Rotarian. He served in various offices, also serving as president of the Jackson Rotary Club 1978-79. He was presented an award from Rotary International for Outstanding Leadership. Jim was a Paul Harris Fellow.

Jim was an avid golfer. His golfing buddies have erected a memorial in his name at the Kimbeland Country Club. After several years fighting heart disease, Jim passed away on Dec. 21, 1991, at the age of 53.

Dixie Moore was a member of Zion United Methodist Church (Gordonville), belonging to the United Methodist Women, Anita Allison Circle, and she held various other offices. She also was a Sunday School teacher and Bible School teacher, and sang in the choir. She is now a member of the New McKendree Methodist Church as was Jim at the time of his death.

Dixie was a den mother for four years with Pack 12, Den 3. She served one year as Pack 12's secretary. PTA was also on her list of activities; she served in various offices, including one year as president.

Dixie worked numerous jobs over the years as a salesperson at Priests; office worker at LaPierre Sawyer Handle Company; and secretary at Jackson RII School District; she was also an aide in the Title III Learning Disability Program, an aide for a Muscular Dystrophy child for five years, and a substitute teacher. She also helped in different capacities at Brennecke Chevrolet.

Dixie returned to Southeast Missouri State University. She graduated June 14, 1985, with a Bachelor of Science degree in Education. She made the Dean's Honor List the last semester with straight As.

Music was always a love of Dixie's. She was a member of the Girardot Rose Chorus – Sweet Adeline International for a couple of years. Dixie is a past member of the Jackson Heritage Association. She loved being a tour guide at the Oliver House, especially with the school age children.

Dixie is a member of the Noon Optimist Club in Jackson, working toward her ten-year perfect attendance pin. She has received numerous Appreciation Awards but is most proud of the President's Citation 1992-93 (her first year as a club member), Optimist of the Year 1995-96, the Always Buckle Children in the Back Seat Award for coming in second internationally in the collection of signatures in support of this program, and the Optimist International Life Member presented to her by the club members at the end of her presidency 1999-2000.

Jeffrey James Moore, the first born on Jim and Dixie, is vice-president of Ross Furniture in Jackson and Perryville. Jeff married Cynthia Ann Brim on Oct. 1, 1988. To this union were born Jennifer Leann Moore, born Sept. 13, 1991, and Jameson Jeffrey Moore, born April 26, 1994.

These are among the awards Jeff has received: Distinguished Service Award presented by the Jackson Jaycees 1995, Jackson Chamber of Commerce, president 1996-1997, and Community Service Award presented by the Jackson Rotary Club.

The marriage of Cindy and Jeff was dissolved. Later Jeff married Terry Lynn Rapp on Feb. 2, 2001. This marriage brought another grandchild, Sydney Marie Rapp, into Dixie's life.

Jay Joseph Moore, second son of Jim and Dixie, is employed full-time at Co B 1140th Engr. BN MO ARNG in Jackson. Various awards received were ribbons: Army Service, Army NCO Professional Development, MO Commendation, State of Emergency and (six) Army Reserve Components Overseas Training. Medals received were: Armed Forces Reserve, National Defense Service, Army Commendation, three Army Achievement and three Army Service Components Achievement.

Jay married Lynette Sue Nitsch on Sept. 8, 1990. From this union a son, Landry James Moore, was born Oct. 7, 1997. Although Dixie did not get into the history of her daughters-in-law, she has been blessed to have such wonderful daughters-in-law and loves them very much. The grandchildren are already making their mark with various awards in sports and other areas. They are also very much loved.

Dixie's final words were a quote of Jackie Robinson: "A life is not important except in the impact it has on other lives." It is her hope that she and her family have made a positive impact on the lives of the people of the Jackson area.
Submitted by Dixie Moore

MORTON - Robert Pinkney Morton was born May 2, 1908 on a farm halfway between Fruitland and Leemon, MO. He was the youngest child of George Pink, born Aug. 4, 1866, died April 4, 1952, and Ollie Corinne McNeely Morton, born Sept. 13, 1870, died July 30, 1960.

Robert lived all his life on this farm. His father bought 40 acres from his wife's aunt, Dovey McNeely Blair, who had homesteaded it with her husband, William, plus 40 more acres from neighbors, and Robert bought it from his father. When he was in the eighth grade at Sawyer School he quit school to help his father farm since his oldest brother, Linus, was away fighting in WWI. His five older sisters, Della, Irma, Mattie, Blanche and Bessie, doted on him.

On Jan. 13, 1929 he married a former schoolmate, Paulene Estell Wallace, born Feb. 7, 1908, died July 22, 1982. She moved into the house with Robert, his parents and an old aunt who was blind. After Aunt Sally died it was decided that "Pink" and "Ollie" should move "to town" (Fruitland). Robert and Estell borrowed money from the Land Bank and his parents carried part of the loan to buy the farm. They worked side by side during the depression, keeping a detailed record of every penny spent and their slight income. During the years 1935-36 their total income was $1,008.03 from the farm and their total living and farm expenses were $1,094.49. On Dec. 31, 1934, Estell's father, Louis, died leaving her a legacy of $2,772.49. They used that money to pay off the Land Bank and repay Robert's parents what they owed them. They felt very fortunate to own their farm free and clear.

All was not happy for them that year though. On Dec. 2, 1934 they had a baby boy, Bradley Wallace, who was born dead. Due to a difficult delivery performed at home Dr. Seabaugh told them they would probably never have any more children.

Robert Pinkney Morton and Paulene Estell Wallace Morton

They continued to put all of their energies into milking cows, raising pigs, and farming their 80 acres. No hired help was needed; Robert "swapped work" with his close neighbors, Clarence Pender and Leslie Schweer. He was also an avid coon hunter.

They were active in the Pleasant Hill Presbyterian Church Robert had been brought up in. In 1937 they were surprised to find out they were expecting again. Ruth Coleen was born Aug. 13, a very happy day for Robert and Estell.

No one was more happy to pay into Social Security than Robert when the IRS decided farmers could pay Self-Employment Tax. He planned toward that end every year. He began to lose interest in farming when the government started telling him how much wheat and corn he could plant. He didn't like those controls. In 1955 he started driving a school bus for Jackson R-2 School District so that he could supplement his Social Security payments from the farm, a job he continued for 12 years.

When he began to have health problems, Robert sold his milk cows and changed to beef cows, and sold his coon dogs and bought fox hounds which didn't require as much walking. He was having to go to the hospital periodically for blood transfusions, never clearly diagnosed until after his death, July 9, 1969. Dr. Jaeger later told his family that it had been discovered that pesticides and herbicides used by farmers got into their bloodstream, causing health-related problems identical to Robert's. He had used them liberally to keep fleas and ticks off his hunting dogs and to keep his fence rows clean. He drew one Social Security check. *Written by Ruth Coleen Morton Tinnin*

MORTON - Robert James "Bob" Morton was born July 10, 1933 in Fruitland, MO. He was the third child of Clarence P. (Aug. 11, 1900-1965) and Dorothy (Webb) Morton (Feb. 22, 1908-1996). He lived in Poplar Bluff and Zalma before moving back to Fruitland when he was in the fourth grade. Bob had four brothers: William; Ronald; Nelson and John. John died in infancy. His three sisters were Marjorie, Margaret and LaFern. Margaret died when she was 13. Robert attended Fruitland Grade School and Jackson High School. In 1950 he joined the U.S. Marines. He served his country during the Korean conflict, spending a year in Korea. He drove a bulldozer to help build campsites and roads, and he also drove an ammunition truck.

Robert Morton family: Mary, Mike, Sherrie and Robert

In August 1954 he married Mary Ella McDowell, daughter of Robert and Ilda McDowell. Mary was born on Nov. 17, 1932. Robert and Mary made their home in Jackson. Robert worked in the construction business until 1965 when he started Morton Bricklaying. He worked in this business until his death, May 25, 1997. Mary taught school in the Jackson R-II School District until her retirement in 1992. They were both active in church, school, and community activities. The family was affiliated with the First Presbyterian Church in Jackson.

Robert and Mary became the parents of Michael Robert and Sherrie Lynn. They have five grandchildren: Matthew Michael Morton; and Steffan, Alex Anne, Kristian and Kyleigh Troxel.

Michael works in the bricklaying business and teaches martial arts. He lives in the Fruitland Community. Sherrie teaches music and she and her husband Matthew "Bo" Troxel live in the Fruitland Community with their four children. *Submitted by Mary Morton*

MOUSER - Vertis Vena Sitze was born Dec. 12, 1908 to Robert Lee Sitze(s), a farmer, and Virginia "Jennie" Elizabeth Cloninger Sitze(s). Their family lived just south of Marquand in Bollinger County, MO. As she grew up she attended school at Moore's Chapel for grades one through five and Trace Creek for grades six through eight.

Vertis married Glen Allen Mouser at the home of Rev. Estel Mouser, who also performed the ceremony. Glen was the son of Andrew "Drew" Jackson Mouser and Susan Ida Sawyer Mouser. He was born Dec. 26, 1907 in Bollinger County, MO. Glen and Vertis lived in the Trace Creek community for several years before moving to Cape Girardeau County.

Glen and Vertis had four children. Willard Allen was born April 14, 1930 and married Wanda Burns. Verna Marie was born Jan. 1, 1934 and married Arnold "J. R." Drum. Kenneth Jackson Robert was born Sept. 8, 1940 and died Aug. 30, 1960 while serving in the U. S. Marine Corps. Sharon Kay was born Nov. 16, 1951 and married Johnny William Cureton.

The Mouser family: front row left to right: Vertis, Sharon, Glen; back row: Kenneth, Willard, Verna

Glen worked at different jobs throughout his life. When they moved to Cape Girardeau County they lived on Three Mile Creek Road near Cape Girardeau and he worked on a dairy farm for Bill Masters. There are two distinct remembrances of the time he worked for Alvin Cotner. One is of Kenny, as a small baby, being wrapped in a blanket and placed in his bushel basket bed. Another remembrance is of Glen and Vertis feeding cattle when their home burned to the ground. The children had been home alone but managed to escape unharmed. They lost everything but the clothes on their back. When Glen went to work for Superior Electric in Cape Girardeau, the family moved to a farm near Burfordville. Glen suffered a heart attack, and died on July 22, 1962. At this time, Vertis and Sharon moved to Jackson where they bought a house on Highland Drive. Vertis, in her fifties, had never driven before but was determined to do so. She took the test numerous times before she finally succeeded. She admits she probably exhausted the examiner into letting her pass.

Vertis engaged in babysitting and ironing as a means of income. There were several Jackson families who frequently called upon her to babysit. She was also a paid nursery worker for years at the First Baptist Church in Jackson where she was a faithful member. *Submitted by Lisa Drum*

MUELLER - Paul Alexander Mueller, the son of H. H. Mueller and his wife Ida Braas Ermertz,

Paul Mueller Sr. and brothers and sisters, except Julia. Little girl is Nellie

was born in 1893. He, with his three brothers and father, worked for and in the H. H. Mueller pork packers and butchers business. He attended the old Jackson Military Academy and later graduated from Jackson High School. He attended the University of Missouri and Washington University in St. Louis but returned home to take up his place in the family business.

World War I interrupted this occupation when he, along with others, was in the first draft called up from Cape Girardeau County. He became a bugler in the Army and was shipped overseas where he served until discharged. After the war he came back to Jackson and again took his place in the business. He married Edna Riley of New Madrid and they had two children, Paul Alexander Jr. and Harriet Ida. He built a home on the family property on East Main and there he resided until his death.

Paul Mueller was an active member of the community and also a member of the City Council of Jackson and a past Commander of the American Legion. He was a member of the Chamber of Commerce and active in helping to bring business to the town.

After the death of his father, H. H. Mueller and two of his brothers, in the midst of the Depression in 1934, Paul moved the existing meat business into Ideal Grocery with August Freidrich and Henry Sievers. This business was located one block north of the Courthouse square on High Street. He continued in the business until he retired in 1958. He died in 1982, three years after the death of his wife. He was the adored grandfather of his seven grandchildren and never failed to find fun in all he did. *Submitted by Harriet Mueller Howard*

Paul Mueller Sr., 1912

MUELLER - This family begins when Herman and Henrietta Taeger Mueller, in 1864, emigrated with their family from Germany to rural Cape Girardeau County. Herman, also known as Henry, owned a cheese factory near Berlin. He fought under Bismarck to form the German Empire but as he saw the Franco-Prussian War approaching he did not intend to fight again. So he, with his family, came to America. With family in the Cape Girardeau County area he settled here.

Herman Henry Godfrey Mueller (H. H.), their son, was born Aug. 2, 1857, in Hermsdorf, Germany. When both of his parents died by 1870, he lived with the Julius Vasterling family in Cape Girardeau. At an early age he was apprenticed as a mud-shipping-clerk to Sebastian Albert. This company later became the Meyer-Albert Grocery Company. A "mud" clerk met the riverboats as they docked and checked the arrival and departure of the merchandise for the Grocery Company. In 1882 he began work for Henry Meystedt as a butcher and packer. In 1884 he moved to Jackson and established the pork packers and butcher business, H. H. Mueller & Co. He operated this business until his death on May 2, 1934. This was a flourishing business with three retail meat markets. Two were located in Cape Girardeau and one in Jackson. He butchered, smoked and shipped hams and other pork products throughout America and some overseas.

H. H. Mueller married Ida Braas Ermertz of St. Louis in 1882. They had 10 children with nine surviving into adulthood. Four of his sons worked in the business, either in the packing and smoking part or the retail side.

Their sons were: 1. Albert, who married Gussie and had two sons and two daughters: Robert; Leo; Virginia and Katherine. 2. Hugo Julius, who married Sadie and had four sons: Hugo; Henry; Joe; and David. 3. H. H. Jr., who married Rilla and had one daughter, Millicent. 4. Adolph William, known as "Butch, " who never married. 5. Paul Alexander, who married Edna Riley and had two children, Paul Alexander Jr. and Harriet. 6. Henry Edward, who also never married. They had three daughters: 1. Clara Cornelia who never married. 2. Henrietta, who married Horatio Tragett and had two children, H. N. III and Henrietta. 3. Julia Lilly, who married Guild LaPierre and had two daughters, Susan J. and Julia Margaret.

H. H. Mueller was a self-made man of little formal education, but a successful businessman and community leader. He was President of People's National Bank until it was merged with the former Jackson Exchange Bank. He was a founder and officer of the Board of Directors of the Jackson Saving and Loan. He served on many local and civic committees and boards.

H. H. Mueller Sr.

The Muellers - all 11 of them - moved in 1900 into the large home on East Main located in the 700 block. He bought this property from the Tiedeman family - of the Cape County Milling Company founding interest. This property comprised the entire south side of the block. Upon this property were later located the homes of H. H. Jr. and Paul. He also owned much uptown Jackson property plus Cape Girardeau lots and businesses. H. H. Mueller died in May of 1934, and shortly thereafter two of his sons followed him in death. *Submitted by Marybelle Mueller (Mrs. Paul A.)*

MUELLER - Paul A. Mueller, Jr. was the son of Paul Alexander Mueller and Edna Riley Mueller. Born and raised in Jackson, he never lost his love of the town. He was born in 1921 in New Madrid County - because that was where the Riley family lived - but was soon brought home to Jackson. He graduated from Jackson High School. He was attending the University of Missouri at the outbreak of WWII and so joined the Army Air Corp. He served all over the southern European and Southeastern Theater and returned home in 1945.

He returned to the University of Missouri to complete his degree and then graduated from the Law School in 1950. He again returned home to Jackson and opened his law office. He practiced law in Jackson first as a solo practitioner and later as the law firm of Mueller and Statler. He continued in that practice until his death in 1986.

In 1951 he married Marybelle Dailey Mueller, also a lawyer, who became one of the first women Judges in the State of Missouri. They had five children.

Paul Mueller, Jr. was active in Jackson Community affairs as were the previous generations before him. He too was a past Commander of the American Legion, Past President of the Jackson Chamber of Commerce, a member of the Jackson School Board and Jackson City Attorney for some time. He was President of the Jackson Saving and Loan - as his grandfather had been. He was always active in the New McKendree Methodist Church and served on many of its boards and committees. He was active in his profession and served as past president of the Cape County Bar Association. He was an active member of the Democratic Party and served as Treasurer of the County Organization

Paul Mueller Jr.

He had five children. Paulette married Dr. Lewis Frazee and they have two daughters, Sarah and Laura; Dr. Janet, of Tucson, AZ; Mary Harriet married Greg Talbut and they have one son, Riley; and twins Barbara, married to Cody Fulkerson, and Dr. Robert, married to Elizabeth Bergen. The latter have two sons, Paul Alexander and Jeffrey Lee. Mary Harriet and her family and Barbara and her husband live in Jackson along with retired Judge and widow Marybelle, to carry on the long tradition of love of this town. *Submitted by Paulette Mueller Frazee*

MUSTER – Johann Heinrich Gemeins Eifert (b. March 3, 1814), was married in Germany to Anna Marie Roth (b. Nov. 6, 1821). Most likely searching for religious freedom, this young couple came to America and settled in Scott County, MO. To this union were born nine children: David; Heinrich; Katharina Elisabeth; Sophia; Casper; Eva; Juliana; John and Elisa. The Eifert family were members of Eisleben Lutheran Church, Illmo, MO, now Scott City, MO.

Juliana Eifert (b. March 6, 1855 in Illmo, MO) was united in marriage with Heinrich Voss Jr., who was the only son of Heinrich Johann Ludwig Voss and Johanna O. A. Steinmann. Juliana and Heinrich Voss Jr. lived on a farm southwest of Gordonville, MO in Hubble Township. In those days, large families were common because lots of chores needed to be done on the farm. Juliana and Heinrich Voss, Jr. were parents of nine children: Anna W.; Maria Wilhelmina; Caroline Sophie; Johann August; Maria Emma Elizabeth; Herman Fredrich; Henry George; Edwin Heinrich August and Juliana Madalene. Maria Emma and Juliana Madalene didn't live to adulthood. The other children became adults and attended the rural Liberty School. Heinrich Voss Jr. and his family were members of Zion Lutheran Church, Gordonville, MO. In the early 1900s, about 1913, Juliana and Heinich Voss Jr. moved from the farm and lived in the same house in Cape Girardeau, South Ellis Street, where he was raised as a young child. Juliana passed away Jan. 1, 1928 and Heinrich Voss Jr., June 25, 1930.

Caroline "Sophie" Voss was born Feb. 15, 1883 and was married to Henry Muster. They were life-long members of Zion Lutheran Church, Gordonville, MO. Henry and Sophie farmed in the Allenville and Gordonville area and were the parents of Johanna "Anna," Albert, Lydia, Emil, Amanda, Henry, Edwin, Edna and Marie. The children married and remained in southeast Missouri except Albert, Amanda, Henry, and Edna who relocated in central Illinois. In later years, Henry and Sophie moved to Gordonville, MO. Emil, a son of Henry and Sophie, married Bertha "Alma" Meier Aug. 3, 1938. They lived on a farm southwest of Gordonville and north of Whitewater until 1986, when they moved to Jackson. Emil and Alma were the parents of two daughters, Carolena and Dorothy.

Carolena and Dorothy have fond memories, when they were children, of visiting the grandparents' home, and all the cousins, aunts and uncles, and other relatives would be there. As youths, Carolena and Dorothy attended Poplar Ridge School and were active in church and local 4-H club. They are graduates of Jackson High School.

Carolena and her husband, W. Dean Galloway, are residents of the Tilsit Community. They are active members of St. James UCC Church. Dean is retired from the Cape County Highway Department. Carolena and Dean enjoy their children, Larry and Bonnie, their spouses and granddaughters.

Henry Muster family, left to right, front row: Henry and Caroline Sophie Voss Muster. Middle row: Marie, Edna, Amanda, Lydia and Johanna "Anna." Back row: Edwin, Henry, Albert and Emil, ca. 1940

Dorothy and her husband were the parents of one daughter, Julie Kaye Crites. In 1973 Dorothy and Julie moved to Jackson. At that time, Dorothy was employed by Brennecke Chevrolet Company and Julie was attending kindergarten. As a student, Julie participated in several school activities, was a member of the Honor Society, FBLA, marching "Chiefs" and concert band. She is a 1986 graduate of Jackson High School. She continued to play the clarinet with the Jackson Muny Band and the Golden Eagles while attending Southeast Missouri State University. After receiving a B. A. degree from Southeast Missouri State University in 1990, Julie received a degree from the Paralegal Institute of Nashville. Julie and her husband are currently living in St. John, MO. *Submitted by Dorothy Rowley*

MYER – Betty Jean Birk was born Aug. 11, 1927, the daughter of Adeline Isabelle "Addie" (Bennett) Birk.

In the spring of 1806 her ancestors began a long trip from Georgia to establish new homes in Missouri. They traveled by ox-wagons, horseback and foot. Among this group was John and Nancy Sheppard with nine children and their slaves. He was among the five Commissioners who purchased 50 acres of land from Colonel William H. Ashley and his wife Mary Able for a new Cape County Seat on Feb. 8, 1814. Jackson was laid out in 1815. He served as Sheriff of Cape Girardeau County from 1830 to 1834.

The John Sheppard farm, south of Jackson, was to become the Bennett family farm, now known as the Elmer Schaper farm. Joseph and Agnes Bennett, as well as James N. and Sarah Bennett, were laid to rest in the family cemetery on the farm.

Lee Edward "Ebby" Myer holding Michael Joe Myer and Betty Jean (Birk) holding John William Myer, Jan. 9, 1954.

In 1818, Joseph Bennett who was born Nov. 12, 1775 and who died Nov. 7, 1858, arrived in Madison County from Tennessee with his wife Agnes. He was a farmer and a Judge of County Court in the Madison County area from 1821 to 1827. He was also a deacon of the Bethel Baptist Church. Two of Joseph Bennett's sons married John Sheppard's daughters.

Joseph's son, James N. Bennett, was born Sept. 10, 1806 and died May 13, 1857. He married Sarah Sheppard on Jan. 16, 1829, and served as Constable and Sheriff of Cape Girardeau County.

James' son, William Bennett, was born Nov. 14, 1833 and died March 6, 1898. He married Margaret E. Sheppard on Nov. 26, 1857.

William's son, James Elisha Bennett, was born Oct. 23, 1862 and died Jan. 28, 1917. He married Lenora Romboutz who was born Sept. 17, 1870 and who died May 7, 1957. She was orphaned at age 6, raised and educated in a convent on Good Hope and Spanish Street in Cape Girardeau. Her father was a Gardner from Holland. They were married in 1886. After James E. passed away, the family farm was sold and Lenora moved to Cape Girardeau in 1920.

Their daughter Adeline Isabelle, who was born Feb. 1, 1895 and who died Aug. 18, 1954, married Therodore Charles Birk in 1920. He was born Dec. 27, 1888 and he died April 7, 1982.

Betty (Birk) Myer was born and educated in Cape Girardeau County, and she married Lee

Edward "Ebby" Myer on June 10, 1950. He served in the U. S. Navy on Okinawa and in the Pacific, attached to a PT outfit, serving on a motor torpedo boat from 1942 to 1946. His father Joe Myer worked at the Cash Book Journal for 45 years. Ebby died in an automobile accident on March 25, 1956.

They are the parents of three sons, Michael Joe, born April 30, 1952; John William, born Dec. 27, 1953; and Mark Edward, born and died July 3, 1955. Michael has one daughter, Rachel Leigh, and John has three sons: Justin Lee, Tyson Eugene, and Jonathan Forrest.

Betty began to work in the Mental Health Unit at the Old St. Francis Hospital on Good Hope in Cape Girardeau in 1975. She helped move to the new hospital on I-55 and Route K and continued with Mental Health until it closed in 1987. She then worked with Medical Records until her retirement on June 21, 1997. She is an active member of St. Paul Lutheran Church and does volunteer work for many causes and organizations. *Submitted by Betty J. Myer*

MYER - Joseph Myer "Joe" was born Oct. 22, 1895 and died in 1963. He was the son of William Myer, who was born Feb. 3, 1863 and who died in 1941, and Nora Webb Myer, who was born April 3, 1877 and who died in 1952.

At the age of 20, Joe began his apprenticeship with Charles Oliver. After serving his county during WWI, he returned to Jackson and bought the Cash-Book from Charles Oliver and later sold the paper to R. K. Wilson, but stayed on and worked for 45 years until retiring in 1960.

Joe married Josephine Nitsch on Aug. 17, 1919, and to this union were born 10 children: Mary (1920-1991); Dorothy (1922-1986); Joe Wilson (1924-1980); Lee Edward "Ebby" (1925-1956); Mildred (Mitze) (1927-); Daisy (1930-); Robert "Bob" (1932-1998); Richard "Dick" (1934-); Donold (1936-1937) and Paul (1939-2000). The family spent its most happy years at 301 N. High, which is now part of the Cape County Jail. All the children graduated from Jackson High School.

Raising a large family during the Depression made it necessary to have a garden. They had not one but two large gardens in which they raised everything they needed, except bread, milk and meat. A garden requires a lot of work. Josephine would be working in it from 6:00 a.m. until it got too hot. No self-respecting weed grew very long in her garden. All the hard work paid off, because they would have food all winter, that she had canned during the summer.

Although Joe had an eighth grade education, he was a self-made educated man. Being a newspaper man for over 45 years with the Jackson Cash-Book, a weekly newspaper, he could look at a tray of type and find a misspelled word upside down. By today's standards, Joe was a workaholic, spending 10 to 12 hours a day at the Cash-Book, helping Josephine with the garden during the summer, and being very active in the American Legion Post #158, where he held the position of Commander twice. He read the Legion Magazine from cover to cover. When he spoke at a Legion meeting everyone listened intently, because they knew Joe knew what he was talking about. He received many awards for signing 100 or more members a year. He was sent as a delegate to many Legion Conventions, and was a member of the 40-8 Club, which is a special group inside the Legion.

Joe didn't have to raise his voice very often to get his point across, because when he gave you that look, you knew to quit doing what you were doing. He loved his family and they loved him. *Submitted by Mildred (Myer) Abbott, Daisy (Myer) Koch and Dick Myer*

NELSON – James R. "Jim" Nelson was born in 1921 in St. Joseph, MO. At the age of 12 he moved to his grandparents' home and graduated from Monticello High School in 1939. He attended Kirksville Teachers College and enlisted in the Air Force in June 1942. He and Evelyn Campen were married in February 1943. In service Jim graduated from Pilot's School and was then trained as a flying instructor in the B-25 aircraft. Released from military service in 1947, Jim returned to Kirksville and graduated in June 1948. He taught school at Macon High School until 1950. He then attended Missouri University, getting his Master's Degree. He then moved to teach in Jackson in 1951.

James R. and Evelyn Campen Nelson

Daughter Janet was born in 1945 at Quincy, IL, and son Kent was born in 1956 in Cape Girardeau. Both graduated from Jackson High School. Janet married David Ludwig in 1968. They have two children, daughter Tracy and son Jason. She teaches Business Education in Jackson High School. Kent married Jean Anderson in 1985 and is a pharmacist and owns Nelson Pharmacy in Ste. Genevieve.

Jim was a long time principal of Jackson High School from 1964 to 1986. This was the longest tenure of a principal in Jackson High School. After retiring in 1986 Jim again renewed his interest in amateur radio and has passed all tests to obtain the top license to operate amateur radios. He has been very active in the American Legion, being commander in 1991. He regularly calls bingo for the post and is the Historian and Publicity chairman for the post. He was president of the Frederick Air Force Reunion group until it disbanded. He is a life member of the V.F.W. and the American Legion as well as a member of two Air Force reunion groups. *Submitted by James R. Nelson*

NISWONGER - Dallas Edward Niswonger was born on Oct. 4, 1928, the son of Harlan Waldo Niswonger (born Oct. 25, 1901; died Sept. 5, 1996) and Reta Marie Turner (born Dec. 19, 1902; died April 27, 1965). Dallas married Juanita Criddle (born Sept. 4, 1934) on July 2, 1951. The couple has three sons, Lynn, Donald and Robert.

Dallas has spent his entire life in the Jackson area. He was employed for 20 years at the local International Shoe Factory where his father was also employed. He then was a salesman for Harris Motor Company in Cape Girardeau, MO. His last years of employment were spent at Proctor and Gamble before retiring in 1991. He spends his retirement days enjoying going to auctions and collecting collectibles and antiques.

The Niswongers have been tracked back to Switzerland, coming to America in the early 1700s, and settling in Virginia and North Carolina. The Joseph Niswonger family, along with a group of 20 other families, left North Carolina in the fall of 1799 by wagon train, arriving in Illinois across from Ste. Genevieve in the winter. Here they waited for the Mississippi River to freeze so that they could cross over to Missouri. After crossing the river on New Year's Day 1800, they came down the bottom lands and settled along the Whitewater River north of Millersville, MO, where they farmed. Dallas' great-grandfather Peter Niswonger (born 1846; died 1938) served a short time in the Civil War and returned to the farm.

In 1847 Dave Niswonger donated some ground along what is now Highway 72, west of Millersville, to build a church, known as the Niswonger Church. Services were held there for many years by the families, and many ancestors are buried in the cemetery beside the church. Others are buried in the old original cemetery located on a farm about a mile from the church. Services are no longer held at the church but it is the gathering place for the Niswonger families and friends at the annual Homecoming the third Sunday in September.

Dallas is one of the many Niswongers remaining in this area. He has seen many spellings of his last name. The original was Neuenschwander; other spellings are Neiswanger and Neiswonger. *Submitted by Dallas Niswonger*

NOLAND - Carl Noland was born in Cape Girardeau County on March 14, 1895, the youngest son of James William Noland and Cornelia Dora McLaird. He served in France during WWI. He and Kathleen Bray were married Sept. 17, 1919. They had nine children. Carl was active in serving on the school board (Indian Creek), doing volunteer work for McLain's Chapel cemetery, and working to obtain telephone, electrical, and school bus services for the community. He died on Dec. 28, 1951.

Kathleen, daughter of Sterling Price and Agnes Cotter Bray, was born on March 21, 1898. She taught school before her marriage to Carl and was active in church and community until her death on Sept. 14, 1992. Children of Carl

The Myer family, left to right, front row: Dick Myer, Paul Myer, Josephine Myer, Joe Myer. Back row: Bob Myer, Daisy Myer, Mildred Myer, Lee Edward "Ebby" Myer, Dorothy Myer.

and Kathleen Noland include: Virginia (1920-) who married Thomas Daniel, and who lives in Fort Smith, AR; Gerald "Bud" (1922-) who married Noma Lee Crites, and who lives in Jackson, MO; Leslie (1924-1986) who married Mary Bynum and who served in the Philippines and Japan during WWII; Harold (1926-1968) who served in Japan during WWII; Ruth (1929-) who married George Schweer and who lives in Jackson, MO; Barbara (1931-1931); James (1933-) who married Joan Brainerd and who lives in Connecticut; Joseph (1935-), who married Norma Lei Chang and who lives in Hawaii; and Judith (1940-) who married Edward Rapp and who lives in Wisconsin.

Carl's father, James William Noland, was born in 1859 in Cape Girardeau County, the son of William Carl and Permelia Garner. Carl's mother, Cornelia McLard Noland, was born in 1860, the daughter of Daniel S. and Eliza Bayliss McLard. James and Cornelia had 12 children. Cornelia died in 1900. "Aunt Nancy", widow of Cornelia's cousin George Pierce, cared for the younger children and lived with the family until her death in the 1930s. Carl's children called her "Mammie." James died in 1931. Carl and Kathleen remained on the farm until his death in 1951. Their son Leslie and his family lived on the farm with Kathleen until his death in 1986 and her death in 1992. After Kathleen's death her share of the farm was purchased by Leslie's children, Vickie Noland and Nancy Noland McNeely.

Carl Harry Noland, ca. 1917

James' grandfather, Ebineezer Noland, was born around 1788 in Cecil County, MD. Ebineezer's wife, Mary Ann Robertson, was born in Virginia around 1790. After marrying in Kentucky, Ebineezer and Mary Ann moved to Indiana, then to Cape Girardeau County where they built a house in the community of Oriole. The homeplace and a family cemetery are located at the foot of the hill holding the KFVS television tower.

James' father, William Carl Noland, was born in 1825 in Davis County, IN. William married Permelia Garner, the daughter of James and Melinda King Garner. They had nine children. William and Permelia Noland, as well as Ebineezer and Mary Ann Noland, are buried in the family cemetery. *Submitted by Pam Schulte*

NOLAND - The Noland family was always short on money, but they had an abundance of love and laughter. There were seven children, six girls and one boy. The girls were Leith (1891-1918); Ada (1893-1975); Zola (1895-1966); Willie (1897-1950); Cecil (1900-1992); and Pearl (1901-1992). The last three girls were given names that could be either sex. John said he would have children until he had a boy to help on the farm. John Eb (1903-1977), his son, was the last child.

They lived most of their lives in this beautiful rural area between Oriole and Egypt Mills. Their children were born in a log house that had been a sheep shed which they rebuilt, adding a lean-to kitchen. The children slept in a loft. They would sometimes awaken with a covering of snow that had blown between the cracks in the logs.

Most of their food was produced on their land, even the wheat. It was taken to Pocahontas to be milled into flour. Chickens and eggs were used to buy sugar, coffee, salt and crackers. Meat was slaughtered from their own cattle and hogs. Neighbors moved from one family to another to help with the "hog killin." They made their own sausage and smoked their own hams. Nothing was wasted. They made headcheese and pickled pigs' feet. The fat was rendered into lard and used to make soap.

After their children were married, they built an eight-room house nearby. Their ancestors had settled in that community. John Wesley Noland (1863-1957) was the son of William (1825-1897) and Permelia (Garner) (1838-1919). John's grandfather, Ebeneezer, had come here from Maryland before 1850. "Nancy" Jane (Reynolds) Noland was the daughter of Dudley Reynolds (1826-1915) and Sally (King) (1840-1902). The old Eb Noland house was sold to Jane's family, the Reynolds. It still stands, a neighboring house to John and Jane's home, on Route 177.

Jane (Reynolds) Noland and John Wesley Noland raised seven children on their farm between Oriole and Egypt Mills. Picture taken about 1935.

John and Jane made everything the family needed. Jane sewed all their clothes. Flour sacks were stitched together for sheets, dishtowels and underwear. Printed sacks were used for dresses and shirts. Jane knitted socks, hats, gloves and scarves. John made their shoes. Each family had large and small iron shoe lasts, an iron stand where different sized shoes would fit on them. When the shoes began to wear, leather strips were soaked in water to make them pliable; then, the shoe was placed on the leather and the correct size was cut. The shoe was placed on the last, holes were hammered in the leather sole with a shoe peg, and shoe tacks were hammered to connect the two. Imagine the discomfort if a tack would come through. Most often, except during very cold weather, the children went barefoot to save their shoes (and probably their feet).

They were respected, giving citizens. They worked to help the school, the church, and their neighbors. John was a constable and helped string the phone lines in the area. Jane, risking her own life, helped by nursing other families during the flu epidemic of 1918. She had lost her oldest daughter to the dreaded disease.

Their last days were spent in Cape Girardeau. After Jane's death, John lived with his daughters, Cecil Schatte and Pearl McLain, and a granddaughter, Ann Davidson Phelps. During their lifetimes they had little, but they had everything that mattered. They were pioneers who loved their family and their God. *Submitted by LaFern McLain Stiver*

NOLAND - Kathleen Bray Noland's father was Sterling Price Bray, born in St. Louis in October 1861. He was named after Confederate General Sterling Price, and was the son of James M. and Lovicy Hood Bray. James Noland was born in Kentucky in 1821. Lovicy Hood was born in Pelham County, MA. James and Lovicy are buried in Pleasant Hill Cemetery in Fruitland, MO.

Kathleen Bray's great-great-grandfather was Thomas Neely. He married Rebecca Hays in 1788 in Pennsylvania. Rebecca was the daughter of Christopher Hays, a Revolutionary War colonel who came to Missouri after the war and became a surveyor of the Louisiana Territory under Don Louis Lorimier. Christopher Hays served as Cape Girardeau County's first presiding justice. Rebecca's brother John served as the first sheriff of Cape Girardeau County. John is buried in Hays cemetery in Neely's Landing where many of the Cotter and Bray family are buried.

Jacob Neely, son of Thomas and Rebecca Hays Neely, married Elizabeth Walls in 1827. They had five children: Lutiscia (grandmother of Kathleen Bray); Tallice; Charles; James and David. After Rebecca's death when David was an infant, Jacob remarried and had another son, William. Jacob Neely died around 1862.

Kathleen Bray's grandfather Edward Cotter was born in Cork, Ireland, in 1812. Family tradition holds that he was traveling in America to regain his health. While traveling aboard a steamboat on the Mississippi River, he became ill and had to disembark at Neely's Landing After leaving the ship, he stayed at the home of Jacob Neely, where he fell in love with and married Jacob's daughter Lutiscia. Edward and Lutiscia Neely had eight children: Charles; Josephine; Eva; Katherine; Mary; Caroline; Agnes Clare (mother of Kathleen Bray) and Pierce.

Kathleen Bray's parents, Agnes Clare Cotter and Sterling Price Bray, were married in Neely's Landing, MO on March 15, 1884. Their ten children included: James (1886-1953); Jewel Clare (1888-1977) who married Oliver "Doc" Miller; Sterling Price (1891-1968), who married Esther Peterson; Pierce Cotter (1893-1956); Bertrude (1895-1981); Gertrude (1895-1983); Kathleen (1898-1992), who married Carl Noland; Mary (1900-1987), who married Grover Waldon; Varena (1903-1960), who married Frank Huck and then married Roy Adams; and Carrie (1906-1996), who married Ernest Droeste and then married Charles Van Ronzalen.

Kathleen Malinda Bray, ca. 1917

Kathleen, born in 1895, married Carl Noland (1895-1951) in 1917 (See Carl Noland family). She died in 1992. Both Kathleen and Carl Noland are buried in McLain's Chapel Cemetery near Oriole, MO. *Submitted by Pam Schulte*

NOTHDURFT - Heinrich Karl (Henry Carl) Nothdurft was born in 1818 in Grössen Rhüden, Germany, near the Kingdom of Hanover. Germany experienced several famines and floods between 1825 and 1845. In addition, there was a great deal of political turmoil. Heinrich registered for the draft at age 18, but decided to avoid having to serve in the Prussian army for three years by escaping to the United States in 1843, at the age of 25. To escape Germany, he constructed a wooden box labeled "dry goods." Heinrich arranged for his cousin to place the box on a ship sailing for America. The box was 52 inches x 23 inches x 23 inches, just large enough for him to hide within under a false bottom. His cousin secretly brought food and water to him during the early days of the voyage. When the ship had sailed outside of the waters claimed by Germany into international waters, the cousin let him out of the box. The ship sailed to New Orleans, and then Heinrich Karl traveled up the Mississippi River to Cape Girardeau. He met some relatives (the Deneke family) when he arrived. He settled near the small town of Tilsit and began to farm. He became a naturalized U. S. citizen in 1848.

The box he came over in was partitioned off and used to store cornmeal, flour and a rolling pin; it has remained in the family and is now located at the Gerald and Jane (Nothdurft) Shinn family home near Gordonville.

Front row, left to right: Heinrich Karl Nothdurft, Caroline (Kempe) Nothdurft, Fredericka (Helibreck) Brase and Hy Brase. Back row: Aug Nothdurft and Minnie (Brase) Nothdurft. In circle: Rev. Chas. Neumeyer, his wife Mary (Nothdurft) Neumeyer and Hilda (Neumeyer) Lindenmeyer.

The Heinrich Karl grave is located in the cemetery of the Zion United Methodist Church near Gordonville and the original farmhouse still stands near Tilsit. Many grandchildren and great-grandchildren of Heinrich Karl Nothdurft still reside in the Jackson area.

This account is based on family oral history and the "Henry Carl Nothdurft Family Genealogy and History" written by Rudolph "Rudy" J. Nothdurft Jr., November 1995. *Submitted by Robert R. Nothdurft and Jane Nothdurft Shinn.*

NOWAK - Lawrence A. "Larry" Nowak was born July 10, 1908 in Nashville, IL, son of Frank E. and Frances Bonk Nowak. He and Mabel M. Klieneberg were married June 1, 1938, at St. Mary's Catholic Church in Chester, IL. In 1939 the Nowaks moved from Chester to Jackson, where Larry was supervisor at the Jackson Hosiery Mill.

Mr. Nowak was active in the Jackson community. He joined the Jackson Optimist Club in 1944; he served as president in 1948, chaplain from 1992 to 2000, and lieutenant governor, and had a 49 year perfect attendance record. In 1968 he joined the Southeast Missouri Medical Center, Inc., a not-for-profit corporation for health services in the Jackson area, and was treasurer for the group from 1971 to 2000. He also served on the Jackson Industrial Development Authority. He was a member of the Jackson Chamber of Commerce from 1955 until his death. In 1982, he received the Chamber's "R. A. Fulenwider Award," the city's highest civic honor.

Mabel and Larry Nowak, 1983

Larry played a prominent role in Jackson government for over 50 years. He served on the Jackson Board of Aldermen from 1949 to 1957, while also serving as chairman of the Power and Light Committee. He was mayor of Jackson from 1957 to 1961, and again from 1963 to 1969. He contributed to the development of the power plant expansion, major street paving, and improvement of waterworks and sewage systems.

Larry and Mabel were longtime members of Immaculate Conception Catholic Church in Jackson. Larry had been a member of the Parish Council and was a 4th Degree Knight in the Knights of Columbus. Mabel passed away Dec. 5, 1997. After Larry's death on July 13, 2000, the flag at the Jackson City Hall was flown at half-mast in honor of the former mayor described as "a true American gentleman and a never-ending ambassador to Jackson." *Submitted by Cathi Stoverink*

NUSSBAUM - Dewey John Nussbaum was born in Cape Girardeau, MO on April 26, 1940 to George William and Theta Clifta (Sebastian) Nussbaum. He married Gwendolyn McSpadden of Mammoth Springs, AR in Burfordville, MO on Jan. 29, 1961, and they made their home in Cape Girardeau. Their three children were born in Cape Girardeau: Kevin Paul, born Sept. 28, 1962; Stephen Douglas, born Feb. 17, 1965; and Katina Marie, born Aug. 31, 1972. The family moved to Sesser, IL in 1973 due to a job change, and all three children graduated from Sesser High School and all three graduated from college, Kevin from Southern Illinois University-Carbondale, Stephen from the University of Missouri at Rolla, and Katina from the University of William Woods.

Dewey and his sisters, Katherine Ann (Lynn) and Mary Emma (King), grew up on the family farm in Gordonville, and attended the Zion Lutheran Church in Gordonville. Their father, George, died March 21, 1957 in a St. Louis Hospital; it is believed that he died as a result of chemical poisoning due to all the chemicals he used on their dairy farm. Theta died at the Lutheran Nursing Home in Cape Girardeau on Feb. 1, 1993.

Dewey and Gwendolyn Nussbaum

Dewey's grandparents were Martin Albert and Annie Emma (Bartels) Nussbaum. Martin was born March 1, 1886 in Gordonville, MO. Annie was born Sept. 4, 1889 in Gordonville. They were married April 25, 1909. After Martin's untimely death on Feb. 18, 1922 of botulism (from home-canned green beans), Annie was left to raise their three sons; Emil Paul, George William and Herbert Martin, plus her sister's son, Ed Sander, on their small family farm in Gordonville. Annie Nussbaum died June 1, 1977 in Cape Girardeau, MO.

Martin Nussbaum was the son of Rudolph and Caroline (Siemers) Nussbaum. Rudolph was born Dec. 1, 1851 in Switzerland and died Aug. 30, 1911. Caroline was born Aug. 26, 1851 and died Oct. 30, 1895. They were married Jan. 30, 18__ and had six children: Herman William; Lewis or Louis; Robert George; Martin Albert; Lydia Derena; and Rudolph. Rudolph's parents were Samuel and Anna Marie (Dubs) Nussbaum. Samuel was born Feb. 15, 1826 in Switzerland. Anna Marie was born Aug. 8, 1830 in Kettigan, Switzerland. They were married in Switzerland on March 4, 1849. It is believed that three of their children were also born in Switzerland; Caroline, Rudolph, and Elizabeth, with Mary probably being born in the United States. Samuel is buried on the Nussbaum family farm in Gordonville while Anna Marie is buried at Dutchtown, MO.

Samuel was the son of Johannas "Hofes" and Magdalena (Senn) Nussbaum of Asp, Switzerland. Johannas was the son of Jacob and Elizabeth Stierli (Von Vrittman) Nussbaum. There are still members of the Nussbaum family living in Asp, Switzerland today. It is not known just when the Nussbaums migrated to Switzerland nor what caused them to flee Germany. The origins of the name "Nussbaum" in records show the family name as being "Nussbaumer." The name was altered in the United States to simply "Nussbaum." The name in English means walnut tree. The "er" added means a "dweller among or at."

Dewey started his banking career in 1960 at Cape State Bank in Gordonville, MO. In 1973 he was employed by the Bank of Sesser and became president in 1991. He retired from the First National Bank of Steelville, IL in 2002 and moved to Jackson, MO in September 2001. *Submitted by Gwen Nussbaum*

OCHS – Theodore Ochs, the son of H. P. and Barbara Popp Ochs, was born in Longtown, MO, on March 3, 1873. He was educated at the State Normal School and at the Gem City Business College. He was a member of the Lutheran Church and a Republican in politics. On May 3, 1896, he married Bertha Popp. They had one son, Henry, and three daughters, Mildred, Lenora, and Laura.

Theodore began his business career in Longtown in a general store. In 1898 he moved to Cape Girardeau and worked in the Vogelsanger Hardware Store, where he remained until 1901. He helped organize the Union Lumber Company, becoming its secretary, and became the manger upon the absorption of the Western Manufacturing and Lumber Company, the largest lumber and veneer plant between St. Louis and Memphis. He bought the lumber company and later sold the business.

Theodore turned his business expertise into building apartments and acquiring prime property along the fringes of Cape Girardeau. He built a brick home, Maple Lawn, on North Sprigg Street. Here he had about 40 acres that he used to raise trees and shrubs for landscaping. Pioneer Orchards Company, Inc. was started in 1923, east of Silver Springs Road.

William Henry Beggs was born in Illmo, MO, and attended Southeast Missouri State Teachers' College. His parents had a butcher shop and grocery store in Illmo. In 1932 he married Laura H. Ochs, Theodore's youngest daughter, and joined Theodore in the orchard and landscaping business. Three children were born to them: William J. (1934), Stanley K. (1936), and Sammy K. (1943).

In 1947 the Pioneer Orchards Company purchased 109 acres west of Jackson and planted 50 acres of peaches and 50 of apples. This was the start of Pioneer Orchards Company, Inc. in Jackson. In 1952 the first roadside market was built, a small, poultry wire-enclosed stand selling farm-fresh fruit during the harvest season.

William H. Beggs managed and operated both the Cape Girardeau and Jackson Orchards until 1971, when he divided the original Pioneer Orchards Company into three new separate corporations. The original Cape Girardeau site was now owned by William J. Beggs and titled Pioneer Land and Development Company. The Jackson site was divided between Sam K. Beggs and Stanley K. Beggs into two new corporations, Sam owning Pioneer Market Company and

Stanley owning Pioneer Orchards Company of Jackson.

William J. and Shirley (Sievers) Beggs raised a daughter and three sons. Today William owns and operates a peach and nectarine orchard and the Pioneer Mobile Home Court on the Cape Girardeau site, and his oldest son, William Walter Beggs, manages the orchards and their farm market.

Sam K. and Margaret (Decker) Beggs raised two daughters and one son. He built Pioneer Market into one of Missouri's finest farm orchard markets. He owns and operates the Pioneer Orchards Market in Jackson along with his youngest daughter Sarah.

Stanley K. Beggs married LaDonia Faye Bock in 1955. He attended the University of Missouri at Columbia and graduated in 1958 with a B. S. degree in agriculture. LaDonia and Stanley have three sons, Dean Stanley, Scott Alvin, and Layton Allen. The original Jackson acres were replanted in apples during 1976 and 1977, and an additional 200 acres were acquired in 1973 and planted in apples. Today Pioneer Orchard Company of Jackson is the largest apple orchard in southeast Missouri. Scott Beggs is now the manager.

O'LOUGHLIN - Civilization is the offspring of cities, we are told, and the organization and event of the urban attests this. But, it is also claimed, there is society where none intrudes: by the deep sea and music in its roar.

A strain of the Celtic attests to the later. Perhaps it was the noted historian, Will Durant, who speculated that the accumulated experience of the 17th century "planting" of Ireland after Cromwell's conquest and subsequent displacements (the defeated were given the choice of "Hell or Connaught," Connaught being the rugged land west of the Shannon River), the dispossessions and resulting uprisings over the next 300 years, and the famine in Ireland during the first half of the 19th century, all accentuated this "land-defined" rather than "town-defined" expression of self. An expression to the point that it seems the marked tendency had a genetic origin. An expression of what is called the clan.

Perhaps. But wideness and expanse in surroundings has deeper, metaphysical origins that beckon beyond the clan.

Ireland to America

Michael O'Loughlin (pronounced O-Lock-lyn) was of the wild Connaught land west of the Shannon River in County Clare on the west face of Ireland, bordering the wide and at times wild North Atlantic. He was born of the union of Matthew O'Loughlin and Ellen Keane near the village of Broadford, a peaty steep land dotted with lakes ("loughs" as they are called in Ireland, or as the same word is spelled in Scotland, "lochs"), about 1815 or so, just as the War of 1812 was ending between Britain and the United States. The English did not allow Catholics to hold public offices, and Irish immigration to America resumed in earnest after the war and grew steadily over the next 30 years. Catholic Emancipation at last began in Ireland in 1829, but Michael and his younger brother went to America. With the vast Atlantic ahead, the teenaged Michael sailed eventually through the Antilles (historical destination of many displaced Irish), arriving after four months in the southern culture of New Orleans in the Louisiana Territory. For three years as a riverman, he continued his voyage, this time up and down the "Father of Waters" which lastly settled him as a merchant in the gateway to the westward migration, St. Louis. Michael's brother drowned in the Mississippi after falling overboard in the night.

Gateway to the West

Michael was locally known as the "Irish Postmaster," as his supply establishment at Main and Spruce, was a point of contact and written communication for the immigrant Irish coming up the Mississippi and moving west. Known for his "generosity of heart and mind," and fine Irish manner, he was "guide, philosopher, and friend" to many. Thus in those immigrant days Michael became the most widely known Irishman in Missouri. Some immigrants arriving in St. Louis were acquaintances from Ireland, such as Thomas King and his wife Katherine McNamara, who came through St. Louis (via Charleston, SC and New Orleans) with their three children around 1847, likely escaping the potato famine (1845-1849) now underway in Ireland. It is said Michael O'Loughlin carried the 4-year old daughter of Thomas King off the river boat when Thomas arrived in St. Louis. Thomas and Katherine's daughter was named Johanna,. After a brief stay, the King family continued up the Missouri River and disembarked at Arrow Rock for the "Irish Settlement" in Saline County where he purchased a section of land from Miles McSweeny who was returning to South Carolina. Such a large tract was likely farmed with slaves.

On May 28, 1854 Michael O'Loughlin wed 19-year old Mary Quinlivan. In 1859, as the Civil War seemed imminent, Michael purchased a half-section of land far up the Merrimac River in what is now Dent County. The contingency of abandoning St. Louis during the Civil War, however, never occurred. Mary Quinlivan died Dec. 30, 1870. One child of the six born, Mary Celestine, survived and married James Brady of St. Louis.

Michael's old friends from Ireland, the King family, had prospered in the Irish settlement in Saline County, now known as Shackelford. Their daughter Mary King (born 1853) attended the Loretto Academy in Florissant, MO. Occasionally Mary's older sister, Johanna, would accompany her in her journey to the St. Louis area. As the O'Loughlin family was the only acquaintance in St. Louis of the King family, it was natural that they would visit. On Thanksgiving day 1872, Michael O'Loughlin married Johanna King at the rectory of the Catholic Church in Shackelford. They resided at Main and Spruce in St. Louis.

Of the six children born of this union, three survived; Solomon (1874-1925), Agnes (1876-1968), and Michael E. (Oct. 9, 1877-1953). Baptisms were at the Old Cathedral and, given the reality of infant mortality, quickly followed birth (Michael E., Oct. 11, 1877). Uncle Sol never married. In October 1898 Aunt Aggie married Jerome Prior from the "Irish Settlement" and returned west to her mother's adopted Saline County. Aggie had attended St. Savior's Academy for Girls in Marshall, MO (staffed by French Notre Dame nuns), and while away at school had met Jerome. Jerome took the entire wedding party along for the honeymoon at the Nebraska State Fair. Johanna King O'Loughlin (died 1923) spent her last 15 years with her daughter in Marshall, MO and is buried with the King family in Mount St. Mary's Cemetery in Shackelford.

The dynamics of immigration, as the frontier moved west and as the railroads replaced the Mississippi as the "path of least resistance" to the frontier, changed the fortunes of Michael O'Loughlin. He moved his store to 14 and Spruce and eventually declared bankruptcy. The "Irish Postmaster" died in 1906 and was interred in the O'Loughlin burial plot of St. Louis' Calvary Cemetery (Section 7, Lot 96) next to Mary Quinlivan.

The Native Generation

Michael E. O'Loughlin was my grandfather and I can remember meeting him only once. I traveled to St. Louis with my father one rainy cool day, and among the many young cousins, seated at the far end of the room, was a fit-looking white-haired man with a square jaw who did not say much and to whom I refused to say anything or to approach.

Michael E. attended, as a boarder, Christian Brothers College at Academy and Easton in St. Louis where he excelled at track and football. A 1894 football teammate was Shapleigh Hunter of New Madrid County. Michael E. graduated in 1895 and worked with his father. In June 1908 Michael E. married Mary Guerin Walsh (1884-1964), a local parish girl whose interest in tennis was the occasion of her friendship with Michael. Mary Guerin Walsh had her own tennis court in the rear of her parents' home. Mary was well-educated (had taken Latin, Greek and German), had two years of teacher training past high school, and taught in the Riddick and Marshall schools in St. Louis. Mary was the only surviving child of Thomas Walsh and Bridget Guerin. Thomas Walsh was from a farm on Lough Derg near the village of Mt. Shannon, County Clare, Ireland. The Guerin family had moved to St. Louis from New Orleans during Reconstruction following the Civil War. Guerin is a Norman name (France), and came to Ireland with the 1169 A. D. invasion led by Richard FitzGilbert de Clare (Strongbow). Of the seven grown children of the Guerin family, only Bridget married, and that was after a two-year delay requested by her mother who was in ill health.

Michael E. O'Loughlin and Mary Guerin Walsh reared six children: Mary Elizabeth (1909-1972); Jane Agnes (1911-1995); Virginia Ann (1914-1976); Thomas King (1915-); Marianne Roberta (1917-2001); and Emily Guerin (1922-). All the O'Loughlin children eventually married and Michael and Mary totaled 17 grandchildren. Michael worked as an appraiser for an asphalting company; he worked for 15 years at the U. S. Post Office, was corporate secretary for the Funsten Fur Company, and was an independent real estate broker for 20 years. Michael E. once suggested to Mary Guerin Walsh that they should move to the wooded half-section of land his father had purchased just prior to the Civil War in Dent County. Mary, a St. Louisan to the bone, was horrified, and, of course, the move to the wooded wilderness never occurred. But some innate orientation to the land is evident in this episode.

Return to the Land

My father, Thomas King O'Loughlin, came to Cape Girardeau in the mid 1930s to attend Southeast Missouri State College. He earned a Bachelors Degree in Science. He also met the lovely Agnes Schmuke of uptown Jackson. She was Sagamore Queen at the college. According to some contemporaries, it was a high romance. Thomas and Agnes were married in the little Catholic Church at Adams and Hope in Jackson just a year before the attack on Pearl Harbor. At their wedding Michael E. O'Loughlin ran into Agnes Schmuke's Uncle Shap. Shapleigh Hunter of New Madrid, from Michael's football days, visited extensively with his old high school chum at the wedding reception.

Thomas was a flight instructor in the Army Air Corps during the war. After the war he started a dairy products distribution company in Jackson, occasionally taught school, and was a Captain in the Army National Guard. After the war (1946) Tom and Ag built a brick home on 1010 West Main in Jackson. There are seven children: Thomas King (1943); Joseph Michael (1947); Timothy Charles (1949); John Patrick (1950); Martha Schmuke (1952); Mary Ann (1954); and Daniel Guerin (1959). The three middle lads attended St. Vincent's College in Cape Girardeau, as their grandfather Joseph Schmuke had. All the children earned university degrees, including one PhD, two Jurist Doctors, and a Masters of Science. But the most unusual aspect of this family is that in 1953 they moved to a farm near Highway 61, north of Fruitland. In this, Thomas King O'Loughlin actualized a tendency evident in his lineage. Against the strongest demographic trends evident in America, he returned to the land. Of course, he had to promise Agnes that she could drive to Jackson each day to visit her mother. She and all her brood drove the seven miles to Jackson many a time to visit Mary Ann Hunter of New Madrid who the children all knew as "Gran" and who had married Joseph Schmuke of Jackson in February 1909.

The history of the Scot-Irish Hunters of New Madrid contains this historical observation of the Celts when they first settled in Cumberland County, PA, before migrating west (written by Sec Logan in 1730). "I must own from my own experience in the land office that the settlement of five families from Ireland gives me more trouble than 50 of any other people." Logan was an Irishman himself. The return to the land meant for the four oldest O'Loughlin boys, early mornings, and long days of farm work and school. The scraps and camaraderie of the brothers left, as the land itself had, an imprint of time and place that tied them to their forebears far beyond memory and written record. The land is thus not merely the physical, but a touchstone of the metaphysical. Not merely economic livelihood (a reality rare today), but an analogy of union. And this brings us to the point and ending of this story.

Land is not really about possession, as the civil law might lead one to believe but rather about union. Union of family to one another. Where spatial openness begets personal openness and generosity. Where the family together helps one another in the struggle, rather than set out against one another. This is the true character of the land. The real value of estate.

And then there is that pleasure in the pathless wood. There is that society where none intrudes. There is rapture on the lonely shore. As if one were by the deep sea, where the music of the Almighty is glassed in its roar.

In the end, we all return to the land. And some across the sea. Home. *Submitted by Tim O'Loughlin*

PEETZ - The Peetz family is very fortunate to have had the original passport of Henrich Patz, wife Henrietta nee Bolm and three children. The writing at the top of the passport beside the two lions is DUKEDOM OF BRAUNSCHWEIG, which establishes the fact that they, at the time of immigration, were living in that small country, and were subjects to the Kingdom of Hanover.

Heinrich Peetz was born in and a resident of Schlewecke, and from there went to Hanover and northwest to Bremen, on the Aller River. They went from Bremen to Bremerhaven, into the North Sea, then across the Atlantic ocean to the Gulf of Mexico and up the Mississippi River to New Orleans. From New Orleans they continued up the Mississippi River by steamboat to Cape Girardeau, MO.

The Peetz family settled about five miles southwest of Jackson, near Tilsit. They purchased the first part of the present 220-acre farm on Feb. 12, 1852. The original farm is presently owned by a fourth generation great-granddaughter.

Johann Henrich Gottlieb Peetz and wife Johanna Sophie Henrietta nee Bolm were both born in Schlwecke, Germany, Kingdom of Hanover. They are buried at St. James United Church of Christ Cemetery at Tilsit, near Jackson, MO. Their oldest son, Henrich (Henry Peetz) married Wilhelmine "Minnie" Meier and both are buried at the Kelso, MO Cemetery. Henrich was born in Schlwecke, Germany, and was the 7-year-old son listed on the passport. Carl Henrich Peetz was born in Schlwecke, Germany and was the 5-year-old son listed on the passport. Marie Madgalene Henriette Peetz was born in Schlwecke, Germany, and was the 4-week-old child mentioned on the passport. Both of these are buried at St. James United Church of Christ Cemetery at Tilsit, near Jackson, MO.

Henrietta Peetz was married to Jacob Brennecke on Feb. 6, 1877. They are buried at Russel Heights Cemetery in Jackson, MO. Carolina Peetz was married to Charles Dralle on April 2, 1888. They are buried at Seward, Stafford County, KS in the Hudson Evangelical Cemetery. August Frederick Peetz was married to Caroline Meier on Jan. 13, 1881. They are buried at St. James United Church of Christ Cemetery at Tilsit, near Jackson, MO. "Wilhelm" William Peetz was married to Augusta Johanna Wilhelmine Meier on June 5, 1890. They are buried at St. James United Church of Christ Cemetery at Tilsit, near Jackson, MO.

This is a very brief overview of the original Peetz family. There is more detailed information on some of the descendants found elsewhere in the book. *Submitted by Patsy Sue Peetz Voshage*

PEETZ – William "Wilhelm" Peetz was born on March 15, 1862 and was married to Augusta Johanna Wilhelmine Meier on June 5, 1890. William died March 29, 1941 and Augusta died on July 10, 1951. Both are buried at St. James United Church of Christ at Tilsit near Jackson. To this union were born 11 children; five died in infancy. They are all buried at St. James Church at Tilsit. Five sons and one daughter that survived were a great help to their parents, as they were farmers. The first part of the 220-acre farm was acquired by Henrich Peetz on Feb. 12, 1852 and William Peetz acquired the farm on April 30, 1890. The Missouri Century Farm is presently owned by one of the granddaughters, Patsy Sue Peetz Voshage.

Leo Peetz, the oldest son, and Amanda Meyer were married on Nov. 27, 1921, both are buried at St. James Church at Tilsit. They were the parents of four daughters. Wilma Vera Peetz married Howard William Nations (deceased). Wilma presently lives in St. Charles, MO. Norma Peetz married Walter Sewing on July 28, 1946, and they reside in Jackson, MO. Esther Peetz married Frank Roberts and they reside in Flippin, AR. Charleen Maxine Peetz married Luther Dean Statler on Dec. 30, 1953 and they reside in Edwardsville, IL.

Alvin Peetz married Lena Sperling on Oct. 4, 1922. Both are buried at St. James Church at Tilsit near Jackson. They had one son, Ervin Peetz. Ervin married Della Mae Maag (deceased). Ervin lives on the family farm west of Gordonville.

Anna Peetz, the only daughter, married Daniel Meyer on Dec. 10, 1921. They had no children. Anna lived to the age of 101, and she passed away on Feb. 28, 2000. They are both buried at Russell Heights Cemetery in Jackson, MO.

Joseph Peetz married Minnie A. Voges on Dec. 3, 1924. Both are buried at St. James Church at Tilsit. They had two sons and one daughter. Earl William Peetz married Dorothy Maag (deceased). Earl lives south of Jackson, MO. Marvin Henry Peetz married Barbara Jean Friedrich on May 23, 1951. Marvin and Barbara live in Jackson, MO. Lorene Marie Peetz married Gilbert N. Gross (deceased). Lorene lives in Gordonville, MO.

Benjamin Peetz and Mae Emily Sachse were married on Aug. 1, 1937. Both are deceased. They are buried at Russell Heights in Jackson, MO. Ben and Mae hd no children.

Emil Herman Peetz and Stella Marie Sachse were married on Dec. 16, 1934. Both are deceased and are buried at Russell Heights at Jackson, MO. Emily and Stella had two children, Robert William Peetz (deceased), who is buried at Russell Heights in Jackson, MO and Patsy Sue Peetz, who married Jerry Lee Voshage on Nov. 22, 1968. They live near Jackson, MO.

The rest of the descendants, children of the 10 grandchildren, are not mentioned. The two large barns are presently standing on the original farm. *Submitted by Patsy Sue Peetz Voshage*

PENNY - The Reverend Charles Cullen Penny (1812-1852) was born in Lincoln County, NC, and immigrated to Missouri in 1831 where he lived in Perry County for one year then moved to Cape Girardeau County. He was an itinerant minister of the Methodist Episcopal Church and died at age 40 while holding a meeting at York Chapel in Longtown, MO. He was married to Mary Dorcas Sides, also born in North Carolina, and they had four sons and four daughters. John Monroe Penny was the oldest son, and he married Susannah Drum who was the daughter of John Drum and Mary Polly Fulbright. The John Drum family settled in the Oak Ridge Area when John was 11 years old. He settled on his own farm near Oak Ridge in 1833 and owned a lot of land. He served as Judge and assessor in Cape County and as state representative.

John and Susannah Penny had 12 children and one son was George Columbus "Lum" Penny (1855- 1921), born near Daisy, MO, who married Julie Johnson. The Penny family was believed to be of Pennsylvania Dutch ancestry. Susannah Drum was of Hunsaker and Drum families and was of German ancestry. John Monroe Penny and his brother, George, were very active in the Methodist Church in Oak Ridge, MO. George was one of the first trustees of the church.

George "Lum" and Julia Penny had four sons and four daughters. George "Lum" played a fiddle and several other family members played musical instruments. The third son was Stephen Marshall Penny (1882- 1942) who married Catherine Laura Proctor. Stephen worked for construction and owned property in the Cape Girardeau area. He was killed in an accident while working on the Mississippi River bridge at Cape Girardeau.

Stephen Marshall Penny and wife, Laura Catherine (Proctor) Penny, with children, Lloyd, Ruby, and Lyman, taken about 1920. Another daughter, Ruth, was born later.

Stephen and Laura Penny had two sons, Lloyd William (1910-1976) and Lyman (1918-1959), and two daughters, Ruby and Ruth. Lloyd married Cora Belle Bowman (1911-1964) and had three sons; Jackie (1934-1946), Floyd (1939) and Eugene (1942). Floyd has three sons, Stephen, Terry and Scott. Stephen has two sons, Stephen and Sam.

This is a chronicle of eight generations of males in the Penny family since they came to Cape Girardeau County and the research is on-going for generations before coming to Cape Girardeau County. There is information of people by the name of Penney coming to Cape Girardeau about 1805 and some believe them to be related to the Penny family of Oak Ridge and some do not. *Submitted by Loine Penny*

PENSEL - The Pensel family immigrated to the United States from Dochenan, Byron, Germany, on the vessel *Rein* in approximately 1889. Wolfgang, along with his wife Maria Magdalene Mueller Pensel, arrived at the port of Maryland and traveled inland to establish a new home. Their 12-year-old son Christian later told stories of the difficult travel on ship and their oppression on the home country. They encountered a severe storm while on the ship and were thrown off course leaving them lost and wandering for a period of time. Sickness became common and death followed leaving others to face severe malnutrition and near starvation. Christian told of boiling leather for soup, and loved ones who died were put overboard, creating much sorrow. Wolfgang led his family to a 57 acre tract of land along Horrell Creek southeast of Oak Ridge. They established a home on a limestone bluff overlooking the creek. A strong spring, which continues to flow today at the base of the bluff, was a prime attraction for the home site not only as a source of fresh water, but also as a place to keep perishable foods cool.

Christian married Caroline Hannah Fredricks and settled on an adjoining tract of land which previously belonged to the Wolfenkoehler and Russell families. This union produced two children, Louis Robert and Linda Marie Pensel Malone. The family was very instrumental in the development of the Saint John's Evangelical and Reformed Church, now the St. John's United Church of Christ, located nearby. A German school, which Louis attended, was located on the property. All instruction was in German and only German was spoken in the home. The German Bible is still in possession of the family.

Louis married Edna Catherine Kasten from Old Appleton. They purchased the farm from Christian and his wife and later added an 80-acre tract on the northeast corner of the original tract from the Ella Anderson family. The original tract has been in the family for more than a century and continues to be operated by the family. Louis and Edna reared five children on the farm. They are Carl Robert, Raymond Ernest, twin sons Harold Lee and Gerald Lynn, and Mary Catherine Feemster. Louis and Edna were very active in the community and added much to the life of the St. John's church. Louis held most every leadership position within the church, taught Sunday School, and on occasion led the worship when a pastor was not available. Louis was a strong supporter of public education and served many years as a director of the Three Director Schoenebeck School. He saw the need and gave strong support for the reorganization of the many smaller districts into a larger district for better efficiency and improved quality of education. He believed that the ideals of 4-H held much potential for developing social and leadership skills and gave generously of his time to assure that each youth of the community had the opportunity to develop their full potential. Several first, second and third generation descendants of Louis and Edna continue to reside in the Jackson area.

PENZEL - The Penzel family ancestors came to Jackson in 1853. Johann Gottlieb, his wife, Christina Zapf Penzel, and their six daughters came from Gettengrün in Saxony. Their son, Gustave, was born here in 1855. Johann Gottlieb Penzel bought a farm a few miles north of Jackson and the family lived there until 1867. Then he bought a large lot near Jackson on what is now Missouri and Cherry Streets and built a brick house on that street corner. That house burned later. Lots were also sold on Cherry Street west to Russell Street.

The daughters all married a few years after they arrived here. Their married names were Christiane Hoffman, Augusta Doering, Ernestine Kromann, Fredericke Scheppelmann, Emilie Kaufmann and Antonia Reitzel. All of them lived in or near Jackson except Fredericka who lived in Cape Girardeau.

In 1881 Johann sold a lot next to his house on Missouri Street to his son Gustave and Gustave's wife, Caroline Brennecke. Caroline Brennecke Penzel's father, George Henry Brennecke, and her grandfather, Johann August Brennecke, died in August and October 1856, presumably from cholera, when Caroline was only 1 year old. Caroline's mother remarried and they lived near Tilsit. Caroline wanted more education than she could get at a church school, so she talked to Linus Sanford, who was president of the Jackson School Board, to see if she could attend the Jackson school. He and his wife let Caroline stay with them and help with the housework. At that time, with none of our modern conveniences such as electricity and running water, people with large houses had someone to help them with their work. Mrs. Sanford taught her many things and often advised her.

Johann was a carpenter and brought some of his carpenter tools with him from Germany. His son Gustave was also a carpenter and built a number of houses, store buildings, and country schools, and a Lutheran Church.

Penzel brothers: Linus, Alvin, Robert, Emil, about 1910

Gustave and his wife had four sons, Linus, Robert, and twins Alvin and Emil. Linus became a contractor and builder. He built many houses in Jackson and the vicinity as well as many larger schools, business buildings, churches, and then bridges and culverts in southeast Missouri. He and his son Carl founded Penzel Construction Company after Carl became a partner in the business. Later Carl's son Gene and grandsons, Philip and Chris, joined the business. The company has built many buildings and larger bridges and continues yet today.

The second son of Gustave and Lena Fenzel was Robert. He met his wife-to-be at the *Cape County Post* newspaper office. She was from Chicago. They married and moved to Chicago. Alvin, one of Gustave's twins, married Eula Miller. He became a banker at Cape County Bank. They had three children, Helen Miller Ritgerod, George and Charles. Emil, the other twin, received a law degree from the University of Michigan, graduating with the highest grades in his class. He later was a Missouri State Senator.

There were also four daughters in the Linus Penzel family. They were Margaret Beaver, Miriam Wallenmeyer, Elizabeth Shinaberry, and Eloise Kroell. *Submitted by Miriam Wallenmeyer*

PHILLIPS - Moses Phillips and his wife Nancy were settlers in the early 1800s along Sexton Creek in Alexander County, IL. Moses was an early justice of the peace and one of the first school teachers at McRaven School House there. He and his family are listed on the 1830 and 1840 census of Alexander County, IL.

Moses and Nancy had two known daughters, Sarah and Lucinda Caroline Phillips. Lucinda was born Dec. 25, 1829 and married Medad Masterson on Jan. 1, 1850 in Cape Girardeau County. They settled on his farm in the Cape La Croix Creek area on the Perryville Road. They had a family of eight children.

Sitting: William Rilet Whittaker, Margaret Minerva Sadler Whittaker, Homer Behymer, Cornelia Louise "Stacy" Whittaker Behymer. Standing: Ed English, Nettie Whittaker English, Ed Whittaker, Ellen Whittaker Walsh and Ed Walsh. Occasion: Margaret Minerva Sadler Whittaker's 75th birthday, Sept. 11, 1921.

Sarah Phillips was born in Illinois May 28, 1827 and married Christopher W. Whittaker on Aug. 6, 1843 in Cape Girardeau, MO. They settled in Neely's Landing, MO. Christopher died Jan. 2, 1870 and was buried in the Neely's Landing Cemetery. Sarah's second marriage was to John Bonney on Oct. 22, 1878. Sarah died Dec. 17, 1902, and is buried in the Shiloh Cemetery, Pocahontas, MO.

Sarah Phillips and Christopher W. Whittaker's children were: William Rilet was born April 8, 1845 and married Margaret Minerva Sadler; Martha was born about 1847; John was born May 1, 1849; James Richard was born April 5, 1850 and married Emily Johanna Garner; Mary E. was born Dec. 13, 1852; Sarah Jane was born about 1855; Cornelia Louise was born 1857 and married James Homer Behymer; Maria Catherine was born about 1859; Edward C. was born about 1862 and married Susan E. Samuels; Nettie M. was born about 1864 and married Ed English; and Ellen Eleanor was born Oct. 5, 1868 and married Edward Walsh.

William Rilet Whittaker was a carpenter by trade. He served in the Civil War as a private in Co. E 8th Regiment Provisional Missouri Militia. For nearly two years Whittaker was stationed with the Federal forces near Allenville and helped bury the dead following the massacre at Round Pond when Gen. Marmaduke raided a Federal supply train company there and killed all of the members. For a time Whittaker was stationed at Fort D, near the present site of the May Greene school. He was also stationed at Ironton and it is believed that he took part in the battle of Pilot Knob, at the foot of which mountain was located Fort Davidson. After the surrender of the South, Whittaker received his discharge at Iron Mountain, the Federal soldiers in that vicinity being disbanded there. William died March 4, 1929.

William Rilet Whittaker and Margaret Minerva Sadler were parents of 11 children: Sara Ann was born July 6, 1865; Charles Christopher was born Dec. 19, 1866 and married Alice May Fulbright; William Elza was born March 28, 1869 and married Sallie Carter Simpson; Arthur C. was born Feb. 24, 1871; Rosa Lee was born Sept. 18, 1873 and married first Ernst Wagner on April 2, 1893 and second to Louis Stoll in October 1933; Joseph Russell was born Sept. 22, 1876 and married Dora B. Lynn; Mary E. was born July 1, 1879; Maggie I. was born Sept. 14, 1881 and married a Copeland; Samuel Vinyard was born Dec. 11, 1883; Effie was born April 29, 1886; and Emma Serena was born July 24, 1888 and married Edgar Wilson. *Submitted by JoAnn Caldwell Wilson, granddaughter of Ernst and Rosa Lee Wagner*

PHILLIPS – Calvin Phillips was born in Perry County, MO, in 1929, to Cleve and Viola McFarland Phillips. His parents and other ancestors were farmers. One of his maternal ancestors was a Boyd who emigrated from England in 1754 and his wife was from Wales. One of their children served in the Revolutionary War. The Boydville Inn in Martinsburg, WV, is situated on 10 acres containing majestic old trees. General Boyd's law office still remains on the property where strategy for the War of 1812 was planned. The manor house, now Inn, was saved from burning during the Civil War by the direct intervention of President Lincoln. Boydville has welcomed presidents, generals, ambassadors, senators, and many other fine folks for nearly 200 years. One of Calvin's paternal ancestors was an American Indian.

Calvin and Dorothy Phillips, July 2000, 50th Wedding Anniversary.

In 1950 Calvin married Dorothy Bangert who was born in 1931 in Bollinger County. Her parents were William and Myrtle Blaylock Bangert, and three of her brothers, Dewey, Wilbur, and Pervis, served in WWII. Calvin and Dorothy's' first home was in Cape Girardeau County. In 1952 they moved into the city of Jackson where they lived until 1987 when they moved back to rural Cape Girardeau County. They had three daughters: Judy (Snyder), Cynthia Phillips, and Holly (Drum). Calvin and Dorothy started an excavating and trucking business in 1955, which they operated for nearly 40 years, and they continue to operate a silica gravel pit on their land.

Dorothy's paternal genealogy finds the Bangerts coming from Germany in the mid 1800s and they were farmers. The maternal ancestry includes the Blaylock lineage, which came to America from Cumberland County, England, in 1622. Thomas Blalock, as it was spelled then, settled in Accomac County on the Peninsula of Virginia, known as the Eastern Shore. The descendants gradually moved westward through Virginia, North Carolina, and on to Missouri with some continuing on to California. Dorothy's maternal grandmother was a Barks and they emigrated from Germany in the early 1720s.

Dorothy has been very active over the years as a volunteer. Many hours were spent working with youth, scout troops and church groups. She also served on the Girl Scout Council for many years and served as President of the Council for five years. Dorothy was also a member of the Jackson School Board, serving terms as Treasurer and President. She has been active in First Presbyterian Church as Session Clerk, Financial Secretary, and as an ordained Elder and Deacon, as well as serving on the Council of Giddings Lovejoy Presbytery.

Calvin and Dorothy both have enjoyed outdoors activities over the years and traveled a lot with their children as they were growing up. Many summer weekends were spent camping with the children near Castor River. This was an escape from the business, which was run out of the home. They continue to spend much of their "retirement" time as volunteers and enjoy RVing, fishing, hunting, gardening, and tending to the acreage surrounding their rural home built in 1987, but their biggest joy is spending time with their four grandchildren. *Submitted by Dorothy Phillips*

PIERCE – Walter M. Pierce was born Aug. 8, 1940 in Natoma, KS, the son of Orval Hollan and Glenn (Stokes) Pierce. Orval was born in 1900 and passed away in 1970. Glenna was born Sept. 24, 1906 and died on Sept. 20, 1990. Ten children were born of this union: Rosemary; Marjorie; Velna; Clyta; Delores; Raymond; Richard; Walter; Iva and Donna.

Walter grew up in the northwest Kansas community of Morland from age 4 through high school. At age 14 he left home for work on a nearby farm which offered room and board and the opportunity to attend high school. Walt graduated as salutatorian of his class in 1958. Upon graduation he worked for K & E Drilling of Wichita, KS, as a roughneck on a wildcat drilling rig; he became a driller at age 21. In 1963-65 he served in the U. S. Army, with basic training at Fort Leonard Wood and advanced training in materials testing at Fort Belvoir, VA, and he served 16 months overseas with the 94th Engineering Battalion in Esslingen, Germany. Upon release from the military, Walt worked for the Department of Defense at Tinker Air Force Base, Oklahoma City, as a sheet metal mechanic on B-52 bombers, while attending the University of Oklahoma. Walt received his B.S.M.E. degree in mechanical engineering in December 1970. He immediately was hired by Procter and Gamble to assist in management of their new diaper plant located north of Cape Girardeau, and he moved into the Cape Girardeau-Jackson area.

Sally Kaye (Galbraith) Pierce's parents were Joe L. (b. March 25, 1915; d. March 29, 1947) and Helen (b. March 19, 1917; d. Dec. 24, 1999) (Squibb) Galbraith. Sally was born on Feb. 1, 1943, in Springfield, MO. Sally's father died when she was 4, so she and her mother lived with her beloved great-aunt and great-uncle, Eurith and Bruce Pickering, on a farm north of Republic. In 1951 her mother, Helen, married Emerson E. Taylor (b. July 31, 1912; d. May 30, 1991) who had three sons; Jim, Bill and Bob. Sally grew up on the Taylor farm and graduated from Republic High School in 1961. She then attended Southwest Missouri State University in Springfield, graduating with a B.S.Ed. in 1965. Sally taught English in two different southwest Missouri communities before becoming an elementary librarian in Ava. During summers she attended the University of Oklahoma and received her Masters Degree in Library Science in 1972.

Walter M. and Sally K. Pierce

Walt and Sally met in 1970 while both were attending Oklahoma University and dated until their marriage on June 7, 1974, in Springfield. Sally and Walt purchased their home at 2812 Hilltop Drive in Jackson in early 1974 and moved there upon their marriage. Walt continued work at Procter and Gamble, and Sally began working in 1976 as a library assistant at Jackson Public Library, then located at 225 S. High; she became director of Jackson Public Library in March 1988.

The Pierces adopted two children, Teresa and Randy, who both graduated from Jackson High in 1991 and 1994 respectively. Teresa is now the mother of Taylor, Kay-Tee-Lyn, and BilLeigh. Randy and his wife Michelle are parents of Gavin.

Sally has had horses since she was a child, so the Pierces now keep their horses (Arabians and Quarter Horses) on land (purchased in 1985) on Highway 25 South, which was a portion of the old Adolph Kies estate. Walt and Sally are both active in New McKendree United Methodist Church, the Jackson Optimist Clubs, and other civic organizations.

Walt and Sally purchased their current home at 1145 Shady Lane, Jackson, in 1998. In 2000 Walt retired from Procter and Gamble. Sally continues as director of Jackson Public Library. *Submitted by Sally Pierce*

POE - Jessie Marvin Poe was the youngest of nine children born to Isaiah Haiston and Martha Elizabeth (Williams) Poe. Marvin was born April 6, 1891, when his father and mother were managing Cape County Poor Farm from 1884 until 1906. They moved from there to a farm east of Jackson and he attended Kage Elementary School. Later they moved to the "Old Toll Gate" house on Old Cape Road and Marvin went to Jackson High School.

On May 31, 1914, Marvin married Lula Maud Cavaner (born Aug. 17, 1891), daughter of George Washington Cavaner and Mahala Katherine (Crites) Cavaner from Lutesville. At the age of 16 she came to Burfordville to live with Mr. and Mrs. J. R. Bowman and later when they moved to Jackson, she came with them; the house was across the street from Marvin Poe and his parents.

Marvin worked for McAtee Mercantile Company and drove a team of horses to take grocery orders and delivered them later in the afternoon; telephones were scarce. He became acquainted with Lula when he took orders for the Bowman family - thus began a courtship. They were married in the Methodist Parsonage on Florence Street in Jackson by Rev. Clarence Burton, on a Sunday morning before church; they

Lula Maud (Cavaner) and Jessie Marvin Poe

drove there in his father's horse and buggy. They had bought a home on 220 North Missouri Street (torn down recently to make room for an addition to the county jail as of 2000).

From 1925 - 1931 he was part owner of McAtee Mercantile Company. For 20 years Marvin was a member of the Volunteer Fire Department, a member of the Home Guard during WWI, a 56-year member of the Masonic Lodge, and a life-long member of New McKendree Methodist Church.

Marvin never owned a car; he always lived uptown and was close to all his needs. Every Sunday afternoon he walked out to Old Cape Road to visit his parents while they lived there. His mother died in 1928 and his father in 1930. In 1945 Marvin was badly injured in an accident and spent many weeks hospitalized and in bed; thereafter he used a cane.

Lula and Marvin had four children: Mary Louise (born April 29, 1915) married John R. Smith on Jan. 4, 1936 and they have two sons, Mike and Tim; Leo Elwood "Pete" (born Feb. 8, 1920) married Marjorie Blumer (deceased) on Feb. 14, 1941 and they had three children, Betty, Emily and David; Betty Jane (born March 29, 1924 - now deceased) married Frank Garratt on Nov. 1, 1953 and they had four children: Bart; David; Janet and Nancy; and John Wm. "Bill" (born June 3, 1926) married Mary Lou Seabaugh (deceased) on July 1949 and they had one child, John Wm. Jr.

Lula Poe became a member of the Methodist Church on March 9, 1914, and in later years all the children and spouses except one became members. Lula was a long-time member of the Wesleyan Service Guild. Marvin died in 1975 and Lula in 1991. Marvin was a humble person but proud of his parents and ancestors. He was a fifth generation of William Williams, who gave two acres of land for Old McKendree Chapel and was actually "the founder" of the Chapel near Jackson. Mr. Williams arrived in Cape Girardeau County from Kentucky ca 1797 and died in 1838. The line of descent from William Williams was Isaac, Jacob, Martha Elizabeth Williams (Mrs. I. H. Poe), and then Marvin. *Submitted by Doris Brennecke Davault with information furnished by Mrs. John (Mary Louise Smith)*

PROBST – Henry Conrad Bartels, Louise Lohkamp, John Probst and Dorothea Voges all emigrated from Germany to Missouri in the 1840s and 1850s with their parents. The stories of these four people would become entwined through their descendants.

Henry Bartels was born on Feb. 2, 1826 in Sende, Germany, and immigrated at the age of 18. He resided first near Commerce and later in Cape Girardeau where he ran a cooper shop for nearly half a century. On April 16, 1863 he married Louise Lohkamp (Oct. 20, 1840-Jan. 9, 1913), daughter of William and Henrietta Maria (Han) Lohkamp, who resided near Egypt Mills. Henry died on Feb. 28, 1918 at the age of 92. The Bartels had eight children: Carolyn Louise (March 2, 1864-May 23, 1931, married Robert Probst); Henry J. (July 1867, later lived in Primrose, IA); Fredonia "Dena" (Feb. 5, 1870-May 28, 1926, married John C. Randol, Cape Girardeau); Emma (June 5, 1872-Feb. 5, 1925, married Dr. Silas W. Morgan, lived at Shawneetown); William Gustav (Jan. 19, 1875-Aug. 22, 1947); Clara Alma (July 26, 1877-1931); Meta (Nov. 5, 1879-May 6, 1905); and Dr. Leo W. G. (March 13, 1884-January 1970, lived in St. Louis).

John Probst was born on July 6, 1826 in Germany and immigrated prior to 1858. He met and married Dorothea Voges (Oct. 7, 1835-Oct. 28, 1910), daughter of Johanne Louise Christina (Vasterling) Voges Sperling. The Probsts had five children, two daughters of whom little is known and three sons. The eldest, Robert, was born July 1, 1858 in Pilot Knob; the other two boys were Frederick "Fritz" (Dec. 16, 1863-Sept. 18, 1890) and Heinrich Carl "Charlie" (Feb. 6, 1866-1924). Only Robert married and he met his future wife as a boy when his family moved back to Cape Girardeau and lived in the same duplex as the Bartels family. Robert's parents would later move to a farm southwest of Gordonville.

Robert Probst married Carolyn Bartels on Feb. 25, 1886. They resided on the Probst farm, raising a family of nine children: Louis (Jan. 23, 1887-Jan. 23, 1995, Kansas City); Walter (Oct. 3, 1889-Nov. 13, 1966, Perryville); Emil (Nov. 3, 1891-April 1, 1973, Milwaukee, WI); Arnold (Dec. 4, 1893-July 12, 1963, Santa Monica, CA); Louise (Dec. 31, 1895-Oct. 31, 1982, Clem Kinder); Alma (March 26, 1898-April 11, 1981, Jake Koch); Robert (Feb. 28, 1900-Feb. 2, 1972, Hayward, CA); Clara (July 21, 1902-July 15, 1986, Arthur Hager); and Dorothy Elsie (Oct. 22, 1906-June 11, 1999).

Dorothy married Albert Henry Macke (Dec. 21, 1905-Dec. 23, 1957) on Oct. 23, 1929. They lived in Gordonville where they operated Macke's Store until Dorothy retired in 1974, selling part of the business. Dorothy was a faithful member of Christ Lutheran Church of Gordonville, worked with 4-H for 40 years and was active in the local Homemakers. The couple had three children, Henry Weldon (Aug. 16, 1930), Dorothy Ann (Aug. 11, 1932) (see Ueleke/Schlueter entry), and Alberta Louise (Nov. 5, 1945). Alberta attended Jackson High School, graduating in 1963. She received a B.S. degree in Education in 1967 from Southeast Missouri State College. She received her Masters Degree from the University of Missouri in 1971 and taught at the University High School. She married Robert Neil Dougan (April 30, 1945) on July 17, 1971. She received her PhD from Indiana University, Bloomington, and is currently a professor in the Department of History at Southeast Missouri State University. She served as chair of the History Department from 1991-2001. Neil is a pipefitter with Pipe Fitters Local 562 and the couple currently resides in Jackson. *Submitted by Alberta Macke Dougan*

PULS – Adrian J. Puls was born in 1840, a native of the Netherlands. At age 28 he became a citizen of the United States in Iron County, MO on Sept. 18, 1869. He was appointed Justice of the Peace in the township of Arcadia on Jan. 22, 1874, and County Surveyor on Feb. 14, 1870. He received his Missouri state teachers certificate, high qualifications on Feb. 17, 1871.

Annie Louise Behrens (born Aug. 15, 1851) married Adrian J. Puls on Dec. 21, 1871; he was a civil engineer of Iron County, where they made their home until his death. They had four children: Henry Puls, born Oct. 9, 1872; Annie Puls (Mrs. John Hallisburton), born May 18, 1875; Clara Puls (Mrs. H. H. Hope), born March 5, 1877; and Oliver H. Puls, born 1879, died 1913; and they had five grandchildren: Henry Puls Jr.; Edwin Puls; Clara Louis Hope, died Oct. 17, 1972; Mrs. Ruth Hunt and Adrian Puls. Annie had two brothers, Charles Behrens and A. P. Behrens. As a small child living in Pilot Knob, MO, Annie Behrens hid in a cave with her family during the Civil War.

Henry Puls, son of Adrian J. and Annie Behrens Puls, was born in Pilot Knob, MO on Oct. 9, 1872. He moved to Jackson with his mother when he was 7 years old. He attended Jackson schools and a business college in St. Louis. In financial and political circles he was considered one of the best. It can be said he was a product of the school of thrift and investments, whether it was business or a personal nature. He also was Jackson Postmaster, City Clerk, County Clerk and President of Cape County Savings Bank until his death. He was a member of the Evangelical Church of Jackson. He married Addie Russell on March 5, 1914; to their union was born two sons. Henry Puls Jr. was born March 4, 1916 and Edwin Russell Puls was born Oct. 3, 1918. Henry married Doris Long on July 3, 1948. They had four children: Mary; Linda; Henry Charles and Carol.

Edwin Russell Puls was born Oct. 3, 1918 and died Dec. 22, 1998. Edwin was a long-time banker. Edwin married Evelyn Burk who was born Aug. 1, 1921. Their children were Van Henry Puls, born June 23, 1948 and Russell Edwin Puls, born Aug. 16, 1952 and died Aug. 5, 1993.

Van Henry Puls married Patricia Wulff on Nov. 15, 1967. Their children were Shannon Van Puls, born June 16, 1969 and Drew Hayes Puls, born Oct. 11, 1976.

Shannon Van Puls married Katrina Bolen on Dec. 22, 1990. Their children were Gabriel Miles Puls, born June 10, 1991 and Megan Lynley Puls, born Nov. 25, 1997. Drew Hayes Puls married Traci Miller on Aug. 17, 1996. She was born Aug. 27, 1975. They are divorced. Their children were Gage Hayes Puls, born March 3, 1997 and Addison Renee Puls, born Feb. 13, 1999. *Submitted by Evelyn Puls*

Standing: Henry Puls Sr., Edwin Russell Puls holding Van Henry Puls; seated, Anna Behrens and Addison Puls, Oct. 16, 1949

PUTZ - Henry William Putz, son of Joseph Putz and Josefa (Reisenbichler-Kain) Putz, was born a few miles east of Pocahontas, MO on Nov. 11, 1871. He received his elementary education in the St. John Lutheran parochial school and worked on the parental farm until he entered the employ of Landgraf and Kieninger, building contractors, as a carpenter's apprentice at the age of 18 years. In 1889 he began working as a salesman in the Schoen Brothers Mercantile business in Pocahontas. On Dec. 27, 1893 he was married to Christiana Johana Ruehling. Five children would be born to this union: Fredrick; Elmer; Olga; Hugo; and Dillman.

He resigned the position at Schoen Brothers Mercantile in 1905 when he was appointed as the first Rural Free Delivery mail carrier out of Pocahontas. For the 11 years he held this position, he never missed a single day, summer or winter, delivering the mail to the area farmers. His green buggy and the well-groomed horse was always a welcome site to the farmers in the rural area, and many of them would go to their

Henry W. Putz

mail box waiting for Henry to bring them their mail. They never had to wait very long as they knew their mailman would arrive about the same time every day. During this time he lived on the family farm, but after a short time he found that farming and the mail route was too much, so he moved back to Pocahontas. Then he purchased the mercantile business of C. A. Morton in Leemon. The family then moved back to Pocahontas, and then Henry found work in a powder plant in Nashville, TN. During this time, Mr. and Mrs. Putz and their son Dillman lived in a rental apartment. In the spring of 1918, during WWI, he began working in a shipyard in Jacksonville, FL. Mrs. Putz and her son had moved back to Pocahontas, where he joined them in 1919.

He resumed work as a carpenter and builder, in which vocation he remained until he was appointed Deputy County Welfare officer, which position he held until he was elected County Treasurer in 1923, holding this office for eight years. Following his service as County Treasurer, he resumed work as a carpenter and painter. He loved the outdoors and spent much time in his truck patch and orchard. Mrs. Putz was the Pocahontas telephone operator and Henry assisted her at the switchboard. As he became more familiar with telephones, he served the area as a telephone repairman. Many phones were brought to his home, which he usually repaired without charge. He was commissioned as Notary Public and as such wrote many wills for his friends and neighbors, these too without charge. On July 31, he was appointed as Secretary of the Board of Education at Pocahontas Public School, and for 20 plus years he held the office of Secretary of St. John Lutheran Church. He was Pocahontas Correspondent for the Jackson weekly papers. He was generous to a fault and was always ready to serve in any capacity and anywhere that his assistance was needed. He, along with A. B. Mueller, developed the small park in the center of the town of Pocahontas.

Henry W. Putz died at his home in Pocahontas Feb. 7, 1952. Mrs. Putz died March 31, 1965. *Submitted by Dillman Putz*

PUTZ - The family history of John G. Putz and Henry W. Putz, based on information available, has its beginning Jan. 9, 1829. It was then that the father of the Putz brothers, Joseph Putz, was born in the small Village of Goisorn in the Carpathian Mountains in upper Austria. He was the son of Leopold and Maria Putz.

At the age of 29 years he, with others, decided to embark on a new life and come to the United States. They emigrated in November 1858. The trip across the Atlantic lasted seven weeks, during which time water and rations became exhausted. The vessel finally docked at Baltimore, MD, and the emigrants proceeded to St. Louis, MO by railroad. There they took passage on a Mississippi River steamer to Neely's Landing in Cape Girardeau County. As there were no railroads in that part of the Missouri at that time, friends who had preceded them to this country awaited them and took them to their homes near the present site of Pocahontas.

The search for land began immediately, and Joseph Putz found a 40-acre tract, about one and one-half miles east of the present site of Pocahontas. On Jan. 1, 1859 Joseph Putz was married to Katherina Pilz, who had come over on the same sailing vessel. Two children were born to them, Maria Theresia and Joseph Frank. Joseph Putz enlisted and fought in the War Between the States. On his return home following the war, he found his wife gravely ill and she died in 1866, leaving the young farmer with two motherless children. On Jan. 28 he was married the second time. His second wife was Mrs. Josephine Kain, the widow of John Kain. She was the daughter of Mathias and Johanna Reisenbichler and was born on June 1, 1844. Two sons were born to them, John G. and Henry W. The modest farm home was their birthplace.

Now the brothers' lives would change. John G. Putz, having lived on the farm and roamed the surrounding hills, acquired the love of nature. He attended the Lutheran parochial school and the public school at Pocahontas. At the age of 20 years he was employed by the Litzenfelner Brothers at Neely's Landing in the General Mercantile business. After leaving that position he entered the employ of James C. Thompson at Pocahontas, where he worked as a clerk in the general store. He also worked as Second Miller in the flour mill, as a lumber jack in the saw mill and as a general roustabout on the farm. When the village of Pocahontas was incorporated in 1893, he became the first town clerk. He also served as a member of the town band, secretary of the creamery company and secretary of St. John Lutheran church. In this church he was the organist for many years and also the director of the choir.

John G. Putz

John G. Putz and Selma Bertha Koenig were married Oct. 29, 1893, and lived in a small house on Abernathy Street. They returned to the home farm in 1895 and remained there until he was elected County Treasurer in 1904, and moved to Jackson Jan. 3, 1905. He was elected to another two-year term November of 1906. The terms of County Treasurer was then changed to four years, and he was elected to the first four-year term in 1908, serving until 1912 as County Treasurer. He was then appointed as Deputy Recorder by G. F. Siemers, serving under him for four years and then 12 years under Siemers' successor, F. H. Schrader. During that time he also served as Justice of The Peace and as such married over 2000 couples. Most of these marriages were performed without charge. Although John Putz was very busy serving the county in the various positions he held, he was identified with and most interested in many civic and cultural developments of the city of Jackson. He was always among the first to volunteer anywhere he could be of service. He helped plan and assisted in the promotion of Jackson's first Homecomers reunion in 1908. He was in charge of the local weather bureau for 53 years. His interest in the County Historical Society resulted in him being the custodian of many valuable papers and records. He was a staunch supporter and promoter of the city library. He loved and was an authority on flowers. He wrote many articles for the *Southeast Missourian* and the *Cape County Post*.

Mr. Putz never owned a car and anytime he wanted to take a trip or take his family on an outing, he would engage the service of the city taxi. On one of these outings, he had Rev. Walter Keisker and his wife join him. This outing would take the group to a wooded area that is now part of the Trail of Tears Park. It was here that John Putz told his friends that "this would be an excellent place for a state park – nothing will ever come of it though." Fifteen years later, on April 24, 1956, the Trail of Tears park board issue was passed, authorizing the purchase of 3000 acres for park purposes.

The family continued to grow and soon their first home in Jackson became too small, so a larger home on 208 West Washington was purchased. This would be the home of many of the 12 children of John G. and Selma Putz. He was an early riser and was always the first person to arrive in the courthouse office, many times before the custodian arrived. Mr. Putz never amassed a great amount of wealth, yet he always provided all of the necessities for his large family. This home on West Washington would be his last Jackson residence as he died on Thursday, Oct. 9, 1945 having reached the age of 75 years. Mrs. Putz died on May 18, 1956. *Submitted by Dillman Putz*

QUINN - Hugh R. Quinn was born July 27, 1857 in St. Louis, MO, the son of Dr. Hugh R. Quinn and Bridget Duffy Quinn. His father, Dr. Quinn, died while he was an infant. Bridget Duffy was born in Ballymote, Ireland, on Dec. 25, 1825, and came to the United States as a young girl along with her sisters, Margaret and Catherine. Catherine Duffy is buried in the City Cemetery, Jackson, MO. She was never married. Margaret Duffy was married to Patrick Quinn and they are also buried in the City Cemetery. Bridget Duffy and Dr. Quinn were married in Cincinnati, OH and three sons were born to them, only one of whom, Hugh R. Quinn, survived childhood.

On April 25, 1860, at St. Vincent's Catholic Church in Cape Girardeau, Bridget Duffy Quinn was joined in marriage to Phillip A. Reilly. The family resided in Jackson, MO where Phillip Reilly was working as a wagon-maker. On Aug. 8, 1862, Phillip Reilly was enrolled in Company B, 29th Regiment of Missouri Volunteers at Cape Girardeau. He was captured by the Confederate Army at Ringgold, GA, and sent to the Andersonville prison where he died May 24, 1864. Phillip and Bridget Reilly had one son, Martin, who died in early childhood.

After the death of Phillip Reilly, Bridget was left poor and had to struggle along as best she could, taking in washing and doing such other work as was necessary to support herself and her child. When Hugh Quinn became old enough to work, he learned the harnessmaker's trade in the Joseph M. Schmuke's saddle and harness shop in Jackson. When Henry R. English was elected circuit clerk and recorder, he made Hugh Quinn his deputy. He was in the circuit clerk and recorder's office with Mr. English for about 16 years. In 1894, Hugh Quinn and Henry English founded the Jackson Exchange Bank and Mr. Quinn was cashier when he died on June 30, 1909. His mother, Bridget Reilly, died May 17, 1906, and was buried in the City Cemetery, Jackson, MO.

Hugh Quinn lived all of his life in Jackson, MO, with the exception of a short time on a farm with his uncle. His homeplace, where he resided during his lifetime, is described as "Lot No. 3 of Flentge's Addition to the City of Jackson, as the same is laid down on the plat of said addition on in the Recorder's Office of Cape Girardeau County, Missouri." Hugh Quinn was never married. His mother was an invalid for many years prior to her death and during her lifetime, Hugh was a most dutiful and affectionate son. Mr. Quinn was a member of the Catholic Church and his funeral services were held in the church on Saturday, July 3, 1909, conducted by his pastor, Father M. D. Collins, after which his remains were buried by his mother's grave in the City Cemetery. A large red granite monument marks the site of their graves. *Submitted by Jane Reilly Purcell*

255

RAFFERTY – James Paul Rafferty's family came to this country from Ireland. James Paul married Mary Duffy. They both died at an early age. Upon their death, their children were placed in several different homes in the area. Mrs. Reilly, mother of H. R. Quinn, reared Thomas Patrick Rafferty.

Thomas Patrick married Lenora "Nora" Franklin Rafferty on Jan. 15, 1893. Shortly after their marriage, they built the house located at 200 Kies in Jackson, MO. Thomas learned the saddlery and harness business under C. H. Wolter and later worked for E. Milde, whose business he later bought. He sold the business to D. Klein and continued working with him until the business closed. Thomas later conducted a store in Burfordville, MO. While conducting that business he was appointed the first rural mail carrier out of Jackson, MO.

Thomas Patrick and Lenora Franklin Rafferty in front of their home at 200 Kies Avenue.

Thomas and Lenora lived their entire life at 200 Kies Avenue in Jackson. They were blessed with eight children. Their first daughter died at birth. Their other children were: Mary Madane Rafferty who married Edwin Mecker; Hugh Quinn Rafferty, who served in World War I; Thomas Franklin Rafferty; Lenora Philomene Rafferty who married William Mezger (Lenora was the librarian at State Teachers College, Cape Girardeau, MO for several years, prior to her marriage. She assisted Mr. Otto Kiene in opening the first Riverside Regional Library in Jackson, MO.); Cathryn Rafferty who married O. O. White; Clarabell Ann Rafferty who married William Harry Brewer; and Robert Edward Rafferty who married Mary Margaret Mollenhour on May 24, 1930 at Jackson, MO.

Robert and Mary lived at Sikeston, MO, and Millersville, MO, prior to buying the "home place," Oakhurst, now 200 Kies Avenue in Jackson, MO, in 1953, which was constructed around 1894. They gave their home the name of Oakhurst because of the many oak trees that grew there. They continued to live there until their deaths, Robert on October 14, 1996 and Mary on November 21, 2001. The family continues to own the home. Robert was employed as a meat cutter for the Kroger Company in uptown Jackson for many years. He served as City Collector for the city of Jackson for two terms and served as an Alderman for the city of Jackson for several years. Bob and Mary owned and operated the A & W Root Beer business on Old Cape Road in Jackson in the 1960s. This business was one of the first in Jackson employing curb hops to wait on customers. Bob and Mary were both active in the Democratic Party. Mary was committeewoman for Ward I for many years. They were lifelong member of Immaculate Conception Catholic Church in Jackson. Mary was active in the St. Ann's Sodality, serving as president. She was a housewife and mother who loved being around her children and their friends. She belonged to the Suburban Garden Club and was a member of the Eastside Homemakers Club.

Mary and Bob were parents of four children: Mary Sue Rafferty who married Donald D. Ludwig; Roberta "Bert" who married Bill Birk; Ann who married Joseph P. Donnelly; and Robert Jr. who married Susan Schulte.

Mary Margaret Mollenhour Rafferty's parents were Peter Earl Mollenhour and Ersie Points Mollenhour. Pete was a native of the state of Indiana. He and his family resided in Jackson for a number of years where he was employed as an automobile mechanic. He operated an auto repair shop in Cape Girardeau for several years prior to his death. There were eight children: Thelma Ilene, Mary Margaret, Elizabeth Honor, Althea Janice, Vern Marie, Richard, Fred Albert and Henry Francis, who died at age 2 on June 25, 1917. *Submitted by Robert Rafferty Jr.*

RAMPLEY – The first Rampley came to America from England and settled on a farm in Hartford County, MD, around 1790. Five generations later, Raymond Rampley was born September 3, 1932 in Stoddard County, MO. He was the fifth child of Leonard and Verbie Morris Rampley of Bell City. He had seven brothers and two sisters. After graduating from Bell City High School in 1952, he enlisted in the Army. He was sent to Fort Bliss, TX, to leadership training and then served his remaining two years in Korea. Raymond received the Korean Service medal with two Bronze Service Stars, United Nations Service Medal, National Defense Service Medal, and the Good Conduct Medal.

After returning from Korea he started courting Betty Sue Eakin. They were married on June 8, 1956. Raymond moved to Jackson in 1954 at the recommendation of Hughs Davault, his former agriculture teacher. He and Dr. Marvin Brennecke formed a partnership and Raymond farmed the land. The farm was formerly known as the George Jenkins farm, located 3.5 miles out of Jackson on Route D. When Dr. Brennecke died, Washington University inherited the farm. Raymond continued to rent it until his death in October 2001. Betty still lives on the farm, which is now owned by Michael Keith Rampley and Thomas Lynn Hecht.

Raymond was a member of Garden Ridge Baptist Church, member and past Master of Excelsior Lodge # 441, Altenthal-Joerns American Legion Post 158, Jackson VFW Post, Co-Op Board of Directors, Byrd Township Road District, and Jackson R2 School Board. In addition, he volunteered at the Missouri Veterans Home, was a member of the Country Club Western Dancers Board and the Southeast Missouri District Fair Board, and served as the chairman of the R&R Tent. He also served as president of the Cape County Farm Bureau.

Betty and Raymond Rampley

Betty was born Nov. 30, 1938 in Atkins, Arkansas, the oldest daughter of Othel Lee and Mary Alice Reed Eakin. Betty had two sisters and three brothers. The Eakins moved to Bell City, MO, in 1941 where they farmed and operated a service station. Betty graduated from Bell City High School in 1956.

Betty was employed at the Hosiery Mill in Jackson from 1965-1970. Then she went to work at Lohmans Shoe Store from 1970- 1981 and at Roziers from 1987-1997.

Betty has served on the Board of Country Club Western Dancers and as co-chairman of the R&R Tent of the Southeast Missouri District Fair. In addition, she is a member of Chapter #91 Order of Eastern Star and was the Worthy Matron in 1976. She was the Bethel Guardian of Bethel #60 of Jobs Daughters. She is also a member of the American Legion Auxiliary and Shawnee Hills Baptist Church.

Raymond and Betty have four children: Stephen Kelly (July 22, 1957), now divorced, has two children, Elizabeth Renee and Stephen Eric. Michael Keith (Aug. 20, 1958) married Mayumi Fukumitsu and has two stepchildren, Yoshikazu and Takako. Kevin Lee (March 15, 1960) married Leigh Guemmer and has two sons, Kremer Lee and Kamden Lee. Kathy Sue (Oct. 20, 1962) married Thomas Lynn Hecht and has two children, Raymond Rampley and Leah Kathryn. *Submitted by Betty S. Rampley*

RANDOL – Narvol Arthur Randol Sr. is a fifth-generation descendant of Enos Randol who settled in Cape Girardeau County in 1797. Born in Whitewater, MO, in 1916, he distinguished himself as a tireless leader in banking, the military, and service to his community and church. Mr. Narvol A. Randol died Aug. 27, 1999, at Southeast Missouri Hospital in Cape Girardeau at the age of 83. Bank president, Brigadier General in the Missouri National Guard, mayor of Cape Girardeau, and a member of 17 boards and foundations during his working life, Mr. Randol was a "leader's leader," held in the highest respect by those who knew him. His parents, Arthur Jackson Randol and Hazel Grace Allen, were married in October 1915. His father died in Whitewater during the Spanish Flu epidemic of 1918 and his mother struggled to raise her two children.

Before attending and graduating from Southeast Missouri State Teachers College, he enlisted in the infantry as a private in 1934, and retired in 1971 as a brigadier general and assistant adjutant general of the Missouri National Guard. He was a lieutenant colonel and battalion commander with the U.S. Army during WWII, fighting at the Battle of the Bulge in Belgium. Mr. Randol was elected mayor of Cape Girardeau in 1954 and served for two years. President Dwight Eisenhower appointed Randol as the city's postmaster at the same time he was offered a job at Farmers and Merchants Bank. He took the bank job, he said in an interview when he retired, because he'd loved it since working part-time as a teller at First National Bank during a college summer. "I enjoy visiting with the people and working out loans so they can go into business and work out problems," he said. "We have supplied funds to put hundreds of people in business over the years." Randol became president of Farmers and Merchants Bank in 1968, remained as president when the bank was purchased by Boatmen's Bank, and retired in 1982. In 1996 he received the Rush Limbaugh Sr. Award, the area's highest business honor. Mr. Randol served as presi-

Narvol A. and Dorothy Randol, 1994

dent of the Southeast Hospital Board, was on the board for 31 years, and was an original incorporator of the hospital foundation. "He was involved in almost every major hospital activity," Hospital Administrator James Wente said. "He was decisive, honest, a man of great personal integrity. He led by example."

He also believed in going to church, starting in Grace Methodist at the age of 7. He and his wife, Dorothy, met at church. He joined Grace Methodist Church in 1931 and was one of the church's oldest members. Mr. Randol was a former president of the Cape Girardeau Kiwanis Club, one of the club's founding members in 1942, and had a perfect attendance record. He helped form the Southeast Missouri State University Foundation and established a scholarship at the university. He received the university's Alumni Merit Award in 1987. The Cape Girardeau School Board, Cape Girardeau Historical Society, Masonic Lodge #672, the Capaha Scottish Rite Club, the Red Cross Council, the United Way, the Girl Scouts, Boy Scouts, and the Crippled Children's Society are just some of the organizations he was involved in, most often as chairman of the board. "He did the work of three people," said his daughter, Jane Randol Jackson.

He and Dorothy Louise Kiehne married in 1939 and raised a family of four children: Carolyn, Jane, Margaret, and Narvol A. Randol Jr. His son continued in the banking business, serving his community on many boards and foundations. Margaret built a national career as a professional artist with paintings, murals, and drawing to her credit. Jane retired from 34 years teaching in Cape Girardeau and Scott County public schools and is director of the Cape Girardeau County Archive Center. Carol, who passed away in 2000, was active as a volunteer in the Red Cross and her church. Narvol Arthur Randol Sr. had eight grandchildren and four great-grandchildren to carry on the Randol tradition. *Submitted by Jane Randol Jackson*

RAUH – My grandfather, John Rauh, was born in 1814 and died in 1890. He emigrated from Germany in 1840, from the province of Byern or Bavaria. The capital city was Muchen or Munich. Two of his nine children were born in Germany and seven were born in the United States, four sons and five daughters. He settled on a farm three miles east of Perryville in Perry County. He was one of the first settlers of that neighborhood. He helped organize the first Lutheran church; he was a good church worker, always seeking the one thing needed, the kingdom of God.

My father's name was also John Rauh. He was born Oct. 5, 1842. At the time of the Civil War, he forested, and at the age of 17 years, he joined our soldiers, guided by the gallant man President Lincoln, and served in the war until the end. Afterward he was chosen by the state militia, and served his time out for eight months. After the war, on Jan. 3, 1865, he married Mary Lang, a daughter of another old German family then living in a neighborhood now called Longtown. John Lang, pronounced "Long" in English, gave the name to Longtown, as he was one of the first settlers there.

Charles Frederick Rauh

My father's family numbered 12; five were lost in infancy, leaving seven to grow up. I am the oldest of five brothers and am still the oldest, for they have all passed away. I am the only one left out of the family, and up to this date, I am sorry to say, no one reached the age of 80. I have outlived them all by ten years.

My father lived on a farm containing 240 acres, three miles east of Perryville, MO, close to the old homestead of his father, until 1902. He sold out and moved to the Cherokee Strip in Oklahoma, I stayed in old Missouri and got by too. Up to this date the Rauhs that are left now own thousands of acres of good farmland; some are fortunate to have oil wells on some of the land...so now we will get to the last part of my story.

Charles F. Rauh Sr. was born March 3, 1873. I grew up on my father's farm. On Nov. 27, 1894, I married a lady of a nearest neighbor, Miss Louise Bergmann, a descendent of another old German emigrant who came to the United States in 1840. John Bergmann was her father. We settled on a farm in the eastern part of Perry County, lived there until 1916, then moved on a farm in Cape Girardeau County, ten miles north of Jackson, the county seat.

In 1923 came a hard blow to the family and me. I lost my dear wife, and the children their mother. We were blessed with 12 children; we lost four in infancy. We also took in an orphan boy, 6 years old, when our oldest son was 1. The two oldest children were married at their mother's death, but I still had six to see after, two of them still minors. We gave up the farm and moved to Cape Girardeau, as four of my children were already employed there. I took up public work, three years at Cape Girardeau and six years in St. Louis, MO.

In 1932 I met a lady who owned a farm. We both agreed to marry and take up farming again on her farm. That has been 31 years ago. It was a mixed life, but I always put my trust in the Lord and asked Him daily to be my counsel and my guide. It all came true. What the Lord doeth is well done. My children are all married and have families, they are well educated, and they are all good Christians and good citizens. I have 48 grandchildren and 50 great-grandchildren.

I was baptized (confirmed in 1885), got my Christian training, and was married at Peace Lutheran Church in Friedenburg. I held my membership there. In 1898 Longtown organized, and I moved my membership to Longtown Zion Lutheran Church. In 1916 I moved to Pocahontas and held membership there until 1924. From 1924 until 1926 my membership was with Trinity Lutheran Church in Cape Girardeau, then to Markus Lutheran Church in St. Louis. In 1932 I returned to Pocahontas Zion congregation, to the present time. I have served as elder and treasurer nearly continuously, and served a number of times on building committees for churches and schools.

I have always been blessed with good health. I lived to see my children's children, six generations (my grandparents, parents, my own generation, my children, their children, and the great-grandchildren). I am happy and thankful to the Lord for this bountiful blessing, but I must say with St. Paul when he once praised: "Not I, not I, but it is Christ that dwelleth within me, that gives me willingness and power to be what I am. Praise and thanks to the Lord."

I have cast my 15th ballot for president in the last election. Harrison was the first president I voted for when he ran the second time; I have never changed my ticket. My reason was not plain politics, but for the honor of my father and many others, and President Lincoln who waved the battle to keep our United States together. God bless our native land; may she forever stand. *Charles F. Rauh, 1963, age 90 years old; Submitted by Marjorie Swan*

RAUH – Elsa Anita Gerler was born March 17, 1901, in Pocahontas, MO, the daughter of Frederick Ludwig Gerler (1873-1960) and Bertha Lehner Gerler (1875-1967). She attended Zion Lutheran Church and school. On Sept. 24, 1922 she was married to Oscar E. Rauh.

Mr. Rauh was born Sept. 28, 1895, in Longtown, MO, the son of Charles F. Rauh (1873-1968) and Louisa Berg-mann Rauh (1874-1923). His elementary education was received at Zion Lutheran School in Longtown, MO. He then attended St. Paul High School and College in Concordia, MO. In 1916 he moved to a farm near Poca-hontas. In 1918 he volunteered for the army and served a tour of duty in France during World War I.

Oscar E. and Elsa Anita Gerler Rauh, Sept. 24, 1922.

He and Elsa resided in Pocahontas their entire married life. Their marriage was blessed with three daughters, Virginia who married Paul Winter, Mildred who married E. C. Younghouse, and Evelyn who married Eugene Kasten.

Mr. Rauh was manager of Bowman Milling Company for 45 years until ill health forced his retirement. Bowman Milling Company, established in 1858, is still a progressive business and is managed by a grandson, Richard Winter.

Both Mr. and Mrs. Rauh took an active part in Zion Lutheran Church, serving in many capacities. Mr. Rauh was a civic-minded person, serving several terms as mayor of Pocahontas. He was instrumental in obtaining electric power for the town of Pocahontas. This became a reality in 1938.

Oscar Rauh died Aug. 9, 1969. Elsa Rauh died Aug. 22, 1974. *Submitted by Evelyn Kasten*

REISENBICHLER – Gottlieb Reisenbichler was born on July 7, 1844 to Leopold and Teresa (Grillen) Reisenbichler in the valley region of the Danube River, a northern Austrian village known as Bad Goisern. The Reisenbichler family remained in this beautiful mountainous section of Austria until 1858 when they took the tumultuous journey to the United States. Courageously, Leopold and Teresa (Grillen) Reisenbichler left their homeland with their three children: George (b. March 25, 1939, d. 1926), Leopold Jr. (b. Sept. 8, 1842, d. July 12, 1863) and my grandfather, Gottlieb, who was fourteen at that time. They stopped in St. Louis, MO and later ended up in the rolling farmlands of Pocahontas, MO.

Gottlieb, which means, "God loved" in the German language, spent his teenage years and all the way up to his death on a farm that is still in the Reisenbichler family. Barely married, Gottlieb lost his mother, Teresa (Grillen) Reisenbichler, on May 2, 1868. This was two years after his father's death, which was on Sept. 1, 1866, and only a month after his marriage to Anna Maria Putz on April 12, 1868. Gottlieb's wife, Anna Maria (b. July 24, 1847) was also a native of Bad Goisern, Austria. Shortly after their marriage, Anna Maria died on Feb. 27, 1870 at the young age of 23. Gottlieb was left with two young children, Henry John Theodore (b. Jan.

22, 1869) and another child, born on Dec. 26, 1869, named Alois Gottlieb Reisenbichler.

Gottlieb's son, Henry Reisenbichler, lived his adult life in Jackson where he ran a tavern and raised two sons, Ervin and Billy Harold. Alois Reisenbichler, Gottlieb's other son from his first marriage, was married and blessed with five children. Alois and his wife had two boys, William A. and Leo G., and three beautiful girls, Adella (Reisenbichler) Gemeinhardt, Cora (Reisenbichler) Black, and Rita (Reisenbichler) Bruhl.

Within three years after Anna Maria (Putz) Reisenbichler's death, Gottlieb had married another Anna Maria, but with the maiden name of Piltz. Anna Maria (Piltz) Lindorer, a widow, and Gottlieb Reisenbichler were married on Sept. 27, 1871 and remained on Gottlieb's farm just east of Pocahontas. Along with Henry and Alois Reisenbichler, the couple added seven more children.

First was a girl, who was given the name Josephine Christina Reisenbichler, born on Oct. 14, 1872. Josephine only lived to be 26, dying on Nov. 4, 1898. She was never married. A boy came to them on Halloween of 1874. Christian Ernst Reisenbichler married Marie Hermann and took over the operation of the Putz-Reisenbichler Funeral Home in Pocahontas until his death on July 4, 1941. They had one daughter, Lorene. The second girl, Ida Maria, came to Gottlieb and Anna Maria almost as a Valentine's present. She was born Feb. 20, 1878, only six days after Valentine's Day. Ida went on to marry Ben Schmidt and have a daughter that they named Vanita (Schmidt) Winter. Ben Schmidt and Ida stayed in Pocahontas where he was the owner of a blacksmith shop. Rudolf Bernhart was born on April 4, 1887 over ten years after Ida was born. He died (March, 1969) in his hometown of Pocahontas, leaving behind his wife, Lena (Danz) Reisenbichler, and four children: Elmer, Marvin, Melvin, and Wilma (Reisenbichler) Kramer. Another girl appears on Oct. 17, 1888, Bertha Alwina. She lived to be 73 and like Josephine, she also was never married. She was buried in Pocahontas after her death in March of 1962. Adding to the growing family was Adolf Herman, born on Dec. 20, 1890. He married a woman by the name of Hedwig Kutscher. Together they raised three boys, Wilbert, Dillman and Lennert. Adolf carried on the family tradition of farming all his life until his death on July 13, 1965.

The last child of Gottlieb and Anna Maria was my father, William Joseph. He was born on Sept. 20, 1893. He married my mother, Elsie (Bachmann) Reisenbichler, in Uniontown, MO. I was still in my teenage years when my father passed away at the age of 53. He was laid to rest in Pocahontas after his death on Dec. 9, 1946. My sister, Lorna (Reisenbichler) Roth, and I, Doloris Emilie (Reisenbichler) Meyr, were the only two children of William and Elsie Reisenbichler.

Many of the descendants of Gottlieb Reisenbichler have remained in the area of southeast Missouri. The majority remained as farmers in and around Pocahontas. The Reisenbichler descendants have remained strong in their Lutheran roots, and many are active members of Zion Lutheran Church in Pocahontas. Gottlieb Reisenbichler's original farm is now owned by his great-grandson, Donald Reisenbichler. *Submitted by Doloris Reisenbichler Meyr and her granddaughter, Elizabeth Meyr*

RHYNE – Marie Rhyne married Johann Heinrich (Brul) Bruhl April 15, 1903 in Perry County, MO, son of Johann Bruhl and Elizabeth Lehner. He was born Aug. 31, 1859 in Cape Girardeau County, MO, and died Nov. 9, 1903 in Frohna, Perry County, MO.

The following was found in the Recorder of deeds, Jackson, Cape Girardeau County, MO: 1871- Personal Property, #1397- Land valued at $650, three horses- $100, two cattle- $20, 14 hogs- $25, other property- $105 for a total value of $900.

More about Johann Heinrich (Brul) Bruhl:
Baptism: Sept. 11, 1859, Immanuel Lutheran Church, New Wells, MO, sponsors- Gottlieb Wunderlich, Joseph Meyer, Fru Marie Mirly; record # 3, third name down
Burial: Nov. 11, 1903 Frohna, Perry County, MO (Record 6, Row G, Grave 47, Concordia Lutheran Cemetery Records).
Census: 1900, Brazeau Township, Perry County, MO (Ed 72, sheet 21, family 392, a boarder living with A. L. Fararrer family.
Confirmation: 1873, Immanuel Lutheran Church, New Wells, MO, record #62.
Medical Information: was 44 years, 2 months, 8 days old when he died (per tombstone information), died from dropsy.
Marriage license- Johann Bruhl (Brul) and Marie Rhyne, Book 7, page 52, Marriage Records, Perry County Recorder's office, Perryville, MO. *Submitted by Carol Bruhl*

RICHTER – Johann Christian and Johanne Sophie Richter were born in Germany. They decided to leave their homeland so they could establish a home where both might enjoy religious, political, and economic freedom. They left Bremerhaven, Germany, on Nov. 18, 1838 on the ship *Olbers*. Their destination was New Orleans and then St. Louis, MO. According to the ship's passenger list, Johann was 53 and Johanne was 54.

After 64 days they arrived in New Orleans on Jan. 31, 1839. On April 26, 1839 they arrived in Perry County. Johanne Sophie died shortly after arriving in America. Johann remarried on July 5, 1840 to Johanna Christiana Theilig, daughter of Michael and Eva Marie (Forester) Theilig. They had four children: Ehregott J. (April 4, 1841); Elias Fuerchtegott (May 23, 1843); Wilheimine Christine (Aug. 23, 1845); and Johanna Gottlob (Sept. 15, 1847). Johann died on March 16, 1848 and Christiana died Oct. 8, 1887 in Perry County, MO.

Erwin William Ehregott Richter, Eleanor Ann (Bultemeyer) Richter 1982, Jackson, MO

Ehregott Johann was raised in Perry County, MO. On April 7, 1863 he married Elizabeth K. Hartung from Cape Girardeau, the daughter of Michael and Sara (Stephan) Hartung. To them were born eight children: Anna C. (May 19, 1866); Martin Christian (April 3, 1869); Emma Marie Caroline (Oct. 8, 1871); Matilda (Sept. 26, 1873); Hulda (Dec. 15, 1875); Arthur Johann August (March 18, 1878); Theodore F. (May 20, 1880); and Joseph William (June 7, 1883). Death called Ehregott on April 23, 1918 and Elizabeth on July 8, 1928. They are buried at St. Paul Cemetery at Wittenberg.

Joseph William was married to Bertha Hulda Emilie Vogel, born May 6, 1866, daughter of William and Emma Hoehne Vogel. He died Nov. 13, 1921 after a short illness of pneumonia and abscess of the liver and is buried in St. Paul Lutheran Cemetery. To them were born four sons: Erwin Ehregott William (Aug. 10, 1908); Arnold Joseph (Dec. 25, 1910); Enno Herbert (May 6, 1913); and Melvin Adolph (Sept. 1, 1915).

After Joseph's early death at 38 years old, Bertha and the children moved to Fort Wayne, Allen County, IN. She was married on Jan. 2, 1929 to Otto B. Lueders, who was from Wittenberg. They enjoyed 35 years of marriage before he died May 14, 1964. She died Nov. 24, 1985 and is buried in Roselawn Cemetery in Auburn, IN, beside Otto.

Erwin Ehregott William was raised in Perry County, MO, and came to Fort Wayne with his mother. On Oct. 7, 1933 in Adams County, IN, he married Eleanor Ann Bultemeyer, daughter of Edward and Caroline Wischmeyer Bultemeyer, being born Jan. 12, 1909. To them were born: Robert Erwin (July 28, 1938); Lynn David (Aug. 13, 1941); Sue Ann (Dec. 29, 1946); and Jo Ann (Dec. 29, 1946).

Upon retirement, Erwin and Eleanor moved to Jackson until failing health forced them to move back to Fort Wayne. Erwin died Dec. 18, 1993 and Eleanor died Feb. 7, 1994. They are buried at Lindenwood Cemetery, Fort Wayne.

Robert Erwin was born in Fort Wayne, IN. On Aug. 22, 1959 he married Judith Elaine Ormsby, daughter of Argus Luster and Edna Chloe Mann Ormsby, born Jan. 10, 1941 in Fort Wayne. To them were born: Karen Lynette (Feb. 28, 1960); Kelly Renee (July 3, 1962); and Kevin Lee (June 26, 1963). Now they live in Albion, IN, and are retired, enjoying their six grandchildren. *Submitted by Judy Richter*

RISTIG – Freddie R. Ristig was born June 1, 1915 near Jackson, a son of Louis Ristig (b. Sept. 28, 1891; d. Dec. 23, 1957) and Ida Zschille Ristig (b. Dec. 7, 1893, at Friedheim; d. Nov. 20, 1991). Louis Ristig and Ida Zschille were married on Aug. 27, 1914. Louis Ristig was the son of Frederick (b. Jan. 24, 1863; d. Dec. 23, 1957) and Amanda Haas Ristig, who were married on April 10, 1890. Ida Zschille Ristig was the daughter of Reinhold and Johanna Lowes Zschille. Freddie had one sister, Norma Ristig Brothers of Jackson. He was a lifelong member of Emanuel United Church of Christ in Jackson, MO.

On Dec. 23, 1939 Freddie was married to Edith Elizabeth Woeltje (b. Feb. 24, 1917, near Byrd's Creek and Oak Ridge, MO). She was the daughter of Oscar Godfrey Woeltje and Dolly Louise Hamilton Woeltje, and had five brothers, Howard, Dale, Walter, Henry and Glenn W. Woeltje.

Freddie R. and Edith Woeltje Ristig

She had attended Roberts's one-room school on Route D between Jackson and Oak Ridge, MO, and also attended Jackson High School. She worked at the shoe factory in Cape Girardeau for several years and helped milk cows and other work on the dairy farm they owned. She attended

Emanuel United Church of Christ in Jackson, MO. She died at St. Francis Medical Center in Cape Girardeau, MO, on Friday, Dec. 24, 1999.

Freddie was employed as a shop foreman by Brennecke Chevrolet in Jackson for 15 years, and was a dairyman for many years. They had started out with 33 acres and expanded their dairy farm to 413 acres. Their dairy farm was a "Showcase Operation" in the Jackson area. He was also manager of Mid America Dairy, a holding and hauling milk operation, for 20 years, retiring in November 1997. He died Feb. 20, 1998 at his home on County Road 618 near Jackson, MO.

Ristigs sold their farm on County Road 618 to Southeast Missouri State University in 1976. School officials said at the time that the Ristigs made a substantial donation to the university because the dairy farm was worth more than the purchase price. Before their death, the farm was changed from a dairy farm to strictly a beef-cattle operation. The Ristigs tried to block the school's decision to dump the dairy operation, but discovered that their agreement with the university only stipulates the land be used for agriculture. They lived on the farm until their death and then the farm was completely turned over to the university.

They had three foster sons, Donald Thompson, John Wachoski and Marcus Wachoski. They were all living in Gulf Port, MS, at the time of Freddie's death. John Wachoski and his wife Laurie Wachoski moved in with Edith after Freddie's death and were her caregivers until her death. John and Laurie Wachoski now live on County Road 347 west of Jackson.

Three of Edith's step-nephews also lived with them for some time, Ron, Glenn and Dale Huffman. Ron Huffman and Freddie ran the dairy farm many years together. After Freddie sold the dairy farm to the university he helped Ron start another dairy farm on County Road 620 near the other farm.

They had several other nieces and nephews, as well as friends and neighbors, who miss them very much. *Submitted by Marilyn Mayfield*

RITTER – Clarence Joseph Ritter's father, Clarence Johann Ritter, emigrated from Germany to the Unied States in 1883. He was 28 years old and had come because of the political situation at the time. He changed his name to John upon his arrival in America. Arriving in Jackson, he lived with a cousin Jacob H. Schaefer. He met, fell in love and married Marie Christine Schmidt. Ten children were born to this union. The ones who reached adulthood were: Martin (1885-1929), Lydia (1893-1963), Amelia (1890-1990), Leo (1893-1975), Hilda McBryde (1897-1977) and Clarence (1899-1976). Clarence and Amelia always lived at the home place. The others left home to establish their own homes and lives.

Johnann "John" Ritter was a stonemason by trade. Many stone foundations and walls around Jackson are his handiwork. He was elected Jackson city commissioner of streets for two terms in 1903 and 1905. He built his own home at 209 East Adams and it became "the home place." Clarence "Brick"

Mary Sue Niemann, "Brick" Ritter, Mabel Ritter, John Ritter, June 27, 1955.

Ritter was born in that home. He later purchased it from remaining heirs and lived with his wife Mabel (Kurre) and two children, Mary Sue Niemann and C. John Ritter, until his death in 1997.

Clarence "Brick" started working at the post office in 1915 and worked through the ranks until he became Assistant Postmaster. Retiring from the post office in 1961, he became active in the Heritage Savings and Loan, which is on North Main (now Union Planters). In 1930 when Clarence and Mabel were married, her teaching ended because married ladies were not allowed to hold teaching positions. That changed with WWII and she returned to the classroom, teaching in Fruitland, Gordonville and Millersville. Besides teaching and raising Mary Sue and John, Mabel was very active in Emmanuel United Church of Christ, devoting many years to the junior high department.

One accomplishment of which she was extremely proud of happened after WWII. Clothing was being sent to the War Relief in Germany. A dress that was received by the Rev. Triebe family contained the name and address of the UCC pastor, Rev. and Mrs. Herman Borne. A correspondence began. Over the years the junior department continued the mission project by sending clothing and other gifts to this family who shared them with others. Years later in 1969, a member of the Triebe family, Ruth, now grown, had a chance to visit America. She paid a visit to Mabel to thank her personally for her help during those difficult times.

As is the custom in many families, an unmarried person might live with a married couple. This was true in the Ritter household. Amelia Ritter, the oldest sister living, remained on the home place with Clarence and Mabel. Amelia worked as a telephone operator. Her employment spanned the time from operators personally taking calls to the automated age. At home she was a wonderful built-in babysitter and mentor for Mary Sue and John.

Mary Sue and John both attended Southeast Missouri State University, Mary Sue becoming a teacher and John going on to medical school. Each had three children, each lost their first spouse, and each remarried. Now retired, Mary Sue and her husband Steve Niemann enjoy life in Jackson and Florida. Dr. John retired from private practice in Cape Girardeau. He and his wife Marcia have done volunteer missionary work in Africa, Mexico, the Caribbean and Honduras. *Submitted by C. John Ritter*

ROLOFF – Albert W. Roloff was born on Dec. 16, 1880, son of Henry Roloff and Johanna Hunnecke. He grew up on a farm near Burfordville, MO. Albert attended the Evangelical Parochial School in Tilsit, MO, the Burfordville Public School, and the Jackson Military Academy. He graduated from the academy in 1902. Upon graduation, Albert served a term as Second Lieutenant of Company F, N.G.M.

Albert went to work as a clerk for McAtee Mercantile Company in Jackson, MO. In 1910 Mr. McAtee sold his interest in the business, and Albert became a stockholder, as well as secretary-treasurer for the firm. Business was brisk. In the early 1900s the firm employed ten clerks and had four

Emma Rose Roloff and Albert Roloff

delivery wagons. Eventually Albert became the sole owner; Roloff's Red-and-White Store prospered and grew.

It was at the military academy that Albert received a thorough indoctrination in music, art and education. He took music lessons and learned to play a wide variety of musical instruments. The Jackson Chamber of Commerce asked Albert to organize a community band, so in 1920 Albert recruited 29 boys

Louise Roloff Kuehle, Helen Roloff Mill and Leo Roloff

for the band. They met each week in Roloff's wood shed for practice. The Jackson Junior Band first performed on Nov. 11, 1921. This group evolved into the Jackson Municipal Band. Albert was also instrumental in starting the first band at Jackson High School, and was its first director.

On May 10, 1906 Albert married Emma Emelie Rose. The couple had three children: Leo Albert was born on July 24, 1907; Louise Johanna was born on July 13, 1908 and Helen E. was born on Feb. 23, 1914. Leo married Opal Lewis Barks on May 25, 1930. Louise wed Lawrence Kuehle on Sept. 20, 1931. Helen married Wilbert "Bill" Moll on Jan. 24, 1932. The family were members of the Evangelical Church in Jackson, MO.

Emma Roloff was born on Oct. 14, 1883; she died Feb. 18, 1957. Albert died on July 14, 1972. Both are buried in Russell Heights Cemetery in Jackson, MO. *Submitted by Donald Kuehle*

ROLOFF – Henry Julius Roloff was born in Bockeman, Germany, on Dec. 10, 1847; he was the son of Julius Roloff and Johanna Hunnecke. Henry grew up in times of war and unrest in Germany. On the night before he was to be drafted into the German Army, Henry left the country. He gave his last $50 to a ship's captain, and set sail for America. Henry arrived in New York with no money and nowhere to go. He slept under a pier for three days, hungry and homeless. A stranger found him and hired him to work on a farm in northern New York State. There, Henry slept in the barn for several months. He was finally able to contact his brother, Albert, who worked as a barber in downstate New York. Henry went to live with his brother, and worked as a barber. Some time later, Albert and Henry journeyed to Missouri to visit a sister, Johanne Hennecke. Misfortune struck, and Albert died while in Missouri. Henry returned to his barbering business in New Jersey. While in Missouri, Henry met Johanna M. H. Nothdurft; when he had saved up enough money, Henry returned to Missouri. Henry and Johanna were married on May 20, 1875; they lived on a farm near Burfordville, MO.

Seven children were born to that union. Alvine Marie was born March 4, 1876; she married Wilhelm Henry Voges on May 6, 1897. Johanna C. was born on Feb. 5, 1879; she wed Henry Illers on May 16, 1901. Albert W. was born Dec. 16, 1880; he married Emma Emelia Rose on May 10, 1906. Wilhelmine was born Jan. 28, 1883; she wed Carl August Wilhelm Schaper on Nov. 3, 1912. Henry Ferdinand was born June 29, 1885; he married Ida Marie Peetz on April 7, 1907. Herman W. was born June 17, 1888; he wed Elilie Rust on May 20, 1913.

Front row: Henry J. Roloff and Johanna M. H. Nothdurft Roloff
Second row: Alvina Roloff Voges, Johanna Roloff Illers, Wilhelmine "Minnie" Roloff Schaper, Caroline "Lena" Roloff Schaper, Herman Roloff, Henry F. Roloff and Albert W. Roloff

Caroline Marie "Lena" was born July 29, 1891; she wed Leo William Henry Schaper on Sept. 6, 1914.

Johanna Roloff was born on a farm near Tilsit, MO; she was the daughter of Julius Nothdurft and Johanna Sophia Brennecke. Johanna died on May 26, 1928; Henry Julius Roloff died July 24, 1934. They are both buried in Russell Heights Cemetery in Jackson, MO. *Submitted by Donald Kuehle*

ROWLEY – Heinrich Gottfried Dralle (b. June 21, 1818) and wife, Johanne Marie Christine Wolters Dralle (b. Aug. 12, 1822), with their two sons, Heinrich Carl Julius (b. Feb. 23, 1845) and Conrad August (b. Aug. 24, 1847), left their home in Bockenem, Germany, and arrived in New Orleans Nov. 2, 1853. Shortly thereafter they settled on a farm southwest of Houck, MO. Later two more children were born, Christine in 1854 and Charles in 1857.

During the Civil War, a sad and turbulent time in American history, Heinrich Carl Julius Dralle enlisted and served in Company K 5th Regiment Missouri Cavalry. After the war, Heinrich was united in marriage Feb. 8, 1872 with Auguste Wilhelmina Grumbrecht (b. Oct. 8, 1853), daughter of Johann Frederick and Johanna Dorothea Schluter Grumbrecht. To this union nine children were born: Heinrich, Alvine Henrietta, Rubine, Ottilie, Martin, Gerhard, Rosine, August and Gustav.

Alvine Henrietta Dralle (b. Feb. 2, 1876) married Wilhelm August "Herman" Meier (b. May 3, 1877), the son of Heinrich Wilhelm and Eva Rehkopf Meier. Alvine and Herman Meier were the parents of seven children: Frieda, Ida, Lena, Wilhelm, Herman, Linda and Alma (b. Sept. 2, 1915).

Ken and Dorothy Rowley, April 22, 2001

There was great sorrow for the parents because several of the small children did not live to adulthood. On April 23, 1925 Herman Meier died, leaving Alvine, his wife, and daughters Ida, Lena and Alma, to manage the family farm. The four women, Alvina and her three daughters, continued to manage the farm until Alvina's death Sept. 14, 1935. For a time after the death of their mother, the three sisters operated the farm.

On Aug. 3, 1938 Alma Meier was married to Emil Herman Muster (b. June 3, 1908), son of Henry and Caroline Sophie Voss Muster. Alma and Emil continued to live on the family farm and were the parents of two daughters, Carolena and Dorothy.

Dorothy was born in Cape Girardeau, MO. She lived with her parents on the same farm that Heinrich and Christine Dralle settled on after arriving in America. For the first five years of primary education, Dorothy attended Poplar Ridge, a one-room rural grade school. After the rural school districts were reorganized, she attended Tilsit Grade School for one year. The seventh through twelfth grade she attended school in Jackson, graduating from Jackson High School in 1962. She moved to Jackson in 1973. Dorothy was employed over 25 years at Brennecke Chevrolet Company, retiring as office manager in 1997. Currently she is office manager for the local H & R Block franchise. She has attended some classes at Southeast Missouri State University, is an enrolled agent and continues her tax preparation education yearly. She has one daughter, Julie Kay Crites Dyer. Dorothy's husband, Kenneth Rowley Sr., son of Roy and Winifred Opal Edwards Rowley, is the father of Kenneth Rowley Jr. Dorothy's ancestors were lifelong residents of Cape Girardeau County and member of St. James United Church of Christ. She and her husband are active members of the same church. They are also members of Cape Girardeau County Genealogical Society and Cape Girardeau County Historical Society. Dorothy serves as treasurer of the German Evangelical Church and Cemetery Association of Dutchtown, MO.

The farmland settled by Heinrich and Christine Dralle had been passed down through the generations and is presently owned by Dorothy and her sister. Kenneth Sr., who is a Proctor and Gamble retiree, enjoys spending time "down on the farm." Dorothy enjoys and has done extensive ancestral research. *Submitted by Dorothy Rowley*

RUESTER – B. Marie (Allen) Ruester was born Jan. 14, 1934 the first child of Clarence W. and Noma M. (Crites) Allen, in the country in the Whitewater-Crump-Crossroads area. Dr. Finney was called and he came by horse and buggy to help with the delivery. They moved to the Jackson area in 1935. She attended grade school in Jackson until her parents moved to a farm seven miles west of Jackson in the Big Springs School District. She attended school there until she started to Jackson High School, graduating in 1951. She worked part time at Cox's 5 & 10 Variety Store while in high school, and after graduation she went to work at the Hosiery Mill in Jackson.

In 1952 she married Thomas V. Turner, son of Elva and Maude Turner, at the Baptist Church in Burfordville. Tom served in the army in Korea from 1952 to 1954. They had three children, Gary L. (b. Feb. 13, 1953), Vern A. (b. May 28, 1955) and Susan E. (b. Dec. 18, 1956). They lived at a home on Highway 72 in Jackson. They moved to Farmington for a few years and in 1960 Marie and the children moved to Cape Girardeau and she went to work for Southwestern Bell Telephone. The children attended Jefferson Grade School. Marie was a member of First Baptist Church in Cape Girardeau where she also taught a Sunday school class.

On Feb. 14, 1970 she married John T. Ruester (b. April 15, 1936), son of Theodore and Edna E. (Steinheimer) Ruester of Marissa, IL, at First Baptist Church in Cape Girardeau. He was a graduate of the University of Missouri at Rolla in 1959 with a degree in mechanical engineering and was employed by Southeast Missouri State University. He has two daughters, Valerie (b. May 26, 1960) and Diana (b. Oct. 19, 1961). They moved to Ballwin, MO in 1970 where John worked for Layne Western and Marie continued to work for Southwestern Bell Telephone.

When Marie retired from "Bell Telephone" in 1985, after working for 25 years, they moved back to Jackson into the John Von Priest home at 924 West Main. John had already moved in and had started doing extensive remodeling. After moving back to Jackson, Marie made a lot of new friends and got to visit her old friends she had known while attending school there. She was an active member of First Baptist Church, Suburban Garden Club and Thursday Study Club. Marie and John worked very long hours planning and remodeling their new "old" home and they did a remarkable job. They did a wonderful job of remodeling the yard also. They always had something in bloom and loved to share flowers and plants with anyone she came in contact with. "Spring just makes you feel better," Marie asserted. "When it starts getting green and things start popping up, you can look out and think about what God created." It was a home she very much enjoyed sharing with her family and friends.

Family of John and Marie Allen Turner Ruester, 30th Wedding Anniversary, February 2000.

Their five children are all married now and they have ten grandchildren. Gary married Kathy Schweer on Feb. 14, 1976. They have two boys, John was born May 28, 1978 and married Jennifer Peters on Sept. 22, 2001; and Ben who lives on the McBride-Schweer "Century" family farm on County Road 439 in Jackson. Vern married Angela Macke in 1988 and with their daughter Angeline, born March 20, 1989, now live in Farmington, MO. Susan White and her two children, Kayla (b. Sept. 17, 1988) and Bobby (b. Nov. 18, 1993) live in O'Fallon, MO. Valerie married Sam Kursar in 1980 and lives in Jackson, MS with Nicky (b. Sept. 24, 1980) and Christopher (b. Sept. 12, 1984). Diana married Andy Lasky on Sept. 13, 1986, and lives in Corydon, IN with Alexander (b. July 23, 1988) and twins Teddy and John (b. Oct. 8, 1989). At holidays and lots of other times, their house was full of good food and lots of good times. Marie passed away on April 30, 2000 after a battle with cancer. *Submitted by Marilyn Mayfield*

RUFF – The Ruffs moved to Jackson in 1991, having lived in the Chicago area for the previous 27 years. Ken, born near Waterloo, IL, met Shirley Wagner while attending Southeast Missouri State University after being discharged from the Naval Air Force, having served in the Korean War. The two were married in 1954 while in college. Shirley retired as head of the home economics department at Medinah Middle School. Ken is a retired Sears executive, spending the last 27 years in corporate headquarters. Their two sons, John and David, and their families, live in the Chicago area.

They chose to retire in Jackson as Shirley has deep roots here. While their daughter, Mrs. Vernon (Stephanie) Kasten Jr., and granddaughter, Chloe', also live in Jackson, Shirley's parents, Carson and Margaret Wagner, were lifelong citizens. With Carson's love for guns, cars and anything mechanical, it wasn't unusual for Carson, known to many as the "Metropolitan Man," to be asked to adjust a homemaker's sewing machine while collecting an insurance premium. His talent to diagnose and repair guns and automobiles was outstanding. He often created his own tools or the needed part at the Wagner Machine Shop where his father Alvin "Boots" did his gunsmith work. Shirley's brother Carson Jr. "Corky" made a career in the U.S. Army. A graduated of West Point, he retired as a four-star general.

Alvin "Boots" Wagner at work in his gunsmith shop, rifling the bore of a gun being made.

Shirley's grandfather Alvin Wagner, a renowned gunsmith featured in *The American Rifleman*, specialized in manufacturing muzzle-loading rifles used by marksmen throughout this and other countries. One such gun was a 25 Caliber muzzle-loader made for Carson Jr. for his first birthday. "Boots" was quite a marksman, continually supplying the table with meat won at rifle matches. Alvin's father, Christian, known as Henry, was a marksman as well and served several years at the town Marshal (see Roland Wagner history). Alvin's wife was Bessie Niblack, daughter of Benedict and Anita (Rose) Niblack. Benedict's parents, Milas and Louisa, at one time owned most of the land on both sides of Highway 61 in east Jackson. The property the Ruff home sits on was part of that land.

Margaret Wagner, Shirley's mother, taught in numerous country schools throughout the area and for many years in the local Immaculate Conception School. She was one of three daughters of Charles Grover and Bertha Olga (Illers) Macke. Charles, born in 1887 and son of John H. and Bertha (Hoffmeister) Macke, was "considered by one and all as one of the most pleasant men in Jackson." He served as Circuit Clerk, Deputy United State Marshall, and Postmaster during his last 12 years of life. He was responsible for planting the two oaks that adorned the front of the post office. The Indian statue is made from the trunk of one of those trees. Charles' father, John, had also been a United States Marshal for the area. Charles' wife, Olga, spent her life as a fastidious homemaker. Her father, August Illers, was one of six founders of St. Paul Lutheran Church (see Aleen Illers Sander for more history). *Submitted by Ken Ruff*

SACHSE – August Robert Sachse was born March 18, 1873 near Old Appleton, MO. He was united in marriage on Dec. 16, 1877 to Dora Martha Bedwell at Zion Methodist Church near Old Appleton, MO. August, like his grandfather, Julius Sachse, was a carpenter and farmer. August and his wife Dora lived near Oak Ridge, MO. August and Dora had five children.

Mae Emily Sachse was united in marriage to Ben F. Peetz on Aug. 1, 1937. They lived on the family farm near Oak Ridge, MO. In October 1971 they retired and moved to Jackson, MO. Mae and Ben had no children.

Earl Bedwell Sachse was united in marriage to Evelyn Hawn on Oct. 27, 1929. They have two daughters, JoAnna Dee Sachse and Dortha Jane Sachse. Earl died on Sept. 21, 1938. Evelyn Hawn Sachse was united in marriage to Adolph Albert Borgfield. Evelyn and Adolph operated the Western Auto Store on West Main Street in Jackson, MO for a number of years, until they were retired. JoAnna Dee Sachse was united in marriage to John Ambrose Peek Jr. on March 23, 1958. JoAnna and John have two daughters, Sandy Sue Peek and Kandy Lue Peek. Dortha Jane Sachse was united in marriage to Harold Albert Strack on June 2, 1957. Dortha worked for many years at Sunny Hill Garden Store in Cape Girardeau, MO. She was also very active in the Kage Homemakers Club, and was a 4-H leader for many years. She was also active with the Southeast Missouri District Fair Board. Dortha and Harold have three sons, Alan Dale, Jay Mark and Jo Wayne Strack.

Roy Sachse was united in marriage to Mayme Penny on Feb. 15, 1931. They farmed the Penny farm near Daisy, MO. They have one son, Grover Gene Sachse. Grover was united in marriage to Edith Scholz on Aug. 7, 1955. Grover and Edith have three children, Gene Sachse, Donna Sachse Vernon and Tom Sachse. We are all wishing Tom the best as he is running for State Representative on the Republican ticket for the 157 District, which comprises Cape Girardeau County and the city of Jackson, MO.

Stella Marie Sachse was united in marriage to Emil Herman Peetz on Dec. 16, 1934. Stella and Emil farmed the Peetz family farm near Jackson, MO. Stella and Emil have two children, Robert William Peetz and Patsy Sue Peetz Voshage who is fourth generation owner of the Missouri Century farm. Patsy was united in marriage to Jerry Voshage on Nov. 22, 1968. They have one son, Douglas Robert Voshage, along with Jerry's three sons, Ronnie, Rodney Joe and David Voshage.

Henry August Sachse was united in marriage to Lula Crites on April 23, 1927. Henry and Lula worked until retirement from the International Shoe Factory in Jackson, MO. They had one daughter, Anna Lee Sachse. Anna Lee Sachse was united in marriage on June 12, 1960 to Thomas Kane. Anna Lee has two daughters, Susie Lee Kane and Karie Lee Kane. *Submitted by Patsy Sue Peetz Voshage*

SACHSE – Theodore Sachse, a substantial merchant of Old Appleton, MO was born on April 27, 1841 in Germany. He was the son of Julius and Rosa (Schultz) Sachse, both of whom were born in Germany in 1810. They immigrated to America in 1849. They first located in St. Louis, MO, before they moved to Old Appleton, MO. The father was a cabinetmaker by trade. In April 1862 Theodore enlisted in the Union Army and was assigned to the Fifth Missouri Cavalry, which he served until his discharge in April 1865. After his discharge from the army he was engaged in the mercantile business, which he continued. On Dec. 24, 1865, he was united in marriage to Mehitabel Whiteldge. She died on May 22, 1873 survived by her four small children, Cora, Edward, Emma and August. Theodore married his second wife, Victoria Unterreiner. She died in March 1885, leaving two children, Rosa and Louisa. Theodore married his third wife, Martha Fisher, and they had five children, Theodore J., Nora, Franklin, Herbert, Edna and Florence Sachse.

Many older residents of Jackson will remember Rosa and Louisa Sachse as they were very good seamstresses. Herbert Sachse married Edna Illers and they operated the A&P Store in Jackson, MO for many years. Cora Sachse married August Dickman and resided near Jackson, MO. They had four children; Earp Theodore, Alvin, Roscoe and Mildred. The Dickmans farmed and operated an orchard near Jackson, MO for many years.

August Robert Sachse married Dora Martha Bedwell. They had five children, May Emily, Earl Bedwell, Roy, Stella Marie and Henry August Sachse.

This is a very brief overview on the Sachse family. There is more detailed information on some of the descendents found elsewhere in the book. *Submitted by Patsy Sue Peetz Voshage*

SALZMANN – Dr. Douglas Warren Salzmann and Paula (Strickland) Salzmann came to Jackson, MO, on Labor Day weekend, 1958. At the time of their move from Kansas City where Dr. Salzmann had recently graduated from Cleveland Chiropractic College, the family consisted of Donna Lynn, age 9, Warren, age 3, and Diana, age 1. Dr. Salzmann was a native of the state of Wisconsin and Paula hailed from the Lone Star state called Texas. Each had chosen Kansas City as the place to obtain their higher education, Doug at Cleveland Chiropractic College and Paula at St. Joseph's Hospital in their nursing program affiliated with the College of St. Theresa. As fate would have it, they met and were married in the Linwood Baptist Church. The story of how this family came to locate in the southeast portion of our state is a rather interesting example of serendipity.

Dr. Salzmann obtained his Missouri state license to practice as a Doctor of Chiropractic in the spring of 1958. He and his wife Paula desired a small community, between 5,000 and 10,000 population, as they preferred the advantages a smaller community of that size would afford their growing family. So they sectioned the state into four areas and proceeded to visit and investigate all communities within that population category during the summer of 1958. Jackson was not on their list because at that point in time its population was a mere 3,700. Southeast Missouri was the last of the four areas they visited. Sikeston, Charleston, Poplar Bluff, Kennett, Crystal City and Festus were the communities that fit into that population requirement. While traveling to the cities on their list they came through Jackson and instantly fell in love with it's well-kept homes, businesses, parks and cleanliness, and actually felt it was the prettiest town in the whole state of Missouri. However, they had no appointments and did not have time to stop and talk with any of the business people so they proceeded on to Festus and Crystal City as previously planned, but they entered Jackson into their notebook as looking like a wonderful place to live.

Upon their return to Kansas City, and as they discussed and pondered where they should go, they were intellectually drawn to Fulton or Rolla, but the beautiful town of Jackson kept coming into their minds. One day a neighbor, Cotton Olson, in visiting inquired where they intended to go. Paula replied that they were thinking about Fulton or Rolla but just couldn't get a little town in southeast Missouri out of their heads. Cotton quickly asked which town. Paula replied, "Jackson." Cotton quickly said, "My Dad is a judge there." Paula inquired if Cotton was from Jackson and she explained the family actually lived in Cape Girardeau and her father, Roland Busch, was Magistrate Judge at the county seat, which was located in Jackson. Paula asked Cotton if she would mind writing to her father to inquire if there was a need for a chiropractor in Jackson and Cotton agreed to do so.

Perhaps a week later, Cotton knocked on Paula's door. She had just received a call from Judge Busch and he had immediately inquired when she had written that letter. She gave the day and time and this was Judge Busch's reply, "Cotton, you're not going to believe this but the only chiropractor in town dropped dead unexpectedly of a heart attack at just that time. Jackson does indeed need the service of a chiropractor." Judge Busch supplied the name of the widow's attorney and within a few weeks the Salzmann family moved to Jackson on Labor Day weekend of 1958.

The Salzmann family, first row left to right: Warren, Deborah, David and Donna. Back row left to right: Dr. Douglas Salzmann, Dr. Diane Salzmann and Paula Salzmann

Dr. Salzmann served the community as a Doctor of Chiropractic from 1958 until January of 1997, at which time he retired. Paula was active in community services and the Parent-Teacher Association, she served as a girl scout leader and a Four-H leader, and was president of the Community Betterment Association the year Jackson obtained its Five Star status.

Two more children were born to this family after their move to Jackson, Deborah Lane in 1961 and David in 1968. Their oldest daughter Donna Catt is a special education teacher with the New Madrid School District and is working on her master's degree in school administration. Donna and Dr. William Catt have two sons: Anthony, a trained chef now employed by Sysco Foods, and Matthew, who just recently graduated from Southeast University with a Bachelor of Fine Arts degree. The Salzmanns' eldest son, Warren (now deceased) graduated from the United States Military Academy at West Point in 1978 and served in the armed forces for five years, reaching the rank of captain. He was working for Texas Instruments in Dallas, TX as an engineer at the time of his death. Their daughter Diana also became a Doctor of Chiropractic, graduating from her father's alma mater, Cleveland Chiropractic College of Kansas City in 1983. She later taught at Life Chiropractic College in Marietta, GA, and has a large chiropractic practice in the Atlanta area. She is married to Dr. Neale Martin, PhD, and lives in Marietta with their daughter Miranda. Deborah married Dr. John D'Onofrio and they live in the Little Rock, AR, area and the parents of three children, Anthony, Stasia and Vittoria. Deborah boards and trains horses and riders in that area. Their son, David, also lives in Little Rock, AR. David is a finish carpenter and has a year old son, Devon.

The Salzmanns realize that something greater than chance directed their steps to Jackson, and they are appreciative of the opportunities it has offered them to contribute to the betterment of this community and to serve it with their talents and presence and to partake of its beauty and opportunity. Thank you, Jackson!
Submitted by Dr. Doug Salzmann

SANDER – Christian Sander (b. Nov. 10, 1797; d. March 13, 1870), his wife Johanna (b. March 2, 1803; d. Feb. 9, 1873) and sons John Henry (b. Nov. 11, 1826; d. Sept. 1, 1905) and William (b. Aug. 11, 1838; d. Nov. 10, 1916) emigrated from Klein Rhueden, Germany, aboard the *Bark Diana*. They arrived in New Orleans on Nov. 11, 1844 and settled near Tilsit in Cape Girardeau County. Christian's occupation was listed as a wheelwright.

On Aug. 29, 1849 John married Louise Wilhelmine Macke (b. July 5, 1826; d. Jan. 23, 1893) (See Macke/Ahrens); they had six children, one of whom was Franklin "Frank" John Sander (b. Feb. 11, 1860; d. Sept. 27, 1959). Frank was married three times with his first wife being Martha Louise Bartels (b. April 9, 1862; d. Feb. 17, 1904), daughter of Charles and Sophia Caroline (Hueneke) Bartels. Mr. Bartels' parents, Christian and Elizabeth, emigrated from Schleweke, Germany, arriving on June 3, 1845, in New Orleans on the *Bark Diana*. They were part of a German immigration from the 1840-1860s that came directly to Cape Girardeau County. The Bartels are listed among the charter members of Zion United Methodist Church located west of Gordonville, MO.

Franklin and Martha were married April 27, 1882 and they had eight children. Frank later married Maria Louise Voshage Lange and Martha Bohnsack Neumeyer.

Wesley Benjamin Sander (b. Dec. 16, 1900; d. Dec. 29, 1994) was the youngest child of Frank and Martha (Bartels). He graduated from Southeast Missouri State Teachers College in 1928 with a Bachelors Degree. His first teaching position was in Tilsit, MO. On Dec. 24, 1922 he married Linda Minnie Macke (b. June 2, 1902; d. Aug. 8, 1982). Linda's parents were Herman Macke (b. Feb. 26, 1864; d. June 16, 1933) and Mathilda Augusta Illers (b. March 25, 1869; d. Oct. 5, 1948) and they were married on Dec. 4, 1891. Mathilda was the daughter of William August (b. Nov. 5, 1839; d. Oct. 11, 1914) and Hannah (Koechig) Illers (b. 1846; d. Sept. 16, 1920), who were married on April 16, 1862. All were German immigrants. Linda's grandfather, Henry Wilhelm Macke, was a brother to Wesley's grandmother, Louise Macke Sander.

Wesley and Linda had one daughter, Dorothy Marie Sander (b. Nov. 16, 1923), who married Marion Charles "Jack" Johnson (b. May 3, 1923, Fairfax, MO; d. Oct. 20, 1968). The couple was married Dec. 17, 1949 in Piggott, AR, and resided primarily in Sikeston, MO. Jack was employed by the Parks Air College at Sikeston until entering the service in February 1943. He served in WWII as a member of the Army Company B 324th Infantry Regiment 44th Armored Division. Service included the campaigns in the European Theatre. He was awarded three bronze stars, a good conduct medal, and the Purple Heart with one oak leaf cluster, and was discharged on Dec. 26, 1945. He returned home to manage the Jewell Coal Company until 1953. He was then employed by the Sikeston Fire Department until 1961. From January 1962 until his death he was employed as a safety engineer for Miller's Mutual General American Insurance Company and Travelers' Insurance Company. Dorothy was employed by the Division of Welfare from 1942-1953. After Jack's death she returned to work for the Division of Employment Security until her retirement in December of 1987. She currently resides in Sikeston, MO.

The Johnsons had two children, Linda Kathryn Johnson (b. Nov. 17, 1954) and Stanley Charles Johnson (b. April 13, 1956). Linda married William Russell Lashmet (b. April 10, 1949) on June 17, 1978 and they have a daughter Kathryn Marie (b. Sept. 11, 1985). Stanley married Pamela Macke (b. June 8, 1955) they have two children and reside near Gordonville in Cape Girardeau County (see Wicker/English entry).
Submitted by Dorothy Sander Johnson

SANDER – Johann Christian and Johanna Dorothee Behrens Sander emigrated from Bremen with their two sons Johann Heinrich (1826-1905) and Johann Christian Wilhelm Sander (1838-1916) on the ship *Bark Diana*. They arrived on Nov. 11, 1844 at the Port of New Orleans with many other Germans who settled in the German area of southern Cape Girardeau County. The father, Christian, was born in Klein Rhüden, Germany, on Oct. 26, 1798. His occupation was listed as wheelwright. The mother, Johanna, was born Jan. 21, 1804. It is likely that several small children died in Germany since there is a 12-year difference in their sons' ages. They settled in Tilsit, MO.

Johann Heinrich Sander was born on Nov. 11, 1826 in Klein Rhüden, Germany. "John Henry" Sander married Johanna Louisa Macke on Aug. 29, 1849 in Cape Girardeau County. Louisa was born July 5, 1826 (See Tilsit Lutheran Church records). They had the following children: Johanna (1851-1915) who married Friederich Schlimme; Mary (1853-1926) who first married Albert Bohnsack and then married William Woeltje; William F. (1856-1932) who married Molly Georgens; Henry John (1858-1895) who married Wilhelmia Bartels; Franklin John (1860-1959) who married Martha L. Bartels, Mary L. Voshage, and Martha Bohnsack; and Dorothea Louise (1863-1909) who married Henry John Bierschwal (See Bierschwal sketch). This family lived in Iron County in the mid 1850s before returning to Tilsit, MO, by 1860. It is believed that John Henry Sander worked in the iron mines there.

Johann Christian Wilhelm Sander was born on Aug. 21, 1838 also in Klein Rhüden, Germany. He married Wilhelmina Friederica Nienstedt on Sept. 1, 1861 in Cape Girardeau County. "Mina" was born on Feb. 7, 1843 in Gross Rhüden. They had the following children: Carolena (1863-1941) who married Henry Heimberg and lived in St. Louis, MO; Sophia Johanna (1864-1959) who married William Heinrich Deneke; Maria (1868-1931) who married Henry W. Bartels and moved to Howell County, MO; William A. (1870-1957) who married Mary Minnie Oehlschlager; John Henry (1872-1952) who married Hannah M. Deneke; Albert Martin (1875-1953) who married Anna Theresia Kies; and Wilhelmina Lydia (1879-1947) who married Arthur William Woeltje.

Many Sander descendants live in the Jackson area today. This family always spells their surname as "Sander," not Sanders. *Submitted by Dawn Dement Detring*

SANDER – Leonard F. Sander Sr. was born Dec. 21, 1918 in Cape Girardeau County, the son of Charles H. Sander and Olga Meyer Sander. His great-great grandparents, Johann Christian and Johanna Brehrens Sander, emigrated from Bremer, Germany, on the ship *Bark Diana*, arriving in New Orleans on Nov. 11, 1844. Johann was a wheelwright and they settled in the German area of southern Cape Girardeau County. The family farmed in the Tilsit area. His grandfather, William H. Sander, also became involved in the farm implement business and was elected a county judge. His father and mother moved to Jackson in 1926. Charles "Charlie" Sander opened "The Sander Sales Company" in 1934 with the help of his son, Leonard, and brother Charles W. Sander. It was the depth of the depression and the family built the hardware, appliance, paint and bottled gas business on a shoestring. Leonard was especially interested and active in radio repairs while still a student at Jackson High School.

Mr. and Mrs. Leonard F. Sander, 1943. Leonard served as a Radar Technician to U.S. Naval Air Force during WWII.

On March 20, 1938 he married Ruby Aleene Illers, daughter of William and Mabel Rice Illers, who operated a large dairy farm one mile south of Jackson. Leonard was a member of the volunteer fire department and told of turning a hose on the crowd at the sawmill fire to move the people away from an area where a smoke stack fell only a few moments later.

His interest and skill in electronics grew, and when WWII began, he volunteered for service in the Airborne Coordinating Group attached to the U.S. Navy. He was one of about 20 original technicians who installed and serviced radar in U.S. aircraft. At the time, radar was new and top secret. He taught classes in the technology at Temple University and various other locations. He served about seven months in the Aleutian Islands and about six months in the South Pacific. While overseas he was in areas that lacked many of the amenities we take for granted today. Socks and other clothing were in short supply. He decorated a Christmas tree obtained from a passing ship with string lights made from salvaged aircraft instrument lights and ornaments made from tin cans. Aleene remembers the tree was on the cover of *Life Magazine*. When he wrote Aleene in late 1943 and told her not to send any Christmas gifts, she knew he would be home in the near future.

After the war, he rejoined his brother and father in the business, which had been renamed C. H. Sander Sales Company. Hard work and honesty brought success to the company.

He and Aleene started their family with the birth of Leonard Fritz Sander Jr., in 1947. They moved to a new home on North High Street in 1953 and their second son, Paul William Sander, was born in 1955. Aleene became very active in community service work. While Fritz and Paul were in grade school, she served as room mother for every class. She organized the first community-wide cancer fund crusade. She also served in various service clubs and on the board of trustees at New McKendree United Methodist Church.

Leonard served on the Jackson City Council and 17 years on the Jackson Park Board. He was one of a few men responsible for organizing little league baseball in Jackson and was instrumental in the effort to put lights on the field by the armory at the City Park. It was one of the first lighted fields in the area. The field was later named after him in his memory. He also served on the board of trustees and the administrative board of New McKendree.

Stephen Sander

Left to right: Marsha Sander, Trentis Sander, Frank Miller, and L. Fritz Sander Jr., in background.

In 1965 Leonard left the family business and started the Sander Appliance Company on East Adams Street. In 1970 he was elected county circuit clerk and served through 1974. In 1976 he was elected county judge. His father and grandfather had also served in this position. While serving as county judge the position became county commissioner. During his 16 years of service, he supervised the construction of over 40 bridges and the numbering of all roads in the county. In 1992 he retired to private life and passed away in 1998.

Fritz returned to Jackson in 1998 after living in Minnesota for 23 years. He continues to develop his business, Sander Financial Services, helping people with their insurance and investment needs. He has two children, Stephen E. and Lindsay N. Sander. He married Marsha D. Miller in 1999. Marsha has two sons, Frank E. and Trentis E. Miller.

Paul married Pam Hahn in 1982. They have two sons, Paul Samuel and Spencer Joseph Sander. Paul was elected mayor of Jackson in 1993 and continues to serve in that position. He is also a real estate broker with Century 21 Heartland Realty.

Aleene remains active in service organizations. *Submitted by Fritz Sander Jr.*

SANDER – Public service has always been a tradition in the Sander family starting in the early 1920s when William A. Sander was elected Cape County Associate Judge and followed that with another term as Presiding Judge. He retired from the post and elected office in the latter part of that decade.

William's son, Charles H. Sander, was elected Mayor of Jackson on 1941 and served four years. He was elected Cape County Associate Judge and served from 1954 through 1956. Charles and his wife, Olga, had three children, Charles W., Leonard F., and Shirley Sander Dippold. Charles H. Sander passed away in 1984 and Olga in 1997.

The third generation of public service came from Leonard F. Sander who was first elected Clerk of the Circuit Court in Cape County. After serving one term in that office, Sander sought the position of Associate County Court Judge in District 1 in 1976. He was elected in a three-way primary race and went on to serve eight two-year terms in that office. During his tenure, the name of the position was changed from County Judge to County Commissioner.

The Sander family has been in public office since the early 1920s. The first Sander to be elected to public office was W. A. Sander, age 85, who is holding the current Mayor of Jackson Paul W. Sander, age 9 months, when this photograph was snapped in 1956. Behind W. A. Sander is Leonard Fritz Sander Jr., age 9. Next to him are the late Leonard F. Sander Sr., age 38, and the late Charles H. Sander, age 64.

Leonard served 24 years in public office and retired in 1992. Leonard and Aleene Sander had two children, Leonard F. Sander Jr. and Paul W. Sander. Leonard passed away in 1998 and his wife, Aleene, still resides in Jackson.

Paul is the fourth and current generation Sander in public service. He was first elected to the Jackson Board of Aldermen in 1986 and served four two-year terms. In 1993, he ran for Mayor of Jackson and defeated the long-time incumbent to win the office. Paul has since been reelected four more times and is currently serving his fifth two-year term. His service to the Jackson community to date totals 16 years. Paul and his wife, Pam, have two children, Paul

Left to right: Sam Sander, Leonard Sander, Aleene Sander, and Spencer Sander. Second row: L. Fritz Sander Jr., Lindsay Sander, Pam Sander, and Paul Sander.

Samuel, 13, and Spencer, 9. The family resides in Jackson.

The Sander family moved from the Tilsit area in 1926 and all generations have since grown up in Jackson. Aleene, Leonard Fritz Jr., Paul, Pam, Sam and Spencer all reside in Jackson still today.

The four generations of consecutive public service by the Sander family is thought to be one of the longest in the Jackson area and quite possibly in Missouri.

This long commitment to public service could continue with the Mayor's sons, Sam and Spencer. The next few years will tell. *Submitted by Paul Sander*

SAWYER – My grandmother always spoke so fondly of Cape Girardeau and how she stood along the river as a girl to watch the Mississippi steamboats. In the past few years, I visited the Cape to do just that and, for a moment, imagined the past as my grandmother knew it.

My grandmother, Willie Marie Sawyer, was the fourth child of William "Will" Franklin Sawyer and Minerva Adeline "Addie" Martin Sawyer and was born in Gravel Hill, MO, on July 22, 1896. Her father, Will, was born April 6, 1858 on his father's homestead just six miles north of Jackson, where he recalled that everybody worked hard clearing the land, building cabins, and mauling rails to fence the cleared land. There was a long two-mile trek through the woods to school, and neighbors were few and far between.

On Oct. 9, 1883 Will married Addie Martin in Pocahontas. They were married for over 50 years, and when they celebrated their 50th Golden Anniversary, they laughingly recalled in an interview that day that "their honeymoon vehicle was a shiny new black buggy, with large red roses painted on the sides. Mr. Sawyer owned a handsome black horse named 'Charley,' and the bride and groom felt just as classy as a modern bride and groom would feel in a brand new automobile." Mr.

Minerva Adeline Martin Sawyer and William Franklin Sawyer

Sawyer was a schoolteacher at the time of their marriage, but he and Mrs. Sawyer spent a large part of their time in the hotel business and always worked together. They operated a hotel in Cape Girardeau, but in 1914 Mr. Sawyer's health failed, and they moved to the Ozarks.

Judge John J. Sawyer, father of Will, was born in Caswell County, NC, in 1833. His parents were Stephen and Louisa (Weeden) Sawyer. In the fall of 1850, Judge Sawyer's parents settled near Jackson on a farm. The judge served as county treasurer and represented Cape Girardeau in the state legislature for three terms. He was a member of the Farmers' Mutual Benefit Association. In 1854 he married Nancy Matilda Templeton, daughter of Oni Sinclair Templeton, who was born in North Carolina, and Emily Boone Templeton, who was born in Tennessee.

The parents of Addie Martin were John Matthews Martin, a staunch southern Democrat and prominent pioneer farmer and stockman of

Judge John James Sawyer and Nancy Matilda Templeton Sawyer, others unidentified.

Cape Girardeau, and Catherine Reck Martin, daughter of George and Catherine Reck, German immigrants who came to this country in 1838 and settled near Appleton. George Reck was a farmer and shoemaker.

The children of Will and Addie Sawyer were musical. My grandmother, Willie Marie "Marie", and her sister Nellie "Nelle" Lucile were piano players. Many a time, I sat next to my grandmother on the piano bench while she played, and we both sang. My grandmother's two brothers, Eber Paul and Roswell Roscoe, played musical instruments and performed in traveling shows. At one time they had their own show, The Sawyer Show. Eber's wife Ruth was a trapeze artist.

On June 8, 1918 my grandmother, Marie Sawyer, married Edward Dawson Dawson-Watson, son of English artist Dawson Dawson-Watson. My mother, Marilyn Jeanne, was born Dec. 16, 1922 in St. Louis, MO. The family then moved to San Antonio, TX, where many years later I was born. *Submitted by Cheri Hamilton*

Marie Sawyer

SCHADE – Conrad (1869-1953) and Maria Louisa (Engelhart) [1876-1966] Schade moved from the Altenburg area to Jackson in 1906. To this union were born nine children: Herbert H. (1903-1994); Ruben R. (1905-1986); Dora B. (1907-1980); Benjamin B. (1910-1974); Leo L. (1910-1991); Irene M. (1911-1911); Arthur A. (1913-1987); Clarence C. (1915-) and Gilbert G. (1917-).

Conrad worked on the construction of the Courthouse, completed in 1908. He then opened a saloon in partnership with Silas Lail immediately west of Hotel Jackson on West Main Street. Many years later, his sons Clarence and Arthur had a men's clothing store at the same location. About 1910, he opened another saloon on South High Street. He sold this business shortly after and briefly worked in the shoe factory, then operating in the old Methodist Church building immediately north of the Courthouse where the County Jail is now located. In 1915, he opened the Gem Café on South High Street. He operated this business until the early 1930s.

The Schades first home in Jackson was near Hubble Creek near the colored school in west Jackson. Their second home was the Malloy (Willie Lewis) house just northeast of the Courthouse. Their third and final home where all the little Schades grew up was the Kneibert house on Cherry Street. In 1923, they added a second story, bath and extra clothes storage included.

The senior Schades were members of St. John's Lutheran Church in Pocahontas, while the children were all active members of St. Paul's Lutheran Church in Jackson.

Herbert had a brief stint at Milde Bottling Works, then Wagner Bakery and then he joined his father and brothers in Schade's Café. Ruben started work at the Cape County Post newspaper, and graduated from Cape State College. He later served as sheriff of Cape Girardeau County, then worked in the advertising department at the Southeast Missourian. He served as chairman of the county and district Republican committees. Dora worked for many years at Rozier's Department Store and later owned a ladies shop with brother Arthur. She also worked a number of years at Schade's Café. Twins Ben and Leo briefly worked at Milde Bottling. Leo started at the Cape County Post and for many years was owner and editor of same. Ben worked briefly at Kerstner Pharmacy, then joined in purchase of Schade's Café on West Main Street. He was later a successful sole owner for many years. Arthur served as Jackson City Collector for a number of years, then County Recorder for two terms, later joining brother Clarence in the men's clothing business. Clarence spent approximately 51 years in the mercantile and men's clothing business. He worked at Rozier's and Priest's and later owned Schade's Men's Wear stores in Cape Girardeau and Jackson. He lost a close race for County Assessor. Gilbert attended Cape State College and graduated from Missouri University with a degree in journalism. After a brief stint with a newspaper, he organized and ran a life insurance company. Most of the Schades were very active in county and district politics in behalf of the Republican Party. Brothers Herbert, Clarence and Gilbert served in the U.S. Army during WWII. The Schades' last year in Jackson was 1987. *Submitted by Clarence Schade*

Conrad Schade Home, 204 Cherry St., Jackson, MO, about 1926. Background: Conrad Schade and wife Mary Louise. Front row left to right eight children according to age: Herbert H., Ruben R., Dora B., Leo L., Ben B., Arthur A., Clarence C., Gilbert G.

SCHAEFER – William B. Schaefer was born in Cape Girardeau County on Sept. 14, 1862, his parents being Henry and Marie Hopfer Schaefer. On Sept. 22, 1892 he married Anna Schmuke. They had one son, William B., and four daughters, Marie, Katherine, Louisa and Margaretha.

Mr. Schaefer was educated in the parochial schools, the public schools, the Cape Girardeau Normal School, and West Point. After leaving school he began his business career in his father's store, and afterwards served as his father's deputy as county collector. While living in Appleton he served as postmaster for several years. In August 1891, Mr. Schaefer moved to Jackson and entered the mercantile business, in which he continued until 1912. Mr. Schaefer served as judge of the county court and as the presiding judge. He was mayor of the city of Jackson, an alderman for eight years, a member of the Jackson School Board, a member of the Commercial Club, and an energetic worker for the development and growth of Jackson. Active in banking circles, he organized the People's National Bank of Jackson, and was also a charter member of the First National Bank of Cape Girardeau, eventually becoming president of that institution. He also took an interest in agriculture, being a partner with J. C. Clippard in the ownership of a 2300-acre cotton plantation in Arkansas. Judge Schaefer passed away July 21, 1922.

William Schaefer's nephew, G. A. Schaefer Jr. of Old Appleton, MO, married Frieda Boehme, daughter of prominent Jackson farmer, Charles and Bertha Boehme, in 1932. In 1955, they moved to Jackson, where first-born daughter Jacqueline Schaefer Guth (wife of Vernon H. Guth, owner of Guth Bros. Block and Brick Company) graduated from Jackson High School in 1959. G. A. Schaefer III, a son, graduated from Jackson High School in 1965. He married Mary Sue Reiminger, daughter of Ray and Joann Reiminger, founder of Overhead Door of Jackson. G. A. and Mary Sue have three children, Derek Schaefer of Crystal, MO; Dana (Schaefer) White, married to Timothy White of Jackson; and Tyler Schaefer, currently attending Southeast Missouri State and working for Sam Beggs at Pioneer Orchard, Jackson, MO. *Submitted by Jacqueline Guth*

SCHAPER – Bernard Schaper was born May 5, 1916 in Jackson, MO. He was the son of Julius Schaper, who was born in 1884 and who died in 1971, and Frieda Kipping Schaper, who was born in 1889 and who died in 1979. In about 1914, Julius Schaper became associated with the McAtee Mercantile Company in Jackson. In 1921, Julius sold his interest in the store and became a partner in a grocery in Cape Girardeau. Consequently, Bernard's school years were in Cape Girardeau except for his final two years in Jackson High School.

When Bernard was about 9 years old, the family lived in an apartment on Broadway in Cape Girardeau. His parents didn't want him to become a "street kid" during summer vacations so they arranged for him to stay with his grandmother, two aunts and two uncles on the Schaper family farm southwest of Jackson on the Snider's Mill Road.

Grandmother Schaper had been left with nine children and two stepchildren when her husband, Carl, died in 1894. Aside from the farm, her only income came from a small Civil War pension. The three hundred acre farm was mostly wooded or suitable only for pasture and hay. It soon became evident that the land was being overcropped and it would be necessary to rent land to support the family. Grandmother Schaper's father, William Rose, had farmed land west of the Williams' plantation known as "Big Hill." Since she was known by the Williams family, it was natural she would rent land from them. Bernard remembered how his grandmother would tell how her father rented slaves from the Williams. Over the years, Grandmother Schaper's children left the farm except for Alvin, the youngest, Albert, Meta and Bertha, and they, during the summers, took care of the little city boy, Bernard. When threshing teams came to the farm, it was Bernard's job to carry water in jugs on an old horse, "Old Beaut," to the men who would pitch bundles of wheat to the wagons.

Aunt Bertha Schaper, Grandmother Carolina Schaper, Bernard Schaper and Aunt Meta Schaper.

Bernard graduated from Jackson High School in 1933, and from Southeast Missouri State Teacher's College in 1938 with degrees in business and industrial arts. After college he served in the Army and the Air Corps as a supply officer in the military for four years, first in Texas and later in Okinawa. After the military he returned to work in his father's grocery store, which had become the first self-serve store in Jackson. In 1947, Bernard and Dorothy Fulbright were married. They had two daughters, Nancy and Teri. Bernard and Dorothy were active members of the New McKendree Methodist Church and many other civic organizations. In 1947, he became a partner in the store. The Schapers built the first supermarket in Jackson in 1948. The store would continue to grow with additions in 1968 and 1970. He retired from the grocery business in 1976. Dorothy Schaper passed away in 1992.

After retirement, Bernard Schaper began a second career with his work as one of the original member of the Jackson Heritage Association and the renovation of the Oliver House in Jackson, MO. *Submitted by Bernard Schaper*

SCHATTAUER – Lloyd Schattauer was born Sept. 6, 1924 on the family farm one and one-fourth miles northeast of Pocahontas, MO. He was the son of August Schattauer, born 1889 and died 1967, and Ella Schroeder Schattauer, born 1898 and died 1969, and a brother of Lillie Schattauer Schilling, born 1927. Lloyd was baptized and confirmed at St. John's Lutheran Church in Pocahontas. He attended St. John's Parochial School, Pocahontas Public School and Jackson High School. He was a member of the 4-H Club and Future Farmers of America.

Lloyd worked on the family farm until he was called into military service on March 1, 1945. After six weeks of naval training at Great Lakes, IL, he was sent for military replacements to the southwest Pacific and landed in Okinawa on July 24, 1945. He received an honorable discharge from the U.S. Naval Service on Aug. 20, 1946. He received the Asiatic Pacific and Victory Medals. Lloyd retained his membership in the American Legion for over 56 years and was also a member of the Veterans of Foreign Wars.

Father August Schattauer, Lloyd Schattauer, sister Lillie Schattauer, mother Ella Schattauer. Picture taken in 1946 at time of military discharge.

Shortly after his military discharge, Lloyd went to work for the Pocahontas Mercantile, specializing in general grocery and propane products. In 1948 a small restaurant and grocery in Pocahontas because available for sale and Lloyd purchased the combined business. In 1950 the postmaster of Pocahontas died. At that time, postmaster appointments were made by the recommendation of the political party serving in power. Since Lloyd owned a centrally located business in Pocahontas, he was contacted by the Democratic party and asked if he was interested in serving as postmaster. He was appointed the position in 1950 and served as postmaster for 40 years at the Pocahontas office.

Lloyd and Erna Meyr were married on April 14, 1950. They had two children, Sandra and Keith. The couple built a new home in Pocahontas in 1957. Lloyd's Grocery was damaged beyond repair on May 11, 1963, when the building next door caught on fire. A vacant office building housed the post office for approximately one year until Sept. 30, 1964 when they rebuilt a corner grocery and post office.

Picture taken around 1957, in original post office and grocer store in Pocahontas, MO. Lloyd Schattauer in foreground.

In his spare time, Lloyd dealt in livestock and real estate, and maintained the family farm. An avid game hunter, Lloyd began deer hunting in 1967 and made the Missouri Show-Me Big Bucks Deer Club in 1968 with a 10-point buck. Lloyd sold the grocery store in 1975 and built the post office next door, where he continued as postmaster until his retirement in 1990. *Submitted by Lloyd Schattauer*

SCHEARF – On June 3, 1995 Kevin Schearf and Debbie Judd, who had been dating and planning their future together, went to an auction of the their dream house which was located at 425 North High. Both share a love of antiques and Victorian homes. They had spent time in the year before the auction sitting in the car together across the street just admiring the house when the owner put up a "For Sale" sign. They had even looked at the house during that time, but felt it would be too much to take on.

A year later the couple noticed a sign advertising an auction was to be held which would include the sale of the house and its contents. A few weeks before the auction, Kevin and Debbie brought their families with them to preview the house. In the weeks before the auction, it was clear to Kevin and Debbie that their families were less then enthusiastic about the possibility of them buying the house as it would require a great deal of work. The couple started to lose some of their excitement of possibly buying the house. By the day of the auction, they were basically resigned to the fact that the house would sell for more than they could afford, so they would just go to watch the auction.

At the auction, another couple that own a Victorian home began reminding them of all the possibilities the house had. By the time the house came up for bid, the couple began to regain some of their excitement. Unexpectedly, the bidding started at a level the couple felt was reasonable, so Kevin bid. In the end he was the final bidder. Since the house did not bring what the owner wanted, negotiations were held with a final price being agreed upon. At last they owned the house of their dreams. Kevin moved into the house a few months later. He lived in two rooms while beginning the restoration. The house needed to completely redone from floor to ceiling.

Kevin and Debbie Schearf 1996

About a year later, Kevin and Debbie were married. Kevin's parents are Betty (Fenimore) Schearf Ulrich of Scott City and Donald Schearf of Delta. His grandparents were Phillip and Myrtle Schearf and Thomas and Altha Fenimore. Kevin has no siblings.

Debbie is the daughter of the late Clinton H. Judd II and La Fern (Farrow) Judd of Jackson. Her grandparents are the late Clinton H. and Hazel (Steager) Judd and Vera (Davis) Farrow and the late Arnold Farrow. Debbie has one sister, Michele (Judd) Housman.

Kevin and Debbie have been working to restore the house to the early 1890s time period in which it was built by Joseph Welling Williams. He and his wife, Mary Catherine (Pace) Williams, raised six children in the home. One of those children, Helen Gladys Williams, had a granddaughter, Judith (Crowe) Renwick, who contacted Kevin and Debbie about a year after the auction. She has provided the couple with pictures of the Williams family, which the Schearfs display in their home, as well as information about the family history. She keeps in contact with the couple and has visited periodically to see the progress the couple has made. The Schearfs also had the opportunity to meet Mary Kate (Williams) Johnson and her husband, Daniel. Mary Kate's great-uncle was Joseph William.

Kevin has been employed at Proctor and Gamble in Cape Girardeau, MO for the past 16 years. Debbie works for the Sikeston Regional center. The Schearfs are members of the Jackson Heritage Association. *Submitted by Kevin and Debbie Judd Schearf*

SCHMID – Eugene "Gene" Frederick Schmid was born June 16, 1915 in Edwardsville, IL. He was the son of John and Lena (Steelinger) Schmid and had two brothers and two sisters, Walter, Esther, Bernice and Edward. He grew up in Edwardsville and graduated from Edwardsville High School in 1935. On July 25, 1937 Gene married Selma Idabelle (she did not like her middle name and later changed it to Isabelle) Fagg. When they were first married, they rented a house for $12 a month and he worked at a filling station. Then in 1941 he began working for American Oil. On June 1, 1945 he left for Fort Bragg, NC, to serve in the Army during WWII. He returned to Edwardsville in 1947 and resumed his job at the oil company. Gene and Selma had two children, Jeannie Marie (1939) and Thomas John (1947). Gene retired from American Oil in 1977, after 36 years. They moved to 423 Marrose Ann #6 in Cape Girardeau, MO, in 1986. Selma passed away at St. Francis Hospital on Sept 8, 1994.

Thomas "Tom" John married Ella Kathleen "Kathy" Skaggs (see Skaggs) on Aug. 31, 1968. In 1969, Tom graduated from Southern Illinois University at Edwardsville with a B.S. degree in business marketing/management and began work as the men's department manager for JCPenney at St. Louis' South County Mall. In 1978 he took a job in Cape Girardeau, MO, as a sales representative for Commerce Clearing House (CCH). Tom and Kathy lived in Cape Girardeau until July 25, 1982 when they moved to Jackson (Fruitland), MO. After 10 years with CCH, Tom decided to start his own business in advertising specialties, TJS Enterprises. Later he changed the name to Advertising Specialty Consultants, and in 1995 he moved the business to Jackson. He added his own full-service screen-printing in 1998, and in 1999 he bought the printing equipment from Cashbook Printing (a business that had been in Jackson for 127 years) and continued printing in the same, but newly remodeled location as ASC Printing and Promotional Products. In 2001 he added embroidery to his shop. His business is located at 104 South High Street in downtown Jackson.

Seated: Kathy and Tom Schmid. Standing left to right: Josh and Lisa Barrett, Bryan Schmid, Andrew Schmid, Julia and Eric Pitts, Dec. 9, 2001.

Tom and Kathy have four children, identical twins Lisa Michelle and Julia Renee (1976), Bryan Thomas (1981) and Andrew John (1987). Lisa and Julia graduated from Jackson High School in 1995. On July 27, 1996 Lisa married Josh Barrett of Harrison, AR, at First Baptist Church in Jackson. In 1999 Lisa graduated from Southwest Baptist University in Bolivar, MO, with a B.S. degree is psychology, and Julia graduated from Missouri Baptist College in St. Louis, MO, with a B.S. degree in psychology. Julia married Eric Pitts of Selah, WA, on Aug. 12, 2000 at Cape Bible Chapel in Cape Girardeau. They live in St. Louis, MO, and Josh and Lisa live in Jackson. Bryan graduated from Jackson High School in 1999, and currently attends Southeast Missouri State University in Cape Girardeau. Andrew will graduate from Jackson High School in 2006. *Submitted by Lisa Barrett*

SCHMUKE – Joseph E. Schmuke was born on March 16, 1870 in Jackson. He lived his entire life in Jackson. He died on Feb. 3, 1947 at age 76. His father was Joseph M. Schmuke and his mother was Catherine Elizabeth Spaulding Schmuke.

The elder Joseph was born in Switzerland on July 27, 1828. He immigrated to America with two of his brothers. The three traveled up the Mississippi River. One brother disembarked somewhere in the state of Mississippi; another in Washington, MO; and Joseph M. got off in Cape Girardeau and settled in Jackson. Shortly after the Civil War, on March 30, 1864 and at age 35, Joseph M. married Catherine Elizabeth "Kate" Spaulding of Cape Girardeau. She was of English descent. Joseph M. and Kate had four children, Joseph E. "Joe", John, Albert and Annie. Annie migrated to California. John died as a young man, unmarried at age 23. Albert went to Wichita, KS, raised a family and died there at age 78. Only Joe stayed and lived his allotted years in Jackson.

Mary Ann Hunter Schmuke age 20, about 1904

In 1908 Joe's work took him to New Madrid, MO. One of his Democratic colleagues arranged a blind date for a local dance with Mary Ann Hunter, daughter of Furgeson and Eva Hunter. Mary Ann was born March 7, 1884 and was nearly 14 years younger than Joe. About a year later, on Feb. 3, 1909 they married in Mary's hometown, New Madrid. Mary Ann died Feb. 13, 1970 at age 85. The elder Schmukes, Joseph M. and Kate, are buried in the Old Jackson Cemetery. Joe and Mary Ann are buried in the "New" Cemetery on Route PP.

Joe was a politician, businessman and avid quail hunter. He served as mayor of Jackson (giving his first campaign speech from the back of a truck parked on High Street), circuit clerk and recorder of deeds. There was reportedly great rejoicing among the Schmukes, the R. K. Wilson family and other Jackson Democrats upon the election of FDR and his promise of the end of the Great Depression. Joe's family owned a farm, the boundaries of which begin on the east side of High Street and extend to the old water tower near Jackson's water treatment plant. The Schmuke family donated the land upon which the old post office was erected (now the license office), donated land for a railroad depot (to entice the railroad to come to town) and developed commercial buildings along the east side of High Street (the old Rozier's Building to the old Albert Sanders Hardware location). Schmukes' addition to Jackson was platted early in the 1900's and sold primarily for residential development. Kate and other streets in the subdivision were designated by family member first names. Joe and the Kasten family purchased the assets of a local bankrupt brickyard and established the Kasten-Schmuke Brickyard. Joe started and operated Jackson Oil Company and ran it until well after WWII and until shortly before he died. Joe's favorite bird dog was "Bob." Family lore says Bob would wag his tail against the front porch floor shortly before 12 p.m. and

5 p.m. (well before Joe could be seen or heard by human eye and ear) walking home for lunch or after work. Bob was reputed to have gone on point for Joe while jumping a barbed wire fence.

Joe and Mary lived in the two-story, Victorian brick house at 122 East Adams Street. It was built about 1902. The home was sold to Jackson and razed about 1974. A sign of these times, the old homestead is now the parking lot behind the commercial buildings on the east side of High Street.

Joe and Mary had eight children: one son and seven daughters. The son, Joseph E. Schmuke Jr., died at about 3 months of age. The Schmuke name was destined to die with the infant, but not the family progeny. The seven daughters: Catherine S. Statler (Nov. 19, 1909 to May 31, 1991); Mary Hunter Schmuke (June 6, 1911); Laura S. Lewis (Sept. 1, 1912 to April 2, 1997); Martha A. Penzel (Sept. 1, 1914 to Oct. 2, 1950); Agnes O'Loughlin (Dec. 29, 1917); Betty S. Seabough (Oct. 8, 1922); and JoAnn S. Hill (July 29, 1924), They had 20 children. Those 20 children had, at last count, 48 great-grandchildren of Joe and Mary's.

The Schmuke family on the date of Martha's wedding, Sept. 2, 1944. Seated: Mary, Joe and Martha. Standing: Agnes, Laura, Joann, Mary Hunter, Betty and Catherine.

Mary (affectionately known as "Gran" to her grandchildren), like most women of her generation, did not drive an automobile and devoted her life to the raising of and caring for her children and grandchildren. Her home became a second home to all of her grandchildren. It was a staging ground for forays to Home-comers and Jackson's swimming pool. Joe and Mary's children regularly came home for summer vacations, Thanksgiving and Christmas. The grandchildren found a home away from home. The breadbox and the icebox were always full. Clean, starched sheets in the then vacant, spare bedrooms welcomed all who came. During this time (late 1940s and 1950s), Jackson had one policeman, 2,800 people and no one locked their doors at night. The children and grandchildren were, for the most part; free to roam the city on foot or on their bicycles at will, so long as they returned in time for meals. Warm evenings were spent in conversation on the front porch in the swing and chairs. The home was the family center of great happiness upon birth, marriage and other important occasions and a place of solace and strength in times of trial and tribulation.

Though death took Joe and Mary's Jackson citizenship, and the Schmuke name is not to be readily found, they nevertheless have left a distinct and wide footprint across the great country of which Jackson is an important part. From Montana to Florida, Michigan to Mississippi, Joe and Mary's first, second, third and fourth generations produced first-class mothers and fathers, business persons, teachers, school administrators, veterinarians, farmers, land surveyors, nurses, ministers, engineers, judges and lawyers. Though they are gone for many years, the succeeding generations' roots were begun, nurtured, widely and well-grown by Joe and Mary and their hometown, Jackson. The Schmukes are truly the now-gone, Norman Rockwell, classic tale of small-town America characterized by honesty, integrity, patriotism and a keen sense of right and wrong. To be a member of Joe and Mary's class of descendants is to be blessed. We shall ever be grateful. *Submitted by Tom O'Loughlin*

SCHWACH – Adolph P. Schwach was born June 4, 1862, in St. Louis, MO. His parents were Jacob and Anna Panoske Schwach. His parents moved to Cape Girardeau County by 1870 with his older brother Casimer and Barbara, his younger sister. Adolph married Maria Anna Frick Lohrum on May 9, 1899 in Immaculate Conception Catholic Church in Jackson, MO. Maria was the daughter of Alois and Barbara Hoef Frick. Maria was born Feb. 2, 1875 in Brewersville, near Prairie du Rocher, IL.

Adolph and Maria had nine children with only four surviving to become adults. Their children were: Anna Marie, born Aug. 9, 1901 and died Aug. 14, 1901. Anna was baptized and buried at St. Edward's Catholic Church in Dutchtown, MO. Francis Paul Schwach was born Oct. 5, 1902 and died two days later. A baby girl was born Aug. 4, 1904 and twin boys Peter and Paul Schwach were born June 29, 1905. They also did not survive.

Elizabeth Caroline Marie Schwach was born June 21, 1907 and was baptized June 30, 1907 at Immaculate Conception Church in Jackson, MO. Elizabeth married Harry H. Watkins on March 23, 1928 in Edwardsville, IL, and died on July 18, 1988. Rose Mary Schwach was born on Feb. 24, 1909 in Cape Girardeau County and was also baptized at Immaculate Conception Church in Jackson. Rose married Roby Kight on Sept. 29, 1926 in St. Louis, MO. Roby was the son of John and Elizabeth Hitt Kight. Roby was born Sept. 18, 1902 in Arbor, MO. Roby and Rose Schwach Kight had two children, Roby Jr. and Doris. Alexander Aloysius Schwach was born June 6, 1911 and was baptized at St. Mary's Catholic Church in Cape Girardeau, MO on June 11, 1911. His godparents were Ferdinand Steimle and Elizabeth Schwartz. He died on Jan. 11, 1943 in St. Louis, MO, of heart disease. Carolyn Christine Marie Schwach was born June 14, 1913 in Cape Girardeau, MO. She married Francis T. Maloney in St. Louis on Oct. 18, 1944. They moved to Niagara Falls, NY, to settle and raise their family. They had two girls, Carol Ann and Mary-Ann, and one son, Timothy.

Adolph and Maria Schwach

Adolph Schwach passed away on Jan. 23, 1935 in Cape Girardeau. He worked in teaming and other work. He was 72 years old and suffered from heart disease. He and his family had lived on a farm near Dutchtown until 1911 when they moved to Cape Girardeau, MO. Maria Schwach died on May 7, 1943 in St. Louis, MO. Adolph and Maria Schwach were members of St. Mary's Catholic Church in Cape Girardeau, MO and are buried in the church cemetery next to their son, Alexander Aloysius.

The descendants of Adolph and Maria Schwach carry on the good works of these two people and desire to pass this heritage on to their children in the future. *Submitted by Teresa Jansen*

SCHWEER – George Bryce Schweer was born on Oct. 7, 1930 the son of Otto Schweer (see Otto Schweer family) and Mollie McBryde (see Mollie McBryde Schweer family), in Jackson, MO. George graduated from Jackson High School. He was stationed in Japan during the Korean War. On Feb. 22, 1951 prior to leaving for the service, he married Ruth Elaine Noland. After leaving the service, George sold life insurance and worked for the Coca Cola Bottling Company. The family settled in Cape Girardeau. After the death of his father, Otto Schweer, in 1965, George and Ruth built a home on the family farm where he was born, about three miles north of Jackson, MO.

Ruth Elaine Noland was born on Feb. 22, 1929, the daughter of Carl Noland (see Carl Noland family) and Kathleen Bray (see Kathleen Bray Noland family). She attended high school at College High in Cape Girardeau and graduated from Southeast Missouri State College with a teaching degree in math and science. She later received a master's degree from the University of Missouri. Prior to her marriage, Ruth taught at Brick Scool and in Portageville. While George was in the service, she taught at Diehlstadt High School and Jackson High School. After her children were born, Ruth returned to teaching at Kelly High School in Benton, MO. She later taught math and science for Cape Girardeau Public Schools and then for Jackson High School. She retired from Jackson High School after 30 years of teaching. George and Ruth are members of Emanuel United Church of Christ in Jackson, MO.

Children of George Schweer and Ruth Noland Schweer include Pamela Ruth, Kathryn Sue, Cheryl Ann and Jeffrey Lynn.

Pamela Ruth (1952-) married Thomas Schulte. Pamela is a science teacher employed by Cape Girardeau Public School. Thomas is employed by U.S. Senator Christopher "Kit" Bond. They live in Gordonville, MO. Tom and Pam have two daughters, Samara Lee (1972-) and Janna Kathleen (1986-), and one grandson, Hunter Thomas Asher (1997-).

George and Ruth (Noland) Schweer, 1981.

Kathryn Sue (1954-) married Gary Turner. Kathryn is employed by Courtesy Cleaners in Cape Girardeau. Gary is an engineer for Burlington Northern Railroads. They live on the family farm purchased from her parents when they retired into Jackson. Kathy and Gary have two sons, Joshua Lynn (1978-) and Benjamin Bryce (1980-). Joshua married Jennifer Peters in 2001.

Cheryl Ann (1957-) married Clarence Bodenstein (later divorced). Cheryl is employed as a teacher aide for Jackson School District.

They have two children, Thor Jeffrey "T. J." (1992-) and Shelly Ann (1994-). Cheryl and her family live in Jackson, MO.

Jeffrey Lynn (1958-1991). After his graduation from Southeast Missouri State University, Jeffrey moved to Alameda, CA, where he was employed by the *San Francisco Chronicle* newspaper until his death in 1991. He is buried in the church cemetery of St. John's United Church of Christ near Fruitland, MO. *Submtited by Pam Schulte*

SCHWEER – Mollie McBryde's great-grandfather Archibald McBryde was born in Scotland around 1768, the son of James McBryde and Janet McMiken. He sailed to America with his parents, settling in North Carolina in 1775. Archie married Rebecca Coffee. Their son, James W. III (1822-1895), left for Tennessee at the age of 14, where he worked as a carpenter. He and Harriet Baker Gordon (1820-1895) married in 1848 and moved to Cape Girardeau County where they farmed land along Cane Creek north of Jackson, MO. James and Harriet are both buried in the Jackson City Cemetery.

Edward Baker "E. B." McBryde, son of James and Harriet, was born in 1854. He married Margaret Summers in 1879. Together they had two daughters and three sons. After Margaret's death, E. B. married Laura Kathryn "Kate" Yoder in 1898. They had two children, Mollie, born in 1900, and Clarence "Butch" born in 1902. E. B. McBryde died in 1906 and is buried in the Jackson City Cemetery. Kate died in 1913 as a result of a hemorrhage, which occurred as she was traveling to town in a buggy. Mollie went to live with her half-sister Annie (McBryde) Wolfenkoehler until her marriage to Otto Schweer in 1917.

Kate Yoder was the daughter of Andrew Franklin "Frank" Yoder and Mary "Mollie" Browning. Frank's great-grandfather Conrad Yoder arrived in America from Switzerland around 1746 and settled in Pennsylvania, where he married Christina Klein. They migrated to North Carolina in the 1750s and settled near what was at the time the Indian frontier. Skirmishes with the Cherokees were common occurrences. Conrad became an ardent supporter of the American Revolution. His son David (1770-1864) was a farmer, brickmaker and cabinetmaker. David married Elizabeth Reep and fathered at least ten children. One of his sons, Eli Yoder, married Elizabeth Detter and became the father of Frank Yoder.

Otto Schweer and Mollie McBryde on their wedding day, 1917

Mollie Browning Yoder was a direct descendant of Captain John Browning, born in England around 1548. He arrived in Virginia with his son William in 1622, where he lived on a plantation about three miles from Williamsburg and served as a burgess in Virginia City. William settled in Jamestown. William's son, grandson, great grandson and great-great grandson, all named John, continued to live in Virginia. John Browning IV had a son Charles, who moved to Tennessee after serving in the War of 1812. Charles' son William, born around 1820, was a carpenter and joiner in Tennessee. He married Elizabeth Elliot in 1846. Their oldest child was Mollie.

Mollie Browning married Frank Yoder in Tennessee. They settled in Cape Girardeau County on a farm near Jackson where they raised a family of 14 children. Frank died in 1926 of a throat hemorrhage from a malignant growth on his neck. Mollie died in 1927 of a heart attack, which she mistook for colic. Both are buried in Russell Heights Cemetery in Jackson, MO. *Submitted by Pam Schulte*

SCHWEER – Otto Schweer was born July 30, 1895 the son of George Albert and Emma Marie (Friedrich) Schweer, on the family farm near Fruitland, MO. On Oct. 4, 1917 he married Mollie McBryde. They moved into the family home built by her late father, Edward Baker McBryde, along Cane Creek north of Jackson, MO. Here they resided, farming and raising a family, until his death in 1965. Mollie remained on the farm for several years following his death, then sold the farm to her son George and bought a house in Jackson. She died in 1992. Both Otto and Mollie Schweer are buried in the church cemetery at St. John's United Church of Christ near Fruitland, MO.

Otto Schweer family, 1965. Seated: Otto Schweer, Mollie (McBryde) Schweer. Standing: Berniece (Schweer) Bogenpohl, Olga (Schweer) Reitzel, Gary Schweer, George Schweer, Betty (Schweer) Baxter and Fern (Schweer) Schlimme.

Children of Otto and Mollie Schweer include: Olga (1918-) who married Earl Reitzel, and who lives in Jackson, MO; Berniece (1920-1990) who married Ruben Bogenpohl; Fern (1922-) who married Millard Schlimme, and who lives in Cape Girardeau, MO; Betty (1925-) who married Clyde Baxter, and who lives in Florida; Helen (1927-1938); George (1930-) who married Ruth Noland, and who lives in Jackson, MO; and Gary (1939-), who married Betty Franck.

Otto Schweer's great grandparents, Johann Dietrich (ca. 1795-1875) and Sophia (ca. 1808-1859) Schweer, were born in Hanover, Germany. They sailed for America with their three children in October 1845, arriving at the port in New Orleans in December, and then settling near Fruitland, MO. In 1848 their youngest son William (grandfather to Otto) was born.

William Schweer married Canzada Walker (daughter of Silas Walker and Caroline Wills) around 1869. They had five children. William, known as "Grandpa Billy," died in 1932 after being bedridden for three years following a severe stroke. Canzada preceded him in death by a number of years. Both are buried in Apple Creek Presbyterian Cemetery.

William's oldest son, George Albert, was the father of Otto. He was born in 1869 in Cape Girardeau County. In 1891 he married Emma Friedrich, the daughter of Henry and Hannah (Kleinswonger) Friedrich. George and his brother Amos were victims of the 1918 flu epidemic. Emma died in 1943. George, Emma, and her parents are buried in St. John's United Church of Christ Cemetery. *Submitted by Pam Schulte*

SEABAUGH – Dr. Dayton Isadore Layton Seabaugh was born Aug. 27, 1882 and died March 16, 1969. Lillie Lucretia Limbaugh was born Aug. 18, 1884 and died June 18, 1984. Dayton Isadore Layton was one of eight children of Christian and Sarah Seabaugh. His siblings were Noah, who died in infancy, Wilbert, Columbus, Odie, Autie, Loy and sister Pricilla. They lived on a large farm in Bollinger County and attended school in the local rural school. After 8th grade, D. I. L. went to Sedgewickville Academy for four years. Upon graduation he enrolled in Barnes Medical College in St. Louis for four years (1901-1905), graduating on May 3, 1905 with a doctor of medicine degree. In June of 1905 he opened his practice of medicine in Millersville, MO, and remained there until July 13, 1922 when he moved his practice to Jackson until 1966. During this time he served on the school boards of both Millersville and Jackson, and the Board of Jackson Exchange Bank. He was a member of Jackson Rotary Club, Cape County Medical Society, the State and American Medical Societies and New McKendree Methodist Church.

Lillie Lucretia Limbaugh was a daughter of Joseph and Susan Presnell Limbaugh. She had four brothers, Arthur, Burette, Roscoe and Rush, and two sisters who died young, Hattie and Jennie. They lived on a farm in the Sedgewickville area. She attended grade school in that area and after 8th grade, four years at the Sedgewickville Academy. After graduation she taught in Scopus School. Dr. D. I. L. and Lillie were married Sept. 10, 1905 and lived in Millersville until July 13, 1922 when they moved to Jackson. They were parents of two sons, Dayton Rusby "Rusby" and Loy Rush "L. R." While living in Jackson she was active in many organizations: Cape County Medical Auxiliary, Jackson PTA, Jackson Library Board, Federated Women's Club, Homemaker Club and many activities of New McKendree Methodist Church.

Dr. and Mrs. D. I. L. Seabaugh on their 50th Wedding Anniversary.

On Sept. 15, 1965 they celebrated their 60th wedding anniversary. They had over 63 years of happy marriage. They had two sons, seven grandchildren, 20 great-grandchildren and four great-great grandchildren. Dr. D. I. L. had several relatives who were medical doctors: brother O. L., two sons, D. Rusby and L. R., a nephew William O. L., cousin Dewey, and two grandsons, D. Rusby Jr. M.D. and Stephen D.M.V.

During the early years of his practice D. I. L. delivered many babies in the homes. He traveled by horse and buggy or horseback to his patients' homes. In 1912 he owned a car, but many of the roads were not fit for cars so he used his horse and buggy. In the early days there were no drug stores. The doctors made their own medicines and Dr. D. I. L. did this. There were not a lot of medicines in his early years of practice. The flu epidemic of 1918-1919 was very hard on doctors and families. He worked many hours of the day and into the night. During this time he hired a driver so he could sleep while riding between the sick homes. D. I. L. saw many changes in the medical world from 1905 until his retirement in 1966. *Submitted by Betty Seabaugh*

SEABAUGH – I, Eugene Seabaugh, started and operated, with my wife Hazel, in 1953 what came to be known as the "Seabaugh Christmas Tree Farm."

At my age of 33, while employed at the Jackson Hosiery Mill for 13 years, I had just received a copy of the *Capper's Weekly* newspaper in which a small article stated that "Iowa farmer makes good growing his own Christmas trees." After due consideration, I decided to proceed by planting several varieties of evergreens through a state-sponsored agricultural program. I was also a 20-year charter member of the Missouri Christmas Tree Growers Association.

Eugene and Hazel Seabaugh

After leaving the hosiery mill, we operated Seabaugh I.G.A. Supermarket for 20 years in Oak Ridge, MO, concurrently to the operation of the tree farm for 39 years, which was the first tree farm south of St. Louis, MO.

Also, at the tree farm we built, in 1976, one of the first new log homes in our area. Our forty-acre farm was located five miles north of Oak Ridge on County Road 510 and one mile from Highway 61.

What was started as a more or less family venture of the tree business with my wife and I and our three children, Cindy, Ron and Keith, came to an end after my 26 years of a growing disability of a loss of strength. The decision was made to discontinue my operation after a farm auction and sale of the farm in 1992. The new owner's operation of the farm was insufficient and lax and after his operation a few years it was shut down.

After my disability was triggered from an unknown origin (either a damaged spinal cord or MS), I and my helpmates continued planting evergreens for up to a quarter of a million trees during our 39 years of growing them. Shearing, shaping and controlling the insects were an endless task along with a continuing fight with the survival rate of the trees.

Gene and Hazel Seabaugh Tree farm and log home, 1977.

However, the one final plus sign of this tree-growing venture was that of marketing. This joyous time of the years packed with the excitement of choosing and cutting of the customer's trees made it all a very worthy and satisfying accomplishment. *Submitted by Gene Seabaugh*

SEABAUGH – A United States Office of Geographic publication shows two population centers in East Germany named Seebach, four more population centers in West Germany and one population center in Switzerland named Seebach, which is the German and/or Swiss spelling of Seabaugh. The first known ancestor of the Seabaugh family was Eckerhardue de Sebecki, who took the route from Switzerland down the Rhine River to Cowes, England, on to America with service in Washington's Army.

The earliest known record of a Seabaugh in America shows a Christopher Seabaugh on an original tax list in Middleton/Paxton, PA, in 1750, occupation hatter. He traveled the great Philadelphia wagon road to Lincoln County, NC. His descendants, including Christian Seabaugh, arrived in 1809 at a Cape Girardeau territory trading post at Lot #99 in Jackson, MO, also listed as a hatter. He eventually settled in Bollinger County with his 15 children, one of whom was Jesse Seabaugh from whom the John O. Seabaugh family descended.

John O. Seabaugh married Sally Caroline Green in 1913. In the fall of 1927, John Seabaugh purchased a 175-acre farm on the Oak Ridge Road, where they reared their seven children: Otto, Bill, Maxine, Hazel, Eugene, J. B. and Jerry, all of whom attended the Jackson public school system, for the most part walking daily at two miles to school. Droughts and depression years took their toll until the WWII era cattle raising helped bring the family to prosperity.

Each of the seven children took their own routes. Otto married Della Seivers and graduated from college at Southeast Missouri Teachers College, received a masters degree at University of Missouri, then went to Small Arms Plant in St. Louis and on to New Haven, CT, with the Olin Corporation to retirement back home in Jackson. Bill served in WWII in the European theater and returned to Jackson to the Ford Tractor Implement business. Maxine married John Fred Hartle and resided in Jackson. Hazel married Joseph Vincent Haynes and as an Air Force officer's wife, traveled the globe. Eugene and his wife Hazel Jones, after a stint at the Jackson Hosiery Mill, purchased the IGA and Seabaugh Tree Farm in Oak Ridge, MO. J. B. married Odetta Cobble and worked at Pocahontas Lumber. Jerry married Phyllis Schwartz and spent 43 years with Southwestern Bell Telephone Company.

John O. and Sallie Caroline Green Seabaugh.

It is with much pride that the Seabaugh family can look back at their family home and now see the Broadridge Subdivision, Jackson Middle School, Orchard Elementary School and bus garages, Jackson Manor, offices of Drs. Asher

The children of John Otto Seabaugh and Caroline Green Seabaugh: left to right on front row: Maxine Seabaugh Hartle and Hazel Seabaugh Haynes. Back row: J. B. Seabaugh, William B. Seabaugh, Otto G. Seabaugh, Eugene Seabaugh and Jerry L. Seabaugh.

and Downey, duplexes, apartments, a retirement complex, as well as residential homes. *Submitted by Phyllis Seabaugh*

SEABAUGH – The Seabaugh family started in Germany. Christopher Seabaugh immigrated to Pennsylvania in the 1700s. They settled in Lancaster County, PA. The records show he had a wife but no name is given. They had one son. They named him Christian Seabaugh.

Christian Seabaugh married in 1772 to Christina Statlar. They together had 15 children: Joseph, Elizabeth, Catherine, Jacob, Christian Jr., Christopher, Adam, Peter, Christina, Emanuel, Daniel, Barbara, David, Sarah and Jesse.

The family left Pennsylvania. They moved to North Carolina sometime after the war, between 1783 and 1787. Christian and family moved from North Carolina to Missouri. The land was cheaper in the early winter of 1809. Christian and family lived in Jackson, MO for a short time. Then they moved to a German Township. Early settlers were of German heritage. The town was renamed Scopus, MO.

Christian Seabaugh died around December 1835. Christina died January or February 1837.

One of Christian and Christina Seabaughs children, Christian Seabaugh Jr., married Catherine Smith in 1811 and she died. Christian Jr. remarried Feb. 15, 1831 to Christina Hayden. Their children were: Allen; Christina; Matilda; Francis; Barbara; Christian III; Thomas; Sarah and Melvina.

Allen Seabaugh married Barbara Statler on June 25, 1835. Their children were: Jesse; Conrad; Catherine; Bennet; Carline; Thomas Allen; Aleline; Melvina; Allen Jr. and Julia Ann.

Bennet Seabaugh married Frances "Fanny" Crites on Feb. 5, 1868. One of their children was William Edward Seabaugh. William married Barbara Ellen Seabaugh on Aug. 7, 1890. They had 10 children: Ellis Elmer, Lena Luecreshie, Joseph "Joey" Bennet, Annie Myrtle, Toney Edward, Minnie Jane, Elizza Esther, Ida Mae, Dale David and Ella Ether.

Lena Luecreshie Seabaugh married Henry Charles Maintz on May 10, 1928. They lived between Millerville and Daisy on County Road 471. Henry was a farmer and Lena stayed home and helped on the farm. They lived on 329 acres of ground. This was Henry Maintz' mother and father's house. They had four children: Hoover Dempsy, Geraldine Esther, Marie Roselee and Dorothy May.

Hoover Maintz married Lurena Niswonger on Nov. 22, 1947. They had three children: David Lee, Kathryn Dell and Carol Ann. Hoover died Jan. 24, 1981. David died on March 6, 1995.

The William and Barbara Seabaugh family
Left to right, first row: Dale, Lena, Barbara, Ella, William, Joey's wife Laurie and daughter and Ellis. Second row: Mae, Myrtle, Minnie, Toney's wife Roxie, Toney, Esther and Joey.

Both are greatly missed. Geraldine Esther married Leroy Seabaugh on Aug. 29, 1953. They had one son, Gary Edward Seabaugh. Marie Roselee married John Moneyhun on May 15, 1954. They had one daughter, Connie Sue Moneyhun. Dorothy May married Truman Horn on July 12, 1968. They had two children, Vickie and Teresa Horn.

They sold the farm in 1978 to move closer into the town of Jackson. They sold the farm to the Missouri Conservation. They also bought Henry's uncle's farm. They combined and made Maintz Preservation on the land. They moved on West Lane in Jackson. Lena's brother Dale David Seabaugh lived up the street from them.

Henry died on Sept. 30, 1992. Lena died on Oct. 15, 1999. She was the last of her brothers and sisters to live the longest. Henry and Lena Maintz had four children, seven grandchildren, 10 great grandchildren, and six great-great grandchildren. *Submitted by Vickie (Horn) Ford*

SEABAUGH – Woodrow W. Seabaugh was born on Jan. 6, 1914. He was the son of Francis Emerson Seabaugh (May 3, 1886-April 30, 1959) and Jane Seabaugh Seabaugh (May 18, 1888-Sept. 18, 1961). The family owned and operated a farm near Sedgewickville, MO. Woodrow, commonly known as Woodie, graduated from Jackson High School in May of 1931 along with his older sister Ollie Louise Seabaugh Friedrich. Because there was only a two-year high school in the town of Sedgewickville, the parents opted to send the children to Jackson High School to graduate. The other siblings, twins Mildred "Sis" and Milford "Bud," graduated from Jackson High School in 1943.

Woodrow, after substituting as a teacher in Bollinger County schools, served in the Civilian Conservation Corps near Little Rock, AR. Upon completion of that period he returned to Jackson and worked with this brother-in-law, Robert Friedrich, who operated a Shell station on West Main Street in Jackson.

Woodie and Jean Seabaugh, Aug. 20, 1942.

In 1940 Woodie enlisted in the Air Force and was sent to Morris Field, CA, for basic training. In May of 1941 he was sent to Scott Air Force Base in Belleville IL, for training as a radio operator. His training there had been completed, as well as a leave following graduation, on the day of Pearl Harbor, Dec. 7, 1941. As ordered, he immediately left to report to his new assignment at March Field in California. In May of 1942 he was accepted as a candidate for officers' training and later graduated from the school at Fort Monmouth, NJ, in August of 1942.

Woodie and Jean Smith, daughter of W. C. and Ada Robinson Smith of the Old McKendree-Williams Creek Community, were married Aug. 20, 1942 at the Sedgewickville Lutheran Church. Jean continued her employment in the office of International Shoe Company in Jackson until a call from Woodie "ordered" her to report to Orlando, FL, where he was stationed. They lived in Florida until November 1942 when Woodie was ordered to serve outside the United States.

Woodie left the United States in November 1942, serving in North Africa, Italy, Sicily, France and Germany until November 1945 and then returning to the United States via England. By chance, Woodie and his brother-in-law Robert Friedrich met in Germany in 1944. During those three years, Jean spent her time writing daily to Woodie and was employed again in the office of International Shoe in Cape Girardeau, scheduling orders for combat boots.

Woodie and Jean Seabaugh home, Sanford Addition, North High Street, Jackson, MO.

Upon his return, Woodie and Jean bought property in the Sanford Addition on North High Street, built their home and lived there until 1994. While the home was being constructed they lived in the old Sanford house in the city park just across the street. Jean would sit on the tiny upstairs porch and watch the building progress on their home. Two children, James Michael, born Oct. 3, 1946 and Marie Michelle, born Nov. 26, 1949 have each opted to make their homes in Jackson with their families.

In March 1946 Woodie and his brother-in-law, Robert Friedrich, began an electrical contracting business with an appliance store called Jackson Electric. This was located in the dining room of Hotel Jackson on West Main. In 1957 Woodie sold his interest and entered into politics. He was elected in 1958 and served as Clerk of the Circuit Court from 1959 through 1970. Following that he was with Employment Security of the State of Missouri, retiring in 1979. Jean served as Probate Clerk from 1953 through 1987.

In 1947 Woodie, along with a group of former servicemen, was instrumental in obtaining a Missouri National Guard Unit in Jackson, which is still an active unit with an Armory in Jackson.

The local roller skating rink, located at the west intersection in Jackson, was placed on the market in March of 1954. Feeling that the place for recreation was needed locally, the decision to purchase resulted from a Sunday afternoon conversation on the way to visit Woodie's parents. The business flourished and in 1960 the building was enlarged. A lunch counter, bowling machines, and a special room for teen dances were added. There are many cherished memories of the years spent there and many good times are remembered by the teems (now adults) who had fun at the Roll O' Fun. The business was sold in 1983 and still continues to this date.

Woodie and Jean were active citizens of Jackson and members of New McKendree United Methodist Church. Woodie served on the Board of Trustees and Jean as secretary to the Administration Board. Both served with Boy Scouts and Girl scouts as leaders. Woodie was a member of the Jackson Rotary Club, serving as president. Woodie built a boat for family recreation. Many scouts and other young people learned to ski behind that boat, even Jean who was not a swimmer.

Woodie and Jean continued a happy retirement at 718 North High, enjoying their grandchildren: Spencer, Jeremy, Heather, Cass, Kerri and Blake. In June of 1993 Woodie suffered a stroke and was hospitalized until November 1993. He was transferred to the Missouri Veterans Home in Cape Girardeau where he passed away on Jan. 19, 1994. Jean sold their home to her son Michael and moved into an apartment. She continues to be active with part-time employment in the jewelry department at the local Wal-Mart store where she enjoys seeing her friends. She is active in her church, and enjoys spending special times with her two sisters Vickie and Mary Lou. She and Woodie now have six great-grandchildren. *Submitted by Jean Seabaugh*

SEBASTIAN – Hermann Sebastian was born April 14, 1838, in Altenburg, Germany and married Elizabeth H. Barbaroski (Warbresky) on March 3, 1856. They had the following children: Henry (Heinrich) (b. April 5, 1858; d. March 7, 1902); Emil or Emelia (b. Dec. 14, 1859); John William (b. Jan. 3, 1863 at Appleton, MO); Emma; Phillip; and Hermann (b. Sept. 8, 1872).

John Sebastian's first marriage was to Mathilda Catharine Kester (b. July 21, 1870; d. March 9, 1892; buried in the Zion Lutheran Church in Gordonville, MO). They were married on April 12, 1892, and had one child, Bertha Helene Sebastian (b. March 8, 1892; d. April 8, 1968), who was married on Nov. 2, 1913, to Henry Michael Sailer and had four children: Ruth, Dorothy, Grace and Calvin.

John W. Sebastian's second marriage was to Caroline "Carrie" Ehelebe of Warsaw, IL, in 1893. John and Caroline are both buried in Memorial Park in Cape Girardeau. They lived on a farm near Gordonville, MO, where the following children were born: Herman Christian (b. Aug. 11, 1894; d. July 7, 1968), who never married; Lulu Katherine (b. Aug. 2, 1896; d. July 27, 1965), who never married; Myra Emma (b. Feb. 22, 1899; d. Feb. 19, 1967), who never married; John "Jack" William (b. April 14, 1902; d. May 15, 1956), who married Anna Ethel Snyder on Sept. 1, 1928, at Pontiac, MI, and had four children: John, Phyllis, George, Sally and Gloria; Rudolph Arnold (b. Aug. 26, 1905; d. Nov. 13, 1968), who married Helen Mae Inman on Feb.

22, 1935, at Gordonville, MO, and had three children: Wesley, Dorthy, and Caroline; Theta Clifta (b. April 13, 1908; d. Feb. 1, 1992), who married George William Nussbaum on April 13, 1939; and Carroll "Hawkshaw" Milton (b. May 14, 1911; d. Feb. 23, 1952 in Michigan), who was married in Jonesboro, IL, on Aug. 15, 1932 to Eula Gladys Goza, and had one child, Barbara Jean.

Caroline Ehelebe's parents are Christian Ehelebe (born in Germany around 1825) and Katherine Hehner Ehelebe (born in 1831 in Germany).

Back row, left to right: Bertha Seiler, Dorothy Seiler, Henry Seiler, Jack Sebastian, Myra, Lulu, and Herman Sebastian. Front row: Rudolph, John Sebastian, Carroll, Theta, and Carolina Ehelebe Sebastian.

George Nussbaum and Theta Clifta Sebastian were married in Cape Girardeau, MO, and lived in Gordonville, MO, on the family farm. They had three children: Dewey J. Nussbaum (b. April 26, 1940) married Gwendolyn McSpadden of Burfordville, MO, on Jan. 29, 1961; Katherine Ann (b. Sept. 29, 1941) married Donald Gene Lynn of Benton, MO, on Oct. 17, 1970; and Mary Emma (b. April 28, 1944) married Michael Wayne King of Oak Ridge, MO, on June 25, 1966.

A few years after George's death Theta moved to the Sebastian family home on Lorimier Street in Cape Girardeau and resided in Cape Girardeau until her death in 1992. *Submitted by Gwen Nussbaum*

SEITZ – Seitz, Sitz, Sites or Sides. These are variations of the same name. Johann Henrich "John Henry" Seitz at the age of 26 arrived in America on the *Queen Elizabeth* ship on Sept. 16, 1738. He came from Rhineland-Palatinate, Germany. The Seitz' settled in North Carolina for a while. Records show these hardy pioneers moved westward. By the mid 1800s, some members of the Seitz family had moved to Missouri, settling in the Leemon area of Cape Girardeau County. It is from these settlers that we descended. The spelling of the family name was Americanized to Sides. The Sides family multiplied and many descendants live in Cape Girardeau County today. Some of the local cemeteries that provide information on the Sides are: Apple Creek in Pocahontas, MO, Darby in Leemon, MO and Sides in Arnsberg, MO.

John Alexander (1852-1927) and Sarah Jane Martin Sides (1848-1919) had six children. The youngest, Samuel Price Sides (1885-1955), was first married to Lula Mae Gordon (1888-1919). This union produced six children. After Lula died, Price married Nancy Hargraves (1899-1942) and had eight more offspring. From the two marriages, twelve children lived to adulthood: Agnes Odessa, Ada Ruth, Norma Marie, Wilson Gordon, Lloyd Eldon, Roy Eugene, Dorothy Jane, Betty June, Rose Mary, Robert Jerry, Nancy Mae and Virginia Lou.

As of this writing, three of the five daughters still living, live in Missouri. These pioneers were hardy Germans with Irish and Indian mixed to help create a new nationality called Americans. *Submitted by Barbara Scheper*

SEARCEY – Robert William Searcey was born June 6, 1847/51 in Gilmer County, GA, the son of Robert and Nancy Telitha Tucker Searcy. His father was born in 1810 in Rutherford County, NC and died on Nov. 19, 1861 in Wayne County, MO. His mother, Nancy, was one-fourth Cherokee Indian, the daughter of John "Big Head" and Ruby Holloway Tucker. Nancy was born Aug. 7, 1828 in North Carolina and died the winter of 1880.

Robert William Searcey married Lucy Ann Knott on Dec. 22, 1870 near Jackson, MO. She was born Nov. 25, 1855 the daughter of Benedict B. and Ann Elizabeth Elliot Knott. They had the following eight Searcey children: William John (1871-1952) who married Clara Smythe; Elizabeth Jennie (1874-1892) who married Wade Strong; Nellie G. (1877-1910) who married James A. Barks; Charles Russell (1879-1960); Stephen Linder (1881-1961) who married Emma Bierschwal; Andrew Glen (1882-1946); Effa E. (1886-1887); and Margaret E. (1889-1924) who married Ellis W. Wissman.

Stephen L. and Emma Bierschwal Searcey

Robert Searcey died Dec. 4, 1909 at their home on Perryville Road in Cape Girardeau and is buried in Fairmont Cemetery there. Lucy died on Oct. 23, 1922 after being struck by a Ford truck rounding a corner in downtown Cape Girardeau. She had gone to surprise a son who was traveling through the area by train. The train left after making its stop with her son not knowing about his mother's accident.

Stephen Linder Searcey was born March 8, 1881 near Jackson, MO. Family legend says that Linder was an important family name. Stephen worked with his father at a flour mill later known as the Whitewater Milling Company. They made White Rose and Elkhorn flour. Stephen married Emma Mary Bierschwal on Aug. 31, 1905, the daughter of Henry John and Dorothea Sander Bierschwal. He operated a small grocery store in the Whitewater Bank building for 46 years. The bank had closed during the depression. Steve and Emma had the following children: Doraretta Marie (1906-1984) who married Wilson Blumenberg; Robert Henry (1908-1908); Ralph Linder (1909-1909); and Ray Milton (1910-1948) (see Blumenberg sketch for Wilson and Doraretta's children). Around 1918, Emma contracted tuberculosis. Doraretta took over all the household chores including caring for her mother and her young brother. In later years, Steve Searcy built a small house at 628 South Sprigg Street, Cape Girardeau, MO. They lived there during the 1950s. It was torn down in fall of 2000, making room for commercial development for the new Emerson Bridge.

Steve died July 16, 1960 of cancer of the esophagus, likely from years working in the mills. Emma died April 26, 1965 at a hospital in Farmington. Both are buried at the Whitewater Methodist Church Cemetery along with their three sons. *Submitted by Dawn Dement Detring*

SEYLLER – Steven Edward Seyller was born on Feb. 17, 1957 in Elgin, IL. His parents were Donald and Barbara (Johnson) Seyller of Elgin. He married Susan Mae Matthis of Elgin, IL on April 26, 1974 while they both attended Larkin High School in Elgin. She was born on June 6, 1956 to Kenneth and Janice (Kremke) Matthis of West Helena, AR. Steven and Sue had four children: Steven Kenneth born Aug. 21, 1974; Christina Ann born Oct. 20, 1978; Jessica Marie born July 24, 1991; and Jason Michael born April 11, 1994. Steven Kenneth moved to Gunnison, Colorado and Christina, Jessica and Jason all reside in the Jackson area.

Steve's paternal great-grandparents were Michael (who came over to this country from Alsace-Lorraine when he was 12 years old) and Kathryn Seyller, and Joseph and Victoria Sester (who both came over from Alsace-Lorraine). His paternal grandparents were Frank and Louise (Sester) Seyller of Burlington, IL.

Steve joined the Marine Corps on Sept. 5, 1974 and was discharged honorably from active duty in December 1979. He remained in the Marine Corps Reserve, reporting to Headquarters and Headquarters Squadron 48, Marine Air Control Group 48, Naval Air Station Glenview, IL. Later he was transferred to Marine Wing Communications Squadron 48, Marine Air Control Group 48, Ft. Sheridan, IL near Chicago, IL. He completed another 26 years in the reserves, obtaining the rank of Master Gunnery Sergeant. He was activated briefly on Feb. 13, 1991 for Desert Storm.

Steve started working for the United States Postal Service in October 1980 at the North Suburban Processing and Distribution Center in River Grove, IL. Later he was moved to the Carol Stream Processing Center on Carol Stream, IL. Susan started working at St. Joseph Hospital in Elgin, IL in May of 1980.

The Seyller family: (clockwise) Steve, Susan, Jessica, Christina, Jason and Steven.

They lived in Elgin most of their lives both before and after Steve's military service. The family decided to move a little farther south and get away from the fast pace of the big cities. During their job and house hunting, they made their way though southeast Missouri and really enjoyed the friendly people, good schools, and affordable living the area had to offer. Steve took a job transfer on Feb. 17, 1996 while working for the United States Postal Service. His move

Price Sides and Nancy Hargraves Sides, circa 1920.

brought him to the Processing Center in Cape Girardeau, MO. Susan was later employed at St. Francis Hospital in Cape Girardeau, MO. After a brief stay in Chaffee and Cape Girardeau, they Seyllers had a home built and took up residence in the Jackson area. *Submitted by Steve Seyller*

SHANER – George Monroe Shaner was born Nov. 12, 1832 in Brazeau, MO, the son of Jacob Shaner and Elizabeth Seibert Shaner. George married Roena Elizabeth McCombs of Jackson, MO. Roena (Aug. 14, 1842-Oct. 28, 1873) was the daughter of Eli McCombs and Martha Beal McCombs. They made their home in the Brazeau Community and were the parents of Randolph, William, Lawrence, Mollie, Minnie and Roena. Roena Elizabeth died in childbirth when her daughter Roena was born. Dr. John McCombs and his wife took baby Roena into their home on North High Street in Jackson.

George moved his family to Jackson after the death of his wife and they lived in a large white house called the Sanford House. It was on a hill next to where the old swimming pool was in the Jackson City Park. George later moved his family to a large farm northeast of Jackson on Greensferry Road. He was killed in a farming accident on his farm in 1884 and his family was left without parents. The older children helped to raise the younger ones.

Lawrence Shaner family: Lawrence, Howard, Ilda and Ella.

George's son Randolph married Ella Belle Hensley. They made their home and raised their family on a farm near the home place. After Ella's death, he married Bertha Harris. Lawrence, William, Rosebud, Corrine and Lillian were the children of this union.

Lawrence M. Shaner married Ella Heuer and they made their home on a farm that was connected to the home place on the north. They had two children, Howard and Ilda.

William also reared his family on a farm nearby. He married Daisy Steward and they had three daughters: Dale, Carrie and Willie.

Mollie, the oldest daughter, married Douglas Hensley. They lived on land adjacent to the home place as well. The names of their children were: George, Cline, Harry, Glenn, Joe, Robb, Roena and Martha.

Minnie married Jefferson McClain and moved to the Oriole community where they owned and operated a store. Their children were Maude and Lawrence.

Roena Shaner never married. She lived on North High Street in Jackson until her death. She was an active member of the New McKendree Methodist Church. Roena was a part of the WCTU temperance movement. *Submitted by Mary Morton*

SHEPPARD – Located about four and a half miles northwest of Jackson on County Road 450 (R.F.D. 2 then), the 'home place' was built around 1851 by Isaac Newton Sheppard (1816-1881) whose wife was Mary Frances Randol (1824-1898).

The farm itself was purchased in the fall of 1811 by Isaac Sheppard (1775-1839) whose first wife was Margaret Cox and second wife was Mary Stout Lambert. Isaac Sheppard was Isaac Newton's uncle. In 1834 he sold it to William Howard, who in 1841 sold it to Isaac Newton Sheppard (1871-1926). The farm remained in the Sheppard/Ford family until 1964 when it was sold by Wilson "Bill" Ford (1912-1997), husband of Edna Jessie Kasting (1913-), and great-grandson of Isaac Newton Sheppard, to Ora Lee Hopkins west of Jackson.

Sheppard/Ford Homestead 1851-1964

The house (still standing) is a two-story brick. The clay bricks were made on site, and rocks from the creek carried by slaves and horse-drawn wagon were used for the foundation. A log barn was built across the creek at the time the house was built. At a later date a very large barn (still standing) and grainery were built by Bill's grandpa, Albert Chesley Ford (1844-1931), whose wife was Eunicia Rebecca Sheppard (1850-1936). The barn was built from popular trees cut from the field across from what was then Lewis Chapel. A springhouse and two silos were erected later. Both silos still stand.

Bill learned to farm the land from his grandpa A. C. and his father, Newton Dilworth Ford (1870-1942), husband of Ella Florence Sheppard (1871-1924). They raised various crops (corn, wheat, beans) and registered Hereford cattle. Edna raised a huge garden and chickens. Together they raised nine children, five of whom attended Robert's School, where their daddy attended through the eighth grade. The four youngest attended Jackson R#2 schools. Most all were active in Robert's 4-H Club and attended First Baptist Church in town. Bill was a member of Missouri Cattleman's Association, Cape County Shipping Association and Farm Bureau. When farming became less profitable for the Ford family, they decided to sell out, moving to town where Edna still resides today, with eight of the children living nearby: Wilson Dilworth "Billy" Ford (1938-1986); Margie Lee Welker (1936-); Carol Jane Lamb (1943-); Carla Deane Ford (1951-) and Joe Don Ford (1956-) of Cape Girardeau; Martha Lynne (Nick) Stoyanoff (1946-) of Troy; Dana Sue Ford (1940-); Ella Jean Pleasant (1949-); and Barbara Kaye (Sam) Sides (1953-)of Jackson; along with 16 grandchildren, 22 great-grandchildren and one great-great grandchild.

Bill, Edna and all of their nine children were employed by Jackson Hosiery (Wayne Knitting Mills) at one time or another. From 1966 up to his retirement in 1979, Bill was supervisor of Klaus' Park and Cape County Park (north), and was instrumental in their development. *Submitted by Ella Jean Plesant*

SIDES – Sides is a name with many derivatives including Sides, Seitz and Sitz. The Sides family is believed to have been from Germany, Switzerland and Holland. They came to America to flee from war, harsh winters, and heavy taxation and for religious freedom. They arrived in Pennsylvania in 1738 aboard the *Queen Elizabeth*. Twelve years later they were found in North Carolina. Levi Sides came to Missouri about 1814 in a two-horse wagon. His brother-in-law came first and found a spring just north of Fairview Church near what is now known as Leemon, MO. This church was built later on land donated by Levi. Levi built a log house near his spring. He lived there for the rest of his life with his wife Susan until he passed away at the age of 84. Susan lived to be 80, and they had five children named: Henry; Vicy; Dan; Dicy and John Franklin Sides.

Henry Sides married Elizabeth Miller. He lived to be 80 and had seven children. One of his sons was named James Harvey Sides. James married Jane Emily and later married a second wife named Luella Cordelia Noland. They had four children named: Pearl; Charles Franklin; Oscar and Cary Sides.

Charles Franklin Sides married Dora Ella Trickey and they lived in Leemon, MO. Charles Franklin was the second child of James Harvey and Luella Noland Sides. Charles and Dora had nine children: Garrent; Cecil; Dennis; Ruby; Lillian; William; Chester; Clyde and Charles Jr. Most of these children and their descendants have remained in Cape Girardeau. Dennis moved to Arkansas and William moved to Utah. Five of Charles and Dora's sons were called to serve in WWII at the same time. William was the only one wounded and he lost his leg during the Battle of the Bulge.

During Charles Franklin's married life he farmed 80 acres of land where he grew tobacco, wheat, corn and sugar came. He liked to hunt and he caught opossum, squirrel and other wild animals. He always butchered his own meat and he worked as a butcher at a meat market along with his farming. He died on Oct. 5, 1969 at the age of 87.

Charles and Dora Sides family, Leemon, MO. First row: Cecil, Lillian (Bowers) and Clyde. Second row: Chester "Tag," Dora "Granny," Garnett "Bud," Howard, Charles "Charlie," Dennis "Salty," Ruby (Jones) and Charles Jr.

Dora was the eighth child of ten. She was born to Velar Monroe Trickey and Matilda Ellen Knight. She was a devout member of the Fairview Methodist Church. She raised her family in a four-room farmhouse where the drinking water was saved in a rain barrel or from a cistern. She was a hard-working mother. She raised chickens and sold the eggs. Family socials were a Sunday tradition. She died on Feb. 1, 1970 at the age of 82. The descendants of the Sides family come from a heritage of hard working individuals. Many of them were farmers and valued the land they worked. I'm proud to be a descendant of this great family and treasure the example and heritage they left me. *Written by Vickie Sides Carrier (daughter of William Sides) and submitted by Nina Sides Dickerson (daughter of Charles Sides Jr.)*

SIDES – The Sides family members were early residents of north Cape Girardeau County. Pearl

The Pearl and Jeffie Sides family: back row: Claude, Helen, Tom, Jim and Gene. Row two: Juanita, James Oliver and Hazel. Seated: Pearl Sides and Jeffie Sides. Ca. 1933

Sides was born Aug. 20, 1888 and Jeffie Abernathy Sides was born Sept. 22, 1878. They were married Feb. 12, 1902 by Ivy McClain, Justice of the Peace. The witnesses were J. H. Young and Fred Abernathy. Pearl and Jeffie were the parents of eight children: Claude; Helen; Tom; Jim; Gene; Hazel; J. O. and Susie. As of the year 2001, three are still living: Gene, Hazel and J. O.

The family lived on a farm near Indian Creek and they attended McLain Chapel at Indian Creek. Here they lived a simple life. Having no indoor plumbing, they bathed in the nearby creek. There was a large front yard where many games of croquet were played in the summer evenings. There was horseshoe pitching and usually the loser would get to milk the cows. Hazel and one of her brothers would compete by shooting basketball goals to see who would carry in the wood for the stoves. Basketball was the favorite game for the boys. They became good players and played on the Fruitland High School team. Tom and Jim played on the Jackson High School team when the team won the state championship in 1927. Gene was a member of the Southeast Missouri College team in the 1930s.

Hazel and William "Bill" Schloss were married May 27, 1938. They became members of New McKendree Methodist Church where Bill was active in the Methodist Men's Club. He was an active member of American Legion Post 158 and served as commander in 1956-1957. He also directed the Homecomers talent show for 20 years. Bill was a veteran of WWII and served in the Air Force at Fiji Island, Hawaii, and Travis Air Base in California. In California Hazel and Bill enjoyed a visit with Jacksonians Herman Lee and Doris Hardy. After the war they returned to 217 Elmwood and resumed their hobbies of fishing and bowling.

Bill died in November 1994 and mother Jeffie died May 30, 1967. Father Pearl Sides died July 24, 1951. *Submitted by Hazel Sides Schloss*

SIDES – Rusby Sherman Sides, the oldest of ten children, was born Dec. 28, 1939 on the Sides family homestead located near Lemon, MO the son of Norman Sides and Minnie E. Dalton-Sides. Siblings in order of birth are: Nelda Ruth; Norma Jean; Emma Jane; Marvin Dale (Marvin is currently Jackson's Chief of police); David Paul; Mary Francis; Steven Sylvester; Geneva Kay and Sherry Lynn.

The Sides family settled on this 160-acre farm in the middle of the 19th century, having journeyed from North Carolina en route to the Oregon territory. The family crossed the Mississippi River at Neeleys Landing. Finding suitable farming land available, they homesteaded 160 acres in a narrow creek watered valley north of Lemon, MO. The family set about clearing to enlarge the arable land. The family grew oats, barley, timothy and sorghum. The family also made molasses from the sorghum for their neighbors. They raised livestock and fed the animals grains and hay they were raising. The animals were in turn sold for cash, or bartered for needs.

The family of Norman Sides sold the family farm in 1949 with the proceeds divided between Norman, his mother and two sisters. Norman moved his family to Jackson, MO, enrolling Sherman and Nelda in public school that same year. A strong work ethic and love of family was instilled in the children.

Sherman worked as a paperboy, pinsetter at the local bowling alley, a dishwasher and a waiter while attending Jackson High School. Sherman developed a passion for flying while in high school. He would hitchhike to the Cape Girardeau airport where he would pay for short flights, and learned as much as possible about aviation. He joined the Air Force in 1957, serving first as a mechanic. While stationed in Tucson, AZ he married Hedy Kiras. They have two sons, Rusby and Raymond, and five grandchildren. In 1967 he was accepted for flight training, graduating with honors, and became a C-141 flight engineer stationed at McChord Air Force Base in Washington. He flew between the United States and South Vietnam the mission logistical supply. He was upgraded to instructor, then with nine months remaining in 1969, drew an assignment called Ranch Hand, flying the C-123 configured to spray Agent Orange. Not wishing to be part of such an undertaking, he elected to leave the Air Force after 12 years and nine months. He worked for the Boeing Airplane Company for a short time, and then returned to Cape Girardeau where he was parts manager for Mid West Diesel. Then in 1971 the DOD Federal Civil Service offered him a position as an instructor engineer training Air Force Reservists, again at McChord Air Force Base. Subsequent promotions led to check airman. In 1987 he was promoted to Chief Engineer for the 97th Airlift Squadron. His unit was recalled to active duty during Desert Shield, Desert Storm for nine months. In 1994, after completing 35 years combined federal service, he retired from Civil Service with the rank of GS-11 and from the Air Force Reserves with the rank of Chief Master Sergeant. Three months later he purchased a small landscape company in Gig Harbor, WA and set about growing its base of operations. The company is now managed by oldest son Rusby Sides Jr.

Sherman and Hedy Sides

The younger son Raymond does research work on thoroughbred racehorses at Washington State University. Sherman missed flying so his wife Hedy purchased a Mooney Airplane for the two of them to fly and visit their scattered family. Sherman and Hedy reside in Sequim, WA during the summer and Mesa, AZ during the winter. Jackson frequently beckons and they return to visit Sides family members as much as possible. He credits the Jackson school system for instilling the love of learning, and the value of having an open mind. Sherman is active in the Aircraft Owners and Pilots Association, Mooney Pilots Association and the Experimental Aircraft Association. He has logged over 12,000 accident-free flying hours. *Submitted by Russ Sides*

SIEMERS – Heinrich Conrad Siemers Sr. was born April 14, 1793 in Germany, and died Dec. 28, 1854 in Cape Girardeau County, MO. He married Anna Marie Dorothea Greten. She was born June 7, 1801 in Germany and died March 19, 1892 in Cape Girardeau County, MO.

Heinrich, thought to be the first of his line to immigrate to America, lived in the Kingdom of Hannover, German Confederation (now a Province of Germany). He processed their immigration papers at Celle, but obituaries from two of the sons indicate they were born in Meitze. Heinrich, Anna and their four children departed Germany from Bremen on the ship *Friedrich Leo* Oct. 14, 1845 and arrived in America at the Port of New Orleans, LA Dec. 2, 1845. This nearly two-month ordeal was lengthened by the lack of winds to sail the ship. After arrival in New Orleans, the family proceeded, via boat, up the Mississippi to Cape Girardeau, MO where Daniel Bertling greeted them. Daniel immigrated earlier and was apparently friends with the Siemers in Germany. Daniel arranged for Heinrich to purchase about 32 acres of land in 1835, ten years before his arrival.

Heinrich settled near Gordonville and purchased his first farm containing about 235 acres from William Thompson and John Lewis. On April 12, 1853 he received from the US Government 55.35 acres of land in Township 31. No accurate accounting had been made of the total amount of land Heinrich owned.

After living in America only about ten years, Heinrich passed away in 1854. He leaves many descendents many of whom still reside in Cape Girardeau County, MO.

Heinrich Conrad Siemers and Anna Marie Greten's children:

George Conrad Siemers, born Sept. 16, 1827, Meitze, Amt Bishendof, Hannover, Germany; died July 20, 1914, Jackson, MO; married first Eva Catharina Keller, July 15, 1852, Cape Girardeau County, MO; born May 10, 1831, Weingarten, Rheinbaiern, Germany; died Dec. 28, 1853, Cape Girardeau County, MO; married second Johanna Maria Sophie Sander, Aug. 17, 1854, Evangelical Whitewater Church, Cape Girardeau County, MO; born Oct. 20, 1833, Braunschweig, Germany; died November 1921, Jackson, MO.

Heinrich Conrad Siemers Jr., born April 8, 1829, Meitze, Amt Bissendorf, Hannover, Germany; died Jan. 28, 1904, Cape Girardeau County, MO; married first Hermine Friderica Bertling, Oct. 11, 1855, Cape Girardeau County, MO; born Aug. 15, 1839, Cape Girardeau County, MO; died Dec. 8, 1891; married second Caroline Lena Lorberg, Jan. 2, 1893, Cape Girardeau County, MO; born Oct. 15, 1839; died Oct. 18, 1912.

Phillip Ludwig Louis Siemers, born Feb. 13, 1833, Hannover, Germany; died March 7, 1902,

Cape Girardeau County, MO; married Anna Maria Charlotte Grossheider, May 20, 1858, Cape Girardeau County, MO; born Aug. 1, 1841, Friedheim, MO; died Feb. 19, 1916.

Sophia G. Siemers, born Sept. 8, 1838, Hannover, Germany; died Nov. 2, 1878, Cape Girardeau County, MO; married Herman Noeninger, March 22, 1860; born April 15, 1837, Baden, Germany; died July 20, 1906, Cape Girardeau County, MO. *Submitted by Charlotte Ainsworth*

SIEVERS – Dennis Sievers was born in Jackson on Feb. 17, 1945 to Mary (Dickerson) and Emil Sievers. He attended rural Schoenebeck Elementary School through fifth grade. Following the reorganization of the Jackson Public Schools, he completed elementary and high school at Jackson Public School, graduating in 1963. While in high school, he was active in athletics, playing fullback on the football team, throwing shot and discus with the track team, and playing on the basketball team. He lettered in all three sports. He was also active in other extracurricular activities.

Cathy was born in Jackson on Aug. 28, 1945, the second of three girls born to Catheryn (Macke) and Charles W. Sanders. Cathy attended Jackson Elementary and High School, graduating in 1963. While in high school, Cathy was a member of Jackson Chiefs Marching Band grades seven through 12. She was also a member of Mixed Chorus, Debate Team, French Club, FTA, History Club and National Honor Society.

The Sievers family. Back row, left to right: Doug, Denny, David and Paul. Front row: Dennis, Cathy and Darrell, 1985.

Cathy and Dennis began dating their sophomore year in high school. These high school sweethearts married on Aug. 25, 1963. Several years and two sons later, they purchased their first home at 212 Morgan. During this time, Dennis worked as a route salesman for Hart's Bread. He accepted a job with Coca-Cola in January 1968, as a relief driver. He spent the rest of his life working with Coca Cola, achieving the position of General Sales Manager.

Cathy and Dennis gave birth to four sons and later adopted a fifth son. Their oldest son, Dennis, was born March 5, 1964. He was an outstanding football player and wrestler, earning a football scholarship to Southeast Missouri State University. He and his wife, the former Chris Allen, have three children and currently reside in Southlake, TX. The second son, David, was born May 23, 1965. He was an all-state wrestler and lettered in football. He also received a football scholarship to Southeast Missouri State University. He and his wife, the former Julie Francis, reside in Poplar Bluff, where David teaches and coaches football. They are the parents of a daughter. A third son, Doug, was born Dec. 20, 1967. Doug, also a talented athlete, lettered three years in football and wrestling. He graduated from Southeast Missouri State University. He and his wife, the former Eileen Oberle, have two children and reside in Jackson. The fourth son, Darrell, was born Jan. 19, 1971. Darrell lettered in football and wrestling in high school, and enlisted in the Air Force following graduation. Following his tour of active duty, he attended the police academy at Southeast Missouri State University. He and his wife, the former Shannon Brown, are the parents of two children. They currently reside in Jackson where Darrell is on the Jackson Police force. Paul became a member of the Sievers family when he was 15 years old. He was born Nov. 13, 1968. Paul was active in sports and choral music. He and his wife, the former Tricia Lauterwasser, have two children and live in Cape Girardeau.

Cathy was a homemaker for the family and operated a daycare in the home for over 17 years. She now works with the Activities and Social Services Department at the Lutheran Home.

Dennis was very active in the Jackson community, serving on the City Council and School Board. He was also a member of the Jaycees, Optimist, Rotary Club, Benchwarmers, and a member of the Governing Board of the Emanuel United Church of Christ. Both Cathy and Dennis were very actively involved in many of the activities in which their sons participated. Dennis died Nov. 1, 1989 while at work. *Submitted by Cathy Sievers*

SIMMONS – Alexander Simmons, birth date unknown, died Nov. 20, 1922, age about 77 or 78 years, at Oriole, MO. His parents were born in North Carolina. Alexander was born in Nashville, TN. His mother and father were drowned when their horse and buggy was washed down a swollen stream. He was then cared for and raised with the black family that lived on the Simmons plantation.

Left to right: Charley McLain, Lizzie Hughes McLain Simmons, Mattie Simmons (Marlin), Kate Simmons (Noland), Alexander Simmons and salesman

As he grew up he drifted through Tennessee, Arkansas, Missouri and into St. Louis, where he had a Simmons Stove Company. As a salesman through southeast Missouri, he met and married Elizabeth "Lizzie" Hughes McLain on Aug. 30, 1886. They lived in the Indian Creek, Oriole Community until his death, Nov. 20, 1922. He is buried in the McLains Chapel Cemetery. The above picture is at Neelys Landing, MO. The stove had been shipped by boat to Neelys Landing (you can see the boat in the background) and Simmons is signing for the stove. This stove was polished and used in the Simmons home at Indian Creek until their deaths. *Submitted by Mary Beth Vogt.*

SKAGGS – William "Carl" Skaggs was born Feb. 26, 1923 in Patton, MO, the oldest son of Harry Everett and Ella Mae (Cook) Skaggs. He and his five siblings (Rose, Ed, Mary, Don and Helen) grew up on the farm that his great-grandfather, James Skaggs, a Union veteran of the Civil War, had homesteaded. His family visited Jackson several times when he was growing up. In the fall of 1935, Carl's father moved his family to a 160-acre farm just north of Chaffee. The owner, Loy Yount, needed someone to farm it while he was gone for a year. Harry loaded their things in a wagon with two horses, and started out at four in the morning. Later Carl (age 13) drove his mother and siblings to the Chaffee farm in a 1928 Model-A Ford. They passed Harry in the wagon, and took Highway 25 to Chaffee from Jackson. Harry arrived at eight that night. When the year was up, they moved back to Patton.

Carl went to Patton High School for three years. In June 1942 he moved to Detroit, MI to work while staying with relatives, and in November he received a draft notice for WWII. He was assigned to the Air Force as an auto mechanic, and served from November 1943 to July 1945 in Tunis, Tunisia (Africa). After the war, he returned to Detroit and worked for Detroit Lubricator Company.

On Nov. 10, 1947 he married Grace Melton. They had two children, Ella Kathleen "Kathy" (1949) and Robert Lee (1956). In 1950 they moved back to Missouri. Between 1950 and 1964 the Skaggs moved to various towns and jobs in the Lead Belt area. During this time Carl finished his last year and graduated from Bonne Terre High School. He also completed a machinist program at the vocational school in Desoto. In 1964 they settled in Edwardsville, IL and Carl worked for Young Metal Company. Carl and Grace moved to Flat River (now Park Hills) after the metal company closed in 1978, and then to Poplar Bluff in 1981, before finally settling in Jackson, MO in July 1985. In October they bought their home at 609 Odus. Carl worked as a custodian at West Lane Elementary in Jackson for 11 years, and retired in May 1996. Carl and Grace are members of Mount Auburn Christian Church in Cape Girardeau, MO and are enjoying their retirement.

Carl and Grace Skaggs

Kathy married Thomas John Schmid (see Schmid) on Aug. 31, 1968. They have four children: Lisa and Julia (identical twins), Bryan and Andrew. Kathy graduated from Southern Illinois University at Edwardsville with a B.A. in education in 1971. She was employed by the school district in Woodriver, IL and then Bismarck, MO before moving to Cape Girardeau, MO in 1979. On July 25, 1982 Tom and Kathy moved to their home in Jackson (Fruitland), MO. Kathy was employed by Jackson R-2 in 1985, and currently teaches second grade at Orchard Elementary. She received her M.A. in teaching from Webster University in 1999. *Submitted by Lisa Barrett*

SLINKARD – Richard Dean Slinkard was born Nov. 19, 1945 in Cape Girardeau and he is single. He was a waiter for 29 years for Drury, and in the floral business almost as long. He was a member of the Whitewater Methodist Church. He belonged to the Sons of the American Revolution and put up the first Revolutionary War monument for his ancestor, Thomas English, in Cape Girardeau. He is 9/16 Cherokee Indian.

Richard's brother, Donald Ray Slinkard, was born July 14, 1940 in Jackson, MO. He worked many years at the Delta High School and is now retired. He was married in November 1966 to Carol Marie Picou, born May 6, 1947 in St. Mary's, MO, the daughter of Adrian and Helen Cleary Picou. Donald and Carol have three sons. Jeffrey Allen, born Oct. 26, 1967, is single, and graduated from Southeast Missouri State College. Mark Wayne was born Oct. 31, 1969 and was married Sept. 21, 1991 to Julie Marie Lueder, born Dec. 16, 1970, the daughter of Arthur Lueder and Marion Pierce. Mark and Julie have three daughters: Amanda Marie born June 27, 1992; Ashleigh Lauren born Feb. 14, 1995; and Andrea Nicole born Dec. 27, 2001. Christopher Boyd Slinkard was born March 12, 1978 and is single.

Donald and Richard Slinkard are sons of Boyd Loren "Dick" Slinkard who was born Oct. 16, 1915 in Crump, MO and died Dec. 31, 1966. He is buried in Russell Heights Cemetery. He was 1/4 Cherokee Indian. He was a carpenter and was in the first quartet at the Whitewater Methodist Church. He loved to fish and hunt, and he raised dogs. He was married on Aug. 19, 1939 to Hattie Ferne "Hap" Allen, who was born Nov. 25, 1919 in Jackson, MO. She had a beauty shop for 34 years at Whitewater.

Hattie was the daughter of William Lynn and Alta "Hall" Allen. Boyd was the son of Ora Cleveland Slinkard who was born Nov. 19, 1888 and who died July 18, 1975. He was married on May 16, 1912 to Arra Mae McGuire who was born July 12, 1893 in Burfordville and who died Feb. 26, 1968. Both are buried at Memorial Park Cemetery. Arra was the daughter of William Franklin McGuire and Artelda Berry. Artelda was the daughter of Robert Berry and Nancy Allen. Robert was the son of George Berry and Martha Lincoln, a cousin to Abraham Lincoln, the President of the United States. Ora and Arra's children were Woodrow W., Boyd L., and Glenda A. DeVore.

Ora Slinkard was the son of Daniel Franklin Slinkard who was born Oct. 27, 1856 and who died Feb. 19, 1935. He was married Dec. 22, 1887 to Mary Catherine "Kate" Henley who was born July 4, 1871 in Bollinger County and who died April 10, 1930. Both are buried in Lessley Cemetery. Mary, a midwife, read her Bible each day. She was the daughter of Thomas Henley and Sarah Jane Rice.

Daniel Slinkard was the son of John Slinkard who was born Dec. 28, 1813 in Scopus, MO, and who died Jan. 14, 1877. He ran a sawmill and wheat-threshing mill. He was married Feb. 9, 1851 to Sarah Margaret Fox who was born Jan. 30, 1832 near Gravel Mill, MO, and who died Dec. 21, 1916. Both are buried in Lessley Cemetery. Sarah was a very religious woman, a full-blooded Cherokee Indian who made her own herbs and smoked a pipe. She was the daughter of William Isaac Fox and Mary Warren Coyler, both buried in Lessley Cemetery.

John Slinkard was the son of Daniel Franklin Slinkard who was born in 1786 in Lincoln County, NC, came to Missouri in 1802, and settled on Whitewater Creek. He is buried on the family home place. He was married in 1812 to Hannah Kinder who was born in North Carolina and who died in 1831/1835. She was the daughter of Adam Kinder.

Daniel Slinkard was the son of Jacob Slinkard, the pioneer of this family who migrated to Missouri from Lincoln County, NC. He came on the first wagon train here on Jan. 1, 1800 and filed for land survey #675 in January 1800. The Slinkard family was of German descent. Jacob was born in 1765 in Lancaster County, PA, and died Nov. 1, 1803 in Cape Girardeau. He was married in 1784/1786 in Lincoln County, NC, to Catherine Crites who was born in 1764/1765 and who died before 1816 in Cape Girardeau. She was the daughter of Davault Critz and Sophia, who may have been a Barks or a Limbaugh.

Jacob Slinkard was in the Revolutionary War and enlisted on Jan. 28, 1781. Jacob Slinkard-Schlunker-Schlenkered, the son of Frederick Wilhelm Schlenker, came on the ship *Leathley* to Philadelphia on Sept. 19, 1753. The Slinkard name seems to be of either Swiss origin, which is really Germanic, or of Palatine origin. It is stated that names beginning with Schl- are from the Palatine region, which were Germanic areas.

Boyd Slinkard was 1/4 and his wife 5/8 Cherokee Indian. I am proud to be Cherokee Indian. *Submitted by Richard Dean Slinkard*

SMITH – Mabel Hutson Smith devoted most of her life educating children in southeast Missouri. She taught with love and caring. She believed in education as a most important need in preparing people for life.

Mabel Hutson Smith was born Aug. 17, 1911 at Jackson, near Burfordville, MO. She is the daughter of S. O. Hutson of Millersville and Iva Craig Hutson of Jackson, MO. She married Luther R. Smith of Oak Ridge, MO on Aug. 10, 1953. Mrs. Smith attended Link and Burfordville Schools. She graduated from Jackson High School in 1931. She attended Southeast Missouri State College. She graduated from Missouri University at Columbia, MO.

Mrs. Smith taught elementary school for 43 years. She taught at Burfordville, Link, Needmore, Hickory Ridge, McFerron and Council Ridge, all in Cape Girardeau County. She also taught at Chaffee in Scott County and at Anniston in Mississippi County. She finished her years of teaching at Jackson R2 at Millersville. She retired in May 1975.

Mrs. Smith had two stepchildren. Mrs. Robert (Lawana) Bell was a teacher. Her husband was a teacher and an assistant principal at Perryville, MO. Her son Carl was a high school math teacher and later became a CPA in Jackson. Carl's wife, Amy, was a high school language arts teacher. Carl is deceased. Mrs. Smith has seven step-grandchildren and two step-great grandchildren. She had three brothers: Billy, who is deceased; Pink and Bob. She had four sisters: Ruth, who is deceased; Ruby Clifton (Earl); Inez Starzinger (Alvin G.); and Ella Mae Cook (Raymond). She and her three sisters get together every Tuesday to visit. The brothers and sisters celebrate each others' birthdays by going to a restaurant for breakfast together.

Mrs. Smith belongs to the Burfordville Baptist Church. She is a member of the Missouri State Teachers Association, the Missouri Retired Teachers Association, the Cape Girardeau Area Retired Teachers Unit and the Jackson R-2 Elementary Retired Teachers Unit of which she is a charter member.

Mabel Smith

Mrs. Smith's husband was a high school superintendent. He retired from Oak Ridge School in 1969. He is deceased.

She is a member of the Eastern Star at Whitewater, MO. She was matron in 1948 and District Deputy of the 49th District in 1953 and 1954. She is a member of the Past Matron's Club of the Order of Eastern Star. Mrs. Smith has been a Sunday school teacher for many years, an active WMU member, a Bible School worker, and a faithful attendee of worship services. She was a member of the Cane Creek Homemakers Club for several years. Mrs. Smith has been active in all the above organizations. She missed very few days of school while teaching those 43 years. She loved and enjoyed teaching and hopes that she helped many children get started in their education.

Mrs. Smith resides near Jackson. She enjoys cooking and has most of her recipes memorized. She loves giving baked goodies to friends. *Submitted by Lawana Bell*

SMITH – Ora Lea Smith was born Ida Leora Smith to Thomas Burrel and Maud Muller (Dunn) Smith in Benton, IL on Jan. 21, 1910. When Ora Lea was about six years old her family moved to Powhatan, AR in an oversized wagon her father had made that was pulled by two horses. On their journey they took along a cow, tethered to the back of the wagon, to supply milk for the family. The children took turns riding in the wagon and walking. One of the highlights of the trip was crossing the Mississippi River on the ferry at Cape Girardeau and the cobblestone streets. After living in Powhatan about four years, the family then moved to Grassy, MO.

It was while they were living in Grassy that Ora Lea met and married Russell Marvin Kirkpatrick, son of Charles Monroe and Mary Eunice (Hill) Kirkpatrick, born April 12, 1908. Russell provided for his family by farming and operating a sawmill. Russell is fondly remembered for his practical jokes and his love of boxing.

Russell and Ora Lea Smith

Through the years, six children were born to Russell and Ora. Jean Daphine was born April 10, 1928 and married Lyndall Ledo Liley. James Russell was born Sept. 6, 1929 and married the former Ora Mae Ede. Jerry Dewain was born Dec. 29, 1930 and died Jan. 5, 1931. Betty Jo was born Aug. 25, 1932 and married William Jack Lindsay. Dean Wilson was born Dec. 5, 1935 and married the former Shirley Janice Cooper. Lynn David was born June 16, 1946 and married the former Janet Lynne Henson. Russell and Ora were also blessed with 18 grandchildren.

During WWII, Ora had five brothers in the war. Patriotism was very high and five stars were displayed in the window, one star for each boy. It was a time of seemingly constant prayer. In 1944, Ora's brother John was killed at Normandy. While serving in the war, the boy's paths would occasionally cross.

After a year of sickness and when the youngest child, David, was only a few months old, Russell was admitted to St. Francis Hospital in Cape Girardeau where he died on Sept. 1, 1946.

After Russell's death, friends and family members continued to cut the timber and sell it to provide income for the family. It was a very hard existence.

With five of the six children married, Ora sold their farm and she, along with her son David, moved to Jackson in 1953. In 1955 Ora began to work at the Hosiery Mill, where she worked for about five years. She was also a very talented seamstress and was called upon by many people in the town of Jackson to sew for them.

Ora Lea remained in excellent health for many years with the aid of regular visits to her chiropractor and daily doses of vitamins. She never had a driver's license so she walked everywhere she went, which also contributed to her healthy lifestyle. In January of 1985 heart problems became apparent. She had quadruple bypass surgery and later died on April 29, 1985 at Baptist Memorial Hospital in Memphis, TN.

Ora Lea was a devout Christian woman and a faithful member of First Baptist Church in Jackson. Her devotion to God was evident in every aspect of her life. *Submitted by Lisa Drum*

SMITH – The Steven W. Smith family of Jackson, MO consists of Steve, Brenda and Stephanie. Steve and Brenda made their home in Jackson after marrying in Poplar Bluff, MO on April 28, 1990. The Smiths chose Jackson, MO to raise their family for several reasons. Both Steve and Brenda grew up in a small town atmosphere and were very happy there. Jackson has a family environment, friendly people, wonderful shops, a small town atmosphere and the city is kept clean. These things are important to their family and they have been very satisfied living in Jackson.

Steve was born Dec. 4, 1961 in Elgin, IL to Ray and Dorothy Smith. The family lived in St. Charles, IL at that time but later moved to Festus, MO. After living there a short time, the family relocated to East Prairie, MO when Steve was about eight years old. This is where Steve grew up.

Steve, Brenda and Stephanie Smith, December 2000.

In 1988 Steve took a job with Schwan's Enterprises, servicing customers on the Cape Girardeau route. While working on this route in the Doctors' Park area, a redheaded young lady, who was employed in one of the offices, caught Steve's attention. He decided to find out more about her. The young lady's name was Brenda Pennington. Steve called her up and asked her out for a date. They continued to date and after approximately a year of dating decided to get married. Shortly before getting married, Steve took a job at Hutson's Furniture. He worked there a few months and then started working for Safety-Kleen Corporation. Steve has been employed at Safety-Kleen Corporation since 1990 and now works in the capacity of Special Markets Sales representative.

Brenda is a native of Poplar Bluff, MO born Sept. 19, 1962 to Rayburn and Ernestine Pennington. She lived with her parents in Poplar Bluff until November of 1985. At that time, Brenda decided to spread her wings and move to Cape Girardeau. She took a full-time medical transcriptionist position at St. Francis Medical Center. After working there for approximately a year, she took a transcription position at the office of Dr. Karen Yates. While working there, she met Steve. Brenda worked for Dr. Yates until the birth of Stephanie. Following Stephanie's birth Brenda worked at home as a self-employed transcriptionist so she could take care of her new baby. When Stephanie was 3-1/2 years old, Brenda took a full-time transcription job at the office of Gregory Tobin, M.D. and has been employed there since that time.

Stephanie Rae Smith was born into the family on Sept. 2, 1991. She is a fourth grade student at West Lane Elementary in Jackson, MO.

Steve, Brenda and Stephanie are members of Dayspring Missionary Baptist Church located in Jackson, MO. They are involved with many activities of the church and enjoy spending time together as a family. *Submitted by Brenda Smith*

STANARD – Vida (Loberg) Stanard was born on May 18, 1941 in Sedgewickville, MO. Her parents were Denver Clyde Loberg (1923-1944) and Marjorie (Sample) Loberg (1923-).

Vida's father, Army Sgt. Denver Loberg, was killed in action as a gunner aboard a B-24 bomber bound for Germany on Dec. 24, 1944. After his death, Vida moved with her mother and sister, Roxie Tina Loberg (Druckenmiller), to her Sample grandparents' Bollinger County farm west of Sedgewickville. She has pleasant memories of living on the farm. In the fall of 1946, her mother married Norman R. Swan and the family moved to Pocahontas. Mr. Swan and Vida's mother had three children: Norman R. "Sam" Swan Jr.; William Reginald Swan and Nina Christine Swan-Kohler.

Ironically, Vida's Loberg family owned and operated a Chevrolet dealership in Sedgewickville. Her "new" Swan family had the Chevrolet dealership in Pocahontas.

Vida recalls the strong German influence in Pocahontas was reflected in some of her young friends speaking that language at play. She became a member of St. John's Lutheran Church, and attended eight years at the Pocahontas School, where teacher Louise Godwin greatly influenced her. Vida and her four siblings participated in most of the Pocahontas 4-H Club projects. Her mother, Marjorie, now has recorded more than 50 years as a 4-H leader.

After graduating in 1959 from Jackson High School, Vida enrolled in the University of Missouri at Columbia. She earned a B.S. in education with a major in home economics in 1963. She was active in the Marching Mizzou band and served as state 4-H secretary.

On July 7, 1963 Vida married John R. Stanard of Poplar Bluff, whom she met four years earlier in Marching Mizzou. Vida taught home economics at the Dixon, MO high school year while John completed duty as an Army bandsman and trombone instructor at Fort Leonard Wood. After spending a year in Minnesota, where John was an editor on the *Minneapolis Star*, the couple returned to Poplar Bluff and John's family newspaper, *the Daily American Republic*. Vida taught home economics at Poplar Bluff junior and senior high schools before becoming an instructor in Fashion Merchandising at Three Rivers Community College. She later coordinated marketing, special projects and recruitment at TRCC, retiring in 2001 as Director of Admissions and Recruitment after 30 years of service to the college.

Vida and John have two children, Michael John Stanard (July 1, 1966) and Christina Louise Vogel (Aug. 10, 1969). Their three grandchildren are William Louis "Will" Vogel (March 6, 1999), Audrey Nicole Stanard (Feb. 22, 2001) and Grace Margaret Vogel (Aug. 7, 2001).

Vida Loberg Stanard

Vida was named Outstanding Young Woman of Poplar Bluff in the 1970s and served on the Missouri Governor's Advisory Council on Vocational Education. She has been a member of the Missouri 4-H Foundation Board, Chapter MF of P.E.O., District 10 Missouri Selective Service (draft) Board, the Missouri Youth Initiative Policy Committee, Poplar Bluff Arts and Museum Advisory Board, University Extension Advisory and Long-Range Planning Committee, Poplar Bluff Crime Stoppers Board, Monday Literary Club, Community Concert Association, Poplar Bluff Public Library Friends, Friends of the Margaret Harwell Art Museum, First United Methodist Church Choir, Nature Conservancy, Women Aware, Inc., Mizzou and Missouri 4-H Alumni Associations and many other civic and community organizations. *Submitted by Marjorie Swan*

STATLER – Swiss-German ancestors of Louis W. and Emma Lilly Victoria Conrad Statler landed in Philadelphia in 1734 and 1737 and finally settled in North Carolina. Louis Statler's great-great grandfather, Conrad Statler, and Emma's great-great grandfather, Henry Bollinger, were part of the group of 20 families who made the arduous trek to Missouri from North Carolina and crossed the Mississippi River on Jan. 1, 1800. They settled on tracts of land in Cape Girardeau County (the area becoming Bollinger County in 1851) and established farms and several mills on the Whitewater River.

Louis W. Statler, son of Polly and John Franklin Statler, was born on Feb. 16, 1877 and after his father's death when he was a small boy he was raised by his grandfather, Conrad Statler. Conrad's father, Peter Statler, also lived with his son Conrad, and had been on the journey from North Carolina and recounted many stories of that trip to Louis. Peter lived an active life up until his death at the age of 104, riding horseback to a party shortly before he died. Conrad Statler and Alfred Conrad both served in the Civil War for the North.

Emma Conrad, daughter of Elizabeth and Alfred Conrad, was born Feb. 2, 1879 and married Louis W. Statler on Sept. 11, 1898. As a wedding present Louis' grandfather gave them 40 acres of land with a house and barn, a cow, some pigs, chickens, geese, sheep and a feather bed and two feather pillows, and a cook stove. Being a skilled carpenter as well as a farmer, the farm soon grew to 160 acres with a big white house

Louis W. and Emma Conrad Statler, 1942

and a new barn. The family also grew as first Lawrence was born Oct. 7, 1899, then Ray, Lester, Virgia, Nola Loni (died in infancy), Mysie and Hirschel. Only Mysie and Hirschel are still living and residing in Jackson.

Wanting better school for his children and liking carpentry better than farming (though he was always interested in agriculture and owned farms the remainder of his life), the family moved to Cape Girardeau in 1920. Louis became a well-known contractor of attractive very well built houses and small business buildings in Cape Girardeau and Jackson. Lester joined his father in the construction business and continued it after his father's death on Oct. 11, 1944.

Emma was an avid gardener who delighted in growing both flowers and vegetables. She was extremely knowledgeable about the proper methods of propagation of the many plants she grew as well as knowing the name and properties of a tremendous number of wild plants. In season the dinner table was always loaded with vegetables fresh from her garden and the shelves in the walled in fruit room in the basement held hundreds of jars of home canned fruits and vegetables for winter. Emma died July 1, 1958.

In the early 1930s the family moved to a farm they owned adjacent to the city limits of Jackson. Louis later built a home on Park Street in Jackson for the family. They became very active members of New McKendree Methodist Church where various members of the family served as Sunday school teachers, played piano, sang in the choir, joined women's groups, etc. Mysie and Hirschel are still members of the church, having joined in 1935.

Hirschel started his education at Franklin School in Cape Girardeau and graduated from Jackson High School in 1948. He entered the military on Jan. 26, 1943 and served until Oct. 23, 1945. He was in the 465th Bomb Group, 782nd Bomb Squadron, 15th Air Force in B-24 bombers in Europe before the war ended in Europe. When he returned home after his discharge on Oct. 23, 1945, he attended Southeast Missouri State College. He and Shirley Smith were married in 1948 and have a son, Mark. He is retired from Gerber Company. *Submitted by Hirschel Statler*

STECK – The Steck name was well known in the history of Jackson. Henry Steck was born in Ste. Genevieve, MO on Aug. 14, 1859, and moved to Jackson as a young boy with his parents. Henry was a "cooper" by trade at the Cape County Milling Company. He bought and sold walnut timber to the federal government during WWI. After retiring from the timber business he became a constable for Jackson until his death on June 20, 1929. On June 8, 1884 he married Elizabeth Matilda Blackwendt in Jackson. Five children were born: William, Charles F., Phillip, Lenora and Marie.

Charles F. Steck lived and attended school in Jackson. At the age of 16 Steck moved to Cape Girardeau to become an apprentice of William Vogel, to learn the sheet metal trade and to continue learning the business. He returned to Jackson in 1912 to begin his own business and to open a shop on Court Street across from the county courthouse. He was well known as a master craftsman of sheet metal in Jackson and the surrounding area. He often made copper crosses, which he placed on top of church steeples. This was quite a feat in those days.

He founded Jackson Volunteer Fire Department in 1912 when the pump and water tank wagon was still in use. The firemen worked the pumps by pushing long handles up and down to force the water from a cistern or nearby stream into the hose and onto the fire. Some years later the city installed water for public usage and also purchased a hook and ladder truck, eliminating the hand pump fire wagon. For 25 years Steck served as fire chief for the Volunteer Fire Department. He took great pride in taking care of the new fire truck. During the Homecomers, a celebration blocking the streets of uptown Jackson and the entrance to the fire station, Steck moved the fire truck to his home. After 45 years of service, he retired in 1957. He was presented a letter of honor from the mayor, John Mabrey, recognizing his many years of dedicated service to the city.

Jackson Fire Department in 1935
Fire Chief Charles F. Steck (Driver), Joe Allen, F. A. Schneider, Eldon Roberts, J. R. Mabrey, W. T. Ruff, Norman Illers, H. L. Jones, T. H. Obermiller, Henry Sievers, J. G. Kies, J. M. Poe, Otto Hanschen, A. W. Roloff.

Steck was a member of Excelsior Lodge No. 441 AF&AM, receiving his 50th years lodge emblem in 1963. He also was a 32nd degree Scottish Rite Mason.

Charles F. Steck (b. Oct. 1, 1888 d. Aug. 26, 1965) married Clara (b. April 2, 1888, d. Dec. 2, 1978), daughter of Emanuel and Caroline Illers Milde, on Aug. 10, 1910 in Jackson. They were members of the First Presbyterian Church. Four children were born: Milde, Charles Wilson, Lucille Eydmann and Betty Holley. They had four grandchildren and four great-grandchildren. *Submitted by Charles W. Steck*

STEARNS – Sarah Jean Stearns was born Aug. 15, 1873 in Millersville, MO, and died Nov. 30, 1927. She is buried in Russell Heights Cemetery. She was married on June 14, 1895 to William Harve Allen who was born Nov. 6, 1862 in Gravel Hill, MO, and who died July 2, 1949 in Moline, IL. Harve Allen was a farmer and raised horses; he owned a farm outside Jackson on Highway D. He was the son of Benjamin F. Allen who was born in 1829 in North Carolina, and Mary J. Bast who was born Nov. 5, 1830 and who died Aug. 18, 1923. Harve and Sarah Allen's children were George, Effie Barrett, Molly (single), Oscar, and William Lynn, who married Alta Idler Hall. Their children were J. C., Tommy Gene, George W., Lee Roy, Joe L., Oscar R., Anna Rumfelt, Mary J. Niswonger, and Hattie Ferne, who married Boyd L. Slinkard.

Sarah Jean Allen was the daughter of Charles B. Stearns who was born Feb. 8, 1844 in Bollinger County, MO, and who died Feb. 8, 1921. He is buried in Snider Cemetery. He was married to Mary J. Baker who was born July 2, 1848 near Millersville, MO, and who died Sept. 21, 1921. Charles Stearns was in the Civil War in Captain Cochran's Volunteer Missouri Militia; he was discharged in July 1865. Charles received a good education. He had 260 acres, an orchard of 200 trees, and a beautiful two-story home. In the year 1990 only the kitchen stands.

Mary J. Stearns was the daughter of Joseph Baker Jr. who was born Nov. 2, 1806, a twin, and who died Jan. 7, 1849. He is buried in Baker Cemetery. He was married Dec. 15, 1831 to Anne Young who was born July 24, 1814 and who died Dec. 21, 1893.

Charles B. Stearns was the son of Joseph Marion Stearns, who was born Oct. 20, 1820 and who died Jan. 15, 1897. He was married on Dec. 18, 1842 to Sarah S. Seabaugh who was born March 26, 1826 in Bollinger County and who died March 31, 1877. Both are buried in Hartle Cemetery.

Joseph M. Stearns was the son of William S. Stearns who was born in 1782 in Washington County, VA and who died in 1842 in Cape Girardeau. He was married about 1805 to Mary A. Pinkston or Downey, who was born in 1784 in Rowan County, NC and who died in 1836 in Cape Girardeau. William S. Stearns was the son of Jacob Stearns who was born in 1750. He was married April 16, 1798 to Elizabeth Strode who was born about 1752.

Sarah S. Stearns was the daughter of Christian Seabaugh Jr. who was born in 1791 in Lincoln County, NC and who died March 31, 1879; he is buried on the home place. He married Catherine Smith who was born in 1792. She was the daughter of Daniel K. Smith/Schmidt and Elizabeth Hahn.

Christian Jr. was the son of Christian Seabaugh/Seebach who was born in 1749 in Pennsylvania, and Christina Statler/Stollar who was born Aug. 24, 1765 and who died in February 1837.

Daniel Smith was born in 1754 in Pennsylvania and died in 1807 in Cape Girardeau. He was married in Lincoln County, NC to Elizabeth Hahn who was born in 1778 in Lincoln County, NC and who died Dec. 25, 1843. Both are buried in Holt Cemetery.

Elizabeth Smith was the daughter of Johann J. Hahn who was born Dec. 17, 1747 and who died Nov. 1, 1801 in Lincoln County, NC. He married Rosina Neigh who died after 1831 in Clark County, IN. She was the daughter of Christian Nigh.

Johann J. Hahn was the son of Johanes Hahn who was born in 1712 in Frechenfeld, Germany and Elizabeth M. Foster who was born about 1720.

Christina Seabaugh was the daughter of Hans P. Statler/Stotlar who was born in 1735/1737 in Pennsylvania, and who died in Lincoln County, NC. He was married Jan. 1, 1756 in Pennsylvania to A. Catherine Hallwein-Holwein, and they were the parents of Christopher, Conrad, Ann, Peter, Susanna, Eva Catharine Niswonger, and Christina Seabaugh. *Submitted by Amanda Marie Slinkard*

STEVENSON – James Stevenson left Mecklenburg County, North Carolina and headed for Missouri in the early 1800s with his wife Jane Fleming and their ten-year-old son, Alexander K. They settled in the north end of Cape Girardeau County around the Shawneetown/New Wells area. The attraction to Missouri-the promised land- was a land grant for Revolutionary War veterans.

Alexander Kennedy Stevenson was reared on his parents' farm. He was married twice; his first wife was Margaret Hill and his second wife was Elizabeth L. Clodfelter. Elizabeth was a native of Cape Girardeau County. She was born June 24, 1824 and died Nov. 28, 1901. Alexander K. and Elizabeth settled on the farm where he resided until his death on Dec. 16, 1881. He and Elizabeth reared a family of seven children: five sons and two daughters.

The Stevenson family left to right: Hugh Roy Stevenson, Lula Gladish Stevenson, Jerry Stevenson, Meredith Stevenson, John Stevenson, twins Roberta Stevenson McDowell and Robert Stevenson.

Their third son, Alpheus Cowan Stevenson, was born on Feb. 3, 1852 and grew to manhood on his father's farm. He received a good education at the Fruitland High School and the common schools with a supplementary commercial course at Cape Girardeau. After finishing his education he taught school for four years. On Jan. 6, 1876 he was united in marriage with Miss Julia Boren, daughter of Hiram Boren of Cape Girardeau County. After Julia and Alpheus were married they resided for two years at Neely's Landing, after which he moved to Pocahontas, and served as clerk in a store during the winter and spring of 1879. They moved to the family farm where he resided until his death. They had seven children, three living to healthy adulthood: Hugh Roy (Jan. 2, 1885), Arthur Lang (Sept. 18, 1891) and Maple Oren (March 12, 1894). Alpheus and Julia were members of the Presbyterian Church, workers in the Sunday school at Shawneetown and members of the Grange.

Hugh Roy "H. R." Stevenson graduated with the class of 1907 at Cape Girardeau Normal School. While going to school and teaching he had met a girl, Lulu Gladish. When the diplomas were handed out in the spring of 1907, he applied for and got the school at Shawneetown and Lulu got a school at Haiti. On June 24, 1908 he and Lulu Gladish were married. They had five children: Roy Gladish "Jerry", Lars Meredith, John Alpheus, Roberta Louise and Robert Louis. H. R. taught school at Shawneetown for a couple of years, then at the Pocahontas school until 1916. He decided to quit teaching and go into the dairy business on the old farm that was deeded to him in 1908 by Amos Stevenson.

H. R. and Lulu moved to Fruitland in 1941 and lived close to Roberta "Patty" and her husband Roy McDowell (deceased). H. R. Stevenson died in 1977. Roberta and Roy McDowell had two children: Joe and Katherine.

By 1949 John was in California with his wife Grace Englehart where they raised their eight children: Donna, John Keith, Donald, Robert Roy, Ted, Tom, Ann and Jerry, until the death of his wife, Grace. He now resides in Fruitland with his second wife, Evelyn Gilmore. Roy G. "Jerry" married Margaret Smith and after farming for many years in Missouri moved his family west in 1950 and eventually settled in Albuquerque, NM with their four children: Marjorie, Janet, Barbara and Gene. Jerry and Margaret are both deceased. Robert L. "Bob" married Joanna Laney and had two boys, Robby and Judd. They still reside in Jacksonville, FL. Lars M. "Mose" married Wanda Garrett and served 20 years in the U.S. Army retiring as a master sergeant. They currently reside in the Fruitland area. The names of spouses, grandchildren and great-grandchildren are too numerous to list.

The Stevensons, including the direct linage as well as spouses and children, have always been caretakers of the land. Through agriculture or just the love of open spaces… we care. Our love of family and friends is the cornerstone of our heritage. The golden rule, in the Stevenson clan, has always been taught and observed with reverence. *Submitted by Erma McDowell*

STONE – The Nelson Stone family moved to Jackson in November 1956 to fill in for a local veterinarian who had been injured in a car accident and needed help with his practice until he recovered, about six weeks. At that time they had a 2-year-old daughter, Mara Beth, and a 6-week-old baby, Barry Nelson.

The six weeks passed with Dr. Stone becoming acquainted with many aspects of veterinary medicine he had not been doing before, while working in government meat inspection in downtown St. Louis, after graduating from Missouri University in 1955. During the next few years a statewide program to eliminate brucellosis in cattle and an outbreak of hog cholera among the swineherds occurred. All cattle had to be blood tested and cleared of brucellosis and all swine vaccinated to protect them from cholera. Those were long workdays, along with the regular workday of a veterinarian, making routine farm calls and treating small animals.

Front row left to right: Libby Stone, Barry Stone and Mara Beth Stone Webster. Back row: Nelson Stone and June Stone.

Nelson and June liked this area so well that after Dr. Wills was able to start work again, they stayed in Jackson to work with him in practice. In 1972 Dr. Stone became owner of the clinic, worked 37 years in his practice, also doing sale barn work for several years, and retired in 1994 because of health problems, and continues to live here. June did the bookkeeping for several years for the business after the children were in school. Before marriage she had attended Southwest Baptist College and taught school at Cross Roads in St. Francois County.

Another daughter, Libby Carol, was added to the family in 1958, and a baby boy, Alan James, was stillborn in 1965.

The children received a good education in Jackson Schools and liked to live here. Mara Beth often expressed the hope that Jackson would stay a small town; of course it has grown considerably these past years, as progressive towns do.

Mara Beth graduated from Southeast Missouri State University with a degree in music, received her Master's Degree from Southern Illinois University, and teaches in the Anna-Jonesboro schools. She is married to Randell Webster and they have two boys, Jared and Damon.

Barry graduated from Rolla, majoring in computer science, got his Master's Degree at Purdue University, and is a computer programmer and consultant. He married Elaine Fayard of New Orleans and they have two boys, Justin and Jordan, and a daughter, Melody.

Libby attended Murray State in Kentucky and received a degree in hotel and motel management, with a minor in French. She now works at the University of Arizona in Tucson in public relation as a liaison between the school and community.

In 1967 Nelson's parents, Orville and Anna Stone, moved to Jackson in their retirement years. They lived on Highway 72 until 1986, then moved to Harmony Lane and lived there until their deaths.

The Stones have been active workers in Jackson, in the First Baptist Church in many aspects, PTA, Chamber of Commerce, and the SEMO Medical Board, and they have worked with boy and girl scouts and FFA students in animal care. Dr. Stone served the Missouri Veterinary Association as secretary-treasurer for 12 years, and continues to be an active member.

An older house on Georgia Street was their first home, and then in 1965 a new house was built on Harmony Lane, where they still reside. Jackson seemed the ideal place to work and raise a family, and they are sure they made the right choice. *Submitted by Dr. and Mrs. Nelson Stone*

STOVERINK – Alphonse Herman Stoverink was born Oct. 30, 1918 in the small town of Leopold, in Bollinger County, MO, the seventh of ten children born to Anthony and Rose Van Doren Stoverink. Anthony's father, Anton, made wooden shoes in Holland and turned to farming after coming to Leopold in 1882. Rose Van Doren, daughter of Henry and Elizabeth Van Doren, was of Dutch and Cherokee lineage.

Irene Anna Thiele was born in Leopold on March 21, 1922, the eldest daughter of seven children of Frederick and Helena Elfrink Thiele. The Thiele and Elfrink families were originally from Germany and emigrated in the 1850s.

When Alphonse and Irene were married March 18, 1943, during Alphonse's military leave, little did they know they would eventually become the parents of 11 children, 39 grandchildren, and seven great-grandchildren- at last count. 1. Carol Jean: born Jan. 9, 1945; married Jerry Dirnberger, Sept. 10, 1966; two children-Donna Kay, Janis Marie. 2. James Edward: born Nov. 1, 1946; married Susan Welker, June 5, 1970; five children- James Edward Jr., Thomas Frederick, Christina Susan, Luke Patrick, Tyson Dean. 3. Gerald Eugene; born Oct. 19, 1947; married Catherine Marie Quatmann, Sept. 2, 1972; four children- Frederick Anthony, Kathleen Marie, Rebecca Ann, Anna Cecelia. 4. Daniel Raymond: born Nov. 12, 1948; married Paula Jean Gerard, Aug. 11, 1973; three children-

Lynnette Marie, Jill Kathleen, Mark Daniel. 5. David Frederick: born Sept. 10, 1950; married Linda Lou Manternach, Sept. 4, 1971; two children- Mathew David, Adam Christopher. 6. Michael Anthony; born May 19, 1953; married Candice Marie Kolkovich, May 30, 1981; three children- Stephanie Ann, Bethany Suzanne, Courtney Joanne. 7. Alvin Marion: born Nov. 4, 1954; married Carol Maureen Flori, Aug. 6, 1977; six children- Julie Irene, Jennifer Marie, Jean Elizabeth, John Anthony, Joseph Michael, Jadie Catherine. 8. Mary Helen: born Jan. 10, 1956; married John Anthony Seiler, April 24, 1976; four children- Carolyn Suzanne, Helena Irene, Virginia Marie, Anthony James. 9. Theresa Rose: born April 12, 1958; married Randy Marion Kern, Aug. 26, 1978; four children- Nicole Irene, Ashley Marie, Cassandra Lashea, Cody Dylan. 10. Rita Ann: born June 5, 1961; married Dan Lynn Koeppel, June 4, 1983; two children- Andrew Christopher, Nicholas Alexander. 11. Linda Sue: born Sept. 14, 1962; married Thomas Lee Essner, Oct. 19, 1984; four children- Marissa Renee, Dana Lynn, Kelly Suzanne, Megan Michele. The family continues to grow with the blessing of many great-grandchildren.

The Alphonse and Irene Stoverink family, 1969. Left to right first row: Theresa, Linda and Rita. Second row: Alphonse, Irene and Carol. Third row: Michael, Alvin and Mary Helen. Fourth row: Gerald, James, Daniel and David.

Alphonse and Irene farmed land in Bollinger, Scott and Cape Girardeau Counties. In the early 1950s, the family moved to a farm south of Gordonville, MO, on County Road 214. Alphonse farmed soybeans and raised cattle and hogs. Irene tended the house and large garden, canned the produce from the garden, and watched over the active household. The family was active in the Immaculate Conception Parish where the children attended the grade school. Alphonse worked at Proctor and Gamble from 1969 to 1982. In 1977, the Stoverinks sold the farm and moved into Jackson. Alphonse passed away Aug. 27, 1998. Irene is a member of the Immaculate Conception Church Quilting Club, and is busy with all of the activities of the extended family. *Submitted by Cathi Quatmann Stoverink*

STOVERINK – Gerald Stoverink was born Oct. 19, 1947 in Cape Girardeau, MO the third of 11 children of Alphonse and Irene Thiele Stoverink originally from Leopold, MO in Bollinger County. In the early 1950s, the family moved to a farm south of Gordonville, MO on County Road 214. The children received their early education at Immaculate Conception School in Jackson, MO. Gerald attended high school at St. Vincent's College in Cape Girardeau. After graduating from Southeast Missouri State College in 1970, he moved to Jefferson City, MO and worked as a chemist for the Missouri Highway Department. On Sept. 2, 1972 Gerald married Catherine Marie Quatmann, born Sept. 3, 1951, the youngest of seven children of Joseph (1913-2000) and Marian Haas (1912-1987) Quatmann IV, of Cape Girardeau. In 1975, the Stoverinks moved to Jackson, where Gerald started Gerald E. Stoverink Construction Company, specializing in residential construction. From 1982 to 1995, Gerald and Catherine owned and operated Stoverink Carpet and Interiors, a retail flooring and paint store located at 503 South Hope Street in Jackson. During the 1990s, Gerald continued building homes while developing real estate: Stoverink Subdivision on Adams Street; Parkwood Place on Morgan Street, and Rosewood Estates on Independence Street.

Gerald E. Stoverink family: Jerry, Cathi, Fred, Katy, Becky and Annie, May 1988.

Catherine grew up in Cape Girardeau, attending St. Vincent's Grade School and Notre Dame High School. She graduated from Fontbonne College in St. Louis in 1972 and later received a Master's Degree in History from Southeast Missouri State University. Catherine has worked as bookkeeper for the family businesses, volunteered at Immaculate Conception Church and School, served on the board of the Jackson Heritage Association, and studied in the field of archives and historic preservation.

Gerald and Catherine are the parents of four children: Frederick Anthony "Fred" born Sept. 14, 1973; Kathleen Marie "Katy" born April 23, 1975; Rebecca Ann "Becky" born Oct. 17, 1979, and Anna Cecelia "Annie" born May 13, 1981. They attended Immaculate Conception Grade School and Jackson High School. Fred graduated from University of Missouri-Columbia in 1997 and is employed as a computer/electrical engineer in St. Louis. Katy graduated from University of Missouri-Rolla in 1997 and is a civil engineer for Koehler Engineering and Surveying in Cape Girardeau. Katy married Jason Scot Liley on Jan. 10, 1998. They are the parents of Mikala Marie, born Nov. 12, 2000. Becky attended Shawnee Community College and is employed as a customer service representative for a communications company in Cape Girardeau. Becky married Christopher Lynn Moore on Oct. 20, 2001. There are three children in their family: their daughter Kari Jo, born Oct. 8, 1999, Ali Nicole, born July 26, 2002 and Christopher's son, Christopher Lynn Moore II, born July 4, 1997. Annie is enrolled at the University of Missouri at Rolla in the civil engineering program. *Submitted by Catherine Marie Stoverink*

Clockwise: Fred Stoverink, Becky Stoverink Moore, Katy Stoverink Liley and Annie Stoverink, 2001.

STOVERINK – Susan Welker was born Feb. 10, 1948 at the old St. Francis Hospital in Cape Girardeau, MO. She is the oldest daughter of Wilbert Welker, born 1920, and Stella Brands Welker, born 1920. Susan grew up on a farm south of Gordonville and attended Needmore School for the first two years. It was a one-room school where one teacher taught all eight grades. She spent the next four years of school at Gordonville. The old Needmore School was bought by Wilbert and Stella, moved down the hill and became the family home until 1969.

Susan attended school at Jackson her seventh and eighth grade years in the same building as the high school. She graduated from Notre Dame High School in 1966 and attended Southeast Missouri University, graduating with a teaching degree in social studies.

In 1970 she married James E. Stoverink, the second child of 11 born to Alphonse and Irene Stoverink. At the time of his birth Jim's folks lived in Jackson on the second floor of his uncle's house. From 1947 to 1953 Jim's family made three more moves before settling near Gordonville on a farm. Jim attended Immaculate Conception Grade School and Notre Dame High School. He graduated from Southeast Missouri University in 1969, with a teaching degree in physical education.

The James Stoverink family seated left to right: Jim holding Tyson, Luke and Susan. Standing left to right: Tom, Christy and James Jr., 1993.

Jim and Susan lived in Petersburg, VA while Jim finished serving in the army. They then lived a short time in the Jackson area while Jim went back to school. Their first son, James Jr. was born during this time. In the fall of 1971, the couple moved to Cuba, MO where Jim taught school for eight years. During this time Susan did substitute teaching in between giving birth to two more children, Thomas and Christina.

Jim and Susan moved back to Jackson in 1979. Susan took on a full-time teaching job at Guardian Angel School in Oran and Jim went into construction work. Two years later Jim obtained a teaching job at Delta, MO. Another child, Luke, was born to the couple in 1981. After four years of teaching at Oran, Susan stayed home and operated a day care in the home. Two years later she began teaching at Immaculate Conception in Jackson. She taught there for six years. In 1991 the couple's youngest son, Tyson was born.

Jim has been teaching in the Jackson School District since 1983 and Susan has been substitute teaching since 1992. While coaching cross-country at Jackson High School Jim has taken runners to state competition every year. He also coached junior high track. Jim and Susan have also worked together running the Jackson Track Club for children ages 14 and under since 1983. For the last five years the couple has spent their summers running the concession stand at the Jackson Swimming Pool.

All five of Jim and Susan's children attended Immaculate Conception Grade School and Jackson High School where they were all active in sports. James Jr. is married to Debbie Schaffer and is teaching school at Pacific, MO. They have two children, Kyle born in 1990 and Whitten born in 1996. Whitten was adopted from Russia. Tom is married to Laura Smith and is working for T. G. Missouri in Perryville. They have one son, Tom Jr., born January 2002. Christy is married to Matt Margrabe and is a physical therapist. Luke works for S&W Cabinets in Chaffee and Tyson is in fourth grade at Immaculate Conception School. *Submitted by Susan Stoverink.*

STOVERINK – Thomas Frederic Stoverink was born May 7, 1973 in Rolla, MO, the son of James Edward (1946) and Susan Veronica Welker (1948). In 1979 Thomas moved to Jackson, MO with his family. He attended Immaculate Conception Elementary School from grades K-8. He then attended Jackson public schools and graduated in 1991. After graduation he attended Southeast Missouri State University where he received a B.S. degree in industrial technology manufacturing in May of 1998.

Tommy, Laura and T. J. Stoverink, Feb. 28, 2002.

While attending Southeast Missouri State University he met his future wife Laura Ellen Smith. She was born May 16, 1976, in Poplar Bluff, MO, to Clifford Lee (1941) and Naomi Bertsell Bowman (1943). She and her family moved to Jackson in 1987. Laura attended Jackson public schools and graduated in 1994. After graduation she attended Southeast Missouri State University, obtaining a degree in elementary education/exceptional child in May of 1998. She then received a Masters degree in elementary administration in August of 2001.

After graduation Thomas began working at TG Missouri in Perryville, MO as a quality engineer. Laura began teaching special education at Delta R-5 School District in Delta, MO.

Thomas and Laura were married on July 3, 1999 at the First General Baptist Church in Jackson, MO. Their first child, Thomas Frederic Stoverink Jr., was born Jan. 3, 2002. They currently live in Jackson, MO. *Submitted by Laura Stoverink*

STRODER – The Stroder family came from North Carolina in the early 1800s and settled in the Crump area in southwestern Cape Girardeau County. The farmed in this area for 150 years before later generations moved to nearby Jackson.

Alex Stroder had a son, Franklin, who married Josie Austin, and they had a son, Willie (b. Oct. 4, 1879). He married Maggie Darthulla Estes in 1897. Maggie's parents were Jim Estes and Alice Dunklin Estes. Willie and Maggie had a son Dale who was born on May 24, 1901. Dale married Grace Aline Hosea (b. Nov. 14, 1906) on Sept. 6, 1923. Grace Aline's parents were Cirgus Hosea (b. July 23, 1879) and Josie Proffer Hosea (b. Nov. 2, 1881), and her grandparents were Robert Lail and Lucy Allen Lail who were married in 1846.

Dale and Aline had nine children: Gertrude (b. March 19, 1924); Richard "Bud" (b. Dec. 13, 1925); Roxie (b. Feb. 12, 1929); W. D. "Dub" (b. March 5, 1931); Roy (b. Dec. 18, 1932); Shelby (b. Dec. 1, 1934); Harold (b. July 6, 1939) and Franklin McArthur (b. April 25, 1942). One child died at birth. Dale and Aline raised their large family during the Great Depression and "times were hard." They tell many stories of how they lived and managed to survive. All six sons served their country in the Army and Navy.

Shelby married Anna Marie Hennecke (b. Sept. 14, 1937) on Oct. 12, 1956 and they had four children: Angela who died at birth in 1963, Ann Christine (b. Jan. 18, 1965), Jeffrey Cirgus (b. Sept. 26, 1970) and Holly Lynn (b. Sept. 18, 1972). Shelby and his brother Roy were bricklayers and laid brick on many buildings in Jackson. Anna Marie taught school for 25 years and retired from Meadow Heights R-2 in 1995.

Ann Christine married Christopher Bess (1965) on June 20, 1987 and they have three children: Ashley (1991), Caitlyn (1994) and Caleb (1998). They live near Millersville. Anne Christine and Chris graduated from Southeast Missouri State University in May 1987 and were married one month later. He is employed at Proctor and Gamble and she is employed as a part-time secretary at First General Baptist Church in Jackson and as a substitute mail carrier.

Jeffrey married Barbie Macke (1969) and they live in Jackson. They graduated from Southeast Missouri State University in May 1992 and were married on Feb. 27, 1993. Barbie is a teacher in the Woodland R-IV school district and Jeffrey is an audit manager with Beussink, Hey and Roe, P.C.

The Stroder family

Holly married Todd Brand (1967) and they live near St. Louis. Holly graduated from Southeast Missouri State University in 1994 and from St. Louis University in 1999. She teaches at Missouri Baptist College. Todd received both his bachelor's and master's degrees from Baylor University in Texas, and is now president of AMG Brand/Russell, an investment advisor firm in Chesterfield. *Submitted by Anna Marie Stroder*

SUEDEKUM – Andreas "Andrew" Suedekum was born Oct. 27, 1821 near the Harz Mountains in the Duchy of Braunschweig, Germany, and died Feb. 26, 1885 in Gordonville, Cape Girardeau County, MO. Both he and his wife are buried in the Suedekum Private Cemetery on their farm near Dutchtown, which is presently the Russ Obermann Farm. He married Johanne Sophie "Conradine" Amelunke on March 2, 1848 in Cape Girardeau, MO, daughter of Heinrich "Christian" Amelunke and Johanne Marie Friederike Klusmann. She was born Feb. 27, 1827 in Seesen-Rhüden, Braunschweig, Germany, and died Sept. 4, 1883 in Gordonville, MO.

Andrew and Conradina (Amelunke) Suedekum

Andrew Sudecum is listed as one of the original founders of the Evangelical Lutheran Church in Dutchtown, also known as the Swampgemeinde congregation. During the winter, when the leaves have fallen off the trees, one can see the Dutchtown Church from the Suedekum farm.

Andrew and Dina had the following children all of whom resided in the Gordonville area. 1. William Suedekum was born in 1850 and died before 1859.

2. Louise Suedekum was born Oct. 31, 1852 and died Oct. 22, 1871 in Dutchtown, MO. She married Benedict Schwab Jr. on May 16, 1871, in Cape Girardeau County and died only a few months later. Benedict was born Jan. 29, 1849 and died Nov. 12, 1883. His first wife, Ervine (Alvina) B. Wagoner, also died shortly after their marriage on April 17, 1870. He married third, Mary D. H. Siemers on Sept. 17, 1872 and she bore him six children.

3. Sophie Suedekum was born in 1855. She married John Heinrich Keller on Dec. 14, 1876 and had a daughter, Amanda.

4. Heinrich Suedekum was born March 14, 1857 and died July 11, 1945 (buried in the Zion Lutheran Cemetery in Gordonville.) He married first Maria Schwab on Feb. 20, 1879; she was the daughter of John C. Schwab and was born March 26, 1857 and died Aug. 29, 1881. They had two children, Louis and Rosena. He married second Louise Schlegel on May 29, 1882. She was born April 14, 1862 and died Nov. 21, 1936 of pneumonia. She gave him seven children: Henry August, Friedrich "Wilhelm", Ernest Otto, Heinrich, Herman, Ida and Alvin Suedekum.

5. William Suedekum was born May 26, 1859 and died Feb. 10, 1945. He married first Albertine Schwab on Jan. 9, 1883. She was born Oct. 4, and died Oct. 7, 1887 and they had one daughter, Tillie Suedekum. He married second Mena Maria Siemers on Oct. 12, 1888. She was born Nov. 30, 1867. They had a boy and a girl, Andrias and Hermine Suedekum. He married third Anna Witzel on Jan. 26, 1898. She was born Oct. 20, 1869 and died Feb. 13, 1924. They had Mathilde, Wilhelm and Theodor Suedekum.

6. August Suedekum was born September 1868. He married Rosena Schlegal on Nov. 14, 1889, and she was born February 1868 in Scott County, MO. They had nine children: Arthur, Lilie, Emma, Edna, Edwin, August, Alma, Louise and Margie Suedekum. *Submitted by Marcine Lohman*

SUMMERS – Ira Thomas Summers was born Sept. 17, 1833 in Tennessee and came to Missouri with his family around 1840. On Nov. 17, 1859 he married Sophia Elizabeth Baker. She died on Feb. 11, 1860. On March 2, 1865 he married Maria Louisa "Lou" Criddle, daughter of William Criddle and Elvira Robinson.

Their children were: John William, b. April 11, 1866, m. Bertie Ellen Scivally; Franklin Lee, b. July 8, 1867, m. Mary Ellen Knupp; Arizona, b. March 1870, m. William Welty; Virginia Tennessee, b. March 1872, m. John Limbaugh; Minnie White, b. Jan. 2, 1874, never married; Clarence Criddle, b. Dec. 15, 1876, m. Emma Criddle; Alabama, b. 1878, m. Andrew Runnels; Sylvester Pinkney, b. June 1882; Edna, b. July 16, 1888, m. James R. Limbaugh; M. G., b. 1879; Infant, born and died Jan. 15, 1881; Infant, born and died Jan. 24, 1885.

Ira died on Nov. 17, 1901 and Maria died Feb. 13, 1933. Both are buried at Fairview Methodist Church Cemetery along with many other members of their family. According to his obituary, Ira embraced religion, serving in many areas of church work- class leader, steward, and a faithful worker in Sunday school. He was loved and respected by many in the community. Ira and Maria donated the land for Fairview Methodist Church near Millersville in February 1892. The marriage of Virginia Tennessee to John Limbaugh was one of the first marriages performed in the church. *Submitted by Marilyn Fronabarger*

SUTTON - James Sutton married Absey Brown about 1768 and later served in the Revolutionary War. Their son, James Simpson Sutton, born in 1795, married Mary Pauline Cornwell in 1819. James Simpson and Mary Pauline's son, James Terrell Sutton was born in 1821 and he married Catherine Hart Draper in Smith County, TN, in 1843. James Terrell and Catherine settled in Jackson County, TN, and later came to southeast Missouri in the 1850s. They came in two covered wagons to Jackson where the family stayed for a short time. They moved on to Wayne County and homesteaded land, east of Coldwater, on Cedar Creek. James Terrell Sutton was a skilled carpenter and blacksmith, and was also a farmer. He built a two-pen log home with a dog trot (breezeway) and also several barn buildings on a sloping hillside above the creek bottom. He and Catherine raised a family of eight children: Simpson Clay; Benjamin Franklin; Mary Elizabeth; James Napoleon; William Jasper; Martha Susan; Joel Warren; and Nancy Jane.

During the Civil War James Terrell Sutton was a member of Wayne County Company A, 47th Infantry and served as First Lieutenant at Fort Davidson in Pilot Knob. He was there in September 1864, during the battle with Confederate General Sterling Price. He was with those who worked to set a charge of explosives to destroy the powder magazine and munitions before they abandoned the outnumbered fort. During the night they padded their wagon and cannon wheels and managed to slip away, marching north toward Caledonia. The over 20 tons of gunpowder and munitions blew a large hole, still visible today, in the center of the deserted earthen fortifications. After the war James Terrell Sutton received his pension but died in 1869 at the age of 47 due to exposure and injuries received in the Pilot Knob Battle, the subsequent escape and further skirmishes. He and his wife are buried in the Dixon-Sutton Cemetery on route EE, east of Coldwater, in the garden area of his homestead.

His son, William Jasper Sutton, married Susan Ann Bennett from Wayne County and settled in Jackson. William Jasper worked as a carpenter for many years. They had four sons. Louie Walter Sutton was one of the last millers to operate the Bollinger Mill in Burfordville. Louie wrote the history of the Sutton family and related many stories his grandfather told of the Civil War and their early life in Tennessee and Wayne County. He left several sketches on the walls of the Bollinger Mill that are still visible, one of a riverboat he had seen on the Mississippi. He painted the name "Cape County Milling Company" above the front porch of the mill and placed his initials "L.W. S." below. The initials are now very faded. William Jasper and Susan Ann Sutton later moved to a farm just south of Burfordville. Their other sons were John Sherman, William Grant and Benjamin Franklin. Benjamin Franklin Sutton married Annie Mae Acre, an orphan girl, and their children were Lloyd Quincey, Lindsay Franklin, Gladys Ailene and Mildred Gail. The two boys died when young children and Mildred Gail married Russell Bazzell of Jackson

Gladys Ailene married Joseph Sciortino of Cape Girardeau. Joseph and Gladys had four children. Jo Ann Sciortino married Roger Schnur of St. Charles; Jane Francis Sciortino married Gerald Meesey of Des Peres; Mary Susan Sciortino married Elroy Kinder of Cape Girardeau; and James Michael Sciortino married Lana Marie Brewer of New Madrid.

Elroy and Mary Susan Kinder have four children: David Frederick who married Cheryl Lynn nee Pogue; John Joseph, Kathy Jane; and Jill Suzanne who married Chris Haman. They have one grandson, Jared Eli Kinder. Elroy retired from the Cape Girardeau Public Schools in 1992 and Mary Susan from the nursing profession. Elroy is now Parish Assistant at Hanover Lutheran Church and is also involved in genealogy and historic preservation activities. Mary Susan received her R.N. degree from St. John's Hospital in St. Louis in 1961. She retired from working as an R.N. in the Cape Girardeau Public Schools and area hospitals. She also worked a number of years for the Cape Girardeau Public Library. *Submitted by Mrs. Elroy, Mary Susan (Sciortino) Kinder*

The children of Elroy and Mary Susan Kinder, left to right, back row: John Kinder and David Kinder. Front row, Kathy Jane Kinder and Jill Suzanne Kinder, 1987

SWAN – Marjorie Bernice (Sample) Swan was born on May 16, 1923 at her Niswonger grandparents' farm home near Patton, MO. Her parents were William Rudolph and Reva (Niswonger) Sample.

Marjorie and her four siblings, Clovis Eugene, George David, Shirley Ann and Roger William, were raised on their parents' farm west of Sedgewickville, MO, in Bollinger County. She attended Flatwoods School, where she later taught, and Patton High School. In 1941 she graduated from Sedgewickville High School. She married her high school sweetheart, Denver Clyde Loberg, son of Jesse J. and Metta (Barks) Loberg of Sedgewickville, on June 22, 1940. The couple had two daughters, Vida Loberg (Stanard) and Tina Loberg (Druckenmiller), born respectively on May 18, 1941 and Sept. 4, 1943. On Christmas Eve 1944, U.S. Army Air Corps Sgt. Denver Loberg was killed in action as a nose gunner aboard a B-24 Liberator bomber bound for Germany.

After the death of Sgt. Loberg, Marjorie moved with her two daughters back to her parents' Bollinger County farm. She graduated from the Cape Girardeau School of Cosmetology and supported her children as a hairdresser.

On Oct. 6, 1946, Marjorie married Norman Raymond Swan, also a WWII veteran of the U.S. Army Air Corps. He was the son of Reginald and Alma (Schoen) Swan of Pocahontas, MO. To that union were born Norman R. "Sam" Swan Jr. (July 5, 1948), William Reginald Swan (Feb. 13, 1950) and Nina Christine Swan-Kohler (Jan. 18, 1852). After marrying Norman Swan, Marjorie moved to Pocahontas, where Mr. Swan owned and operated a Chevrolet dealership. He later was general manager of Interstate Radial Tire in McClure, IL, served for over three decades as Pocahontas City Clerk and town board member, and was a member of the Jackson R-II Board of Education for nine years. He also was known for overseeing the "kettle beef" dinners at St. John's Lutheran Church. Mr. Swan died on July 1, 1984.

After raising her five children, all of whom are college educated, Marjorie attended Southeast Missouri State University. At the time of publication, Marjorie had nine grandchildren and seven great-grandchildren. Having become an adult 4-H leader when Vida was 9 years old in 1950, Marjorie continues as an assistant leader of the Pocahontas 4-H Club, and has served for more than 50 years. In 1995 she was honored by the Missouri 4-H foundation with the Naomi Crouch State Leadership Award. Marjorie has been an active member of St. John's Lutheran Church for more than 50 years, and led a campaign to restore the church's original cemetery. She has been active in the Missouri Extension Homemakers association (now Family Community Education Association) for many years serving as Cape Girardeau County president and district director on the state board. She also has worked many years as a Pocahontas precinct election official and has been an active member (no. 697983) of the Daughters of the American Revolution since 1986. One of her proudest achievements was the publication of the 435-page history and genealogy book titled *Conrads: 1750-1986*, of which she was editor and Conrad historian.

Marjorie Swan

SWAN – Dr. Norman R. "Sam" Swan Jr. was born July 5, 1948, the son of Norman R. Swan (b. July 9, 1919) and Marjorie Sample Loberg Swan (b. May 16, 1923). His grandparents were Reginald and Alma (Schoen) Swan, and William Sample and Reva (Niswonger) Sample.

Dr. Swan attended Pocahontas Public School and Jackson High School, where in his senior year he was student body president. He graduated from Southeast Missouri University in 1970. He received a master's degree from Central Missouri State University in Warrensburg, MO, in 1974, and a PhD in communications at the University of Missouri at Columbia in 1978.

As a youth he was very active in the 4-H program, serving as president and a Cape Girardeau County junior leader. He became an I.F.Y.E. exchange member to Sri Lanka in 1970 for six months. He also served as national president of the I.F.Y.E. association from 1974-1977. While in college at Southeast Missouri University, he worked as an anchor at KFVS television. He also taught at Notre Dame High School, and worked as a 4-H youth agent in Lafayette County, MO, in 1974.

In 1976 Dr. Swan married Sheriann Campbell (b. Sept. 30, 1953) in Columbia, MO. She is the daughter of Buel and Ann Webb Campbell, and she is a graduate of the University of Missouri with a degree in education. Their daughter, Leslie Anne, was born Nov. 14,

Dr. Norman Swan Jr.

1978 in St. Paul, MN, and graduated from the University of Tennessee at Knoxville in 2001. Their son, Nicholas, was born June 7, 1981 in Carbondale, IL.

After graduating, Dr. Swan first went to the University of Minnesota at St. Paul, then to Southern Illinois University in Carbondale, IL. Then he became the department head at the University of Tennessee at Knoxville in the College of Communications.

Dr. Swan also teaches and oversees for the "Voice of America." He has taught in the following third-world countries: Angola, Bosnia, Bulgaria, Croatia, Czech Republic, Ghana, India, Latvia, Macedonia, Nigeria, Pakistan, Romania, Russia, South Africa, Tanzania, Ukraine, Yugoslavia, and Trinidad and Tobago; he has made a total of 28 trips overseas to 18 different countries. In these countries the government controls radio and television. He teaches them how to open their own stations and make it profitable. He also trains radio and television journalists. *Submitted by Marjorie Swan*

SWAN – Alma Rosalie Schoen was born Aug. 4, 1894 in Pocahontas, MO, the daughter of Emmanuel Gustav and Maria Theresa Haberfeller Schoen. She was married on June 4, 1916, to Reginald Otto Swan, born Oct. 16, 1893 at Whittenburg, MO, the son of Charles and Emilie Palisch Swan.

Four children lived to adulthood. Norman Raymond was born July 9, 1919 and married Marjorie Sample Loberg on Oct. 6, 1946. Leonard Nelson was born Nov. 18, 1921, and married Louise Morton on April 23, 1944. Dorothy Lavern was born Jan. 3, 1928 and married George Vernon on Nov. 6, 1948. Kathryn Marie was born Nov. 21, 1936; she married first, Carlos Garcia on May 1, 1974, and second, Frank Noble on April 6, 2002.

The Reginald Swan family.

Mr. and Mrs. Swan lived for a time in Whittenburg where he was a farmer, before moving to Pocahontas. He opened a garage in the center of town and later it became a Chevrolet dealership, which he operated until his death in 1947. At this time his sons Norman and Leonard had the dealership for a number of years.

Mr. Swan was active in St. John's Lutheran Church E.L.C.A., holding many offices including chairman. He was known as a baseball enthusiast; he played catcher and later became an umpire. When he was a young man, he attended State Normal College in Cape Girardeau, MO. He served as mayor of Pocahontas and also served on the school board and had been appointed to the County Highway Commission.

Alma Schoen Swan descends from St. John's founders Joseph Haberfeller Sr., born Jan. 31, 1819, in Austria, and Joseph Haberfeller Jr., born Dec. 25, 1848, in upper Austria. Both are buried in the old cemetery at St. John's near Pocahontas.

Mrs. Swan was known as an excellent cook. She cooked several years at Pocahontas Public School, where some of her grandchildren were attending. It was not too unusual for an extra cookie to find its way onto their lunch tray. *Submitted by Marjorie Sloan*

SWAN – William Reginald Swan was born Feb. 13, 1950, the son of Norman R. Swan (b. July 9, 1919) and Marjorie Sample Loberg Swan (b. May 16, 1923). His grandparents were William Sample (b. Dec. 2, 1896) and Reva Niswonger Sample (b. Dec. 13, 1903), and Reginald Swan (b. Oct. 16, 1893) and Alma Schoen Swan (b. Aug. 4, 1894).

Reg attended Pocahontas Public School and graduated from Jackson High School in 1968. He was active in debate, marching band, and football. He graduated from Southeast Missouri University in 1972 with a degree in industrial arts. As a teenager he was very active in the 4-H program, earning all three top trips offered by 4-H; he was also the first of three Cape Girardeau County 4-H members to be elected state president in 1968. Reg is an avid car enthusiast and enjoys off-roading on mountain trails.

Kathryn Johnson Swan and W. Reginald Swan, owners of JCS/Tel-Link, displayed plaque marking the 40th anniversary of the Cape Girardeau business, August 1999.

Reg married Kathryn Johnson (b. Nov. 9, 1950) on April 17, 1971. She is the daughter of Charles Johnson (b. Aug. 28, 1920) and Marie Nenninger (b. Oct. 2, 1920). Their son, William Reginald "Regan" Swan Jr. was born July 16, 1973, and their daughter, Maria Kathryn, was born June 2, 1977. Both graduated from college, Regan at Southeast Missouri University and Maria at the University of Missouri at Columbia.

Reg and Kathy own Johnson Communications J.C.S./Tel-Link in Cape Girardeau and received the "Small Business of the Year" award by the Cape Girardeau Chamber of Commerce in 1997 on their 40th anniversary of the business. The company is the largest locally owned paging company in the area, and owns stores in Cape Girardeau, Jackson, and Arnold in Missouri, and Chester and Anna in Illinois. Reg served as chairman of the board of "Great Lakes MSS Association" in 1996. Kathy has been elected for the year 2002.

Kathy received her associate of arts in nursing at Southeast Missouri University in 1970 and her bachelor's degree in 1975. She is active in many community organizations. She is a current board member of St. Francis Medical Center Foundation, American Cancer Society, American Heart Association, Vision 2020 Community Relations Council, and Great Lakes MMS (Motorola Service Station) Association; she is chairman of United Way, president of Zonta Club of the Cape Girardeau area, and board secretary of the Lambda Theta Chapter of Southeast Missouri State University; she is a member of the Sigma Theta Tau International Honorary Nursing Society, a committee member of Governor Holden's Business Education Roundtable, Education Council Administrative Committee, Missouri Chamber of Commerce Government and Public Policy Committee, Cape Girardeau Chamber of Commerce Leadership Development Committee, and various other boards and committees.

SWAN/KOHLER – Nina Christine Swan was born Jan. 18, 1952, in Cape Girardeau, MO, and is the daughter of Norman Swan (b. July 1, 1919, in Wittenburg, MO) and Marjorie Sample Loberg Swan (b. May 16, 1923, in Patton, MO). Nina, the youngest of five, grew up in a wonderful Christian family where her parents loved each other and they loved her and her siblings. Nina learned much later in life how rare this family situation was, since so many people do not have close family ties. Nina's parents made many sacrifices to provide a happy and loving environment for the family. Nina was somewhat spoiled by her two older sisters (Vida and Tina) who both taught her many things. Her brothers, Sam and Reg, picked on her at home but protected her when outside the home. They paved the way for her through high school and college. Nina says it was great, being the little sister and the youngest in the family.

Nina lived in Pocahontas, MO from 1952 until 1975. Nina attended Pocahontas Elementary School for six years. She was sent home for wearing shorts to school in the second grade. Nina joined the Pocahontas 4-H Club at age 8 and enrolled in a food class, although she had attended 4-H meetings with her mother and siblings since birth. Nina attended Jackson Junior High School for grades seven though nine. She wore a ponytail and was a cheerleader during grades seven and eight. She attended grades ten through twelve at Jackson High School, where she was active in band, chorus, Future Homemakers of America, Student Council, and debate.

After high school graduation, Nina attended Southeast Missouri State University in Cape Girardeau, MO, where she majored in Vocational Home Economics Education. She was active in Southeast Missouri 4-H, Missouri Student Home Economics Association, and the Golden Eagles Marching Band, where she "played" in the Super Bowl in 1971. She graduated in 1974. She attended the University of Missouri in Columbia and graduated in 1978 with a master's degree in foods, nutrition and communications.

Nina Swan-Kohler

Active in the 4-H program in her youth, Nina was State 4-H Council Secretary, a state and national winner in Home Improvement, and an International 4-H Youth Exchange (IFYE) representative to Trinidad and Tobago, where she lived with 11 families during the five-month cultural exchange program to promote world peace and understanding.

Her career path follows: Home Economist/Program Director, St. Louis District Council, Springfield, MO (1975 to 1978); International Marketing Specialist, Missouri Department of Agriculture, Jefferson City, MO (1978 to 1979); Nutrition/ Media Coordinator, St. Louis District Dairy Council, St. Louis, MO (1979 to 1981); Director of Consumer Relations, National Oats Company, Inc., Cedar Rapids, IA (1981 to 1984); and Account Executive and Account Supervisor, CMF&Z Advertising and Public Relations Agency, Cedar Rapids, IA (1984 to 1991). Presently she is President/ Owner of Swan-Kohler & Associates, Cedar Rapids, IA. She founded the marketing, public relations and promotions agency in 1991, specializing in the marketing of food and consumer products, and the communications business. Swan-Kohler & Associates has a network of experienced and creative associates (art directors/ graphic designers, copy writers, media planners and buyers, home economists, and clerical support) "standing by" to assist with the execution of any plans presented to and approved by clients of Swan-Kohler & Associates.

Professional Organizations include: Member of Consumer Science Business Professional since march 1999; member of International Association of Culinary Professional (IACP), 1995-2002; former member of the American Association of Family and Consumer Sciences, AAFCS Business Section; chairperson of Iowa State University's college of Family and Consumer Sciences Advisory Board, 1994-1996; member of The Cedar Rapids Salvation Army Advisory Board, 1991-2001; trustee on the Iowa 4-H Foundation Board 1995-2000; and member of the Cedar Rapids Birthright Advisory Board 1997-2002.

Her awards include: named "Outstanding Junior Alumna" in 1984 and received one of only six "Alumni Merit Awards" given in 1999 from Southeast Missouri State University. Nina was named "Home Economist In Business of the Year" by the Iowa Home Economists in Business (1990), and twice awarded the prestigious "Drumbeater Award" by The Cedar Rapids Salvation Army (1994 and 1996). Nina also initiated the "free breakfast program" for The Cedar Rapids Salvation Army in 1991 to provide a hot breakfast to all needy people in Cedar Rapids, IA.

Today Nina and her husband of 16 years (married Oct. 19, 1985) Ronald Kohler, reside in Cedar Rapids, IA. Ronald, a 1969 graduate of Loras College in Dubuque, IA, is General Adjuster for GAB/ Robins-North America, an independent insurance adjustment firm. Nina is a very committed aunt who loves and adores her nieces and nephews and great-nieces and great-nephews. She takes her role as aunt very seriously and enjoys each and every moment she gets to spend time with them. Nina enjoys organizing and hosting many parties for her friends and family members. She finds it extremely rewarding and fun to "customize" her parties to fit the guest of honor or the theme of the party. Her lifetime goal is to bring joy and blessings to those around her. Nina's hobbies include gourmet cooking, entertaining, walking, needlepoint, traveling, and collecting teddy bears and heart-shaped "treasures." *Submitted by Marjorie Swan*

TALLENT – I was born near Millersville, next door to the Niswonger church on Highway 72, at my grandfather's house. Dr. D. I. L. Seabaugh was the doctor. It was near dinnertime and my dad invited him to eat with them. I was the fifth child with two older brothers and two older sisters, Jewel, Ruby, Harlan and Jesse and they named me Opal.

I started school at Old Salem School with Miss Hester Dalton as the teacher. My dad had a heart attack and we moved to Jackson. By that time I had two more brothers, Glenn and Woodrow. I started second grade at Jackson Grade School, which was a little strange since at Old Salem all grades were in one room.

We lived on the Greensferry Road and I walked a mile to school. We lived in a rock house, which I liked very much because there was no other house like that. We lived there until I was in the fourth grade, when we moved to Main Street where now is the former Cracraft-Miller store in a small white house. I remember crossing the footbridge over Hubble Creek to get to school. After several years we moved back to Greensferry Road and our next-door neighbor was Wilma Walters. We became very good friends and walked to school together. My family moved back to west Jackson on Bast Street when I was ready for high school.

I graduated from high school in 1932 and went to work at the International Shoe Company. At the age of 25 I met my future husband, Willie "Bill" M. Tallent. I met him through some friends, Shelby and Mildred Brown. We met in April 1939 and married in November the same year.

Bill owned a small farm in Scopus, 20 miles from Jackson, and was a mail carrier. We lived there until that job was over and moved back to Jackson and lived on the Bainbridge Road. Bill worked for Kroger. Our first daughter, Mary Catherine, was born May 20, 1942 and our second daughter, Margaret Sue, was born Dec. 11, 1945, while we lived there. We moved to Colorado Street when Margaret started first grade. While in that home our third daughter, Martha Leah, was born Aug. 30, 1952. We lived there until we moved to 931 West Main, which was our home for over 40 years.

W. M. "Bill" and Opal Niswonger Tallent and daughters: left to right Margaret Morgan, Mary Hill and Martha Garrett.

Bill worked for Elfrink Construction Company, ABF Trucking and Cracraft Miller until he retired. Bill passed away in 1996. I now reside at the Monticello Residential House.

My years in Jackson were spent being very active at the First Baptist Church, Eastside Homemakers, and spending 15 years working at Jackson School District in food services.

Jackson has been a great place to live and raise our family. Our daughters have many memories and always looked forward to coming home. Mary lives in Lawson, MO, Martha lives in Louisville, KY and Margaret lives in Scopus on the Tallent home place. *Submitted by Margaret Morgan*

TALLEY – Carl Talley and his wife, Mary, have lived and raised their three children on Old Cape Road in Jackson, MO, since their marriage in 1959. Their first daughter, Andrea Lea, was born in 1960. In 1962 their son, Douglas Kent, was born. Their third child, Susan Jeanne, was born in 1966.

Carl Lee Talley was born in 1936 near Byrds Creek, about three miles west of Jackson, the son of Harry Lee and Carrie Edna Statler Talley. The family moved to Jackson, MO, when Carl was 2 years old. A daughter, Ruth Ann, was born in 1940. Carl's father, Harry, was a livestock dealer.

Mary Louise Milde Talley was born in 1939, the first of four children of Frank Albert Sr. and Louise Anna Schaper Milde. Mary's sister and brothers included: Frances Kay, Frank Albert Jr., and Louise Mark. The family lived about two miles south of Jackson on a family-operated dairy and grain farm, which Frank Sr. and Louise operated with his parents, Albert J. and Lucy Milde.

Carl attended Jackson High School and Southeast Missouri State University. He was employed by the City of Jackson for 38 years. He was the City Administrator from 1972 to 1994, and has continued as a consultant since that time. Carl has been active in the Jackson community over the years. He has been a member of the Jackson Optimist Club, serving as a past president and active in its youth programs. He has been a member of the Jackson Chamber of Commerce, the Jackson Industrial Development Committee, the Southeast Missouri Port Authority Board, the Jackson Community Betterment Association, and the Jackson Heritage Association. He has coached flag football, girls' and boys' basketball, AAU basketball and track, Little League baseball, and Junior Babe Ruth baseball.

Mary and Carl Talley

Mary graduated from Jackson High School and Southeast Missouri State University. She was employed as a school speech/language therapist. Mary's community activities have included: Girls Scouts, serving as a troop leader, Jackson neighborhood chairman, day camp director, Otahki Girl Scout Council board of directors, Jackson R-2 PTO president, Progressive FCE Extension Club, Jackson Community Betterment Association, and the Jackson Heritage Association.

The three children of Carl and Mary are graduates of Southeast Missouri State University and are presently residents in the Jackson area. Andrea is an art teacher at Jackson R-2, Doug is employed in manufacturing, and Susan is a dental assistant. Susan is married to Robert M. Englehart, the son of Dr. John D. and Jean Englehart of Marble Hill, MO. Susan and her husband Bob are the parents of two children: Callie Elizabeth, born March 21, 1998, and Robert Case, born Feb. 16, 2001.

Carl's family has traced its lineage in the Jackson area to Carl's great-grandfather, David E. Talley, born in Tennessee in 1857, who came to Missouri when he was 16 years old. He married Elizabeth B. Knott in 1881. David E. and Elizabeth's first home was located about six miles west of Jackson near Big Spring, west of Byrds Creek, where Walter B. Talley, Carl's grandfather, was born on Jan. 30, 1885. The family later moved to a farm two miles northwest of Jackson on Oak Ridge Road. Walter Talley married Flora May Browning Blackman, a widow, in 1905. He was a livestock dealer. Their children included: Hugh, Willard, Mabel, Eula, Dorothy, Harry, and Helen. Walter and Flora moved to Jackson in 1933. Harry, the youngest son of Walter and Flora Talley, and Carrie Edna Statler, the daughter of Malachi and Bertha Alice "Allie' Statler, were married in 1933. Carrie's father farmed in the Sedgewickville, MO area. Carrie's parents, Chi and Allie Statler, married in 1907, and were the parents of four children: Della, Carrie, Coy and Thurman. Harry and Carrie Statler Talley were Carl's parents.

Mary's family has traced its lineage, on both her mother and father's sides, to Germany. The

Milde family's beginnings in the Jackson area occurred when Joseph Milde, born Oct. 3, 1820, and Rosalia Herrmann, born June 20, 1822, came to this country in 1858. They, with their four sons, Frank X., Ignatz, Emanual, and Daniel, emigrated from Bohemia to the United States because of all the military activities going on in Europe at the time. Joseph Milde bought 150 acres of land two and one-half miles south of Jackson where he farmed, made furniture and raised bees. Mary's great-grandfather, Franz Xavier (Frank X.), the oldest son of Joseph and Rosalia Milde, was born Sept. 11, 1845, in Bohemia. Frank X. and Anna Guenther, a widow, born March 1, 1843, in Bohemia, were married in 1868. Frank and Anna built a home on the Milde farm where they raised nine children: Charles Guenther, Alfred, Robert, Bertha, Emma, Henry, Mary, Albert, and Anna. Frank engaged in farming, sawmilling, and organizing and directing a musical band- the Milde Band. Frank and Anna's son, Albert Joseph Milde, born Sept. 1, 1880, married Lucy Brugger of the Gordonville area. Albert and Lucy were the parents of one son, Frank Albert Milde, born July 10, 1914. Albert remained on the family farm. In 1917, Albert and Lucy built a home on the farm, the place that Frank and Louise Milde's family, Mary's parents, called home. Frank A. Milde Sr. married Louise Anna Schaper on June 7, 1938. She was the daughter of Louis and Anna Brennecke Schaper, who farmed between Jackson and Gordonville. Louis, born July 7, 1878, was one of the nine children of Carl and Caroline Schaper, who farmed southwest of Jackson on the Snider's Mill Road. Anna Brennecke Schaper, born Jan. 26, 1881, was one of six children of Jacob and Henrietta Peetz Brennecke, who farmed in the Gordonville-Tilsit area. Mary's grandparents, Louis and Anna Schaper, were the parents of three children: Elmer, a farmer; Herbert, a teacher in Cape Girardeau County rural schools; and Louise, who married Frank A. Milde Sr., Mary's parents. *Submitted by Mary Talley*

TANT – In 1859 a young lad of 13 years came to Cape Girardeau County. He was Andrew Jackson Tant born in 1846 near Nashville, TN. His parents died when he was quite young and he was "taken in" by a neighbor. This neighbor brought Andrew to Missouri.

At the age of 15 he tried to enlist in the Civil War. For three years he rounded up cattle to be shipped east to feed the southern troops. When he reached 18 years he enlisted in Col. Jeffer's 8th Missouri Confederate Cavalry and served until the war ended.

After the war he returned to Cape Girardeau County and finished high school at the Pleasant Hill Academy near Fruitland, MO. There he met and fell in love with Mary Adelaide McNeely. They were wed Dec. 9, 1869. In 1871 he bought a farm located on the Jackson-Pocahontas road near Fruitland and lived there until his death in 1920.

Six children were born to this union. The four daughters married and established homes elsewhere. Eula wed Dr. B. W. Hays, a prominent Jackson physician. Grace and Robert L. Daniels, a teacher, established a home in Ellington, MO. Della and husband James P. McNeely lived many years in Texas. Myrtle and A. C. Hope settled down on a farm in Pocahontas, MO.

Two sons, Tilden and Victor, lived in the Fruitland Community all of their lives. They bought a farm and worked together for many years. Tilden remained single. Victor met Amy Barber, a teacher, from Brazeau, MO. A church picnic at Wilkinson's Mill, Altenburg, MO was where they met. They were married on Oct. 12, 1907 at the home of the bride by the Rev. E. S. Brainard, Presbyterian minister.

Two daughters, Mildred and Esther, were born to this union. Both were teachers. Mildred wed C. Wilson McDowell on Oct. 14, 1928 and Esther and Walter P. Been were married May 23, 1940 in Jackson, MO by Rev. S. H. Salmon, with Mrs. Eula Hays a witness. Each of the daughters had children. The sons Byron W. and Kenneth T. McDowell served in the U.S. Army and Rodney K. Been with the U.S/ Navy.

From the arrival of Andrew Jackson Tant to Missouri in 1859 to the passing of Amy Barber Tant in 1974, 115 years passed and during that time there was always a Tant family in the Fruitland Community. The main characters in this family history are now gone. With no Tant male heirs the family name is found only as a middle name for two surviving great-grandsons of Andrew Jackson Tant, namely Donald Tant McNeely and Kenneth Tant McDowell.

Victor and Amy Tant, 50th wedding anniversary, 1957.

Pleasant Hill Presbyterian Church has always been a special place of worship for the Tant family. Andrew Jackson and sons Tilden and Victor were deacons and elders. Amy, a Sunday school teacher, was still teaching a class at age 80. Many of the Tant family are at rest in the cemetery near the church.

One of the old Fruitland landmarks that still stand is the Houck Train Depot, now someone's home. Gone are Winter Bros. Store, Leimer's Blacksmith Shop, Germinhardt's Flour Mill and Fruitland High School. With the passing of time changes come but memories linger on. *Submitted by Esther Tant Been*

TAYLOR – On June 27, 1923 Vera Gale Taylor walked briskly towards his sister-in-law's home. A little smile hovered on his lips. He was going to take his children, Sarah Berniece and Robert Henry, home to Dallas Street where a surprise awaited. His wife Zelma had given birth to twin girls! After the first surprise, Bobby asked, "Can we keep both of them?"

Catherine Louise and Dorothy Lucille rounded out the Taylor family. Taylor was a local businessman, a plumbing and heating contractor. He was the son of Henry Taylor and Berniece Shepherd Taylor. He had worked with his father Henry at the stone quarry (located on highway 61) until Henry's death. Henry was fatally burned when a gasoline motor exploded.

Vera, the oldest son in the family, which included Alvin, Bess and Erna, became responsible for looking after his mother. He apprenticed to a local plumber and later was able to set up his own place in the "old Wagner building" on Main Street which houses the Wagner Bakery and Huckstep Shoe Repair, as well as V. G. Taylor Plumbing and Heating.

Zelma Catherine Talley was the daughter of Dr. Robert Talley and Sarah Elizabeth Ford Talley. He had moved his medical practice from Millersville to Jackson. Being members of First Baptist Church of Jackson brought these two, Vera Taylor and Zelma Talley together and afforded them opportunities to be together in church activities. Zelma related to her children how they with other young couples used to visit the covered bridge in Burfordville where they had carved their initials in a beam of the old bridge. Lucille relates her futile attempts to find those initials many years later. V. G. and Zelma married in December 1914.

The Depression years were difficult for Taylor. He remained a man of integrity in his business and Zelma was a loving, faithful wife and mother to their four children. Taylor's dream was that all his children might have a college education, which was realized, although he did not live to see that accomplished for all four. He died in February 1947. Sarah "Sally", the eldest, attended two years in Hannibal-Lagrange College in Hannibal, MO. She married Guy Edzel Brown, a minister to many rural churches in Missouri. Robert "Bob" also attended Hannibal-Lagrange, a junior college, and finished his college education at what is now Southeast Missouri State University. WWII interrupted his life plans for a period as he served in the army-armored division in Europe where he was awarded the Purple Heart and the Bronze Star. Before he shipped overseas he and his college sweetheart, Sara Norris, were married. Upon his return he began teaching music in the lead belt. Later he went to Southwestern Baptist Theological Seminary where he received his degree in music ministry and a PhD in Theology. He served in Texas first as minister of music and later as a pastor. Later they returned to Missouri and he is now retired in Lebanon, MO, which was his last pastorate.

Louise and Lucille attended college in Cape Girardeau after high school graduation in 1941. They both began teaching in the boot heel. Louise also taught in Union and Springfield, MO, and finally in the North Kansas City School District. She retired after more than 37 years in which she had been a classroom teacher, then an art supervisor. She earned a Master's degree at Columbia University in New York City. She now makes Jackson her home and finds joy in continuing in the production of art.

Taylor family ca. 1930. Front row left to right: Lucille Taylor (Ford) and Louise Taylor. Back row: Robert Taylor, Sarah Taylor, Zelma and V. G. Taylor.

Lucille taught in Jackson, Peoria, IL and Springfield, MO, before going to Southwestern Theological Seminary in Ft. Worth, TX. There she committed to missionary work overseas, which led her to Nigeria, West Africa. In Abeokuta, Nigeria, she taught in a training school for young African girls aspiring to be teachers. Charles S. Ford was a single missionary from Florida teaching in Baptist Boys High School in Abeokuta. Lucille and Charles became romantically involved and were married in Abeokuta on Dec. 6, 1954. Added to this marriage were five children. Charles Taylor "Chuck" Ford was born in Jacksonville, FL, on Feb. 12, 1956, while his parents were in the states on furlough. During their next tour of service in Nigeria, Stephen Patterson was born March 19, 1957, in Ogbomosho, Nigeria and John William was born Nov. 16, 1958 in Eku, Nigeria. During another furlough, Cathleen Louise was born in Hartfield, CT., May 24, 1961. During another tour of service, the Fords did linguistic work among a tribe with an unwritten language. During the next furlough, Robert Gale was born in Ocala, FL on Jan. 28, 1967. At the end of furlough the Fords resigned as international missionaries. They lived in Charles' native state of Florida before moving to Jackson. Charles taught 20 years in R. O. Hawkins Junior High and Lucille taught eight years in West Lane Elementary before retiring.

Recently the whole family gathered for Thanksgiving. Chuck is coach and teacher in Fredericktown, MO, where he resides with his wife Paula and son Heath. Steve, Sherri and girls Alison and Emily traveled from Franklin, TN, where Steve is owner of Bolden Construction Company in Nashville. John recently relocated in Jackson from Wisconsin. He is an artist whose work is exhibited in galleries in the United States, Ireland and continental Europe. Cathleen, a teacher in Kansas City Magnet schools for 16 years, has transferred to Garden City, MO, where she and son Cody reside. At present she is pursuing a Master's degree in technology in education. Robert is an environmental engineer employed in a research lab of the E.P.A. located in Ada, OK, where he resides with wife Amy and son Bryce.

What started in Jackson in the 1800s has come full circle for several members of Taylor/Ford families back to Jackson. It is reassuring to realize God's providential care has brought this about. *Submitted by Lucille Taylor Ford*

THIELE – Edwin and Evelyn Thiele established residency in Jackson following their marriage in August 1946 in Leopold, MO. Edwin is the eldest son of the late Fred William and Helena Elfrink Thiele. Evelyn is the youngest daughter of the late Henry and Mina Stoverink Holweg. Both Ed and Evelyn grew up in Bollinger County. Ed attended school in Leopold while Evelyn attended school in Glennon.

Ed was self-employed for many years as a residential building contractor, constructing single-family homes, and was employed as a carpenter by area contractors. Some of the local area projects that Ed contributed to include Interstate 55, Jackson swimming pool, KFVS TV headquarters building, Chateau Girardeau retirement center, and St. Francis Medical Center and Southeast Missouri Hospital additions. He retired from the Penzel Corporation.

The Thiele family left to right front row: Charles, Ed, Evelyn and Tim; back row: Diane, Jody, Ed, Angie, Rick, Gerri, Larry and Nancy.

Ed and Evelyn are the parents of ten children: Angie (Ken) Mirly, Issaquah, WA; Gerrie (Don) Sandin, Jackson; Jody (Richard) Hahn, Advance; Diane (Lee) Moore, Perryville; Edwin (Doris McCall), Jackson; Nancy (Rick) Stearns, Perryville; Larry, Cape Girardeau; Rick, Jackson; Tim (Sandy Malone), Benton; and Charles (Donna Fowler), Birmingham, AL. Four sons, Virgil, Kenneth, LeRoy and Ronald died as infants and were buried in Russell Heights Cemetery.

Ed and Evelyn are members of the Immaculate Conception Catholic Church in Jackson. Ed drove the elementary school bus for a few years. They participated in the Home and School Association, the Holy Name Society, and the St. Ann's Sodality. Ed is a member of the Knights of Columbus Council 6405.

Ed is a woodworker. One can find Ed in his workshop creating another treasure from the local woods of Missouri; his roll-top desks and porch swings grace many Jackson homes. Ed is a vegetable gardener and has enjoyed experimenting with a variety of species. Evelyn is a housewife and flower gardener with a very green thumb. She has crocheted for years and creates many lovely keepsakes. If a great-grandchild is visiting you can be assured the "little one" is helping Grandpa or Grandma in their latest endeavor. These days, Ed and Evelyn keep up with family and observe their grandchildren and great-grandchildren's progress by e-mail.

The Thiele family's growth has continued through the years. Ed and Evelyn's extended family of grand- and great-grandchildren include Maureen Mirly (Raymond) Noble and son Adrian, Federal Way, WA; Joe Mirly and Theresa (McDonald) and son Spencer, Everett, WA; Stacey Sandin (Steve) Money and son Garrett, Bridgton; Willie Sandin and Melissa (Bea) and son Devin, Columbia; Vance Boyer and Angela (Dippold) and sons Brent and Braydon Boyer, Perryville; Jeff Boyer, Chicago; David and Dotty O'Leary and daughter Roslyn, Fort Belvoir, VA; Mark Hahn and Angel Atchley, Detroit, MI; Tara Hahn (Shawn) King, Cape Girardeau; Travis Moore and Erin (Marler), Kansas City; Leigha Moore, Deslodge; Megan and Fallan Thiele, Jackson; Andy Stearns, Perryville; Danielle, Joe and Alex Thiele, Jackson; Leigha and Jon Stewart, Steelville, IL; and Jessica Jeffries, Birmingham, AL. *Submitted by Angie Mirly*

THOMPSON – Billy Joe Thompson was born July 12, 1925, near Leemon, MO, in an old house by Kneebow Hill on Indian Creek. He was the oldest of three children of Anna Mabel McDonald (1908-1993) and Sylvester Udee Thompson (1904-1942). Sylvester worked as a pile driver on the Missouri and Mississippi Rivers, causing the family to move up and down the river going where work would take him.

Anna was one of eight children and her father, John Pitts McDonald (1872-1948), was a Methodist circuit rider preacher. They moved often while John was preaching with only a few days' notice of his transfer, so she knew the life of moving frequently. Often she would be "privileged" to ride up front in the buggy, watching the two oxen pulling them along, while the other children sat in back watching out for the milk cow that followed behind.

Sylvester's father, Fielding Thompson (1859-1929), was one of five children of John A. Thompson (1815-1882), who came from North Carolina to this area in the early 1800s to settle. Most of Sylvester's early relatives are buried in the Apple Creek Cemetery near Pocahontas, MO.

Billy Joe's family settled down when he was in the third grade. They moved to Fruitland to live with Sylvester's parents, Fielding and Sheba Thompson. Sylvester continued to work on the Mississippi River. Being in ill health with asthma, the family moved to Jackson in 1941 to be near the doctor. A year later he caught pneumonia and died in April of 1942.

Anna, still having three children to care for, moved to St. Louis where she got a job in the McDonald's plant as a "rivet girl." It was decided that Billy Joe would stay in Jackson since he was doing well in school and soon to graduate. He was about 14 years old at the time.

Billy Joe lived in the Jackson Hotel, sweeping floors before and after school, serving food at Ott's Tavern and working evenings and Saturdays at Fulenwiders' soda fountain. Billy Joe graduated from Jackson High School in 1943 with letters in football and basketball. He then worked selling clothes at Priest Clothing Store, later becoming the store manager.

In June of 1944, Billy Joe married a popular Jackson girl, Alice Faye Mason (1926-1999), who had just graduated from Jackson High School. During high school she was a band majorette and a member of the choir. Singing was Alice Faye's passion and she performed at many occasions. She was the daughter of E. A. and Alice Faye (Burdette) Mason. Mr. Mason was a prominent Jackson attorney.

They had their first of six children in 1945, the same year they bought Charlie's Grill on the square on Jackson. They changed the name to Thompson's Grill. Alice would work during the day and Billy Joe would work in the evenings after getting off work from Priest's. They sold the grill in 1952 and purchased the first of three houses they would live in. This was the first house Billy Joe had lived in that was not rented. In 1953 they became owners of the Dairy Queen, then sold it to Billy Joe's brother Jim in 1957. In 1956 they bought Deal Nursing Home from his stepfather, Nelson Deal. His mother, Anna, had remarried in 1951 and moved back to Jackson. In 1962, Billy Joe graduated from Southeast Missouri College, the first male with an RN degree. They owned Deal Nursing Home for 42 years before retiring.

Alice Faye Mason Thompson and Billy Joe Thompson

Billy Joe and Alice Faye, in addition to raising their six lively children, also enjoyed being active in the community. They were involved in numerous civic, business and church organizations. *Submitted by Susan Thommpson Hahs*

TOMLIN – One of the first settlers in Howard County, MO, was John Tomlin. He was born in Tennessee and died in 1826 in Lexington, MO. He was married to Hannah Cook, who died at the age of 91 in 1862. The Tomlins had 12 children: Mary, who married Urial Jackson; Elizabeth, who married William Woolsey; Lucinda, who married Thomas Field; William C., who married Susan McCrary; James B., who married Lucy Howell; Nancy, who married Harvey Dillon; Joshua J., who married Nancy Powell; John L., who married Millie Sisk; Christian S., who married Alcey Hood; Deborah, who married Henry Gray; Hannah, who died in infancy; and Michael, who married Eliza Williams.

Christian and Alcey Tomlin resided in Carroll County, MO, and are thought to have had seven children: Hester, born about 1838; Charles, born about 1840; Calmet, born about 1843; Emiline, born about 1846; Cordelia, born about 1848; Joshua born about 1850; and Spencer, born Sept. 24, 1852. Christian died in 1858.

Spencer Tomlin married Rebecca Adeline "Addie" Standley, daughter of Ingram and Sarah Hale Standley, on Feb. 21, 1878. They had 13 children: Mathal (Mag Ethel), born in 1878 and died in 1880; Thomas Alfred, born in 1880 and died in 1881; Emeline, born in 1882 and died in 1883; Louis Standley, born March 9, 1883; Allen and Blackwell, twins born in 1885; Harriett "Hattie", born in 1887; Alcy Ann, born in 1888; Blanche, born in 1891 and died in 1896; Mary Elizabeth, born in 1894; Naomi Spencer, born in 1897; Eugenia Frances, born in 1900 and died in 1910; and Eliza Jane, born in 1902. Spencer Tomlin died Sept. 9, 1923, and Addie died July 24, 1936. Both are buried in the Powell Cemetery in Carroll County, MO.

Louis Standley Tomlin married Rosa Ethel Comeford in Des Moines, IA on Sept. 10, 1905. They had four children: Malcolm Royce, born Sept. 10, 1906; Marguerite; Travis; and Milton. Louis Tomlin died Sept. 13, 1962, and Rosa died Feb. 9, 1968. Both are buried in Powell Cemetery in Carroll County, MO.

Malcolm Royce Tomlin was a graduate of Central Methodist College and played on the championship football teams of 1929 and 1930. He met Mildred Anna Zimmerman, daughter of Lloyd and Jeanette Green Zimmerman, who was a graduate of Culver Stockton College and played the violin. They were married in Quincy, IL, on June 29, 1936. Malcolm served on the Missouri State Highway Patrol for 31 years and Mildred was an elementary teacher for 27 years in Jefferson City, MO. They had three children: David Lloyd, Michael Louis, and John Milton. Malcolm Tomlin died May 24, 1990, and Mildred died Jan. 16, 2001. Both are buried in Hawthorn Cemetery in Jefferson City, MO.

Michael, born on Jan. 9, 1943, in Marshall, MO, is an insurance agent and moved from Jefferson City to Cape Girardeau County, MO in 1967. He married Terri Gohn on Sept. 16, 1978, at Old McKendree Chapel, near Jackson. They have one son, Josh Michael, born Nov. 13, 1982. Michael also has two daughters: Suzanne Lynne, born March 27, 1965, and Michelle Dawn, born Sept. 3, 1974. Suzanne married Mark Beall and they have three daughters: Regan, Camryn and Kendall. Michelle married Brett Turner and they have one son, Alexander William. *Submitted by Terri Gohn Tomlin*

TUSCHHOFF – Christian Tuschhoff I was born in 1809 and came from Waldeck, Germany. He first married Elizabeth Clement of Feb. 12, 1842, and they had two children. Christian Tuschhoff I then married Philippinee Richter before 1847. She was born July 1, 1819, in Prussia, and is buried at Arnsberg, MO. They had five children: Henry, Henrietta, Mary, Christian II, and Daniel Tuschhoff.

Christian II was born Nov. 4, 1853, died March 14, 1898, and is buried at Arnsberg, MO. He married Johanette Bruene on Sept. 23, 1886. She was born Nov. 30, 1863, at Rhenegg, Waldeck, Germany, and died Feb. 1, 1938. She is buried at Friedheim, MO. She came to America with two brothers, Carl and Ernst Bruene, and left four siblings in Germany.

Christian II and Johanette Bruene farmed near Arnsberg, MO, and had six children: Emma, Blanch (died as a baby), Mathilda, Bertha, Monroe and Martha. Christian Tuschhoff died before Martha was born, thus leaving Johanette with five small children. The strain was more than she could bear and she became very ill, and was not able to care for her children. Emma (the eldest) was 11 years old when her father died and at the age of 16 (when her mother was seriously ill) she was left to raise these children on her own. There were no social services in those days; therefore these children had to do all the work on the farm to earn their living. Emma taught them to cook, clean, sew, and do gardening. They butchered hogs (with help of neighbors). They hauled hay and did whatever had to be done.

The children attended Arnsberg Public School for six years, attended Trinity Lutheran School (German School) at Friedheim, MO, for two years, then returned to the Arnsberg Public School in order to complete grades seven and eight, thereby attending school for ten years. They attended Trinity Lutheran church at Friedheim every Sunday that services were held.

Left to right seated: Philippnee (Richter) Tuschhoff, Johanette (Bruene) Tuschhoff holding baby, Bertha Louise Tuschhoff (Villhard), girl between mother and father is Mathilda Hannah Tuschhoff (Neislein), Christian Tuschhoff II. Young girl standing in back is Emma Whillamina Bertina Tuschhoff (Kassel). Photo taken circa 1895.

Martha at age 16 rode the train (Houck Railroad) from Daisy, MO to Cape Girardeau, where the Leming family employed her. While working there she became acquainted with Lydia Bock of Allenville, MO. Lydia had a brother, Otto Bock, who later became Martha's husband. They were married at Trinity Lutheran church, Friedheim, MO, on Oct. 21, 1923. They had four children: Nora Nelda (Seabaugh), Whitewater, MO; Wesley Bock, Advance, MO; Lela (Hahn), Advance, MO; and Vera, who married Loyd Birk of Jackson, MO. Loyd and Vera had two children, Christine and Philip, who attended Jackson High School at Jackson, MO. Christine married Richard Buttram and had two children, Nathaniel and Rachel. Philip married Patti Peel and had three children: Chastity, Alexandria and Keaton.

Martha and Otto Bock lived on the Sparfeld-Bock home place on Hickory Ridge, and at the time their address was Route #1, Allenville, MO. At one time, "bushwhackers," who killed several Union soldiers at the nearby "Round Pond Massacre" during the Civil War, had occupied their log home. The Bock children attended Oak Valley Grade School, a one-room school that stood nearby. *Submitted by Christine Diane (Birk) Buttram*

UELEKE – Johann Heinrich Jacob Ueleke was born July 31, 1779 at Ruhen near Vorsfelde, Germany. He was a second son and took up teaching at Volkersheim where he met and on June 9, 1807 married Johanne Sofie Dorothea Becker (b. Oct. 20, 1784). The couple had a son and a daughter, Johanne Sofie Antionette Christine Ueleke (b. April 10, 1808), who married Gottfried Heinrich Kuster and remained in Germany. The son, Johann Heinrich "Henry" Julius Christian Ueleke (b. March 21, 1811, d. Feb. 24, 1884), was a model joiner employed at the Wilhelmshutte 2 Iron mill at Bornum. On Dec. 10, 1843, he married Johanne Wilhelmine Schuppman (Schubmann) (b. April 22, 1819, d. Feb. 14, 1875) and their first son Heinrich "Henry F." Friedrich Carl Ueleke was born Oct. 26, 1844. The Uelekes immigrated to Missouri in 1846 and located near Dutchtown. The couple had seven more children that include Johanna (b. Oct. 18, 1848, d. Dec. 3, 1886), William (b. 1851), Albert (b. 1853), Augusta (b. Feb. 21, 1854, d. July 22, 1892, m. William Blank), Mary (b. 1857, m. Andrew Geron), Wilhelmie (b. 1859) and Lydia (b. 1866).

Alvin Ueleke, ca. 1945

Henry learned the carpenter's trade and on July 15, 1873, he married Louise Eggiman, who died April 17, 1874. Henry was married on Sept. 30, 1875, to Anna Schlueter (b. Dec. 26, 1854, d. July 29, 1934), daughter of Andrew and Caroline (Schlimme) Schlueter, both of whom were born in the Hanover province of Germany and immigrated in the 1840s. Henry and Anna had seven children. Henry Alvin (b. June 5, 1876, d. February 1962) married Bertha Karger (b. Aug. 7, 1877, d. March 8, 1945) and they had one son, Alvin. Henry and Alvin owned a clock repair and jewelry shop in uptown Jackson. Rosena Caroline (b. Aug. 28, 1877, d. Nov. 14, 1915) was married on May 29, 1904, to Henry Wesley Macke (b. March 5, 1882, d. Nov. 13, 1918). Johanne W. (b. Oct. 18, 1878, d. Dec. 3, 1886) died young, and Emilia A. (Feb. 1, 1881, d. March 20, 1956) became the second wife of Henry Macke on Aug. 31, 1916. Albert John (b. Sept. 10, 1883, d. Sept. 12, 1935) married Marie Hartman (b. Sept. 9, 1889, d. March 23, 1976), Otto Benjamin (b. Dec. 24, 1886, d. June 15, 1960) married Louise Hager, and Fred William (b. May 8, 1892, d. December 1984) married Verna Simmons Barger Clark.

Henry and Rosena Macke had a son, Albert Henry (b. Dec. 21, 1905, d. Dec. 23, 1957), who married Dorothy Elsie Probst (b. Oct. 22, 1906, d. June 11, 1999) on Oct. 23, 1929. They had three children, Henry Weldon (b. Aug. 16, 1930) {see Macke/Ahrens entry}, Dorothy Ann (b. Aug. 11, 1932) and Alberta Louise (b. Nov. 5, 1945){see Probst/ Bartles entry}. Dorothy Ann graduated from Jackson High School (JHS) in 1950. She obtained her B.S. degree in elementary education from Southeast Missouri State College in 1954. Dorothy Ann was first married on June 8, 1957, one son, Thomas Kirk Wilson (b. April 9, 1958), was born to this union. She later married Charles Ramsey (b. Jan. 17, 1927) on July 10, 1970. Dorothy Ann has taught kindergarten in Highland, IL; Fargo, ND; and Jackson R-2, retiring with 31 years of service in Jackson. Her husband, Charles, is retired from Southwestern Bell Telephone. The couple currently resides in Jackson. Tom graduated from Jackson High School in 1976, went on to graduate from the University of Missouri-Columbia (UMC) in 1980 as a 2nd lieutenant in the army, and later earned an MBA. He married Christine Emily Dietz (b. Sept. 26, 1961) who graduated from the University of Missouri-Columbia in 1983 with a B.S. degree in nursing. Tom and Chris have three children, Andrew Thomas (b. April 21, 1987), Matthew Joseph (b. Nov. 15, 1990), and Katherine Emily (b. July 8, 1993). Tom is a lieutenant colonel, a career military officer, and is scheduled to return to St. Louis in 2002 to teach ROTC. *Submitted by Dorothy Ann Macke Ramsey*

ULRICH – Eugene Russel Ulrich was born Feb. 7, 1919 on Sprigg Street, the house is still standing. Reared in Cape Girardeau, he was the son of Benjamin Franklin Ulrich and Flora Belle Kinder Ulrich. His paternal grandparents were Frederick "Fritz" Ulrich and Emma A. E. Miller Ulrich of the Whitewater area, and his great-grandparents were Johann Carl Ulrich and Christina Hille Ulrich, who arrived in the United States on Jan. 18, 1847 on the ship *Columbus*. Johann was naturalized in 1855. His paternal great-great grandfather was Kostassen Frederick Ulrich, who in 1818 married Ilse Sophia Schaper in Berel, Germany. Gene's maternal grandparents were Joel Franklin Kinder and Barbara Liley Kinder, and his great grandparents were Adam Kinder and Mary Linebarger from the southern area of Germany, near the border of Liechtenstein.

Gene attended seven grade schools and graduated from Central High School in 1935. He went to Missouri State Teacher's College (SEMO) for two years; then moved to Memphis and lived with Courtney Terrell and Bloomie Kinder Chron for five or six years, working for his uncle in the Acme Woodcarving Business. He went to Business College while working. He then enlisted in the Army Air Corps, training at Montgomery, AL Air Force Base, and then went to Officer's Candidate School, graduating as a second lieutenant at Kelly Field in San Antonio, TX. He was assigned to bomber duty in the 301st Bomb Group, 352nd Bomb Squadron, and trained all over the United States. He met Jane Collins in El Paso, TX while stationed at Alamogordo Air Force Base, New Mexico. He picked up a new B-17F in Dayton, OH and shipped out, to be sent overseas from Florida. He flew from there to South America and then to North Africa to take part in liberating North Africa from the "Desert Rat" Rommel. He flew 50 missions from different airfields, being the right-wing plane in the lead group, when Rome, Italy was bombed. When Italy surrendered, Italian prisoners who had been captured were returned to Italy and some of our boys came home on those Navy ships landing in New York in September 1943. He received the Purple Heart for a mission over Pantelleria Island, receiving shrapnel in his head and cheek, where it still remains. He also received the Distinguished Flying Cross and many other medals for Unit performances.

Benjamin and Flora Ulrich on their wedding day

Gene and Jane were married at Grace Methodist Church on the corner of Sprigg and Independence on Sept. 29, 1943. The Cape Girardeau Fire Station (2001) is there now. They had four children, Eugene Russel II, born 1944; Carolyn Jane "Kandy" Ulrich, born 1946; Elwood Randolph "Randy" Ulrich, born 1950; and Constance Lanier "Connie" Ulrich, born 1957. All were born in El Paso, TX. All attended school in northeast El Paso, graduating from Irvin High School. Gene II served in the U.S. Navy for 30 years aboard submarines, retiring in 1993 in Honolulu, HI. Kandy is Public Relations Vice President for Union Planter's Bank. Randy lives in El Paso and is employed by Raytheon. Connie is employed by a major law firm in St. Louis, where she and her sister reside. Both boys live in Texas. Gene and Jane have eight grandsons and two great-granddaughters. They have traveled for over 20 years, Gene being Past President of Good Sam Club (local) and the local "Paso del Norte" Unit of the Airstream Club. *Submitted by Gene and Jane Ulrich*

Gene and Jane Ulrich, May 1983

UNTERREINER – James Louis Unterreiner was born August 1972 in Cape Girardeau, MO to Robert Walter Unterreiner (who grew up in Apple Creek, MO), born February 1943, and Dolores (Buchheit) Unterreiner (who grew up in St. Louis, MO), born October 1942. James' siblings were Laura Lincoln of Cape Girardeau, born April 1965; Robert Jr. Unterreiner of Cape Girardeau, born June 1967; Susan Koch of Cape Girardeau, born February 1969; and Diana Schreiner of Jackson, born October 1970.

James attended Immaculate Conception in Jackson and graduated in 1990 from Jackson High School. James attended Southeast Missouri State University where he was a member of the Alpha Sigma Lambda National Honor Society. James worked for Saint Francis Medical Center in Cape Girardeau, MO, in the Heart Institute and Information Systems.

James met Tammy (Hendrix) Harris Unterreiner while they both worked at St. Francis in 1997. They were married in April 1998. They have two children. Their first child, Stephen Harris, was born in Illinois in July 1989, from a previous marriage; and Dominique Louis Walter Unterreiner was born in St. Louis in December 1999. Tammy was the daughter of Gary Don Hendrix of Jackson, born November 1944, and Donna Jean (New) Hendrix of Jackson, born October 1946. Tammy and her siblings were born in Sikeston, MO. Tammy's siblings were Kimberlee (Hendrix) Powell of Jackson, and Jeffery Don Hendrix of Jackson, born March 1978. Tammy graduated in 1988 from Civic Memorial High School in Bethalto, IL. Tammy attended Southeast Missouri State University where she was a member of the Alpha Sigma Lambda National Honor Society. *Submitted by James Unterreiner*

VENABLE – Genealogy tells us that people with the name of Venable originally came to America from a village, town, or community named Venables in Normandy, France. Venables hold reunions in Venables, France. Fenton Venable's ancestors came to Maryland, we understand, but have no proof of arrival or date.

Benjamin Venable, Fenton's great-great-grandfather, and family were in Posey County, Indiana, in 1840. In 1850 Benjamin is in White County, IL. Benjamin's son Stanford S. Venable was Fenton's great grandfather. Stanford's son, the first Fenton Lum Venable, was his grandfather. His son James Henry named his son Fenton Lum Venable and he moved to Jackson, MO.

His son Gerald Fenton of Jackson always wondered how his father had been named Lum. Was it after Lum of Lum and Abner or radio fame long before television? A minister of the Springerton, IL Christian Church was named Fenton Lum. Great grandfather Stanford S. Venable respected him so he named his son Fenton Lum Venable. Then his son James Henry named his son after his father. So Fenton Lum Venable of Jackson, MO was the second Fenton Lum Venable in this branch of the family of Venables from France. The name Fenton was passed on to his son Gerald. It was given to his son Daryl and Stuart Wayne, Gerald's son, gave it to his son Major Venable.

Fenton Lum Venable was born in Sikeston, MO on June 22, 1905, to James Henry and Martha Jane (Haynes) Venable. He married Margaret Lucile Medley at Sikeston, MO, Dec. 11, 1926. She was the daughter of Francis "Frank" Newton Medley and Emaline "Lina" Shorter of Jackson, MO. Living in Akron, OH, the depression sent them to Jackson to live with her parents Frank and Lina Medley. The lived in Dexter, Hayti and Flint, MI prior to Akron. He was assistant store manager for Kroger in Flint. In Akron Fenton worked for Firestone Tire.

After returning to Jackson he had a store or worked at 507 West Main Street. In 2001 this is Estes Deli & BBQ. After that Fenton worked at Cities Service Station located at 113 West Jackson Blvd. In 2001 it is Rhodes 101 Shop. He then had his own Phillips 66 service station located on the corner of Washington and North High Street behind the courthouse. Fenton worked with his brother-in-law Frank Korossy in Frank's Shoe Repair shop at 120 East Adams where Accent Security is in 2011. He worked at International Shoe Company. His last employment until retirement was Jackson Hosiery Mill.

Returning to Jackson during the Depression, Lucile worked as a telephone operator. She worked as a receptionist and secretary for Gold Leaf Flour Mill. I believe it was called Mill A. Their office was located near the corner of South Georgia and Adams Streets. She worked in the office for MFA and retired after working in the Lenco office.

Fenton's hobbies were building/flying miniature airplanes, bowling, golf and square dancing. He sold and serviced Toro lawn mowers/gardening equipment from their home. Lucile enjoyed square dancing as well. She crocheted as a hobby. She was an organist for Immaculate Conception in Jackson prior to marriage. Her sister Elsie B. Medley followed her as organist. They lived their remaining years in their home built at 323 East Adams Street, Jackson, MO.

Fenton Lum and Margaret Lucile (Medley) Venable with son Gerald.

Margaret Lucile (Medley) Venable passed away Jan. 9, 1975. Fenton Lum Venable passed away Dec. 8, 1985. Fenton and Lucile were put to rest in Russell Heights Cemetery in Jackson, MO. *Submitted by Gerald F. Venable*

VENABLE – Gerald Venable was born Nov. 26, 1927 in the Francis/Emaline Medley home in Jackson. His parents were Fenton Lum and Margaret Lucile (Medley) Venable. Susan was born in Southeast Missouri Hospital in Cape Girardeau. Her parents were Guild Mazuret and Julia (Mueller) La Pierre.

Both graduated from Jackson elementary and

high school. Both were promoted into the high school band while in elementary school. Mr. LeRoy Mason came to teach band and chorus at Jackson High School in 1939. He started many new students. The high school band was very small when he came to Jackson. Gerald was one of seven clarinet students in his group. Susan was one of three flutes in her group. It is not known how many groups he started, maybe only one of each due to all the other instruments he had to start to enlarge the band. Gerald was always proud of being one of the first two new students to be promoted to the high school band. He was 12 years old at the time. However, Susan was moved into the band at age 10. Mr. Mason' band became an example for all schools in southeast Missouri. Several years the band excelled the Southeast Missouri State University band.

As a boy and teenager Jerry found jobs. He worked for Dalton Grocery, Cape County Post, Palace Theatre, Lewis Delivery of Globe Democrat, Priest's (clothing) and as a lifeguard for the city of Jackson. While attending college he worked as a laborer in construction; at the handle factory; laid AT&T cable from St. Louis to Memphis; and worked at Charlie's Grill and the Probst Café.

The Gerald Venable family: Gerald, Susan, Daryl, Eric, Stuart, Linda and Steven.

Jerry enjoyed a lot of firsts during his life in Jackson. They were enjoyable even if not significant by some standards. However he enjoyed being one of the first school boy patrols; in the first soap box derby race; a first coach in Optimist Little League baseball, flag football and basketball; first Explorer Post leader of Boy Scouts in Jackson; and a charter member of Company E Missouri National Guard organized in November 1946, and recognized in January 1947. His rank when discharged was Master Sergeant. He was charter member and charter president of Junior (J.C.'s) Chamber of Commerce.

Susan graduated from MacMurray College in Jacksonville, IL in 1952. She taught at Lutesville High, which is called Woodland High in 2001. She started their band and taught music. She has given piano lessons since 1955. She started with six students and had as many as 34 during a years. She has been active in First Presbyterian Church. She served as choir director for 20 years and also served as an elder. She raised a family of five children in addition to her teaching and services to her church.

Jerry attended Southeast Missouri State University for three years. He went to work at Jackson Hosiery Mill in February 1950. He worked as shipping clerk at the La Pierre-Sawyer Handle Factory. He sold insurance for Metropolitan Life Insurance. He was Transportation Director fro Jackson R-II. He was sales representative for Coca-Cola Bottling Company of Southeast from June 19, 1978 until retirement on Aug. 3, 1991.

The home location in 2001 is 524 North Maryland, in Jackson. Their children are Daryl Fenton, Eric Guild, Stuart Wayne, Linda Susan and Steven Mark Venable. *Submitted by Gerald F. Venable*

VINYARD – George Washington Vinyard was born in Jefferson County on a farm near Victoria, MO, on March 5, 1850, the son of Charles and Susan Vinyard.

Charles Vinyard was a native Virginian and Susan Cross Vinyard was a Pennsylvanian. Charles and Susan first settled in Washington County, MO, and later moved to Jefferson County, MO. There Charles Vinyard hauled lead for Jack Smith Tee from the Mine La Motte mines to Herculaneum where a shot tower was located. For this work he received 25 cents per day with which he paid for 200 acres of land at 12-1/2 cents per acre.

George Washington was the sixth child in a family of nine children, five daughters and four sons. The oldest son drove a team in the wagon trains going over the Santa Fe and Oregon Trails. George Washington Vinyard was educated in the public and private schools of Jefferson County and received his medical degree in the Missouri Medical College, now Washington University, of St. Louis, MO, in March 1875. He practiced medicine in southeast Missouri, most of the time in Jackson, MO. He married Imogene Amy Brown on July 26, 1874, and was the father of nine children, five daughters and four sons, two of which were medical doctors. Dr. Vinyard passed away July 2, 1941, in his 91st year.

These were 91 full and busy years and are worthy of further comment. He first located at Longtown, Perry County, MO, a small village in a farming community where the population was largely German. He had to learn the German language to be able to converse with his patients, which he was able to do quite well when he moved from Longtown.

When he began his practice, southeast Missouri was rather wild. Animals roamed the woods and riding in the country was not a pleasure. Often roads were impassable for the buggy. Horseback riding with saddlebags was the only way to reach his patients. In those early years, the most prevalent diseases were malaria and typhoid fever. Typhoid was common because families depend on springs and branch water for their drinking water and homes were located nearby. The heavy timber and swamps of southeast Missouri furnished plenty of mosquitoes and fortunate was the household that escaped long sieges of malaria.

Dr. Vinyard entertained his children by telling them what the frogs said. The big frogs said: "Malaria, Malaria, Malaria." The little frogs said: "Quinine, Quinine, Quinine. Double the dose, double the dose, double the dose."

Dr. G. W. Vinyard, who practiced medicine for over 50 years, is shown returning to his home in Jackson after making his house calls in the early 1920s.

The Southeast Missouri Medical Association was organized in 1877. Dr. Vinyard was one of the charter members. He was elected president in the early days and again in 1924. A newspaper, in giving a report of the meeting of the Southeast Missouri Medical Association in 1924 said: "Tuesday evening was devoted to a banquet in honor of Dr. G. W. Vinyard who is the only living charter member of the association and the only member who has had the honor of being elected president of the organization a second time and who is this year celebrating his half century in the practice of medicine."

He was also a member of the State Medical Association and the American Medical Association. He was a registered pharmacist, as well as a doctor, and filled his own prescriptions. Doctors had to in the horse and buggy days. His office shelves were lined with bottles of all sizes

Front row left to right: Jack M. Hoffman, Sam Vinyard, A. D. Hoffman, Bob Vinyard, Dick Vinyard, Dorothy Jean Hoffman Long, Sue Kies Horne, Virginia Kies, Dorothy Vinyard Dunn, Mary Hoffman Pollard, Jean Marie Vinyard Brown, Dr. Paul Vinyard and Ruth Summers Mullaly. Second row left to right: Stella Cassell, George Vinyard and Bob, Hester Vinyard and Jim, Marie Vinyard, Lula Vinyard, Imogene Vinyard Hoffman, Ben Vinyard, Blanche Vinyard Luten, Grace Vinyard Kies, Alice Vinyard, Dr. G. W. Vinyard, Maud Vinyard Summers, Dr. Robert Vinyard and Charles Vinyard. Third row left to right: Mrs. Truitt Vinyard, Marian Vinyard Disse Bailey, Inez Luten Williams, Harriett Kies Abbott, Virginia Vinyard Bailey, Jane Vinyard, Charlotte Vinyard Seyers, Miriam Kies, Imogene Luten Wilson, Virginia Luten Bazaar, Betty Hoffman Walton, Dr. Vinyard Kies, Elizabeth Vinyard Looney, Mary Vinyard Hoffman, George Summers, Alice Summers Hulett and Imogene Summers Montgomery. Fourth row left to right: Truitt Vinyard, Lura Vinyard, Lin Vinyard, Genevieve Vinyard Taylor, Charlotte Cassell Mathis, Lorene Gephart, Louis Gephart, Jack R. Hoffman, Robert Hoffman, Alice Luten Long Roland, Dr. J. B. Luten and Frank Summers.

filled with curious tinctures and powders. This was true when he lived in the village of Longtown where there was no drug store.

The time came when he began to think of educating his children. Longtown, for a short time, had a private school in which one-half day was given to teaching German and one-half day to English. The public school was one or two miles away. So Dr. Vinyard moved his family to Jackson, MO, and began practicing there in 1889. For a few years he was a partner of Dr. R. T. Henderson but soon built up a practice of his own.

During his busy years, he not only had a large practice but he also took a great interest in civic affairs. He was on the city council when the town prepared to install water works. There were those on the council who wanted to use the creek water, having a mercenary design as to location. Dr. Vinyard fought for a deep well to supply pure water. The argument became so hot that the question was left up to the voters to decide in a special election and they backed the well by a heavy note.

He served on the school board and was a member of the Draft Board and examining physician during WWI. It was a big job well done. There were 4,171 men in the service from Cape Girardeau County, MO. He was a member of the First Baptist Church and was on the Building Committee when they replaced the original building with a more modern one.

His faculties began to fail. He said: "Nature was closing the doors, and he must quit the practice of medicine for a doctor needed good eyes and keen ears." In 1930 he moved to his farm just outside of town and in a quieter atmosphere viewed life's problems. He read his magazines and kept in touch with the great changes made in medicine. He attended the conventions when he could. He was toastmaster at one convention at the age of 82. Year after year, he supplied the Necrology Report, which was printed in the State Medical Journal.

He had his typewriter and took a great deal of pleasure in writing letters. Often times he spent several days writing one letter, putting in literary quotations, comments on politics and up-to-date witty observations. When a letter was finished, it was a masterpiece, highly prized by the receiver.

His children were: Maud Vinyard-Summers 1875-1969; Charles Vinyard 1876-1961; Alice Vinyard 1878-1971; Benjamin Vinyard 1880-1950; Paul Vinyard M.D. 1882-1969; Blanche Vinyard Luten 1884-1969; Robert Vinyard M. D. 1890-1955; Imogene Vinyard Hoffman 1892-1983; and Grace Vinyard Kies 1895-1986.

This biography closes with a quotation from his obituary that appeared in the *Missouri Medical Journal*: "Dr. Vinyard was a truly remarkable man with a keen sense of humor and a deeply religious spirit." The following, which was read at the Southeast Missouri Medical Association, is quite characteristic: "If I had to live my life over again, I would devote it to the practice of medicine, notwithstanding its physical hardships of exposure in inclement weather, midnight toil, its sadness and disappointments. However, there are many roses along the pathway of the faithful physician. When he deserves it, he has the respect and trusting confidence of the community in which he lives and labors." *Submitted by Virginia Kies*

VOGEL – When speaking of earlier years, I will particularly be thinking of the 1930s and 1940s, which were part of "growing-up" years and/or the time I spent around Pocahontas.

I have fond memories of my grandfather, Joseph Engelhart Sr., who lived with us and read and wrote letters until shortly before his death at 92. The Engelhart grandparents had come to America from Austria in 1875 and bought land and property one mile west of Pocahontas. My father, Joseph Engelhart Jr., also known as Joe or J. C., was the second youngest of a family of nine children. He later lived on the old homestead, which is the place where I grew up. My mother's parents were Charles and Amalia Landgraf Gerharter of nearby Shawneetown. She was from a family of eight children. Later generations had fewer than five. I came from a family of three children.

My husband's parents, Alfred and Ida Steiner Vogel, and their four children were all born in or near Pocahontas. The family moved to Cape Girardeau shortly after the Vogel creamery burned. Mel and brother, Richard, recalled looking out the window early one morning and seeing the fire. It is of interest, too, that in that time period, babies were all born at home, and Dr. R. D. Blaylock, who practiced medicine at Pocahontas, was the attending physician. His office building still stands in the heart of the town.

There are vivid memories of the Great Depression of the 1930s. There have been other so-called depression periods, recessions, but none had such an impact as that great one. Our farmhouse was a short distance from Highway 25 (now 61) that was the main highway to St. Louis. People left the cities because of job losses. Many times someone came to our house and offered to work just for something to eat. Our mother would always give them food without having them work for it. We didn't have much money but we usually had enough to eat. Our house looked so bad because it needed to be painted. I remember my floppy shoes; shoes that needed soles. Our father told us to be patient, that soon he would have money to buy paint and shoes for me. At age 15 I had chronic appendicitis and finally surgery was absolutely necessary. My dad borrowed $75 so that he could pay the surgeon.

Then there was the feed sack era. Feed at the Pocahontas Mill came in sacks that were colored and patterned fabrics. Mom would ask Pop to try to get feed sacks that would match sacks that we had. She made pillowcases, aprons, tablecloths, and even dresses. I remember the time when Miss Bedford in my college art class had me model a dress to show the class what could be made of various fabrics. It was a pretty dress and I liked it but, nevertheless, I was embarrassed. After all, it was a feed sack dress.

WWII in the early 1940s brought many changes to families. People were united in the war efforts to help our country's armed forces. I was teaching during that time and helped many people with the rationing book registration. Various items such as: gasoline, kerosene, tires, coffee, sugar, meat, etc., were rationed. Children bought war stamps in their classrooms. Families lost loved ones. Three Pocahontas boys lost their lives in service. They were Melvin Kieninger, Norbert Kuecker, and Edmund Landgraf. Churches, school, and the community were the stabilizing forces during those tumultuous times. *Submitted by Verna Vogel*

VOGT – Harry C. Vogt was born May 19, 1915, at Friedheim, MO, the son of Frederick "Fritz" Vogt (b. 1878, d. 1966) and Marie Brune Vogt (b. 1881, d. 1920). He married Mary Beth Marlin (b. July 3, 1915) on May 24, 1941. They had two children, Frederick Ivan Vogt (b. Feb. 26, 1947) and Harriet Elizabeth Vogt Martin (b. Sept. 18, 1950). Frederick is a C.P.A. in Cape

Girardeau and Harriet is a third grade teacher in Jackson Orchard Elementary School. There are four grandchildren, Eric Vogt, Erin Vogt, Matthew Martin and Patrick Martin, and one great-grandchild, Colten Vogt. Eric Vogt graduated from medical school in Columbia, MO in May 2001.

Harry graduated from Southeast Missouri University and had one year of post-graduate work in Agricultural Economics at the University of Missouri in Columbia. Harry taught school at Daisy and Oak Ridge for eight years. He worked one year in Baltimore, MD for Social Security, and 40 years for the U.S.D.A. with Farmers Home Administration (Fm.H.A.) as a county supervisor and district director, serving counties from St. Louis to Springfield, MO. He received many awards with his work. He drove a million miles on the roads of the Ozarks without trouble.

The Vogt family: Harriet, Frederick, Harry and Mary Beth, Dec. 31, 1965.

Harry joined Rotary on Sept. 9, 1949, in Ellington, MO and was a member of the Jackson Rotary Club at the time of his death on May 18, 1996. In 1965 he became a Rotary District Governor of District 609, receiving training for this in Lake Placid, NY. He made visits to the 42 clubs of District 609. He attended 16 international conventions and was a Paul Harris Fellow.

Harry was a member of the Missouri Farm Managers and Rural Appraisers and the American Society of Farm Managers and Rural Appraisers, and past president of both societies.

Harry was in the 140th Missouri National Guard for five years. He spent three and a half years in WWII in England, France and Germany, and was at Normandy during the big invasions as WWII ended.

In 1983 Harry retired and moved to Jackson from Ellington and became active with farm management until his death. Mary Beth lives in Jackson and still maintains her farm in Cape Girardeau County, which had been in her family since about 1840. She is active in church and community activities. *Submitted by Mary Beth Vogt*

VOSIN/FOSSE – The Vosin family received its release from its pledge of loyalty to Royal Bavaria on June 16, 1836, in order to immigrate to the United States. Samuel Vosin (48), a farmer, and his wife Anna Maria (47) and four children, Elizabeth (14), Michael (7), Martin (14) and Wilhelm (22), boarded the vessel *Henry IV* at Lehavre, France, on Aug. 8, 1836, bound for New York.

The Vosin family apparently spent very little time getting to St. Clair County, MO, where they resumed farming, because the family appears in the 1850 census of St. Clair County, MO. Both Samuel and Anna Maria passed away sometime after 1860.

William Vosin, son of Samuel Vosin, married Elizabeth Wedel on March 11, 1851, and settled in St. Clair County, MO. The couple had five children: Louis, Charles, William, Caroline "Carrie", and Katherine. After William Vosin Sr. died from one of the cholera epidemics that hit St. Louis, MO, in 1862, Louise was sent to be reared by his Uncle Adam Wedel. Elizabeth Vosin passed away in St. Louis during the year 1917.

The Vosin name was changed to Fosse, because in the community where Louis grew up, the people had some difficulty in pronouncing his name. This difficulty arose out of the German alphabet being applied to the French name Vosin; so when Louis applied for a marriage license he took the liberty of changing his name, and his father's name, to Fosse.

Louis Fosse (Vosin) and Louisa Metzger were married on April 18, 1881. They settled on a farm in Marion, IL, in 1884. The couple had four children: William Louis, Edward Phillip, Erwin Adam, and Fred Louis. Louis passed away in St. Louis in 1929, and Louisa died in 1935 in Marion.

Fred Fosse married Bertha Scheltenberger. Fred worked in the Southern Illinois coalfields until he retired. After retirement from the coalfields Fred started farming on a farm east of Marion. The family was recognized as Farm Family of the week on July 11, 1951. The couple had four children: Wilsie, Edward, Leon, and Loren Lee. After Fred's death in 1960 Bertha sold the farm and moved into Marion, IL. A modular home was placed in the back yard of Loren Fosse's house for Bertha to live in. She remained there until she passed away in 1976.

Loren Fosse married Mary Elizabeth Smith on May 20, 1945. Loren worked on the family farm, served in the army during WWII, and became a meat cutter for the Kroger and I G A grocery stores until he retired. The couple had three sons: Frederick Bruce, John Patrick, and Jay Michael (twins). John Patrick was five minutes older than Jay Michael. They are identical twins and looked so much alike that when most people called them, they would just say PatMike. Loren, Mary, and their family resided at 710 North Vicksburg, until 1980, when they moved into their newly built house located at 12728 Rt. 37, Whitash, IL. After retirement Loren gardened as a hobby. Mary passed away at home on Nov. 2, 1998, in Marion. Loren passed away at home on Jan. 17, 2000, in Marion, IL.

John Patrick moved to Cape Girardeau, MO, in 1985, after graduating from Southern Illinois University in Carbondale with degrees in Radiological Technology and Marketing and Mid Management. On Oct. 10, 1987, John Patrick "Pat" and Jane Ann Scherer (daughter of Theon and Leona Scherer) were married at St. Augustine Church in Kelso, MO. The couple moved into their new house located in Jackson, MO, on May 1, 1992. Pat and Jane have two children, Nicholas John and Mathew Patrick. Pat has been employed at Southeast Missouri Hospital in Cape Girardeau since 1985, in the Radiology Department. Jane also works in Radiology at St. Francis Hospital in Cape Girardeau, MO. Pat currently serves as president of The Jackson Heritage Association. *Submitted by Pat Fosse*

WAGNER – Johann Heinrich Wagener left Germany in 1845 with his family, sailed to America, and settled in Cape Girardeau County. During the winter of 1864-1865, both Johann and wife Augusta died, leaving eight children: Fredericka, Wilhelmina, Wilhelm, Heinrich, August, Ernst, Ferdinand and Anna. The children were taken into Jackson homes to be raised.

Christian Heinrich "Henry" Wagner was 11 when he went to live with the Fred Reinecke family, working as a farmhand. At an early age, he became a blacksmith's apprentice. Completing his training in Jackson, he worked for Hoffman, Macke & Milde. Henry was successful as a blacksmith and being mechanically gifted as well, developed into one of the best gun- and locksmiths to be found, his reputation extending far beyond this county.

From youth into middle age, Henry Wagner, a superior marksman, loved hunting. On one occasion he borrowed a Springfield rifle from the Jackson Light Guards organization and went hunting in the swamps below Dutchtown. Coming upon a flock of wild turkeys, he patiently waited behind a log until two of them were in line. A single bullet went through the heads of both birds.

Henry served several years as City Marshal, maintaining law and order in the Jackson Community. He was described as a splendid officer.

On Christmas Day, 1877, Fredericke Rasche and Henry Wagner were married. They were blessed with six children: Alvin, who became an excellent gunsmith, specializing in muzzle-loading rifles; Louis, a professional baseball player; Lawrence, an electrician; Frederick, who died in infancy; and Ruby, who became clerk of the Common Pleas Court, Jan. 1, 1931, the first woman to be elected to this position.

Henry Joseph, known as Harry, married Florentine Wolgast of High Ridge, MO, on Nov. 26, 1914. They made their home in Jackson and were parents of three children: Kenneth, Jeanette, and Roland. Harry's five grandchildren called him "Poppy" and playing with them was his delight.

Florentine and Harry Wagner, 50th Wedding Anniversary, Nov. 26, 1964.

Like his father before him, Harry had a mechanical nature, which could lead to Florentine's frustration. An idea would strike, Harry would sequester himself in the basement to ponder and create, but first he searched the kitchen for any likely utensil, which might be needed for the experiment. Luckily, Florentine possessed a sense of humor, and Harry had a lot of charm. They were happily married for 58 years.

Harry was a skilled machinist and in 1922, he and his brother Alvin took over the blacksmith shop, started by their grandfather and later owned by their father, and turned it into a machine shop. Harry provided custom work for many local factories and in some surrounding communities. He developed and patented a design for electric welding holders and later manufactured welding accessories.

Harry Wagner passed away Dec. 16, 1972, at age 82. Florentine Wagner died Oct. 25, 1998, at age 105, blessed with bright memories of her life with "Poppy." *Submitted by Roland Wagner*

WAGNER – Johann Heinrich Wagner was born in 1806 in Germany and died in early January 1865. Heinrich came to America on the ship *Charlemagne* from the port in Hamburg, arriving Nov. 29, 1845, in New Orleans, LA. Listed as passengers on the *Charlemagne* were Heinrich Wagner, 39, smith from Langesheim, Germany; Henriette Sprengel Wagner, 34, wife, Braunschweig; Dorothea Wagner, 70, mother; Frederike Wagner, 4, daughter; and Wilhelmina Wagner, 1/2, daughter, who died on the journey from Germany to America.

Johann Heinrich Wagner was a gunsmith and founded the Wagner Machine Shop in 1848 in Jackson, MO. His wife died shortly after their arrival here. Heinrich went back to Germany and married for the second time on Feb. 8, 1847, Johanna Wihelmine Auguste Sprengel, his first wife's sister. She was born in 1825 in Germany and died Dec. 16, 1864. Both Heinrich and Johanna are said to be buried in the Evangelical Cemetery in Tilsit, MO.

Ernst F. Wagner, Baby Flay and Rosa Lee Wagner, 1894.

Children by Heinrich's second wife were: Katherine Dorothea Wilhelmina Wagner who married Frederick Friedrich Gerichs; Heinrich Fredrich "William" Wagner who married Caroline Altenthal and established Wagner's Bakery in 1884; Christian "Heinrich" Friedrich Wagner who married Fredericha Rasche and was City Marshall of Jackson, MO, for many years; Johann Ferdinand Christian "August" Wagner who first married Emma Boss and second married Annie Toensmann Klinkman; Ernst Fred Aaron Wagner, a blacksmith, who married Rosa Lee Whittaker; Ferdinand Wagner, a blacksmith, who married Bertha Friedrich; and Anna Wagner who was about 7 weeks old when her father died.

Ernst Fred Aaron Wagner was born Feb. 1, 1858, and married April 2, 1893, in Oak Ridge, MO, Rosa Lee Whittaker, who was born Sept. 18, 1873, daughter of William Rilet Whittaker and Margaret Minerva Sadler. They became parents of 11 children: William Flay Wagner was born Feb. 9, 1894, died Sept. 9, 1938, and married Clara Koeppel on Aug. 8, 1916; Flora was born Jan. 3, 1896, and died Jan. 16, 1896; Maude Myree was born Feb. 2, 1897, died Sept. 21, 1980, and married Edgar Francis Huhn on May 3, 1924; Esther Irene was born June 12, 1899, died Jan. 12, 1993, first married Andward S. Owens on Dec. 25, 1919 and second married Aquilla S. Reed; Opal Emma was born Nov. 15, 1901, died Jan. 13, 1975 and married James Marvin Langford on Dec. 31, 1927; Wilmer Othel was born June 16, 1904 and died Feb. 6, 1972; Ruby May was born May 8, 1907, died April 23, 1951, and married Dec. 22, 1928, Elvis L. Caldwell; Albert Gordon was born Nov. 27, 1909 and died March 21, 1914; Chester Martell (twin) was born Feb. 27, 1914 and died Oct. 6, 1920; Lester Odell (twin) was born Feb. 27, 1914, married first Florence Wolf, and married second Priscilla Carter, was born Oct. 7, 1991, and married Dec. 7, 1941, Dolores Thixton.

Ruby May Wagner and Elvis L. Caldwell became parents of two children. Jo Ann married Clyde Wilson Jr. and their children are Gregory Miles, Kimberly Ann and John Bradley. Jerry Lee married Ruby Lee Wilson and their children are

Timothy Lee and Cynthia Lynn. *Submitted by Jo Ann Caldwell Wilson*

WAGNER – Richard Wagner, son of Martin Wagner and Bessie Henry Wagner, was born May 25, 1909, and died Dec. 27, 1967. He and Esther Chandler Hacker were married June 6, 1942; she was born Aug. 29, 1906, the daughter of G. L. and Mattie Hill Chandler of Marble Hill. They had one daughter, Jane Wagner of San Diego, CA. Richard has one living sister, Martha, and two brothers (deceased), the Rev. Joseph "Joe" Wagner and Martin Wagner Jr.

Richard lived all his life in Jackson where he graduated from high school and worked in the Wagner Bakery. He first worked for his grandfather William Wagner Sr., then his father Martin, and when his father died, he bought his father's share and became the sole owner of the bakery.

Esther attended Marble Hill public school and Will

Esther and Richard Wagner

Mayfield College, graduated from Jackson High School, and received her B.S. degree in education from Southeast Missouri State University where she was a member of the Kappa Delta Pi Honorary Education Organization. She taught in the R-2 School District, mainly Jackson High School, for nearly 40 years. Esther was first married to Ernst C. Hacker June 24, 1929. He died Feb. 10, 1932. They had one son, Jean Hacker of Houston, TX. Esther was a member of New McKendree United Methodist Church for years. Mrs. Wagner had served on its administrative board and taught Sunday school classes. She was a life member of the church's United Methodist Women's organization and the Esther circle. She was active in numerous clubs and community organizations. She was a 50-year member and past worthy matron of the Jackson Chapter Order of Eastern Star, member and past regent of the John Guild Chapter of Daughters of the American Revolution, member and past president of Thursday Sunday Club, a member of the Jackson Public Board and the Jackson Heritage Association. She also was a volunteer for the Southeast Missouri Hospital Auxiliary.

Mrs. Wagner has two living sisters, Olga Hill of Jackson and Elinor Fenner and husband Otto of Webster Groves; one deceased sister, Mary Kate James and three brothers. She also has two living sisters-in-law, Vera Wagner and Martha Wagner, both of Jackson (...Vera Wagner passed away Jan. 6, 2002).

Esther said her husband loved being a baker and couldn't have imagined being anything else. Even though he was allergic to wheat flour, he continued until his death in 1967. The bakery had been relocated in 1958 to South High Street. Esther managed to stay in business for another three years after her husband's death before having to sell the business. *Submitted by Doris Brennecke Davault with material furnished by Martha Wagner*

WAGNER – Vera Seabaugh Wagner was born Nov. 20, 1913, the oldest daughter of Loy and Ester Morton Seabaugh. Vera was a graduate of Jackson High School and earned a B. S. degree in education from Southeast Missouri State University in 1940. She taught English and art in Jackson and Jefferson City, MO. During WWII she served in the United States Waves Medical Corps and was stationed in New Orleans for two years. In 1948 Vera graduated from Columbia University in New York with a Master's Degree in art.

On June 21, 1948, Vera married the Reverend Joseph Wagner of Jackson. The couple served Methodist churches in Salisbury, Fulton, Hannibal and Sikeston, MO. They were the parents of three daughters: Rebecca Wagner Burns, Patricia Wagner Corcoran, and Mary Esther Wagner Farris. After Reverend Wagner passed away on March 6, 1972, Vera returned to Jackson.

Vera Seabaugh Wagner

Mrs. Wagner taught art at Southeast Missouri State University from 1972 to 1978, retiring in 1978 as professor emeritus of fine arts. Mrs. Wagner served on the Jackson Park Board for 20 years and was instrumental in turning the old swimming pool into a playground and in establishing Litz Park. She also designed and painted animals in the park. She had been an active member of American Legion Post 158 Altenthal-Joerns Auxiliary. She was on the Southeast Missouri State University's Wesley Foundation Board. She received honors from many of the organizations in which she participated. The Jackson Heritage Association presented her with the "Unsung Hero Award" in 1995, and the "Heritage Association Award" in 1996. As a volunteer with the Salvation Army, she became known as the "Gravy Lady" for her many years of service during the annual Thanksgiving meal. Mrs. Wagner was also honored for her "Hard Work and Dedication" for the Veterans of All Wars memorial at Brookside Park. She served six years on the board of directors of Gambrill Gardens Methodist Retirement Home in St. Louis.

Mrs. Wagner was a member of New McKendree United Methodist Church where she served on the church's administrative board, taught Sunday school, was Sunday school superintendent and past president of the United Methodist Women, and a member of the Dorcas Circle. Vera Seabaugh Wagner passed away on Jan. 6, 2002. *Submitted by Grace Wille and Cathi Stoverink*

WAGNER – William Wagner Sr., reared and schooled in Cape Girardeau County, was the son of a wagonmaker from the Black Forest of Germany; he made his appearance into the world on Feb. 17, 1851, and died Jan. 15, 1923. At the age of 13, young Wagner traveled to Cape Girardeau to become a baker's apprentice to French baker, Monsieur Taraque. In February 1876 he married Carolina Altenthal who was born March 2, 1856, and who died July 18, 1940. Shortly thereafter he bought a farm.

Still with the desire of becoming a baker, Wagner decided the county seat of Jackson needed a good bakery. He sold his farm and purchased property in Jackson and he and his wife started a bakery in 1883; he later sold that property to the city. Using skills he acquired from his father, he enlarged a building on the corner of West Main and Missouri Streets. Mr. Wagner and 10-year-old Will cleared away flower beds and shrubbery and put up a fine two-story building (still standing in 2001.) The bakery was appropriately advertised as "The Home of Good Bread" and it opened in 1888.

William and Carolina's six children and spouses were: William H. (Nov. 10, 1877- April 13, 1966) married Jennie Henry Oct. 1, 1902; Louis F. (Nov. 20, 1878- Aug. 29, 1939) married Hester Peterman April 11, 1901; Martin H. (Dec. 25, 1883- Nov. 13, 1953) married Bessie Henry April 18, 1908; Anna (Feb. 6, 1881-April 6, 1976) married William H. Besel Jan. 3, 1901; Alma (April 26, 1887- March 10, 1974) married Henry Brennecke June 21, 1930; and Linda (Aug. 15, 1891-?) married Theodore W. Ade Nov. 15, 1931. William, Carolina, and children first lived above the bakery but later built a two-story brick home, which is now New McKendree United Methodist Church west parking lot.

Wagner's sons, William and Martin, took a great interest in their father's business and he taught them the fine points of baking. In 1907, William Wagner retired and sons William and Martin carried on the family legacy. William, Martin, and their families worked hard for several years but in 1943 Will sold his interest to Richard Wagner, Martin Wagner's son. Martha Wagner (living in Jackson), who is also Martin's daughter, started working in the bakery when she was in the seventh grade. Martha and her three brothers all worked there; her brothers were Richard (wife Esther Chandler Hacker), Joe (wife Vera Seabaugh), and Martin Jr. (wife Maria Christina Rodriquez). When Martin Wagner died, Richard bought his father's share and became sole owner of the bakery. Familiar over the years at the counter of the bakery besides Martha were Esther, Richard, Mrs. Alma Brennecke (daughter of William), and the rest of the earlier family. One also remembers Mrs. Emma Malone and Mrs. Rhoda Reiman.

William and Carolina Wagner Sr.

Richard married Esther Chandler Hacker June 6, 1942. Their story will be found on a later page. *Submitted by Doris Brennecke Davault with material furnished by Martha Wagner*

WALKER/HENDERSON – My Missouri story begins with the knowledge of my grandfather Cicero Walker who was the son of Frank Walker and Emily Hall, both of Missouri. Cicero was born April 25, 1893 in Fruitland, Cape Girardeau County. He joined the army and was stationed in Jefferson City, MO. While in the service he met Agnes Henderson (1901-1964) from Jackson, Cape Girardeau County. Agnes was a schoolteacher in Jackson before moving to St. Louis, where they met.

Cicero and Agnes were married in St. Louis on July 15, 1918. Agnes' parents were Edward Henderson and Mabel Daugherty. Cicero was one of three children. His siblings were Frank Jr. and Mary Jane. Agnes was also one of three children. Her siblings were Alma and Ralph.

Cicero was a truck driver who delivered coal to the community. My fondest memory of my Grandfather Cicero was that he was tall in stature and had a beautiful smile. He was a family man; his family always came first. In his back yard he raised chickens and ducks for the family's table. Even though he was a driver of a coal truck, he always kept the truck polished and shined. He was of fair complexion and when he came home from work with all the soot from the coal on him, he was a funny sight. Cicero in the winter would make us ice cream out of the snow. He told me that his father taught him how to make beer so he would make his own beer.

Agnes' lifelong dream was to be a teacher and she taught for a wile until her family began to grow. Cicero and Agnes were the parents of seven children: Cornelius, Maxine (my mother), Lois, Earl, Clarice, Franklin and Edith. The family resided in St. Louis on Wells Street before moving to Wagner Avenue in Wellston. They were of the AME faith, attending church in Wellston.

I, Ronald William Higgins, am the first of seven children born to Fletcher Higgins and Maxine Walker. With four children, my family moved to California. I was about 7 years of age. *Submitted by Ronald Williams Higgins*

WALKER – Mildred Elizabeth Walker (1919-1998) married Jackson Riley Faries in 1942 and three children were born to the marriage. Those children all have children and grandchildren. Mildred was a great-granddaughter of William Addison Walker who came to Cape Girardeau County from Virginia at a young age after being born in North Carolina in 1811. He was a son of another William Walker who might have been born in America or in England where the Walkers originated. They probably settled in the Oak Ridge area around 1820.

The Walkers were engaged in farming and other crafts at varied levels of skills and came to the area in a time totally different from today. If they needed a house, barn, or other building, they built it, often with the help of neighbors, and each returned favors in the same way. The raised nearly all the food they had, usually buying only coffee, salt, pepper, sugar, and maybe a few other things. They raised wheat and corn to be ground into flour and cornmeal. The old-timers would tell of wheat threshing day when just about everyone in the area would participate. The men would follow the wheat threshing machine from farm to farm threshing the wheat and the women would travel with them to provide a dinner to feed all the workingmen. Many years later many of them would refer to a big meal as a "wheat threshing dinner." Men seldom left the farm for public work and even fewer women did. The women sewed clothing for all family members and made all the quilts and other dry goods for the household. Later on men would wear bib "overhalls."

There was a William A. Walker who fought in the Civil War from September 1861 to February 1862 and that was probably him.

The Walkers were of Methodist faith and some were active participants in the church. William Addison Walker had at least one brother, Reverend Jesse Walker (1815) who was a Methodist minister and traveled as a circuit-riding preacher several years before Oak Ridge Methodist Church was established in 1874. Dr. John H. Walker was probably a son of Jesse Walker. John was born in Cape Girardeau County and fought in the Civil War with the Confederate Army.

William Addison Walker had five sons and four daughters. One son, Richard Alexander Walker (1837-1920), born in North Carolina, was married to Nancy Susan Crow (1842-1931), also born in North Carolina. Nancy was a daughter of Richard Crow (1816-1858) and Frances Abernathy Crow. The Crows were originally from Ireland. There were several Methodist preachers in the Crow family, including Nancy's brother David Crow (1842-1923) who served as pastor of churches in Bloomfield, Joplin, Marble Hill, Farmington, and DeSoto, MO. David Crow and brother, Richard Watson Crow, served in the Civil War with the Union Army.

Mildred Elizabeth Walker and Jackson Riley Faries on their wedding day April 17, 1942

Richard Alexander Walker and Nancy Susan Crow Walker had seven daughters and five sons. One son, Marvin Harwood Walker (1886-1930), married Lula Caroline Buehler (1890-1973), who was a daughter of John and Caroline (Stamm) Buehler, and born in Glen Allen, MO. Marvin and Lula had two sons and three daughters: Earnest Hubert Walker (1911-1989) married Esther Slinkard and they had two sons (Lowell and Winfred) and one daughter (Carol Jean Walker Estes). Edith Cora Walker (1914-1993) and Ernest Rhodes had three sons, (Jerry, Larry and Richard). Mildred Elizabeth Walker (1919-1998) married Jackson Riley Faries and had two sons, (Jackson W. and Marvin Edward) and one daughter (Loine Faries Penny). Glenda Veda Walker (1924-1972) married Robert Jordan and had two sons (Robert and Claude) and one daughter (Linda Jordan Wallace). Curtis Waldo Walker was born in 1926 and died of appendicitis at age 4.

William Addison Walker married Mary Ann Cobb and Reverend Jesse Walker married Elizabeth Cobb, both were daughters of Sterling Cobb and Nancy Penny Cobb. *Submitted by Loine Penny*

WALLACE – William W. Wallace was born in 1766 in North Carolina, probably in Mecklenburg County; and married on Dec. 1, 1792 in Mecklenburg County, NC to Jean/Jane Moffett, born in 1768 in North Carolina, the daughter of John Moffett and Ann Watson. William W. was the son of James Wallace and Jean/Janet Baird/Beard who lived in Mecklenburg County in the part that became Cabarrus County. James' will of 1795 names children and divides land in North Carolina and 800 acres in Wilson Valley, on the Duck River in Middle Tennessee; also willed are black velvet breeches, silver shoe buckles, and slaves. Jean Beard was the daughter of Francis Baird (will dated 1789, Lincoln County) and John Baird (will dated 1782, Lincoln County, NC) and John was the son of William Beard of Franklin County, PA. James Wallace had nine known children. William W. Wallace inherited land from James that he sold in 1819 to R. W. Smith in order to move to Missouri territory. Jane descended from John Moffett of Revolutionary War fame (see Draper papers).

The *St. Louis Globe Democrat* newspaper dated July 2, 1887, on the occasion of William W.'s son John's 90th birthday, states, "John came to this county (Cape Girardeau) with a younger brother at the age of 22, and was joined two years later by his parents and a party of 72 Carolinian emigrants." These North Carolina people lived close together and worshipped together for years. Most of this family worshipped at Apple Creek Church in Pocahontas, MO, and William and Jane, William Jr., John, and James were among the charter members listed on May 21, 1821.

David Crawford Hope, in his reflection in the Cape Girardeau County Archives wrote, "Nearer Jackson was Capt. Ebenezer Flinn, War of 1812, Elijah Harris, John Gilliland, William Wallace known as Red Billy, near Apple Creek was William Wallace known as Black Billy, and John Wallace who is living near Pocahontas at the advanced age of 88, James Hope, and Robert Hope, Mrs. Jennie Little …(this was probably written in 1885.)

The Collage of Cape Girardeau, Volume 17 #3, states, "Wallace place was bottom land along the creek between the Quary Place and the 80 acres that Mitchell Fleming gave to Robert McFarland when McFarland married his daughter Agnes." The following land purchases were made: William W. Wallace, 80 acres Sept. 11, 1820; 80 acres Jan. 5, 1822; 80 acres March 23, 1822; John Wallace, Aug. 10, 1822 80 acres; Mathew Smith Sept. 19, 1821 80 acres.

William W. Wallace owned slaves; on July 5, 1822 he sold a boy named Bob for $180 and John Wallace sold a boy named Jimmy for $150, both sold to John Harrass. Bob had been purchased from Robert Steel, deceased. William's estate sold one slave for $650.

The Wallace brothers, 1911. Left to right: Joseph Cicero Wallace (1826-1920), John Newton Wallace (1841-1927), James Albert Wallace (1838-1916), Alonzo Moffitt Wallace (1847-1928), William Franklin Wallace (1833-1920). Another brother, Adison Metherie Wallace (1844-1865), died from effects of the Civil War.

William W. died May 14, 1834; Jane died Jan. 6, 1836; the estate files of each are in Cape Girardeau County. They both ran an account at Kimmel and Taylor and he had one at Apple Creek Mill Store. At Jane's death all children lived in Cape Girardeau County except Rachel who lived in Brazeau Township, Perry County, MO.

The following are children of Jane Moffett and William W. Wallace: most of these dates of born and married come from a family Bible printed in 1817 and owned by Ivy Modde Baebler.

Margaret Wallace was born in 1793 and married on Sept. 29, 1819 in Cabarrus County to Mathew Smith, born June 28, 1798. This couple was in the Missouri territory for the birth of their twins on June 11, 1820. They sold land in 1845 in Cape Girardeau County and moved to Perry County, MO, and had ten children.

James was born Sept. 17, 1795 and married on March 20, 1823 to Mary Patty Abernathy, sister of Elizabeth and daughter of Joseph and Glaffira Abernathy; he is buried in the Apple Creek Church Cemetery. The couple had seven children.

John was born July 6, 1797 in Cabarrus County, NC and married in 1824 to Elizabeth

Turner Abernathy, born in 1806 in Lincoln County, NC. Both are buried at Apple Creek Church Cemetery; his stone still stands and says he died at 90 years and 9 months. The couple had nine children.

William Beard Wallace was born May 5, 1799 in North Carolina and married on Sept. 30, 1824 to Nancy Hope. He is buried at Apple Creek Church Cemetery. The couple had four children.

Rachel was born March 26, 1801 and married Oct. 12, 1824 to William Anderson Bull; both are buried at Brazeau Presbyterian Church Cemetery. The couple had seven children.

Jane Wallace was born Jan. 11, 1803 and married on March 6, 1822 to Royal Thompson. No children's names have been found.

Abner was born May 5, 1805 in North Carolina and died on Oct. 30, 1823.

Ruth E. was born Aug. 26, 1807 and died Nov. 17, 1823; this is 18 days after her brother Abner died.

Elizabeth "Betsy" was born May 11, 1809 in North Carolina and married Archibald L. Reid; he is buried at Apple Creek Church Cemetery.

"Polly" Mary Wallace was born Sept. 28, 1812 in North Carolina and married Robert McCombs; the couple had eight children.

Robert M. Wallace was born May 28, 1815 in North Carolina and married on Dec. 23, 1834, Eliza E. Reid, sister of Archibald and daughter of Alexander Reed/Reid by his second marriage on Feb. 24, 1843, to Mary E. Hope. The couple had five children. *Submitted by Ivy Modde Baebler, great-great-great granddaughter of William Wallace and Jane Moffett*

WALLENMEYER – Kermit Wallenmeyer was not a native of southeast Missouri but came from Jamestown in central Missouri. I, Miriam Penzel Wallenmeyer, met Kermit in New Madrid, MO. I was a teacher; he was a foreman in the CCC Camp.

The 1930s were years of deep depression. Many people lost jobs and were very poor. People came past the house and asked for food. Farmers were especially hit hard. They had food that they raised but very little money. My husband had raised beautiful corn in the Missouri River bottoms but it didn't pay to haul it to market. The government started the Conservation Corps when Franklin Roosevelt was President, and many farmers' sons and others joined. It was a method to fight soil erosion and declining timber supplies. Unemployed young men, ages 18-26, were enrolled- housed, fed and clothed, and put to work. By the end of 1935, 505,782 enrollees occupied 2,650 camps in all states. There was a CCC Camp on Old Cape Road in Jackson.

The Wallenmeyer family: Kermit, Miriam (Penzel) W., Janet and Steve

Kermit and I were married in 1938. We had two children, Janet who later married Frank Szofran, and Stephen. In the early 1940s Japan bombed Pearl Harbor; our country was involved in WWII.

Kermit was inducted into the Marine Corps. A few months later I saw a small article in the *Southeast Missourian* that the Marine Corps needed heavy equipment operators. Since that was his work in the CCC, I sent the article to him. He then showed it to his commander. The commander gave him a weekend pass to San Francisco to investigate. There he was told they needed him at once, so Kermit spent two years there, until the war ended, getting heavy equipment ready to send overseas. My sister Margaret, Janet, who was 1 year old, and I drove to San Francisco to visit. We stayed there until the war ended two years later. We then came back to Jackson, but my sister stayed in California.

I was born in Jackson, one of five children of Linus and Mathilda Kies Penzel. My sisters were Margaret, Elizabeth and Eloise. Margaret married Herbert Beaver in California. Elizabeth, who was a WAC in WWII, married Cliff Shinaberry and moved to Toledo, OH. Eloise met Walton Kroell in Chillicothe, MO Business School. He was from Alabama. They were married and have lived there for over 60 years. My brother Carl was the oldest in the family. He became a builder and worked with Dad in the construction business.

I have many memories of growing up in Jackson. The Puls and Cracraft boys were our neighbors on High Street. We often played together. South of us lived the older Williams family and the Presbyterian minister's families. North of us was the large Sanford estate, which is now the Jackson City Park. Our house, which Dad built, is still there, but the upstairs burned after our family left, so it looks different. We lived some distance from school but we always walked to school, as did all children, rain or shine. We went home for lunch and back to school by 1:00. I have wonderful memories of Jackson, a great place to live. *Submitted by Miriam Wallenmeyer*

WALLMAN – This is the history of three brothers who came to the United States in 1850. First was Joseph Wallman, b. November 1823 in Goisern, Austria, d. Aug. 28, 1903, buried St. John's Lutheran Church Cemetery, Pocahontas, MO. Second was John Wallman, b. April 26, 1826, in Goisern, Austria, d. Dec. 2, 1874, buried Apple Creek Church Cemetery east of Pocahontas, MO, is one of the founders of St. John's Lutheran Church, Pocahontas, MO. Third was Carl Wallman, b. July 19, 1836, in Goisern, Austria, d. July 29, 1914, buried Immanuel Lutheran Church Cemetery, New Wells, MO.

In the 1840s and 1850s revolutions broke out in the Austrian Empire; this is why they migrated to the United States of America. They found the hills around Pocahontas, MO and New Wells, MO quite attractive, not because of their richness of soil - for there was none - but because the wooded hillsides and the creek-bottomed valley reminded them of the land from which they had come. New Wells, MO was named after Wells, Austria. These Austrians were Lutherans by birth. Most all of Austria was German-speaking and they opposed the Roman church in their old homeland.

Carl Wallman (b. July 19, 1836, d. July 29, 1914) married on Sept. 1, 1863 Rebecca Christian Stirewald (b. Feb. 20, 1844, d. Aug. 6, 1911). Children: Ambrosius J.; Solome E.; Heinrich Carl Christian; Marie T; and Ida L.

Heinrich Carl Christian Wallman (b. Aug. 13, 1872, d. March 26, 1956) married Emma Emilie Hoehl (b. Sept. 23, 1877, d. Dec. 24, 1953) on March 31, 1902. Children: Carl; Fredrich; Andreas; Rudolph; Magdalena and Leona.

Carl John Wallman (b. July 2, 1903, d. Aug. 9, 1975) married Ora E. Bollinger on March 31, 1932. Children: Melvin W., Carl R., Mary E., Melva M. and Paul E.

Melvin W. (b. Nov. 22, 1933, d. Nov. 14, 1977) married Wyonia S. Poe (b. Feb. 23, 1942) on Nov. 4, 1961. Children: 1) Rodger D. (b. Aug. 11, 1962). 2) Tony L. (b. Nov. 29, 1963) married on March 9, 1991 to Sandra C. Swift (b. June 18, 1968). Children: Heather D. Swift (b. Sept. 22, 1985); Krysty L. Baker (b. Nov. 13, 1987); Michael L. McIntire (b. Jan. 14, 1988); Joshua D. McIntire (b. Jan. 27, 1989); Tiffany C. Wallman (b. March 6, 1992); and Cassie M. Wallman (b. March 12, 1993). 3) Robert E. (b. Sept. 1, 1965). 4) Patricia A. (b. May 19, 1967) married on Jan. 11, 1986 to Raymond Pulliam. Children; Raymond (b. July 8, 1986), Bradley (b. March 1, 1992) and Stacey (b. Nov. 1, 1995). 5) Dennis R. (b. Aug. 27, 1969) married on Nov. 7, 1992 to Lera Ussery. Children, Marinda D. (b. Aug. 19, 1993) and Cynthia M. (b. Aug. 6, 1994).

Carl R. (b. July 24, 1940) married Evelyn Crader (divorced). Children: 1) Debbra A. (b. July 9, 1964) married Timothy Heise on Sept. 20, 1986. Children: Kristra (b. April 12, 1989) and Nicholas (b. March 15, 1991). 2(Lisa G. (b. Oct. 11, 1966) married Roy Reeves (divorced), married second Mark Mirly. Child: Casey Reeves (b. July 23, 1988). 3) Danny C. (b. Sept. 20, 1972) married Tiffany Cook. Child: Andrea Cook (b. Oct. 28, 1993).

Mary E. (b. Aug. 25, 1941) married on Nov. 3, 1960 to Elmer Pinkerton. Children: 1) Darrel E. (b. August 1961). 2) Miranda K. (b. Nov. 17, 1962), children: Ashley N. Pinkerton (b. Sept. 18, 1984) and Charley J. Williams (b. Aug. 23, 1987). 3) Marsha K. (b. July 4, 1965), children: Amanda M. (b. Sept. 17, 1983) and Amber D. M. (b. Oct. 8, 1996).

Melva M. (b. Nov. 14, 1943) married on March 26, 1965 to Gary Baker. Children: 1) Tonia A. (b. Dec. 25, 1970) married on Nov. 13, 1993 to Johnny Hendrix; children: Jon T. (b. Dec. 27, 1992) and Paige T. (b. Jan. 24, 1997). 2) Timothy L. (b. Dec. 26, 1972).

Paul E. (b. Dec. 15, 1945).

WALPERSWILLER – Benedict Walperswiller Sr. was born May 1827 in Seedorf, Switzerland, and died in 1909 in Cape Girardeau County, MO. He is buried in the German Evangelical Lutheran Cemetery in Dutchtown, MO. Benedict married Johanna S. W. Amelunke on Feb. 3, 1865, daughter of heinrich Amelunke and Johanne Klusmann. She was born Feb. 17, 1842, in Klein-Rhüden, Braunschweig, Germany, and died Feb. 11, 1884, in Gordonville, MO.

Jackson Missouri Cash Book Newspaper, Feb. 21, 1884, Page 4. Walperswiller - Near Gordonville, MO on Wednesday, Feb. 13, 1884. Mrs. Benedict Walperswiller, aged about 45 years.

Their children were: first unknown Walperswiller who died Aug. 18, 1867, in Gordonville, MO. Second Benedict Walperswiller Jr. who died Dec. 11, 1888, in Gordonville, MO. Third William Arnhold Walperswiller Sr. who was born Dec. 15, 1865, and died April 8, 1938, in Gordonville, MO.

Maria, Bertha and Sophia Walperswiller

He married Emma W. S. Diamund on April 9, 1885. She was born March 1867 and died Aug. 29, 1935, in Gordonville.

Cape Girardeau Southeast Missourian Newspaper, April 8, 1938, Page 6. Wm. Walperswiller, Gordonville Farmer, Succumbs at 72. Wm. Walperswiller, 72 years old, a farmer, died of infirmities of age at his home southwest of Gordonville at 4 a.m. today. He had been sick for 11 days. He was born on the same farm, Dec. 15, 1865 and lived all his life in the Gordonville Community. Mr. Walperswiller was married to Miss Emma Diamund more than 50 years ago, and Mrs. Walperswiller died Aug. 29, 1935. Of five children born to the couple only one, a son, William Jr., living as home, survives. Surviving also are two sisters, Mrs. Bertha Sachse of Oak Ridge and Mrs. Mary Amelunke of near Dutchtown. The body was to be taken from the Haman Funeral Home to the family home late today and funeral services will be conducted from the home at 1:30 p.m. Sunday and at the Zion Lutheran Church, near Gordonville, of which he was a member, at 2 p.m. The pastor, Rev. Seabaugh, will be in charge. Pallbearers, all nephews, will be Leo and Albert Amelunke, Albert and Charles Dankel, Ed Diamund and Alvin Commiski.

Fourth was Sophia Walperswiller born September 1870 and died after 1922. She married Carl Dankel on March 6, 1901, in Cape Girardeau County. Carl was born Oct. 11, 1854, and died after 1922. Fifth was Henry Walperswiller, born October 1875 in Missouri. Sixth was Maria W. Walperswiller, born Feb. 16, 1877, in Gordonville, MO, and died April 12, 1948, in Dutchtown, MO. She married August Amelunke on April 12, 1896, in Gordonville, MO. He was born May 3, 1866, to Heinrich Andreas Amelunke (no relation to Maria's mother's family) and Karoline Krueger in Gordonville, MO. August died May 31, 1941, in Dutchtown, MO. Seventh was Auguste Rosine Walperswiller, born Oct. 29, 1879, and died Dec. 10, 1888, in Gordonville, MO. Eighth was Bertha Rosette Walperswiller, born Nov. 24, 1882, in Gordonville, MO. She married a Sachse. *Submitted by Marcine Lohman*

WALTER – During the Civil War, Charles Cecil Walter was born in Fairfield, IL. He married Mary Terrell and they had three children, the middle one being Gilbert Gilmore who was born in 1900. Gilbert married Eva Bernice Fleming in May 1919 in Caraway, AR. Calvin Gilbert was born on Feb. 13, 1924, in Campbell, MO. Eva had gone to visit her brother, Roy, and his wife, Colleen, when she went into labor and delivered her third child.

Calvin grew up mainly in the cotton and truck patch fields of northeast Arkansas near Monette. His grandfather Walter had a cotton gin and a general store so Calvin and his two older brothers worked the fields and in the gin. They grew up strong, enjoyed school, and enjoyed living in the community. When WWII started in the 1940s, the older two boys joined the Navy; being alone to work the fields and anxious to serve, Calvin soon followed. He became a signalman on a Patrol Craft, which served in the Gulf of Mexico and was eventually sent to the Philippines. It was near the end of the war, in 1944, in the Leyte Gulf, that a large battle with the Japanese ensued. Calvin was seriously wounded; however, a nearby hospital ship saved his life. The following two years proved to be a personal battle for Signalman Walter. Repeated surgeries in Navy hospitals throughout the Pacific, then in California and Tennessee, repaired torn organs and tissues; however, it drained the young man of his strength. A couple of extended visits back to the farm helped him build and regain that strength until he could be discharged in the autumn of 1946.

The following year, on June 13, 1947, Calvin married Lorene Lincoln of Scopus, MO (see Lincoln/Long history). They lived in the Jackson/Cape Girardeau area for two years, and then bought a home in Marble Hill where they worked for the Deevers Shoe Company. In 1951 they had Patricia (see Wischmann/Walter history), and in 1953, Judy Leigh was born.

Lorene, Judy, Calvin and Patricia Walter, 1970.

They decided to try farm life, so they bought a 60-acre plot near Scopus where they lived and worked the farm for six years. Calvin had gone to work for the Natural Gas Pipeline and with working "swing" shifts and farming, it proved to be too much, so they sold the farm and bought an older home in Burfordville. They remodeled the house and remained there for 10 years. Lorene was a homemaker and both the Walters were and still are avid flower and vegetable gardeners.

The two girls attended grade school in Burfordville where Lorene was involved with PTA. Calvin had gone to work for Lohman Restaurant Supply in Cape Girardeau and remained there for eight years.

In 1969 they purchased a home on Priest Street in Jackson and a year later sold the house in Burfordville to the state. It became the home for the superintendent of the new Bollinger Mill State Historic Site.

In 1971 Calvin was hired by the city of Jackson as a building inspector and remained in that position for 19 years. The Walters have been active in helping establish the Westside Church of Christ where Calvin has served as a lay minister. Lorene has assisted and still privately assists senior citizens in Jackson. Patricia lives in Jackson and Judy lives in Dexter. *Submitted by Patricia Wischmann*

WEDEKIND – Charles Wedekind (1856-1937), son of Frederich and Maria, married Louise Nabe (1867-1949) and had four children, Emil (1899-1986), Laura (1900-1931), Meta (1902-1991) and Lydia (1905-1995). They all attended Oak Grove School through the sixth grade, which was over a mile away. Starting at seventh grade, they attended Hanover Lutheran School. This was about a four-mile walk each way. They had to cross many farm fields with dogs and at times bulls giving chase. To get to school they had to cross Cape La Croix Creek by way of the Cape Girardeau Northern Railroad trestle. Lydia always spoke about how scary and dangerous it was when it rained and the water was high. Emil, being one of the older boys at the school, was often given the responsibility of building the fire in the stove that heated the school. Emil had to quit school after the seventh grade to help his mother Louise do her butter, cream, and egg route in Cape Girardeau. Emil helped by churning butter, hitching up the horse, and driving the buggy for his mother. They

The Wedekinds: Laura, Meta, Lydia and Emil.

would go into Cape Girardeau about twice a week and it would take all day to complete their route. Emil would also help his dad drive the team of horses that pulled a wagon loaded with hogs or other livestock to the Jackson Railroad Stock Yard. While in Jackson they would pick up groceries and supplies uptown, and barrels of flour and livestock feed at the mills in Jackson. This was a nine-mile round trip for them.

In 1918 Emil was called to report to the Army for WWI and was to leave from Jackson Depot. On the day of departure, the entire family was at the Depot to see him off. Emil was about to board the train with his cardboard suitcase when word came over the telegraph that the war with Germany was over and no one had to report to the Army camps. The family, very relieved that the war was over, went home to the farm.

In the 1920s, the state cut though the Wedekind farm again for the new Highway 61. At this time, Charles and Louise gave the state of Missouri over seven acres of land lying between Highway 61 and the old Cape Girardeau-Jackson Road for a roadside park. The state named the piece of ground "Wedekind Roadside Park." Donald's family has wonderful memories of picnics in this park. The farm, being about equal distance from Jackson and Cape Girardeau, was also in the center of the famous ten-mile rose garden, which was planted along the side of Highway 61 by the State Highway Department. In 1960 the Interstate Highway 55 came along and split the Wedekind property again from north to south, taking over 50 acres.

Other than going to Cape Girardeau or Jackson for shopping, or to Hanover Lutheran Church for the Sunday service, Emil and Meta stayed on the Wedekind farm until the cities of Jackson and Cape Girardeau came to them. Now the Wedekind farm is again in "the middle," about half in the city of Cape Girardeau and half in Jackson. Lydia found her way back to the farm once her children were grown.

Donald still owns property on the southwest side of the intersection of I-55 and Highway 61, which is part of the original Wedekind farm. Donald purchased the land and the barn (now identified as the Rainbow Auction Barn) from his Uncle Emil and Aunt Meta in 1980. *Submitted by Donald Kuntze*

WEISS – William G. Koerber, born in 1830, immigrated to America from Brunswick-Hanover provinces in Germany to escape the German Army draft. He arrived in New Orleans, then traveled north to Cape Girardeau. He farmed until he was drafted into the Union Army and served in the Missouri Militia, 56th regiment, Company B, as a private. Their main duties were at first guarding railroad bridges and public buildings in Cape Girardeau and Jackson. Company B was also in action at the battles of Cape Girardeau, Jackson, Pocahontas, and northeast Arkansas.

His son, William F. Koerber, established a dairy of registered Guernsey cattle obtained from Wisconsin. His son, George Koerber, continued the dairy. They sold and delivered milk to homeowners and their surplus to the St. Vincent's Seminary in Cape Girardeau. They quit the dairy farming in 1958.

George and Ruby Masters Koerber had two children, Viola Marie Koerber, who married Norman Weiss; and Julia Mathilda Koerber, who married Billy Dean Hoffmeister, a lineman for the Missouri Electric Company. Julia worked for the Southwestern Bell Telephone Company. Viola worked for the International Shoe Factory.

Antone Jacob Weiss and family emigrated from the Province of Braunschweig, Germany. They settled in Cape Girardeau because they had friends there. George Weiss Sr. stayed on the farm and after his parents died he bought out the heirs' shares. He married Wilhelmina Lowes. They had eight children and continued buying land until his holdings were over 800 acres. As their boys married, he helped them acquire a farm.

Henry Weiss married Lula Heuer Weiss and had four sons, Clarence, Arnold, Louis and Norman. Their first son, Clarence Weiss, helped on the farm through his years at Central High School and Southeast Missouri State University. He received his Ph. D. in chemical engineering and worked at Buckeye Cellulose in Memphis, TN, until his retirement. Their second son, Arnold Weiss, also continued his education through Southeast Missouri State University, and received his M.S. from the University of Missouri-Columbia. He taught several years, his last years at Fruitland High School. He then worked as an auditor for the Missouri State Department of Liquor. Their third son, Louis Weiss, also continued his education through Southeast Missouri State University. He taught several years and his final teaching was at Jackson High School. He was an avid baseball player. He played semi-professional ball for three years in Texas. He played and managed the Capahas many years. He married Paula Wittrock and they had one son, Paul Louis Weiss, who lived in Cape Girardeau. Their fourth son, Norman H. Weiss, worked on the farm until college, served in the Air Force for three years, came home, graduated from Southeast Missouri State University, married and bought the farm.

Henry Weiss holding Louis Weiss on lap, and Arnold Weiss seated on the running board of a 1913 Model-T Roadster.

Henry and Lula Weiss farmed until their retirement. During their farming careers, Lula in a buggy would peddle their surplus eggs and butter in Jackson; this would take an entire day. When they bought their first automobile in 1913, a Model "T" Ford, she used it to deliver eggs and butter. This cut her time to half a day.

Lula was quite a prankster- here are two examples. When one of the boys wanted a button sewn on a shirt she would sew it on while they were wearing the shirt. Sewing lightly, she hit them in the stomach with her sewing hand. If you didn't jump, then the next time she would turn the needle in; you would jump that time! She also was an excellent rifle shot, better than all four of the boys. The three boys were target shooting. She came out and asked what they were doing. She took a shot and hit the target dead center at 35 feet. She asked for a smaller target. Arnold put a wooden match in the fence and she shot it in two at 35 feet! She had him do it again. This time, she struck the match and it lit. She handed the rifle to her sons and went into the house to fix lunch.

Henry was an avid foxhunter. He had excellent dogs and loved "running" foxes with friends, not to catch the fox, but for the music the dogs made. Lula was scared of mice. She kept traps set. If they didn't work she would take the .22 rifle and shoot them in the head. There are still several bullet holes on the quarter rounds in the house.

During Norman Weiss' first two years of high school at Jackson High School, the "bus" was a Model A Ford driven by Oscar Schweer. He would come out of the Clover Hill Road (now County 614) and go back in the "Lower Road" (now County 616). He loaded eight students in the Model A; it was somewhat crowded.

Norman Weiss married Viola Marie Koerber in 1949; they bought his father's farm. He farmed and worked for the USDA ASCS for 30 years. In 1933, their farm was certified by the Missouri Extension Service as a "Century Farm," one that had been in the family for over 100 years. Norman and Viola had three children: Mike, Chris and Carolyn.

Their first son, Mike W. Weiss, graduated from Rolla Engineering School as a petroleum engineer. He married Debbie Sebastian. He first worked in Texas; then Cairo, Egypt; Chicago; Kogland, Russia; and now in Louisiana. They have two children, Elizabeth and Jason. Their second son, Chris N. Weiss, graduated from Southeast Missouri State University and Missouri University. He married Lesa Holland. He worked in agriculture sales for two years, then went to Missouri University and obtained a law degree. He joined the Lichtenegger law firm and is now a full partner. They are located in Jackson, Marble Hill, St. Louis, and Vail, CO. Their daughter, Carolyn M. Weiss, went to Jackson High School. In her senior year she was killed in an auto accident in December 1976. *Submitted by Norman Weiss*

WEISS – Marie Bodenstein Weiss was born on Jan. 23, 1908, on a farm one mile west of Jackson. Her great-grandparents bought the land in the late 1850s. Her grandfather, Phillip, purchased it from his mother following the death of her husband, also named Phillip. Marie loved to tell how her grandmother Fredericka served fresh bread from her kitchen to hungry Civil War soldiers as they passed by. If they had any money they would leave a coin. In this way she increased the family income. Her husband served as a private in the Union Army. After his death in 1890 she received a widow's pension of $30.00 a month.

Marie's mother, Minnie, was born Jan. 11, 1873. She married August Bodenstein at the age of 18 and became a widow with three children, Alvin, Frieda and Edna, at the age of 30. A year later, in 1903, she married her first husband's cousin, William Bodenstein. They had three children, William, Marie and Mildred. Following the death of Marie's father in 1924, her mother continued to live on the farm until her death in May 1937.

Marie graduated as valedictorian of her high school class in 1926 and was elected to teach at Campster School for $75.00 a month starting in the fall. She was offered a summer job in the Jackson Exchange Bank for $1.00 a day, making her its first female employee. During August she was asked to continue working at the bank.

Marie Bodenstein Weiss in front of brother Bill's first car, 1924.

Her decision was easy to make, as she was concerned with teaching eight grades in a one-room country school. She remained with the bank for approximately 11 years and never made more than $75.00 a month.

In 1929 she bought a new Ford Sedan for $718.00 and began dating Walter Weiss. They were married Sept. 23, 1935, and moved in with Walter's father and stepmother on a farm south of Jackson. While living there they had two daughters, Rosemary Weiss Gasper and Martha Weiss Maxton. Marie frequently recalled memories of the Great Depression. Arriving at the bank one morning the door was locked. Using her key, she let herself in and was told to go home. President Roosevelt had closed every bank in the United States. When the bank reopened she saw men crying over losing farms, businesses and homes.

In 1941 Marie and Walter bought a farm three miles north of Jackson on Highway 61. With the poor economy and the nation on the brink of war, friends and family thought they were crazy. But with lots of hard work their mortgage was paid off in six years.

Marie was well known in the community for her musical talent. She mastered the piano and sang in her church, school, and community choirs and frequently sang solos at weddings and funerals.

Marie and Walter moved to Jackson in 1987 after selling their beloved farm. Walter passed away on May 24, 1990, and Marie on Dec. 28, 1995, at Chateau Girardeau in the Health Center where their daughter, Martha, worked as a registered nurse. *Submitted by Martha Maxton*

WELKER – Lisa Emaline Davault, daughter of Polly Rhodes and James Davault, married Jacob Welker on July 2, 1868. Lisa Emaline was born Oct. 21, 1850, and died Oct. 17, 1920. Jacob Welker, son of Leonard Welker and Patience Cheek, was born Aug. 26, 1842, and died April 24, 1924. They are both buried at Mount Zion Cemetery in Bollinger County, MO.

Children of Lisa Emaline and Jacob were: Amanda Elizabeth, born June 20, 1873, married Peter LeRoy Rhodes. Adam Lee, born Feb. 16, 1879, married Fannie James. Mahala Frances married John T. Hanners. Elmine, born April 21, 1877, married George H. Moore. Mary E., born May 23, 1881, married Henry Luther Angel. Lillie Bell, born Aug. 1, 1885, married Charles Leadbetter. Ilonia "Lonie" married Jessie L. Estes. Aaron, born July 12, 1889, married Iva Ridings. Jacob W., born May 2, 1887, married Effie Jane Shrum. Naaman, born July 12, 1891, married Flora Brown. Sarah Ellen was born Feb. 28, 1894.

On Dec. 24, 1922, Sarah married Elijah Cornelius Hahn, son of John and Lucinda Stroder

Hahn. Cornelius was born Dec. 9, 1887, and died July 27, 1974. Sarah died Sept. 28, 1973. Both are buried in Russell Heights Cemetery in Jackson, MO. They were the parents of four children: 1) Wilma Eileen, born March 9, 1924, married Lloyd R. Summers on April 21, 1944. They have one daughter, Marilyn R., born Feb. 1, 1949, who married Glenn Wayne Fronabarger on Dec. 19, 1970. Wayne and Marilyn have two children, Kelly Nicole, born July 31, 1970, and Darin Wayne, born Aug. 19, 1980. 2) Lela Lorene, born Aug. 28, 1925, married Charles Pinkson Hutson on March 1, 1958. 3) Johnny Jacob, born Aug. 21, 1930, married Joann Jones on April 2, 1955. 4) Virginia Lou, born May 27, 1934, married Larry Dean Sides on Sept. 17, 1955. *Submitted by Marilyn Fronabarger*

WELKER – Wilbert Welker, the son of Jesse Welker (1886-1975) and Francis Shumer Welker (1884-1965), was born April 6, 1920, in Perryville, MO. Wilbert was the seventh of ten children. He had three brothers, Lawrence, Floyd and Glennon. His sisters included Ida, Beulah, Veronica, Clara, Frances and Hilda. Wilbert grew up on a farm near Perryville, MO. He attended school for only a few years before quitting to help out on the family farm. At the age of 18, he worked as a water boy during the construction of the old St. Francis Hospital in Cape Girardeau, MO. He later worked in maintenance at the hospital. His next job was at the Cape Girardeau Shoe Factory where he worked until he was drafted into the army. During WWII he was stationed in Hawaii and the Philippines where he served as a radar operator.

Stella Marie Brands, the daughter of John Brands (1883-1978) and Bernadette Brauer Brands (died in 1940), was born March 3, 1920, in Leopold, MO. She was the sixth of seven children. Her brothers included Henry, Frank and Ted. She had three sisters, Louise, Gertrude and Ann. She lived in Leopold, MO, until the age of 5, at which time the family moved to Portageville, MO, where her dad farmed. As a young girl, Stella worked as a child-care provider. At the age of 19 she moved to Cape Girardeau, MO, and obtained a job at St. Francis Hospital. She worked there for seven years taking care of newborn babies. She tells how there were so many babies that they fashioned beds for them out of drawers.

During WWII everyone was encouraged to write to the "boys" serving in the armed forces. Stella wrote to Wilbert for three years before actually meeting him. They were married April 7, 1947, at St. Mary's Catholic Church in Cape Girardeau, MO.

Wilbert and Stella's first home was located near Sedgewickville on a small farm. Less than a year later they bought a farm near Gordonville, MO, where they have lived ever since. When they first moved to this farm they lived in an old two-story farmhouse, part of which was made of logs. A one-room school, called Needmore School was located just up the hill from the Welker farm. When the school was closed in 1955, the Welkers bought it, moved it down the hill and remodeled it into the home

The Welker family, clockwise: Wilbert, Stella, Susan, Wib, Jim, Ed and Mary Anne, circa 1960.

where they lived until 1969. At that time a new modern home was built.

Wilbert and Stella had five children. Susan (born 1848) became a teacher and married James Stoverink. They have five children and three grandchildren. Mary Anne (born 1949) became a nurse and married Jack Martin. They have three children and one grandchild. Edwin (born 1951) works for the Farm Home Administration and married Kathy Reynolds. They have three children and two grandchildren. Wilbert Jr. (born 1952) took over the home farm and married Ann Ansberry. They have three children. James (born 1955) became a teacher and is presently the assistant superintendent of the Jackson School District. He married Teri Weber and they have three children.

On the 160-acre farm the Welkers raised cattle, hogs and chickens and grew crops. They eventually turned their farm into a dairy farm. They presently still live on the farm but their son, Wilbert Jr, farms it. *Submtited by Susan Welker Stoverink*

WELLS – Jacob K. Wells was a teacher and a fellow with an ability to capture images of rural Missouri. He produced numerous watercolors, a few oil paintings and filled up stacks of sketchbooks during his life. In 1970 he began a three-year project to design and paint a mural measuring 40 feet by 21 feet at Kent Library on the campus of Southeast Missouri State University. In 1977 he collaborated with his friend Dr. George Suggs, a professor of history at the university, to provide watercolor illustrations to accompany George's text for the book *Water Mills of the Missouri Ozarks*. As a boy, his grandfather, Jacob Simmerman, intro-

Jeanette and Jake Wells, wedding photo, 1943.

duced him to the workings of water mills in Bollinger County. It kindled a fascination for the beauty of the locations, sounds and mechanics of mills that never left him. He listed his hobbies as fishing, hunting Indian artifacts, observing nature, painting and drawing.

He was born in 1918, to Jesse King and Ibbia Simmerman Wells, in Marble Hill, MO, preceded in birth by his brothers Zahn and Webster, and sisters Marguerite and Myra Jean. In 1930 the Wells family moved from Marble Hill to Cape Girardeau, where Jake graduated from Central High School in 1936. He completed a Bachelor of Science in education from Southeast Missouri State Teachers College with a major in Fine Art and later earned his master's Degree in Art from George Peabody College in Nashville, TN (now a part of Vanderbilt).

He worked as a lineman for a telephone company and taught at Dogwood School in Mississippi County prior to enlisting in the Army in 1942. He served in the Signal Corps in the Aleutian Islands in Alaska. An injury sidelined him for a while to Fitzsimmons Hospital in Denver, CO. While on leave in February of 1943 he caught a train from Denver to St. Louis where he and his Jackson sweetheart, Jeanette Leone Wagner, were married. After his discharge from the Army in 1945, he returned to Jackson to work for the Wagner Machine and Welding Works and began working part time in the Cape Girardeau County R-2 School District. He was hired full time in 1947 and for the next 13 years taught elementary and secondary level art and social studies, was supervisor of elementary art, and assistant football and basketball coach and baseball coach. He was hire in 1960 by Southeast Missouri State College and the Wells family moved to Cape Girardeau. For the next 20 years Jake taught in the art department and was department chair for four years. He was a member of a number of teacher's associations and served terms as president of both the Southeast Missouri State University District Teachers Association and the Southeast Missouri State University District Art Teachers Association. History was another lifelong interest and he was a member and supporter of the River Heritage Museum Association, and the Bollinger County Historical Society. He was a recipient of the Dingeldein Award for Achievement in the Arts, Distinguished Service in Education, Excellence in Painting and Teaching and Alumni Merit Award from Southeast Missouri State University.

Jeanette was born in 1917 in St. Louis, the second child of Henry J. and Florentine Wolgast Wagner. She gradated from Jackson High School in 1935 and attended Southeast Missouri State College for one year. In 1942 she and some of her friends headed for California to enlist their womanpower in the war effort. Her aptitude for geometry and experience from her father's machine shop got her a position in the drafting department of Consolidated Vultee, an aircraft manufacturer in San Diego, CA. She returned to Jackson with Jake in 1945.

She and Jake had two children, Bert Nelson, born in 1946, and Jeanie Diane, born in 1952. Bert married Margaret Boos, daughter of Lee and Raymond Boos of Cape Girardeau, in 1974. Their two sons are Jesse David, born in 1979, and Jacob Lee, born in 1981. In 1984, Jeanie married Jack Troy, son of William and Kathryn Troy of Dyersburg, TN.

Jeanette was a caseworker for the State Welfare Office in Cape Girardeau for several years. For 20 years she weathered the intrusions and recessions of cancer by concentrating on things she enjoyed. She played piano and organ and she sang. She was active in the choir at Emanuel United Church of Christ in Jackson, was a member of the Cape Choraliers and music director of the Evangelical United Church of Christ in Cape Girardeau. Her eye for design and color and proficiency in geometry made her an extremely skilled seamstress. Bowling and cultivating roses were favorite hobbies and she was probably among the first people in Cape Girardeau County to take up yoga exercise.

Jeanette died Feb. 6, 1977; Jake joined her Aug. 1, 1999. They are buried in Russell Heights Cemetery in Jackson. *Submitted by Jeanie Troy*

WERNER – Vernon and LaWanda Werner with their grandchildren, Whitney, Kylie and Tanner Werner, children of Randy and Connie Werner of Jackson, Mo; Dakota and Clayton Werner, children of Mark Werner of Jackson, MO; and Jordan, Taylor and Ali, children of Beth and Rob Janet of Cape Girardeau, MO.

Vernon and LaWanda reside at 521 Bainbridge Road in Jackson, MO. They are natives of Cape Girardeau County, having both been in the area and having lived here all of their lives except for the time Vernon served in the Korean War. Vernon was founder and owner of Dutch Enterprises, Inc., until his retirement. They are members of St. Paul

Front row: Dakota, Ali, Clayton and Taylor.
Middle row: Kylie, Jordan, Tanner and Whitney.
Back row: Vernon and LaWanda.

Lutheran Church in Jackson, MO. "Taking time for our grandchildren brings love, joy and lasting significance." *Submitted by LaWanda Werner*

WICKER – Henry Whicker received his property in Colyton Parish, Devonshire, England, from King Henry the VII or VIII for services rendered. Five generations later, his descendant, Thomas, left England in the fall of 1685 and arrived in Virginia Dec. 1, 1685, aboard Capt. Walter Lyle's ship. Thomas' grandson, Thomas Oscar, was born in New Kent County, VA, on Aug. 11, 1717. He married Mary Hester (b. 1722 in Virginia) in 1736-36 at Chatham County, North Carolina. Thomas received land grant #458, 100 acres in return for his patriotic service of running supplies from Granville and Chatham County, NC, for the revolutionary case. Both Thomas and Mary died in 1784 in Chatham County, NC. Their son Robert, one of seven children, was born about 1738 in Louisa County, VA, and about 1757-8 he married Hannah Simmons Holley, daughter of Nathaniel and Jane Simmons Holley (b. 1742 in Edgecomb County, NC). Twelve children were born to this marriage. The family lived in Granville and Anson County, NC (1765), Chesterfield County, SC (1776), Columbia and finally Washington County, GA. Robert's daughter Jane (b. May 27, 1760) married Thomas English (b. Oct. 13, 1754, Virginia) about 1776 in Washington County, GA. Robert, his son William and his son-in-law Thomas English served at the battle of Eutaw Springs during the Revolutionary War.

As the Wickers seemed prone to moving, it should not came as a surprise that in 1806 they moved from Georgia to Cape Girardeau County, MO. Thomas and Jane (Wicker) English moved with her parents and their own children, which included six sons and six daughters. They became members of the Old Bethel Baptist Church, which was constituted on July 19, 1806, with Thomas English as a deacon. Hannah Wicker died Aug. 12, 1818, followed by Robert on Jan. 2, 1821; son-in-law Thomas English died May 16, 1829 and his wife Jane died April 5, 1842. All are buried in Cape Girardeau County and have many descendents still living in the region. This family's history is continued in the Howard/Webb entry. This is but a small part of the "goodly heritage" that Pamela Macke Johnson began researching in 1972 as a class subject.

Her parents are Henry Weldon Macke and Bonnie Sue Bierschwal, both natives of Cape Girardeau County, who still live near Gordonville, MO. Pamela was born June 8, 1955, and is the oldest of three daughters. She graduated from Jackson High School in 1973, Southeast Missouri State University in 1977 with a B. S. degree in chemistry, and again in 2000 with a Master's of science in administration. On Aug. 6, 1977 she married Stanley Charles Johnson (b. April 13, 1956), son of Marion Charles "Jack" and Dorothy (Sander) Johnson, of Sikeston, MO. Stan received his B. S. degree in civil engineering from the University of Missouri-Rolla in December of 1977. The couple moved to northwest Indiana in 1978 where they resided in Chesterton, IN. Their children Elizabeth Kathleen (b. Dec. 12, 1982) and Jack Thomas (b. June 22, 1985) were born in Valparaiso, IN, and in 1986 the family moved back to Jackson, MO. Stan is currently employed at the Missouri Department of Transportation assigned to the Cape Girardeau area and is involved with the construction of the new Bill Emerson Memorial Bridge. Pam is employed as a forensic chemist at the Southeast Missouri State University Regional Crime Lab. The family members are active with Zion Methodist Church of Gordonville, various Masonic organizations, Troop 311 Boy Scouts, and John Guild Chapter, NSDAR. *Submitted by Pamela Macke Johnson*

WILLER – As a young boy Alpha Willer desired to learn the art of leather craft, which required perfection in cutting, bending, and polishing the leather. He moved to Jackson in 1905, learning the trade from Herman Wolters, owner of the harness store on Main Street in Jackson. As an apprentice Willer earned $10 a month. His salary increased after learning the art and sales.

They buggy and wagon pulled by horses was the mode of transportation; thus the need for leather equipment was in demand. The unassembled buggies were delivered to the wide basement door of the store. After assembly a large hand-operated elevator transferred the buggies to the display floor for sale of $40 to $60 depending on style. Around the 1920s automobiles replaced buggies. Willer encouraged a change to selling farm seed. Later a large garden seed and plant center was added.

Willer purchased the business and building from Wolters in 1945 and changed the name to The Willer Seed Company. In 1948 Raymond Willer became a partner. The store became well-known for seed sales. In early spring the store was a hub for farmers and gardeners wanting to purchase seed and also receive valuable advice from the owners who experimented with seed, learning information to better serve their customers.

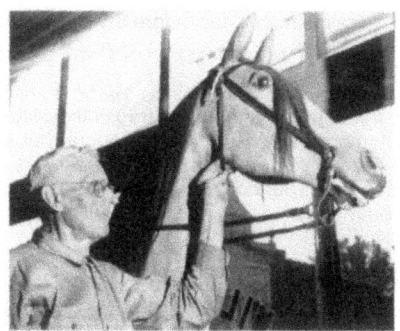

Alpha W. Willer

A trademark was the dapple-gray horse, made of plaster, paper and frame, in the front window, which had been purchased by Wolters in 1898. The arrival caused much glee and excitement. News of the large handcrafted horse was told. Visitors made a special trip to view the horse. The seed store became known as "The Store With the Horse in the Window." The horse was often used in parades and festivals. Children were delighted to sit in the saddle on the horse and hold the straps of the bridle. Oh, if this "Horse in the Window" could talk, many interesting stories would it tell.

Saddles for riding horses continued for sale after buggies were no longer used. Some of the saddles and bridles were ornate and attractive in a style made especially for "show." One of these was an old sidesaddle especially designed for the female, who in the 1800s and early 1900s wore dresses or skirts.

Alpha Willer retired in 1963. The business was sold, but Raymond retained ownership of the building.

Alpha (Jan. 8, 1885 – Jan. 6, 1968), son of Joe and Christine Reinecke Willer, and Minnie Louise (March 4, 1889 – Jan. 6, 1967), daughter of Henry and Lydia Deneke Rasche, were married in the parlor of the bride's home on Oct. 28, 1914. Three children, Frances Heimbaugh Oswald, Raymond and Bernice Steck, were born to the couple. Grandchildren and great-grandchildren were greatly loved and enjoyed.

The Willer family were members of Emmanuel United Church of Christ and participated in many activities of the church. They were interested in the advancement of Jackson and surrounding areas. *Submitted by Bernice Steck*

WILLIAMS – The family has owned the Big Hill farmstead for over 200 years. It is a part of the original Spanish land grant to William Daugherty, who had fought in the American Revolution, and who was from the western part of Virginia. He married Elizabeth Ramsay; daughter of Andrew Ramsay, and in 1796 came to the Cape Girardeau area with his father-in-law and other family members. Ramsay had been out to the Spanish territory the year before and was the first American settler to receive land in the area from the Spanish government. Daugherty started settling land for himself northeast of Cape Girardeau and received official confirmation of it in 1799 when he was granted 440 arpens of land along Hubble Creek: 300 arpens for his service as captain of a Company of Rangers in Houck's Spanish Regiment and the other 140 arpens for his service on the local legislative council. The U.S. Government confirmed the original 440 arpens in 1806. William Daugherty gave the name Big Hill to this property. His granddaughter Berenice Daugherty Williams and her husband built the house at Big Hill. She was given the plantation from the estate of her other grandfather George Frederick Bollinger, one of the early leaders of Missouri who is remembered by the Bollinger Mill State Historic Site and by Bollinger County and Fredericktown, MO. He had obtained the land from Berenice's father Ralph Daugherty, son of William, in 1830, and his daughter Sarah Bollinger Daugherty gave it to Berenice in 1849.

Berenice Daugherty was born in 1830 at Cape la Croix near Cape Girardeau. Berenice completed her education at Mrs. Guild's school in Philadelphia, PA. Berenice married Harrison Harvey Minton Williams at Bollingers' in January of 1847. Williams (H.H.M.) was also from a well-known pioneer family whose land on Indian Creek was near what is now the town of Oriole, MO. He was the son of Jane Minton and George Harvey Williams. As his mother died soon after he was born in 1821, his grandparents, Colonel Charles and Mary Harvey Williams, raised him. Colonel Williams had been Master Armorer at Harpers Ferry and was appointed the Chief Arms Inspector for the U.S. government.

H.H.M. as a teenager was sent to the Catholic School operated in Perryville, MO, by the Vincentian order and then to the college operated by them in Emmitsburg, MD. He returned to Jackson and read law in the office of Col. Thomas Ranney. At the age of 21 he was admitted to the bar and began his practice throughout the district. At age 25 when the Mexican War began in 1846, he was elected Lieutenant Colonel of a regiment of volunteers. Though the unit was never called to active duty, the title stayed with him for the rest of his life.

H.H.M. farmed the land given to his wife, then owned a general mercantile store in Jackson for over 40 years and was one of the most successful businessmen of the county. He was County Treasurer and Public Administrator for 15 years and was the treasurer of the Baptist church in Jackson for 50 years. In 1852 he was president of the Cape Girardeau McAdamizing and Plank Road Company that built the road from Cape Girardeau to Jackson and on to Bollinger Mill, facilitating the movement of commerce in the area. He chaired the committees to obtain depots to get the railroad to come into the area and to find a place for a Normal School. He was an organizer of the public school system and was president of the school board.

Bill Hill Farmstead

H.H.M. and Berenice had six children who lived to adulthood: Sarah Conway, Samuel Daugherty, Minnie Berenice, George Harvey, Joseph Welling and Harrison Ralph. Their eldest son, Samuel, also a Jackson merchant, and his wife Frederica Welling moved into the house in 1883 and were the next generation to raise a family here. They had seven sons and one daughter: Samuel Daugherty Jr., Berenice Elizabeth, Manning George, Conway Guild, Earle Bollinger, Homer Richards, George Frederick and Miller. The two unmarried children, Berenice and Manning, a civil engineer, were the ones living at the farm after the death of their parents. In 1965 the son of George Frederick, who had an insurance agency in Miami, FL, and his wife Katrina Worley, acquired Big Hill from the rest of the family. In 1971, their daughter Mary Kate and her husband Colonel Daniel F. Johnson, U.S. Army, moved to the farm upon his retirement. They worked to restore the house for comfortable living. Their children Christine and Daniel Mebane are the seventh generation of the same family on the land.

Big Hill Farmstead is listed on the National Register of Historic Places. It in now owned by Mrs. Mary Kate W. Johnson and her brother George Frederick Williams Jr., a retired electrical engineer. *Submitted by Mary Kate Johnson*

WILSON – The patriarch of the Wilson family, Robert Kent Wilson, was born Nov. 26, 1883, in Jackson, the son of Robert Pinkney and Lillian Seibert Wilson. He was married to Miss Anita Helmkampf of Jackson, who passed away in October 1942.

Kent Wilson attended the Jackson Public Schools and the old Jackson Military Academy. After attending Westminster College at Fulton, he retuned to Jackson and became the city's youngest mayor at the age of 21. In 1915 he was appointed by President Woodrow Wilson to serve as postmaster. In 1923 he purchased the *Missouri Cash-Book* and was known for his fiery editorials. He served for many years on the Board of Education and was its president for 15 years. While he was a member, the stadium and elementary school building were erected. He was an active member of the Presbyterian Church and president of the Jackson Building and Loan Association.

Kent's immediate family suffered many illnesses. His wife, Anita, was physically impaired after being stricken with encephalitis. Daughter Irene was stricken with spinal meningitis during her junior year in high school. Son Robert died at age 39 from a malignant brain tumor.

Kent and Anita's son, Robert, familiarly known as Bob, was born in 1908. Following graduation from the Missouri University of Journalism, he returned to Jackson and joined his father at the newspaper as a cub reporter. In 1930 he married Marian Frances Fenimore. In 1935 he purchased the Palace Theater, which he operated until his death in 1947. During WWII he served as a lieutenant in the Navy. Bob and Marian were the parents of four children: Marilyn, Anita, Kent and Jim.

Marian Fenimore Wilson was born in 1908. She attended Synodical College in Fulton and came to Jackson as an elementary school teacher. She was active in church, community and club affairs and was a longtime member of the Presbyterian Church choir. She operated the movie theater with the assistance of her father-in-law during her husband's military service.

Robert Kent Wilson

Irene Louise was born in 1912, and although paralyzed on her left side, never let her affliction keep her from being active in community activities. For many years she was chairman of the March of Dimes program and well known for her witty "So I Heard" column in the *Cash-Book*.

Following the death of his son Bob, Kent again assisted his daughter-in-law Marian in the operation of the Palace Theater and became an advisor and confidante to his grandchildren. There were pleasure rides before Sunday church services, fatherly lectures, and advice when requested.

Returning from St. Louis on March 4, 1955, Kent, Irene, and Marian were tragically killed in an automobile accident. The outpouring of assistance and compassion from the citizens of Jackson was evidence of a closely knit and caring community. *Submitted by Marilyn Wilson Proffer*

WILSON – Margie Wilson was born Sept. 23, 1928, on a farm now located on County Road 522. Margie is the daughter of Leo and Imogene Snider Wilson.

Margie attended Pocahontas Grade School where she was a member of the girl's basketball team and the Pocahontas 4-H Club. Margie graduated from Pocahontas High School in 1944. Margie was the valedictorian of her graduating class. Margie then attended Jackson High School and graduated in 1946. She was very active in Secretarial Club activities and was secretary to the assistant principal.

After high school Margie met and married Raymond Rastl, a farmer from the Oak Ridge area. Raymond was the son of Henry and Agneta Rastl. A daughter, Maryln was born to them on July 24, 1950. Raymond Rastl died on July 10, 1953, after a brief illness.

We then moved back to the farm to live with my grandparents, Mr. and Mrs. Leo Wilson. Margie went to work in 1953 at Bowman Milling Company as a secretary; while working there she met Wib Reisenbichler, son of Adolph and Hattie Reisenbichler who lived east of Pocahontas. Wib attended Zion Lutheran Elementary School and graduated from Pocahontas High School in 1943.

Margie and Wib were married on May 14, 1955. A son, Vernon was born to them on Nov. 20, 1957. Vernon is now married and lives in St. Louis County and has two children, Christopher and Godiva.

Our parents taught at a very early age the importance of faith and being involved at Zion Lutheran Church in Pocahontas, they both served on various boards and organizations in the church. We attended worship and Sunday school regularly.

Both Margie and Wib were very involved in the activities of the community. Wib has served on the Pocahontas Town Board for many years and still is on that board. Wib was the mayor of Pocahontas for many of those years. He also was actively involved in the Public Water District Board and the Fruitland Fire Department Board. Margie has been active in the Ladies Aid at Zion for a number of years, Adult Club, and many other church committees.

Both Margie and Wib are still involved in church and community activities as time and health allow them to be. They have been wonderful role models for their children, in the area of caring for others. They are respected and looked up to by the entire community. *Submitted by Marilyn Rastl*

WINTER – Catharina or Katie Winter (nee Gieschen) was born Oct. 14, 1877, in Germany, and was baptized at Kirchtimbeke at Hepstedt, Hanover in Germany. She entered school when she was six. In August 1884 she started her trip to America; after 11 weeks on the ship they arrived in New York. They stayed three weeks with relatives, and then went by train to Concordia, MO. There she entered the Christian Day School. Her first teacher was Teacher Hamm, then Teacher Wilk. She got confirmed March 22, 1891, at St. Paul's Lutheran Church, by Pastor F. J. Bultz. There were 50 in the class. The girls wore black long dresses and a ribbon on top of their heads, and one at the end of their braid, as well as a ribbon around the neck with a bow on the shoulder.

Catharina "Katie" Winter

She married Paul B. Winter in 1904. They lived in Fruitland and ran a general store and the post office. She moved to Pocahontas after Paul died. They had four boys: Lamar, Raymond, Hugo, and Paul G. She settled in Pocahontas for the remainder of her life. She died at the age of 96. She had written the story of her life.

WINTER – Virginia Viola Rauh Winter was born to Oscar and Elsie Gerler Rauh on Aug. 11, 1923, in Pocahontas. She was the oldest of three children; her sisters were Evelyn and Mildred. She attended elementary school at Zion Lutheran Church, where she was also a life-long member. She taught Sunday school, sang in the choir, and was a member of the Ladies Aid. She graduated from Jackson High School, after which she worked for her father as a secretary at Bowman Milling Company, Inc. until 1980. Virginia's grandparents were Charles and Louisa Rauh and Fred and Bertha Gerler.

Paul Gerhardt Winter was born April 28, 1916, at Fruitland, MO. Pastor Flies at Pocahontas, MO, baptized him on May 7. He entered the public school at Fruitland in 1922. In 1923 he entered the Christian Day School at Pocahontas. Pastor Hilmer was his teacher until December 1927 when Rev. Kueoker came, who also confirmed him on March 24, 1929. In the fall, he entered Fruitland School to make it to the eighth grade. In September 1930 he entered high school, but he had to quit in December 1931 because of his father's illness.

Paul and Virginia Winter

In September 1933, he started school again but just for a few months before he quit for good. He then worked in the Winter Brothers store in Fruitland until his family sold their share. For some time he bought cream at Uniontown and Pocahontas. He worked Saturdays at the Jackson cream station.

By this time, his number came up and he was examined for the army. He passed the examination and was sent to Texas for basic training. He served in the Pacific area in WWII and in New Guinea and the Philippines. Upon his discharge from the army, he married Virginia Viola Rauh on Aug. 11, 1946. He went to work for Sugar Creek Creamery in Cape Girardeau. After it closed, he went to work for Kurre Creamery in Jackson, MO. After it closed, he became a salesman for Bowman Milling Company, Inc. in Pocahontas, MO.

Virginia and Paul had three children: Gary, who was born Aug. 4, 1951; Gregory, who died at birth; and Richard, who was born Dec. 24, 1958. They built a new home in Pocahontas, MO, where they reared their two boys. Virginia died in 1980 and Paul died in 1984. *Submitted by Marjorie Swan*

WISCHMANN – Richard A. Wischmann was born in Pipestone, MN, in 1919. Hilda Marie Fisher was born in Frankfurt, East Germany (Prussia), and came through Ellis Island in 1929 when she was 6 years old. They met in Pipestone and were married in 1941; 12 years later the family moved to Holbrook, AZ, where their children grew up. The fourth child was Gustav Herman, who came to Jackson in April of 1970 to marry Patricia Paulette Walter, daughter of Calvin and Lorene Walter (see Walter/Lincoln Family History). Patricia was a 1969 Jackson High School graduate and had been employed in uptown Jackson. After the wedding, the young couple went overseas to Budingen, West Germany, where Specialist Wischmann was stationed in the U.S. Army.

A year later, upon discharge from the service, Gus and Trisha settled in Winslow, AZ, where their first son, Richard Gustav, was born Sept. 13, 1971. Later they moved on to Flagstaff, but within a year they came back to Jackson. Their second child and only daughter, Natasha Yvette, was born June 13, 1974. Gus had been transferred to Anna, IL, where he was a meat cutter with the Kroger Company. However, Jackson kept beckoning this family, so in April of 1977, they purchased "Ideal Grocery" in uptown Jackson and operated it for three and one-half years. Two more additions to the family came in the early 1980s with Derek Walter and Ashley Brent.

The family experienced "county life" west of Millersville for five years, and then returned to Jackson once again. All of the sons were in Boy Scout Troop 311 and played little League Baseball. Richard completed Jackson High School in 1989. While a student at Southeast Missouri State University and Rolla, he served as a sergeant in the Missouri National Guard. With a double major in science and technology and civil engineering, he is an engineer for the city of O'Fallon, MO. He and his wife, Linda (Feise), have a young son, Gustav Anthony.

"Tasha" was a Jackson elementary student, 4-H member, and an active member of the Westside Church of Christ where the whole family worshipped. Unfortunately, her life was cut short when she was involved in an automobile accident on Oct. 6, 1984. She will always remain in the hearts and minds of the Wischmann family and friends.

Derek Walter entered the world on Dec. 15, 1980. After his 1999 high school graduation, he completed Army advanced training and obtained an ROTC scholarship. He was commissioned as a 2nd Lieutenant in July of 2001. In addition, he is a secondary social studies major at Central Missouri State University at Warrensburg; Derek is also a combat engineer platoon leader in Lexington, MO.

The Wischmanns: Gustav, Patricia, Richard (standing in back), Derek and Ashley, 1989.

The youngest of the children, Ashley Brent, was born March 18, 1982, at home in Jackson. A 2000 Jackson High School graduate, he was a light wheel mechanic at the Jackson National Guard unit. He and his wife, Melissa (Wooster), will soon move to Ft. Rucker, AL, where he will train as a helicopter pilot for the Missouri Guard.

Gus retired with honors as a master sergeant from the Army National Guard in January of 2000; he served 31 years with the military. He is currently driving for Genesis Transportation Company. He and Trisha opened the first bed and breakfast in southeast Missouri, right here in Jackson at 203 Bellevue Street, which was originally the H. H. Mueller Jr. home. Since 1988 they have continued to operate the lodging facility with its private tearoom and gift shop. Trisha is a past board member and volunteer with the St. Louis Iron Mountain Railway, and is a past president and board member of the Jackson Heritage Association. *Submitted by Patricia Wischmann*

WISSMANN – John Ferdnan Wissmann was born in Hanover, Germany, in 1817. In 1849 John and his brother Henry came to America on a sailing ship, landing in New Orleans, LA. They came up the Mississippi River into this area where they settled on some ground in the Jackson area. They worked clearing the ground during the summer with one of them returning to Louisiana during the winter months to work as a longshoreman. In 1850 John met Rosa Shott at Kelso and was later married. Rosa was born in Alsace-Lorraine, France, and came to America on a sailing ship, landing on the east coast. After they were married they moved to the farm west of Jackson on Greensferry Road on what is now Highway Y. They were land-granted this farm of 80 acres on Oct. 10, 1856, signed by President Franklin Pierce. They built a two-story log house on the farm. There they raised their family of 13 children of which John David, born March 13, 1875, was the last child. The log house they were raised in stood there for over 100 years. John Ferdnan died Feb. 4, 1900, and Rosa Wissmann died Oct. 6, 1907.

John David married Lora Belle Ellis in 1900. They had two children, Alma and Clyde. Lora Belle died April 19, 1905. On June 27, 1907, he married Ethel Perry at Moccasin Springs, now located in the Trail of Tears State Park. Ethel Perry's family lived on a farm in the park located about a half-mile northwest of Princess Otaki's grave. Ethel's parents were John Edmund and Panther Etta Perry. John David and Ethel had nine children. Those nine children were: John Lester, Carl Vernon, Rose Etta, Emma Marie, Herman David, Jesse Eugene, Mabel Elzina, Lulu Maxine and Jewell Aline.

John David and Ethel (Perry) Wissmann

They also adopted Mary Olivia Perry, daughter of Ethel's brother Frank Perry. The children attended Plainview School on Highway Y. John David was an overseer for the Cape Girardeau County road district. He was an avid fox and coon hunter in the area. They lived in a log house on part of the original land grant. The log house is still standing on Highway Y. John David died July 4, 1964, and Ethel died Jan. 13, 1965. *Submitted by Mark Wissmann*

WITTKE – Erna Leona Schoen Wittke was born Sept. 10, 1906, the daughter of Emmanuel Schoen (b. Jan. 30, 1874) and Maria Louisa Gratz Schoen (b. Dec. 6, 1874).

Erna grew up in Pocahontas, MO, and was a member of St. John's Lutheran Church. She was the organist for many years. A young minister, Rev. Gastav Wittke, came to pastor the church. They fell in love and were married June 21, 1931. In 1944 they moved to Herron, MI, where her husband Paul Wittke.

Erna Schoen Wittke, Rev. Gastav Wittke, and son Paul Wittke.

served the St. Matthew and Salem congregations until his death in July 1959. Erna died March 20, 2002.

They had one son, Paul Edward, born July 16, 1936 in Cape Girardeau, MO. He is a physician in Knoxville, TN.

INDEX

A

Abbott 213, 247, 288
Abel 154, 165
Abelunke 156
Abernathy 11, 31, 77, 81, 101, 135, 154, 175, 204, 210, 214, 223, 224, 234, 246, 273, 292, 293
Able 12, 154, 246
ACF 54
Achterman 100
Achtermann 163, 213, 226
Ackermann 112
Ackman 63, 116, 175, 176, 185
Acre 281
Acup 24
Adams 120, 132, 136, 138, 141, 142, 145, 154, 248
Ade 291
Afholter 23
Aftenthal 166
Aguilar 129
Ahrens 27, 42, 65, 101, 115, 229, 262, 286
Ainsworth 125, 274
Albers 110
Aldrich 208
Alexander 63, 169, 174, 180
Alford 212
Allard 176, 198, 199, 200
Allen 24, 46, 66, 91, 98, 127, 130, 132, 136, 147, 154, 155, 156, 157, 158, 172, 186, 189, 191, 194, 203, 214, 218, 232, 233, 237, 242, 243, 256, 260, 274, 275, 277
Allen House 145
Allers 100, 226
Allgier 173
Allgood 126, 127
Alligood 172
Allison 115, 213
Allmon 137
Alsop 37, 132, 201
Altenthal 128, 290, 291
Amelung 156, 163
Amelunke 156, 280, 293, 294
American Legion 119, 123, 128, 129, 130, 144, 147, 158
American Red Cross 130
Amos 64, 166, 179, 208
Amtrak 142
Anderson 26, 27, 83, 97, 104, 137, 165, 247, 252
Angel 295
Angle 194
Ansberry 296
Antonsen 115
Antwerpen 164
Appleton 42
Arbor 4
Arington 167
Armagost 176
Armor 19
Armour 19, 173
Armstrong 19, 81, 82, 83, 126, 156, 157, 177, 202, 204, 227, 236, 241
Arnhart 126
Arnold 217, 234
Arnsberg 22, 81
Arnzen 134, 159
Asborn 220
Ashcroft 64, 188
Asher 267, 269
Ashley 12, 13, 14, 154, 246
Ashton 99
Ashworth 168
Atchison 212

Atchley 159, 285
Ates 24
Athey 137
Atwell 189
Aufdenberg 91, 160, 161, 177
Augilar 128
Austin 185, 204, 218, 219, 280
Autry 193
Avakian 233
Aylett 201

B

Babcock 79
Bachmann 258
Backler 155
Bacon 86
Bader 208
Badger 139
Baebler 181, 292, 293
Baidy 99
Bailard 213
Bailey 22, 192, 288
Baird 292
Baker 62, 81, 90, 98, 99, 132, 138, 157, 172, 207, 212, 277, 280, 293
Bald Knobbers 140
Baldwin 198
Bales 243
Ball 238
Ballew 11, 97, 185
Bandy 185
Bangers 138
Bangert 27, 34, 62, 130, 136, 157, 206, 235, 239, 253
Banks 90, 91
Baptist Bible College 99
Barbaroski 270
Barber 98, 202, 284
Barger 286
Barker 223
Barks 98, 99, 154, 157, 182, 191, 192, 253, 259, 271, 275, 281
Barnes 137, 157
Barnett 222
Barnhouse 99
Barr 85, 189
Barret 220
Barrett 128, 187, 266, 274, 277
Barringer 176
Bartels 45, 66, 83, 114, 115, 138, 139, 157, 158, 160, 162, 181, 226, 229, 249, 254, 262
Bartles 45, 160, 162, 208, 286
Bartlett 136
Basel 112
Bast 155, 158, 242, 277
Bates 206
Battery F 118
Battle of Cape Girardeau 119
Battle of Horse Shoe Bend 13
Battle of New Orleans 12, 13
Battle of the Bulge 34
Battle Row 121
Baudendistl 218
Baugh 98, 127, 132, 190, 218, 219
Baumann 161
Baumgardt 160
Baumgarth 165
Baxter 268
Bayliss 248
Bazaar 288
Bazzell 281
Beal 164, 272
Beale 28
Beall 286
Bean 32, 189
Beard 292
Beasley 141
Beattie 130, 185
Beatties 120

Beauteau 28
Beaver 252, 293
Becker 136, 157, 286
Bedford 289
Bedhe 186
Bedwell 261
Been 284
Beers 100
Beeson 139
Beggs 132, 133, 158, 162, 249, 250, 265
Begley 97
Behrens 230, 254, 262
Behymer 252
Beiser 163
Beissink 128
Belarrus 103
Bell 158, 275
Belmont 142
Below 132, 133, 167
Bendel 216
Bender 190
Benkendoerfer 110
Bennett 135, 161, 193, 246, 281
Bentley 100
Berberich 184
Bergen 246
Bergfeld 240
Bergmann 228, 257
Berkbigler 150
Berry 18, 203, 213, 235, 275
Bertling 273
Besel 291
Bess 99, 280
Best 22, 46, 66, 160, 161, 182
Bethe 100
Bethel Baptist Church 12, 97, 103
Beussink 51, 128, 129, 138, 139, 158, 159, 160
Bibb 212
Bickett 237
Biegner 166
Bierschwal 65, 115, 125, 160, 203, 229, 262, 271, 297
Bierschwale 160
Bierschwalen 160
Bierschwall 160
Bill Wallace Ins. 75
Billings 43
Billingsley 173
Bingenheimer 22, 86, 210
Bingo World 140
Biri 52
Birk 130, 132, 136, 141, 142, 160, 161, 162, 175, 193, 218, 242, 243, 246, 256, 286
Birkner 112
Bishop 136, 238
Black 45, 181, 258
Black Forest 48
Blackman 62, 136, 283
Blackwendt 277
Blair 132, 244
Blalock 253
Blank 100, 286
Blatner 126
Blattel 159
Blattner 43, 100, 125, 202, 222, 224
Blaylock 29, 157, 161, 162, 218, 219, 253, 289
Blease 99
Bledsoe 161
Blevens 62
Blomeyer 4, 81
Bloom 6
Blount 13, 14
Blow 193
Blumberg 58
Blumenberg 58, 162, 167, 181, 271
Blumer 254
Bock 160, 161, 162, 229, 250, 286
Bodenstein 127, 130,

156, 162, 163, 164, 209, 267, 295
Bodie 230
Boehme 123, 163, 265
Boeller 179
Boettcher 114, 115
Bogan 199
Boganpohl 216
Bogenpohl 216, 268
Bogy 238
Bohnenkamp 99
Bohnert 29
Bohnsack 100, 112, 138, 220, 262
Boitnott 138, 139
Bolen 90, 161, 254
Boles 173, 222
Bollerslev 60, 61
Bollinger 10, 11, 16, 17, 19, 23, 37, 38, 79, 92, 97, 98, 128, 129, 130, 132, 133, 157, 163, 164, 168, 169, 176, 182, 188, 194, 197, 201, 212, 241, 276, 293, 297
Bollinger Mill 16, 21, 23, 24, 38, 123
Bolm 251
Bomar 141
Bond 91, 195
Boner 11
Bonk 249
Bonner 205
Bonney 252
Boohnsack 230
Boohnsacker 230
Boon 93
Boone 165, 194, 195, 237, 264
Boos 296
Boren 47, 48, 278
Boresove 166
Borgfield 18, 110, 137, 140, 209, 222, 261
Borne 97, 102, 259
Bose 101, 229
Boshart 189
Boss 41, 44, 45, 46, 66, 77, 104, 120, 121, 141, 207, 234, 290
Boucher 237
Boudinot 52
Boutin 145
Boutwell 99
Bowers 29, 83, 89, 99, 144, 162, 164, 166, 169, 272
Bowman 15, 24, 28, 31, 37, 39, 84, 116, 141, 223, 251, 253, 280
Box 104
Boy Scouts 140, 141
Boyd 11, 97, 253
Boyer 285
Bracher 190
Braddock 156
Bradford 138, 139, 197
Bradley 11, 173
Bradshaw 206
Bradsher 224
Brady 173, 250
Braig 231
Brainard 284
Brainerd 248
Brakebusch 100, 160
Brakebush 160
Brame 237
Brand 184, 280
Brandenburg 110
Brands 231, 279, 296
Brandt 112
Branscum 138
Branson 140
Brase 115, 126, 136, 164, 165, 178, 226, 249
Brass 220
Brauer 296
Braun 165
Braunschweig 114
Bray 45, 66, 234, 247, 248, 267

Brazeau Presbyterian Church 117
Brazel 136
Brazil 106, 141
Breakfast Optimist Club 140
Breckenridge 29
Breeze 222
Brehrens 263
Brenecke 99
Brennecke 101, 121, 165, 166, 167, 169, 176, 179, 213, 216, 251, 252, 254, 256, 260, 284, 291
Brennecke Chevrolet Co. 46, 145
Brevard 20
Brewer 256, 281
Brick School House 81
Bright 37, 234
Brightwell 212
Brim 244
Brimmer 229
Brinkman 160, 226
Brinkopf 186, 226
Britt 167
Britzman 90
Broadway 194
Brock 132, 167, 168
Brockett 54, 91, 204
Brommer 42
Brooks 15, 77, 81, 86, 221, 234
Brooks House 15
Brookside 22, 23, 83
Brookside 4-H Club 23
Brookside Park 119, 136, 148
Broshius 138, 159, 168
Broshuis 168
Brothers 258
Brothers of the Brush 144, 145
Brotherhon 46, 66
Broussard 89
Brown 54, 65, 80, 82, 83, 90, 91, 96, 98, 99, 119, 125, 132, 133, 137, 142, 162, 166, 167, 168, 169, 175, 176, 180, 183, 194, 196, 207, 222, 274, 281, 283, 284, 288, 295
Browning 199, 268, 283
Brudl 169, 170
Brue 234
Bruegging 214
Bruene 286
Bruening 96, 123, 127, 141, 144
Bruening Company 144
Brugger 284
Bruhl 30, 169, 170, 171, 258
Bruihl 28, 162, 220
Brul 169, 170, 171, 258
Brune 25, 173, 289
Brunke 30
Brunner 100
Bruns 162
Brunswich School Pharmacy 42
Brunswick 114
Brusse 229
Bryan 135, 194
Bryant 174, 237
Buchanon 28
Buchheit 287
Buchterkirchen 226
Buckeye 81
Buckner 14, 16, 146
Budlong 102, 110
Buehler 292
Buerkle 48
Buessink 65
Buetiger 100
Bull 12, 97, 100, 101, 133, 226, 293
Bullinger 41
Bultemeyer 258
Bultz 298
Bums 172

Burch 83
Burdette 231, 285
Burford 23, 37, 125, 195
Burfordville 4, 10, 21, 23, 24, 36, 37, 50, 79, 81, 85, 144, 214
Burfordville Covered Bridge 23
Burgett 238
Burk 91, 254
Burke 141
Burnette 136
Burns 171, 172, 181, 221, 245, 291
Burress 138
Burtles 190, 215
Burton 253
Busch 211, 262
Bush 177
Butcher 237
Butler 138, 174
Buttram 161, 286
Butz 100, 133
Buxton 180
Bynum 248
Byrd 10, 11, 12, 14, 20, 36, 37, 83, 84, 85, 86, 89, 99, 133, 157, 172, 173, 178, 190, 234
Byrd Creek 22, 23, 28, 82, 110, 121
Byrd Township 44
Byrds Creek 13
Byrne 208

C

C. H. Sander Sales 70, 48, 143, 145
C. H. Wolter Buggy and Harness Shop 19
C. O. Snider Restaurant and Saloon 28
Cagle 212
Caillot 133
Cain 11
Caldwell 82, 83, 117, 128, 130, 146, 161, 173, 174, 221, 222, 223, 253, 290, 291
Caldwell-Snider Post 115 128
Calvary Baptist Church 98, 99
Calvin Phillips Excavating 62
Cameron 38, 116
Camp 198
Camp Enterprise 141
Camp Fremont 118, 119
Camp Funston 119
Camp Lewallen 127
Campbell 16, 45, 66, 170, 188, 232, 234, 281
Campen 247
Campster 81, 82, 126
Campster 4-H Club 82, 125, 126
Campster District 82
Campster Ladies Club 125
Campster School 81, 82, 125, 126
Campster Welfare Club 82
Canada 10, 44
Cane Creek 81, 121
Cannon 14, 16, 19, 120, 174, 206
Cantrell 125
Cape Christian Academy 94
Cape County Milling Company 20, 23, 24, 36, 37, 38, 45, 111
Cape Girardeau County Central School 91, 92
Cape Girardeau County Historical Society 12, 23, 38

Cape Girardeau Presbyterian Church 104
Cape Normal School 84
Cardell 189
Carlisle Training School 85, 86, 92
Carlton 91
Carlton College 92
Carmack 201
Carnett 103
Carondelet 10
Carr 98
Carrier 272
Carrington 84
Carron 29
Carson 89, 127
Carter 119, 194, 290
Carvey 24
Carvin 126
Casper 189
Cassell 288
Cassidy 132
Cates 228
Cato 199
Catt 262
Cattron 91
Cauble 189
Cauvey 81
Cavaner 253
Cavender 11
Central Elementary 85, 86, 87
Central Hotel 29
Ceylon 125
Chaferman 116
Chamber of Commerce 51, 54, 131, 144
Chamberlain 97
Chandler 291
Chang 248
Chapman 231
Chappel 99
Charlton 99
Chasteen 63
Chastner 174
Cheatam 196
Cheatum 195
Cheek 233, 295
Chequer 211
Chesley 202
Chester 41
Chicago World's Fair 37
Child Development Center 109
Childs 116
Chiles 6, 109, 174, 175
Chilton 237
China 45, 52, 80
Chostner 100, 167, 179
Christ Lutheran Church 27
Chron 287
Chronister 175
Chu Lai 19
Chubboy 12
Civil Defense 34, 35
Civil War 19, 20, 22, 23, 24, 25, 27, 28, 30, 65, 85, 97, 103, 107, 108, 109, 112, 115, 118, 119, 142
Clark 11, 212, 286
Clausmann 156
Clay 20, 157, 198, 241
Cleary 275
Clement 286
Cleveland 201
Clery 172
Clifton 128, 147, 174, 175, 275
Clingingsmith 175, 176, 218, 220
Clingsmith 130
Clinton 225
Clippard 28, 29, 36, 81, 82, 83, 84, 132, 138, 154, 164, 176, 180, 195, 196, 198, 204, 238, 265
Clodfelter 120, 277
Cloninger 245
Clover Hill 81
Cobb 138, 292
Cobble 104, 154, 164,

269
Cochran 14, 21, 141, 154, 174, 277
Coffee 268
Coker 28, 81, 84
Cole 52, 120
Coleman 15
College of Mortuary Science 46
Collier 90
Collins 19, 20, 21, 118, 119, 255, 287
Collins-Moore 81
Collishonn 154
Colman 176
Columbia 94
Columbian Bible Society 97
Colyer 86, 182
Combs 99
Comeford 286
Comer 236, 237
Commiski 294
Community Chest 130
Company A 118
Company C 118
Company K 118
Compas 81
Condor 168
Confederate Army 37
Conley 89
Connecticut 67
Conner 41, 42, 89, 126
Conquest 125
Conrad 130, 132, 133, 141, 211, 276, 281
Conway 298
Cook 55, 58, 99, 132, 133, 137, 154, 155, 162, 165, 178, 242, 274, 275, 285, 293
Cooke 133
Cooper 64, 176, 177, 200, 275
Copeland 253
Copman 53
Corbin 99, 109
Corcoran 291
Cordell 120, 185
Corinth 11
Corinthian Baptist Church 121
Corning 57
Cornwallis 172
Cornwell 281
Corola 32
Cosby 198, 200
Costner 120, 132
Cotner 23, 245
Cotter 247, 248
Cottner 175, 176, 179
Cousins 12
Covenant Christian Center 26
Covington 64
Cowan 29, 82, 106
Cowell 137
Cowen 120
Cox 82, 106, 109, 126, 173, 174, 179, 183, 190, 191, 272
Cox Memorial Hall 97, 109
Coyler 201, 275
Cozby 154
Crabtree 63, 92
Cracraft 36, 52, 62, 64, 92, 127, 128, 130, 137, 144, 145, 177, 293
Cracroft 177
Crader 91, 128, 293
Crafford 28
Craft 30, 175, 176, 190
Crafton 203
Craig 138, 275
Craiglow 137
Cramer 28, 156, 220
Crawford 89, 176
Craycraft 177
Craycroft 177
Creacraft 177
Creamer 231
Crecraft 177

Creicraft 177
Cresap 220
Creycraft 177
Criddle 14, 15, 16, 19, 29, 81, 85, 99, 166, 177, 227, 247, 280
Crimmins 132
Crites 24, 25, 33, 34, 35, 89, 92, 129, 132, 137, 155, 173, 176, 177, 178, 179, 186, 195, 218, 219, 220, 232, 242, 246, 248, 253, 260, 261, 269, 275
Critesville 81
Critz 275
Croll 38
Cromer 136
Cromwell 250
Cronester 175
Crook 176
Crooke 99
Crosby 174
Cross 98, 99, 156, 288
Crouch 138
Crouse 221
Crow 184, 292
Crowe 266
Crowell 170
Crump 4, 11, 81
Crutsinger 96
Crytes 23
Culbertson 106
Cummins 194
Cunningham 24, 109, 125, 126
Cupples 19
Cureton 245
Currin 11
Curry 29, 63
Curtis 201
CWA 147

D

Dailey 246
Daley 128
Dallas 52
Dalton 121, 167, 212, 243, 273, 283
Dambach 22, 128
Daniel 120, 137, 169, 248
Daniels 53, 89, 169, 284
Dankel 160, 294
Dankels 187
Danridge 201
Danz 258
Darnell 129
Daugherty 23, 37, 101, 104, 120, 214, 291, 297, 298
Daughtery 214
Daume 22, 23, 81, 82, 100, 110, 164, 179
Davault 132, 133, 137, 165, 166, 167, 176, 178, 179, 213, 254, 256, 291, 295
Davenport 89, 137, 232
Davey 63
Davidson 90, 132
Davies 161
Davis 12, 14, 49, 92, 97, 101, 102, 104, 120, 127, 128, 130, 156, 179, 180, 181, 183, 184, 185, 191, 204, 215, 223, 224, 242, 266
Dawson 160
Day 173
Deal 285
Dean 17, 132
Dearmont 85, 120
DeBakey 195
DeBrock 168
Deck 92
Decker 41, 94, 96, 180, 181, 250
DeClue 137, 138
Declue 137
Deevers 165
Deimund 83
Delap 19, 79, 181
Delapp 181
Delesser 37
DeLisle 165
Dellinger 190
Delporte 224
Delvean 102
Dement 160, 162, 175, 181, 184, 215, 241, 263, 271
DeMolay 123
Dempsey 190
Deneke 114, 115, 136, 217, 249, 262, 297
Denman 57
Denmark 60, 125, 141
Dennis 120
Dennison 120
Desert Storm 119
Desha 221
Desloge 91
Desselman 166
Detring 58, 160, 162, 175, 181, 184, 215, 263, 271
Detter 268
Deuschle 110
Deutscher Voksfreund 57
Devault 169
Devenport 128
DeVore 53, 235, 275
Devore 33, 52, 53, 154, 198, 199, 200, 213
Devore's Feed Store 33, 34
Dial 213
Diamund 293, 294
Dibrell 133
Dickerson 130, 221, 272, 274
Dickey 38, 202
Dickman 261
Dickmann 22, 83
Dickson 45, 99
Diebold 240
Diefenbach 25, 123
Diehlstadt 92
Dietz 286
Dillard 237
Dillon 285
Dinkins 106
Dippold 263, 285
Dirnberger 77, 181, 182, 278
Disse 288
Dittlinger 119, 198
Dixon 173
Doberenz 141
Dobron 167
Dockery 226
Dockins 24, 27, 46, 66, 168, 169, 182, 198
Dockter 169, 170
Dodson 99
Doederlein 112
Doemel 219
Doere 114
Doering 163, 252
Doerris 115
Dohn 41
Dohogne 139
Donaldson 231
Doniphan 144
Donnell 234
Donnelly 256
Donner 138
D'Onofrio 262
Dooley 167
Doolittle 173
Dormeyer 225
Dorrie 216
Dost 58, 91, 113
Dougan 6, 10, 15, 254
Dougherty 10, 11, 19, 232
Douglas 221
Douglass 154
Dousay 200
Dow 91, 154, 155
Dowdy 106
Downey 269, 277
Dowty 101
Dralle 115, 251, 260
Draper 203, 281
Dresden 32
Droeste 248
Druckenmiller 182, 183, 276, 281
Drum 24, 25, 29, 38, 81, 84, 173, 183, 222, 236, 243, 245, 251, 253, 276
Drum Town 24
Drury 142, 206
Drusch 142
Dryden 224
Dubs 81, 249
Duden 114
Dudley 176
Duffey 106
Duffy 255, 256
Duhaime 190, 224
Dunbar 63
Duncan 173
Dunklin 174, 206, 280
Dunlap 194
Dunn 12, 26, 30, 106, 148, 183, 184, 185, 214, 275, 288
Duperier 63
Duplissey 175
Dupuis 169
Durant 250
Durham 237
Dutzow 114
DuVal 110
Dyer 260

E

Eagle Ridge Christian School 94
Eaglin 225
Eaker 178, 212, 241
Eakin 256
Eakins 53, 89, 178
Earhart 175
Earles 11
Eastern Star 33, 137
Eastin 63
Eatherton 111
Eaton 194
Ebson 161
Eckhardt 19
Eddleman 126
Ede 275
Edel 179
Edell 164
Eden Seminary 102
Eden Theological Seminary 116
Edinger 242
Edmundson 99
Edwards 19, 54, 136, 142, 212, 260
Eftink 200
Eggers 184, 185, 204, 232, 238
Eggiman 27, 94, 100, 137, 286
Eggimann 100, 167
Ehelebe 270, 271
Eichhorn 170
Eichmeyer 157
Eifert 90, 246
Eighth Infantry 118
Eighth Missouri Cavalry 118
Eisenberg 82
Eisenhower 256
Elders 99
Elfrink 51, 134, 139, 158, 159, 168, 278, 285
Ellenberger 166
Elliot 184, 215, 268, 271
Elliott 106, 184, 186
Ellis 16, 29, 83, 126, 164, 221, 233, 299
Elmore 238
Eltzroth 205
Emanuel Evangelical Church 116
Emanuel United Church of Christ 116
Emery 63, 99
Enbrecht 229
Enderle 100
Engelhart 30, 82, 107, 140, 184, 185, 264, 289
Engelmann 22, 123, 164, 179
Engineer Regiment 118
England 44, 141
Englehart 82, 83, 184, 185, 235, 278, 283
Englemann 179
English 20, 54, 86, 101, 120, 133, 185, 203, 221, 226, 229, 235, 238, 252, 255, 262, 274, 297
Eps 163
Epworth League 115
Ermertz 245
Ernst 175
Ervin 81, 190, 234
Eschenfeld 83, 110
Eshbaugh 47
Essmann 141
Essner 279
Estes 82, 91, 137, 145, 223, 241, 242, 280, 292, 295
Etherton 126
Eubank 132
Evangelical Lutheran St. John Church 22
Evangelical Synod of North America 102, 110
Evangelical United Church of Christ 19, 116
Evans 14, 84, 139, 174, 209, 218
Evening Optimist Club 140
Ewing 184
Excelsior Lodge 441 137
Eydmann 277

F

F.C.E. 31
Fadler 58
Fagg 266
Fairview United Methodist Church 99
Falk 175
Fararrer 258
Faries 292
Faris 104
Farmer 16, 132, 243
Farmstead 298
Farrar 126
Farris 291
Farrow 180, 185, 186, 191, 192, 215, 266
Fassold 225
Fayard 278
Feemster 252
Feeney 63
Feiner 90
Feise 299
Fellows 192, 193, 198, 200
Felts 212
Felty 99, 158, 198, 199
Fenimore 266, 298
Fennell 234
Fenner 132, 291
Fenzel 252
Ferguson 20, 98, 135, 198, 199
Ferst 161, 193
Feszold 65
Fette 238
Fetterhoff 64
Feuerhahn 100
Ficken 239
Fiedler 225
Fiehler 128, 129
Field 285
Fielder 225
Fiesler 22
Fiftieth Regiment 118
Fikuart 212
Filer 194
Finch 38
Finland 125, 141
Finley 161
Finney 204, 260
First Apple Creek Presbyterian Church 104
First Baptist Church 101, 103
First Federal Savings and Loan Association 76
First Military District 118
First Presbyterian Church 104, 117
Fisher 100, 205, 261, 299
Fishler 112
Fismer 110
Fitzpatrick 132, 201
Flachsbart 111
Flannery 138
Flat River 48, 91
Flat River Optimist Club 140
Fleming 97, 98, 133, 201, 277, 292, 294
Flenge 158
Flenzi 120
Fliege 89
Flies 299
Flin 98, 120
Flinn 117, 292
Flint 97, 194
Flintge 101
Flori 279
Florida 63
Flowers 120
Floyd 180
Fluegge 32, 68, 127, 136, 160, 161, 179, 198, 230
Flynn 238
Folenweider 189
Folk 144
Forbis 184
Ford 24, 29, 67, 83, 84, 101, 116, 230, 270, 272, 284, 285
Forester 258
Formosa 99
Fornkahl 225, 226
Fornkohl 237, 239
Forrest 154, 155
Fort A-D 118, 119
Fort Mims 13
Fort Wayne, IN 41
Fosse 5, 135, 289, 290
Foster 277
Fountain 28, 100
Fourth Missouri Infantry 22
Fowler 137, 285
Fox 83, 201, 275
France 10, 37, 103, 119, 141
Francis 135, 157, 274
Franck 268
Franke 110, 140
Franklin 76, 256
Frankmore 170
Frary 117
Frazee 246
Frederick 136
Fredricks 252
Freeburg 62
Freeland 176
Freeman 57, 200, 221
Freeza 156
Freeze 105
Freidrich 245
Fremont Rangers 118
French 132, 160
Frentzel 190, 224
Frenzel 39
Freund 154, 155, 186
Frey 100
Frick 267
Friedel 222
Friedheim 4
Friedhof 226
Friedhoff 225
Friedrich 49, 110, 127, 130, 132, 134, 137, 139, 168, 178, 186, 187, 188, 201, 227, 251, 268, 270, 290
Friend 156
Friese 29, 164
Frisch 32
Frissel 84
Frissell 83
Fritsche 58
Frizel 16, 17, 19, 96, 133, 188, 220
Frizell 97
Frizzell 28
Froemsdorf 127, 215
Fronabarger 29, 72, 83, 99, 191, 194, 242, 281, 296
Fronaberger 29, 59, 82
Fruitland Community Church 26
Fruitland Methodist Church 25
Fuehler 193
Fuerth 178
Fuhrman 39
Fukumitsu 256
Fulbright 22, 28, 81, 99, 188, 189, 243, 251, 253, 265
Fulenwider 24, 120, 121, 138, 189, 285
Fulenwider Drugs 145
Fulkerson 246
Futrell 28, 29, 189, 190
Fylenwider 19, 79

G

Gable 138
Gaebler 113
Gaines 102, 133
Gaither 213
Galbraith 253
Galloway 99, 246
Gambill 66
Gammon 98, 133
Gannon 156
Garcia 282
Gardiner 85
Garland 136, 220
Garner 51, 190, 214, 231, 248, 252
Garratt 254
Garrett 278, 283
Garris 91
Garrison 99
Gartung 98
Gartz 227
Garvey 225
Gasche 156
Gasper 295
Gassner 111
Gast 27
Gatlin 222
Gebhard 224
Geisendoerfer 30
Geiser 100, 125
Gellately 138
Gemeinhardt 258
Georgens 262
Georgia 27, 103
Gephart 288
Gerard 278
Gerecke 112, 130
Gerharter 219, 289
Gerichs 290
Gerlach 111
Gerler 30, 113, 170, 257, 298, 299
German Evangelical Church 100, 101, 110
German Methodist Church 115
German Reformed Church 97
Geron 286
Gerth 113
Geske 113
Getts 136
Gholson 82, 221
Gibbs 94, 135
Giboney 108, 238
Gibson 164
Giddings 97, 98
Gideon 92
Gieschen 298
Gilbert 204, 225, 236
Gillespie 39, 172, 191
Gillette 132
Gilliland 97, 98, 175, 292
Gillispie 173
Gilmore 136, 185, 278
Gladish 39, 52, 89, 128, 191, 195, 196, 197, 278
Glass 90, 94, 99
Glasscock 19, 108
Glassey 182
Glenallen 33
Glenn 138
Gluckhertz 190
Glueck 41
Glueckhertz 42
Gluekhertz 100
Gnatt 14
Gneissl 171
Gober 28
Gockel 15, 19, 42, 92, 121, 204
Godair 221
Godsey 132
Godwin 38, 83, 91, 92, 116, 154, 178, 218, 276
Goehman 98, 164
Goehmann 110
Goertner 110
Goforth 81, 224
Gohn 94, 137, 190, 224, 232, 238, 286
Golden 81, 90, 94
Goldman 194
Golightly 116, 190, 191, 223
Gonce 175
Goode 201
Goodin 93
Goodson 29, 90, 187
Goodspeed 11, 12, 14, 19, 20, 100, 118, 119, 181, 198
Goodwin 38, 39, 96, 168, 191, 212
Gorman 185
Gorski 225
Gorton 140
Gosche 182
Goshen 81, 116
Goslin 141
Goza 128, 130, 195, 271
Graden 120
Graeve 225
Graff 208
Grahm 205
Grandstaff 193
Grange 26
Grange Stock Company 28
Granger 16, 96, 104, 188
Grant 96, 133, 141, 143, 147
Grass 168
Gratz 179, 299
Graulich 163
Graves 98
Gray 191, 285
Grayson 120
Grebe 29, 50, 154, 160, 226, 229
Grebing 127, 141, 225
Green 11, 30, 31, 97, 101, 102, 103, 120, 126, 127, 157, 165, 173, 186, 191, 192, 195, 269, 286
Greene 165, 242
Greenlee 158
Greenwell 224
Greenwood 180
Greer 132, 184, 226
Gregg 125, 243
Gregory 85
Greten 273
Griffing 221
Griffith 132, 208
Griffy 132
Grillen 257
Grimm 175
Grindstaff 46, 66, 128, 130, 157, 161, 182, 192, 193, 233
Grojean 225
Gross 94, 136, 251
Grossheider 125, 126, 166, 190, 239, 274
Grossman 233
Grosvenor 180
Grout 23
Groves 236
Gruenloh 209
Gruhne 163
Grumbrecht 260
Grutz 227
Guemmer 256
Guenter 115
Guenther 284
Guerin 250
Guild 132, 133, 188, 297
Guilliams 66, 182
Gumplemeyr 184
Guth 193, 265
Guthing 11

H

Haake 216
Haas 258, 279
Haase 111, 239
Habekost 156
Haberfeller 282
Hacker 62, 291
Haddock 234
Hadjuk 165
Haertling 229
Hafernik 165
Hagans 41, 118, 126
Hager 51, 89, 98, 112, 120, 160, 254, 286
Hahn 24, 162, 193, 197, 201, 263, 277, 285, 286, 295, 296
Hahs 24, 25, 29, 85, 98, 99, 130, 136, 137, 194, 195, 208, 232, 285
Haines 166
Hale 28, 98, 120, 241, 286
Hall 26, 142, 169, 172, 194, 230, 232, 275, 277, 291
Hallerweger 184
Hallisburton 254
Hallwein 277
Haman 125, 126, 213, 281
Hambright 132, 133
Hamilton 176, 221, 226, 258, 264
Hamlin 86
Hamm 77, 298
Hampton 178
Han 254
Hanesworth 99
Hankinson 132
Hanlin 241, 242
Hanna 99
Hanners 195, 232, 295
Hanover 114
Hanover Church 111
Hanschen 178, 219, 277
Hansel 224
Hanselmann 110
Hanson 126
Happel 239
Happle 160
Harbison 150, 156
Hard 178
Hardin 221
Hardy 24, 127, 141, 205, 273
Hargens 217
Hargraves 271
Harkelrode 11
Harmon 123, 163
Harper 176
Harrass 292
Harries 204
Harris 24, 28, 29, 83, 84, 97, 98, 120, 132, 133, 137, 177, 178, 194, 199, 204, 272, 287, 292
Harrisburg 107
Harrison 11, 92, 126, 184, 206, 257
Hart 29
Hartle 6, 16, 62, 77, 86, 92, 118, 127, 128, 129, 155, 163, 195, 196, 197, 200, 203, 204, 229, 233, 269
Hartline 200
Hartman 98, 102, 110, 286
Hartmann 186
Hartsfield 16, 133, 188
Hartung 203, 258
Harvey 46, 216, 297
Hary 91
Hatler 28, 84
Hauenschild 158
Haupt 198, 218, 230
Haw 109
Hawke 213
Hawkins 15, 62, 137, 180, 233
Hawn 261
Hawthorne 134, 221
Hayden 269
Hayes 28, 29, 98, 223
Haynes 99, 136, 164, 197, 269, 287
Hays 10, 11, 15, 42, 98, 143, 144, 172, 248, 284
Hazelwood 137
Head 126, 190
Headen 181
Headrick 99
Hearn 99
Heartling 30
Heath 133
Hebron Church 101
Hecht 41, 256
Hecker 62, 166
Heckt 137
Hedge 179
Hedwig 219
Hehner 271
Heidelbarger 218
Heider 110
Heimbaugh 297
Heimberg 262
Heise 43, 44, 179, 226, 239, 293
Helderman 74, 81, 184, 195
Helibreck 249
Helmkampf 298
Hempstead 14
Hemsdale 171
Hency 208
Henderson 38, 39, 44, 91, 93, 104, 109, 128, 130, 132, 133, 137, 141, 182, 191, 194, 197, 198, 201, 289, 291
Hendricks 203
Hendrix 100, 176, 177, 196, 198, 199, 200, 201, 203, 287, 293
Henley 201, 228, 235, 275
Hennecke 82, 111, 259, 280
Hennig 112
Henrich 111
Henry 44, 84, 109, 133, 137, 138, 291
Hensley 188, 272
Henson 98, 99, 236, 275
Hente 125
Henze 112, 162
Herman 100
Hermann 22, 110, 258
Herold 51
Herrman 240
Herrmann 284
Hersinger 198
Hertel 102, 110
Herzog 162

Hess 6, 63, 135, 201
Hessenflow 239
Hester 203, 297
Heuer 132, 235, 238, 272, 295
Hey 160
Heyde 37, 38, 46, 62, 130, 133, 150, 201, 202, 234
Hickman 120
Hicks 92, 221
Hickson 190
Higgins 292
High Hill 81
Highway 25 Diner 141
Hildebrand 227
Hilderbrand 81
Hill 63, 101, 132, 133, 136, 220, 237, 267, 275, 277, 283, 291
Hille 287
Hillier 24
Hilmer 299
Hilpert 27, 169, 170, 226
Himmelsbach 118
Hinchey 154
Hinck 166, 178
Hinderberger 202, 227
Hines 84, 86, 96, 127, 128, 130, 141, 145, 204
Hinkebein 128, 129, 130, 134, 138, 139
Hinkle 28, 29, 36, 84, 181
Hinkler 29
Hinze 90
Hitt 12, 52, 89, 94, 101, 126, 147, 184, 225, 232, 234, 267
Hobbs 81, 175, 222
Hobeck 25, 138
Hockenberry 132
Hoeckele 165
Hoef 267
Hoeger 171
Hoehl 293
Hoehne 258
Hoelscher 67, 161
Hoffman 22, 50, 57, 86, 89, 121, 175, 179, 186, 210, 252, 288, 289, 290
Hoffmann 23, 140, 145
Hoffmeister 76, 128, 129, 145, 175, 261, 294
Hoffstadter 169
Hohler 98, 130
Holcomb 101
Holden 38, 202
Holland 141, 185, 200, 295
Hollenbeck 231
Holley 185, 238, 277, 297
Hollister 98
Hollman 114
Holloway 137, 271
Holly 203
Holman 203
Holmes 22, 24, 96, 195
Holt 133, 234
Holweg 285
Holwein 277
Holzum 158, 159, 168
Homburg 100
Hood 248, 285
Hooper 133
Hope 30, 31, 97, 98, 130, 133, 202, 203, 207, 242, 254, 284, 292, 293
Hopfer 265
Hopkins 130, 167, 199, 239, 240, 272
Hopper 132, 190
Horn 21, 28, 230, 239, 270
Hornberg 162
Horne 213, 288
Horner 99
Horrell 20, 36, 81, 82, 83, 86, 89, 120, 139, 234
Horst 158
Horvath 165
Hosea 280
Hoskey 241
Hosking 241
Houck 10, 11, 12, 13, 14, 19, 20, 25, 29, 32, 79, 85, 97, 109, 181, 194, 238, 297
Houghton 175
Houk 195, 198
Housman 186, 266
Hovis 89
Howard 28, 41, 45, 76, 85, 90, 127, 132, 160, 177, 198, 203, 205, 229, 235, 239, 245, 272, 297
Howell 132, 200, 285
Hrabik 138
Hubbard 28
Hubbell 10, 11, 27
Hubble 10, 79
Hubble Creek 10, 11, 13, 16, 27, 37, 51, 65, 79, 102, 121, 122, 146, 147
Huck 90, 138, 248
Huckstep 130, 145
Huckstep Springs 34
Hudgins 213
Hudson 162
Huebel 186, 196, 203, 204
Hueneke 262
Huffman 29, 259
Hufstedler 206
Hughes 137, 204, 236, 274
Hughey 120, 175
Huhn 290
Hulett 288
Hulsey 218
Hulshof 134, 139
Humes 136, 138
Humphry 132
Hunnecke 259
Hunsaker 133, 251
Hunt 132, 133, 176, 199, 213, 254
Hunter 34, 37, 121, 132, 133, 172, 207, 250, 251, 266
Huntley 234
Hunze 166, 226, 239
Hurst 138, 237
Huston 203
Hutchinson 221
Hutchison 221
Huter 161, 210
Hutson 128, 129, 132, 133, 242, 275, 296
Hutteger 229
Hutton 204
Hyson 129

I

Idell 168, 179
Illers 28, 39, 40, 49, 91, 111, 127, 128, 130, 132, 133, 163, 204, 205, 212, 226, 229, 240, 241, 259, 260, 261, 262, 263, 277
Illspach 158
Immaculate Conception Catholic Church 94, 96, 105, 120, 123, 134
Immanuel Lutheran Church 32, 113
Inman 270
Innman 120
Institute of Political Studies, Paris, France 141
International Exposition 37
International Order of Job's Daughters 125, 137, 138
Iona 81
Irby 194
Isaac 138
Isbell 141
Ische 115

J

Jackman 90
Jackson 6, 12, 13, 46, 52, 102, 103, 175, 257, 285
Jackson Academy 85
Jackson and Southern Railroad 19, 142
Jackson Church of Christ 106
Jackson Heritage Association 2, 5, 135
Jackson Memorial VFW Auxiliary #10495 136
Jackson Military Academy 45, 85, 86, 92, 104
Jackson Pioneer 57
Jackson Post 119, 128, 158
Jacksonian Day 145
Jaco 90, 175
Jacob 237
Jacoby 115
Jaeger 22, 205, 244
Jahn 113
James 82, 99, 121, 126, 137, 142, 157, 177, 178, 191, 194, 205, 206, 223, 291, 295
James Earl Survey 14
Janet 296
Jank 229
Jankowsky 110
Jansen 206, 225, 267
Janson 55
Jarvis 225
Jean 38, 191
Jeffer 284
Jeffers 118, 119, 175, 206, 223, 242
Jefferson 11, 83
Jeffries 285
Jenkins 26, 29, 49, 121, 124, 126, 150, 174, 179, 197, 206, 207, 215, 218, 226, 256
Jensen 138
Jocob 224
Joerns 128, 207
Johannes 136
Johnson 27, 91, 97, 111, 132, 133, 138, 144, 156, 161, 174, 175, 234, 251, 262, 266, 271, 282, 297, 298
Johnston 232
Jones 51, 54, 57, 91, 109, 132, 133, 136, 138, 141, 154, 173, 177, 185, 200, 201, 207, 208, 209, 238, 269, 272, 277, 296
Jordan 183, 292
Jordon 227
Joyce 185, 238
Judd 186, 265, 266
Juden 14, 19, 81, 101, 221
June's 29
Junk 213
Jurick 110

K

Kage 81
Kain 254, 255
Kaiser 22, 25, 128
Kalkbrenner 102
Kallies 184
Kaminiski 102
Kaminsky 32
Kammrath 189
Kamp 10, 41, 74, 164, 175, 179, 209, 210, 242
Kane 261
Kansas City 25
Kanter 215, 216
Kanzler 102
Kapp 170
Karben 227
Karger 286
Karondo 126
Karrillon 205
Kaschner 160
Kassel 207, 286
Kasten 23, 30, 31, 51, 52, 54, 62, 74, 89, 107, 123, 127, 130, 132, 133, 137, 140, 187, 210, 211, 225, 233, 252, 257, 261, 266
Kasting 24, 272
Kaufman 211
Kaufmann 83, 110, 252
Kauntan 115
Kayser 22, 83
Keane 250
Keaster 237
Keathly 44
Kec 169
Keeble 231
Keeling 201
Keen 206, 222
Keene 145, 211, 212, 235
Keesee 206
Keisker 96, 111, 179, 212, 242, 255
Keller 27, 64, 81, 82, 100, 112, 126, 138, 156, 177, 213, 226, 273, 280
Kellett 48, 241
Kelley 34
Kelly 35
Kelpe 160
Kempe 249
Kendell 99
Kenne 206
Kennett 48, 51
Kennon 197
Kenny 169
Kern 279
Kerr 25
Kerstner 27, 31, 32, 42, 65, 190
Keslar 184
Kessler 130
Kester 157, 214, 270
Kesterson 184
Kettner 218
Key 212, 213
Keyser 141
Kibler 127, 128
Kiehl 107
Kiehne 33, 96, 125, 126, 257
Kiene 211, 256
Kieninger 81, 113, 145, 254, 289
Kiepe 22, 23, 226, 227
Kies 36, 43, 57, 83, 102, 116, 127, 141, 143, 144, 201, 202, 206, 213, 253, 262, 277, 288, 289, 293
Kiesel 102
Kight 213, 226, 267
Kilbues 190
Kilby 200
Kimbel 43, 44, 62, 63, 83
Kimbeland 63
Kimble 62
Kimbrell 92
Kincaid 99, 171
Kinder 24, 25, 32, 45, 53, 66, 84, 88, 89, 99, 124, 126, 138, 176, 194, 198, 199, 200, 213, 214, 226, 254, 275, 281, 287
King 90, 98, 136, 137, 173, 214, 215, 248, 249, 250, 271, 285
Kinnard 237
Kipping 32, 33, 86, 265
Kiras 273
Kirchdoerfer 126
Kirchmeyr 184
Kirk 88, 233
Kirkpatrick 157, 176, 183, 200, 222, 275
Kirn 89, 128, 129
Kistner 81
Kitchen 195
Klaproth 130
Klaus 22, 226
Klein 198, 256, 268
Kleinswonger 268
Klempe 22
Klieneberg 249
Klinkman 290
Klob 136
KluBmann 156
Kluender 162
Kluesner 138, 197
Klugsherz 190
Klunder 162
Klusmann 156, 162, 280, 293
Knaup 203
Knehans 195, 197
Kneibert 57, 83, 101, 132, 155, 184, 198, 264
Kniebert 155
Knight 272
Knights of Columbus 138, 139
Knoll 231
Knott 136, 184, 190, 215, 271, 283
Knowlan 64
Knowles 172
Knox 44, 51, 104, 128
Knupp 280
Kobler 100, 101
Koch 67, 90, 164, 208, 247, 254, 287
Kochititsky 135
Koeberl 30, 138
Koeberle 107
Koechig 110, 226, 262
Koehler 34, 45, 99, 110, 134, 139, 184, 190
Koeneke 114
Koenig 81, 113, 229, 239, 255
Koepel 113
Koeppel 279, 290
Koerber 126, 294, 295
Kohler 182, 276, 281, 282, 283
Kohlfeld 142
Koletschke 100
Kolkovich 279
Korea 119
Korossy 287
Kostal 169
Kothe 100, 160
Kracke 136
Kraegel 179
Kraemer 180, 185, 191, 215
Kraft 186, 203
Kramer 96, 258
Kranawetter 113, 215, 216
Krattli 179
Krauss 193
Kremke 271
Kreuter 112
Kroell 252, 293
Kroger 145
Kroman 22
Kromann 252
Krueger 213, 225, 226, 294
Kruger 170
Krummenacher 170
Krutz 63
Kubb 159
Kuecker 229, 289
Kuehle 81, 101, 115, 120, 166, 216, 217, 229, 259, 260
Kuehler 82
Kuellmer 76
Kueoker 299
Kugler 102
Kuntze 137, 149, 190, 217, 218, 294
Kurre 91, 92, 128, 132, 145, 155, 218, 220, 259
Kurreville 81
Kursar 260
Kuss 100
Kuster 286
Kutscher 258

L

Lacey 210
Lacy 87
Ladreiter 89, 162, 174, 206, 207, 218, 219
LaDue 220
Lages 215, 216
Lail 121, 264, 280
Lake 133, 239
Lakenan 77
Lakner 240
Lamar 190
Lamb 46, 238, 272
Lambert 272
Lampley 195
Landewe 159
Landgraf 30, 91, 113, 128, 129, 142, 215, 254, 289
Landon 132
Lane 135, 172, 194, 210, 219, 220
Laney 278
Lang 100, 163, 220, 257
Langdon 132, 133
Lange 157, 158, 160, 161, 262
Langehennig 111, 210
Langenhennig 205
Langford 138, 290
Langston 90
Lansmon 23, 198
Lape 130, 137
LaPierre 44, 47, 85, 104, 122, 132, 133, 141, 143, 144, 220, 245, 287
LaRue 138
Lashmet 262
Lasky 261
Lasten 15
Latham 104, 171
Lathem 11
Latimer 128, 136, 220
Lattimer 129
Latvia 141
Laurentius 128, 129, 134
Lauterwasser 274
Law 128, 136
Lawbaugh 238
Lawrence 210
Leadbetter 136, 295
Lebanon 99
Lebrid 173
Lee 71, 94, 142, 174, 220, 221
Leeman 112
Leemon 4
Leggett 224
Lehman 209
Lehmann 110, 116, 209
Lehner 113, 169, 257, 258
Leimer 30, 184, 220, 243
Leine 25
Leist 88, 89, 127, 233
Leming 286
Lemly 213
Lenderink 168
Leonard 15, 67, 157, 189
LeRoy 222
Lesotho 103
Lessley 154
Lett 173, 174, 190, 221, 222
Leuthold 195
Leutje 224
Lewis 6, 11, 15, 101, 126, 128, 129, 134, 177, 189, 190, 219, 235, 267, 273
Liberty 81
Liberty School 82
Lichtenegger 30, 64, 128, 141, 142, 295
Lichtenegger AG Store 145
Lichtenegger and Knowlan 64
Lichtenegger, Weiss & Fetterhoff, LLC 64
Light 176
Lightener 173
Lightner 173, 174, 221, 222
Lihn 125, 126
Liley 87, 183, 200, 222, 275, 279, 287
Limbaugh 11, 15, 23, 86, 99, 120, 137, 168, 201, 222, 223, 268, 275, 280
Lincecum 181
Linch 120
Lincoln 83, 89, 118, 205, 221, 223, 253, 257, 275, 287, 294, 299
Lindbergh 228
Lindenmeyer 249
Lindorer 258
Lindsay 175, 275
Linebarger 200, 287
Lineberger 213
Lingle 223, 224
Lingo 136
Link 81, 96, 191
Linkhorn 223
Linkogel 62
Linnenbringer 180
Linton 207
Lion's Club 51
Lischer 220
Little 292
Little German Methodist Church 34
Littleton 30, 190, 224
Litvay 63
Litz 62, 91, 148
Litzelfelner 86, 92, 93, 96, 224, 225, 234
Litzenfelner 137, 204, 255
Livers 238
Liztelfelner 168
Lloyd 173, 176
Loberg 182, 276, 281, 282
Lochart 133
Lockhart 19
Loebs 163
Loffel 190
Loftis 133
Logan 251
Lohkamp 254
Lohman 137, 145, 156, 163, 229, 280, 294
Lohmann 136
Lohr 5, 6, 89, 90, 94, 135, 206, 225
Lohrum 267
Long 14, 22, 130, 159, 190, 223, 254, 257, 288, 294
Longwell 189
Looney 34, 41, 42, 62, 101, 288
Loos 39, 44, 45, 92, 98, 110, 122, 125, 127, 128, 142, 145, 184, 241, 243
Lorberg 142, 225, 226, 273
Lorh 225
Lorimier 10, 11, 14, 23, 27, 79, 105, 172, 176, 241, 248
Lorimont 11
Loss 162
Louden 137
Love 90
Lowes 22, 100, 119, 137, 163, 164, 165, 225, 226, 239, 258, 295
Loyd 218
Luber 155
Lucke 100
Ludwig 30, 81, 82, 83, 100, 110, 126, 127, 156, 157, 166, 178, 179, 188, 203, 218, 226, 227, 228, 229, 248, 256
Ludy 234
Luecker 112
Lueder 172, 225, 275
Lueders 258
Luehrs 136, 157, 225, 239
Luetje 52, 96, 127, 227, 228
Lukow 213
Lund 12
Lupkes 27
Luscombe 106
Luten 288, 289
Lutge 227
Luttrull 228
Luytenaar 159
Lyle 297
Lynch 42, 164
Lynn 249, 253, 271
Lynwood Baptist Church 26

M

Maag 251
Mabrey 15, 37, 93, 128, 140, 144, 277
Mabuce 135, 228
MacArthur 207
Macke 27, 31, 65, 101, 124, 135, 137, 141, 160, 203, 217, 228, 229, 254, 260, 261, 262, 274, 280, 286, 287, 290, 297
Mackey 133
Madare 166
Madden 190
Madison 136
Maevers 50, 73, 136, 197, 229, 230, 242
Magill 133
Mahanney 175
Mahy 204, 237
Maintz 22, 29, 230, 269, 270
Makins 138
Malay Islands 115
Malloy 264
Malone 29, 57, 84, 182, 252, 285, 291
Maloney 98, 267
Manes 141
Mangels 29
Manley 161
Mann 113, 229, 258
Mansfield 221
Mantel 130
Manternach 279
Mantia 137
Mantz 33, 110, 128, 230
Maple 171
March 147
Margrabe 136, 218, 280
Marks 133, 241
Marler 285
Marlin 204, 230, 231, 236, 274, 289
Marmaduke 118, 119, 252
Marr 221
Marshall 91, 94
Martens 166
Martin 98, 99, 109, 139, 158, 159, 204, 218, 228, 231, 237, 262, 264, 271, 289, 296
Martindill 175
Maryville College 92
Maschka 179
Mason 88, 89, 91, 96, 127, 150, 193, 231, 233, 285, 288
Masons 28, 33, 123, 137
Massey 101
Masters 93, 142, 157, 195, 218, 245, 294
Masterson 120, 137, 138, 161, 190, 222, 224, 232, 234, 252
Mathis 288
Matthis 271
Matvy 213
Mautino 139
Maxton 295
Maxwell 97
Mayer 110, 111, 117, 218, 227
Mayfield 28, 130, 133, 137, 154, 155, 187, 188, 192, 195, 207, 232, 233, 259, 261
Mayor 164
McAdam 43
McAfee 66
McAlister 106
McAllister 184
McAtee 49, 57, 259
McBee 99
McBride 154, 240, 260
McBryde 259, 267, 268
McCain 116, 175, 176
McCall 285
McCallister 208
McCanless 177
McCarty 228
McCauley 25, 136
McClain 98, 229, 272, 273
McClard 77, 130, 138
McClary 233, 234
McClintook 161
McCombs 36, 37, 45, 46, 66, 70, 96, 120, 141, 144, 145, 201, 202, 234, 272, 293
McCrary 285
McCrate 165
McCune 63
McDonald 99, 141, 155, 224, 234, 235, 285
McDowell 94, 104, 126, 142, 178, 181, 184, 208, 234, 235, 244, 278, 284
McElrath 44
McElroy 81
McFarland 194, 253, 292
McFarlin 98
McFerron 11, 14, 81, 83, 85, 215
McGee 84, 86
McGivney 139
McGuffey 28
McGuire 16, 19, 24, 57, 79, 94, 104, 121, 130, 136, 143, 172, 201, 203, 235, 236, 275
McIntire 293
McKendree 97, 108
McKenney 83
McKibben 202
McLain 34, 130, 184, 204, 215, 236, 237, 248, 274
McLaird 237, 247
McLard 83, 248
Mclard 214
McLaughlin 236
McLemore 136
McManus 128, 130, 182
McMiken 268
McMillan 35
McMillian 169
McMillin 12
McMullen 45
McNamara 159, 250
McNeely 46, 47, 48, 49, 120, 122, 127, 128, 183, 211, 232, 244, 248, 284
McNeil 119
McRaven 221, 222
McSpadden 237, 249, 271
McSweeny 250

McWilliams 79, 133
Mech 184
Mecherle 75
Mecker 157, 256
Medley 16, 24, 27, 37, 85, 86, 104, 120, 121, 128, 132, 133, 237, 238, 287
Medlock 116, 175, 190
Meehan 146, 147
Meesey 281
Mehl 170
Mehrle 184, 238
Meier 80, 92, 127, 128, 158, 238, 239, 246, 251, 260
Meir 163
Melton 81, 200, 274
Merrill 184
Methodist Episcopal Church 24, 97, 104, 115
Metzger 290
Mexican War 119
Meyer 15, 20, 45, 46, 53, 54, 66, 82, 97, 100, 111, 114, 115, 128, 129, 133, 135, 137, 138, 141, 157, 166, 175, 182, 217, 225, 226, 232, 233, 234, 239, 251, 258, 263
Meyers 241
Meyr 89, 224, 239, 258, 265
Meystedt 190, 245
Mezger 256
Mick 137
Mier 139, 239, 240
Mifflin 221
Miinch 228
Mikesch 166
Milas 176
Milde 48, 51, 138, 141, 144, 165, 240, 241, 256, 277, 283, 284, 290
Mill 259
Mill Hill 140, 145, 146
Miller 23, 27, 28, 29, 35, 44, 46, 48, 52, 76, 91, 100, 104, 128, 130, 138, 141, 142, 143, 157, 161, 174, 177, 178, 184, 192, 195, 198, 204, 205, 214, 218, 221, 241, 242, 248, 252, 254, 263, 272, 287
Mills 10, 12, 14
Milner 92, 224
Milster 22
Miltenberger 224
Ministerial Alliance 97, 123
Minton 297
Mirly 30, 90, 155, 156, 214, 239, 258, 285, 293
Mitchell 19, 99, 170, 181, 183
Mitkos 111
Mitter 234
Mitze 247
Mizell 173, 242
Mobile River 13
Mobius 228
Modde 292, 293
Model Grocery 145
Modern Woodmen of America 25
Moeller 130, 157, 242, 243
Moffett 292, 293
Mogler 238, 239
Moll 46, 51, 127, 128, 133, 217, 259
Mollenhour 256
Money 285
Moneyhun 29, 230, 270
Montgomery 137, 204, 288
Moody Bible College 116
Moon 223
Mooney 221
Moore 70, 82, 86, 125, 130, 141, 172, 190, 222, 226, 228, 243, 244, 279, 285, 295
Mooreland and Tobler 45, 66, 70
Morgan 119, 189, 194, 203, 223, 224, 254, 283
Moritz 102, 110
Morris 15, 41, 256
Morrison 19, 89, 185, 190
Mortiz 179
Morton 21, 24, 25, 28, 45, 46, 66, 86, 126, 128, 137, 176, 200, 211, 215, 234, 235, 244, 245, 255, 272, 282, 291
Mosley 133
Mothershead 19
Mount Tabor School 85
Mouser 91, 96, 136, 183, 228, 238, 245
Mowery 83, 145, 184
Moyers 138
Muehleim, MO 22
Mueller 15, 16, 17, 18, 62, 65, 77, 93, 96, 110, 127, 128, 133, 145, 170, 220, 229, 231, 242, 245, 246, 252, 255, 287, 299
Mullaly 288
Muller 128, 170
Mullet 100
Munden 219
Mungle 214
Murdoch 118
Murphy 139
Murphysboro 89
Murray 184, 228
Musgraves 46, 66
Musgroves 184
Muster 246, 260
Myer 57, 128, 129, 130, 136, 161, 175, 176, 246, 247
Myers 83, 173, 178, 190, 242
Myracle 157

N

Nabe 160, 294
Nagel 160, 161, 229
Nance 83, 185
Nations 128, 136, 251
Naumeyer 217
Neace 214
Neader 154
Neal 237
Neal Creek 121
Neale 19
Nebels 100
Needmore 81
Neeley 11
Neely 248
Neelys 30
Neigh 277
Neighswonger 157
Neilson 126, 137
Neinstaedt 166
Neislein 22, 286
Neiswanger 23, 247
Neiswonger 247
Nelson 90, 91, 128, 129, 150, 154, 198, 247
Nenninger 159, 282
Nesslein 63
Netherlands 125
Neuenschwander 247
Neumann 110
Neumeyer 23, 91, 127, 160, 161, 166, 217, 230, 249, 262
New 199, 200, 287
New Bethel Baptist Church 116
New Bethel Church 97
New Salem Methodist Church 24
New Wells 4, 31, 81, 107, 111, 113
Newell 137
Newman 90
Newton 99, 201
Neyswanger 241
Niblack 44, 190, 215, 261
Nicholas 189
Nicolls 201
Niederkorn 51, 158, 159
Niemann 163, 218, 259
Niemeier 35, 226
Nienstedt 99, 262
Nigh 277
Nischwitz 190
Niswonger 10, 81, 92, 137, 157, 172, 175, 179, 182, 191, 194, 208, 225, 230, 241, 247, 269, 281, 282, 283
Niswonger Church 103
Nitch 128
Nitsch 129, 130, 136, 220, 244, 247
Noble 282, 285
Noe 96
Noel 213
Noeninger 274
Noland 96, 204, 234, 235, 236, 247, 248, 267, 268, 272, 274
Nolde 190
Nolte 110
Nordenia 54
Norman 90, 94
Norris 284
Northcutt 109
Norville 106
Nothdurft 92, 101, 166, 173, 216, 217, 248, 249, 259, 260
Notre Dame 51, 94, 105
Nowak 15, 41, 140, 249
Nurls 181
Nussbaum 100, 112, 136, 160, 213, 226, 237, 249, 271
Nussbaumer 184, 249

O

Oak Ridge Baptist Church 119
O'Bannon 14
Oberbeck 115, 154, 239
Oberdorff 190
Oberle 274
Obermann 100, 280
Obermiller 86, 121, 127, 141, 180, 277
Obermiller Floor Co. 145
Oberndoerfer 184
O'Brien's Store 34
Ochs 249
Oehlschlager 262
O'Henry 221
Ohman 12
O'Laughlin 129
Old Apple Creek Presbyterian Church 117
Old Appleton 81, 107
Old Bavarian Sausage 60, 61
Old Bethel 12, 31, 100, 101, 103
Oldenhoener 210
Oldenhoener Company 54
O'Leary 285
Oliver 19, 57, 84, 86, 135, 137, 247
Oliver House Museum 5, 45, 123, 135
Ollar 186
O'Loughlin 128, 231, 250, 251, 267
Olson 162, 233, 262
O'Neal 133, 213
O'Neill 137
Orchard Elementary 87
Oriole 4
Ormsby 258
Orrell 98
Osborn 175, 183
Osborne 222
Oster 206
Oswald 297
Overbeck 154, 178
Overfert 156
Owens 83, 211, 232, 290

P

P.E.O. 96
Paar 15, 111, 130
Pace 166, 266
Pagano 6
Page 201
Pahl 102
Painter 19
Pair 47, 184, 188, 189
Palezewski 238
Palisch 42, 169, 170, 282
Palmer 137, 175
Palo 170
Panoske 267
Parker 101, 189, 224, 227, 236
Parks 198
Parmenter 28
Parrish 165
Parson 228
Parsons 133
Partridge 89, 127, 233
Patchin 172
Pate 200
Patrick 233
Patten 219
Patterson 11
Patz 251
Paubel 186
Paul 126
Peabody College 141
Peak 134
Pearson 100
Pechmueller 239
Peck 14
Peek 261
Peel 161, 286
Peerman 57, 133
Peetz 136, 166, 251, 259, 261, 284
Peil 41
Pender 64, 180, 183, 244
Penn 194, 234
Pennebaker 25, 200
Penney 252
Pennington 276
Penny 28, 29, 82, 161, 164, 251, 252, 261, 292
Pennybaker 199, 200
Pensel 83, 110, 165, 182, 210, 252
Penzel 21, 27, 33, 49, 52, 83, 104, 142, 241, 252, 267, 293
Pepper 15, 84
Perdue 48
Perkins 132
Pernambuco 106
Perrin 67
Perry 96, 102, 110, 173, 206, 299
Pershing 128
Peterman 291
Peters 24, 27, 260, 267
Peterson 28, 98, 133, 167, 198, 248
Petterson 169
Pettifer 175
Petzoldt 83, 110
Pew 11
Pfeiffer 177, 184, 193
Pflantz 111, 112
Phelps 24, 29, 214, 248
Philadelphia 22, 67
Philipp 179
Philippines 52
Philipps Carpet and Decorating 6
Philips 160
Phillips 63, 83, 115, 137, 157, 158, 203, 232, 233, 252, 253
Philpott 210
Phoris 221
Phy-Cat Air Base 119
Pickering 253
Picou 172, 275
Piepenbrok 110
Pierce 28, 96, 128, 140, 172, 227, 243, 248, 253, 275, 299
Pilot Knob 118, 119, 142
Piltz 258
Pilz 255
Pink 244
Pinkert 102
Pinkerton 30, 174, 293
Pinkston 138, 277
Pitman 138
Pittman 137
Pitts 266
Plagge 115
Plainview 81
Pleasant 101, 272
Pleiman 138
Plesant 272
Pletcher 164
Plumer 102
Plunk 188
Poe 57, 67, 77, 96, 101, 128, 132, 133, 253, 254, 277, 293
Pogue 213, 281
Pohlman 157, 179
Pohlmann 22, 239
Point Lookout, MO 38
Points 256
Polack 112
Polk 217
Pollard 288
Popp 161, 170, 175, 190, 249
Post 38
Poston 158, 190, 243
Potashnick 201
Powell 22, 90, 199, 285, 287
Preslar 106
Presnell 268
Press 100
Preston 238
Price 119, 195, 234, 248, 281
Prichard 99, 179
Pridemore 193
Priest 19, 41, 74, 126, 127, 133, 141, 198, 209, 260
Prill 137
Primm 47
Prior 250
Probst 29, 65, 99, 130, 198, 229, 254, 286
Proctor 24, 128, 129, 130, 251
Proffer 57, 128, 137, 138, 145, 208, 280, 298
Prokopf 139
Propst 27, 28, 81, 137, 193
Prudl 170, 171
Pruitt 192
Puchbauer 82, 83, 110, 128
Puhbauer 130
Pulliam 293
Puls 44, 77, 127, 132, 133, 141, 143, 161, 221, 254, 293
Puntmann 22
Purcell 255
Putnam 188
Putz 12, 13, 30, 33, 143, 180, 218, 254, 255, 257, 258

Q

Quade 184, 213
Quatmann 243, 278, 279
Query 145, 174
Quinlivan 250
Quinn 106, 224, 255, 256

R

Rabold 123, 226
Rafferty 256
Ragsdale 238
Rahm 54
Rainey 99
Rains 237
Ralph 99
Rampley 90, 136, 137, 138, 166, 256
Ramsay 10, 85, 156, 297
Ramsey 28, 32, 89, 126, 156, 157, 191, 227, 286, 287
Randall 44
Randall Creek 13, 97, 121
Randles 4, 81
Randol 11, 30, 101, 120, 132, 134, 139, 221, 254, 256, 257, 272
Randolph 160
Raney 222
Ranney 19, 85, 120, 132, 133, 185, 215, 297
Rapp 22, 23, 110, 244, 248
Rasche 50, 51, 101, 290, 297
Rash 43
Rastl 298
Rauh 30, 211, 228, 229, 257, 298, 299
Rawlings 195
Ream 140
Recife 106
Reck 264
Redman 166
Redrick 190
Reed 86, 128, 130, 137, 145, 158, 242, 256, 290, 293
Reep 268
Reeves 120, 170, 293
Rehahn 111
Rehkopf 184, 260
Reid 29, 81, 133, 293
Reiger 173
Reilly 255, 256
Reiman 291
Reimann 82, 164
Reiminger 89, 90, 139, 190, 265
Reinecke 50, 163, 290, 297
Reinemer 22
Reinert 102
Reisenbichler 30, 91, 113, 146, 147, 203, 205, 254, 255, 257, 258, 298
Reiter 195
Reither 171
Reitman 126, 166, 198
Reitmann 101
Reitzel 187, 188, 252, 268
Rendleman 189
Renfroe 185
Renne 136
Rentfloe 242
Renwick 266
Rese 229
Retherford 33, 53
Reuter 171
Reutzel 157
Revelle 175
Reynolds 161, 191, 214, 248, 296
Rhea 201
Rheingold 105
Rhodes 33, 34, 41, 127, 136, 142, 173, 178, 179, 184, 194, 208, 209, 228, 292, 295
Rhyne 22, 169, 170, 179, 258
Rice 39, 40, 109, 201, 205, 263, 275
Richardson 99, 201
Richey 193
Richter 22, 82, 89, 187, 258, 286
Rider 100
Ridings 295
Riehn 98, 100, 136, 138
Rieman 27
Riemann 81
Rigdon 141, 159
Riley 245, 246
Riney 89, 94
Ringwald 100
Risha 195
Ristig 162, 258, 259
Ritgerod 252
Ritter 121, 218, 259
Roach 15
Robb 84, 121
Roberts 28, 84, 128, 130, 219, 251, 277
Robertson 33, 238, 248
Robins 129, 157, 228
Robinson 97, 133, 175, 244, 270, 280
Rockwell 267
Rodgers 194, 212
Rodney 11
Rodney's Mill 100
Rodriquez 291
Roe 160
Roerts 81
Roesner 111
Roesnor 111
Roethemeyer 116
Rogers 15, 92, 185, 193, 223
Rogler 186
Roglin 102
Rohlfs 140
Roither 171
Roland 127, 288
Rolfe 201
Roloff 123, 127, 146, 192, 217, 259, 260, 277
Romboutz 246
Ronzalen 248
Roosevelt 128, 293, 295
Rose 22, 57, 217, 229, 259, 261, 265
Roseborough 28
Roshek 89
Ross 70, 104, 133, 137, 170, 238
Roth 49, 169, 246, 258
Rouse 115
Roussell 203
Rowan 71
Rowe 178
Rowland 88, 89, 189, 233
Rowley 100, 102, 246, 260
Rubel 184, 215
Ruddell 172
Ruddle 173
Rudert 32, 33, 79
Rudolf 110
Ruehling 30, 216, 254
Ruesler 129, 130, 157
Ruester 154, 155, 260
Ruff 45, 52, 85, 124, 132, 210, 261, 277
Ruffner 207, 208
Rukkila 173
Rumfelt 194
Runnels 47, 99, 192, 280
Ruppel 22, 224
Rushin 240
Rushing 98, 154
Russel 84
Russell 15, 20, 82, 83, 120, 172, 173, 178, 185, 252, 254
Rust 57, 216, 259

S

Sachse 141, 144, 229, 251, 261, 294
Sackman 65
Sadler 82, 176, 220, 230, 252, 253, 290
Sailer 270
Sain 106
Salinger 102
Salmon 104, 284
Salzmann 261, 262
Sample 82, 83, 132, 133, 182, 211, 276, 281, 282
Samples 233
Sampson 167
Sams 119
Samuel 29
Samuel Pew Survey 14
Samuels 29, 81, 252
Sander 15, 16, 40, 42, 48, 78, 101, 112, 132, 133, 137, 143, 160, 161, 205, 217, 225, 229, 241, 243, 249, 261, 262, 263, 264, 271, 273, 297
Sanders 48, 145, 160, 163, 165, 237, 274
Sandin 137, 285
Sanford 85, 133, 144, 252, 270, 293
Santner 110
Santos 221
Sauer 22, 139
Saupe 68
Savers 140
Sawyer 44, 81, 83, 100, 123, 220, 245, 264
Scates 127, 130
Schabbing 125, 126
Schade 42, 57, 144, 218, 264
Schaefer 15, 76, 89, 111, 144, 163, 169, 170, 171, 193, 259, 265
Schafer 170
Schaffer 279
Schaffner 110
Schaper 5, 6, 33, 49, 50, 82, 83, 118, 127, 135, 146, 165, 166, 188, 189, 207, 246, 259, 260, 265, 283, 284, 287
Scharenborg 139
Scharlott 100
Schattauer 136, 265
Schatte 248
Schearf 15, 135, 186, 265, 266
Scheffer 134, 138
Schell 133, 195
Scheltenberger 290
Scheper 271
Scheppelmann 252
Scherer 159, 290
Scherrer 185
Schilling 265
Schirl 171
Schlage 184
Schlegal 280
Schlegel 42, 100, 205, 280
Schleger 186
Schlemmer 186
Schlenker 275
Schlenkered 275
Schlick 90, 91
Schlimme 160, 262, 268, 286
Schlimpert 49, 216, 239
Schloss 39, 91, 123, 128, 136, 162, 204, 236, 273
Schlosser 233
Schlueter 114, 223, 229, 254, 286
Schlunker 275
Schluter 260
Schmeiser 102
Schmid 266, 274
Schmidt 22, 29, 30, 82, 145, 258, 259, 277
Schmie 156
Schmiechen 110
Schmitt 186
Schmuke 12, 15, 45, 54, 121, 133, 141, 210, 250, 251, 255, 265, 266, 267
Schneider 57, 78, 100, 112, 113, 156, 187, 190, 277
Schnur 281
Schnurbusch 128
Schnurr 166
Schoen 29, 145, 182, 281, 282, 299
Schoen Construction 29
Schoenebeck 81, 83, 110, 179, 227
Schoenebeck School 23, 82, 83
Scholl 172, 194
Scholz 261
Schonoff 81
Schrack 160
Schrader 100, 125, 133, 255
Schreiner 90, 91, 137, 226, 287
Schriner 187
Schriners 82
Schrock 163, 164
Schroeder 102, 265
Schrumpf 239
Schubmann 286
Schuch 67
Schuessler 35
Schuette 32, 216
Schuknecht 145
Schulenburg 100
Schulte 42, 54, 55, 62, 188, 248, 256, 267, 268
Schultz 74, 102, 220, 261
Schumann 133
Schumke 66
Schuppman 286
Schwab 27, 47, 81, 82, 93, 100, 112, 125, 127, 128, 138, 229, 280
Schwach 267
Schwane 185
Schwartz 96, 128, 129, 130, 134, 141, 267, 269
Schwarz 185
Schweain 88, 89, 192
Schweer 83, 156, 184, 230, 238, 244, 248, 260, 267, 268, 295
Schweiger 239
Schwent 63, 89, 127
Schwepker 81, 82
Schwerdtfeger 22
Schwiesow 112
Sciortino 213, 226, 281
Scivally 148, 280
Scotland 43, 104
Scott 11, 90, 96
Scripps 19, 85
Scully 180
Seabaugh 6, 13, 25, 28, 29, 89, 96, 100, 118, 123, 127, 128, 135, 137, 141, 145, 154, 155, 157, 160, 162, 172, 177, 188, 190, 192, 195, 196, 197, 198, 205, 231, 232, 234, 235, 237, 246, 255, 268, 269, 270, 277, 283, 286, 291, 294
Seabough 267
Searcey 160, 162, 271
Searcy 215, 271
Sebastian 128, 129, 217, 249, 270, 271, 295
Sebaugh 25, 217
Sebecki 269
Seboldt 112
Second Artillery 118
Second Illinois Light Artillery 118

Second Infantry 118
Sedalia 48
Sedare 242
Sedgewickville 84, 85, 106
Seebach 269, 277
Seefeld 92
Seibert 85, 272, 298
Seiler 271, 279
Seitz 271, 272
Seivers 89, 269
Selves 97
Senn 100, 249
Sester 271
Settle 126
Sewing 128, 157, 251
Seybold 128, 130, 188
Seyer 89, 126
Seyers 288
Seyller 271, 272
Shaffer 175
Shaner 76, 235, 236, 272
Shannon 181
Shaper 57
Shaw 176
Shelby 108, 119, 133, 173, 178, 221
Shell 12, 195
Shelton 130, 173, 204
Shepard 19
Shepherd 284
Sheppard 12, 101, 185, 226, 238, 246, 272
Shepper 34
Sheridan 11, 44
Sherrow 99
Shields 133, 174
Shiloh 118
Shinaberry 252, 293
Shinn 88, 249
Shirley 132
Shively 238
Shoe Factory 36
Shorb 176
Short 91, 104, 120, 128, 130, 133, 178
Shorter 238, 287
Shott 299
Shoults 163
Shrum 157, 295
Shultz 136, 141
Shuman 133
Shumate 212
Shumer 296
Shurm 99
Sibley 15, 76
Sides 29, 30, 89, 127, 130, 154, 160, 161, 196, 197, 204, 215, 235, 236, 237, 252, 271, 272, 273, 296
Siebert 25, 62, 84, 128, 129, 130, 136, 175, 218
Siemer 48
Siemers 65, 100, 112, 123, 125, 126, 225, 249, 255, 273, 274, 280
Siermers 100
Siervers 127
Sievers 82, 83, 90, 91, 110, 123, 140, 141, 179, 245, 250, 274, 277
Sillivan 128
Simmerman 296
Simmons 106, 185, 201, 204, 230, 236, 274, 286, 297
Simpson 63, 82, 171, 253
Sinden 204
Sink 89, 90, 94
Sisk 285
Sites 271
Sitton 173, 174
Sitz 271, 272
Sitze 176, 183, 200, 245
Sivia 41
Skaggs 266, 274
Skelton 90
Skinner 136, 184
Slack 93, 128, 221
Slater 213
Slinkard 23, 53, 81, 124, 130, 132, 136, 157, 158, 172, 173, 175,
194, 195, 201, 203, 235, 274, 275, 277, 292
Sloan 282
Slovensky 99
Smally 185
Smart 133
Smith 24, 29, 72, 81, 83, 84, 89, 91, 98, 99, 126, 127, 128, 129, 130, 136, 137, 156, 158, 175, 181, 189, 192, 195, 200, 201, 213, 218, 222, 227, 233, 239, 254, 269, 270, 275, 276, 277, 278, 280, 290, 292
Smoot 24
Smythe 271
Sneathen 92, 133, 136
Sneed 42, 138
Sneider 187
Snider 19, 20, 21, 27, 28, 29, 81, 100, 118, 119, 120, 124, 126, 128, 141, 150, 174, 175, 176, 185, 223, 235, 237, 241, 298
Snow 133
Snyder 185, 253, 270
Soelberg 228
Sokolowski 133
Solado 4
Sommer 170
Sommerhauser 94, 97
Southard 74, 122
Southwood 158
Spanheimer 200
Spanish-American War 119
Spann 222
Sparfeld 162, 286
Sparfield 161
Sparkman 77, 78
Spaulding 266
Spears 136
Sperling 128, 215, 239, 251, 254
Spiegel 193
Spradling 93
Sprengel 290
Sprenger 125
Springfield 84
Spurrier 133
Squibb 253
St. Andrews Lutheran Church 94
St. Ildefonso 10
St. Jacobi (James) German Evangelical Church 101
St. James Church 101
St. James Congregation 102
St. James Evangelical Church 32
St. James United Church of Christ 23, 101, 102, 110, 116, 117
St. John African Methodist Episcopal Church 102
St. John Evangelical Lutheran Church 22, 23, 31, 45, 83, 107
St. John's Evangelical and Reformed Church 31, 83, 110, 107
St. Mary's 122
St. Paul Lutheran Band 123
St. Paul Lutheran Church 42, 43, 94, 111, 122
St. Paul Lutheran School 42, 94, 95, 113
Stalcup 144
Stallings 200
Stamm 292
Stamper 99
Stanard 31, 182, 276, 281
Stancik 169
Standley 286
Stanfield 77
Stanfill 217
Stanley 84
Stants 175
Starzinger 113, 216, 239, 275
Statlar 269
Statler 23, 28, 29, 46, 64, 66, 82, 84, 100, 128, 133, 157, 161, 162, 182, 192, 193, 194, 196, 211, 212, 222, 223, 235, 236, 243, 246, 251, 267, 269, 276, 277, 283
Steager 266
Stearns 24, 25, 58, 157, 172, 194, 241, 242, 277, 285
Steck 48, 104, 127, 128, 277, 297
Steel 98, 292
Steele 83, 84, 128, 130
Steelinger 266
Steimel 100
Steimle 126, 167, 267
Steinberg 137, 181
Steinborn 225, 226
Steiner 113, 141, 289
Steinheimer 260
Steinhoff 38, 100, 127, 190
Steinmann 246
Steinmeyer 104, 138
Stephan 258
Stephenson 98
Sterling 141
Sternberg 158
Sterner 138
Stevens 139
Stevenson 154, 184, 277, 278
Steward 175, 272
Stewart 19, 96, 99, 108, 222, 285
Sticka 169
Stickler 38, 126, 130
Stiegemeyer 91
Still 204
Stirewald 293
Stiver 237, 248
Stockton 91
Stoerker 100
Stoffregan 217
Stoffregen 114, 115, 225, 226
Stokes 253
Stoll 126, 253
Stollar 277
Stolle 134
Stone 189, 278
Stoner 200
Stotlar 277
Stout 272
Stovall 192, 193
Stoverinks 279
Stoyanoff 272
Strack 91, 225, 226, 239, 261
Straedey 138
Strange 20
Strickland 261
Stricklin 194
Strieker 138
Stringham 110
Strode 277
Stroder 66, 81, 160, 193, 201, 203, 238, 280, 295
Stroderville 81
Stroner 169
Strong 27, 52, 195, 199, 200, 203, 207, 271
Strongbow 250
Strube 179
Strunz 186, 187
Struthers 220
Struwe 22
Stubblefield 43
Stueve 136, 216
Stumpp 186
Stutts 217
Sudecum 280
Suedekum 100, 156, 164, 179, 280
Suffold 99
Suggs 296
Sullivan 129
Summers 10, 24, 99, 129, 177, 194, 198, 268, 280, 288, 289, 296
Suppe 102
Surrell 19
Surretts 101
Sutherland 174
Sutter 186
Sutton 91, 121, 281
Suzuki 81
Swamp Rangers 118, 119
Swan 28, 30, 31, 84, 132, 133, 182, 211, 257, 276, 281, 282, 283, 299
Swann 34, 212, 213
Sweden 141
Swift 293
Switzer 137
Switzerland 27, 37, 125
Symanski 102
Szofran 293
Szwabo 184

T

Taake 125, 217
Tacke 22, 119, 220, 238
Tackey 224
Tado 154
Taeger 245
Taggert 41
Talbert 83
Talbut 246
Tallent 283
Talley 12, 15, 28, 52, 88, 91, 92, 136, 215, 283, 284
Tanabe 161
Tandy 212
Tant 284
Taplin 206
Taraque 291
Taylor 11, 86, 93, 104, 120, 121, 132, 158, 202, 222, 223, 253, 284, 285, 288
Tee 288
Teets 15
Templeton 25, 110, 264
Tennille 185
Tenth Cavalry 118
Terrell 294
Thaal 100
Theilig 258
Thiele 25, 158, 182, 278, 279, 285
Third Cavalry 118
Third Company 118
Thirty-ninth Regiment 118
Thixton 290
Thoma 91, 119
Thomas 14, 24, 90, 101, 145
Thomen 162
Thommpson 285
Thompson 56, 58, 62, 63, 81, 84, 100, 101, 109, 117, 118, 127, 128, 134, 137, 138, 140, 141, 161, 177, 202, 211, 213, 225, 232, 234, 238, 255, 259, 273, 285, 293
Thomure 22
Thorne 160
Thurman 186
Tibbs 130, 154
Tiedeman 245
Tiedemann 36, 76, 201
Tierney 231
Tillman 99
Timenstien 111
Timon 105, 237
Timpkins 58
Tindal 127
Tinnin 26, 244
Tlapek 238
Tobago 125
Tobin 276
Tobler 45, 66, 101, 135
Todd 106
Toensmann 290
Tolson 92
Tomlin 108, 132, 133, 190, 224, 232, 285, 286
Tomlinson 166
Tompson 154
Tooke 171, 203
Torbitzky 110
Torrence 41
Townsend 27, 28, 220
Tragett 245
Trankler 139
Trapp 219
Travis 97
Trickey 49, 213, 272
Triebe 259
Triller 115
Trimble 24, 154
Trinity 112
Triplett 236
Trischler 137
Trost 202
Trotter 235
Troxel 244, 245
Troy 296
Tucker 177, 203, 214, 271
Turley 222
Turnbaugh 120
Turpin 216
Turner 84, 99, 226, 247, 260, 267, 286
Tuschhoff 22, 83, 110, 162, 215, 220, 286
Tuschoff 130, 138
Tussey 99
Twelfth Cavalry 118
Twenty-ninth Infantry 118
Twogood 234
Tyler 167

U

Ude 239
Ueleke 50, 65, 76, 100, 229, 254, 286
Ulrich 100, 136, 137, 266, 287
Umbeck 101
Umfleet 34
Unbeck 100
Underwood 22, 137
Unger 83, 137, 238
Union Church 100
United Church of Christ 102, 107, 110
Unterreiner 261, 287
Unterriner 199
Urbann 115
Ussery 293

V

Vallacher 161
Van Doren 278
Van Dyke 132
Van Metre 132
Vanamburg 200
VanCleve 195
Vandivort 15, 23, 37, 38, 133, 136, 141
Vangilder 89
Vanhorn 14, 19
Vargas 184
Vasterling 33, 115, 245, 254
Venable 16, 44, 94, 147, 220, 222, 238, 287, 288
Vernon 261, 282
Vickrey 225
Viehe 102
Villhard 286
Vinyard 91, 119, 213, 288, 289
Vogel 63, 113, 133, 184, 229, 258, 276, 277, 289
Vogelsang 154
Voges 102, 217, 251, 254, 259, 260
Vogt 204, 231, 236, 274, 289
Volkerding 27, 65, 112
Volksfreund 144
Volz 29
Von Vrittman 249
Voshage 33, 130, 158, 251, 261, 262
Vosin 289, 290
Voss 246, 260
Vrbosky 158
Vrielink 159

W

Wachoski 65, 259
Wachter 31, 89, 90, 94
Wade 102, 109
Wagener 290
Wagner 48, 50, 67, 96, 124, 130, 132, 133, 136, 141, 143, 144, 146, 147, 150, 160, 166, 173, 180, 186, 253, 261, 290, 291, 296
Wagoner 280
Wahlco D. W. Tool 54
Walburg 173
Walder 189
Waldon 248
Waldron 64
Wales 125
Walker 28, 29, 63, 81, 92, 97, 98, 109, 116, 133, 137, 141, 175, 176, 181, 190, 218, 227, 238, 242, 268, 291, 292
Wallace 25, 75, 190, 244, 292, 293
Wallenmeyer 126, 252, 293
Waller 11, 130
Wallis 89, 126, 232
Wallman 30, 293
Walls 248
Walperswiller 156, 293, 294
Walsh 250, 252
Walter 223, 294, 299
Walters 283
Walthers 112
Walton 288
Wampler 63, 173
Warbresky 270
Ward 100, 118
Wardron 138
Ware 132, 174, 206, 207, 218, 219
Warneke 162
Warner 217, 235
Warren 120, 141, 185, 229
Washington 13, 201, 235
Wathen 215, 237, 238
Wather 41
Wathern 85
Watkins 15, 98, 118, 135, 213, 236, 267
Watson 90, 125, 199, 264, 292
Watts 212
Wead 137
Webb 158, 160, 203, 229, 244, 247, 281, 297
Webber 89, 90, 94, 172
Weber 110, 180, 216, 296
Webster 278
Wedekind 101, 149, 217, 218, 294
Wedekinds 294
Wedel 289, 290
Weeden 264
Weekender 57
Weeks 44
Weiberg 194
Weidmann 162
Weis 91, 111, 212
Weisbrod 134
Weise 111
Weiss 64, 92, 226, 294, 295
Weith 90
Welch 174
Welker 23, 83, 90, 99, 160, 166, 194, 231, 272, 278, 279, 280, 295, 296
Welling 16, 17, 28, 96, 104, 120, 121, 188, 220, 298
Wells 88, 193, 204, 296
Weltecke 232
Weltge 102
Welty 28, 185, 195, 215, 280
Wencewicz 240
Wendel 89, 90, 136, 200
Wente 257
Werner 33, 44, 77, 110, 154, 161, 296, 297
Wesch 229
Wessel 89, 238
Wessell 52, 65, 92, 100, 112, 180
Westenberger 31
Westenburger 107
Westover 220
Wettengel 239
Weyberg 97
Wheeler 102, 120, 176, 242
Whicker 297
Whitaker 11
White 87, 98, 256, 260, 265
Whiteldge 261
Whitely 166
Whitener 129, 132, 133, 176
Whitewater 4, 16, 17, 32, 33, 34, 53, 81
Whitford 137
Whitledge 31
Whitney 94, 133
Whittaker 252, 253, 290
Wicker 132, 133, 185, 203, 229, 238, 262, 297
Wickham 88
Wier 224
Wiggins 136, 175
Wike 221
Wilburn 100
Wilcox 133, 137
Wilcoxin 126
Wilcoxson 161
Wiley 105
Wilferth 28, 241
Wilhelm 23, 82, 83, 92, 110, 204, 227, 230, 237
Wilk 298
Wilke 22, 33, 89
Wilkening 83, 220
Wilkerson 82, 221, 222
Wilkinson 11, 81, 130, 154, 222, 238, 239
Will 120
Willa 110, 156, 162
Willard 99
Wille 135, 136, 175, 291
Willer 28, 100, 129, 130
Williams 15, 34, 44, 63, 76, 81, 86, 90, 91, 97, 98, 101, 104, 108, 128, 130, 132, 159, 194, 233, 253, 254, 265, 266, 285, 288, 293, 297, 298
Williamson 77, 120, 137, 141, 161, 175, 176, 237
Willis 212
Willmann 23
Wills 25, 29, 82, 84, 214, 268, 277
Wilson 15, 24, 28, 29, 31, 39, 41, 57, 84, 89, 96, 123, 128, 133, 147, 156, 168, 175, 176, 188, 192, 201, 208, 220, 224, 247, 253, 266, 286, 288, 290, 291, 298
Windeknecht 239
Windisch 191
Windsor 180
Wingert Pottery 52
Winkler 27, 115
Winningham 43, 136
Winter 257, 258, 298, 299
Winterich 110
Winterick 102
Winters 26, 27, 120
Winton 224
Wischmann 18, 294, 299
Wischmeyer 258
Wisconsin Cavalry Regiment 119
Wise 154
Wiseman 90, 201
Wissman 204, 237, 271
Wissmann 237, 299
Witt 212
Wittke 299
Wittrock 295
Witzel 280
Wm. A. Illers Dairy 145
Woeltje 128, 179, 258, 262
Wofford 195
Wolf 290
Wolfenhoehler 30
Wolfenkoehler 22, 23, 30, 83, 110, 187, 252, 268
Wolfenkoehler Blacksmith Shop 22
Wolfenkoehler Shop Community 22
Wolfenkoehlers Shop 23
Wolgast 290, 296
Wolkenkoehler 22
Wolter 19, 256
Wolters 127, 141, 260, 297
Women's Foreign Missionary Society 115
Women's Mite Society 97
Women's Society of Christian Service (WSCS) 115
Wonderworkers Extension Homemakers 31, 119
Wood 137, 198
Woodard's Restaurant 44, 126
Woodland 133
Woodman Hall 25
Woods 117, 204
Woolsey 285
Wooster 299
Work Projects Administration 36
World War I 20, 44, 57, 104, 114, 115, 119, 120, 130, 144
World War II 27, 34, 39, 40, 41, 49, 52, 65, 119, 130, 144
World's Fair 44
Worley 298
WPA 82, 86
Wright 90, 137, 175, 241
Wubker 159, 168
Wulff 62, 161, 254
Wunderlich 91, 258
Wyatt 201
Wynn 184
Wyoming 103

Y

Yamintz 157
Yamnitz 155
Yancey 98, 154
Yarbro 160
Yates 276
Yoder 268
Yoes 109
York 194
Young 22, 88, 90, 132, 133, 157, 169, 172, 203, 236, 273, 277
Young Americans 4-H Club 122
Younghouse 257
Young's Pharmacy 37
Yount 110, 195, 202, 202, 234, 274

Z

Zapf 190, 252
Ziegler 51, 158, 159
Zimmer 39, 49
Zimmerman 22, 286
Zimmith 23
Zion 111, 112
Zion Lutheran Church and School 31, 112, 113
Zion United Methodist Church 114, 115
Zoellner 22
Zoffuto 133
Zoll 109
Zschille 258

304

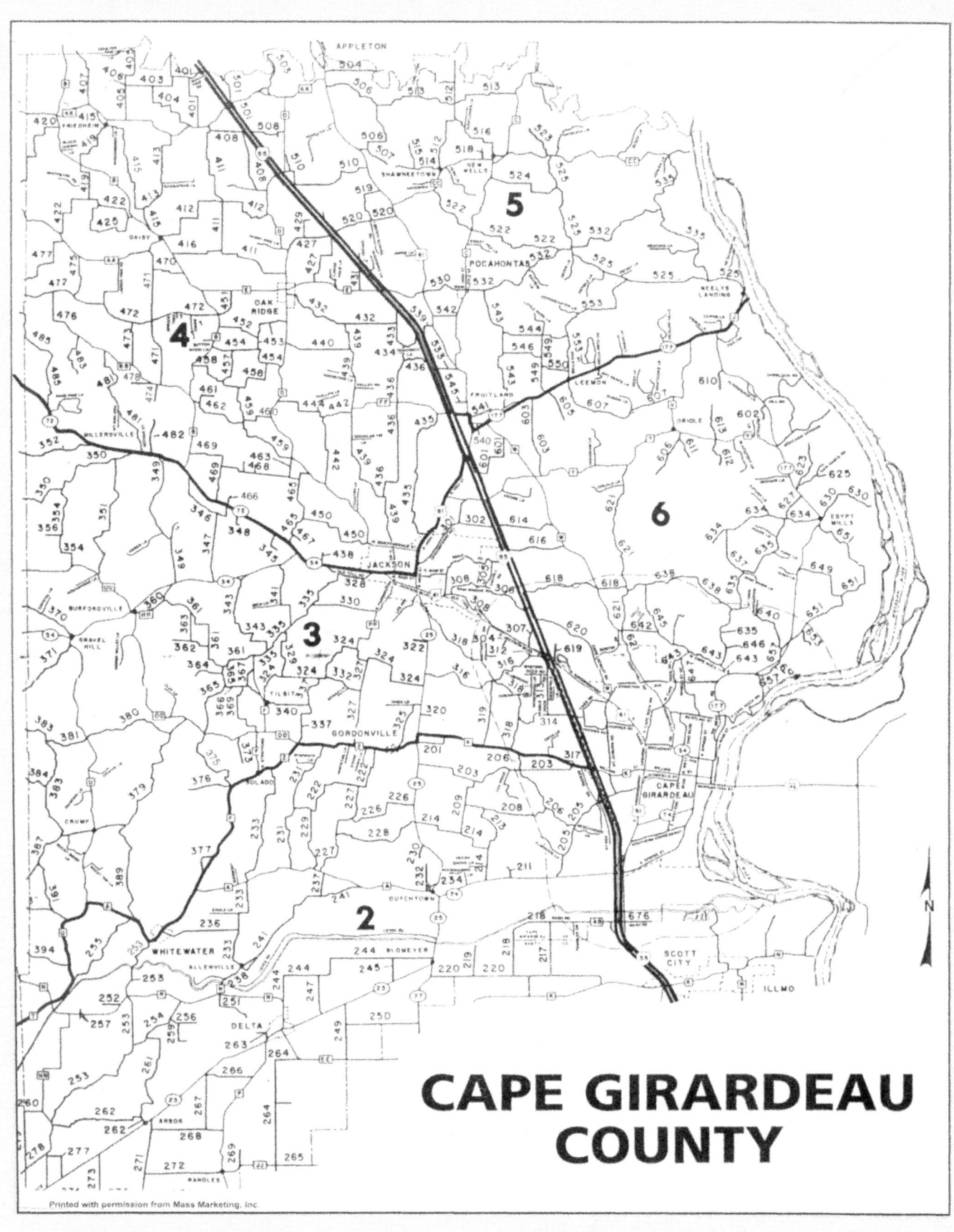

CAPE GIRARDEAU COUNTY